Lecture Notes in Computer Science 8274

Commenced Publication in 1973
Founding and Former Series Editors:
Gerhard Goos, Juris Hartmanis, and Jan van Leeuwen

Samik Basu   Cesare Pautasso   Liang Zhang
Xiang Fu (Eds.)

Service-Oriented Computing

11th International Conference, ICSOC 2013
Berlin, Germany, December 2-5, 2013
Proceedings

 Springer

Volume Editors

Samik Basu
Iowa State University, Ames, IA, USA
E-mail: sbasu@iastate.edu

Cesare Pautasso
University of Lugano, Switzerland
E-mail: cesare.pautasso@usi.ch

Liang Zhang
Fudan University, Shanghai, China
E-mail: lzhang@fudan.edu.cn

Xiang Fu
Hofstra University, Hempstead, NY, USA
E-mail: xiang.fu@hofstra.edu

ISSN 0302-9743   e-ISSN 1611-3349
ISBN 978-3-642-45004-4   e-ISBN 978-3-642-45005-1
DOI 10.1007/978-3-642-45005-1
Springer Heidelberg New York Dordrecht London

Library of Congress Control Number: 2013953384

CR Subject Classification (1998): D.2, C.2, H.4, H.3, H.5, J.1, F.3

LNCS Sublibrary: SL 2 – Programming and Software Engineering

Typesetting: Camera-ready by author, data conversion by Scientific Publishing Services, Chennai, India

Printed on acid-free paper

Springer is part of Springer Science+Business Media (www.springer.com)

Preface

Welcome to the proceedings of the 11th International Conference on Service-Oriented Computing (ICSOC 2013), held in Berlin, Germany, December 2–5, 2013. These proceedings contain high-quality research papers that represent the latest results, ideas, and positions in the field of service-oriented computing.

Since the first meeting more than ten years ago, ICSOC has grown to become the premier international forum for academics, industry researchers, and practitioners to share, report, and discuss their ground-breaking work. ICSOC 2013 continued along this tradition, in particular focusing on emerging trends at the intersection between service-oriented, cloud computing, and big data.

This year's call for papers attracted 205 submissions from 29 countries and five continents. The submissions were rigorously evaluated by three reviewers followed by a meta-review by a senior Program Committee (PC) member, which in turn was followed by discussion moderated by the senior PC member. The decision for acceptance/rejection was based on all the above aspects. The PC is composed of world-class experts in service-oriented computing from 30 different countries. The ICSOC 2013 program featured a research track with 26 full papers and 26 short papers (giving an acceptance rate of 13% and 25%, respectively). Concerning the industry track, we received 15 submissions for the industry track, out of which three full papers and one short paper were accepted for these proceedings. The conference program was highlighted by two invited keynotes (by Carlo Ghezzi and by Richard Hull), two invited tutorials (by Jian Yang and by Manfred Reichert), a lively panel discussion on big data (moderated by Mathias Weske), many demonstrations, the PhD Symposium, and a record number of workshops.

We would like to express our gratitude to all individuals, institutions, and sponsors that supported ICSOC 2013. The high-quality program you are about to experience would have not been possible without the expertise and dedication of our PC and in particular of our senior PC members. We are grateful for the guidance of the General Chairs (Wolfgang Reisig and Jianwen Su), the effort of the external reviewers, the Proceedings Chair (Xiang Fu), and the local organizers, and last but not least to the distinguished members of the ICSOC Steering Committee. All of them helped to make ICSOC 2013 a success. Finally, a special word of thanks goes to all researchers and students who contributed with their presentations, questions, and active participation in the conference. We hope you enjoy these proceedings!

September 2013

Samik Basu
Cesare Pautasso
Liang Zhang

ICSOC 2013 Organization

General Co-chairs

Wolfgang Reisig	Humboldt University of Berlin, Germany
Jianwen Su	University of California at Santa Barbara, USA

Program Co-chairs

Samik Basu	Iowa State University, USA
Cesare Pautasso	University of Lugano, Switzerland
Liang Zhang	Fudan University, China

Workshop Co-chairs

Alessio R. Lomuscio	Imperial College London, UK
Surya Nepal	CSIRO, Australia

Demonstration Chairs

Roman Vaculin	IBM T.J. Watson Research Center, USA
Marco Montali	Free University of Bozen-Bolzano, Italy

Panel Chair

Mathias Weske	University of Potsdam, Germany

PhD Symposium Chairs

Boualem Benatallah	University of New South Wales, Australia
Ivona Brandi	Vienna University of Technology, Austria
Fabio Patrizi	Sapienza University of Rome, Italy

Publicity Co-chairs

Domenico Bianculli	University of Luxembourg, Luxembourg
Zhongnan Shen	Bosch Research and Technology Center, USA

Corporate Sponsor Chair

Hua Liu	Xerox Research Center, USA

Publication Chair

Xiang Fu   Hofstra University, USA

Web Chair

Cagdas Evren Gerede   Google, USA

Steering Committee

Asit Dan   IBM Research, USA
Bernd Krämer   FernUniversität in Hagen, Germany
Boualem Benatallah   UNSW, Australia
Fabio Casati   University of Trento, Italy
Mike Papazoglou   Tilburg University,
                                  The Netherlands - Acting Chair
Paco Curbera   IBM Research, USA
Paolo Traverso   ITC-IRST, Italy
Winfried Lamersdorf   University of Hamburg, Germany

Program Committees

Senior PC Members

Athman Bouguettaya   RMIT, Australia
Boualem Benatallah   UNSW, Australia
Barbara Pernici   Politecnico di Milano, Italy
Fabio Casati   University of Trento, Italy
Flavio De Paoli   Università di Milano Bicocca, Italy
Gustavo Rossi   UNLP, Argentina
Heiko Ludwig   IBM T.J. Watson Research Center, USA
Jian Yang   Macquarie University, Australia
Lin Liu   Tsinghua University, China
Mathias Weske   HPI / University of Potsdam, Germany
Michael Maximilien   IBM Research, USA
Michael Q. Sheng   Adelaide University, Australia
Mohand-Said Hacid   Universite Claude Bernard Lyon 1, France
Schahram Dustdar   TU Wien, Austria
Stefan Ta   KIT, Germany
Zahir Tari   RMIT University, Australia

PC Members

Abdelkarim Erradi   Qatar University, Qatar
Aditya Ghose   University of Wollongong, Australia
Alvaro Arenas   Instituto de Empresa Business School, Spain
Andrea Zisman   City University London, UK
Andreas Friesen   SAP AG, Germany
Antonia Bertolino   ISTI-CNR, Italy

Antonio Ruiz Cortes	University of Seville, Spain
Artem Polyvyanyy	Queensland University of Technology, Australia
Bernhard Holtkamp	Fraunhofer ISST, Germany
Carlo Ghezzi	Politecnico di Milano, Italy
Cesare Pautasso	University of Lugano, Switzerland
Christian Perez	Inria, France
Christoph Bussler	Analytica, Inc., USA
Claudio Bartolini	HP Labs, Palo Alto, USA
Colette Roland	Université Paris Pantheon Sorbonne, France
D. Janakiram	IIT Madras, India
Daniel Gmach	HP Labs
Daniela Grigori	University of Paris-Dauphine, France
Dimka Karastoyanova	University of Stuttgart, Germany
Dragan Gasevic	Athabasca University, Canada
Ebrahim Bagheri	Athabasca University, Canada
Emmanuel Coquery	Université de Lyon, France
Florian Daniel	University of Trento, Italy
Florian Rosenberg	IBM Research, USA
Francesco Lelli	European Research Institute on Service Science, Tilburg, The Netherlands
Frank Leymann	University of Stuttgart, Germany
Frank Puhlmann	inubit AG, Germany
Fu-ren Lin	National Tsing Hua University, R.O.C.
G.R. Gangadharan	IDRBT, Hyderabad, India, India
George Spanoudakis	City University London, UK
Gerald Kotonya	Lancaster University, UK
Gregor Engels	University of Paderborn
Guiling Wang	North China University of Technology, China
Hai Jin	HUST, China
Haluk Demirkan	Arizona State University, USA
Helen Paik	UNSW, Australia
Ignacio Silva-Lepe	IBM, USA
Ingo Weber	NICTA, Australia
Jian Yu	Swinburne University of Technology, Australia
Jianwu Wang	University of California, San Diego, USA
Joao E. Ferreira	University of Sao Paulo, Brazil
Jos van Hillegersberg	University of Twente, The Netherlands
Jun Han	Swinburne University of Technology, Australia
Jun Li	HP Labs, USA
Karthikeyan Ponnalagu	IBM Research, India
Khalil Drira	LAAS Toulouse, France
Lai Xu	Bournemouth University, UK
Larisa Shwartz	IBM T.J. Watson Research Center, USA
Lars Moench	University of Hagen, Germany
Lawrence Chung	The University of Texas at Dallas, USA
Liang Zhang	Fudan University, China

Luciano Baresi	Politecnico di Milano, Italy
Manfred Reichert	University of Ulm, Germany
Manuel Carro	UPM and IMDEA Software Institute, Spain
Marcelo Fantinato	University of Sao Paulo, Brazil
Marco Pistore	Fondazione Bruno Kessler, Italy
Markus Kirchberg	National University of Singapore
Massimo Mecella	Sapienza Università di Roma, Italy
Michael Mrissa	University of Lyon, France
Mikio Aoyama	Nanzan University, Japan
Nanjangud C. Narendra	IBM India Software Lab, Bangalore, India
Olivier Perrin	Lorraine University, France
Paolo Giorgini	University of Trento, Italy
Patricia Lago	VU University Amsterdam, The Netherlands
Paul Grefen	Eindhoven University of Technology, The Netherlands
Peng Han	Chongqing Academy of Science and Technology, China
Qi Yu	Rochester Institute of Technology, USA
RadhaKrishna Pisipati	Infosys Technologies Limited, India
Rafael Accorsi	University of Freiburg, Germany
Rama Akkiraju	IBM/USA, USA
Raman Kazhamiakin	Say Service s.r.l., Italy
Rania Khalaf	IBM T.J. Watson Research Center, USA
Rik Eshuis.	Eindhoven University of Technology, The Netherlands
Roman Vaculin	IBM, USA
Salima Benbernou	Université Paris Descartes, France
Sami Bhiri	DERI, Ireland
Sergey Smirnov	SAP Research, Germany
Shiping Chen	CSIRO ICT, Sydney
Shuiguang Deng	Zhejiang University, China
Surya Nepal	CSIRO, Australia
Sven Graupner	HP Labs, Palo Alto, USA
Vincenzo D'Andrea	University of Trento, Italy
Walter Binder	University of Lugano, Switzerland
Weiliang Zhao	University of Wollongong, Australia
Wing-Kwong Chan	City University of Hong Kong, SAR China
Woralak Kongdenfha	Naresuan University, Thailand
Xumin Liu	Rochester Institute of Technology, USA
Yan Wang	Macquarie University, Australia
Yan Zheng	Aalto University/Xidian University, Finland
Ying Li	Zhejiang University, China
Zaki Malik	Wayne State University, USA
Zhongjie Wang	Harbin Institute of Technology, China
Zibin Zheng	The Chinese University of Hong Kong, SAR China

Additional Reviewers

Saeed Aghaee	University of Lugano, Switzerland
Masiar Babazadeh	University of Lugano, Switzerland
Alessio Gambi	University of Lugano, Switzerland
Zachary J. Oster	University of Wisconsin-Whitewater, USA
Achille Peternier	University of Lugano, Switzerland
Ganesh Ram Santhanam	Iowa State University, USA

Sponsors

IBM Research
SOAMED
Berlin's First University
SerTech
ACM

Table of Contents

Keynotes

Research Track

Research Track Short Paper

Industry Track

Industry Track Short Paper

Demo Track

Data-Centricity and Services Interoperation

Richard Hull

IBM T. J. Watson Research Center, New York, USA
hull@us.ibm.com

Abstract. This position paper highlights three core areas in which persistent data will be crucial to the management of interoperating services, and highlights selected research and challenges in the area. Incorporating the data-centric perspective holds the promise of providing formal foundations for service interoperation that address issues such as providing a syntax-independent meta-model and semantics, and enabling faithful modeling of parallel interactions between multiple parties.

1 Introduction

Services-oriented computing has been evolving, from its roots in orchestration and choreography to the recent tremendous growth in usage stemming from the Software-as-a-Service paradigm and the pragmatism of open REST APIs. Strong notions of "type" have been dropped in favor of message-based API's that refer to data objects with flexible and possibly nested structure. However, as we embrace a world of rich and rapidly created combinations of SaaS-based services from massive numbers of third-party sources, we face challenges of ontology mismatch, entity resolution, and correlation confusion. These challenges must be addressed if we are to find formal and syntax-independent abstract models of service interoperation, systematic design methods for large-scale service compositions, and approaches to support intuitive and formal reasoning about them. Solving these challenges will involve multiple techniques and new advances, but a key element will rely on a shift towards *data-centricity*, that is, enabling data to be at the heart of conceptual modeling, design, and reasoning for interoperating services.

This position paper highlights the need for data-centricity, and overviews research progress and challenges in the area. In particular, the next three sections overview issues and relevant research to date on shared vocabularies and ontologies, entity resolution, and entity correlation; and the concluding section highlights selected research challenges raised and and opportunities enabled by incorporating a data-centric perspective into services interoperation.

2 Shared Vocabulary

Service interoperation involves the exchange of information between services; this is predicated on the assumption that the services involved have an agreed upon meaning for the information. As outlined briefly below, the general solution to enabling rapid

S. Basu et al. (Eds.): ICSOC 2013, LNCS 8274, pp. 1–8, 2013.

compositions of services from multiple sources will require access to ontology mappings, which in turn will rely on both stored information and description-logic style reasoning.

Under the traditional solution, a standard is established that a large body of services are to follow, e.g., see the work of the United Nations Economic Commission for Europe that maintains standards for Electronic Data Interchange (EDI) relating to commercial activities [30]. In the services realm, the SA-WSDL standard [20] enables specification of the ontologies to be used for interpreting values of parameters mentioned in service APIs. Importantly, recent work such as [21] is developing extensions of SA-WSDL to apply to REST APIs, and enabling matchmaking techniques to be applied on them.

In many application areas, however, it is not possible to enforce a universal standard with regards to the vocabulary or ontology used by services. This is acknowledged in the data management literature, for example, [9] provides a survey of problems and techniques for integrating data stored according to different vocabularies and ontologies. Citation [16] argues that we must live with such heterogeneity in the healthcare domain, and [18] argues similarly for education. More generally, [10] provides a comprehensive discussion of techniques to semi-automatically develop mappings between ontologies, and how the results are used in a variety of applications.

From the perspective of service interoperation, simply having the ability to semi-automatically compute ontology matchings is not sufficient. In particular, mechanisms are needed to access such matchings, either from a locally stored ontology or through a service. A rich example of the latter is found in OntoCAT [2], which provides APIs for going between multiple ontologies in the bioinformatics field. Tools such as the Karlsruhe Ontology (KAON) infrastructure [17] and the Ontology Mapping Store [25] provide generic access to ontology mappings.

To summarize, although ontology mappings are not in practical use to support modern service interoperation, much of the foundational research and several research tools have been developed in recent years. In the coming years requirements from industry will help to determine the application, business models, and evolution of these techniques.

3 Entity Synonym Repositories

Entity resolution, that is, the problem of extracting, matching, and resolving occurrences of entity names in structured and unstructured data has a history going back to the 1950's. This topic has become important again in recent years because of the interest in so-called "big data" and applications in advertising, marketing, and personalized services that attempt to mine social data for useful, entity-specific information. A survey of the field, including recent advances that use advanced machine learning techniques, is provided in the recent tutorial [11].

On the positive side, many successful techniques are in place to achieve relatively accurate entity resolution. But in practical systems that need a very high degree of precision it is typical to augment the automated techniques with manual validation activity. Although not scalable in a true sense, this can provide a pragmatic approach to incrementally build up near-certain information that augments the automated techniques.

To illustrate, consider applications that attempt to find sales leads for business-to-business (B2B) companies, by searching through news articles, blogs, and other social media for events that suggest that a given company might be helped through the purchase of a given product. Although there are pseudo-standards for company names, e.g., the Dunn and Bradstreet database, companies are often referred to by a handful of synonyms in the media. As a result, a viable service in this space will augment automated techniques by storing a dictionary of manually determined synonyms. Whether this is stored as part of the service, or is accessed from an external service, it is nevertheless a persistent data store.

Increasingly, interoperating services will be accessing unstructured data and/or data from multiple repositories. As a result they will need to rely on entity resolution, and on associated repositories of entity synonyms. It is likely that multiple proprietary and externally accessible services will become available that provide access to synonym repositories, to enable uniform entity reference across interoperating services.

4   Managing Entities across Services

In many service interoperation scenarios there are multiple entities, either physical or conceptual, that are being managed or manipulated through time by different services. This requires precise management of the relationships between the entities, called *correlation* in the early literature on orchestration and choreography of web services. That early literature does not provide mechanisms for explicitly modeling or specifying such correlations. Recently, [29] has developed a framework for such explicit modeling, based on the notion of business artifacts This includes a declarative language for intuitive yet systematic specification of correlations across entities along with constraints on the correlations, and also supports the possibility of formal reasoning about them. This section briefly explores some of the ways that the business artifact perspective can support the management of correlations.

Since their introduction in 2003 [26,19], business artifacts have been shown useful for several aspects of business process modeling. Briefly, a business artifact type is used to represent a class of (physical or conceptual) entities that evolve as a business process unfolds. An artifact type includes both an *information model*, that provides room to hold (possibly nested) data about an artifact instance that may change over time, and a *lifecycle model*, that holds a specification of the possible ways that the artifact instance might evolve. (The lifecycle model might be specified in a procedural paradigm such as finite state machines or Petri nets, or a more declarative paradigm such as DECLARE [27] or Guard-Stage-Milestone [13,8]). Applications of the artifact perspective include enabling a cross-silo view of business processes [28], providing a coherent integrated view of multiple similar but different business processes [7], business process performance monitoring [23] and enabling data-centric service interoperation [15]. Further, artifacts are closely related to "cases" in the sense of Case Management, and the recent OMG Case Management Modeling and Notation (CMMN) standard [6] embodies a merging of these two streams of conceptual modeling [24]. We believe that the artifact approach will bring numerous advantages to our understanding, design, and deployment of service compositions, including those just mentioned. We focus here on the issue of correlation because it provides the single most easily motivated application of the artifact perspective to services interoperation.

To illustrate the basic form of correlation, consider the "make-to-order" example as described in [14] and elsewhere. In this scenario, a "Customer Purchase Order" is sent to an "assembler", who in turn creates several "Line Items" that must be obtained in order to fulfill the customer order. The assembler researches the problem of which suppliers to use to obtain the line items, and eventually creates multiple "Supplier Purchase Orders", each of which may request multiple line items from a given supplier. Furthermore, in some cases a supplier may reject a Supplier Purchase Order, which means that the affected Line Items must be grouped again to generate additional Supplier Purchase Orders. Importantly, the specific relationships evolve over time, e.g., as, Line Items are created, as Supplier Purchase Orders are created, and as Supplier Purchase Orders are fulfilled or rejected. It is easy to see that in the general case, there are $1{:}n$ relationships between Customer Purchase Orders and Line Items. If we consider Line Items and Supplier Purchase Orders over time, then $n{:}m$ relationships may arise, e.g., if a Supplier Purchase Order is rejected and then one of its Line Items is placed into a second Supplier Purchase Order. Business artifacts were used in 2005 in support of an application with similar kinds of correlations involving 1000's of interrelated objects [5]. The application, based on the pharmaceutical drug discovery process, was centralized in that study, but would most likely be distributed across multiple services if developed today.

As mentioned above, [29] shows that a natural approach for explicitly modeling correlations in a services interoperation context is through the use of business artifacts. In the make-to-order example, three artifact types can be used, one each for Customer Purchase Order, Line Item, and Supplier Purchase Order. It is straightforward in this context to maintain the correlations between artifact instances, e.g., in a deployment where each artifact type is maintained by a separate service. This approach can be extended to situations where one or more artifact types is managed by multiple services, rather than by just one. The approach can be used in a choreography-based setting, as illustrated in [29], or in an orchstration-based setting such as [15,22].

A richer form of correlation arises when entities can be split apart or merged. One example of this arises in the context of Collaborative Decision Processes. These are processes that involve multiple stakeholders who together explore a variety of ideas and initiatives in order to reach a (typically multi-faceted) decision over a period of time (e.g., weeks or months). An example application is when members of a community decide on the characteristics that should be embodied in a new shopping mall. This may include several investigations into traffic impact, watershed impact, etc., and also the exploration of numerous alternatives. In some cases these initiatives may split (e.g., consideration of a recreational shop for the mall may split into considerations for adult recreation and for youth recreation) or iniatives may merge (e.g., separate initiatives around a movie theater and something for art lovers might merge into an initiative for an independent film theater). As described in [31], it is natural to model and implement such processes using the business artifact approach, using an artifact instance for each idea or initiative that is explored. This simplifies the use of multiple interoperating services when implementing the core of the decision process, and also when incorporating new services, e.g., to solicit opinions from a crowd or to conduct polls.

An application area that involves a broad array of stakeholder enterprises and where conceptual entities can transform is in tracking food in the supply chain "from farm to fork". For example, with a potato in a frozen stew, multiple interrelated "lots" (i.e., collections of goods treated as a unit for shipping or processing activities) come into being, as the result of combining potatoes from different harvests, mixing different ingredients, and finally the packaging and delivery. Monitoring the overall process and enabling adjustments to it (including recalls) is vastly simplified if a data model is deployed as the backbone for the interoperation. In this case, the lots are naturally modeled as business artifacts, and systematic correlation between lots is easily managed, even as the underlying goods are processed.

As illustrated by the examples above, the artifact perspective can provide a natural and comprehensive modeling framework for managing entities and their correlations in service compositions. At the core of the approach is the understanding that the various services are manipulating a common set of conceptual entities. Multiple approaches can be used for the actual storage of associated information, e.g., maintaining full artifact instances within a single service, distributing their storage across multiple services, or passing partially completed artifact instances from one service to another (cf. [1]).

5   The Challenges Ahead

Data has always been fundamental in service interoperation, but until recently it has not been emphasized in the research on conceptual models, in specification languages, or in the study of foundations. With the dramatic increase in SaaS offerings and the anticipation that many business processes will be performed using rapidly created service compositions, the systematic and intuitively natural management of the data aspect along with the process aspect will become essential. As discussed above, there are three main components to the data aspect, namely, access to ontology matchings, access to synonym repositories, and the management of entity correlations. Three broad research areas are now highlighted.

One broad challenge area concerns extensions of "keep it simple" approaches such as REST and noSQL (e.g., as embodied by JSON) to incorporate data more explicitly. As noted above, the piece-parts to support such extensions are now available in the research literature. But finding ways to combine them in simple ways that become widely adopted remains open. Here the ontology matching and entity name synonyms can be viewed as more-or-less stand-alone services giving access to essentially static data, In contrast, entity correlation involves dynamic data and traditional database considerations such as transactional consistency, maintenance of equivalence across copies of data held in different services, and preservation of integrity constraints across updates. Such issues become more intricate in cases where the underlying implementation for one or more services is parallelized and/or distributed for performance reasons.

A second challenge area involves developing mechanisms for reasoning about service interoperation, reasoning that incorporates the data aspect along with the process aspect. Promising formal work in this direction is provided by, e.g., [4], which develops formal verification techniques for distributed artifact-based systems, and by, e.g., [12] and related papers, which develop a rich theoretical basis for formal verification of systems that involve ontology, data, and the evolution of data reminiscent to that found in artifact systems. The latter work is especially relevant to service interoperation where ontology matching is involved, since those matchings may include a combination of fixed data and description logic based reasoning. More broadly, this work will help to pave the way for practical (possibly semi-automatic) verification tools that enable faster and more automated development and testing of service compositions, and also for debugging systems that can help to explain why errors are occurring.

A third area where the data-centric perspective may have useful application for service interoperation is to address concerns around foundations for the orchestration and choreography standards, as raised in [3] and elsewhere. In particular, the artifact perspective holds the promise of providing a formal grounding for both orchestration and choreography, precisely because it can faithfully represent not only the process aspects but also the data aspects. Reasoning about the interactions between entities can be explicit, as already demonstrated in [29]. More broadly it appears that these techniques can be extended to reason about both the parties involved in a service composition and the conceptual entities being manipulated on their behalf. The artifact perspective can be extended to provide an explicit formal meta-model underlying the BPEL and WS-CDL standards, which would enable rich styles of formal verification for specifications in those standards, styles that incorporate the data aspects as well sa the process aspects. Multi-party interactions, and in particular managing multiple interactions that may happen in parallel, can be formalized and studied, as illustrated by the work on entity correlation [29] described above, and by research on artifact-centric interoperation hubs [15]. Finally, the artifact perspective may provide a workable basis for developing a theory around the integration of multiple service compositions, including an understanding of compositions of compositions, an area that will be increasingly important as the use of service compositions continues to grow.

References

1. Abiteboul, S., Benjelloun, O., Milo, T.: The Active XML project: An overview. Very Large Databases Journal 17(5), 1019–1040 (2008)
2. Adamusiak, et al.: OntoCAT simple ontology search and integration in Java, R and REST/-JavaScript. BMC Bioinformatics 12(218) (2011),
   http://www.biomedcentral.com/1471-2105/12/218
3. Barros, A., Dumas, M., Oaks, P.: Standards for web service choreography and orchestration: Status and perspectives. In: Bussler, C.J., Haller, A. (eds.) BPM 2005. LNCS, vol. 3812, pp. 61–74. Springer, Heidelberg (2006)
4. Belardinelli, F., Lomuscio, A., Patrizi, F.: Verification of agent-based artifact systems. CoRR, abs/1301.2678 (2013)
5. Bhattacharya, K., et al.: A Model-driven Approach to Industrializing Discovery Processes in Pharmaceutical Research. IBM Systems Journal 44(1) (2005)
6. BizAgi, Cordys, IBM, Oracle, SAP AG, Singularity (OMG Submitters), Agile Enterprise Design, Stiftelsen SINTEF, TIBCO, Trisotech (Co-Authors).: Case Management Model and Notation (CMMN), FTF Beta 1 (January 2013), OMG Document Number dtc/2013-01-01, Object Management Group

7. Chao, T., et al.: Artifact-based transformation of IBM Global Financing. In: Dayal, U., Eder, J., Koehler, J., Reijers, H.A. (eds.) BPM 2009. LNCS, vol. 5701, pp. 261–277. Springer, Heidelberg (2009)
8. Damaggio, E., Hull, R., Vaculín, R.: On the equivalence of incremental and fixpoint semantics for business artifacts with guard-stage-milestone lifecycles
9. Doan, A., Halevy, A.Y.: Semantic-Integration Research in the Database Community. AI Magazine 26(1) (2005)
10. Euzenat, J., Shvaiko, P.: Ontology matching. Springer, Heidelberg (2007)
11. Getoor, L., Machanavajjhala, A.: Entity resolution: Theory, practice & open challenges. Proc. of the VLDB Endowment (PVLDB) 5(12), 2018–2019 (2012)
12. Hariri, B.B., Calvanese, D., De Giacomo, G., Deutsch, A., Montali, M.: Verification of relational data-centric dynamic systems with external services. In: Proc. Intl. Conf. on Principles of Database Systems (PODS), pp. 163–174 (2013)
13. Hull, R., et al.: Introducing the guard-stage-milestone approach for specifying business entity lifecycles. In: Bravetti, M., Bultan, T. (eds.) WS-FM 2010. LNCS, vol. 6551, pp. 1–24. Springer, Heidelberg (2011)
14. Hull, R., et al.: Business artifacts with guard-stage-milestone lifecycles: Managing artifact interactions with conditions and events. In: ACM Intl. Conf. on Distributed Event-based Systems, DEBS (2011)
15. Hull, R., Narendra, N.C., Nigam, A.: Facilitating workflow interoperation using artifact-centric hubs. In: Baresi, L., Chi, C.-H., Suzuki, J. (eds.) ICSOC-ServiceWave 2009. LNCS, vol. 5900, pp. 1–18. Springer, Heidelberg (2009)
16. Iroju, O., Soriyan, A., Gambo, I.: Ontology matching: An ultimate solution for semantic interoperability in healthcare. International Journal of Computer Applications 51(21), 7–14 (2012)
17. KAON2 Home Page (2005), http://kaon2.semanticweb.org/
18. Kiu, C.-C., Lee, C.-S.: Ontology mapping and merging through ontodna for learning object reusability. Educational Technology & Society 9(3), 27–42 (2006)
19. Kumaran, S., Nandi, P., Heath III, F.F. (T.), Bhaskaran, K., Das, R.: Adoc-oriented programming. In: SAINT, pp. 334–343 (2003)
20. Farrell, L., Lausen, H.: Semantic Annotations for WSDL and XML Schemas. W3C Recommendation (August 2007), http://www.w3.org/TR/sawsdl/
21. Lampe, U., Schulte, S., Siebenhaar, M., Schuller, D., Steinmetz, R.: Adaptive matchmaking for restful services based on hrests and microwsmo. In: Proceedings of the 5th International Workshop on Enhanced Web Service Technologies, WEWST 2010, pp. 10–17. ACM, New York (2010)
22. Limonad, L., Boaz, D., Hull, R., Vaculín, R., Heath, F.(T.): A generic business artifacts based authorization framework for cross-enterprise collaboration. In: SRII Global Conference, pp. 70–79 (2012)
23. Liu, R., Vaculín, R., Shan, Z., Nigam, A., Wu, F.: Business artifact-centric modeling for real-time performance monitoring. In: Rinderle-Ma, S., Toumani, F., Wolf, K. (eds.) BPM 2011. LNCS, vol. 6896, pp. 265–280. Springer, Heidelberg (2011)
24. Marin, M., Hull, R., Vaculín, R.: Data centric BPM and the emerging case management standard: A short survey. In: La Rosa, M., Soffer, P. (eds.) BPM 2012 Workshops. LNBIP, vol. 132, pp. 24–30. Springer, Heidelberg (2013)
25. Marte, A., Fuchs, C.H.: OMS - Ontology Mapping Store (2013), Available on Source Forge, http://sourceforge.net/projects/om-store/

26. Nigam, A., Caswell, N.S.: Business artifacts: An approach to operational specification. IBM Systems Journal 42(3), 428–445 (2003)
27. Pesic, M., Schonenberg, H., van der Aalst, W.M.P.: Declare: Full support for loosely-structured processes. In: IEEE Intl. Enterprise Distributed Object Computing Conference (EDOC), pp. 287–300 (2007)
28. Strosnider, J.K., Nandi, P., Kumaran, S., Ghosh, S., Arsanjani, A.: Model-driven Synthesis of SOA Solutions. IBM Systems Journal 47(3) (2008)
29. Sun, Y., Xu, W., Su, J.: Declarative choreographies for artifacts. In: Liu, C., Ludwig, H., Toumani, F., Yu, Q. (eds.) ICSOC 2012. LNCS, vol. 7636, pp. 420–434. Springer, Heidelberg (2012)
30. United Nations Economic Commission for Europe (UNECE). Introducing UN/EDIFACT (2013), http://www.unece.org/trade/untdid/welcome.html
31. Vaculín, R., Hull, R., Vukovic, M., Heath, T., Mills, N., Sun, Y.: Supporting collaborative decision processes. In: Intl. Conf. on Service Computing, SCC (2013)

QoS-Aware Cloud Service Composition
Using Time Series

Zhen Ye[1], Athman Bouguettaya[2], and Xiaofang Zhou[1]

[1] The University of Queensland, Australia
[2] Royal Melbourne Institute of Technology, Australia

Abstract. Cloud service composition is usually long term based and economically driven. We propose to use multi-dimensional Time Series to represent the economic models during composition. Cloud service composition problem is then modeled as a similarity search problem. Next, a novel correlation-based search algorithm is proposed. Finally, experiments and their results are presented to show the performance of the proposed composition approach.

1 Introduction

Cloud computing is increasingly becoming the technology of choice as the next-generation platform for conducting business [1]. Big companies such as Amazon, Microsoft, Google and IBM are already offering cloud computing solutions in the market. A fast increasing number of organizations are already outsourcing their business tasks to the cloud, instead of deploying their own local infrastructures [2]. A significant advantage of cloud computing is its economic benefits for both users and service providers.

Compared to traditional service composition, cloud service composition is usually long-term based and economically driven. Traditional quality-based composition techniques usually consider the qualities at the time of the composition [3]. For example, which composite service has the best performance at present? This is fundamentally different in cloud environments where the cloud service composition should last for a long period. For example, which composite cloud service performs best in the next few years, despite it may not be the best one at present? This paper presents a novel cloud service composition approach based on time series. Time series databases are prevalent in multiple research ares, e.g., multimedia, statistics etc. Many techniques [4], [5] have been proposed to effectively and efficiently analyze economic models in cloud computing [] [].

We identify four actors in the cloud environment (Fig. 1): *End Users, Composer, SaaS (Software as a Service) Providers* and *IaaS (Infrastructure as a Service) Providers*. Platform as a Service (PaaS) layer is omitted as we assume that it is included in the IaaS layer. *End Users* are usually large companies and organizations, e.g., universities, governments. The composer in this paper represents the proposed composition framework. SaaS providers supply SaaS [6] to end users. IaaS providers supply IaaS [6], i.e., CPU services, storage services, and network services, to SaaS providers and end users. The composer acts on

S. Basu et al. (Eds.): ICSOC 2013, LNCS 8274, pp. 9–22, 2013.

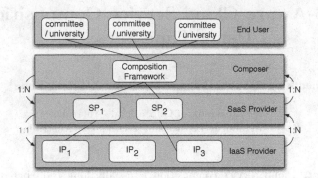

Fig. 1. Four actors in cloud computing

the behave of the end users to form composite services that contains services from multiple SaaS providers and IaaS providers (Fig. 1).

Similar to traditional service composition [7], cloud service composition is conducted in two steps. First, a composition schema is constructed for a composition request. Second, the optimal composition plan is selected. A composition plan is formed by choosing concrete cloud service providers for each abstract SaaS and abstract IaaS in the composition schema.

Our research focuses on the selection of composition plans based solely on non-functional (Quality-of-Service, or QoS) attributes [8]. On one hand, we model the requirements of end users as a set of time series. On the other hand, cloud service providers market their services (SaaS or IaaS) using a set of time series. Each time series represents the values of a corresponding QoS attribute over a long period. Hence, cloud service composition problem becomes a similarity search problem whose query is a set of desired time series.

Traditional techniques seldomly handle complex time series queries which require the correlation between the time series to be used during similarity matching. The correlation, however, are prevalent during service composition where each QoS attribute is correlated with several other QoS attributes. For example, considering that we will select the best composition plan by leveraging two QoS attributes, response time and cost. The cost of a cloud service may decrease during a period, while the response time of the cloud service is also decreasing. We can easily observe the correlations that exist between time series. If we process each time series independently, we will not be able to make use of the inherent correlations.

We refer to groups of time series with correlations as Time Series Groups (TSG). Given a query TSG object $Q = \{q_1, q_2, \ldots, q_l\}$, where l is the number of the time series in Q and each time series $q_i = \{(x_m, t_m)|m = 1, 2, \ldots, L_i\}$, where x_m is the value of the time series at time t_m, and a TSG set $D = \{TSG_1, TSG_2, \ldots, TSG_N\}$. The similarity search on TSG is to find the most similar TSGs from set D via a predefined function $dist(Q, TSC_i)$, where

$$result = argmin_{i=1,\ldots,N}(dist(Q, TSC_i)). \tag{1}$$

The main contributions of the paper include: (1) Cloud service composition problem is considered as a similarity search problem. Specifically, this paper proposes algorithms that leverages time series correlations to effectively and efficiently compute the distance between two TSGs. (2) We propose two data structures for Time Series Group processing, which leverage the principal components and the relations of time series. A key difference between TSG and existing time series similarity search is that the former requires the use of relations between time series. (3) Analytical experiments are presented to show the performance of the proposed approach. The empirical results show that the proposed approach is superior compared with other similarity search approaches.

The remainder of the paper is structured as follows: Related work are presented in section 2. Section 3 presents a use case for cloud service composition. Section 4 gives a detail analysis of the research challenges and then elaborates the proposed composition approach. Section 5 evaluates the proposed approaches and shows the experiment results. Section 6 concludes this paper and highlights some future work.

2 Related Work

Service composition is an active research topic in service-oriented computing [9]. During the last decade, many QoS-aware composition approaches are proposed. QoS-aware service composition problem is usually modelled as a Multiple Criteria Decision Making [3] problem. The most popular approaches include integer linear programming and genetic algorithms. An Integer Linear Program (ILP) consists of a set of variables, a set of linear constraints and a linear objective function. After having translated the composition problem into this formalism, specific solver software such as LPSolve [10] can be used. [11] and [12] use Genetic Algorithms (GA) for service composition. Individuals of the population correspond to different composition solutions, their genes to the abstract component services and the possible gene values to the available real services. While GAs do not guarantee to find the optimal solution, they can be more efficient than ILP-based methods (which have exponential worst-case time complexity). Most of the traditional Web service composition approaches are not well suited for cloud environment [12]. They usually consider the qualities at the time of the composition [9]. [8] adopts Nayesian Network and Influence diagram to model the economic models and solve the cloud service composition problem. However, they assume conditional probability relationship among multiple QoS attributes, which is not a general case in reality. This paper considers a general case where QoS attributes can be described using time series.

Existing work on time series query can be categorized into two categories, time series matching and pattern and correlation mining on multiple time series. In existing similarity search over time series databases, the time series is transformed from its original form into a more compact representation. The search algorithm leverages on two steps: dimensionality reduction [4], [13], [14], [15] and data representation in the transformed space. Various dimensionality reduction techniques have been proposed for time series data transformation. These includes: Discrete Fourier Transform (DFT), Singular Value Decomposition (SVD)

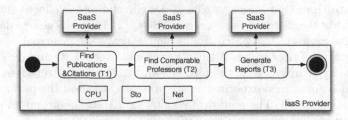

Fig. 2. Tenure application for University A

[13], Discrete Wavelet Transform (DWT)[14], and Piecewise Aggregate Approximation (PAA) [13]. Another approach for dimensionality reduction is to make use of time series segmentation [4].

Existing multiple time series research have focused on pattern mining and finding correlation between multiple time series, over patterns and observed values from group of individual time series. Papadimitriou et al. [16] proposed the SPIRIT system, which focuses on finding patterns, correlations and hidden variables in a large number of streams. SPIRIT performs incremental Principal Component Analysis (PCA) over stream data, and delivers results in real time. SPIRIT discovers the hidden variables among n input streams and automatically determines the number of hidden variables that will be used. The observed values of the hidden variables present the general pattern of multiple input series according to their distributions and correlations. These existing approaches cannot be easily extended for the TSG similarity search problem because of the lack of a clearly defined similarity measure. Most importantly, existing approaches are unable to deal with the relations that exist between the multiple time series.

3   Use Case

Let us consider a simple use case, university A requires a composite cloud service to aid the tenure process every year. Suppose the university outsources three main tasks to the clouds during 2012 and 2015. The aim of cloud service composition in this example is to find and select a set of component cloud services to form a tenure application. Specifically, the tenure application (Fig. 2) has three abstract SaaS. Tenure application will first search and find the publication and citation records of a candidate (task 1, T_1). It will then find the the publication and citation records of the comparable professors (task 2, T_2). Finally, the tenure application will generate the evaluation report (task 3, T_3). Besides these abstract SaaS, the composite tenure application also needs CPU, network and storage resources from IaaS providers. CPU services (denoted as CPU) are used to do computations on data. Storage services (denoted as Sto) are used to keep intermediate data. The whole tenure application should be as fair as and as transparent as possible. Therefore, all the input and output data, should be stored in case some appeals arise. Network services (denoted as Net)

are needed to transfer data between end users and the application, and between components in the composite application.

University A has different QoS requirements (e.g., the number of tenure cases that the composite service can process at once, the cost of the service and the reputation of the service) on the composite tenure application over a period of time. These preferences are presented through a set of time series data. Each time series denotes the requirement of the university on a specific QoS attribute. All the cloud service providers also advertise their services using time series with the same time frequency. Hence, there are multiple candidate composition plans, which are also represented as a set of time series data by aggregating all the component services together. The composition problem, therefore, becomes a query problem that aims to find the most similar sets of time series to meet the university's requirements.

4   Time Series Group Search Approach

There are two requirements when designing our composition approach. First, a time series representation is needed to describe and measure the general information extracted from a TSG. Second, the similarity search algorithm must be more scalable compared to other approaches, since cloud environment is more scalable than other existing platforms.

This section first presents the QoS model for cloud service composition. Two data structures, denoted as QA and QR are then introduced to represent time series during cloud service composition. The proposed composition approach is finally presented at the end of this section.

4.1   QoS Model

To differentiate composition plans during selection, their non-functional properties need to be considered. For this purpose, we adopt a QoS model that is applicable to all the SaaS and IaaS. Without loss of generality, we only consider the QoS attributes listed as follows. Although the adopted QoS models have a limited number of attributes, they are extensible and new QoS attributes can be added. We assume IaaS are homogeneous. One unit of IaaS, i.e., *CPU, network* or *storage*, possess the same resources.

Three QoS attributes are considered for component services and composite services: throughput, reputation, and cost.

- Throughput. Given an SaaS provider SP, the throughput of its SaaS $q_{sr}(SP)$ is the number of requests the SaaS provider is able to process per second. Given an IaaS provider IP, the service rate of its IaaS $\overrightarrow{q_{sr}(IP)} = [q_{sr}^{CPU}(IP), q_{sr}^{Net}(IP), q_{sr}^{Sto}(IP)]$ is a three-attribute vector, where $q_{sr}^{CPU}(IP)$ ($q_{sr}^{Net}(IP)$, $q_{sr}^{Sto}(IP)$) represents the number of CPU (network, storage) requests the IaaS provider is able to process per second.

- Reputation. Given an SaaS provider SP, the reputation $q_{rt}(SP)$ is a value between $(0, 1)$. Given an IaaS provider IP, the reputation of its IaaS $\overrightarrow{q_{rt}(IP)} = [q_{rt}^{CPU}(IP), q_{rt}^{Net}(IP), q_{rt}^{Sto}(IP)]$ is a three-attribute vector, where $q_{rt}^{CPU}(IP)$ $(q_{rt}^{Net}(IP), q_{rt}^{Sto}(IP))$ is the reputation for processing a computation (data transfer, storage) request.
- Cost. Given an SaaS provider, the execution cost $q_{cost}(SP)$ is the fee that a customer needs to pay for the SaaS. Given an IaaS provider IP, the cost for using IaaS is denoted as a three-attribute vector $\overrightarrow{q_{cost}(IP)} = [q_{cost}^{CPU}(IP), q_{cost}^{Net}(IP), q_{cost}^{Sto}(IP)]$, where $q_{cost}^{CPU}(IP)$, $q_{cost}^{Net}(IP)$ and $q_{cost}^{Sto}(IP)$ are the price for using CPU IaaS, unit network IaaS and unit storage IaaS correspondingly.

The quality criteria defined above are in the context of elementary cloud services. Aggregation functions are used to compute the QoS of the composite service.

- Throughput. The throughput of a composite service denotes the number of requests it serves per second. For an abstract composite service aCS, the throughput $q_{sr}(aCS)$ is the minimal service rate of the selected SaaS providers $q_{sr}(SP)$ and the IaaS provider $q_{sr}(IP)$.
- Reputation. The reputation $q_{rt}(aCS)$ of an abstract composite service aCS is computed by multiplying the selected SaaS providers and IaaS providers.
- Cost. The cost of an abstract service is the sum of execution cost of all the selected SaaS and IaaS.

4.2 QoS Attribute of TSG

One of the key challenges of performing TSG similarity search in cloud service composition is to efficiently match the QoS attribute (QA) of multiple time series in TSGs. Using a compact representation can avoid the need to perform pairwise comparisons of the time series, which is computationally expensive.

Principal Component Analysis (PCA) is commonly used in time series analysis [16] to reduce dimensionality, and to facilitate query retrieval. The essential idea in PCA is to transform a set of observed values in the high-dimensional vector space into a smaller new vector space. Given a data matrix X, and a transformation matrix W. Each column of X corresponds to a data vector in the original space. Each row of W corresponds to a transformation vector. The transformation vector transforms the data vectors from the original space to the value of certain principal components (PCs). The PCA transformation is given as: $Y = X \times W$. Y denotes the data matrix in the new vector space. In the new vector space, each dimension corresponds to the principal component of the original space. It is generated from the original dimensions based on the statistical distribution of the observed values.

We adopt PCA to produce QA, a compact representation of the patterns of multiple time series in a TSG. Each QA consists of one or several time series of the principal components extracted from the original TSG. Given a TSG, which consists of n time series $T_1, T_2, \ldots, T_n$, for each time series T_i, the observed value in time t_j is x_{t_j}. Assume the number of time slots is denoted as l, the TSG can also be represented as a $ln-$dimensional vector. We build a n-dimensional vector $X_j = (x_{1_j}, x_{2_j}, \ldots, x_{n_j})$ for each time slot. Each dimension refers to a time series in $T_1, T_2, \ldots, T_n$. We perform PCA transformation on these n-dimensional vectors to identify the first few principal components. In the implementation, we choose the first n' principal components as the QAs ($n' \leq n$). These n' PCs can capture the most dominant information of the original data, even if $n' \ll n$. We only consider these PCs and their associated observed values which have been transformed in PCA dimensions. The new observed values of time slot t_j on the dimensions of transformed PCA space are:

$$\overline{X_j} = X_j \times W = (X_j \times W_1, X_j \times W_2, \ldots, X_j \times W_n). \qquad (2)$$

where W_i is a n-dimensional transformation vector. The derived values in each time slot t_j in QA are the first n' principal components of X_j, which are the first n' dimensions of $\overline{X_j}$. The transformation matrix which transforms the origin vector space into first n' dimensions is: $W' = (W_1, W_2, \ldots, W_{n'})$. Hence, QA can be represented as:

$$QA = X \times W' = (X_1 \times W', X_2 \times W', \ldots, X_l \times W'), \qquad (3)$$

where l is the length of time series. The $l \times n'$ data matrix in this equation represents n' time series which are generalized form the multiple patterns of original n time series.

Comparing to Brute-Force method (mentioned in Sec. 5), which finds the best matches between every time series pair, QA is a more general feature and is easier to measure the similarity, though information will be lost by only reserving the first few principal components. The lost information can be compensated using QoS Relation (QR) which will be introduced in the next section.

4.3   QoS Relation for TSG

This section shows how we can generate relations among time series in a TSG. Relations between multiple time series can be complex. Similar to "Relation Vector" in [17], a QoS Relation (QR) of a TSG is a multidimensional vector, which can be used to describe the relations among multiple time series in a TSG. QR consists of a set of signatures, which are extracted from a relation matrix. The relation matrix is obtained based on the relation descriptors of every time series pair in TSG.

QR can be generated in mainly two steps:

- First, a relation descriptor is used to capture the intrinsic relationship for any two time series in a TSG.
- Second, PCA transformation is used to transform the high-dimensional relation descriptors into a smaller space.

The relations between T_m and T_n refer to the differences between the QoS values in the time series and the associated time slots. Hence, we introduce two basic relations defined by [17], i.e., variance in QoS values (VIQ) and variance in time (VIT). The VIQ is a high-dimensional vector, each dimension of which captures the difference between the sampled observed QoS values of T_m and T_n:

$$(|x_{m_{s1}} - x_{n_{s1}}|, |x_{m_{s2}} - x_{n_{s2}}|, \ldots, |x_{m_{sl}} - x_{n_{sl}}|), \tag{4}$$

where $x_{m_{si}}$ is the sampled QoS values of T_m, and $x_{n_{sj}}$ is the sampled QoS value of T_n. VIT is a descriptor of the relation between intervals of T_m and T_n denoted as a 4D vector $VIT(T_m, T_n)$ [17]:

$$VIT(T_m, T_n) = (t_{m1} - t_{n1}, t_{ml} - t_{nl}, t^3_{m,n}, t^4_{m,n}), \tag{5}$$

where t_{m1} and t_{n1} are the first time ticks of T_m and T_n, t_{ml} and t_{nl} are the last time ticks. $t^3_{m,n}$ and $t^4_{m,n}$ are used to describe the overlap status between two time series' interval. They are defined as:

$$t^3_{m,n} = \begin{cases} 0, m = n, \\ t_{m1} - t_{nl}, t_{m1} \geq t_{n1}, \\ -(t_{n1} - t_{ml}), t_{ml} < t_{n1}. \end{cases} \tag{6}$$

$$t^4_{m,n} = \begin{cases} 0, m = n, \\ t_{ml} - t_{n1}, t_{m1} \geq t_{n1}, \\ -(t_{nl} - t_{m1}), t_{ml} < t_{n1}. \end{cases} \tag{7}$$

In summary, the relation descriptor of T_m and T_n is the combination of two components, i.e., the differences between QoS values and intervals.

The relation descriptors of each time series pair in TSG are vectors in a high-dimensional vector space. Given a TSG object which has n time series $T_1, T_2, \ldots, T_n$, we can generate n^2 relation descriptors R_{ij} of each pair of time series T_i and T_j from the TSG object, where $R_{ij} = \{VIQ(T_i, T_j), VIT(T_i, T_j)\}$. Using these n^2 vectors, we perform PCA to find the Principal components according to the datas latent correlation and distribution on these dimensions. Set r as the dimensionality of each R_{ij}, and $r \times r$ transformation matrix W for PCA as $(W_1, W_2, \ldots, W_r)$, we reserve only first few PCs which contain the majority information. The number of PCs remained is denoted as r'. Thus, we obtain the transformed relation descriptors $\overline{R_{ij}}$

$$\overline{R_{ij}} = (R_{ij} \times W_1, R_{ij} \times W_2, \ldots, R_{ij} \times W_{r'}). \tag{8}$$

4.4   Similarity Search of Time Series Groups

Given two TSG objects which are represented by aforementioned features, e.g., $TSG_i = \{QA_i, QR_i\}$ and $TSG_j = \{QA_j, QR_j\}$, we define the distance function between two TSGs $dist(TSG_i, TSG_j)$ based on the similarity measure for QA, i.e., $DIS(QA_i, QA_j)$ and relation vector QR, i.e., $DIS(QR_i, QR_j)$. For simplicity of presentation, we deploy the euclidean Distance as the default distance function. The distance between two QAs can be calculated by the following equation:

$$DIS(QA_i, QA_j) = \sqrt{\sum (qc_i^k - qc_j^k)^2} \qquad (9)$$

where qc_i^k and qc_j^k are the values for the k principal components of TSG_i and TSG_j.

The distance between two QRs can be calculated:

$$DIS(QR_m, QR_n) = \sqrt{\sum (\overline{R_{ij}^m} - \overline{R_{ij}^n})^2} \qquad (10)$$

According to the distance functions defined on the two features, the overall distance between two TSG objects $dist(TSC_i, TSC_j)$ can be calculated by the geometric value of the two distances:

$$dist(TSC_i, TSC_j) = \sqrt{DIS(QA_i, QA_j) \times DIS(QR_i, QR_j)}. \qquad (11)$$

By using these two components for TSG similarity evaluation, we solve the two challenges of effectively evaluating relations and measuring the patterns of multiple time series in TSG; therefore, our approach can perform effectively and efficiently for similarity search in TSG databases.

5   Experiments and Results

We conduct a set of experiments to assess the performance of the proposed approach. We measure both the query effectiveness and the execution time for TSG retrieval. We compare our proposed approach named TSG with the Brute-Force approach, and the QA-only approach. QA-only approach is the same with the proposed approach in Sec.4 except that it only consider QAs when computing the distance between two TSGs. All experiments are conducted using Matlab. We run our experiments on a Macbook Pro with 2.2 GHz Intel Core i7 processor and 4G Ram under Mac OS X 10.8.3. Since there is no testbed available, we focus on evaluating the proposed approach using synthetic cloud services.

5.1   Brute-Force Approach

To show the performance of the proposed approach, we first present a Brute-Force approach for solving the TSG matching problem, which exhaustively compares the time series in TSGs. In such a Brute-Force approach for TSG similarity matching, the distances between all the QoS attributes in the query time series and the candidate plan's time series are computed. The maximum similarity (i.e., minimum distance) is then used to represent the similarity between two TSGs. Here, we computing the similarity between TSG_1 and TSG_2 by calculating the euclidean distances. The Brute-Force approach guarantees the minimum of

$$\sum_{T_i \in TSG_1 \wedge T_i' \in TSG_2} DIS(T_i, T_i'), \qquad (12)$$

where $T_i' \in TSG_2$ and T_i in TSG_1 are QoS attributes. In summary, by enumerating all pairs between the time series in two TSGs, we can calculate the minimum distance of Brute-Force approach by the following equation:

$$dist_{BF}(TSG_1, TSG_2) = min_k(\sum(DIS(T_m, T_n))), \qquad (13)$$

The Brute-Force TSG similarity matching approach is an exhaustive matching-based algorithm. The approach is very costly, as it requires an enumeration between all pairwise single time series. Meanwhile, this method can measure the patterns between time series in two TSGs well, but ignores the correlations of time series inside the TSG.

5.2 Data Description

To generate the synthetic data sets, we first randomly generate 5 time series. Each time series is denoted as $\{(QoS_i, t_i)|i = 1, 2, 3, \ldots, l\}$, where the length l is equal to 150. These five time series form the seed TSG. For each time series in the seed TSG, we add some normally distributed random noise to create another 199 TSGs. Using the 200 TSGs as seeds, we expand them to 200 TSG categories, each of which is with 80 TSGs. We produce variations of TSGs by adding small time warping (e.g., 5 percent of the series length), and some normally distributed random noise. Consequently, our synthetic data set contains 200 categories and each has 80 similar TSGs, i.e., the TSG database has 16,000 TSGs in total. We use the first 200 TSGs as the query set.

We generate two dataset to evaluate the proposed approach. Time series in *RAND* dataset are generated randomly in Matlab, while time series in *GAS* dataset are generated with Gaussian distribution. For each TSG in the query set, we search the similar TSG in the whole dataset using three approaches: TSG, QA-only and the brutal force approach. Each approach will return a sorted list of the most similar TSG to the query.

We use *recall* and *precision* to compare different algorithms. We denote the first 100 results returned by the brutal force approach as the *relevant results*. Hence, the precision and the recall can be calculated using:

$$precision = \frac{\{relevant\} \bigcap \{retrieved\}}{\{retrieved\}} \qquad (14)$$

$$recall = \frac{\{relevant\} \bigcap \{retrieved\}}{\{relevant\}} \qquad (15)$$

5.3 Performance

In the first experiment, we investigate two important parameters of the proposed TSG retrieval method. The first parameter is the number of PCs reserved in QA feature generation. We extract QA feature by using first n' PCs of multiple time series. The second parameter is the reduced dimensionality of Relation

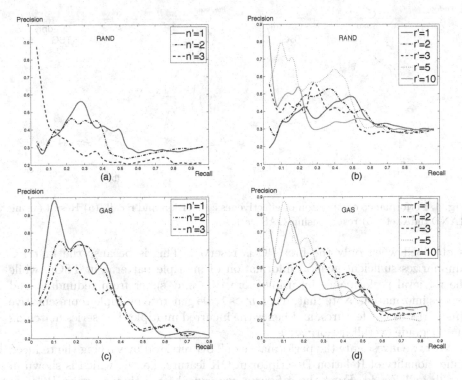

Fig. 3. Performance on parameter tuning. (a) varying the number of PCs in QA using RAND data set. (b) Varying the number of PCs in QR using RAND data set. (c) varying the number of PCs in QA using GAS data set. (b) Varying the number of PCs in QR using GAS data set.

Descriptor in QR , i.e., r', which is used to capture the relations among the time series in a TSG.

We first evaluate the effect of QA feature on TSG retrieval performance by varying the number of PCs n'. As the maximum number of PCs in QA generation is the number of time series in TSG, we conduct the experiments by varying n' from 1 to 5. The results of precision/recall for TSG retrieval are shown in Fig. 3. Each line in the graph represents the performance of a corresponding approach. Each node on a line represents the precision and the recall when the first num ($num \geq 100$) results are returned. For example, in the first graph in Fig. 3, the first node on the green line represents the precision and the recall when the first 100 results are returned.

According to Fig. 3a and Fig. 3a, the TSG approach performs best when $n' = 1$, although when it comes to RAND data set, $n' = 3$ performs better than $n' = 1$ when the recall is less than 0.16. The approach performs similarly when the recall is high. This can be explained by that when almost all the relevant results are retrieved, the precision tends to be the same. To sum up, the best performance

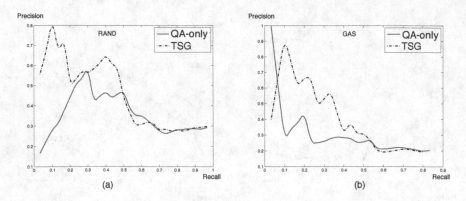

Fig. 4. Performance comparison of effectiveness: precision and recall. (a) Results using RAND data set. (b) results using GAS data set.

is obtained when only the first PC is reserved. This is because the first PC summarizes sufficient general information of multiple patterns in TSGs, while the retrieval performance by using more PCs may suffer from redundant and useless information. Note that, when $n' > 1$, we generate multiple representative time series as QA features, and hence the incurred multiple time series matching may degrade overall performance.

Next, we investigate the performance of TSG retrieval by varying the reduced dimensionality of Relation Descriptor in QR feature, i.e., r', which is shown in Fig.3b and Fig.3d. From these figures, we can observe that as more PCs are used, the performance is improved. This is because more information is included in the relation descriptor of the QR. Notice that when the recall is higher, the approach performs more similarly. Therefore, in the following experiments, we fix the two parameters for performance comparison, i.e., $n' = 1$ and $r' = 5$.

5.4   Comparison with Other Methods

In this experiment, we compare the retrieval performance of our approach with the the QA-only method. As we can see from Fig. 4, the proposed TSG approach performs similarly as the QA-only approach when the recall is bigger than 0.5 for RAND data set and 0.55 for GAS data set. This is because that when recall gets larger, more relevant results are retrieved. However, we can still observe that when the recall is small, i.e., retrieving a few most similar results, which is more common in the similarity query area, TSG still preforms better than QA-only approach. This is because the compact representation of multiple time series in QA-only approach, can only capture the limited pattern information, while ignore the intrinsic relations between the multiple time series in the TSG, which are more valuable to distinguish different TSCs. QA feature matches the similarity of group of time series by generalizing their characteristic patterns, and the QR information can capture the natural relations among time series in TSGs. The TSG approach can take both factors into effect for TSG retrieval, and hence improve the retrieval effectiveness in TSG databases.

5.5   Scalability and Robustness

In this section, we investigate the scalability and robustness of the proposed approaches. We first evaluate the time efficiency for the three approaches in terms of the scalability of the database size. We vary the size of TSG data set by utilizing 50, 100, 150, 200 categories of TSGs, which results in the data size from 4,000 to 16,000 TSGs.

Fig. 5 shows the average time cost of these different approaches for one TSG retrieval. We can observe that QA-only approach and the proposed approach are comparable and perform much better than the Brute-Force method. Our TSG approach explores both QA and QR for similarity computation, and the extra computation on QR feature is needed compared with QA-only approach. While the Brute-Force algorithm performs badly by two orders of magnitude. This is because the Brute-Force algorithm needs to calculate all the matches for each time series pair in the group.

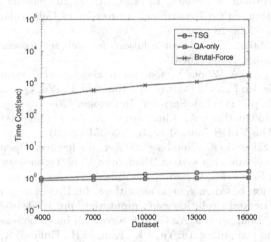

Fig. 5. Time efficiency of different approaches

6   Conclusion

This paper proposes a cloud service composition approach to aid end users selecting and composing SaaS providers and IaaS providers in the cloud environment. Compared to traditional service composition framework in SOC, the proposed approach considers service composition from a long-term perspective. Cloud economic models for both end users and cloud service providers are leveraged during the composition. Specially, we propose to use time series to represent the economic models. Cloud service composition is then modeled as a similarity search problem in the multiple time series database. We use two structure QoS attribute and QoS relation to further improve the effectiveness and the efficiency of the similarity search approach.

References

1. Motahari-Nezhad, H., Stephenson, B., Singhal, S.: Outsourcing business to cloud computing services: Opportunities and challenges. IEEE Internet Computing (2009)
2. Youseff, L., Butrico, M., Da Silva, D.: Toward a unified ontology of cloud computing. In: Grid Computing Environments Workshop (2009)
3. Zeng, L., Benatallah, B., Ngu, A., Dumas, M., Kalagnanam, J., Chang, H.: QoS-aware middleware for web services composition. IEEE Transactions on Software Engineering 30(5), 311–327 (2004)
4. Keogh, E., Chu, S., Hart, D., Pazzani, M.: Segmenting time series: A survey and novel approach. Data Mining in Time Series Databases 57, 1–22 (2004)
5. Bashir, F.I., Khokhar, A.A., Schonfeld, D.: Real-time motion trajectory-based indexing and retrieval of video sequences. IEEE Transactions on Multimedia 9(1), 58–65 (2007)
6. Armbrust, M., Fox, A., Griffith, R., Joseph, A., Katz, R., Konwinski, A., Lee, G., Patterson, D., Rabkin, A., Stoica, I., et al.: Above the clouds: A berkeley view of cloud computing. EECS Department, University of California, Berkeley, Tech. Rep. UCB/EECS-2009-28 (2009)
7. Milanovic, N., Malek, M.: Current solutions for web service composition. IEEE Internet Computing, 51–59 (2004)
8. Ye, Z., Bouguettaya, A., Zhou, X.: QoS-aware cloud service composition based on economic models. In: Liu, C., Ludwig, H., Toumani, F., Yu, Q. (eds.) ICSOC 2012. LNCS, vol. 7636, pp. 111–126. Springer, Heidelberg (2012)
9. Medjahed, B., Bouguettaya, A., Elmagarmid, A.: Composing web services on the semantic web. The VLDB Journal 12(4), 333–351 (2003)
10. Berkelaar, M., Eikland, K., Notebaert, P., et al.: lpsolve: Open source (mixed-integer) linear programming system. Eindhoven U. of Technology (2004)
11. Canfora, G., Di Penta, M., Esposito, R., Villani, M.: An approach for QoS-aware service composition based on genetic algorithms. In: Proceedings of the 2005 Conference on Genetic and Evolutionary Computation, pp. 1069–1075 (2005)
12. Ye, Z., Zhou, X., Bouguettaya, A.: Genetic algorithm based qoS-aware service compositions in cloud computing. In: Yu, J.X., Kim, M.H., Unland, R. (eds.) DASFAA 2011, Part II. LNCS, vol. 6588, pp. 321–334. Springer, Heidelberg (2011)
13. Keogh, E., Chakrabarti, K., Pazzani, M., Mehrotra, S.: Dimensionality reduction for fast similarity search in large time series databases. Knowledge and Information Systems 3(3), 263–286 (2001)
14. Kahveci, T., Singh, A.: Variable length queries for time series data. In: Proceedings of the 17th International Conference on Data Engineering, pp. 273–282. IEEE (2001)
15. Wu, Y.-L., Agrawal, D., El Abbadi, A.: A comparison of dft and dwt based similarity search in time-series databases. In: Proceedings of the Ninth International Conference on Information and Knowledge Management, pp. 488–495. ACM (2000)
16. Papadimitriou, S., Sun, J., Faloutsos, C.: Streaming pattern discovery in multiple time-series. In: Proceedings of the 31st International Conference on Very Large Data Bases, pp. 697–708. VLDB Endowment (2005)
17. Cui, B., Zhao, Z., Tok, W.H.: A framework for similarity search of time series cliques with natural relations. IEEE Transactions on Knowledge and Data Engineering 24(3), 385–398 (2012)

QoS Analysis in Heterogeneous Choreography Interactions

Ajay Kattepur, Nikolaos Georgantas, and Valérie Issarny*

Equipe ARLES, Inria Paris-Rocquencourt, France
firstname.lastname@inria.fr

Abstract. With an increasing number of services and devices interacting in a decentralized manner, *choreographies* are an active area of investigation. The heterogeneous nature of interacting systems leads to choreographies that may not only include conventional services, but also sensor-actuator networks, databases and service feeds. Their middleware behavior within choreographies is captured through abstract interaction paradigms such as *client-service*, *publish-subscribe* and *tuple space*. In this paper, we study these heterogeneous interaction paradigms, connected through an *eXtensible Service Bus* proposed in the *CHOReOS* project. As the functioning of such choreographies is dependent on the Quality of Service (QoS) performance of participating entities, an intricate analysis of interaction paradigms and their effect on QoS metrics is needed. We study the composition of QoS metrics in heterogeneous choreographies, and the subsequent tradeoffs. This produces interesting insights such as selection of a particular system and its middleware during design time or end-to-end QoS expectation/guarantees during runtime. Non-parametric hypothesis tests are applied to systems, where QoS dependent services may be replaced at runtime to prevent deterioration in performance.

Keywords: Heterogeneous Choreographies, Quality of Service, Interaction Paradigms, Middleware Connectors.

1 Introduction

Choreographies, unlike centrally controlled orchestrations, involve a decentralized service composition framework where only the participants' functionality and associated message passing are described [1]. Service Oriented Architectures (SOA) allow choreography components to interact via standard interfaces, with the enterprise service bus (ESB) [3] providing a common middleware protocol to convey the messaging interactions. However, these are principally based on the *client-service* interaction paradigm, as, for instance, with RESTful services [20].

Heterogeneous choreographies that involve conventional services, sensor networks and data feeds, such as those seen in the *Internet of Things* [12], require

* This work has been partially supported by the European Union's 7th Framework Programme FP7/ 2007-2013 under grant agreement number 257178 (project CHOReOS, http://www.choreos.eu).

S. Basu et al. (Eds.): ICSOC 2013, LNCS 8274, pp. 23–38, 2013.

additional paradigms to ensure interoperability. Heterogeneous applications are handled at the middleware level with varied interactions, data structures and communication protocols made interoperable. In particular, platforms such as REST [20] based *client-service* interactions, *publish-subscribe* based Java Messaging Service [19] or JavaSpaces [9] for *tuple space* are made interoperable through *middleware protocol converters*.

Studies that characterize the Quality of Service (QoS) in web services orchestrations have conventionally been done at the application level; heterogeneous choreographies consisting of services and sensor networks require further QoS analysis of paradigms, unless they can rely on QoS aware middleware [18]. An intricate analysis of QoS at the abstract level of interaction paradigms, in addition to the application level, would enable analysis of heterogeneous choreographies.

In this paper, we use the *eXtensible Service Bus (XSB)* proposed by the *CHOReOS* project [4,10] in order to deal with the heterogeneous aspects of choreographies. The common protocol of XSB preserves the interaction paradigms of the individual components, while still allowing interoperability. It supports interoperability among the three aforementioned, widely used, middleware paradigms: *client-service*, *publish-subscribe* and *tuple space*.

We enhance the middleware paradigms that are employed inside heterogeneous choreographies with QoS composition frameworks. While our previous work [15] studies the effect of choreography topology on the QoS, by fine-grained analysis of message interactions, we evaluate the performance of choreography participants in relation to heterogeneous paradigms. This methodology enables: 1) Design-time selection of interaction paradigms to match required functional and QoS goals, and 2) Runtime analysis of composed choreographies to prevent deterioration of end-to-end QoS of participants. Interesting facets include the use of non-parametric Kolmogorov-Smirnov hypothesis testing to replace an interaction paradigm with another, when abstracted with a particular QoS metric.

The rest of the paper is organized as follows. An overview of heterogeneous interaction paradigms and XSB is provided in Section 2. The QoS domains, metrics and algebra for composition are studied in Section 3. The methodology of measuring and propagating QoS increments across various domains are analyzed in Section 4. The results of our analysis through experiments are presented in Section 5, which includes an analysis of tradeoffs and interaction substitution. This is followed by related work and conclusions in Sections 6 and 7, respectively.

2   Interconnecting Heterogeneous Interaction Paradigms

In this section, we briefly describe the three interaction paradigms that may be abstractly applied within our QoS analysis framework. The functional semantics of these paradigms are abstracted into a set of corresponding *middleware connectors* proposed by the *CHOReOS* project. After that, we provide an overview of the *eXtensible Service Bus (XSB) connector*, which ensures interoperability across these connectors and the represented paradigms.

Table 1. APIs of Interaction Paradigms

Interaction	Primitives	Arguments
Client-Service	send	destination, operation, message
	receive_sync	↑source, ↑operation, ↑message, timeout
	receive_async	source, operation, ↑callback(source, operation, message), ↑handle
	end_receive_async	handle
	invoke_sync	destination, operation, in_msg, ↑out_msg, timeout
	invoke_async	destination, operation, in_msg, ↑callback(out_msg), ↑handle
Publish-Subscribe	publish	broker, filter, event, lease
	subscribe	broker, ↑filter, ↑handle
	get_next	handle, ↑event, timeout
	listen	handle, ↑callback(event)
	end_listen	handle
	unsubscribe	handle
Tuple Space	out	tspace, extent, template, tuple, lease
	take	tspace, extent, template, policy, ↑tuple, timeout
	read	tspace, extent, template, policy, ↑tuple, timeout
	register	tspace, extent, template, ↑callback(), ↑handle
	unregister	handle

2.1 Interaction Paradigm Connectors

In order to let choreographies include services (typically, client-service interactions), service feeds (publish-subscribe), and sensor-actuator networks (shared tuple spaces), it is a requirement to allow heterogeneity. We briefly review in the following the relevant interaction paradigms [10], and discuss the Application Programming Interfaces (APIs) of corresponding connectors [4]. These APIs are depicted in Table 1. Their primitives and arguments are provided, with ↑ representing an out or in-out return argument of a primitive.

- *Client-Service (CS)* - Commonly used paradigm for web services. The client may send a message with send; the receiving service blocks further execution until synchronization or timeout, with a receive_sync. Alternatively, asynchronous reception can be set up with receive_async; then, a callback is triggered by the middleware when a message arrives. The two-way request-response invocation procedure is further captured by the invoke_sync and invoke_async primitives. CS represents tight *space coupling*, with the client and service having knowledge of each other. There is also tight *time coupling*, with service availability being crucial for successful message passing.
- *Publish-Subscribe (PS)* - Commonly used paradigm for content broadcasting/feeds. Multiple peers interact using an intermediate *broker* service. Publishers publish events that may be forwarded to peers via the broker until a lease period. Filtering (filter) of messages may be done with respect to subscriptions (subscribe) of the peers. Besides synchronous reception (get_next with timeout) of an event, asynchronous reception of multiple events is procured via listen and callback. PS allows *space decoupling*, as the peers need not know each other. Additionally, *time decoupling* is possible, with the disconnected peers receiving updates synchronously or asynchronously when reconnected to the broker.
- *Tuple Space (TS)* - Commonly used for shared data with multiple read/write users. Peers interact with a *data space*, with participants having write (out),

read and data removal (**take**) access. The peers can retrieve data whose value matches a **tuple** pattern (**template**), either synchronously with a **timeout** or asynchronously via **register** and **callback**. A peer may connect to the space at any time and procure data before the **lease** period. TS enables both space and time decoupling between interacting peers.

2.2 eXtensible Service Bus (XSB)

CHOReOS [4] uses the following abstractions to deal with large scale choreographies that connect heterogeneous participants:

- *Components*: The heterogeneity of services and devices encountered are modeled as *service interface abstractions*, which represent groups of alternative services that provide similar functionalities through varied interfaces.
- *Connectors*:This definition relates to the introduction of a new multi-paradigm *eXtensible Service Bus (XSB) connector*, which allows components to interoperate even if they are based on heterogeneous interaction paradigms. XSB extends the conventional ESB system integration paradigm [10].
- *Coordination Delegates*: These are used to enforce the realizability of choreographies despite the autonomy of the composed services. They ensure that the choreography specifications, such as message ordering integrity, are adhered to by the participating entities.

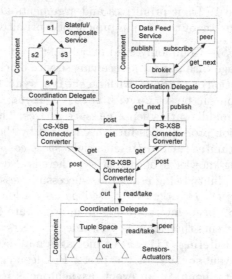

Fig. 1. *CHOReOS* Choreography Model

The generic representation of the *CHOReOS* model is shown in Fig. 1, with services/devices represented by *components* abstracting their functional behavior. At the choreography level, the *coordination delegates* wrap such services and adapt their roles to message passing specifications. The *XSB connector* ensures

Table 2. XSB connector API

Primitives	Arguments
post	scope, data
get_sync	↑scope, ↑data, timeout
get_async	scope, ↑callback(scope, data), ↑handle
end_get_async	handle
post_get_sync	scope, in_data, ↑out_data, timeout
post_get_async	scope, in_data, ↑callback(out_data), ↑handle

interoperability across a host of middleware protocols (following the CS, PS, TS paradigms). Note that there are multiple types of components that may participate: *Atomic/Composite Services* (CS requests-responses); *Data Feed Services* (they publish PS events, which are then passed to subscribers); *Sensor Actuator Networks* (TS-based interaction).

The semantics of the XSB connector is elicited as the *greatest common denominator* of the semantics of the CS, PS and TS connectors. As the latter semantics are incompatible in certain aspects, some enforcement by the applications employing the heterogeneous connectors may be necessary. For example, the two-way, time-coupled, CS interaction has no equivalent in the PS and TS paradigms. In this case, the PS and TS applications interacting with a CS application will have to complement the semantics of their underlying connectors with the lacking behavior (e.g., ensure that a PS peer receiving a published event will respond by publishing a correlated event that will be received by the initial publishing peer). Hence, the XSB connector can abstractly represent any of the three CS, PS and TS connectors. The XSB API is depicted in Table 2. It employs primitives such as **post** and **get** to abstract CS (**send, receive**), PS (**publish, get_next**), and TS (**out, take/read**) interactions. The **data** element can represent a CS **message**, PS **event** or TS **tuple**. The **scope** argument is used to unify space coupling (addressing mechanisms) across CS, PS and TS. Two-way interaction is enabled with the **post-get** primitive. Additionally, XSB is the *common bus protocol* employed for the interconnection of CS, PS and TS systems, as seen in Fig. 1. Finally, XSB represents also the *end-to-end interaction protocol* among such interconnected systems.

3   Modeling Quality of Service

While conventional middleware connectors focus on heterogeneity and functional interoperability, choreographies include additional non-functional metrics during design/runtime. This specifically involves analysis of constraints on QoS performance of individual participants (at the application/middleware level) and their side-effects on choreography enaction. QoS metrics being probabilistic and multi-dimensional, accurate analysis of increments and composition rules are crucial. In this section, the QoS domains that are of interest for interactions and the corresponding algebra for their composition are analyzed.

3.1   QoS Domains

We review the basic domains of QoS that require analysis for heterogeneous choreography interactions. We identify three basic domains [6]:

- δ: *Timeliness* incorporates aspects such as latency and reliable message delivery. For the case of client-service interactions, timeliness concerns one-way message or two-way request-response latency. In case of publish-subscribe, the latency between publication to a broker and subsequent coupled or decoupled delivery to peers is examined. With tuple space, the latency between writing to a tuple and coupled or decoupled access to the data is analyzed.
- S: *Security/Data Integrity* incorporates the trustworthiness of the interaction paradigms with respect to the confidentiality of information. This especially holds in publish-subscribe systems, where there is an intermediate broker, or tuple spaces, where there is an intermediate space and multiple peers have access to the same data. For example, a peer in the tuple space may remove and modify the data before they are procured by the other peers.
- λ: *Resource Efficiency* incorporates multiple aspects, such as efficiency in bandwidth usage and protocol message passing. In the case of publish-subscribe, for instance, the additional resources needed for subscription messages are to be included. Generally, this may be traded off with timeliness: greater bandwidth usage/active sessions help in timely delivery of messages. Analysis of these tradeoffs will help understand the pros and cons of a particular interaction paradigm.

3.2   QoS Algebra

In order to aggregate metrics available from heterogeneous interactions, we make use of an algebraic framework as introduced in [21]. This can handle random variables drawn from a distribution associated with a lattice domain. A *QoS metric* q is a tuple:

$$q = (\mathbb{D}, \leq, \oplus, \bigwedge, \bigvee) \tag{1}$$

1. $(\mathbb{D}, \leq)$ is a QoS domain with a corresponding partially ordered set of QoS values.
2. $\oplus : \mathbb{D} \times \mathbb{D} \to \mathbb{D}$ defines how QoS gets incremented by each new *action* or *operation*, like sending a message or receiving an event. It satisfies the following conditions:
    - $\oplus$ possesses a *neutral element* q_0 satisfying $\forall q \in \mathbb{D} \Rightarrow q \oplus q_0 = q_0 \oplus q = q$.
    - $\oplus$ is *monotonic*: $q_1 \leq q_1'$ and $q_2 \leq q_2'$ imply $(q_1 \oplus q_2) \leq (q_1' \oplus q_2')$.
3. $(\bigwedge, \bigvee)$ represent the lower and upper lattice, meaning that any $q \subseteq \mathbb{D}$ has a unique greatest lower, least upper bound $(\bigwedge_q, \bigvee_q)$. When taking the *best* QoS with respect to the ordering $\leq$, we take the lowest QoS value, with $\bigwedge$. When synchronizing (for instance, with fork-joins), the operator $\bigvee$ amounts to taking the *worst* QoS as per the ordering $\leq$.

Table 3. Basic classes of QoS domains

QoS Metric	$\mathbb{D}$	$\leq$	$\oplus$	$\bigwedge$	$\bigvee$
δ: Timeliness	$\mathbb{R}_+$	$<$	$+$	min	max
$\mathcal{S}$: Security/Data Integrity	finite set $\mathbf{Q}$	$>$	$\bigvee$	max	min
λ: Resource Efficiency	finite set $\mathbf{Q}$	$<$	$+$	min	max

Basic classes of QoS domains are displayed in Table 3 and composed according to rules specified in Eq. 1. The use of this algebraic framework allows us to reason, in an abstract way, about the behavior of interaction paradigms and their effect on choreography performance. The framework may be invoked by any choreography description language to incorporate QoS composition. It specifies calculation of the QoS increments via the associated algebra with domains $\mathbb{D}$, partial order $\leq$, and operations $(\oplus, \bigvee, \bigwedge)$. Note that the algebra is "general" enough to incorporate multiple units for each domain. For metric $\mathcal{S}$, the domain $\mathbf{Q}$ can be subjective to scaled preferences such as $\{low, medium, high\}$. The operation $\oplus$ is treated as $\bigvee$, modeling instances where "high" security data is passed to a "low" security service.

4 QoS Analysis of Interactions

In order to upgrade choreography interactions with QoS assessment, we equip every *atomic transaction* $\mathcal{T}$ in a client-service, publish-subscribe, or tuple space interaction with a QoS increment; $\mathcal{T}$ represents an end-to-end interaction enabling sending and receiving of data. From Fig. 1, $\mathcal{T}$ includes end-to-end data transfer between components enabled by the XSB connectors. This produces a tuple of $(\mathcal{T}, q)$ that may be propagated along the choreography. As the choreography does not have a centralized QoS control mechanism, this propagation of tuples can be combined with the algebraic operators to aggregate these increments. As the QoS values are random variables, the collected increments may be used either at *design time* (using statistical data) or for *run-time* monitoring.

4.1 QoS Model for Generic XSB Transactions

The XSB connector can represent end-to-end transactions for any one of the CS, PS, TS connectors. One-way interaction can be abstracted as follows: a sender can **post** *data* – representing a *message, event* or *tuple* – with a validity period **lease**; this is procured (using **get**) within the **timeout** period at the receiver side. The peers initiate their actions independently.

Model for Timeliness. Fig. 2 depicts an one-way XSB transaction as a correlation in time between a **post** action and a **get** action. The **post** and **get** operations are asynchronous and have individual time-stamps. The **post** operation is initiated at t_{post_0}. At t_{med}, the posted data arrive at the intermediary *medium*; we introduce this notion to represent the broker/data space in the case

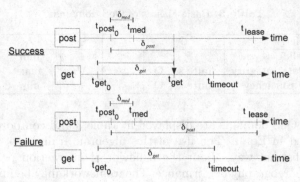

Fig. 2. Analysis of post and get δ increments for success and failure

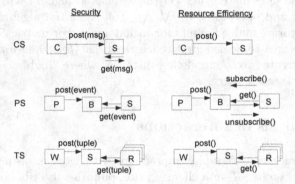

Fig. 3. Analysis of post and get $\mathcal{S}$ and λ increments for success and failure

of PS/TS, or the remote CS middleware entity. A timer is initiated at t_{med}, constraining the data availability to the lease period t_{lease}. Note that the lease period may be set to 0, as in the case of CS messages. Similarly at the receiver side, the get operation is initiated at t_{get_0}, together with a timer controlling the timeout period $t_{timeout}$. If get returns before the timeout period with valid data (not exceeding the lease), then the transaction is successful. We consider this instance also as the end of the post operation. Hence, if the transaction is successful, the overall QoS increment is:

$$\delta = \bigvee(\delta_{post}, \ \delta_{get}) \tag{2}$$

where δ_{post} and δ_{get} represent the durations of the two corresponding actions. In the case of failure, there is no overlapping in time between the two actions. In other words, only one of them takes place, and goes up to its maximum duration, i.e., δ_{med} + lease for post or timeout for get, while the other's duration is 0. Hence, the QoS output is once again as in Eq. 2. Finally, we note that, while we present the synchronous data reception case, the case with asynchronous get and callbacks follows similar timeliness composition models.

Model for Security/Data Quality. In order to model the data security level associated with each transaction, we equip the *data-carrying* post and get operations, depicted in Fig. 3, with a security level. Note that the post operation here refers to the interaction between the sender and what we called above the *medium*, i.e., the PS broker, TS data space, or remote CS middleware entity. Locally executed actions, such as get(msg) in the case of CS schemes, come equipped with good security levels. In case of TS schemes, as there is a shared channel between peers (unlike the exclusive channel of CS, PS), the security levels are worse than, for example, PS. For a successful transaction, the supremum of the security levels linked with the actions are taken, which means the worst security level among the supported ones:

$$\mathcal{S} = \bigvee (\mathcal{S}_{post}, \mathcal{S}_{get}) \tag{3}$$

In the case of failure, Eq. 3 still holds, with the operation that did not take place carrying a null security level. Finally, for asynchronous data reception, the security level composition is similar to the synchronous case presented here.

Model for Resource Efficiency. When measuring resource efficiency, we include the subset of all *networked* primitives related to the post and get operations, as in Fig. 3. In the case of PS, for instance, the subscription level primitives are taken into account. Note that we only consider synchronous data reception in our evaluation; for asynchronous callbacks, resource efficiency can be evaluated in a similar fashion. In case of success, the resultant resource efficiency is:

$$\lambda = \lambda_{post} \oplus \lambda_{get} \tag{4}$$

In case of failure, Eq. 4 still holds, with the missing operation contributing a null value to the metric.

4.2   Upgrading the API

We append the API arguments of Table 2 with *QoS parameters* that may be either self-measured by the peers or aggregated through a third party service. The QoS increments and composition are presented in Table 4. The post operation is given an initial QoS value q_post. This is, for the example of timeliness, the timestamp t_{post_0} (see Fig. 2), which is then used at the receiver to calculate the final returned output QoS increment. For a successful get_sync, the value specified in Eq. 2 is returned with q_get_sync. In the case of failure, the resulting timeliness value can be measured either by the receiver (timeout) or by a probe installed at the medium (δ_{med} + lease).

4.3   Model for QoS Propagation

The QoS model for generic XSB transactions and the related API introduced in Sections 4.1 and 4.2 can be applied for measuring QoS in heterogeneous choreographies where CS, PS and TS systems are interconnected via an XSB bus (see Fig. 1). In particular, the model and API introduced for XSB can be easily transcribed to the corresponding primitives and transactions of CS, PS and TS. Additionally, they can be used directly for the transactions performed on the

Table 4. Extending the XSB API for QoS Analysis

Primitives	Arguments
post	scope, data, q_post
get_sync	↑scope, ↑data, timeout, ↑q_get_sync
get_async	scope, ↑callback(scope, data), ↑handle, ↑q_get_async
end_get_async	handle, q_end_get_async
post_get_sync	scope, in_data, q_post, ↑out_data, timeout, ↑q_post_get_sync
post_get_async	scope, in_data, q_post, ↑callback(out_data), ↑handle, ↑q_post_get_async

XSB bus interconnecting heterogeneous systems. For multiple sequential choreography transactions, QoS increments can be propagated along with the transaction data and be passed from one transaction to the following one. Hence, QoS values can be calculated, propagated and aggregated along end-to-end choreography links, such as the ones depicted in Fig. 1. For example, in the case of timeliness for an one-way CS-XSB-PS transaction, we need to aggregate the three involved transactions:

$$\delta = \bigvee(\delta_{send}, \ \delta_{receive}) \oplus \bigvee(\delta_{post}, \ \delta_{get}) \oplus \bigvee(\delta_{publish}, \ \delta_{getnext}) \qquad (5)$$

In a similar fashion, for timeliness or other QoS metrics, QoS increments can be composed for both one-way and two-way interaction.

5   Results: QoS in Choreography Interactions

Choreographies involve heterogeneous interactions between services, things (sensors/actuators), computational entities and human participants. The use of our QoS analysis enables the following:

1. *Bottom-up Choreography Designs*: where the interactions are fixed but the choreography enaction and the expected QoS can be modified. The composition models take into account the nature of the interaction and their effect on the composed QoS. This is primarily done at *design-time* with previously collected statistics.
2. *Top-down Choreography Designs*: fixed choreography specifications that may be implemented by varied interaction paradigms. At *runtime*, similar functionality may be replicated by services/things in a registry – leading to late binding. Focusing on QoS, we study the possibility of replacing an interaction with another to prevent deterioration of output QoS.

For example, an improvement in performance δ by the interactions is traded off with deteriorating λ. Thus, if cost of bandwidth is to be taken into consideration, a choice can be made at design time to select a particular interaction paradigm over another. This involves discovering services that are implemented with specific interaction paradigms. In case this is not exposed, the worst case performance for each domain must be expected at design time. At runtime, if re-configuration [15] or replacement/late-binding occurs, changes that may be expected through varied interaction paradigms may be evaluated. For instance, reduced $\mathcal{S}$ may be traded off with improvements in δ.

5.1 Comparison of Tradeoffs

To compare the effect of CS/PS/TS paradigms on QoS metrics such as timeliness, security and message efficiency, simulations were performed according to the models provided in Section 4.1. As any particular implementation is affected by the network load, middleware and individual applications' QoS increments, we assume some general characteristics in our simulations. The interactions are assumed to follow tight space-time coupling for CS/PS/TS to prevent failed transactions (even though our analysis in Section 4.1 can handle this). The details for the specific interactions are:

- *Client-Service* - At (t_{post_0}), every client posts a message to a single server. Two measurements are made: the QoS increments associated with one-way post-get messages; the QoS increments with round-trip two-way request-response invocations. CS assumes tight space-time coupling and that the server is available and connected to the client. The response get(msg) is linked with the end-to-end QoS increments.
- *Publish Subscribe* - At (t_{post_0}), a publication to a broker is initiated, which is then forwarded to the peers. We assume that the broker is efficient and that it forwards the messages to all subscribed peers synchronously (get_next). The broker intermediary adds some latency δ_{broker} and has some effect on the security level S_{broker}. The subscription level messages subscribe, unsubscribe are considered during message efficiency calculations. While PS schemes typically allow only one-way publisher to subscriber messaging, to compare with the two-way CS case, we assume that the applications may behave as a publisher+subscriber for the two-way interaction.
- *Tuple Space* - At (t_{post_0}), data is written to a tuple, which may be read by peers. Synchronous write-read scenarios are studied, with the data space being efficient in matching tuples. Note that there may be QoS increments introduced between writing and reading from the tuple, captured by $\delta_{tuplespace}, S_{tuplespace}$. Of particular interest is the data integrity/security of the tuples, as these may be modified/removed by any of the peers. Two-way interaction is additionally studied, with a writer to a tuple later functioning as a reader.
- *XSB* - When converting between these schemes via a common bus protocol provided by the XSB, QoS increments are produced. These are appended for various domains using δ_{post}, S_{get} and so on. The conversion also increases the bandwidth resource usage that must be taken into account.

Based on [7], the QoS random variables are modeled as follows: δ as a *heavy-tailed* (nctrnd) distribution; S as a *uniform* (randi) distribution; λ as an *exponential* (exprnd) distribution. The simulations are done in MATLAB with increments and random variables provided as in Table 5. We assume uniform performance of the interactions, with $\delta_{send}, \delta_{post}, \delta_{pub}$ drawn from distributions with similar mean and variances. Slight variations are provided, with faster response times pertaining to the broker, tuple space and bus protocols. The security level of the tuple space is set to be lower than other interaction paradigms, as the data can be maliciously modified by peers. These values can differ according to the implementations, network load and resource management accorded.

Table 5. Simulation Parameters in MATLAB

QoS Increments	MATLAB call
δ_{send}, $\delta_{receive}$, δ_{pub}, $\delta_{getnext}$, δ_{out}, δ_{read}	nctrnd(1,10)
δ_{broker}, $\delta_{tuplespace}$, δ_{post}, δ_{get}	nctrnd(1,2)
S_{send}, $S_{receive}$, S_{pub}, $S_{getnext}$, S_{out}, S_{read}, S_{broker}, S_{post}, S_{get}	randi(3)
$S_{tuplespace}$	randi(2)
λ_{send}, $\lambda_{receive}$, λ_{pub}, $\lambda_{getnext}$, λ_{out}, λ_{read}, λ_{sub}, λ_{endsub}, λ_{post}, λ_{get}	exprnd(5)

As shown in Fig. 4, there are differences in performance of these schemes for the evaluated QoS metrics. The cases considered were: *one-way interaction*: CS send-receive, PS publish-subscribe, TS write-read; *two-way interaction*: CS invocation, PS publish-subscribe-(re)publish-subscribe, TS write-read-(re)write-read. In case of *timeliness* δ, the one and two-way CS schemes performed superiorly to corresponding TS and PS schemes. For *security* S, as an intermediate broker or data space are employed by the PS/TS schemes, the levels are consistently lower than that of the CS scheme. The security level of the TS scheme is lower than that of the PS scheme due to the ability of peers to access common data. *Message efficiency* λ considers individual subscriptions needed by the PS scheme, which increases the number of messages per interaction.

We continue this evaluation in Fig. 5 with the effect of using the intermediate XSB connectors on these metrics. The increments are studied for two-way interaction across connectors. While there are not significant differences in domains δ and S for the CS-PS-TS interconnection, the CS-TS interconnection has lower message efficiency λ. Having these statistics in mind, it is possible to study the runtime replacement of a particular connection with another, as we see in the next section.

5.2   Substituting Interactions

In large spaces of services and devices [12], late-binding and replacement procedures are commonly employed. The replacement of heterogeneous systems in such cases should take into account the interaction paradigms and their corresponding QoS. A level of control is to check if the replacement would not affect the particular QoS metric in hand. In order to compare the statistics provided by two interaction paradigms, we employ nonparametric hypothesis tests.

The two-sample *Kolmogorov-Smirnov* test [5] is a nonparametric hypothesis test that evaluates the difference between the cumulative distribution functions of two sample data sets. This statistic may also be used to test whether two underlying one-dimensional probability distributions differ:

$$\mathbf{KS}_{n,n'} = \bigvee_q \mid F_{1,n}(q) - F_{2,n'}(q) \mid \tag{6}$$

where $F_{1,n}$ and $F_{2,n'}$ are the empirical distribution functions of the first and the second sample data sets with n and n' elements in the vectors, respectively. The hypothesis test result is returned as a logical value: $\mathbf{h} = 0$ indicates an acceptance of the null hypothesis at α significance level: that the data in vectors q_1 and q_2 are from the same distribution; $\mathbf{h} = 1$ indicates the rejection of the

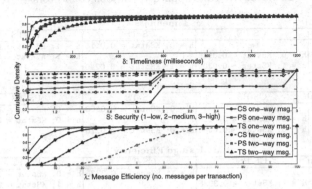

Fig. 4. QoS composition with CS, TS, PS paradigms

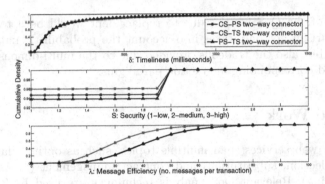

Fig. 5. QoS composition across the XSB connector

null hypothesis at α significance level: the alternative hypothesis that q_1 and q_2 are from different distributions. The null hypothesis is accepted at level α if:

$$\sqrt{\frac{nn'}{n+n'}}\mathbf{KS}_{n,n'} \leq K_\alpha \tag{7}$$

We make use of this test on the observations of the CS, TS, PS schemes when applied to connectors, such as in Fig. 5. This is to determine whether a particular scheme can be replaced with another when querying for a particular QoS metric $(\delta, \mathcal{S}, \lambda)$. We set this tests in MATLAB with $\alpha = 1\%$ as [h,KSstat] = kstest2(q1,q2,0.01) in Table 6.

This provides some interesting insights: assuming certain distributions on the underlying interactions (as in Fig. 5), for timeliness δ, the CS-PS interaction can be suitably replaced by the CS-TS interaction; for security $\mathcal{S}$, all interactions are replaceable with the 1% confidence interval selected; for message efficiency λ, the CS-PS interaction can be suitably replaced by the PS-TS interaction. Though this can change according to measurements and collected statistics, this procedure can be applied in general cases to safely replace interactions. For example, if contractual obligations and SLAs need to be met in certain domains,

Table 6. KS Tests applied to various connectors

δ: **Timeliness**

Connectors	CS-PS	CS-TS	PS-TS
CS-PS	–	h = 0; KSstat = 0.0115	h = 1; KSstat = 0.0309
CS-TS	h = 0; KSstat = 0.0115	–	h = 1; KSstat = 0.0240
PS-TS	h = 1; KSstat = 0.0309	h = 1; KSstat = 0.0240	–

S: **Security**

Connectors	CS-PS	CS-TS	PS-TS
CS-PS	–	h = 0; KSstat = 0.0128	h = 0; KSstat = 0.0088
CS-TS	h = 0; KSstat = 0.0128	–	h = 0; KSstat = 0.0216
PS-TS	h = 0; KSstat = 0.0088	h = 0; KSstat = 0.0216	–

λ: **Message Efficiency**

Connectors	CS-PS	CS-TS	PS-TS
CS-PS	–	h = 1; KSstat = 0.3335	h = 0; KSstat = 0.0102
CS-TS	h = 1; KSstat = 0.3335	–	h = 1; KSstat = 0.3413
PS-TS	h = 0; KSstat = 0.0102	h = 1; KSstat = 0.3413	–

deterioration of the QoS metrics due to replacement would be deterred. This sort of comparison not only takes into account the probabilistic nature of the QoS metrics, but also the tradeoffs provided due to the multi-dimensional QoS evaluation and corresponding interaction paradigms.

6   Related Work

QoS issues in web services span multiple topics, such as optimal late-binding (discovery, selection, substitution) and contract management (SLAs, negotiation, monitoring). Relevant QoS analysis techniques are used by Zeng et al. [23] for optimal decomposition of global QoS constraints into local constraints for composition in the case of service orchestrations. An algebraic formulation based on multi-dimensional probabilistic models is proposed in [21] to compose QoS metrics in the case of web services orchestrations. This has been used to support optimization problems for decision making in orchestrations [14]. In our work, we make use of this algebraic framework and provide an extension for the case of heterogeneous choreography QoS composition.

While QoS issues in composite services based on centralized control (orchestrations) have received some attention, the metrics relevant to choreographies are an active area of research. In [17], Mancioppi et al. provide a structured overview of the possible metrics to be incorporated within choreographies. A generalized stochastic Petri net model is proposed in [8] to compose QoS in choreographies. In [2], the MOSES framework is proposed as an efficient and flexible technique for runtime self-adaptation in service oriented systems. Adaptive and self-healing choreographies have been studied with the survey by Leite et al. [16] providing a systematic overview of model, measurement, agent and formal methods driven techniques for adaptation. In [11], Goldman et al. use a linear programming framework to predict the QoS of BPMN based web services choreographies. A constraint based model for QoS dependent choreographies is proposed in [13]. However, these techniques assume typical client-service interactions for analysis.

With an increasing number of devices being interconnected through the Internet of Things [12], extensions to the standard (client-service interaction based) ESB middleware adapters [3] are required. In the *CHOReOS* project [4][10], the XSB connector is provided, which incorporates multiple interaction paradigms including PS and TS schemes. In order to extend such middleware with QoS, in [18], metrics are integrated in the middleware architecture for discovery, configuration and deployment analysis. In [6], the characteristics of publish-subscribe interactions that are crucial to QoS composition are studied in considerable detail. In [22], the publish-subscribe middleware interaction is upgraded with the *Harmony* overlay messaging to prevent runtime QoS deterioration. Our work builds on heterogeneous interaction paradigms and enhances them with QoS composition rules. While QoS in the typical web services setting is done at the application level, capturing the fine-grained interactions within heterogeneous paradigms provide us with a detailed outlook of QoS aggregation policies. These may be exploited during design-time selection or runtime replacement.

7   Conclusions

QoS analysis in choreographies typically considers homogeneous client-service interactions and is performed at the application level. Choreographies of heterogeneous devices, such as those in the Internet of Things, require further fine-grained QoS analysis of underlying interaction paradigms. In this paper, we study the effect of heterogeneous middleware connectors, interconnected via the *extensible service bus* from the *CHOReOS* project, on choreography QoS metrics. Using multi-dimensional, probabilistic QoS metrics and an algebraic model for composition, this procedure reveals some interesting results. The tradeoffs in particular QoS domains may be studied along with interactions, for efficient selection during design-time. Through hypothesis tests, such as Kolmogorov-Smirnov, runtime replacement of a particular interaction paradigm with another can be performed. In the near future, we intend to apply these analysis techniques on real-world implementations of large scale heterogeneous choreographies, like the ones currently being developed in the *CHOReOS* project.

References

1. Barker, A., Walton, C.D., Robertson, D.: Choreographing web services. IEEE Trans. on Services Computing 2, 152–166 (2009)
2. Cardellini, V., Casalicchio, E., Grassi, V., Iannucci, S., Presti, F.L., Mirandola, R.: MOSES: A framework for QoS driven runtime adaptation of service-oriented systems. IEEE Trans. on Software Engineering 38(5) (2012)
3. Chappell, D.A.: Enterprise Service Bus. O'Reilly Media (2004)
4. CHOReOS. Final CHOReOS architectural style and its relation with the CHOReOS development process and IDRE. Technical report, Large Scale Choreographies for the Future Internet (2013),
   http://www.choreos.eu/bin/Download/Deliverables
5. Conover, W.J.: Practical Nonparametric Statistics. Wiley (1999)

6. Corsaro, A., Querzoni, L., Scipioni, S., Piergiovanni, T.S., Virgillito, A.: Quality of service in publish/subscribe middleware. Global Data Management 8, 1–19 (2006)
7. Cremonesi, P., Serazzi, G.: End-to-end performance of web services. In: Calzarossa, M.C., Tucci, S. (eds.) Performance 2002. LNCS, vol. 2459, pp. 158–178. Springer, Heidelberg (2002)
8. Diaz, A.P., Batista, D.M.: A methodology to define QoS and SLA requirements in service choreographies. In: 17th Intl. Wksp. on Computer Aided Modeling and Design of Communication Links and Networks (2012)
9. Freeman, E., Hupfer, S., Arnold, K.: JavaSpaces Principles, Patterns, and Practice. Addison-Wesley Professional (1999)
10. Georgantas, N., Bouloukakis, G., Beauche, S., Issarny, V.: Service-oriented Distributed Applications in the Future Internet: The Case for Interaction Paradigm Interoperability. In: Lau, K.-K., Lamersdorf, W., Pimentel, E. (eds.) ESOCC 2013. LNCS, vol. 8135, pp. 134–148. Springer, Heidelberg (2013)
11. Goldman, A., Ngoko, Y., Milojicic, D.: An analytical approach for predicting QoS of web services choreographies. In: Middleware for Grid and eScience (2012)
12. Guinard, D., Karnouskos, S., Trifa, V., Dober, B., Spiess, P., Savio, D.: Interacting with the SOA-based internet of things: Discovery, query, selection, and on-demand provisioning of web services. IEEE Trans. on Services Computing 3, 223–235 (2010)
13. Ivanović, D., Carro, M., Hermenegildo, M.V.: A constraint-based approach to quality assurance in service choreographies. In: Liu, C., Ludwig, H., Toumani, F., Yu, Q. (eds.) ICSOC 2012. LNCS, vol. 7636, pp. 252–267. Springer, Heidelberg (2012)
14. Kattepur, A., Benveniste, A., Jard, C.: Optimizing decisions in web services orchestrations. In: Kappel, G., Maamar, Z., Motahari-Nezhad, H.R. (eds.) ICSOC 2011. LNCS, vol. 7084, pp. 77–91. Springer, Heidelberg (2011)
15. Kattepur, A., Georgantas, N., Issarny, V.: QoS composition and analysis in reconfigurable web services choreographies. In: Intl. Conf. on Web Services (2013)
16. Leite, L.A.F., Oliva, G.A., Nogueira, G.M., Gerosa, M.A., Kon, F., Milojicic, D.S.: A systematic literature review of service choreography adaptation. In: Service Oriented Computing and Applications, pp. 1–18 (2012)
17. Mancioppi, M., Perepletchikov, M., Ryan, C., van den Heuvel, W.-J., Papazoglou, M.P.: Towards a quality model for choreography. In: Dan, A., Gittler, F., Toumani, F. (eds.) ICSOC/ServiceWave 2009. LNCS, vol. 6275, pp. 435–444. Springer, Heidelberg (2010)
18. Nahrstedt, K., Xu, D., Wichadakul, D., Li, B.: QoS-aware middleware for ubiquitous and heterogeneous environments. IEEE Communications Magazine 39, 140–148 (2001)
19. Richards, M., Monson-Haefel, R., Chappell, D.A.: Java Message Service, 2nd edn. O'Reilly (2009)
20. Richardson, L., Ruby, S.: RESTful Web Services. O'Reilly (2007)
21. Rosario, S., Benveniste, A., Jard, C.: Flexible probabilistic QoS management of transaction based web services orchestrations. In: IEEE Intl. Conf. on Web Services, pp. 107–114 (2009)
22. Yang, H., Kim, M., Karenos, K., Ye, F., Lei, H.: Message-oriented middleware with QoS awareness. In: Baresi, L., Chi, C.-H., Suzuki, J. (eds.) ICSOC-ServiceWave 2009. LNCS, vol. 5900, pp. 331–345. Springer, Heidelberg (2009)
23. Zeng, L., Benatallah, B., Ngu, A.H., Dumas, M., Kalagnanam, J., Chang, H.: QoS-aware middleware for web services composition. IEEE Trans. on Software Engineering 30, 311–326 (2004)

Improving Interaction with Services via Probabilistic Piggybacking*

Carlo Ghezzi[1], Mauro Pezzè[2], and Giordano Tamburrelli[2]

[1] Dipartimento di Elettronica e Informazione. Politecnico di Milano, Italy
carlo.ghezzi@polimi.it
[2] Faculty of Informatics. University of Lugano, Switzerland
{mauro.pezze,giordano.tamburrelli}@usi.ch

Abstract. Modern service oriented applications increasingly include publicly released services that impose novel and compelling requirements in terms of scalability and support to clients with limited capabilities such as mobile applications. To meet these requirements, service oriented applications require a careful optimisation of their provisioning mechanisms. In this paper we investigate a novel technique that optimises the interactions between providers and clients called probabilistic piggybacking. In our approach we automatically infer a probabilistic model that captures the behaviour of clients and predicts the future service requests. The provider exploits this information by piggybacking each message toward clients with the response of the predicted next request, minimizing both the amount of exchanged messages and the client latency. The paper focuses on REST services and illustrates the technique with a case study based on a publicly available service currently in use.

1 Introduction

Service oriented applications (SOC) [16] support the integration and collaboration among internal entities of the same organisation and enable industrial partnerships across distinct organisations, independently from their technological stacks. Recently, software services are increasingly released to the general public allowing independent developers and external software organisations to create new software artifacts that leverage them.

The increasing popularity of openly accessible services introduces novel software engineering challenges that affect the way clients exploit services as well as the mechanisms adopted by service providers to offer them. From the service provider perspective, SOC applications need to meet new compelling requirements in terms of scalability, being concurrently accessed by large and unpredictable populations of distinct clients. Indeed, the massive stream of requests that service providers have to deal with may hamper their capability to operate efficiently,

* This research has been funded by the EU, Programme IDEAS-ERC, Project 227977-SMScom and FP7-PEOPLE-2011-IEF, Project 302648-RunMore.

S. Basu et al. (Eds.): ICSOC 2013, LNCS 8274, pp. 39–53, 2013.

potentially violating existing service level agreements. For example, the Twitter REST services[1] serve several billions of requests per day and several thousands calls per second. Moreover, from the client perspective, the interactions with the service providers need to be as efficient as possible for example in terms of number of exchanged messages and latency. Indeed, an increasing percentage of existing clients is represented by mobile applications that are typically characterised by limited bandwidth, unreliable connectivity, and limited computational power. To effectively support the required scalability and to optimise the interactions with clients characterised by limited capabilities, modern SOC applications require efficient service provisioning mechanisms. This paper addresses this issue and introduces a technique that focuses on REST services [8,22] called *probabilistic piggybacking*.

Probabilistic piggybacking consists of an inference algorithm that monitors at runtime all the requests issued by a client and incrementally infers a probabilistic model of its behaviour in terms of service invocations. Given a certain service invocation currently issued by a client, the inferred probabilistic model predicts the next service invocation it may issue next. The service provider exploits this information by piggybacking each message towards the client with the response to the predicted request. Probabilistic piggybacking brings two distinct advantages, (1) reduces client latency since responses to predicted invocations are immediately available to the client, and (2) optimises the interaction among clients and service providers since each correctly predicted invocation reduces the number of exchanged messages. In addition, as discussed later on in Section 5, the proposed solution is transparent to the client, requires a minimum modification to the server implementation, and is complementary to other existing related techniques such as caching.

This paper contributes to current research in service engineering in two distinct ways. First, it defines an inference algorithm for SOC applications that captures the usage profiles of clients and predicts their service invocation patterns. Second, it proposes a novel probabilistic piggybacking technique based on the inference algorithm to optimise REST service provisioning mechanisms. The inference algorithm and the proposed technique have been validated with experiments and simulations extracted from a case study of a set of REST services currently in use.

The remainder of the paper is organized as follows. Section 2 overviews the probabilistic piggybacking technique. Section 3 introduces the running case study, namely a set of REST services publicly available online and currently in use that we use throughout the paper to exemplify and validate the approach. Section 4 provides a detailed description of the approach through the case study, while Section 5 presents the results of our analytical and experimental evaluation of the proposed approach and its applicability. Section 6 discusses the related work. Section 7 summarizes the main contributions of the paper, and illustrates the ongoing research work.

---

[1] https://dev.twitter.com

2   Probabilistic Piggybacking: An Overview

Piggybacking [17] is a well-known data transmission technique that belongs to the network layer and improves transmission efficiency. In this technique, the acknowledgements to data received from an emitter by a sender are attached to the messages emitted in the opposite direction. More precisely, piggybacking implies that an acknowledgement sent by a receiver, instead of being sent in an individual message, is piggybacked on a data frame going toward the sender. In this paper we conceived a probabilistic technique inspired by the basic principle of piggybacking that optimises service provisioning. Although the proposed technique is in principle applicable to many different SOC styles, we refer to services implemented according to a REST architectural style. REST is an increasingly popular[2] architectural style in which requests and responses flow through the *stateless* transfer of resources via http urls that uniquely identify the state of the conversation between clients and servers. A complete discussion of the REST architectural style is beyond the scope of this paper, the interested readers can find additional details in [8,22].

The probabilistic piggybacking technique includes two fundamental components: (1) the *inference engine* and (2) the *piggybacking engine*. The former is deployed to the client, while the latter is deployed to the service provider. The technique is articulated in four main steps that we introduce below. The first step occurs at design time, while the others take place at runtime.

1. *Specifying Endpoints:* At design time providers specify the service endpoints using a lightweight service description language. This description integrates the service documentation and is publicly released to clients.

2. *Inferring the model:* The inference engine monitors the service requests issued by a client and infers a discrete time Markov chain (DTMC) [18]. DTMCs are finite state automata augmented with probabilities. The Markov model is built incrementally as soon as new requests are issued to the service provider.

3. *Predicting requests:* The inference engine uses the inferred model to predict the next most likely service invocation, given a currently issued service request. The prediction is sent, together with the request currently issued, to the provider.

4. *Instantiating request parameters:* The service provider serves the requests as soon as they are issued and receives with each of them the endpoint predicted by the inference engine deployed on the client side. The piggybacking engine – deployed on the service provider – exploits this information, instantiates the actual parameters of the predicted endpoint, and prepares the corresponding response to be sent to the client via piggybacking (i.e., attached to the response of the request issued by the client). The response piggybacked to the client is cached. If the prediction made by the inference engine is correct the cached response will be immediately available thus reducing the latency and avoiding otherwise the client to issue a new service invocation to the provider.

---

[2] According to ProgrammableWeb, the largest directory of publicly available services, the percentage of publicly available REST services listed in their platform is gradually increasing and recently reached 68%. http://www.programmableweb.com

Table 1. Flixster Movie REST Api

Name	Type	Service Endpoint	Description	Url Parameter (default value)
search	GET	/movies.json	The movies search endpoint for plain text queries	q: query to search (-) page_limit: results per page (30) page: selected page (1)
info	GET	/movies/<id>.json	Detailed information on a specific movie specified by the <id>	-
cast	GET	/movies/<id>/cast.json	Retrieves the complete cast for a movie specified by the <id>	-
clips	GET	/movies/<id>/clips.json	Retrieves the trailer for a movie specified by the <id>	-
similar	GET	/movies/<id>/similar.json	Retrieves similar movies for a movie specified by the <id>	limit: max number of results (5)

3   Motivating Example

In this section we introduce an example of popular REST services that we use through the paper to illustrate and motivate our research. The case study refers to the Flixster movie REST api[3] that gives access to the Flixster movie database, allowing independent developers or external organisations to build applications and widgets containing movies data. Using these api users can search for movies, retrieve detailed movie information like cast or directors, and access movie trailers. The Flixster movie REST api includes other endpoints (related to upcoming movies, dvd, etc) that we omit due to the limited space. Service endpoints return responses in the JSON[4] standard format: a lightweight data-interchange format alternative to XML increasingly popular for REST services. Table 1 lists the service endpoints with a brief textual description. The proposed solution focuses on optimising GET requests and ignores other kinds of messages (e.g., POST). Indeed, GET requests correspond to requesting specific resources and retrieving data without any side-effect on the server [7]. In other words GET requests are idempotent read requests that can be predicted and served by our piggybacking mechanism without hampering the semantics of the interaction between client and server. In addition, GET requests represent, in practice, the most frequent class of messages exchanged among clients and REST service providers.

In REST services, GET requests may have two distinct classes of parameters: *structural parameters* and *url parameters*. Structural parameters refer to parametric fragments of the path of a certain endpoint used to customise requests issued by the clients. For example, clients parametrize the path of the *similar* service endpoint with respect to the id of the movie they are interested in. Url parameters refer to parameters appended at the end of the endpoint in the form *name=value* and interleaved by an ampersand. For example, the *similar* service endpoint may be parametrized with the *limit* url parameter as reported in the

---

[3] http://developer.rottentomatoes.com
[4] http://www.json.org

```
 1  {
 2    "name": "search",
 3    "url":  "/movies.json?apikey={}&q={}&page_limit={30}&page={1}",
 4    "response":
 5    [
 6      {
 7        "name":"id",
 8        "select":  "$.movies[0].id"
 9      }
10    ]
11  }
```

Listing 1.1. RDL endpoint definition with response field

fourth column of Table 1. The fourth column of the table reports the default value of url parameters (i.e., the value of the parameter if omitted in the request). All the endpoints reported in Table 1 require the additional mandatory url parameter *apikey* used by the service provider to identify the clients. The following url is an example of a valid service request to the *similar* endpoint:

/movies/77/similar.json?apikey=798&limit=30

In this case the client has an apikey equal to 798, the movie targeted by the request has an id equal to 77, and the request will return at most 30 movies.

As introduced in Section 1, thousands of clients may simultaneously access these endpoints and an increasing number of these accesses is performed by client with limited capabilities such as mobile applications. As a consequence, the service provisioning mechanisms should be as efficient and scalable as possible.

4 Probabilistic Piggybacking Explained

In this section we explain in details the probabilistic piggybacking approach and how it optimises the service provisioning mechanisms referring to the four steps previously introduced and to the Flixster movie services.

4.1 Specifying Endpoints

Providers describe the endpoints with a lightweight service description language in the JSON format called RDL[5]. We conceived RDL specifically for probabilistic piggybacking, not with the goal of designing a new service specification language that could replace existing standards, such as WSDL [5]. Indeed, the scope of RDL is limited to supporting the piggybacking operations and not to specifying or documenting the endpoints.

---

[5] *REST Description Language*

The RDL service description consists of a list of JSON objects. Each of them contains the description of an endpoint in terms of its name and its url. The url representation includes its parameters as follows. Structural parameters in the url are specified by a name within curly brackets ({*parameter_name*}), while url parameters are specified by their name followed by an equal sign and curly brackets that may contain the default value of the parameter (*parameter_name={default_value}*). As an example, let us consider Listing 1.1, which shows the RDL representation of the Flixster *search* endpoint. The *response* field in the RDL description may be used to select a string fragment of the endpoint response and to assign to it a name. For this task RDL relies on a JSONPath[6] expression. JSONPath is a path expression syntax, which can select parts of JSON documents in the same way as XPath [1] expressions select nodes of XML documents. For example, in the case of the *search* endpoint specified in Listing 1.1, we may want to select the id of the first movie in the response by labelling it with the string *"id"*. The index 0 indicates we are interested in the first item of the array of the movies returned in the response. We clarify the meaning of an RDL response field in the context of probabilistic piggybacking in Section 4.4.

The provider of Flixster movie services may easily translate all the endpoints illustrated in Table 1 to RDL obtaining a complete description to be publicly released to the clients.

4.2   Inferring the Model

Clients invoke service endpoints by issuing http requests to the endpoint urls. In our approach, each request issued by a client is intercepted by the inference engine and used to incrementally infer a discrete time Markov chain (DTMC) [18] used to predict the next request by the client. DTMCs are finite state automata augmented with probabilities. In our setting each state corresponds to a service endpoint, while probabilistic transitions among states represent the probabilities of sequences of invocations. Formally:

A DTMC is a tuple $\langle S, s_0, P, N, L \rangle$ where:

S : is a non empty finite set of states, where $s_0 \in S$ is the initial state;

$P : S \times S \to [0, 1]$ is a stochastic function representing the probabilistic edges that connect the states in S. An element $P(s_i, s_j)$ represents the probability that the next state will be s_j given that the current state is s_i;

N: is the set of endpoint names extracted from the RDL file;

$L : S \to N$ is a labeling function associating each state to an endpoint name;

The inference engine uses the RDL specification of endpoints to identify and label states. The inference process starts from a DTMC with a set of states S that contains only the initial state s_0 and the initial labelling function $L(s_0) = start$. The inference engine builds the DTMC incrementally by processing the service requests as they are issued by the client adding new states to DTMC and inferring *transitions* between states in S. For each request the inference engine

---

[6] http://goessner.net/articles/JsonPath/

```
1   /movies.json?apikey=798&q=Psycho&page_limit=30&page=1
2   /movies/17355.json?apikey=798
3   /movies/17355/similar.json?apikey=798&limit=30
4   /movies.json?apikey=798&q=Vertigo&page_limit=30&page=1
5   /movies/22490.json?apikey=798
6   /movies/22490/cast.json?apikey=798
```

Listing 1.2. A list of REST requests

infers a transition following a 3-step process: extracting the destination state, extracting the source state, and computing the probabilities.

1. *Extracting the destination state.* The inference engine examines the current request r and maps the request to its corresponding endpoint name n exploiting the RDL file. Thus the engine associates a destination state $d \in S$ to r such that $\mathcal{L}(d) = n$. If d does not belong to S yet, the inference engine adds the new state d to S and updates the labelling function $\mathcal{L}$ accordingly.

2. *Extracting the source state.* The engine associates the destination state of the last invoked service request to the source state of r and associates the first service request issued by the client to the initial state s_0.

3. *Computing the probabilities.* The engine uses the intercepted service invocations to update two sets of counters that are initially set to zero: a set of counters $c_{i,j}$ for each pair of states $(s_i, s_j) \in S \times S$, and a set of counters t_i for each state $s_i \in S$. The inference engine increments both the counter $c_{i,j}$ for each transition from state s_i to s_j and the counter t_i for each transition whose source state is s_i, independent of its destination state. The counter t_i represents the number of times the clients exited state s_i, while the counter $c_{i,j}$ represents the number of times the clients moved from state s_i to state s_j. The inference engine updates the counters for each request that corresponds to a transition in the model, and uses these counters to calculate the (i, j) entry of the stochastic function $\mathcal{P}$ that represents the probability of traversing the edge from state s_i to state s_j, by computing the following frequency:

$$\mathcal{P}(s_i, s_j) = \frac{c_{i,j}}{t_i}$$

for all pairs of states s_i and s_j. The probability $\mathcal{P}(s_i, s_j)$ computed as the ratio between the number of traversals of the transition from the state s_i to s_j and the total number of traversals for all the transitions exiting state s_i corresponds to the *maximum likelihood estimator* for $\mathcal{P}(s_i, s_j)$ [6]. Notice that the probabilities can be recomputed incrementally after adding any number of transitions or states to the DTMC.

Figure 1 illustrates the inference process described so far, by referring to the sequence of invocations of a given client reported in Listing 1.2. We start from

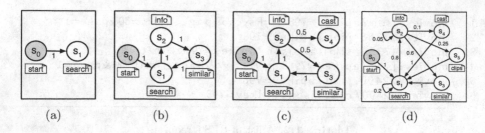

Fig. 1. DTMC inference process

the initial DTMC shown in Figure 1(a), and proceed incrementally through the invocations. The first invocation is associated with the endpoint *search*. Since S does not contain any state s such that $\mathcal{L}(s) = search$, the engine adds a new state s_1 to S, and extends the labelling function with $\mathcal{L}(s_1) = search$. Being this the first service invocation of the client, the engine considers state s_0 as the source state for the inferred transition $(\langle s_0, s_1 \rangle)$. The engine increments the counters t_0 and $c_{0,1}$, and consequently $\mathcal{P}(s_0, s_1)$ is set to 1. The resulting DTMC is shown in Figure 1(a). The second request corresponds to a request of detailed information on a specific movie with id equal to 17355 and is associated with the endpoint *info*. The inference engine associates the new destination state s_2 to this request and updates the labelling function: $\mathcal{L}(s_2) = info$. The engine identifies the destination state of the last invoked service request as the source state yielding to a transition $\langle s_1, s_2 \rangle$. The engine increments the counters related to the new transition: $t_1 = 1$ and $c_{1,2} = 1$. Consequently, $\mathcal{P}(s_1, s_2)$ is set to 1.

Similarly, the third request is associated with a new destination state s_3 such that $\mathcal{L}(s_3) = similar$. The source state is associated again with the destination state of the last transition generated (s_2) and results in transition $\langle s_2, s_3 \rangle$. The engine increments the counters t_2 and $c_{2,3}$, and consequently sets $\mathcal{P}(s_2, s_3) = 1$. The fourth request results in the transition $\langle s_3, s_1 \rangle$. The resulting DTMC is reported in Figure 1(b). The fifth request represents again a request to the *info* endpoint and is treated as previously shown. The sixth request infers a new destination state s_4, where $\mathcal{L}(s_4) = cast$, and a new transition $\langle s_2, s_4 \rangle$. The engine increments the counters t_2 and $c_{2,4}$, and consequently sets $\mathcal{P}(s_2, s_4) = 0.5$ and $\mathcal{P}(s_2, s_3) = 0.5$. Figure 1(c) shows the resulting DTMC.

By applying the inference algorithm to the requests issued by a client we eventually obtain a DTMC that probabilistically captures its usage profile. For example, if a client issued 350 requests to the *search* endpoint and 280 of these requests were followed by a request to the *info* endpoint, in the inferred DTMC the transition $\langle s_1, s_2 \rangle$ would be associated with probability 0.8. An example of a possible inferred DTMC for the Flixster services is shown in Figure 1(d).

In this paper we refer to client applications that deal with only one service provider. This is not always the case if we consider for example applications that organise and exploit multiple services such as service mashups or service compositions. The proposed technique is applicable seamlessly also to these multi-provider examples by simply instantiating several inference engines, one for each provider, that independently infer distinct client behaviours.

4.3 Predicting Requests

The inference engine intercepts all the outgoing service requests issued by the client to infer the DTMC model as explained above. At each intercepted service request, the engine uses the inferred model to predict the service endpoint that the client will invoke in the next service request.

Given a request r to a certain service endpoint e, the engine analyzes the state in the DTMC representing e and selects the outgoing transition with the highest probability. If the transition probability is greater than a given threshold (the *piggybacking_threshold*) the engine considers its destination state as a valuable prediction of the most likely next service request. The engine communicates this information to the server by appending an additional url parameter (called *piggyback*) to the outgoing request r that indicates the predicted endpoint name as specified in the RDL file. If the transition probability is less than the piggybacking_threshold, the engine does not append the additional parameter and the probabilistic piggybacking simply does not occur for this request.

Let us consider the case where a client issued a request to the *info* endpoint for the movie with id equal to 77. In the scenario in which the DTMC indicates that the most likely service endpoint invoked next is the *similar* endpoint, the url actually issued by the client is the following:

```
/movies/77.json?apikey=798&piggyback=similar
```

The prediction process starts only after the inference engine has collected a significant number of requests obtaining a DTMC that well represents the client's behaviour. This minimum number of requests is a parameter that can be tuned for each client to meet its specific characteristics.

4.4 Instantiating Request Parameters

The service provider serves the received requests and computes their responses ignoring the piggyback parameter appended to them. Before sending the responses back to client, for each request that contains the piggyback parameter the provider invokes the piggybacking engine forwarding to it the following elements: (1) the request including its piggybacking parameter and (2) the computed response. The piggybacking engine is in charge of transforming the predicted endpoint (the piggybacking parameter) to a concrete service request: a valid url with its appropriate parameters. To this end the engine looks up in the RDL file the url structure of the predicted endpoint, extracts the parameters it contains composing a set of parameters $\mathcal{M}$. To instantiate a valid url for the predicted endpoint, the piggybacking engine finds a suitable value for all the elements in $\mathcal{M}$ relying on the following heuristics:

1. The engine extracts all the parameter values contained in the client request. The engine relies on these extracted values to instantiate the corresponding parameters in $\mathcal{M}$.

2. The engine examines the response to the current request and extracts the parameters specified in the response field as defined in the RDL file (see for example Listing 1.1). The engine relies on these extracted values to instantiate the corresponding parameters in $\mathcal{M}$.

3. The engine considers the most recent past requests of the predicted endpoint and uses their parameter values to instantiate the parameters in $\mathcal{M}$.

4. If by applying the above steps the engine could not instantiate all the parameters in $\mathcal{M}$, the engine relies on their default value if available.

The engine proceeds with the piggybacking process if and only all the parameters in $\mathcal{M}$ have a corresponding value for their instantiation obtained through the heuristics described above. Otherwise the engine aborts the piggybacking process for this request. Let us consider the case in which the client issued the url exemplified in the previous paragraph where the model prediction corresponds to the *similar* endpoint. Given the structure of the *similar* endpoint as specified in the RDL file we have that $\mathcal{M} = \{id, apikey, limit\}$. The id as well as the apikey parameters are collected from the url request issued by the client (i.e., id= 77, apikey= 798), while the limit parameter is extracted from previous *similar* requests issued to the server or using its default value (limit= 5). Considering this second case the predicted request to the *similar* endpoint is instantiated as:

/movies/77/similar.json?apikey=798&limit=5

Similarly, let us consider the case in which the client issued a request to the *search* endpoint where the prediction corresponds to the *info* endpoint. In this case we have that $\mathcal{M} = \{apikey, id\}$. The apikey parameter is collected as in the previous case. However, the id parameter is not present in the request issued by the client (the *search* endpoint does not contain any id parameter). The piggybacking engine collects it from the response to the search request computed by the service provider. Indeed, the engine applies step 2 of the heuristics and relies on the JSONPath expression reported in Listing 1.1 to instantiate the id parameter. This process yields the following url (assuming the result of the search request produced an array in which the first item has id equal to 48):

/movies/48.json?apikey=798

As shown by this example, the RDL response field may be used to exploit regularities in the usage profile of the clients to instantiate the predicted url. In this case, we rely on the fact that the first result in the movie returned by the search is the most relevant result and thus the most likely parameter for the predicted *info* endpoint. If the piggybacking engine successfully instantiates a url corresponding to the predicted endpoint, the provider serves it as if it was a request issued by the client. At this stage the service provider has two responses: the response computed for the request issued by the client and the response computed from the url instantiated by the piggybacking engine. The provider sends back to the client a unique response message that encapsulates the second one in a specific field. On the client side the inference engine intercepts the response message sent from the service provider and forwards the first response to the client, while caching internally the response to the predicted endpoint. A subsequent request of the client to the predicted endpoint with the same parameters used by piggybacking engine will result in a cache hit. In such a case, the result is available to the client with zero latency and without exchanging any additional message. The effectiveness of the heuristics described in this section is application specific, and thus the piggybacking engine is open to possible extensions and customisations to fit the specific requirements of applications.

5   Evaluation of Probabilistic Piggybacking

Efficiency. Let us consider two endpoints A and B offered by a provider and let us consider the case of a client that, after invoking A, invokes B with probability to p_{AB}. By relying on the maximum likelihood estimator, see Section 4.2, the transition between the states representing A and B will eventually be labelled with probability p_{AB}. If p_{AB} is greater than the piggybacking threshold, each response to requests to A is piggybacked with a response to B. Thus, the overall probability for a client to experience a cache hit is: $p_{hit} = p_{AB} \times p_{param}$, where the first term indicates the probability of having a request to B after a request to A, while the second term indicates the probability that requests to B are correctly instantiated by the piggybacking engine. Notice that, for every cache hit, the client and the server exchanged only two messages (request and response), while in the case of a cache miss the client and the sever exchanged four messages (two requests and two responses). Thus the average number of messages exchanged (m_p) can thus be estimated as follows:

$$m_p = p_{hit} \times 2 + (1 - p_{hit}) \times 4 \tag{1}$$

Since p_{hit} is a probability ($0 \leq p_{hit} \leq 1$) we have that $m_p \leq 4$, while the number of messages exchanged by implementations without piggybacking is four. This indicates that the average number of message exchanged with piggybacking is always less than or equal to the number of messages exchanged by an implementation that does not rely on it and the difference among these two values depends on the probability of cache hits. We measured approximately these results by considering the Flixster movie services. We extended an existing Java client[7] with our inference engine and we produced sequences of invocations to the the *similar* and to the *info* endpoint. We also built a proxy of the Flixster movie services to serve these requests relying on our piggybacking engine. We artificially generated the client requests with an increasing value of $p_{info,similar}$ and a fixed value of p_{param}. Running the client, we measured the average number of messages exchanged with and without the probabilistic piggybacking.

---

[7] JTomato: http://giordano.webfactional.com/?page_id=22

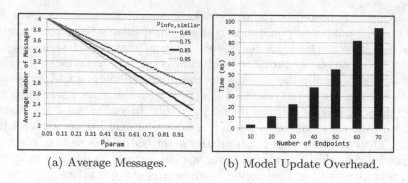

(a) Average Messages.   (b) Model Update Overhead.

Fig. 2. Simulation results

If piggybacking is disabled, we measured a constant number of exchanged messages equal to four. Enabling piggybacking – with a piggybacking threshold equal to 0.6 – we obtained an average number of messages always less than or equal to four as illustrated in Figure 2(a). In particular, the average number of messages depends linearly on the parameters $p_{info,similar}$ and p_{param} as indicated in Equation 1. In general, the larger their product is (i.e., p_{hit}), the more efficient the interaction among the client and the service provider is. In addition to the increased efficiency in terms of exchanged messages, probabilistic piggybacking also brings an additional advantage to the client side in terms of latency. Indeed, each cache hit corresponds to a service invocation issued by the client that can be resolved locally and thus immediately without any network latency. Probabilistic piggybacking introduces an overhead which may be relevant on the client side, in particular in the specific case of mobile clients. To measure this overhead we ran our inference engine on an Android[8] client measuring the average time required by the inference engine to process a service request updating an inferred model of increasing dimension. Figure 2(b) shows that the overhead is negligible. For example the average time required to update a DTMC of 40 states – corresponding to a service with 40 endpoints – is only 40ms. In this evaluation we measured the increased efficiency in terms of exchanged messages and not in terms of generated network traffic. Indeed, in this domain, a real bottleneck is the number of connections opened with clients (see for example the well known C10K problem [10]), which directly depends on the number of service requests invoked by them. Similarly, from the perspective of mobile clients, the metric to be minimised is the number of messages since, because of their mobile nature, each additional message may potentially require a new connection (and thus a new TCP/IP handshake) that is a considerable overhead in terms of radio (i.e., battery) usage and latency. Due to the lack of space we cannot report other relevant scenarios. To support the replicability of results we released our current prototype as an open source artefact[9].

---

[8] HTC Wildfire, Android 2.1.

[9] http://giordano.webfactional.com/?page_id=22

Adaptability to Multiple Usage Profiles. The inferred DTMC captures two distinct usage profiles: (1) the *application profile*, and (2) the *user profile*. The application profile refers to patterns in service requests caused by the structure of the client application. Let us consider for example a mobile application that relies on the Flixster movie services. Let us imagine that this mobile application includes a frame that: (1) displays the details of a given movies and (2) lists a set of recommended similar movies. To develop this frame the developers invoke the *info* endpoint to retrieve the detail of the movie and subsequently the *similar* endpoint to display the recommended movies. The causal correlation among these two requests is captured by the inferred DTMC as a transition between the states corresponding to these endpoints labelled with an high probability of occurrence (equal to one if the application invokes the *info* endpoint only in this application frame). In this case the probabilistic piggybacking is extremely effective since the client's behaviour is easily predictable. Indeed, in this case, the correlation between the invocations is hardcoded in the client application. The user profile refers instead to patterns in service requests caused by frequent behaviours of the final users of the client application. For example, as previously exemplified in Section 4.4, given a request to the *search* endpoint the user may subsequently select – in the majority of cases – the first item in the result set returned by the search. Our solution seamlessly captures also this kind of usage patterns by piggybacking the appropriate response.

Transparency to Clients. Clients typically issue requests to service endpoints using http libraries that are available off the shelf for all the commonly adopted programming languages. The inference engine is an extension of these libraries that issues the requests, handles the responses, infers a DTMC, and caches the responses piggybacked by the provider. From this viewpoint, probabilistic piggybacking is totally transparent to the clients that invoke requests through the inference engine instead of invoking them through the standard http library. Our current implementation of the inference engine consists of an extension of the popular Java http library Apache HttpComponents[10].

Complementarity to Caching Techniques. Efficient service provisioning is so crucial in modern service oriented applications that clients always try to optimise the way in which they use services, for example adopting caching mechanisms to reduce the number of interactions with the providers. An additional advantage of the probabilistic piggybacking technique is its complementarity with respect to the traditional caching of requests. Indeed, while caching minimises the interactions with the service provider by exploiting recurrent *past* service invocations, probabilistic piggybacking minimises the interactions by predicting and anticipating *future* service requests, similarly to server-side active caches [3]. These techniques are orthogonal and complementary. Indeed, the piggybacked responses may be stored in the same cache used by traditional caching solutions.

---

[10] http://hc.apache.org

6 Related Work

The problem of inferring and analysing the client behaviours has been address by many approaches for several distinct goals. For example, Liu and V. Kešelj combine the analysis of Web server logs with the contents of the requested Web pages to predict users future requests [13]. They capture the content of Web pages by extracting character N-grams that are combined with the data extracted from the log files. Alternatively, Schechter et al. use a tree-based data structure to represent the collection of paths inferred from the log file and predict the next page access [20]. Markov models are the most commonly adopted framework to represent clients interactions. Indeed, such models provide an approximate abstraction of client behaviours that, when applicable in a given domain [4], balance well complexity and expressiveness. Borges and Levene propose a Markov model for representing user navigation sessions inferred from log files and modelled with hypertext probabilistic grammars whose higher probability strings correspond to the users navigation patterns [2]. Sarukkai relies on Markov chains for predicting links and analysing paths by using an inference mechanism similar to the one proposed in this paper [19]. Considering the specific problem of optimising the service provisioning mechanisms we can mention the work by Krashinsky [11] that investigates how to optimise the final critical link between a mobile client and a stationary base station by compressing http request and response messages. Similarly, Tian et al. [21] discuss the benefits obtained by compressing the messages in XML. Krishnamurthy et al. [12] categorises instead the set of clients communicating with a server in order to optimise the communication for example optimising the interactions with clients characterised by a limited connectivity altering the caching policies. In [14] Papageorgiou et al. analyse the factors that affect the consumption of services by mobile devices in terms of efficiency by comparing different approaches and protocols. Papageorgiou et al. [15] discuss the effectiveness of client side cache for services and mobile clients. Finally, concerning specifically the REST architectural style we can mention the work by Hamad et al. [9] that evaluates the efficiency of REST against SOAP services. Probabilistic piggybacking differs and complements these solutions since it focuses on optimising the service provisioning mechanisms minimising the number of exchanged messages and exploiting a probabilistic approach specifically conceived for mobile clients.

7 Conclusions and Future Work

In this paper we discussed a novel technique to optimise the flow of service requests and the client latency. The proposed solution is transparent to the client and complementary to other existing related techniques such as caching. Future work includes a larger validation campaign based on logs of real service invocations and an extension to support services implemented with other architectural styles.

References

1. Berglund, A., Boag, S., Chamberlin, D., Fernandez, M.F., Kay, M., Robie, J., Siméon, J.: Xml path language (xpath) 2.0. W3C recommendation, 23 (2007)
2. Borges, J., Levene, M.: Evaluating variable-length markov chain models for analysis of user web navigation sessions. IEEE Transactions on Knowledge and Data Engineering 19(4), 441–452 (2007)
3. Cao, P., Zhang, J., Beach, K.: Active cache: Caching dynamic contents on the web. Distributed Systems Engineering 6(1), 43 (1999)
4. Chierichetti, F., Kumar, R., Raghavan, P., Sarlós, T.: Are web users really markovian? In: WWW. ACM (2012)
5. Chinnici, R., Moreau, J., Ryman, A., Weerawarana, S.: Web services description language version 2.0 part 1: Core language. W3C Recommendation, 26 (2007)
6. DeGroot, M.H., Schervish, M.J.: Probability and Statistics-International Edition. Addison-Wesley Publishing Company, Reading (2001)
7. Fielding, R.T., Gettys, J., Mogul, J., Frystyk, H., Masinter, L., Leach, P., Berners-Lee, T.: Hypertext transfer protocol–http/1.1 (1999)
8. Fielding, R.T., Taylor, R.N.: Principled design of the modern web architecture. ACM Transactions on Internet Technology (TOIT) 2(2), 115–150 (2002)
9. Hamad, H., Saad, M., Abed, R.: Performance evaluation of restful web services for mobile devices. International Arab Journal of e-Technology (2010)
10. Kegel, D.: The c10k problem (2006), http://www.kegel.com/c10k.html
11. Krashinsky, R.: Efficient web browsing for mobile clients using http compression (2003), http://www.cag.lcs.mit.edu/~ronny/classes/httpcomp.pdf
12. Krishnamurthy, B., Wills, C.E.: Improving web performance by client characterization driven server adaptation. In: Proceedings of the 11th International Conference on World Wide Web, pp. 305–316. ACM (2002)
13. Liu, H., Kešelj, V.: Combined mining of web server logs and web contents for classifying user navigation patterns and predicting users future requests. Data & Knowledge Engineering 61(2), 304–330 (2007)
14. Papageorgiou, A., Blendin, J., Miede, A., Eckert, J., Steinmetz, R.: Study and comparison of adaptation mechanisms for performance enhancements of mobile web service consumption. In: Services. IEEE (2010)
15. Papageorgiou, A., Schatke, M., Schulte, S., Steinmetz, R.: Enhancing the caching of web service responses on wireless clients. In: 2011 IEEE International Conference on Web Services (ICWS), pp. 9–16. IEEE (2011)
16. Papazoglou, M.P.: Service-oriented computing: Concepts, characteristics and directions. In: Proceedings of the Fourth International Conference on Web Information Systems Engineering, WISE 2003, pp. 3–12. IEEE (2003)
17. Postel, J.: Rfc 793: Transmission control protocol, september 1981 (2003)
18. Ross, S.M.: Stochastic processes. Wiley Series in Probability and Mathematical Statistics, EUA (1983)
19. Sarukkai, R.R.: Link prediction and path analysis using markov chains. Computer Networks 33(1), 377–386 (2000)
20. Schechter, S., Krishnan, M., Smith, M.D.: Using path profiles to predict http requests. Computer Networks and ISDN Systems 30(1), 457–467 (1998)
21. Tian, M., Voigt, T., Naumowicz, T., Ritter, H., Schiller, J.: Performance considerations for mobile web services. Computer Communications 27(11), 1097–1105 (2004)
22. Wilde, E., Pautasso, C.: REST: From Research to Practice. Springer (2011)

Runtime Enforcement of First-Order LTL Properties on Data-Aware Business Processes

Riccardo De Masellis[1] and Jianwen Su[2]

[1] SAPIENZA Università di Roma, Italy
demasellis@dis.uniroma1.it
[2] University of California at Santa Barbara, United States
su@cs.ucsb.edu

Abstract. This paper studies the following problem: given a relational data schema, a temporal property over the schema, and a process that modifies the data instances, how can we enforce the property during each step of the process execution? Temporal properties are defined using a first-order future time LTL (FO-LTL) and they are evaluated under finite and fixed domain assumptions. Under such restrictions, existing techniques for monitoring propositional formulas can be used, but they would require exponential space in the size of the domain. Our approach is based on the construction of a first-order automaton that is able to perform the monitoring incrementally and by using exponential space in the size of the property. Technically, we show that our mechanism captures the semantics of FO-LTL on finite but progressing sequences of instances, and it reports satisfaction or dissatisfaction of the property at the earliest possible time.

Keywords: data-aware business processes, runtime monitoring, formal verification.

1 Introduction

A common pattern in computer science is the constantly increasing complexity of systems, therefore a main challenge is to provide formalisms, techniques, and tools that enable the efficient design and execution of correct and well-functioning systems, despite their complexity. Such a challenge is tackled by business process management (BPM) in the context of business processes. When interested in checking the correctness of a process w.r.t. some properties, two orthogonal approaches can be put in place: *(i)* given a dynamic model of the process, checking *offline*, i.e., before the process is executed, whether every possible execution satisfies the properties, or *(ii)* checking *online* (or *at runtime*) if the current execution satisfies the properties. The first problem is generally called *verification*, and model checking [7] has been the major breakthrough, while the second is called *runtime verification* [20], and it occupies the middle-ground between verification and testing. While both of the aforementioned techniques have considered almost entirely propositional properties, in recent years the emerging of data-aware approaches to business process modeling [24,5] pushed the

S. Basu et al. (Eds.): ICSOC 2013, LNCS 8274, pp. 54–68, 2013.
© Springer-Verlag Berlin Heidelberg 2013

verification and database community to explore more expressive formalisms for specifying the properties of interest [11,19,4,8]. The key idea of data-aware approaches is to elevate design of data to the same level as design of activities and their control flows, enriching the classical approaches which lack the connection between process and data. Unfortunately, data-aware business process systems are very challenging to be verified. Indeed, on the one hand, languages for specifying properties are very expressive since they merge the capability of querying a rich structure (e.g., relational) with temporal operators, and on the other hand the presence of data makes such systems infinite state. Unless several restrictions to both the language and possible system evolutions are posed [19,4,8], the classical verification techniques, which check offline all possible evolutions of the systems, are, in general, undecidable. In many practical scenarios, however, it is not necessary to verify all possible executions of the system, but just the current one. For instance, a formal description of the system to be analyzed can be missed, e.g., because unknown, or because highly unstructured (hence an offline analysis cannot be performed) but nonetheless, there are underlying data changing and temporal properties over such data should be enforced.

A representative scenario is health care. Governments have general *guidelines* which do not describe a precise process, but rather a set of cases in which some activities have to be performed. As an example, when a head injury happens, the patient may be rushed to a hospital. During the transportation and upon arrival in emergency room, a crude assessment of the vitals are measured, using the Glasgow coma scale (GCS), injury severity score (ISS) and other test results. *Physicians make decisions on diagnostics and treatments based on collected data and protocols.* Treatment protocols are formulated based on analysis of past patient records and change often. For example, a protocol may state that lightly injured (low ISS score) patients over 65 years old with decreasing GCS scores should have additional tests. After analyzing data, the condition in the protocol may be revised to lightly injured patients over 79 with decreasing GCS or increasing heart rate. In such a scenario, *runtime monitoring of data would help physicians to adhere to the protocol and assists their decisions.*

A further motivation for runtime verification is that it monitors a *concrete* execution of the process, while offline verification is performed on a model of the process (not on the process itself) which, in order to achieve decidability of verification or to cope with the state explosion problem, is usually an approximation of the original process (obtained, e.g., through predicate abstraction or bit state hashing techniques), leading to sound but not complete verification procedures.

In this paper, we focus on the support for runtime enforcement of first-order LTL formulas for data-aware process executions and study the problem of how to incrementally evaluate them. Technically, properties are specified in a first-order language extended with (future time) linear-time logic (LTL) operators and we check them on a sequence of relational data instances incrementally.

The paper makes the following technical contributions. We initiate the study on incremental evaluation of first-order temporal properties over data instances evolving over time, by proposing an automata-based approach: we extend the runtime verification technique presented in [3] to a first-order setting by constructing a first-order Büchi automaton. Such an automaton, along with auxiliary data structures evolving together with the data evolution, is able to monitor the property in an incremental fashion and in exponential space in the size of the property, while using existing propositional techniques would require exponential space in the size of the domain. More generally, this paper provides an alternative way of performing formal verification of artifact-centric models [17,8] and other business process models such as [14,21].

The paper is organized as follows. Section 2 defines our first-order LTL language and its formal semantics; Section 3 illustrates the automata-based approach and the auxiliary data structures needed for the monitoring; Section 4 describes the space and time complexity; Section 5 provides a picture of the related works and Section 6 concludes the paper.

2   First-Order LTL

We assume the data schema to be relational. We define the *data schema* as a tuple $\mathcal{S} = (R_1 \dots R_n, \Delta)$ where $R_1 \dots R_n$ are relation symbols with an associated arity and Δ is a *fixed* a-priori and *finite* set of constants. An instance I of $\mathcal{S}$ interprets each relation symbol R_i with arity n as a relation $R_i^I \subseteq \Delta^n$. Values in Δ are interpreted as themselves, blurring the distinctions between constants and values. Following the tradition of artifact-centric models, we use the terms instance, snapshot or interpretation interchangeably. Given a schema $\mathcal{S}$, symbol $\mathcal{I}$ denotes all possible interpretations for $\mathcal{S}$.

The analysis we perform consists in checking temporal properties while data evolve. In particular, we provide the theoretical foundations for building a module that takes as input a first-order temporal property and, each time data changes, it inspects the new instance and checks whether the temporal property is verified, is falsified or neither of the previous. If the property is falsified, the new instance is rejected, and the execution must continue starting from the previous one, i.e., we rollback to the previous state. Otherwise, the new instance is accepted. In such a scenario we need to recognize a violation at the earlier possible time, in order to be sure that before the last update, i.e., from the previous snapshot, a possible execution that satisfies the formula does exist.

We present a first-order LTL language that merges the capabilities of first-order logic for querying the instance with the LTL temporal operators.

Definition 1 (First-order LTL Language $\mathcal{L}$ Syntax). *Given a data schema $\mathcal{S}$, the set of closed first-order LTL formulas Φ of language $\mathcal{L}$ are built with the following syntax:*

$$\Phi^\ell := true \mid Atom \mid \neg\Phi^\ell \mid \Phi_1^\ell \wedge \Phi_2^\ell \mid \forall x.\Phi^\ell$$
$$\Phi^t := \Phi^\ell \mid \mathbf{X}\Phi^t \mid \Phi_1^t \mathbf{U}\Phi_2^t \mid \neg\Phi^t \mid \Phi_1^t \wedge \Phi_2^t$$
$$\Phi := \Phi^t \mid \neg\Phi \mid \forall x.\Phi$$

where x is a variable symbol and Atom is an atomic first-order formula or atom, i.e., a formula inductively defined as follows: true is an atomic formula; if t_1

and t_2 are constants in Δ or variables, then $t_1 = t_2$ is an atomic formula and if $t_1 \ldots t_n$ are constants or variables and R a relation symbol of arity n, then $R(t_1 \ldots t_n)$ is an atomic formula. Since Φ is closed, we assume that all variables symbols are in the scope of a quantifier.

We call *local* formulas the set Φ^ℓ because they do not include any temporal operators. In fact, a formula in Φ^ℓ is a first-order formula with equality but no function symbols and, by expressing a local constraint, it can be checked by looking at a single snapshot. The set of formulas in Φ^t are *temporal* formulas, and indeed they include **X** and **U** logic symbols that are the usual LTL *next* and *until* operators. Satisfiability of temporal formulas cannot be established by looking at a single snapshot only. Notice that formulas in Φ^t do not include any quantifier for variables occurring in the scope of temporal operators. Finally, the set Φ is made up by formulas that have quantifiers for variables that occur in the scope of temporal operators. We call such variables *across-state* variables. Such formulas are hard and costly to be monitored, because, in general, they require the whole history of snapshots seen so far to determine their truth value. Notice also that the scope of the quantifiers is required to be the entire formula. In other words, our language is not full first-order LTL, since we require all across-state variables to appear in the front of the formula. As an example, $\forall x.(R_1(x)\mathbf{U}(\neg \forall y.(R_2(x,y) \land \mathbf{X}R_3(y))))$ is not allowed, since variable y is across-states (because in the scope of **X**) but its quantifier is not in the front.

We define the propositional symbols $\lor$ and $\exists$ as $\Phi_1 \lor \Phi_2 := \neg(\neg\Phi_1 \land \neg\Phi_2)$ and $\exists x.\Phi := \neg\forall x.\neg\Phi$ respectively. Moreover the "finally" **F** and "globally" **G** LTL operators are defined as $\mathbf{F}\Phi := true\mathbf{U}\Phi$; $\mathbf{G}\Phi := \neg\mathbf{F}\Phi$.

Every formula in $\mathcal{L}$ can be translated into an equivalent formula in *prenex normal form*, i.e., with all quantifier in the front. From now on we assume formulas to be in such a form.

Before showing the semantics of $\mathcal{L}$, we need to introduce the notion of assignment. Let I be a first-order interpretation, i.e., a snapshot for $\mathcal{S}$, an *assignment* η is a function that associates to each free variable x a value $\eta(x)$ in Δ. Let η be an assignment, then $\eta_{x/d}$ is the assignment that agrees with η except for the value $d \in \Delta$ that is now assigned to the variable x. We denote by $\Phi[\eta]$ is the formula obtained from Φ by replacing variables symbols with values in η.

Our analysis is performed at runtime, and hence its semantics is based on finite-length executions, also called paths. Such a semantics is defined starting from the usual infinite-length paths semantics, therefore we first show the latter, and then we turn to the former. An infinite *path* is an infinite sequence of snapshots $I_0, I_1 \ldots$, i.e., given a schema $\mathcal{S}$, it is a function $\pi : \mathbf{N} \to \mathcal{I}$ that assigns a snapshot I_i to each time instant $i \in \mathbf{N}$.

Definition 2 (Infinite path $\mathcal{L}$ Semantics). *Given a formula $\Phi \in \mathcal{L}$ over a schema $\mathcal{S}$, an assignment η, a path π and an instant of time i we have that:*

- $(\pi, i, \eta) \models \Phi^\ell$ *iff* $(\pi(i), \eta) \models \Phi^\ell$, *where* $(\pi(i), \eta) \models \Phi^\ell$ *is the usual first-order logic evaluation function;*
- $(\pi, i, \eta) \models \mathbf{X}\Phi^t$ *iff* $(\pi, i+1, \eta) \models \Phi^t$;

$-$ $(\pi, i, \eta) \models \Phi_1^t \mathbf{U} \Phi_2^t$ iff for some $j \geq i$ we have that $(\pi, j, \eta) \models \Phi_2^t$ and for all $i \leq k < j$ we have that $(\pi, k, \eta) \models \Phi_1^t$;

$-$ $(\pi, i, \eta) \models \neg \Phi$ iff $(\pi, i, \eta) \not\models \Phi$

$-$ $(\pi, i, \eta) \models \Phi_1 \wedge \Phi_2$ iff $(\pi, i, \eta) \models \Phi_1$ and $(\pi, i, \eta) \models \Phi_2$;

$-$ $(\pi, i, \eta) \models \forall x. \Phi$ iff for all $d \in \Delta$ we have $(\pi, i, \eta_{x/d}) \models \Phi$;

Further, $(\pi, \eta) \models \Phi$ *iff* $(\pi, 0, \eta) \models \Phi$ *and, since every formula in* $\mathcal{L}$ *has no free variables, we can simply write* $\pi \models \Phi$.

Note that when a formula does not contain any temporal operators, i.e., when it is local, its semantics corresponds exactly to the usual first-order semantics. Indeed, in order to evaluate a local formula, we do not need the whole path, but the current snapshot only. Moreover, the domain Δ is the same for each instant of time (see [15] for a dissertation on different semantics for first-order modal logics).

We now turn to the finite-path semantics. Since the first introduction of LTL by Pnueli [25], several different semantics for finite-path LTL have been proposed, see e.g., [23,13,9]. Here we adapt the one in [3] to our first-order setting. Such a semantics is strongly related with the notion of bad prefixes, that has been established in [22]. Given a formula Φ in $\mathcal{L}$, a *bad prefix* for Φ is a finite path such that any infinite extension of it does not satisfy Φ. In other words, no matter the continuation of the prefix, the formula Φ will be always evaluated to false. As an example, safety properties such as "*p* holds forever" always have a bad prefix that violates them, that is, a finite path containing a state where *p* does not hold. Analogously, a *good prefix* can be defined as a finite path which, no matter its continuation, it will always satisfy the property Φ. Eventualities, such as "eventually *p* holds", always have a finite path that satisfies them. Notice that there are several LTL properties that cannot be satisfied nor falsified by any finite trace, e.g., "infinitely often *p* holds" as any finite path can be extended to an infinite one satisfying the formula as well as falsifying it. Such formulas are called in [3] *non-monitorable*.

Definition 3 (Finite path $\mathcal{L}$ Semantics). *Given a formula Φ over a schema $\mathcal{S}$ and a finite path of length k, written as $\pi[k]$, the truth value of a formula Φ on $\pi[k]$, denoted by $[\pi[k] \models \Phi]$, is an element of the set $\mathbb{B}_3 = \{true, false, ?\}$ defined as follows:*

$-$ $[\pi[k] \models \Phi] := true$ *iff* $\pi[k]$ *is bad prefix for* $\neg \Phi$;

$-$ $[\pi[k] \models \Phi] := false$ *iff* $\pi[k]$ *is bad prefix for* Φ;

$-$? *otherwise.*

Notice that a bad prefix for $\neg \Phi$ is a good prefix for Φ. The core technical issue of our problem can now be re-formulated as recognizing the bad and good prefixes. Indeed, when a new snapshot I_i is presented as input, we have to check if $I_0 \ldots I_i$ is a bad, good prefix or neither of the two, i.e., we have to compute the relation $[I_0 \ldots I_i \models \Phi]$. In the classical, propositional version, the problem of recognizing a bad prefix for a propositional formula Ψ can be solved by building a so-called *monitor* for Ψ (see, e.g., [3,9]). The procedure is centered on the construction of a Büchi automaton for Ψ (e.g., following the procedure in [1] or [16]) which is an automaton on infinite strings representing the language $L(\Psi)$ whose accepting condition requires that a final state is visited infinitely often.

Given a propositional formula Ψ over a set of atomic propositions AP, the Büchi automaton $\mathcal{A}$ for Ψ is the automaton such that the language it accepts, denoted by $L(\mathcal{A})$, is the language $L(\Psi)$. Technically, a Büchi automaton is a tuple $\mathcal{A} = (2^{AP}, Q, \delta, Q_0, F)$ where Q is a set of states, $\delta : Q \times 2^{AP} \to 2^Q$ the (possibly nondeterministic) transition function, Q_0 the set of initial states and F is the set of final states. A *run* of $\mathcal{A}$ on an infinite word $\alpha = a_0, a_1 \ldots$ (or ω-word) is an infinite state sequence $r(0), r(1) \ldots$ where the following holds: (i) $r(0) = q_0$ and (ii) $r(i) \in \delta(r(i-1), a_i)$ for $i \leq 1$ if $\mathcal{A}$ is nondeterministic or $r(i) = \delta(r(i-1), a_i)$ for $i \leq 1$ if $\mathcal{A}$ is deterministic. An infinite word α is accepted by $\mathcal{A}$ iff there exists a run $r(0), r(1) \ldots$ which visits one of the states in F infinitely often. In other words, α is accepted if the run $r(0), r(1) \ldots$ cycles in a set of states containing a final state.

Given a propositional formula Ψ, the monitor for Ψ is constructed as follows: (1) the automaton for Ψ is generated and (2) states of the automaton that do not satisfy the Büchi condition, i.e., from which a path that leads to a cycle containing an accepting state does not exist, are marked with "bad". The analysis in (2) is called *emptiness check*. To monitor an execution of a system, it is enough to navigate the automaton's transitions while instances are presented as inputs. When a bad state is reached, the last instance must be rejected. In fact from each bad state there is no way to accept any infinite words belonging to $L(\Psi)$, meaning that Ψ is falsified. Notice that the monitor outputs the truth value ? in any other no bad states, because from them there exists a path leading to the acceptance condition, but the formula can still be falsified later on. Indeed, by using the automaton for Ψ we can recognize the bad prefixes only, but not the good ones. To fully capture the three-valued semantics presented before, two automata have to be used: one for Ψ for recognizing the bad prefixes and one for $\neg\Psi$ recognizing the good ones. We propose an approach that is grounded on the aforementioned technique but that introduces some novelties needed when dealing with first-order properties.

Before entering into the details of our methodology, we point out that our first-order formulas can be translated into an equivalent propositional formula. Indeed, given that no function symbols are in the language and we assume finite domain, the first-order syntax is just a shortcut for the propositional one. Given a first-order formula $\Phi \in \mathcal{L}$, we can build an *equivalent* propositional formula.

In what follows, we refer to [28] for the classical, i.e., on infinite paths, LTL propositional semantics and to [3] to the LTL$_3$ semantics, i.e., on finite propositional paths.

Lemma 1 (Propositionalization). *Let $\mathcal{L}$ be the language defined before, $\mathcal{L}^p$ a propositional LTL language and Δ a finite domain. Then we can build a mapping $\mathsf{p} : \mathcal{L} \to \mathcal{L}^p$ such that, given a formula $\Phi \in \mathcal{L}$, an infinite path π, and a finite path $\pi[k]$:*

- $\pi \models \Phi \equiv \mathsf{p}(\pi) \models \mathsf{p}(\Phi)$;
- $[\pi[k] \models \Phi] \equiv [\mathsf{p}(\pi[k]) \models \mathsf{p}(\Phi)]$

where, with abuse of notation, $\mathsf{p}(\pi)$ is the natural extension of p to paths, i.e., the path obtained from π by applying function p at the first-order interpretation $\pi(i)$ seen as a logic formula[1], for each time instant $i \in \mathbf{N}$.

Proof (Sketch). Function p is inductively defined over $\mathcal{L}$ formulas and, as base case, it associates propositional symbols to first-order atoms. When applied to formulas with a universal quantifier, p returns the conjunction of each assignment for the variables. Given that the domain is finite, we get the claim.   □

Notice that there are several ways to map atoms to propositional symbols, hence there are several different propositionalization functions, all equivalent modulo propositional symbol renaming. In the rest of the paper we assume to set one, say function p.

Given a formula $\Phi \in \mathcal{L}$, the size of the formula $\mathsf{p}(\Phi)$ is exponential in the number of universal variables, hence, in the worst case, on the length of Φ. More precisely, its size is $|\Delta|^{|\Phi|}$.

3   First-Order Automaton

Every formula $\Phi \in \mathcal{L}$ can be propositionalized. Therefore it is easy to see that to monitor Φ we could first propositionalize it, obtaining $\mathsf{p}(\Phi)$, and then we could use existing techniques for monitoring propositional formulas. However, building a monitor requires the construction of the Büchi automaton for $\mathsf{p}(\Phi)$ (see, e.g., [1,16] for the actual procedure) that is exponential in the size of the formula, which, in turn, is exponentially bigger than the original Φ. Given that the automaton construction is $c^{|\mathsf{p}(\Phi)|}$, where c is a constant, we obtain an overall space complexity of is $c^{|\Delta|^{|\Phi|}}$, that is, exponential in the size of the domain and double exponential in the size of the formula.

In this Section we illustrate how to monitor a first-order formula in exponential space in the size of the formula. We make use of a first-order automaton plus some data structures. As it will be clear later on, the auxiliary data structures are used to keep track of assignments to variables. The advantage of this methodology is to decouple the cost of building the automaton from the size of the domain.

Given a formula $\Phi \in \mathcal{L}$, in order to build the first-order automaton for Φ, we first drop all quantifiers from Φ, obtaining an open first-order formula $\hat{\Phi}$ and then we build the automaton for $\hat{\Phi}$. Indeed, given that $\hat{\Phi}$ contains no quantifiers, we can consider the atomic formulas of $\hat{\Phi}$ as propositional symbols and use a standard propositional procedure, e.g., the one in [1], for building the automaton for $\hat{\Phi}$. The formal procedure would require to first propositionalize the atoms of $\hat{\Phi}$, then build the automaton, and lastly use p^{-1} to translate back the propositional

---

[1] We can represent an interpretation I as the conjunction of all positive facts $R_i(d_1, \ldots, d_n)$ when $(d_1, \ldots, d_n) \in R_i^I$ and the conjunction of all negative facts $\neg R_i(d_1, \ldots, d_n)$ when $(d_1, \ldots, d_n) \notin R_i^I$, for all relation symbol $R_i \in \mathcal{L}$ and tuple $(d_1, \ldots, d_n) \in \Delta^n$.

symbols into first-order formulas. To ease the presentation we skip the propositionalization step. Indeed, given that $\hat{\Phi}$ does not have quantifiers, function p turns out to be a syntactic renaming of atoms (cf. Lemma 1).

The automaton $\mathcal{A}(\hat{\Phi})$ is likewise a propositional one, except for its transitions and states that are labeled with *open* first-order formulas.

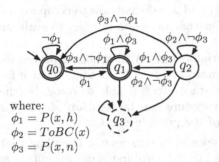

where:
$\phi_1 = P(x, h)$
$\phi_2 = ToBC(x)$
$\phi_3 = P(x, n)$

Fig. 1. Graphical representation of the first-order automaton for the formula in Example 1.

Example 1. As an example of the first-order automaton construction, let us consider an hospital that keeps track of the vitals of its patients.

Table P stores information about patients and its attributes are the identifier of the patient and the blood pressure. Moreover, we have a $ToBC$ table with a single attribute storing information about patients which need to be checked by a nurse. We assume possible values for the blood pressure to be normal (n), high (h) or low (l). We want to monitor the property that, for each patient, anytime his blood pressure changes to high, then, in the next instant, a check is needed until his pressure goes back to normal. Such a property can be expressed in $\mathcal{L}$ as:

$$\Phi := \forall x. \mathbf{G}(P(x, h) \rightarrow \mathbf{X}(ToBC(x)\mathbf{U}P(x, n)))$$

The first-order automaton for Φ is graphically represented in Figure 1, and it is obtained by: (1) dropping the quantifiers in the front of the formula getting $\hat{\Phi} = \mathbf{G}(P(x, h) \rightarrow \mathbf{X}(ToBC(x)\mathbf{U}P(x, n)))$ and (2) building the Büchi automaton of $\hat{\Phi}$ according to the procedure in [1] by considering atoms as propositional symbols. Double-circled states q_0 and q_1 are final states, q_0 is the only initial state and the dashed state q_3 is a sink, i.e., *bad* state. To keep the picture readable, labels on transitions to the sink state are omitted, but, intuitively, from each state q_i the bad state is reached whenever any other outgoing transition cannot be executed, hence we have $\delta(q_1, \neg((\neg\phi_1 \wedge \phi_3) \vee (\phi_3 \wedge \neg\phi_1) \vee (\phi_2 \wedge \neg\phi_3))) = \{q_3\}$, $\delta(q_2, \neg(\phi_2 \wedge \neg\phi_3) \vee (\phi_1 \wedge \phi_3) \vee (\phi_3 \wedge \neg\phi_1)) = \{q_3\}$ and $\delta(q_3, true) = \{q_3\}$.

Automaton $\mathcal{A}(\hat{\Phi})$ can be used to recognize bad prefixes of Φ. In general, in order to capture the three-valued semantics in Definition 3, we have to recognize the good prefixes as well, and hence we need the automaton $\mathcal{A}(\neg\hat{\Phi})$. In our example, however, being Φ a safety property, it has no good prefixes because it can be verified by an infinite trace only. The automaton for $\neg\Phi$ is therefore not needed, because it would always return ?.   □

Our approach is grounded on the fact that a first-order automaton $\mathcal{A}(\hat{\Phi})$ along with some data structures, is capable of effectively simulating the propositional automata $\mathcal{A}(\mathsf{p}(\Phi))$ needed for recognizing the bad prefixes of $\mathsf{p}(\Phi)$. When using automaton $\mathcal{A}(\neg\hat{\Phi})$ we can recognize also the good prefixes of $\mathsf{p}(\Phi)$. In the rest of the section we are going to show how to use both $\mathcal{A}(\hat{\Phi})$ and $\mathcal{A}(\neg\hat{\Phi})$ for monitoring Φ according to the finite path semantics in Definition 3. To ease the presentation, we proceed in two steps: we first illustrate how, given an assignment η for the variables in Φ, we can recognize the bad prefixes of $\Phi[\eta]$, where $\Phi[\eta]$ denotes the formula obtained from Φ by ignoring the quantifiers and by assigning variables according to η. We then generalize the procedure by showing how to concurrently monitor all possible assignments using $\mathcal{A}(\hat{\Phi})$ and $\mathcal{A}(\neg\hat{\Phi})$ and how to compose the results obtained for each assignment and for each automata in order to evaluate the original formula.

Let us assume an assignment η for the variables of Φ. We now show a procedure that, given as input: *(i)* a first-order automaton $\mathcal{A}(\hat{\Phi})$; *(ii)* an assignment η for the variables and *(iii)* the snapshots (as data evolve), is able to recognize the bad prefixes for $\mathsf{p}(\Phi[\eta])$ (an analogous procedure can be used on $\mathcal{A}(\neg\hat{\Phi})$ for recognizing the good prefixes). The steps of the procedure follow:

1. we propositionalize the automaton $\mathcal{A}(\hat{\Phi})$ with assignment η. Recalling that a first-order automaton has transitions labeled with first-order formulas, its propositionalization consists in first substituting the variables with values in η and then using function p to obtain propositional formulas in the transitions. We denote such an automaton with $\mathsf{p}(\mathcal{A}(\hat{\Phi})[\eta])$;
2. We define a marking $M' := Q_0$ as the set of initial states and a marking $M := \emptyset$.
3. At runtime, when a new snapshot I is presented as input:
   (a) $M := M'$ and $M' := \emptyset$;
   (b) for each state $q \in M$ if there exists a transition $(q, \mathsf{p}(\gamma[\eta]), q')$ such that $\mathsf{p}(I) \models \mathsf{p}(\gamma[\eta])$, then $M' := M' \cup q'$.
   (c) we check the emptiness for all $q \in M'$. If at least one state in M' satisfies the Büchi condition, then we return ?, otherwise *false*.

The markings are needed to follow the execution of the snapshots over the automaton which is, in general, nondeterministic, hence more than one state can be contained in the current marking. If from none of the states in the marking it is possible to reach a cycle containing an accepting state, then the sequence of snapshots seen so far is a bad prefix for Φ, and the procedure returns *false*.

By running the same procedure in parallel on the automaton for $\neg\Phi$ (except for step 3(c) where we output *true* if none of the states satisfies the Büchi condition) we recognize also the good prefixes of Φ.

We now prove that this procedure capture exactly the semantics in Definition 3. To this purpose, we reduce to the propositional case where the same result has been proved to hold in [3] and, as a first step, we show that the automaton $\mathsf{p}(\mathcal{A}[\eta])$ and the propositional one for $\mathsf{p}(\Phi[\eta])$ recognize the same language.

Theorem 1. *Given a formula $\Phi \in \mathcal{L}$, let $\hat{\Phi}$ be the (open) formula obtained from Φ by dropping the quantifiers and $\hat{\Phi}[\eta]$ the formula obtained from $\hat{\Phi}$ by substituting all variables with the value given by assignment η. Let moreover:*

- *$\mathcal{A}(\hat{\Phi})$ be the first order automaton for $\hat{\Phi}$;*
- *$\mathcal{A}(\mathsf{p}(\hat{\Phi}[\eta]))$ the propositional automaton for $\mathsf{p}(\hat{\Phi}[\eta])$;*

- $\mathsf{p}(\mathcal{A}(\hat{\Phi})[\eta])$ *the automaton obtained from* $\mathcal{A}(\hat{\Phi})$ *by substituting variables with values given by assignment* η *and by propositionalizing first order formulas with function* p;

then $L(\mathsf{p}(\mathcal{A}(\hat{\Phi})[\eta])) = L(\mathcal{A}(\mathsf{p}(\hat{\Phi}[\eta])))$.

Proof (Sketch). We prove that the two languages are the same by showing that automata $\mathsf{p}(\mathcal{A}(\hat{\Phi})[\eta])$ and $\mathcal{A}(\mathsf{p}(\hat{\Phi}[\eta]))$ are the same automaton. As a first step, since formula $\hat{\Phi}$ has no quantifiers, we abstract from p that trivially associates atoms of the form $R(x, y)$ to propositional symbols $R_{x\text{-}y}$. Then we notice that an assignment η can be viewed as a syntactic manipulation of the formula which changes the name of the variables. Two cases are possible: *(i)* η assigns each variable symbol to a different constant, and *(ii)* η assigns two (or more) variable symbols to the same constant. First case is trivial, while the second one is more involved since two different atoms, e.g., $R(x, y)$ and $R(x, x)$ can become identical, e.g., when $\eta = \{x/a, y/a\}$. If we assume to have two variables only, this requires to prove that $\mathcal{A}(\hat{\Phi}(x, y))|_{y/x}$ and $\mathcal{A}(\hat{\Phi}(x, x))$ are indeed the same automaton, where with $\mathcal{A}(\hat{\Phi}(x, y))|_{y/x}$ we denote the automaton obtained from $\mathcal{A}(\hat{\Phi}(x, y))$ by syntactically replacing each occurrence of y with x. Intuitively, $\mathcal{A}(\hat{\Phi}(x, x))$ shares with $\mathcal{A}(\hat{\Phi}(x, y))$ some states and transitions but it has some less because substituting y to x in Φ may generate contradictions in sub-formulas of Φ (see automaton construction in [1]). Such additional states and transitions, however, are ruled out in $\mathcal{A}(\hat{\Phi}(x, y))|_{y/x}$ after the substitution of y with x. $\qquad\square$

Since *(i)* $\mathcal{A}(\mathsf{p}(\phi[\eta]))$ and $\mathsf{p}(\mathcal{A}(\hat{\Phi})[\eta])$ recognize the same language and *(ii)* the monitoring procedure checks the emptiness per state at each step, we are guaranteed that $\mathsf{p}(\mathcal{A}(\hat{\Phi})[\eta])$ recognizes *minimal* bad prefixes for $\hat{\Phi}[\eta]$.

We now show the key idea for monitoring the whole formula Φ, i.e., all assignment concurrently. Since Φ is in prenex normal form, formula $\mathsf{p}(\Phi)$ has the structure $\bigwedge_{d_1 \in \Delta} \bigvee_{d_2 \in \Delta} \cdots \bigwedge_{d_{n+m} \in \Delta} \mathsf{p}(\Phi[x/d_1, y/d_2 \ldots z/d_{n+m}])$. We can look for the bad (or good) prefixes of such a formula by monitoring $\mathsf{p}(\Phi[x/d_1, y/d_2 \ldots z/d_{n+m}])$ for each assignment $\{x/d_1, y/d_2 \ldots z/d_{n+m}\}$ separately and then composing the results. Indeed, from Definition 3 and the semantics of LTL, it follows that:

- $[\pi[k] \models \phi_1 \wedge \phi_2] = true$ iff $[\pi[k] \models \phi_1] = true \wedge [\pi[k] \models \phi_2] = true$;
- $[\pi[k] \models \phi_1 \wedge \phi_2] = false$ iff $[\pi[k] \models \phi_1] = false \vee [\pi[k] \models \phi_2] = false$;
- $[\pi[k] \models \phi_1 \wedge \phi_2] =?$ otherwise

and analogously for $[\pi[k] \models \phi_1 \vee \phi_2]$.

Given a first order automaton $\mathcal{A}(\hat{\Phi})$, the procedure for recognizing the bad prefixes of Φ is as follows:

1. We define a marking $m : Q \to 2^\eta$ (where η is the set of possible assignments for Φ) as a function which takes as input a state q of $\mathcal{A}(\hat{\Phi})$ and returns the set of assignments q is marked with; we assign $m'(q) := \eta$ for each $q \in Q_0$ and $m'(q) := \emptyset$ for each $q \notin Q_0$.
2. When a new snapshot I is presented as input:
   (a) $m := m'$ and $m'(q) := \emptyset$ for each $q \in Q$;

(b) for each state q and for each assignment $\eta \in m(q)$, if there exists a transition (q, γ, q') such that $I \models \gamma[\eta]$ (recall that γ is an open first-order formula) then $m'(q') := m'(q') \cup \eta$;

(c) for each assignment η we assign a truth value $t(\eta)$ as follows: if there exists at least one state q such that $\eta \in m'(q)$ and the emptiness check from q w.r.t. η (see later) returns true, then $t(\eta) = ?$, otherwise $t(\eta) = false$.

(d) recalling that $\Phi := \bigwedge_{d_1 \in \Delta} \bigvee_{d_2 \in \Delta} \cdots \bigwedge_{d_{n+m} \in \Delta} \mathsf{P}(\Phi[x/d_1, y/d_2 \ldots z/d_{n+m}])$, we output the truth value $\bigwedge_{d_1 \in \Delta} \bigvee_{d_2 \in \Delta} \cdots \bigwedge_{d_{n+m} \in \Delta} t(x/d_1, y/d_2 \ldots z/d_{n+m})$.

Notice that the emptiness check is now more complex (step 2(c)), because (unlike the previous case) transitions are first-order formulas. In order to find the minimal bad prefixes, for each q and η such that $\eta \in m'(q)$, we have to substitute values given by η to all transitions involved in paths starting from q. The emptiness check cannot be computed once and for all for a state q because it also depends on the value of η, that is, there can be a transition (q, γ, q') that is first-order satisfiable, i.e., there is at least one assignment that satisfies γ, but $\gamma[\eta]$ is unsatisfiable. We have indeed to be sure that $\mathcal{A}(\hat{\Phi})$ is suitably pruned from unsatisfiable transitions for a given assignment η, before checking for emptiness for q.

By reducing to the previous case, and by running the algorithm in parallel on both $\mathcal{A}(\hat{\Phi})$ and $\mathcal{A}(\neg \hat{\Phi})$ we capture the semantics of Definition 3 for a first-order formula Φ so we recognize minimal good and bad prefixes, i.e., we report a violation or satisfaction at the earliest possible.

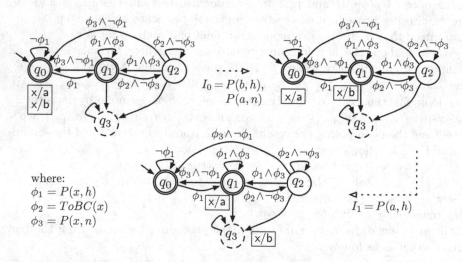

Fig. 2. Graphical representation of the monitoring described in Example 2

Example 2. We continue Example 1 by showing the evolution of marking m as new instances are presented as inputs. We assume a domain $\Delta = \{a, b\}$. Figure 2 illustrates graphically the assignments $m(q_i)$ inside boxes next to q_i for each $q_i \in Q$. In the initial time instant, according to step 1 of the monitoring procedure, the initial state is marked with all assignments for the free variables, that is, $\eta_1 = x/a$ and $\eta_2 = x/b$. When instance $I_0 = P(b, h), P(a, n)$ is presented as input, we check if it satisfies any of the outgoing transitions from q_0 with substitutions η_1 and η_2 (recall transitions are labeled with open formulas). The automaton has two outgoing transitions from q_0, namely $\delta(q_0, \neg P(x, h)) = \{q_0\}$ and $\delta(q_0, P(x, h)) = \{q_1\}$. Given that $I_0 \models \neg P(x, h)[x/a]$ and $I_0 \models P(x, h)[x/b]$, following step 2(b) of the procedure, the new marking is $m'(q_0) = \{\{x/a\}\}$ and $m'(q_1) = \{\{x/b\}\}$. We then check the emptiness condition for every state marked with an assignment (step 3(c)) and we get $t(x/a) =?$ and $t(x/b) =?$ because both q_0 and q_1 are not bad states and, indeed, from both of them there exists a path leading to a loop containing a final state. Since the original formula is $\bigwedge_{x \in \{a,b\}} \hat{\Phi}(x)$, we get $? \wedge ? =?$, meaning that the formula is not yet falsified.

Next instance $I_1 = P(a, h)$ satisfies transitions from q_0 to q_1 with assignment $\{x/a\}$ and from q_1 to q_3 with assignment $\{x/b\}$. Given that q_3 is a bad state, we get $? \wedge false = false$ and the monitoring can be stopped since any prosecution will violate the formula.

4 Time and Space Complexity

The number of states of the Büchi automaton for a formula Φ is $c^{|\Phi|}$. During the runtime monitoring we keep $|\Delta|^n$ number of assignments where n is the number of variables, hence, in the worst case $|\Delta|^{|\Phi|}$. Given that the automaton is nondeterministic, each state can be marked with all assignments, hence we get a space complexity of $c^{|\Phi|} \cdot |\Delta|^{|\Phi|}$ which is exponential in the size of the formula. For the sake of readability, we presented markings as containing substitutions to both across-state and local variables. Actually, in order to evaluate a formula in $\mathcal{L}$ we do not need to keep assignments for local variables across the execution. Indeed, they are used to check local conditions only. Therefore we can mark states of the automaton with the across-state variables only and use a refined (but trivial) mechanism for computing the markings at each step. Therefore, we get an exponential space approach in the number of across state variables only, which, in many practical cases, is much smaller than the length of the formula. Recall that the naive approach costs $c^{|\Delta|^{|\Phi|}}$ in space.

This gain does not come for free. Indeed, while in the naive approach the emptiness per state can be done offline and once for all after the construction of the automaton, in our case checking the Büchi condition is more involved, because we have to perform it for each assignment separately. As described in the previous Section, we perform such an analysis on the fly. Assuming we use nested depth first search, that is linear time in the size of the automaton, each time a new instance is presented as input, we have to check the emptiness $|\Delta|^{|\Phi|}$ times. We get $|\Delta|^{|\Phi|} \cdot c^{|\Phi|}$ time complexity at each step. We could also check the emptiness for each assignment offline, paying the time cost once for all. This, however, would require to keep, for each state q and for each assignment η information about the badness of q for η, leading to another $c^{|\Phi|} \cdot |\Delta|^{|\Phi|}$ in space.

Since the major constraint of this problem is the space rather than the time, we prefer to perform the analysis online.

5   Related Work

Our work stands in the middle-ground between databases and verification, hence it has been influenced by both fields.

Concerning databases, works on incremental evaluation of queries inspired our approach. The work in [12] addresses the problem of efficiently evaluating a datalog query to a database that is being updated. The solution amounts to compute differences between successive database states which, along with the old query answer, can be used to reduce the cost to re-evaluate the query in the new state. Derived (auxiliary) relations are stored to solve the problem. Chomicki [6] focuses on an "history less" approach for checking database integrity temporal constraints. Such constraints are FO-LTL formulas with past-tense operators (*previous time* and *since*). This impacts the verification procedure that is not *runtime* and does not account the undefined ? truth value. An incremental solution, which makes use of auxiliary relations to store intermediate results, is proposed and complexity results are similar. Toman [27] investigated techniques for historical query evaluation in warehouse systems, which, knowing all queries to be asked in advance, physically delete irrelevant past databases. The query language includes temporal variables. Besides, how to evaluate temporal queries over databases has been extensively studied in database literature and ad-hoc query languages has been proposed, such as TSQL2 [26]. Such approaches, however, explicitly represent time in the data, hence they deeply differ from the incremental approach used here. All the aforementioned solutions do not employ automata.

On the other side, the verification community has proposed several techniques for checking dynamic properties of data-aware business processes, all of them based on model checking [7]. Since the presence of data makes the system infinite-state, distinct approaches differ over restrictions used to achieve decidability. In [4] decidability results for verifying temporal properties over data-aware systems are shown, and they are obtained by abstraction and by bounding the size of the so-called *deployed* instances. In [11,19,8] decidability is achieved by constraining the actions that specify how the system evolves. Given that in general several restrictions should be put in place to achieve decidability, our work distances itself from (offline) verification by proposing runtime verification as an alternative to evaluate temporal properties on dynamic systems.

In the runtime verification literature, different formalisms for specifying admissible executions has been proposed, such as ω-regular languages [9], LTL [3] or even μ-calculus [10], but all of them uses propositional languages. In [2] open first-order temporal properties are monitored, and the technique proposed returns assignments that falsify the formula. However, the logic is too expressive for supporting satisfiability and, more important, there is no "lookahead" mechanism of possible future evolutions (automata are not used indeed) so the bad prefixes recognized are not minimal. The work in [18] is the closest to ours, but a naive solution is adopted and no emphasis on complexity is placed.

6 Conclusions and Future Work

This paper initiates the study of runtime monitoring of temporal properties over data evolution using an automata-based technique. We have presented a property specification language $\mathcal{L}$, that consists in a first-order language with LTL operators, fixed domain and quantification across-state. To achieve decidability we constraint the interpretation domain to be finite. From a formula $\Phi \in \mathcal{L}$ we have shown how to build a first-order automaton that, along with auxiliary data structures, can be used for monitoring data evolutions of finite and unknown length. In order to do so, we use the finite path semantics during the runtime evolution of snapshots for recognizing both bad prefixes and good prefixes of a formula. Given that some LTL properties can be violated or satisfied only by infinite paths, such a semantics accounts the truth value ?. The evaluation of the property is based on the traditional emptiness checking and our mechanism captures the semantics of finite paths.

We believe the theoretical complexity results we have obtained justify a deeper investigation of the topic. As a first step in this direction we plan to practically validate our approach. We think that implementing our procedure by making use of symbolic data structures, such as binary decision diagrams, can further improve space and time performances. Besides, an analysis of structural properties of both formulas and automata can reveal ways for implementing optimized data structures for assignments in order to save space. From the theoretical viewpoint, we plan to relax some of the assumptions we have made in this paper, such as the fixed and finite domain assumptions. It would be also of interest to investigate extensions of the temporal component of the language, such as regular expressions, or more powerful logics such as μ-calculus.

Acknowledgments. The authors would sincerely like to thank G. De Giacomo, C. Di Ciccio, D. Firmani, F. Leotta and A. Russo for the interesting discussions and suggestions about the paper.

References

1. Baier, C., Katoen, J.P.: Principles of model checking. MIT Press (2008)
2. Basin, D., Klaedtke, F., Müller, S.: Policy monitoring in first-order temporal logic. In: Touili, T., Cook, B., Jackson, P. (eds.) CAV 2010. LNCS, vol. 6174, pp. 1–18. Springer, Heidelberg (2010)
3. Bauer, A., Leucker, M., Schallhart, C.: Runtime verification for ltl and tltl. ACM Trans. Softw. Eng. Methodol. 20(4), 14:1–14:64 (2011)
4. Belardinelli, F., Lomuscio, A., Patrizi, F.: Verification of deployed artifact systems via data abstraction. In: Kappel, G., Maamar, Z., Motahari-Nezhad, H.R. (eds.) ICSOC 2011. LNCS, vol. 7084, pp. 142–156. Springer, Heidelberg (2011)
5. Bhattacharya, K., Gerede, C., Hull, R., Liu, R., Su, J.: Towards formal analysis of artifact-centric business process models. In: Alonso, G., Dadam, P., Rosemann, M. (eds.) BPM 2007. LNCS, vol. 4714, pp. 288–304. Springer, Heidelberg (2007), http://www.springerlink.com/content/w31j312311x6310j
6. Chomicki, J.: Efficient checking of temporal integrity constraints using bounded history encoding. ACM Transactions on Database Systems 20(2), 149–186 (1995)
7. Clarke, E.M., Grumberg, O., Peled, D.A.: Model checking. The MIT Press, Cambridge (1999)

8. Damaggio, E., Deutsch, A., Hull, R., Vianu, V.: Automatic verification of data-centric business processes. In: Rinderle-Ma, S., Toumani, F., Wolf, K. (eds.) BPM 2011. LNCS, vol. 6896, pp. 3–16. Springer, Heidelberg (2011)
9. D'Amorim, M., Roşu, G.: Efficient monitoring of ω-languages. In: Etessami, K., Rajamani, S.K. (eds.) CAV 2005. LNCS, vol. 3576, pp. 364–378. Springer, Heidelberg (2005)
10. D'Angelo, B., Sankaranarayanan, S., Sánchez, C., Robinson, W., Finkbeiner, B., Sipma, H.B., Mehrotra, S., Manna, Z.: Lola: Runtime monitoring of synchronous systems. In: TIME, pp. 166–174 (2005)
11. De Giacomo, G., De Masellis, R., Rosati, R.: Verification of conjunctive artifact-centric services. Int. J. Cooperative Inf. Syst. 21(2), 111–140 (2012)
12. Dong, G., Su, J., Topor, R.: Nonrecursive incremental evaluation of datalog queries. Annals of Mathematics and Artificial Intelligence 14, 187–223 (1995)
13. Eisner, C., Fisman, D., Havlicek, J., Lustig, Y., McIsaac, A., Van Campenhout, D.: Reasoning with temporal logic on truncated paths. In: Hunt Jr., W.A., Somenzi, F. (eds.) CAV 2003. LNCS, vol. 2725, pp. 27–39. Springer, Heidelberg (2003)
14. Fahland, D., Favre, C., Jobstmann, B., Koehler, J., Lohmann, N., Völzer, H., Wolf, K.: Instantaneous soundness checking of industrial business process models. In: Dayal, U., Eder, J., Koehler, J., Reijers, H.A. (eds.) BPM 2009. LNCS, vol. 5701, pp. 278–293. Springer, Heidelberg (2009)
15. Fitting, M., Mendelsohn, R.L.: First-Order Modal Logic. Kluwer Academic Press (1998)
16. Gastin, P., Oddoux, D.: Fast LTL to Büchi automata translation. In: Berry, G., Comon, H., Finkel, A. (eds.) CAV 2001. LNCS, vol. 2102, pp. 53–65. Springer, Heidelberg (2001)
17. Gerede, C.E., Su, J.: Specification and verification of artifact behaviors in business process models. In: Krämer, B.J., Lin, K.-J., Narasimhan, P. (eds.) ICSOC 2007. LNCS, vol. 4749, pp. 181–192. Springer, Heidelberg (2007), http://www.springerlink.com/content/c371144007878627
18. Hallé, S., Villemaire, R.: Runtime monitoring of message-based workflows with data. In: EDOC, pp. 63–72 (2008)
19. Hariri, B.B., Calvanese, D., De Giacomo, G., De Masellis, R., Felli, P., Montali, M.: Verification of description logic knowledge and action bases. In: ECAI, pp. 103–108 (2012)
20. Havelund, K., Rosu, G.: Foreword - selected papers from the first international workshop on runtime verification held in paris, july 2001 (rv'01). Formal Methods in System Design 24(2), 99–100 (2004)
21. Klai, K., Tata, S., Desel, J.: Symbolic abstraction and deadlock-freeness verification of inter-enterprise processes. In: Dayal, U., Eder, J., Koehler, J., Reijers, H.A. (eds.) BPM 2009. LNCS, vol. 5701, pp. 294–309. Springer, Heidelberg (2009)
22. Kupferman, O., Vardi, M.Y.: Model checking of safety properties. Formal Methods in System Design 19(3), 291–314 (2001)
23. Manna, Z., Pnueli, A.: Temporal verification of reactive systems - safety. Springer (1995)
24. Nigam, A., Caswell, N.S.: Business artifacts: An approach to operational specification. IBM Systems Journal 42(3), 428–445 (2003)
25. Pnueli, A.: The temporal logic of programs. In: FOCS, pp. 46–57 (1977)
26. Snodgrass, R.T. (ed.): The TSQL2 Temporal Query Language. Kluwer (1995)
27. Toman, D.: Expiration of historical databases. In: TIME, pp. 128–135 (2001)
28. Vardi, M.Y.: An automata-theoretic approach to linear temporal logic. In: Moller, F., Birtwistle, G. (eds.) Logics for Concurrency. LNCS, vol. 1043, pp. 238–266. Springer, Heidelberg (1996)

QoS-Aware Service VM Provisioning in Clouds: Experiences, Models, and Cost Analysis

Mathias Björkqvist[1], Sebastiano Spicuglia[2], Lydia Chen[1], and Walter Binder[2]

[1] IBM Research Zürich Laboratory
Rüschlikon, Switzerland
{mbj,yic}@zurich.ibm.com
[2] University of Lugano
Lugano, Switzerland
firstname.lastname@usi.ch

Abstract. Recent studies show that service systems hosted in clouds can elastically scale the provisioning of pre-configured virtual machines (VMs) with workload demands, but suffer from performance variability, particularly from varying response times. Service management in clouds is further complicated especially when aiming at striking an optimal trade-off between cost (i.e., proportional to the number and types of VM instances) and the fulfillment of quality-of-service (QoS) properties (e.g., a system should serve at least 30 requests per second for more than 90% of the time). In this paper, we develop a QoS-aware VM provisioning policy for service systems in clouds with high capacity variability, using experimental as well as modeling approaches. Using a wiki service hosted in a private cloud, we empirically quantify the QoS variability of a single VM with different configurations in terms of capacity. We develop a Markovian framework which explicitly models the capacity variability of a service cluster and derives a probability distribution of QoS fulfillment. To achieve the guaranteed QoS at minimal cost, we construct theoretical and numerical cost analyses, which facilitate the search for an optimal size of a given VM configuration, and additionally support the comparison between VM configurations.

Keywords: QoS, cloud services, VM provisioning, Markovian models.

1 Introduction

Service systems are increasingly deployed in clouds due to the advantages of scalability and ease of management. In the cloud, a set of preconfigured VM instances is available at different costs (e.g., small, medium, large, and very large instances in Amazon EC2 [1]), and their corresponding hardware-related performance metrics are provided at best effort [15]. Meanwhile, service providers face ever more stringent QoS demands from users, in particular regarding the tail performance, e.g., 95th percentile or higher response times. The difficulties of service management in clouds (i.e., selecting a VM configuration and dimensioning the system correctly) are further exacerbated when aiming at providing

S. Basu et al. (Eds.): ICSOC 2013, LNCS 8274, pp. 69–83, 2013.

QoS guarantees for both average and tail performance [8], while retaining the cloud advantages at the same time.

Several empirical studies [6, 16, 20] point out a common pitfall in clouds that the performance variability — in this case the response time of services — fluctuates significantly and tail latency degrades due to the heterogeneity of the underlying hardware and the workloads collocated on the same physical hosts. Although virtualization enables the efficient multiplexing of workloads across the ample hardware resource, performance isolation is limited [7], especially for applications that are not CPU intensive. While the performance variability persists in cloud platforms, little is known about the sensitivity of services on different VM configurations in terms of capacity[1] i.e., the maximum number of service requests that can be processed sustainably, and the aggregate impact of the capacity variability of a single VM on the QoS of the entire service cluster.

VM provisioning of service systems is typically based on the average capacity, which in turn is a good indicator for systems experiencing low variability and providing simple QoS guarantees [22], such as average throughput over a certain threshold. To avoid performance penalties due to variability in the cloud, selecting VMs with desirable performance becomes of paramount importance not only to reduce performance variability [9], but also to optimize cost [3, 5]. Consequently, empirical approaches are proposed to acquire VMs with higher capacities. However, due to the empirical nature of the proposed VM selection strategies, a QoS promise of satisfying a given target throughput is only attained at best effort. Moreover, the resulting cost minimization may be arbitrary, depending on the workload dynamics of the underlying cloud platform.

Our study aims to find the optimal VM provisioning for a service system, i.e., composed of an ideal VM configuration using a minimum number of VM instances, such that the required QoS properties are guaranteed for a certain fraction of time at minimal cost (e.g., 90% of the time the sustainable throughput should be at least 30 requests per second). To such an end, we study a wikipedia service [19] and first empirically quantify its capacity variability on different VM configurations, in the presence a daemon VM executing various benchmark workloads in a private cloud. Leveraging our empirical experience, we build a Markovian model which explicitly models the capacity variability of an entire cluster, and we derive the *probability distribution* of the delivered QoS for a given number of VMs of a certain configuration. Based on analytical solutions regarding the QoS fulfillment, we construct theoretical and numerical analyses to evaluate the tradeoff between cost and the fulfillment of QoS promises, (1) by comparing optimal provisioning to simple pessimistic and optimistic provisioning; (2) when provisioning based on the average capacity fails; and (3) when choosing a VM configuration that returns the best cost/service-availability ratio.

This paper is organized as follows: The capacity variability of a VM hosting a wiki service on different VM configurations is discussed in Section 2. The proposed

---

[1] In this paper, we use the terms capacity and sustainable maximum throughput interchangeably.

Markovian model and VM provisioning optimization is described in Section 3. Section 4 presents our cost analysis. Related studies are summarized in Section 5. Section 6 concludes this paper.

2 Capacity Variability of Service VM Configuration

In this section, we use a controlled cloud environment to study the capacity variability of service hosting on different VM configurations, i.e., the fluctuation of capacity, against single neighboring VMs executing various workloads. To such an end, our target service is a wikipedia deployed on a set of VM configurations and collocated with a daemon VM executing Dacapo benchmarks [2] in a private cloud. Essentially, we use the daemon VM to synthesize interference that can be encountered by a wiki VM in the cloud and parametrize the capacity variability, which is then used to build the QoS model for a service cluster in Section 3.

2.1 Experiment Setup

From our private cloud environment, we chose two IBM System x3650 M4 machines, *gschwend* and *nussli*, each with 12 Intel Xeon E5-2620 cores running at 2.00GHz, and 64 and 36 GB of RAM, respectively, for running our experiments. We use KVM on gschwend for hosting our target and daemon VMs, and nussli for generating the Apache JMeter workload requests for our target wiki VM.

The target wikipedia system is based on a subset of 500000 entries from a *pages-articles.xml* dump downloaded on October 12, 2012. The wiki VM is a Debian 7.0 system running an Apache 2.4.4 web server, the PHP 5.4.15 server-side script engine, MediaWiki 1.21 as the web application, and the MySQL 5.5.31 database. The number of threads employed by Jmeter is configured such that the maximum throughput of the wiki VM is reached. As for the workload on the daemon VM, we selected the following benchmarks from the Dacapo benchmark suite: (1) `fop`, a lowly threaded CPU-intensive benchmark; (2) `luindex`, a lowly threaded IO-intensive benchmark; (3) `sunflow`, a highly threaded CPU-intensive benchmark; (4) `lusearch`, a highly threaded CPU- and IO-intensive benchmark; and (5) `tomcat`, a network-intensive benchmark. We refer readers to [7] for the detailed threading behaviors and characterization of the Dacapo benchmarks.

We consider four types of VM configurations, with CPUs and memory sizes as listed in Table 1, which are comparable to VM offerings in Amazon EC2 [1]. We use three configurations for the wiki VM (bronze, silver, and gold), and two configurations for the daemon VM (gold and platinum). Based on experimental evaluation, we use two, four, and eight threads when running Jmeter against a wiki running on a bronze, silver, and gold VM instance, respectively. In total, we evaluate the amount of performance interference experienced by the wiki under 36 scenarios, i.e., three configurations of wiki VMs × six types of daemon workloads (5 DaCapo benchmarks and no workload) × two daemon VM configurations.

Table 1. VM configurations and naming conventions

	Bronze	Silver	Gold	Platinum
No. processing units	1	2	4	8
RAM (GB)	4	8	16	32

The target wiki performance statistics are collected from the Apache log files which record the current time, the requested URL, and response time for each request. After a warmup period for the wiki VM, Jmeter, the daemon VM and the DaCapo benchmark, we start collecting statistics for five minutes for each of the 36 scenarios, each of which is repeated ten times. We summarize the results of $36 * 10 = 360$ runs using box plots in Fig. 1. One can straightforwardly find that the capacity variability of the wiki, i.e., the difference between no workload and different DaCapo benchmarks running on the daemon VM, can vary significantly depending on VM configurations and the characteristics of the DaCapo benchmark.

For further analysis, we take the median of the repeated runs of all scenarios and compute the average of the normalized throughput, compared to the scenario with no daemon VM neighbor. We thereafter categorize the results by target VM type, daemon VM type, and benchmark.

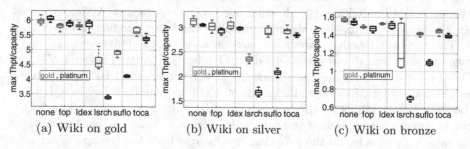

(a) Wiki on gold   (b) Wiki on silver   (c) Wiki on bronze

Fig. 1. Capacity variability of a wiki running on different VM configurations against `fop`, `luindex`, `lusearch`, `sunflow`, and `tomcat`, hosted on gold and platinum VMs: box plots based on 10 repetitions

2.2   (In)Sensitivity of Capacity Variability

To compare the robustness of different target VM configurations, we normalize the throughput of the wiki VM by the throughput of the wiki without any neighbor for gold, silver, and bronze VMs. In Fig. 2(a), we present the average normalized throughput, a higher value of which means less interference is observed and the wiki VM is more robust. When collocated with a gold daemon VM, the difference between wikis running on different VM configurations is almost negligible. However, in our setup, when the daemon VM is more dominant, i.e., a platinum VM, a wiki on a silver VM seems to be slightly more robust than when on a gold or bronze VM. Such an observation can also be made for individual daemon workloads, see Fig. 1. Overall, our experiments show that a wiki running on a silver VM is slightly more robust to noisy neighbors, and the capacity of the wiki can be throttled by 10-20% on average due to interference from neighboring VMs.

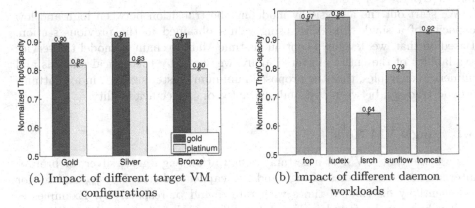

(a) Impact of different target VM configurations

(b) Impact of different daemon workloads

Fig. 2. Average analysis of normalized throughput of target wiki

2.3   A Really Noisy Daemon

We try to identify which type of workload represents the noisiest neighbor and causes high capacity variability for a wiki service collocated on the same physical machine. We compute the average normalized throughput across all target VM configurations for each benchmark, as presented in Fig. 2(b). One can clearly see three levels of performance variability: (1) mild interference from `fop`, `luindex`, and `tomcat`, where the capacity degradation is within 10%; (2) medium interference from `sunflow`, where the capacity is degraded by roughly 20%; and (3) high interference from `lusearch`, where the capacity degradation can be up to 35%. Clearly, `lusearch` is the noisiest neighboring VM for our wiki service, as they both compete for a similar set of resources, i.e., both CPU and IO. As both `fop` and `luindex` have limited concurrent threading, only limited performance interference is observed.

Up to this point, our experiments have addressed the variability of a wiki service hosted on a single VM. In the next section, we leverage Markovian modeling to capture the capacity variability of a wiki cluster consisting of multiple VMs.

3   Markov Chain Model for Service Cluster

In this section, our objective is to derive a rigorous mathematical analysis for answering the question, "what is the minimum size of a cluster whose VMs experience capacity variability such that the probability of achieving a target QoS is guaranteed?". We define the service capacity $C(n)$ as the total number of requests processed by a cluster of $n \in \mathbb{Z}$ VMs, its QoS target as C^*, the fulfillment of which should be above a certain threshold ξ. Using Markov chain modeling, we obtain the steady-state distribution of QoS of a cluster with n VMs, and further search for the minimum n that satisfies the desired availability, $Pr[C(n) > C^*] > \xi$.

We start out the analysis by modeling the transition between high and low capacity of a single wiki VM, using values obtained in the previous section. Based on that, we develop a continuous-time Markov chain to model the service availability of the entire cluster. Finally, we show, by theoretical analysis and numerical examples, that the proposed minimum cluster size, n^*, indeed attains a good trade-off between cost and guarantee of service availability.

3.1 Single VM Node

We assume that a VM of a certain configuration (e.g., gold, silver, or bronze) alternates between states of high and low capacity, denoted by μ_h and μ_l, for exponentially distributed times with rate α and β, respectively. Examples of such values can be found in Fig. 1 for different VM configurations. We term the difference between μ_h and μ_l the capacity variability, and (α, β) the intensity of the variability. Fig. 3 illustrates the state transitions and time series of such a model. To capture the maximum variability possibly experienced by a VM, we only adopt two states of capacity, namely high and low, for different VM configurations. Their parameterizations can be carried out by our empirical analysis in Section 2. On the contrary, the values of α and β depend on the workload dynamics of the underlying cloud, and thus are assumed invariant to VM configurations. Note that one may find intermediate states in reality, i.e., the capacity is between $[\mu_l, \mu_h]$. Our proposed model can be further refined to accommodate multiple levels of capacities, albeit with a higher computation overhead for obtaining steady-state probability of service availability (see the next subsection).

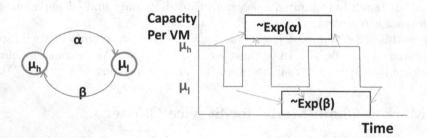

Fig. 3. Capacity variability of a VM: state diagram of high and low capacity (left) and illustration of time series (right)

3.2 Continuous Markov Chain Modeling of the Cluster

The single VM model naturally leads us to use a continuous-time Markov chain (CTMC) to describe the dynamics of available capacity in a cluster consisting of n VMs, experiencing high and low capacity. In the proposed CTMC, a state $i \in I = \{1, 2, \ldots n\}$ is defined as the number of VMs having low capacity, while the rest of $n - i$ VMs in the cluster have high capacity. Consequently, the corresponding capacity of state i in the systems is

$$C_i(n) = i\mu_l + (n - i)\mu_h.$$

Note that $C_i(n) \geq C_j(n)$, for $i \leq j$ — essentially, $C_i(n)$ monotonically decreases in i. When there are i VMs with low capacity, the system transpositions to state $i + 1$ with the rate $(n - i)\alpha$, and to state $i - 1$ with the rate $i\beta$. Fig. 4 illustrates such a Markov chain for a cluster of n VMs.

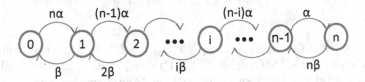

Fig. 4. Markov chain of aggregate VM capacities, where the state denotes the number of VMs experiencing low capacity

We let $\pi = [\pi_0, \pi_1 \ldots \pi_n]$ denote the steady-state probability that the system has a service capacity of $C_i(n)$. One can solve the Markov chain in Fig. 4 by a set of balance equations [13], i.e.,

$$(n - i)\alpha\pi_i = (i)\beta\pi_{i+1} \; \forall i,$$

$$\sum_i \pi_i = 1.$$

Substituting all π_i as a function of π_n, we can then obtain the closed formed solution of π

$$\pi_n = \frac{1}{(1 + \frac{\alpha}{\beta})^n} \tag{1}$$

$$\pi_i = \binom{n}{i}(\frac{\alpha}{\beta})^{n-i}\pi_n, \; 0 \leq i < n.$$

Consequently, we can derive the probability that the service capacity is greater than the target

$$\mathbf{Pr}[C(n) > C^*] = \sum_{i \in \{I : C_i(n) > C^*, i \leq n\}} \pi_i. \tag{2}$$

To compute $\mathbf{Pr}[C(n) > C^*]$ for all $n \in \mathbb{Z}$, one shall first compute the values π_i, $\forall i$ using 1 for a given n, and the sum of π_i for the states i where the resulting capacity is greater than C^*, and then iterate the computation procedure for all values of n.

3.3   Trade-Off between Cost and Service Availability

To find a minimum cluster size that ensures that a service capacity greater than the target capacity, $C > C^*$, is guaranteed for $\xi\%$ of time, we can formulate the following optimization after substituting Eq. 1 into the constraints and re-arrangements:

$$
\begin{aligned}
&\text{minimize} \quad n \\
&\text{subject to} \quad (n - i)\mu_h + i\mu_l \geq C^* \\
&\qquad \sum_i \binom{n}{i}(\frac{\alpha}{\beta})^{n-i}\frac{1}{(1 + \frac{\alpha}{\beta})^n} \geq \xi \\
&\qquad i \leq n
\end{aligned}
$$

For given values of α, β, μ_h, and μ_l, $Pr[C(n) > C^*]$ is a function increasing in n, i.e., when $n_1 \geq n_2$, $\mathbf{Pr}[C(n_1) > C^*] \geq \mathbf{Pr}[C(n_2) > C^*]$, as self-explained in the second constraint in the above optimization. Consequently, one can straight-forwardly find the optimal n^* by linearly searching through the possible values of $n \in \mathbb{Z}$ in an increasing order.

Note that the optimization is constructed implicitly depending on the workload intensity via the value of C^*. For a given period of time when the workload intensity is predicted as λ requests per second, one may want to keep the system 80% utilized, and set the target capacity to $C^* = \lambda/0.8$. The choice of the target capacity is out of scope of this work, and we direct interested readers to our prior work [4, 5].

n^* **vs. Simple Solutions.** Herein, we illustrate how n^* obtained through our proposed methodology attains a good trade-off between the cost and the guaranteed service availability, compared to simple optimistic and pessimistic solutions. One may optimistically think that all VMs have high capacity and only purchase $n^{opm} = \lceil C^*/\mu_h \rceil$ VMs by simply dividing the target capacity with the value of high capacity of a single VM. In contrast, a pessimistic solution would be to assume that all VMs have low capacity and purchase $n^{psm} = \lceil C^*/\mu_l \rceil$. As $\mu_h > \mu_l$, n^{psm} is greater than n^{opm}.

We compute the service availability curves by Eq. 2 for all values of n that fulfill the target capacity of $C^* = 60$ requests per second, using $\alpha = 60$, $\beta = 50$ and two sets of μ_h and μ_l, respectively. Fig. 5 summarizes the numerical results. Additionally, we also graphically illustrate the optimal provisioning of VMs (n^*) that fulfill the desired service availability, i.e., the cluster capacity is greater than 60 for $\xi = 90\%$ of the time, compared with pessimistic (n^{psm}) and optimistic (n^{opm}) solutions. We consider service availability curves in two cases of capacity variability, namely with smaller and bigger difference between the high and low capacity of a VM. One can easily see that the optimal cluster size grows with the variability, indicated by a higher value of n^* in Fig. 5(b) than (a). When the variability of capacity is higher, the service availability curve increases slower in n than in the low variability case. Moreover, the pessimistic and optimistic allocations are even further away from the optimal one.

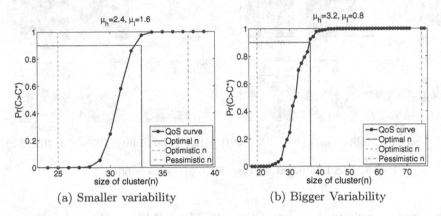

(a) Smaller variability   (b) Bigger Variability

Fig. 5. Service availability curve, $Pr[C(n) > 60]$: the optimal number of VMs to achieve $\xi = 90\%$, the pessimistic, and the optimistic solution

To proceed to cost comparison, we assume the cost of a cluster, $cost(n)$, is a strictly increasing function in n, i.e., $cost(n_1) \geq cost(n_2)$ when $n_1 \geq n_2$. Furthermore, due to the monotonicity of $Pr[C(n) > C^*]$ and $n^{opm} \leq n^* \leq n^{psm}$, we reach the following corollary:

Corollary 3.1.

$$cost(n^{opm}) \leq cost(n^*) \leq cost(n^{psm}),$$
$$\mathbf{Pr}[C(n^{opm}) > C^*] \leq \mathbf{Pr}[C(n^*) > C^*] \simeq \xi \leq \mathbf{Pr}[C(n^{psm}) > C^*]. \tag{3}$$

Though the optimistic solution incurs lower cost, the QoS fulfillment threshold is not met. On the contrary, the pessimistic solution can achieve the service availability with 100% guarantee, but at a higher cost. The optimal provisioning of VMs, n^*, indeed achieves a good trade-off between cost and QoS fulfillment, compared to simple optimistic and pessimistic solutions. Note that n^* can result in a slightly higher value of $\mathbf{Pr}[C(n^*) > C^*]$ than ξ, due to the discrete choice of the number of VMs.

We further numerically illustrate how such a trade-off is affected by different levels of variability in capacity of a single VM. Using a simple linear cost function, i.e., $cost(n) = 1.2 \cdot n$, we construct two numerical examples in Fig. 6, following the parameters discussed in Fig. 5. Note that the cost here is defined as the cost per time unit, which can be aligned with the billing periods used in commercial clouds, e.g., one hour. One can see that n^* can improve the QoS fulfillment drastically by increasing cost, compared to n^{opm}, and reduce cost significantly by allowing a fractional capacity degradation, compared to n^{psm}. The advantage of n^* in attaining a good trade-off is even more prominent in the case of bigger variability.

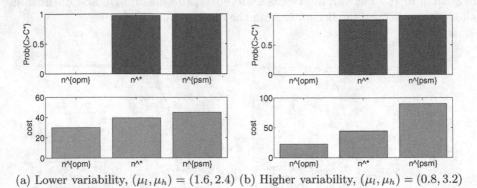

(a) Lower variability, $(\mu_l, \mu_h) = (1.6, 2.4)$ (b) Higher variability, $(\mu_l, \mu_h) = (0.8, 3.2)$

Fig. 6. QoS fulfillment vs. cost: $\mathbf{Pr}[C(n) > C* = 60] > \xi = 0.9$

Why Not Consider Average Capacity of a VM?. In this subsection, we show that choosing n based on the average capacity of a VM cannot reach the optimal values nor guarantee QoS fulfillment at the target capacity level, using numerical examples. Recalling the state transition of a VM depicted in Fig. 3(a), the average capacity of a single VM, μ, and the VM provisioning based on the average capacity, n^{avg} are

$$\mu = \frac{\mu_h \alpha + \mu_l \beta}{\alpha + \beta}, \text{ and } n^{avg} = \frac{C^*}{\mu},$$

respectively. Fig. 7 demonstrates that a cluster size based on the average capacity is not a reliable solution under three scenarios of (α, β), namely (a) often experiencing low capacity (b) alternating between high and low capacity equally, and (c) often experiencing high capacity. We let $\mu_h = 2.4$ and $\mu_l = 1.6$, as used in the case of small variability. Shown in Fig. 7(a), when $\alpha < \beta$, n^{avg} tends to overestimate and $\mathbf{Pr}[C(n) > C^*]$ is over the required values, $\xi = 0.9$. When $\alpha > \beta$, n^{avg} tends to underestimate and $\mathbf{Pr}[C(n) > C^*]$ is below the required values, indicated by the horizontal line overlapped on the x-axis in Fig. 7(c).

As for $\alpha = \beta$, we want to highlight that n^{avg} can achieve the target capacity roughly 50% of the time, for any capacity variability and target values. This observation can be explained by Eq. 1. When $\alpha = \beta$, the steady state of QoS fulfillment is greatly simplified to $\pi_n = 1/2^n$ and $\pi_i = \binom{n}{i}(1/2^n)$. Thus, substituting $n^{avg} = \lceil 1/2\mu_h + \mu_l \rceil$ can result in $\mathbf{Pr}[C(n) > C^*] = (50 + \epsilon)\%]$, where ϵ is a small positive fluctuation due to the ceiling operator on n^{avg}.

Observation 3.2. *When $\alpha = \beta$, n^{avg} can achieve $C(n) > C^*$ roughly 50% of the time, i.e., $Pr[C(n) > C^*] = 50 + \epsilon\%$, where ϵ is a small positive value.*

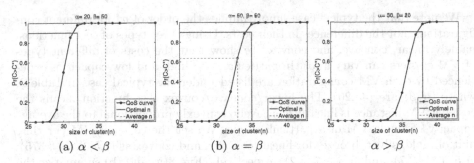

Fig. 7. QoS fulfillment curves based on n^{avg} and n^*, under $\mu_h = 2.4$ and $\mu_l = 1.6$

4 Choosing a VM Configuration

In this section, we compare different VM configurations in terms of their optimal cluster sizes and total cost, based on our proposed Markov chain model. Using theoretical and numerical analysis, we study if a cluster composed of more powerful VMs is always smaller than a cluster of weaker VMs. Due to the large number of parameters considered, we focus on providing a condition where weaker VMs imply a bigger cluster, and numerical counter examples where a cluster of weaker VMs can provide better service availability than a cluster of more powerful VMs.

4.1 Typical Case: Weaker VM Means a Bigger Cluster

Following the convention in Section 2, we consider three types of VM instances, namely gold, silver, and bronze. A gold instance is more powerful and implies a higher average computational capacity than a silver instance, whose average capacity is more than that of a bronze instance. All VM configurations experience high ($\mu_{h,type}$) and low capacity ($\mu_{l,type}$) for exponentially distributed durations with means equal to α and β, respectively. We can show the necessary condition for the *typical case*, meaning clusters of weaker VMs are bigger than clusters of more powerful VMs when achieving the same target of service availability.

Theorem 4.1. *When experiencing the same α and β and aiming at the same service availability threshold, the cluster sizes of gold, silver, and bronze instances are*

$$n^*_{gold} \leq n^*_{silver} \leq n^*_{bronze}, when$$

$$\mu_{h,gold} \leq \mu_{h,silver} \leq \mu_{h,bronze}, and \; \mu_{l,gold} \leq \mu_{l,silver} \leq \mu_{h,bronze}.$$

The theorem follows straightforwardly from the monotonicity of $Pr[C(n) > C^*]$ in n. Due to the lack of space, we skip the proof. The theorem tells us that to guarantee the same level of service availability, one should definitely acquire a higher number of weaker VMs than powerful VMs, when the low and high capacity of weaker VMs are inferior to the low and high capacity of powerful VMs, respectively.

We note that the typical case simply implies the order of n^* for different configurations, not the differences in their costs. Using three types of cost functions, namely linear, concave, and convex, we show that the costs of different types of VM clusters can vary a lot. In particular, the high and low capacities experienced by each VM configuration are listed under the typical case in Table 2, where (α, β) are (40,20). The linear/concave/convex cost function means the cost per VM instance is linearly/concavely/convexly proportional to the average capacity of single VM of a particular type. We set the cost per VM per time unit of (gold, silver, bronze) for linear, concave, and convex as (1.5, 2.25, 3.375), (1.5, 1.95, 2.7), and (1.5, 2.7, 4.2), respectively. Fig. 8(a) and (b) summarize the resulting service availability curves of different VM types and the resulting costs under different cost functions. One can see that although the bronze cluster is much bigger than the gold, the cost can still be lower when the cost per VM is linearly and convexly proportional to their average capacity. On the contrary, when there is a discount on computational capacity, i.e., when the cost per unit of computation decreases for gold, a gold cluster can be a cheaper option as shown by the case of a concave cost function.

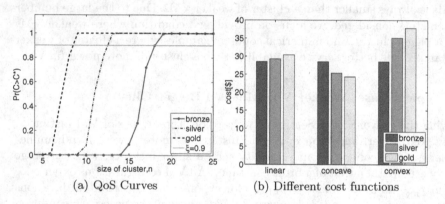

(a) QoS Curves   (b) Different cost functions

Fig. 8. QoS fulfillment and cost comparison for a typical case: comparison of gold, silver and bronze VMs

4.2   Counter Example: A Cluster of Weaker VMs Can Be Smaller

Here, we show by some counter examples that the optimal size of a cluster with weaker VMs is not necessarily larger. The capacity parameters of gold, silver, and bronze instances used are listed under the counter example in Table 2. The average capacity, μ, is the average of high and low capacity, and grows with the VM configuration. However, the capacity variability, i.e., the difference between high and low capacity, is higher for more powerful VMs.

Fig. 9 summarizes the curve of QoS fulfillment of the three VM configurations. One can see that the QoS curve of the three types of VMs cross each other at $n = 15$. For a given size, the QoS of a gold VM is not necessarily higher than that of a silver or bronze VM. In particular, for $n \geq 15$, the QoS of a silver VM is higher or equal to a gold VM. As a result, depending on the threshold of

Table 2. Capacity parameters of single VM for all VM types

	Typical Case			Counter Example		
	μ_l	μ	μ_h	μ_l	μ	μ_h
Gold	3.75	4.5	5.62	0.26	2.65	5.03
Silver	2.25	3.00	3.75	0.95	2.30	3.64
Bronze	1.50	2.00	2.50	1.80	2.00	2.20

QoS, ξ, the optimal cluster size of bronze VMs can be bigger, or smaller than that of gold VMs. To guarantee $Pr[C(n) > 30] \geq 0.85$, the optimal cluster size of all three types of VMs is 16. When such a threshold is higher than 0.85, the number of VMs in a gold cluster should be higher than in a bronze cluster. This leads us to conclude that not only the average, but also the variability in VM throughput is crucial in choosing and sizing VM clusters in the cloud.

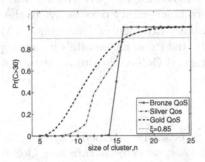

Fig. 9. QoS curve of different types of VMs, under $\alpha = \beta = 20$, $Pr[C > 30] > 0.85$

Our proposed Markov model and solution provide an efficient means to explore a large number of parameters encountered, such as different cost functions, and exogenous variabilities and their intensity, when choosing the right VM configuration and deciding the cluster size. Numerical examples serve the purpose of illustrating how our solution robustly attains an optimal trade-off between cost and QoS fulfillment across different system parameters and VM configurations.

5   Related Work

Recent studies on QoS analysis for cloud services [18, 21, 22] are mainly driven by service compositions and service selection, using a Markovian decision process [14] or a Baysian network model [21]. In contrast, studies focusing on constant QoS value, e.g., Zheng [22] proposed a calculation method to estimate the probabilistic distribution of QoS. However, the impact on the QoS due to the underlying performance variability of the cloud is to a large extent overlooked.

Most existing studies on the performance variability of applications hosted in the cloud are based on empirical experiments, especially in terms of average and 95th response time [16, 20], and aim to discover the root cause of such a phenomenon [10–12]. The observations made from cloud experiments are mainly based on a single type of configuration and simple benchmarks. A few studies [16, 17, 20] focus on multiple types of VM configurations and try to quantify the variability in their response times. Moreover, the variability in throughput is largely evaluated under a particular workload intensity, instead of using the maximum sustainable throughput, i.e., the capacity.

Meanwhile, another set of studies focus on developing solutions to reduce the performance variability in a best effort manner, from the perspective of service providers. Particularly, both [5,9] propose opportunistically selecting VMs which have high capacity, while discarding VMs with low capacity. Another type of solution is to try to figure out the underlying hardware and neighboring workloads, so as to select similar physical hosts [16] and influence the neighboring VMs [15]. As the methodology is trial and error, the QoS of the target application, e.g., the service availability, is not always guaranteed. Moreover, the cost analysis is over-simplified, without considering the performance variability.

Our study provides a complementary perspective to the related work by characterizing capacity variability experienced by a single VM, with respect to different types of workloads, and rigorously models its aggregate effect on multiple VMs in fulfilling sophisticated QoS while aiming at minimizing cost.

6   Conclusion

Using empirical experiments with a wikipedia system, as well as a Markovian model and numerical analysis, we demonstrate how QoS fulfillment can be best guaranteed with a minimum number of correctly configured VMs deployed in a cloud where VMs suffer from high capacity variability. Our experimental results show that different VM instance sizes can have varying degrees of capacity variability from collocated VMs and that workloads on collocated VMs can impact the capacity of the service VM by up to 35%. Our analytical and numerical results provide not only insight on how an optimal number of VMs should be chosen for a service cluster, but also give counter examples on why simple pessimistic, optimistic, and average-based provisioning of VMs cannot strike an optimal balance of cost and QoS fulfillment in the cloud where performance variability persists. Overall, we provide a systematic and rigorous approach to explore several crucial aspects of VM provisioning for service clusters, i.e., capacity variability, cost structure, and guarantees regarding QoS fulfillment.

Acknowledgements. The research presented in this paper has been supported by the Swiss National Science Foundation (project 200021_141002) and by the European Commission (Seventh Framework Programme grant 287746).

References

1. Amazon EC2, http://www.amazon.com/
2. DaCapo suite, http://dacapobench.org/

3. Björkqvist, M., Chen, L.Y., Binder, W.: Cost-driven Service Provisioning in Hybrid Clouds. In: Proceedings of IEEE Service-Oriented Computing and Applications (SOCA), pp. 1–8 (2012)
4. Björkqvist, M., Chen, L.Y., Binder, W.: Dynamic Replication in Service-Oriented Systems. In: Proceedings of IEEE/ACM CCGrid, pp. 531–538 (2012)
5. Björkqvist, M., Chen, L.Y., Binder, W.: Opportunistic Service Provisioning in the Cloud. In: Proceedings of IEEE CLOUD, pp. 237–244 (2012)
6. Casale, G., Tribastone, M.: Modelling Exogenous Variability in Cloud Deployments. SIGMETRICS Performance Evaluation Review 40(4), 73–82 (2013)
7. Chen, Y., Ansaloni, D., Smirni, E., Yokokawa, A., Binder, W.: Achieving Application-centric Performance Targets via Consolidation on Multicores: Myth or Reality? In: Proceedings of HPDC, pp. 37–48 (2012)
8. Dean, J., Barroso, L.: The Tail at Scale. Commun. ACM 56(2), 74–80 (2013)
9. Farley, B., Juels, A., Varadarajan, V., Ristenpart, T., Bowers, K.D., Swift, M.M.: More for your Money: Exploiting Performance Heterogeneity in Public Clouds. In: SoCC, pp. 20:1–20:14 (2012)
10. Jackson, K.R., Ramakrishnan, L., Runge, K.J., Thomas, R.C.: Seeking Supernovae in the Clouds: A Performance Study. In: Proceedings of HPDC, pp. 421–429 (2010)
11. Kossmann, D., Kraska, T., Loesing, S.: An Evaluation of Alternative Architectures for Transaction Processing in the Cloud. In: SIGMOD Conference, pp. 579–590 (2010)
12. Mao, M., Humphrey, M.: A Performance Study on the VM Startup Time in the Cloud. In: IEEE CLOUD, pp. 423–430 (2012)
13. Nelson, R.: Probability, Stochastic Processes, and Queueing Theory: The Mathematics of Computer Performance Modeling. Springer (2000)
14. Ramacher, R., Mönch, L.: Dynamic Service Selection with End-to-End Constrained Uncertain QoS Attributes. In: Liu, C., Ludwig, H., Toumani, F., Yu, Q. (eds.) ICSOC 2012. LNCS, vol. 7636, pp. 237–251. Springer, Heidelberg (2012)
15. Ristenpart, T., Tromer, E., Shacham, H., Savage, S.: Hey, You, Get Off of My Cloud: Exploring Information Leakage in Third-Party Compute Clouds. In: Proceedings of ACM CCS, pp. 199–212 (2009)
16. Schad, J., Dittrich, J., Quiané-Ruiz, J.-A.: Runtime Measurements in the Cloud: Observing, Analyzing, and Reducing Variance. PVLDB 3(1), 460–471 (2010)
17. Spicuglia, S., Chen, L.Y., Binder, W.: Join the Best Queue: Reducing Performance Variability in Heterogeneous Systems. In: Proceedings of IEEE CLOUD (2013)
18. Tsakalozos, K., Roussopoulos, M., Delis, A.: VM Placement in non-Homogeneous IaaS-Clouds. In: Kappel, G., Maamar, Z., Motahari-Nezhad, H.R. (eds.) ICSOC 2011. LNCS, vol. 7084, pp. 172–187. Springer, Heidelberg (2011)
19. Wikipedia, http://www.wikipedia.org/
20. Xu, Y., Musgrave, Z., Noble, B., Bailey, M.: Bobtail: Avoiding Long Tails in the Cloud. In: Proceedings of NSDI (April 2013)
21. Ye, Z., Bouguettaya, A., Zhou, X.: QoS-aware cloud service composition based on economic models. In: Liu, C., Ludwig, H., Toumani, F., Yu, Q. (eds.) ICSOC 2012. LNCS, vol. 7636, pp. 111–126. Springer, Heidelberg (2012)
22. Zheng, H., Yang, J., Zhao, W., Bouguettaya, A.: QoS analysis for web service compositions based on probabilistic qoS. In: Kappel, G., Maamar, Z., Motahari-Nezhad, H.R. (eds.) ICSOC 2011. LNCS, vol. 7084, pp. 47–61. Springer, Heidelberg (2011)

Personalized Quality Prediction for Dynamic Service Management Based on Invocation Patterns

Li Zhang[1,2], Bin Zhang[1], Claus Pahl[2], Lei Xu[2], and Zhiliang Zhu[1]

[1] Northeastern University, Shenyang, China
{zhangl,zhuzl}@swc.neu.edu.cn, zhangbin@ise.neu.edu.cn
[2] Dublin City University, Dublin, Ireland
{cpahl,lxu}@computing.dcu.ie

Abstract. Recent service management needs, e.g., in the cloud, require services to be managed dynamically. Services might need to be selected or replaced at runtime. For services with similar functionality, one approach is to identify the most suitable services for a user based on an evaluation of the quality (QoS) of these services. In environments like the cloud, further personalisation is also paramount. We propose a personalized QoS prediction method, which considers the impact of the network, server environment and user input. It analyses previous user behaviour and extracts invocation patterns from monitored QoS data through pattern mining to predict QoS based on invocation QoS patterns and user invocation features. Experimental results show that the proposed method can significantly improve the accuracy of the QoS prediction.

Keywords: Service Quality, Web and Cloud Services, QoS Prediction, Invocation Pattern Mining, Collaborative Filtering, Personalized Recommendation.

1   Introduction

Service QoS (Quality of Service) is the basis of Web and Cloud service discovery [1-4], selection [5,6] and composition [7-9]. For services located in open environments such as the Web or the Cloud, QoS may vary depending on the network, the service execution environment and user requirements. Additionally, a *personalized QoS evaluation* of services for different service users is necessary in particular in these open environments, as users more and more expect the customisation of publically provided services used by them. Generally, service QoS information is derived in three ways: delivered by services providers, evaluated based on user feedback and predicted based on monitoring information. Prediction based on monitoring is more objective and reliable in untrusted Web and Cloud contexts and more suitable for these *dynamically changing environments*. There are two types of prediction based on monitoring: one is based on statistical, the other is personalized prediction. Many implementations [1,5,7,9,10] adopt the statistical approach for usage (QoS) prediction. The statistical method is simple and easy to implement, e.g., response-time is usually calculated based on the average response time. This method ignores the users' personalized requirements, network conditions and execution features. For example,

S. Basu et al. (Eds.): ICSOC 2013, LNCS 8274, pp. 84–98, 2013.
© Springer-Verlag Berlin Heidelberg 2013

for an on-demand cloud-based movie/video processing service, the size of the video has a significant influence on the response time. Different users, accessing the service through the cloud, may experience different response times. In [11,12,13], collaborative filtering methods are proposed, predicting QoS for a user by referring to past information of similar users. The influence of the user environment and input can also be considered to provide a user with a more personalized QoS prediction.

Moreover, even the same user does not experience the same QoS values for different invocations at different times and with different invocation parameters – which is something that current cloud services, whether multimedia on-demand for end users or commercial applications in the cloud, highlight as a problem. If a user invokes a service many times, then the QoS cannot be determined by collaborative filtering, which is inefficient for QoS prediction for every invocation. A Bayesian network-based QoS assessment model for web services is proposed in [13]. It predicts the service performance level depending on the user requirements level, but how to define the performance level is still a problem. Most QoS prediction methods of services do not consider the impact on service performance by environmental factors. The *prediction performance* becomes a critical aspect in dynamically managed service and cloud environments, where monitored QoS data is taken into account.

Our experiments and analyses show that user inputs, network conditions and Web server performance impact on QoS significantly. Assume three services s_1, s_2 and s_3 with similar functions. Take input data size, network throughput and CPU utilization as representatives of input, network and Web server characteristics. Table 1 shows an invocation log of these services. It records information for every invocation: network throughput (MB), data size (MB), Web server CPU utilization and response-time(s).

Table 1. Services Usage Information

Service name	1st invocation	2nd invocation	3rd invocation	4th invocation	5th invocation
s_1	<2, 10, 0.2, 0.5>	<1.5,20, 0.5, 2>	<2.5,10,0.1,0.2>	<2,30, 0.3, 0.8>	<2, 8,0.2, ?>
s_2	<1.5,10,0.3, 0.3>	<2,20, 0.4, 1.8>			
s_3	<2, 20, 0.3, 3 >	<1, 20, 0.2, 6 >	<1.5,20, 0.3, 4 >	<2,15,0.2, 2.4 >	

In the third invocation of s_1, network throughput is 2.5MB, data size is 10MB, Web server CPU utilization is 0.1 and response time is 0.2sec. Now, if there is another user wanting to invoke s_1, the network throughput is 2MB, data size is 8MB and CPU utilization is 0.2. Then, predicting the response time for this user depends on history information (cf. Table 1). The three services were invoked 5 times, 2 times or 4 times. The average response times are 0.875s, 1.05s and 3.85s. This is independent of invocation parameters. No matter what the situation of the next invocation, the traditional prediction results will be the same, but according to Table 1, the real result is dependent on input, network and Web server factors. The prediction in our previous work [15,16] is based on collaborative filtering. It predicts QoS through calculating the similarity of invocation parameters and parameters in past invocations. The prediction is more accurate than an averaging method, but needs to calculate the similarity of target invocation and all past invocations, resulting in too many repeated calculations and low efficiency, which needs to be addressed for dynamic contexts like the cloud.

An important observation is that most services have relatively fixed *service invocation patterns* (SIPs). A SIP consists of ranges of input characteristics, network characteristics and Web server characteristics and reflects relatively stable, acceptable variations. The service QoS keeps steady under a SIP. If we can abstract the SIP from service usage, the prediction can be based on usage information for the matched pattern. If there is no usage information for the matched pattern, the prediction needs to be calculated using past log information of other similar services. We propose constructing SIPs by analysing user input, network environment and server status factors. We *adapt collaborative filtering prediction to be based on SIPs and pattern mining*, improving prediction accuracy and performance. Thus, our contributions are:

- Firstly, we propose the novel concept of Service Invocation Pattern and an aligned method for *mining and constructing SIPs* (Sections 2 and 3). It considers the influence of environmental characteristics on the quality of a Web service.
- Secondly, we propose a collaborative filtering QoS prediction algorithm based on SIPs (Sections 4 and 5). This approach can *predict QoS based on personalized user requirements*. It improves the prediction accuracy and computational performance.

2   Service Invocation Pattern SIP

Services QoS characteristics are related to user input, network status and server performance. It means that a certain range of input, network status and server status determines a relatively fixed service invocation pattern. A SIP reflects that the QoS remains steady under this pattern, i.e., predicting QoS this way is beneficial. We analyse the characteristics which impact Web service execution and define the SIP.

Definition. 1. *Service Invocation Characteristic* (SIC). $C = <$ ***Input, Network, Server*** $>$ is the characteristic model of one invocation. ***Input, Network*** and ***Server*** represent user input characteristics, network characteristics and Web server characteristics, respectively. We take input data size, network throughput and CPU utilization as examples. In invocation characteristic $<30, 1.5, 0.2>$, the input data size is 30MB, throughput between server and user is 1.5MB and server CPU utilization is 0.2.

Definition. 2. *Input Characteristic* (IC). ***Input*** $=< In^1, In^2, ..., In^P>$ is the input characteristics vector. It describes the input characteristics that have an influence on QoS. I^k $(1 \leq k \leq p)$ is the *k-th* input characteristic.

Definition. 3. *Network Characteristic* (NC). ***Network*** $=< net^1, net^2, ..., net^r>$ is the network characteristics vector. It describes the network characteristics that have an influence on QoS. n^k $(1 \leq k \leq r)$ represents the *k-th* network characteristic.

Definition. 4. *Web Server Characteristic* (WSC). ***Server*** $=< se^1, se^2, ..., se^q>$ is the server characteristics vector. It describes the Web server characteristics that have an influence on service QoS. se^k $(1 \leq k \leq q)$ represents the *k-th* server characteristic.

Definition. 5. *Service Invocation Pattern* (SIP). A SIP is a group of service invocation characteristics SIC. In a SIP, the value of invocation characteristics is a range. The QoS is meant to be steady under a SIP. We describe it as $M = <$ ***Input**_{low}* ~ ***Input**_{high}*,

$Network_{low} \sim Network_{high}$, $Server_{low} \sim Server_{high} >$, **Input**, **Network** and **Server** are input characteristics, network characteristics and Web server characteristics.

Definition. 6. *Invocation Pattern-QoS matrix.* If the QoS of services keeps steady or have a fixed relation to a SIP, then this relation can be expressed as a matrix **MS**:

$$MS = \begin{array}{c} \\ M_1 \\ M_2 \\ \cdots \\ M_l \end{array} \begin{array}{cccc} s_1 & s_2 & \cdots & s_m \\ \begin{bmatrix} q_{1,1} & q_{1,2} & \cdots & q_{1,m} \\ q_{2,1} & q_{2,2} & \cdots & q_{2,m} \\ \cdots & \cdots & \cdots & \cdots \\ q_{l,1} & q_{l,2} & \cdots & q_{l,m} \end{bmatrix} \end{array}$$

The matrix **MS** shows the QoS information of all the services s under all the patterns M. q_{ij} ($1 \leq j \leq l$, $1 \leq i \leq m$) is the QoS of service s_j under the pattern M_i.

with

$$q_{i,j} = \begin{cases} \phi & \text{Service } s_j \text{ has no invocation history under pattern } m_i. \\ low_{i,j} \sim high_{i,j} & \text{Service } s_j \text{ has invocation history under pattern } m_i \text{ with range '}\sim\text{'.} \end{cases}$$

If a pattern is <20-30*MB*, 0.5-0.6, 0.2-0.4, 30-40*MB*>, then the input data size is 20-30*MB*, CPU utilization is 0.5-0.6, memory utilization is 0.2-0.4 and server throughput is 30-40*MB*. We can search for the QoS of a service based on information related to this pattern. If there is corresponding information and the value keeps steady in a range, then it is returned to the user. If the value is not consecutive, it means the service is not only affected by the characteristics of the invocation pattern. It then needs further calculation based on history information. If there is no invocation history, this value will be null. In that case, prediction is done for a user invocation requirement. Below is an example of an Invocation Pattern-QoS Matrix. There are 4 invocation patterns. We introduce how to abstract/mine SIPs and predict in Sect. 3.

$$\begin{array}{c} M_1 \\ M_2 \\ M_3 \\ M_4 \end{array} \begin{array}{cccc} s_1 & s_2 & s_3 & s_4 \\ \begin{bmatrix} 0.2 \sim 0.5s & & 1 \sim 1.3s & \\ 0.8 \sim 1.1s & 1.1 \sim 1.5s & & \\ 0.4 \sim 0.5s & & 2 \sim 2.4s & 0.3 \sim 0.5s \\ & 3 \sim 4s & & \end{bmatrix} \end{array}$$

Some services have no usage information within a pattern range – e.g., since s1 has an invocation history for pattern M1, it returns this range of values, but as s2 has no invocation history, it needs collaborative filtering for prediction.

3   Service Invocation Pattern Abstraction and Mining

The values of user invocation characteristics are spread across a certain range. Obtaining these value ranges significantly helps QoS prediction, but the number of SIPs that reflect these cannot be decided in advance and all usage information is multi-dimensional. Density-based spatial clustering of applications is used to achieve this. DBSCAN (density-based spatial clustering of application with noise) [17] is a density-based clustering algorithm. It analyses the density of data and allocates them into a cluster if the spatial density is greater than a threshold. DBSCAN can find clusters of any shape. The DBSCAN algorithm has two parameters: ε and *MinPts*. If the distance between two points is less than the threshold ε, they can be in the same cluster. The minimum number of points in a cluster must be greater than *MinPts*. DBSCAN clusters the points through spatial density. The main steps of DBSCAN:

1. Select any object p from the object set and find the objects set D in which the object is density-reachable from object p with respect to ε and *MinPts*.
2. Choose another object without cluster and repeat the first step.

A SIP Extraction Algorithm based on DBSCAN shall now be introduced. A SIP is composed of user input, network and server characteristics. For these aspects, we take throughput, input size and CPU utilization as representatives, respectively. We consider the execution time as the representative of QoS here.

- An execution log records the input data size and execution QoS.
- A monitoring log records the network status and Web server status.

We reorganize these two files to find the SIP under which QoS keeps steady. A SIP extraction algorithm is shown in Alg. 1 (see also the SIP format in Definition 5).

Algorithm 1.   SIP Extraction Algorithm based on DBSCAN

Input: Service Usage Information *InforSet* (execution+monitoring log), ε,   *MinPts*.

Output: SIP Database *PatternBase*, Pattern-QoS information *PatternQoS*.

```
1  for ( Infori<DataSize, CPU, ThroughPut, time> ∈ InforSet )
2  {
3    if ( Infori does not belong to any exist cluster ) {
4      Pj= newPattern(Infori) // create a new pattern withInfori as seed.
5      Add( Pj, PatternBase )
6      InforSet = InforSet - Infori
7      SimInfor = SimilarInfor(InforSet, Infori, ε) // SimInfor is the infor-
8          mation set which includes all the similar usage information of
9          Infori. Differences between the information in SimInfor and
10         Infori on the charac-teristics value except execution time are
11         less than ε. n is the number of information items in SimInfor.
12     InforSet = InforSet - SimInfor
13     if ( n>MinPts ) { // MinPts is min number of exec inform in cluster.
14       (S1, S2, … ,Sm) = Divide(SimInfor) // Divide SimInfor into different
15            groups. Group S1 includes all information of servs1.
16       for(k=1; k≤m; k++){
17         for(Inforj∈Sk) {
18            SimInfor = SimilarInfor(InforSet, Inforj, time, MinPts, ε)
19            // Search similar info of Sk in execution information set. If
20            the number of similar information item is less than MinPts,
21            then the density will turn low and top the loop.
22            Sk = Sk + SimInfor
23            InforSet = InforSet - SimInfor
24         }
25         PatternCharacteristics(Sk) // Organizes the information in the
26            cluster and statistics for the ranges of characteristics.
27            Completes the pattern-QoS matrix.
28       }
29    }
30  }
31 }
```

The distance calculation between two objects in this algorithm is different from the traditional DBSCAN. It includes two types of distance:

- Firstly, when we initialize a cluster, we randomly select an object without cluster. We take it as the seed to find the cluster it belongs to. In this cluster, the response time of different services may differ, but the performance of different invocations of the same service keeps steady. The distance between the other information and seed information is computed based on all characteristics except response time.
- Secondly, when the cluster has been constructed, we need to check whether the information does not belong to any cluster or belongs to the given cluster. We need to compare this information with others of the same service in the cluster and calculate the distance of this information with the cluster. Then, the distance computation is dependent on all the characteristics of the two information items.

4   The QoS Prediction Based on SIP

This section will introduce the Web Service QoS prediction approach. It uses Service Invocation Patterns and the Invocation Pattern-QoS Matrix to carry out the prediction. It fully considers the requirements of every invocation.

4.1   The QoS Prediction Procedure Based on SIP

In order carry out the prediction, we assume that the SIP database has been created.

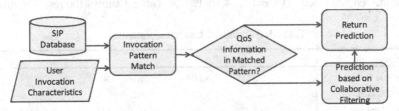

Fig. 1. QoS Prediction Procedure

The steps of the prediction procedure in Fig. 1 are as follows. Firstly, we match the target invocation characteristics with the SIPs in the database. We match the characteristics of target service s_j with the characteristics of stored patterns. If there is a pattern that can be matched directly, then we return it. Otherwise, we employ the Gray Relevance Analysis to get the matched pattern. Assume that the matched pattern is m_i. Then, we search information about a matched pattern in the QoS matrix. If there is QoS information of the target service in pattern m_i, then we return it directly. Finally, if there is no related QoS information, then we predict QoS by collaborative filtering.

4.2   Matching User Invocation Characteristics with Patterns

A characteristics vector of a user invocation is $C = < Input, Network, Server>$. Here *Input*, *Network* and *Server* represent input, network and server characteristics, respectively. The Service Invocation Pattern is defined as $M = <Input_{low} \sim Input_{high}$, $Network_{low} \sim Network_{high}$, $Server_{low} \sim Server_{high} >$. During the matching process, we compare the user invocation characteristics and the respective component in the pattern. Matching is successful if $Input_{low} \leq Input \leq Input_{high}$, $Network_{low} \leq Network \leq Network_{high}$ and $Server_{low} \leq Server \leq Server_{high}$. Assume the matched pattern is m_i.

If there is no matched pattern, adopt the *Gray Relevance Analysis* method to calculate the association degree between QoS and invocation characteristics to *a)* find the ordering of characteristics that have greater impact on QoS and *b)* match the pattern based on the order. Table 2 shows the n times invocation information of service s.

Table 2. Usage Information of Service s

Features	1	......	I	......	n
Response Time	T_1	......	T_i	......	T_n
Input Datasize	$Data_1$	......	$Data_i$	......	$Data_n$
Throughput	TP_1	......	TP_i	......	TP_n
CPU utilization	CPU_1	......	CPU_i	......	CPU_n

1. Take response time as the reference sequence $x_0(k)$, $k = 1,\ldots, n$, and other characteristics as comparative sequences. Calculate the association degree of the other characteristics with response time. First, take the characteristics of an invocation as standard and carry out normalization of the other characteristics. The reference sequence and comparative sequence are handled dimensionless. Assuming the standardized sequence $y_i(k)$, $i=1,\ldots,4$, $k=1,\ldots,n$, Table 3 shows the result matrix.

Table 3. Normalized Usage Informaiton

Features	1	......	I	......	n
Response Time	1	......	$y_1(i)$	......	$y_1(n)$
Input Datasize	1	......	$y_2(i)$	......	$y_2(n)$
Throughput	1	......	$y_3(i)$	......	$y_3(n)$
CPU utilization	1	......	$y_4(i)$	......	$y_4(n)$

2. Calculate absolute differences for Table 3 using $\Delta_{0i}(k) = |y_0(k) - y_i(k)|$. The resulting absolute difference sequence is:

$$\Delta_{01} = (0, y_{01}(1), \cdots, y_{01}(n)), \quad \Delta_{02} = (0, y_{02}(1), \cdots, y_{02}(n)), \quad \Delta_{03} = (0, y_{03}(1), \cdots, y_{03}(n))$$

3. Calculate a correlation coefficient between reference and comparative sequence:

$$\zeta_{0i}(k) = \frac{\Delta_{\min} + \rho\Delta_{\max}}{\Delta_{0i}(k) + \rho\Delta_{\max}}$$ is the correlation coefficient of the Gray Relevance.

Here $\Delta_{0i}(k) = |y_0(k) - y_i(k)|$ is the absolute difference and $\Delta_{\min} = \min_i \min_k \Delta_{0i}(k)$ is the minimum difference value between two poles, and $\Delta_{\max} = \max_i \max_k \Delta_{0i}(k)$ is the maximum difference value. $\rho \in (0,1)$ is the distinguishing factor.

4. Calculate the correlation degree: Use $r_{0i} = \frac{1}{n} \sum_{k=1}^{n} \zeta_{0i}(k)$ to calculate the correlation degree between characteristics. Then, sort the characteristics based on the correlation degree. If r_0 is the largest, it has the greatest impact on response time and will be matched prior to others. Assume usage information of s as in Table 4.

5   QoS Prediction Based on Collaborative Filtering

If there is no related QoS within matched patterns, we need to predict QoS based on collaborative filtering. In the Invocation Pattern-QoS Matrix, there are a usually a number of null values. The prediction accuracy will be affected if we ignore these null values. We need to fill the null values for the information items of similar services.

5.1   QoS Prediction Process Based on Collaborative Filtering

Assume that the target service is s_j, and the matched pattern is m_i. When service s_j has no QoS information in pattern m_i, the prediction process is as follows:

1. For any service s_v, $v \neq j$, if there is information of s_v under pattern m_i. then calculate the similarity between service s_j and service s_v.
2. Get the k neighbouring services of service s_j through the similarity calculated in step 1. The set of these k services is $S = \{s_1\text{'}, s_2\text{'}, \cdots, s_k\text{'}\}$. We fill the null QoS values for the target invocation using the information in this set.
3. Using the information in S, calculate the similarity of m_i with other patterns that have the information for target service s_j.
4. Choose the most similar $k\text{'}$ patterns of m_i, and use the information across the $k\text{'}$ patterns and S to predict the QoS of service s_j .

5.2   Service Similarity Computation

Assume that m_i is the matched pattern and s_j is the target service. If there is no information of s_j in pattern m_i, we need to predict the response time $q_{i,j}$ for s_j. Firstly, calculate the similarity of s_j and services which have information within pattern m_i ranges. For a service $s_v \in I_i$ where I_i is the set of services that have usage information within pattern m_i, calculate the similarity of s_j and s_v. Vector similarity calculation commonly adopts cosine similarity, correlation similarity or correction cosine similarity. However, these 3 methods do not consider the impact of user environment differences, i.e., the methods are not suited for service similarity computation directly. We need to improve the similarity calculation. We define service similarity as follows:

Definition. 7.   The similarity of two services s_j and s_v is defined by

$$sim(s_v, s_j) = \alpha \cdot sim_{sum}(s_v, s_j) + \beta \cdot sim_{data}(s_v, s_j) \tag{1}$$

where

- $sim_{sum}(s_v, s_j)$ is the similarity of the numbers of invocation patterns which are invoked by services s_v and s_j together. Two services are more similar if they have more used invocation patterns in common.
- $sim_{data}(s_v, s_j)$ is the similarity of the usage information of services s_j and s_v. Two services are more similar if their usage information is more similar.
- α and β are adjustable balance parameters. They can be changed based on different user requirements.

For services s_j and s_v, $P(s_j/s_v)$ is the probability of the coexistence of services s_j and s_v within a pattern. This probability can be used to measure the similarity of s_j and s_v:

$$sim_{sum}(s_v, s_j) = \frac{num(s_v s_j)}{num(s_j)} \tag{2}$$

Here, $num(s_v, s_j)$ is the number of the common pattern-based invocations by two services. $num(s_j)$ is the number of pattern-based invocation by service s_j. Based on formula (1), $sim_{sum}(s_v, s_j)$ is between 0 and 1.

Our definition of the similarity of invocation information adopts the correction cosine similarity method. It is shown in formula (3). M_{vj} is the set of invocation pattern models which have the usage information of s_v and s_j.

$$sim_{data}(s_v, s_j) = \frac{\sum_{m_c \in M_{vij}} (q_{c,v} - \overline{q_v})(q_{c,j} - \overline{q_j})}{\sqrt{\sum_{m_c \in Mvj} (q_{c,v} - \overline{q_v})^2} \sqrt{\sum_{m_c \in Mvj} (q_{c,j} - \overline{q_j})^2}} \tag{3}$$

Here, $\overline{q_v}$ is the average of the usage information for service s_v, $\overline{q_j}$ is the average of the usage information for service s_j.

From formula (3), we can obtain all similarities between s_j and others services which have usage information within pattern m_i. The more similar the service is to s_j, the more valuable the data of it is. Formulas (2) and (3) are two aspects of service similarity. Formula (1) provides the sum of these two different similarities.

5.3   Predicting Missing Data

Missing data will have a negative impact on the accuracy of QoS prediction. We calculate the similarity between two services and get the k neighbouring services. Then, we establish the k neighbours matrix T_{sim} and fill the missing data in T_{sim}.

Assume the k neighbouring services form the set $S = \{s_1{}', s_2{}', \cdots, s_k{}'\}$. Here, s_1' has the highest similarity with service s_j and so on. Then, these k services are more valuable and their usage information is defined as follows in matrix (4) below. Matrix T_{sim} shows the usage information of the k neighbouring services of s_j within all invocation patterns. The data space is reduced to k columns and the computational effort required is consequently also reduced. In this matrix, there are still many missing data items $t_{i,j}$. We need to fill these empty spaces before prediction. Firstly, we fill the missing data references to the services similarity.

$$
T_{sim} = \begin{array}{c} \\ M_1 \\ \\ \cdots \\ M_i \\ \cdots \\ M_l \end{array}
\begin{array}{cccccc}
s_j & s_1 & s_2 & \cdots & s_k \\
\left[\begin{array}{ccccc} t_{1,j} & t'_{1,1} & t'_{1,2} & \cdots & t'_{1,k} \\
\cdots & \cdots & \cdots & \cdots & \cdots \\
\Phi & t'_{i,1} & t'_{i,2} & \cdots & t'_{i,k} \\
\cdots & \cdots & \cdots & \cdots & \cdots \\
t_{l,j} & t'_{l,1} & t'_{l,2} & \cdots & t'_{l,k} \end{array}\right]
\end{array}
\tag{4}
$$

We fill $P_{i,p}^{ser}$, which is the data of service s_p under pattern m_i. The method is:

$$
P_{i,p}^{ser} = \bar{t'}_p + \frac{\sum_{n \in S'} sim_{n,p} \times (t'_{i,n} - \bar{t'}_n)}{\sum_{n \in S'} (\mid sim_{n,p} \mid)},
\tag{5}
$$

Here $\bar{t'}_p$ is the average QoS of service s_p, and $sim_{n,p}$ is the similarity between service s_n and s_p. For any service $p \in S'$, every service has usage information within all the pattern ranges in m_i after this process.

5.4   Calculating the Pattern Similarity and Prediction

There is QoS information of k neighbouring services of s_j in matrix T_{sim}. Some of them are prediction values. We can calculate the similarity of pattern m_i and other patterns using the correction cosine similarity method:

$$
sim_{model}(m_i, m_j) = \frac{\sum_{s_k \in S} (t'_{i,k} - \bar{t'}_i)(t'_{j,k} - \bar{t'}_j)}{\sqrt{\sum_{s_k \in S} (t'_{i,k} - \bar{t'}_i)^2} \sqrt{\sum_{s_k \in S} (t'_{j,k} - \bar{t'}_j)^2}},
\tag{6}
$$

After determining the pattern similarity, the data of patterns with low similarity are removed from T_{sim}. The set of the first k patterns is $M' = \{M_1, M_2, \cdots M_k\}$. The data of these patterns are retained for prediction.

As described above, if $p_{i,j}$ is the data to be predicted as the usage data of service s_j within pattern M_i, it is calculated as:

$$
p_{i,j} = \bar{t'}_i + \frac{\sum_{n \in M'} sim_{n,i} \times (t'_{n,j} - \bar{t'}_n)}{\sum_{n \in M'} (\mid sim_{n,i} \mid)}
\tag{7}
$$

Here $\bar{t'}_i$ is the average QoS of the data related to pattern m_i and $sim_{n,i}$ is the similarity between patterns M_n and M_p.

6   Experimental Analysis

We have designed a simulation environment to evaluate the efficiency and accuracy of the approach proposed. First, we implemented 100 Web services. These services belong to 3 categories, which are sensitive to data size, network throughput and CPU utilization separately. They are distributed over different network environments. All Web servers provide an open SNMP service and we installed a monitoring program for network monitoring. We gathered user input data size, server CPU utilization and server port throughput. The monitor submits environment information to the monitoring log recorder, which is responsible for cleaning the monitor log and storing data in the database. We generated a 200*100 invocation pattern-QoS matrix, restricted to the response time characteristics. Fig. 2 shows the experimentation architecture.

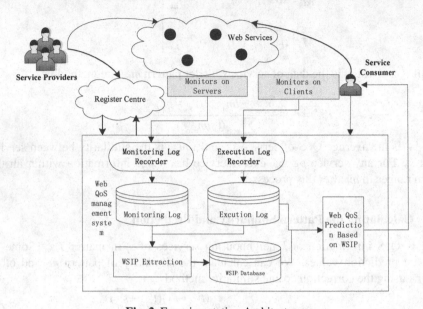

Fig. 2. Experimentation Architecture

Service providers register their Web service with a registry centre. Monitors for server and client are responsible for submitting the monitoring data to the Monitoring Log Recorder and the Execution Log Recorder. The Service Invocation Pattern Extraction module is responsible for extracting the service invocation patterns from the monitoring log and the execution log. When user requirements need to be processed, the QoS Management System will predict service QoS for a user according to their requirements. Then, the user can decide to invoke this service or not.

Accuracy Analysis. *MAE* (Mean Absolute Error) is the normal standard to measure the prediction accuracy. Here *MAE* is the mean absolute error between prediction and real response time. The smaller the *MAE*, the more accurate is the prediction. Assuming p_{ij} is the prediction value and t_{ij} is the real value, then *MAE* can be calculated as follows, where N is the total number of predictions:

$$MAE = \frac{\sum_{i,j} |t_{ij} - p_{ij}|}{N} \tag{8}$$

Different characteristics of QoS have different ranges. Consequently, we use *NMAE* (Normalized Mean Absolute Error) instead of *MAE*. The smaller the *NMAE*, the more accurate is the prediction. *NMAE* is the normalized *MAE*:

$$NMAE = \frac{MAE}{\sum_{i,j} t_{i,j} / N} \qquad (9)$$

The accuracy of the prediction is important. Web QoS prediction algorithms usually are statistics-based and collaboration method-based. Average-based methods do not consider the users' personalized requirements and the impact of the network. Thus, they calculate the same prediction for all users. Collaboration-based methods need to use all historic data, i.e., the computation takes too long. We analysed these three approaches and tried different settings of k, α and β to assess the result.

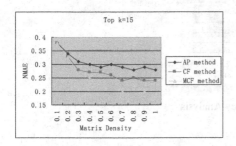

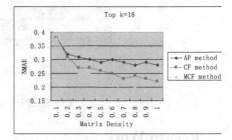

Fig. 3. NMAE of $k=15$ **Fig. 4.** NMAE of $k=18$

Different ks have different impacts on the result. If k is too large, there will be too much unnecessary information. The prediction result will be affected. However, if k is too small, useful information will be ignored and the data will not be sufficiently large enough for prediction. The similarity of the first k patterns maybe different under different data condition. Thus, a fixed k is not the objective. We tested different numbers of neighbouring patterns. We took the square root of the number of patterns first. Then, considering the pattern similarity, we fixed 0.5 as the critical value of similarity. If similarities between the target pattern and all other patterns exceed 0.5, then we increase k, otherwise decrease k. After testing, when k is 15 or 18, the performance is better in our environment. α and β in Formula (1) have also different impacts in different datasets. For our dataset, the performance is best when α is 0.2. We use AP to represent the average method. CF is the abbreviation of the collaboration-based algorithm. MCF is the abbreviation of the approach in this paper. As indicated in Figures 3 and 4, an increase of the dataset size improves the accuracy significantly.

Efficiency Analysis. If the target invocation can be matched in the service invocation pattern database and if there is QoS of the target service within the matched pattern, we can predict QoS directly. Only if there is no related data, collaborative computation is needed. The dataset for collaborative computation is related to service invocation patterns, but the number of patterns is far less than the number of usage information items. We used DBSCAN to obtain the service invocation patterns. We determined 150 invocation patterns from 2400 usage recordings. Compared to work in [11,12], the matrix for collaborative computation is reduced from 2400*100 to 150*100. Here, only when the matched pattern has no information of the target service, the calculation for prediction is required. Thus, the computation effort is decreased to a large extent. We tested the algorithm on many datasets. For each dataset, 50 predictions were taken and we averaged the response time. The comparison between the methods is shown in Figure 5. When the size of the dataset grows, time consumption in normal collaborative cases increases quickly. Our approach (MCF) is not much affected by data size.

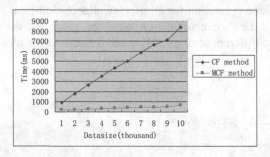

Fig. 5. Efficiency Analysis

7   Related Work

Different types of Web or cloud services [26] usually have different QoS characteristics [1-12]. The normally used ones are response time, execution cost, reliability, availability, security and reputation. There are many factors that impact on QoS [18]. Some factors are static, some are run-time static, the others are totally dynamic. Run-time static and dynamic factors are uncertain. They are client load, server load, network channel bandwidth or network channel delay. Most factors can be obtained by monitoring, but not all. Then, their impact cannot be calculated.

QoS-based service selection has been widely covered [1-10]. Many service prediction methods are proposed. There are three categories of prediction. The first one is statistic, which is normally adopted [1,2,7,8,9]. This method is simple and easy to implement. The second category is based on user feedback and reputation [19,20]. It can avoid malicious feedback, but these methods do not consider the impact of user requirements and the environment and cannot personalize prediction for users. The third category is based on collaborative filtering [11-14]. Collaborative filtering is a widely adopted recommendation method [21-24,28]. Zeng [22] summarizes the application of collaborative filtering in book, movie and music recommendation. In this paper, collaborative filtering is combined with service invocation patterns, user requirement and preferences. This considers different user preferences and makes prediction personalized, while maintaining good performance results.

Some works integrate user preferences into QoS prediction [11-15], e.g. [11-13] propose prediction algorithms based on collaborative filtering. They calculate the similarity between users by their usage data and predict QoS based on user similarity. This method avoids the influence of the environment factor on prediction. Even the same user will have different QoS experiences over time or with different input data, but these works do not consider user requirements and generally show low efficiency.

The proposed method in this paper takes full account of user requirements, the network and server factors. It abstracts the service invocation pattern to keep the service

QoS steady. When user requirements are known, prediction can be done based on matched patterns. This approach is efficient and reduces the computational overhead.

8   Conclusion

Service management in Web and Cloud environments [26,27], e.g. public clouds, requires service-level agreements (SLA) for individual users to be managed continuously, based on monitored QoS data. (Cloud) service managers take care of this for the users. Dynamic, personalised prediction of QoS is an essential component of reliable service provisioning that makes service lifecycle management more reliable. The need to personalise services dynamically is highlighted by e.g. cloud requirements for efficient service quality management adapted to user-specific requirements and situations across a range of end-user and business solutions offered as cloud services.

This paper proposes a service QoS prediction technique to satisfy personalized requirements. It considers not only the impact of the network, but also the Web server environment, and especially the individual user requirements. Based on historic information, we can abstract past user invocation pattern (mined from monitored log data) in order to predict future QoS of potential services to be utilised. The pattern approach provides independent reliability for the prediction of SLA-relevant aspects. When there is no information about the target pattern, we utilize collaborative filtering to predict according the data of other patterns. The results show that this approach is more accurate and personalized, and also demonstrates good prediction performance, which allows for dynamic utilisation of the technique.

Acknowledgement. This research has been supported by the National Natural Science Foundation of China (grant 61073062), the *Technology Project of LiaoNing Province* (2011216027) and the *Irish Centre for Cloud Computing and Commerce*, an Irish national Technology Centre funded by Enterprise Ireland and the Irish Industrial Development Authority.

References

1. Cardoso, J., Sheth, A., Miller, J., Arnold, J., Kochut, K.: Quality of Service for Workflows and Web Service Processes. Journal of Web Semantics 1(3), 281–308 (2004)
2. Kritikos, K., Plexousakis, D.: Requirements for QoS-based Web service description and discovery. IEEE Transactions on Services Computing 2(4), 320–337 (2009)
3. Zheng, K., Xiong, H.: Semantic Web service discovery method based on user preference and QoS. In: Intl. Conf. on Consumer Electr., Comms. and Netw. CECNet 2012, pp. 3502–3506 (2012)
4. Ali, R.J.A., Rana, O.F., Walker, D.W.: G-QoSM: Grid service discovery using QoS properties. Computing and Informatics 21(4), 363–382 (2012)
5. Wang, P.: QoS-aware web services selection with intuitionistic fuzzy set under consumer's vague perception. Expert Systems with Applications 36(3), 4460–4466 (2009)
6. Huang, A.F.M., Lan, C.W., Yang, S.J.H.: An optimal QoS-based Web service selection scheme. Information Sciences 179(19), 3309–3322 (2009)
7. Ye, Z., Bouguettaya, A., Zhou, X.: QoS-Aware Cloud Service Composition based on Economic Models. In: Liu, C., Ludwig, H., Toumani, F., Yu, Q. (eds.) ICSOC 2012. LNCS, vol. 7636, pp. 111–126. Springer, Heidelberg (2012)

8. Alrifai, M., Skoutas, D., Risse, T.: Selecting skyline services for QoS-based web service composition. In: Proc. Intl. Conf. on World Wide Web, pp. 11–20. ACM (2010)
9. Zeng, L., Benatallah, B., Ngu, A.H.H., et al.: QoS-Aware middleware for Web services composition. IEEE Trans. on Software Engineering 30(5), 311–327 (2004)
10. Yu, T., Lin, K.J.: Service Selection Algorithms for Web Services with End-to-end QoS constraints. Information Systems and E-Business Management 3(2), 103–126 (2005)
11. Shao, L., Zhang, J., Wei, Y., et al.: Personalized QoS prediction for Web services via collaborative filtering. In: IEEE Intl. Conference on Web Services, ICWS 2007, pp. 439–446 (2007)
12. Zheng, Z., Ma, L.M.R., et al.: Qos-aware web service recommendation by collaborative filtering. IEEE Transactions on Services Computing 4(2), 140–152 (2011)
13. Zheng, Z., Ma, H.: WSRec: A Collaborative Filtering Based Web Service Recommender System. In: Proc IEEE Intl. Conference on Web Services, pp. 437–444 (2009)
14. Wu, G., Wei, J., Qiao, X., et al.: A Bayesian network based QoS assessment model for web services. In: Proc IEEE Intl. Conference on Service Computing, pp. 498–505 (2007)
15. Li, Z., Bin, Z., Ying, L., et al.: A Web Service QoS Prediction Approach Based on Collaborative Filtering. In: IEEE Asia-Pacific Services Computing Conf APSCC 2010, pp. 725–731 (2010)
16. Li, Z., Bin, Z., Jun, N., et al.: An Approach for Web Service QoS prediction based on service using information. In: Intl Conference on Service Sciences, ICSS 2010, pp. 324–328 (2010)
17. Ester, M., Kriegel, H.P., Sander, J., et al.: A density-based algorithm for discovering clusters in large spatial databases with noise. In: Proc. Intl. Conf. on Knowledge Discovery in Databases and Data Mining (KDD 1996), pp. 226–232. AAAI Press (1996)
18. Lelli, F., Maron, G., Orlando, S.: Client Side Estimation of a Remote Service Execution. In: IEEE International Symposium on Modelling, Analysis, and Simulation of Computer and Telecommunication Systems, MASCOTS (2007)
19. Vu, L.H., Hauswirth, M., Aberer, K.: QoS-based Service Selection and Ranking with Trust and Reputation Management. Computer Science 3760(2005), 466–483 (2005)
20. Yan, L., Minghui, Z., Duanchao, L., et al.: Service selection approach considering the trustworthiness of QoS data. Journal of Software 19(10), 2620–2627 (2008)
21. Sarwar, B., Karypis, G., Konstan, J., et al.: Item-based collaborative filtering recommendation algorithms. In: Proc 10th Int'l World Wide Web Conf., pp. 285–295. ACM Press (2001)
22. Chun, Z., Chunxiao, X., Lizhu, Z.: A Survey of Personalization Technology. Journal of Software 13(10), 1852–1861 (2002)
23. Hailing, X., Xiao, W., Xiaodong, W., Baoping, Y.: Comparison study of Internet recommendation system. Journal of Software 20(2), 350–362 (2009)
24. Ailing, D., Yangyong, Z., Bole, S.: A Collaborative Filtering Recommendation Algorithm Based on Item Rating Prediction. Journal of Software 14(9), 1621–1628 (2003)
25. Balke, W.T., Matthias, W.: Towards personalized selection of Web services. In: Proc. Intl. World Wide Web Conf., pp. 20–24. ACM Press, New York (2003)
26. Pahl, C., Xiong, H., Walshe, R.: A Comparison of On-premise to Cloud Migration Approaches. In: Lau, K.-K., Lamersdorf, W., Pimentel, E. (eds.) ESOCC 2013. LNCS, vol. 8135, pp. 212–226. Springer, Heidelberg (2013)
27. Pahl, C., Xiong, H.: Migration to PaaS Clouds - Migration Process and Architectural Concerns. In: IEEE 7th International Symposium on the Maintenance and Evolution of Service-Oriented and Cloud-Based Systems, MESOCA 2013. IEEE (2013)
28. Huang, A.F., Lan, C.W., Yang, S.J.: An optimal QoS-based Web service selection scheme. Information Sciences 179(19), 3309–3322 (2009)

Open Source versus Proprietary Software in Service-Orientation: The Case of BPEL Engines

Simon Harrer, Jörg Lenhard, and Guido Wirtz

Distributed Systems Group, University of Bamberg, Germany
{simon.harrer,joerg.lenhard,guido.wirtz}@uni-bamberg.de

Abstract. It is a long-standing debate, whether software that is developed as open source is generally of higher quality than proprietary software. Although the open source community has grown immensely during the last decade, there is still no clear answer. Service-oriented software and middleware tends to rely on highly complex and interrelated standards and frameworks. Thus, it is questionable if small and loosely coupled teams, as typical in open source software development, can compete with major vendors. Here, we focus on a central part of service-oriented software systems, i.e., process engines for service orchestration, and compare open source and proprietary solutions. We use the Web Services Business Process Execution Language (BPEL) and compare standard conformance and its impact on language expressiveness in terms of workflow pattern support of eight engines. The results show that, although the top open source engines are on par with their proprietary counterparts, in general proprietary engines perform better.

Keywords: open source, SOA, BPEL, patterns, conformance testing.

1 Introduction

The comparison of open source and proprietary software is a topic that, depending on the audience, can quickly turn from a moderate discussion to a heated debate. Although it has been investigated a number of times, see for instance [10, 15, 26, 27], a definite answer is seldom found. Studies often focus on software such as operating systems [26] and despite the wide academic interest in such comparisons, little work on comparing open source and proprietary service-oriented software can be found. In the services ecosystem, highly specialized and inherently complex software that differs from operating systems in nature and level of abstraction prevails. Especially when it comes to middleware, vendors established large projects and created highly priced products and it is unclear whether open source alternatives can compete. This makes the comparison of open and proprietary service-oriented software especially interesting. What is more, direct comparisons of open source and proprietary software are typically impeded by the fact that truly comparable software is hard to find [26, p.260]. In the area of service-oriented computing, however, there exists a large set of detailed international standards that describe required functionality for Web

S. Basu et al. (Eds.): ICSOC 2013, LNCS 8274, pp. 99–113, 2013.

Services. Hence, a meaningful and precise comparison becomes feasible in this area. Here, we compare service-oriented middleware for service orchestration [23], in particular BPEL engines.

The BPEL 2.0 specification [20] defines a language to implement executable processes as interactions of Web Services in XML. A series of control- and data-flow activities are used to specify the order of the interactions, thereby orchestrating invoked Web Services [23]. A typical example for a BPEL process is that of a travel agency service which books accommodation, flight and transportation in a single transaction by reusing multiple external services. BPEL is tightly integrated into the Web Services ecosystem and relies heavily on other standards, e.g., the Web Service Description Language (WSDL), XPath, and SOAP. As such, BPEL is a natural choice for implementing processes within a Web Services-based service-oriented architecture (SOA) [22]. It is frequently used in scenarios such as business-to-business integration where multiple partners participate in cross-organizational business processes. Within such scenarios, service choreographies define the global perspective of a shared process by specifying the public collaboration protocol, whereas orchestrations implement the local perspective of a single partner [23]. BPEL particularly fits to implement these orchestrations due to its inherent usage of vendor-independent technologies such as Web Services and XML, and has been used in industry standards, for example [24], and various studies, e.g., [9,11].

These approaches rely, among other criteria, on the existence of fully conformant BPEL engines, which provide two of the key selling points of BPEL, namely platform independence and portability of process definitions. Therefore, standard conformance is a highly relevant selection criterion for projects in industry or academia that leverage BPEL. For this reason, we use standard conformance as the central comparison factor in this study. A comparison of additional quality factors, such as performance, is also valuable, but we defer this to future work. Directly related to standard conformance and potentially more insightful is the factor of expressive power. Expressive power refers to the ease with which concepts typically needed in a language or system can be expressed in that system. The more concepts supported and the easier they can be expressed, the more suitable the system is. For process languages such as BPEL, expressiveness is typically measured in terms of workflow pattern support [30]. Such patterns are derived from real world systems and usage scenarios, describing features of processes that are repeatably used. Thereby, patterns can provide meaningful insights into the capabilities of engines. If an engine is not fully standard conformant and lacks several features, it may also suffer from a reduction of expressiveness. Hence, we consider expressiveness of engines as the second comparison factor. In previous work [8], we evaluated the standard conformance of five open source engines and could show that it varies strongly among them. Here, we complement this evaluation by extending the comparison to a) proprietary engines and b) workflow pattern support. These proprietary engines often claim to excel in terms of performance and are part of large and optimized middleware solutions. We evaluate three proprietary engines and contrast the results to [8]. Furthermore, we present a test suite for automatically evaluating workflow patterns [30] support to determine the effects of standard conformance of engines on their expressiveness. In summary, we pose two research questions:

RQ1: Do proprietary BPEL engines outperform open source engines in terms of standard conformance?

RQ2: How do variances in standard conformance influence the expressiveness of the language subsets supported by the engines?

The rest of the paper is structured as follows: First, we discuss related work and, thereafter, outline our testing approach with a focus on the testing of expressiveness. In section 4, we evaluate, analyze, and discuss the test results and their implications, and answer both research questions. Last, a summary and an outlook on future work is given in section 5.

2   Related Work

Related work is subdivided into four different areas: i) alternative process and workflow languages and systems, ii) testing and verification of BPEL, iii) evaluations of the expressiveness of process languages using patterns, and iv) approaches for comparing the quality of open versus proprietary software.

i) Process languages: Although BPEL has received immense attention in the last decade, there are a variety of other process or workflow languages and engines. Yet Another Workflow Language (YAWL) [29] is a formally defined workflow language based on Petri nets with direct support for workflow patterns [30]. At this time, only one implementation, namely, the YAWL workflow engine exists. Another notable competitor to BPEL is the Windows Workflow Foundation [4]. For this language, there is also only a single implementation, but it is closed source and does not ship with an accompanied specification. In recent years, the Business Process Model and Notation (BPMN) 2.0 [21] has gained rising attention. Although the focus of BPMN resides on its visual notation for business processes, it ships with a mapping to BPEL 2.0 [21, pp. 445–474]. Today, several implementations of BPMN have arrived. However, nearly all of them only provide *modeling conformance* [21, p.1], meaning they can be used for visualization, but not *execution conformance*, required for constructing executable processes. What is more, the BPMN specification offers a lot of room for interpretation concerning executable processes models. This makes it more easily adaptable to a different technological context, as opposed to BPEL which is tailored to Web Service orchestration, but complicates the construction of processes that can be executed on more than a single engine [6]. Last, the XML Process Definition Language (XPDL) 2.2 [31] from the Workflow Management Coalition (WfMC) is a serializable meta model to exchange process definitions between different products. As opposed to BPEL, XPDL includes and serializes visual information and is well suited for exchanging BPMN models but does not provide execution semantics. In summary, we focus on BPEL here, as it provides, in contrast to other process languages, precisely defined execution semantics, as well as a variety of open source and proprietary implementations, which are directly comparable.

ii) Testing of BPEL: Testing and verification of SOAs and Web Services has been extensively studied. See for instance [3] for a comprehensive overview. When it comes to conformance testing, a distinction has to be made between approaches that assert the conformance of concrete services, possibly implemented in BPEL, to a communication protocol, such as [5, 14], and the testing of an engine to a language specification, which we do here. Concerning BPEL, research primarily focuses on unit testing, performance testing, or formal verification of BPEL processes, and not engines. When it comes to unit testing, BPELUnit is of most importance [17]. Performance testing approaches for services, such as SOABench [1], which also benchmarks BPEL engines, and GENESIS2 [13], are based on generating testbeds from an extensible domain model which can then be used to gather performance metrics. Here, we conduct standard conformance testing, thus, instead of testing the correctness of a BPEL process, we test the correctness of a BPEL engine, and focus on different kinds of metrics. We build upon the tool *betsy*[1], which we also use in [8], but extend it with capabilities for testing several proprietary engines and a test suite for the evaluation of workflow pattern support.

iii) Expressiveness and patterns: Workflow patterns aim to "provide the basis for an in-depth comparison of a number of commercially available workflow management systems" [30, p.5]. Patterns capture a distinct feature or piece of functionality that is frequently needed in workflows and processes and which should therefore be supported as directly as possible in process languages. The more patterns a language or system supports, the more expressive it is. The original pattern catalog [30] consists of 20 workflow control-flow patterns (WCPs) which are subdivided into *basic* control-flow, *advanced branching and synchronization, structural, state-based, cancellation,* and *multi-instance* patterns. Although the appropriateness of these patterns is not undisputed [2], they have been extensively used for benchmarking, designing and developing languages and systems, as demonstrated by a large array of additional pattern catalogs and studies, for instance [16, 19, 28]. For this reason, the usage of the workflow patterns here facilitates the comparison of this study to related work. The Workflow Patterns Initiative[2] already provides evaluations of the expressiveness of BPEL 1.1 and two proprietary BPEL 1.1 engines. Here, we focus on BPEL 2.0 only, as it is the latest published version of the standard for six years. In [19], multiple pattern catalogs, including the workflow patterns, have been implemented for WF, BPEL 2.0 and the BPEL 2.0 engine OpenESB. We base our work on [19] by adapting these BPEL 2.0 implementations of the original 20 workflow patterns to allow for an automatic and repeatable benchmark of eight BPEL engines and thereby evaluate the effects of BPEL standard conformance on language expressiveness.

iv) Comparing quality: Software quality comparisons typically focus on *internal quality* [26, 27], for instance by computing and comparing source code metrics for different pieces of software, or *external quality* [15], by investigating

---

[1] This tool can be found at https://github.com/uniba-dsg/betsy.
[2] See the project page at http://www.workflowpatterns.com/.

the usefulness of the software for its end users. Here, we do not look at source code, which in case of proprietary engines is not available. Instead, we focus on conformance as an external quality attribute. Conformance determines the degree to which prescribed functionality is available to the users of an engine. This has a direct effect on the kinds of patterns that can be implemented on an engine, and thereby its expressiveness. The more standard-conformant an engine is, and the more patterns it directly supports, the higher its external quality is.

3   Testing Approach

To be able to compare different engines and answer the research questions, we need a mechanism for an in-depth and isolated analysis of each engine. The approach for achieving this kind of analysis is described in this section. Thereafter, the results are aggregated for the comparison in the following section.

The testing approach consists of the testing setup in general and the expressiveness test suite in particular. Within the testing setup, we list the engines under test, elaborate on the standard conformance test suite, and the steps of a typical test run.

3.1   Testing Setup

Our testing setup is an adapted and extended version of the setup proposed in [8] which relies on the publicly available testing tool betsy. The tool can be used to automatically manage (download, install, start and stop) several open source engines. Moreover, it provides a conformance test suite which comprises more than 130 manually created test cases, in the form of standard-conformant BPEL processes. Since the publication of [8], three open source engines received major or minor updates. Here, we updated betsy to use the latest versions of these engines, namely, Apache ODE 1.3.5, bpel-g 5.3, OpenESB v2.3, Orchestra 4.9.0 and Petals ESB 4.1[3]. Furthermore, we added support for testing the conformance of three proprietary BPEL engines. These engines come from major global SOA middleware vendors that also participated in crafting the BPEL specification. Due to licensing reasons, we cannot disclose the names of the proprietary engines, and, therefore, refer to them as $P1$, $P2$ and $P3$.

The tests are derived manually from the normative parts of the BPEL specification which are indicated with the keywords MUST and MUST NOT, as defined in [12]. The test suite is subdivided into three groups resembling the structure of the BPEL specification, namely, basic activities [20, pp. 84–97] (e.g., assign, empty, exit, invoke, and receive), scopes [20, pp. 115–147] (e.g., fault-, compensation-, and termination handlers) and structured activities [20, pp. 98–114] (e.g., if, while, flow, and forEach). The various configurations of the BPEL activities of each group form the basis of the test cases, including all BPEL faults. Hence, every test case of the standard conformance test suite asserts

---

[3] Download links available at https://github.com/uniba-dsg/betsy#downloads

the support of a specific BPEL feature. Every test case consists of a test definition, the BPEL process and its dependencies (WSDL definitions, XML Schemas, etc.), and a test case configuration, specifying the input data and assertions on the result. All processes are based upon the same process stub, which is shown in Listing 1, and implement the same WSDL interface containing a one-way and two request-response operations for exchanging basic data types via the document/literal binding over HTTP[4]. To assert the correctness of the process execution, each test must provide observable output, which is implemented via a receive-reply pair.

```
1 <process>
2     <partnerLinks/>
3     <variables/>
4     <sequence>
5         <receive createInstance="true" />
6         <!-- feature under test -->
7         <assign /> <!-- prepare reply message -->
8         <reply />
9     </sequence>
10 </process>
```

Listing 1. Process stub for conformance tests adapted from [8, p.4]

The tests aim at checking the conformance of a feature in isolation. This is not completely possible, as the basic structure depicted in Listing 1 and basic input and output is always required, otherwise the correctness of a test cannot be asserted. However, all features in the stub could be verified to work in a basic configuration on all engines and therefore have no impact on the test results.

During a full test run, our tool automatically converts the engine independent test specifications to engine specific test cases and creates required deployment descriptors as well as deployment archives. Next, these archives are deployed to the corresponding engines and the test case configurations are executed. At first, every test case configuration asserts successful deployment by determining whether the WSDL definition of the process has been published. Next, the different test steps are executed, sending messages and asserting the responses by means of correct return values or expected SOAP faults. When all test cases have been tested, an HTML report is created from the test results.

The quality and correctness of the conformance test cases were ensured by validating them against the XML Schema files of their specifications, e.g., BPEL 2.0, WSDL 1.1 and XML Schema 1.1, and by reviewing them within our group. In addition, all test cases are publicly available and, as a result, already have been improved by the developers of two of the engines, Apache ODE and bpel-g. Finally, only 4 of the test cases fail on all engines, hence, approx. 97% of all test cases succeed on at least one engine, indicating their correctness.

---

[4] This is the preferred binding for achieving interoperability, as defined by the WS-I Basic Profile 2.0.

3.2   Pattern Test Suite

Table 1 shows the test case implementations for the automatic testing of work-flow patterns support of the original 20 workflow patterns from [30]. According to [30] and related studies, a pattern is *directly* supported (denoted as +) in a language or system, if at least one direct solution using a single language construct (activity in BPEL) for the pattern can be found. If the solution involves a combination of two constructs, it is counted as *partial support* (denoted as +/−) for the pattern, otherwise, there is *no direct support* (denoted as −). The BPEL 2.0 column in Table 1 shows the workflow patterns support by the specification [19][5].

Table 1. List of workflow patterns from [30] along with number of test cases and degree of support

Basic Control Flow Patterns		BPEL 2.0	Tests
WCP01	Sequence	+	1
WCP02	Parallel Split	+	1
WCP03	Synchronization	+	1
WCP04	Exclusive Choice	+	1
WCP05	Simple Merge	+	1
Advanced Branching and Synchronization Patterns		BPEL 2.0	Tests
WCP06	Multi-Choice	+	2
WCP07	Synchronizing Merge	+	2
WCP08	Multi-Merge	-	0
WCP09	Discriminator	-	0
Structural Patterns		BPEL 2.0	Tests
WCP10	Arbitrary Cycles	-	0
WCP11	Implicit Termination	+	1
Patterns with Multiple Instances		BPEL 2.0	Tests
WCP12	Multiple Instances Without Synchronization	+	3
WCP13	Multiple Instances With a Priori Design Time Knowledge	+	2
WCP14	Multiple Instances With a Priori Runtime Knowledge	+	1
WCP15	Multiple Instances Without a Priori Runtime Knowledge	-	0
State-based Patterns		BPEL 2.0	Tests
WCP16	Deferred Choice	+	1
WCP17	Interleaved Parallel Routing	+/-	1
WCP18	Milestone	+/-	1
Cancellation Patterns		BPEL 2.0	Tests
WCP19	Cancel Activity	+/-	1
WCP20	Cancel Case	+	1

The BPEL implementations used here are adopted from [18, 19] and modified to be automatically testable with betsy, that is, to use the same WSDL definition and partner service as the conformance test suite. The pattern implementations work similar to the other test cases and are based on the process stub presented in Listing 1. Each pattern test case contains an implementation of a workflow pattern in BPEL. Given an engine successfully deploys the process and returns the asserted result on invocation, it demonstrates that it supports

---

[5] The pattern support evaluation from [19] differs from [25] which evaluates BPEL 1.1. Please refer to [19] or the technical report [18] for explanatory details.

the related workflow pattern. Four of the patterns, *Multi-Merge*, *Discriminator*, *Arbitrary Cycles* and *Multiple Instances Without a Priori Runtime Knowledge*, are left untested. These patterns cannot be implemented directly in BPEL (i.e., they would require the usage of too many constructs), due to the structuredness of its control-flow definition and the inability to create cycles using links [19]. Moreover, the tests for three patterns, *Interleaved Parallel Routing*, *Milestone*, and *Cancel Activity* provide at most partial support, as there is no single activity in BPEL that directly implements these patterns. Four of the patterns, *Multi-Choice*, *Synchronizing Merge*, *Multiple Instances Without Synchronization* and *Multiple Instances With a Priori Design Time Knowledge* are implemented in more than one test case. The reason for this is that multiple alternative implementations of the pattern, with a differing degree of support, are available in BPEL. For instance, the *Multi-Choice* pattern is typically implemented in BPEL using `links` in a `flow` activity to activate different parallel control-flow paths at the same time. However, `links` are not supported by all engines under test and these engines would consequently fail to support that pattern. An alternative implementation of the *Multi-Choice* pattern that grants partial support can be achieved by nesting multiple `if` activities in a `flow` activity. By including such alternative tests, we can provide a precise classification of all engines under test.

In summary, if an engine passes a test case, it provides either direct or partial support depending on the type of the test case. If there are multiple test cases, the engine is granted the degree of support of the most direct test case.

4   Results and Implications

In this section, we present the test results of a full test run evaluating the standard conformance and the expressiveness test suite on both, proprietary and open source engines[6]. The results are subdivided into standard conformance results in Table 2 and expressiveness evaluations in Table 3. In the following, we first discuss the conformance results of the three proprietary engines. Next, we compare these to the results of the five open source engines and discuss the implications of this comparison. Last, based on workflow pattern support, the effects of standard conformance on expressiveness are evaluated and presented for both engine types.

4.1   Commercial Engines

The conformance results in Table 2 consist of the aggregated number of successful tests per BPEL activity for each engine as well as the percentage and average values per engine, engine type, and activity group. In addition, the *deployment rate*, the percentage of successfully deployed test cases, is given at the bottom of the table.

---

[6] We executed this test run on a Windows 7 64 bit system with 16 GB of RAM and an i7-2600 processor.

Engine P1: Engine $P1$ ranks first place when compared to the other proprietary products and conforms to the BPEL specification to a degree of 92%, failing only in eleven of 131 test cases. Nine of these failed tests concern basic and two concern structured activities, respectively. Language features related to scopes are fully supported. The major shortcomings of this engine lie in fault handling and detection. Faults that are expected to be thrown under certain circumstances are not thrown. For example, the engine does not throw the expected `invalidExpressionValue` fault when the `startCounter` of the `forEach` activity is too high or its `completionCondition` is negative. In addition, XSL transformations and the invocation of Web Service operations that do not expect input are not implemented in a standard-conformant fashion.

Table 2. Number of successfully passed conformance tests, aggregated by activity, group, and engine

Activity	Prop. E.				Open Source Engines							
	P1	P2	P3	Ø	bpel-g	ODE	OpenESB	Ø	Orch.	Petals	Ø	Σ
Basic Activities												
Assign	15	7	15		15	10	13		11	8		19
Empty	1	1	1		1	1	1		1	1		1
Exit	1	1	1		1	1	1		1	1		1
Invoke	11	6	7		11	7	3		8	5		12
Receive	4	3	3		4	3	1		1	1		5
ReceiveReply	8	6	6		8	5	6		5	1		11
Rethrow	3	0	1		3	2	1		0	0		3
Throw	5	0	4		5	5	4		0	0		5
Validate	2	0	2		2	0	2		0	0		2
Variables	3	1	1		3	2	2		1	1		3
Wait	3	2	3		3	3	3		2	1		3
Σ	56	27	44		56	39	37		30	19		65
	86%	41%	68%	65%	86%	60%	57%	68%	46%	29%	56%	
Scopes												
Compensation	5	5	5		5	4	5		2	0		5
CorrelationSets	2	0	2		2	2	1		0	0		2
EventHandlers	8	5	7		8	6	6		6	0		8
FaultHandlers	6	5	6		6	6	6		2	5		6
MessageExchanges	3	1	1		3	1	1		1	0		3
PartnerLinks	1	0	1		1	1	1		1	0		1
Scope-Attributes	3	2	3		3	2	3		1	1		3
TerminationHandlers	2	0	0		2	0	2		2	0		2
Variables	2	2	2		2	2	2		2	0		2
Σ	32	20	27		32	24	27		17	6		32
	100%	63%	84%	82%	100%	75%	84%	86%	53%	19%	66%	
Structured Activities												
Flow	9	6	7		9	9	2		7	0		9
ForEach	9	4	6		9	3	9		0	2		11
If	5	4	4		5	4	4		4	4		5
Pick	5	5	5		5	5	4		4	1		5
RepeatUntil	2	2	2		2	1	2		2	0		2
Sequence	1	1	1		1	1	1		1	1		1
While	1	1	1		1	1	1		1	1		1
Σ	32	23	26		32	24	23		19	9		34
	94%	68%	76%	79%	94%	71%	68%	77%	56%	26%	62%	
Σ of Σ	120	70	97		120	87	87		66	49		131
	92%	53%	74%	73%	92%	66%	66%	75%	50%	26%	62%	
Deployment Rate	98%	88%	100%		98%	92%	100%		95%	57%		

Engine P2: The second engine is the lowest-ranking proprietary product, as it only supports roughly half of the test cases. Although it supports approximately two third of the scope and structured activity test cases, less then half of the basic activities are implemented correctly. This is mostly due to the way faults are propagated in engine $P2$. If a fault is not handled at root level, the process fails silently and does not propagate the fault to external callers that are still waiting for a response. Thus, an external caller gets no hint on the cause of the error. This contradicts common fault handling principles known in higher level programming languages and hampers distributed fault handling [7]. As a consequence, $P2$ fails all fault related tests, e.g., for the throw, rethrow, and validate activities, the handling of incoming faults from invoked services, and tests for standard BPEL faults. This amounts to ten tests for structured activities, two for scopes and 30 for basic activities, and adds up to 32% of all tests in total. Another factor that impacts its standard conformance rating is its deployment rate. Twelve percent of the standard-conformant test cases are rejected by $P2$ during deployment resulting in an upper bound of 88% for its conformance rating. Furthermore, multiple features of the assign activity seem to be unimplemented: the XPath extension functions for BPEL, getVariableProperty and doXslTransform, the assignment of a partnerLink or a property, as well as the keepSrcElementName attribute of a copy element. Invoke activities cannot be used with correlationSets or empty messages, and the same applies to embedded fault handlers. Engine $P2$ does not implement terminationHandlers and the definition of correlationSets or partnerLinks at the level of a scope is unsupported, although both constructs work when used on the process level. Event handling is supported in a basic fashion. However, the onEvent activity does not support the fromParts syntax and the onAlarm activity does not support the until element. The initiation of a correlationSet with an asynchronous operation leads to a failure to correlate on this set in an onEvent message handler. If used within a scope or at root level, faultHandlers work in most cases. The only exception to this is the failure to catch a fault that carries additional fault data using a faultElement. The forEach activity is implemented but lacks support for configuration related to the completionCondition. In a similar fashion, the flow activity supports links, but no conditional activation with joinConditions.

Engine P3: The proprietary engine with the second highest degree of standard conformance, successfully completing 74% of the tests, is engine $P3$. It supports all structured activities in their basic configuration but fails to support several special cases, such as links in a flow activity that use joinConditions, and forEach activities that use a completionCondition with successful-BranchesOnly. In addition, the forEach activity is always executed sequentially even if the parallel attribute is set. $P3$ does not support terminationHandlers, throwing or re-throwing faultData, the keepSrcElementName option of the copy element and the specification of toParts for messaging activities. Moreover, embedded fault- or compensation handlers for the invoke activity are not supported. Finally, the remaining tests fail, because certain standard faults, such as `correlationViolation` or `missingReply`, are not thrown as required.

4.2   Comparison of Proprietary and Open Source Engines

This section compares the standard conformance and its effects on expressiveness of open source engines with that of proprietary engines and answers the two research questions posed in the introduction. The results of the five open source engines presented in Table 2 vary slightly from previous analyses [8], because the engines under test as well as the conformance test suite were updated.

Proprietary engines successfully pass between 53% and 92% of the conformance tests. For open source engines, these numbers vary from 26% to 92%. On average, proprietary engines pass 73% of the conformance test suite, whereas the open source engines only achieve 62%. We used a binomial test to verify if this difference is significant. We tested if the number of successfully passed tests for open source engines is equal to the corresponding value for proprietary engines at a significance level of 5%. With a p-value of $2.5e^{-9}$, this hypothesis can be safely rejected in favour of the alternative: Open source engines pass significantly less tests than their counterparts. A reason for this observation may be that our test set of open source engines includes engines that could be considered experimental or premature. This is supported by the fact that the lowest ranking engine only deploys 57% of the tests and passes 26%. But because we lack market data on engine usage, we are unable to make a clear distinction on this issue. The overall situation changes, however, when looking at the top three open source engines which, to our experience, also are the ones most widely used in practice. Considering the top three open source engines, standard conformance ranges at 75%, two percentage points above the corresponding value for proprietary engines. Using binomial tests as before, we could confirm that there is no significant difference between the proprietary and the top three open source engines. The number of successful tests is clearly not lower (p-value of 0.81), but also not significantly higher (p-value of 0.23) for open source engines. In summary, based on this data, the answer to $RQ1$, whether proprietary engines outperform open source ones, has to be confirmed. In total, proprietary engines provide a higher degree of support, although the difference balances when only considering mature open source engines.

Table 3 details the results for workflow pattern support based on the expressiveness test suite using the trivalent rating described in section 3.2. Insights on pattern support can be gained by comparing the engines with the workflow pattern support of BPEL 2.0 shown in the BPEL column. We consider the number of times an engine is *compliant* to BPEL (i.e., the engine has the same degree of pattern support as BPEL), the engine *deviates* (i.e., the engine only provides partial support while BPEL directly supports the pattern) and the engine fails to directly support the pattern, in relation to the total number of patterns. We exclude the four patterns that cannot be implemented directly in BPEL from these calculations, as we cannot diagnose support for them in the first place. The results show that compliance to BPEL in pattern support ranges from 56% to

Table 3. Workflow patterns support per engine, aggregated by pattern, pattern group and engine

Pattern	BPEL	Comm. Eng.			Open Source Engines					
		P1	P2	P3	bpel-g	ODE	OpenESB	Orch.	Petals	
Basic Control-Flow Patterns										100%
WCP01 Sequence	+	+	+	+	+	+	+	+	+	100%
WCP02 Parallel Split	+	+	+	+	+	+	+	+	+	100%
WCP03 Synchronization	+	+	+	+	+	+	+	+	+	100%
WCP04 Exlusive Choice	+	+	+	+	+	+	+	+	+	100%
WCP05 Simple Merge	+	+	+	+	+	+	+	+	+	100%
Advanced Branching and Synchronization Patterns										88%
WCP06 Multi-Choice	+	+	+	+	+	+	+/-	+	+/-	75%
WCP07 Synchronizing Merge	+	+	+	+	+	+	+/-	+	+/-	75%
Structural Patterns										100%
WCP11 Implicit Termination	+	+	+	+	+	+	+	+	+	100%
Patterns with Multiple Instances										50%
WCP12 MI Without Sync.	+	+	+	+/-	+	+	+/-	+/-	+/-	50%
WCP13 MI W. Design T. Know.	+	+	+	-	+	+	+/-	+/-	+/-	50%
WCP14 MI W. Runtime Know.	+	+	+	-	+	+	-	-	-	50%
State-based Patterns										90%
WCP16 Deferred Choice	+	+	+	+	+	+	+	+	+	100%
WCP17 Interl. Parallel Routing	+/-	+/-	+/-	+/-	+/-	+/-	-	-	-	63%
WCP18 Milestone	+/-	+/-	+/-	+/-	+/-	+/-	+/-	-	-	75%
Cancellation Patterns										100%
WCP19 Cancel Activity	+/-	+/-	+/-	+/-	+/-	+/-	+/-	+/-	+/-	100%
WCP20 Cancel Case	+	+	+	+	+	+	+	+	+	100%
compliance		100%	100%	81%	100%	100%	63%	69%	56%	84%
deviation				6%			25%	13%	25%	9%
no direct support				13%			13%	19%	19%	8%
Ø of compliance per engine group			94%			88%		72%		

100% for open source engines, wheras proprietary engines excel their competitors with support ranging from 81% up to 100%. Two open source engines, Apache ODE and bpel-g, and two proprietary engines, P1 and P2, are completely compliant to BPEL in terms of support. P3 ranks second, whereas the remaining open source engines Orchestra, OpenESB, and PetalsESB come last.

All engines share the degree of support with BPEL for nine patterns (WCP01-WCP05, WCP11, WCP16, WCP19-20). For three patterns, several engines deviate from BPEL, whereas five patterns are not directly supported by at least one engine. As shown in the right-most column in Table 3, engines comply with BPEL for the basic control-flow patterns, the structural patterns, and the cancellation patterns. Patterns with multiple instances show most deviations and only in 50% of the cases, the engines achieve the same rating as BPEL. For advanced branching and synchronization and state-based patterns, engines provide 88% and 90% of compliance, respectively. What is more, support for advanced branching and synchronization patterns is in place for all engines, although two open source engines only support the patterns using a workaround solution. A similar situation applies to the the *Multiple Instances* patterns, where two patterns, WCP12 and WCP13, can be implemented by workaround solutions by three engines. One proprietary engine fails to support two of the *Multiple Instances* patterns (WCP13 and WCP14), and deviates from BPEL for the third *Multiple Instance* pattern (WCP12). Several open source engines also fail to support three patterns, namely, the *Multiple Instances With a Priori Runtime Knowledge* pattern (WCP14), the *Interleaved Parallel Routing* pattern (WCP17) and the *Milestone* pattern (WCP18). Interestingly, the patterns for which open source and proprietary engines deviate from BPEL are almost disjunctive, only WCP14 is not directly supported in both groups on at least one engine. Moreover, WCP14 is the least supported pattern as the corresponding test case fails on four engines. In total, the proprietary engines implement more workflow patterns (94%) than their open source counter parts (72%). As before, when comparing the three proprietary engines with the top three open source engines, this difference shrinks to an insignificant level (94% vs. 88%). The proprietary engines provide no direct support in two cases and deviate from BPEL in one case, whereas the top three open source engines provide no direct support in two cases and deviate from BPEL in four cases. These results reinforce the answer to $RQ1$.

The 21 cases of deviation from BPEL are caused by a lack of support for the flow activity in combination with links (six times), the forEach activity (three times) in combination with parallel execution (nine times), message correlation (twice) and isolated scopes (once). These results let us answer $RQ2$, concerning the impact of standard conformance on workflow pattern support. All in all, 18 cases of deviation (or 86% of the deviations) are a result of the lack of a standard conformant implementation of the flow and the forEach activity. Put differently, the lack of truly parallel execution in an engine is the biggest obstacle to pattern support. Nevertheless, the impact of standard conformance on pattern support seems little. Apache ODE, with 66% of successful conformance tests, supports all workflow patterns that can be directly implemented in BPEL. Even the worst engine in terms of standard conformance, PetalsESB with only 26% of successful conformance tests, provides direct or partial support for 13 out of 16 workflow patterns (81%). To frame an answer to $RQ2$: *Workflow patterns can be directly implemented with only a moderate degree of standard conformance, but support for truly parallel execution of activities is a decisive factor.*

5   Conclusion and Future Work

In this paper, we presented a comparison of open source and proprietary BPEL engines in terms of standard conformance and language expressiveness. The results demonstrate, that proprietary engines provide a slightly higher degree of standard conformance and language expressiveness than their open source counterparts, and thus are of higher quality. This observation changes when considering the top three open source engines which are equal to their proprietary counterparts. The effect of standard conformance on language expressiveness turned out to be moderate, although parallel execution is a crucial factor.

Future work comprises two aspects: i) adding additional conformance and expressiveness test suites to get a more precise picture and ii) enhancing the test suite for testing other criteria, to provide a more comprehensive comparison of open source and proprietary products. Firstly, the BPEL specification [20, appendix B] contains a list of 94 static analysis rules specifying which BPEL processes must be rejected by a standard conformant engine. A test suite based on these rules that helps to verify if erroneous processes are correctly rejected would be desirable. Concerning language expressiveness, as outlined in section 2, many additional pattern catalogs do exist for which automatic testing would be beneficial. Secondly, in addition to standard conformance and expressiveness, performance is also a very important selection criteria for a process engine and a major quality criterion. The existing infrastructure could be used to provide valuable insights on the performance of certain activities and combinations thereof, as well as of workflow pattern implementations.

References

1. Bianculli, D., Binder, W., Drago, M.L.: Automated Performance Assessment for Service-Oriented Middleware: a Case Study on BPEL Engines. In: Proceedings of the 19th International World Wide Web Conference (WWW), Raleigh, North Carolina, USA, pp. 141–150 (April 2010)
2. Börger, E.: Approaches to modeling business processes: a critical analysis of BPMN, workflow patterns and YAWL. Software & Systems Modeling 11(3), 305–318 (2012)
3. Bozkurt, M., Harman, M., Hassoun, Y.: Testing & Verification In Service-Oriented Architecture: A Survey. Software Testing, Verificaton and Reliability, 1–7 (2012)
4. Bukovics, B.: Pro WF: Windows Workflow in .NET 4. Apress (June 2010) ISBN-13: 978-1-4302-2721-2
5. Geiger, M., Schönberger, A., Wirtz, G.: Towards Automated Conformance Checking of ebBP-ST Choreographies and Corresponding WS-BPEL Based Orchestrations. In: 23rd International Conference on Software Engineering and Knowledge Engineering, Miami, Florida, USA, July 7-9, KSI (2011)
6. Geiger, M., Wirtz, G.: BPMN 2.0 Serialization - Standard Compliance Issues and Evaluation of Modeling Tools. In: 5th International Workshop on Enterprise Modelling and Information Systems Architectures, St. Gallen, Switzerland (September 2013)
7. Guidi, C., Lanese, I., Montesi, F., Zavattaro, G.: On the Interplay Between Fault Handling and Request-Response Service Interactions. In: 8th International Conference on Application of Concurrency to System Design (ACSD), Xi'an, China, pp. 190–198 (June 2008)
8. Harrer, S., Lenhard, J., Wirtz, G.: BPEL Conformance in Open Source Engines. In: Proceedings of the 5th IEEE International Conference on Service-Oriented Computing and Applications (SOCA2012), Taipei, Taiwan, December 17-19. IEEE (2012)
9. Harrer, S., Schönberger, A., Wirtz, G.: A Model-Driven Approach for Monitoring ebBP BusinessTransactions. In: Proceedings of the 7th World Congress on Services 2011 (SERVICES 2011). IEEE, Washington, D.C. (2011)
10. Hoepman, J., Jacobs, B.: Increased Security Through Open Source. Communications of the ACM 50(1), 79–83 (2007)
11. Hofreiter, B., Huemer, C.: A model-driven top-down approach to inter-organizational systems: From global choreography models to executable BPEL. In: Join Conf. CEC, EEE, Hong Kong, China (2008)
12. IETF. Key words for use in RFCs to Indicate Requirement Levels (March 1997), RFC 2119
13. Juszczyk, L., Dustdar, S.: Programmable Fault Injection Testbeds for Complex SOA. In: Maglio, P.P., Weske, M., Yang, J., Fantinato, M. (eds.) ICSOC 2010. LNCS, vol. 6470, pp. 411–425. Springer, Heidelberg (2010)

14. Kaschner, K.: Conformance Testing for Asynchronously Communicating Services. In: Kappel, G., Maamar, Z., Motahari-Nezhad, H.R. (eds.) ICSOC 2011. LNCS, vol. 7084, pp. 108–124. Springer, Heidelberg (2011)

15. Kuan, J.: Open Source Software as Lead User's Make or Buy Decision: A Study of Open and Closed Source Quality. In: Proceedings of the 2nd Conference on The Economics of the Software and Internet Industries, Toulouse, France (January 2003)

16. Lanz, A., Weber, B., Reichert, M.: Workflow Time Patterns for Process-Aware Information Systems. In: Bider, I., Halpin, T., Krogstie, J., Nurcan, S., Proper, E., Schmidt, R., Ukor, R. (eds.) BPMDS 2010 and EMMSAD 2010. LNBIP, vol. 50, pp. 94–107. Springer, Heidelberg (2010)

17. Lübke, D.: Unit Testing BPEL Compositions. In: Baresi, L., Nitto, E.D. (eds.) Test and Analysis of Service-oriented Systems, pp. 149–171. Springer (2007) ISBN 978-3-540-72911-2

18. Lenhard, J.: A Pattern-based Analysis of WS-BPEL and Windows Workflow. Bamberger Beiträge zur Wirtschaftsinformatik und Angewandten Informatik, no. 88, Otto-Friedrich Universität Bamberg (March 2011)

19. Lenhard, J., Schönberger, A., Wirtz, G.: Edit Distance-Based Pattern Support Assessment of Orchestration Languages. In: Meersman, R., et al. (eds.) OTM 2011, Part I. LNCS, vol. 7044, pp. 137–154. Springer, Heidelberg (2011)

20. OASIS. Web Services Business Process Execution Language v2.0 (April 2007)

21. OMG. Business Process Model and Notation, v2.0 (January 2011)

22. Papazoglou, M.P., Georgakopoulos, D.: Service-oriented Computing. Communications of the ACM 46(10), 24–28 (2003)

23. Peltz, C.: Web Services Orchestration and Choreography. IEEE Computer 36(10), 46–52 (2003)

24. RosettaNet. MCC Web Services Profile, R11.00.00A (June 2010)

25. Russell, N., ter Hofstede, A.H.M., van der Aalst, W.M.P., Mulyar, N.: Workflow Control-Flow Patterns: A Revised View. Technical report, BPM Group, Queensland University of Technology; Department of Technology Management, Eindhoven University of Technology (2006)

26. Spinellis, D.: Quality Wars: Open Source Versus Proprietary Software. O'Reilly Media, Inc., Making Software (2011) ISBN: 978-0-596-80832-7

27. Stamelos, I., Angelis, L., Okionomou, A., Bleris, G.L.: Code quality analysis in open source software development. Information Systems Journal 12(1), 43–60 (2002)

28. Thom, L.H., Reichert, M., Iochpe, C.: Activity Patterns in Process-aware Information Systems: Basic Concepts and Empirical Evidence. International Journal of Business Process Integration and Management (IJBPIM) 4(2), 93–110 (2009)

29. van der Aalst, W., ter Hofstede, A.: YAWL: yet another workflow language. Information Systems 30(4), 245–275 (2005)

30. van der Aalst, W.M.P., ter Hofstede, A.H.M., Kiepuszewski, B., Barros, A.P.: Workflow Patterns. Distributed and Parallel Databases 14(1), 5–51 (2003)

31. WfMC. XML Process Definition Language, v2.2 (August 2012)

Detection of SOA Patterns

Anthony Demange, Naouel Moha, and Guy Tremblay

Département d'informatique, Université du Québec à Montréal, Canada
anthonydemange@gmail.com,
{moha.naouel,tremblay.guy}@uqam.ca

Abstract. The rapid increase of communications combined with the deployment of large scale information systems lead to the democratization of *Service Oriented Architectures* (SOA). However, systems based on these architectures (called SOA systems) evolve rapidly due to the addition of new functionalities, the modification of execution contexts and the integration of legacy systems. This evolution may hinder the maintenance of these systems, and thus increase the cost of their development. To ease the evolution and maintenance of SOA systems, they should satisfy good design quality criteria, possibly expressed using patterns. By *patterns*, we mean good practices to solve known and common problems when designing software systems. The goal of this study is to detect patterns in SOA systems to assess their design and their Quality of Service (QoS). We propose a three steps approach called SODOP (Service Oriented Detection Of Patterns), which is based on our previous work for the detection of antipatterns. As a first step, we define five SOA patterns extracted from the literature. We specify these patterns using "rule cards", which are sets of rules that combine various metrics, static or dynamic, using a formal grammar. The second step consists in generating automatically detection algorithms from rule cards. The last step consists in applying concretely these algorithms to detect patterns on SOA systems at runtime. We validate SODOP on two SOA systems: *Home-Automation* and *FraSCAti* that contain respectively 13 and 91 services. This validation demonstrates that our proposed approach is precise and efficient.

Keywords: Service Oriented Architecture, Patterns, Specification and Detection, Software Quality, Quality of Service (QoS), Design.

1 Introduction

Service Oriented Architecture (SOA) is an architectural style increasingly adopted because it offers system architects a high level solution to software design. SOA systems are based upon loosely coupled, autonomous and reusable coarse-grained components called services [22]. Each service provides a domain specific behavior, and services can be composed as composite to fulfill high level business processes requirements. Various technologies have emerged to implement this style, among them, Web Services [14] and SCA [6]. Google, Amazon, Microsoft are well-known businesses that have successfully based their information

S. Basu et al. (Eds.): ICSOC 2013, LNCS 8274, pp. 114–130, 2013.

systems on SOA. Software systems evolve rapidly due to the addition of new functionalities and the integration of legacy systems. Well designed systems tend to reduce maintenance effort and costs in the long term [4,21]. However, designing such systems becomes far more complex with the increasing use of distributed and service-based systems. To ease evolution and maintenance, it is important that systems satisfy good design and Quality of Service (QoS) criteria. These concerns were first assessed in the object-oriented (OO) world. For instance, the "Gang of Four" (GoF) [12] proposed several good practices, known as design patterns, to solve common and recurring design problems. In the SOA context, various catalogs [7,9,22] have been published in the last few years to provide similar good patterns to follow. For example, a *Facade*, also referred by the same name in the catalog of OO patterns, correspond to a service that hides complex implementation details. The implementation is decoupled from the service consumer and therefore can evolve independently. A *Router* is another typical SOA pattern [19], which provides an additional layer to service consumers to preclude strong coupling with business services. However, due to their own structural and behavioral properties, SOA and OO patterns remain different.

Various interesting approaches have been proposed to assess software systems quality and efficiency. Many of them focus on automatic design pattern detection in OO systems [3,8,13,15,17]. These are either based on static or dynamic analysis, even sometimes on trace execution mining for architectural style recovery. Thus, they provide a consistent and mature way to assess the quality of OO systems.

Unfortunately, to our knowledge, no such approach exists in the SOA context; that's why we are exploring the SOA patterns detection area. The only closely related work corresponds to our previous work for the detection of SOA antipatterns, which are bad practices by opposition to SOA patterns, which are good practices [20]. A domain specific language provided by the Service Oriented Framework for Analysis (SOFA: http://sofa.uqam.ca) allows system analysts to describe bad design practices with a high level expressive vocabulary. Each antipattern, derived from the literature, is specified with rule cards, which are sets of rules that use specific metrics [20]. These can either be static, and thus provide information about structural properties like cohesion or coupling, or dynamic, and provide information about response time or number of service invocation. An automatic generation process converts rule cards into detection algorithms, that can then be applied on the SOA systems under analysis.

In this paper, we extend the existing SOFA framework to consider the detection of SOA patterns at runtime. Until now, no automatic approach for the detection of such patterns has been proposed, making the approach proposed in this paper original. The proposed approach is called SODOP (Service Oriented Detection Of Patterns) and consists in the following three contributions. (1) A thorough domain analysis from different catalogs led us to compile and categorize the best practices in SOA systems and their underlying technologies. (2) This analysis resulted in the specification of five significant SOA patterns using rule cards. We selected these five SOA patterns because they represent technology-agnostic, common and recurrent good quality practices in the design and QoS of SOA systems. (3) Specifying the appropriate rule cards required us to extend SOFA's existing set of metrics with eight new metrics. We validated the proposed approach with two SOA systems: *Home-Automation*, a system that provides services for domotic tasks, and *FraSCAti*, an implementation of the *Service Component Architecture* (SCA) standard [24]. We show that our SODOP approach allows the specification and detection of SOA patterns with high precision values. More detailed information on our approach and the analyzed systems can be found through the SOFA website (`http://sofa.uqam.ca/sodop`).

Overall, the paper is organized as follows. Section 2 describes related work in SOA patterns and their automatic detection. Section 3 presents the proposed approach for the specification and detection of SOA patterns based on metrics. Section 4 describes experiments and results on the two SOA systems mentioned above. Finally, Section 5 concludes and presents future work.

2   Related Work

Automatic detection of design patterns has already been highly investigated for assessing the quality of OO systems. Antoniol *et al.* proposed one of the first approach for design pattern recovery in OO programs [3]. The first step of this approach consists in mapping source code in an intermediate representation with an abstract object language. In the second step, several static metrics, like the number of attributes, methods or associations, are then computed on this abstract language. The final pattern recognition process is executed by examining relations between classes and matching them with GoF design patterns. However, as in many other work, behavioral patterns were omitted because of the focus on static analyses.

Tsantalis *et al.* proposed an interesting way to recover behavioral patterns through a data-mining process based on execution traces [25]. The process consists in extracting graphs or matrices for each of the following OO concepts: association, generalization, abstract classes and abstract method invocations. Based on design patterns definition from the literature, they identify the best matching results from each matrix and identify candidate patterns. Ka-Yee Ng *et al.* gave an alternative solution based on a dynamic pattern recovery process [18]. They begin with the specification of scenario diagrams for each design pattern to consider. Based on execution traces, the system under analysis is then reverse-engineered based also on a scenario diagram. This program scenario diagram is finally assigned to the initial design pattern scenario diagram with an explanation-based constraint programming to identify potential matches. Wendehals *et al.* combined static and dynamic approaches to recover both structural and behavioral patterns. Their dynamic approach is based on transforming execution calls between objects to finite automata. A matching process between these automata and design patterns templates returns the best patterns candidates.

The majority of the community tends to say SOA was first introduced in 1996 by Schulte and Natiz in their Gartner technical report [23]. SOA patterns catalogs only appeared starting around 2009 [7,9,22]. Galster *et al.* identified most of the patterns specified in Erl's *SOA Patterns* [9] and showed the positive impacts of patterns on quality attributes [11]. Their approach, manual, consists in specifying quality attributes on each pattern and then identifying them manually in real service-based systems.

Despite the emerging interest in SOA, the literature is not really consistent with respect to SOA pattern definition and specification. Indeed, the available catalogs use different classification, either based on their nature, scope or objectives. After an in depth review, we identified the available patterns and the three main categories in which they fall. The first category describes structural patterns which focus on how services are designed to assess common concerns like autonomy, reuse, or efficiency. The second category represents integration and exchange patterns, and describes how service composition and orchestration are used to answer high level business application needs. This category includes how services communicate with each other using different messaging capabilities like synchronous or asynchronous exchanges. The last category can be seen as specific QoS objective patterns such as scalability, performance or security requirements.

To our knowledge, the only related work investigating design and quality of service-based systems is from Yousefi *et al.* [27]. Their recent work proposed to recover specific features in SOA systems by mining execution traces. By executing specific scenarios provided by a manager, they collect the distributed execution traces. A bottom-up data mining algorithm analyzes the traces to build closed frequent item-sets graphs. A filtering and feature recovering process finally eliminates noises and omnipresent calls. This process allows the extraction of specific scenario features based on call frequency and utilization. The obtained results tend to help maintainers by focusing on the most important service providers to improve the QoS of SOA systems and ease their evolution.

Finally, Hohpe, in his report *SOA Patterns: New Insights or Recycled Knowledge?* [16], explained that SOA is more than "a new fancy technology." It is really a new programming model that requires specific approaches and therefore interests in SOA patterns. Thus, OO software systems cannot be directly compared to SOA systems because they both have their own structural and behavioral properties. Therefore, OO design patterns recovery cannot be directly applied to SOA pattern detection. This is why our approach aims at providing a specific technique to recover SOA patterns in an automated manner.

3   Our Approach SODOP

We propose the SODOP approach (*Service Oriented Detection Of Patterns*) that aims at the specification and automatic detection of SOA patterns. SODOP is an extension of a previous approach proposed by Moha *et al.* [20] called SODA (Service Oriented Detection for Antipatterns). In the following, for the sake of clarity, we first describe the SCA standard key concepts and the SODA approach. Then, we present the SODOP approach and the specification of five SOA patterns as defined with SODOP.

3.1   About the Service Component Architecture

Before introducing the SODA and SODOP approaches, it must be stressed that
the following experiments were made with the Service Component Architecture
(SCA) standard. A description of the SCA standard and its vocabulary is thus
useful to better understand how specific metrics are computed. A software application built with SCA contains one or many components as shown in Figure 1.
A component is a logical building block implementing a specific business logic,
which is why we consider a component as a high level SOA service in this paper.
Each component can expose services, which declare methods potentially called
by clients, and references to other services the component depends on. The link
between two components is called a wire. A component could potentially nest
other components and become a composite. This composite can expose nested
components behaviors by promoting their services or references.

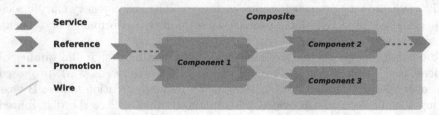

Fig. 1. Key Concepts of the SCA Standard

3.2   Description of the Earlier SODA Approach

SODA proposes a three steps approach for the detection of SOA *antipatterns*—
an antipattern corresponds to bad design practices, by opposition to patterns.
The first step consists in specifying SOA antipatterns using a Domain Specific
Language (DSL) that defines "rule cards", which are set of rules matching specific QoS and structural properties. Figure 3 shows this DSL's grammar, in
Backus-Naur Form. A rule describes a metric, a relationship, or a combination
of other rules (line 3) using set operators (line 6). A metric can either be static
(line 11) or dynamic (line 12)—computed at runtime. Examples of static metrics
include number of methods declared (NMD) or number of outgoing references
(NOR). Examples of dynamic metrics include response time (RT) or number
of incoming calls (NIC). A metric can optionally be defined as an arithmetic
combination of other metrics (lines 8 and 9). Each metric can be compared to
one ordinal values (line 7)—a five value Likert scale from very low to very high
(line 12)—or compared to a numeric value (line 8) using common arithmetic
comparators (line 13). A metric value is calculated for each service in the set
to populate one box-plot per metric. Figure 2 describes how ordinal values are
mapped to box-plot intervals.

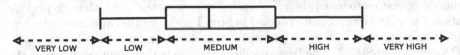

Fig. 2. Mapping between ordinal values and box-plot intervals

The second step consists in generating automatically the detection algorithms corresponding to the rule cards specified. These algorithms were generated with the EMF [2] meta-model combined with the Acceleo [1] code generation tool. The third and final step consists in applying these algorithms on real SOA systems to detect candidate services that match antipattern rule cards. In our case, SCA joint points were woven on each service so that every call trigger an event. Each event is caught so that the computation of metrics is done on the called service.

1	*rule_card*	::= RULE_CARD: *rule_card_name* { (*rule*)⁺ };
2	*rule*	::= RULE: *rule_name* { *content_rule* };
3	*content_rule*	::= *metric* | *set_operator rule_type* (*rule_type*)⁺
4		| RULE_CARD: *rule_card_name*
5	*rule_type*	::= *rule_name* | *rule_card_name*
6	*set_operator*	::= INTER | UNION | DIFF | INCL | NEG
7	*metric*	::= *metric_value comparator* (*metric_value* | *ordi_value* | *num_value*)
8	*metric_value*	::= *id_metric* (*num_operator id_metric*)?
9	*num_operator*	::= + | - | * | /
10	*id_metric*	::= ANAM | ANIM | ANP | ANPT | COH | NID | NIR | NMD | NOR | NSC | TNP
11		| A | DR | ET | NDC | NIC | NOC | NTMI | POPC | PSC | SR | RT
12	*ordi_value*	::= VERY_LOW | LOW | MEDIUM | HIGH | VERY_HIGH
13	*comparator*	::= < | ≤ | = | ≥ | >
14	*rule_cardName*, *ruleName* ∈ string	
15	*num_value* ∈ double	

Fig. 3. BNF Grammar for Rule Cards

3.3   Description of the SODOP Approach

The SODA approach is flexible and relatively easy to extend for SOA *patterns* instead of antipatterns. Indeed, the DSL and the underlying SOFA framework allow the integration of new metrics required for the specification of patterns. The approach proposed in this paper, called SODOP, introduces five new patterns, that we identified from the SOA literature. These patterns have been specified with rule cards by combining existing metrics along with eight newly defined ones—those are underlined in Figure 3 and are briefly described below. SODOP's three steps are described in Figure 4, and are similar to SODA's ones. The DSL grammar has been extended to allow more flexibility in the rule card specification. We add the possibility of combining two existing metrics with numeric operators to avoid the proliferation of new metrics and, thus, to provide ratios. The pattern rule cards specified in Step 1 are generated automatically into detection algorithms in Step 2, followed by the concrete detection of patterns on SOA systems in Step 3. The first specification step is thus manual, whereas the second and third are automated.

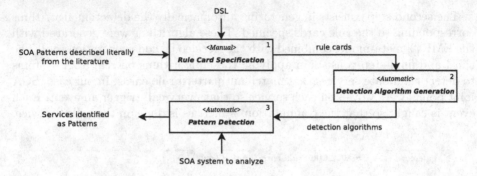

Fig. 4. The Three Steps of the SODOP Approach

The following eight new metrics were defined. The *Execution Time (ET)* represents the time spent by a service to perform its tasks; it differs from the response time as it excludes the execution time of nested services. The *Number of Different Clients (NDC)* is the number of different consumers, thus multiple incoming calls from the same consumer are counted only once. By contrast, the *Number of Incoming Calls (NIC)* and *Number of Outgoing Calls (NOC)* refer to dynamic calls, thus possibly counting several times the same service. The *Delegation Ratio (DR)* represents the ratio of incoming calls that are relayed by a service. The *Service Reuse (SR)* is a dynamic metric that computes to what extent a service is reused; it is the ratio between the incoming calls (NIC) and the total number of calls in the system. The *Proportion of Outgoing Path Change (POPC)* computes the proportion of outgoing paths that change for a given incoming call. In other words, this proportion is zero if the incoming call and its underlying outgoing calls are always the same. Finally, the *Proportion of Signature Change (PSC)* computes the proportion of method signature change for a pair of incoming/outgoing calls. In other words, this metric represents the dissimilarity level between an incoming and outgoing method call; it is computed with the Jaro-Winkler similarity distance between method names [26].

3.4   Basic Service Pattern

When dealing with SOA pattern specification and detection, we want to specify the best fundamental characteristics every system designer or architect should take into account. Several principles, some of which are described in *SOA Patterns* [9], have to be considered for service design. Components reusability (SR) as well as high cohesion (COH) are common requirements in the design of general systems such as OO systems [5]. The dynamic nature of SOA systems introduces new non-functional requirements such as high availability (A) or low response time (RT). These metrics are combined in the rule card shown in Figure 9(a) for the specification of this *Basic Service* pattern.

3.5   Facade Pattern

A *Facade*, as illustrated in Figure 5, is used in SOA systems to get a higher abstraction level between the provider and the consumer layers. Fowler and Erl describe the pattern respectively as *Remote Facade* [10], *Decoupled Contract* or *Service Decomposition* [9] and give as example using it to wrap legacy systems. This pattern is similar to the *Facade* in OO systems because it hides implementation details [12] such as nested compositions and calls. It also provides loosely coupled relationships with consumer services and let the implementation evolve independently, without breaking the client contract. Using this pattern, it is possible to decompose SOA systems following the principle of *separation of concerns*. It will thus be easier to reuse the different layers in other systems. A *Facade* can be responsible for orchestration, and can describe how composition of subsequent services can fulfill the client requirements. Given that the *Facade* acts as a front layer to several clients, we characterize its response time (RT) as high. Such a pattern is defined to hide implementation details from many services. Thus, its incoming outgoing calling ratio (NIC/NOC) is low because for one incoming call, the components tends to execute multiple outgoing calls. Finally, we assume that such a service has a high delegation ratio (DR) because it does not provide business logic directly but, instead, delegates to other services. Figure 9(b) shows the rule card specification for the *Facade* pattern.

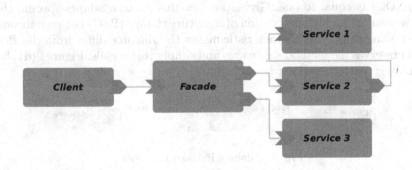

Fig. 5. Facade Pattern Example

3.6   Proxy Pattern

The *Proxy* pattern, represented in Figure 6, is another well-known design pattern from OO systems, that adds an additional indirection level between the client and the invoked service. Its objective differs from a *Facade* because it can, for example, add new non-functional behaviors, which can cover security concerns

Fig. 6. Proxy Pattern Example

such as confidentiality, integrity or logging execution calls for accountability goals. Different kinds of *Proxy* patterns exist, such as *Service Interceptor* [7] or *Service Perimeter Guard* [9], and they could all be specified with several distinct rule cards. Instead, we choose to specify a generic version of this pattern with the following characteristics. The proportion between incoming and outgoing calls (NIC/NOC) has to be equal to one because it acts only as a relay. Moreover, this relay property implies that incoming and outgoing method signatures have to be the same. The fact that the *Proxy* pattern generally adds non-functional requirements to SOA systems also means that it can be involved in several scenarios. Thus, it has a high service reuse (SR) compared to other services. Figure 9(c) shows its underlying rule card.

3.7   Adapter Pattern

The *Adapter* pattern, shown in Figure 7, is also close to the *Adapter* as found in OO systems. Its goal is to adapt the calls between the destination service and the clients. The integration of legacy systems into a SOA system often requires adaptations to perform type transformations and preserve the functionality of the legacy systems. Daigneau gives the example of a *Datasource Adapter* [7] pattern as a solution that provides data access to specific different platforms. In general, the number of incoming and outgoing calls are identical, thus the ratio (NIC/NOC) is equal to one. Given the fact this pattern adapts specific client calls, we can infer a high proportion of signature change (PSC) between incoming and outgoing calls. This characteristic makes the *Adapter* differ from the *Proxy*, which preserves the method signatures and simply relays calls. Figure 9(d) shows the *Adapter* pattern rule card.

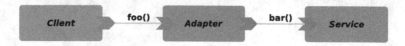

Fig. 7. Adapter Pattern Example

3.8   Router Pattern

The *Router* pattern, as illustrated in Figure 8, is similar to a network router that forwards packets according to different paths. A SOA *Router* distributes incoming calls to various destinations based on different criteria, which can be either the client identity or the call parameters. Some smart routers either detect paths on dynamic metrics such as availability or previous calls history and forward calls to the best matching service. The main criterion to consider is a

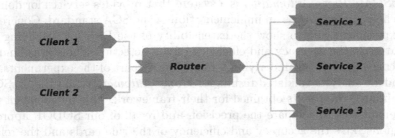

Fig. 8. Router Pattern Example

change of outgoing paths for a specific incoming call, so a high proportion in path changes (POPC) can be significant. It may be interesting to see if some specific clients use specific paths and then make the correlation with incoming parameters. Figure 9(e) shows the *Router* pattern rule card.

```
1 RULE_CARD: Basic Service {
2   RULE: Basic Service {INTER HighSR
3   HighCOH HighA LowRT};
4   RULE: HighSR {SR ≥ HIGH};
5   RULE: HighCOH {COH ≥ HIGH};
6   RULE: HighA {A ≥ HIGH};
7   RULE: LowRT {RT ≤ LOW};
8 };
```
(a) Basic Service

```
1 RULE_CARD: Facade {
2   RULE: Facade {INTER HighDR
3   LowIOCR HighRT};
4   RULE: HighDR {DR ≥ HIGH};
5   RULE: LowIOCR {NIC/NOC ≤ LOW};
6   RULE: HighRT {RT ≥ HIGH};
7 };
```
(b) Facade

```
1 RULE_CARD: Proxy {
2   RULE: Proxy {INTER EqualIOCR
3   HighSR LowPSC};
4   RULE: EqualIOCR {NIC/NOC = 1.0};
5   RULE: HighSR {SR ≥ HIGH};
6   RULE: LowPSC {PSC ≤ LOW};
7 };
```
(c) Proxy

```
1 RULE_CARD: Adapter {
2   RULE: Adapter {INTER EqualIOCR
3   HighPSC};
4   RULE: EqualIOCR {NIC/NOC = 1.0};
5   RULE: HighPSC {PSC ≥ HIGH};
6 };
```
(d) Adapter

```
1 RULE_CARD: Router {
2   RULE: Router {HighPOPC};
3   RULE: HighOPC {POPC ≥ HIGH};
4 };
```
(e) Router

Fig. 9. Rule Cards for SOA Patterns

4   Experiments

To show the usefulness of the SODOP approach, we performed some experiments that consisted in specifying the five SOA patterns presented in the previous section and detecting them automatically on two SCA systems, *Home-Automation* and *FraSCAti*. *Home-Automation* is a system that provides services for domotic tasks, whereas *FraSCAti* is an implementation of the SCA standard. Concretely, these experiments aim to show the extensibility of the DSL for specifying new SOA patterns, the accuracy and efficiency of the detection algorithms, and the overall correctness of the underlying framework. As part of the experiments, two independent analysts validated results for *Home-Automation* and the FraSCAti team validated the results obtained for their framework. This independent validation enables us to compare the precision and recall of our SODOP approach and demonstrates the accuracy and efficiency of the rule cards and the related detection algorithms.

4.1   Assumptions

The experiments aim at validating the following three assumptions:

A1. Extensibility: *The proposed extended DSL is flexible enough to define SOA patterns.* Through this assumption, we show that although the DSL and the SOFA framework were initially dedicated to the specification and detection of SOA antipatterns, they are sufficiently extensible to handle SOA patterns thorough the use of metrics.

A2. Accuracy: *The services identified as matching our SOA patterns must attain at least 80% of precision and 100% of recall.* We want to guarantee the accuracy and the efficiency of the rule cards and the related detection algorithms by identifying all patterns present in the analyzed systems while still avoiding too many false positives with a high precision value.

A3. Performance: *The time needed by the detection algorithms must not impact the performance of the analyzed system.* We want to keep the detection time required by the SODOP approach and the underlying SOFA framework very low to avoid efficiency issues in the analyzed system.

4.2   Analyzed Systems

The experiments have been performed on two different SCA systems that are in conformance with the SOA principles: *Home-Automation*, composed of 13 services and executed with 7 different scenarios, and *FraSCAti*, an open-source implementation of the SCA standard. *FraSCAti* fully uses SCA service composition as it includes 13 composite components, themselves encapsulating components, for a total of 91 components. The experiment with this system involves the bootstrap and launch of six SCA applications developed within *FraSCAti* to simulate the scenarios.

4.3   Process

The process used for these experiments follows the three steps of the SODOP approach presented in Section 3. We first specified the rule cards representing the five SOA patterns described previously. Then, we generated automatically the detection algorithms in the second step. Finally, we applied them respectively on *Home-Automation* and *FraSCAti* to detect the SOA patterns specified. We validated the results by computing the precision—the proportion of true patterns in the detected patterns— and the recall—the proportion of detected patterns in all existing patterns. These validations were made through a manual and static analysis of each service in the systems under analysis. The computations were performed by two external software engineers to ensure the results were not biased. An additional feedback was given by the *FraSCAti* core team itself to strengthen the results.

4.4   Results

In the following, we first discuss the results obtained on the two SCA systems. Tables 1 and 2 respectively present the detection results on each system. For each SOA pattern listed in column one, column two describes the services detected as patterns. Columns three, four and five give respectively the value of metrics involved in the rule card of the pattern, the time required for applying the detection algorithms and the system execution time. The two last columns provide the precision and the recall values. The last row gives average values (detection time, execution time, precision and recall).

Details of the Results on *Home-Automation*
Four of the five specified SOA patterns were detected on *Home-Automation*— the *Adapter* pattern was not detected. The *patientDAO*, *communication* and *knxMock* components are detected as *Basic Service* pattern with a maximal cohesion (COH $\geq$ 0.34), high reuse values (SR $>$ 0.10) and very low response time (RT $<$ 0.25ms). According to the definition of the *Basic Service* pattern, these three components thus represent the services in the system that are the most well designed, as they appear to satisfy common software design principles. The *mediator* component is considered both a *Facade* and a *Router*. The *Facade* represents a service acting as a front layer to clients to hide a complex subsystem. Indeed, the delegation metric (DR = 1) of the *mediator* component always acts as a relay and tends to have six times more outgoing calls for each incoming one (NIC/NOC = 0.17), thus this traduces its high response time (RT = 2.8ms). The *mediator* has also been detected as a *Router* because of its high dynamic metric (POPC = 0.5). This value means that the *mediator* distributes to different outgoing paths half of its incoming calls. The *patientDAO* also matches the *Proxy* pattern because of its high reuse (SR = 0.24 compared to the median value of 0.06) and systematic incoming calls relay (NIC = NOC) with the same method signatures (PSC = 0). We can also observe that the time required for the detection of each pattern is on average 25ms, whereas the average execution time on a given set of scenarios is 6.73s. These values demonstrate the low impact of the pattern detection on the system execution, and thus on the results. Finally, the validation performed by the two experts lead to a 93.3% precision and 100% recall, which indicates that all existing patterns in *Home-Automation* have been detected, with high precision.

Table 1. SOA Pattern Detection Results on the Home-Automation System

PatternName	DetectedServices	Metrics	DetectTime	ExecTime	Precision	Recall
Basic Service	*patientDAO* *communication* *knxMock*	COH RT SR 0.49 0.25ms 0.24 0.34 0.24ms 0.10 0.38 0.16ms 0.11	80ms	6.82s	[3/2] 66.6%	[2/2] 100%
Facade	*mediator*	NIC/NOC DR RT 0.17 1.0 2.8ms	10ms	6.66s	[1/1] 100%	[1/1] 100%
Proxy	*patientDAO*	NIC/NOC SR PSC 1.0 0.24 0.0	13ms	6.74s	[1/1] 100%	[1/1] 100%
Adapter	n/a	n/a	10ms	6.76s	[0/0] 100%	[0/0] 100%
Router	*mediator*	POPC 0.5	11ms	6.67s	[1/1] 100%	[1/1] 100%
Average			25ms	6.73s	93.3%	100%

Details of the Results on *FraSCAti*

As shown in Table 2, the detection of patterns on *FraSCAti* returns more results than *Home-Automation*, i.e. more components are detected as patterns. This is partly explained by the size of *FraSCAti*, which is almost ten times larger than *Home-Automation*. Five components have been detected as matching the *Basic Service* pattern, because of their very high reusability (SR > 0.1 compared to the median value of 0.003), high cohesion (COH > 0.48) and mostly very low response time (RT < 0.7ms). The core framework components, *FraSCAti*, *assembly-factory* and *composite-parser*, are detected as *Facade* as they are main entry points of the framework that relay every incoming calls (DR = 1). Their incoming outgoing call ratio (NIC/NOC = 0.46, 0.25 and 0.63) remains low compared to the median value of 1. They act as a *Facade* because they have among the highest response times (respectively 571ms, 181ms and 10ms) mainly due to their massive under-lying calls. The *Proxy* pattern is involved in the three following components: *sca-interface*, *sca-implementation* and *component-factory*. The components have been identified as *Proxy* because they represent highly reused (SR > 0.5) relay services (NIC/NOC = 1) and they include the same method calls (PSC = 0). The only missing SOA pattern in *Home-Automation* and discovered in *FraSCAti* is the *Adapter*, seen in the *BindingFactory* component. It acts as an *Adapter* because it relays all its incoming calls (NIC/NOC = 1) and adapts the method calls to the underlying components (PSC = 1, which indicates a high proportion of signature change). Unlike in *Home-Automation*, no *Router* pattern has been detected. The average detection time required for our experiments is 97ms on average for a total time average of 10.9s. As for *Home-Automation*, the detection represents only 1% of the total system execution, and thus does not affect its performance, even with a relatively larger system. We reported those results to the *FraSCAti* core team and they confirmed all components detected as pat-terns. This leads to a precision of 100% for this detection. However, the recall

Table 2. SOA Pattern Detection Results on the FraSCAti System

PatternName	DetectedServices	Metrics			DetectTime	ExecTime	Precision	Recall
Basic Service	sca-interface sca-interface-java sca-impl. sca-impl.-java sca-comp.-service	COH 0.48 0.50 0.48 0.50 0.48	RT 0.09ms 0.02ms 0.67ms 0.59ms 0.25ms	SR 0.11 0.11 0.05 0.04 0.48	241ms	11.34s	[5/5] 100%	n/a
Facade	FraSCAti assembly-factory composite-parser	NIC/NOC 0.46 0.25 0.63	DR 1.0 1.0 1.0	RT 571ms 181ms 10ms	57ms	10.62s	[3/3] 100%	[3/16] 18.7%
Proxy	sca-interface sca-impl. component-factory	NIC/NOC 1.0 1.0 1.0	SR 0.11 0.05 0.11	PSC 0.0 0.0 0.0	65ms	10.72s	[3/3] 100%	[3/14] 21.4%
Adapter	BindingFactory	NIC/NOC 1.0	PSC 1.0		57ms	10.96s	[1/1] 100%	[1/14] 7.1%
Router	n/a	n/a			67ms	10.88s	[0/0] 100%	[0/7] 0.0%
Average					97ms	10.90s	100%	11.8%

value of 11.8% is low. Our detection algorithms thus failed at detecting all the existing components involved as patterns in the *FraSCAti* system.

4.5 Discussion

We now discuss the three assumptions mentioned earlier to show the usefulness of the SODOP approach.

A1. Extensibility: *The proposed extended DSL is flexible enough to define SOA patterns.* This first assumption is positively supported because we show through the experiments that the DSL allows designers to define different kinds of rule cards and add new metrics that can be either static or dynamic. Indeed, the specification of SOA patterns required the addition of eight dynamic metrics and the reuse of the 14 existing ones. In addition to the new metrics, the DSL has been extended with numeric operators (+,-,*,/) to allow the combination of metrics and, thus, avoid introducing new metric specifications, keeping the language as simple and flexible as possible.

A2. Accuracy: *The services identified as matching our SOA patterns must attain at least 80% of precision and 100% of recall.* The detection results demonstrate the high precision of the SODOP approach, respectively 93.3% and 100% for *Home-Automation* and *FraSCAti*. The recall for *Home-Automation* is 100% but the one for *FraSCAti* is about 12%. This result is related to the highly dynamic detection of patterns, which is based on a set of scenarios that do not cover all the system execution paths. In these experiments with *FraSCAti*, unlike with *Home-Automation*, it is quite difficult to reach 100% coverage because of the system size.

A3. Performance: *The time needed by the detection algorithms must not impact the performance of the analyzed system.* As shown in Tables 1 and 2, no matter which

SOA patterns or how many metrics are computed, the detection time remains low compared to the execution time and thus does not impact the system under analysis. As a first analysis, we find the only affecting property is the number of services involved in the SOA system under analysis, because all the metrics are computed against each of them. *FraSCAti* has around eight times more components than *Home-Automation*, which explains the proportional time needed to run the metrics computation (around 1% of the execution time). Because the experiments are run locally, the execution time is also highly dependent on the computer computational power. In these experiments, an Intel E5345 CPU with 4GB of RAM was used.

4.6   Threats to Validity

Several threats can be considered as counter-measures to the validity of our study. First, the external reliability, i.e., the repeatability of our experiments, is guaranteed under the condition that the same computational facilities are used. This is still guaranteed by the automatic detection algorithms generation, which will be identical for the same input rule card. We provide the details of our results as well as the systems analyzed in the SOFA website (http://sofa.uqam.ca/sodop). The main possible external validity threat may come from the fact we only focus on two SCA systems. Although they are representative of small as well as big systems, SOA technologies often have specific characteristics, which is why we plan to extend our study in the future. We tried to minimize the potential construct validity of our approach by providing the most representative execution scenarios for each system under analysis. However for FraSCAti, the scenarios were not exhaustive as highlighted by the recall of 11.8%. Because of the size of the system, we will consider it in our next future experiments. The other construct validity potentially questionable may come from the rule cards subjectivity. Indeed, this depend heavily on the designer specifying them, but we tried as much as possible to remain close and faithful to the SOA patterns described in the literature. Moreover, although we only defined five SOA patterns in the form of rule cards, they are representative according to the literature. Indeed, even if SOA catalogs mainly define patterns for specific technologies, we tried to specify meaningful technology-agnostic SOA patterns.

5   Conclusion and Future Work

SOA patterns are proven good practices to solve known and common problems when designing software systems. Indeed, our three steps SODOP approach consists in the specification and detection of SOA patterns to assess the design and QoS of SOA systems. The first step consists in specifying rule cards—set of rules, combining static and dynamic metrics—for each pattern. Five patterns were described in our study, involving 22 different static and dynamic metrics, including eight newly defined dynamic metrics. The second step consists in generating automatically detection algorithms from rule cards, and applying them on SOA systems in the third step. We validated our approach using two SCA systems, *Home-Automation*—a system that provides 13 services for domotic tasks—and

FraSCAti—a SCA standard implementation that provides 91 components. The experiments showed that we can obtain high precision and recall values under the condition that execution scenarios are exhaustive.

Various lines of future work are currently being explored by our research group. First, we will expand the SODOP approach by specifying more SOA patterns and applying them on other SOA systems. We also plan to extend our approach to other SOA technologies, such as Web Services and REST, as they share many common properties. Our approach remain however applicable to these other technologies to the condition we wrap them in specific SCA containers.

Acknowledgments. The authors would like to thank the FraSCAti core team, and in particular Philippe Merle, for the validation of the results on FraSCAti and their valuable discussions on these results. This work was partially supported by *Research Discovery* grants from NSERC (Canada).

References

1. Acceleo code generator tool, http://www.acceleo.org/
2. Eclipse modeling framework project, http://www.eclipse.org/modeling/emf/
3. Antoniol, G., Fiutem, R., Cristoforetti, L.: Design Pattern Recovery in Object-Oriented Software. In: 14th IEEE Intl. Conf. on Prog. Comprehension, pp. 153–160 (June 1998)
4. Banker, R.D., Datar, S.M., Kemerer, C.F., Zweig, D.: Software complexity and maintenance costs. Comm. of the ACM 36(11), 81–94 (1993)
5. Basili, V., Briand, L., Melo, W.: A validation of object-oriented design metrics as quality indicators. IEEE Transactions on Software Engineering 22(10), 751–761 (1996)
6. Chappell, D.: Introducing SCA (2007),
   http://www.davidchappell.com/articles/introducing_sca.pdf
7. Daigneau, R.: Service Design Patterns. Addison-Wesley (2011)
8. De Lucia, A., Deufemia, V., Gravino, C., Risi, M.: Improving Behavioral Design Pattern Detection through Model Checking. In: 14th European Conf. on Soft. Maintenance and Reengineering, pp. 176–185. IEEE Comp. Soc. (March 2010)
9. Erl, T.: SOA Design Patterns. Prentice Hall PTR (2009)
10. Fowler, M.: Patterns of Enterprise Application Architecture. Addison-Wesley Professional (2002)
11. Galster, M., Avgeriou, P.: Qualitative Analysis of the Impact of SOA Patterns on Quality Attributes. In: 12th Intl. Conf. on Quality Software, pp. 167–170. IEEE (August 2012)
12. Gamma, E., Helm, R., Johnson, R., Vlissides, J.: Design Patterns - Elements of Reusable Object-Oriented Software. Addison-Wesley (1994)
13. Guéhéneuc, Y.G., Antoniol, G.: DeMIMA: A Multilayered Approach for Design Pattern Identification. IEEE Trans. on Soft. Eng. 34(5), 667–684 (2008)
14. Hansen, M.D.: SOA Using Java Web Services. Prentice Hall (2007)
15. Heuzeroth, D., Holl, T., Hogstrom, G., Löwe, W.: Automatic design pattern detection. In: Intl. Symp. on Micromechatronics and Human Science, pp. 94–103. IEEE Comp. Soc. (2003)

16. Hohpe, G., Easy, C.: SOA Patterns New Insights or Recycled Knowledge. Tech. rep. (2007)
17. Hu, L., Sartipi, K.: Dynamic Analysis and Design Pattern Detection in Java Programs. In: 20th Intl. Conf. on Soft. Eng. and Data Eng., pp. 842–846 (2008)
18. Ka-Yee Ng, J., Guéhéneuc, Y.G., Antoniol, G.: Identification of Behavioral and Creational Design Patterns through Dynamic Analysis. In: 3rd Intl. Work. on Progr. Comprehension through Dynamic Analysis, pp. 34–42. John Wiley (2007)
19. Milanovic, N.: Service Engineering Design Patterns. In: Second IEEE Intl. Symp. on Service-Oriented System Eng., pp. 19–26 (October 2006)
20. Moha, N., Palma, F., Nayrolles, M., Conseil, B.J., Guéhéneuc, Y.-G., Baudry, B., Jézéquel, J.-M.: Specification and Detection of SOA Antipatterns. In: Liu, C., Ludwig, H., Toumani, F., Yu, Q. (eds.) ICSOC 2012. LNCS, vol. 7636, pp. 1–16. Springer, Heidelberg (2012)
21. Oman, P., Hagemeister, J.: Metrics for assessing a software system's maintainability. In: Proc. Conf. on Soft. Maint., pp. 337–344. IEEE Comp. Soc. Press (1992)
22. Rotem-Gal-Oz, A.: SOA Patterns. Manning Publications (2012)
23. Schulte, R.W., Natis, Y.V.: Service Oriented Architectures, Part 1. Tech. rep., Gartner (1996)
24. Seinturier, L., Merle, P., Fournier, D., Dolet, N., Schiavoni, V., Stefani, J.B.: Reconfigurable SCA Applications with the FraSCAti Platform. In: 2009 IEEE Intl. Conf. on Services Computing, pp. 268–275. IEEE Computer Society (September 2009)
25. Tsantalis, N., Chatzigeorgiou, A., Stephanides, G., Halkidis, S.: Design Pattern Detection Using Similarity Scoring. IEEE Trans. on Soft. Eng. 32(11), 896–909 (2006)
26. Winkler, W.E.: String Comparator Metrics and Enhanced Decision Rules in the Fellegi-Sunter Model of Record Linkage (November 1989)
27. Yousefi, A., Sartipi, K.: Identifying distributed features in SOA by mining dynamic call trees. In: 27th IEEE Intl. Conf. on Soft. Maint., pp. 73–82. IEEE (September 2011)

Optimal Strategy for Proactive Service Delivery Management Using Inter-KPI Influence Relationships

Gargi B. Dasgupta, Yedendra Shrinivasan, Tapan K. Nayak, and Jayan Nallacherry

IBM Research, Bangalore, India

Abstract. Service interactions now account for major source of revenue and employment in many modern economies, and yet service operations management remains extremely complex. To lower risks, every Service Delivery (SD) environment needs to define its own key performance indicators (KPIs) to evaluate the present state of operations and its business outcomes. Due to the over-use of performance measurement systems, a large number of KPIs have been defined, but their influence on each other is unknown. It is thus important to adopt data-driven approaches to demystify the service delivery KPIs inter-relationships and establish the critical ones that have a stronger influence on the business outcomes. Given a set of operational KPIs and SD outcomes, we focus on the problem of (a) extracting inter-relationships and impact delays among KPIs and outcomes, and building a regression-based KPI influence model to estimate the SD outcomes as functions of KPIs. (b) Based on the model we propose a schedule of action plans to transform the current service delivery system state. (c) We also build a visualization tool that enables validation of extracted KPIs influence model, and perform what-if analysis.

1 Introduction

A *Service System (SS)* is an organization composed of (a) the resources that support, and (b) the processes that drive service interactions so that the outcomes meet customer expectations [8]. Service interactions now account for a major source of revenue and employment in many modern economies, and yet service operation management remains extremely complex and unpredictable. Due to the labor intensive processes, their complex inter-dependencies, and the large variation in the tasks and skills required, these human provided Service Delivery Systems (SDS) are often at the risk of missing performance targets.

Conforming with the underlying philosophy of "what gets measured, gets done", every SS has now defined a set of key performance indicators (KPIs) in accordance with standardized process frameworks such as ITIL [1], Lean[13], Six Sigma [2]. These KPIs serve as management aids to evaluate the present state of operations. Consider an incident management process measured by the MTTR (mean time to resolve) as well as incidents resolved within target time. Or, a work assignment process measured

---

[1] http://www.itil-officialsite.com/home/home.aspx
[2] http://asq.org/learn-about-quality/six-sigma/
overview/overview.html

S. Basu et al. (Eds.): ICSOC 2013, LNCS 8274, pp. 131–145, 2013.

by the mean waiting time for an incident and mean utilization of service workers. A special category of KPIs are the service delivery outcomes of customer satisfaction and quality of service. These are measured against the Service Level Objectives (SLO) (e.g., availability, throughput, response time, etc) agreed between the service provider and the customer. Inter-relationships between KPIs and business outcomes are critical for business decisions. Consider an example where the MTTR in a SS is seen to improve, it alone may not indicate an improving system. At the same time if overall customer satisfaction drops, this is likely to indicate that irrespective of the tickets being closed quickly, the real problem still exists in the customer environment. Hence same issues are being re-opened (can be measured by a rework KPI) and satisfaction scores are plummeting.

The increasing KPI population poses a challenge for managers to use manual methods for understanding KPI alignments and implications to outcomes, especially given the large number of performance measurement systems and hundreds of KPIs use in current service delivery. It is hence important to drive data-driven methods that analyzes the critical KPIs and can help move the system to a desired optimal state. However demystifying the impact of operational KPIs is non-trivial due to the following reasons:(1) each KPI relation can have multiple attributes of direction, strength and polarity [1]. Negative polarities imply that improving some KPIs could worsen others. (2) a KPI's impact on an outcome may not be visible instantly, taking effect only after a lag (3) due to the high number of KPIs, their different polarities and lags, the possible paths to affect business outcomes is exponentially large.

Measurement frameworks for IT service systems is a well-established need and in the last couple of years a fair amount of research is focusing on service quality [4]. In the paper [1] authors discuss a validation approach for KPI relationships and a regression model for predicting the values of outcome KPIs. However the work uses an aggregated KPI measure and complexity of different lags is not addressed. The problem of selecting the right set of KPIs, such that the desired outcome state is attained within a time and a budget constraint has also not been addressed in the service system domain. Building up on previous work [1], we outline the following:

Contributions: Given a complex network of operational KPIs and Service Delivery Outcomes, both of which can be represented as time-varying datasets, we focus on the problem of: (1) Adopting a data driven approach for detecting inter-relationships and impact delays among KPIs and business outcomes. (2) Building an analytical model to estimate the SD outcomes as functions of KPIs.(3) Using the model to compute a optimal plan of scheduled actions such that transformation of outcome KPI performance can happen within a time and a budget.(4) Building a visualization tool that helps the user to explore and tune the proposed plan using what-if analysis.

The rest of the paper is organized as follows. Section 2 presents background of the data center management domain and describes some KPIs used in our analysis. Section 3 presents our KPI data analysis and influence estimation while Section 4 introduces our prediction model and the transformation planning algorithm. Section 5 presents an interactive visualization system that can be used by experts for relationship visuals, *what-if* type of analysis and plan exploration. Related work is summarized in Section 6 and we conclude with Section 7.

2   Data Center Management Services

This section gives background on the domain of data center management services, the nature of work and the role of KPI management. In the domain of data center management, the customers own data centers and other IT infrastructures supporting their business. The service provider manage the data centers from remote locations called *delivery centers* where groups of service workers (SW) skilled in specific technology areas support the corresponding service requests (SR). Each SR from the customer arrives with an associated priority (e.g. High, Medium or Low) and skills required to solve it. SWs also have associated skill levels and can work on matched SRs. Every priority of work has an associated service level objective (SLO) that is derived from the contract agreed between customer and provider.

The primary focus of this business is to make sure customer SLOs are not violated. To ensure this and continuously improve the efficiency of the service delivery teams, multiple KPIs have been defined with the purpose of measuring the SD operations. Some of the representative KPIs and their measures are given in Table1. Also is shown a business outcome measured by SLO misses of a particular priority of work. The problem at hand is to understand which of these KPIs have a major impact on SLO misses. Consider an example of the workload distribution KPI that is an indicator of how evenly work gets distributed among SWs and is measured by the mean utilizations of different groups of people. But does improving this KPI impact the business goal of reducing SLO Misses? If yes, what is the expected time of benefit realization? These are the questions we attempt to address with our model in section 3.

3   KPI Analysis and Influence Estimation

KPI relationships can be captured by direction and polarity. For example, the rework KPI in a service system maybe impacted by the workload complexity KPI. In this case the *direction* of this causal relationship is from workload complexity to rework. Additionally, an increase in one KPI may imply a decrease in another. In such cases, the *polarity* of the causal relationship is negative. Further, the *degree* of influence one KPI has on another varies — some KPIs are independent implying no influence. Lastly, the influences among KPIs do not occur instantaneously, the performance of one process influences another with a certain delay. Thus each causal relationship has a *lag* associated with it. Assessing the direction, polarity, degree of influence, and impact delay among the KPIs is a prerequisite to predicting their impact to the business outcomes.

A possible approach for assessing the KPI relations is to depend on domain expertise for identifying the major KPIs of interest and their intuitive relationships. Shrinivasan et al.[1] outline a method for validating expert opinion and leveraging it to understand relations. However it may not be feasible to identify all the relations using domain experts, especially their strength of influence or how soon the causal effects of one be seen on the other. Hence, there needs to be a data driven method for estimating the strength of the relation as well as the impact delay between the relationships.

Table 1. Example Data Management KPIs and their measurements

Data Management KPIs	Measured As:
A. Central Assignment: SRs should be centrally assigned to SWs	Fraction of SRs dispatched via dedicated dispatchers.
B. Workload distribution: Achieve even distribution of workload among SWs in each skill group.	Proximity among utilizations of all SWs of all skill groups.
C. Planned Upskilling: SRs are assigned to SWs with lower skills in a planned manner to up-skill them.	Fraction of higher-skill SRs assigned to lower-skilled SWs as per skill plan.
D. Skills Under-Utilization: SRs are assigned to SWs with higher skills to control backlogs.	Fraction of low-skill SRs assigned to higher-skilled SWs.
E. Cross Customer work SWs should work on SRs from multiple customers.	Fraction of SWs working for multiple customers.
F. Rework: Number of attempts required to resolve SRs.	Fraction of SRs resolved in the first attempt.
Business Outcomes	Measured As:
G. SLO Misses for Priority p, p $\in$ High, Med, Low :	Number of Misses on the work of type Priority p

3.1 KPI Data Analysis

We now analyze real KPI data for the datacenter management domain and establish some observations based on its statistical properties. While the specific observations may be domain-specific, the analysis methodology remains same for data collected in a different domain.

The KPIs are collected from different data sources such as work hours claim catalogues, human resource management, and customer works process management tools deployed in a large service delivery organization. These datasets are refreshed at daily, weekly and monthly frequencies. We use data for real 57 service systems collected over 60 weeks of duration in the year 2012. We use the weekly frequency data for analysis. For each week of data, KPIs are computed and results are stored in a database. Since the management tools are often deployed on production system, the data was noisy in parts due to routine system maintenance (server reboots, performance troubleshooting etc.). Thus, the traces had missing or incorrect data for many time intervals during the trace period. We used a simple interval graph technique to identify the longest contiguous interval, where all the KPIs in one SS had monitored data available. Hence, for each SS we identified a smaller period of 56 weeks which had accurate monitored data available and used this 56 periods for our analysis.

Fig.1 shows the timeseries plot of each KPI over time. The ones marked in red are the outcome KPIs (i.e., KPI 9 and 10). We observe that there exists a wide variation both across the time dimension and among the individual KPIs. This is reinforced by looking at the Cumulative Probability Distributions (CDF) plot that shows the large skew in the distributions. Many KPIs achieve the maximum performance value of 1 at some point of time. Due to the skewness, statistical measures like mean, median, percentiles may not be useful. Also since the distributions are so widely varied, statistical properties of a single distribution will not be effective for outcome prediction. This has an important implication on our method.

Observation 1:*The impact of KPIs on outcomes is not easily deducible from visuals. Aggregation measures like mean, median or percentiles cannot be used for representing the KPI distribution.*

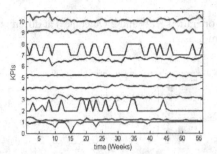 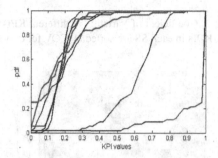

Fig. 1. Operational KPIs and Outcomes as functions of time (CDF of KPI 3 and 8 are omitted to improve the clarity as these are close to step functions)

We next measure the variability in each individual KPI and compute the coefficient of variation (COV) for each. The coefficient of variation is a normalized measure of dispersion of a probability distribution. and is defined as: COV $= \frac{\sigma}{\mu}$ where σ is the standard deviation and μ is the mean of the distribution.

COV is a useful statistic for comparing the degree of variation and equals to 1 for exponential distribution. Distributions with $COV > 1$ (such as a hyper-exponential distribution) are considered high-variance, while those with $COV < 1$ are considered low-variance. The coefficient of variations for all the KPIs are shown for three different service systems in Fig.2 We observe that for each SS there are a few KPIs with heavy-tailed distributions with $COV > 1$. If the outcome is hyper-exponential (as in the second SS) then the individual KPIs that have higher variation is more likely to influence the outcome. In the third SS there is very little variation in the outcomes. This leads to our second important observation.

Observation 2: *For outcome metrics that are heavy-tailed, KPI metrics with low COV may have low influence and vice versa. Statistical measures that ignore the variation in the distribution i.e. the tail of the individual KPIs will be unlikely to accurately estimate the influence.*

As a consequence of the above observation rule, we use it as a filtering mechanism to identify the influential KPIs which show statistically similar variation as the outcome(s) KPI.

Next the relationship between a pair of KPIs is studied, using the cross-correlation measure. The cross-correlation function between the KPIs with timeseries $\{x_1, x_2, \ldots, x_N\}$ and $\{y_1, y_2, \ldots, y_N\}$ is represented by the *normalized covariance function*,

$$\rho_{xy}(k) = \frac{\sum_t (x_t - \bar{x})(y_{t+k} - \bar{y})}{\sqrt{(\sum_{t=1}^{N}(x_t - \bar{x})(\sum_{t=1}^{N}(y_t - \bar{y}))}}, \quad k = 0, \pm 1, \pm 2, \ldots \qquad (1)$$

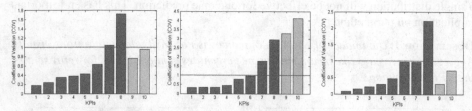

Fig. 2. Coefficient of Variation of different KPIs (8 operation KPIs and 2 Outcomes) at different SS. KPIs in each SS are sorted by COV for easy comparison

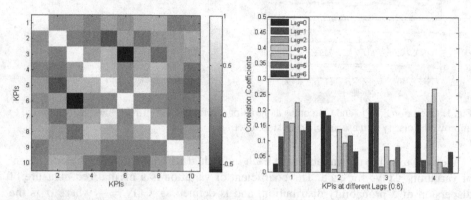

Fig. 3. (a)KPI-KPI and Outcome-KPI correlations Matrix (KPI 9 and 10 correspond to outcomes) and (b) Outcome-KPI correlation magnitudes at different lags (0 to 6 weeks)

where $\bar{x}$ and $\bar{y}$ are the means of $\{x_t\}$ and $\{y_t\}$, respectively, and k is the lag. Fig. 3 shows the cross-correlation matrix between the KPIs in a SS at lag=0. We observe that there exists both positive and negative correlations among the KPIs. The uncorrelated KPIs may be ignored from the influence model perspective.

We note that while one KPI can positively affect an outcome (i.e. KPI 4 and outcome 9), it can simultaneously negatively affect a different outcome(i.e. KPI 4 and outcome 10). This adds to the complexity of the model and the model should consider these inter-KPI dependencies. Again the correlations are also dependent on time lags. Fig.3(b) shows the correlations of 4 KPIs with an outcome with lag varying from 0 to 6 weeks. It is seen that though KPI 1 may appear uncorrelated at lag 0, the correlation increases at lag of 1 week and is maximum at week four. In contrast, KPI 3 affects the outcome instantaneously. This brings us to our third observation.

Observation 3: *Correlation is a significant indicator of influence and a KPI may have both the positive and negative impacts simultaneously on different set of outcomes. KPI relations which may have transitive influence on the outcome needs to be considered. Also due to the possible delayed response of influence, correlations at all reasonable lags need to be studied. Thus cross-correlation among KPIs as well as with the outcomes are both important for the influence model.*

3.2   Influence Estimation

Correlation with lags is a characteristic of many physical systems and we use it as statistical measure for KPI influence on service delivery outcomes. After calculating the cross-correlation between two KPIs, we compute the time-lag at which this maximum correlation occurs. The maximum of the cross-correlation function indicates the point in time where the signals are best aligned with respect to the delay between the KPIs. Hence the maximum impact delay or impact delay between a pair of KPIs can be estimated by the argument of the maximum of cross-correlation,

$$k_{impact} = \arg\max_{k} \rho_{xy}(k), \ 0 \le k \le k_{max}, \tag{2}$$

where k_{max} is the upper bound on the lag in weeks. We fix the upper bound $k_{max} = 8$ as the impact delay rarely exceeds over 8 weeks. The KPIs whose maximum cross-correlation value among each other and with the outcome is above a threshold are considered for the influence model, described in section4.1.

Among multiple KPIs with the same correlation value, the one which affect the outcome quicker is considered as more crucial. For this purpose we define the weekly rate of influence between two KPIs as $\gamma_{xy} = \rho_{xy}(k_{impact})/k_{impact}$.

Intuitively, the rate of influence between any two KPIs reflects how influence flows from a source KPI to a target when there is a stimulus at the source KPI. In the SD domain, possible stimuli for changing performance of a KPI are budget investments that improve the overall process.

4   Outcome Prediction and System Transformation Model

In this section, we develop a model to predict the system outcomes as a function KPI variables and subsequently formulate an optimization model to solve the investment scheduling problem so as to meet the service level objectives while minimizing the cost and delay for system transformation.

4.1   Outcome Prediction Using Multi-variate Regression Model with Time-Lag

A multivariate regression model is formulated to represent the system outcomes as a linear function of KPI variables with appropriate time-lags. For multiple outcome prediction, the prediction model is applied separately for each outcome since the impact delays between the KPI variables and each outcome could be different.

Assume $x_1(t), \ldots, x_M(t), t = 1, \ldots, N$ are the M KPI variables related to the outcome $y(t)$. The linear regression model for the dependent variable $y(t)$ has the form

$$y(t) = \beta_0 + \beta_1 x_1(t - k_1) + \beta_2 x_2(t - k_2) + \ldots + \beta_M x_M(t - k_M) + \epsilon(t), \tag{3}$$

where $k_i, \ i = 1, \ldots, M$ is the impact delay of KPI variable x_i on the outcome y, $\epsilon(t)$ is a random error and $\beta_i, \ i = 0, 1, \ldots, M$ are the unknown regression coefficients. The accuracy of the prediction depends on the sample values of the KPI variables as well as the corresponding delay of impact on the outcome. To estimate the impact delay, we develop a model based on user's suggestion and fine tune it around the suggested value with observed data. For each KPI, we select a range of time delay around the suggested value and set the lag of maximum correlation as the impact delay (see eqn. 2).

The above model estimates the impact delays $k_1, k_2, \ldots, k_M$ for all the KPIs. Aggregating the sample points, we have

$$\mathbf{Y} = \beta_0 + \beta_1 \mathbf{X_1} + \beta_2 \mathbf{X_2} + \ldots + \beta_M \mathbf{X_M} + \epsilon = \mathbf{X}\beta + \epsilon, \tag{4}$$

where $\mathbf{Y} = [y(1) \ldots y(n)]^T, \mathbf{X_i} = [0 \ldots x_i(1) \ldots x_i(n - k_i)]^T, \mathbf{X_0} = [1, \ldots, 1]^T,$ $\mathbf{X} = [\mathbf{X_0 X_1} \ldots \mathbf{X_M}], \beta = [\beta_0 \beta_1 \ldots \beta_M]^T$ and $\epsilon = [\epsilon(1)\epsilon(2) \ldots \epsilon(n)]^T$.

To estimate the unknown regression coefficients $\beta_0, \beta_1, \ldots, \beta_M$, the least squares estimation method is used that minimizes the sum of squared residuals $(\mathbf{Y} - \mathbf{X}\beta)^T(\mathbf{Y} - \mathbf{X}\beta)$. The least square estimate of regression coefficients $\hat{\beta} = (\mathbf{X}^T\mathbf{X})^{-1}\mathbf{X}^T\mathbf{Y}$.

The outcome estimate as a linear function of lagged KPI variables given by:

$$\hat{y}(t) = \hat{\beta}_0 + \hat{\beta}_1 x_1(t - k_1) + \hat{\beta}_2 x_2(t - k_2) + \ldots + \hat{\beta}_M x_M(t - k_M) \tag{5}$$
$$= f(x_1(t - k_1), x_2(t - k_2), \ldots, x_M(t - k_M)). \tag{6}$$

4.2   Budget Allocation Model

In this section, we address the budget allocation problem for system transformation. Given a service delivery system SS1 that has the following properties:

1. SS1 has J outcomes and the desired values of outcomes are $y_j^d, j = 1, 2, \cdots, J$.
2. Assume B denotes the available budget and T represents the time limit to complete the system transformation.
3. Investment can be applied to a given set of leaf nodes and without loss of generality, assume the nodes are $1, 2, \ldots, p$. Let Q_i be the investment required to improve the KPI value of node i, x_i by unit amount, $i = 1, 2, \ldots, p$.
4. A outcome j can be improved at time t by improving one or more of the KPI values $x_1, x_2, \ldots, x_p$ at the leaf nodes provided the impact delay of the KPI is less than t. Thus a KPI node i is a candidate for investment if the impact delay on j-th outcome k_{ji} is smaller than t. Let A_{ji} denotes the case that KPI node i is an investment candidate for improving the outcome j.

A system outcome y_j can be estimated as a function of lagged KPI variables as shown in eqn. (6). After investment at $t = 0$, KPI values will be increased from x_i^0 to x_i, $i \in \{1, 2, \ldots, p\}$ at selected set of nodes and the rest of KPI values will remain unchanged. From eqns. (6), we can also estimate any outcome as a function of investment-ready KPI variables $(x_1, \ldots, x_p)$ only as the impact of remaining leaf nodes is unchanged. Hence the modified prediction function will be

$$y_j = F\left(A_{j1}x_1 + (1 - A_{j1})x_1^0, \ldots, A_{ji}x_i + (1 - A_{ji})x_i^0, \ldots, A_{jp}x_p + (1 - A_{jp})x_p^0\right) + \eta_j, \tag{7}$$

where η_j is a constant. Note that the investment-ready leaf node i is an investment candidate if the improvement in KPI value x_i causes improvement in the outcome value y_j and is represented as $A_{ji} = 1$. Considering all the outcomes, an investment-ready leaf node will be an investment candidate if it has the ability to improve any of the system outcomes within the time limit T. A binary variable H_i is defined to represent the KPI node i as an investment candidate. Hence $H_i = 1$ if and only if there exists at least one $A_{ji} = 1$ or $H_i = 1 - \prod_j (1 - A_{ji})$. The total cost of investment to improve the candidate KPI values from x_i^0 to x_i is $\sum_{i=1}^p Q_i H_i (x_i - x_i^0)$.

Given the KPI network and relation among the nodes, we need to decide the investment amount at each candidate node so as to meet the desired outcome requirements within an overall budget and time. The general problem is to choose the investment-ready nodes ($H_i = 1$) and the corresponding KPI values x_i, so as to minimize the weighted combination of normalized transformation time t/T and normalized cost $\sum_{i=1}^p Q_i H_i (x_i - x_i^0)/B$, subject to the constraints that the outcome values are greater than the desired levels, required transformation time is bounded by the upper limit T and the total investment does not exceed the overall budget B.

The problem is stated formally as a *mathematical program*.

Objective function: $\quad \min \; w_t \dfrac{t}{T} + w_c \dfrac{1}{B} \sum_{i=1}^p Q_i H_i (x_i - x_i^0) \hspace{2cm}$ (8)

subject to

$$y_j = F\big(A_{j1}x_1 + (1 - A_{j1})x_1^0, \ldots, A_{jp}x_p + (1 - A_{jp})x_p^0\big) + \eta_j \geq y_j^d, \; \forall j, \tag{9}$$

$$\sum_{i=1}^p Q_i H_i (x_i - x_i^0) <= B, \tag{10}$$

$$t <= T, \tag{11}$$

$$x_i^0 \leq x_i \leq x_i^M, \; \forall i, \tag{12}$$

$$0 \leq A_{ji} \leq I_{\{t > k_{ji}\}}, \; \forall i, j, \tag{13}$$

$$H_i = 1 - \prod_j (1 - A_{ji}) \in \{0, 1\}, \; A_{ji} \in \{0, 1\}, \; \forall i, j, \tag{14}$$

where w_c and w_t are the weights corresponding to transformation cost and time, x_i^M is the upper bound on KPI value x_i and I is an indicator function defined as $I_{\{x\}} = 1$, if $x \geq 0$, else $I_{\{x\}} = 0$. Note that transformation time minimization for a given budget B and transformation cost minimization for a given time limit T are special cases of the above general formulation with ($w_t = 1, w_c = 0$) and ($w_t = 0, w_c = 1$), respectively.

This is an example of *mixed integer nonlinear program* or MINLP. Although some efficient algorithms are known for solving *nonlinear programs* (NLPs), no efficient algorithms are known for the solution of arbitrary MINLPs which are extremely hard [18]. Hence we develop a heuristic to find the optimal solution under certain conditions using an iterative approach over t. Observe that the integer complexity arises due to the transform time optimization and it has the same level of complexities as the weighted combination. However, if we fix the transformation time $t = t^L$, the integer variables $A_{ji} = I_{\{t^L > k_{ji}\}}$ becomes constant for all $i = 1, \ldots, p$, and $j = 1, \ldots, J$ and we need to solve only the reduced cost optimization problem as following:

Objective function: $\quad \min \; \sum_{i=1}^p Q_i H_i (x_i - x_i^0) \hspace{2.5cm}$ (15)

subject to

$$y_j = F\big(A_{j1}x_1 + (1 - A_{j1})x_1^0, \ldots, A_{jp}x_p + (1 - A_{jp})x_p^0\big) + \eta_j \geq y_j^d, \; \forall j, \tag{16}$$

$$\sum_{i=1}^p Q_i H_i (x_i - x_i^0) <= B, \tag{17}$$

$$x_i^0 \leq x_i \leq x_i^M, \; \forall i, \; H_i = 1 - \prod_j (1 - A_{ji}) \; \forall i, j. \tag{18}$$

The above mathematical problem (eqns. (15)–(18)) is a linear optimization problem as all the constraints and objective functions are linear and it can be solved by the algorithms for linear constrained minimization [18,19]. Statistical toolboxes like MATLAB, SPSS provide such facilities. However, this solves the *investment optimization problem* for a given time limt t^L. We select integer values for t^L as $1, 2, \ldots, T$ and solve the above problem (eqns. (15)–(18)) iteratively to compute the minimum investment required $\sum_{i=1}^{p} Q_i H_i(x_i^* - x_i^0)$ at each iteration. The optimum weighted combination is obtained by comparing the results at all iterations. Note that the integer assumption of transformation time limit t is a valid assumption as impact delays are generally measured as integers in terms of weeks or days and hence the iterative approach will lead to an optimal solution. For the optimal solution t^*, assume x_i^* is the optimal value of KPI x_i. We now compute the week-wise transformation schedule for each x_i based on the weekly rate of modification.

4.3   Transformation Schedule

If every KPI can be increased to their optimal values without any constraint, then in order to find the schedule, we update every KPI at the beginning of the first week, and due to the respective lags, they converge to the optimal values within t^* weeks. However in reality, increasing a KPI value instantaneously without any limit is not feasible, since improving a KPI usually involves process or people changes or both. Thus typically every KPI will have a limit beyond which it cannot be changed in one week. In that case we use a heuristic to modify a schedule:

Let x_i^c be the maximum improvement that can be made to x_i in one week

1: **if** $\frac{(x_i^* - x_i^0)}{x_i^c} + \max_j (k_{ji}) \leq t^*$ **then**
2:      Increment x_i by x_i^c every week till it reaches x_i^*
3: **else**
4:      Update upper limit of $x_i, x_i^M = x_i^0 + x_i^c \times (t^* - \max_j (k_{ji}))$.
5:      Redo Iterative Optimization (eqns. (15)–(18))
6: **end if**

5   Model Validation Using Interactive Visualization

We build an interactive visualization system to enable managers/analysts of a service system to (a) explore and validate KPI relationships; (b) interactively conduct what-if analysis, and (c)choose the right action plan for improvement. The tooling is Html5 based with the backend supported by Java Server and IBM DB2. KPI datasets from 57 real service systems across 60 weeks are stored, visualized and analyzed by the system. For the backend statistical models (i.e., distributions, COV, correlation, regression, solver) we use standard MATLAB/SPSS packages.

5.1   Relationship Visualization

KPI relationships in the tool are captured using a graph notation, where nodes represent the KPIs. Directed edges connecting two KPIs represents the influence relationship between them. The label pair along the edge represent maximum relationship intensity

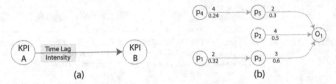

Fig. 4. A KPI relationship representation

and the lag at which it occurs as shown in Fig. 4(a). Blue edges represent positive polarity and those in orange represent negative polarity. Fig. 4(b) shows relationships among process KPIs (p_i) and their relationships to an outcome (o_1). The outcome node (o_1) is placed in the far right. Process KPI nodes are arranged in columns left to (o_1) based on the directness of influence to KPIs. For instance, KPIs p_5, p_2 and p_3 are placed in the first column left to (o_1) since they directly affect the outcome. KPIs p_1 and p_4 are placed in the second column left to (o_1) because they are one-hop away and so on.

5.2   Relationship Validation and Prediction

In order to validate the KPIs relationships, tool users start with selecting both the service system for investigation and an outcome through 'service system and outcome selection' panel (see Fig. 5a). Users can also select the process KPIs to be included for the relationship analysis (see Fig. 5b). To assist them in the selection of the outcome KPI for analysis, we show a series of trend graphs, the CDFs and the CoV values for the outcome KPIs for different service system. This view, as shown in Fig. 5c, enables users to select the outcome by investigating its behavior over time. As discussed in section 3, outcomes that demonstrate variation are more suited for this kind of influence analysis.

Next, the KPI relationships are extracted by individual setting of the parameters of lag and minimum pairwise relationship strength (Fig. 5d).

(a)Lag analysis: Users can study the impact of lag on relationships by either fixing a lag period (in weeks) or selecting a range of lag periods. This helps to explore the degree of influence among KPIs at any given lag. In Fig. 6, a user explores and validates KPIs relationship based on only the degree of influence by fixing lag at 2 and 5 weeks respectively. On selecting a range of lags on the UI, the lag at maximum correlation is associated with the relationship. A KPI relationship map extracted using this option is shown in Fig. 5e with a lag range of 0 to 8 weeks.

(b)Degree of influence analysis: Users can study the impact of pairwise relationship strength by varying a minimum threshold on the strength parameter with a given lag setting. This filters out any relation with strength below the threshold. Fig. 6 shows a dense and a sparse KPI relationship based on threshold values of 44.3% and 51.3%, respectively. The extracted KPI relationship is visualized in Fig. 5f, with the settings in (Fig. 5e) and can be accordingly modified by users (Fig. 5g). The validated relationships are saved for future use.

Prediction Model Validation. The validated relationships are used to build the multivariate regression model with time lag (Section 4.1). Fig. 7 shows regression co-efficients for 3 SS and their normalized RMSE. In this example 40 weeks of data was used for building the model and the next 17 weeks was predicted. In each case the outcome was dependent on $4-10$ influence KPIs. We note that for 2 out of 3 service systems the RMSE

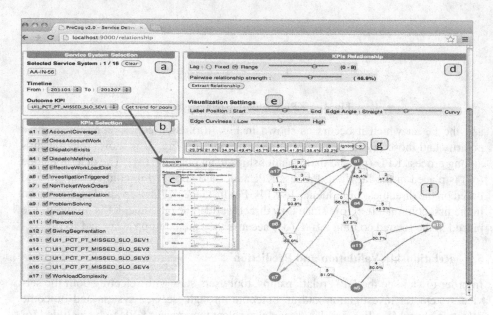

Fig. 5. An interactive visualization system to validate KPIs relationship in a service system. (a) Service System and outcome Selection, (b) KPIs selection, (c) Outcome KPI trends for service systems, (d) KPIs relationship extraction settings, (e) Graph drawing settings, (f) KPIs relationship visualization using representation discussed in Fig. 4b, and (g) Relationship validation panel.

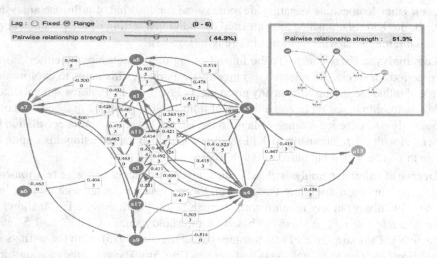

Fig. 6. KPI relationship validation by varying minimum threshold for pairwise relationship strength and lag. The dense KPI network is obtained by setting low threshold for pairwise relationship strength and high lag range. The sparse KPI network (shown in the inset) is obtained by setting high threshold for pairwise relationship strength for the same lag range.

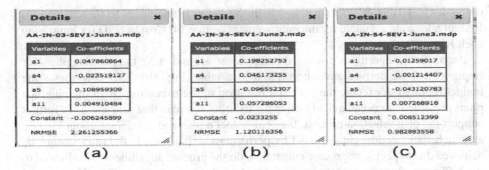

Fig. 7. (a)-(c) Regression results for models from 3 Service Systems

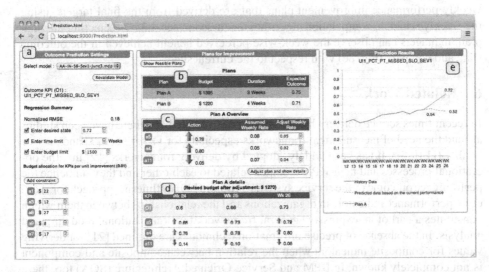

Fig. 8. An interactive user interface for exploring possible plans for improvement. (a) Outcome prediction settings panel. (b) Possible plans. (c) Selected plan details with options for adjusting weekly rates. (d) Weekly plan details. (e) Prediction graph showing the improvement in the outcome using the recommended plan. Red dashed line represents the current outcome and green line represents the improvement achievable by the suggested plan A.

errors is within 1%. Hence it seems that having a linear model of outcome prediction may work reasonably well for service systems, where the dependent KPI relations affecting each outcome is under 10. For a larger number of KPI relationships other models will have to be explored. For each service system, users can either accept the error of prediction (NRMSE) or choose to re-validate with a different set of parameter settings. Once a prediction model is accepted (Fig. 8a), the next step is to explore possible plans for system improvement.

5.3 Exploring Improvement Plans

In this state, the user is ready to explore different transformation plans. The following inputs are required (as shown in bottom part of Fig. 8a):(1) Desired state of the outcomes, (2) Time in weeks within which the desired state needs to be achieved,(3) Budget allocation available for the improvement actions,(4) Cost in USD for improving each KPI by 0.01 (1%).

Based on the algorithms discussed in Sections(4.2 and 4.3), the possible plans for improvement are derived and summarized in a table (Fig. 8b). The table shows the budget required to execute the plan and duration of the execution. With the alternate plans presented, users can quickly compare and choose a plan that suits them. To further support the plan selection process, they can select a plan and get details about the rate at which they need to change a KPI's performance (Fig. 8c). If the rates cannot be achieved due to people or process constraints on the ground, adjustments are allowed to the KPI rates. Recomputations are performed on the revised targets (based on method in sec 4.3, thereby producing a new set of expected outcomes. Fig. 8d gives the detailed weekly performance improvement plans that are derived from the final targets, using the weekly schedule computation algorithm discussed in sec 4.3. On selecting the final plan, managers can observe the week-wise perceived benefit achieved in the outcome state and compare (Fig. 8e) with respect to the current state.

6   Related Work

In recent times service delivery has been highly IT oriented and there have been studies around the need of measurement frameworks especially for IT services [3] and service quality ([14],[4]). It has been widely adopted by delivery frameworks [12] that the operational processes and their KPIs are inter-related to each other and they influence the performance outcome of the service systems. Authors [20] outline an approach for modeling performance indicators in organizations and the relationships between them which constitutes a part of an expressive general framework for organizational modeling and analysis. In the absence of precise information techniques are outlined [21] for deriving values for composite indicators when the relation between composite and component is not completely known. In BPM and Service Oriented Architecture (SOA) too, there is work [6] on automated monitoring of KPIs and developing dependency trees using machine learning. Authors in [2] detail methods for preventing KPI violations based on decision tree learning and proactive runtime adaptation.

Process based performance analysis has been addressed before([7][15], [5]), but not in the particular flavor of service delivery outcomes. Lag selection using regression for high dimensional data is addressed in [10]. Authors refer to budgeting for the service transformation in [17]. However, none of them address the combined problem of creating influence models and using it for a budget constrained transformation schedule.

7   Conclusions and Future Work

We present a KPI influence model that can be used by managers for outcome state prediction, as well as system state transformation. We also provide visualization system supported by statistical models for managers to perform what-if type of analysis and iterative refinements before producing a consolidated final plan. During our model validation we find that a linear relationship may not suffice for all service systems. As part of future work we propose to investigate non-linear influence models.

References

1. Shrinivasan, Y.B., Dasgupta, G.B., Desai, N., Nallacherry, J.: A method for assessing influence relationships among kPIs of service systems. In: Liu, C., Ludwig, H., Toumani, F., Yu, Q. (eds.) ICSOC 2012. LNCS, vol. 7636, pp. 191–205. Springer, Heidelberg (2012)
2. Prashanth, L.A., Prasad, H.L., Desai, N., Bhatnagar, S., Dasgupta, G.: Stochastic optimization for adaptive labor staffing in service systems. In: Kappel, G., Maamar, Z., Motahari-Nezhad, H.R. (eds.) ICSOC 2011. LNCS, vol. 7084, pp. 487–494. Springer, Heidelberg (2011)
3. Lepmets, M., Ras, E., Renault, A.: A quality measurement framework for it services by marion lepmets. In: SRII Global Conference (2011), 9. Lin, S.P., Chen, L.F., Chan, Y.H.: What is the valuable
4. Rajamani, N., Mani, D., Mehta, S., Chebiyyam, M.: Quality, Satisfaction and Value in Outsourcing: Role of Relationship Dynamics and Proactive Management. In: ICIS 2010 (2010)
5. Motta, G., Pignatelli, G., Barroero, T., Longo, A.: Service level analysis method - SLAM. In: Proceedings of ICCSIT, pp. 460–466 (2010)
6. Wetzstein, B., Leitner, P., Rosenberg, F., Brandic, I., Dustdar, S., Leymann, F.: Monitoring and analyzing influential factors of business process performance. In: Proceedings of EDOC. IEEE Computer Society (2009)
7. Han, K.H., Kang, J.G., Song, M.: Two-stage process analysis using the process-based performance measurement framework and business process simulation. Expert Systems with Applications 36(3, pt. 2), 7080–7086 (2009)
8. Alter, S.: Service system fundamentals: Work system, value chain, and life cycle. IBM Systems Journal 47(1), 71–85 (2008)
9. Johnston, R., Clark, G.: Service operations management: improving service delivery. Financial Times Prentice Hall, Harlow (2008) ISBN 9781405847322
10. Simon, G., Verleysen, M.: Lag Selection for Regression Models Using High-Dimensional Mutual Information: ESANN 2006 proceedings. In: European Symposium on Artificial Neural Networks, Bruges (Belgium), April 26-28 (2006)
11. Settas, D., Bibi, S., Sfetsos, P., Stamelos, I., Gerogiannis, V.: Using Bayesian Belief Networks to Model Software Project Management Antipatterns. In: Proceedings of the Fourth International Conference on Software Engineering Research, Management and Applications (2006)
12. Grembergen, W.V., Haes, S.D.: Cobits management guidelines revisited: The kgis/kpis cascade. Information Systems Control Journal 6(1), 1–3 (2005)
13. Apte, U.M., Goh, C.H.: Applying lean manufacturing principles to information intensive services (2004)
14. Schneider, B., White, S.S.: Service Quality: Research Perspectives (Foundations for Organizational Science). Sage Publications (2003)
15. Linard, K., Fleming, C., Dvorsky, L.: System dynamics as the link between corporate vision and key performance indicators. In: System Dynamics Conference, pp. 1–13 (2002)
16. Foster, I., Kesselman, C.: The Grid: Blueprint for a New Computing Infrastructure. Morgan Kaufmann, San Francisco (1999)
17. Abedian, I., Strachan, B., Ajam, T.: Transformation in Action: Budgeting for Health Service Delivery. University of cape town press, ISBN 1-919713-26-3
18. Bertsekas, D.: Nonlinear Optimization. Athena Scientific (1995)
19. Nash, S., Sofer, A.: Linear and Nonlinear Programming. McGraw-Hill, New York (1996)
20. Popova, V., Sharpanskykh, A.: Modeling organizational performance indicators. In: Inf. Syst. 2010. Elsevier Science Ltd. (2010)
21. Barone, D., Jiang, L., Amyot, D., Mylopoulos, J.: Reasoning with Key Performance Indicators. In: Johannesson, P., Krogstie, J., Opdahl, A.L. (eds.) PoEM 2011. LNBIP, vol. 92, pp. 82–96. Springer, Heidelberg (2011)

On-the-Fly Adaptation of Dynamic Service-Based Systems: Incrementality, Reduction and Reuse

Antonio Bucchiarone, Annapaola Marconi,
Claudio Antares Mezzina, Marco Pistore, and Heorhi Raik

Fondazione Bruno Kessler, Via Sommarive, 18, Trento, Italy
{bucchiarone,marconi,mezzina,pistore,raik}@fbk.eu

Abstract. On-the-fly adaptation is where adaptation activities are not explicitly represented at design time but are discovered and managed at run time considering all aspect of the execution environments. In this paper we present a comprehensive framework for the on-the-fly adaptation of highly dynamic service-based systems. The framework relies on advanced context-aware adaptation techniques that allow for i) incremental handling of complex adaptation problems by interleaving problem solving and solution execution, ii) reduction in the complexity of each adaptation problem by minimizing the search space according to the specific execution context, and iii) reuse of adaptation solutions by learning from past executions. We evaluate the applicability of the proposed approach on a real world scenario based on the operation of the Bremen sea port.

1 Introduction

One of the key advantages of the service oriented paradigm is the possibility to reduce the development and maintenance cost of software applications without loosing the control of their quality and the capability of managing their lifecycle. A key enabling factor to fully exploit these advantages, is the capability of service oriented applications to *adapt*, i.e., to modify their behavior and to evolve in order to satisfy new requirements and to fit new situations. Addressing this problem is not at all easy, especially considering the challenges posed by the Internet of Services [13], where applications need to deal with a continuously changing environment, both in terms of the context in which the applications operate, and of the services, users and providers involved. In such a setting, the same application shall operate differently for different contextual situations, deal with the fact that involved services are not known a priori, and be able to dynamically react to changes to better fit the new situations.

Despite the considerable effort dedicated in recent years to investigate approaches for the adaptation of service-based systems, we are still far from effective solutions. As we will discuss in depth in the related work, most adaptation approaches require to analyze all the possible adaptation cases at design-time, and to embed the corresponding recovery activities in the system model, and can hardly be used in dynamic settings; or only deal with very limited forms of "local" dynamic adaptation, e.g., service replacement.

In recent work [4], we have proposed a comprehensive framework for the on-the-fly adaptation of service-based application. This approach exploits the concept of process fragments [9] as a way to model reusable process knowledge and to allow for an *incremental* and context-aware composition of such fragments into adaptable service-based

S. Basu et al. (Eds.): ICSOC 2013, LNCS 8274, pp. 146–161, 2013.

applications. The framework allows for processes that are only partially specified at design time, and that are automatically refined at run-time taking into account the specific execution context. This refinement exploits the available fragments, which are provided by the other actors and systems to describe the services and capabilities that are offered to the process in the specific context. The framework also supports on-the-fly adaptation to unexpected or improbable context changes that may affect the execution of the application. Also in this case, available fragments and current context are exploited to solve the problem.

Since highly dynamic systems generates a large number of adaptation problems (both in terms of process refinements and of other forms of adaptation), this paper investigates a potential problem of on-the-fly adaptation for such system: is it feasible to solve large number of adaptation problems at run time, each involving a potentially very large set of other actors and available fragments? We answer to this question by extending the framework of [4] in two directions: first, we show that it is possible to *reduce* the complexity of each adaptation problem by minimizing the search space so that it only includes fragments and properties that are relevant for the problem; second, we show that it is possible to store and *reuse* previously discovered adaptation solutions, thus learning from past executions and reducing the number of adaptations to be effectively computed at run time. These two extensions are complementary and integrated: by reducing the adaptation problems to their minimal versions, we increase the number of adaptation problems that turn out to be equal, and we hence increase the possibility of reusing previous solutions.

We evaluate the proposed approach on a real world scenario based on the operation of car logistics in the Bremen sea port [3]. We show that it is effective in reducing the number of requested adaptations: the experiments show that, while the situation where new adaptation are not needed is never reached (thus witnessing the need of dynamic adaptation), the number of such new adaptations decreases over time (thus making reuse more and more efficient). We also show that the approach seamlessly accommodates situations where previous adaptations are not valid anymore, e.g., due to changes in the requirements or in the available fragments: these changes are reflected in changes in the context that make the past solutions not reusable; the approach computes new solutions suited for the new requirements and fragments; and the overhead in terms of performance of this computation of new plans is very limited.

The rest of the paper is structured as follows. Following, we shortly introduce the Bremen harbor car logistic scenario that is used as a reference throughout the paper. Section 2 presents the proposed framework for on-the-fly adaptation; Section 3 gives a formal specification of the framework, while Section 4 shows the definition and implementation of adaptation reduction and reuse within the framework. Finally, Section 5 describes how we have evaluated our solution using the car logistic demonstrator while Section 6 presents some related works, and conclusions.

1.1 Motivating Scenario: Car Logistics

The reference scenario is based on the operation of the sea port of Bremen, Germany [3], where nearly 2 million new vehicles are handled each year in order *to deliver them from manufacturers to retailers.*

Our goal is to develop a system (the Car Logistic System (CLS)) to support the management and operation of the port, where numerous actors (i.e., cars, ships, trucks, treatment areas, etc.) need to cooperate in a synergistic manner respecting their own procedures and business policies. The system needs to deal with the dynamicity of the scenario, both in terms of the variability of the actors' involved and of their procedures (customizable processes), and of the exogenous context changes affecting its operation.

Considering for instance the delivery process of each car, customization means that the delivery procedure of each car needs to be customized according to the car brand, model, retailer-specific requirements, etc. Moreover new car models, having specific requirements and procedures, have to be able to be easily integrated in the system. Similarly, the system needs to flexibly deal with changes in the procedures of external actors such as ships and trucks. Concerning *context dynamicity*, examples of environment conditions to be taken into account are the unavailability or malfunctioning of the different port facilities, accidental damages of cars and trucks, human errors (e.g., a car is parked in the wrong parking lot).

2   General Framework and Approach

In this section we present our framework for creating and running adaptive context-aware service-based systems like the CLS described above.

2.1   Modeling Artifacts

In our framework, we model the real-world system under consideration as a set of *entities* that can collaborate with each other in order to accomplish their business goals (e.g., in the CLS scenario such entities might be cars, ships and other port facilities). In turn, the entity model includes 1) *entity context* capturing key characteristics of the entity, 2) business *process* determining entity behaviour and 3) a set of *process fragments* (from now on, simply *fragments*) that can be exploited by external partners (i.e., other entities) in order to collaborate with the fragments owner.

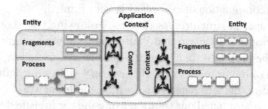

Fig. 1. Modeling Artifacts

Entity context is modeled as a set of *context properties*, each capturing some relevant characteristic of an entity (e. g., car location, car status, etc.). A context property is represented by a context property diagram, a state transition system containing all possible property values (states) and value changes (transitions labeled with events).

For instance, car location may be changed from *storage* to *mechanical station* when the car moves around the harbour area. The overall application context is composed of context properties of all constituent entities (see Figure 1).

Entity process and fragments are modeled as Adaptable Pervasive Flows (APFs) [5], that is an extension of classical workflow languages that 1) adds the possibility to model special types of process activities (most interestingly, *abstract activities*), and 2) introduce contextual annotations that connect processes to their operational context. Abstract activities let us include in a process some task whose actual implementation cannot be efficiently provided at design time and needs to be dynamically determined (or generated) at run time. Contextual annotations include preconditions, effects, goals and compensations. Activity *precondition* shows in which contextual situations (states) the activity execution is allowed. Activity *effect* indicates which contextual events are triggered when the activity is executed. Abstract activity *goal* expresses an abstract task associated with the abstract activity in terms of goal contextual situations. Finally, activity *compensation* specifies how the activity can be compensated after execution (similarly to goals, it is expressed as a set of context situations in which activity effects are considered to be compensated).

The proposed set of modeling artifacts is able to capture the key characteristics of dynamic context-aware systems since i) abstract activities expressed in terms of goals allow for run-time selection of fragments according to their availability and further fragment composition in compliance with the execution context, ii) the context-awareness of processes allows us to detect execution problems at run time (e. g., by detecting precondition violations) and produce solutions to them dynamically (using fragment composition tools), iii) entities can join/leave the system at run time without interrupting its operation.

2.2   On-the-Fly Adaptation Approach

Our approach enables on-the-fly adaptation of context-aware systems by combining the four key features: i) incremental resolution of complex adaptation problems by interleaving problem solving and solution execution, ii) reduction in the complexity of each adaptation problem (by using the search space that contains only information that is relevant for a given problem and context), iii) reuse of adaptation solutions by learning from past executions, and iv) exploitation of advanced AI planning techniques [2] to solve adaptation problems by appropriately composing available fragments. The general idea of the approach consists in constantly monitoring process execution, detecting various forms of inconsistencies (for now, these includes unrefined abstract activities and precondition violation) and resolving them through composition of available fragments. In Figure 2 we show the approach life-cycle and in the rest of this section we explain it in detail.

Incremental Adaptation. As described in Section 2.1, a key feature of the framework is the possibility of partially specifying the process logic at design-time, leaving the refinement of abstract activities and resolution of most problems to run time. The advantage of performing process adaptation at run time is twofold. First, efficient adaptation heavily depends on run-time status of the execution environment (e.g., on the set of available fragments and actual context), which often is unknown at design time. Second, availability of automated adaptation tools significantly simplifies the work of process designer, who now does not need to consider all special cases and to implement all tasks at design time.

Abstract activity refinement consists in producing fragment composition that satisfies abstract activity goal and thus can be used as an activity implementation. Since fragments used in refinement may also contain abstract activities, the resulting process instance has a multi-layer structure, where the top layer is the initial process and intermediate layers correspond to incremental refinements. Consider, for instance, the abstract activity *Store* of the main car process in Figure 3. During the execution, the activity is automatically refined and composes four available fragments (i.e., Registration, StorageAssignment, StoreToA, StoreToB) provided by different entities (i.e, *Storage Manager*, *Storage Area A*, *Storage Area B*). The abstract activity *BookA* within this refinement is further refined with fragments provided by *StorageAreaA* entity.

Considering another form of on-the-fly adaptation (i. e., reaction to precondition violation), the aim of the composition produced is to bring the system to a context where the process execution can be resumed (i.e., precondition is not violated anymore). This is the case of adaptation *A1* in Figure 3, where the car has been damaged and violates the precondition of the *Registration* fragment. The framework supports different adaptation mechanisms to tackle this problem, among which: *local adaptation*, where the aim is to bring the system to a context configuration satisfying the violated precondition; *on-the-fly compensation*, that can be used to dynamically compute a compensation process for an activity or a set of already executed activities; *re-refinement*, combining

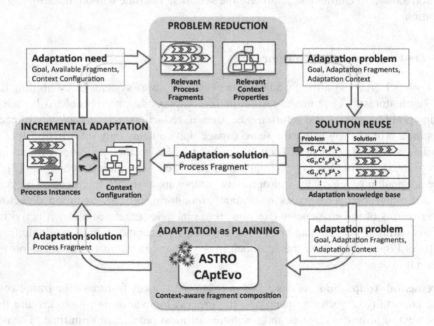

Fig. 2. Overview of the On-the-Fly Adaptation Approach

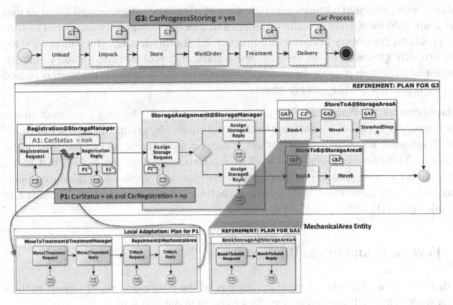

Fig. 3. Process Adaptations in action

compensation and refinement mechanisms to re-compute the refinement of an abstract activity considering the new execution context. A complete description and definition of all the adaptation mechanisms and strategies provided by the ASTRO-CAptEvo Framework is presented in [4].

To summarize, this phase can deal with two different *adaptation needs*: the need for refining an abstract activity and the need to resolve precondition violation. In both cases, an adaptation problem is formally specified, in terms of the goal to be reached, the available fragments, and the current context configuration. Then, it is passed as input to the problem reduction phase.

Problem Reduction. The aim of this phase is to optimize an adaptation problem in order to reduce search space for further planning. The point is that while the whole system can be rather complex (including dozens of facilities and thousands of cars), only its small portion is relevant for a particular inconsistency resolution (e. g., if we need to plan car unloading, we need to consider only this particular car and only the actors participating in unloading). This is done in two steps. First, we identify the range of entities (participants) that are relevant for the adaptation problem in hands. Second, we reduce preselected fragments and context properties taking into account the current context state of the system (e.g., remove all transitions and state that can never be reached from the current state). These two steps are further explained in Section 4.1.

It is worth to mention that the reduction phase is key not only for the *Adaptation as Planning* phase, but also for the *Solution Reuse* phase, since it allows for better characterization of the adaptation problem.

Solution Reuse. Given an adaptation problem, this phase checks whether absolutely the same problem has already been solved in the past. Though simple from a conceptual point of view, this step requires generalization of a specific adaptation problem so that it is abstracted away from specific instances and can be conceptually compared to similar problems previously resolved (see Section 4.2 for the details). If a solution exists, it is properly grounded to the instance-level adaptation problem and passed to the *Incremental Execution* phase to be executed. Otherwise, the adaptation problem is passed to the *Adaptation as AI Planning* phase.

Adaptation as AI Planning. This phase is responsible for finding a solution to the adaptation problem (i.e., a new fragment), by automatically composing the set of available fragments, according to the current context configuration and to the goal to be achieved. This phase exploits the ASTRO-CAptEvo adaptation engine [14] that transforms an adaptation problem into a planning problem and applies to it advanced planning techniques capable of dealing with asynchronous nondeterministic domains and complex goals ([2,10]).

3 Formal Framework: Background

In this section we introduce formal definitions of the core elements of our adaptation framework. They will be used in Section 4 to present our solution.

3.1 Elements

Definition 1 (Context Property Type). *A context property type is a state transition system* $c = \langle L, l^0, E, T \rangle$, *where:*

- *L is a set of context states and $l^0 \in L$ is the initial state;*
- *$E = E_{unc} \cup E_{cnt}$ is a set of context events, where E_{unc} is a set of uncontrollable and E_{cnt} is a set of controllable events, such that $E_{cnt} \cap E_{unc} = \emptyset$;*
- *$T \subseteq L \times E \times L$ is a transition relation.*

The *context model* of a system is composed by a set of context property types $C_M = \{c_1, \ldots, c_n\}$ such that $c_i = \langle L_i, l_i^0, E_i, T_i \rangle$ and $L_i \cap L_j = \emptyset$ and $E_i \cap E_j = \emptyset$ if $i \neq j$. For each context property type c_i there may exist zero or more instances at run time, hence we define the *runtime context state* as a set of the states of the all the instances.

Definition 2 (Runtime Context State). *A runtime context state is a set* $C = \{(l_{i,j})\}$ *such that* $l_{i,j} \in L_i$ *for some* $c_i = \langle L_i, l_i^0, E_i, T_i \rangle \in C_M$.

Since we want to relate multiple states of the same context property c_i with different instances, we define the set of all possible states of an instance j of type i as the set $L_j^i = \{(j, l) \mid l \in L_i\}$.

We denote with $\mathbb{L} = (\prod_{\forall i \mid c_i \in C_M} L_i)$ and $\mathbb{L}_C = (\prod_{\forall i \forall j \mid l_{i,j} \in C} L_i^j)$.

Set $\mathbb{L}$ represents the set of all the possible configurations (in terms of states) in which the context model C_M can be, while $\mathbb{L}_C$ represents the set of all the possible configurations in which the runtime context C can be. In the same way sets $\mathbb{E}$ and $\mathbb{E}_C$ are defined, representing respectively all the possible combinations of events of the model and of the runtime context.

Processes (and fragments) are modeled as state transition systems, where each transition corresponds to a particular process activity. In particular, we distinguish four kinds of activities: input and output activities model communications among processes; concrete activities model internal elaborations by the process; and abstract activities correspond to the abstract activities of the process. In the following we will indicate with A^* either the set A or $\emptyset$. Abstract activities can be annotated with goals, while input, output and concrete activities can be annotated with preconditions, effects, and compensations. We define a *process instance* as follows:

Definition 3 (Process Instance). *A process instance defined over the runtime context state C is a tuple $p = \langle S, s^0, A, T, Ann \rangle$, where:*

- *S is a set of states and $s^0 \subseteq S$ is a set of initial states;*
- *$A = A_{in} \cup A_{out} \cup A_{con} \cup A_{abs}$ is a set of activities, where A_{in} is a set of input activities, A_{out} is a set of output activities, A_{con} is a set of concrete activities, and A_{abs} is a set of abstract activities. A_{in}, A_{out}, A_{con}, and A_{abs} are disjoint sets;*
- *$T \subseteq S \times A \times S$ is a transition relation;*
- *$Ann = \langle Pre, Eff, Goal, Comp \rangle$ is a process annotation, where $Pre : A_{in} \cup A_{out} \cup A_{con} \to \mathbb{L}_C^*$ is the precondition labeling function, $Eff : A_{in} \cup A_{out} \cup A_{con} \to \mathbb{E}_C^*$ is the effect labeling function, $Goal : A_{abs} \to \mathbb{L}_C$ is the goal labeling function, and $Comp : A \to \mathbb{L}_C^*$ is the compensation labeling function;*

We denote with $S(p)$, $A(p)$, etc. the corresponding elements of p.

Definition 4 (Process Fragment). *A process fragment defined over the context model C_M is a tuple $f = \langle S, s^0, A, T, Ann, En \rangle$, where:*

- *S, s^0, A, T are as Definition 3;*
- *Ann is as Definition 3 but on set $\mathbb{L}^*$ and $\mathbb{E}^*$*
- *En is a set of entity types that can use the process fragment f.*

Let $a \in A(f)$ an activity of a process fragment f and $l = Ann(a) \subset \mathbb{L}^*$ its annotation. To understand if l contains states of a certain context property type $c_i \in C_M$ we define the projection of the annotation l onto context property type c_i as $l \downarrow_{c_i} = l_i$. In the same way we define an instance based projection on $\mathbb{L}_C$, written $\mathbb{L}_C \downarrow_{i,j}$ to capture all the possible states of an instance j of type c_i.

As described in Section 2, the system operation is modeled through a set of entities (e.g., ships, cars, trucks, etc..), each specifying its behavior through a process and offering their services through a set of process fragments. Formally an entity type is defined as:

Definition 5 (Entity Type). *An entity type $\mathcal{E}$ is a tuple $\mathcal{E} = \langle p, \mathcal{F}, C_{\mathcal{E}} \rangle$ where p is the entity behaviour (i.e., process), $\mathcal{F}$ is a set of process fragments provided by the entity and $C_{\mathcal{E}} \subseteq C_M$ is a set of context property types that characterize the entity itself (i.e., CarLocation, etc..). We denote with $p(\mathcal{E})$, $\mathcal{F}(\mathcal{E})$ the corresponding elements of an entity $\mathcal{E}$.*

3.2   Execution Model

As illustrated in Section 2, an adaptable process is a multi-layer process, where the top layer is the initial process and the intermediate layers correspond to the adaptations (i.e, incremental refinements, local adaptations and compensations). For this reason we model the *process execution* of an adaptable process as a stack of pairs process-state. In the pair, *process* is a fragment as defined in Definition 4, while *state* is the current state of the process instance. The bottom (first) pair refers to the core process and all the others refers to adaptation processes. The top (last) pair in the stack is the one that is currently under execution. Pairs can be pushed to the stack when process adaptation is performed and can be popped from the stack when, e.g., the process instance of the top pair terminates.

Definition 6. *(Process Execution) A process execution is a non-empty stack of pairs* $\phi = (p_1, s_1), (p_2, s_2), \ldots, (p_n, s_n)$, *where:* $p_i = \langle S_i, s_i^0, A_i, T_i, Ann_i, E_{n_i} \rangle \in \phi$ *is a process fragment, while* $s_i \in S_i$ *is the current state in the corresponding process fragments.*

Following Definition 5, we define *entity instance* as follows:

Definition 7   (Entity Instance). *An entity instance e of type $\mathcal{E}$ is a tuple $e = \langle p_e, \mathcal{F}, C_e \rangle$ where p_e is an instance of the process $p(\mathcal{E})$, $\mathcal{F} = \mathcal{F}(\mathcal{E})$ is a set of process fragments provided by the entity and $C_e = \{(i, j)\}$ s.t. $c_i \in C_{\mathcal{E}}$ and $l_{i,j} \in C$ is a set of pairs indicating the context property instances that characterize the entity instance.*

The running configuration of the whole system is defined by the runtime context state, by the process instances in the system, and by the set of available fragments.

Definition 8. *(Running System Configuration) A running system configuration is a tuple $S = \langle C_M, \mathcal{F}, C, \Omega \rangle$, where: C_M is the context model, $\mathcal{F}$ is the set of fragments available in the system, C is the runtime context state, and Ω is a set of pairs $(p_i, \mathcal{E}_j)$ where p_i is a process instance of $p(\mathcal{E}_j)$.*

3.3   Adaptation Need and Solution

Our framework can deal with two different adaptation needs [4,14]: the need for refining an abstract activity within a process instance, and the violation of the context precondition of an activity that has to be executed. The *refinement adaptation* is triggered whenever an abstract activity in a process instance needs to be refined. The aim of this mechanism is to automatically compose available process fragments taking into account the goal associated to the abstract activity and the current context

An adaptation need captures all the runtime system information at the time of the violations. We formalize it as follows:

Definition 9   (Adaptation Need). *An adaptation need is a tuple $\xi = \langle C_M, \mathcal{F}, C, \mathcal{G}, (p_i, \mathcal{E}_j) \rangle$, where: C_M is the context model, $\mathcal{F}$ is a set of process fragments available in the system annotated over context model C_M, C is the runtime context state, $\mathcal{G}$ is an adaptation goal over C, and $(p_i, \mathcal{E}_j)$ is the process instance p_i that needs to be adapted and $\mathcal{E}_j$ is the type of the entity to which the process instance belongs.*

We denote with $C(\xi)$ and $\mathcal{F}(\xi)$ the corresponding elements of an adaptation need ξ.

For expressing the adaptation goals, we exploit EAGLE [7] that allows the definition of goals as sets of context configurations, $\mathcal{G} \subseteq C$.

An *adaptation solution* is a process fragment f_{adapt} that is obtained as the composition of a set of fragments in $\mathcal{F}$. When executed from the current system configuration $\mathcal{S}$, and in absence of exogenous events corresponding to unpredicted situations, f_{adapt} ensures that the resulting runtime context state C satisfies the goal $\mathcal{G}(\xi)$ of the adaptation need ξ.

4 Formal Framework: Solution

The aim of this section is to present how the on-the-fly adaptation framework works. Starting from the elements introduced in the previous section we present: (i) how an adaptation problem is generated from an adaption need, (ii) how an adaptation problem is optimized, and (iii) how we can reuse or find a solution for that problem.

4.1 Adaptation Problem

With respect to an adaptation need, an *adaptation problem* captures all the relevant system information needed to resolve it. In our approach it is generated by calling first the function *reduce* of Figure 4 and then function *optimize* of Figure 5.

The *reduce* function takes as input an adaptation need ξ and returns a first version of an adaptation problem with the set of relevant fragments $\mathcal{F}_{rd}$ and context properties C_{rd} that can be used to satisfy the need. It is computed in two steps: **Step 1** (lines 3-5) analyzes each fragment $f \in \mathcal{F}$ and selects only those that can be used by the entity e_i ($e_i \in E_n(f)$); **Step 2** (lines 6-15) analyzes each fragment $f \in \mathcal{F}_{rd}$ and for each activity a that belongs to f it retrieves its annotations l (line 8). From all the context properties instances $l_{i,j} \in C$ the algorithm first selects only those whose type is part of the annotation l and that are defined by the entity e_i (lines 10-11). Afterwards, it selects all the context property instances that are used by the fragments provided by the entities that eventually can collaborate with e_i (lines 13-15).

Once a reduced version of the adaptation problem is obtained, we further optimize it by eliminating all states (transitions) in the context properties and process fragments that a priori will never be reached (triggered). The optimization algorithm is shown in Figure 5. The main function *optimize* (lines 27-40) takes as input an adaptation problem and returns its optimized version. The function repeats two optimization steps (lines 32-39) until the fixed point is reached.

```
1   function reduce(⟨C_M, F, C, G, (p_i, e_i)⟩)        9    foreach(l_{i,j} ∈ C)
2     F_rd = ∅; C_rd = ∅; C_{M_rd} = C_M;              10     if (l ↓_{c_i} ∈ l ∧ (i, j) ∈ C_e(e_i))
3     foreach(f ∈ F)                                   11       C_rd = C_rd ∪ {(l_{i,j})};
4       if(e_i ∈ E_n(f))                               12     else C_{M_rd} = C_{M_rd} \ {c_i}
5         F_rd = F_rd ∪ {f};                           13     foreach (ℰ ∈ E_n(f))
6     foreach(f ∈ F_rd)                                14       if(c_i ∈ C_ℰ(ℰ))
7       foreach(a ∈ A(f))                              15         C_rd = C_rd ∪ {(l_{i,j})};
8         l = Ann(a);                                  16   return (⟨C_{M_rd}, F_rd, C_rd, G⟩);
```

Fig. 4. Reduction algorithm

```
1  function fwdCntx(⟨L, l⁰, E, T⟩, ℱ, l₀)        21   A = A \ {a ∈ A : ∄(s, a, s') ∈ T : s, s' ∈ Sⁿᵉʷ};
2    Lⁿᵉʷ = {l₀};                                 22   T = T \ {(s, a, s') ∈ T : a ∉ A};
3    do                                            23   S = Sⁿᵉʷ;
4      Lᵒˡᵈ = Lⁿᵉʷ;                                24   return ⟨S, s⁰, A, T, Ann⟩;
5      Lⁿᵉʷ = Lⁿᵉʷ ∪ {l' ∈ L : ∃(l, e, l') ∈ T :  25
6             l ∈ Lⁿᵉʷ ∧ effVal(e, ℱ)};          26
7    while (Lᵒˡᵈ ≠ Lⁿᵉʷ);                          27   function optimize(⟨C_M, ℱ, l⁰_C, 𝒢⟩)
8    E = E \ {e ∈ E : ∄(l, e, l') ∈ T :           28     ℱⁿᵉʷ = ℱ; Cⁿᵉʷ_M = C_M;
9             l, l' ∈ Lⁿᵉʷ};                       29     do
10   T = T \ {(l, e, l') ∈ T : e ∉ E};            30       ℱᵒˡᵈ = ℱⁿᵉʷ; Cᵒˡᵈ_M = Cⁿᵉʷ_M;
11   L = Lⁿᵉʷ;                                     31       ℱⁿᵉʷ = ∅; Cⁿᵉʷ_M = ∅;
12   return ⟨L, l⁰, E, T⟩;                         32       foreach(c ∈ Cᵒˡᵈ_M)
13                                                  33         Cⁿᵉʷ_M = Cⁿᵉʷ_M ∪
14 function fwdFrgm(⟨S, s⁰, A, T, Ann⟩, C_M)       34           {fwdCntx(c, ℱᵒˡᵈ, l⁰_C ↓c))};
15   Sⁿᵉʷ = {s⁰};                                  35       foreach(f ∈ ℱᵒˡᵈ)
16   do                                            36         f' = fwdFrgm(f, Cⁿᵉʷ_M);
17     Sᵒˡᵈ = Sⁿᵉʷ;                                37         if(!hasEffect(f'))
18     Sⁿᵉʷ = Sⁿᵉʷ ∪ {s' ∈ S : ∃(s, a, s') ∈ T :  38           ℱⁿᵉʷ = ℱⁿᵉʷ ∪ {f'};
19            s ∈ Sⁿᵉʷ ∧ precVal(a, ℱ, C_M)};     39     while(ℱⁿᵉʷ ≠ ℱᵒˡᵈ ∨ Cⁿᵉʷ_M ≠ Cᵒˡᵈ_M);
20   while (Sᵒˡᵈ ≠ Sⁿᵉʷ);                          40     return ⟨Cⁿᵉʷ_M, ℱⁿᵉʷ, l⁰_C, 𝒢⟩;
```

Fig. 5. Optimization algorithm

Step 1 (lines 32-34) is the reachability analysis of context properties ($l^0_C \downarrow_c$ returns a state of context property c for context configuration l^0_C using set-based projection). We remark that context model C_M is the reduced one take form algorithm in Fig.4. The core of this step is function fwdCntx(c, $\mathcal{F}$, l_0) (lines 1-12), which figures out the portion of the original context property c that can be reached from the current state l_0 by executing fragments $\mathcal{F}$. It is implemented as a largest fixed point loop (lines 3-7), in which it is assumed that a context property can evolve only through transitions that can be triggered by available fragments (in lines 5-6 function effVal($e, \mathcal{F}$) is used to identify if there exists at least one action among $\mathcal{F}$ that triggers e). All the irrelevant elements are removed from the original context property (lines 8-10);

Step 2 (lines 35-38) is the reachability analysis for fragments exploiting fwdFrgm function (lines 13-23). Function fwdFrgm(f, C) figures out the portion of the original fragment f that can be reached from its current state in compliance with context C. It is implemented as a largest fixed point loop (lines 16-20), in which it is assumed that a fragment can evolve only through transition that can be executed in the current context model without violating their preconditions (in lines 18-19 function precVal(a, $\mathcal{F}$, C) is used to identify if action a belonging to some fragment among $\mathcal{F}$ can ever have its precondition satisfied in context model C). All the irrelevant elements are removed from the original fragment (lines 21-23). After fwdFrgm is called, we check (line 37) if the resulting fragment f' obtained can produce any contextual affect in the current contextual situation (using function hasEffect(f') we check if fragment f still contains at least one action that is either abstract or can potentially produces some affect). If it is the case, f' is added to the collection of fragments, if not, it is considered as useless (it by now means can change the context) and is filtered out.

We remark that any optimization in Step 1 may enable further optimization in Step 2 and vice versa. This is why the optimization process have to continue until a fixed point is reached.

4.2   Plan or Reuse

After that an adaptation problem has been optimized, the next step is to check if a solution for it has already been found in the past or not. Since the context C and the goal $\mathcal{G}$ of an adaptation problem are expressed in terms of property instances, we have to abstract them in a way that they refer to context model. To this end we define an *abstract adaptation problem* as:

Definition 10 (Abstract Adaptation Problem). *An* abstract adaptation problem *is a tuple* $\xi_{abs} = \langle C_M, C_{abs}, \mathcal{F}, C, \mathcal{G}, \mathcal{G}_{abs} \rangle$, *where:*

- C_M, $\mathcal{F}$, C, $\mathcal{G}$ *are as Definition 9 ;*
- C_{abs} *is a set of pairs of the form* $(i, l_{i,j})$ *where* c_i *is a property model (type), while* $l_{i,j}$ *is the state of its instance;*
- $\mathcal{G}_{abs}$ *is a set of pairs of the form* $(i, l_{i,j})$ *indicating that a context property of type* c_i *should reach the state* $l_{i,j}$.

We indicate with the symbol $\xi_{abs}\bullet$ the triplet $\langle C_{abs}, \mathcal{F}, \mathcal{G}_{abs} \rangle$ belonging to a abstract problem ξ_{abs}.

```
1   function abs (C_M, F, C, G)              10  function find((⟨C_M, C_abs, F, C,
2     C_abs = ∅;  G_abs = ∅;                 11                     G, G_abs, Ψ))
3     foreach( l_i,j ∈ C )                   12    ξ_abs• = ⟨C_abs, F, G_abs⟩;
4       C_abs = C_abs ∪ {(i, l_i,j)};        13    if( Ψ(ξ_abs•) == ⊥ )
5     foreach(l ∈ G)                         14      solution = planner(C_M, F, C, G);
6       foreach(l_i,j ∈ C )                  15      Ψ = Ψ[ξ_abs•, solution];
7         if(l ↓ c_i ∈ l}                    16      return solution;
8           G_abs = G_abs ∪ {(i, l_i,j)};    17    else
9     return ⟨C_abs, G_abs⟩;                 18      return Ψ(ξ_abs•);

19  function grnd(f, C_M, C)                 26    A(f)=A';
20    A' = ∅;                                27    return f;
21    foreach(a ∈ A(f))                      28
22      l = Ann(a);                          29  function reuse(C_M, F, C, G)
23      foreach c_i,j ∈ C                    30    ⟨C_abs, G_abs⟩ = abs(C_M, F, C, G);
24        if( l ↓ c_i ∈ l ∧ (j, l ↓ c_i) ∈ 𝕃_C ↓_i,j)  31    f = find((⟨C_M, C_abs, F, C, G, G_abs, Ψ⟩));
25          A' = A' ∪ {j, l ↓ c_i};          32    return grnd(f, C_M, C);
```

Fig. 6. Reuse Algorithm

Figure 6 shows the reuse algorithm (lines 29-32). It is composed by three steps: problem abstraction, finding a general solution and then grounding the solution to the actual runtime context. Once the abstract adaptation problem has been computed (function *abs* of Figure 6), then the function *find* checks if a solution for it has already been calculated in the past. To this end, we use a lookup function Ψ from abstract problems to fragments. If an abstract problem does not belong to the domain[1] of Ψ (e.g. the abstract problem is a new one) then the solution is calculated by invoking the adaptation engine and then Ψ is augmented with the new solution (line 15 of Figure 6). We define $\Psi[\xi_{abs}\bullet, f](\xi^1_{abs}\bullet)$ as:

$$\Psi[\xi_{abs}, f](\xi^1_{abs}\bullet) = \begin{cases} \Psi(\xi^1_{abs}\bullet) & \text{if } \xi^1_{abs}\bullet \neq \xi_{abs}\bullet \\ f & \text{otherwise} \end{cases}$$

---

[1] The function returns $\perp$ if a problem is not in its domain.

Solutions returned by the function *find* (and by the planner) are fragments, whose annotations are on context models and not on instances. We need then to ground the found solution to the level of the process that rose the adaptation, in terms of context property instances used by the process itself. To this end the function *grnd* that substitutes all the (context model) annotations of a fragment with runtime context state annotations.

5   Experiments and Results

The proposed framework has been implemented as an extension of the ASTRO-CAptEvo framework [14] and evaluated on a real world scenario based on the operation of car logistics in the Bremen sea port [3]. We show that it is effective in reducing the number of requested adaptations: while the situation where new adaptation are not needed is never reached (thus witnessing the need of dynamic adaptation), the number of such new adaptations decreases over time (thus making reuse more and more efficient). We also show that the approach seamlessly accommodates situations where previous adaptations are not valid any-more, e.g., due to changes in the requirements or in the available fragments. The specification of the CLS we used to evaluate our approach contains 29 entity types, 69 process fragment models and 40 types of context properties.

During the experiments[2], we collected the number of adaptation cases and the time to generate an adaptation solution for each case. We remark that preliminary optimization steps described in Section 4 require significantly less time than planning itself and thus do not contribute dramatically to the overall solution search time.

In the first experiment we measure the effectiveness of the proposed optimization approach, i.e., of the possibility to reuse previous solutions. We conducted four simulations in different configurations, each one differing from the others in terms of frequency of ship arrivals, car damages and delivery orders. The chart in Figure 7 plots on the X-axis the number of adaptation cases (the first 2500 for each simulation) and on the Y-axis the number of unique adaptation problems (i.e., number of adaptations actually computed in the presence of our reuse mechanism). The dashed curve represents the old (naive) approach without the reuse mechanism. Indeed the curve is linear for all the experiments, meaning that for each adaptation problem that comes a solution is calculated from scratch. The other curves correspond to the four simulations with the reuse. In the worst case, we have 118 unique adaptation problems out of 2500 adaptation cases, that is in 94.3% of the cases we are able to reuse existing solutions. On average for the four simulations, the reuse rate was 95.5%. In terms of time (not shown in the figure), the computation of all 2500 adaptations solutions *without* adaptation problem optimization required 4821 seconds, while the optimization mechanism reduced this time to 306 seconds (6.34% of the non-optimized time). Figure 7 also shows that new adaptation problems (where reuse was not possible) keep emerging through all the simulation, even though their rate reduced over time. This indicates the importance of on-the-fly adaptation as opposed to static predefined solutions. Indeed, after the initial phase (first 1000 adaptation cases) new adaptation problems emerge quite rarely, but

---

[2] All the experiments were executed on a Linux machine with 4-core Intel i7 CPU running at 2.3GHz with 16GB of memory.

even after 2500 cases they do not disappear completely (i.e., the complete reuse was not possible).

In order to see how the new framework can deal with highly dynamic systems, we measure the impact of various dynamic factors (in particular, changes in requirements and fragments) on its operation and performance. More precisely, we compare the normal simulation of the system with the one where two dynamic factors are enabled. These factors are (i) the introduction of a new type of entity (in our case, the luxury car) and (ii) the change in a single fragment (in our case, we change the procedure for storing cars in the consignment area). In the first case, all the adaptation solutions involving luxury cars have to be generated anew (no reuse is possible). In the second case, all the adaptation cases involving the changed fragment have also to be regenerated. Both dynamic changes result in increase of a number of unique adaptation cases (and in additional workload for the composition engine). To reflect this in figures, through the simulation we measure the number of calls to the composition engine for the last 40 adaptation cases (thus reflecting the number of new adaptation problems for which reuse is not possible). These data are shown in Figure 8. The solid red line reflect the rate of new adaptation problems attributed to the normal run of the system, while the dashed blue one reflects only those new adaptation cases that were triggered by dynamic factors. From the red line it can be seen that the high rate of new adaptation cases is common for the initial phase of the simulation (first 800 − 1000 adaptation cases) but even after 2000 cases into the simulation it is still non-zero. From the blue

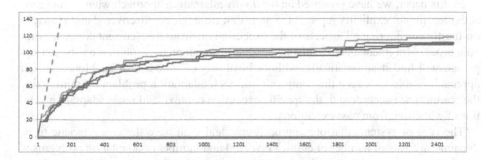

Fig. 7. New adaptation problems versus total number of adaptation needs

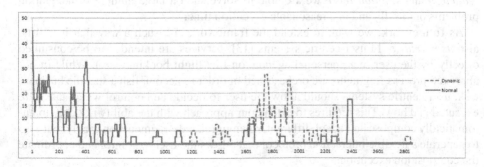

Fig. 8. Impact of dynamic factors on the number of new adaptation problems

line, it is evident that new adaptation problems start to emerge after 1200 cases (which actually corresponds to the introduction of a new entity type) and has a prominent peak around 1700-th case (which corresponds to the change in the fragment). It is worth to note that introducing a new entity brings immediately just a small amount of new adaptation problems (three peaks between the 1200-th and 1600-th problem) while the change in the fragment that is involved in many various adaptations produces considerable immediate surge. Again, after having computed the new problems brought by the changes, the system behaves as the normal execution (e.g. the ratio of new problems keeps decreasing but never reaches 0).

6 Related Work and Conclusion

In the community of Service Oriented Computing (SOC), various approaches supporting adaptation have been defined, e.g., triggering repairing strategies as a consequence of a requirement violation [15], and optimizing QoS of service-based applications [11,17,19], or for satisfying some application constraints [8,16]. Repairing strategies could be specified by means of policies to manage the dynamism of the execution environment [1,6]. The aim of the strategies proposed by the aforementioned approaches range from service selection to rebinding and application reconfiguration [12,18]. These are interesting features, but cannot deal with complex and dynamic service-based systems where context-awareness and adaptivity are key characteristics.

In this paper, we have proposed an *on-the-fly* adaptation approach where adaptation activities are not explicitly represented at design time but are discovered and managed on-the-fly considering all aspects of the execution environment (current context, available process fragments, etc.). This means that if an adaptation solution exists, our approach will find it automatically, without involving off-line activities. Moreover, our approach is able to reduce the complexity of each adaptation problem by minimizing the search space according to the specific execution context, and reuse adaptation solutions by learning from past executions.

The type of systems that our approach can deal with have the characteristic to be dynamic in terms of number of entities involved and number of adaptation problems to consider. At the same time each adaptation problem involves a potentially very large set of available fragments. Thanks to the two steps defined in our approach: *problem reduction* and *solution reuse* we are able to solve such a large number of adaptation problems on-the-fly and in a reasonable execution time.

As future work, we want to extend the framework in a such a way that it will be also *user-centric*. In user-centric systems [13], services are intended to be consumed directly by the user (e.g., personal agenda, on-line flight booking, etc.). While in our approach process fragments are orchestrated in order to accomplish a specific business task, user centric systems should allow the user to decide and control which tasks are executed and how. This requires to extend our approach with the ability not only to automatically compose and adapt different, often unrelated, fragments on the fly, but also to generate a flexible interaction protocol that allows the user to control and coordinate the composition execution.

Acknowledgment. This work is partially funded by the 7th Framework EU-FET project 600792 ALLOW Ensembles.

References

[1] Baresi, L., Guinea, S., Pasquale, L.: Self-healing BPEL processes with Dynamo and the JBoss rule engine. In: Proc. of ESSPE 2007, pp. 11–20. ACM (2007)

[2] Bertoli, P., Pistore, M., Traverso, P.: Automated composition of web services via planning in asynchronous domains. Artif. Intell. 174(3-4), 316–361 (2010)

[3] Böse, F., Piotrowski, J.: Autonomously controlled storage management in vehicle logistics applications of RFID and mobile computing systems. International Journal of RT Technologies: Research an Application 1(1), 57–76 (2009)

[4] Bucchiarone, A., Marconi, A., Pistore, M., Raik, H.: Dynamic Adaptation of Fragment-based and Context-aware Business Processes. In: Proc. of ICWS 2012, pp. 33–41 (2012)

[5] Bucchiarone, A., Antares Mezzina, C., Pistore, M.: Captlang: a language for context-aware and adaptable business processes. In: Proc. of VaMoS 2013, pp. 12:1–12:5. ACM (2013)

[6] Colombo, M., Di Nitto, E., Mauri, M.: SCENE: A service composition execution environment supporting dynamic changes disciplined through rules. In: Dan, A., Lamersdorf, W. (eds.) ICSOC 2006. LNCS, vol. 4294, pp. 191–202. Springer, Heidelberg (2006)

[7] Dal Lago, U., Pistore, M., Traverso, P.: Planning with a Language for Extended Goals. In: Proc. of AAAI 2002 (2002)

[8] de Leoni, M.: Adaptive Process Management in Highly Dynamic and Pervasive Scenarios. In: Proc. of YR-SOC, pp. 83–97 (2009)

[9] Eberle, H., Unger, T., Leymann, F.: Process fragments. In: Meersman, R., Dillon, T., Herrero, P. (eds.) OTM 2009, Part I. LNCS, vol. 5870, pp. 398–405. Springer, Heidelberg (2009)

[10] Marconi, A., Pistore, M., Traverso, P.: Automated Composition of Web Services: the ASTRO Approach. IEEE Data Eng. Bull. 31(3), 23–26 (2008)

[11] Mirandola, R., Potena, P.: A qos-based framework for the adaptation of service-based systems. Scalable Computing: Practice and Experience 12(1), 63–78 (2011)

[12] Pfeffer, H., Linner, D., Steglich, S.: Dynamic adaptation of workflow based service compositions. In: Huang, D.-S., Wunsch II, D.C., Levine, D.S., Jo, K.-H. (eds.) ICIC 2008. LNCS, vol. 5226, pp. 763–774. Springer, Heidelberg (2008)

[13] Pistore, M., Traverso, P., Paolucci, M., Wagner, M.: From software services to a future internet of services. In: Proc. of FIA 2009, pp. 183–192 (2009)

[14] Raik, H., Bucchiarone, A., Khurshid, N., Marconi, A., Pistore, M.: Astro-captevo: Dynamic context-aware adaptation for service-based systems. In: Proc. of SERVICES 2012, pp. 385–392 (2012)

[15] Spanoudakis, G., Zisman, A., Kozlenkov, A.: A service discovery framework for service centric systems. In: Proc. of IEEE SCC 2005, pp. 251–259 (2005)

[16] Verma, K., Gomadam, K., Sheth, A.P., Miller, J.A., Wu, Z.: The METEOR-S approach for configuring and executing dynamic web processes. Technical report, University of Georgia, Athens (2005)

[17] Wang, C., Pazat, J.L.: A two-phase online prediction approach for accurate and timely adaptation decision. In: Proc. of SCC 2012, pp. 218–225. IEEE Computer Society (2012)

[18] Yan, Y., Poizat, P., Zhao, L.: Self-adaptive service composition through graphplan repair. In: Proc. of ICWS 2010, pp. 624–627 (2010)

[19] Zhai, Y., Zhang, J., Lin, K.: Soa middleware support for service process reconfiguration with end-to-end qos constraints. In: Proc. of ICWS 2009, pp. 815–822 (2009)

WT-LDA: User Tagging Augmented LDA for Web Service Clustering

Liang Chen[1], Yilun Wang[1], Qi Yu[2],
Zibin Zheng[3], and Jian Wu[1]

[1] Zhejiang University, China
[2] Rochester Institute of Technology, USA
[3] The Chinese University of Hong Kong, HK
{cliang,yilunwang,wujian2000}@zju.edu.cn, qi.yu@rit.edu,
zibinzheng@cse.cuhk.edu.hk

Abstract. Clustering Web services that groups together services with similar functionalities helps improve both the accuracy and efficiency of the Web service search engines. An important limitation of existing Web service clustering approaches is that they solely focus on utilizing WSDL (Web Service Description Language) documents. There has been a recent trend of using user-contributed tagging data to improve the performance of service clustering. Nonetheless, these approaches fail to completely leverage the information carried by the tagging data and hence only trivially improve the clustering performance. In this paper, we propose a novel approach that seamlessly integrates tagging data and WSDL documents through augmented Latent Dirichlet Allocation (LDA). We also develop three strategies to preprocess tagging data before being integrated into the LDA framework for clustering. Comprehensive experiments based on real data and the implementation of a Web service search engine demonstrate the effectiveness of the proposed LDA-based service clustering approach.

1 Introduction

The explosive growth of Web services poses key challenges for Web service discovery. Existing service discovery approaches rely on either UDDI (*Universal Description Discovery and Integration*) or Web service search engines to locate matching services. As many service providers choose to publish their Web services through their own websites instead of using public registries, the number of Web services in public UDDI registries decreases significantly. A recent study shows that more than 53% of the UDDI business registry registered services are invalid, whereas 92% of Web services cached by Web service search engines are valid and active [1]. Therefore, using search engines to search and discover Web services becomes more common and effective than UDDI service registries [17].

Existing Web service searching engines primarily focus on keyword-based matching on names, input/output parameters, and bindings defined in the Web service description file [1]. In this case, if a service description does not match

S. Basu et al. (Eds.): ICSOC 2013, LNCS 8274, pp. 162–176, 2013.
© Springer-Verlag Berlin Heidelberg 2013

the query term, it won't be discovered even though the service may provide the user desired functionality. As it is difficult for a casual user to choose keywords that match the terms in a service description, keyword-based search usually suffers from low recall, where services containing synonyms or concepts at a higher (or lower) level of abstraction will not be discovered. As an example, a service named "Mobile Messaging Service" may not be returned for the query term "SMS" submitted by a user even though they describe the same concept. To handle this issue, service clustering has been recently exploited to improve the search quality [19,20]. By clustering Web services together, services in the same cluster are expected to provide similar functionalities so that they can be discovered together as a group. However, existing service clustering algorithms mainly rely on the WSDL descriptions of services, which usually contain very limited terms, some of which are even not proper words. Hence, these algorithms may lead to low clustering quality, which will negatively affect the accuracy of service discovery.

Recently, some real-world Web service search engines, such as *Seekda!*, have allowed users to manually annotate Web services using tags. Tags provide meaningful descriptions of objects and allow users to organize and index their contents. Tagging data has been proved to be very useful in many domains such as multimedia, information retrieval, data mining, and so on. Figure 1 shows two examples of Web service tags in *Seekda!* service search engine. *MeteorologyWS* in Fig. 1(a) is a weather forecasting Web service, which has two tags, *weather* and *waether*. However, there is no word *weather* in its service name or WSDL document. Thus, it is hard for this service to be clustered into the weather cluster. Further, this service will be hard to be retrieved without utilizing the tag information, if the query term is *weather*. Besides, the tag *waether* is also useful as some users may make a mistake in the typing process and use *waether* as the query term. As a service provider, one may have different naming convention and prefer to use *Meteorology* instead of *weather* in the generated WSDL file, as shown in Fig. 1(a). On the other hand, service users are likely to use the same tag to annotate services with similar functionality. Therefore, leveraging the tagging information along with the WSDL can help improve the quality of service clustering.

(a)   (b)

Fig. 1. Example of Web Service Tags

In this paper, we propose to augment the Latent Dirichlet Allocation (LDA) model [3,13], referred to as *WT-LDA*, to seamlessly integrate WSDL documents and service tags for service clustering. LDA has been demonstrated to be an effective tool in topic modeling and document clustering in the text domain. Specifically, *WT-LDA* models each service as a distribution of a set of topics and functionally similar services are expected to be represented by a similar distribution of topics. Service tags are also used to determine the topics of the services. We assess the effectiveness of the proposed *WT-LDA* via real-world Web services collected from Seekda!. Preliminary experimental results reveal that the performance of *WT-LDA* is affected by Web service with few tags or many meaningless tags. To tackle this issue, we propose three strategies to preprocess service tags before being used by *WT-LDA*. The experiment results in Section 5 demonstrate that our tag preprocessing strategies help improve the performance of *WT-LDA*. The major contributions of this paper can be summarized as follows:

1. We propose a novel Web service clustering approach *WT-LDA* based on a probabilistic graphic model (i.e., LDA), in which both the WSDL documents and service tags are effectively utilized.
2. We propose three tag preprocessing strategies to improve the performance of *WT-LDA*.
3. We crawl 15,968 real Web services to evaluate the performance of *WT-LDA* and three tag preprocessing strategies.

The rest of this paper is organized as follows. Section 2 gives an overview of the related work on Web service discovery and clustering. Section 3 details the proposed *WT-LDA*, while Section 4 presents the tag preprocessing strategies that help improve the performance of *WT-LDA*. Section 5 shows the experimental results and Section 6 concludes the paper.

2   Related Work

With the wide adoption of service computing and cloud computing, Web service discovery becomes a popular research topic that attracts significant attention. Recently, Web service clustering [8,10,21] has been demonstrated as an effective tool to boost the performance of Web service discovery. Most service clustering algorithms rely on the computation of similarity between services, which can be (1) semantic based and (2) non-semantic based. Ontology is utilized to compute the semantic similarity between Web services in many studies [2,6,11,15]. Specifically, Cristina et al. [11] propose to use an ant-based method to cluster Web services based on semantic similarity. Sun et al. [15] propose to adopt Petri net as the modeling language for the specification of a service process model, and cluster services based on functional similarity and process similarity. In this paper, we focus on the clustering of non-semantic Web services as most services are described using the WSDL standard, which focuses on the syntactic description of services.

Several approaches have been developed for the calculation of similarity between non-semantic Web services [7,16]. Liu et al. propose to extract 4 features, i.e., *content, context, host name, and service name*, from the WSDL document to cluster Web services [16]. They take the process of clustering as the preprocessor to discovery, aiming to building a search engine that crawls and clusters non-semantic Web services. Khalid et al. also propose to extract features from WSDL documents to cluster Web services [7]. Different from the work in [16], a set of different features, including *content, types, messages, ports, and service name* are extracted from the WSDL documents. SVD based and matrix factorization based approaches are adopted to achieve the co-clustering of services and operations in [19,20]. Co-clustering exploits the duality relationship between services and operations to achieve better clustering quality than one-side clustering.

Despite WSDL-based clustering being widely adopted, the clustering performance is rather limited as only WSDL documents are employed. With the development of Web service community, more and more tags are annotated to Web services by users. These tags can be employed to enhance the accuracy of service discovery. However, limited work has exploited tagging data for service discovery. In our preliminary work [4,5,18], we investigated the benefits of utilizing both WSDL documents and tagging data to cluster Web services. The findings motivate our present study. In this paper, we improve the performance of Web service clustering by introducing a novel LDA based approach to explore the knowledge behind WSDL & tags and by proposing three tag preprocessing strategies to improve the performance of service clustering.

3   WT-LDA Based Service Clustering

In this section, we first describe the proposed architecture for Web service discovery framework in Section 3.1, and then introduce data preprocessing component and the probabilistic graphic model of *WT-LDA* in Section 3.2 and Section 3.3, respectively.

3.1   Web Service Discovery Framework

Figure 2 shows the proposed architecture for Web service discovery framework, which consists of two major components: data preprocessing and service discovery. In the first component, both WSDL documents and tags of Web services are crawled from the Internet, which will be used for service clustering. Specifically, we use the meaningful words in WSDL documents as the feature words to construct a probabilistic graphic model, i.e., *WT-LDA*. After we extract feature words and tags from Web services, the *WT-LDA* is used to cluster Web services. Since data preprocessing and service clustering are conducted offline, the efficiency of service discovery can be guaranteed. Hence, the focus will be placed on accuracy. In the second component, clustered result of *WT-LDA* will be used to improve the search result of a Web service search engine. When a query term is sent to the Web service search engine, it can return a more accurate search result by leveraging the clustered result.

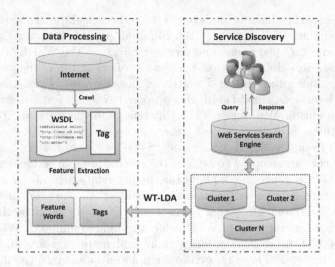

Fig. 2. Framework for Web service Discovery

3.2   Data Preprocessing

As discussed above, we extract the meaningful words from WSDL documents as the feature words, then jointly model these feature words and tags for the purpose of clustering of Web services. In this part, we describe the details in data preprocessing component.

1. **Building an original vector**. In this step, we perform tokenization over the entire WSDL document to produce the original content vector.
2. **Suffix Stripping**. Words with a common stem will usually have the same meaning, for example, *connect*, *connected*, *connecting*, *connection*, and *connections* all have the same stem *connect* [16]. We strip the suffix of all these words that have the same stem by using the Porter stemmer [12]. After the step of suffix stripping, a new content vector is produced.
3. **Pruning**. In this step, we remove two kinds of words from the content vector. The first kind is XML tags, such as *s:element*, *s:complexType*, and *wsdl:operation*, which are not meaningful for the comparison of content vectors. Content words are typically nouns, verbs or adjectives, and are often contrasted with function words which have little or no contribution to the meanings of texts. Therefore, the second kind of word to be removed is function word. Church *et al.* state that the function words could be distinguished from content words using a Poisson distribution to model word occurrence in documents [9]. Typically, a way to decide whether a word w in the content vector is a function word is by computing the degree of overestimation of the observed document frequency of the word w, denoted by n_w using Poisson distribution. The overestimation factor can be calculated as follows.

$$\Lambda_w = \frac{\hat{n_w}}{n_w}, \tag{1}$$

where $\hat{n}_w$ is the estimated document frequency of the word w. Specifically, the word with higher value of Λ_w has higher possibility to be a content word. In this paper, we set a threshold Λ_T for Λ_w, and take the words which have Λ_w higher than threshold as content words. The value of threshold Λ_T is set as follows:

$$\Lambda_T = \begin{cases} avg[\Lambda] & \text{if}(avg[\Lambda] > 1); \\ 1 & \text{otherwise} \end{cases} \tag{2}$$

where $avg[\Lambda]$ is the average value of the observed document frequency of all words considered. After the process of pruning, we can obtain a new content vector, in which both XML tags and function words are removed.

4. **Refining**. Words with very high occurrence frequencies are likely to be too general to discriminate between Web services. After the step of pruning, we implement a step of refining, in which words with too general meanings are removed. Clustering based approaches were adopted to handle this problem in some related work [7,16].

After the above four steps, we obtain the meaningful words in a WSDL document.

3.3   WT-LDA

The proposed *WT-LDA* model extends Latent Dirichlet Allocation and takes both the content of WSDL documents and the user-contributed tagging data into consideration. *WT-LDA* can find short description of members of a collection that enable efficient processing of large collections of WSDL documents while preserving the essential statistical relationship that are useful for Web services clustering. Main advantages of the proposed *WT-LDA* model are listed below:

1. It provides a generative probabilistic graphic model of WSDL documents and a probabilistic view to extract latent variables from WSDL documents which can significantly improve the clustering result of Web services
2. It measures the word co-occurrence from heterogeneous service description in WSDL documents, infer the topic distribution of each WSDL document and the result topic vectors can contribute to Web services clustering.
3. It takes tagging data of WSDL documents into consideration while unique tag has its own distribution of topics. Tags with similar meaning or function have similar distribution of topics. Thus the content of WSDL documents as well as tagging data can contribute to the clustering of Web services.

In the model of *WT-LDA*, tag related to one document is chosen uniformly at random for each word in that document. Each tag has its own distinct contribution to the topic distribution of the documents. Thus, the topic distribution corresponding to each tag of Web service is drawn from Dirichlet hyper-parameter α. The word distribution specific to each topic is drawn from the Dirichlet hyper-parameter β. Then, a topic is drawn from the topic distribution according to the chosen tag in the document, and the word is generated from that chosen topic.

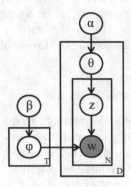
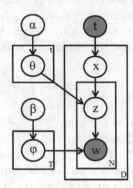

Fig. 3. Probabilistic graphical models of LDA and WT-LDA: the nodes denote random variables, while the edges indicate conditional dependencies. The shaded nodes are observed variables (words); the unshaded nodes are latent variables (topics). The outer rectangles, or "plates", indicate repeated samples.

WT-LDA is a generative model of user-contributed tagging data and words in the WSDL documents. The generative process can be described as follows:

1. Draw T multinomial ϕ_z from a Dirichlet prior β, one for each topic z
2. For each tag t_d in document d, draw a multinomial θ_{t_d} from a Dirichlet prior α
3. For each word w_{di} in document d:
   (a) Draw a tag x_{di} uniformly from tags t_d in document d;
   (b) Draw a topic z_{di} from multinomial $\theta_{x_{di}}$;
   (c) Draw a word w_{di} from multinomial $\phi_{z_{di}}$;

The probabilistic graphical model corresponding to *WT-LDA* is shown in Fig. 3. As a Web service clustering model, each topic is associated with a distribution ϕ over words, drawn independently from a Dirichlet prior β. x indicates the tag responsible for a given word, chosen from t_d, and each tag has a distribution θ over topics generated from a Dirichlet prior α. The topic distribution of tags and the word distribution of topics is combined to generate a topic z_{di}, then a word w_{di} is drawn from the chosen topic.

As shown in the above process, the posterior distribution of topics depends on the information from both content of the WSDL documents and the tags. *WT-LDA* parameterization is given as follows:

$$
\begin{aligned}
\theta_x | \alpha &\sim \text{Dirichlet}(\alpha) \\
\phi_z | \beta &\sim \text{Dirichlet}(\beta) \\
x_{di} | t_d &\sim \text{Uniform}(t_d) \\
z_{di} | \theta_{x_{di}} &\sim \text{Multinomial}(\theta_{x_{di}}) \\
w_{di} | \phi_{z_{di}} &\sim \text{Multinomial}(\phi_{z_{di}})
\end{aligned}
$$

We employ Gibbs sampling as a common means of statistical inference to infer *WT-LDA*. Note that Gibbs sampling provides a simple and effective method to estimate the latent variables under Dirichlet priors and observed variables given by the content of the WSDL documents and the user-contributed tagging data of corresponding documents. There are four latent variables in *WT-LDA* model: the word distribution of topic ϕ_z, the topic distribution of tag θ_x, the tag assignment x_{di} of each word, and the topic assignment z_{di} of each word. Gibbs sampling construct a Markov chain that calculate the conditional distribution $P(z_{di} = j, x_{di} = k|w_i = m, z_{-di}, x_{-di}, t_d)$ where z_{-di} represents the topic assignments for all tokens except w_{di}, x_{-di} represents the tag assignments for all tokens except w_{di}, the conditional probability is shown below:

$$P(z_{di} = j, x_{di} = k|w_i = m, \mathbf{z}_{-di}, \mathbf{x}_{-di}, \mathbf{t}_d) \propto \frac{m_{x_{di}z_{di}} + \alpha_{z_{di}}}{\sum_{v=1}^{V}(m_{x_{di}v} + \alpha_v)} * \frac{n_{z_{di}w_{di}} + \beta_{w_{di}}}{\sum_{v=1}^{V}(n_{z_{di}v} + \beta_v)} \tag{3}$$

where n_{zw} is the number of tokens of word w are assigned to topic z, m_{xz} represent the number of tokens in tag x are assigned to topic z.

In Gibbs Sampling, we sample z_{di} and x_{di} by fixing z_{-di} and x_{-di}. The other two latent variables: the word distribution of topic ϕ and the topic distribution of tag θ are estimated from samples by:

$$\theta_{xz} = \frac{m_{x_{di}z_{di}} + \alpha_{z_{di}}}{\sum_{v=1}^{V}(m_{x_{di}v} + \alpha_v)}, \phi_{zw} = \frac{n_{z_{di}w_{di}} + \beta_{w_{di}}}{\sum_{v=1}^{V}(n_{z_{di}v} + \beta_v)} \tag{4}$$

For document d, we sum over all the θ_x where $x \in t_d$ to compute the topic distribution of document d. Therefore, we can cluster web service by θ and get the detail information of each cluster by ϕ.

4 Tag Preprocessing Strategies

Some inherent properties of Web service tagging data, e.g., uneven tag distribution and noisy tags, impact the reliability of tagging data. In this section, we introduce three tag preprocessing strategies to make the tagging data more reliable and suitable for the proposed *WT-LDA* model to further improve the service clustering accuracy.

4.1 Tag Recommendation

Through our observation, some Web services, especially those newly deployed ones, do not have tags. In this case, we have to assign some initial tags from the textual features of the services first by using approaches such as TF-IDF, and then use a tag recommendation approach to improve the quality of the tagging data. For the Web services with few user-contributed tags, tag recommendation approaches could be directly employed. Typically, an initial set of tags $\mathcal{I}_s$ associated with a Web service s is provided to the recommendation method, which outputs a set of related tags $\mathcal{C}_s$, where $\mathcal{I}_s \bigcap \mathcal{C}_s = \emptyset$. Tag co-occurrence is a commonly used method for tag recommendation.

Figure 4 shows an example of tag co-occurrence based recommendation framework, in which it first generates candidate tags based on original tags by using tag co-occurrence, and then obtains the recommended tags by using some tag ranking strategies, e..g, *Sum* and *Vote* [14]. Due to the space limitation, we do not give the details of tag recommendation. In this paper, tag co-occurrence and *Vote* ranking strategy are employed for recommendation.

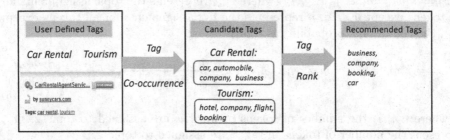

Fig. 4. An Example of Framework for Web Service Tag Recommendation

4.2   High-Frequency Tags

In order to cluster Web services into the exact cluster they belong to, we expect tags of Web services provide accurate information of distinct property between different clusters and common property shared among the Web services in same cluster. As a result, we believe high-frequency tag, which means the unique tag of one Web service that occurs with a high frequency among all tags of the Web service, as an important evidence for Web service clustering.

4.3   Tag Preprocessing Strategies

Based on the above analysis, we present three tag preprocessing strategies to improve the performance of *WT-LDA*

1. **Original tags**. In this strategy, only the original user-contributed tags are provided for *WT-LDA* based Web service clustering.
2. **Original tags + Recommended tags**. In this strategy, we mix original tags with recommended tags generated by the proposed approach in Section 4.1.
3. **High-frequency tag**. In this strategy, we select the high-frequency tag of each Web service for clustering.

5   Experiments

In this section, we first compare the performance of different Web service clustering approaches and then study the performances of tag preprocessing strategies.

Table 1. Experimental Data Description

WSDL Document	185
Word	62,941
Token	1481
Tag	888
Recommended Tag	799

5.1 Experiment Setup

To evaluate the performance of Web service clustering approaches and tag pre-processing strategies, we crawl 15,968 real Web services from the Web service search engine Seekda!. For each Web service, we get the data of service name, WSDL document, tags, and the name of service provider. We publicize the crawled dataset via http://www.zjujason.com. Further, to implement the overall process of service discovery, we build a Web service search engine *Titan*, which could be accessed via http://ccnt.zju.edu.cn:8080.

As the manual creation of ground truth is an expensive process, we randomly select 185 Web services from the dataset we crawled to evaluate the performance of Web service clustering. We perform a manual classification of these 185 Web services to serve as the ground truth for the clustering approaches. Specifically, we distinguish the following categories: "Weather", "Stock", "SMS", "Finance", "Tourism", and "University". There are 28 Web services in "Weather" category, 21 Web services in "Stock" category, 37 Web services in "SMS" category, 21 Web services in "Finance" category, 31 Web services in "Tourism" category, 27 Web services in "University" category. 20 Web services are randomly selected from other categories as noise in our experiment. Limited by space, we don't show the detailed information of these Web services. The experimental data description is given in Table 1.

All experiments are implemented with JDK 1.7.0-10, Eclipse 3.6.0. They are conducted on a Dell OptiPlex 390 machine with an *3.10 GHZ Intel Core I3 CPU* and *2GB RAM*, running *Windows 7*.

5.2 Evaluation Metric

To evaluate the performance of Web service clustering, we introduce two metrics: Precision and Recall, which are widely adopted in the information retrieval community.

$$Precision_{c_i} = \frac{succ(c_i)}{succ(c_i) + mispl(c_i)} \tag{5}$$

$$Recall_{c_i} = \frac{succ(c_i)}{succ(c_i) + missed(c_i)}, \tag{6}$$

where $succ(c_i)$ is the number of services successfully placed into cluster c_i, $mispl(c_i)$ is the number of services that are incorrectly placed into cluster c_i,

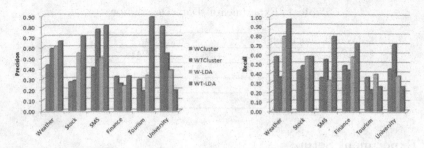

Fig. 5. Performance Comparison of Four Web Service Clustering Approaches

and $missed(c_i)$ is the number of services that should be placed into c_i but are placed into another cluster.

5.3 Performance of Web Service Clustering

In this section, we compare the performance of four Web service clustering approaches, including two state-of-the-art clustering approaches and two versions of the proposed *WT-LDA* approach. The details of these algorithms are given below:

1. **WCluster**. In this approach, Web services are clustered according to the semantic WSDL-level similarity between Web services. This approach has been adopted in some related works [4,7,16].
2. **WTCluster**. In this approach, both WSDL documents and the tagging data are employed to cluster the Web services according to the composite semantic similarity [4].
3. **W-LDA**. In this approach, we extract feature words from WSDL documents and cluster Web service without any additional information using traditional LDA approach.
4. **WT-LDA**. In this approach, we utilized both feature words from WSDL documents and the user-contributed tagging data, then cluster Web services using *WT-LDA* approach proposed in Section 3.

Figure 5 shows the performance comparison of above 4 Web service clustering approaches. Empirically, we set $\alpha = 0.01$, $\beta = 0.01$ and run Gibbs-sampling for 1000 iterations in the proposed *WT-LDA* approach. It can be discovered that the proposed *WT-LDA* outperforms the other three approaches in most cases in terms of precision and recall, respectively. Further, it can be found the addition of tagging data improves the performance of service clustering, as *WT-LDA* outperforms *W-LDA*, and *WTCluster* outperforms *WCluster* in most cases.

Table 2 shows the average precision and recall values of the above four service clustering approaches. It can also be found that the proposed *WT-LDA* has the best performance in terms of average precision and average recall. Further, we can also find that *WTCluster* outperforms *WCluster*, and *WT-LDA* outperforms

Table 2. Average Precision and Recall of Four Web Service Clustering Approaches

Clustering Approach	Precision	Recall
WCluster	0.4219	0.4378
WTCluster	0.4387	0.4553
W − LDA	0.4350	0.5017
WT − LDA	**0.5966**	**0.5919**

Fig. 6. Word Distribution of Two Clusters: the left cluster is about weather forecast, while the right cluster is about stock

W-LDA. As we discussed above, the user-contributed tagging data of Web services contains a lot of information, such as service function, location, and other semantical information. Utilizing these information improves the performance of Web service clustering.

Figure 6 shows the word distribution of two clusters, for each of which we pick words with top ten probability in each cluster and the size of word in Fig. 6 is corresponding to its probability. After observing the services in each cluster, we find the services in the first cluster are most about weather forecast, which matches the word distribution in the left figure. And the services in the second cluster are most about stock, which also matches the word distribution in the right figure. Thus, the proposed *WT-LDA* is quite effective. Compared with traditional unsupervised clustering approach, one additional advantage of *WT-LDA* is that user could directly know the main functionality of services in one cluster, instead of observing all services in the cluster.

5.4 Evaluation of Tag Preprocessing Strategies

In this section, we compare the performance of the proposed three tag preprocessing strategies with the one without tagging data. The four clustering approaches for comparison are detailed as follows:

1. *No Tag.* In this approach, Web services are clustered according to word features from WSDL documents. We cluster Web services using the traditional LDA approach.
2. *Original Tag.* In this approach, we utilize both the WSDL documents and the original tags, and cluster the Web services using the proposed *WT-LDA*.

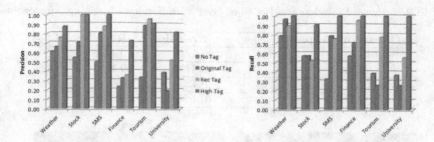

Fig. 7. Performance Comparison of Tag Preprocessing Strategies

Table 3. Average Precision and Recall of Four Tag Strategies

Clustering Approach	Precision	Recall
No Tag	0.4350	0.5017
Original Tag	0.5966	0.5919
Rec Tag	0.7442	0.7426
High Tag	**0.8882**	**0.9841**

3. **Rec Tag.** In this approach, we utilize the WSDL documents, the original tags, and the recommended tags. Then we cluster the Web services using the proposed *WT-LDA*.
4. **High Tag.** In this approach, we utilize both the WSDL documents and the high-frequency tags, and cluster the Web services using *WT-LDA*.

Figure 7 shows the performance comparison of the above four approaches. It can be found that the *High Tag* approach outperforms the other three ones in most cases in terms of precision and recall, respectively. This is because the high-frequency tags are helpful for distinguishing services, while the addition of low-frequency tags has a negative effect. From Fig. 7, it can also be found that the *Rec Tag* approach outperforms *Original Tag* approach in most cases, which means the recommended relevant tags improves the performance of service clustering.

Table 3 shows the average precision and recall values of the above four clustering approaches. It can be found that the *High Tag* has the best performance in terms of both average precision and recall, while the performance of *No Tag* is the worst. This can be easily understood because *No Tag* does not utilize tagging data, which contains a lot of meaningful information. Similarly, it can be observed that *Rec Tag* outperforms *Original Tag*. Therefore, it can be found that the *High Tag* strategy is the best strategy for *WT-LDA* clustering.

6   Conclusion

In this paper, we propose a probabilistic graphical model based approach, referred to as *WT-LDA*, which explores the knowledge behind WSDL documents and user-contributed tagging data to cluster Web services. Three tag preprocessing strategies are also developed to improve the service clustering performance. Extensive experiments conducted over real Web services demonstrate the effectiveness of the proposed *WT-LDA* approach and tag preprocessing strategies.

In our future work, we plan to use an online version of *WT-LDA* to improve the efficiency of Web service clustering, which allows the algorithm to scale to a massive number of services and service tags contributed by a large number of users.

Acknowledgements. This research was partially supported by the National Technology Support Program under the grant of 2011BAH16B04, the National Natural Science Foundation of China under the grant of No. 61173176, National High-Tech Research and Development Plan of China under the Grant No. 2012AA02A604 and No. 2013AA01A604, the Shenzhen Basic Research Program (Project No. JCYJ20120619153834216).

References

1. Al-Masri, E., Mahmoud, Q.H.: Investigating web services on the world wide web. In: International World Wide Web Conference, pp. 795–804 (2008)
2. Bianchini, D., Antonellis, V.D., Pernici, B., Plebani, P.: Ontology-based methodology for e-service discovery. ACM Journal of Information Systems 31(4), 361–380 (2006)
3. Blei, D.M., Ng, A.Y., Jordan, M.I.: Latent dirichlet allocation. The Journal of Machine Learning Research 3(1), 993–1022 (2003)
4. Chen, L., Hu, L., Zheng, Z., Wu, J., Yin, J., Li, Y., Deng, S.: WTCluster: Utilizing tags for web services clustering. In: Kappel, G., Maamar, Z., Motahari-Nezhad, H.R. (eds.) ICSOC 2011. LNCS, vol. 7084, pp. 204–218. Springer, Heidelberg (2011)
5. Chen, L., Zheng, Z., Feng, Y., Wu, J., Lyu, M.R.: WSTRank: Ranking tags to facilitate web service mining. In: Liu, C., Ludwig, H., Toumani, F., Yu, Q. (eds.) ICSOC 2012. LNCS, vol. 7636, pp. 574–581. Springer, Heidelberg (2012)
6. Dasgupta, S., Bhat, S., Lee, Y.: Taxonomic clustering of web service for efficient discovery. In: Proceedings of International Conference on Information and Knowledge Management, pp. 1617–1620 (2010)
7. Elgazzar, K., Hassan, A.E., Martin, P.: Clustering wsdl documents to bootstrap the discovery of web services. In: International Conference on Web Services, pp. 147–154 (2009)
8. Hao, Y., Junliang, C., Xiangwu, M., Bingyu, Q.: Dynamically traveling web service clustering based on spatial and temporal aspects. In: Hainaut, J.-L., et al. (eds.) ER Workshops 2007. LNCS, vol. 4802, pp. 348–357. Springer, Heidelberg (2007)
9. Church, K., Gale, W.: Inverse document frequency (idf): a measure of deviations from poisson. In: Proceedings of the ACL 3rd Workshop on Very Large Corpora, pp. 121–130 (1995)
10. Platzer, C., Rosenberg, F., Dustdar, S.: Web service clustering using multidimensional angles as proximity measures. ACM Transactions on Internet Technology 9(3), 1–26 (2009)

11. Pop, C.B., Chifu, V.R., Salomie, I., Dinsoreanu, M., David, T., Acretoaie, V.: Semantic web service clustering for efficient discovery using an ant-based method. In: Essaaidi, M., Malgeri, M., Badica, C. (eds.) Intelligent Distributed Computing IV. SCI, vol. 315, pp. 23–33. Springer, Heidelberg (2010)
12. Porter, M.F.: An algorithm for suffix stripping. Program 14(3), 130–137 (1980)
13. Rosen-Zvi, M., Griffiths, T., Steyvers, M., Smyth, P.: The author-topic model for authors and documents. In: Proceedings of the 20th Conference on Uncertainty in Artificial Intelligence, pp. 487–494 (2004)
14. Sigurbjrnsson, B., van Zwol, R.: Flickr tag recommendation based on collective knowledge. In: Proceedings of the 17th International Conference on World Wide Web, pp. 327–336 (2008)
15. Sun, P., Jiang, C.: Using service clustering to facilitate process-oriented semantic web service discovery. Chinese Journal of Computers 31(8), 1340–1353 (2008)
16. Liu, W., Wong, W.: Discovering homogenous service communities through web service clustering. In: Kowalczyk, R., Huhns, M.N., Klusch, M., Maamar, Z., Vo, Q.B. (eds.) SOCASE 2008. LNCS, vol. 5006, pp. 69–82. Springer, Heidelberg (2008)
17. Wu, J., Chen, L., Xie, Y., Zheng, Z.: Titan: A system for effective web service discovery. In: 21st International World Wide Web Conference, pp. 441–444 (2012)
18. Wu, J., Chen, L., Zheng, Z., Lyu, M.R., Wu, Z.: Clustering web services to facilitate service discovery. International Journal of Knowledge and Information Systems (2012) (to appear)
19. Yu, Q.: Place semantics into context: Service community discovery from the WSDL corpus. In: Kappel, G., Maamar, Z., Motahari-Nezhad, H.R. (eds.) ICSOC 2011. LNCS, vol. 7084, pp. 188–203. Springer, Heidelberg (2011)
20. Yu, Q., Rege, M.: On service community learning: A co-clustering approach. In: Internatonal Conference on Web Services, pp. 283–290 (2010)
21. Zheng, Z., Ma, H., Lyu, M.R., King, I.: QoS-aware Web service recommendation by collaborative filtering. IEEE Transactions on Service Computing 4(2), 140–152 (2011)

Does *One-Size-Fit-All* Suffice for Service Delivery Clients?

Shivali Agarwal, Renuka Sindhgatta, and Gargi B. Dasgupta

IBM Research India
{shivaaga,renuka.sr,gdasgupt}@in.ibm.com

Abstract. The traditional mode of delivering IT services has been through customer-specific teams. A dedicated team is assigned to address all (and only those) requirements that are specific to the customer. However, this way of organizing service delivery leads to inefficiencies due to inability to use expertise and available resources across teams in a flexible manner. To address some of these challenges, in recent times, there has been interest in shared delivery of services, where instead of having customer specific teams working in silos, there are cross-customer teams (shared resource pools) that can potentially service more than one customer. However, this gives rise to the question of what is the best way of grouping the shared resources across customer? Especially, with the large variations in the technical and domain skills required to address customer requirements, what should be the service delivery model for diverse customer workloads? Should it be customer-focused? Business domain focused? Or Technology focused? This paper simulates different delivery models in face of complex customer workload, diverse customer profiles, stringent service contracts, and evolving skills, with the goal of scientifically deriving principles of decision making for a suitable delivery model. Results show that workload arrival pattern, customer work profile combinations and domain skills, all play a significant role in the choice of delivery model. Specifically, the complementary nature of work arrivals and degree of overlapping skill requirements among customers play a crucial role in the choice of models. Interestingly, the impact of skill expertise level of resources is overshadowed by these two factors.

1 Introduction

Service-based economies and business models have gained significant importance over the years. The customers (a.k.a. clients) and service providers exchange value through service interactions with the goal of achieving their desired outcomes. Given the focus on the individual customer's value and uniqueness of the customer's needs, the service providers need to meet a large variety of expectations set by the customers with due diligence. At the same time, they need to continuously evolve better methods of operations to minimize cost of delivery in order to be competitive in the market. In this paper, we focus on how to organize IT (software) service delivery for diverse customer workloads under strict contractual agreements.

Services in software service industry are typically delivered by specialized Service Workers (SW) or human resources who are teamed together in order to serve the

S. Basu et al. (Eds.): ICSOC 2013, LNCS 8274, pp. 177–191, 2013.

Service Requests (SR) or work of the customer. The structure of this team and the flow of customer work across multiple teams define a Service Delivery Model (SDM). A service provider typically caters to multiple customers belonging to different industry domains that require multiple business functions, applications and technologies to be supported. For example, it is possible to service clients from banking, telecom and insurance domain at the same time by a service delivery organization. In spite of belonging to different verticals, customers may share common business functions like payroll, HR etc. Analogously, it is possible that all these functions for all the customers require common set of technical skills like Storage, Database, and Mainframes etc. In such situations, it becomes important to identify the optimal way of grouping customers and forming SW teams to service them such that service provider can minimize resource costs without compromising customer satisfaction.

A customer's work could be potentially mapped to one or more teams in accordance with one of the following service delivery models: (a) Customer focused (b) Business Function focused and (c) Technology-focused. Figure 1 shows a relationship among business functions, technologies and teams for each of the three models. The legend for technology, business and customer in the figure is as follows: technologies are denoted by colors, the business functions are denoted by the shape of the boxes and the customers are denoted by the different patters in the boxes. A customer has systems based on different technologies (Unix, Windows, Transaction Server, etc.) catering to different business functions (Payroll, Billing, Marketing,etc.). In the **Customer focused (CF)** SDM, all service interactions of a customer, across all business functions are served from single customer dedicated team. While this model is believed to have high customer satisfaction levels, the practical challenges involve scalability (since every new customer on-boarded now needs a dedicated team). In the **Business focused (BF)** model, business functions of multiple customers are served from the common pool. The resources in such a pool have the desired domain knowledge in addition to the required technical skills required to carry out the tasks. This model addresses the utilization issue of the dedicated scenario by supporting multiple customers with similar business functions and also maintains no fragmentation within the business function of a customer. However since business functions may map to different technologies, the common pool again requires expertise in multiple technologies, which results in higher labor costs. In **Technology-focused (TF)** SDM, multiple customers using similar technologies are grouped into a team which is served by highly skilled people in the relevant technologies. There are dedicated teams for each required technology in this model and it carries out work related to that technology from multiple business functions across different customers. In this model single skilled people are needed which is easier to hire and train. The drawback of this model is that customer work is split by technology and tends to get very fragmented. This may result in complex situations taking longer to resolve, as they traverse through the multiple teams, thereby causing customer dissatisfaction.

Given the choice of the types of SDM and their associated merits and de-merits, it becomes challenging for an organization to decide which model to adopt. The situation is further aggravated by the fact that various client specific factors, that may be static and dynamic, play a role in accentuating or diminishing the merits/de-merits of the SDMs. Section 2 of this paper, describes some of the key factors that impact SDM performance. A static one-time decision that is universally applied to all customers may not suffice for the design of a large-scale service provider. Especially with services business revenue being close to a billion USD for major providers, its success is strongly related to the trust and satisfaction of its existing customers. This necessitates a superior decision process regarding which customer workload, service contracts and skill distributions effectively map best to which SDM and optimize cost to the provider. In this paper, we aim to analyze the three SDMs from the perspective of performing highly diverse and complex clients' workload and focus on the multiple performance parameters of SLA, cost, throughput and utilization. The goal is to not only establish the best SDM under a subset of specific circumstances, but also understand the Pareto improvements that can be made to any SDM parameter. The simulation analysis presented here can be used by organizations to find the most appropriate delivery model for a client portfolio. It can also be used to find the appropriate customers groupings for a given SDM type.

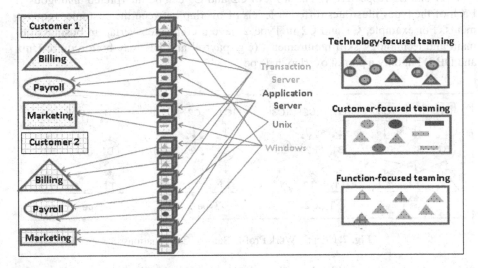

Fig. 1. Customer processes to SDM mapping

Rest of the paper is organized as follows: Section 2 describes the different factors specific to customers that affect the choice of SDM. Section 3 introduces our simulation model and the various operational parameters of interest. Section 4 presents the experimental analysis and section 5 presents a review of the related work.

2   Why One Model May Not Fit All

In this section, we describe the key factors that should be considered in choosing a service delivery model for diverse customer group. Each of these factors capture some aspect of the customer and its' workload. A combination of these factors defines the clients' work portfolio being serviced by the service provider. Different portfolios will typically suit different delivery models. Portfolios are dynamic in nature as existing customers can undergo changes and new customers may get on boarded. A service provider has to deal with different work portfolios at different points in time making it difficult to have a de-facto model because it can perform in a very sub-optimal manner for portfolios that it does not correspond to.

Customer Work Profiles - Work profile of a customer defines the nature of SRs that arrive in that customer's workload. It is a mapping of the customer's business functions to the technologies that are required to carry it out. The combined profiles of customers determine the required skills for the service delivery. Fig 2 provides the combined profiles samples that are studied in this paper. These are representative samples of the actual profiles and capture the key features relevant for simulation. The Type 1 profile in Fig 2 depicts a case where the provider is catering to three customers, C1, C2, C3 such that C1 has work that belongs to business functions of type B1 and B2. The business function B1 needs the technologies T1 and T2 both, while B2 requires T2 and T3 both. The label x1 and y1 denote the percentage of work of type B1 and B2 respectively. The work of C2 and C3 can be interpreted analogously. Each of the types illustrates different levels of overlap between the customer requirements. For example, C1 and C2 in Type 2 have a complete overlap in business domain and technology skill requirements (e.g. payroll and HR may both require Unix and DB2) but only a partial overlap in Type 1.

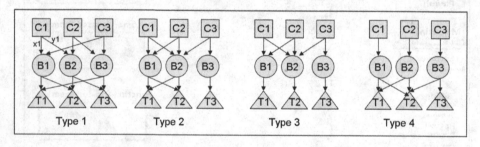

Fig. 2. Clients' Work Profile Sample Combinations

In some cases the combined profiles may look obviously tailored for a certain type of shared model, for example, because of the higher sharing of business functions in Type 3, it is intuitive that sharing of resources at business function level may benefit Type 3. This is less clear in Type 1 and Type 2, where it is possible that TF outperforms BF. A detailed analysis is required to develop the insight into the effect of different overlapping patterns that may occur in customer work profiles.

Workload Arrival Patters – It may be a myopic strategy to make decisions about shared delivery models solely based on customer work profiles, because the work arrival patterns also play a role in accentuating the benefits of sharing. The benefits of sharing will be visible most when customers have complementary workload arrival patterns. That is, the peaks and crests of one customer do not coincide with the others who are being serviced from the same pool. Then the question arises that how are the comparative performances of CF, TF and BF models in case of non-complementary workloads. It is also important to understand the role of overlapping business functions and technical skill requirements in the performance of the three SDMs in case of complementary arrivals.

Business Function Complexity – Some complex SRs may need deep domain knowledge and customer knowledge while the others may be relatively simple to handle. Consequently, the service times for a request involving a complex function will be different in the case where it is handled by a SW with less domain knowledge vs. one with high domain knowledge. As mentioned in section 1, resources in TF SDM will typically have lower level of domain and customer knowledge. This can potentially lead to SLA misses for service requests and thus skill levels become an important factor in choosing the model.

We resort to simulation based analysis for studying the interplay of these factors in mapping the class of portfolios that are best suitable for each of the three SDMs.

3   Formalizing the Service Delivery Model

We now formalize the SDM and present the framework that models the various customer and workload related factors. Each SDM is typically characterized by:

- A finite set of customers, denoted by C, to be supported.
- A finite set of W *S*ervice *W*orkers (SW).
- A finite set of teams consisting of a mutually exclusive subset of W,
  - denoted by CT, if *C*ustomer *F*ocused SDM
  - denoted by BT, if *B*usiness function *F*ocused SDM
  - denoted by TT, if *T*echnology *F*ocused SDM
- A finite set of domain skills, denoted by BD, with L levels in each skill.
- A finite set of technical skills, denoted by TD, with L levels in each skill.
- A finite set of skills pertaining to customer knowledge, denoted by CK.
- A finite set of priority levels, denoted by the set P.
- A finite set of service requests (SR) raised by the customers that arrive as work into the system.
- A   map   of   service   requests   to   required   skills,   defined   by $SR \rightarrow CK \cup BD \cup TD$.
- A map of service workers to skills,
  - One-to-many map, defined by $W \rightarrow CK \cup BD \cup TD$, if CT
  - One-to-many map, defined by $W \rightarrow BD \cup TD$, if BT
  - One-to-one map, defined by $W \rightarrow TD$, if TT
- A finite set of Key Performance Indicators, denoted by KPI.

In CF model, each customer team has a dedicated set of SWs for each business function, such that they have the customer knowledge, business domain knowledge and are skilled in the required technologies for that function. In BF model, the SWs working in a team are shared across customers and are knowledgeable about the business domain handled by that team as well as skilled in the required technologies for servicing that business function. The workers may acquire customer knowledge in the process of servicing customers for a long period of time, In TF model, the SWs are skilled in a particular technology and may acquire domain and customer knowledge over a period of time by virtue of servicing multiple customers. It is possible to have delivery models that are a combination of CF, BF and TF but such models are outside the scope of this paper. The goal of this work is to fundamentally understand the suitability of specified models for specific type of workloads.

We next discuss the operational aspects like customer SLAs of the SR, service times and evolving skills of workers, and how SRs are dispatched to service workers. We also discuss the specifics of performance indicators.

3.1   Service Level Agreements

SLA constraints, given by the mapping $\gamma : C \times P \rightarrow (r_1, r_2), r_i \in \Re, i = 1,2$ is a map from each customer-priority pair to a pair of real numbers representing the SR resolution time deadline (time) and the percentage of all the SRs that must be resolved within this deadline within a month (pct). For example, $\gamma(Customer_1, P_1) = \langle 4, 95 \rangle$, denotes that 95% of all SRs from customer$_1$ with priority P_1 in a month must be resolved within 4 hours. Note that SLAs are computed at the end of each month and hence the aggregate targets are applicable to all SRs that are closed within the month under consideration. Also the SLAs are on the entire SR itself, which means the targets apply to resolution across multiple domains.

3.2   Service Time

The time taken by a SW to complete an SR is stochastic and follows a lognormal distribution for a single skill, where the parameters of the distribution are learned by conducting time and motion exercises described in [6]. Service time distributions are characterized by the mapping $\tau : P \times D \rightarrow \langle \mu_1, \sigma_1 \rangle$, where $D = BD \cup TD \cup CK$ and μ_1, σ_1 are the mean and standard deviation parameters of the lognormal distribution and represent the longest time a worker usually takes to do this work. The distribution varies by the priority of a SR as well as the minimum skill-level required to service it. For complex work requiring multiple skills $(D_1, \ldots D_i)$ the total service time is an additive component of the individual work completions and follows a shifted lognormal distribution [16].

However with some learning in the environment and with repeated use of skills, these service times become lower according to a power law equation given by LFCM [13]. Also since complex work takes more time to complete, for the sake of maintaining throughput, it becomes imperative to assign some work to people skilled below the minimum skill-level. When lower skilled people (s_w) do higher skilled work (s_r), where $s_r > s_w$, the service times become higher. This increase in service time is obtained from an adaptation of the LFCM algorithm [17], where the service time $\mu_n(s_w, s_r)$ to finish the nth repetition of work requiring skill s_r by worker with skill level s_w is given by:

$$\mu_n(s_w, s_r) = \mu_1 n^{-\beta\left(1-\frac{\log\left(1+\gamma/t_n\right)}{\log n}\right)} \tag{1}$$

where μ_1 is the mean service time to execute the higher skilled work for the *first* time, β is the learning factor, γ is the skill gap between levels s_w and s_r, t_n is the time spent by worker at level s_r. Higher the gap γ, and lower the time spent t_n, higher is μ_n. μ_1 represents the longest time to do this type of work, but with work repetitions, expertise is gained and μ_n decreases. In practice we bound the minimum value of μ_n at μ_{min}, which is the lowest service time work s_r can take. The parameters $\langle \mu_1, \beta, \gamma, \mu_{min} \rangle$ are learned by conducting time and motion studies [6] in real SS to measure the exclusive time spent by a SW on a SR. As given by Eqn. (1), slower learning rates and bigger gaps in the skill required of a SR and skill possessed by a SW, both contribute to longer service times.

3.3   Dispatching

The Dispatcher is responsible for diagnosis of the faulty component(s) as well as work assignment to a suitable worker. During work assignment, SRs are assigned in order of their work priorities to SWs of the matching skill-level requirements. When matching skill levels are not available, higher or lower skilled SW may be utilized for servicing a SR. For fault diagnosis the dispatcher intercepts the SR to determine the most likely faulty component(s) and maps them to appropriate skill domains (from BD,TD). In case of CF model, it ensures that it maps to the right customer team as well. In TF model, a SR dispatched with $\{TD_1, TD_2\}$, needs to traverse through teams that support TD_1 and TD_2. When multiple domains of customers are supported, solving the fault-diagnosis without ambiguity is non-trivial [24] and may result in misroutes. We assume no misrouting in our model, without loss of generality.

3.4   Key Performance Indictors

Cost: The cost of delivery is directly related to the cost of the resources working in the teams. Let C_l be the base cost of the resource in TF model with single skill expertise at level l. The base cost is assumed to be higher for higher skilled people (i.e., $C_{l1} > C_{l2}, \forall l1 > l2$). In contrast BF/CF model has multi-skilled people who would need training for each additional skill. Let l_H be the highest skill level of a resource in this model. We assume that the base cost of a multi-skilled resource is dominated by the base cost of her highest expertise. She also has N additional skills, out of which n_i skills are at level l_i. Let the cost for training each skill to level l_i be given by δ_{l_i}.

Assuming a linear cost model of skills, the cost incurred for training a multi-skilled resource is given by:

$$C = C_{l_H} + \sum_i n_i * \delta_{li}, where \sum_i n_i = N \tag{2}$$

It can be seen that a resource in a BF/CF model is much more expensive than in the TF model.

Utilization: If a resource works for x hours out of available H hours, then the utilization is x/H. A SDM with higher utilization of SWs is indicative of good staffing.

Throughput: Ratio of the amount of work completed and the amount of incoming work is defined as the throughput. A model with higher throughput will typically lead to improved chances of SLA adherence.

4   Simulation Based Evaluation

In this section, we describe the simulation set up for SDM according to its definitions in Section 3 and present the experimental analysis.

Workload Parameters

- *Customer Work Profiles* : The workload is generated as per the customer work profiles given in Fig. 2. These are a very small scale representation of the actual clients' profiles but capture all the essential attributes required for simulation. The values of distributions, x1 and y1 are simulated with either of the two distributions: (i) uniform distribution, (ii) an extremely biased distribution where 90% work is of one business function type and 10% of the other.
- *Work Arrivals* : According to existing body of literature in the area of Service Delivery systems [6,8], work arrives into the system at a finite set of time intervals, denoted by T , where during each interval the arrivals stay stationary. Arrival rates are specified by the mapping $\alpha : C \times T \to \Re$, assuming that each of the SR arrival processes from the various customers C_i are independent and Poisson distributed with $\alpha(C_i, T_j)$ specifying the rate parameter. Customers can have complementary patterns of work arrival where peaks and troughs complement each other, or it can be amplifying workload with overlapping peaks or the work arrival can be a simple uniform pattern without much variation in time.

Simulation Parameters

- T contains one element for each hour of week. Hence, |T| = 168. Each time interval is one hour long.
- Priority Levels P = {P1, P2, P3, P4}, where, P1 > P2 > P3 > P4.
- Customer Skills CK={C1,C2,C3}, Business Domain Skills BD={B1,B2,B3}, Technology Skills TD={T1,T2,T3}

- *Skill Levels and Service Times*: We assume $L = 3$. The three different levels of expertise simulated are {Low, Medium, High}, where, High > Medium > Low. Each level of expertise has a least service time distribution $(\mu_{min}, \sigma_{min})$ associated with it, which characterizes the minimum time this work type could take. The estimates are obtained from real life, time and motion studies [6].
- *Learning Factor:* We assume a learning rate of $\beta = 0.1$ for each SW with high skill level, 0.08 for medium and 0.06 for low.
- *Transfer Time*: In case of work requiring multiple skills, the work gets handed over from one team to another. The teams could be geographically co-located (transfer time ~20min) or dispersed (> 20min).
- *Cost:* A blended rate (across skill levels) of 80K USD per SW and an additional cost of 10K USD per specialized skill or customer knowledge is assumed.

4.1　Experimental Analysis

We employ the AnyLogic Professional Discrete Event simulation toolkit [4] for the experiments. We simulate up to 40 weeks of simulation runs with the aforementioned parameters and dispatching as described in section 3.3. Measurements are taken at end of each week. No measurements are recorded during the warm up period of first four weeks. In steady state the parameters that were measured include:

- SLA measurements at each priority level
- Completion times of work in minutes (includes queue waiting times, transfer times, and service times)
- Throughput (work completed/week)
- Resource utilization (captures the busy-time of a resource)
- Number of resources that is an indication of cost

For all the above parameters the observation means and confidence intervals are reported. Whenever confidence intervals are wider, the number of weeks in simulation is increased and reported values in the paper are within $\pm 5\%$ confidence intervals. We seed the simulation with a good initial staffing solution from the Optimizer kit [15] which returned the optimal number of resources that can meet the contractual SLAs (we assume SLA adherence as a required condition for a model). Table 1 shows the distribution of work across priorities, the target resolution times and the percentage of SRs that need to be completed within the target resolution time. These values are defined based on our analysis of the real life data collected from projects at IBM.

Table 1. Work Distribution and SLA Target Times and Percentages

Priority of SR or Work	% Distribution	SLA Target Times (minutes)	% Meeting Target Time
1	10	240	90
2	20	480	90
3	40	720	100
4	30	1440	100

Simulation Results for Studying the Impact of Arrival Patterns and Skills on SDM

For the first set of experiments we take the work profiles with substantial overlap like Type 1 as shown in Fig. 2, and vary the workload arrival patterns. We have two type of arrival patterns, i) non-complementary workload for all customers and ii) complementary workload for customer C1 and C2 and uniform for C3. For the purpose of experiments, we differentiate resources with specialized customer knowledge (CK) and technical skills (TD). Specialized customer knowledge includes fair amount of knowledge of customer specific details of the business functions in addition to adequate relevant BD skills. The effect of skills is captured by differentiating the service times as described in section 3.2. We simulate non-complementary workload by simulating simultaneous peaks in the customer workload. In this case as shown in Table 2, we see that when all SDMs have equally skilled people with high customer knowledge (CK), then the optimal staffing required by CF, BF teams is very similar. Since the service workers have similar skills, the average completion times for work and the resource utilizations are comparable. We next simulate the environment where the skills of people in the SDMs vary. We assume in CF, people are highly well-versed with the customer domain while the people in BF and TF have comparatively lower customer knowledge. The results in Table 2 show the trend that with increasingly different levels of customer knowledge between the three models, CF increasingly tends to outperform the other two delivery models. Thus we conclude, without loss of generality, that the CF focused SDM is actually the best choice among all SDMs, when the workload arrivals offer no real benefit of work multiplexing especially when customer knowledge is an important part of the work environment.

Table 2. KPI Performance for Non-complementary, Type1 work profile

Non-complementary workload, Type 1 profile	Same Customer Knowledge			Specialized Customer Knowledge		
	CF(HI CK)	BF(HI CK)	TF(HI CK)	CF (HI CK)	BF (Med CK)	TF (Med CK)
Num Resources	105	107	120	105	108	124
Cost (USD)	9.4M (@80K/SW)	9.6M (@90K/SW)	9.6M (@90K/SW)	9.4M (@90K/SW)	9.7M (@90K/SW)	9.9M (@80K/SW)
Utilization %	49%	50%	44%	49%	56%	51%
Completion Time	141	120	130	141	130	170

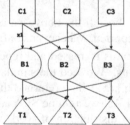

Type 1

We next simulate the scenario, when the workload arrivals are complementary. The customer knowledge is still assumed to be an important part of the environment, i.e., CF has a higher customer knowledge skill. However the fact that the workload peaks are now staggered and no longer happen simultaneously, changes the landscape of the results. Table 3 shows that in this case BF and TF show big improvements when compared to CF in terms of resource cost and utilization. The CF suffers from low resource utilization in this scenario. Both BF and TF perform well, with BF having the lowest cost, and completion times. The TF completion times are slightly higher, even though both have the same level of skills (medium CK). This can be explained due to the effect of transfer times on multi-skill work requirements in the TF model. Recall that the work coming to these teams require multiple skills for resolution. Workers in BF SDMs typically have multiple skills and work on tickets for a longer amount of time. In contrast the TF workers only work on their specific specialized skill and pass it on to the next expert resulting in higher completion time.

We conclude that when workloads have some complementary behavior, either BF or TF should be the SDM of choice; and the impact of complementary behavior overrides the requirement of customer knowledge in the SDM KPIs. The simulations for other profile types follow suite and for sake of brevity, results are not presented here.

Table 3. KPI Performance for Complementary, Type1 and 2 work

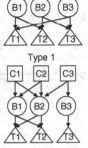

Type 1

Type 2

Complementary workload	Specialized Customer Knowledge Type 1 Profile			Specialized Customer Knowledge Type 2 Profile		
	CF (HI CK)	BF (Med CK)	TF (Med CK)	CF (HI CK)	BF (Med CK)	TF (Med CK)
Num Resources	115	103	124	115	100	112
Cost (USD)	9.9M (@90K/SW)	9.3M (@90K/SW)2	9.9M (@80K/SW)	9.9M (@90K/SW)	9.0M (@90K/SW)	8.9M (@80K/SW)
Utilization %	46%	59%	50%	46%	60%	50%
Completion Time	141	152	173	147	147	151

Simulation Results for Studying the Impact of Work Profiles on SDM

We simulate different work profiles on SDM that captures the level of sharing that can be achieved at the customer, business or the technical domains. We restrict to complementary workloads to study BF vs. TF. It was seen that BF clearly outperforms others in most KPIs, as shown in Table 3, where there is sufficient overlap between business functions of customers with complementary workloads. Note that this is true even though people in CF have higher skills and lower completion times when compared to BF.

We next simulate scenario for type 4 where the customers do not have many overlapping business functions, but a high technology overlap. In this case customers have a very diverse set of business functions but they all require common technologies. In this case, Table 4 shows that the TF model performs the best in terms of resource cost, completion time and utilization. This is when we assume that customer knowledge is still higher with the CF SDM. Since TF builds specialized skills, it is often believed that workers in TF are highly skilled in the technical areas of expertise. With this assumption we simulate the case where TF workers have higher skills in their individual domains but lower customer knowledge skill. In this scenario, while transfer times are reasonable (~10 to 20 minutes) TF is remains the best SDM.

The biggest drawback of the TF model in case of multi-skill work is the *hand-off* between teams, causing transfer delays. We next analyze the sensitivity of the TF performance with respect to transfer times. Fig. 3 and Fig. 4 show that TF performance degrades, both in terms of completion time and number of resources deteriorate as transfer times increase beyond 30 min. Hence, while TF is a good model for type 2 customer profiles, its sensitivity to transfer times needs to be considered. Especially when the teams are geographically distributed and transfer times are naturally higher due time-zone shifts, the benefit of using TF in a high technology overlap customer profile may be overridden.

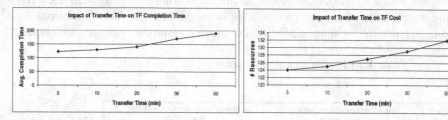

Fig. 3. Transfer time Vs Completion time (TF)   **Fig. 4.** Transfer time Vs Cost (TF)

Table 4. KPI Performance for Complementary, Type4 work

Complementary workload, Profile Map Type 4	Specialized Customer Knowledge			Specialized Customer Knowledge And Specialized Technical Domain Knowledge		
	CF (Hi CK)	BF (Med CK)	TF (Med CK)	CF (Hi CK + Med TD)	BF (Med CK + Med TD)	TF (Med CK + Hi TD)
Num Resources	110	110	120	110	110	116
Cost (USD)	9.9@(90K/SW)	9.9M@(90K/SW)	9.6M@(80K/SW)	9.9@(90K/SW)	9.9M@(90K/SW)	9.2M@(80K/SW)
Utilization %	49%	55%	52%	49%	55%	55%
Completion Time	157	155	154	157	155	150

Type 4

In the last profile experiment, we simulate the profile type 3 when technology requirements are very distinct even though a lot of business function sharing is present. In this case, BF is the clear choice, even when customer skills are higher in CF and technology skills are higher in TF as show in Table 5.

Table 5. KPI Performance for complementary, Type3 work

Complementary workload, Profile Map Type 3	Specialized Customer Knowledge			Specialized Customer Knowledge And Specialized Technical Domain Knowledge		
	CF (Hi CK)	BF (Med CK)	TF (Med CK)	CF (Hi CK + Med TD)	BF (Med CK + Med TD)	TF (Med CK + Hi TD)
Num Resources	110	105	130	110	104	128
Cost (USD)	9.9@(90K/SW)	9.4M@(90K/SW)	10.4M@(80K/SW)	9.9@(90K/SW)	9.3M@(90K/SW)	10.2M@(80K/SW)
Utilization %	49%	55%	47%	49%	57%	50%
Completion Time	157	155	154	157	155	150

Type 3

We conclude that customer profile maps are a very prominent factor in deciding the SDM of choice and has a bigger impact than skills (customer knowledge or technical domain expertise) on SDM KPIs. For most profiles, that have some degree of commonality in business functions, BF is the best SDM choice. When customers have diverse business requirements but common technology requirements, TF outperforms other models, as long as transfer times are reasonable (~20 min).

A note on Utilization: With respect to the utilization of resources, we realize that the averages may not accurately represent the distributions that have a lot of skew. Hence, we look at the distributions of the utilization across the three scenarios to draw conclusions on their utilization pattern. Fig 5 shows the box-plots for CF, BF and TF utilization, when sharing is high at both business and technology levels. The whiskers represent the min and max of the distributions while the '+' indicates the median. In the high sharing case for all distributions, the median lies in the centre of the box. In CF the box is equally placed between the whiskers indicating normally distributed utilization. The smaller inter-quartile range shows similar utilizations among the resources in TF, but varied in case of BF to CF. Overall Fig. 5 shows that in each scenario, peoples' utilization distributions are more symmetric. In Fig. 6 for a profile like type 4, where the business function sharing is low, the CF and BF utilizations are skewed. In CF, the median is closer to the first quartile value, indicating that more people are lowly utilized. For BF, the median is closer to the third quartile value indicating a left skew with a larger clustering of higher values in that section. However the median of the TF is centrally located indicating a more uniform distribution. This shows that from the utilization perspective, TF focused teams exhibit uniform utilization patterns irrespective of the amount of sharing available. BF shows uniform utilizations with high business function sharing customer profiles.

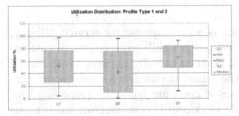 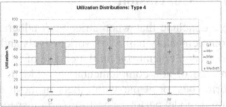

Fig. 5. Utilization Distribution: Type 1   **Fig. 6.** Utilization Distribution: Type 4

5   Related Work

The concept of shared service has existed for a long time, for e.g., multiple departments within an organization shared services like HR, finance, IT etc. A recent study [23] of global service delivery centers revealed that shared services not only reduces costs, but also improves quality. There is also work on organizational design principles underlying an effective service delivery model [1,3,5] and resource hiring, cross-training in such models [20]. However, there is no work on generalizing the service delivery models and evaluating the pros and cons when presented with different kinds of workloads and work arrival patterns. Learning and forgetting curves in production and manufacturing industry [13] have received a lot of attention.

The service delivery work, being repetitive in nature can benefit from these results in modeling the effect of learning and forgetting on service times. This paper incorporates some of the manufacturing domain results. One of the interesting results in this body of work is [14] where the authors demonstrate that forgetting by workers in an establishment or line of production as a substantive characteristic of actual production processes is overstated and that although important and interesting, is not as influential as previous work for labor productivity has suggested. There is another line of work that studies the effects of task assignment on long term resource productivity. This is because the task assignment impacts mean learning rate, mean forgetting rate, mean prior expertise, variance of prior expertise etc and thus has a direct consequence on productivity. The work in [18] presents a heuristic approach for assigning work by taking into account all these factors. We have modeled productivity differences between various skill levels for the same skill type. How to staff, cross-train them and utilize multi-skill resources have also received adequate attention in the past and especially in the context of call-centers [7,9]. The work in [12] advocates that a flexible worker should process a task s/he is uniquely qualified for before helping others in shared tasks. This is advocated in work-in-process constrained flow-lines staffed with partially cross-trained workers with hierarchical skill sets. The effect of collaboration between teams has also been studied in work in [21] which proposes the concept of social compute unit. The work in [10] theorizes how task/team familiarity interact with team coordination complexity to influence team performance. They find that task and team familiarity are more substitutive than complementary in: Task familiarity improves performance more strongly when team familiarity is weak and vice versa. The work in [2] elaborates on the impact of high transfer times on SLAs and deals with minimizing the transfer times in the context of service tickets.

6   Conclusion

We conclude that when strict SLA adherence is a pre-requisite for service delivery, complementary nature of work arrivals and overlapping skill requirements of customers play a crucial role in the choice of SDM. Domain knowledge plays a role mainly in case of non-complementary workload. The business function focused model performs best or at par with others in most cases if costs are ignored. Technology focused model performs best for certain specific work profile combinations and is at par with BF in most cases if labor cost is the primary KPI. TF model also exhibits more uniform utilization, but suffers from high sensitivity to transfer times. Such kind of detailed analysis will give useful insights in choosing the delivery model. An interesting extension of this study would be to evaluate the conditions for hybrid SDMs.

References

1. Agarwal, S., Reddy, V.K., Sengupta, B., Bagheri, S., Ratakonda, K.: Organizing Shared Delivery Systems. In: Proc. of 2nd International Conference on Services in Emerging Markets, India (2011)
2. Agarwal, S., Sindhgatta, R., Sengupta, B.: SmartDispatch: enabling efficient ticket dispatch in an IT service environment. In: Proc. of the 18th ACM SIGKDD International Conference on Knowledge Discovery and Data Mining, KDD 2012 (2012)

3. Alter, S.: Service System Fundamentals: Work System, Value Chain, and Life Cycle. IBM Systems Journal 47(1), 71–85 (2008)
4. Anylogic Tutorial, How to build a combined agent based/system dynamics model in Anylogic. In: System Dynamics Conference (2008),
   http://www.xjtek.com/anylogic/articles/13/
5. Assembly Optimization: A Distinct Approach to Global Delivery, IBM GBS White Paper (2010)
6. Banerjee, D., Dasgupta, G.B., Desai, N.: Simulation-based evaluation of dispatching policies in service systems. In: Winter Simulation Conference (2011)
7. Cezik, M.T., L'Ecuyer, P.: Staffing multi-skill call centers via linear programming and simulation. Management Science Journal (2006)
8. Diao, Y., Heching, A., Northcutt, D., Stark, G.: Modeling a complex global service delivery system. In: Winter Simulation Conference 2011 (2011)
9. Easton, F.F.: Staffing, Cross-training, and Scheduling with Cross-trained Workers in Extended-hour Service Operations. Robert H. Brethen Operations Management Institute (2011) (manuscript)
10. Espinosa, J.A., Slaughter, S.A., Kraut, R.E., Herbsleb, J.D.: Familiarity, Complexity, and Team Performance in Geographically Distributed Software Development. Organization Science 18(4), 613–630 (2007)
11. Franzese, L.A., Fioroni, M.M., de Freitas Filho, P.J., Botter, R.C.: Comparison of Call Center Models. In: Proc. of the Conference on Winter Simulation (2009)
12. Gel, E.S., Hopp Wallace, J., Van Oyen, M.P.: Hierarchical cross-training in work-in-process-constrained systems. IIE Transactions, 39 (2007)
13. Jaber, M.Y., Bonney, M.: A comparative study of learning curves with forgetting. Applied Mathematical Modelling 21, 523–531 (1997)
14. Kleiner, M.M., Nickelsburg, J., Pilarski, A.: Organizational and Individual Learning and Forgetting. Industrial and Labour Relations Review 65(1) (2011)
15. Laguna, M.: Optimization of complex systems with optquest. OptQuest for Crystal Ball User Manual Decisioneering (1998)
16. Lo, C.F.: The Sum and Difference of Two Lognormal Random Variables. Journal of Applied Mathematics 2012, Article ID 838397, 13 pages (2012)
17. Narayanan, C.L., Dasgupta, G., Desai, N.: Learning to impart skills to service workers via challenging task assignments. IBM Technical Report (2012)
18. Nembhard, D.A.: Heuristic approach for assigning workers to tasks based on individual learning rates. Int. Journal Prod. Res. 39(9) (2001)
19. Ramaswamy, L., Banavar, G.: A Formal Model of Service Delivery. In: Proc. of the IEEE International Conference on Service Computing (2008)
20. Subramanian, D., An, L.: Optimal Resource Action Planning Analytics for Services Delivery Using Hiring, Contracting & Cross-Training of Various Skills. In: Proc. of IEEE SCC (2008)
21. Sengupta, B., Jain, A., Bhattacharya, K., Truong, H.-L., Dustdar, S.: Who do you call? Problem resolution through social compute units. In: Liu, C., Ludwig, H., Toumani, F., Yu, Q. (eds.) ICSOC 2012. LNCS, vol. 7636, pp. 48–62. Springer, Heidelberg (2012)
22. Spohrer, J., Maglio, P.P., Bailey, J., Gruhl, D.: Steps Toward a Science of Service Systems. IEEE Computer 40(1), 71–77 (2007)
23. Shared Services & Outsourcing Network (SSON) and The Hackett Group, Global service center benchmark study (2009)
24. Verma, A., Desai, N., Bhamidipaty, A., Jain, A.N., Barnes, S., Nallacherry, J., Roy, S.: Automated Optimal Dispatching of Service Requests. In: Proc. of the SRII Global Conference (2011)

Runtime Evolution of Service-Based Multi-tenant SaaS Applications

Indika Kumara, Jun Han, Alan Colman, and Malinda Kapuruge

Faculty of Information and Communication Technologies
Swinburne University of Technology, Melbourne, Australia
{iweerasinghadewage,jhan,acolman,mkapuruge}@swin.edu.au

Abstract. The Single-Instance Multi-Tenancy (SIMT) model for service delivery enables a SaaS provider to achieve economies of scale via the reuse and runtime sharing of software assets between tenants. However, evolving such an application at runtime to cope with the changing requirements from its different stakeholders is challenging. In this paper, we propose an approach to evolving service-based SIMT SaaS applications that are developed based on Dynamic Software Product Lines (DSPL) with runtime sharing and variation among tenants. We first identify the different kinds of changes to a service-based SaaS application, and the consequential impacts of those changes. We then discuss how to realize and manage each change and its resultant impacts in the DSPL. A software engineer declaratively specifies changes in a script, and realizes the changes to the runtime model of the DSPL using the script. We demonstrate the feasibility of our approach with a case study.

Keywords: SaaS, Evolution, Multi-tenancy, SPL, Compositional, Feature.

1   Introduction

The Software as a Service (SaaS) models for service delivery offer software applications as a utility over the Internet. In particular, the Single-Instance Multi-Tenancy (SIMT) model hosts different tenants in a single application instance, increasing runtime sharing and hence reducing operational cost [1]. In this model, the functionality for all the tenants is integrated into a single application, and the differentiation of the varied support for tenants is realized at runtime.

After an SIMT application is successfully developed and deployed, its evolution takes place. During this phase, the application can be modified, for instance, to cope with a changed need of a tenant or the SaaS provider or a change in a partner service's capability. Evolving an SIMT application is a complex problem. Firstly, the application should support *different classes of changes* that can potentially occur during its lifetime. Secondly, the application needs to enable the identification and control of the *impacts of a change* on the application. Finally, a change and its impacts need to be *realized and managed at runtime* without disturbing the operations of those tenants unaffected by the change.

S. Basu et al. (Eds.): ICSOC 2013, LNCS 8274, pp. 192–206, 2013.

To date, there is little support for runtime evolution of a multi-tenant SaaS application [2-4]. Some efforts have considered such issues as tenant on-boarding [2] and tenant-specific variations [3, 4]. However, they do not sufficiently support two key activities of change management [5]: identifying a change and its impacts, and designing and implementing the change and impacts.

In [6], we have proposed to realize a service-based SIMT SaaS application as a Service-Oriented Dynamic Software Product Line (SO-DSPL) that supports runtime sharing and variation across tenants/products. Our approach utilizes the DSPL's capability to share and differentiate product features, but all achieved at *runtime*.

In this paper, we discuss the above-mentioned *two key activities of change management* (main contributions) for service-based SIMT applications developed using our product line based model. We first identify the different types of changes to our SO-DSPL and their potential impacts. Second, we discuss our approach to realizing each change and managing each change impact. In particular, we support the identification of the potential impacts of a change on the products (tenants), and the management of such impacts without disturbing the operations of the unaffected products. An initial modification and its consequential impacts can be specified and realized through the runtime representation of the product line created based on the *models@runtime* concept [7]. With a case study that implements common SPL evolution scenarios, we demonstrate the feasibility of our approach. We analyze the case study results to assess change impacts and the programming effort for the scripts that specify changes. We also quantify the time taken to realize such changes at runtime.

In this paper, we start by providing the motivation, background, and overview of our approach to realizing an SIMT application as an SO-DSPL (Sections 2, 3, and 4). Section 5 presents our approach to the identification and management of the runtime changes and their impacts. In Sections 6 and 7, we discuss our prototype implementation and evaluation results respectively. Section 8 presents related work, and Section 9 concludes the paper while providing directions for future research.

2   Motivating Scenario and General Requirements

To motivate this research, let us consider a business scenario from SwinRoadside, a company offering roadside assistance to its customers such as Travel Agencies (TA) and Truck Sellers (TS) by utilizing external partner services such as Garage Chains (GC) and Towing Companies (TC). SwinRoadside manages both the roadside assistance business and the supporting IT infrastructure, which adopts the *SIMT SaaS model*. The customers use their own variants of this roadside assistance service to serve their users such as travelers and truck buyers. In this IT-enabled business scenario, we can identify three key requirements for SwinRoadside.

(Req1) Runtime Sharing with Variations. To achieve economies of scale, SwinRoadside expects to share the roadside business process and services across its customers (tenants). However, these customers have varying needs. For instance, TA1 needs onsite vehicle repair and accommodation, while TS1 prefers repairing at a garage. SwinRoadside needs to support sharing with variations at runtime.

(Req2) Managing Runtime Changes to the SaaS Application. The requirements of the tenants, the SaaS provider, and the external services can change over time. For instance, six months into operation, TA1 needs support for renting a vehicle instead of accommodation, as travelers prefer continuing their journey. After one year, SwinRoadside decides to enhance repair notification by supporting the direct notification of a motorist by the garage. The towing company starts to offer accident towing that SwinRoadside and some of its customers want to utilize. The roadside application needs to evolve at runtime to respond to or utilize these changes.

(Req3) Managing Change Impacts. A change in the roadside process can affect the application as well as individual tenants. For example, modifying the towing capability to tow a rented vehicle (for TA1) can affect TS1 that uses it to tow a vehicle to a garage. The roadside application needs to identify and control these impacts.

3   Software Product Lines and Feature Model

An SPL is a family of software systems developed from a common set of core assets [8]. Compared to an SPL, a dynamic SPL (DSPL) creates and adapts products at runtime [9]. The realization of a variant-rich application with the SPL approach can yield significant improvements in business drivers such as time to market, cost, and productivity. There are two main ways to implement an SPL: *annotative approach* and *compositional approach* [10]. The former embeds the features of the SPL in the application code using explicit annotations (e.g., '#ifdef' and '#endif' statements of C style) or implicit annotations (e.g., hooks or extension points), supporting fine-grained variability, but reducing flexibility and maintainability [10]. The latter realizes the features as modular units and creates products by composing these modular units. It can potentially reduce the aforementioned drawbacks of the annotative approach [10].

A feature model [11] captures the commonality and variability in a product line at a higher abstraction level. It supports activities such as asset development and product creation. Figure 1 shows the cardinality-based feature model [12] for the motivating example. The *Composed of* relationship arranges features in a *hierarchy*. For instance, the features *Accommodation* and *TechAdvice* are the children of *ExtraServices*. The feature cardinality specifies how many instances of a feature can be included in a feature configuration or product. The cardinality of an *optional* feature is [0-1], and that of a *mandatory* feature is [1-1]. The cardinality of a feature group specifies how many features the group can include. For example, the group cardinality ([1-2]) of *ExtraServices* implies that *at least one* of its two children must be selected. The constraints define dependencies among features. For instance, the constraint *AtGarage includes Tow* indicates that if *AtGarage* is selected, *Tow* must also be selected. By selecting the features respecting these constraints, a feature configuration is created.

Fig. 1. The feature model for the motivating example

4 Product Line-Based Realization of SIMT SaaS Applications

Design-Time Representation. In [6], we have introduced a service-oriented DSPL (SO-DSPL) based approach to realizing service-based SIMT SaaS applications that supports runtime sharing among products/tenants while allowing product/tenant-specific variations (*Req1*). This section provides an overview of our DSPL based approach, which comprises four layers, as shown in Fig. 2(a).

At the bottom is the *service asset layer*, including all the partner services used by the product line or SaaS application. The *structure layer* provides an abstraction over *service assets* and their interactions needed to realize the *features* of the product line. The *roles* are abstract representations of service assets (referred as *players*), making roles and players loosely coupled. The *contracts* capture the allowed interactions between the players playing roles, and make roles loosely coupled. The *role-contract topology*, consisting of roles and contracts, models the structure of the product line. A role defines its *responsibility* as a set of *tasks* that encapsulate the *capabilities* of a service. A contract consists of a set of *interaction terms*, defining the allowed interactions between the relevant roles (players). The input and output of a task are defined based on interaction terms. Messages flow between services via roles and contracts.

Consider the structure layer for the motivating example (see Fig. 2(a)). The role-contract topology comprises the roles MM, SC, HC, GC, TC and the contracts among them. The role GC, an abstract garage service, is realized by the service (player) FastRepair. The role SC represents the Support Center and is realized by the service 24by7. The contract SC_GC defines the expected interactions between the players 24by7 and FastRepair in playing the roles SC and GC. Lines 13-14 in Fig. 3 show the task *tRepair* of the role GC. The task's input (*UsingMsg*) uses the interaction *iOrderRepair* from SC. Its output (*ResultingMsg*) refers to the interactions *iPayRepair* to SC and *iAckRepair* to *MM* (representing the member, i.e., the user or motorist).

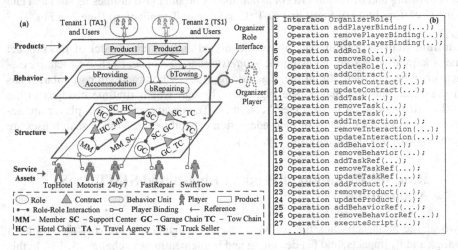

Fig. 2. (a) An overview of the SO-DSPL for the motivating example, (b) part of the organizer

```
1  ProductDefinition Product1 {
2    CoS "eProduct1Reqd"; CoT "ePaidRepair * ePaidRoomRent * eAckedMM";
3    BehaviorRef  bRepairing; BehaviorRef  bProvidingAccommodation; ... }
4  Behavior bRepairing {
5   TaskRef GC.tRepair     { InitOn "eRepairReqd"; Triggers "eRepaired"; }
6   TaskRef SC.tPayRepair { InitOn "eRepaired"; Triggers "ePaidRepair"; }
7   TaskRef MM.tAckRepair { InitOn "eRepaired"; Triggers "eAckedMM";     } ...}
8  Behavior bProvidingAccommodation { ... }
9  Contract SC_GC { A is SC, B is GC;
10    ITerm iOrderRepair(String:msg) withResponse (String:ack)from AtoB; ITerm iPayRepair(..);..}
11 Contract GC_MM { ITerm iAckRepair(...) ...}
12 Role GC {
13    Task tRepair { UsingMsgs SC_GC.iOrderRepair.Req;
14               ResultingMsgs SC_GC.iPayRepair.Req,GC_MM.iAckRepair.Req; } ...}
15 Role MM { Task tAckRepair{...} ...}, Role SC { Task tPayRepair{...} ... }
16 PlayerBinding gcPlayer "www.fastrepair.com/GCService" is a GC;
```

Fig. 3. Part of the configuration for the product line depicted in Fig. 2(a)

The *behavior layer*, consisting of *behavior units*, encapsulates the control flow and regulates the message flow between service assets. To provide a *feature*, a behavior unit realizes a collaboration among a subset of services by coordinating the tasks of the roles that these services fulfill. The topology of the collaboration (referred to as *local topology*) is defined using references to the tasks of the participating roles. The *control flow* is specified as the dependencies between the tasks using their *InitOn* and *Triggers* clauses (pre- and post-conditions) based on events that are generated by interpreting role-role interactions. For example, consider the behavior unit *bRepairing* (lines 4-7 in Fig. 3). It groups and coordinates the tasks of *GC.tRepair*, *SC.tPayRepair*, and *MM.tAckRepair*. The task *GC.tRepair* depends on the task that creates the event *eRepairReqd*. Its completion generates the event *eRepaired* that triggers (as the preconditions for) the consequent tasks, e.g., *SC.tPayRepair* and *MM.tAckRepair*.

At the *product layer*, a product models a tenant's product configuration and composes the related behavior units by referring to them (*aka*, the *compositional approach*). Products *share* behavior units for their commonality and use different behavior units for their variability, i.e., achieving the *SIMT model*. As depicted in Fig. 2(a), Product1 and Product2 use the behavior unit *bRepairing*, and one of the behavior units *bTowing* and *bProvidingAccommodation*. A product also defines its start and end using CoS (Condition of Start) and CoT (Condition of Termination) (line 2 in Fig. 3).

Runtime Representation. The above-mentioned architecture model of the product line is kept alive at runtime using the *models@runtime* concept [7]. As such, its elements can be modified at runtime, e.g., adding roles or contracts. In particular, it has an organizer role and player (see Fig. 2(a)) through which runtime changes to the product line can be performed (see Section 5). The organizer role and player are generic to our approach. Some of their adaptation capabilities that this research uses are shown as adaptation operations in Fig. 2(b).

5   Runtime Evolution of Product Line-Based SIMT SaaS Applications

Two of the main activities for software change management are: (1) identifying a change and its impacts, and (2) designing and implementing the change [5, 13]. In this paper, we consider these activities *at runtime* for service-based SIMT SaaS applications developed using our DSPL based model (*Req2* and *Req3*). Section 5.1 identifies the *changes* to the DSPL and their *potential direct impacts*. Section 5.2 discusses the realization and management of the identified changes and impacts in the DSPL.

5.1   Identification of Changes and Impacts

A change request and the current system are key inputs to a change process [5]. In our approach, external service providers consider changes at the service-level, such as service addition and removal. The SaaS provider and tenants identify changes at the feature-level as addition, removal and modification of features. The SaaS provider can also consider architectural changes, e.g., for the purpose of optimizing the product line architecture. In general, each layer of the product line can be potentially modified to realize a change (see Fig. 4).

Service Asset Layer. The changes at the service asset layer include: adding, removing, replacing, and modifying a service asset, service capability changes, and service interface changes. The capability changes include adding, removing, and modifying capabilities and the control relations between them. The interface changes include adding, removing, and modifying operations and the control relations between them.

A new service asset (to be used) requires a role, a player binding for that role, and a set of contracts to capture the expected relationships between the new service asset and the relevant existing service assets in realizing that role. It also introduces new capabilities. The removal of a used service asset makes the related player binding, role, and contracts invalid since the player binding refers to a nonexistent service, the realization of the role is removed, and the contracts represent nonexistent relationships. Moreover, the used capabilities of the deleted service asset are removed. The replacement of a used or an existing service asset requires updating the related player binding. Additionally, the mismatch/difference between the new service and the replaced one can result in capability and interface changes (see below for their impacts). A modification to a used service asset can involve capability and interface changes.

A new service capability (to be used) requires a task to represent it. The removal of a used capability makes the related task invalid since there is no realization for it. The modifications to used capabilities (e.g., merging capabilities) can result in the same types of changes to the relevant tasks. Generally, to use or realize a capability, service

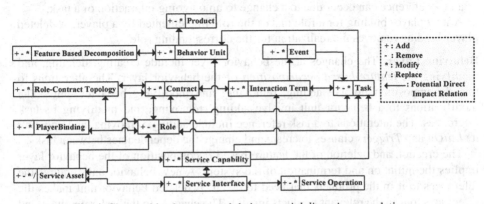

Fig. 4. Changeable elements and their *potential direct impact* relations

assets need to interact with each other, and thus a capability change can also have impacts on contracts and interaction terms. A change to a control relation between used capabilities can affect the dependencies among the corresponding tasks captured in relevant behavior units. A capability change can also involve an interface change.

An interface change related to an unused capability does not affect the product line. The impacts of an interface change related to a used capability (unchanged) are unwanted by the product line, and thus should be controlled (see Section 5.2). An interface change that alters a used capability has the same impacts of a capability change.

Structure Layer. The changes at the structure layer include adding, removing, and modifying the role-contract topology and the player bindings. The modifications to a role-contract topology include adding, removing, and modifying roles and contracts. Altering a role involves adding, removing, and modifying tasks. Altering a contract involves adding, removing, and modifying interaction terms. The modifications to a player binding include updating its endpoint and role reference.

The addition and removal of the role-contract topology implies the initiation and termination of the system. A new role may need a set of tasks, a player binding, and the contracts with the other roles that the new role should interact. The removal of a role deletes its tasks, and makes its contracts and the references to the role in behavior units and player bindings invalid. A new contract between two roles relates the two roles, and may require a set of interaction terms to be used by the tasks of the two roles. A deletion of a contract removes its interaction terms and the association between the related roles, and makes the references to it by the related tasks invalid.

A new task may use a subset of existing interaction terms, and require the references to it in the behavior units that need to use it. If an interaction term used in a task is not shared by other tasks, the removal of the task makes the interaction term isolated. A deleted task also makes the reference to it in the related behavior units invalid.

A new interaction term may require adding the references to it in the tasks that need to use it. A deleted interaction term makes the references to it in the related tasks invalid. Moreover, the changes to interaction terms that alter the events they create can affect the representations of the dependencies between tasks (*InitOn/Triggers* of a task reference). A new incoming interaction of a task may require adding the relevant events to the *InitOn* of the related task references. A removed incoming interaction makes the references to the related events invalid. The similar impacts on the *Triggers* of a task reference can occur due to a change to an outgoing interaction of a task.

A new player binding for a role makes the role implemented by a player. A deleted player binding removes the realization for the corresponding role.

Behavior Layer. The changes at the behavior layer include creating, deleting, and modifying the *feature-based decomposition* of the behavior layer. The alterations to this decomposition involve adding, removing, and modifying behavior units. The modifications to a behavior unit involve adding, removing, and modifying its task references. The alterations to a task reference include adding, removing, and updating its *InitOn* and *Triggers* clauses to create and change the dependencies between tasks.

The creation and deletion of the feature-based decomposition of the behavior layer implies the initiation and termination of the system. A new behavior unit requires the references to it in the products that need to use it. A deleted behavior unit makes the references to it in the relevant products invalid. The changes to the task references and task dependencies captured in a behavior unit can alter the service collaboration (the feature implementation) realized by the behavior unit. This in turn can modify the feature (an end-user experienced functionality/behavior) offered by the behavior unit.

A change to a feature implementation can introduce unintended behaviors to one or more different features as well as to a subset of the products that use the feature. As an example for the first case, consider that the feature *AtGarage* uses the feature *Tow* to carry a vehicle to a garage (used by Product2), and the new feature *VehicleHire* also needs the feature *Tow* to tow a rented vehicle (to be used by Product1). Changing the collaboration related to the feature *Tow* can affect the feature *AtGarage*. As an example for the second case, suppose that Product2 needs a periodic repair notification. Modifying the collaboration for the shared feature *Repair* for this purpose adds an unwanted behavior to Product1. These effects need to be reduced (see Section 5.2).

Product Layer. The changes at the product layer include: adding, removing, and modifying products. The modifications to a product involve adding and removing the references to behavior units, and updating its CoT and CoS. Since the events used in the CoT and CoS of a product depend on the behavior units that the product uses, the inclusion and exclusion of a behavior unit in the product as well as the change to a behavior unit used by the product can affect the CoT and CoS of the product.

5.2   Realization of Changes and Impacts

In this section, we describe how the identified changes and impacts can be realized in the SO-DSPL, and how the change impacts are managed and realized.

Solutions for Changes. The change primitives supported by the organizer (see Fig. 2 (b)) are used to perform the changes to the runtime model of the product line.

Using the operations *[add/remove/update][Role/Contract]()*, the role-contract topology can be altered. The methods *[add/remove/update]PlayerBinding()* can be used to realize player binding changes. To change tasks, interaction terms, and their relations, the operations *[add/remove/update][Task/Interaction]()* can be used.

The operations *[add/remove]Behavior()* need to be used to add or remove a behavior unit. By changing the task references of a behavior unit using the methods *[add/ remove]TaskRef()*, the local topology of a collaboration captured in a behavior unit can be modified. The control flow can be altered by modifying dependencies among tasks via changing their *InitOn* and *Triggers* using the operation *updateTaskRef()*. For example, to ensure a repair notification (*MM.tAckRepair*) follows a repair payment (*SC.tPayRepair*), the *InitOn* of the taskref *MM.tAckRepair* in the behavior unit *bRepairing* (Fig. 3) can be replaced by the *Triggers* of *SC.tPayRepair*. Figure 5 shows this variation with an EPC (event-driven-process chain) diagram [14].

Fig. 5. Changing the control flow via altering task dependences (a) initial, (b) modified

A product can be created and removed using the methods *[add/remove]Product()*. The operation *updateProduct()* can be used to alter the CoS and CoT of a product. A created product can be reconfigured using the operations *[add/remove]BehaviorRef()*.

Solutions for Impacts. The general approach to realize an impact of a change is as follows. If a change E causes a change F as a direct impact, then to propagate this impact, the techniques for realizing the change F need to be used (see above). For example, the removal of a role requires the removal of its contracts since there are invalid, and the operation *removeContract()* can be used to propagate this effect. Note that we assume that the initial change made by a developer is an intended one. Due to limited space, we do not describe each propagation link using the general approach.

However, there are two cases that require specific techniques to control the propagation of impacts. First, the service interface changes related to a used capability (unchanged) should not be propagated to the product line. Such changes include: operation signature changes, and operation granularity (e.g., split) and transition (control relation) changes. By changing the transformations between role-role interactions and role-player interactions, the propagation of the operation signature changes can be avoided. To cope with the operation granularity and transition changes, sub-service composites that act as *adapters* need to be created. A sub-composite (an adapter) for handling the interface changes of the player C of the role B becomes the new player (the realization) for the role B. In [15], different service composite-based adapters are presented, and thus we will not further discuss these issues in this paper.

Second, the feature changes that add unwanted behaviors to one or more different features or to a subset of products need to be controlled. For this purpose, we create *variations* of the affected feature implementations (collaborations). Such variations are captured in the behavior layer by *specializing* the related behavior units. Note that a variation in a collaboration may require structural changes, e.g., new tasks. A behavior unit can be specialized to create new child behavior units by adding new elements or overriding its existing elements. The parent represents common behaviors, and the children represent variations. For instance, to support towing a rented vehicle, the behavior unit *bTowing* can be extended to create *bTowingRentedVehicle* (Fig. 6). The task *VC.tGetLocation* is created (VC - vehicle renting company), and a reference to it is added to *bTowingRentedVehicle*. The *InitOn* of *TC.tTow* is overridden to ensure that the towing starts after *VC.tGetLocation* gave the destination. Now, Product1 uses *bTowingRentedVehicle*, while Product2 continues using *bTowing* (no impact).

Note that, due to limited space, the use of the proposed techniques to solve feature implementation dependency types that can make products invalid, e.g., operational dependency [16] and feature interaction [17] is not discussed. To address these issues, the works in [16, 17] used (class) inheritance and coordination, which we also adopt.

```
1 Behavior bTowing {
2    TaskRef TC.tTow { InitOn "eGCLocKnown"; Triggers "eTowed"; } ...  }
3 Behavior bTowingRentedVehicle extends bTowing {
4    TaskRef VC.tGetLocation { InitOn  "eTowReqd"; Triggers "eVCLocKnown"; }
5    TaskRef TC.tTow { InitOn "eVCLocKnown"; Triggers "eTowed"; } ...  }
```

Fig. 6. Extending the collaboration for the feature *Tow* for the feature *VehicleHire*

Realization of Changes and Impacts to the Running Application. Upon receiving a change request, the software engineer identifies the initial changes to realize the change request as well as the further impacts of each change. The solutions for the identified changes and impacts are designed and then specified in a form of a change script. A unit in such a script is a *change command*, which comprises a name and a set of parameters as name-value pairs. For example, *addBehavior* is a command name, and *bId = "bRentingVehicle"* is a parameter (line 18 in Fig. 7). These change commands are the representations of the change primitives of the organizer at the script-level. The changes defined in a change script can be applied to the running system using the operation *executeScript()* of the organizer role. The organizer creates the executable change commands (in Java) from a change script, and applies those commands to the runtime model of the system created using the *models@runtime* concept.

An Example. Bellow, we present the process of designing a change script using an example: *add feature VehicleHire* whose implementation creates a new collaboration among a subset of services to implement the feature *VehicleHire* for use in Product1.

1. *Identifying and defining role-contract topology and service changes*: A developer identifies the differences between the expected topology and the initial one, and specifies the differences in a change script. For instance, the collaboration for *VehicleHire* requires a topology consisting of the roles MM, VC (vehicle renting company) and SC, and contracts SC_MM, SC_VC and VC_MM. The roles MM and SC, and contract SC_MM are in the initial system so the required changes concern the role VC, and contracts SC_VC and VC_MM. The player *TomAuto* is required to play role VC. Lines 3, 8, and 15 in Fig. 7 define part of these changes.

2. *Identifying and defining role-role interaction changes*: Next, a developer designs the changes to interaction terms. In our example, we add the interaction terms *iOrderVehicle* and *iPayVehicleFare* to the contract SC_VC, and the interaction term *iAckVehicleBooking* to the contract VC_MM. Lines 9-10 and 12 in Fig. 7 specify part of these changes.

```
1   AddFeatureVehicleHire{              rId : role id  cId : contract id  bId  : behavior id
2   // Roles related changes            tId : task id  tmId : term id     pdId : product id
3   addRole rId="VC";
4   addTask rId="VC" tId="tRentVehicle" usingMsgs="SC_VC.iOrderVehicle.Req"
5     resultingMsgs="SC_VC.iOrderVehicle.Res, VC_MM.iAckVehicleBooking.Req";
6   ...
7   // Contracts related changes
8   addContract cId="SC_VC" rAId="SC" rBId="VC";
9     addInteraction tmId="iOrderVehicle" cId="SC_VC" direction="AtoB" ...;
10    addInteraction tmId="iPayVehicleFare" cId="SC_VC" direction="BtoA" ... ;
11  addContract cId="VC_MM" rAId="VC" rBId="MM";
12    addInteraction tmId="iAckVehicleBooking" cId="VC_MM" direction="AtoB" ...;
13  ...
14  // Player-bindings related changes
15  addPlayerBinding pbId="vcPb" rId="VC" endpoint="www.tomauto.com/VCService";
16  ...
17  // Behavior units related changes
18  addBehavior bId="bRentingVehicle";
19  addTaskRef tId="VC.tRentVehicle" bId="bRentingVehicle"
20     initOn="eRentVehicleReqd" triggers="eVehicleRented";
21  ...
22  // Products related changes
23  addBehaviorRef pdId="Product1" bId="bRentingVehicle"; ... }
```

Fig. 7. Part of the change script for adding the feature *VehicleHire*

3. *Identifying and defining task definition changes*: Next, a developer identifies and designs the changes to the task definitions in the related roles. In our example, we create the definitions for the tasks *VC.tRentVehicle, SC.tPayVehicleFare,* and *MM.tAckVehicleBooking*. Lines 4-5 in Fig. 7 define part of the task *tRentVehicle*.

4. *Identifying and defining behavior unit changes*: In the next step, the changes to the local topologies, control flow, and behavior layer decomposition are designed. In our example, the behavior unit *bRentingVehicle* needs to be created with the references to the above-mentioned tasks. Lines 18-20 specify part of these changes.

5. *Identifying and defining product changes*: Next, a developer reconfigures the affected products. In our example, Product1 needs the feature *VehicleHire*. Thus, a reference to the behavior unit *bRentingVehicle* is added to it (line 23 in Fig. 7).

6   Prototype Implementation

To realize SO-DSPL based SaaS applications in our approach, we adopt and further improve the ROAD/Serendip framework [18, 19], which supports development and management of adaptive service orchestrations. In doing so, we treat the SO-DSPL realization for an SIMT SaaS application as an adaptive service orchestration. We presented this implementation in [6] in detail. For this work, we have used this prototype to analyze the changes and impacts presented in Section 5 and to implement the proposed solutions. We have also formulated and implemented the change commands required for this work, which are generic to our approach and independent from a particular case study.

We provide Eclipse plugins to specify (the change script editor) and perform (the adaptation tool) changes discussed in Section 5. The former can highlight and detect errors of the syntax of change commands. The latter allows executing a change script, shows the status of the execution, and if it fails, the details required to correct and rerun it. The organizer role is exposed as a Web service to allow providing change scripts remotely. We adopt the Serendip language to specify the SO-DSPL architecture and the evolutionary changes. Figure 8 shows a screenshot of the adaptation tool, executing the change script for removing the feature *Accommodation*. The snippets of the change script and the logs of the execution of the script are shown.

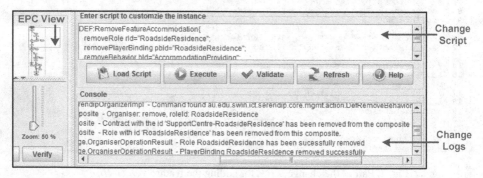

Fig. 8. A screenshot of the adaptation tool running the script for removing *Accommodation*

7   Evaluation

We demonstrate our approach's feasibility by realizing 10 SPL evolution scenarios (adapted based on [20, 21]) (Table 1). For each scenario, we create a change script capturing the difference between the initial system configuration and the expected configuration after an evolution. A change script is enacted at runtime on the system with the initial configuration. To validate an evolution, we first analyze logs for all the expected changes. Second, we compare the responses and logs for requests to the products after evolution with those of the system having the expected system configuration (manually created). The case study resources are in http://tinyurl.com/d5xlaom.

Change Impact Analysis. We assessed the effectiveness of our support for evolution by doing a change impact analysis. The complexity of each scenario was intentionally kept low to make it easier to identify change impacts. Due to limited space, we present the results for three scenarios related to addition, removal, and modification of a feature. The results for other scenarios are in the case study resources (see above).

To add the feature *BankTransfer* (CS3), we create a collaboration consists of the roles BK (Bank), AF (AccountingFirm), and MM. The last two roles and the contract between them (AF_MM) are part of the initial system. Two new contracts BK_AF and BK_MM are created. The tasks and interactions required to implement the bank transfer functionality are added/modified. A new player for realizing the role BK, and the player-binding is added. Finally, the behavior unit *bPayingByBankTransfer,* to capture this collaboration is created, and the related products are updated to use it.

The removal of the feature *BankTransfer* (CS6) is realized by deleting the elements of the collaboration for that feature, which are the same elements introduced in CS3.

Scenario CS10 is implemented by removing the interaction term *iNotifyCompletion* from the contract SC_MM, and adding a new contract GC_MM with the same interaction term. Additionally, the tasks *GC.tOrderRepair* and *SC.tAckRepair* are updated to reflect the interaction term changes, and the new task *MM.AckRepair* is added. These modifications are confined to the collaboration for the feature *Repair*.

As per the above analysis, units of change at the feature-level and the service-level are confined to their explicit representations in the SO-DSPL architecture, i.e., collaborations and abstract representations of services, their interactions and the control flow among them. This is a key requirement to support effective evolution [22].

Table 1. Change scenarios for the roadside assistance case study

No:	Type of Change	Example
CS1	Inclusion of a mandatory feature	Supporting the reimbursement of costs met by a member
CS2	Inclusion of an optional feature	Supporting renting a vehicle as an alternative transport
CS3	Inclusion of an alternative feature	Supporting paying by credit card or bank transfer
CS4	Mandatory to optional conversion	Allow using towing or expert advice without repairing
CS5	Removal of an optional feature	Discontinuing providing accommodations
CS6	Removal of an alternative feature	Dropping the bank transfer payment option
CS7	Splitting one feature into two	Separating legal assistance from the accident towing
CS8	Merging two features	Merging technical advice and vehicle test reports
CS9	Feature implementation changes	Extending fuel delivery by using an external service center
CS10	Feature implementation changes	Direct notification by a garage instead via a support center

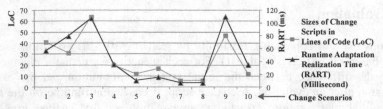

Fig. 9. Runtime adaptation realization time and change script size for change scenarios

Programmer Effort. We have used lines of code (LOC) as the metric to measure the size of a change script to approximate the effort for developing the change scripts for the case study (similar to [23]). We ignored blank lines and comments. The length of a line is approximately 120 characters. Figure 9 shows the sizes of the change scripts.

Runtime Adaptation Realization Time (RART). We have measured the *runtime adaptation realization time (RART)* for each scenario. It is the time difference between the system receiving a script and its being ready for use after changes. The framework was run on an Intel i5-2400 CPU, 3.10GHz with 3.23 GB of RAM and Windows XP. As shown in Fig. 9, the RART is within 6-110 milliseconds. We believe that this is reasonable. In addition, we observed a correlation between the RART and the size (LoC) of a change script, which approximately corresponds to the number of atomic adaptation steps included in the script. We also observed that the time taken for the removal of a feature (CS3) is low compared to its addition (CS6).

8   Related Work

We discuss below the existing research efforts from the perspectives of (D)SPLs and SaaS applications that consider *service-based systems* and support *runtime* changes.

In general, the *runtime* changes to a product line fall into two categories: adaptation of a product, and evolution of the product line [9]. Most existing works studied only the first issue [9]. We also considered it in [6] and thus focus on the second issue in this paper. In a product line, the problem space (e.g., the feature model), the solution space, and the mapping between them can evolve [20]. Within the scope of this paper, we consider the solution space for an SO-DSPL. Among the works focused on the solution space, Morin et al. [7] and Baresi et al. [21] supported modifying a business process at a set of *predefined* variation points to create products. They used SCA (Service Component Architecture) and BPEL (Business Process Execution Language) to realize their SO-DSPLs, and AOP (Aspect-Oriented Programming) to realize changes. Bosch and Capilla [24] supported, in a smart home SPL, feature-level changes by mapping a feature to a device that offers a particular service.

Studies on runtime changes to SaaS applications considered issues such as tenant on-boarding [2] and tenant-specific variants [3, 4]. Ju et al. [2] proposed a formal model to assess the cost of tenant on-boarding. In the context of *component-based systems*, Truyen et al. [3] proposed the tenant-aware dependency injection to bind tenant-specific variants to the variation points of the application' component model. Moens et al. [4] proposed a feature-model based development of services where a one-to-one mapping between a feature and a service is used. These services are deployed in a cloud environment and composed based on the selected features.

Table 2. A summary of the comparative analysis of the related works

Criterion \ Approach		[7]	[21]	[24]	[3]	[4]	we	
Req1	Runtime Sharing	-	-	-	+	-	+	+ Supported
	Variations	+	+	+	+	+	+	- Not
Req2 : Managing Changes		~	~	~	-	-	+	Supported
Req3 : Managing Change Impacts		-	-	-	-	-	+	~ Limited
Explicit Representations of Units of Change		~	~	-	-	-	+	Support

In analyzing the above works, the studies that allow modifying the product line or SaaS application at the predefined variation points did not consider the changes to the base model and its variation points, and the studies that used a compositional approach assumed a feature as a component service. None of them considers change impacts on variants. The underlying technologies used (i.e., SCA and BPEL) do not sufficiently represent the structure and behavior of services or modular service collaborations, and thus offer little support to explicitly represent units of change at the feature-level or the service-level. Moreover, the works in DSPLs usually create physically separated variants, which do not meet the requirements of the SIMT model.

In comparison with the above approaches (Table 2), we use a compositional technique to realize the variability by treating collaboration as the unit of composition. A collaboration provides a better abstraction to modularize a feature compared to a service or an arbitrary process fragment [6]. Moreover, we consider the runtime changes to an SO-DSPL that supports runtime sharing, and the management of the impacts of those changes. Our product line architecture provides an abstraction over the service asset space and explicitly represents features as modular units.

9   Conclusions and Future Work

We have addressed the runtime evolution of single-instance multi-tenant SaaS applications that are realized based on SO-DSPLs and support runtime sharing and tenant-specific variations. We have identified different types of changes to the SaaS application and their potential impacts, and proposed techniques to realize those changes and impacts at our SO-DSPL based SaaS applications. In particular, we have presented solutions to control the impacts of a change on tenants (products). A change is realized on the runtime model of the product line created based on the models@runtime concept. We have evaluated our approach with a case study and related analysis concerning change impacts, effort of developing change scripts, and time to realize a runtime change. The results have shown that our approach is feasible and beneficial.

In future, we plan to extend FeatureIDE (http://fosd.de/fide) to provide direct support for feature-based evolution, to study change impacts on ongoing transactions, and to explore the performance variability in a service-based SaaS application.

Acknowledgements. This research was partly supported by the Smart Services Cooperative Research Centre (CRC) through the Australian Government's CRC Program (Department of Industry, Innovation, Science, Research & Tertiary Education).

References

1. Chong, F., Carraro, G.: Architecture Strategies for Catching the Long Tail, MSDN Library. Microsoft Corporation (2006)
2. Ju, L., Sengupta, B., Roychoudhury, A.: Tenant Onboarding in Evolving Multi-tenant Software-as-a-Service Systems. In: ICWS, pp. 415–422 (2012)
3. Truyen, E., et al.: Context-oriented programming for customizable SaaS applications. In: SAC, pp. 418–425 (2012)
4. Moens, H., et al.: Developing and managing customizable Software as a Service using feature model conversion. In: NOMS, pp. 1295–1302 (2012)
5. Bohner, S.A.: Impact analysis in the software change process: a year 2000 perspective. In: ICSM, pp. 42–51 (1996)
6. Kumara, I., et al.: Sharing with a Difference: Realizing Service-based SaaS Applications with Runtime Sharing and Variation in Dynamic Software Product Lines. In: SCC, pp. 567–574 (2013)
7. Morin, B., et al.: Models@ Runtime to Support Dynamic Adaptation. Computer 42, 44–51 (2009)
8. Bass, L., Clements, P., Kazman, R.: Software Architecture in Practice. Wesley (2003)
9. Bencomo, N., Hallsteinsen, S., Almeida, E.S.: A View of the Dynamic Software Product Line Landscape. Computer 45, 36–41 (2012)
10. Kastner, C., Apel, S., Kuhlemann, M.: Granularity in Software Product Lines. In: ICSE, pp. 311–320 (2008)
11. Kang, K.C., Lee, J., Donohoe, P.: Feature-oriented product line engineering. IEEE Software 19, 58–65 (2002)
12. Czarnecki, K., Kim, C.H.P.: Cardinality-based feature modeling and constraints: a progress report. In: International Workshop on Software Factories, pp. 16–20 (2005)
13. Han, J.: Supporting impact analysis and change propagation in software engineering environments. In: STEP, pp. 172–182 (1997)
14. Scheer, A.W., Thomas, O., Adam, O.: Process Modeling using Event-Driven Process Chains. In: Process-Aware Information Systems, pp. 119–145 (2005)
15. Benatallah, B., Casati, F., Grigori, D., Nezhad, H.R.M., Toumani, F.: Developing Adapters for Web Services Integration. In: Pastor, Ó., Falcão e Cunha, J. (eds.) CAiSE 2005. LNCS, vol. 3520, pp. 415–429. Springer, Heidelberg (2005)
16. Lee, K., Kang, K.C.: Feature Dependency Analysis for Product Line Component Design. In: Dannenberg, R.B., Krueger, C. (eds.) ICOIN 2004 and ICSR 2004. LNCS, vol. 3107, pp. 69–85. Springer, Heidelberg (2004)
17. Weiss, M., Esfandiari, B.: On feature interactions among Web services. In: ICWS, pp. 88–95 (2004)
18. Colman, A., Han, J.: Using role-based coordination to achieve software adaptability. Science of Computer Programming 64, 223–245 (2007)
19. Kapuruge, M.K.: Orchestration as organization. PhD Thesis. Swinburne University (2013)
20. Seidl, C., Heidenreich, F., Aßmann, U.: Co-evolution of models and feature mapping in software product lines. In: SPLC, pp. 76–85 (2012)
21. Baresi, L., Guinea, S., Pasquale, L.: Service-Oriented Dynamic Software Product Lines. Computer 45, 42–48 (2012)
22. Tarr, P., et al.: N degrees of separation: multi-dimensional separation of concerns. In: ICSE, pp. 107–119 (1999)
23. Hihn, J., Habib-agahi, H.: Cost estimation of software intensive projects: A survey of current practices. In: ICSE, pp. 276–287 (1991)
24. Bosch, J., Capilla, R.: Dynamic Variability in Software-Intensive Embedded System Families. Computer 45, 28–35 (2012)

Critical Path-Based Iterative Heuristic for Workflow Scheduling in Utility and Cloud Computing

Zhicheng Cai[1], Xiaoping Li[1], and Jatinder N.D. Gupta[2]

[1] Computer Science and Engineering, Southeast University, Nanjing, China
[2] College of Business Administration, University of Alabama in Huntsville, Huntsville, USA

Abstract. This paper considers the workflow scheduling problem in utility and cloud computing. It deals with the allocation of tasks to suitable resources so as to minimize total rental cost of all resources while maintaining the precedence constraints on one hand and meeting workflow deadlines on the other. A Mixed Integer programming (MILP) model is developed to solve small-size problem instances. In view of its NP-hard nature, a Critical Path-based Iterative (CPI) heuristic is developed to find approximate solutions to large-size problem instances where the multiple complete critical paths are iteratively constructed by Dynamic Programming according to the service assignments for scheduled activities and the longest (cheapest) services for the unscheduled ones. Each critical path optimization problem is relaxed to a Multi-stage Decision Process (MDP) problem and optimized by the proposed dynamic programming based Pareto method. The results of the scheduled critical path are utilized to construct the next new critical path. The iterative process stops as soon as the total duration of the newly found critical path is no more than the deadline of all tasks in the workflow. Extensive experimental results show that the proposed CPI heuristic outperforms the existing state-of-the-art algorithms on most problem instances. For example, compared with an existing PCP (partial critical path based) algorithm, the proposed CPI heuristic achieves a 20.7% decrease in the average normalized resource renting cost for instances with 1,000 activities.

Keywords: Cloud computing, workflow scheduling, utility computing, critical path, dynamic programming, multi-stage decision process.

1 Introduction

Cloud computing is a new economic-based computational resource provisioning paradigm, in which customers can outsource their computation and storage tasks to Cloud providers and pay only for resources used. At present, only simple pricing models (posted prices) are applied in cloud computing and resources for a task are usually from a single cloud provider. However, there is a trend towards the use of complex pricing models (such as spot-pricing) and a federated architecture (which spans both Cloud and Grid providers) [1]. That is to say, a Utility

S. Basu et al. (Eds.): ICSOC 2013, LNCS 8274, pp. 207–221, 2013.

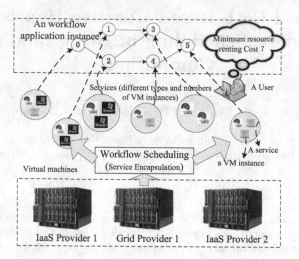

Fig. 1. Architecture of the Utility Computing Environments

Computing based global market (such as Federated Cloud) containing different types of computing and storage resources with different prices is established. For example only in the commercial Amazon Cloud, there are many types of Virtual Machines (VM), each of which provides different levels of services (number of virtual cores, CPU frequency, memory size and I/O bandwidth) with various prices per hour.

Many complex applications such as commercial data analysis, scientific earthquake prediction, weather forecast, are usually modeled as workflow instances and executed on Utility Computing based platforms. Workflows are always denoted by Directed Acyclic Graphs (DAG), in which nodes represent activities and arcs represent precedence relations between activities. Most workflow applications have deadlines. It is desirable to select appropriate services (appropriate type and right number of VM instances) for each activity to get a balance between the task execution time and resource costs. For DAG based task scheduling, there have been many related works such as in homogeneous [2] and heterogeneous distributed systems [3]. They usually try to maximize the utilization of fixed number of resources from the perspective of the service providers. In this paper, we consider the minimization of resource renting cost over unbounded dynamic resources (such as Clouds) for executing a workflow with a given due date from the perspective of customers. For customer-oriented resource renting cost minimization, Byun et al. [4] allocates fixed number of resources to the whole lifespan of the workflow. But in this paper, resources can be acquired at any time and released when they are idle, saving renting cost.

Exact methods, heuristics, and meta-heuristics are commonly used for the DAG-based scheduling problems. Since the workflow scheduling considered in this paper is known to be NP-hard [5], exponential amount of computation time is required for exact algorithms, such as dynamic programming, Branch and Bound, and Benders Decomposition. The three available heuristics for these

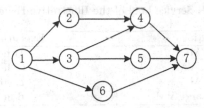

Fig. 2. An Illustrative Example for the Workflow

problems, MDP [6], DET [7], and PCP [8] are single or partial critical-path based. Meta-heuristics, such as [9,10,11] are time-consuming for complex applications (such as workflows with thousands of activities).

DET [7] and PCP [8] schedule activities of a workflow by partitioning them into different types of critical paths and assigning a priority to each critical path. The procedures used to assign services to activities and to schedule (partial) critical paths immensely impact the performance of a scheduling algorithm. Therefore, in this paper, CPI (Critical Path based Iterative) heuristic is developed. CPI heuristic generates complete critical paths as opposed to the partial ones produced by PCP. The proposed CPI heuristic iteratively generates multiple critical paths, which is distinct from the single critical path way adopted in DET. All unscheduled activities are assigned to the longest services. Assignment of all scheduled activities are kept unchanged to generate new complete critical paths. As soon as a new critical path is found, its cost is minimized. In order to simplify the optimization process, the critical path optimization problem is relaxed to the Multi-stage Decision Process (MDP) problem, which can be solved by a dynamic programming algorithm in pseudo-polynomial time.

The rest of the paper is organized as follows. Section 2 describes the workflow scheduling problem in detail and constructs its mathematical model. Section 3 presents the proposed CPI, the complexity analysis and an illustrative example. Experimental results are given in Section 4, followed by conclusions in Section 5.

2 Problem Description

Workflows in Utility and Cloud Computing environments can be depicted by a Directed Acyclic Graph (DAG), $G = \{V, E\}$ where $V = \{V_1, V_2, \ldots, V_N\}$ is the set of activities of the workflow, $E = \{(i, j)|i < j\}$ is the precedence constraints of activities, which indicates that V_j cannot start until V_i completes, P_i and $\mathcal{L}_i$ represents the immediate predecessor set and the immediate successor set of V_i, and $path(i, j) = 1$ means that there exists a path from V_i to V_j, otherwise, $path(i, j) = 0$. Figure 2 depicts a workflow example with five activities (V_1 and V_7 are dummy source and sink nodes).

As shown in Figure 1, different types of Virtual Machines (with distinct price per hour) are provided by different IaaS or even Grid providers. For every activity, there are several candidate services, each of which has different types and numbers of VMs with distinct execution times and costs. The candidate services

Table 1. Service Pool of the Illustrative Example

Services	Configurations	Execution time	Cost
S_2^1	1 Small VM	24 hours	$1.44
S_2^2	1 Medium VM	15 hours	$1.8
S_2^3	1 Large VM	8 hours	$1.92
S_2^4	1 Extra Large VM	6 hours	$2.88
S_3^1	1 Extra Large VM	18 hours	$8.6
S_3^2	2 Extra Large VM, 1 Large VM	9 hours	$10.8
S_3^3	4 Extra Large VM	6 hours	$11.52
S_4^1	1 Large VM	30 hours	$7.2
S_4^2	1 Extra Large VM	20 hours	$9.6
S_4^3	1 Extra Large VM, 1 Medium VM	18 hours	$10.8
S_5^1	1 Small VM	35 hours	$2.1
S_5^2	2 Small VM	20 hours	$2.4
S_5^3	4 Small VM	13 hours	$3.12
S_6^1	1 Medium VM	25 hours	$3
S_6^2	2 Medium VM	20 hours	$4.8

for activity V_i form the service pool $S_i = \{S_i^1, S_i^2, \cdots, S_i^{m_i}\}$, $m_i = |S_i|$. And, the service is denoted as $S_i^k = (d_i^k, c_i^k)$, in which d_i^k means the execution time (contains VM set up time and data transfer time) and c_i^k represents the resource renting cost. Shorter activity execution time needs higher resource renting cost. The cost function for the activity execution time may be concave, convex and hybrid. For example, the candidate services for each activity of the workflow in Figure 2 are illustrated in Table 1.

Appropriate services must be selected for each activity to make a balance between execution time and cost. The binary variable $\chi_i^k \in \{0, 1\}, 1 \leq i \leq N, 1 \leq k \leq m_i$ is used to demonstrate whether the service S_i^k is chosen for V_i. Each activity is allocated to the most appropriate service to minimize the total resource renting cost, under the constraint of a given deadline D, i.e., the objective of the problem is to find the activity-service mapping for all activities and services to minimize the total cost within deadline D. This problem can be modeled as a mixed integer linear programming (MILP) problem as follows.

$$\text{Min} \quad \sum_{i \in V} \sum_{k=1}^{m_i} c_i^k \chi_i^k \tag{1}$$

$$\text{S.t.} \quad \sum_{k=1}^{m_i} \chi_i^k = 1, 1 \leq i \leq N \tag{2}$$

$$f_i \leq f_j - \sum_{k=1}^{m_i} d_j^k \chi_j^k, \forall (i,j) \in E \tag{3}$$

$$f_1 \geq \sum_{k=1}^{m_1} d_1^k \chi_1^k \tag{4}$$

$$\chi_i^k \in \{0, 1\}, 1 \leq k \leq m_i \tag{5}$$

$$d_i^k \in I^+, 1 \leq i \leq N, 1 \leq k \leq m_i \tag{6}$$

$$Max\{f_i\} \leq D, 1 \leq i \leq N \tag{7}$$

The objective function (1) is to minimize the total cost. One and only one service (mode) is assigned to each activity according to constraint (2). Constraint

(3) and (4) guarantee the precedence constraints. Constraint (5) denotes a binary decision variable. The execution times of activities are integers according to constraint (6). The deadline is met according to the constraint (7).

3   Proposed Heuristics

Though critical paths are commonly calculated in DAG-based scheduling methods, only single critical path or partial critical paths are utilized to distinguish critical activities from the activity set. For the grid workflow scheduling considered by Yuan et al. [7], the criticality of non-critical activities is measured by activity floats after the activities on the single critical path have been scheduled. For the workflow scheduling in IaaS Clouds and Utility Grids considered by Abrishami et al. [12,8], partial critical paths are obtained by setting all unscheduled activities with the shortest services. Path structure information is not fully used in these two methods. In this paper, a novel critical path construction method and a new critical path optimizing method are investigated.

3.1   Multiple Complete Critical Path Construction

Let $\mathcal{F}$ and U denote the set of scheduled and unscheduled activities respectively. $\mathcal{Q}_{[j]}$ denotes the index of the selected services for scheduled activity V_j in partial solution $\mathcal{Q}$ and $EFT^L(V_i)$ denotes the earliest finish time of the activity V_i, calculated by assigning all activities in U to the services with the longest execution times while keeping the scheduled activities in $\mathcal{F}$ unchanged. If the activity V_i has been scheduled, i.e., $V_i \in \mathcal{F}$, the execution time of the V_i remains $d_i^{\mathcal{Q}_{[i]}}$, the same as the assigned service in $\mathcal{Q}$. Otherwise, the execution time of V_i is set as $\max_{k=1}^{m_i}\{d_i^k\}$. $EFT^L(V_i)$ for each activity V_i is calculated from V_1 to V_N sequentially according to the above procedure. Initially, the sink activity V_N is chosen as the last node of the critical path (CP) and set as the current activity. The activity with the largest EFT^L among immediate predecessors of the current activity, denoted as V_b, is inserted at the head of CP. V_b is set as the current activity and the activity with the largest EFT^L among its immediate predecessors is denoted as V_b and inserted at the head of CP. The procedure is repeated until V_1 is inserted into CP and the final CP is constructed. The construction process is formally described in Algorithm 1.

Multiple complete critical paths are generated iteratively during the whole optimization process. To ensure that the whole workflow can finish before D, the latest finish time $LFT^S(V_i)$ of V_i is calculated by keeping the scheduled activities unchanged and assigning the unscheduled activities to their shortest execution times, i.e., $\min_{V_j \in \mathcal{L}_i}\{\{LFT^S(V_j) + d_j^{\mathcal{Q}_{[j]}}, V_j \in \mathcal{F}\}, \{LFT^S(V_j) + \min_{k=1}^{m_j}\{d_j^k\}, V_j \in U\}\}$. The solution of the workflow is feasible if and only if the finish time of every V_i is not greater than $LFT^S(V_i)$. Then, the length of CP is $\ell_{CP}^L = \sum_{V_i \in \mathcal{F} \cap CP}\{d_i^{\mathcal{Q}_{[i]}}\} + \sum_{V_i \in U \cap CP}\{\max_{1 \le k \le m_i}\{d_i^k\}\}$. If ℓ_{CP}^L is less than D, the current solution is cheapest because all unscheduled activities take their

---

Algorithm 1. CP Construction using Longest services

1: $EFT^L(V_1) \leftarrow 0, CP \leftarrow (V_N), V_b \leftarrow V_N$.
2: **for** $j = 2$ to N **do**
3:    **if** $V_j \in \mathcal{F}$ **then**
4:        $EFT^L(V_j) \leftarrow \max\limits_{V_i \in P_j} \{EFT^L(V_i)\} + d_j^{Q[j]}$.
5:    **else**
6:        $EFT^L(V_j) \leftarrow \max\limits_{V_i \in P_j} \{EFT^L(V_i)\} + \max\limits_{k=1}^{m_j}\{d_j^{m_j}\}$.
7: **while** $(V_b! = V_1)$ **do**
8:    $V_b \leftarrow \arg\max\limits_{V_k \in P_c} \{EFT^L(V_k)\}$.
9:    Insert V_b at the head of CP.
10: **return** CP.

---

cheapest services. The whole algorithm terminates. Otherwise, some activities on CP should be assigned to shorter execution times at higher cost services, which may result in new critical paths. In other words, unscheduled activities on CP are reassigned to services in order to minimize the total cost C_{CP} of CP while all activities in V meet their LFT^S constraints, i.e, all unscheduled activities on CP are reassigned to the most appropriate services to minimize C_{CP}. The details of the critical path optimization process is described in Section 3.2 below. The critical path of the workflow would be changed and a new one could be obtained by Algorithm 1 again. The process is iterated until the length of the newly found critical path is not greater than D.

3.2 Critical Path Optimization

The model of the critical path optimization problem is as follows:

$$\text{Min} \quad C_{CP} = \sum_{i \in CP} \sum_{k=1}^{m_i} c_i^k \chi_i^k \qquad (8)$$

$$\text{S.t.} \quad \sum_{k=1}^{m_i} \chi_i^k = 1, \forall V_i \in U \qquad (9)$$

$$\chi_i^k \in \{0, 1\}, \forall V_i \in U, 1 \leq k \leq m_i \qquad (10)$$

$$\chi_i^k = y_i^k, i \in \mathcal{F}, 1 \leq k \leq m_i \qquad (11)$$

Equations $(3),(4),(6),(7)$

where $y_i^k = 1$ if activity $V_i \in \mathcal{F}$ and 0 otherwise.

The objective (8) is to minimize the total cost C_{CP} of the critical path CP, Constraints (9), and (10) are similar to the constraints (2) and (5) of the original problem respectively. Constraint (11) means that the scheduled activities keep their services assignments unchanged.

In this paper, a Dynamic Programming based Pareto Method (DPPM) is proposed to simplify the critical path optimization problem. For each activity V_i, $EFT^S(V_i)$ is the earliest finish time in terms of the scheduled activities, i.e., execution time of the scheduled activities remain $d_i^{Q[i]}$. At first, the critical path optimizing problem is relaxed to a Multi-stage Decision Process (MDP) problem

---

Algorithm 2. Dynamic Programming for MDP_i

1: Initialize the $PS_1 \leftarrow \{< 0, 0, 0 >\}, i \leftarrow 1$;
2: **for** i=1 to $|CP|$ **do**
3:    **for** each $s \in PS_i$ **do**
4:       **for** k=1 to $|S_{i+1}|$ **do**
5:          Generate a solution s' for SSP_{i+1}, $C(s') \leftarrow C(s) + c_{i+1}^k$;
6:          $T(s') \leftarrow T(s) + d_{i+1}^k, s' \leftarrow < T(s'), C(s'), I_{(1,i)}(s), k >$;
7:          $PS_{i+1} \leftarrow PS_{i+1} \bigcup \{s'\}$;
8:    Update PS_{i+1}, remove solutions which are dominated by others or the finish time is already greater than D;
9: **return** $PS_{|CP|}$;

---

by temporarily deleting activities and precedence constraints not on the critical path CP Then, the MDP problem can be formulated as follows:

$$\text{Min} \quad [\sum_{i \in CP} \sum_{k=1}^{m_i} c_i^k \chi_i^k, \sum_{i \in CP} \sum_{k=1}^{m_i} d_i^k \chi_i^k]^T \tag{12}$$

$$\text{S.t.} \quad \sum_{k=1}^{m_i} \chi_i^k = 1, \forall V_i \in U \cap CP \tag{13}$$

$$f_i \leq f_j - \sum_{1 \leq k \leq m_i} d_j^k \chi_j^k, \forall (i,j) \in CP \tag{14}$$

$$\chi_i^k \in \{0,1\}, \forall V_i \in U \cap CP, 1 \leq k \leq m_i \tag{15}$$

$$\chi_i^k = y_i^k, i \in \mathcal{F} \cap CP, 1 \leq k \leq m_i \tag{16}$$

$$d_i^k \in I, V_i \in CP, 1 \leq k \leq m_i \tag{17}$$

$$Max\{f_i\} \leq D, V_i \in CP \tag{18}$$

Function (12) means that it is a multi-objective optimization problem to find Pareto optimal solutions. Only precedence relations on CP are considered, which are represented in Constraints (14) and (18).

Then, a Dynamic Programming (DP) algorithm is proposed to optimize the MDP problem in pseudo-polynomial time. Sub-problems should be defined before a DP algorithm can be used. In this paper, the ith sub-problem SSP_i of the MDP is defined to get a Pareto solution set for partial critical path $PCP_i = \{CP_1, CP_2, CP_3, \ldots, CP_i\}$. Solutions of current sub-problem SSP_i are constructed by combining the Pareto solutions of the immediate former sub-problem SSP_{i-1} and services of the ith activity CP_i. Solutions, which are dominated by others or the solutions with the total execution time larger than the deadline, are removed from the Pareto set. Pareto solutions of the SSP_i can be represented with a set $PS_i = \{< T(s), C(s), I_1(s), I_2(s), I_3(s), \ldots, I_i(s) >, \ldots\}$. Each element of the PS_i is a $(i+2)$-tuple. The first and second elements of the tuple represents the finish time and the total cost of the PCP_i. The element $I_i(s)$ of the tuple represents the index of the selected service for the ith activity of the SSP_i in solution s. The $I_1(s), I_2(s), I_3(s), \ldots, I_i(s)$ can be denoted with $I_{(1,i)}(s)$. Since SSP_{i+1} can be solved based on the solutions of SSP_i directly, SSP_1 to SSP_L are solved one by one. At last, a Pareto optimal solution set $PS_{|CP|}$, in which there are at most D solutions, is found. The formal description of this DP procedure is given in Algorithm 2.

Algorithm 3. DPPM(SP_i)

1: Relax the critical path optimizing problem to MDP;
2: Call Algorithm 2 to get a Pareto solution set PS for MDP;
3: Sort solutions of PS by the total cost in non-decreasing order;
4: **for** each $s \in PS$ **do**
5:     **for** $j = 1$ to N **do**
6:       **if** $V_j \in CP_i$ **then**
7:         $EFT^S(V_j) \leftarrow \max_{i \in P_j}\{EFT^S(V_i)\} + d_j^{s[j]}$;
8:       **else if** $V_j \in \mathcal{F}$ **then**
9:         $EFT^S(V_j) \leftarrow \max_{i \in P_j}\{EFT^S(V_i)\} + d_j^{Q[j]}$;
10:       **else**
11:         $EFT^S(V_j) \leftarrow \max_{i \in P_j}\{EFT^S(V_i)\} + \min_{k=1}^{m_j}\{d_j^{m_j}\}$
12:       **if** $EFT^S(V_j) > LFT^S(V_j)$ **then**
13:         Goto Step 4;
14:     $s_{best} \leftarrow s$, break;
15: **return** s_{best};

After MDP is solved by Algorithm 2, the cheapest feasible solution should be distinguished from $PS_{|CP|}$. Firstly, solutions of $PS_{|CP|}$ are sorted by the total costs $T(s)$ in non-decreasing order. Then, their feasibility is verified by checking whether $EFT^S(V_i)$ is less than $LFT^S(V_i)$ for all activity $V_i \in V$. Once a feasible solution is found, the feasibility verification process stops. Finally, $LFT^S(V_i)$ are recalculated once a critical path is scheduled. The formal description of the DPPM procedure is shown in Algorithm 3, in which $s[j]$ is the services index of activity V_j in solution s.

3.3 The Proposed CPI Heuristic

The proposed CPI heuristic can be described as follows: Initially, $U \leftarrow V$ and $\mathcal{F}$ are set as empty. $LFT^S(V_i)$ is calculated one by one with all activities being assigned the shortest services. A new critical path CP is generated by assigning all unscheduled activities to the longest services while keeping the assignment of scheduled activities in $\mathcal{F}$ unchanged. If the total duration of the CP is less than the deadline D (i.e., $\ell_{CP}^L \leq D$), the algorithm stops because the partial solution Q (unscheduled activities select the longest durations) is feasible. Otherwise, CP is optimized by DPPM. $U \leftarrow U/\{V_j \in CP\}$ and $\mathcal{F} \leftarrow \mathcal{F} \cup \{V_j \in CP\}$. s_{cp} is appended to Q. LFT_i is recalculated in terms of Q. The steps of the CPI heuristic are formally described in Algorithm 4.

3.4 An Illustrative Example for CPI

Take the workflow in Figure 2 for example. Set deadline $D = 35$.

(1) *Calculate* $LFT^S(V_7) = 35$, $LFT^S(V_6) = 35$, $LFT^S(V_5) = 35$, $LFT^S(V_4) = 35$, $LFT^S(V_3) = 17$ *and* $LFT^S(V_2) = 17$. *Since no activities has been scheduled in*

Algorithm 4. CPI

1: Set $U \leftarrow V, \mathcal{F} \leftarrow NULL, LFT^S(V_N) \leftarrow D$.
2: Assign V_i the service with $\min_{k=1}^{m_i}\{d_i^k\}, V_i \in V$.
3: **for** $i = N - 1$ to 1 **do**
4:     Calculate $LFT^S(V_i)$;
5: **while** $U \neq Null$ **do**
6:     $CP \leftarrow$ Call Algorithm 1.
7:     **if** $\ell_{CP}^B \leq D$ **then**
8:         Set $V_i \in U$ with the longest services, Update $\mathcal{Q}$, Go to step 11.
9:     $s_{cp} \leftarrow$DPPM(CP).
10:    $U \leftarrow U/\{V_j \in CP\}, \ \mathcal{F} \leftarrow \mathcal{F} \cup \{V_j \in CP\}$. Append s_{cp} to $\mathcal{Q}$. Recalculate $LFT^S(V_i), 1 \leq i \leq N$ in terms of $\mathcal{Q}$.
11: **return** $\mathcal{Q}$.

---

the first iteration, all activities are allocated to their longest services. Calculate $EFT^L(V_2) = 24, EFT^L(V_3) = 18, EFT^L(V_4) = 54, EFT^L(V_5) = 53$ and $EFT^L(V_6) = 25$ one by one . Initially, V_7 is added to the CP first, then, immediate predecessor V_4 with largest $EFT^L(V_4) = 54$ is added to the front of CP and set as the current activity. Later, V_2 is added. At last the first critical path $CP_1 = (V_1, V_2, V_4, V_7)$ is constructed. Since $\ell_{CP_1}^L = 54 > D$, CP_1 should be optimized. In Algorithm 3, a Pareto solution set $PS_{CP_1} = \{(35, 11.4, S_2^2, S_4^2), (28, 11.52, S_2^3, S_4^2), (33, 12.6, S_2^2, S_4^3), (26, 12.48, S_2^4, S_4^2), (24, 13.68, S_2^4, S_4^3)\}$ is generated by Algorithm 2. Later, the cheapest feasible solution $s = (35, 11.4, S_2^2, S_4^2)$ for the CP_1 is distinguished from PS_{CP_1}. Update $\mathcal{Q} = \{\chi_2^2 = 1, \chi_4^2 = 1\}$, $LFT^S(V_7) = 35$, $LFT^S(V_6) = 35$, $LFT^S(V_5) = 35$, $LFT^S(V_4) = 35$, $LFT^S(V_3) = 15$ and $LFT^S(V_2) = 15$. $\mathcal{F} = \{V_1, V_2, V_4, V_7\}, U = \{V_3, V_5, V_6\}$.

(2) *After $EFT^L(V_2) = 15, EFT^L(V_3) = 18, EFT^L(V_4) = 38, EFT^L(V_5) = 53$ and $EFT^L(V_6) = 25$ are calculated in terms of the solution of CP_1, a new critical path $CP_2 = (V_1, V_3, V_5, V_7)$ is generated. Since $\ell_{CP_2}^L = 53 \geq D$, CP_2 still needed to be optimized. At first, a Pareto solution set $PS_{CP_2} = \{(31, 11.72, S_3^1, S_5^3), (29, 13.2, S_3^2, S_5^3), (22, 13.92, S_3^3, S_5^3), (26, 13.92, S_3^3, S_5^3), (19, 14.64, S_3^3, S_5^3)\}$ for the MDP is generated. Later, each solution of PS_{CP_2} is checked to find if $EFT^S(V_i) \leq LFT^S(V_i), V_i \in V$. For the first solution $(31, 11.72, S_3^1, S_5^3)$, $EFT^S(V_2) = 18 > LFT^S(V_2)$. So, it is infeasible. Considering the second solution $(29, 13.2, S_3^2, S_5^3)$, $EFT^S(V_2) = 15, EFT^S(V_3) = 9, EFT^S(V_4) = 35, EFT^S(V_5) = 29, EFT^S(V_2) = 18$ is calculated. Since $EFT^S(V_i) \leq LFT^S(V_i)$, for all $V_i \in V$, the second solution is the cheapest feasible solution for CP_2.*

(3) *Update $\mathcal{Q} = \{\chi_2^2 = 1, \chi_4^2 = 1, \chi_3^2 = 1, \chi_5^2 = 1\}, \mathcal{F} = \{V_1, V_2, V_4, V_3, V_5, V_7\}, U = \{V_6\}$. Then calculate $EFT^L(V_2) = 15, EFT^L(V_3) = 9, EFT^L(V_4) = 35, EFT^L(V_5) = 29$ and $EFT^L(V_6) = 25$. The $CP_1 = (V_1, V_2, V_4, V_7)$ is got again and $\ell_{CP_1}^L = 35 \leq D$, which demonstrate that the left unscheduled activities need not to be optimized again, i.e., $\chi_6^2 = 1$ is added to $\mathcal{Q}$. The CPI algorithm terminates.*

3.5 Complexity Analysis

Let N is the number of activities and $M = \max_{i=1}^N\{m_i\}$. In step 2 of Algorithm 2, there are $|CP| \leq N$ iterations. And in step 3, the Pareto solution set PS_i has at most D Pareto non-dominated solutions. That is because the finish time of solutions can only be an integer in the interval [1,D] and for each finish time there can be only one Pareto non-dominated solution. For step 4 of Algorithm 2, $|S_{i+1}| \leq M$ services are available. And the complexity of generating a solution is O(N). So the complexity of Algorithm 2 is $O(N^2DM)$. The complexities of the step 3 and 4 of the Algorithm 3 are $O(D^2)$ and $O(DN)$ respectively. So, the complexity of Algorithm 3 is $O(N^2D^2M)$. It now remains to find the number of times step 5 of algorithm 4 is executed. The following theorem helps to do that.

Theorem 1 (Unequal critical path property in CPI). *In the CPI, if $\ell^L_{CP_i} > D$, at least one activity in the new generated critical path CP_i is unscheduled, i.e., CP_i has never been found in previous steps.*

Proof. In each iteration step $j, j < i$, the critical path $CP_j, j < i$ is scheduled, while the LFT^S is not violated, i.e., ℓ^S of all paths is less than D. Assuming that all activities of CP_i have been scheduled after iteration $k, k \leq i-1$, we can conclude that in each iteration step $j, j > k$, $\ell^S_{CP_i} = \ell^L_{CP_i}$ and $\ell^S_{CP_i} < D$. Therefore, $\ell^L_{CP_i} < D$ is obtained, which is conflict with $\ell^L_{CP_i} > D$. □

In view of the above theorem, there are at most N iterations of step 5 of Algorithm 4. And the complexity of Algorithm 1 is $O(N^2)$. Therefore, the overall complexity of the proposed CPI heuristic is $O(N^3D^2M)$.

4 Computational Results

We now describe the computational tests used to evaluate the effectiveness of the proposed CPI heuristic in finding good quality workflow schedules. To do this, the proposed CPI heuristic is compared with three existing state-of-the-art algorithms (DET heuristic [7], PCP_F heuristic where PCP heuristic with fair policy is used [8], and PCP_D heuristic in which PCP heuristic deploys the decrease cost policy [8]. For comparison purposes, we also included the ILOG CPLEX v12.4 with default settings to solve the MILP model of the workflow problem formulated in Section 2 earlier. All four algorithms (CPI, DET, PCP_F and PCP_D) were coded in Java. Computational experiments for all four algorithms and ILOG CPLEX v12.4 were performed on Core 2 computer with one 3.1GHZ processor, 1G RAM, and Windows XP operating system.

4.1 Test Problems

Since parameters exert influence on the performance of an algorithm, they should be tested on different values. Existing test problem instances used by Abrishami et al. [12] only have paths with at most 9 activities. However, in practice, paths of workflow have much more activities. In our computational experiments, therefore, parameters of the problem instances are as follows:

- the number of activities, N in a workflow takes a value from {200, 400, 600, 800, 1000};

- the number of services for each activity i, m_i is generated from a discrete uniform distribution $DU[2, 10], DU[11, 20]$, or $DU[21, 30]$;
- the complexity of the network structure, measured by OS according to [13], takes a value from $\{0.1, 0.2, 0.3\}$;
- the cost function (CF), denoting the functional type of cost to duration, is concave, convex, or hybrid;
- deadlines are generated by $D = D_{min} + (D_{max} - D_{min}) * \theta$ where D_{min} is the minimal total duration (using shortest duration of each activity), D_{max} is the maximal total duration of the workflow, and θ is the Deadline Factor, which takes a value from $\{0.15, 0.3, 0.45, 0.6\}$. This ensure the existence of at least one feasible solution.

The services alternatives for each activity are generated according to [14] and details are as follows: First the number of services, m_i, is generated from DU[2,10] (i.e., discrete uniform distribution with parameters 2 and 10), DU[11,20] or DU[21,30]. Then, the execution time of these services are randomly generated between 3 and 163 as follows: The range [3, 163] is divided into intervals of size 4 and a simple randomized rule is used to decide whether one of the services will have an execution time within that interval. If so, the execution time is generated within the interval using Discrete Uniform distribution. After all the m_i number of execution times are determined, the costs of the services are generated sequentially, starting with that of the minimum-cost services, c_{m_i}, which comes from U[5,105]. Given the execution time, cost pair (d_k, c_k), for services k and d_{k-1} for service $k-1$, c_{k-1} is calculated as $c_k + s_k(d_k - d_{k-1})$, where s_k is the randomly generated slope. For convex cost functions, s_{k-1} is generated from U$(s_k, s_k + S)$, where S is the maximum change in slope per service and generated from U(1,2). s_{m_i-1} (the minimum slope) is set to be 0.5. For the concave functions, s_{m_i-1} is randomly generated as $1 + u(m_i - 1)S$, where u is generated from U[0.75,1.25] (so that the initial slope is large enough to allow for smaller slopes for the other services), and then s_{k-1} is generated from U[max(1,$(s_k-S))$),s_k]. For the hybrid functions, we randomly determine the number of times the slope will increase/decrease compared to the previous one.

The paths connecting various activities are randomly generated, during which the redundant arc avoiding method given by [15] are adopted. The details are shown in Algorithm 5. $path(i, j) = 0$ means that there is no path from V_i to V_j. Step 1 of Algorithm 5 generates the node number of activities with ascending integer numbers. Then, in step 2, random arcs are added to the network one by one where an arc is accepted only if it does not produce redundancy [15].

Using the above test problem generation schemes, for each combination of m_i, OS, and CF, 10 problem instances are generated. Thus, a total of 1,350 problem instances (= 5(N) * 3(m_i)*3(OS)*3(CF)*10) are generated and used in our computational experiments.

4.2   Comparison with Existing Algorithms

To compare the effectiveness of the proposed CPI algorithm with existing algorithms, several measures are used. Let C_b^* be the total cost if all activities of

---

Algorithm 5. Random Instance Generating Algorithm

Generate activities $V = \{1, 2, \ldots, N\}$;
while $OS_c \leq OS$ **do**
    Generate a non-existed arc $(i, j), i < j$ randomly;
    if $(\forall V_{t_1} \in P_j \forall V_{t_2} \in \mathcal{L}_i \forall V_{t_3} \in P_i \forall V_{t_4} \in \mathcal{L}_j)(path(i, j) = 0 \wedge path(t_1, i) = 0 \wedge path(j, t_2) = 0 \wedge path(t_3, t_4) = 0)$ **then**
        Accept the arc (i, j), recalculate Order Strength OS_c.
return

---

a problem instance b select the cheapest services. Let $best_b$ and $worst_b$ be the best and worst solutions among all compared algorithms on instance b. For the convenience of reporting, let W_p be the total number of all problem instances for parameter p which are grouped together (shown in Count column of Table 3). Further, let $C_b(A)$ be the total cost of instance b obtained by algorithm A. Then, the ANC (average normalized resource renting cost), ARDI (Average Relative Deviation Index), and VAR (variance of RDI), are defined as follows:

$$ANC = (\sum_{b=1}^{W_p} C_b(A)/C_b^*)/W_p \tag{19}$$

$$RDI_b = (C_b(A) - best_b)/(worst_b - best_b) \tag{20}$$

$$ARDI = (\sum_{b=1}^{W_p} RDI_b)/W_p \tag{21}$$

$$VAR = (\sum_{b=1}^{W_p} (RDI_b - \sum_{b=1}^{W_p} RDI_b/W_p)^2)/W_p \tag{22}$$

Due to the excessive computational time requirements, CPLEX cannot optimally solve most of the random instances with the above parameters. Therefore, to fairly compare the algorithms, the computation time of CPLEX is set to be identical to that of CPI on the same instance and the best solution obtained within this time is taken as the solution by CPLEX.

Table 2 illustrates that CPI outperforms PCP_F, PCP_D and DET on average normalized renting cost (ANC) and ARDI for all cases. The percentage number in the ANC column for the CPI heuristic in Table 2 shows the decreased percentage of average normalized renting cost, comparing the CPI and PCP_F. CPI gets better performance (lower renting cost) than CPLEX when $N > 400$ or $OS \geq 0.2$. As N increases, Both ANC and ARDI of CPI decease faster than the other heuristics, which implies that CPI is more suitable than the compared heuristics for complexity network structure instances, i.e., great N and big OS. As m_i and OS increase, ANC of all algorithms increases because the problems become more and more complex. ANC of the compared algorithms with concave CF is significantly bigger than those with convex and hybrid CF because the concave CF has fewer cheap service candidates than the other two.

From VAR column of Table 3, it can be observed that the CPI heuristic generates solutions with the lowest VAR for all cases except for $N = 200$. This illustrates that proposed CPI heuristic is more robust than the compared existing algorithms. VAR of CPI decreases as N increases, which means that the robustness of the CPI heuristic increases with the increase in the size of the problem instance. As m_i becomes larger, VAR of each algorithm increases. Among

Table 2. ANC and ARDI(%) of the Random Instances

ParasVals		CPLEX		DET		PCP_F		PCP_D		CPI	
		ANC	ARDI	ANC	ARDI	ANC	ARDI	ANC	ARDI	ANC(Perc en)	ARDI
N	200	5.27	0	12.45	95.6	7.74	33.2	8.15	51.2	7.43(4%↓)	26.2
	400	3.78	1.7	8.53	91.7	4.99	27.9	5.27	48	4.25(14.8%↓)	15.2
	600	5.67	10.6	8.76	87.9	5.02	26.7	5.27	47.1	**4(20.3%↓)**	8.4
	800	7.32	16.7	8.9	86.1	4.88	24.6	5.14	44.4	**3.84(21.5%↓)**	6.7
	1000	5.77	14.8	7.34	85.7	4.16	23.3	4.41	42.7	**3.3(20.7%↓)**	6.1
m_i	[2,10]	1.44	1.6	3.03	99.2	1.75	23.5	1.76	30.6	1.55(11.4%↓)	10.5
	[11,20]	4.4	8	8.04	89.1	4.71	29.6	4.98	54.1	**4.09(13.2%↓)**	15.5
	[21,30]	11.11	14.4	18.07	80.5	10.63	30.5	11.28	58.6	**9.11(14.3%↓)**	15.4
OS	0.1	3.63	2.1	7.29	87.1	4.68	30.8	5.03	55.3	3.95(15.6%↓)	13.2
	0.2	5.69	9	9.67	89.8	5.57	26.3	5.87	46.5	**4.78(14.2%↓)**	13
	0.3	7.65	15.3	10.93	90.8	5.93	23.9	6.17	39.4	**5.05(14.8%↓)**	11.6
CF	convex	2.77	3.6	5.81	97.8	3.65	34.1	3.84	38.1	2.87(21.4%↓)	12.6
	concave	12.4	11.7	20.92	93.9	11.67	27.5	11.95	28.2	**10.22(12.4%↓)**	16
	hybrid	1.31	8	1.73	78.2	1.36	21.4	1.8	75.3	**1.3(4.4%↓)**	12.5
θ	0.15	8.84	14.1	12.2	89.8	9.4	40.8	9.68	56.5	**8.47(9.9%↓)**	23.3
	0.3	6.59	10.5	10.03	89.3	6.37	33.5	6.7	51.5	**5.4(15.2%↓)**	16.4
	0.45	4.24	4.8	8.38	90.3	4.02	23.4	4.33	44.4	**3.28(18.4%↓)**	10.1
	0.6	2.34	1.8	7.25	90.4	2.42	13	2.68	36.2	**2.01(16.9%↓)**	4.9

Table 3. VAR(%) and Time (s) of the Random Instances

Paras Vals		Count	CPLEX		DET		PCP_F		PCP_D		CPI	
			VAR	Time	VAR	Time	VAR	Time	VAR	Time	VAR	Time
N	200	270	0	12.9	1.9	0.83	2.7	0.31	7.8	0.27	3.62	14.05
	400	270	1.67	20.4	3.65	1.06	3.02	1.65	9.69	1.41	**1.48**	21.18
	600	270	9.26	27.0	4.93	2.28	3.52	4.89	10.72	4.20	**0.73**	27.74
	800	270	13.77	38.5	5.38	4.78	3.31	10.25	10.48	8.93	**0.61**	39.58
	1000	270	12.45	40.9	5.84	6.43	3.32	13.34	10.95	11.82	**0.54**	41.17
m_i	[2,10]	450	1.55	14.3	0.41	2.32	1.55	3.08	3.26	2.88	**1.09**	15.18
	[11,20]	450	7.28	29.3	4.18	3.28	3.46	6.82	10.71	5.81	**2.67**	30.28
	[21,30]	450	12.09	36.2	6.78	2.77	4.66	6.46	11.44	5.59	**2.83**	37.50
OS	0.1	450	2.0	23.6	5.7	2.96	3.7	4.18	10.5	3.72	**1.7**	24.58
	0.2	450	8.0	29.7	4.0	3.14	2.9	5.57	10.0	4.90	**2.0**	30.86
	0.3	450	12.9	27.9	3.8	2.71	2.8	7.85	8.5	6.74	**2.2**	28.89
CF	convex	450	3.48	24.0	1.15	2.84	4.61	4.79	6.55	5.16	**1.96**	25.08
	concave	450	10.26	21.4	3.13	2.22	2.54	4.71	3.19	4.67	**2.71**	22.15
	hybrid	450	7.13	33.3	6.39	3.26	1.82	6.63	7.43	4.25	**1.89**	34.41
θ	0.15	1350	11.8	37.1	4.0	2.48	3.4	4.72	6.9	3.90	**3.7**	37.98
	0.3	1350	9.2	29.5	4.4	2.61	2.8	5.26	7.8	4.52	**2.0**	30.17
	0.45	1350	4.5	22.9	4.2	2.82	1.7	5.64	9.8	5.00	**0.9**	23.61
	0.6	1350	1.8	15.5	4.5	3.19	0.8	5.88	12.4	5.35	**0.3**	17.10

the compared algorithms, as N and m_i increase, VAR of CPLEX increases the fastest and that of CPI increases the slowest. This demonstrates that the stability of CPLEX decreases rapidly as the complexity of the problem increases. VAR of CPLEX and CPI on concave instances is bigger than that on convex and hybrid instances. As the deadline factor θ increases (the deadline becomes looser), the performance of CPLEX, CPI and PCP_F becomes more stable.

Time columns of Table 3 show that CPI and CPLEX consume more computation time than the other algorithms. DET is the fastest algorithm. As N, m_i, and OS increase, more computation time is needed by all algorithms. CF exerts little influence on computation time. Instances with bigger θ consume less computation time for CPI and CPLEX whereas it is reverse situation for PCP and DET. However, computational time to solve a problem by any heuristic is less than one minute, which is reasonable and acceptable in practice.

5 Conclusions

In this paper, services with different time and cost attributes are allocated to workflows in Utility Computing environments by the proposed Critical-Path based Iterative (CPI) heuristic. All activities are grouped and scheduled by iteratively constructed critical paths. In every iteration, a new critical path is generated by keeping the activity-service mapping of the scheduled activities and temporarily assigning the unscheduled activities to the longest services. Dynamic programming based Pareto method is developed for the renting cost minimization of critical paths, in which the workflow is relaxed to a Multi-stage Decision Process (MDP) problem by removing the activities and relations not on the critical path. CPI heuristic is compared with the state-of-the-art algorithms (PCP, DET, and CPLEX) for the considered problem. Experimental results show that the proposed CPI heuristic outperforms the PCP and the DET algorithms for all cases. CPI heuristic is better than CPLEX for most instances and is more stable than CPLEX. Though CPLEX outperforms the CPI heuristic on small size and simple structure problems, the stability of CPLEX is much worse than that of CPI. While computational time required to solve the workflow scheduling problem using the CPI heuristic is more than that required for the PCP and DET algorithms, it is never more than one minute, which is reasonable and acceptable in practice.

In the future, it is worth developing more effective methods for critical path optimization, introducing new decomposition methods for workflows, and investigating the bounds of the problem during the search process.

Acknowledgment. This work was supported in part by the National Natural Science Foundation of China (61003158 and 61272377) in part by the Research Fund for the Doctoral Program of Higher Education of China (20120092110027) and in part by the Southeast University (CXLX12_0099).

References

1. Chard, K., Bubendorfer, K.: High performance resource allocation strategies for computational economies. IEEE Transactions on Parallel and Distributed Systems 24(1), 72–84 (2013)
2. Kwok, Y.K., Ahmad, I.: Static scheduling algorithms for allocating directed task graphs to multiprocessors. ACM Computing Surveys (CSUR) 31(4), 406–471 (1999)
3. Bajaj, R., Agrawal, D.P.: Improving scheduling of tasks in a heterogeneous environment. IEEE Transactions on Parallel and Distributed Systems 15(2), 107–118 (2004)
4. Byun, E.K., Kee, Y.S., Kim, J.S., Deelman, E., Maeng, S.: Bts: Resource capacity estimate for time-targeted science workflows. Journal of Parallel and Distributed Computing 71(6), 848–862 (2011)
5. De, P., Dunne, E., Ghosh, J., Wells, C.: Complexity of the discrete time-cost trade-off problem for project networks. Operations Research 45(2), 302–306 (1997)
6. Yu, J., Buyya, R., Tham, C.: Cost-based scheduling of scientific workflow applications on utility grids. In: First International Conference on e-Science and Grid Computing, p. 8. IEEE (2005)
7. Yuan, Y., Li, X., Wang, Q., Zhu, X.: Deadline division-based heuristic for cost optimization in workflow scheduling. Information Sciences 179(15), 2562–2575 (2009)
8. Abrishami, S., Naghibzadeh, M., Epema, D.: Cost-driven scheduling of grid workflows using partial critical paths. IEEE Transactions on Parallel and Distributed Systems 23(8), 1400–1414 (2012)
9. Yu, J., Buyya, R.: Scheduling scientific workflow applications with deadline and budget constraints using genetic algorithms. Scientific Programming 14(3), 217–230 (2006)
10. Chen, W.N., Zhang, J.: An ant colony optimization approach to a grid workflow scheduling problem with various qos requirements. IEEE Transactions on Systems, Man, and Cybernetics, Part C: Applications and Reviews 39(1), 29–43 (2009)
11. Wu, Z., Liu, X., Ni, Z., Yuan, D., Yang, Y.: A market-oriented hierarchical scheduling strategy in cloud workflow systems. The Journal of Supercomputing 63(1), 256–293 (2013)
12. Abrishami, S., Naghibzadeh, M., Epema, D.: Deadline-constrained workflow scheduling algorithms for iaas clouds. In: Future Generation Computer Systems (2012)
13. Demeulemeester, E., Vanhoucke, M., Herroelen, W.: Rangen: A random network generator for activity-on-the-node networks. Journal of Scheduling 6(1), 17–38 (2003)
14. Akkan, C., Drexl, A., Kimms, A.: Network decomposition-based benchmark results for the discrete time–cost tradeoff problem. European Journal of Operational Research 165(2), 339–358 (2005)
15. Kolisch, R., Sprecher, A., Drexl, A.: Characterization and generation of a general class of resource-constrained project scheduling problems. Management Science 41(10), 1693–1703 (1995)

REFlex: An Efficient Web Service Orchestrator for Declarative Business Processes

Natália Cabral Silva, Renata Medeiros de Carvalho,
César Augusto Lins Oliveira, and Ricardo Massa Ferreira Lima

Center for Informatics (CIn),
Federal University of Pernambuco,
Recife – PE, Brazil
{ncs,rwm,calo,rmfl}@cin.ufpe.br

Abstract. Declarative business process modeling is a flexible approach to business process management in which participants can decide the order in which activities are performed. Business rules are employed to determine restrictions and obligations that must be satisfied during execution time. In this way, complex control-flows are simplified and participants have more flexibility to handle unpredicted situations. Current implementations of declarative business process engines focus only on manual activities. Automatic communication with external applications to exchange data and reuse functionality is barely supported. Such automation opportunities could be better exploited by a declarative engine that integrates with existing SOA technologies. In this paper, we introduce an engine that fills this gap. REFlex is an efficient, data-aware declarative web services orchestrator. It enables participants to call external web services to perform automated tasks. Different from related work, the REFlex algorithm does not depend on the generation of all reachable states, which makes it well suited to model large and complex business processes. Moreover, REFlex is capable of modeling data-dependent business rules, which provides unprecedent context awareness and modeling power to the declarative paradigm.

Keywords: declarative business process, business process flexibility, business rules, web services orchestrator, context awareness.

1 Introduction

Processes change very often in some business areas. Customer demands are volatile and business partners change frequently as new opportunities arise. To remain competitive, organizations need to be prepared to confront unforeseen situations. This requires flexible processes that can be adapted to cope with changes in the environment [10]. Such flexibility requirements motivated the development of the *declarative* business process paradigm. The declarative approach differs from most traditional, imperative modeling approaches because they model *what* must be done but do not prescribe *how* [13] to do it. In this way,

S. Basu et al. (Eds.): ICSOC 2013, LNCS 8274, pp. 222–236, 2013.

declarative business processes allow the participants to decide which activities are more appropriate for each particular situation.

Service Oriented Architecture (SOA) is a well-established software architecture for the design of enterprise applications. In SOA, a number of business activities may be performed by mature services provided by partners and third-party enterprises. These services deliver functionalities that can be shared and reused across the enterprise. Web service orchestration is an essential feature of most business process enactment frameworks. They enable the construction of automated workflows that explore the benefits provided by SOA. However, current technologies for declarative business process enactment (Declare and DCR Graphs) are focused in the modeling of manual activities. They lack adequate support for web service integration. This impairs their use in more complex applications in which both manual and automated activities are necessary.

The purpose of this paper is to introduce an approach for integrating the declarative paradigm with SOA. Our tool, called **REFlex** (*Rule Engine for Flexible Processes*), is a declarative process management system that provides a rule engine for declarative processes and a language for service orchestration [4][14].

REFlex is based on an efficient algorithm that does not rely on state-space generation [4]. Moreover, it offers support for data manipulation and data-dependent rules, which improves its context awareness and increases the range of modeling capabilities.

This paper is organized as follows. An overview of background and related work is presented in Sections 2 and 3, respectively. REFlex rule engine is described in Section 4. Next, Section 5 describes the orchestration mechanism and architecture. To demonstrate the use of the proposed approach, a case study is presented in Section 6. Finally, Section 7 discusses conclusions and future work.

2   Declarative Processes

When the company tasks are less repetitive and predictable, workflows are not able to properly represent the possible flows of work [10]. They often are either too simple, thus unable to handle the variety of situations that occur; or they are too complex, trying to model every imagined possible situation but being hard to maintain. In both cases, they may cause several problems to the company. To tackle these limitations, flexible processes surged as a shift paradigm from traditional workflow approaches [15].

Declarative business processes define the process behavior by *business rules* described in a declarative language. Traditional workflows take an "inside-to-outside" strategy, where all the executions alternatives must be explicitly represented in the process model. On the other hand, a declarative process takes an "outsite-to-inside" strategy, where the execution options are guided by constraints [13]. Adding new constraints reduces the number of execution options.

In this constraint-based approach, a process model is composed of two elements: activities and constraints. An activity is an action that updates the enterprise status and is executed by a resource. A constraint is a business rule that must be respected during the entire process execution. Thereby, the permission to execute activities is controlled by business rules. Each activity has its execution enabled only if and when the business rules allow it.

3   Related Work

In this section we discuss some important works in the areas of declarative processes and web service composition.

3.1   Declarative Processes

Declare is a rule engine system proposed by Pesic et al. [12] for modeling and executing declarative processes through an extensible graphical language called **ConDec** [13]. This language offers a set of graphical representations to describe control-flow rules that constrain the execution of process activities. Declare uses Linear Temporal Logic (LTL) as its formalism for the internal representation of business processes. Process enactment requires the construction of a Büchi automaton that contains all possible states of the process. This strategy leads to the well known problem of *state space explosion*, which limits the size and complexity of the business processes that can be executed using Declare.

Hildebrandt and Mukkamala [8] propose a graph-based model called *DCR Graphs* to specify business process rules. At runtime, DCR Graphs control the dynamic evolution of the process' state. Since the states of the process are updated dynamically, this approach does not require a prior generation of all possible states.

In a previous work, we proposed an approach for declarative processes that is based on event-driven programming [11]. This approach aims to minimize the gap between the business rules and their implementation by systematically moving from business rules described in natural language towards a concrete implementation of a business process. We use complex event processing (CEP) to implement such a process. CEP is more expressive than the above mentioned languages. It can describe both control-flow and data dependencies. However, this approach is not based on an underlying formal model that guarantees the correctness of the resulting process models.

Except from our former approach using CEP, none of the aforementioned declarative approaches are data-aware, i.e., the activities and rules do not have the concept of context data. Furthermore, none of these works are integrated with SOA concepts, i.e., the activities are not executed by web service invocation.

Works on process mining have already considered data-aware rules in declarative processes. Through the SCIFF Checker [1], a set of execution traces can be classified as compliant or not compliant with a group of business rules. However, SCIFF's algorithm is only useful for verification purposes and is not applicable for business process enactment.

3.2   Web Service Composition

None of the current tools that support the execution of declarative processes [8][12] employ Service-Oriented Computing (SOC) concepts. In all these systems, the activities are manual. The user only informs when the activity starts, concludes, or is canceled. There is no built-in support for activity automation.

The *Business Process Execution Language* (BPEL) [2], is the *de facto* standard for web services orchestration. However, it is static and not easy to adapt [16]. In this regard, a number of works propose flexible alternatives to BPEL, to allow for the construction of more flexible and adaptable business processes [9][5][7][17].

VxBPEL [9] is an extension to the standard BPEL language that provides VariationPoint, which is a container of possible BPEL codes available for selection at runtime.

AO4BPEL [5] is another BPEL extension that improves the business process flexibility using aspect-oriented concepts. The BPEL structure is expanded to include aspects, which define fragments of business processes that can be inserted into one or more process models at runtime.

CEVICHE [7] is a tool that employs the AO4BPEL. CEVICHE's users do not activate the aspects. Instead, the aspects are activated when event patterns are recognized by a Complex Event Processing (CEP) engine. Thus, CEVICHE can automatically decide *when* and *how* to adapt the system by analyzing events with the CEP technology.

Xiao *et al.* [17] propose a constraint-based framework that employs process fragments. A process fragment is a portion of a process that can be reused across multiple processes. These fragments are selected and composed based on some business constraints and policies. The resulting process is a standard BPEL process, deployable on standard BPEL engines.

Another dynamic composition proposal is the SCENE service execution environment [6]. It allows the BPEL to be changed at runtime by choosing the correct service to be invoked based on business rules. These rules are used to realize the correct bindings between the BPEL engine and the services. For this purpose, there is a rule engine that makes the decisions about the services selection.

All the aforementioned works are extensions to BPEL aiming at making it more adaptive. However, none of them provide ways to execute declarative processes. Since declarative processes do not have any predefined structure, it is not possible to execute them using BPEL or its extensions. Therefore, integrating web services and the declarative approach requires the development of novel engine technology.

4   REFlex Rule Engine

In this section, we describe the rule engine used by REFlex to control the execution of declarative processes.

The declarative business process engines primary task is to guarantee that all process instances adhere to the business rules defined for that process. To accomplish this, the engine must prevent the user from executing activities that violate the rules and must also oblige the execution of pending activities. Moreover, the engine should not let the user execute a sequence of activities that blocks the completion of the process. In other words, the engine must guarantee that the process never reaches a deadlock state, in which pending activities cannot be executed.

The REFlex rule engine is an efficient declarative process engine. It does not have the state explosion problem that is exihibited by DECLARE, since it does not require the previous generation of the complete set of reachable states [4]. The state of the process is updated dynamically. To avoid deadlocks, REFlex uses a *liveness-enforcement* algorithm that guarantee that a deadlock state is never reached.

REFlex models are *directed graphs* in which **nodes are activities** and **arcs define the relationship** between activities. Table 1 describes the rule types of REFlex, as well as their graphical representation (arcs) and semantics. An example of REFlex model can be seen in Section 6.

Observe that several ConDec rules can be implemented using REFlex rule types. The translation from ConDec to REFlex rules is shown in Table 2.

During runtime, activities change their state. An activity may be *enabled*, *disabled*, or *blocked*. An enabled activity may also be *obliged*. An *obliged* activity that has not be executed is called "pending activity". Activities that are *disabled* or *blocked* cannot be executed by the user. Moreover, the process can not be concluded if there are *pending activities* left.

When the user executes an enabled activity X, an *exec(X)* event is issued. This event causes an update in the state of the system according to the process rules (Table 1). Furthermore, certain rules are valid only at the first execution of an activity (see, for example, precedence). In such cases, the rule is *removed* from the process after its conditions have been fulfilled.

To guarantee deadlock freedom, i.e., that the process instance never reaches a deadlock state, REFlex inserts liveness-enforcing rules in the model. The objective of these rules is to disable execution paths that would certainly result in a deadlock in a future step of execution. As an example, consider a process with three activities (A, B, C) and two rules: *response*(A, B) and *not after*(C, B). Clearly, after the execution of A, the activity C can not be executed until B is executed. This is because if C executes between A and B it would make activity B both obliged and blocked, which configures a deadlock. A similar situation occurs if A executes after C. Indeed, A can *never* execute *after* C in such a process.

The idea behind the liveness-enforcing algorithm is to avoid all situations that cause an activity to be simultaneously *blocked* and *obliged*. To accomplish that, we analyze the model statically and (transparently) insert new rules that are specific to control such situations. The model can execute only after applying the algorithm to analyze the model and inserting the rules to remove deadlock threats. The rules inserted by the algorithm do the following: 1) "propagate" blocking states (e.g., if A obliges B and B obliges C, when C is blocked, so are A and B); 2) disable blocking when the activities that would be blocked are

Table 1. REFlex rule types

Existential Rules	
at least(A, n)	
Behavior	**Semantics**
A is initialy obliged and remains obliged until it is executed n times.	when *exec(A)* do if $(n > 0)$ then $n = n - 1$
at most(A, n)	
Behavior	**Semantics**
After n executions of A, it is blocked.	when *exec(A)* do if $(n > 0)$ then $n = n - 1$; when $n = 0$ do block A
Relational Rules	
response(A, B)	
Behavior	**Semantics**
After the execution of A, B is obliged.	when *exec(A)* do oblige B
responded existence(A, B)	
Behavior	**Semantics**
The first execution of A obliges B. If B is executed before A, remove the rule.	when *exec(A)* do remove *resp.existence*(A,B), oblige B; when *exec(B)* do remove *resp.existence*(A,B)
precedence(A, B)	
Behavior	**Semantics**
While A is not executed, B is disabled.	when *exec(A)* do remove *precedence*(A,B)
not after(A, B)	
Behavior	**Semantics**
After the execution of A, B is blocked.	when *exec(A)* do block B
Default Rules (valid for all activities in all processes)	
disable(A)	
Behavior	**Semantics**
If exists X such that *precedence*(X, A), A is disabled.	if exists *precedence*(X, A) then disable A
waive(A)	
Behavior	**Semantics**
After the execution of A, if there is an *at least*(A, n), $n > 0$, then A is obliged. If not, A is not obliged.	when *exec(A)* do if not exists *at least(A, n)*, $n > 0$ then A is not obliged else A is obliged

already obliged (e.g., in the previous example, if D blocks C, when A, B, or C are obliged, D is disabled until the obligations are waived); 3) oblige precedences (e.g., if there is a *precedence* (A, B), obliging B also obliges A); and 4) blocking precedences (e.g., if there is a *precedence* (A, B), blocking A also blocks B). A proof for the *liveness* of REFlex models is described by Carvalho et al. [3].

Table 2. ConDec templates X REFlex rule types

Condec Rules	Description	Reflex Rules
Existential Rules		
init(A)	All activities but A are disabled until the execution of A.	For all activities (a_i) except A, *precedence*(A, a_i)
existence(A, n)	A is obliged until it is executed n times.	*at least*(A, n)
absence(A, n)	After $n-1$ executions of A, it can not be executed anymore.	*at most*(A, n-1)
exactly(A, n)	A must be executed exactly n times in a process instance.	*at least*(A, n) and *at most*(A, n)
Relational Rules		
response(A, B)	After the execution of A, B is obliged.	*response*(A, B)
precedence(A, B)	While A is not executed, B is disabled.	*precedence*(A, B)
succession(A, B)	After the execution of A, B is obliged, but it is disabled while A is not executed.	*precedence*(A, B) and *response*(A, B)
coexistence(A, B)	A and B are either both executed or not executed at all.	*responded existence*(A, B) and *responded existence*(B, A)
responded existence(A, B)	The first execution of A obliges B.	*responded existence*(A, B)
Negation Rules		
not response(A, B)	After the execution of A, B can not be executed.	*not after*(A, B)
not coexistence(A, B)	A and B can not be both executed in the same process instance.	*not after*(A, B) and *not after*(B, A)

4.1 Data-Aware Extension

The semantics of REFlex is extended to support data-dependent rules. This kind of rule is applied only if certain conditions hold. Such data-aware extensions provide unprecedented expressive power to declarative business processes. Few engines today are able to model this type of constraints [11]. Yet, data-dependent rules are ubiquous. It is difficult to model large, realistic declarative processes without data-dependencies.

Data-dependent rules are constructed following the pattern:

$$\textbf{IF } predicate \textbf{ THEN } rule \ (...)$$

Graphically, a data-dependent rule is represented by an arc that has an inscription attached. The inscription corresponds to the predicate that is the condition for the rule.

The semantics is the following. If the rule's predicate is true, the rule is part of the process. We say that the rule is *active* in the process instance. If the predicate is false, the engine ignores the rule. We say that it is *inactive*.

Some example of data-dependent rules are:

1. *A reimbursement for expenditure can not be sent after the grant is cancelled, unless the expenditure is prior to the cancellation date*

   IF date of expenditure > date of cancellation
   THEN *not after* ("cancel grant", "send reimbursement")

2. *If a rented car is returned after the expected return date, a charge must be issued*

   IF return date > expected return date
   THEN *response* ("return car", "issue charge")

Liveness-enforcement is a challenge for data-dependent rules. The reason is that it is not always possible to foresee which rules will be activated at runtime. For example, let us assume we have a data-dependent *response (A, B)* and a regular *not after (C, B)*. In the moment that A is obliged, if the *response* rule is active, the engine disables C until A and B execute. However, if the *response* rule is not active at this moment, it is ignored. So the engine lets the user execute C, which blocks B. Suppose that, after the execution of C, the conditions for activating the *response* are met. Now we have a situation that leads to a deadlock, once the execution of A will oblige activity B, which is currently blocked.

The problem just described can be solved if we restrict the action of activity C over the variables of the process. Once C blocks an activity, we can not allow that the execution of C itself creates conditions to oblige that activity.

This solution can be generalized as follows. First, we identify all activities that may be obliged in the next or in a future execution step (Def. 1).

Definition 1 (Possible obligation). *We say that an activity A possibly obliges B in a process instance if:*

- *the process contains the rule* response*(A, B) and the conditions for its activation are satisfied; or*
- *the process contains the rule* responded existence*(A, B) and the conditions for its activation are satisfied; or*
- *there is an activity X that possibly obliges B and A possibly obliges X.*

Next, we restrict the variables that can be affected by certain activities of the process, according to Def. 2.

Definition 2 (Data-Restricted Activities). *An activity A is not allowed to change the value of a process variable x if, for any activity B:*

1. *the process contains a rule* not after *(A, B) and*
   (a) *there is one or more conditional rules in the process that depend on x;*
   (b) *the rules that are conditioned to x affect whether B is* possibly obliged *or not in a process instance.*
2. *or the process contains a rule* at most *(A, 1) and*
   (a) *the rules that are conditioned to x affect whether A is* possibly obliged *or not in a process instance.*

The modeler is responsible for assuring the process's conformance to the data restrictions in Def. 2. With such an approach, we guarantee that, if an activity A blocks another activity B in the process, the latter will never be obliged in the future. If B is obliged before A, the liveness-enforcing rules already inserted into the model will prevent B from executing while A is obliged. The liveness-enforcing rules will also guarantee that no activity will ever oblige B after it has been blocked.

5   REFlex Orchestrator

Amongst the engines for declarative processes, only REFlex has the ability to execute external web services. Such feature allows for the modeling of semi-automated declarative business processes. This section describes how REFlex's orchestration mechanism works.

In most business processes, there are several opportunities for the automation of tasks through the use of web services. For example, we may want to query a database for product or customer information, to schedule an appointment into an on-line calendar, or perhaps to register an authorization for a new employee. We may want to be able to request an operation from a web service, send our process' data to it, and use the data from its response in other activities of the process.

To implement this feature, REFlex allows the user to set up variables and service bindings. *Variables* may be global (accessible in the entire process) or local (accessible in the scope of a single activity). The user can define any number of variables for a process. Currently, the data types supported by REFlex are *int, float, double, String, boolean* and *list* (an array of elements of any of the primitive types).

Service bindings, in turn, enable the linkage between an activity in the process and an external web service. A service binding describes which web service is linked to the activity, the location of its WSDL interface, and the binding, port type, and operation that should be called when the user wants to execute the activity.

REFlex uses the WSDL interface of the web service to automatically construct and interpret SOAP messages that are sent/received to/from the web service. The variables of the process are filled in the SOAP message body according

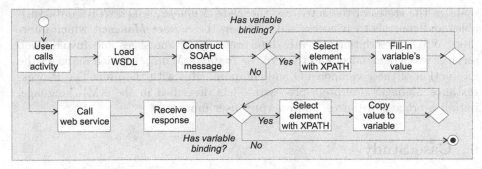

Fig. 1. REFlex orchestration process

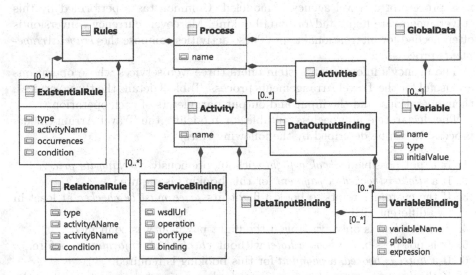

Fig. 2. Elements of a Process Definition XML

to the activity's *data input binding* and *data output binding*. These elements
define *variable bindings*, which map a variable into an element inside the SOAP
body using XPATH expressions. When calling the web service, the values of the
process' variables are copied to the SOAP message. Once the response from the
web service is received, its contents are copied into process' variables, according
to the variable bindings.

The process just described is illustrated in Fig. 1.

The process definition is described in an XML file, which contains all infor-
mation necessary to execute the process and to communicate with web services.
A process definition includes the elements presented in the diagram shown in
Fig. 2.

There are four major components in REFlex architecture [14]: REFlex is
composed of four main components: the *Engine*, which interprets the rules and

updates the states of the activities; the *Data Manager*, which stores data variables and controls their access and updates; the *Service Manager*, which interprets WSDL descriptions, creates/interprets SOAP messages and invokes web services when demanded; and the *Process Instance Manager*, which manages the interaction of these components and communicates with the user. The Process Instance Manager interprets process models described in the XML language, initialize process instances, and interpret user inputs.

6   Case Study

This section presents a case study that demonstrates the use of REFlex. A business process of a travel agency is modeled. Common tasks performed by this travel agency are flight and/or hotel booking. Moreover, currency conversion is often needed for international trips. These activities compose the *Travel Arragements* process.

The agency's information system offers three web services whose operations are useful for the Travel Arrangements process. Table 3 details the three services, their operations, and the input and output parameters of each operation.

The declarative approach is suitable for modeling the Travel Arrangements process. It can be described by the following rules:

1. It is not possible to *book a flight* without previously *checking its price*.
2. If a *flight is booked*, a *payment* for this booking is required.
3. If the customer wants to book a flight, its *price must be checked* at least in two different airlines.
4. The *check-in* is only available if the flight payment was confirmed.
5. It is not possible to *book a hotel* without *checking its information* before.
6. If a *hotel is booked*, a *payment* for this booking is required.
7. If the *booking payment* was confirmed, then a *voucher must be sent* to the costumer email.
8. If the booking payment was not confirmed, then the *costumer must be notified*.
9. A *discount* must be issued to groups of more than 10 persons that book a hotel.

One can notice that the currency service was not mentioned among the business rules. This means that the user can choose currency operations at any time while executing the business process, which characterizes the flexibility provided by declarative processes.

Fig. 3 shows how REFlex rule engine represents these rules graphically. Each node is an activity available in the process. Rules that have any dependency on context data are represented by arcs annotated with conditions. A rule is active only if the condition is evaluated to true. Otherwise, the rule is simply ignored. On other hand, rules that have no data dependency are always active. Thus, rules are enforced or not depending on the context.

Table 3. Services details

Operations	Input Variables	Output Variables
Flight Service		
checkFlightPrice	from, to, price, date, airline	flightId
bookFlight	flightID	bookID
payFlight	bookID, value, creditCard	confirmation, paymentCode
checkIn	bookID, passportNumber, email	-
Hotel Service		
checkHotel	hotelName, checkInDate, checkOutDate	roomsAvailable
bookHotel	hotelName, checkInDate, checkOutDate, persons	bookID, bookValue
payHotelBooking	bookID, value, creditCard	confirmation, paymentCode
sendVoucher	bookID, email	-
notifyCostumer	email, message	-
giveDiscount	bookID, discountPercentage	finalValue
Currency Service		
convertCurrency	value, fromCurrency, toCurrency	newCurrency

To better understand how useful data-aware rules are, note the activities *send voucher* and *notify costumer* are dependent form the result of *pay hotel booking*. This result can only be analyzed at run-time. If the business rules were static, it would not be possible to model this dependency. Thus, in this case, there are two *response* rules that rely on the result of *pay hotel booking* activity. Each rule has a condition that expresses what must be checked at run-time. When this activity is executed, the global data *hotelBooked* is updated. If the payment is confirmed, activity *send voucher* is obliged by the *response* rule while *notify costumer* becomes optional. If the payment is not confirmed, *notify costumer* is obliged and activity *send voucher* will be disabled, due to a precedence on itself. Without data-dependent rules, this behavior would be hard to achieve. Thus, data-aware declarative models are more intuitive and expressive.

After modeling the activities and their relationship, we are able to link activities to their corresponding web service operations. The orchestrator uses this information to perform the service bindings and invoke operations when activities are executed. Listing 1.1 presents an excerpt of the XML definition of our process' variables and activity bindings. It shows how the *Pay Flight* activity is bound to the *payFlightBooking* operation of the *FlightService*. This activity references local variables, whose values are provided by the user prior to its

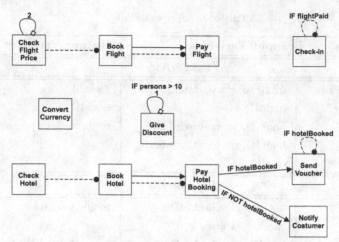

Fig. 3. REFlex model of the case study

execution. It also references global variables, which may be set by the user or by other services. For example the input parameter *bookValue* is the return of the *bookFlight* operation.

```
<process name="TravelProcess">
 <globalData>
   ...
   <variable name="bookID" type="STRING"/>
   <variable name="flightPaid" type="BOOLEAN"/>
   <variable name="flightPaymentCode" type="INT"/>
   ...
 </globalData>
 <activities>
   ...
   <activity name="Pay_Flight">
    <serviceBinding operation="payFlightBooking"
    wsdlUrl="http://...FlightService?wsdl"
    portType="FlightServicePortType"
    binding="FlightServiceSOAP11Binding"/>
    <dataInputBinding>
     <variableBinding variableName="bookID" global="true"
     expression="xpath:/payFB/bookID"/>
     <variableBinding variableName="value" global="false"
     type="DOUBLE" expression="xpath:/payFB/value"/>
     <variableBinding variableName="creditCard" global="false"
     type="STRING" expression="xpath:/payFB/creditCard"/>
    </dataInputBinding>
    <dataOutputBinding>
     <variableBinding variableName="flightPaid"
     expression="//payFB/result/confirmation"/>
     <variableBinding variableName="flightPaymentCode"
     expression="//payFB/result/paymentCode"/>
    </dataOutputBinding>
   </activity>
   ...
 </activities>
</process>
```

XML 1.1. Snipet of the process definition of the case study

7   Conclusions

This work proposes a web-service orchestrator for declarative business processes, called REFlex. This kind of business process rely on business rules to describe the behavior of the process and to control the execution of process instances. Hence, the flow of activities is only determined at run-time.

Current engines for the enactment of declarative processes are not completely integrated with current SOA technologies. On the other hand, all professional engines for traditional workflow execution recognize the necessity for integration with web services. It is our contend that a web service orchestrator capable of interpreting declarative models brings enormous benefits to the field. It allows for the construction of semi-automated, flexible business processes where process participants interact with external tools to exchange data and reuse functionality. In this way, the flexibility of declarative models can be complemented by the efficiency offered by automation.

REFlex adopts both a graphical and an XML-based languages for the description of declarative business models. The graphical notation is useful for communication with business administrators. The XML model is used to model the technical details of the process, such as its data variables and web service bindings. SOAP messages are automatically constructed at run-time to perform the service invocations requested by the user.

REFlex uses a novel rule engine that offers the efficient and deadlock-free execution of declarative business processes [4]. Furthermore, a unique feature of REFlex engine among related work is its capacity to interpret data-aware rules. These rules depend on context information and enhance the expressive power of the modeling language.

To demonstrate our approach, we described a declarative business process modeled in REFlex notation. The process make use of web service bindings and data-dependent rules. Albeit simple, it illustrates the usefulness of such features for real world applications.

References

1. Alberti, M., Chesani, F., Gavanelli, M., Lamma, E., Mello, P., Torroni, P.: Verifiable agent interaction in abductive logic programming: The sciff framework. ACM Trans. Comput. Logic 9(4), 29:1–29:43 (2008)
2. Andrews, T., Curbera, F., Dholakia, H., Goland, Y., Klein, J., Leymann, F., Liu, K., Roller, D., Smith, D., Thatte, S.: et al. Business process execution language for web services (2003)
3. de Carvalho, R.M., Silva, N.C., Oliveira, C.A.L., Lima, R.M.: Reflex: an efficient graph-based rule engine to execute declarative processes. In: Proceedings of the International Conference on Systems, Man and Cybernetics (2013)
4. de Carvalho, R.M., Silva, N.C., Oliveira, C.A.L., Lima, R.M.: A solution to the state space explosion problem in declarative business process modeling. In: Proceedings of the 25th International Conference on Software Engineering and Knowledge Engineering (2013)

5. Charfi, A., Mezini, M.: Ao4bpel: An aspect-oriented extension to bpel. World Wide Web 10(3), 309–344 (2007)
6. Colombo, M., Di Nitto, E., Mauri, M.: SCENE: A service composition execution environment supporting dynamic changes disciplined through rules. In: Dan, A., Lamersdorf, W. (eds.) ICSOC 2006. LNCS, vol. 4294, pp. 191–202. Springer, Heidelberg (2006)
7. Hermosillo, G., Seinturier, L., Duchien, L.: Using complex event processing for dynamic business process adaptation. In: 2010 IEEE International Conference on Services Computing (SCC), pp. 466–473 (July 2010)
8. Hildebrandt, T.T., Mukkamala, R.R.: Declarative event-based workflow as distributed dynamic condition response graphs. In: PLACES, pp. 59–73 (2010)
9. Koning, M., Sun, C.-A., Sinnema, M., Avgeriou, P.: Vxbpel: Supporting variability for web services in bpel. Inf. Softw. Technol. 51(2), 258–269 (2009)
10. Nurcan, S.: A survey on the flexibility requirements related to business processes and modeling artifacts. In: HICSS 2008: Proceedings of the 41st Annual Hawaii International Conference on System Sciences, p. 378. IEEE Computer Society, Washington, DC (2008)
11. Oliveira, C., Silva, N., Sabat, C., Lima, R.: Reducing the gap between business and information systems through complex event processing. Computing and Informatics 32(2) (2013)
12. Pesic, M., Schonenberg, H., van der Aalst, W.M.P.: Declare: Full support for loosely-structured processes. In: 11th IEEE International Enterprise Distributed Object Computing Conference, EDOC 2007, p. 287 (October 2007)
13. Pesic, M.: Constraint-Based Workflow Management Systems: Shifting Control to Users. PhD thesis, Technische Universiteit Eindhoven, Eindhoven, The Netherlands (2008)
14. Silva, N.C., de Carvalho, R.M., Oliveira, C.A.L., Lima, R.M.: Integrating declarative processes and soa: A declarative web service orchestrator. In: Proceedings of the 2013 International Conference on Semantic Web and Web Services (2013)
15. van der Aalst, W.M.P., Pesic, M.: Decserflow: Towards a truly declarative service flow language. In: Leymann, F., Reisig, W., Thatte, S.R., van der Aalst, W.M.P. (eds.) The Role of Business Processes in Service Oriented Architectures, July 16-July 21. Dagstuhl Seminar Proceedings, vol. 06291. Internationales Begegnungs-und Forschungszentrum fuer Informatik (IBFI), Schloss Dagstuhl, Germany (2006)
16. Weigand, H., van den Heuvel, W.-J., Hiel, M.: Business policy compliance in service-oriented systems. Information Systems 36(4), 791–807 (2011), ¡/ce:title¿ Selected Papers from the 2nd International Workshop on Similarity Search and Applications SISAP 2009 ¡/ce:title¿
17. Xiao, Z., Cao, D., You, C., Mei, H.: Towards a constraint-based framework for dynamic business process adaptation. In: Proceedings of the 2011 IEEE International Conference on Services Computing, SCC 2011, pp. 685–692. IEEE Computer Society, Washington, DC (2011)

Task Scheduling Optimization in Cloud Computing Applying Multi-Objective Particle Swarm Optimization

Fahimeh Ramezani, Jie Lu, and Farookh Hussain

Decision Systems & e-Service Intelligence Lab
Centre for Quantum Computation & Intelligent Systems
School of Software, Faculty of Engineering and Information Technology
University of Technology, Sydney, P.O. Box 123 Broadway NSW 2007 Australia
Fahimeh.Ramezani@student.uts.edu.au,
{Jie.Lu,Farookh.Hussain}@uts.edu.au

Abstract. Optimizing the scheduling of tasks in a distributed heterogeneous computing environment is a nonlinear multi-objective NP-hard problem which is playing an important role in optimizing cloud utilization and Quality of Service (QoS). In this paper, we develop a comprehensive multi-objective model for optimizing task scheduling to minimize task execution time, task transferring time, and task execution cost. However, the objective functions in this model are in conflict with one another. Considering this fact and the supremacy of Particle Swarm Optimization (PSO) algorithm in speed and accuracy, we design a multi-objective algorithm based on multi-objective PSO (MOPSO) method to provide an optimal solution for the proposed model. To implement and evaluate the proposed model, we extend Jswarm package to multi-objective Jswarm (MO-Jswarm) package. We also extend Cloudsim toolkit applying MO-Jswarm as its task scheduling algorithm. MO-Jswarm in Cloudsim determines the optimal task arrangement among VMs according to MOPSO algorithm. The simulation results show that the proposed method has the ability to find optimal trade-off solutions for multi-objective task scheduling problems that represent the best possible compromises among the conflicting objectives, and significantly increases the QoS.

Keywords: Cloud computing, Task Scheduling, Multi-Objective Particle Swarm Optimization, Jswarm, Cloudsim.

1 Introduction

Cloud computing provides new business opportunities for both service providers and requestors (e.g. organizations, enterprises, and end users) by means of a platform for delivering Infrastructure as a Service (IaaS), Platform as a Service (PaaS) and Software as a Service (SaaS). A Cloud encloses IaaS, PaaS, and/or SaaS inside its own virtualization infrastructure to carry out an abstraction from its underlying physical assets [1].

Task scheduling problems which relate to the efficiency of the whole cloud computing facilities, are one of the most famous combinatorial optimization problems, and

S. Basu et al. (Eds.): ICSOC 2013, LNCS 8274, pp. 237–251, 2013.
© Springer-Verlag Berlin Heidelberg 2013

play a key role in improving flexible and reliable systems. The main purpose is to schedule tasks to adaptable resources in accordance with adaptable time, which involves establishing a proper sequence whereby tasks can be executed under transaction logic constraints [2]. The scheduling algorithms in distributed systems usually have the goal of spreading the load on processors and maximizing their utilization while minimizing the total task execution time [3]. In the cloud environment, the number of tasks in a workflow as well as the number of available resources can grow quickly, especially when virtual resources are allocated. Calculating all possible task-resource mappings in cloud environment and selecting the optimal mapping is not feasible, since the complexity would grow exponentially with the number of tasks and resources [4]. The use of a heuristic algorithm ensures an acceptable runtime of the scheduling algorithm itself since it significantly reduces the complexity of the search space. This provides a compromise between scheduling runtime and optimality of the assignment. Of the heuristic optimization algorithms, genetic algorithm, fuzzy-genetic algorithm, multi-objective genetic algorithm, swarm optimization and normal best-oriented ant colony have been applied in previous works for optimizing task scheduling, mostly with two main objectives: (1) to minimize the task execution time and (2) to minimize cost in the cloud environment.

Although a significant amount of research has been done in this area, the majority assumed that the objective functions in their multi-objective optimization model are not in conflict with each other and have the same trend. Therefore, they applied single-objective evolutionary algorithms to solve their optimization problem. In this study we develop a comprehensive multi-objective task scheduling optimization model to optimize cloud utilization and QoS, with in the objective functions are in conflict with each other. Considering the supremacy of PSO for solving task scheduling optimization in cloud and grid environments [5-9], we develop an algorithm based on Multi-Objective Particle Swarm Optimization (MOPSO) to solve our model. The feasibility and the advantages of applying MOPSO for task scheduling in any distributed environments, has not been investigated previously in the literature. In the proposed model, the criteria of QoS, including response time and service cost, are considered to determine the optimization objectives for task distribution in cloud computing. To implement and evaluate the proposed optimization model, we extend Jswarm [10] to Multi-objective Jswarm and apply it in the Cloudsim toolkit [11] as the task scheduling algorithm. We analyze the implementation results and compare our method with three other methods to prove its efficiency. Simulation result shows that the proposed model significantly increases the QoS in comparison with previous works. In fact, the proposed model is able to determine good trade-off solutions that offer the best possible compromises among the optimization objectives, and help clouds providers to maintain the expected level of QoS, or to improve it after creating new optimal task distribution schema. The paper contributions can be summarized as:

1) Develop a new multi-objective task scheduling model to minimize both task execution and transferring time, and task execution cost
2) Develop a MOPSO-based algorithm to solve the proposed task scheduling model
3) Extend the Jswarm and Cloudsim packages to evaluate our model

The rest of this paper is organized as follows. In Section 2, related works for task scheduling optimization methods are described. In Section 3, we propose our multi-objective model for optimal task scheduling, followed by a developed MOPSO-based algorithm for solving the proposed multi-objective task scheduling model in Section 4. We evaluate our developed model and analyze the simulation results, in Section 5. Finally we present our conclusion and future works in Section 6.

2   Related Works for Task Scheduling Optimization

The task scheduling problem in distributed computing systems is an NP-hard optimization problem which plays an important role in optimizing cloud utilization. It also effects on QoS in the cloud environment by optimizing service cost and service response time. Song et al. [12] proposed a general task selection and allocation framework to be directly applicable in a dynamic collaboration environment and improve resource utilization for primary cloud provider. Their framework utilizes an adaptive filter to select tasks and a modified heuristic algorithm (Min-Min) to allocate tasks. A trade-off metric is developed as the optimization goal of the heuristic algorithm, so that it is able to manage and optimize the trade-off between the QoS of tasks and the utilization of resources. The authors considered four criteria for resource utilization in their approach, namely: resource requirement of CPU, memory, hard-disk and network bandwidth. In addition they considered two objectives: they tried to allocate tasks to a physical machine by maximizing the remaining CPU capacity, and maximizing the utilization of whole resources. Li et al. [13] applied another heuristic optimization approach to propose an algorithm called Normal Best-Oriented Ant Colony Optimization (NBOACO). They applied their experimental results in a simulation environment to prove that a better scheduling result with shorter total-task-finish time and mean-task finish time, and batter load balance can be achieved by their proposed algorithm in compared to the Ant Colony Optimization algorithm (ACO). To achieve better results in task scheduling, Li et al. [14] took resource allocation pattern into account and proposed a task and resource optimization mechanism. Their approach contains two online dynamic task scheduling algorithms: dynamic cloud list scheduling and dynamic cloud min-min scheduling. These algorithms were designed to schedule tasks for the IaaS cloud system with preemptive tasks and task priorities. They considered tasks map and task types (Advance Reservation or Benefit- effort), to determine tasks priorities. Their algorithms dynamically adjust the resource allocation based on updated actual task execution which can be calculated by applying the information about the resource status. This information is pulled from other clouds and aggregated by clouds' servers managers.

Zomaya et al. [3] and Xiao et al. [2] applied Genetic Algorithm (GA) to develop a load-balancing algorithm whereby optimal or near optimal task allocation can evolve during the operation of the parallel computing system. To enhance the accuracy of GA results for the task scheduling process, Tayal [15] purposed an optimized algorithm based on the fuzzy-genetic algorithm optimization which makes a scheduling decision by evaluating the entire group of tasks in the job queue. To adapt the GA operator's value (selection; crossover; mutation) during the run of the GA, they designed an algorithm for the fuzzy setting of GA parameters. They considered three parameters for the triangular function which are: (1) execution time, (2) work load and (3) objective function[1]. Juhnke et al. [4] proposed a multi-objective scheduling algorithm for cloud-based workflow applications by applying Pareto Archived Evolution Strategy which is a type of GA which are capable of dealing with multi-objective optimization problems. When the constituent workflow tasks in a cloud environment are geographically distributed – hosted by different cloud providers or data centers of the same provider – data transmission can be the main bottleneck. The multi-objective genetic algorithm therefore takes data dependencies between BPEL (Business Process Execution Language for Web Services) workflow steps into account and assigns them to cloud resources based on the two conflicting objectives of execution cost and execution time according to the preferences of the user, and provides additional resources when needed.

Task assignment has been found to be an NP-Complete problem, thus GA has been used for solving this problem. However, GA may not be the best method. Lei et al. [6] and Salman et al. [5] have illustrated that the particle swarm optimization (PSO) algorithm is able to obtain a better schedule than GA in grid computing and distributed systems. Not only is the solution quality of PSO algorithm better than GA in most of the test cases, it also runs faster than GA [7].

Considering that user applications may incur large data retrieval and execution costs. Chen and Tsai [16] suggested that the cost arising from data transfers between resources as well as execution costs, should be taken into account in the optimization of task scheduling. They therefore presented a Discrete Particle Swarm Optimization (DPSO) approach for tasks allocation. They proposed a meta-heuristic optimization approach based on PSO for finding the near optimal tasks allocation with reasonable time. The approach seeks to dynamically generate an optimal task allocation so that tasks can be completed in a minimal period of time while still utilizing resources in an efficient way. Similarly, Guo et al. [7] proposed a PSO algorithm which is based on a small position value rule to formulate a model for task scheduling that would minimize the overall time of execution and transmission. They compared and analyzed PSO with crossover, mutation and local search algorithms based on particle swarm. The experiment results demonstrate that the PSO algorithm converges and performs more quickly than the other two algorithms in a large scale. Hence the authors concluded that the PSO is more suitable for task scheduling in cloud computing. As an expansion of [16] and [7], Liu et al. [8] introduced several meta-heuristic adaptations to the particle swarm optimization algorithm to deal with the formulation of efficient schedules and presented the Variable Neighborhood Search Particle Swarm Optimization (VNPSO) algorithm as a method for solving the resulting scheduling problem. They formulated the scheduling problem for workflow applications with security constraints in distributed data-intensive computing environments and presented a novel security constraint model. They introduced VNPSO as an algorithm which can be applied in distributed data-intensive applications to meet specific requirements, including workflow constraints, security constraints, data retrieval/transfer, job

---

[1] Objective function represents the time that processor i will have finished the previously assigned jobs and E[t][i] is the predicted execution time that task t is processed on processor i.

interaction, minimum completion cost, flexibility and availability. The authors benchmarked the proposed algorithm with a multi-start particle swarm optimization and multi-start genetic algorithm. The empirical results illustrate that VNPSO is more feasible and effective than two other baselines. According to the outputs, VNPSO balances the global exploration and local exploitation for scheduling tasks very well.

Despite the efficiency of PSO-based single objective algorithms, they are not practical for solving a multi-objective task scheduling problems for minimizing both cost and time in a cloud environment, because these two objectives are in conflict with one another and there does not exist a single solution that simultaneously optimizes each of them. To confront with this drawback, MOPSO is applied in this paper to solve such problems and determine the best possible trade-off among the objectives while also providing higher QoS.

3 A Multi-Objective Model for the Optimal Task Scheduling Problem

We develop a multi-objective model for optimizing task scheduling considering three aspects of task scheduling optimization problem including: task execution time, task transferring time, and task execution cost. To determine this problem we combine and improve the methods which are proposed in [7, 8] for formulating task execution time. In this model, to minimize time consumption, not only total tasks execution time is minimized, but also minimize the maximum tasks execution time. Applying this method, the highest level of time consumption for task executing is also restricted. To formulate the multi-objective model, the following variables are defined:

n = The number of arrival tasks

$T = \{t_1, t_2, \ldots, t_n\}$ = Set of arrival tasks

N_{PM} = The number of Physical Machines (PMs) in cloud

m = The number of VMs

VM_j = Virtual Machine j, $j = \{1, 2, \ldots, m\}$

$PM_z = \{k | VM_k \in z \text{ th } PM, z \in \{1, 2, \ldots, N_{PM}\}\}$
$\quad$ = The set of VMs which are located in zth PM

$SP_p = \{k | VM_k \in P \text{th Cloud provider}, P \in \{1, 2, \ldots, cp\}\}$
$\quad$ = The set of VMs which are asigned to Pth provider

B_{ck} = The bandwidth between center and VM_k

cp = Number of cloud providers

$\tilde{C}_p$ = Maximum capacity for provider p

x_{ik} = 1 if task i is assigned to VM_k and x_{ik} = 0, otherwise

DE_{ik} = The amount of data that task i assigns to the VM_k

VMm_k = The amount of memory of VM_k

VMc_k = The amount of capacity of VM_k

$Pcost_j$ = The cost of one unit VM for jth provider (USD per hour)

r_p = The total number of VMs supplied by provider k

      that have executed tasks in the period time pt

Applying these variables, we can calculate the following functions:

$$Texe_k = \sum_{i=1}^{n} x_{ik} * \frac{DE_{ik}}{VMm_k * VMc_k} \tag{1}$$

where $Texe_k$ denotes the task execution time on VM_k. Using this, the total task execution time is calculated as:

$$Texe = \sum_{k=1}^{m} Texe_k \tag{2}$$

The total tasks transferring time is determined as:

$$Ttrans = \sum_{k=1}^{m}\sum_{i=1}^{n} x_{ik} * \frac{DE_{ik}}{B_{ck}} \tag{3}$$

The total task execution cost for providers (USD per hour) is:

$$Cexe = \sum_{p=1}^{cp} (Pcost_p * r_p * (\sum_{k \in SP_p} Texe_k)) \tag{4}$$

and r_p is determined using following equation:

$$r_p = \sum_{k \in SP_p} min(\sum_{i=1}^{n} x_{ik}, 1) \tag{5}$$

Problem:

$$min\, f(Time) = (Texe + Ttrans) + (max_{i=1}^{k} Texe_i) \tag{6}$$

$$min\, f(Cost) = Cexe \tag{7}$$

Subject to

$$\sum_{k=1}^{m} x_{ik} = 1, \forall i = 1, ..., n$$

$x_{ik} \in \{0,1\}, \forall i = 1,..,n\ \&\ k = 1, ..., m$

$0 \leq r_p \leq \tilde{C}_p\ , \forall p = 1,2, ..., cp$

4   MOPSO-Based Algorithm for Solving the Multi-Objective Task Scheduling Problem

In this section we first provide preliminary definition and explanation of MOPSO method. Then, we explain our proposed MOPSO-based algorithm that will be used to solve the proposed model in Section 3.

4.1   Multi-Objective Particle Swarm Optimization Method

Optimization problems that have more than one objective function are rather common in every field or area of knowledge. In such problems, the objective functions are normally in conflict with respect to each other, which means that there is no single solution for these problems. Instead, the aim is to find good trade-off solutions that represent the best possible compromises among the objectives [17]. A multi-objective optimization problem is of the form:

$$\text{Min } \vec{F}(\vec{x}) := [f_1(\vec{x}), f_2(\vec{x}), \dots, f_k(\vec{x})] \tag{8}$$

where $\vec{X} = (x_1, x_2, \dots, x_k)$ is the vector of decision variables; $f_i: R^n \to R, i = 1, \dots, k$ are the objective functions. Let particle $\vec{X}_1 = (x_1, x_2, \dots, x_k)$ represent a solution to (1). A solution $\vec{X}_2$ dominates $\vec{X}_1$ if $f_j(\vec{X}_1) \geq f_j(\vec{X}_2)$ for all $j=1,..,k$ and $f_j(\vec{X}_1) > f_j(\vec{X}_2)$ for at least one $j=1,...,k$. A feasible solution $\vec{X}_1$ is called Pareto optimal (non-dominated) if there is no other feasible solution $\vec{X}_2$ that dominates it. The set of all objective vectors $F(\vec{X}_1)$ corresponding to the Pareto optimal solutions is called the Pareto front (P*). Thus, the goal is to determine the Pareto optimal set from the set F of all the decision variable vectors (particles) [18-21].

In PSO, particles are flown through hyper dimensional search space. Changes to the position of the particles within the search space are based on the social–psychological tendency of individuals to emulate the success of other individuals. The position of each particle is changed according to its own experience and that of its neighbors. Let $\vec{X}_i(t)$ denote the position of particle i, at iteration t. The position of $\vec{X}_i(t)$ is changed by adding a velocity $\vec{V}_i(t + 1)$ to it as follows:

$$\vec{X}_i(t + 1) = \vec{X}_i(t) + \vec{V}_i(t + 1) \tag{9}$$

The velocity vector reflects the socially exchanged information and, in general, is defined in the following way:

$$\vec{V}_i(t + 1) = W\vec{V}_i(t) + C_1 r_1 \left(\vec{x}_{\text{pbest}_i} - \vec{X}_i(t)\right) + C_2 r_2 \left(\vec{x}_{\text{gbest}_i} - \vec{X}_i(t)\right) \tag{10}$$

where C_1 is the cognitive learning factor and represents the attraction that a particle has towards its own success; C_2 is the social learning factor and represents the attraction that a particle has towards the success of the entire swarm; W is the inertia weight, which is employed to control the impact of the previous history of velocities on the current velocity of a given particle; $\vec{x}_{\text{pbest}_i}$ is the personal best position of the particle i; $\vec{x}_{\text{pbest}}$ is the position of the best particle of the entire swarm; and $r_1, r_2 \in$ [0,1] are random values [17]. In MOPSO all Pareto optimal solutions are stored in an archive and $\vec{x}_{\text{gbest}_i}$ is chosen from this archive.

4.2   MOPSO-Based Algorithm

We develop a MOPSO-based algorithm to solve the proposed multi-objective task scheduling problem presented in Section 3. MOPSO finds the optimal task scheduling pattern, minimizing task execution time, task transfer time, and task execution cost. In the task scheduling model, we have n tasks $\{t_1, t_2, ..., t_n\}$ that should be assigned to m VMs $\{vm_1, vm_2, ..., vm_m\}$ to be executed (Table1). All particle positions $\vec{X}_i = (x_1, x_2, ..., x_n)$ determined by MOPSO by applying Equations 9 and 10, are vectors with continuous values, but we need their corresponding discrete values to determine the number of chosen VM for executing tasks. Therefore, we convert the particles' continuous position values vector to discrete vectors $d(\vec{X}_i) = (d_1, d_2, ..., d_n)$ applying the Small Position Value (SPV) rule [7].

Table 1. Task scheduling pattern (task mapping)

Tasks	t_1	t_2	t_3	t_4	t_5	...	t_n
VM number = Particle position	vm_7	vm_4	vm_5	vm_7	vm_3	...	vm_m

Particle position in Table 1 is a possible solution $d(\vec{X}_i) = (d_1, d_2, ..., d_n) = (7, 4, 5, 7, 3, .., m)$ after converting the continuous position values to discrete. According to this possible solution VMs: vm_7, vm_4, vm_5, vm_7, ..., and vm_m are chosen to execute t_1, t_2, t_3, t_4, ..., and t_n respectively. Considering this fact, every particle in our MOPSO model has n dimensions to assign n tasks to m VMs, and this model has two fitness functions: (1) minimizing task execution and transferring time ($f(Time)$), (2) minimizing tasks execution cost: ($f(Cost)$). Every particle will be assessed considering these fitness functions and all Pareto optimal solutions stored in an archive. In this paper we assume:

$$QoS(\vec{X}_i) = \sum_{j=1}^{m} W_j f_j(\vec{X}_i), \{\forall \vec{X}_i \in \text{Archive}\} \tag{11}$$

where m is the number of objective functions and W_j is the preference weight for every objective function ($f_j(\vec{X}_i)$). We then rank Pareto optimal solutions (archive members) on the basis of the number of functions that they minimized, and the maximum value of QoS. Then $\vec{X}_{gbest_i}$ is randomly chosen from the top ten. The MOPSO-based algorithm is summarized as follow:

Step 1.   Initialize population: determine random position and velocity for every particle in the swarm population

Step 2. Initialize archive: archive members are non-dominated solutions (n dimensions particles whose position is a Pareto optimal solution)

Step 3. Convert continuous position values vector of $\vec{X}_i$ to discrete vector $d(\vec{X}_i)$ using SPV rule to determine allocated VM for every arrival task.

Step 4. Determine the value of $DE_{ik}, VMm_k, VMc_k, Pcost_j, r_p$ and B_{ck} based on $d(\vec{X}_i)$ to calculate the value of every fitness function.

Step 5. Evaluate population according to defined fitness functions:
Step 5.1. Minimize tasks execution/transferring time (Equation (6))
Step 5.2. Minimize tasks execution cost (Equation (7))

Step 6. Update the archive contents: delete dominated members from archive and store the Pareto optimal (non-dominated) solutions in the archive.

Step 7. Sort archive members based on the number of function that they minimized and the maximum value of $QoS\,(\vec{X}) = W_1 * f(Time) + W_2 * f(Cost)$

Step 8. Choose $\vec{X}_{gbest}$ from top 10 sorted members in the archive randomly

Step 9. Choose $\vec{X}_{pbest_i}$ for every particle: If the current position of the particle dominates best position of the particle, use current position as new best position for the particle

Step 10. Compute inertia weight and learning factors

Step 11. Compute new velocity and new position of the particles based on MOPSO formulations (Equations (9) and (10))

Step 12. If maximum iteration is satisfied then
    Step 12.1. Output $d(\vec{X}_{gbest})$ position as the best task scheduling pattern (task mapping))
Else
    Step 12.2 Go to Step 3

5   Simulation Results

In this section, we aim to prove the efficiency of our multi-objective task scheduling method. We first describe the simulation environment. Then, we explain how the Jswarm and CloudSim packages are extended to implement the method, and finally the performance and evaluation section is presented.

5.1   Environment Description

We design the simulation by assuming that we have three PMs (data centers), five VMs, five cloud providers and ten arrival tasks (cloudlets). We assume every VM belongs to one provider. Data and information about VMs and tasks (cloudlets) are summarized in Tables 2 and 3:

Table 2. Properties of VMs

VM Id	MIPS	VM image size	VM memory (Ram)	Bandwidth	The number of CPUs	VMM name
0	256	10000	512	10000	4	Xen
1	300	1000	256	1000	1	Xen
2	256	1000	512	10000	2	Xen
3	256	1000	512	1000	1	Xen
4	256	100	256	10	1	Xen

Table 3. Properties of tasks

Task Id	Length	File Size	Output Size	The number of required CPUs
0	250000	300	300	1
1	25000	300	300	1
2	250000	300	300	1
3	25000	300	300	1
4	250000	300	300	1
5	250000	300	300	1
6	25000	300	300	1
7	250000	300	300	1
8	250000	300	300	1
9	25000	300	300	1

5.2　Implementation

To implement the proposed method, we extend Jswarm package [10] to MO-Jswarm by converting the PSO algorithm to MOPSO algorithm. To achieve this goal, we first change the evaluation method in Swarm class by adding four new functions to: determine non-dominated (Pareto optimal) solutions, insert non-dominated solutions in the archive, determine the dominated solutions in the archive, and update achieve. In the first function, for every iteration, the positions of the particles (possible solutions) are assessed considering all the fitness functions (objectives) and the non-dominated solutions are determined, then they are inserted in the archive by applying the second function. Non-dominated solutions in the archive are assessed by the third function to find dominated solutions in the archive, and in the fourth function, dominated solutions in the archive are deleted. The archive members are then sorted. We then change the velocity and position calculation methods in ParticleUpdate class. We also make Particle, Neighborhood, SwarmRepulsive, VariableUpdate classes compatible with the new multi-objective calculations. We then extend the Cloudsim toolkit [11] by applying MO-Jswarm as its task scheduling algorithm. The bindCloudletToVm() method in the DatacenterBrocker class of Cloudsim is responsible for assigning tasks to VMs, and the MO-Jswarm has the ability to determine the optimal tasks arrangement among VMs according to the MOPSO algorithm.

The objective functions in the proposed multi-objective task scheduling model are applied as the fitness functions in MO-Jswarm. In our model, we have 20 particles and the optimal results are obtained after 2000th iteration of the MOPSO algorithm in

MO-Jswarm. Cloudsim allocates tasks to VMs in an optimal way based on the results of the developed MOPSO-based algorithm in MO-Jswarm.

5.3   Evaluation

To evaluate the proposed method, we firs perform the simulation under the environment that we define in Section 5.1.The output results are illustrated in Table 5. As can be seen from the results, cloudlets (tasks) 1, 2, 4, 7, 8 and 9 are assigned to VM_0, and cloudlets 0, 3, 5 and 6 are allocated to VM_2.

Table 4. Cloudsim outputs for the proposed model using MO-Jswarm

Tasks	t_0	t_1	t_2	t_3	t_4	t_5	t_6	t_7	t_8	t_9
VM numbers = Particle position	vm_2	vm_0	vm_0	vm_2	vm_0	vm_2	vm_2	vm_0	vm_0	vm_5

The graphs for task execution/transferring time ($f(Time)$), and task execution cost ($f(Cost)$) using our MOPSO-based algorithm are illustrated in Fig. 1. As can be seen, $f(Time)$ fluctuates from 420 to 60 seconds, and $f(Cost)$ decreases from 37 to around 14 USD per hour, within 2000 iterations. $f(Time)$ decreases while $f(Cost)$ rises dramatically in interval [140, 260] iteration. This shows that some solutions (task scheduling pattern) that minimize one objective can maximize another objective. In the obtained optimal solution at iteration 2000, $f(Time)$ and $f(Cost)$ are equal to 60 seconds and 14 USD respectively.

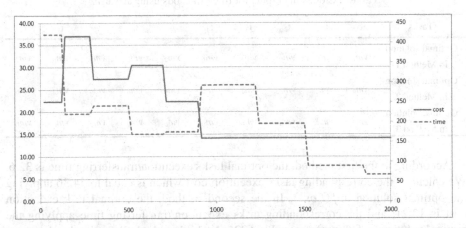

Fig. 1. The value of objective functions: Task execution/transferring time and task execution cost

We compare our proposed multi-objective method of solving task scheduling problem with conflicting objective with three different methods. The defined methods are explained as follows:

- Method 1: in which a single-objective optimization model is applied to minimize tasks execution/transferring time with objective function $f(Time)$. The corresponding value of $f(Cost)$ is simply calculated using the optimal solution of the model in Equation 7.
- Method 2: in which a single-objective optimization model is applied to minimize tasks execution cost with objective function $f(Cost)$. The corresponding value of $f(Time)$ is simply calculated using the optimal solution of the model in Equation 6.
- Method 3: in which a single-objective optimization model is applied to minimize $f(Time)$ and $f(Cost)$, and weighted aggregation of these objectives is considered as the single-objective of the model:

$$W_1 * f(Cost) + W_2 * f(Time) \qquad (12)$$

The PSO algorithm in Jswarm package is used to solve the optimization models in these three methods. In the third comparison, we compare our method with the optimization method proposed by [7] which has two objectives: (1) execution time and (2) execution cost and is solved by PSO-based single-objective algorithms. In this model, the weighted aggregation of the objectives is considered as a single optimization objective, which means the optimal solutions for the single-objective optimization problem are Pareto optimal solutions to the multi-objective optimization problem, and the conflict between the objectives is neglected. Based on the Cloudsim output results, the optimal solutions (best particle position) resulted from every method are illustrated in Table 5.

Table 5. Cloudsim outputs for three methods using Jswarm.

Tasks	t_0	t_1	t_2	t_3	t_4	t_5	t_6	t_7	t_8	t_9
Optimal solution in Method 1	vm_1	vm_3	vm_0	vm_1	vm_0	vm_2	vm_1	vm_3	vm_0	vm_1
Optimal solution in Method 2	vm_0	vm_4	vm_0	vm_4	vm_0	vm_0	vm_0	vm_0	vm_0	vm_0
Optimal solution in Method 3	vm_0	vm_0	vm_0	vm_0	vm_0	vm_0	vm_0	vm_0	vm_0	vm_0

According to the first method, the optimal tasks execution/transferring time is 32.6. We calculate the corresponding tasks execution cost which is equal to 54.36 applying the optimal solution in $f(Cost)$. In the second method, the optimal task execution cost is 12.21, and the corresponding tasks execution/transferring time applying the optimal solution in $f(Time)$ is equal to 6335. In third method, the optimal task execution/transferring time and tasks execution cost is equal to -3235.66 applying weighted aggregation of the objectives. To estimate the QoS which results from every method, the following equation is utilized by assuming the same preference weight (-0.5) for both cost and time:

$$QoS\,(\vec{X}) = (-0.5) * f(Time) + (-0.5) * f(Cost) \qquad (4)$$

The optimal results of all methods are summarized in Table 6.

Table 6. Comparison results

User preference weight Cost weight = Time weight = 0.5	Task execution and transferring time (Seconds)	Task execution cost (USD)	Estimated QoS
PSO in Method 1	32.6	54.36	-43.48
PSO in Method 2	6335	12.21	-3173.6
PSO in Method 3	-3235.66		-3235.66
MOPSO in the proposed Method	60	15.00	-37.5

As can be seen from the comparison results in Table 6, the estimated QoS in Methods 1, 2 and 3 are -43.48, -3173.6 and -3235.66 respectively. The estimated QoS in our proposed method is equal to -37.5, that is significantly increased in contrast to the QoS obtained in Methods 2 and 3. It is also higher than the QoS resulted from Method 1. Although, $f(Time)$ in Method 1 (i.e. 32.6) and $f(Cost)$ in Method 2 (i.e. 12.21) have their minimum values, they did not result the highest QoS. In addition, the QoS has its lowest value in Method 3. In this case, the approaches in Methods 1 and 2 are even better than the multi-objective optimizing approach in Method 3.

As the result, the proposed method determines an optimal trade-off solution for the multi-objective task scheduling problem with objective functions that are in conflict with one another, and determines the best possible compromises among the objectives, thereby significantly increasing the QoS.

6   Conclusion and Future Works

In this paper we propose a multi-objective model for optimizing task scheduling that considers three aspects of the task scheduling optimization problem: task execution time, task transferring time, and task execution cost. We also design a MOPSO algorithm to solve the proposed task scheduling model. To evaluate our proposed method we first extend the Jswarm package, change it to a multi-objective PSO and convert it to MO-Jswarm. Then we extend the Cloudsim toolkit by applying MO-Jswarm as its task scheduling algorithm. The bindCloudletToVm() method in the DatacenterBroker class of Cloudsim is responsible for assigning tasks to VMs, and the MO-Jswarm has the ability to determine the optimal task arrangement among VMs according to the MOPSO algorithm. The experimental results in the simulation environment show that the proposed optimization model has the ability to determine the best trade-off solutions compared to recent task scheduling approaches; it provides the best possible coincidences among the objectives and achieves the highest QoS. The decision support system that we have designed, implemented and validated in our work, could be made part of the virtualization layer. This would enable data center operators to make use of this system for load balancing.

In our future work, we will implement the proposed model in a real cloud environment. We also will consider task priorities and types in our optimization model. In addition, we will extend our model to minimize energy consumption by not choosing VMs on idle PMs as new hosts for executing tasks. Furthermore, we will compare the MOPSO with other multi-objective evolutionary algorithms such as MOGA, to find the most efficient and reliable algorithm that not only determines the optimal task scheduling pattern but also obtains the solution in the shortest possible time.

Acknowledgment. The first author would like to thank Dr. Vahid Behbood for his help and comments.

References

1. Celesti, A., Fazio, M., Villari, M., Puliafito, A.: Virtual machine provisioning through satellite communications in federated cloud environments. Future Generation Computer Systems 28(1), 85–93 (2012)
2. Xiao, Z.J., Chang, H.Y., Yi, Y.: An optimization m ethod of w orkflow dynamic scheduling based on heuristic GA. Computer Science 34(2) (2007)
3. Zomaya, A.Y., Yee-Hwei, T.: Observations on using genetic algorithms for dynamic load-balancing. IEEE Transactions on Parallel and Distributed Systems 12(9), 899–911 (2001)
4. Juhnke, E., Dörnemann, T., Böck, D., Freisleben, B.: Multi-objective scheduling of bpel workflows in geographically distributed clouds. In: 4th IEEE International Conference on Cloud Computing, pp. 412–419 (2011)
5. Salman, A., Ahmad, I., Al-Madani, S.: Particle swarm optimization for task assignment problem. Microprocessors and Microsystems 26(8), 363–371 (2002)
6. Lei, Z., Yuehui, C., Runyuan, S., Shan, J., Bo, Y.: A task scheduling algorithm based on pso for grid computing. International Journal of Computational Intelligence Research 4(1), 37–43 (2008)
7. Guo, L., Zhao, S., Shen, S., Jiang, C.: Task scheduling optimization in cloud computing based on heuristic algorithm. Journal of Networks 7(3), 547–553 (2012)
8. Liu, H., Abraham, A., Snášel, V., McLoone, S.: Swarm scheduling approaches for work-flow applications with security constraints in distributed data-intensive computing environments. Information Sciences 192(0), 228–243 (2012)
9. Behbood, V., Lu, J., Zhang, G.: Fuzzy bridged refinement domain adaptation: Long-term bank failure prediction. International Journal of Computational Intelligence and Applications 12(01) (2013), doi:10.1142/S146902681350003X
10. Cingolani, P.: http://jswarm-pso.sourceforge.net/
11. Calheiros, R.N., Ranjan, R., De Rose, C.A.F., Buyya, R.: Cloudsim: A novel framework for modeling and simulation of cloud computing infrastructures and services. Arxiv preprint arXiv:0903.2525 (2009)
12. Song, B., Hassan, M.M., Huh, E.: A novel heuristic-based task selection and allocation framework in dynamic collaborative cloud service platform. In: 2nd IEEE International Conference on Cloud Computing Technology and Science (CloudCom), pp. 360–367 (2010)
13. Li, J., Peng, J., Cao, X., Li, H.-y.: A task scheduling algorithm based on improved ant colony optimization in cloud computing environment. Energy Procedia 13, 6833–6840 (2011)

14. Li, J., Qiu, M., Ming, Z., Quan, G., Qin, X., Gu, Z.: Online optimization for scheduling preemptable tasks on iaas cloud systems. Journal of Parallel and Distributed Computing 72(5), 666–677 (2012)
15. Tayal, S.: Tasks scheduling optimization for the cloud computing systems. International Journal of Advanced Engineering Sciences and Technologies 5(2), 111–115 (2011)
16. Chen, Y.M., Tsai, S.Y.: Optimal provisioning of resource in a cloud service. IJCSI International Journal of Computer Science Issues 7(6), 1694–1814 (2010)
17. Mahmoodabadi, M.J., Bagheri, A., Nariman-zadeh, N., Jamali, A.: A new optimization algorithm based on a combination of particle swarm optimization, convergence and divergence operators for single-objective and multi-objective problems. Engineering Optimization, 1–20 (2012)
18. Deb, K., Pratap, A., Agarwal, S., Meyarivan, T.: A fast and elitist multiobjective genetic algorithm: NSGA-II. IEEE Transactions on Evolutionary Computation 6(2), 182–197 (2002)
19. Alves, M.J.: Using MOPSO to solve multiobjective bilevel linear problems. In: Dorigo, M., Birattari, M., Blum, C., Christensen, A.L., Engelbrecht, A.P., Groß, R., Stützle, T. (eds.) ANTS 2012. LNCS, vol. 7461, pp. 332–339. Springer, Heidelberg (2012)
20. Gao, Y., Zhang, G., Lu, J., Wee, H.-M.: Particle swarm optimization for bi-level pricing problems in supply chains. Journal of Global Optimization 51(2), 245–254 (2011)
21. Lu, J., Zhang, G., Ruan, D.: Multi-objective group decision making: Methods, software and applications with fuzzy set techniques. Imperial College Press, London (2007)

Verification of Artifact-Centric Systems:
Decidability and Modeling Issues

Dmitry Solomakhin[1], Marco Montali[1],
Sergio Tessaris[1], and Riccardo De Masellis[2]

[1] Free University of Bozen-Bolzano, Piazza Domenicani 3, 39100 Bolzano, Italy
{solomakhin,montali,tessaris}@inf.unibz.it
[2] Sapienza Università di Roma, Via Ariosto, 25, 00185 Rome, Italy
demasellis@dis.uniroma1.it

Abstract. Artifact-centric business processes have recently emerged as an approach in which processes are centred around the evolution of business entities, called *artifacts*, giving equal importance to control-flow and data. The recent Guard-State-Milestone (GSM) framework provides means for specifying business artifacts lifecycles in a declarative manner, using constructs that match how executive-level stakeholders think about their business. However, it turns out that formal verification of GSM is undecidable even for very simple propositional temporal properties. We attack this challenging problem by translating GSM into a well-studied formal framework. We exploit this translation to isolate an interesting class of "state-bounded" GSM models for which verification of sophisticated temporal properties is decidable. We then introduce some guidelines to turn an arbitrary GSM model into a state-bounded, verifiable model.

Keywords: artifact-centric systems, guard-stage-milestone, formal verification.

1 Introduction

In the last decade, a plethora of graphical notations (such as BPMN and EPCs) have been proposed to capture business processes. Independently from the specific notation at hand, formal verification has been generally considered as a fundamental tool in the process design phase, supporting the modeler in building correct and trustworthy process models [17]. Intuitively, formal verification amounts to check whether possible executions of the business process model satisfy some desired properties, like generic correctness criteria (such as deadlock freedom or executability of activities) or domain-dependent constraints. To enable formal verification and other forms of reasoning support, business process models are translated into an equivalent formal representation, which typically relies on variants of Petri nets [1], transition systems [2], or process algebras [19]. Properties are then formalized using temporal logics, using model checking techniques to actually carry out verification tasks [9].

A common drawback of classical process modeling approaches is being *activity-centric*: they mainly focus on the control-flow perspective, lacking the connection between the process and the data manipulated during its executions. This reflects also in the corresponding verification techniques, which often abstract away from the data component. This "data and process engineering divide" affects many contemporary process-aware information systems, increasing the risk of introducing redundancies and

S. Basu et al. (Eds.): ICSOC 2013, LNCS 8274, pp. 252–266, 2013.
© Springer-Verlag Berlin Heidelberg 2013

potential errors in the development phase [13,8]. To tackle this problem, the artifact-centric paradigm has recently emerged as an approach in which processes are guided by the evolution of business data objects, called *artifacts* [18,10]. A key aspect of artifacts is coupling the representation of data of interest, called *information model*, with *lifecycle constraints*, which specify the acceptable evolutions of the data maintained by the information model. On the one hand, new modeling notations are being proposed to tackle artifact-centric processes. A notable example is the Guard-State-Milestone (GSM) graphical notation [11], which corresponds to way executive-level stakeholders conceptualize their processes [7]. On the other hand, the formal foundations of the artifact-centric paradigm are being investigated in order to capture the relationship between processes and data and to support formal verification [12,5,4,3]. Two important issues arise. First, verification formalisms must go beyond propositional temporal logics, and incorporate first-order formulae to express constraints about the evolution of data and to query the artifact information models. Second, verification tasks become undecidable in general.

In this work, we tackle the problem of *automated verification of GSM models*. First of all, we show that verifying GSM models is indeed a very challenging issue, being undecidable in general even for simple propositional reachability properties. We then provide a sound and complete encoding of GSM into Data-Centric Dynamic Systems (DCDSs), a recently developed formal framework for data- and artifact-centric processes [4]. This encoding enables the to transfer in the GSM context the decidability and complexity results recently established for DCDSs with bounded information models (*state-bounded DCDSs*). These are DCDSs where the number of tuples does not exceed a given maximum value. This does not mean that the system must contain an overall bounded amount of data: along a run, infinitely many data can be encountered and stored into the information model, provided that they do not accumulate in the same state. We lift this property in the context of GSM, and show that verification of state-bounded GSM models is decidable for a powerful temporal logic, namely a variant of first-order μ-calculus supporting a restricted form of quantification [14]. We then isolate an interesting class of GSM models for which state-boundedness is guaranteed, introducing guidelines that help to make GSM models state-bounded and, in turn, verifiable.

The rest of the paper is organized as follows. Section 2 gives an overview of GSM and provides a first undecidability result. Section 3 introduces DCDSs and presents the GSM-DCDS translation. Section 4 introduces "state-bounded" GSM models and provides key decidability results. Discussion and conclusion follow.

2   GSM Modeling of Artifact-Centric Systems

The foundational character of artifact-centric business processes is the combination of static properties; i.e., the data of interest, and dynamic properties of a business process, i.e., how it evolves. *Artifacts*, the key business entities of a given domain, are characterized by *(i)* an *information model* that captures business-relevant data, and *(ii)* a *lifecycle model* that specifies how the artifact progresses through the business. In this work, we focus on the Guard-Stage-Milestone (GSM) approach for artifact-centric modeling, recently proposed by IBM [11] and included by the Object Management Group (OMG) into the new standard for Case Management Model and Notation (CMMN) [22].

For the sake of simplicity here we provide a general overview of the GSM methodology and we refer an interested reader to [6] for more detailed and formal definitions.

GSM is a declarative modelling framework that has been designed with the goal of being executable and at the same time enough high-level to result intuitive to executive-level stakeholders. The GSM information model uses (possibly nested) attribute/value pairs to capture the domain of interest. The key elements of a lifecycle model are *stages*, *milestones* and *guards* (see Example 1). Stages are (hierarchical) clusters of activities (*tasks*) intended to update and extend the data of the information model. They are associated to milestones, business operational objectives to be achieved when the stage is under execution. Guards control the activation of stages and, like milestones, are described in terms of data-aware expressions, called *sentries*, involving events with associated data (called *payload*) and conditions over the artifact information model. Sentries have the form **on** *e* **if** *cond*, where *e* is an event and *cond* is an (OCL-based, see [16]) condition over data. Both parts are optional, supporting pure event-based or condition-based sentries. Changes on the artifact state are performed by tasks, which represent atomic operations. They can be used to update the data of artifact instances (e.g., based on the payload of an incoming event), or to add/remove (nested) tuples. Crucially, tasks are used to manage artifacts life cycle. *Create-artifact-instance* tasks enable the creation of new artifact instances of a given type. Creation of artifacts is modelled as a two-way service call, where the returned result is used to create a new tuple for the artifact instance, to assign a new identifier to it, and to fill it with the result's payload. Analogously, tasks may remove existing artifact instances. In the following, we use *model* for the intensional level of a specific business process described in GSM, and *instance* to denote a GSM model with specific data for its information model.

The execution of a business process may involve several *instances* of artifact types described by a GSM model. At any instant, the state of an artifact instance (*snapshot*) is stored in its information model, and is fully characterised by: *(i)* values of attributes in the data model, *(ii)* status of its stages (open or closed) and *(iii)* status of its milestones (achieved or invalidated). Artifact instances may interact with the external world by exchanging typed *events*. In fact, *tasks* are considered to be performed by an external agent, and their corresponding execution is captured with two event types: a *service call*, whose instances are populated by the data from information model and then sent to the environment and a *service call return*, whose instances represent the corresponding answer from the environment and are used to incorporate the obtained result back into the artifact information model. The environment can also send unsolicited (one-way) events, to trigger specific guards or milestones. Additionally, any change of a status attribute, such as opening a stage or achieving a milestone, triggers an internal event, which can be further used to govern the artifact lifecycle.

Example 1. Figure 1 shows a simple order management process modeled in GSM. The process centers around an *order* artifact, whose information model is characterized by a set of status attributes (tracking the status of stages and milestones), and by an extendible set of ordered *items*, each constituted by a code and a quantity. The order lifecycle contains three top-level atomic stages (rounded rectangles), respectively used to manage the manipulation of the order, its payment, and the delivery of a payment receipt. The order management stage contains a task (rectangle) to add items to the

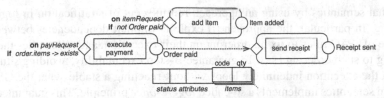

Fig. 1. GSM model of a simple order management process

order. It opens every time an *itemRequest* event is received, provided that the order has not yet been paid. This is represented using a logical condition associated to a guard (diamond). The stage closes when the task is executed, by achieving an "item added" milestone (circle). A payment can be executed once a *payRequest* event is issued, provided that the order contains at least one item (verified by the OCL condition *order.items* → *exists*). As soon as the order is paid, and the corresponding milestone achieved, the receipt delivery stage is opened. This direct dependency is represented using a dashed arrow, which is a shortcut for the condition **on** *Order paid*, representing the internal event of achieving the "Order paid" milestone.

2.1 Operational Semantics of GSM

GSM is associated to three well-defined, equivalent execution semantics, which discipline the actual enactment of a GSM model [11]. Among these, the *GSM incremental semantics* is based on a form of Event-Condition-Action (ECA) rules, called *Prerequisite-Antecedent-Consequent (PAC)* rules, and is centered around the notion of *GSM Business steps (B-steps)*. An artifact instance remains idle until it receives an incoming event from the environment. It is assumed that such events arrive in a sequence and get processed by artifact instances one at a time. A B-step then describes what happens to an *artifact snapshot* Σ when a single incoming event e is incorporated into it, i.e., how it evolves into a new snapshot Σ' (see Figure 5 in [11]). Σ' is constructed by building a sequence of pre-snapshots Σ_i, where Σ_1 results from incorporating e into Σ by updating its attributes according to the event payload (i.e., its carried data). Each consequent pre-snaphot Σ_i is obtained by applying one of the PAC rules to the previous pre-snapshot Σ_{i-1}. Each of such transitions is called a *micro-step*. During a micro-step some outgoing events directed to the environment may be generated. When no more PAC rules can be applied, the last pre-snapshot Σ' is returned, and the entire set of generated events is sent to the environment.

Each PAC rule is associated to one or more GSM constructs (e.g. stage, milestone) and has three components:

- **Prerequisite:** this component refers to the initial snapshot Σ and determines if a rule is *relevant* to the current B-step processing an incoming event e.
- **Antecedent:** this part refers to the current pre-snapshot Σ_i and determines whether the rule is eligible for execution, or *executable*, at the next micro-step.
- **Consequent:** this part describes the effect of firing a rule, which can be nondeterministically chosen in order to obtain the next pre-snapshot Σ_{i+1}.

Due to nondeterminism in the choice of the next firing rule, different orderings among the PAC rules can exist, leading to non-intuitive outcomes. This is avoided in the GSM operational semantics by using an approach reminiscent of stratification in logic programming. In particular, the approach *(i)* exploits implicit dependencies between the (structure of) PAC rules to fix an ordering on their execution, and *(ii)* applies the rules according to such ordering [11]. To guarantee B-step executability, avoiding situations in which the execution indefinitely loops without reaching a stable state, the GSM incremental semantics implements a so-called *toggle-once* principle. This guarantees that a sequence of micro-steps, triggered by an incoming event, is always finite, by ensuring that each status attribute can change its value at most once during a B-step. This requirement is implemented by an additional condition in the prerequisite part of each PAC rule, which prevents it from firing twice.

The evolution of a GSM system composed by several artifacts can be described by defining the initial state (initial snapshot of all artifact instances) and the sequence of event instances generated by the environment, each of which triggers a particular B-step, producing a sequence of system snapshots. This perspective intuitively leads to the representation of a GSM model as an infinite-state transition system, depicting all possible sequences of snapshots supported by the model. The initial configuration of the information model represents the initial state of this transition system, and the incremental semantics provides the actual transition relation. The source of infinity relies in the payload of incoming events, used to populate the information model of artifacts with fresh values (taken from an infinite/arbitrary domain). Since such events are not under the control of the GSM model, the system must be prepared to process such events in every possible order, and with every acceptable configuration for the values carried in the payload. The analogy to transition systems opens the possibility of using a formal language, e.g., a (first-order variant of) temporal logic, to verify whether the GSM system satisfies certain desired properties and requirements. For example, one could test generic correctness properties, such as checking whether each milestone can be achieved (and each stage will be opened) in at least one of the possible systems' execution, or that whenever a stage is opened, it will be always possible to eventually achieve one of its milestones. Furthermore, the modeler could also be interested in verifying domain-specific properties, such as checking whether for the GSM model in Figure 1 it is possible to obtain a receipt before the payment is processed.

2.2   Undecidability in GSM

In this section, we show that verifying the infinite-state transition system representing the execution semantics of a given GSM model is an extremely challenging problem, undecidable even for a very simple propositional reachability property.

Theorem 1. *There exists a GSM model for which verification of a propositional reachability property is undecidable.*

Proof. We represent a Turing machine as a GSM artifact, formulating the halting problem as a verification problem over such artifact. We consider a deterministic, single tape Turing machine $\mathcal{M} = \langle Q, \Sigma, q_0, \delta, q_f, \_\rangle$, where Q is a finite set of (internal) states, $\Sigma = \{0, 1, \_\}$ is the tape alphabet (with $\_$ the blank symbol), $q_0 \in Q$ and $q_f \in Q$ are the initial and final state, and $\delta \subseteq Q \setminus \{q_f\} \times \Sigma \times Q \times \Sigma \times \{L, R\}$ is a transition relation. We assume, without loss of generality, that δ consists of k right-shift transitions

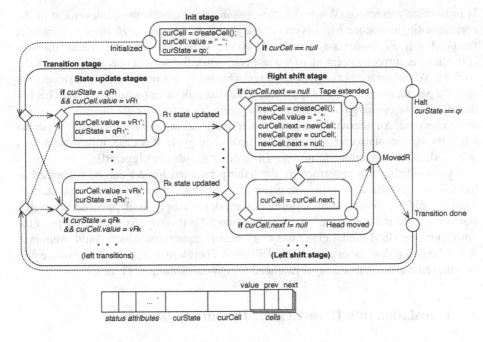

Fig. 2. GSM model of a Turing machine

$R_1, \ldots, R_k$ (those having R as last component), and n left-shift transitions $L_1, \ldots, L_n$ (those having L as last component). The idea of the translation into a GSM model is the following. Beside status attributes, the GSM information model is constituted by: *(i)* a *curState* slot containing the current internal state $q \in Q$; *(ii)* a *curCell* slot pointing to the cell where the head of $\mathcal{M}$ is currently located and *(iii)* a collection of *cells* representing the current state of the tape. Each cell is a complex nested record constituted by a value $v \in \Sigma$, and two pointers *prev* and *next* used to link the cell to the previous and next cells. In this way, the tape is modeled as a (double) linked list, which initially contains a single, blank cell, and which is dynamically extended on demand. To mark the initial (resp., last) cell of the tape, we assume that its *prev* (*next*) cell is *null*.

On top of this information model, a GSM lifecyle that mimics $\mathcal{M}$ is shown in Figure 2, where, due to space constraints, only the right-shift transitions are depicted (the left-shift ones are symmetric). The schema consists of two top-level stages: *Init*, used to initialize the tape, and *Transition*, encoding δ. Each transition is decomposed into two sub-stages: *state update* and *head shift*. The state update is modeled by one among $k + n$ atomic sub-stages, each handling the update that corresponds to one of the transitions in δ. These stages are mutually exclusive, being $\mathcal{M}$ deterministic. Consider for example a right-shift transition $R_i = \delta(qR_i, vR_i, qR_i', vR_i', R)$ (the treatment is similar for a left-shift transition). The corresponding *state update stage* opens whenever the current state is qR_i, and the value contained in the cell pointed by the head is vR_i (this can be extracted from the information model using the query *curCell.value*). The incoming arrows from the two parent's guards ensure that this condition is evaluated as soon as the parent stage opens, hence, if the condition is true, the *state update stage* is immediately executed. When the *state update stage* closes, the achievement of the corresponding milestone triggers one of the guards of the *right shift stage* that handles the head shift. *Right shift stage* contains two sub-stages: the first one extends the tape if the head is currently pointing to the last cell, while the second one just performs the shifting. Whenever a *right* or *left shift stage* achieves the corresponding milestone, then also the parent, *transition stage* is closed, achieving milestone *transition done*. This has the effect of re-opening the transition stage again, so as to evaluate the next transition to be executed. An alternative way of immediately closing the *transition stage* occurs when the current state corresponds to the final state q_f. In this case, milestone *halt* is achieved, and the execution terminates (no further guards are triggered).

By considering this construction, the halting problem for $\mathcal{M}$ can be rephrased as the following verification problem: given the GSM model encoding $\mathcal{M}$, and starting from an initial state where the information model is empty, is it possible to reach a state where the *halt* milestone is achieved? Since $\mathcal{M}$ is deterministic, the B-steps of the corresponding GSM model give raise to a linear computation, which could eventually reach the *halt* milestone or continue indefinitely. Therefore, reaching a state where *halt* is achieved can be equivalently formulated using propositional CTL or LTL.   □

3   Translation into Data-Centric Dynamic Systems

Despite having a formally specified operational semantics for GSM models [11], the verification of different properties of such models (e.g. existence of complete execution, safety properties) is still an open problem. A promising framework for the formalization and verification of artifact systems is the one of data-centric dynamic systems (DCDS), recently presented in [4]. Translating a GSM model into a corresponding DCDS enables the application of the decidability results and verification techniques discussed in [4] to the concrete case of GSM. Additionally, such translation will allow to benefit from the results of the ongoing effort towards execution support for DCDS [20]. First we briefly introduce DCDS and then we present a translation that faithfully rewrites a GSM model into a corresponding formal representation in terms of DCDSs.

Formally, a DCDS is a pair $\mathcal{S} = \langle \mathcal{D}, \mathcal{P} \rangle$, where $\mathcal{D}$ is a data layer and $\mathcal{P}$ is a process layer over $\mathcal{D}$. The former maintains all the relevant data in the form of a relational database together with its integrity constraints. In the artifact-centric context, the database is the union of all artifacts information models. The process layer modifies the data maintained by $\mathcal{D}$, and it is defined as a tuple $\mathcal{P} = \langle \mathcal{F}, \mathcal{A}, \varrho \rangle$ where:

- $\mathcal{F}$ is a finite set of functions representing interfaces to external services, used to import new, fresh data into the system.
- $\mathcal{A}$ is a set of actions of the form $\alpha(p_1, ..., p_n) : \{e_1, ..., e_m\}$, where $p_1, ..., p_n$ are input parameters of an action and e_i are effects of an action. Each effect specification defines how a portion of the next database instance is constructed starting from the current one and has the form $e_i = q_i^+ \wedge Q_i^- \rightsquigarrow E_i$ where:
  - q_i^+ is a union of conjunctive queries (UCQ) over $\mathcal{D}$, used to instantiate the effect with values extracted from the current database.
  - Q_i^- is an arbitrary FO formula that filters away some tuples obtained by q_i^+.

- E_i is a set of effects, specified in terms of facts over $\mathcal{D}$ that will be asserted in the next state; these facts can contain variables of Q (which are then replaced with actual values extracted from the current database) and also service calls, which are resolved by calling the service with actual input parameters and substituting them with the obtained result.[1].

- ϱ is a declarative process specified in terms of a finite set of Condition-Action (CA) rules that determine, at any moment, which actions are executable. Technically, each CA rule has the form $Q \mapsto \alpha$, where α is an action and Q is a FO query over $\mathcal{D}$. Whenever Q has a positive answer over the current database, then α becomes executable, with actual values for its parameters given by the answer to Q.

Example 2. Consider a fragment of an order management process. Once pending, an order can be moved to the ready state by executing a *prepare* action, which incorporates into the system the destination address of the customer associated to the order. A DCDS could encode the executability of the *prepare* action by means of the following CA rule: $order(id, cust) \wedge pending(id) \mapsto$ PREPARE(id). The rule states that whenever an order identified by id and owned by customer *cust* is pending, it is possible to apply action *prepare* on it. The action can in turn be defined as:

$$\text{PREPARE}(id) : \{ \quad order(id, cust) \wedge pending(id) \rightsquigarrow \{ready(id), dest(id, addr(cust))\}$$
$$order(x, y) \rightsquigarrow \{order(x, y)\}$$
$$order(x, y) \wedge pending(x) \wedge x \neq id \rightsquigarrow \{pending(x)\}$$
$$order(x, y) \wedge ready(x) \rightsquigarrow \{ready(x)\} \quad \}$$

The first effect states that the order id becomes ready, and its destination is incorporated by calling a service $addr$, which mimics the interaction with the customer. The other effects are used to determine which information is kept unaffected in the next state: all orders remain orders, all ready orders remain ready, and all pending orders remain pending, except the one identified by id.

The execution semantics of a DCDS $\mathcal{S}$ is defined by a possibly infinite-state transition system $\Upsilon_\mathcal{S}$, where states are instances of the database schema in $\mathcal{D}$ and each transition corresponds to the application of an executable action in $\mathcal{P}$. Similarly to GSM, where the source of infinity comes from the fact that incoming events carry an arbitrary payload, in DCDSs the source of infinity relies in the service calls, which can inject arbitrary fresh values into the system. Despite the resulting undecidability of arbitrary DCDSs, an interesting class of *state-bounded* DCDSs has been recently identified [4], for which decidability of verification holds for a sophisticated (first-order) temporal logic called $\mu\mathcal{L}_P$. Intuitively, state boundedness requires the existence of an overall bound that limits, at every point in time, the size of the database instance of $\mathcal{S}$ (without posing any restriction on which values can appear in the database). Equivalently, the size of each state contained in $\Upsilon_\mathcal{S}$ cannot exceed the pre-established bound. Hence, in the following we will indifferently talk about state-bounded DCDSs or state-bounded transition systems.

Theorem 2 ([4]). *Verification of $\mu\mathcal{L}_P$ properties over state-bounded DCDS is decidable, and can be reduced to finite-state model checking of propositional μ-calculus.*

$\mu\mathcal{L}_P$ is a first-order variant of μ-calculus, a rich branching-time temporal logic that subsumes all well-known temporal logics such as PDL, CTL, LTL and CTL* [14]. $\mu\mathcal{L}_P$

---

[1] In [4], two semantics for services are introduced: deterministic and nondeterministic. Here we always assume nondeterministic services, which is in line with GSM.

employs first-order formulae to query data maintained by the DCDS data layer, and supports a controlled form of first-order quantification across states (within and across runs).

Example 3. $\mu\mathcal{L}_P$ can express two variants of a correctness requirement for GSM:
- it is always true that, whenever an artifact id is present in the information model, the corresponding artifact will be destroyed (i.e., the id will disappear) *or* reach a state where all its stages are closed;
- it is always true that, whenever an artifact id is present in the information model, the corresponding artifact will persist *until* a state is reached where all its stages are closed.

3.1 Translating GSM into DCDS

In this section we propose a translation procedure that takes a GSM model and produces a corresponding faithful representation in terms of DCDSs. This allows us to transfer the decidability boundaries studied for DCDSs to the GSM context[2].

As introduced in Section 2.1, the execution of a GSM instance is described by a sequence of B-steps. Each B-step consists of an initial micro-step which incorporates incoming event into current snapshot, a sequence of micro-steps executing all applicable PAC-rules, and finally a micro-step sending a set of generated events at the termination of the B-step. The translation relies on the incremental semantics: given a GSM model $\mathcal{G}$, we encode each possible micro-step as a separate condition-action rule in the process of a corresponding DCDS system $\mathcal{S}$, such that the effect on the data and process layers of the action coincides with the effect of the corresponding micro-step in GSM. However, in order to guarantee that the transition system induced by a resulting DCDS mimics the one of the GSM model, the translation procedure should also ensure that all semantic requirements described in Section 2.1 are modeled properly: *(i)* "one-message-at-a-time" and "toggle-once" principles, *(ii)* the finiteness of microsteps within a B-step, and *(iii)* their order imposed by the model. We sustain these requirements by introducing into the data layer of $\mathcal{S}$ a set of auxiliary relations, suitably recalling them in the CA-rules to reconstruct the desired behaviour.

Restricting $\mathcal{S}$ to process only one incoming message at a time is implemented by introducing a *blocking mechanism*, represented by an auxiliary relation $R_{block}(id_R, blocked)$ for each artifact in the system, where id_R is the artifact instance identifier and $blocked$ is a boolean flag. This flag is set to $true$ upon receiving an incoming message, and is then reset to $false$ at the termination of the corresponding B-step, once the outgoing events accumulated in the B-step are sent the environment. If an artifact instance has $blocked = true$, no further incoming event will be processed. This is enforced by checking the flag in the condition of each CA-rule associated to the artifact.

In order to ensure "toggle once" principle and guarantee the finiteness of sequence of micro-steps triggered by an incoming event, we introduce an *eligibility tracking mechanism*. This mechanism is represented by an auxiliary relation $R_{exec}(id_R, x_1, ..., x_c)$, where c is the total number of PAC-rules, and each x_i corresponds to a certain PAC-rule of the GSM model. Each x_i encodes whether the corresponding PAC rule is eligible to

---

[2] For the sake of space, we give a general description of the translation and illustrate the technical development by the example in Figure 4. For a full technical specification of the translation, we refer the interested reader to a technical report [21].

$$R_{exec}(id_R, \overline{x}) \wedge x_k = 0 \wedge exec(k) \wedge R_{block}(id_R, true) \mapsto \tag{1}$$

$$a_{exec}^k(id_R, \overline{a}', \overline{x}) : \{ \tag{2}$$

$$R_{att}(id_R, \overline{a}, \overline{s}, \overline{m}) \wedge R_{chg}^{S_j}(id_R, true) \rightsquigarrow \{R_{att}(id_R, \overline{a}, \overline{s}, \overline{m})[m_j/false]\} \tag{3}$$

$$R_{att}(id_R, \overline{a}, \overline{s}, \overline{m}) \wedge R_{chg}^{S_j}(id_R, true) \rightsquigarrow \{R_{chg}^{m_j}(id_R, false)\} \tag{4}$$

$$R_{exec}^M(id_R, \overline{x}) \wedge x_k = 0 \rightsquigarrow \{R_{exec}^M(id_R, \overline{x})[x_k/1]\} \tag{5}$$

$$[\mathsf{CopyMessagePools}], [\mathsf{CopyRest}] \quad \} \tag{6}$$

Fig. 3. CA-rule encoding a milestone invalidation upon stage activation

fire at a given moment in time (i.e., a particular micro-step). The initial setup of the eligibility tracking flags is performed at the beginning of a B-step, based on the evaluation of the prerequisite condition of each PAC rule. More specifically, when $x_i = 0$, the corresponding CA-rule is eligible to apply and has not yet been considered for application. When instead $x_i = 1$, then either the rule has been fired, or its prerequisite turned out to be false. This flag-based approach is used to propagate in a compact way information related to the PAC rules that have been already processed, following a mechanism that resembles *dead path elimination* in BPEL. In fact, R_{exec} is also used to enforce a firing order of CA-rules that follows the one induced by $\mathcal{G}$. This is achieved as follows. For each CA-rule $Q \mapsto \alpha$ corresponding to a given PAC rule r, condition Q is put in conjunction with a further formula, used to check whether all the PAC rules that precede r according to the ordering imposed by $\mathcal{G}$ have been already processed. Only in this case r can be considered for execution, consequently applying its effect α to the current artifact snapshot. More specifically, the corresponding CA-rule becomes $Q \wedge exec(r) \mapsto \alpha$, where $exec(r) = \bigwedge_i x_i$ such that i ranges over the indexes of those rules that precede r. Once all x_i flags are switched to 1, the B-step is about to finish: a dedicated CA-rule is enabled to send the outgoing events to the environment, and the artifact instance *blocked* flag is released.

Example 4. An example of a translation of a GSM PAC-rule (indexed by k) is presented in Figure 3. For simplicity, multiple parameters are compacted using an "array" notation (e.g., $x_1, \ldots, x_n$ is denoted by $\overline{x}$). In particular: (1) represents the condition part of a CA-rule, ensuring the "toggle-once" principle ($x_k = 0$), the compliant firing order ($exec(k)$) and the "one-message-at-a-time" principle ($R_{block}(id_R, true)$); (2) describes the action signature; (3) is an effect encoding the invalidation a milestone once the stage has been activated; (4) propagates an internal event denoting the milestone invalidation, if needed; (5) flags the encoded micro-step corresponding to PAC rule k as processed; (6) transports the unaffected data into the next snapshot.

Given a GSM model $\mathcal{G}$ with initial snapshot S_0, we denote by $\Upsilon_{\mathcal{G}}$ its *B-step transition system*, i.e., the infinite-state transition system obtained by iteratively applying the incremental GSM semantics starting from S_0 and nondeterministically considering each possible incoming event. The states of $\Upsilon_{\mathcal{G}}$ correspond to stable snapshots of $\mathcal{G}$, and each transition corresponds to a B-step. We abstract away from the single micro-steps constituting a B-step, because they represent temporary intermediate states that are not interesting for verification purposes. Similarly, given the DCDS $\mathcal{S}$ obtained from the translation of $\mathcal{G}$, we denote by $\Upsilon_{\mathcal{S}}$ its *unblocked-state transition system*, obtained by starting from S_0, and iteratively applying nondeterministically the CA-rules of the pro-

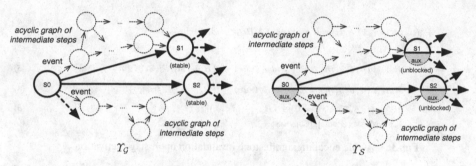

Fig. 4. Construction of the B-step transition system Υ_G and unblocked-state transition system Υ_S for a GSM model G with initial snapshot s_0 and the corresponding DCDS S

cess, and the corresponding actions, in all the possible ways. As for states, we only consider those database instances where all artifact instances are not blocked: these correspond in fact to stable snapshots of G. We then connect two such states provided that there is a sequence of (intermediate) states that lead from the first to the second one, and for which at least one artifact instance is blocked; these sequence corresponds in fact to a series of intermediate-steps evolving the system from a stable state to another stable state. Finally, we project away all the auxiliary relations introduced by the translation mechanism, obtaining a *filtered* version of Υ_S, which we denote as $\Upsilon_S|_G$. The intuition about the construction of these two transition systems is given in Figure 4. Notice that the intermediate micro-steps in the two transition systems can be safely abstracted away because: *(i)* thanks to the toggle-once principle, they do not contain any "internal" cycle; *(ii)* respecting the firing order imposed by G, they all lead to reach the same next stable/unblocked state. We can then establish the one-to-one correspondence between these two transition systems in the following theorem (refer to [21] for complete proof):

Theorem 3. *Given a GSM model G and its translation into a corresponding DCDS S, the corresponding B-step transition system Υ_G and filtered unblocked-state transition system $\Upsilon_S|_G$ are equivalent, i.e., $\Upsilon_G \equiv \Upsilon_S|_G$.*

4   State-Bounded GSM Models

We now take advantage of the key decidability result given in Theorem 2, and study verifiability of *state-bounded GSM models*. Observe that state-boundedness is not a too restrictive condition. It requires each state of the transition system to contain a bounded number of tuples. However, this does not mean that the system in general is restricted to a limited amount of data: infinitely many values may be distributed *across* the states (i.e. along an execution), provided that they do not accumulate in the same state. Furthermore, infinitely many executions are supported, reflecting that whenever an external event updates a slot of the information system maintained by a GSM artifact, infinitely many successor states in principle exist, each one corresponding to a specific new value for that slot. To exploit this, we have first to show that the GSM-DCDS translation preserves state-boundedness, which is in fact the case.

Lemma 1. Given a GSM model G and its DCDS translation S, G is state-bounded if and only if S is state-bounded.

Proof. Recall that S contains some auxiliary relations, used to restrict the applicability of CA-rules in order to enforce the execution assumptions of GSM: *(i)* the eligibility tracking table R_{exec}, *(ii)* the artifact instance blocking flags R_{block}, *(iii)* the internal message pools $R_{data}^{msg_k}$, $R_{data}^{srv_p}$, $R_{out}^{msg_q}$, and *(iv)* the tables of status changes $R_{chg}^{m_i}$, $R_{chg}^{s_j}$. ($\Leftarrow$) This is directly obtained by observing that, if Υ_S is state-bounded, then also $\Upsilon_S|_\mathcal{G}$ is state-bounded. From Theorem 3, we know that $\Upsilon_S|_\mathcal{G} \equiv \Upsilon_\mathcal{G}$, and therefore $\Upsilon_\mathcal{G}$ is state-bounded as well.
($\Rightarrow$) We have to show that state boundedness of $\mathcal{G}$ implies that also all auxiliary relations present in Υ_S are bounded. We discuss each auxiliary relation separately. The artifact blocking relation R_{block} keeps a boolean flag for each artifact instance, so its cardinality depends on the number of instances in the model. Since the model is state-bounded, the number of artifact instances is bounded and so is R_{block}. The eligibility tracking table R_{exec} stores for each artifact instance a boolean vector describing the applicability of a certain PAC rule. Since the number of instances is bounded and so is the set of PAC rules, then the relation R_{exec} is also bounded. Similarly, one can show the boundedness of $R_{chg}^{m_i}$, $R_{chg}^{s_j}$ due to the fact that the number of stages and milestones is fixed a-priori. Let us now analyze internal message pools. By construction, S may contain at most one tuple in $R_{data}^{msg_k}$ and $R_{data}^{srv_p}$ for each artifact instance. This is enforced by the blocking mechanism R_{block}, which blocks the artifact instance at the beginning of a B-step and prevents the instance from injecting further events in internal pools. The outgoing message pool $R_{out}^{msg_q}$ may contain as much tuples per artifact instance as the amount of atomic stages in the model, which is still bounded. However, neither incoming nor outgoing messages are accumulated in the internal pool along the B-steps execution, since the final micro-step of the B-step is designed not to propagate any of the internal message pools to the next snapshot. Therefore, Υ_S is state-bounded. $\square$

From the combination of Theorems 2 and 3 and Lemma 1, we directly obtain:

Theorem 4. *Verification of $\mu\mathcal{L}_P$ properties over state-bounded GSM models is decidable, and can be reduced to finite-state model checking of propositional μ-calculus.*

Obviously, in order to guarantee verifiability of a given GSM model, we need to understand whether it is state-bounded or not. However, state-boundedness is a "semantic" condition, which is undecidable to check [4]. We mitigate this problem by isolating a class of GSM models that is guaranteed to be state-bounded. We show however that even very simple GSM models (such as Fig. 1), are not state-bounded, and thus we provide some modeling strategies to make any GSM model state-bounded.

GSM Models without Artifact Creation. We investigate the case of GSM models that do not contain any *create-artifact-instance* tasks. Without loss of generality, we assimilate the creation of nested datatypes (such as those created by the "add item" task in Example 1) to the creation of new artifacts. From the formal point of view, we can in fact consider each nested datatype as a simple artifact with an empty lifecycle, and its own information model including a connection to its parent artifact.

Corollary 1. *Verification of $\mu\mathcal{L}_P$ properties over GSM models without* create-artifact-instance *tasks is decidable.*

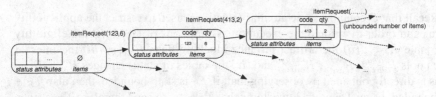

Fig. 5. Unbounded execution of the GSM model in Fig. 1

Proof. Let $\mathcal{G}$ be a GSM model without *create-artifact-instance* tasks. At each stable snapshot Σ_k, $\mathcal{G}$ can either process an event representing an incoming one-way message, or the termination of a task. We claim that the only source of state-unboundedness can be caused by service calls return related to the termination of *create-artifact-instance* tasks. In fact, one-way incoming messages, as well as other service call returns, do not increase the size of the data stored in the GSM information model, because the payload of such messages just substitutes the values of the corresponding data attributes, according to the signature of the message. Similarly, by an inspection of the proof of Lemma 1, we know that across the micro-steps of a B-step, status attributes are modified but their size does not change. Furthermore, a bounded number of outgoing events could be accumulated in the message pools, but this information is then flushed at the end of the B-step, thus bringing the size of the overall information model back to the same size present at the beginning of the B-step. Therefore, without *create-artifact-instance* tasks, the size of the information model in each stable state is constant, and corresponds to the size of the initial information model. We can then apply Theorem 4 to get the result. □

Arbitrary GSM Models. The types of models studied in paragraph above are quite restrictive, because they forbid the possibility of extending the number of artifacts during the execution of the system. On the other hand, as soon as this is allowed, even very simple GSM models, as the one shown in Fig. 1, may become state unbounded. In that example, the source of state unboundedness lies in the stage containing the "add item" task, which could be triggered an unbounded number of times due to continuous *itemRequest* incoming events, as pointed out in Fig. 5. This, in turn, is caused by the fact that the modeler left the GSM model underspecified, without providing any hint about the maximum number of items that can be included in an order. To overcome this issue, we require the modeler to supply such information (stating, e.g., that each order is associated to at most 10 items). Technically, the GSM model under study has to be parameterized by an arbitrary but finite number N_{max}, which denotes the maximum number of artifact instances that can coexist in the same execution state. We call this kind of GSM model *instance bounded*. A possible policy to provide such bound is to allocate available "slots" for each artifact type of the model, i.e. to specify a maximum number N_{A_i} for each artifact type A_i, then having $N_{max} = \sum_i N_{A_i}$. In order to incorporate the artifact bounds into the execution semantics, we proceed as follows. First, we pre-populate the initial snapshot of the considered GSM instance with N_{max} blank artifact instances (respecting the relative proportion given by the local maximum numbers for each artifact type). We refer to one such blank artifact instance as *artifact container*. Along the system execution, each container may be: *(i)* filled with concrete data carried by an actual artifact instance of the corresponding type, or *(ii)* flushed to the initial, blank state. To this end, each artifact container is equipped with an auxiliary flag

fr_i, which reflects its current state: fr_i is false when the container stores a concrete artifact instance, true otherwise. Then, the internal semantics of *create-artifact-instance* is
changed so as to check the availability of a blank artifact container. In particular, when
the corresponding service call is to be invoked with the new artifact instance data, the
calling artifact instance selects the next available blank artifact container, sets its flag
fr_i to *false*, and fills it with the payload of the service call. If all containers are occupied, the calling artifact instance waits until some container is released. Symmetrically
to artifact creation, the deletion procedure for an artifact instance is managed by turning
the corresponding container flag fr_i to true. Details on the DCDS CA-rules formalizing
creation/deletion of artifact instances according to these principles can be found in [21].

We observe that, following this container-based realization strategy, the information
model of an instance-bounded GSM model has a fixed size, which polinomially depends on the total maximum number N_{max}. The new implementation of *create-artifact-
instance* does not really change the size of the information model, but just suitably
changes its content. Therefore, Corollary 1 directly applies to instance-bounded GSM
models, guaranteeing decidability of their verification. Finally, notice that infinitely
many different artifact instances can be created and manipulated, provided that they
do not accumulate in the same state (exceeding N_{max}).

5 Discussion and Related Work

In this work we provided the foundations for the formal verification of the GSM artifact-
centric paradigm. So far, only few works have investigated verification of GSM models.
The closest approach to ours is [6], where state-boundedness is also used as a key property towards decidability. The main difference between the two approaches is that decidability of state-bounded GSM models is proven for temporal logics of incomparable
expressive power. In addition to [6], in this work we also study modeling strategies to
make an arbitrary GSM model state-bounded, while they assume that the input model
is guaranteed to be state-bounded. Hence, our strategies could be instrumental to [6] as
well. In [15] another promising technique for the formal verification of GSM models
is presented. However, the current implementation cannot be applied to general GSM
models, because of assumptions over the data types and the fact that only one instance
per artifact type is supported. Furthermore, a propositional branching-time logic is used
for verification, restricting to the status attributes of the artifacts. The results presented in
our paper can be used to generalize this approach towards more complex models (such
as instance-bounded GSM models) and more expressive logics, given, e.g., the fact that
"one-instance artifacts" fall inside the decidable cases we discussed in this paper.

It is worth noting that all the presented decidability results are actually even stronger:
they state that verification can be reduced to standard model checking of propositional μ-
calculus over finite-state transition systems (thanks to the abstraction techniques studied
in [4]). This opens the possibility of actually implementing the discussed techniques,
by relying on state-of-the-art model checkers. We also inherit from [4] the complexity
boundaries: they state that verification is EXPTIME in the size of the GSM information
model which, in the case of instance-bounded GSM models, means in turn EXPTIME
in the maximum number of artifact instances that can coexist in the same state.

References

1. van der Aalst, W.M.P., Stahl, C.: Modeling Business Processes - A Petri Net-Oriented Approach. Springer (2011)
2. Armando, A., Ponta, S.E.: Model checking of security-sensitive business processes. In: Degano, P., Guttman, J.D. (eds.) FAST 2009. LNCS, vol. 5983, pp. 66–80. Springer, Heidelberg (2010)
3. Bagheri Hariri, B., Calvanese, D., De Giacomo, G., De Masellis, R., Felli, P., Montali, M.: Description logic knowledge and action bases. Journal of Artificial Intelligence Research, 651–686 (2013)
4. Bagheri Hariri, B., Calvanese, D., De Giacomo, G., Deutsch, A., Montali, M.: Verification of relational data-centric dynamic systems with external services. In: Proc. of PODS, pp. 163–174. ACM Press (2013)
5. Belardinelli, F., Lomuscio, A., Patrizi, F.: An abstraction technique for the verification of artifact-centric systems. In: Proc. of KR. AAAI Press (2012)
6. Belardinelli, F., Lomuscio, A., Patrizi, F.: Verification of gsm-based artifact-centric systems through finite abstraction. In: Liu, C., Ludwig, H., Toumani, F., Yu, Q. (eds.) ICSOC 2012. LNCS, vol. 7636, pp. 17–31. Springer, Heidelberg (2012)
7. Bhattacharya, K., Caswell, N.S., Kumaran, S., Nigam, A., Wu, F.Y.: Artifact-centered operational modeling: Lessons from customer engagements. IBM Systems Journal 46(4) (2007)
8. Calvanese, D., De Giacomo, G., Montali, M.: Foundations of data-aware process analysis: A database theory perspective. In: Proc. of PODS, pp. 1–12. ACM Press (2013)
9. Clarke, E.M., Grumberg, O., Peled, D.A.: Model checking. The MIT Press (1999)
10. Cohn, D., Hull, R.: Business artifacts: A data-centric approach to modeling business operations and processes. IEEE Data Eng. Bull. 32(3) (2009)
11. Damaggio, E., Hull, R., Vaculin, R.: On the equivalence of incremental and fixpoint semantics for business artifacts with guard-stage-milestone lifecycles. Information Systems (2012)
12. Deutsch, A., Hull, R., Patrizi, F., Vianu, V.: Automatic verification of data-centric business processes. In: Proc. of ICDT, pp. 252–267. ACM Press (2009)
13. Dumas, M.: On the convergence of data and process engineering. In: Eder, J., Bielikova, M., Tjoa, A.M. (eds.) ADBIS 2011. LNCS, vol. 6909, pp. 19–26. Springer, Heidelberg (2011)
14. Emerson, E.A.: Model checking and the mu-calculus. In: Descriptive Complexity and Finite Models (1996)
15. Gonzalez, P., Griesmayer, A., Lomuscio, A.: Verifying gsm-based business artifacts. In: Proc. of ICWS, pp. 25–32. IEEE (2012)
16. Group, T.O.M.: Object constraint language, version 2.0. Tech. Rep. formal/06-05-01, The Object Management Group (May 2006), http://www.omg.org/spec/OCL/2.0/
17. Morimoto, S.: A survey of formal verification for business process modeling. In: Bubak, M., van Albada, G.D., Dongarra, J., Sloot, P.M.A. (eds.) ICCS 2008, Part II. LNCS, vol. 5102, pp. 514–522. Springer, Heidelberg (2008)
18. Nigam, A., Caswell, N.S.: Business artifacts: An approach to operational specification. IBM Systems Journal 42(3) (2003)
19. Puhlmann, F., Weske, M.: Using the pi-calculus for formalizing workflow patterns. In: van der Aalst, W.M.P., Benatallah, B., Casati, F., Curbera, F. (eds.) BPM 2005. LNCS, vol. 3649, pp. 153–168. Springer, Heidelberg (2005)
20. Russo, A., Mecella, M., Montali, M., Patrizi, F.: Towards a reference implementation for data centric dynamic systems. In: Proc. of BPM Workshops (2013)
21. Solomakhin, D., Montali, M., Tessaris, S.: Formalizing guard-stage-milestone meta-models as data-centric dynamic systems. Tech. Rep. KRDB12-4, KRDB Research Centre, Faculty of Computer Science, Free University of Bozen-Bolzano (2012)
22. The Object Management Group: Case Management Model and Notation (CMMN), Beta 1 (January 2013), http://www.omg.org/spec/CMMN/1.0/Beta1/

Automatically Composing Services by Mining Process Knowledge from the Web

Bipin Upadhyaya[1], Ying Zou[1], Shaohua Wang[1], and Joanna Ng[2]

[1] Queen's University, Kingston, Canada
{bipin.upadhyaya,ying.zou}@queensu.ca, shaohua@cs.queensu.ca
[2] CAS Research, IBM Canada Software Laboratory, Markham, Canada
jwng@ca.ibm.com

Abstract. Current approaches in Service-Oriented Architecture (SOA) are challenging for users to get involved in the service composition due to the in-depth knowledge required for SOA standards and techniques. To shield users from the complexity of SOA standards, we automatically generate composed services for end-users using process knowledge available in the Web. Our approach uses natural language processing techniques to extract tasks. Our approach automatically identifies services required to accomplish the tasks. We represent the extracted tasks in a task model to find the services and then generate a user interface (UI) for a user to perform the tasks. Our case study shows that our approach can extract the tasks from how-to instructions Web pages with high precision (*i.e.,* 90%). The generated task model helps to discover services and compose the found services to perform a task. Our case study shows that our approach can reach more than 90% accuracy in service composition by identifying accurate data flow relation between services.

Keywords: task model, service composition, Web, instructions, UI generation.

1   Introduction

Software is prevalent in all aspects of our lives, such as checking a stock price, finding a doctor and buying a product. Nowadays a significant part of software system is structured using software services and implemented using Web service technologies. Programmable Web[1] alone has indexed more than 9000 services that are used in our daily activities, such as education, dating, shopping, and job search. However, a single service cannot fulfill a user's goal. For example if a user wants to plan a trip, he may require a flight booking and a hotel reservation services. One or more services are combined to fulfill his goal. A service composition is a process that combines a set of logically related services to achieve a given goal. In the current state of practices, the combination process is based on a pre-defined process model that describes the services to accomplish a task, such as planning a travel. A significant amount of effort from industry and academics focuses on providing infrastructures, languages and

---

[1] ProgrammableWeb - Mashups, APIs, and the Web as Platform,
http://www.programmableweb.com/

S. Basu et al. (Eds.): ICSOC 2013, LNCS 8274, pp. 267–282, 2013.

tools to compose the services. However, the complexity of state-of-the-art Web services technology prevents users with limited IT skills from getting easy access to Web services and their offered functionalities. A user has to perform a sequence of tasks to complete a process. From the implementation point of view, a task can be implemented by one or more services. For example, a typical process of buying a movie ticket includes tasks related to "searching for movies", "choosing the date and time", and "paying for the ticket". Web service composition [11] requires the resolution of multiple dependencies between input parameters (IP), output parameters (OP) and non-trivial reasoning about the composition of required functionalities from smaller units of Web services. It is challenging to acquire the complete knowledge of a domain (*e.g.,* hotel booking, flight booking in travel) and then searching, and combining the services found. We envision two challenges for a novice designer or a user to perform service composition (SC) as listed below:

- **Lack of complete knowledge about the tasks involved in order to accomplish a goal.** A user has to repeatedly search the Web to learn and complete different tasks required to achieve a goal. For example, searching for a movie, finding the showtime in a local theater and making online payment are tasks for buying a movie tickets. This process is tedious, error-prone and time consuming. Knowledge from business processes to describe the tasks for achieving a goal, if available, is hard for a novice designer or a user to understand.
- **Difficult to identify a set of services and link the services to execute a process.** There are a large number of services available on the Web. Locating a suitable set of services and linking the identified services are challenging even for experienced developers. Current work in service flow identification [1, 2 and 6] do not help to identify tasks as those methods are solely based on input and output parameters of services. A user communicates with a task through a user interface (UI). Current approaches in UI generation for Web services [10 and 12] are based on technical descriptions and therefore, are difficult to understand and error prone.

In this research, we address the aforementioned challenges. The Web contains a lot of well-written instructions (such as eHow [27] and Wikihow [28]) to teach people how to perform a process (such as how to buy a camera, how to make a restaurant reservation and how to buy a movie tickets). These instructions often describe how to accomplish a sequence of tasks step by step. Our approach understands the human-written instructions and guides a user to complete a process by discovering and integrating different services. Our goal is to build a knowledge base for a process using text mining techniques that exploit the structure of the how-to descriptions. Our approach automatically identifies a task model from written instructions in the Web pages. We use a task model to identify and combine services to execute a process. To complete a process, a user needs a UI. Building a UI for a task is time consuming. We present an approach to generate a UI to execute a task. Our UI generation approach considers data-sharing between services, so a user only needs to provide minimum input for a task.

The remainder of this paper is organized as follows. Section 2 gives an overview of our approach and provides in detail discussion about each step. Section 3 presents our case study. Section 4 discusses the related work. Finally, Section 5 concludes the paper and explores the future work.

2   Background

Our research is primarily focused on extracting knowledge from Web pages with how-to instructions. In this section, we will discuss the basic structure of how-to instruction Web pages, Web services, and task models.

2.1   How-to Instruction Web Pages

How-to instructions in the Web are a knowledge base of human activities. These websites currently store millions of articles on how to do things step by step, which collectively cover almost every domain of our daily lives, such as business, education, and travel. More or less all how-to instruction Web pages have the similar format to present the content. Fig. 1 shows an example of a Web page with how-to instructions from an eHow website. The article describes the steps to buy a movie ticket online. Fig. 1 contains four annotated parts, such as a process; a short description of the process; other related processes; and a list of tasks for completing the process. We observed three types of how-to instruction articles in the Web. First type of how-to

Fig. 1. An annotated eHow article[2]

articles helps a user to perform labor-intensive processes, such as how to clean a TV screen, and how to create a contact group on iPhone. The second type contains particularly descriptive and well-defined processes, such as Web pages related to recipes or hobbies. The third type describes the dynamic processes with many choices since the parameters and choices of a task involved vary from user to user. Examples of these tasks are reserving a seat in a restaurant, and going for a trip to Europe. Our approach cannot help with the first type of labor intensive processes. For the second and the third type of how-to instructions, our approach can assist in finding possible services and integrate services to perform a process.

2.2   Web Services

A Web service is a software module designed to help interoperation between machines over the Web. There are currently two approaches for interfacing to the Web with Web services, namely Simple Object Access Protocol (SOAP) and Representational State Transfer (REST) [20]. REST as the architectural style of the Web improves scalability of the Web applications using statelessness, performance based on caching, and compatibility through content types. RESTful services [21] simplify the development, deployment and invocation of Web services. In this paper, we refer to a

---

[2] How to Buy Movie Tickets Online | Ehow,
    www.ehow.com/how_2106555_buy-movie-tickets-online.html

service as a RESTful resource. If a service is not RESTful, it is transformed into a RESTful service using the techniques described in our earlier work [4]. We model a service in terms of service name, HTTP verb, input parameters and output parameters.

In a service invocation chain, there can be different linkages: user-to-service; service-to-service and service-to-user. When a user invokes a service, the relation is a user-to-service linkage. A service-to-human linkage indicates that a service needs human inputs or confirmation. A service-to-service linkage occurs when a service invokes another service.

2.3   Task Model

A Task model describes the logical tasks that have to be carried out in a process to reach a user's goals. Several task modeling notations exist, such as Hierarchical Task Analysis (HTA), Goals, Operators, Methods, Selection rules (GOMS), and Concur-TaskTrees (CTT). CTT [30] is a graphical notation that supports the hierarchical structure of tasks, which can be interrelated through a powerful set of operators (such as iteration and optional) that describe the temporal relationships (such as choice, interleaving and enabling) between subtasks. CTT describes four types of tasks: the user, the application, their interaction and the abstract tasks. W3C [19] specification for CTT [30] provides complete information on CTT Meta-model and relations among the tasks. We use CTT to model tasks as CTT follows an engineering approach to task models. Moreover, the semantics of CTT are more complete and precise. It can support automated service discovery more effectively than other user task modeling formalisms. CTT is applied in the field of end-user programming. It is easy for end-users to express and understand CTT.

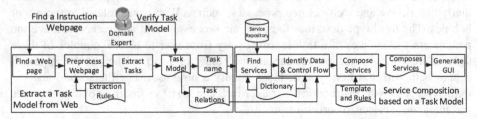

Fig. 2. Overall steps to generate UI for a task from Web services

3   Overview of Our Approach

A user selects one of many how-to instruction Web pages related to his goal. Our approach is to search and compose services based on a user selected Web page. A process is well-defined, concrete action that a user performs to achieve a goal. In order to achieve a user's goal, we break a process into a set of tasks that can be scheduled and completed. Fig. 2 shows the overall steps of our approach. We identify task models from how-to instructions in the Web. We use the task models to find and compose services. We describe each step in details in this section.

3.1   Extracting a Task Model from the Web

In this sub-section, we introduce our approach that automatically extracts a task model from a semi structured Web page.

Find Web Pages
In this paper, we examine two specific Web sites to extract human written instructions (eHow [28] and Wikihow [27]). If a Web page matches the user's scenario, we use this Web page to extract a task model to form service composition.

Preprocess How-to Instruction Web Pages
To analyze Web pages, we parse Web pages to build a Document Object Model (DOM) tree structure. An HTML file may contain mismatched HTML tags although it can be correctly displayed by Web browsers due to the fault-tolerance capability of Web browsers. We use HTML syntax checker [9] to correct the malformed HTML tags. Then we parse the HTML into DOM tree structure. The preprocessor contains two steps: 1) learn rules from the sample Web pages; and 2) apply rules on a Web page to extract tasks. We manually examine and learn the DOM structure of the title and the instruction steps. We use these learned DOM structures to form the rules. This procedure is based on the assumption that the documents collected from an identical source share the common structures. The preprocessor uses wrapper induction approaches to extract the title and the instruction steps from a Web page. The title becomes the root of a task model and the instruction steps become the tasks to complete a process (*i.e.*, extracting tasks).

```
Input: InstructionSteps
Output: Action Object Lists
Algorithm
1. For each step in InstructionSteps
2. step=Instructionsteps[index]
3. List<Segment> seglist=ComputerSegment(step);
4.     For all Seglist sleseglists do
5.         ASegment=POSTagger(sl);
6.         List<ActionObject> aolist=ExtractActionObject(ASegment)
7.         List conjection=ExtractConjuction(Asegment)
8.         Aobj=Order(aolist, conj)
9.     End For
10. End For
```

Fig. 3. An algorithm for identifying tasks from how-to instruction Web pages

Extract Tasks
Each instruction step describes the tasks in a process. We extract functional semantics of an instruction step. Functional semantics express the main intent of a sentence in terms of the action-object pairs. An action-object pairing articulates what action is performed with an object. An action is represented by a verb and objects are described by nouns in a sentence. For example, in a sentence "buy a ticket", the functional semantic pair is {buy, ticket}. "buy" and "ticket" correspond to the action and the object respectively. Our objective is to extract tasks involved in a process (*i.e.*, instruction steps) as action-object pairs. We analyze the instruction steps to extract tasks as

functional semantics. Fig. 3 shows
the algorithm to identify tasks. An
instruction steps may contain
multiple segments. Each segment
is an instruction to perform a task.
A segment is a sentence in the
instruction step containing one or
more verbs and nouns. Line 3 in
Fig. 3 extracts the segments from
an instruction step. We use a
well-stabilized   part-of-speech
(POS) tagger [29] to identify the
syntactic structure of a segment.
Step 2 in Fig. 4 shows a POS
tagged sentence. The number
(*i.e.*, inside small brackets) in
Step 2 indicates the index of the
word as a noun or a verb in a
sentence. For example in Step 2
of in Fig. 4, selection is the first

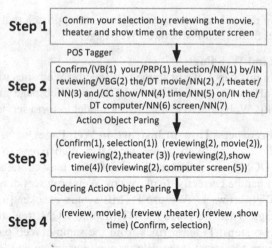

Fig. 4. An example for task extraction steps

noun (NN) and the movie is the second noun (NN). We post-process the generated
data structures to resolve object names consisting of multiple words (*e.g.*, "Computer
screen"), phrasal verbs (*e.g.*, "go to"), and pronominal referrals (*e.g.*, "it"). We assume
"it" always refers to the last mentioned object, which is proved to be a sensible heuristic in most of the cases. For each segment, we extract actionable verb (VB)/verb
phrases (VP) and the related noun phrases (NP). (VB/VP) or (NP) forms a task. Step 3
shows action-object pairs, such as "confirm selection", "reviewing movie", "reviewing theater", "reviewing showtime" and "reviewing computer screen".

$$PMI(domain, task) = \frac{hits(\text{domain } AND \text{ } task)}{hits(task)} \tag{1}$$

where hits (x) is the number of results that a search engine returns for a query 'x'.

We filter irrelevant tasks from the list of tasks extracted. PMI (Pointwise mutual
information) [23] helps identify how two words or phrases are related based on all the
information available in the Web. We use Google Services[3] to calculate PMI. The
PMI score is the number of hits for a query that combines domain and task divided by
the hits for the task alone. This can be viewed as the probability that a domain and a
task can be found on a Web page as shown in equation 1. For example in Step 4, we
compute PMI for each term with the domain "movie" and each object in action-object
pairs. As a result, PMI (movie, review theater) is 0.287; PMI (movie, confirm selection) is 0.197; and PMI (movie, review computer screen) is 2.13415E-05. To identify
the threshold to filter irrelevant tasks, we randomly selected 10 how-to description
Web pages and manually check the result PMI. We empirically set 10^{-3} as the threshold. In line number 6 of Fig. 3, we compute the score. If the score is above the threshold, we consider it as an action-object pair. Hence in Fig. 4, (review, computer

---

[3] https://developers.google.com/web-search/docs/

screen) is filtered out. We convert the verb to the base form. For the extracted pairs, we analyze its occurrence index and compare with clauses, such as before, after, and by, to identify the order of the sequence. We further arranged the remaining action-object (review movie, review theater and review selection) pairs based on the hierarchical relationship among the words. If no relation is found, the arrangement is based on the order of their occurrences in a sentence.

Using the action-object extracted from Fig. 3, we build a CTT task model. Fig. 5 shows a task model to buy a movie ticket online. Only two kinds of temporal relationship exist in how-to instructions. If the two noun phrases are connected through and clauses, there is a sequential enabling info (*i.e.*, []>>) relation. If the noun phrases are connected with or clauses there is a Choice (*i.e.* []).If the same

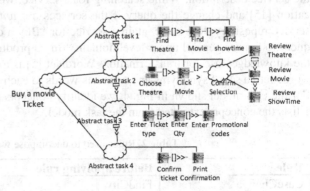

Fig. 5. A simplified task model extracted from Fig. 1

task appears multiple times in a process, we choose the last place where the task had appeared and remove other occurrences. If a step contains multiple tasks, we make an abstract task which connects all the tasks of a step. An extracted model is verified by a user. It is easy to add and modify tasks in a CTT model.

Table 1. Different information extracted from the task model

Field	Heuristic and Explanation	Example
Domain Concept	Noun in the process title	In "How to Buy Movie Tickets Online", movie is the domain of process title.
Service Name	For each task, the first word corresponds a service name.	In "Review movies", review is related to the service name
Input	Noun occurring with the UI related words (Input, Enter, Fill, Click, Submit)	In "Enter Name", name is the word related to input
Output	Noun occurring with the UI related words (show, select, read, confirm, validate, check, review, decide, ensure, choose)	In "Show movie list", movie list is the word related to the output.

3.2   Service Composition Based on the Task Model

In this sub-section, we present our approach to find and compose services based on the task model generated from Section 3.1.

Find Services
In this step, we find the services for each step in CTT task model. We use our previous work in concept-based service discovery [3] to discover services. A concept is a semantic notion or a keyword for describing a subject, *e.g.,* "traveling" or "taxi reservation". Service repository indexes services based on concepts available in the service description documents. Our approach clusters services using the concepts conveyed in the service description. While searching for a service, we perform the entity identification [15] and change the query if the services are not found. For example if our service repository does not contain a service for "Buy a camera" then we change the query to a more general upper level domain "Buy a product". We use WordNet [5] as the knowledge base for transformation. WordNet [5] is a lexical database that groups words into a set of synonyms and connects words to each other via semantic relations. For the task model shown in Fig. 4, we identify concepts to search for services. Table 1 lists the concepts extracted from the task model.

Table 2. Rules used to decompose words

Rule	Before applying rule	After applying rule
CaseChange	FindCity	Find, city
	getMovie	Get, Movie
Suffix containing No.	City1	City
Underscore separator	Customer_Information	Customer, Information
Dash separator	Find-city	Find, City

Identify Control and Data Flows
We consider the task relations from the CTT model as a control flow of a composite service. We find the data-dependency between services and change the control flow based on the data-dependency. A data-dependency graph depicts the collaboration relations between services related to different tasks. Each service has a name and takes input parameters and gives an output. Either input or output of a service can be empty, but, not both. Multiple input and output messages in a composite service are merged into a set of input or output. We exclude fault messages as they seldom contribute to the data flow to the subsequent services. Similarly, access keys for services are excluded as they do not contribute to the data flow.

$$Semantic(p_{s1}, p_{s2}) = \begin{cases} 1 \text{ if } p_{s1} \text{ and } p_{s2} \text{ are identical/synonymous} \\ \dfrac{1}{\#links} \text{ if } p_{s1}, p_{s2} \text{ have hierarchical relation} \\ 0 \text{ otherwise} \end{cases} \quad (2)$$

where, p_{s1} and p_{s2} are the name of parameters of services s1 and s2;
#link is the number of nodes to reach a common parent from the names of p_{s1} and p_{s2} in WordNet

The name of a service and the input/output parameters follow the conventions used in programming languages. Table 2 shows the rules to decompose input parameters and output parameters. After decomposing words, we use porter stemmer [20], which is the process for reducing derived words to their stem, base, or root form. For example, the words "fishing", "fished", "fish", and "fisher" have the same root word, "fish". Equation (2) shows a formula to calculate the semantic similarity. For each word, we calculate the semantic similarity. WordNet helps to identify if two terms are semantically similar and to what degree they are similar. When the words are identical or synonymous, the semantic similarity is 1. If there is a hierarchical relation, it depends on their similarity degree. If the semantic (p_{s1}, p_{s2}) is greater than a threshold (*i.e.*, 0.3), we consider it is a match. We choose a threshold by analyzing different service input and output parameters. For each pair of services, we evaluate the semantic similarity between the input and output parameters. Based on the similarity between parameters, we identify the linkage between different services.

For a set of services, if an output parameter of one service and an input parameter of another service are semantically similar, a data flow relation exists. We compute the semantic weight between the services which is the sum of semantic similarity between all parameters of two services. The semantic weight is normalized in interval 0 to 1. 0 means no data flow. 1 indicates that all the inputs of a service come from the output of another service.

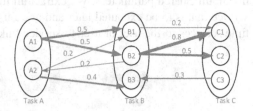

Fig. 6. Dependency graph between different services in three different tasks

Fig. 6 shows a simplified version of the dependency graph containing services of different tasks. Moreover, the direction of the edges between two enclosed nodes dictates the dataflow. The service where the arrow points to takes one output of the preceding service as its input. For example shown in Fig. 6, service B2 of task B has two links between services, C1 and C2 on task C.

Compose Services

We have a task model that defines the steps that a user needs to follow to perform a process. A task model helps us to find relevant services and then gives a logical flow between different services. However, a task is performed by services. The execution order of services can be different from the task model. It depends on the data dependency between services. An executable task is a graph G (V, E) where G is a Directed Acyclic Graph (DAG). Each vertex $v_i \in V$ is a service. Each edge (u, v) represents a logical flow of messages from service u to service v. If there is an edge (u, v), then it means that an output message produced by service u is used to create an input message to service v. Our goal in this step is to combine one or more services in the dependency graph to form a task that can maximize the data sharing properties between services. From Fig. 6, we select A1 between {A1, A2} based on the semantic weight. We select B2 among {B1, B2} because its weight to C2 or C1 is the maximum. Hence the flow will be A1→B2→C1.

The task model from how-to instruction Web pages, such as recipe Webpage is different. Obviously services for the action-object pairs like "Boil Pasta" are not available, and hence there is no flow information. For such Web pages, we define a service composition template and use a rule to invoke predefined template in such a specific domain. We impose a rule to invoke E-commerce templates for recipe related how-to Web pages.

Generate User Interface (UI)

A user needs an interface to provide the data to perform a task. Each task may require more than one service. As mentioned in the background section, three relations among services are defined. We want to increase the service-to-service interaction to minimize the demand for a user to enter information for accomplishing a task. Our service selection approach maximizes data sharing by choosing services with the maximum shared parameters. We extract all the parameters that may be required by a service that is to be executed later and ask a user to fill the information avoiding multiple services-to-the user or user-to-service linkage.

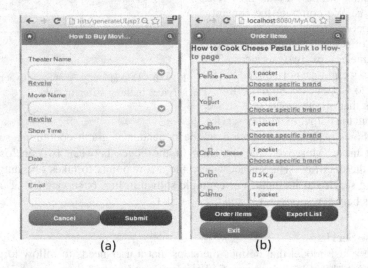

Fig. 7. Screenshot of generated UI

We enhance Kasarda *et al.* [22] approach to generate UI when each service has different input and output parameters. The approach by Kasarda *et al.* is simple and easy to implement. The use of XHTML makes the generated UI adaptable to cross-platforms. Decision for the placement input or output in UI is based on the dependency between the services. The service input and output parameters are represented in XML. We enhance the approach by Kasarda *et al.* to find the relation among different input elements. Our enhancement also helps decide whether the input element should be user editable or not. We enhance the UI generation techniques using the following techniques:

1. If the output of a service is not used as an input parameter to another service, the UI element of the output parameter is not user editable;

2. If the output of a service is a single parameter and used as an input parameter to another service, the UI element of the parameter is not user editable;

3. If the output of a service has multiple values (*i.e.*, array) and one of the elements is used as an input parameter to another service, the UI element of the parameter is user editable;

4. If the input parameter for a service does not come as an output from any other services, we select an appropriate UI element based on the approach described in [22].

5. If a node has multiple paths and if they do not merge to the same node later, the shortest path becomes a new task and used as a link. For example in Fig.7a review movie and theater are tasks used as links.

6. Based on the dependency found in section *Identify Control and Data Flow* step, we link service invocation with UI elements. Unless it's predefined in a template, we add two UI elements (submit and cancel), submit executes all the service invocations and the cancel exits the service composition. For example as illustrated in Fig. 7, the change in theater name alters the values in the selection box for the movie name which in turn modifies the values in the show time selection box.

UI elements for an executable task are dependent on each other. A change in one parameter can trigger a run-time change in another UI element. We also identify the dependency between these parameters. Fig. 7 shows the generated UI. Fig.7a shows a UI of a process to get a movie ticket. Fig. 7b illustrates a UI to order items to prepare a recipe based on pre-defined e-commerce template.

4   Case Study

We conduct a case study to evaluate the effectiveness of our approach. The objectives of our case study include: 1) evaluate if our approach can achieve high precision and recall to extract task models from how-to instruction Web pages; and 2) evaluate the accuracy of our approach to compose services from task models.

4.1   Setup

We collect 40 different how-to instructions from eHow and Wikihow. The collected Web pages were from different domains, such as communication (*e.g.*, send SMS), finance (*e.g.*, find a stock price of a company), and E-commerce (*e.g.*, buy a product). We avoid selecting many processes from the domain to ensure the case study result is not skewed due to this particular. In addition, we collected more than 600 service description files to examine our approach on the service composition capability. The collected service description files have more than 4,000 different services. Our case study specifically answers the following two research questions.

1. How effective is our approach to extract a task model from Web pages?

2. How accurate is our approach of service composition based on task models?

In our case study, the first author evaluated all the result. Our evaluator has two years of experience in developing Web services and composite services.

4.2   Evaluate the Effectiveness of Our Approach to Extract Task Models

We measure the effectiveness of our approach on identifying task models using precision and recall. As shown in equation (3), the precision is the ratio of the total number of tasks correctly extracted by our approach to the total number of tasks in a how-to instruction Web page. Recall, as shown in equation (4), is the ratio of the total number of tasks correctly extracted by our approach to the total number of tasks existing in the how-to description Web pages.

$$precision = \frac{\{\text{relevant tasks}\} \cap \{retrieved\ tasks\}}{\{\text{retrieved tasks}\}} \tag{3}$$

$$recall = \frac{\{\text{relevant tasks}\} \cap \{retrieved\ tasks\}}{\{\text{relevant tasks}\}} \tag{4}$$

Table 3 presents the effectiveness of our approach to extract task models from how-to instruction Web pages. Table 3 shows the effectiveness of task identification of our approach. Our approach has the average precision of 90% and average recall of 59%. The reason for lower recall is due to verb scoping during task extraction step. When two verbs are conjoined, it is not clear whether the noun is associated with both or just the latter one. With "review and buy a camera" and "Go and buy a camera", for example, our approach needs to decide whether the noun (*i.e.,* camera) is associated with either both the verbs or just the one. Our approach could not correctly identify multi-word expressions (MWEs) in the instruction steps. MWEs represent the structure and meaning that cannot be derived from the component words, as they occur independently. Examples of MWEs include conjunctions like 'as well as' (meaning 'including'), and phrasal verbs like 'find out' (meaning 'search').

Table 3. Results for our case study

Domain	Effectiveness of our approach to extract task model			Accuracy of our approach to compose services	
	#Web pages	Precision (%)	Recall (%)	# task Model	Accuracy of SC (%)
Hotel	10	91	57	3	88
Flight	10	89	53	2	85
Ecommerce	8	92	61	4	83
Finance	7	88	58	3	85
Communication	5	93	70	3	95

4.3   Evaluate the Accuracy of Automatic SC Based on the Task Model

We are interested in evaluating the accuracy of service composition based on the task model. Equation (5) gives the measure of our accuracy. Accuracy of our approach is given by the ratio of the correctly identified data and control flow by the total number of data and control flows among services.

$$Accuracy = \frac{\#Correctly\ Identified\ flow\ for\ SC}{\#Flow\ required\ for\ SC} \times 100\ (\%) \tag{5}$$

To check the accuracy of service composition we first made sure that there are services available to perform the service composition for the task models. We selected the task model with at least one candidate service to form the service composition. For this case study, we selected 15 out of 40 task models. We manually verified the services used by our approach and the data and control flows between the services selected. Table 3 presents the result of our case study for automatic service composition based on a task model. Our approach has average accuracy of 85% to identify correct flow different services. The uses of ambiguous words and the words not available in WordNet cause difficulties in identifying semantic similarity. Some element names were misspelled or inconsistently named. e.g., an element conferenceIdentifier was misspelled as conderenceIdentifier in several places in a conference management service. Hence our approach could not identify the data flow between services. Some of the entities are named differently, *e.g.*, *ASIN* and *OfferListingID* were used interchangeably in Amazon Product API. We were unable identify these interchangeable entities.

4.4   Threats to Validity

In this section, we discuss the limitations of our approaches and the threats that may affect the validity of the results of our case study. In our case study, only one of the co-author inspects the results. Our evaluator has experience in developing service composition and has knowledge of the domains used in our case study. The manual verification introduces bias because a single evaluator could make mistakes. We should have recruited additional people for the evaluation. Unfortunately, we were not able to recruit more evaluators with sufficient knowledge about service-oriented applications and who can spend considerable time to manually inspect our results. To generalize our results to task extraction and service composition in other domains, we chose to study systems with a variety of domains to help ensure the generality of our results. Even though we think the case study in still need to enhance to include more domains and a wider variety of tasks from each domain.

5   Related Work

Our work is related to three research areas: mining human activities from the Web, Web service composition and UI generation from Web services.

5.1   Mining Human Activities from the Web

Singh *et al.* [21] collect knowledge about commonsense including daily living is the Open Mind Common Sense project. More than 729,000 raw sentences representing commonsense knowledge collected from the general public through a template-based

Web interface. In our previous work [16], we extract process knowledge by analyzing the menus and forms that are limited to a certain domain. In this work, we extract human activity knowledge automatically from how-to instructions on the Web. We define a process in terms of a sequence of tasks. Our approach is similar to Perkowitz *et al.* [13] who proposed a method for mining human activity models in terms of a sequence of objects involved in an activity and their probabilities. From the definitions of activities obtained in external resources, such as how-to instructions, recipes, and training manuals, they attempted to extract objects by identifying noun phrases and their hyponyms under 'object' or 'substance' categories in WordNet. Unlike their approach, we not only focus on identifying tasks to achieve a goal. We find the corresponding services and link services to execute a task.

5.2   Web Service Composition

For composing services, a user can perform either a manual composition in cooperation with domain experts or automatic composition [2, 6 and 7] conducted by software programs. In the manual approach, human users who know the domain well (*e.g.,* domain ontology) select proper Web services and weave them into a cohesive workflow. Although users may rely on some GUI-based software [24] to facilitate the composition, in essence, it is a labor-intensive and error-prone task. On the contrary, in the automatic composition approach, software programs know if two Web services can be connected or not (*i.e.,* via syntactic matching of Web services parameters or even via semantic matching). The problem with AI based approach is how we can make sure what are the services need to perform a task, such as "planning a holiday in New York". Our approach combines both manual and automatic aspects of SC. We use task models to discover relevant services and define the sequence between services. Instead of relying on data dependencies among service, our approach uses task relations along with data-dependencies to identify service sequences.

Currently available end-users SC [11] tools, such as Yahoo! Pipe [35] and IBM Mashup center [25] provide a user friendly environment for end users to integrate different services. However, those products require end-users to manually identify all the services to form a process. Our approach reduces the workload of end users by automatically generating processes required based on easily available knowledge in the Web. Our approach helps novice programmers and end-users.

5.3   User Interface Generation from Web Services

The creation of user interfaces is still a complex problem. Bias *et al.* [8] state that 50% of time for building an application is due to the UI development. There are some approaches for generating the UI automatically [6, 10 and 12]. These approaches focus on the generation of user interfaces for services. A common way to generate user interfaces for services is their inference from services description, like WSDL [17] or WADL [18] files. Given that data types can be matched to specific graphical controls, the inference mechanism to create UI forms can be straightforward. However, the inference mechanism is limited to a certain degree because the developer may need to include more details to the controls on the form that cannot be inferred from technical descriptions. Some research, such as Dynvoker [12] cannot support composed services. Moreover, a designer cannot edit the resulting forms. We present an approach for task identification that considers the composition as a dynamic hyperlinked environment of services. Our UI is editable making modification easier.

6   Conclusion and Future Work

We provide an approach to build task models from how-to instruction Web pages. Our case study shows that our approach has high precision to identify instructions from Web pages. In most cases, our approach can correctly identify tasks. Similarly, we use the task model to find relevant services to execute tasks based on the data flows between the services.   Given a correct task model, our approach can build an executable process with 90% accuracy. We believe the UI generation process is still a complex issue. The manual creation process is time consuming and complex because it requires the combination of the work from application developers and the UI designers. We designed and developed a tool which intends to ease and enhance the automatic UI generation process. In the future, we plan to conduct a user study to see the effectiveness of UI generation. We would also like to perform a larger case study including different how-to instructions.

References

[1]   Gerede, C.E., Hull, R., Ibarra, O.H., Su, J.: Automated composition of e-services: lookaheads. In: ICSOC, pp. 252–262 (2004)

[2]   Thomas, J.P., Thomas, M., Ghinea, G.: Modeling of web services flow. In: IEEE International Conference on E-Commerce, CEC 2003 (2003)

[3]   Upadhyaya, B., Khomh, F., Zou, Y., Lau, A., Ng, J.: A concept analysis approach for guiding users in service discovery. In: 2012 5th IEEE International Conference on SOCA, pp. 1–8 (2012)

[4]   Upadhyaya, B., Zou, Y., Xiao, H., Ng, J., Lau, A.: Migration of SOAP-based services to RESTful services. In: Proc. of the 13th IEEE International Symposium on WSE, pp. 105–114 (2011)

[5]   Miller, G.A.: WordNet: A Lexical Database for English. Communications of the ACM 38(11), 39–41

[6]   Li, L., Chou, W.: Automatic Message Flow Analyses for Web Services Based on WSDL. In: IEEE International Conference on Web Services (2007)

[7]   Hwang, S.Y., Lim, E.P., Lee, C.H., Chen, C.H.: Dynamic Web Service Selection for Reliable Web Service Composition. IEEE Transactions on Services Computing 1(2), 104–116 (2008)

[8]   Bias, R.G., Mayhew, D.J.: Cost-Justifying usability. Morgan Kaufmann Publishers, San Francisco

[9]   JTidy, http://jtidy.sourceforge.net/

[10]   Kassoff, M., Kato, D., Mohsin, W.: Creating GUIs for web services. IEEE Internet Comp. 7(5), 66–73

[11] Mehandjiev, N., Namoune, A., Wajid, U., Macaulay, L., Sutcliffe, A.: End User Service Composition: Perceptions and Requirements. In: IEEE 8th European Conference on ECOWS, pp. 139–146 (2010)

[12] Spillner, J., Feldmann, M., Braun, I., Springer, T., Schill, A.: Ad Hoc Usage of Web Services with Dynvoker. In: Mähönen, P., Pohl, K., Priol, T. (eds.) ServiceWave 2008. LNCS, vol. 5377, pp. 208–219. Springer, Heidelberg (2008)

[13] Perkowitz, M., Philipose, M., Fishkin, K.P., Patterson, D.J.: Mining models of human activities from the web. In: WWW 2004, pp. 573–582 (2004)

[14] Raphael, B., Bhatnagar, G., Smith, I.F.: Creation of flexible graphical user interfaces through model composition. Artif. Intell. Eng. Des. Anal. Manuf. 16(3), 173–184 (2002)

[15] Poibeau, T., Kosseim, L.: Proper Name Extraction from Non-Journalistic Texts. In: Proc. Computational Linguistics in the Netherlands (2001)

[16] Xiao, H., Upadhyaya, B., Khomh, F., Zou, Y., Ng, J., Lau, A.: An automatic approach for extracting process knowledge from the Web. In: Proc. of ICWS, pp. 315–322 (2011)

[17] Web Service Definition Language (WSDL), http://www.w3.org/TR/wsdl

[18] Web Application Description Language,
http://www.w3.org/Submission/wadl/

[19] World Wide Web Consortium (W3C), http://www.w3.org/

[20] Fielding, R.T., Taylor, R.N.: Principled design of the modern Web architecture, pp. 407–416

[21] Richardson, L., Ruby, S.: RESTful web services (2007)

[22] Ján, K., Necaský, M., Bartoš, T.: Generating XForms from an XML Schema. NDT (2), 706–714 (2010)

[23] Turney, P.D.: Mining the Web for synonyms: PMI-IR versus LSA on TOEFL. In: Flach, P.A., De Raedt, L. (eds.) ECML 2001. LNCS (LNAI), vol. 2167, pp. 491–502. Springer, Heidelberg (2001)

[24] IBM WebSphere Integration Developer,
http://www-01.ibm.com/software/integration/wid/

[25] IBM Mashup Center, https://greenhouse.lotus.com/wpsgh/
wcm/connect/lotus+greenhouse/lotus+greenhouse+next+site/
home/products/ibm+mashup+center

[26] iGoogle, http://www.google.com/ig

[27] wikihow-how to do anything, http://www.wikihow.com/Main-Page

[28] eHow | Discover the expert in you, http://www.eHow.com

[29] Klein, D., Manning, C.D.: Accurate Unlexicalized Parsing. In: 41st Annual Meeting of the Association for Computational Linguistics, pp. 423–430 (2003)

[30] Concur Task Trees (CTT), http://www.w3.org/2012/02/ctt/

[31] Singh, P., Lin, T., Mueller, E.T., Lim, G., Perkins, T., Zhu, W.L.: Open Mind Common Sense: Knowledge acquisition from the general public. In: Meersman, R., Tari, Z. (eds.) CoopIS/DOA/ODBASE 2002. LNCS, vol. 2519, pp. 1223–1237. Springer, Heidelberg (2002)

All URLs are last accesses on 25-July-2013

Batch Activities
in Process Modeling and Execution

Luise Pufahl and Mathias Weske

Hasso Plattner Institute at the University of Potsdam
Prof.-Dr.-Helmert-Strasse 2-3, 14482 Potsdam
{luise.pufahl,mathias.weske}@hpi.uni-potsdam.de

Abstract. In today's process engines, instances of a process usually run independently to each other. However, in certain situations a synchronized execution of a group of instances of the same process is necessary especially to allow the comparison of business cases or to improve process performance. In this paper, we introduce the concept of batch activities to process modeling and execution. We provide the possibility to assign a batch model to an activity for making it a batch activity. As opposed to related approaches, the batch model has several parameters with which the process designer can configure individually the batch execution. A rule-based batch activation is used to enable a flexible batch handling. Our approach allows that several batches can run in parallel in case of multiple resources. The applicability of the approach is illustrated in a case study.

Keywords: batch activity, process modeling, synchronization of instances.

1 Introduction

In today's organizations, modeling of business processes and their execution based on process-oriented systems has a high relevance. Business operations are usually specified by process models with focus on the single business case. A process model describes a set of activities jointly realizing a business goal and the execution constraints between them [16]. At runtime, for each business case, a process instance is created. When designing a process, it is typically assumed that process instances are completely independent from each other [4]. Also in process engines, instances are usually executed individually. Nevertheless, certain dependencies between process instances may require a synchronization. In this paper, we introduce an approach for coordinating the activity execution of different process instances motivated by the following example.

Fig. 1 shows the *Train ticket refund* process of a train company in which passenger claims are received and checked. When a passenger experienced a delay of more than one hour, the company provides a voucher card with an amount of 50% of the train ticket price. A process instance is started when a claim for refund is received from a passenger . Then, for each activity in the process model, an activity instance is created as soon as a process runs. Usually, activity instances are executed independently from each other. For instance, the company enters the data of each claim individually and checks whether the claim is correct. However, activities in process models can be observed for which it is beneficial or even required to synchronize the execution of a group of business cases,

S. Basu et al. (Eds.): ICSOC 2013, LNCS 8274, pp. 283–297, 2013.

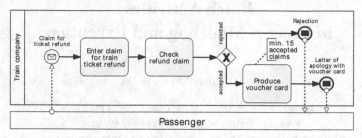

Fig. 1. Train ticket refund process

e.g., the activity *Produce voucher card*. The train company activates the machine for producing the voucher cards only when 15 cards are requested in order to save setup costs. Such a type of activity, we call *batch activity* which is defined as an activity clustering a set of active activity instances together and synchronizing their execution according to pre-defined rules [4, 13]. Currently, the batch activation rule is informally noted as comment on the respective activity (cf. Fig. 1). The goal of this paper is to formalize the design of batch activities and to give a blue print for them. Two types of use cases for which a batch activity is needed, can be differentiated [2]:

- **Achieving an increased process performance**: A process may have an activity with high setup costs, i.e., preparation costs to start an activity (e.g., setups of machines, familiarization periods for a type of work or traveling distances). In our example, we have the setup costs of the voucher card machine. By synchronizing the activity enactment of several cases, the train company can save those costs and can be more efficient in their process execution.
- **Comparing business cases**: A process may have an activity where business cases are ranked according to specific criteria. In order to be able to compare them, several cases have to be grouped together, e.g., a ranking of application candidates.

A common assumption is that batch requirements can be solved with multi-instance patterns [14] which are supported by several modeling languages. For example, the widely applied process modeling language BPMN (Business Process Modeling Notation) provides the concept of multi-instance activities. When a multi-instance activity is started in the context of a process instance, multiple activity instances are initialized simultaneously running independently from each other. Synchronization may be organized with regards to starting the subsequent activity, but their execution is not aligned. Since multi-instance activities have an opposite execution paradigm which splits one instance as opposed to synchronize multiple existing instances, a new concept for a batch handling needs to be developed.

Also, most process modeling languages do not support the design and configuration of batch activities; they are often enacted as batch manually or by special software. Organized manually by human resources, the rules of a batch activity can be unclear or the batch execution may simply be forgotten resulting in lower process performance. Otherwise, a batch activity may be controlled by specific software. Since the batch configurations are then not traceable for the process owner and the participants, the batch activity settings cannot be controlled by them and adaptations result in high efforts.

In this paper, we propose a concept to integrate batch activities in process modeling and execution. The integration has the advantages that (i) rules are clear for the process owner, the participants, and the process engineer, (ii) no manual implementation is required, (iii) batch activities can be included into potential process simulations, and (iv) monitoring as well as analysis of executed batches can be done based on process logs.

The paper is structured as follows. In Section 2, we discuss requirements for integrating the concept of batch activities into process modeling and execution. Then, we present our approach to enable the design, configuration and execution of batch activities in Section 3, where we also discuss the applicability of our approach in a case study. In Section 4, related work is discussed followed by a conclusion in Section 5.

2 Requirements of Integrating Batch Activities

In the following, we present several requirements to integrate batch activities in process modeling and execution, summarized and related to each other in Fig. 2. On the one hand, they arise due to the different execution semantics of a batch activity (cf. path (b) in Fig. 2) in comparison to the regular one (cf. path (a) in Fig. 2) (R1). On the other hand, we collect them based on descriptions of the batch service problem. The batch service problem was investigated by the queuing research, e.g., in [8–10], and is described as follows: "Customers arrive at random, form a single queue in order of arrival and are served in batches" [1], whereby the basic object of investigation is when to start a batch (R2). Queuing researchers investigated it for different configurations of queue (R3) and server (R4-6). In the following, we will discuss the identified requirements in detail.

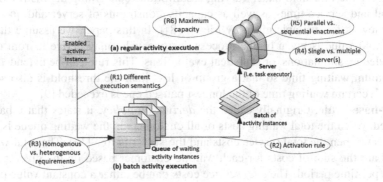

Fig. 2. Requirements regarding integration of batch activities

Requirement R1 - Different execution semantics: A usual activity instance passes different states during its lifetime [16]. In a simplified version, these are *init, ready, running,* and *terminated*. With the start of a process, the activity instance enters the *init* state and changes to the *ready* state when all pre-conditions for the activity are fulfilled. Then, it is immediately offered by the process engine to the respective task executor (cf. path (a) in Fig. 2). The task executor can be either a software service, a human, or a non-human resource. When a resource or service starts the work of the activity instance, it enters the *running* state and with completion, it is in the *terminated* state.

In contrast, the offer of a batch activity instance has to be delayed by the process engine in order to provide the task executor a group of instances being executed as batch. Here, it is required that the process engine collects all enabled activity instances according to a queue discipline, e.g., first-come first-served (FCFS) or last-come first-served (LCFS), and assigns them to a batch as depicted in Fig. 2. In this paper, we choose FCFS as queuing system, because it is a commonly applied policy [8].

Requirement R2 - Activation rule: With a batch activity, the control of starting a group of instances is allocated to the process engine to achieve an increased process performance or to enable the comparison of business cases. The larger the size of a batch, the lower are the average setup costs per activity instance, but the higher are the waiting time per instance. So, costs can be reduced, when the train company waits at minimum for 30 instead of 15 claims for which a voucher card is produced. However, the risk for the train company increases to lose passengers, because of dissatisfaction regarding the service time. Rules have to be specified and enforced in order to achieve an optimal trade-off between setup costs and waiting time. As stated, this optimization problem – when to activate a batch service and provide it to the server – is investigated by the queuing research for which they propose different optimization policies. In this paper, we want to present two often discussed rules [10]:

- **Threshold rule**: Originally called the *general bulk service rule*, it states that a batch is started, when the length of the waiting queue with customers is equal or greater than a given threshold (i.e., a value between one and the maximum server capacity) and the server is free [9]. Several studies investigate how to determine an optimal value for the threshold under varying assumptions concerning the distribution of arrival and service times as well as capacity constraints of server and queue (an overview is for example given by Medhi [8]). In this paper, we assume that the threshold value is given by the process designer who may derive it from expert knowledge, simulations, or statistical evaluations. This rule can be extended by a maximum waiting time so that a group of less than the threshold is also served, when a certain waiting time of the longest paused one is exceeded [9].
- **Cost-based rule**: Originally called the *derivation policy*, it states that a batch is started, when the total waiting costs of all customers in the waiting queue is equal or greater then the total service costs and the server is free [15]. The total waiting costs are the sum of costs for each waiting customer based on the given penalty costs per time period. The total service costs can be either a constant value or they are a function considering the number of customers.

Besides these two, other types of activation rules exist. Thus, it should be possible to provide different types of activation rules from which a process designer can select one for a batch activity and fill it with required user inputs.

Requirement R3 - Homogeneous vs. heterogeneous requirements: In studies from queuing research, it is discussed that arrived customers may be homogeneous or heterogeneous in their demand [10]. If they are heterogeneous, different types of batches have to be formed. Also activity instances can be heterogeneous regarding their inputs respectively required outputs. In our train example, all *Produce voucher card*-instances are currently homogeneous. The activity instances will become heterogeneous concerning their output requirements, for example, if the train company produces two types of voucher cards; white colored ones for amounts lower €150 and better protected once in silver for amounts equal or greater than €150. In this case, two different batch types have to be created. However, we assume in this work that all activity instances are homogeneous.

Requirement R4 - Single vs. multiple server(s): Often, studies from queuing research assume that only a single server is available [8]. Hereby, it is assumed that the availability of the server is controlled and the activation of a batch depends on it. Business process management differentiates between the control flow perspective, where the batch activity is part of, and the resource perspective concentrating on the modeling of resources and the allocation of work. Russell et al. [11] present several resource patterns for offering, allocating, and detouring work after an activity was enabled (e.g., the role-based allocation). We require that the batch activity execution should not interfere with the concepts of the resource perspective. Therefore, we assume the general case that a batch can be provided to multiple available resources. Here, the engine should be able to run several batches in parallel when they are needed.

Requirement R5 - Parallel vs. sequential enactment: Batch processing occurs in two versions: parallel and sequential execution [7]. In parallel batch execution, the activity instances of a batch are processed by the task executor simultaneously, because the server capacity is greater than one. An example for it is the voucher card machine of the train company which can produce more than one card in a run. In sequential batch execution, the task executor enacts the activity instances one after another. They are processed as batch, because they share the same setup, e.g., the setup of a machine, a traveling distance. An example is the task of controlling exams where the examiner needs a certain familiarization phase for each examination question and then checks the answers of all students for one question.

Requirement R6 - Maximum capacity: An often discussed constraint of the batch service problem is the maximum capacity of the task executor respectively the maximum number of cases that the executor can handle in a sequence [8]. For instance, the voucher card machine may be able to produce at maximum 25 cards in a run. This capacity determines the maximum size of a batch, which is 25 for the *Train ticket refund* example. If a batch is activated and offered to its executor, but not yet started, because the executor is not available, it should be still possible to add further activity instances until the maximum is achieved or the batch is started. This leads to an increased process performance.

3   Integrate Batch Activities in Process Modeling and Execution

In this section, a general approach to model and configure a batch activity in process modeling languages is presented. The de facto standard BPMN is used to illustrate it. For the approach, we augmented the process meta model by Weske [16] with the required concepts for batch activities which is explained in detail in Section 3.1. For the enactment of batch activities in a process engine, an enhanced engine architecture and execution semantics is proposed in Section 3.2. We evaluate the applicability of our approach based on a case study in Section 3.3.

3.1   Modeling and Configuration of a Batch Activity

In this work, we want to provide the possibility to design and configure a specific activity as batch activity in order to synchronize the execution of its instances. Therefore, we extended the process meta model by Weske [16]. The meta model describes that a process model consists of nodes and edges. A process model acts as blueprint for a set of process instances which are related to exactly one process model. A node in a process model can represent an event, a gateway, or an activity model. Similar as the node, the activity model is associated to an arbitrary number of activity instances (see Fig. 3(a)) for which it describes the key characteristics, e.g., resource assignment, input and output data. An activity model can be a system, user interaction, or manual activity.

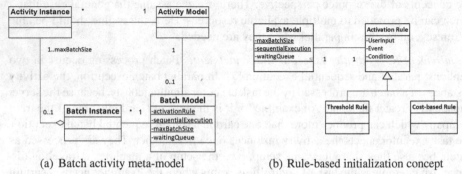

(a) Batch activity meta-model   (b) Rule-based initialization concept

Fig. 3. Extension of process meta model for batch activities. In (a), we show that a batch activity can be designed by assigning a batch model with several configuration parameters to an activity model. In (b), we show that each batch model gets assigned an activation rule which can be from different types (here from type threshold or cost-based) to enable a rule-based batch initialization.

We extend these concepts by the batch model (see class diagram of Fig. 3(a)); an activity becomes a batch activity, if its activity model is associated to a batch model which in turn can only be associated with exactly one activity model. A batch model describes the conditions for batch execution and can be configured based on the parameters *activationRule*, *sequentialExecution*, and *maxBatchSize* by the process designer.

- The *activationRule* provides the possibility to specify a policy when a batch is enabled and offered to the task executor. Therefore, the process designer selects an activation rule type (e.g., threshold rule) and provides required user inputs (see R2).
- The *sequentialExecution* is of type boolean. In case of *false*, all instances of a batch are provided at once to task executor for parallel execution. In case of *true*, instances are provided one after another to the executor for sequential execution (see R5).
- The *maxBatchSize* is of type integer and represents the maximum capacity of the task executor. It specifies the number of instances which can be at maximum in a batch. It can be limited by user input or unlimited without user input (see R6).

In Fig. 4, we show an exemplary configuration by means of the batch activity *B* in the example process *P*. In this context, we illustrate a batch activity in BPMN by a double framed activity. For the batch activity *B*, the process designer selected the threshold rule as activation rule with a threshold of two and a maximum waiting time of one hour (i.e., the batch is offered to the task executor latest after an hour). The batch activity was configured such that at maximum three instances of *B* can be in a batch and they are all executed in parallel, because the *sequentialExecution* is set to false.

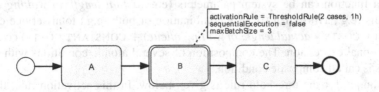

activationRule = ThresholdRule(2 cases, 1h)
sequentialExecution = false
maxBatchSize = 3

Fig. 4. Example process *P* with three activities whereby *A* and *C* are usual single case activities and *B* is a batch activity illustrated here with a double border

In summary, a batch model associated to an activity model describes with its configurations the behavior for an arbitrary set of batch instances. A batch instance represents one batch and is responsible for its initiation and execution. Several batch instances being associated to exactly one batch model can exist simultaneously to allow the parallel execution of batches (see R4). Thus, when a batch instance is currently executed, another instance can already be initiated when it is required, and can be allocated, e.g., to an alternative resource. We will give more details on how the parallel run of batch instances can be organized and implemented in the next section.

Enabled activity instances are associated to a batch instance. Each batch instance has its own waiting queue where all its assigned activity instances are collected in order of their arrival (see R1). At minimum, the queue has the size of one, because a batch instance is only initialized when it is required by at least one instance, and at maximum it has a size of the user-specified *maxBatchSize*. A batch instance also passes the states *init*, *ready*, *running* and *terminated*. Thereby, a batch instance changes from the *init* to *ready* state as soon as the predefined activation rule is fulfilled. Then, the batch of activity instances is offered to the task executor. When a resource accepts it, the batch instance enters the *running* state and as soon as the batch work is completed, it changes into the *terminated* state. Additionally, we extended the life cycle for batch instances so that they can also be in state *maxloaded* after being *ready* and before being *running* when it reaches the specified maximum size of a batch. After a batch instance is initialized and as long as it does not enter the *maxloaded* or *running* state, activity instances can be bound to it. So, we ensure that an optimal number of activity instances is added to a batch instance.

As described, the process designer selects an activation rule type for a batch model and configures it with the required user inputs. Thus, each batch model is associated with an activation rule as shown in Fig. 3(b). We assume that process engine suppliers provide different types of activation rules in advance, e.g., the threshold rule or cost-based rule from queuing research presented in Section 2. In general, an activation rule relies on the concept of ECA (Event Condition Action) rules. Basic elements of an ECA rule are an event E triggering the rule, a condition C which has to be satisfied, and an action A being executed in case of fulfillment of the condition [3].

Thus, we define an activation rule as a tuple $E \times C \times A$, whereby the action A is always the enablement of the associated batch instance. An event E is either an atomic event (e.g., a state change of the batch waiting queue or a specific time event) or a composite event being a composition of atomic events through logical operators, as for instance *AND* or *OR*. A condition C is a boolean function. The input elements to such a function can be system parameters (e.g., *actual length of waiting queue*), user inputs (e.g., THRESHOLD), or a combination of both (e.g., total service costs = (VARIABLE COSTS * *actual length of waiting queue*) + CONSTANT COSTS) connected by a relational expression. The composition of several atomic conditions with logical operators is called composite condition.

An example for the threshold rule is given below. In this activation rule, the user inputs are indicated by capitals and the system parameters are italicized. It consists of a composite event saying that the rule is triggered when a new activity instance was added to the waiting queue of the associated batch instance b or when no new one was added for a specific period, i.e., the user-specified maximum waiting time divided by ten. With triggering the rule, the given composite condition is checked. It states that either the length of the waiting queue has to be equal or greater than the user-specified threshold or the lifetime of b has to be equal or greater than the user-specified maximum waiting time. If the condition evaluates to true, b gets enabled.

```
ActivationRule Threshold rule
  On Event      (Instance added to b.waitingQueue) OR
                   (No instance since MaxWaitingTime/10)
  If Condition (b.waitingQueue.length ≥ Threshold)OR
                   (b.lifetime ≥ MaxWaitingTime)
  Do Action     Enable batch instance b
End ActivationRule
```

We enable the integration of batch activities into process modeling with few extensions on the existing process meta model. In the next section, we propose an architecture and execution semantics for batch activities.

3.2 Execution of a Batch Activity

In Fig. 5, we present an abstract architecture of a usual process engine (cf. white elements). Process models are saved in a repository on which the process engine has read access. As soon as a start event occurs for a process, the engine initializes an instance of this process. Thereby, the process instance controls the initialization and enablement of each of its activity instances based on the control flow specification in the process model. Exemplary, we show in Fig. 5 process instances of our example process P with its activity instances. The process engine is able to offer and allocate the work of activity instances to task executors. For service activities, the respective service is invoked by the engine. User interaction activities are provided via a task management component with a graphical interface to the process participants. This approach aims at relating a batch configuration to any activity type (i.e., system, user interaction, or manual activity). Thus, we abstract from the service invocation and task management components.

In order to execute a batch activity, the architecture is extended with batch instances and a batch factory (cf. shaded elements in Fig. 5 for the example batch activity *B*). For each batch activity, a batch factory exists which is responsible for mapping activity instances to batch instances and for initializing new batch instances when required. Thus, activity instances request the batch factory – in Fig. 5 the instances of the batch activity *B* – for being associated to a batch instance. A batch instance in turn communicates with one or more associated activity instances as well as with the process engine which can offer the batch to the executor.

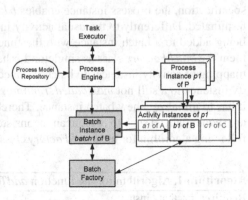

Fig. 5. Process engine architecture (white elements) with extensions for batch activity execution (shaded elements)

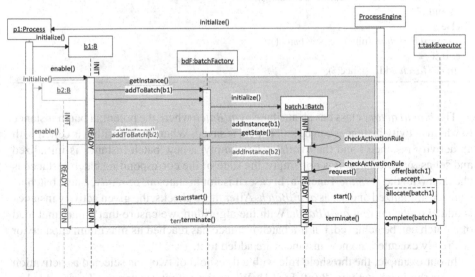

Fig. 6. Execution semantics of a batch activity

An example scenario of the activity instance *b1* of the batch activity *B* being part of the process instance *p1* and associated to the batch instance *batch1* is represented in the sequence diagram of Fig. 6. It illustrates the execution semantics of an activity instance of a batch activity which is a refinement (cf. shaded box in Fig. 6) of the common activity instance execution. The main difference is that instead of offering the activity directly to the task executor after its enablement, it is added to a batch instance which then controls its start and termination. In the sequence diagram, we label the activation line of the *activity instance* and *batch instance* entities with the states they are currently in. Next, we discuss the sequence diagram in detail.

As usual, the process engine initializes the instance *p1* of the process *P* and the instance initializes all its activity instances including *b1*. Based on the control flow specification, the process instance enables *b1* as soon as the preceding activity *A* was terminated. Differently to the usual activity instance, *b1* requests the *batchFactory* for being added to a batch instance with the function *addToBatch*. We propose to implement the *batchFactory* class as singleton for having only one responsible object for the mapping of activity instances to batch instances. It decides whether it can add an activity instance to a still not *maxloaded*, *running*, or *terminated* batch instance or whether it has to initialize a new batch instance. Thereby, the requests by the activity instances are sequentialized such to prevent an inconsistent state of the system. We developed the following algorithm for the *batchFactory* class:

Algorithm 1. Algorithm for the function *addToBatch*

Require: *i*:activity instance
  if *availBatch* not null **then**
    if *availBatch*.getState ! = INIT || READY **then**
      availBatch = initialize new batch();
    end if
  else
    availBatch = initialize new batch();
  end if
  availBatch.addInstance(*i*);

The *batchFactory* class has an attribute *availBatch* where the potential batch instance to which activity instances can be still added, is saved. When the algorithm is called with an activity instance *i* and the *availBatch* is empty, a new batch instance is initialized and set as *availBatch*. If it is not empty, the state of the corresponding batch instance is checked with the *getState*-function. In case, it is not in state *init* or *ready*, a new batch instance is initialized and set as *availBatch*. After these checks, the given activity instance is added to the current *availBatch*. With the algorithm, we ensure that a maximal load of a batch can be achieved, but if a batch instance has reached its maximum capacity or is already executed, no new instances are added to it.

In our example, the threshold rule with a threshold of two was selected as activation rule for the batch activity *B* (cf. Fig. 4). When the activity instance *b1* was added to the waiting queue of *batch1*, its activation rule is checked, because it is an event which triggers to check the condition. Due to the waiting queue length of one, the condition is evaluated to false and the action is not executed. For reason of complexity reduction, we represent the activation rule in Fig. 6 as function and not as own object. With the second added activity instance *b2*, *batch1* enters the *ready* state, because now the condition that the waiting queue length is greater or equal to the threshold is fulfilled. Then, the process engine is requested to offer *batch1* to the task executor. With acceptance of the task executor, the engine allocates the work of all associated activity instances at once and starts the batch instance. Having entered the *running* state, the batch starts all its activity instances of its waiting queue. At some time, the task executor completes the batch. Then, the engine terminates the batch and *batch1* in turn terminates its activity instances *b1* and *b2*. In case that the sequential execution was selected for a batch activity, the engine acts slightly different compared to the parallel execution: After the batch was accepted by a resource, the engine starts the batch instance. The batch instance provides in a loop its associated activity instances one after another over the engine to the task executor. The currently provided activity instance is then started and terminated by it.

After we presented the architecture and execution semantics of a batch activity, we will illustrate our approach using a case study in the next section.

3.3 Case Study

We already provided some insights into the *Train ticket refund* process in the introduction on which we will focus in our case study. Fig. 7 shows a variant of it as BPMN model.

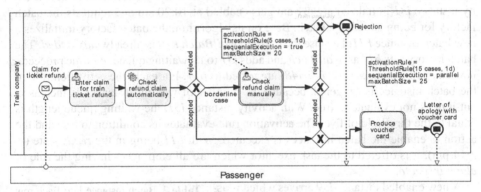

Fig. 7. Train ticket refund process with manual claim check

After a claim by a passenger is received in a form, the data of the form is entered into the process system of the train company. We assume that our company receives 150 claims per day on average. Based on the entered data, the process system runs an automatic check whether the passenger claim is accepted or rejected. Some claims – in average 5% – are classified as borderline cases where the system check could not result in a clear decision, e.g., when a passenger experienced a delay of 56 minutes instead of an hour. An employee has to check them manually a second time.

We assume that the employee needs a familiarization phase of approximately four minutes for this task to get afresh familiar with proceeding guidelines and rules. In order to save setup time, the employee shall process at minimum a set of five cases. The employee can organize this for her-/himself. However, the employee may get disturbed from each case arriving in the work list while working on other tasks. We propose to install a batch activity so that the employee gets offered the work only when necessary. The requirements are that at minimum five cases should be processed in a sequence, but not more than 20 cases due to the risk of decreased motivation, and no case should wait longer than one day until being provided to task executor to ensure short response time for passengers. We capture them in our batch activity (cf. *Check refund claim manually* in Fig. 7).

Table 1. Activity instance log of *Check refund claim manually*: Each row presents an activity instance, i.e., when it entered a certain state and its relating batch instance

id	init	ready	running	terminated	batch
...	...	...	...	...	
i31	13/03/11 09:31 am	13/03/11 10:20 am	13/03/11 03:40 pm	13/03/11 03:51 pm	11
i37	13/03/11 09:58 am	13/03/11 11:01 am	13/03/11 03:51 pm	13/03/11 03:57 pm	11
i40	13/03/11 12:01 am	13/03/11 12:17 am	13/03/11 03:57 pm	13/03/11 04:02 pm	11
i48	13/03/11 02:33 pm	13/03/11 02:46 pm	13/03/11 04:02 pm	13/03/11 04:09 pm	11
i51	13/03/11 02:54 pm	13/03/11 03:14 pm	13/03/11 04:09 pm	13/03/11 04:16 pm	11
i59	13/03/11 03:07 pm	13/03/11 03:32 pm	13/03/12 04:16 pm	13/03/12 04:23 pm	11
i64	13/03/11 04:02 pm	13/03/11 04:13 pm	14/03/12 04:13 pm	14/03/12 04:25 pm	12
i76	14/03/12 10:21 am	14/03/12 10:45 am	14/03/12 04:25 pm	14/03/12 04:31 pm	12
i83	14/03/12 02:40 pm	14/03/12 02:49 pm	14/03/12 04:31 pm	14/03/12 04:36 pm	12
...	...	...	...	...	..

In Tables 1 and 2, we show exemplary extracts of the activity and batch log of *Check refund claim manually* in order to illustrate the batch activity execution. A new activity instance *i31* initialized at 9:31 am gets enabled at 10:20 am and requests the batch factory for being added to a batch. Base on its algorithm, the batch factory initializes a new batch instance *b11*, because the current *availBatch b10* is already *maxloaded*. The batch factory sets *b11* as *availBatch* and adds *i31* to its waiting queue. As time proceeds, new enabled instances (*i37*, *i40*, *i48*) are added to *b11*. For each, the activation rule of the batch instance is triggered, because the number of waiting instances is increased, but it does not evaluate to true. With activity instance *i51*, the waiting queue length is equal to the threshold of five. The activation rule evaluates its condition to true and the action to enable the batch instances is executed. With *b11* being in the *ready* state (at 3:14 pm), it is offered to the task executor which are all employees having the role of *claim inspector*.

A new enabled instance *i59* arrives which is assigned to *b11* by the batch factory, because *b11* is still in the *ready* state and so still the *availBatch*. At 3:40 pm, a claim inspector accepts the batch and starts it. The batch instance *b11* changes into the *running* state. Due to the choice of sequential batch execution, *b11* triggers the state change of the first assigned activity instance *i31* and provides it over the process engine to the claim inspector. When *i31* is terminated, the batch instances starts the next instance. For the newly enabled activity instance *i64*, a new batch instance *b12* is created, because *b11* is *running* already. With completion of *i59* at 4:23 pm – the last one in the waiting queue of *b11* –, the batch instance changes into *terminated*.

Table 2. Batch instance log: Each row presents moment of state change by a batch instance

id	state	time
...	...	...
b10	maxloaded	13/03/11 10:18 am
b10	running	13/03/11 10:50 am
b10	terminated	13/03/11 11:45 am
b11	init	13/03/11 10:20 am
b11	ready	13/03/11 03:14 pm
b11	running	13/03/11 03:40 pm
b11	terminated	13/03/11 04:23 pm
b12	init	13/03/11 04:13 pm
b12	ready	14/03/12 04:13 pm
b12	running	14/03/12 04:17 pm
b12	terminated	14/03/12 05:05 pm
...	...	...

On the next day, only few enabled activity instances for manual claim check arrive. The activation rule is triggered, because instances are not added to the waiting queue of *b12* for a longer time period. At 4:13 pm, the condition that the lifetime of *b12* is equal or greater than the maximum waiting time of one day is fulfilled and the enablement of *b12* is conducted. Few minutes later at 4:17 pm, the batch is accepted by a claim inspec-tor. Again, the activity instances are started one after another and the batch instance *b12* terminates at 4:36 pm with the end of its last activity instance *i83*.

The batch activity *Produce voucher card* in the process of Fig. 7 is an example for parallel batch execution. As we already discussed parallel execution in detail in Section 3.2, we will omit the discussion here due to space requirements.

4   Related Work

In an early work, Barthelmess and Wainer distinguish activities in work-case based ac-tivities acting exclusively on particular business cases and batch activities for which a set of cases have to be bought together [2]. They argue that batch activities are needed to improve process performance or to compare business cases. Since than, only few at-tempts to integrate batch activities into process modeling and execution were proposed. In Table 3, we show them with respect to their coverage of the requirements of Section 2.

Table 3. Evaluation of related work

	Aalst et al. [13]	Sadiq et al. [12]	Liu et al. [4]	Mangler et al. [6]	This
R1: Different execution semantics	+	+	+	+	+
R2: Activation rule	-	-	o	+	+
R3: Homog. vs. heterog. requirements	-	-	+	+	-
R4: Single vs. multiple server(s)	+	+	-	o	+
R5: Parallel vs. sequential enactment	-	-	-	-	+
R6: Maximum capacity	+	+	+	-	+

fully satisfied (+), partially satisfied (o), not satisfied (-)

One of them is the *proclet* framework by van Aalst et al. [13]. It defines a process as a set of interacting proclets representing process fragments via channels. A batch activity can be realized by a proclet which receives a predefined number of messages by instances of a cooperating proclet, enacts the batch task and sends back messages to the corresponding instances (R1). The other proclet may cover all single-case activities of the process. A sequential batch execution is not possible. Proclets allow different resource allocations (R4), but the size of a batch has to be explicitly given at design time (R6) leading to a inflexible batch execution: The number of cases for comparison cannot be defined dynamically and waiting for specific number of instances can result in decreased process performance. In this work, we provide a flexible batch execution approach by giving the possibility to select an activation rule for a batch activity.

Sadiq et al. [12] propose to establish *compound activities* in workflow systems with a grouping- and ungrouping-function generating one activity instance based on several ones and splitting it after task execution (R1). This activity instance could be provided based on different resource patterns to task executors (R4). The grouping-function can be either auto-invoked with a predefined number of required instances (R6), which has similar drawbacks as proclets, or user-invoked, creating a batch with user-selected in-stances. The user-invocation means a manual batch organization where rules are not explicitly defined and errors can occur. In contrast, our approach offers the possibility to explicitly define the batch execution rules with automatic enforcement of those.

Also, Liu et al. [4] want to integrate a new type of activity for batch execution into workflow systems which is called batch processing activity (BPA). As the BPA is limited to the threshold rule (R2), the process designer defines a threshold and the maximal capacity for a BPA as well as a grouping characteristic. Based on this characteristic, a grouping and selection algorithm (GSA) groups activity instances arrived in the central waiting queue of the BPA and selects a group to submit it to a server (R3). The functionality of the GSA is not further discussed in this work; a proposal can be found in a later work [5]. The authors limit their approach such that each BPA has only one server available. Liu et al. [4] establish a scheduling algorithm for the GSA which observes the state of BPA's waiting queue as well as server and initializes it when the server is idle and the threshold rule is fulfilled. With this algorithm, only one specific case of a direct allocation to one resource is covered. In our work, we allow that several batches can run in parallel so that all patterns of the resource perspective can still be used.

Mangler and Rinderle-Ma [6] provide an approach for a rule-based activity synchronization of instances of the same process as well as of instances of different processes. The synchronization is organized before or after specific rendezvous points. They propose that an external synchronization service can subscribe itself for being informed about the progress of certain process instances. This service can trigger to stop their execution as well as their continuation due to predefined ECA rules. According to their approach, a batch activity can be organized as follows: Before certain process instances start with a specified activity, the subscriber stops them and the references to them are saved in a buffer (R1). When a certain condition is met, the subscriber triggers the continuation of the respective process instances (R2). With several subscribers focusing on same rendezvous points, but different types of instances, also heterogeneous demands by activity instances can be served (R3). However, the authors do not discuss, how this batch of instances is provided to the task executor (R4). Furthermore, advanced technical knowledge is requested for the implementation of the synchronization service and its ECA rules. In this paper, we provided an approach with which a batch activity can be designed without any technical background and then automatically be executed.

5   Conclusion

In this work, we propose an approach to integrate the concept of batch activities into process modeling and execution. Therefore, we first defined several requirements based on the batch service problem in queuing research and the different execution semantics of a batch activity compared to a regular one. Next, we extended the process meta model so that a batch model can be optionally associated to an activity making it a batch activity. With its different parameters, a process designer can configure the batch execution by selecting an activation rule and defining the maximum batch size as well as the way of execution (i.e., parallel vs. sequential). With these configuration parameters, the rules for a batch activity are explicitly documented which facilitates the communication with process stakeholders. The batch model describes the behavior for a set of batch instances where each batch instance manages one batch execution in order to allow that several batches can run in parallel in case of multiple available resources. We presented an architecture and execution semantics to show how the parallel batch execution can be organized and implemented in a process engine. The applicability of our approach was illustrated based on a case study. The study demonstrated that an automatic execution of batch activities by a process engine removes effort from process participants to organize it manually. Furthermore, it improves monitoring and analysis of a batch activity which results can be also used for enhancing batch configurations.

Our approach covers all defined requirements except that activity instances can be heterogeneous in their demands and may have to be grouped into different types of batches. This may be solved by developing an additional configuration parameter for the batch model to express grouping characteristics. Furthermore, our approach assumes that only activity instances of the same process can be grouped into a batch. The BPMN concept of *call activities* can provide a possibility for bringing activity instances of different processes together. When the batch activities are part of the process model, the process designer has an increased responsibility for their correct configuration. In order to support that, further validation and verification techniques should be developed which take into account batch activities. In future work, we want to address these limitations.

References

1. Bailey, N.: On queueing processes with bulk service. Journal of the Royal Statistical Society. Series B (Methodological), 80–87 (1954)
2. Barthelmess, P., Wainer, J.: Workflow systems: A few definitions and a few suggestions. In: Organizational Computing Systems, pp. 138–147. ACM (1995)
3. Laliwala, Z., Khosla, R., Majumdar, P., Chaudhary, S.: Semantic and rules based event-driven dynamic web services composition for automation of business processes. In: SCW, pp. 175–182. IEEE (2006)
4. Liu, J., Hu, J.: Dynamic batch processing in workflows: Model and implementation. Future Generation Computer Systems 23(3), 338–347 (2007)
5. Liu, J., Wen, Y., Li, T., Zhang, X.: A data-operation model based on partial vector space for batch processing in workflow. Concurrency and Computation 23(16), 1936–1950 (2011)
6. Mangler, J., Rinderle-Ma, S.: Rule-based synchronization of process activities. In: CEC, pp. 121–128. IEEE (2011)
7. Mathirajan, M., Sivakumar, A.I.: A literature review, classification and simple meta-analysis on scheduling of batch processors in semiconductor. IJAMT 29(9-10), 990–1001 (2006)
8. Medhi, J.: Stochastic Models in Queueing Theory. Academic Press (2002)
9. Neuts, M.F.: A general class of bulk queues with poisson input. The Annals of Mathematical Statistics 38(3), 759–770 (1967)
10. Papadaki, K.P., Powell, W.B.: Exploiting structure in adaptive dynamic programming algorithms for a stochastic batch service problem. EJOR 142(1), 108–127 (2002)
11. Russell, N., van der Aalst, W.M.P., ter Hofstede, A.H.M., Edmond, D.: Workflow resource patterns: Identification, representation and tool support. In: Pastor, Ó., Falcão e Cunha, J. (eds.) CAiSE 2005. LNCS, vol. 3520, pp. 216–232. Springer, Heidelberg (2005)
12. Sadiq, S., Orlowska, M., Sadiq, W., Schulz, K.: When workflows will not deliver: The case of contradicting work practice. In: BIS, vol. 1, pp. 69–84. Witold Abramowicz (2005)
13. van der Aalst, W.M.P., Barthelmess, P., Ellis, C.A., Wainer, J.: Proclets: A framework for lightweight interacting workflow processes. IJCIS 10(4), 443–481 (2001)
14. van der Aalst, W.M.P., ter Hofstede, A.H.M., Kiepuszewski, B., Barros, A.P.: Workflow patterns. Distributed and Parallel Databases 14(1), 5–51 (2003)
15. Weiss, H.J., Pliska, S.R.: Optimal control of some markov processes with applications to batch queueing and continuous review inventory systems. CMS-EMS, Discuss. Paper (214) (1976)
16. Weske, M.: Business Process Management: Concepts, Languages, Architectures, 2nd edn. Springer (2012)

Multi-Objective Service Composition
Using Reinforcement Learning

Ahmed Moustafa and Minjie Zhang

School of Computer Science and Software Engineering
University of Wollongong, Gwnneville, NSW 2500, Australia
{aase995,minjie}@uowmail.edu.au
http://www.uow.edu.au

Abstract. Web services have the potential to offer the enterprises with the ability to compose internal and external business services in order to accomplish complex processes. Service composition then becomes an increasingly challenging issue when complex and critical applications are built upon services with different QoS criteria. However, most of the existing QoS-aware compositions are simply based on the assumption that multiple criteria, no matter whether these multiple criteria are conflicting or not, can be combined into a single criterion to be optimized, according to some utility functions. In practice, this can be very difficult as utility functions or weights are not well known a priori. In this paper, a novel multi-objective approach is proposed to handle QoS-aware Web service composition with conflicting objectives and various restrictions on quality matrices. The proposed approach uses reinforcement learning to deal with the uncertainty characteristic inherent in open and decentralized environments. Experimental results reveal the ability of the proposed approach to find a set of Pareto optimal solutions, which have the equivalent quality to satisfy multiple QoS-objectives with different user preferences.

Keywords: Web services, multi-objective optimization, reinforcement learning.

1 Introduction

Web service composition is an important and effective technique that enables individual services to be combined together to generate a more powerful service, composite service. When conducting service composition, certain Quality of Service (QoS) constraints have to be considered, namely, QoS-aware Web service composition. This usually refers to the problem of composing a set of appropriate services into a richer service that follows application logics while satisfying certain QoS requirements.

QoS-aware Web service composition has been widely researched in the areas of Service Oriented Architecture (SOA) and Service Oriented Computing (SOC) [4,10,19]. However, existing approaches assume simple service composition models. Also, they give a single objective semi-optimal solution rather than a set of

S. Basu et al. (Eds.): ICSOC 2013, LNCS 8274, pp. 298–312, 2013.

Pareto optimal solutions that exhibit the trade-offs among different objectives. For example, it becomes complex if a client wants to make sure of receiving a service which meets a specific performance within a given cost level and a minimum time delay, but within a higher availability. This is because different dimensional qualities may conflict with one another in the real world. A typical example is the time and cost pair. QoS-aware service composition is then a multi-objective optimization problem, which requires simultaneous optimization of multiple and often competing criteria. Finding the optimal solutions for QoS-aware Web service composition with conflicting objectives and various restrictions on quality matrices is an NP-hard problem.

In the literature, linear weight sum method is employed, and single-objective algorithms are used to solve this problem [22]. However, linear weight sum method has the following problems: 1) solutions are sensitive to the weight vector and stronger prior awareness is required before solving the problem; 2) its number of solutions is small and the distribution of solutions is poor; 3) its time complexity increases exponentially with the increasing problem space size; 4) it will fail to find Pareto optimal solutions which lie in concave regions of the Pareto front.

On the other hand, linear weight sum method offers the user only one solution, while in reality, the user might prefer to see several good solutions, i.e., Pareto optimal, and decide which one is the best for himself. It is more natural to let the user decide the importance of each objective than aggregating the objectives and ask the user to specify a priori his/her preferences which is a demanding task. By using multi-objective optimization, it is no longer necessary for the user to define a priori an aggregation function.

Reinforcement learning (RL) [15] originally stems from the studies of animal intelligence, and has been developed as a major branch of machine learning for solving sequential decision-making problems. RL is concerned with how an agent ought to take actions in an environment so as to maximize some notion of long-term reward. RL has primarily been limited in its applicability to solve only single objective problems. However, many industrial and scientific problems are inherently complex and cannot be expressed in terms of just a single objective. Multi-objective Reinforcement Learning (MORL) combines advances in multi-objective optimization and techniques from reinforcement learning, thus extending RL techniques into the realms of multi-objective problems.

In this paper, an approach based on (MORL) is proposed for multi-objective service composition and adaptation in dynamic uncertain environments. Within the proposed approach, two algorithms are devised to handle different composition scenarios based on user preferences. Experiments have shown the ability of the proposed approach to provide scalable results especially in compositions with multiple quality attributes. The rest of this paper is organized as follows. The problem formulation and basic definitions are introduced in Section 2. Section 3 presents the multi-objective service composition approach. In Section 4, some experimental results are presented for evaluating the proposed approach.

Section 5 gives a brief review of related work and discussions. Finally, the paper is concluded in Section 6.

2   Problem Formulation

In this section, we describe the problem of service composition and give basic definitions related to our approach. In this approach, we employ the concept of Markov Decision Process (MDP) to schematically describe the process of service composition and adaptation. MDP is an AI method to model sequential decision processes under uncertainty and has also been used in different applications [12]. We use Multi-objective Markov Decision Process (MOMDP) to model multi-objective service composition in uncertain dynamic environments. The key concepts used in our approach are formally defined as follows.

In general, Web services can be described in terms of their service ID and QoS. A Web service can be formally defined by Definition 1.

Definition 1: (Web Service). A *Web Service WS* is defined as a tuple $WS =< ID, QoS >$, where ID is the identifier of the Web service, QoS is the quality of the service represented by a n-tuple $< Q_1; Q_2; ...; Q_n >$, where each Q_i denotes a QoS attribute of WS.

Generally, a single objective Markov Decision Process (MDP) can be defined defined as follows.

Definition 2: (Markov Decision Process (MDP)). An *MDP* is defined as a 4-tuple $MDP =< S, A, P, R >$, where

- S is a finite set of states of the world;
- $A(s)$ is a finite set of actions depending on the current state $s \in S$;
- P is a probability value, i.e., when an action $a \in A$ is performed, the world makes a probabilistic transition from its current state s to a resulting state s' according to a probability distribution $P(s' \mid s, a)$; and
- R is a reward function. Similarly, when action a is performed the world makes its transition from s to s', the composition receives a real-valued reward r, whose expected value is $r = R(s' \mid s, a)$.

By extending the single-objective Markov decision process, the multi-objective Markov decision process is defined as follows.

Definition 3: (Multi-Objective Markov Decision Process (MOMDP)). An *MOMDP* is defined where

- There is an environment and an agent which takes an action at discrete time $t = 1, 2, 3, .$
- The agent receives a state $s \in S$ from the environment, where S is the finite set of states.
- The agent takes an action $a \in A$ at state s, where A is the finite set of actions that the agent can select.

- The environment gives the agent the next state $s' \in S$. The next state is determined with the state transition probability $P(s, a, s')$ for state s, action a and the next state s'. The state transition probability can be defined by the mapping:

$$P : S \times A \times S \rightarrow [0, 1] \qquad (1)$$

- There are $(M > 1)$ objectives which the agent wants to achieve, and the agent gains the following reward vector from the environment when it moves to the next state.

$$r(s, a, s') = [r_1(s, a, s'), r_2(s, a, s'), \cdots, r_M(s, a, s')]^T \qquad (2)$$

MOMDP involves multiple actions and paths for each agent to choose. By using MOMDP to model service compositions, the composition agent will be able to find a set of Pareto optimal workflows satisfying the trade-offs among multiple QoS objectives. For each agent i, we call our service composition model as Multi-Objective Markov Decision Process based Web Service Composition ($MOMDP - WSC$), which simply replaces the actions in a MOMDP with Web services.

Definition 4: (MOMDP-Based Web Service Composition (MOMDP-WSC)). An $MOMDP$-WSC is defined as a 6-tuple $MOMDP - WSC =< S^i, s_0^i, S_r^i, A_i(.), P^i, R^i >$, where

- S^i is a finite set of world states observed by agent i;
- $s_0^i \in S$ is the initial state and any execution of the service composition usually starts from this state;
- $S_r^i \subset S$ is the set of terminal states. Upon arriving at one of those states, an execution of the service composition terminates;
- $A^i(s)$ is the set of Web services that can be executed in state $s \in S^i$, a Web service ws belongs to A^i, only if the precondition ws^P is satisfied by s;
- P^i is the probability when a Web service $ws \in A^i(s)$ is invoked when agent i makes a transition from its current state s to a resulting state s', where the effect of ws is satisfied. For each s, the transition occurs with a probability $P^i(s'|s, ws)$; and
- R^i is a reward function when a Web service $ws \in A^i(s)$ is invoked, agent i makes a transition from s to s', and the service consumer receives an immediate reward r^i, whose expected value is $R^i(s'|s, ws)$. Consider selecting Web service ws with multiple QoS criteria, agent i receives the following reward vector:

$$Q(s, ws, s') = [Q_1(s, ws, s'), Q_2(s, ws, s'), \cdots, Q_M(s, ws, s')]^T, \qquad (3)$$

where each Q_i denotes a QoS attribute of ws.

The solution to an MOMDP-WSC is a decision policy, which is defined as a procedure for service selection $ws \in A$ by agent i in each state s. These policies, represented by π, are actually mappings from states to actions, defined as:

$$\pi : S \longrightarrow A. \tag{4}$$

Each policy of MOMDP-WSC can define a single workflow, and therefore, the task of our service composition model is to identify the set of Pareto optimal policies that gives the best trade-offs among multiple QoS criteria.

3   Multi-Objective Reinforcement Learning for Service Composition

In order to solve the above mentioned MOMDP, we propose an approach based on Multi-Objective Reinforcement Learning (MORL). The goal of MORL is to acquire the set of Pareto optimal policies in the MOMDP model. The set π^p of the Pareto optimal policies is defined by:

$$\pi^p = \left\{ \pi^p \in \Pi \middle| \nexists \pi \in \Pi, s.t. \vee^{\pi^p}(s) >_p \vee^{\pi}(s), \forall s \in S \right\}, \tag{5}$$

where Π is the set of all policies and $>_p$ is the dominance relation. For two vectors $a = (a_1, a_2, \cdots, a_n)$ and $b = (b_1, b_2, \cdots, b_n)$, $a >_p b$ means that $a_i \geq b_i$ is satisfied for all i and $a_i > b_i$ is satisfied for at least one i. Moreover, $V^{\pi}(s) = (V_1^{\pi}(s), V_2^{\pi}(s), \cdots, V_M^{\pi}(s))$ is the value vector of state s under policy π and it is defined by:

$$V^{\pi}(s) = \mathbb{E}_{\pi} \left\{ \sum_{k=0}^{\infty} \gamma^k r_{t+k+1} \middle| s_t = s \right\}, \tag{6}$$

where $\mathbb{E}_{\pi}$ is the expected value provided that the agent follows policy π, s_t is the state at time t, r_t is the reward vector at t and γ is the discount rate parameter. We also define the Q-learning [20] vector by:

$$Q_{\pi}(s, a) = \mathbb{E}_{\pi} \left\{ \sum_{k=0}^{\infty} \gamma^k r_{t+k+1} \middle| s_t = s, a_t = a \right\}, \tag{7}$$

where a_t is the action at time t.

The MORL agent works to find the set of Pareto optimal policies under the condition that the agent does not know the state transition probability $P(s, a, s')$ and the expected reward vector $E\{r(s, a, s')\}$.

Current MORL approaches can be divided into two classes based on the number of policies that they learn [11]. The first class aims to learn the single policy that best satisfies a set of preferences between objectives as derived from the problem structure. We will refer to theses as single policy approaches. The second class seeks to find the set of policies which approximate the Pareto optimal front of all possible user preferences. We will refer to these as multiple policy approaches. Inspired by recent works in MORL [11], we propose two algorithms to address multi-objective composition in Web service environments. The first algorithm handles the case of single policy multi-objective service composition and the second algorithm handles the case of multiple policy multi-objective service composition.

3.1 Single Policy Multi-objective Service Composition

In the first algorithm, each QoS-objective is implemented as a separate Q-learning agent. Web services and their relative importance to these objectives are learned rather than predefined and the deployment of multiple QoS-objectives is enabled. At every state s, each agent i selects the candidate web service ws_i that optimizes its relative QoS-objective, then the agents negotiate together to decide which candidate service to execute in this state.

The agents learn to cooperate by negotiation and the agent that wins is the agent that would suffer the most if it did not. Given a state s, the agents suggest their Web service selections with strengths or weights $W_i(s)$. The agent with the largest W values is then allowed to deploy its preferred Web service in this state such that:

$$W_k(s) = Max_{i \in 1, \cdots, n} W_i(s) \tag{8}$$

Therefore, agent k is then a winner and executes Web service ws_k. We call agent k the leader in competition for state s at the moment. The agents then modify their $w_i(s)$ values based on whether they were obeyed, and what happened if they weren't, so the next round there may be a new winner.

Algorithm 1. Single Policy Algorithm

Observe state s
initialize leader k with a random integer between 1 and N
$W_k \leftarrow 0$
$a_k \leftarrow argmax_a Q_k(s, a)$
repeat
  for all agents i except k **do**
    $W_i \leftarrow max_a Q_i(s, a) - Q_i(s, a_k)$
    if the highest $W_i > W_k$ **then**
      $W_k \leftarrow W_i$
      $a_k \leftarrow argmax_a Q_i(s, a)$
      $k \leftarrow i$
    end if
  end for
until converges
return a_k

W values build up on the difference between predicted reward P, which represents what is predicted if the agent was obeyed, and actual rewards A, which represents what actually happened. Therefore, W is calculated by:

$$W = P - A, \tag{9}$$

where p is the anticipated Q-vector if this agent's suggested Web service is executed, and A is the received Q-vector of the execution of another agent's suggested Web service. $(P - A)$ is the loss that the other agent causes to this one by being obeyed in its place. Consider the Q-learning process, when agent k is the winner and has its Web service executed, all other agents except k update their W values as follows:

$$W_i(x) \to (Q_i(x, a_i) - (r_i + \gamma max_{b \in a} Q_i(y, b))), \tag{10}$$

where the reward r_i and the next state y are caused by the agent k than by this agent itself. This process is described by Algorithm 1.

3.2   Multiple Policy Multi-objective Service Composition

In the second algorithm, the multiple policy service composition problem is solved by introducing the concept of the convex hull into Q-learning based Web service composition [8]. The convex hull is defined as the smallest convex set that contains all of a set of points. In this case, we mean the points that lie on the boundary of this convex set, which are of course the extreme points, the ones that are maximal in some direction. This is somewhat similar to the Pareto front, since both are maxima over trade-offs in linear domains. The proposed algorithm exploits the fact that the Pareto optimal set of the Q-vectors is the same as the convex hull of these Q-vectors.

In order to acquire the set of Pareto optimal service selection policies for all the QoS objectives, the set of the vertices in the convex hull of the Q-vectors at state s is updated by the value iteration method:

$$\hat{Q}(s, a) = (1 - \alpha)\hat{Q}(s, a) + \alpha \left[r(s, a) + \gamma hull \bigcup_{a'} \hat{Q}(s', a') \right], \tag{11}$$

where $\hat{Q}(s, a)$ is the vertices of the convex hull of all possible Q-value vectors for taking action a at state s, α is the learning rate, γ is the discount value, r is the immediate reward, the operator hull means to extract the set of the vertices of the convex hull from the set of vectors.

Algorithm 2. Multiple Policy Algorithm

---

initialize $\hat{Q}(s, a)$ arbitrarily $\forall s, a$
while not converged **do**
    for all $s \in S, a \in A$ **do**

$$\hat{Q}(s, a) = (1 - \alpha)\hat{Q}(s, a) + \alpha \left[r(s, a) + \gamma hull \bigcup_{a'} \hat{Q}(s', a') \right]$$

    end for
end while

Given these definitions, now we can rewrite the Q-learning based Web service composition algorithm [8] in terms of operations on the convex hull of Q-values. In the proposed algorithm, an action is selected based on the dominance relation between Q-vectors following the ϵ-greedy exploration strategy. This algorithm can be viewed as an extension to [8], where instead of repeatedly backing up maximal expected rewards, it backs up the set of expected rewards that are maximal for some set of linear preferences. The proposed multiple policy Web service composition algorithm is illustrated in Algorithm 2.

4   Simulation Results and Analysis

Two simulation experiments have been conducted to evaluate the proposed algorithms from different perspectives. The first experiment examines the ability of the single policy algorithm in composing Web services with Multiple QoS criteria and unknown user preferences. The second experiment examines the efficiency of the second algorithm in learning the set of Pareto optimal compositions considering the trade-offs among QoS objectives, simultaneously. Note that terms such as criteria and objectives, qualities and characteristics, solutions and workflows are used interchangeably unless otherwise specified.

We consider using four abstract services (i.e. the typical travel scenario) in both experiment. We assume there are a number of concrete Web services available for each abstract service. The detailed task is to choose the optimal concrete services to achieve better composition results that satisfy three QoS objectives which are *availability*, *response time* and *cost*.

4.1   Experiment Setting

Since there is not any sizable Web service test case that is in the public domain and that can be used for experimentation purposes, we focus on evaluating the proposed algorithms by using synthetic Web services. We assigned each concrete Web service in the simulated MOMDP-WSC model with random QoS vector. The values of the quality parameters in this vector followed normal distribution.

The proposed algorithms run in successive iterations/episodes till reaching a convergence point. Each algorithm converges to a near optimal policy once it receives the same approximate value of average accumulative rewards for a number of successive episodes, those average accumulated rewards are compared episode by episode and the difference is projected against a threshold. For both algorithms, this threshold value is set to 0.001, and the number of successive episodes is set to 1000

To ensure the highest learning efficiency, a number of parameters are set up for both experiments as follows. The learning rate α is set to 1, the discount factor γ is set to 0.8 and the ϵ-greedy exploration strategy value is set to 0.7. These parameter settings are shown in Table 1. The two experiments are conducted on 3.33 GHz Intel core 2 Duo PC with 3 GB of RAM.

Table 1. Parameter Settings

Parameter	Meaning	Value
α	Learning rate	1
γ	Discount factor	0.8
ϵ	Exploration strategy	0.7

4.2   Result Analysis

The results of the two experiments are demonstrated and analyzed in details in the following subsubsections

Experiment 1: Single Policy Algorithm

The purpose of the first experiment is to examine the ability of the single policy algorithm in composing web services with multiple QoS criteria and with no predefined user preferences. The algorithm's ability is measured in terms of the average accumulated reward the composition agent receives when it converges to an optimal policy. This reward value represents the aggregate QoS of the optimal workflow.

For this end, we ran the experiment multiple times and changed the environment scale in every run. The environment scale represents the number of concrete Web services assigned to each abstract service. The average accumulated reward of the single policy algorithm is recorded accordingly and compared with the average accumulated reward of the linear weight Q-learning approach [18]. The linear weight Q-learning approach assumes a predefined user preferences encoded as a weight vector over the multiple QoS attributes. This weight vector is set, in this experiment, to $\omega = (0.3, 0.3, 0.3)$

Fig. 1 depicts the relationship between the average accumulated rewards obtained by running the single policy algorithm and the linear weight Q-learning approach multiple times with various number of concrete Web services.

As shown in Fig. 1, the proposed single policy algorithm yields higher rewards than the linear weight Q-learning approach, every run, apart from the number of concrete Web services. This proves the capability of the single policy algorithm to find higher quality compositions considering multiple QoS objectives. The reward difference becomes more significant as the number of web services increases, i.e., goes beyond 200. This is explained by the ability of the single policy algorithm to better explore the Pareto front. While the linear weight Q-learning approach fails to explore solutions lie on concave regions of the Pareto front, the proposed algorithm is able to scale well with the spread of Pareto front as the environment scale increases. Also, the linear-weight Q-learning approach assumes the usage of a predefined user preferences represented by a given weight vector ω. This weight vector might trip the search process into suboptimal regions of the Pareto surface as the composition agent is biased towards the user preferences. In contrast, the proposed algorithm builds upon the composition structure to derive the relative weights among different QoS preferences. This feature allows the proposed algorithm to adapt efficiently to the dynamics of open environments where many Web services join or leave during run-time.

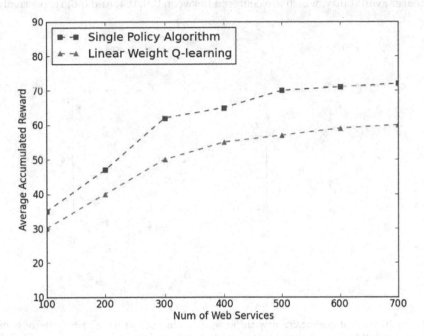

Fig. 1. Single Policy Algorithm

Experiment 2: Multiple Policy Algorithm

The purpose of the second experiment is to assess the ability of the proposed multiple policy algorithm in learning the set of Pareto optimal workflows considering the trade-offs among different QoS criteria. Totally three tests are carried out in this experiment. In the first two tests, each abstract service has been assigned 50 and 100 candidate Web services, respectively. Consequently, this creates an 4×50 matrix and 4×100 matrix for each quality attribute, respectively. The proposed multiple policy algorithm is implemented and tested with the parameters given above. The proposed algorithm runs till convergence and the number of non-dominated solutions/workflows are calculated accordingly.

As shown in Fig. 2, the experimental results indicate that the proposed algorithm is capable of guiding the search towards the Pareto-optimal front efficiently. As the initial attribute matrix data are created randomly, we have no idea where the true Pareto optimal front is. However, we understand that better solutions would be the ones with lower cost, lower response time, but higher availability. The search process should converge towards this direction.

Fig. 2a clearly shows that the optimal solutions have achieved lower cost and response time, but greater availability, which are centered between 0.4, 0.2, and 0.8, respectively. Fig. 2b also supports this statement, regardless of the bigger number of concrete services assigned to each abstract service, as the optimal solutions continue showing the same trend with lower cost and response time, but greater availability, which are centered between 0.3, 0.4, and 0.6, respectively.

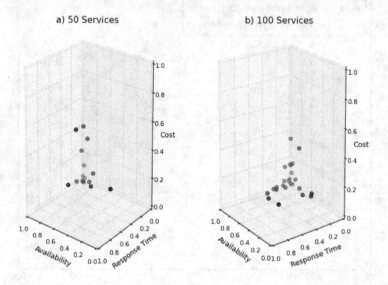

Fig. 2. (a) Results of composition with 50 services in each state; (b) Results of composition with 100 services in each state

The next test is performed to display the convergence property with the presence of different environment scales and various concrete services. Still, four abstract services are considered. We experiment three different cases with the number of concrete Web services varying from 100 to 400 for each abstract service. As shown in Fig. 3, it takes longer to find a set of optimal solutions with the increase of the number of concrete services. For example, in the case of 100 services, the algorithm converges at 400 episodes, while for the cases of 200 services and 400 services, the algorithm finds the non-dominated solutions at 800 episodes and 1000 episodes, respectively. The same tendency is anticipated to continue for any other bigger number of concrete services. As a matter of fact, the three cases generated the same number of non-dominated solutions, 25, at episode 400. The reason for this is currently unknown and is set for future research. In short, the proposed multiple policy algorithm is able to provide a set of Pareto-optimal solutions for service composition problems with different QoS criteria.

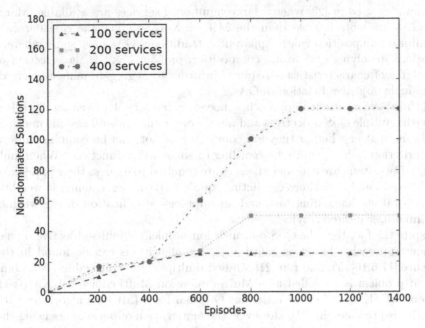

Fig. 3. Multiple Policy Algorithm

5   Related Work and Discussion

The problem of QoS-aware Web service composition is well known in SOC domain and various solutions are proposed based on different approaches[9,22,10,1]. Zeng et al. [22] introduced a QoS model in which aggregation functions are defined in order to aggregate and measure constraints into a single objective function. The major issues of the QoS-driven service selection approach presented in [22] are scaling (amongst objectives) and weighting. Its weighting phrase requires the selection of proper weights to characterize the users preferences, which can be very difficult in practice. Furthermore, the method from [22] cannot always guarantee the the fulfillment of global constraints, since Web service composition is not separable. Wang et al. [19] proposed an efficient and effective QoS-aware service selection approach. It employs cloud model to compute the QoS uncertainty for pruning redundant services while extracting reliable services. Then, Mixed Integer Programming (MIP) is used to select optimal services. Lin [10] aims at enhancing the credibility of service composition plan, taking advantage of a Web services QoS history records, rather than using the tentative QoS values advertised by the service provider, but at last the composition optimization problem is also instantiated into an Integer Programming (IP) problem. However, as pointed out by Berbner et al. in [1], the IP approach is hardly feasible in dynamic real-time scenarios when a large number of potential Web services are concerned. Canfora et al. [2] proposed the use of Genetic Algorithms (GAs) for the problem mentioned above. It has shown that GAs outperform integer programming used in [22] when a large number of services are available. Moreover, GAs are more flexible than the MIP since GAs allow the consideration of nonlinear composition rules. Apparently, traditional GAs have some inherent limitations in solving QoS-aware composition problems as the the selection of the weights of characteristics is required in order to aggregate multi-objectives into a single objective function in GAs.

All the above mentioned approaches, however, cannot solve Web service selection with multiple QoS objectives and multi-constrain. They all assume multiple criteria, no matter whether they are competing or not, can be combined into a single criterion to be optimized, according to some utility functions. When multiple quality criteria are considered, users are required to express their preference over different, and sometimes conflicting, quality attributes as numeric weights. This is a rather demanding task and an imprecise specification of the weights could miss user desired services.

Despite the fact that the QoS optimization problem is multi-objective by nature few approaches based on multi-objective algorithms can be found in the literature [17,6,16]. Yu and Lin [21] studied multiple QoS constraints. The composition problem is modelled as a Multi-dimension Multi-choice 0-1 Knapsack Problem (MMKP). A Multi-Constraint Optimal Path (MCOP) algorithm with heuristics is presented in [21]. However, the aggregation of parameters using the Min function is neglected. Maximilien and Singh [13] describe the Web Service Agent Framework (WSAF) to achieve service selection by considering the preferences of several service consumers as well as the trustworthiness of providers.

Evolutionary Algorithms (EAs) are suitable to solve multi-objective optimization problems because they are able to produce a set of solutions in parallel. A growing interest in the application of EAs to the multi-objective Web service composition in recent years is evident. Claro et al. [5] discussed the advantages of Multi-Objective Genetic Algorithms (MOGA) in Web service selection and a popular multi-objective algorithm, NSGA-II [7], is used to find optimal sets of Web services. Other EAs that have been proposed to solve multi-objective service composition include, Multi-Objective Particle Swarm Optimizer (MOPSO) [3], and Multi-Objective Evolutionary Algorithm based on Decomposition (MOEA/D) [14]. These EAs propose mathematical improvements to solve multi-objective service composition problems. However, as the dimensionality of problems increases, the performance of these EAs significantly deteriorates, since they cannot find a wide range of alternative solutions. In addition, MOGA and MOPSO cannot solve the optimization problems with concave Pareto fronts which are commonly encountered in the real world. In contrast, the proposed MORL based approach is able explore well the Pareto front of multi-objective service composition problems and deliver optimal solutions.

On the other hand, EAs require a level of awareness of the problem domain to setup the initial population through encoding the available combinations as genomes. In contrast, the proposed MORL based approach can learn how to best select Web services in complex environments based on multiple QoS criteria without any prior knowledge regarding the nature or the dynamics of these environment. Up to our knowledge, this is the first approach that' uses MORL to solve this problem.

6 Conclusion

This paper proposes a novel approach to facilitate the QoS-aware service composition problem. By using multi-objective reinforcement learning, we devise two algorithms to enable Web service composition considering multiple QoS objectives. The first algorithm addresses the single policy composition scenarios, while the second algorithm addresses the multiple policy composition scenarios. The simulation results have shown the ability of the proposed approach to efficiently compose Web services based on multiple QoS objectives, especially in scenarios where no prior knowledge of QoS data is available and no predefined user preferences are given. The future work is set to study the performance of the proposed approach in large scale service compositions scenarios.

References

1. Berbner, R., Spahn, M., Repp, N., Heckmann, O., Steinmetz, R.: Heuristics for qos-aware web service composition. In: International Conference on Web Services, ICWS 2006, pp. 72–82 (2006)
2. Canfora, G., Di Penta, M., Esposito, R., Villani, M.L.: An approach for qos-aware service composition based on genetic algorithms. In: Proceedings of the 2005 Conference on Genetic and Evolutionary Computation GECCO 2005, pp. 1069–1075. ACM, New York (2005)
3. Cao, J., Sun, X., Zheng, X., Liu, B., Mao, B.: Efficient multi-objective services selection algorithm based on particle swarm optimization. In: 2010 IEEE Asia-Pacific Services Computing Conference (APSCC), pp. 603–608 (2010)
4. Chiu, D., Agrawal, G.: Cost and accuracy aware scientific workflow composition for service-oriented environments. IEEE Trans. Services Computing (2012)
5. Claro, D.B., Albers, P., Hao, J.K.: Selecting web services for optimal composition. In: SDWP 2005, pp. 32–45 (2005)
6. de Campos, A., Pozo, A.T.R., Vergilio, S.R., Savegnago, T.: Many-objective evolutionary algorithms in the composition of web services. In: 2010 Eleventh Brazilian Symposium on Neural Networks (SBRN), pp. 152–157 (2010)
7. Deb, K., Pratap, A., Agarwal, S., Meyarivan, T.: A fast and elitist multiobjective genetic algorithm: Nsga-ii. IEEE Transactions on Evolutionary Computation 6(2), 182–197 (2002)
8. Dehousse, S., Faulkner, S., Herssens, C., Jureta, I.J., Saerens, M.: Learning optimal web service selections in dynamic environments when many quality-of-service criteria matter. Machine Learning, InTech., 207–229 (2009)
9. Kalasapur, S., Kumar, M., Shirazi, B.A.: Dynamic service composition in pervasive computing. IEEE Trans. Parallel and Distributed Systems 18(7), 907–918 (2007)
10. Lin, W., Dou, W., Luo, X., Chen, J.: A history record-based service optimization method for qos-aware service composition. In: 2011 IEEE International Conference on Web Services (ICWS), pp. 666–673 (2011)

11. Liu, C., Xu, X., Hu, D.: Multiobjective reinforcement learning: A comprehensive overview. IEEE Transactions on Systems, Man, and Cybernetics, Part C: Applications and Reviews PP(99), 1–13 (2013)
12. Mastronarde, N., Kanoun, K., Atienza, D., Frossard, P., van der Schaar, M.: Markov decision process based energy-efficient on-line scheduling for slice-parallel video decoders on multicore systems. IEEE Trans. Multimedia 15(2), 268–278 (2013)
13. Maximilien, E.M., Singh, M.P.: A framework and ontology for dynamic web services selection. IEEE Internet Computing 8(5), 84–93 (2004)
14. Suciu, M., Pallez, D., Cremene, M., Dumitrescu, D.: Adaptive moea/d for qos-based web service composition. In: Middendorf, M., Blum, C. (eds.) EvoCOP 2013. LNCS, vol. 7832, pp. 73–84. Springer, Heidelberg (2013)
15. Sutton, R.S., Barto, A.G.: Reinforcement learning: Introduction (1998)
16. Taboada, H.A., Espiritu, J.F., Coit, D.W.: Moms-ga: A multi-objective multi-state genetic algorithm for system reliability optimization design problems. IEEE Transactions on Reliability 57(1), 182–191 (2008)
17. Wada, H., Suzuki, J., Yamano, Y., Oba, K.: E3: A multiobjective optimization framework for sla-aware service composition. IEEE Transactions on Services Computing 5(3), 358–372 (2012)
18. Wang, H., Zhou, X., Zhou, X., Liu, W., Li, W., Bouguettaya, A.: Adaptive service composition based on reinforcement learning. In: Maglio, P.P., Weske, M., Yang, J., Fantinato, M. (eds.) ICSOC 2010. LNCS, vol. 6470, pp. 92–107. Springer, Heidelberg (2010)
19. Wang, S., Zheng, Z., Sun, Q., Zou, H., Yang, F.: Cloud model for service selection. In: 2011 IEEE Conference on Computer Communications Workshops (INFOCOM WKSHPS), pp. 666–671 (2011)
20. Watkins, C.: Learning from Delayed Rewards. PhD thesis, Cambridge University, England (1989)
21. Yu, T., Lin, K.-J.: Service selection algorithms for composing complex services with multiple qos constraints. In: Benatallah, B., Casati, F., Traverso, P. (eds.) ICSOC 2005. LNCS, vol. 3826, pp. 130–143. Springer, Heidelberg (2005)
22. Zeng, L., Benatallah, B., Ngu, A.H.H., Dumas, M., Kalagnanam, J., Chang, H.: Qos-aware middleware for web services composition. IEEE Transactions on Software Engineering 30(5), 311–327 (2004)

Provisioning Quality-Aware Social Compute Units in the Cloud

Muhammad Z.C. Candra, Hong-Linh Truong, and Schahram Dustdar

Distributed Systems Group, Vienna University of Technology
{m.candra,truong,dustdar}@dsg.tuwien.ac.at

Abstract. To date, on-demand provisioning models of human-based services in the cloud are mainly used to deal with simple human tasks solvable by individual compute units (ICU). In this paper, we propose a framework allowing the provisioning of a group of people as an execution service unit, a so-called Social Compute Unit (SCU), by utilizing clouds of ICUs. Our model allows service consumers to specify quality requirements, which contain constraints and objectives with respect to skills, connectedness, response time, and cost. We propose a solution model for tackling the problem in quality-aware SCUs provisioning and employ some metaheuristic techniques to solve the problem. A prototype of the framework is implemented, and experiments using data from simulated clouds and consumers are conducted to evaluate the model.

Keywords: human-based service, social compute unit, quality of service, service cloud management.

1 Introduction

Recently, we have been seeing on-demand online resource provisioning models being applied not only to hardware- and software-based computing elements but also to human-based counterpart. To date, the provisioning of human-based services (HBS) in the cloud is traditionally used to provision an individual compute unit (ICU) suitable for solving simple and self-contained human tasks. However, for solving more complex tasks, we often require a group of people working in a collaboration. We advocate the notion of a Social Compute Unit (SCU) as a construct for loosely coupled, and nimble team of individual compute units, which can be composed, deployed, and dissolved on demand.

In provisioning an SCU, quality control remains a major issue. Existing quality control approaches are traditionally relies on primitives and hard-wired techniques, which do not allow consumers to customize based on their specific requirements [1]. Still we lack effective HBS management frameworks to manage the socially connected human-based resources for fulfilling the consumers' requests.

In this work, we present a framework that focuses on the provisioning of SCUs containing socially connected ICUs obtained from the cloud, such as crowdsourcing marketplaces. We posit that provisioning SCUs using the underlying ICU

S. Basu et al. (Eds.): ICSOC 2013, LNCS 8274, pp. 313–327, 2013.

clouds could enhance the on-demand provisioning model of human-based services so that it can be utilized for solving more complex tasks. Our contribution in this paper is to provide *a flexible quality-aware SCU provisioning framework*, which is based on consumer-defined quality requirements, using ICUs obtained from the cloud. In particular, our framework provides

- an architecture for quality aware SCU provisioning, which allows different quality control mechanisms to be plugged in using provisioning APIs,
- a tool for modeling quality requirements using fuzzy concepts, and
- solution models which exemplify the quality control strategies for the framework. Specifically, we develop some algorithms, one of them based on the Ant Colony Optimization (ACO) approach, for dealing with the multiobjective quality-aware SCU formation problem.

The proposed framework is particularly useful for, e.g., (i) providing a tool for the human-based services management, which integrates the involved parties in the human-based services ecosystem, and (ii) providing a simulation testbed for studying various quality control technique for human-based services. To illustrate the usefulness of our framework, we study the feasibility of the results and compare with other simpler and common approaches using simulations.

The rest of the paper is organized as follows. Section 2 provides some background for our work. Section 3 discusses the details of our proposed framework. In Section 4, we present a provisioning solution model and describe some algorithms for dealing with the SCU formation problem. Section 5 presents our experiments to study our model. Some related works are presented in Section 6. Finally, Section 7 concludes the paper and outlines our future work.

2   Background

2.1   Human-Based Compute Unit

We define two types of compute units, which are capable of delivering HBS: an individual person, i.e., Individual Compute Unit (ICU), and a composition of socially connected individuals, i.e., Social Compute Unit (SCU). These individuals can be obtained on-demand from ICU clouds. Some examples of ICU clouds include task-based crowdsourcing platforms (e.g., in [2]), collections of experts on social networks (e.g., in [3]), and enterprise ICU pools (e.g., in [4]).

The execution of human tasks may employ different patterns depending on the problem domain and on the runtime systems. Some examples of such patterns include (i) *single unit*, where ICUs works individually on different tasks, (ii) *pipeline*, where the assigned SCU members execute the task sequentially one after another, (iii) *parallel*, where the task is split into subtasks, assigned to SCU members, and the results are merged back after they finish (e.g., in [5]), (iv) *fault-tolerant*, where the task execution is made redundant and the best result is selected from the aggregation of the results (e.g., in [6]), and (iv) *shared artifacts*, where the SCU members works collaboratively over some objects shared among all SCU members (e.g., in [7]).

The effect of these patterns to the SCU provisioning is that each pattern may require different ways to measure the SCU properties. For example, given a task t, and an SCU $\mathcal{V} = \{v_1, v_2, ..., v_n\}$, the response time of the pipeline pattern may be defined as $\sum_{v \in \mathcal{V}} time(v, t)$, while the response time of the parallel pattern may be defined as $\max_{v \in \mathcal{V}} time(v, t)$, where $time(v, t)$ is the time required by the ICU v to execute the task t.

2.2   ICU Properties

We define the following generally common ICU properties: *skill sets, response time,* and *cost*.

Skill Set. A skill of an ICU represents a qualification that the ICU has. An ICU, v, has a set of skills, $Sk^v = \{(s_1, x_1), (s_2, x_2), ..., (s_n, x_n\}$, where $n = | Sk^v |$. The skill type, s_i, of a skill defines the kind of competency that the ICU is endowed with. The skill level x_i may be defined based on different measurement techniques. For example, the skill level can be calculated based on a qualification test or based on a stastical measurement such as the acceptance rate [2].

Response Time. For any ICU v for executing a task t, an estimated response time can be provided, i.e., $time : (v, t) \mapsto \mathbb{R}_{>0}$. This response time is also affected by the job queueing and assignment model, such as based on a maximum number of concurrent job (e.g., [2]), using a work queue approach commonly found in WfMS (e.g., [8]), or using a project scheduling approach considering the time availability of the candidates (e.g., [9]).

Cost. An ICU v may specify its expected cost to perform a task t, which is modeled as a function of the task parameters $cost : (v, t) \mapsto \mathbb{R}_{>0}$. This function, for example, can be simply based on the estimated duration and the hourly cost.

2.3   Social Connectedness

The success of an SCU depends highly on its social connectedness [4]. We define a connectedness graph as an ordered pair $G = (\mathcal{V}, \mathcal{E})$, where $\mathcal{V}$ represents an SCU obtained from ICU clouds, and $\mathcal{E}$ represents a set of weighted undirected edges between two different ICUs in $\mathcal{V}$. We define an edge $e = \{v_1, v_2\} \in \mathcal{E}$ as an indication that v_1 and v_2 have worked together in the past. The weight of the edge, $w(e)$, is an integer number that represents the number of successful task completions substracted by the number of unsuccesful task completions. This weighting approach allows us to give penalty to, for example, malicious workers.

An SCU and its connectedness can be represented as a graph $G' = (\mathcal{V}', \mathcal{E}')$, where $\mathcal{V}' \subset \mathcal{V}$, $\mathcal{E}' \subset \mathcal{E}$, so that $\mathcal{E}'$ is the maximum subset of $\mathcal{E}$ that connects all ICUs in $\mathcal{V}'$. We measure the connectedness of G' as the average weighted degree of all nodes:

$$conn(G') = \frac{\sum_{e \in \mathcal{E}'} 2 \cdot weight(e)}{|\mathcal{V}'|} \qquad (1)$$

3   Quality-Aware SCU Provisioning Framework

3.1   Framework Overview

The core of our framework is the *Provisioning Middleware*, which coordinates interactions among the *ICU Cloud Manager*, the *Provisioning Engine*, and the *Runtime Engine*, as depicted in Figure 1. A scenario for an SCU provisioning starts when a consumer submits a task request to the *Runtime Engine*. This request contains the consumer-defined quality requirements for the task. This quality requirements consists of required skill levels of the SCU members, as well as their connectedness, maximum response time, and total cost. For executing this task, the *Runtime Engine* sends an SCU provisioning request to the *Provisioning Middleware* using the *hybrid service programming API* [10].

The Provisioning Middleware retrieves ICUs' properties from the ICU Cloud Manager, which maintains the functional and non-functional properties of the ICUs, as well as tracking the previous interactions between ICUs, from various ICU clouds. This ICU Cloud Manager encapsulates different APIs provided by different ICU clouds into a unified API. This ICU Cloud Manager also allows the formation of an SCU using many ICUs from different clouds.

The Provisioning Engine is responsible for controlling the quality of the SCU provisioning. A *quality control strategy* for an SCU provisioning is a strategy to control the formation and execution of an SCU, which takes the consumer requirements and the properties of ICUs on the cloud into consideration. There are two types of SCU quality control strategies covering two phases of the task life cycle: pre-runtime and runtime. At pre-runtime, an SCU quality control strategy governs the SCU formation. During runtime, a dynamic adaptation technique is employed to guarantee the required quality. Here we focus on pre-runtime quality control strategies (Section 4), and leave the latter issue for future work.

A pre-runtime quality control strategy is implemented using an algorithm and executed by the Provisioning Engine. To process a task in the queue, the Provisioning Middleware requests the Provisioning Engine to form the SCU. Then, the Provisioning Engine invokes the algorithm to create the formation. Upon receiving this formation, the Provisioning Middleware instructs the ICU Cloud Manager to instantiate this SCU and deploy it to the Runtime Engine. The SCU then executes the tasks using human interfaces provided by the Runtime Engine. When the task finished, the result is returned back to the consumer.

3.2   Consumer Requirements

In our framework, we allow consumers (e.g., human-based application owners, crowdsourcing requesters) to specify their requirements that represent constraints and objectives for the SCU formation and task execution. Our model defines the consumer requirements along four dimensions: *job descriptions*, *connectedness*, *response time*, and *cost*.

Due to imprecise nature of human work, defining a precise constraint can be troublesome for consumers. Here, we propose to model quality requirements

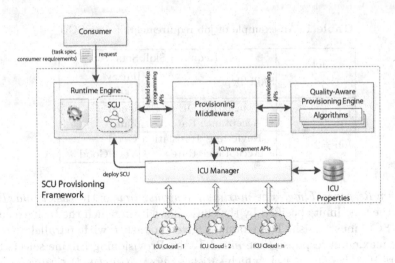

Fig. 1. SCU Provisioning Framework

using *fuzzy concept* [11,12]. For example, instead of saying "I need an ICU with a translation *qualification* ≥ 0.75", the consumer could say "I need an ICU with a *good* translation skill". For a given fuzzy quality q (e.g., *good*), we could measure the *grade of membership* of an ICU using the function $\mu_q : \mathbb{R}_{\geq 0} \to [0..1]$. We apply this fuzzy concept to model the consumer requirements with respect to job descriptions and connectedness.

Job Description. A task request contains a set of *job descriptions*, or *jobs* for short. For each job, the consumer defines the meta-information (e.g., title, description, and presentation) and the required skill set. Our framework provisions an SCU for the task, where each SCU member with the required skill set fulfills a job in the task. Table 1 depicts an example of job requirements for a task, which requires two SCU members: one translator and one reviewer.

Given a task with a set of jobs $\mathcal{J} = \{j_1, j_2, ..., j_n\}$ for an SCU with size n, the Provisioning Engine attempts to find a set of ICUs $\mathcal{V}' = \{v_1, v_2, ..., v_n\}$, which maximizes $\mu_{j_i}(v_i) \ \forall i \in [1..n]$. μ_{j_i} represents the aggregated grade of membership on the *intersection* of the fuzzy sets of all required fuzzy qualities in the job, i.e., given $j_i = \{(t_1, q_1), (t_2, q_2), ..., (t_m, q_m)\}$, $\mu_{j_i}(v) = \wedge_{(t_k, q_k) \in j_i} \{\mu_{q_k}(x_k^v)\}$, where x_k^v is the numerical skill level of ICU v for skill type t_k. Here, we use the min operation as the interpretation of fuzzy set intersection [12].

Connectedness. The required connectedness of the SCU being formed is calculated using Equation 1. This requirement is also defined using a liguistic variable, e.g., the consumer may say "I want to have an SCU with *fair* connectedness". Given a connectedness requirement q_{conn} (e.g., *fair*), the Provisioning Engine composes an SCU $\mathcal{V}' = \{v_1, v_2, ..., v_n\}$ with a connectedness graph $G' = (\mathcal{V}', \mathcal{E}')$, which maximizes $\mu_{q_{conn}}(conn(G'))$.

Table 1. An example of job requirements for an SCU

Jobs	Required Skill Sets	
	Skill Types	Fuzzy SkillLevels
Job #1	– Translating DE to EN – Acceptance Rate	Good Fair
Job #2	– Reviewing Translation – Acceptance Rate	Good Very Good

Maximum Response Time. The *maximum response time* of the task t, $maxRT \in \mathbb{R}_{>0}$, is the time limit specified by the consumer within which the task execution by the SCU must finish. For example, given a task t with parallel subtasks and the maximum response time $maxRT$, the Provisioning Engine selects SCU members $\mathcal{V}' = \{v_1, v_2, ..., v_n\}$, which satisfies $\max_{i=1}^{n} time(v_i, t) \leq maxRT$.

Cost Limit. The consumer defines *cost limit* of the task t, $costLimit \in \mathbb{R}_{>0}$ which represents the maximum total cost payable to the SCU members, i.e., give a task t with cost limit $costLimit$, the composed SCU members $\mathcal{V}' = \{v_1, v_2, ..., v_n\}$, must satisfy $\sum_{i=1}^{n} cost(v_i, t) \leq costLimit$.

Objectives. Furthermore, consumers may also define the objective of the SCU formation. We support the following four goals: *maximizing skill levels*, *maximizing connectedness*, *minimizing maximum response time*, and *minimizing cost*. An *objective* is an ordered 4-tuple, $\mathcal{O} = (w_s, w_{cn}, w_t, w_c)$, each respectively represent the weights of skill levels, connectedness, response time, and cost for measuring the objective value of a provisioning solution, where $w_s + w_{cn} + w_t + w_c > 0$.

Given the aforementioned constructs, we define a task request as a 3-tuple, $t = (\mathcal{J}, \mathcal{C}, \mathcal{O})$, where $\mathcal{J} = \{j_1, j_2, ..., j_n\}$, $j_i = \{(t_1, q_1), (t_2, q_2), ..., (t_m, q_m)\}$, $\mathcal{C} = (q_{conn}, maxRT, costLimit)$, and $\mathcal{O} = (w_s, w_{cn}, w_t, w_c)$.

4   Quality Control Strategies

Here we focus on pre-runtime quality control strategies, which deal with the formation of SCU prior to runtime. We formulate the SCU formation problem, which takes the quality requirements from the consumer into consideration, and propose some algorithms to solve it.

Given an SCU $\mathcal{V}$ socially connected in a graph $G = (\mathcal{V}, \mathcal{E})$, and a task request $t = (\mathcal{J}, \mathcal{C}, \mathcal{O})$, we define the *SCU formation problem* as a problem of finding $\mathcal{V}' \subset \mathcal{V}$ as members of SCU for executing task t which minimizes $\mathcal{O}$ subject to $\mathcal{C}$ and skill set requirements in $\mathcal{J}$. In the following we discuss some building blocks required to solve the SCU formation problem.

4.1   Assignments

The *ICU Cloud Manager* maintains a socially connected ICUs $G = (\mathcal{V}, \mathcal{E})$ obtained from various ICU clouds. Given a task t with a set of jobs $\mathcal{J}$, our goal is to create assignments $\mathcal{A} = \{(j_1, v_1), (j_2, v_2), ..., (j_n, v_n)\}, \forall j_i \in \mathcal{J}, v_i \in \mathcal{V}$.

The goal of an algorithm for solving the quality-aware SCU formation problem is to find $\mathcal{A}$ in the search space $\mathcal{J} \times \mathcal{V}$. Due to the size of $\mathcal{V}$ obtained from ICU clouds, this search space can be extremely huge. Therefore, we filter out non-feasible assignments based on the feasibility of competency, deadline, and cost. Formally, for each job j, we search only in $\mathcal{V}' \subset \mathcal{V}$, where $\mu_j(v) > 0$ and $time(v, t) \leq maxRT$ and $cost(v, t) \leq costLimit, \forall v \in \mathcal{V}'$.

However, this filtering does not guarantee a full feasibility of complete assignments on all jobs. To guide our heuristic algorithms for selecting assignments towards a feasible solution while minimizing the objective, we define two algorithm control mechanisms: *the local fitness* which represents the fitness of an assignment relative to other possible assignments for the same job, and *the objective value of a solution* which represents the fitness of a complete solution. The formulation of these mechanisms is stimulated by the necessity to measure the heuristic factors and solution quality in ACO approaches[13]. However, as we show in Section 4.4, these mechanisms can also be used by other heuristics.

4.2   Local Fitness

The local fitness of an assignment is defined based on a partially selected assignments, starting form an empty set of assignments when the algorithm begins. Given a task t with the objective weighting factors $\mathcal{O} = (w_s, w_{cn}, w_t, w_c)$, a set of selected partial assignments up to job number $i - 1$, $\mathcal{A}_{i-1}$, that already contains a set of ICUs $\mathcal{V}_{i-1}$, and a set of possible assignments for the subsequent job j_i, $\mathcal{A}_i^P$, the *local fitness* λ for an assignment $a_{i,j} = (j_i, v_j)$, $a_{i,j} \in \mathcal{A}_i^P$, is defined as

$$\lambda(a_{i,j} \cup \mathcal{A}_{i-1}) = \frac{\lambda_s \cdot w_s + \lambda_{cn} \cdot w_{cn} + \lambda_t \cdot w_t + \lambda_c \cdot w_c}{w_s + w_{cn} + w_t + w_c} \tag{2}$$

where

$$\lambda_s(a_{i,j} \cup \mathcal{A}_{i-1}) = \mu_{j_i}(v_j),$$

$$\lambda_{cn}(a_{i,j} \cup \mathcal{A}_{i-1}) = \frac{conn(v_j \cup \mathcal{V}_{i-1}) - conn(\mathcal{V}_{i-1})}{\gamma_{conn} + conn(v_j \cup \mathcal{V}_{i-1}) - conn(\mathcal{V}_{i-1})},$$

$$\lambda_t(a_{i,j} \cup \mathcal{A}_{i-1}) = \frac{\gamma_{time}}{\gamma_{time} + time(v_j \cup \mathcal{V}_{i-1}, t) - time(\mathcal{V}_{i-1}, t)},$$

$$\lambda_c(a_{i,j} \cup \mathcal{A}_{i-1}) = \frac{\gamma_{cost}}{\gamma_{cost} + cost(v_j, t)}.$$

where γ is an adjustable parameter, e.g., we can use the consumer-defined $costLimit$ as γ_{cost}. Note that these local fitness values are normalized, i.e., $\lambda : \mathcal{A}^P \mapsto [0..1]$. The elements in $\mathcal{A}_i^P$ can be defined based on the ICUs filtering described in Section 4.1.

4.3   Objective Value of Solution

For each solution, i.e., a complete set of assignments $\mathcal{A}$ for all jobs in $\mathcal{J}$, we could measure the normalized *objective value* returned by the function f : $\mathcal{A}^D \mapsto [0..1]$, $\mathcal{A}^D = \mathcal{J} \times \mathcal{V}$. Given a task t with the objective weighting factors $\mathcal{O} = (w_s, w_{cn}, w_t, w_c)$, the objective function $f(\mathcal{A})$ for $\mathcal{A} = \{(j_1, v_1), (j_2, v_2), ..., (j_n, v_n)\}$, is defined as follows:

$$f(\mathcal{A}) = 1 - \frac{f_s(\mathcal{A}) \cdot w_s + f_{cn}(\mathcal{A}) \cdot w_{cn} + f_t(\mathcal{A}) \cdot w_t + f_c(\mathcal{A}) \cdot w_c}{w_s + w_{cn} + w_t + w_c}, \qquad (3)$$

where

$$f_s(\mathcal{A}) = \wedge_{(j_i, v_i) \in \mathcal{A}} \{\mu_{j_i}(v_i)\},$$
$$f_{cn}(\mathcal{A}) = \mu_{conn}(\mathcal{V}_\mathcal{A}),$$
$$f_t(\mathcal{A}) = \frac{\gamma_{time}}{\gamma_{time} + SCURT(\mathcal{V}_\mathcal{A}, t)}, \text{ and}$$
$$f_c(\mathcal{A}) = \frac{\gamma_{cost}}{\gamma_{cost} + \sum_{(j_i, v_i) \in \mathcal{A}} cost(v_i, t)}.$$

$\mathcal{V}_\mathcal{A}$ is the set of ICUs in assignments $\mathcal{A}$, i.e., for any $\mathcal{A} = \{(j_1, v_1), (j_2, v_2), ..., (j_n, v_n)\}$, $\mathcal{V}_\mathcal{A} = \{v_1, v_2, ..., v_n\}$. For $f_s(\mathcal{A})$, we again apply min function as the interpretation of intersection operation $\wedge$. The function $SCURT(\mathcal{V}_\mathcal{A}, t)$ returns the aggregated response time of all ICUs in $\mathcal{V}_\mathcal{A}$, which determined by, e.g., the response time of each ICU and the SCU pattern employed (see Section 2.1). The goal of an SCU formation algorithm is to minimize $f(\mathcal{A})$.

4.4   Algorithms

We have established the building blocks required for solving the SCU formation problem. Here, we present some algorithms to solve the SCU formation problem.

Simple Algorithms. We present two simple algorithms that can be used to find a solution of the SCU formation problem based on the *first come first selected (FCFS)* and the *greedy* approach.

FCFS Approach. This approach resembles the approach traditionally used in task-based crowdsourcing model: the first ICU who 'bids' wins the task. Assuming that a standby ICU is interested in taking a task, we select the first earliest available ICU for each job. In the case where there are some ICUs with the same earliest availability, we pick one randomly.

Greedy Approach. Initially we construct a solution by selecting assignments for each job that has the highest local fitness value. Afterwards, we gradually improve the solution by changing an assignment at a time. Improvement is done by randomly selecting a job, and randomly selecting another ICU for that job. If the new assignment improve the objective value of the solution, we replace the associated old assignment with this new better one. This procedure is repeated until a certain number of maximum cycle is reached. The greedy approach makes a locally optimized choice for each job at a time with a hope to approximate the global optimal solution.

Ant Colony Optimization. Ant Colony Optimization (ACO) is a metaheuristic inspired by the foraging behavior of some ant species[13]. In the ACO technique, artificial ants tour from one node to another node in the solution space until a certain goal is achieved. The tour is guided by the pheromone trails, which are deposited by the ants to mark the favorable path. The nodes visited in a complete tour represent a solution. Once all ants have finished a tour, the process is repeated for a specified number of cycles or until a certain condition is met. The best solution of all cycles is selected as the solution of the problem.

In our SCU formation problem, given a requested task with a set of ordered jobs $\mathcal{J}$, a node is a tuple (j, v), where $j \in \mathcal{J}$ and $v \in \mathcal{V}$. An ant starts a tour by selecting an initial node (j_1, v_1) and travels to the next nodes $(j_2, v_2), \ldots (j_n, v_n)$ until all jobs $j_i \in \mathcal{J}$ are assigned. Each node has a probability to be selected determined by the pheromone trail and heuristic factor of the node.

Several variants of ACO algorithms have been proposed. Here, we develop our algorithm based on three variants: the original Ant System (AS) [14], $\mathcal{MAX}$-$\mathcal{MIN}$ Ant System (MMAS) [15], and Ant Colony System (ACS) [16]. Generally, the ACO approach is depicted in Algorithm 1.

When traveling through the nodes, at each move i, an ant k constructs a partial solution $\mathcal{A}_i^k$ consisting all visited nodes for job 1 to i. When ant k has moved $i - 1$ times, the probability it moves to another node (j_i, v_j) is given by

$$p_{i,j}^k = \begin{cases} \dfrac{(\tau_{i,j})^\alpha \cdot (\eta_{i,j})^\beta}{\sum_{(j_i, v_w) \in \mathcal{A}_i^{P'}} \left((\tau_{i,w})^\alpha \cdot (\eta_{i,w})^\beta \right)} & \text{if } (j_i, v_j) \in \mathcal{A}_i^{P'}, \\ 0 & \text{otherwise,} \end{cases} \qquad (4)$$

where $\mathcal{A}_i^{P'} = \mathcal{A}_i^P - \mathcal{A}_{i-1}^k$, i.e. the set of possible assignments for job j_i containing only ICUs that are not yet included in $\mathcal{A}_{i-1}^k$; $\tau_{i,j}$ is the pheromone value of the node (j_i, v_j) at current cycle; and the heuristic factor $\eta_{i,j} = \lambda(a_{i,j} \cup \mathcal{A}_{i-1}^k)$ as defined in Equation 2. The relative importance of pheromone and heuristic factor are determined by parameter α and β. ACS variant uses a modified transition rule, so-called *pseudorandom proportional rule* as shown in [16].

At the end of each cycles, pheromone trails on all nodes are updated. At each cycle t, given the number of ants $nAnts$, the basic pheromone update formula for a node (j_i, v_j), which is proposed by the original AS variant [14], is given by

$$\tau_{i,j}(t) = (1 - \rho) \cdot \tau_{i,j}(t - 1) + \sum_{k=1}^{nAnts} \Delta \tau_{i,j}^k \qquad (5)$$

where $\rho \in (0..1]$ is the *pheromone evaporation* coefficient, and $\Delta \tau_{i,j}^k$ is the quantity of pheromone laid by ant k on the node (j_i, v_j), which is given by

$$\Delta \tau_{i,j}^k = \begin{cases} Q / f(\mathcal{A}^k) & \text{if } (j_i, v_j) \in \mathcal{A}^k \wedge \mathcal{A}^k \text{ is feasible,} \\ 0 & \text{otherwise,} \end{cases} \qquad (6)$$

where $\mathcal{A}^k$ is the solution found by ant k and Q is an adjustable parameter. $\mathcal{A}^k$ is feasible if it does not violate any constraints $\mathcal{C}$. We exclude solutions that violate one or more constraints so that only feasible solutions are promoted by the ants. The pheromone update for MMAS and ACS variant has the same principle but different formula as presented in [15] and [16].

Algorithm 1. Ant-based Solver Algorithm

initialize graph and pheromone trails
repeat
$\quad$ $\mathcal{A}_{ants} \leftarrow \varnothing$
$\quad$ **for** $i = 0$ **to** $nAnts$ **do**
$\quad\quad$ $\mathcal{A} \leftarrow$ find a tour for ant_i
$\quad\quad$ $\mathcal{A}_{ants} \leftarrow \mathcal{A}_{ants} \cup \mathcal{A}$
$\quad$ update pheromone trails
until $\exists \mathcal{A} \in \mathcal{A}_{ants} \; f(\mathcal{A}) = 0$ **or** *is stagnant* **or** *max cycles reached*

---

5 Evaluation

5.1 Implementation

We have implemented a prototype of our proposed provisioning framework as depicted in Figure 1. The implementation contains three independent components, namely *Provisioning Middleware*, *Provisioning Engine*, and *ICU Cloud Manager*. The Provisioning Engine is implemented using the quality control strategies discussed in Section 4. For simulation purpose, we populate the ICU cloud with a simulated pool of ICUs. Furthermore, we have also develop a prototype *consumer application* which capable to submit SCUs provisioning requests to the Provisioning Middleware. These components are loosely-coupled and talk to each other through specified APIs implemented using SOAP-based Web services.

In our experiments, we focus on the following aspects of the SCU provisioning: (i) we study our pre-runtime quality control strategy based on the three aforementioned algorithms and analyze the perfomance and result, and (ii) we study the ACO approach to have an insight of (a) the effect of different algorithm parameters (b) the performance and result of the three different ACO variants.

5.2 Experiment Setup

Our prototype ICU manager maintains a work queue for each ICU. Each ICU can only execute a single job at a particular time. We experiment with *parallel* pattern (see Section 2.1), where subtasks, i.e., jobs, are assigned to the SCU members and executed in parallel. We generate 500 ICUs on our simulated cloud. We define 10 types of skills, and each ICU is randomly endowed with these skill types. The consumer application generates task request with random parameters. Each job in a task has some skills set requirements with the required fuzzy quality uniformly distributed over four fuzzy quality levels: *poor*, *fair*, *good*, and *very good*. In this experiment, we use the *trapezoidal* membership functions adopted from [17], which support *over-qualification* when assigning SCU members.

5.3   Experiment Result

To study our pre-runtime quality control strategy, we configure our consumer application to randomly generate and submit 100 task requests. The requests are queued by the Provisioning Middleware in first-in-first-out manner. The Provisioning Middleware then requests the Provisioning Engine to form an SCU for each task request. We repeat the same setup three times to test the Provisioning Engine configured using the three implemented algorithms: the FCFS algorithm, the greedy algorithm, and the original variant of Ant System (AS) algorithm.

Table 2 shows a comparison of average results from all task requests. The AS algorithm outperforms the others with respect to the aggregated objective, i.e., minimizing $f(\mathcal{A})$. The AS algorithm also provides SCU team formation with better skill levels. However, as expected, the FCFS algorithm gives the fastest running time. But considering the nature of human tasks, few seconds running times of the AS algorithm and the greedy algorithm are reasonable. This fast performance is not without cost, since the FCFS algorithm concludes a solution too fast considering the response time only, it results in some constraint violations. Fortunately, due the filtering of the search space (see Section 4.1), violations on skill level constraints do not occur.

Table 2. Results and performance comparison

Algo	Objective Values $\overline{f}$	Skill Levels $\overline{f_s}$	Response Times $\overline{SCURT}$	Violation	Algo Time
FCFS	0.4501	0.0810	6.06	4%	0.9117 ms
Greedy	0.3468	0.2130	11.87	0%	0.1219 s
AS	0.3147	0.3228	10.90	0%	6.6565 s

Furthermore, we are also interested in studying the quality control behavior with respect to the objective weightings, $\mathcal{O} = (w_s, w_{cn}, w_t, w_c)$, as defined by the consumer. Figure 2 shows results of our experiment using task requests with varying objective weightings and SCU size. On each experiment shown on the subfigures, we vary one weight from 0.5 to 8 and fix the others. The results show that the AS algorithm honors the consumer defined weights better compared to the other two. The sensitivity of the FCFS algorithm is flat on all cases, because it does not consider the objective weightings during the formation. The sensitivity levels of the cost weight w_c of the greedy algorithm and the AS algorithm are similar, due to the fact that the local fitness value for cost λ_c contributes linearly to the objective value of the cost f_c. For the connectedness sensitivity, the AS algorithm cannot be seen clearly outperforms the greedy algorithm, because the formed SCU almost reach the upper limit of f_{cn}, i.e., 1.

Knowing that the AS algorithm provides better results in many aspects, we carry out further experiments to understand the behavior of our ACO approach. First, we study the effect of the ACO parameters to the performance and to the quality of the resulted SCU formation. In our experiment, we use the AS variant

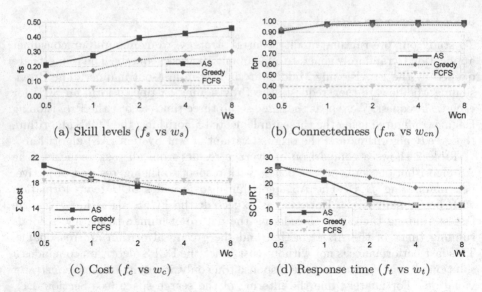

(a) Skill levels (f_s vs w_s)   (b) Connectedness (f_{cn} vs w_{cn})

(c) Cost (f_c vs w_c)   (d) Response time (f_t vs w_t)

Fig. 2. Sensitivity on objective weightings

and fix the pheromone evaporation factor low, $\rho = 0.01$. If ρ is set too high, it will cause the pheromone trails to be negligible too fast. Then, we vary the relative importance of pheromone and heuristic factor, α and β. Figure 3a shows how different α and β yield different results with respect to the average aggregated objective value of the best SCUs formed. Furthermore, we run the experiments for 8 ants in 2000 cycles and see whether a stagnant behavior occurs as shown in Figure 3b. A cycle is said to be stagnant when all ants result in the same SCU formation; hence, causing the exploration of the search space to stop. Our experiments show that the combination of $\alpha = 0.2$ and $\beta = 1$ gives best results.

Furthermore, we extend the experiment further using the same α and β parameters to the other two ACO variants. We are interested in finding out which ACO variants give faster conclusion to a good SCU formation. We run the experiment using 8 ants and 10000 cycles as shown in Figure 4. The result shows

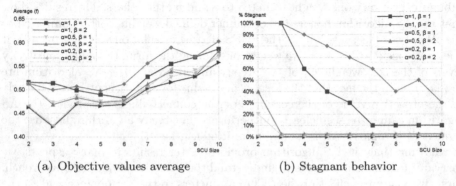

(a) Objective values average   (b) Stagnant behavior

Fig. 3. Influence of α and β

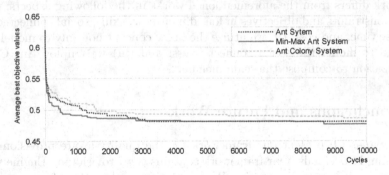

Fig. 4. Comparison on results of ACO variants

that the MMAS variant gives better SCU formations (less objective values) in less number of cycles than the others.

Different quality control strategies implemented by different algorithms cater different needs. Here we show an ACO based algorithm provides better results in some aspects. However, there is no "one size fits all" strategy. For example, the FCFS approach may be preferable in some circumstances where the response time is the most important factor and the consumer only cares about skill constraints, which happens in typical microtask crowdsourcing systems. The usefulness of our framework is therefore also to support multiple strategies.

6   Related Work

HBS Management Framework. Recently, the issue of quality management in human-based services has attracted many researchers. The issue becomes even more crucial when we deal with online and open labor markets such as crowdsourcing marketplaces [1,18]. Several works have also been introduced to deliver managed human-based services frameworks such as [19,20].

Many techniques have also been introduced for executing human tasks in a workflow management system using organizational human-based services, such as [21,22]. Some works such as [23] goes further to allow the execution of workflows or business processes using the cloud of human-based services.

Our work endorses the notion of Social Compute Unit (SCU), which allows the execution of human tasks not only by a single human-based service but also by a composition of socially connected human-based services. Furthermore, we abstract open (e.g., crowdsourcing) and organizational pool of human-based services as ICU clouds, and therefore, we envision the execution of organizational human-based workflow using open ICU clouds such as crowdsourcing platforms.

Formation Techniques. One of the main focus of our work is in the domain of team formation optimization. Some approaches for team formation based on the fuzzy concept have been proposed, e.g., [9,17]. Other works, such as [24,25,26,27], also take the social network of the team member candidates into consideration.

Our work differs from the aforementioned works in the following aspects: (i) we model constraints and objectives in four dimensions: skills, social connectedness, response time, and cost, (ii) we utilize the fuzzy concept not only to model skills but also to model the social connectedness, and (iii) we employ Ant Colony Optimization to compose the team members.

7   Conclusions and Future Work

In this paper we present our framework for the quality-aware provisioning of SCU using ICU clouds. Our framework contains the Provisioning Engine which executes quality control strategies. We propose some algorithms for pre-runtime quality control strategies, which deals with the SCU formation request considering the consumer-defined quality requirements and the ICUs properties obtained from the cloud. We conduct experiments to study the characteristics of the algorithms, which could be utilized to cater different system needs.

Our work presented in this paper is part of our ongoing research in the field of human-based service. We plan to develop other quality control strategies such as runtime adaptation techniques to govern the human-based services during runtime. Furthermore, we are also interested in investigating quality control strategies for human-based tasks on busines processes using the ICU clouds.

Acknowledgements. The first author of this paper is financially supported by the Vienna PhD School of Informatics. The work mentioned in this paper is partially supported by the EU FP7 FET SmartSociety (http://www.smart-society -project.eu/).

References

1. Allahbakhsh, M., Benatallah, B., Ignjatovic, A., Motahari-Nezhad, H.R., Bertino, E., Dustdar, S.: Quality control in crowdsourcing systems: Issues and directions. IEEE Internet Computing 17(2), 76–81 (2013)
2. Amazon: Amazon mechanical turk. Website (2013), http://www.mturk.com/
3. Anagnostopoulos, A., Becchetti, L., Castillo, C., Gionis, A., Leonardi, S.: Online team formation in social networks. In: WWW, pp. 839–848. ACM (2012)
4. Sengupta, B., Jain, A., Bhattacharya, K., Truong, H.-L., Dustdar, S.: Who do you call? problem resolution through social compute units. In: Liu, C., Ludwig, H., Toumani, F., Yu, Q. (eds.) ICSOC 2012. LNCS, vol. 7636, pp. 48–62. Springer, Heidelberg (2012)
5. Kulkarni, A.P., Can, M., Hartmann, B.: Turkomatic: automatic recursive task and workflow design for mechanical turk. In: CHI, pp. 2053–2058 (2011)
6. Varshney, L.: Privacy and reliability in crowdsourcing service delivery. In: IEEE 2012 Annual SRII Global Conference (SRII), pp. 55–60 (2012)
7. Spillers, F., Loewus-Deitch, D.: Temporal attributes of shared artifacts in collaborative task environments (2003)
8. Jin, L.J., Casati, F., Sayal, M., Shan, M.C.: Load balancing in distributed workflow management system. In: ACM SAC, pp. 522–530. ACM (2001)

9. Baykasoglu, A., Dereli, T., Das, S.: Project team selection using fuzzy optimization approach. Cybernet. Syst. 38(2), 155–185 (2007)

10. Truong, H.-L., Dustdar, S., Bhattacharya, K.: Programming hybrid services in the cloud. In: Liu, C., Ludwig, H., Toumani, F., Yu, Q. (eds.) ICSOC 2012. LNCS, vol. 7636, pp. 96–110. Springer, Heidelberg (2012)

11. Zadeh, L.A.: The concept of a linguistic variable and its application to approximate reasoning–i. Information Sciences 8(3), 199–249 (1975)

12. Bellman, R.E., Zadeh, L.A.: Decision-making in a fuzzy environment. Management Science 17(4), B141 (1970)

13. Dorigo, M., Birattari, M., Stutzle, T.: Ant colony optimization. IEEE Computational Intelligence Magazine 1(4), 28–39 (2006)

14. Dorigo, M., Maniezzo, V., Colorni, A.: Ant system: optimization by a colony of cooperating agents. IEEE TSMC 26(1), 29–41 (1996)

15. Stutzle, T., Hoos, H.H.: Max-min ant system. Future Generations Computer Systems 16(8), 889–914 (2000)

16. Dorigo, M., Gambardella, L.M.: Ant colony system: A cooperative learning approach to the traveling salesman problem. TEC 1(1), 53–66 (1997)

17. Strnad, D., Guid, N.: A fuzzy-genetic decision support system for project team formation. Applied Soft Computing 10(4), 1178–1187 (2010)

18. Ipeirotis, P.G., Horton, J.J.: The need for standardization in crowdsourcing. In: Proceedings of the CHI 2011 Conference (2011)

19. Minder, P., Seuken, S., Bernstein, A., Zollinger, M.: Crowdmanager-combinatorial allocation and pricing of crowdsourcing tasks with time constraints. In: Workshop on Social Computing and User Generated Content, pp. 1–18 (2012)

20. Dow, S., Kulkarni, A., Klemmer, S., Hartmann, B.: Shepherding the crowd yields better work. In: ACM CSCW, pp. 1013–1022. ACM (2012)

21. Agrawal, A., Amend, M., Das, M., Ford, M., Keller, C., Kloppmann, M., König, D., Leymann, F., et al.: WS-BPEL extension for people (BPEL4People). V1. 0 (2007)

22. Salimifard, K., Wright, M.: Petri net-based modelling of workflow systems: An overview. EJOR 134(3), 664–676 (2001)

23. La Vecchia, G., Cisternino, A.: Collaborative workforce, business process crowdsourcing as an alternative of BPO. In: Daniel, F., Facca, F.M. (eds.) ICWE 2010. LNCS, vol. 6385, pp. 425–430. Springer, Heidelberg (2010)

24. Rangapuram, S.S., Bühler, T., Hein, M.: Towards realistic team formation in social networks based on densest subgraphs. In: WWW, pp. 1077–1088. ACM (2013)

25. Kargar, M., An, A., Zihayat, M.: Efficient bi-objective team formation in social networks. In: Flach, P.A., De Bie, T., Cristianini, N. (eds.) ECML PKDD 2012, Part II. LNCS, vol. 7524, pp. 483–498. Springer, Heidelberg (2012)

26. Cheatham, M., Cleereman, K.: Application of social network analysis to collaborative team formation. In: CTS, pp. 306–311. IEEE (2006)

27. Lappas, T., Liu, K., Terzi, E.: Finding a team of experts in social networks. In: ACM SIGKDD, pp. 467–476. ACM (2009)

Process Discovery Using Prior Knowledge

Aubrey J. Rembert, Amos Omokpo,
Pietro Mazzoleni, and Richard T. Goodwin

IBM T.J. Watson Research Center
Yorktown Heights NY 10598, USA

Abstract. In this paper, we describe a process discovery algorithm that leverages prior knowledge and process execution data to learn a control-flow model. Most process discovery algorithms are not able to exploit prior knowledge supplied by a domain expert. Our algorithm incorporates prior knowledge using ideas from Bayesian statistics. We demonstrate that our algorithm is able to recover a control-flow model in the presence of noisy process execution data, and uncertain prior knowledge.

1 Introduction

Process discovery is a research area at the intersection of business process management and data mining that has as one of its main objectives the development of algorithms that find novel relationships within, and useful summarizations of, process execution data. These relationships and summarizations can provide actionable insight such as the need for process redesign, organizational restructuring, and resource re-allocation. Control-flow discovery is a sub-area of process discovery concerned with the development of algorithms for learning the dependency structure between activities from process execution data.

In this paper, we consider the problem of learning control-flow models in the form of Information Control Nets (ICN) from the combination of noisy process execution logs, and uncertain prior knowledge encoded as augmented ICNs. Most control-flow discovery algorithms do not incorporate prior domain knowledge. Prior knowledge from domain experts or a repository of process models from the same domain can be a valueable resource in the discovery of control-flow models. This is especially true if there are important process segments that are executed infrequently. For example, in a banking process, if a transaction involving more than $100,000 is performed, a separate part of the banking process is executed. If the underlying control-flow discovery algorithm is designed to handle noise, then important, infrequent process executions may not get reflected in the discovered control-flow model. On the other hand, if the control-flow discovery algorithm is not designed to handle noise, then the discovered control-flow model will incorporate important, infrequent process executions, as well as erroneous, infrequent process executions.

The main contributions of this paper are that we present a control-flow discovery algorithm that uses prior knowledge in the form of an augmented Information Control Net, and process execution data to automatically discover a control-flow

S. Basu et al. (Eds.): ICSOC 2013, LNCS 8274, pp. 328–342, 2013.

model in the form of an Information Control Net. Our control-flow discovery algorithm can deal with noise in the process execution data, and uncertainty in the prior knowledge using ideas from Bayesian statistics. Additionally, our control-flow discovery algorithm can deal with cycles and discovers the semantics of splits and joins.

2   Related Work

The area of process discovery is over fifteen years old. It was first investigated by Cook and Wolf [1] in the context of software processes. Next, process discovery was investigated by Agrawal et. al [2] in the context of business processes. The work of Cook and Wolf, and Agrawal et. al laid a foundation for process discovery. However, their work does not make use of models that can explicitly represent the nature of concurrent and decision splits, and synchronous and asynchronous joins, and does not leverage prior knowledge. The first phase of our algorithm builds on the algorithm developed by Agrawal et. al [2] by incoporating an approach to leverage prior knowledge.

In the paper [3], van der Aalst et al. describe the α-algorithm, a process discovery algorithm that explores the theoretical limits of the WF-Net (a Petri-net variant) approach to process discovery. It is based on a complete and noise-free log of process traces. The authors describe some control-flow patterns that are impossible for the α-algorithm to discover.

The paper by Fahland and van der Aalst [4] proposes an approach to include prior knowledge in process discovery. Their approach takes as input a potentially noisy process execution log and prior knowledge encoded as a Petri net. It produces a Petri net that contains the prior knowledge Petri net with additional sub-models that represent subtraces in the process execution data that did not fit the prior knowledge Petri net. Their approach assumes that the control-flow model provided by a domain expert is accurate and that only the addition of sub-control-flow models to the domain expert supplied control-flow model can be made. Our approach assumes that there is a level of uncertainty associated with provided domain knowledge. This leaves room for a domain expert's control-flow model to be erroneous. In our approach to process discovery using prior knowledge, the resulting control-flow model omits erroneous structures in a domain expert's control-flow model if it is not supported by enough evidence in the process execution data.

In the paper [5], Medeiros et. al. introduce a genetic algorithm for process discovery that takes as input process models represented as Causal Matrices as an initial population. This initial population can be a set of process models supplied by a domain expert. However, the genetic algorithm approach for process discovery uses a global score and search procedure, which makes it difficult to distinguish important, yet infrequent process fragments from noise.

3   Process Execution Logs

Process execution logs are the process execution data that our control-flow discovery algorithm uses to learn control-flow models. A *process instance* is an execution of a process. A *process trace* or simply *trace* is a list of events generated by a process instance. The events in a trace are denoted by the triple, (P, A, X), where P is unique trace identifier, A is the name of the activity, and X is the timestampe of the event. A *process execution log*, denoted by $\mathcal{L}$, is a multiset of process traces.

The dependencies that exist in a process will be implicitly embedded in the process execution log it generates. For instance, if activity b is dependent on activity a in a control-flow model, then, in each trace containing events from activities a and b, the event generated by a will always appear before that of b, unless there are measurement or ordering errors in process execution log generation. By an abuse of notation, we represent activities and events with the same symbol; this abuse of notation will be clear from the context.

Definition 1 (Precede). *Given a trace T containing events a and b, event a precedes event b in T, denoted by $a \prec_T b$, if a occurs before b in T. (The T from $\prec_T$ can be dropped when the context is clear)*

Definition 2 (Dependent). *Let $\mathcal{L} = \{T_1, \ldots, T_{|\mathcal{L}|}\}$ be a process execution log. Activity b is dependent on activity a, denoted by $a \rightarrow b$, if event a precedes event b a statistically significant number of times.*

Definition 3 (Independent). *Let $\mathcal{L}$ be a process execution log. Activity a is independent of activity b (and vice versa), if it is not the case that $a \rightarrow b$, or $b \rightarrow a$.*

Definition 4 (Mutually Exclusive). *Let $\mathcal{L}$ be a process execution log. Activity a is mutually exclusive of activity b, if a and b are negatively correlated in $\mathcal{L}$ (i.e. they hardly ever appear together in the same process trace).*

Given a process execution log, $\mathcal{L}$, we can define a dependency graph, and an independency graph that represent the dependencies between activities. These two graphs implicitly represent the structure and semantics of the underlying control-flow model. The dependency graph represents the structure, and the independency graph represents the semantics of the splits and joins.

Definition 5. *Given a process execution log, $\mathcal{L}$, and a set of unique activities in $\mathcal{L}$, denoted by $A_{\mathcal{L}}$, a directed graph $D_{\mathcal{L}} = (A_{\mathcal{L}}, F)$ is a dependency graph over $\mathcal{L}$, if for each pair of activities $a, b \in A_{\mathcal{L}}$, there exists a path $a \rightsquigarrow b$ in $D_{\mathcal{L}}$ where there exists a dependency relationship, $a \rightarrow b$, between activities a and b in $\mathcal{L}$.*

Definition 6. *Given the process execution log, $\mathcal{L}$, and a set of unique activities, $A_{\mathcal{L}}$, an undirected graph $U_{\mathcal{L}} = (A_{\mathcal{L}}, H)$ is a independency graph over $A_{\mathcal{L}}$, iff there exists an undirected edge between each pair of activities a and b in $U_{\mathcal{L}}$ where there exists an independency relationship between a and b in $\mathcal{L}$.*

4   Information Control Nets

The result of control-flow discovery using prior knowledge is an Information Control Net (ICN). An ICN is an edge-colored, directed graph $G = (A, E, \delta)$ used to model the control-flow of a business process, where A is a finite set of activities, $E \subseteq A \times A$ is a set of control-flow links, and $\delta = \delta_{in} \cup \delta_{out}$ is a set of mappings used to represent edge colors. Sets A and E define the structure of an ICN, while set δ defines the semantics of its splits and joins. Let $a, b \in A$ be activities. The *predecessors* of a are denoted by $pred(a) = \{b | (b, a) \in E)\}$. The *successors* of a are denoted by $succ(a) = \{b | (a, b) \in E)\}$.

Activities can be classified as *simple*, *split* or *join*. A simple activity has at most one predecessor, and at most one successor. A split activity has multiple successors, and a join activity has multiple predecessors. It is important to note that in the ICN model a single activity can be both a split activity and a join activity. There are two unique activities, s and t, called the starting and terminating activities, respectively, in every ICN. Starting activity s has no predecessors, and terminating activity t has no successors.

A control-flow link (a, b) is said to be *activated* if once activity a has finished executing, activity b is eligible for execution. In some instances, where activity a is a split activity, activity a must choose a subset of its control-flow links to activate. If the proper constraints are satisfied, the target activities of activated control-flow links can be executed. We describe those contraints in Section 4.1.

4.1   ICN Normal Form of δ

The ICN Normal form of δ is a canonical representation, invented by Ellis in the paper [6], that enables our edge coloring scheme. The mappings $\delta_{in}(a)$ and $\delta_{out}(a)$ partition the sets $pred(a)$ and $succ(a)$, respectively, in such a way that they describe which activities can execute concurrently and which activities cannot. Let $\mathcal{C}$ be a set of disjoint sets of activities such that $\delta_x(a) = \mathcal{C}$, and let each $C_i \in \mathcal{C}$ be a set of activities. Additionally, let the cardinality of each $C_i \in \mathcal{C}$ be $s(i)$, the cardinality of $\mathcal{C}$ be ℓ, and c_i^j be an activity in the set C_i. The *ICN normal form* of $\delta_x(a)$ is represented by Equation 1, where x can take on either the value *in* or *out*.

$$\delta_x(a) = \{\{c_1^1, \ldots, c_1^{s(1)}\}, \ldots, \{c_\ell^1, \ldots, c_\ell^{s(\ell)}\}\}, \tag{1}$$

In Equation 1, when $x = in$, activity a can execute if and only if each activity c_i^j in exactly one set $C_i = \{c_i^1, \ldots c_i^{s(i)}\} \in \mathcal{C}$ has finished executing and activated control-flow link (c_i^j, a). When $x = out$, activity a can choose only one set $C_i \in \mathcal{C}$. Based on this choice, each activity $c_i^k \in C_i$ is enabled to execute when control-flow link (a, c_i^k) becomes activated. Activities c_i^j and c_i^k in the same set C_i can be executed concurrently. Alternatively, given sets $C_i, C_j \in \delta_x(a)$ such that activities $c_i^k \in C_i$, $c_j^l \in C_j$, and $i \neq j$, it is the case that c_j^k and c_i^l can never be executed concurrently.

We now sketch our edge-coloring scheme. Given an activity a such that $\delta_{out}(a) = C = \{C_1, \ldots, C_\ell\}$, let $E_{succ(a)} = \{(a,b)|b \in succ(a)\}$ be the set of control-flow links to the activities in $succ(a)$ from a. Let each $C_i \in C$ define a color. Each edge in $E_{succ(a)}$ is colored according to the set, $C_i \in C$, its target activity belongs to. However, if a is connected to a join activity j then the color of the (a, j) control-flow link is determined by $E_{pred(j)}$, which is defined analogously to $E_{succ(a)}$. Additonally, in ICNs, some activities are *observable*, while others are *hidden*. Observable activities are executed by (human/machine) actors and generate events that are recorded in process execution data, while hidden activities are not executed by actors and do not generate events that are recorded. Hidden activities are a convention used to represent control-flow patterns that cannot be directly represented in ICN normal form using only observable activities. For purposes of this paper, we substitute edge color for edge slashes (edges with the same number of slashes are the same color).

Example 1. Consider the ICN in Figure 1. Let the hollow circles represent hidden activities $h1$ and $h2$. The figure shows that $\delta_{out}(a) = \{\{b, h1\}\}$ and $\delta_{in}(a) = \{\{\}\}$. This means that a can be executed at any time, and once it has finished executing, the control-flow links (a, b) and $(a, h1)$ are activated. Thus, enabling b and $h1$ to execute concurrently. This figure also shows that $\delta_{in}(h2) = \{\{c\}, \{d\}\}$. This means $h2$ can execute when either the control-flow link $(c, h2)$ is activated as a result of c finishing execution, or when the control-flow link $(d, h2)$ is activated as a result of d finishing execution. After $h2$ executes, the control-flow link $(h2, f)$ is activated. Note that f cannot execute until the both the (e, f) and $(h2, f)$ edges are activated.

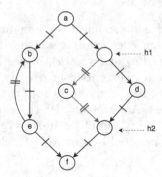

Fig. 1. An Information Control Net (ICN)

4.2   Augmented ICN

The prior knowledge is specified in an augmented ICN. That prior knowledge can be from a domain expert, or a repository of control-flow models from the same domain in which we wish to perform process discovery. An augmented ICN is an ICN with degrees of belief specified on its edges, and edge colors. The degree of belief specified on an edge reflects either how strongly a domain expert believes in the dependency between two activities, or, given a repository of control flow

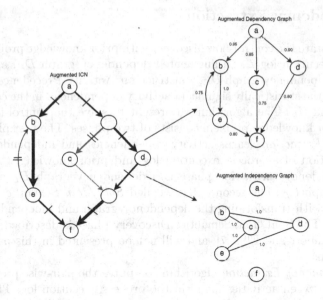

Fig. 2. An Augmented ICN with Corresponding Augmented Dependency Graph and Augmented Independency Graph

models from the same domain, the proportion of control flow models that contain that edge. The degree of belief specified on an edge color signifies the strength of belief in the concurrency of two activities. Degrees of belief can be represented by the thickness of an edge (i.e. the thicker the edge the higher the degree of belief), and the intensity of an edge color (i.e. the more intense the edge color the higher the degree of belief). The thickness of an edge, as well as the intensity of an edge color correspond to a probability in the interval $(0, 1]$.

An augmented ICN can be broken down into its components, which are an augmented dependency graph $D_{\mathcal{K}}$, and an augmented independency graph $U_{\mathcal{K}}$. The augmented dependency graph $D_{\mathcal{K}}$ is a colorless digraph that contains all of the observable activities in the corresponding augmented ICN, and edge labels of the degree of belief. The augmented independency graph is an undirected graph that contains all of the observable activities in the augmented ICN as vertices. An undirected edge in the augmented independency graph represents a concurrency relationship between the incident activities.

In addition to the degree of belief, the experience level of the domain expert, and/or number of control-flow models in the repository must be taken into account. The quantity $n_{\mathcal{K}}$ represents the number of traces that a domain expert's belief is based on or the number of control-flow models in the repository. This experience level will also help in determining how eager our control-flow discovery algorithm is to change the structure and semantics of an augmented ICN. Figure 2 shows an augmented ICN along with its corresponding augmented dependency graph and augmented independency graph.

5   Dependency Extraction

We can now state the control-flow discovery with prior knowledge problem. Given a process execution log $\mathcal{L}$, an augmented dependency graph $D_\mathcal{K}$, and an augmented indenpendency graph $U_\mathcal{K}$, construct an Activity Precedence Graph G, that encodes the statistically significant activity dependencies in the combination of $\mathcal{L}$, $D_\mathcal{K}$, and $U_\mathcal{K}$. The algorithm we present to solve the control-flow discovery with prior knowledge problem consists of two phases. The first phase, called *Dependency Extraction*, learns activity dependencies and independencies from the combination of a process execution log and prior knowledge. The output of the Dependency Extraction phase is a dependency graph $D_\mathcal{L}$ and a independency graph $U_\mathcal{L}$. The second phase, called *Split/Join Semantics Discovery*, is concerned with transforming the dependency graph and independency graph into an ICN. The Split/Join Semantics Discovery phase is described in the 2009 paper by Rembert and Ellis [7], and will not be presented in this paper due to space concerns.

The *Dependency Extraction* algorithm computes the pair-wise precedence relationships between activities found in the process execution log. The input to the Dependency Extraction algorithm is a process execution log $\mathcal{L}$, a user-defined threshold μ, an augmented dependency graph $D_\mathcal{K}$, an augmented independency graph $U_\mathcal{K}$, and a domain expert's experience level $n_\mathcal{K}$.

The outputs of this algorithm are a dependency graph and an independency graph that contain the most probable dependency relationships reflected in both the process execution log and the prior knowledge. The Dependency Extraction algorithm is depicted in Algorithm 5.1

Before we proceed with the description of the algorithm, we first characterize the type of noise we expect to see in process traces. Our characterization is adapted from Silva et. al. [8]. By an abuse of notation, we let a be a binary random variable such that $a = 1$ means that activity a was executed, and $a = 0$ means that activity a was not executed. Let a_R be a binary random variable such that $a_R = 1$ means that the event corresponding to activity a was recorded and $a_R = 0$ means that the event was not recorded. We assume the following type of measurement error. The conditional probability $p(a_R = 1|a = 1) = \omega > 0$, captures the uncertainty associated with an activity executing in a process instance, and its corresponding event being recorded in the appropriate process trace. We assume $p(a_R = 1|a = 0) = 0$, which expresses that an event cannot be included in a process trace if a corresponding activity was not executed. In addition to measurement error (activities being executed but not recorded in a process trace), we consider ordering errors. An ordering error happens in a process instance when an activity a finishes executing before an activity b has, but in the corresponding process trace event b is recorded as finishing before event a has finished. Between each pair of activities, we consider and ordering error rate of ϵ.

The *DependencyExtraction* algorithm is based on ideas presented by Agrawal et. al [2]. The first idea that we leverage from Agrawal is the notion of *cycle unrolling* in the process execution log. Cycle unrolling entails treating events with the same label in a process trace as different events. This is done by relabeling events with an occurence counter. For instance, the first occurence of activity a is relabeled a_1, the second occurence as a_2, and so on. The process execution log $\mathcal{L}$ with unrolled cycles is denoted by $\mathcal{L}^*$.

Mutually exclusive activities can be difficult to detect if they occur within a cycle. This is because cycles can enable mutually exclusive activities to appear in the same process trace. However, we can leverage correlation to determine the strength of association between activities across process traces. In a cycle unrolled process execution log, we can compute the ϕ-coefficient between activities and store the result in the square matrix $\mathbf{M}^\phi = [\phi_{ij}]$. The rows and columns of $\mathbf{M}^\phi$ correspond to unique activities in $\mathcal{L}^*$, and the value ϕ_{ij} corresponds to the ϕ-coefficient of activities indexed by i and j. The ϕ-coefficient of activities a and b is given by Equation 2

$$\phi_{ab} = \frac{(N_{ab}N_{\overline{ab}}) - (N_{a\overline{b}}N_{\overline{a}b})}{\sqrt{N_a N_{\overline{a}} N_b N_{\overline{b}}}}, \tag{2}$$

where:

- N_{ab} is the number of process traces that both activities a and b occurr in,
- $N_{\overline{ab}}$ is the number of traces that don't contain either a or b,
- $N_{a\overline{b}}$ is the number of traces that contain a, but not b,
- $N_{\overline{a}b}$ is the number of traces that contain b, but not a,
- N_a is the number of traces that contain a,
- $N_{\overline{a}}$ is the number of traces that don't contain a,
- N_b is the number of traces that contain b, and
- $N_{\overline{b}}$ is the number of traces that don't contain b.

If activities are found to be negatively correlated, we assume that they are mutually exclusive. It easy to see that if $N_{ab} = 0$ (i.e. activities a and b don't occur in any of the same process traces), then Equation 2 will have a negative value.

Binomial Distribution and Beta Prior. For all the positively correlated pairs of activities, we compute the likelihood that one activity is dependent on another with the results stored in a cycle unrolled dependency graph and a cycle unrolled independency graph. Let $D_{\mathcal{L}^*}$ be a cycle unrolled dependency graph and $U_{\mathcal{L}^*}$ be a cycle unrolled independency graph, both of which contain all of the relabeled activities as vertices. The cycle unrolled dependency graph is a directed graph, and the cycle unrolled independency graph is an undirected graph, both of which are initially edgeless.

To add directed edges to $D_{\mathcal{L}^*}$ and undirected edges to $U_{\mathcal{L}^*}$, we leverage the Binomial distribution and the Beta prior. The binomial distribution is used determine the probability of k successes in N bernoulli trials given a parameter

μ. Let a and b be activities that we wish to discover the dependency relationship between, N be the total number of traces in the process execution log, N_{ab} be the number of traces that both a and b occur in, and $k_{a \prec b}$ ($k_{b \prec a}$) be the number of traces that a precedes b (b precedes a). Additionally, let μ be a user-defined parameter that represents the proportion of times that a must precede b in order for b to be considered dependent on a; μ can be considered an *activity precedence to occurrence ratio*. It is important to note that one should set μ so that a certain amount of ordering error can be effectivly handled.

The binomial distribution can be written

$$p(D_{ab}|\mu) = \binom{N_{ab}}{k_{a \prec b}} \mu^{k_{a \prec b}} (1 - \mu)^{N_{ab} - k_{a \prec b}} \tag{3}$$

, where

$$\binom{N_{ab}}{k_{a \prec b}} = \frac{N_{ab}!}{(N_{ab} - k_{a \prec b})! k_{a \prec b}!}. \tag{4}$$

The conditional probability $p(D_{ab}|\mu)$ is the likelihood of D_{ab} given μ, where $D_{ab} = \{T_1^{a \prec b} = 1, T_2^{a \prec b} = 0, \ldots, T_{N_{ab}}^{a \prec b} = 1\}$ represents the set of traces that activities a and b occur together in. The trace-level precedence indicator $T_i^{a \prec b}$ takes a value of 1, if a was executed before b, and 0 otherwise. It should be noted that $k_{a \prec b} = \sum_{i=1}^{N_{ab}} T_i^{a \prec b}$.

We use the binomial distribution in activity dependency discovery by conducting a binomial test for each pair unique activities in the cycle unrolled process execution log $\mathcal{L}^*$. The null hypothesis of this test is: if $p(D_{ab}|\mu)$ is greater than a user-defined significance level, then $\frac{k_{a \prec b}}{N_{ab}}$ is not significantly different from μ, thus $a \to b$. The first alternative hypothesis is: if $p(D_{ab}|\mu)$ is less than a user-defined significance level in the top tail of the binomial distribution, then $\frac{k_{a \prec b}}{N_{ab}}$ is significantly larger than μ, therefore it is also the case that $a \to b$. The second alternative hypothesis is: if $P(D_{ab}|\mu)$ is less than a user-defined significance level in the bottom tail of the binomial distribution, then $\frac{k_{a \prec b}}{N_{ab}}$ is significantly smaller than μ, therefore b is not dependent on a. The user-defined significance-level is typically 0.05 or 0.025 for two-tailed binomial tests. If the null hypothesis is accepted, or the null hypothesis is rejected and the first alternative hypothesis is accepted, then a directed (a, b) edge is added to the cycle unrolled dependency graph $D_{\mathcal{L}^*}$. If it is found that b is not dependent on a and vice-versa, then an undirected edge (a, b) is added to $U_{\mathcal{L}^*}$.

The approach just described is called the *Likelihood Estimate* approach. The Likelihood Estimate approach is based solely on data and does not take into account the experience and expertise of domain experts when discovering the dependency between activities. In situations where domain expertise is not available, or contains gaps, the Likelihood Estimate approach is used. However, since the Likelihood Estimate approach does not take into account the prior knowledge of a domain expert, we need an approach that does. This can be done using Bayesian statistics.

In Bayesian statistics, we can leverage prior knowledge to help with determining the dependencies between activities. In the Likelihood Estimate approach, the uncertainty is associated with the data. However, in the Bayesian approach, the uncertainty is associated with the activity precedence to occurrence ratio μ. So, instead of calculating $p(D_{ab}|\mu)$, we calculate $p(\mu|D_{ab})$, which according to Bayes' Theorem is:

$$p(\mu|D_{ab}) = \frac{p(D_{ab}|\mu)p(\mu)}{p(D_{ab})}. \tag{5}$$

From Equation 5, we can see that the Bayesian approach leverages the Likelihood Estimate approach. Additionally, since the data is given, $p(D_{ab}) = 1$. For the assesment of $p(\mu)$, we choose the Beta distribution as a prior because it is conjugate to the Binomial distribution. The Beta distribution is defined as

$$p(\mu) = Beta(\mu|v, w), \tag{6}$$

such that

$$Beta(\mu|v, w) = \frac{\Gamma(v + w)}{\Gamma(v)\Gamma(w)}\mu^{v-1}(1 - \mu)^{w-1}, \tag{7}$$

where the Gamma function is defined as $\Gamma(x + 1) = x!$. The quantities v and w are called the hyperparameters of the Beta distribution, and are used to control its shape.

To incorporate prior knowledge, we take both the augmented dependency graph and the augmented independency graph and use the edge labels as priors when trying to determine the dependency relationship between activities. Essentially, the prior knowledge of experts represent virtual occurences of activity pairs occurring in a particular order. Since $k_{b \prec a} = N_{ab} - k_{a \prec b}$, then

$$p(\mu|D_{ab}) = \frac{\Gamma(N_{ab} + v + w)}{\Gamma(k_{a \prec b} + v)\Gamma(k_{b \prec a} + w)}\mu^{k_{a \prec b}+v-1}(1 - \mu)^{k_{b \prec a}+w-1}, \tag{8}$$

where the hyperparameters v and w are based on the prior degree of belief on the domain expert.

We now show how to assess the hyperparameters v and w for a pair of activities, given an augmeneted dependency graph $D_{\mathcal{K}}$ and an augmented independency graph $U_{\mathcal{K}}$. For activities a and b, let there be a directed (a, b) edge in the augmented dependency graph $D_{\mathcal{K}}$. By another abuse of notation, let $a \to b$ be a binary random variable such that $p(a \to b = 1|D_{\mathcal{K}}, U_{\mathcal{K}})$ is the degree of belief specified on the dependency relationship between activities a and b. Additionally, let edge (a, b) be based on $n_{\mathcal{K}}$ process traces, which, as described above, captures the level of experience of the domain expert. Given these assumptions, we set v and w to be: $v = p(a \to b = 1|D_{\mathcal{K}}, U_{\mathcal{K}})n_{\mathcal{K}}$, and $w = p(a \to b = 0|D_{\mathcal{K}}, U_{\mathcal{K}})n_{\mathcal{K}}$. For activities b and c, let there be an undirected (b, c) edge in an augmented independency graph $U_{\mathcal{K}}$. In this case, we assess v and w to be: $v = p(a \to b = 1|D_{\mathcal{K}}, U_{\mathcal{K}}) \cdot 0.5 \cdot n_{\mathcal{K}}$, and $w = v$.

The binomial test is again used to determine activity dependence. The null hypothesis of this test is: if $p(\mu|D_{ab})$ is greater than a user-defined significance level, then there is no significant difference between μ and $\frac{k_{a \prec b} + v}{N_{ab} + v + w}$, and therefore $a \to b$. The first alternative hypothesis is: if $p(\mu | D_{ab})$ is less than a user defined significance level and in the top tail of the distribution, then μ is significantly less than $\frac{k_{a \prec b} + v}{N_{ab} + v + w}$, and $a \to b$. The second alternative hypotheis is: if $p(\mu | D_{ab})$ is less than a user defined significance level and in the bottom tail of the distribution, then μ is significantly greater than $\frac{k_{a \prec b} + v}{N_{ab} + v + w}$, and b is not dependent on a. If the probability returned from the binomial distribution is above a user-defined significance-level, then we accept the null hypothesis, otherwise we reject it and accept the alternative hypothesis. Like the Likelihood Estimate approach, If the null hypothesis is accepted, or the first alternative hypothesis is accepted, we add an directed edge (a, b) in the cycle unrolled dependency graph $D_{\mathcal{L}^*}$, and if b is not dependent on a, and vice-versa, we add an undirected edge (a, b) in $U_{\mathcal{L}^*}$.

When constructing $D_{\mathcal{L}^*}$ and $U_{\mathcal{L}^*}$ using prior knowledge $D_{\mathcal{K}}$ and $U_{\mathcal{K}}$, it is the case that the relabeled activities in the cycle unrolled process execution log $\mathcal{L}^*$ will not match the activities in $D_{\mathcal{K}}$ and $U_{\mathcal{K}}$. To handle this issue, when matching activities from the augmented dependency graph and the augmented independency graph, we ignore the count appended to the activities in $\mathcal{L}^*$. For example, the edge (a, b) in an augmented dependency graph will match the pair of activities a_1 and b_1, as well as the pair a_2 and b_7. If b_7 is found to be dependent on a_2 based on edge (a, b) in the augmented dependency graph and the binomial test, then edge (a_2, b_7) is added to $D_{\mathcal{L}^*}$.

Re-rolling the Cycle Unrolled Dependency and Independency Graphs. Our algorithm re-rolls the cycle unrolled dependency and independency graphs. The first step in this process is to minimize the number of edges in $D_{\mathcal{L}^*}$ without loosing the appropriate dependency information. This is done by using a heuristic proposed by Agrawal et. al. [2], which computes the transitive reduction of each induced subgraph $D_{\mathcal{L}^*}^i$ formed over the activity relabeled process trace T_i. For each $D_{\mathcal{L}^*}^i$, mark all the edges in the transitive reduction. Remove all edges from $D_{\mathcal{L}^*}$ that remains unmarked.

The next step in our process is to collapses $D_{\mathcal{L}^*}$ and $U_{\mathcal{L}^*}$ such that all of the activities that were relabelled to unroll cycles are merged into their original activity in both graphs. For instance, activity a_2 is collapsed into activity a_1, and all of the incoming and outgoing edges of a_2 become incoming and outgoing edges of a_1. This process continues until there are no more activities with an activity counter label greater than 1. The activity counter label, is then dropped from all activities. The collapsed versions of $D_{\mathcal{L}^*}$ and $U_{\mathcal{L}^*}$ are $D_{\mathcal{L}}$ and $U_{\mathcal{L}}$, respectively.

The final step in cycle re-rolling algorithm is the capture of cycles in $D_{\mathcal{L}}$. We capture cycles in $D_{\mathcal{L}}$ because in the split/join semantics discovery phase of the *LearnICN* algorithm activities that are the target of a backegdge are treated slightly different than other activities. Cycles are captured by discovering and marking all backegdes in $D_{\mathcal{L}}$. Backedges are discovered using a simple depth-first search exploration of $D_{\mathcal{L}}$ initiated at the unique starting activity s.

Algorithm 5.1. *DependencyExtraction*($\mathcal{L}$, $D_\mathcal{K}$, $U_\mathcal{K}$, $n_\mathcal{K}$, μ)

1:   $\mathcal{L}^* \leftarrow UnrollCyclesInLog(\mathcal{L})$
2:   $A^* \leftarrow$ unique activities in $\mathcal{L}^*$
3:   $\mathbf{M}^\phi \leftarrow ComputeCorrelation(\mathcal{L}^*)$
4:   $D_{\mathcal{L}*} \leftarrow (A^*, \emptyset)$
5:   $U_{\mathcal{L}*} \leftarrow (A^*, \emptyset)$
6:   **for** each pair of positively correlated activities $a, b \in \mathbf{M}^\phi$ **do**
7:      **if** the pair (a, b) is unmarked **then**
8:        Let N_{ab} be the number of times that a and b occur in the same process trace
9:        $v \leftarrow 0$
10:       $w \leftarrow 0$
11:       **if** edge $(a, b) \in D_\mathcal{K}$ **then**
12:         $v \leftarrow p(a \to b = 1 | D_\mathcal{K}, U_\mathcal{K}) \cdot n_\mathcal{K}$
13:         $w \leftarrow p(a \to b = 0 | D_\mathcal{K}, U_\mathcal{K}) \cdot n_\mathcal{K}$
14:       **else if** edge $(a, b) \in U_\mathcal{K}$ **then**
15:         $v \leftarrow p(a \to b = 1 | D_\mathcal{K}, U_\mathcal{K}) \cdot 0.5 \cdot n_\mathcal{K}$
16:         $w \leftarrow v$
17:       **end if**
18:       **if** $BinomialTest(k_{a \prec b} + v, N_{ab} + v + w, \mu)$ accepts null hypothesis or first alternate hypothesis **then**
19:         add directed edge (a, b) to $D_{\mathcal{L}*}$
20:       **else if** $BinomialTest(k_{b \prec a} + w, N_{ab} + v + w, \mu)$ accepts null hypothesis or first alternate hypothesis **then**
21:         add directed edge (b, a) to $D_{\mathcal{L}*}$
22:       **else**
23:         add undirected edge (a, b) to $U_{\mathcal{L}*}$, if its not already there
24:       **end if**
25:       mark the pair (a, b)
26:      **end if**
27: **end for**
28: **for** each process trace $T_i \in \mathcal{L}^*$ **do**
29:      Let $D_{\mathcal{L}*}^i$ be the trace dependence graph for T_i
30:      Compute the transitive reduction of $D_{\mathcal{L}*}^i$
31:      Mark the edges in $D_{\mathcal{L}*}$ that are in the transitive reduction of $D_{\mathcal{L}*}^i$
32: **end for**
33: Remove all unmarked edges from $D_\mathcal{L}^*$
34: $D_\mathcal{L} \leftarrow Collapse(D_{\mathcal{L}*})$
35: $U_\mathcal{L} \leftarrow Collapse(U_{\mathcal{L}*})$
36: Mark all backedges in $D_\mathcal{L}$
37: Return $D_\mathcal{L}$, $U_\mathcal{L}$

---

6   Experiments

We tested the hypothesis that, in the presence of noise, our process discovery algorithm that leverage prior knowledge learns more accurate APGs than ICN learning algorithms that do not. We tested our algorithm using the telephone repair example process execution log from the ProM example [9]. In our experiments, we let the activity occurrence to precedence ratio be $\mu = 0.90$, and the significance level be 0.05 for a two-tailed test. We experimented with two types of domain knowledge (perfect and imperfect), as well as no domain knowledge. We consider perfect domain knowledge to have the same structure as the reference activity precedence graph and certainty of edges and edge colors between (0.9 and 1.0) We created imperfect domain knowledge by removing and adding edges from the augmented dependency graph and the augmented independency graph. Additionally, the degree of belief for edges in both graphs is drawn uniformly from the range $(0.5, 0.9)$.

We tested the three versions of the algorithm at seven different log sizes (200, 400, 600, 800, 1000, 1200, 1400), three different experience levels (100, 200, 400), and three different measurement error levels (0.95, 0.90, 0.85) and a constant ordering error level of (0.05). To determine how well the control-flow discovery algorithm works, we compared the learned dependency graph and independency graph to the reference dependency graph and reference independency graph. The reference dependency graph and reference independency graphs were computed from the reference ICN. The reference ICN is the true control-flow model.

To compare the learned dependency graph with the reference dependency graph, we computed the edge recall, edge precision, color recall, and color precision. Edge recall is the number of edges that the learned dependency graph and reference dependency graph share divided by the number of edges in the reference dependency graph. Edge precision is the number of edges that the learned dependency graph and reference dependency graph share diveded by the number of edges in the learned dependency graph. Edge F-measure is a combination of edge precision and edge recall. Table 1 shows the edge F-measure for the dependency graphs learned from noisy process execution logs of the telephone repair process with a domain expert experience level of 200 (i.e. $n_K = 200$). As can be seen from the results in Table 1, the control-flow discovery approach that leverages imperfect prior knowledge performs better, in terms of Edge F-measure, than the control-flow discovery approach that does not use prior knowldge. However, as the log size increases, this disparity is reduced because evidence provided by the data will eventually be the main determiner of edge recall and edge precision. Color recall is the size of the intersection between the edges in the learned independency graph and reference independency graph divided by the number of edges in the reference independency graph. Color precision is the number of edges that the learned independency graph and reference independency graph share diveded by the number of edges in the learned independency graph. Table 2 shows the color F-measure for the independency graphs learned from noisy process execution logs of the telephone repair process with a domain expert experience level of 200 (i.e. $n_K = 200$). In Table 2, the color F-measure for Imperfect domain knowledge is slightly smaller than the color F-measure for no prior knowledge. This is primarily due to color recall for Imperfect domain knowledge.

Table 1. Edge F-measure of Learned Dependency Graph with $\epsilon = 0.05$ and $n_K = 200$

| Prior
Traces | Measurement Error | | | | | | | | |
| | 0.85 | | | 0.9 | | | 0.95 | | |
	None	Imperfect	Perfect	None	Imperfect	Perfect	None	Imperfect	Perfect
200	0.744	0.841	0.844	0.778	0.871	0.874	0.870	0.935	0.937
400	0.766	0.846	0.848	0.844	0.904	0.905	0.938	0.980	0.984
600	0.798	0.863	0.867	0.878	0.925	0.927	0.950	0.991	0.993
800	0.831	0.879	0.883	0.900	0.943	0.948	0.950	0.989	0.997
1000	0.827	0.860	0.864	0.902	0.947	0.949	0.952	0.998	1.000
1200	0.821	0.893	0.895	0.915	0.968	0.970	0.952	0.996	1.000
1400	0.854	0.940	0.945	0.925	0.989	0.993	0.952	0.996	1.000

Table 2. Color F-measure of Learned Dependency Graph with $\epsilon = 0.05$ and $n_K = 200$

Prior Traces	Measurement Error								
	0.85			0.9			0.95		
	None	Imperfect	Perfect	None	Imperfect	Perfect	None	Imperfect	Perfect
200	0.809	0.974	0.984	0.777	0.961	0.979	0.789	0.947	0.964
400	0.899	0.971	0.984	0.932	0.957	0.973	0.966	0.958	0.966
600	0.917	0.972	0.980	0.947	0.944	0.953	0.984	0.957	0.984
800	0.955	0.958	0.974	0.960	0.942	0.961	0.996	0.982	0.996
1000	0.970	0.963	0.978	0.956	0.949	0.956	0.999	0.987	0.999
1200	0.887	0.947	0.968	0.953	0.945	0.963	0.990	0.999	1.000
1400	0.875	0.949	0.961	0.946	0.970	0.986	0.998	0.977	1.000

The slightly reduced color recall numbers are due to ordering errors in the log being boosted by reversed edges in the imperfect augmented dependency graph. However, despite the errors in the imperfect domain knowledge, a more correct model was found as more process execution data was provided. Additionally, as can be seen in both the edge F-measure, and the color F-measure, when there are small data sizes, having some prior knowledge increases the edge F-measure and color F-measure. This means that portions of the true process that are executed infrequently can be boosted by the presence of domain knowledge, therefore those infrequent portions of a process trace won't be considered noise. The results of our experiments confirm our hypothesis.

7   Summary and Future Work

In this work, we have presented a process discovery algorithm that leverages prior knowledge in the form of augmented Information Control Nets. We have shown that our process discovery algorithm is robust to noise in the process execution data in the form of measurement errors and ordering errors. Additionally, our process discovery algorithm is able to deal with uncertainty and errors in the prior knowledge it is provided. Through experimentation, we have shown that our approach is useful when important, infrequent portions of a process need to be discovered. Given enough certainty and experience, our approach will not consider the infrequency of those executions as noise. ICNs were developed nearly 30 years ago by Ellis [6]. Since the ICN normal form is nearly identical to the Causal Matrix [5] formalism, for the future, we'd like to explore process discovery with prior knowledge using Causal Matrices, which can be transformed into Petri nets.

References

1. Cook, J.E., Wolf, A.L.: Discovering models of software processes from event-based data. ACM Trans. Software Engineering Methodology 7(3), 215–249 (1998)
2. Agrawal, R., Gunopulos, D., Leymann, F.: Mining process models from workflow logs. In: Schek, H.-J., Saltor, F., Ramos, I., Alonso, G. (eds.) EDBT 1998. LNCS, vol. 1377, pp. 469–483. Springer, Heidelberg (1998)

3. van der Aalst, W., Weijters, T., Maruster, L.: Workflow mining: Discovering process models from event logs. IEEE Transactions on Knowledge and Data Engineering 16(9), 1128–1142 (2004)
4. Fahland, D., van der Aalst, W.M.P.: Repairing process models to reflect reality. In: Barros, A., Gal, A., Kindler, E. (eds.) BPM 2012. LNCS, vol. 7481, pp. 229–245. Springer, Heidelberg (2012)
5. Medeiros, A., Weijters, A., Aalst, W.: Genetic process mining: an experimental evaluation. Data Mining and Knowledge Discovery 14(2), 245–304 (2007)
6. Ellis, C.A.: Formal and informal models of office activity. In: IFIP Congress, pp. 11–22 (1983)
7. Rembert, A.J., Ellis, C(S.): Learning the control-flow of a business process using ICN-based process models. In: Baresi, L., Chi, C.-H., Suzuki, J. (eds.) ICSOC-ServiceWave 2009. LNCS, vol. 5900, pp. 346–351. Springer, Heidelberg (2009)
8. Silva, R., Zhang, J., Shanahan, J.G.: Probabilistic workflow mining. In: KDD 2005: Proceeding of the Eleventh ACM SIGKDD International Conference on Knowledge Discovery in Data Mining, pp. 275–284. ACM Press, New York (2005)
9. Verbeek, H.E., Bose, J.C.: Prom 6 tutorial, reviewexample. (2010)

Mirror, Mirror, on the Web, Which Is the Most Reputable Service of Them All?

A Domain-Aware and Reputation-Aware Method for Service Recommendation

Keman Huang[1], Jinhui Yao[2], Yushun Fan[1], Wei Tan[3],
Surya Nepal[4], and Yayu Ni[1], and Shiping Chen[4]

[1] Department of Automation, Tsinghua University, Beijing 100084, China
[2] School of Electrical and Information Engineering, University of Sydney, Australia
[3] IBM Thomas J. Watson Research Center, Yorktown Heights, NY 10598, USA
[4] Information Engineering Laboratory, CSIRO ICT Centre, Australia
hkm09@mails.tsinghua.edu.cn, jinhui.yao@gmail.com,
fanyus@tsinghua.edu.cn, wtan@us.ibm.com, surya.nepal@csiro.au,
nyy07@mails.tsinghua.edu.cn, shiping.chen@csiro.au

Abstract. With the wide adoption of service and cloud computing, nowadays we observe a rapidly increasing number of services and their compositions, resulting in a complex and evolving service ecosystem. Facing a huge number of services with similar functionalities, how to identify the core services in different domains and recommend the trustworthy ones for developers is an important issue for the promotion of the service ecosystem. In this paper, we present a heterogeneous network model, and then a unified reputation propagation (URP) framework is introduced to calculate the global reputation of entities in the ecosystem. Furthermore, the topic model based on Latent Dirichlet Allocation (LDA) is used to cluster the services into specific domains. Combining URP with the topic model, we re-rank services' reputations to distinguish the core services so as to recommend trustworthy domain-aware services. Experiments on ProgrammableWeb data show that, by fusing the heterogeneous network model and the topic model, we gain a 66.67% improvement on top20 precision and 20%~ 30% improvement on long tail (top200~top500) precision. Furthermore, the reputation and domain-aware recommendation method gains a 118.54% improvement on top10 precision.

Keywords: Heterogeneous Network, Reputation Propagation, Topic Model, Service Recommendation, Service Ecosystem.

1 Introduction

With the wide adoption of service and cloud computing, nowadays we observe a rapidly increasing number of services and their compositions (mashups, workflows) [1]. Internet companies such as Google, Flickr, and Facebook publicly provide the APIs of their services, which effectively motivates individual developers to combine available services (e.g. web services, web APIs) into innovative service-compositions/

S. Basu et al. (Eds.): ICSOC 2013, LNCS 8274, pp. 343–357, 2013.

mashups as a value-add to these existing web services. As a consequence, several domain-specific or general purpose online service ecosystem, such as ProgrammableWeb[1], myExpriment[2] and Biocatalogue[3], have emerged and collected a rapidly increasing number of services and their compositions in recent years. As atomic services are composed into composite ones, they are not isolated but influenced with each other. Thus the services, compositions (mashups, workflows), the service providers and the composition developers together form a complex and evolving service ecosystem. When constructing a composition in the service ecosystem, the straightforward method for the developers is to refer to the related domain and then select the trustworthy services to compose. However, it is difficult to guarantee this trustworthiness in the real practice.

First of all, the querying power in the recent service ecosystems is usually preliminary [2]. Taking ProgrammableWeb as an example, services are registered into a specific category with only a simple word such as "Bookmarks", "Search" and "Social", etc. However, some services naturally belong to multiple domains as they offer different domain-specific functionalities. For example, "del.icio.us" is a famous service for the social bookmarks which also can be used to store the users' bookmarks online and search the bookmarks by tags. Thus it not only belongs to the category "Bookmarks" and "Social" , but also the category "Database" and "Search". Thus in this paper, a topic model based on Latent Dirichlet Allocation (LDA) [3] is used to cluster the services so that we can assign the services into different domains.

Secondly, facing the huge number of services, the developers need to select the desirable services against many other alternatives which are similar to one another. Therefore, the ecosystem should not only list services in different domains but also provide guidelines for selecting the trustworthy ones based on their performance in the past. We define *trust* as the belief that a user has regarded the intention and capability of a service/mashup to behave as expected. We use reputation as a mechanism of establishing the belief about a service's ability to deliver a certain service level objective [4, 14]. The notion underpinning the reputation-based trust models is to capture consumers' perception of the consumed service and use it to evaluate the reputation of the service [5, 20]. Many researches use the quality of service (Qos) combining with the Collaborative Filtering (CF) to calculate the reputation of the services [6-9]. However, it is resource-intensive and sometime impossible to fetch the Qos of the services over time, especially when considering the different Qos metrics that can be applied for different types of services that are deployed remotely. Taking ProgrammableWeb as an example, there is no information about the Qos for most of services. Fortunately, the historical usage information embedded with the related consumers' experiences [10] and the collective perception from the developers can be used to calculate the reputation of services in the ecosystem. In this paper, we present a unified reputation propagation (URP) method to calculate services' reputation so as to facilitate trust-aware recommendations. Furthermore, different services with unique

---

[1] http://www.programmableweb.com
[2] http://www.myexperiment.org/
[3] http://www.biocatalogue.org/

functionalities have specific areas where they can perform better than others [11]. Therefore, combining the services' reputation and the LDA model, we re-rank the services to get a domain-aware recommendation for their specific functionality domains. Based on these, the main contribution of this paper is as follow:

1) We propose a heterogeneous network model of the service ecosystem and the unified reputation propagation (URP) framework is used to calculate the global reputation of various entities in the ecosystem.

2) The LDA model is used to analyze the services in the ecosystem and re-cluster them into different domains. Combing the LDA and the URP-based reputation-ranking method, for the first time, we offer the reputation- and domain-aware service recommendation.

3) Experiments on the real-world dataset, i.e., ProgrammableWeb, show that our method gain a 66.67% improvement on top20 precision and 20%~ 30% improvement on long tail (top200~top500) precision, compared to the methods based on the homogeneous network. Furthermore, the reputation and topic aware recommendation method gains a 118.54% improvement on top10 precision, compared to the domain-only method. Thus our approach can effectively offer trustworthy recommendation for developers.

The rest of the paper is organized as follows. Section 2 introduces a heterogeneous network model and the reputation propagation framework to calculate the global reputation. Section 3 shows the domain-aware recommend method which combines the topic model and the global reputation. Section 4 reports our empirical experiments on the real-world data ProgrammableWeb. Section 5 discusses the related work and Section 6 concludes this paper.

2   Unified Reputation Network Model

2.1   Heterogeneous Network Model

In the service ecosystem, service providers publish services into the ecosystem and then those services are classified into different domains based on their functionalities. Composition developers will choose one or more services and combine them into a composition (i.e. mashup) and publish it into the ecosystem which will be used by consumers. Throughout this paper, we will use "composition" and "mashup" interchangeably as they both combine atomic services to provide added value. Considering these, we can model the ecosystem into a heterogeneous network model which contains developers, mashups, services and providers as well as the relationships among them. Figure 1 shows the schematic diagram of the heterogeneous network and we can formalize it as follow:

Definition 1 (Heterogeneous Network for a Service Ecosystem). A service ecosystem is a heterogeneous network $G = (V, E)$ where $V = \{De, Ma, Se, Pr\}$ refers to the four different types of entities in the ecosystem. De refers to all the developers who publish at least one mashup in the ecosystem. Ma refers to all the mashups. Se refers to the services and Pr refers to the service providers. $E = \{D, Y, P\}$ refers to the three kinds of relationships among the entities. D refers to the developer-mashup network, Y is the mashup-service network and P is the provider-service network. These three networks can be defined in matrix as follows:

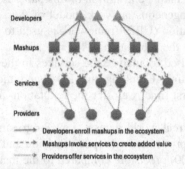

Fig. 1. The heterogeneous network model for service ecosystem which including developers, mashups, services, providers as well as the three kinds of relationships among them

Definition 2 (Developer-mashup Network) The developer-mashup network is used to present the publish relationship between developers De and mashups Ma. It is denoted by a $n \times m$ matrix $D = \left[d_{ij} \right]_{n \times m}$ and the element is

$$d_{ij} = \begin{cases} 1 \text{ if } De_i \text{ develops } Ma_j \\ 0 \qquad otherwise \end{cases}$$ where n refers to the number of developers and m is the number of mashups.

Definition 3 (Mashup-service Network) The mashup-service network is used to present the invoking relationship between mashups Ma and services Se. It is denoted by a $m \times s$ matrix $Y = \left[y_{jk} \right]_{m \times s}$ and the element is $y_{jk} = \begin{cases} 1 \text{ if } Ma_j \text{ invokes } Se_k \\ 0 \qquad otherwise \end{cases}$ where m is the number of mashups and s is the number of services.

Definition 4 (Provider-service Network) The provider-service network is used to present the supply relationship between services and providers. It is denoted by a $p \times s$ matrix $P = \left[p_{ok} \right]_{p \times s}$ and the element $p_{ok} = \begin{cases} 1 \text{ if } Pr_o \text{ provides } Se_k \\ 0 \qquad otherwise \end{cases}$ and p is the number of providers.

Furthermore, based on the definitions shown above, we can get the derivations:

Definition 5 (Service Co-occurrence Network) The service co-occurrence network is denoted by a $s \times s$ matrix $S = [f_{kl}]_{s \times s}$ in which $f_{kk} =$ the number of mashups the service k is invoked and f_{kl} is the number that service k and service l are used together in the same mashup. We denote the main diagonal as $\Lambda = [f_{kk}]_{s \times s}$ and it is easy to get that:

$$f_{kk} = \sum_j y_{jk} \tag{1}$$

Definition 6: Developer reputation is a $n\times1$ vector $R_d = [rd_i]_{n\times1}$ and the element rd_i refers to the reputation of developer i.

Definition 7: Mashup reputation is a $m\times1$ vector $R_y = [ry_j]_{m\times1}$ and the element ry_i refers to the reputation of mashup j.

Definition 8: Service reputation is a $s\times1$ vector $R_x = [rx_k]_{s\times1}$ and the element rx_k refers to the reputation of service k.

Definition 9: Provider reputation is a $p\times1$ vector $R_p = [rp_o]_{p\times1}$ and the element rp_o refers to the reputation of provider o.

2.2 Unified Reputation Propagation Model

It is troublesome to calculate the reputation of the four entities at once in the ecosystem as they are affecting each other simultaneously. However, there are a few basic assumptions that we can take to simplify the calculation:

Assumption 1. **Highly reputable providers will offer many highly reputable services which are invoked in many highly reputable mashups.**

Assumption 2. **Highly reputable developers will develop many highly reputable mashups which invoke the highly reputable services.**

As we known, the evolution of the ecosystem is driven by the enrolling of new mashups and services. However, the services which are never invoked will not affect other services' reputations, including the newly registered one. So the propagation of the reputation in the ecosystem will be activated by the mashup. Thus we get the third assumption in this paper:

Assumption 3. **The reputation of mashups activates the reputation propagation process in the ecosystem.**

Based on these assumptions, we have a simple illustration of the reputation propagation model as Figure 2.

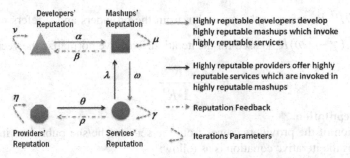

Fig. 2. The unified reputation propagation model for the service ecosystem

Mashup Reputation

The reputation of the mashup is decided by the reputation of the services it invoked and the reputation of its developer. Thus we can get the iterative equation as:

$$R_y^+ \leftarrow \mu R_y + \alpha D^T R_d + \lambda Y \Lambda^{-1} R_x + \xi_y \qquad (2)$$

Here $\mu + \alpha + \lambda \leq 1, \mu \geq 0, \alpha \geq 0, \lambda \geq 0$. $\alpha D^T R_d$ refers to the reputation from its developers; $\lambda Y \Lambda^{-1} R_x$ refers to the reputation from its invoking services, ξ_y refers to the random factors and μR_y is used for iteration. Then the reputation is normalized:

$$R_y^+ \leftarrow \frac{R_y^+}{1 \cdot R_y^+} \qquad (3)$$

Developer Reputation

The reputation of the developer comes from the mashups he/she has ever published in the past. Intuitively, the higher the reputation his/her mashups have, the higher the reputation he/she will gain. Thus the iterative equation can be defined as:

$$R_d^+ \leftarrow v R_d + \beta D R_y^+ + \xi_d \qquad (4)$$

Here $v + \beta \leq 1, v \geq 0, \beta \geq 0$. $\beta D R_y^+$ refers to reputation from the mashups the developers have ever published and ξ_d refers to the random factors. $v R_d$ refers to iteration from the last step. Then the reputation is normalized:

$$R_d^+ \leftarrow \frac{R_d^+}{1 \cdot R_d^+} \qquad (5)$$

Service Reputation

The service reputation comes from the reputation of the mashups it has been invoked in and the reputation of its providers. We define the iterative equation as:

$$R_x^+ \leftarrow (\gamma - \lambda \omega) R_x + \omega Y^T R_y^+ + \theta P^T R_p^+ + \xi_x \qquad (6)$$

Here $\gamma + \omega + \theta \leq 1, \gamma, \omega, \theta \geq 0$. $\omega Y^T R_y^+$ refers to the reputation updating from mashups, $\theta P^T R_p^+$ refers to the reputation from the providers and ξ_x refers to the random factors. $(\gamma - \lambda \omega) R_x$ is used for the iteration. Then we normalize the vector as:

$$R_x^+ \leftarrow \frac{R_x^+}{1 \cdot R_x^+} \qquad (7)$$

Provider Reputation

The reputation of the providers comes from the services he/she published in the ecosystem. Thus the iterative equation is as follow:

$$R_p^+ \leftarrow \eta R_p + \rho P R_x + \xi_p \qquad (8)$$

Here $\eta + \rho \le 1, \eta, \rho \ge 0$. $\rho P R_x$ refers to the reputation from services, ξ_p refers to the random factors and ηR_p is used for iteration. Then we normalize the vector:

$$R_p^+ \leftarrow \frac{R_p^+}{1 \cdot R_p^+} \tag{9}$$

2.3   Model Simplification

Until now, we have proposed the iteration method for the reputation propagation so that we can gain the global reputation of the entities in the ecosystem. By setting different parameter combinations, we can derive three different propagation methods:

Top-Popularity Reputation (TR) Model
Here we set $\alpha = 0, \mu = 1, \lambda = 0, \omega = 1, \theta = 0, \gamma = 0$ and set the random factor $\xi_y = 0, \xi_x = 0$ We can easily get that:

$$R_y = R_y^0 \quad R_x = \frac{Y^T R_y^0}{1 \cdot Y^T R_y^0} = \frac{1}{C} Y^T R_y^0 \tag{10}$$

Where R_y^0 refers to the initial reputation of mashup and $C = 1 \cdot Y^T R_y^0$ will be a constant for different services in the ecosystem. Furthermore, we set $R_y^0 = \left[\frac{1}{m} \right]_{m \times 1}$ which means that the initial reputation for each mashup is equivalent, then we get:

$$R_x(k) \propto \sum_j y_{jk} = f_{kk} \tag{11}$$

This means that the reputations of services are just based on its used frequency.

Page-Rank-Based Reputation (PR) Model
Here we set $\alpha = 0, \mu = 0, \lambda = 1, \theta = 0, \gamma = 0$ and the random factor for mashup's reputation is set as 0, we can easily get that:

$$R_y^+ = \frac{Y \Lambda^{-1} R_x}{1 \cdot Y \Lambda^{-1} R_x} \tag{12}$$

As $1 \cdot Y \Lambda^{-1} R_x = \sum_k r x_k = 1$ we can further get that:

$$R_x^+ = -\omega R_x + \omega Y^T R_y^+ + \xi_x = -\omega R_x + \frac{\omega Y^T Y \Lambda^{-1} R_x}{1 \cdot Y \Lambda^{-1} R_x} + \xi_x \tag{13}$$

$$= \omega (Y^T Y \Lambda^{-1} - I) R_x + \xi_x$$

Setting $\xi_x = (1 - \omega) \left[\frac{1}{n} \right]_{n \times 1}$ we can get that:

$$R_x^+ = \omega(Y^T Y \Lambda^{-1} - I)R_x + (1-\omega)\left[\frac{1}{n}\right]_{n\times 1} \tag{14}$$

$$rx_i^+ = \omega\sum_k \frac{f_{ki}}{f_{kk}}rx_k + \frac{(1-\omega)}{n}, i \neq k \tag{15}$$

Apparently, the reputation of the service is based on the reputation of its neighbors. In this case, our model can be reduced into a page-rank [12] algorithm method just based on the co-occurrence service network.

Developer-Related Reputation (DR) Model

Here we set $\beta = 1, \nu = 0, \mu = 1-\alpha, \lambda = 0, \omega = 1, \gamma = 0, \theta = 0$ and $\xi_y, \xi_d, \xi_x = 0$

which means the reputation of the developers just come from the reputation of mashups, the reputation of the services is decided by the mashups it has been invoked in.

$$R_y^+ = \frac{(1-\alpha)R_y + \alpha D^T R_d}{1\bullet((1-\alpha)R_y + \alpha D^T R_d)} = (1-\alpha)R_y + \alpha D^T R_d \tag{16}$$

$$R_d^+ = \frac{DR_y^+}{1\bullet DR_y^+} = DR_y^+ \quad R_x^+ = \frac{Y^T R_y^+}{1\bullet Y^T R_y^+} \tag{17}$$

Furthermore we can get the reputation for mashups and developers as:

$$R_y^t = (I - \alpha(I - D^T D))^t R_y^0 \quad R_d^t = D(I - \alpha(I - D^T D))^t R_y^0 \tag{18}$$

Here t refers to the number of iterations. If we set $\alpha = 0$, this model will reduce to the TR model.

2.4   Initial Strategy

From the discussion above, we can observe that the global reputation is related to the initial reputation of each mashup. We define two initial reputations as:

1) Equivalent Initial Mashup Reputation (EI): The hypothesis here is that the initial reputation for each mashup is equivalent. We can set that $ER_y^0 = \left[\frac{1}{m}\right]_{m\times 1}$

2) Popularity-based Initial Mashup Reputation (PI): The hypothesis here is that highly reputable mashups will attract consumers' high attention, which will be reflected in their rating and visited number. We define the popularity of the mashup as the product of its rating and visited number. Then we use the normalized popularity as the initial reputation. Thus we can get that $PR_y^0 = \left[prx_i^0\right]_{m\times 1}$

$$prx_i^0 = \frac{Rate(Ma_i)\times Visited(Ma_i)}{\sum_k Rate(Ma_k)\times Visited(Ma_k)} \tag{19}$$

3   Domain-Aware and Reputation-Aware Recommendation

As we discussed in the introduction, the current categorization method for the service ecosystem such as ProgrammableWeb is rather preliminary. Topic model based on LDA performs well for the document analysis, thus we will firstly employ the LDA to analyze the context (tags, description, summary, etc) of the services in the ecosystem and extract different topics from the context. Each topic is considered as a domain and each service will be affixed with the affiliation degree to the domain. Then for each domain, the services with a top-k affiliate degree will be selected and considered as the related services in the domain. Based on the URP framework, we can get the global reputation for each service in the ecosystem which reflects the collective perception from the historical information. Thus we can re-rank the services in each domain by the global reputation so that we can get the top trustworthy services for the developers in each domain. Table 1 shows the detail of our method for the domain-aware and reputation-aware recommendation.

From the algorithm we can see that the topic model is used to cluster the services by their context so that we can get the most related services; then the global reputation is used to re-rank the services by their reputation so that the trustworthy services can be recommended. Thus this method can recommend the highly trustworthy services in each domain for the developers.

Table 1. Combining Topic Model and Reputation for Recommendation

Algorithm: Topic Model with Reputation for Recommend
Input:
(1) Service list Se with the global reputation for each service R_x
(2) Topic/Domain Number: T
(3) Top number of services for each topic: k ; Parameter q
Output:
(1) Top-k services for each Topic
01. Running LDA method to extract the T topics in the service list
02. For each topic, sort the services by its affiliate degree then get the top qk services
03. Sort the qk services by the reputation R_x and then get the top-k services for each topic

4   Empirical Study on ProgrammableWeb

4.1   Experiment Data Set

To the best of our knowledge, ProgrammableWeb is by far the largest online repository of web services, and their mashups. In this paper, we obtain the data regarding services and compositions from June 2005 to March 2013. Each service contains the information such as name, provider, category, publication date, summary and description; each mashup contains the information such as name, creation data, developer, the list of services in it, its description and its visited number as well as the user rating; each developer contains the information including name and the mashups he/she registered.

In order to examine the performance of our method, we separate the dataset into two sets: one set contains the mashups published from June 2005 to August 2012 which we use as the **Training Data** to calculate the global reputation and the topics in the ecosystem; the other set contains the mashups published from September 2012 to March 2013 which we use as the **Testing Data** to test the performance of our approach. Table 2 reports some basic statistics of our experiment dataset.

Table 2. Basic Statistic of the ProgrammableWeb Data for Experiment

	Training Period (2005.6~2012.8)	Testing Period (2012.9~2013.3)
Number of Services	7077	805
Number of Mashups	6726	212
Number of Developer[*]	2383	127
Number of Providers	5905	699

[*]: Only the developers who publish at least one mashup are considered

4.2   Evaluation Metrics

In order to evaluate the performance of each approach, we use the existence of the services in the testing period as the ground truth.

$$y(Se_i) = \begin{cases} 1 & Se_i \ exist \ in \ the \ testing \ period \\ 0 & otherwise \end{cases} \quad (20)$$

As the invoked frequencies of different services during the testing period are different, we can use the frequency $f(Se_i)$ as the ground truth. If a service does not appear in the testing period, then $f(Se_i) = 0$. Based on these, we can consider the precision ($P @ k$), and discounted cumulative gain ($D @ k$) which are defined as:

$$P @ k = \frac{\sum_{Se_i \in top-k} y(Se_i)}{k} \qquad D @ k = \sum_{Se_i \in top-k} \frac{f(Se_i)}{\log(1 + \pi(Se_i))} \quad (21)$$

Here $\pi(Se_i)$ is the position of the service in the reputation ranking list. Furthermore, given an approach as the baseline, we can calculate the difference discounted cumulative gain ($DD @ k$):

$$DD @ k = \frac{D @ k - D @ k(Baseline)}{D @ k(Baseline)} \quad (22)$$

4.3   Performance Comparison

Global Reputation Ranking Based on URP Framework

Based on the discussion shown above, we will consider three propagation models: 1) Top-Popularity Reputation Model (TPR) in which the reputation of each service is just based on its used frequency; 2) Page-Rank-Based Reputation Model (PRR) in which the reputation of each service is related to its co-occurrence services and 3) Developer-related Reputation Model (DRR) in which the reputation of the developers is taken into account. For each model we will consider the two initial strategies (EI and PI) we discuss in Section 2.4. Thus we can get six models such as: TPR+EI, TPR+PI, PRR+EI, PRR+PI, DRR+EI and DRR+PI.

In order to compare the performance of the heterogeneous network, we define two methods which just employ the information of the service co-occurrence network. In fact, the service co-occurrence network is a homogeneous network.

1) Top-Degree Reputation Model (TDR): The reputation of each service is the normalization of its network degree in the service co-occurrence network.

2) Homogeneous Page-Rank Reputation Model (HPRR): The page rank algorithm is run on the service co-occurrence network and then the reputation of each service is the normalization of its page rank value.

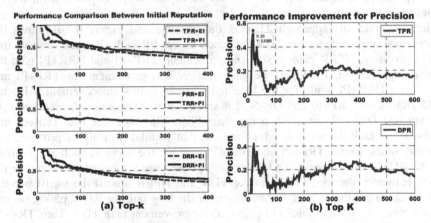

Fig. 3. Performance Comparison. (a) Performance comparison between different initial reputation of mashups. (b) Performance improvement in precision.

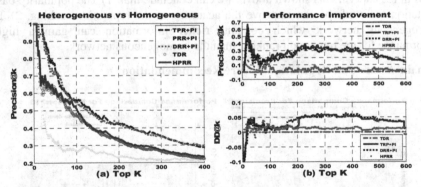

Fig. 4. Performance comparison between heterogeneous network methods and homogeneous network methods

Figure 3 shows the performance comparison between different initial reputations. We can observe that TPR model and DRR model are sensitive to the intitial mashup reputation. For TPR, the precision improvement for the top20 is up to 53.85% while for the long tail (top200~top500) is about 20%; For DRR, the precision improvement for top20 is up to 42.85% while for the long tail (top200~top500) is also about 20%. However for the PRR model, it is not sensitive to the initial mashup reputation and the two models have the extractly same performance. From the result, we can conclude that in practice, taking the mashup's popularity into account can help to improve the performance.

Figure 4 shows the performance comparison between the heterogeneous network and homogeneous network. From Figure 4 (a), we can observe that TPR+PI and DRR+PI gain consistently higher performance than TDR and HPRR. However, PRR+PI is the worst method in our experiment. One reason is that in ProgrammableWeb, the distribution of the service usage frequency meets the power-law distribution and only few services are very popular, for example, "*Google Map*" appears in 2975 mashups. This makes the reputation propagation from service to mashup useless.

Here, we take the approach TDR as the baseline and Figure 4 (b) shows the performance improvement for the approaches except PRR+PI. We can observe that for the precision, HPRR gains a slight improvement; TRP+PI and DRR+PI gain the similar improvement, for top20 we gain a 66.67% improvement for TRP+PI and 61.53% for DRR+PI while for the long tail we gain a 30% improvement. Also the top15 DD@k for TRP+PI and DRR+PI is smaller than TDR while the precision for TRP+PI and DRR+PI are much better than TDR. This indicates that TRP+PI and DRR+PI will rank the services which are not that popular in a higher position. For example, in the top10, TRP+PI and DRR+PI will get the services such as "*Twilio*", "*Twilio SMS*", "*Foursquare*" and "*Box.net*" whose usage frequencies are not in the top10. However, the top10 services for TDR and HPRR are all the top10 popular services in the training period. Furthermore, for the long tail (top200~top500), we can observe that TRP+PI and DRR+PI gain a 5% improvement than TDR. Thus TRP+PI and DRR+PI can gain a higher performance than TDR and HPRR for the services which are not so popular in the past.

From the experiments shown above, we can conclude that: 1) The popularity-based reputation for mashups can improve the accuracy of the reputation ranking. 2) The heterogeneous network which contains richer information can gain a higher performance for the reputation ranking than the homogeneous network.

Domain-Aware and Reputation-Aware Recommendation

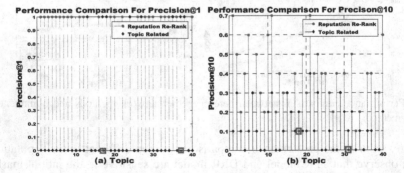

Fig. 5. Effectiveness of Reputation-based Recommendation

Another observation from the experiments is that the TRP+PI and DRR+PI gain higher performances than the others. Thus in this paper, we just employ DRR+PI to generate the global reputations for each services. Then the LDA-based topic model implemented in Mallet[4] is used to extract the different domains from the context of the services in the ecosystem. Here we set the number of domains to be 40. For each domain, we get the top 50 services based on the topic affiliate degree and consider then as the related services in the certain domain. Finally, we re-rank the services in each domain based on the global reputation and get the top-10 services as the recommendation for the providers. For simplicity, we name our approach as "RR".

In order to show the performance of our method, we consider the approach which only based on the domain affiliation degree. For simplicity, we name it as "TR". From Figure 5. We can observe that for the top1 recommendation, RR performances better than TR in 24 (60%) domains and worse than TR only in 2 (5%) domains; For the top10 recommendation, RR still performances better than TR in 60% domains and worse in 5% domains. Furthermore, the average improvement for the precison@10 is up to 118.54%.

5   Related Work

5.1   Reputation Based Trust for Recommendation

The concept of trust is not new. Trust has been studied in many disciplines including sociology, economics, and computer science [13]. In this paper, we consider the reputation based trust [14]. There are three groups of trust models for social networks: graph based trust models, interaction based trust models[7] and hybrid trust models [8]. These models aggregate the opinions of other users in the trust network to generate personalized recommendation for consumers. Recently, some researches employ the Quality of Service (Qos) combining with the Collaborative Filtering (CF) to calculate the reputation of the services for recommendation [6,8].

Recommender systems often exploit explicit trust data to generate recommended list. Explicit data sources include user profiles, articulated friend networks, or group memberships. Recommenders often exploit explicit friendships or linkages to generate recommendation lists [19, 21]. User profile data can be used to identify articles and other content believed to be relevant to users [22].

These approaches can yield good results when the services have complete metadata. However, in practice, most of the service ecosystem will not contain detail feedback from the users and the Qos for each service is resource-intensive to fetch, especially when considering the different Qos over time or at the different location. Thus from a different perspective, we just employ the historical popularity and the topological information to calculate the reputation of the services.

5.2   Complex Network for Service Ecosystem

The increasingly growth of Web services has attracted much attention in recent years. Many works employ the network analysis method to study the web service ecosystem as complex network analysis is a powerful tool to understand the large scale networks

---

4   http://mallet.cs.umass.edu/topics.php

[15]. Yu and Woodard presented a preliminary result in studying the properties in ProgrammableWeb and proved that the cumulative frequency of APIs follows power law distribution [16]. Wang et al emphasized on mining mashup community from users' perspective by analyzing the User-API and User-Tag network in ProgrammableWeb [17]. Our previous work [18] studied the usage pattern of services in ProgrammableWeb based on the social network analysis.

Unlike the existing studies shown above, our work constructs a heterogeneous network for the service ecosystem and then formalizes the reputation propagation in the ecosystem. Furthermore, we take the difference between domains into account so that we can offer a domain-aware and reputation-aware recommendation.

6   Conclusion and Future Work

With the widely adoption of Service Oriented Architecture, we can observe a rapidly increasing number of services and their compositions these days. When exploring a service repository to choose services among those with similar functions, it is important to provide guidelines for the developers to select the trusted services.   To the best of our knowledge, we are the first to: 1) Introduce a heterogeneous network model for a service ecosystem and the unified reputation propagation (URP) framework to calculate reputations in the service ecosystem. 2) Combine the LDA-based topic model with the URP to offer a domain-aware and reputation-aware service recommendation for the developers.

We conducted a comprehensive set of experiments on ProgrammableWeb and the results show the effectiveness of our method: 1) Taking the mashups' popularity into account gains a 40%~50% improvement for top20 precision and about 20% improvement for the long tail (top200~top500); 2) Compared with the method based on the homogeneous network, the heterogeneous network based methods such as TPR with PI and DRR with PI gain at least 60% improvement for top20 precision and 30% for the long tail (top200~top500); 3) Combining the reputation and domain, we get an 118.54% improvement for top10 precision compared to the domain-only method, which indicates that we can offer the trustworthy recommendation for each domain.

In the future, we will further our study on the implications of different parameters in our reputation propagation model, and the approach to find an optimal set of parameters for reputation calculation.

Acknowledgments. This work is partially supported by the National Natural Science Foundation of China (No. 61174169) and the National High Technology Research and Development Program of China (863Program, No. 2012AA040915)

References

1. Al-Masri, E., Mahmoud, Q.H.: Investigating web services on the world wide web. In: Proc. 17th International Conference on World Wide Web, pp. 795–804 (2008)
2. Wang, J., Zhang, J., Hung, P.C.K., Li, Z., Liu, J., He, K.: Leveraging fragmental semantic data to enhance services discovery. In: IEEE International Conference on High Performance Computing and Communications (2011)
3. Blei, D.M., Lafferty, J.D.: Dynamic topic models. In: Proc. 23rd International Conference on Machine Learning, pp. 113–120 (2006)

4. Mollering, G.: The Nature of Trust: From Geog Simmel to a Theory of Expectation, Interpretation and Suspension. Sociology 35, 403–420 (2002)
5. Cook, K.S., Yamagishi, T., Cheshire, C., Cooper, R., Matsuda, M., Mashima, R.: Trust building via risk taking: A cross-societal experiment. Social Psychology Quarterly 68, 121–142 (2005)
6. Cao, J., Wu, Z., Wang, Y., Zhuang, Y.: Hybrid Collaborative Filtering algorithm for bidirectional Web service recommendation. Knowledge and Information Systems, 1–21 (2012)
7. Yao, J., Chen, S., Wang, C., Levy, D.: Modelling Collaborative Services for Business and QoS Compliance. In: Proc. International Conference on Web Services (ICWS), pp. 299–306 (2011)
8. Wang, Y., Vassileva, J.: A review on trust and reputation for web service selection. In: 27th International Conference on Distributed Computing Systems Workshops (2007)
9. Wu, Y., Yan, C., Ding, Z., Liu, G., Wang, P., Jiang, C., Zhou, M.: A Novel Method for Calculating Service Reputation. IEEE Transactions on Automation Science and Engineering 99, 1–9 (2013)
10. Zhang, J., Tan, W., Alexander, J., Foster, I., Madduri, R.: Recommend-As-You-Go: A Novel Approach Supporting Services-Oriented Scientific Workflow Reuse. In: IEEE International Conference on Services Computing, pp. 48–55 (2011)
11. Gupta, M., Sun, Y., Han, J.: Trust analysis with clustering. In: Proc. 20th International Conference Companion on World Wide Web, pp. 53–54 (2011)
12. Page, L., Brin, S., Motwani, R., Winograd, T.: The PageRank citation ranking: bringing order to the web, Technical Report, Stanford Digital Library Technologies Project (1999)
13. Yao, J., Tan, W., Nepal, S., Chen, S., Zhang, J., De Roure, D., Goble, C.: ReputationNet: a Reputation Engine to Enhance ServiceMap by Recommending Trusted Services. In: IEEE Ninth International Conference on Services Computing, pp. 454–461 (2012)
14. Nepal, S., Malik, Z., Bouguettaya, A.: Reputation management for composite services in service-oriented systems. International Journal of Web Services Research 8, 29–52 (2011)
15. Tan, W., Zhang, J., Foster, I.: Network Analysis of Scientific Workflows: A Gateway to Reuse. IEEE Computer 43, 54–61 (2010)
16. Yu, S., Woodard, C.J.: Innovation in the programmable web: Characterizing the mashup ecosystem. In: Feuerlicht, G., Lamersdorf, W. (eds.) ICSOC 2008. LNCS, vol. 5472, pp. 136–147. Springer, Heidelberg (2009)
17. Wang, J., Chen, H., Zhang, Y.: Mining user behavior pattern in mashup community. In: IEEE International Conference on Information Reuse & Integration, pp. 126–131 (2009)
18. Huang, K., Fan, Y., Tan, W.: An Empirical Study of Programmable Web: A Network Analysis on a Service-Mashup System. In: IEEE 19th International Conference on Web Services, pp. 552–559 (2012)
19. Chen, J., Geyer, W., Dugan, C., Muller, M., Guy, I.: Make new friends, but keep the old: recommending people on social networking sites. In: Proceedings of the SIGCHI Conference on Human Factors in Computing Systems, pp. 201–210. ACM, Boston (2009)
20. Massa, P., Avesani, P.: Trust-aware recommender systems. In: Proc. ACM Conference on Recommender Systems (2007)
21. Guy, I., Ur, S., Ronen, I., Perer, A., Jacovi, M.: Do you want to know?: recommending strangers in the enterprise. In: Proceedings of the ACM 2011 Conference on Computer Supported Cooperative Work, pp. 285–294. ACM, Hangzhou (2011)
22. Liu, H., Maes, P.: Interestmap: Harvesting social network profiles for recommendations. Beyond Personalization-IUI (2005)

Service Discovery from Observed Behavior while Guaranteeing Deadlock Freedom in Collaborations

Richard Müller[1,2], Christian Stahl[2],
Wil M.P. van der Aalst[2,3], and Michael Westergaard[2,3]

[1] Institut für Informatik, Humboldt-Universität zu Berlin, Germany
Richard.Mueller@informatik.hu-berlin.de
[2] Department of Mathematics and Computer Science,
Technische Universiteit Eindhoven, The Netherlands
{C.Stahl,W.M.P.v.d.Aalst,M.Westergaard}@tue.nl
[3] National Research University Higher School of Economics, Moscow, 101000, Russia

Abstract. Process discovery techniques can be used to derive a process model from observed example behavior (i.e., an event log). As the observed behavior is inherently incomplete and models may serve different purposes, four competing quality dimensions—fitness, precision, simplicity, and generalization—have to be balanced to produce a process model of high quality.

In this paper, we investigate the discovery of processes that are specified as services. Given a service S and observed behavior of a service P interacting with S, we discover a service model of P. Our algorithm balances the four quality dimensions based on user preferences. Moreover, unlike existing discovery approaches, we guarantees that the composition of S and P is deadlock free. The service discovery technique has been implemented in ProM and experiments using service models of industrial size demonstrate the scalability or our approach.

1 Introduction

Service-oriented design [24] reduces system complexity, and service models are useful to understand the running system, to verify the system's correctness, and to analyze its performance. However, it is often not realistic to assume that there exists a service model. Even if there exists a formal model of the implemented service, it can differ significantly from the actual implementation; The formal model may have been implemented incorrectly, or the implementation may have been changed over time. Fortunately, we can often *observe behavior* recorded in the form of an *event log.* Such event logs may be extracted from databases, message logs, or audit trails. Given an event log, there exist techniques to produce a (service) model. The term *service discovery* [5] or, more general, *process discovery* [3] has been coined for such techniques.

In this paper, we assume a known service model S and an event log L containing observed behavior in the form of message sequences being exchanged between

S. Basu et al. (Eds.): ICSOC 2013, LNCS 8274, pp. 358–373, 2013.
© Springer-Verlag Berlin Heidelberg 2013

(instances of) the implementation of S and (instances of) its environment (i.e., the services S interacts with) to be given. Our goal is to produce a model of the environment of S. As the event log is inherently incomplete (i.e., not all possible behavior was necessarily observed), there are, in general, infinitely many models of the environment of S. Clearly, some models might be more appropriate than others regarding some user requirements. Therefore, service discovery can be seen as a *search process*: We search for a model of the environment that describes the observed behavior "best".

To judge the discovered model we consider two aspects: *correctness* (internal consistency of model, e.g., no deadlocks) and *quality* (ability to describe the underlying observed process well).

Correctness is motivated by the discovery of sound workflow models in [10], where soundness refers to the ability to always terminate [1]. In our service-oriented setting, it is reasonable to require that S and its environment interact correctly. As a minimal requirement of correct interaction, we assume *deadlock freedom* throughout this paper. We refer to such model of the environment of S as a *partner* of S. Thus, we are interested in discovering a partner of S.

Regarding quality, there exist four quality dimensions for general process models [3]: (1) *fitness* (i.e., the discovered model should allow the behavior seen in the event log), (2) *precision* (i.e., the discovered model should not allow behavior completely unrelated to what was seen in the event log), (3) *generalization* (i.e., the discovered model should generalize the example behavior seen in the event log), and (4) *simplicity* (i.e., the discovered model should be as simple as possible). These quality dimensions compete with each other. For example, to improve the fitness of a model one may end up with a substantially more complex model. A more general model usually means a less precise model. We assume that a user guides the balancing of these four quality dimensions. As a consequence, we aim at *discovering a service model that is a partner of S and, in addition, balances the four quality dimensions guided by user preferences.*

The actual challenge is now to find such a model. As a service S has, in general, infinitely many partners, the search space for service discovery is *infinite*. Therefore, we are using a *genetic algorithm* to find a good but possibly not an optimal model of a partner of S. We have implemented this algorithm. It takes a service model S, an event log, and values for the four quality dimensions as input. The output of the algorithm is a model of a partner of S that comes close to the specified values of the quality dimensions. We show its applicability using eight service models of industrial size. Moreover, based on the notion of a *finite* representation of all partners of S [14]—referred to as *operating guideline*—we additionally apply an *abstraction* that reduces the search space to a finite one. Although the abstraction only preserves fitness, our experimental results show that the other quality dimensions do not suffer too much due to this abstraction. An full version of this paper including a more detailed discussion on the abstraction and the experimental results has been published as a technical report in [22].

Summarizing, the main contributions of this paper are:

- *adapting existing discovery techniques* for workflows (i.e., closed systems) to services (i.e., reactive systems);
- *adapting the metrics for the four quality dimensions* to cope with service models;
- presenting an approach to *reduce an infinite search space to a finite one*; and
- *validation of the algorithm* based on a prototype.

We continue with a motivating example in Sect. 2. Section 3 provides background information on our formal service model and process discovery techniques. Section 4 adapts existing discovery techniques and metrics for workflows for service mining and reduces the infinite search space to a finite one. We present experimental results in Sect. 5. Section 6 reviews related work, and Section 7 concludes the paper.

2   Motivating Example

Figure 1 shows a service S modeled as a state machine, and an event log L. A transition label $!x$ ($?x$) denotes the sending (receiving) of a message x to (from) the environment of S. The event log L contains information on 210 traces. There are three types of traces: ac (10 times), ad (100 times), and bd (100 times). Our goal is to produce a model of the environment of S. Two example models are P and R in Fig. 1. P incorporates the frequently observed behavior in L (traces ad and bd) and disregards trace ac, arguing that ac is negligible for a "good" model. R incorporates even more than the observed behavior in L—for example, the trace bc which was not observed in the interaction with S—generalizing the observed behavior in L in account for L's incompleteness.

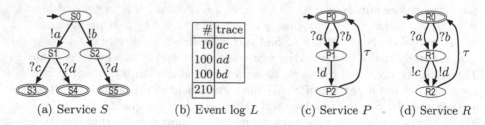

#	trace
10	ac
100	ad
100	bd
210	

(a) Service S (b) Event log L (c) Service P (d) Service R

Fig. 1. Running example: The event log L represents observed communication behavior of S and its environment

The service P is a partner of S—they both interact without running into a deadlock—whereas the service R is not: If S sends a message b, then R receives this message b and may send a message c. However, S cannot receive message c and R does not send any additional messages unless it receives a message a or b. Thus, the interaction of S and R deadlocks. For this reason, we prefer P over R and our discovery algorithm would exclude R. Classical process mining approaches do not take S into account and will allow for models that deadlock when composed.

3   Preliminaries

For two sets A and B, $A \uplus B$ denotes the disjoint union, i.e., writing $A \uplus B$ expresses the implicit assumption that A and B are disjoint. Let $\mathbb{N}^+$ denote the positive integers. For a set A, $|A|$ denotes the cardinality of A, $\mathcal{B}(A)$ the set of all multisets (bags) over A, and $[\,]$ the empty multiset. Throughout the paper, we assume a finite set of *actions* $\mathcal{A}$ such that $\{\tau, final\} \cap \mathcal{A} = \emptyset$.

For a set A, let A^* be the set of finite sequences (words) over A. For two words v and w, $v \sqsubseteq w$ denotes that v is a *prefix* of w. For a ternary relation $R \subseteq A \times B \times A$, we shall use $a \xrightarrow{b}_R a'$ to denote $(a, b, a') \in R$. If any of the elements a, b, or a' is omitted, we mean the existence of such an element. The relation $R^* \subseteq A \times B^* \times A$ is the *reflexive and transitive closure* of R, defined by $a \xrightarrow{b_1 \ldots b_n}_{R^*} a'$ if and only if there are $a_0, \ldots, a_n \in A$ such that $a = a_0$, $a' = a_n$, and, for all $1 \leq i \leq n$, $a_{i-1} \xrightarrow{b_i}_R a_i$. If $a \rightarrow_{R^*} a'$, then a' is *reachable* from a in R.

3.1   State Machines for Modeling Services

We model a service as a *state machine* extended by an *interface*, thereby restricting ourselves to the service's communication protocol. An interface consists of two disjoint sets of input and output labels corresponding to asynchronous message channels. In the model, we abstract from data and identify each message by the label of its message channel.

Definition 1 (State Machine). A *state machine* $S = (Q, \alpha, \Omega, \delta, I, O)$ consists of a finite set Q of *states*, an *initial state* $\alpha \in Q$, a set of *final states* $\Omega \subseteq Q$, a *transition relation* $\delta \subseteq Q \times (I \uplus O \uplus \{\tau\}) \times Q$, and two disjoint, finite sets of *input labels* $I \subseteq \mathcal{A}$ and *output labels* $O \subseteq \mathcal{A}$.

Let $l(t) = a$ define the label of a transition $t = (q, a, q') \in \delta$. We canonically extend l to sequences of transitions. For a state $q \in Q$, define by $en(q) = \{a \mid q \xrightarrow{a}_\delta\}$ the set of labels of outgoing transitions of q. The set $\mathcal{R}(S) = \{q \mid \alpha \rightarrow_{\delta^*} q\}$ denotes the *reachable states* of S. The state machine S is *deterministic* if for all $q, q', q'' \in Q$ and $a \in I \uplus O$, $(q, \tau, q') \in \delta$ implies $q = q'$ and $(q, a, q'), (q, a, q'') \in \delta$ implies $q' = q''$; it is *deadlock free* if, for all $q \in \mathcal{R}(S)$, $en(q) = \emptyset$ implies $q \in \Omega$.

Graphically, we precede each transition label x with ? (!) to denote an input (output) label. A final state is depicted with a double circle (e.g., S_3 in Fig. 1(a)). An incoming arc denotes the initial state (e.g., S_0 in Fig. 1(a)).

For the composition of state machines, we assume that their interfaces completely overlap. We refer to state machines that fulfill this property as *composable*. We compose two composable state machines S and R by building a product automaton $S \oplus R$, thereby turning all transitions into (internal) τ-transitions. In addition, a multiset stores the pending messages between S and R.

Definition 2 (Composition). Two state machines S and R are *composable* if $I_S = O_R$ and $O_S = I_R$. The *composition* of two composable state machines S and

R is the state machine $S \oplus R = (Q, \alpha, \Omega, \delta, \emptyset, \emptyset)$ with $Q = Q_S \times Q_R \times \mathcal{B}(I_S \uplus I_R)$, $\alpha = (\alpha_S, \alpha_R, [\,])$, $\Omega = \Omega_S \times \Omega_R \times \{[\,]\}$, δ containing exactly the following elements:

- $(q_S, q_R, B) \xrightarrow{\ \tau\ }_\delta (q_S', q_R, B)$, if $q_S \xrightarrow{\ \tau\ }_{\delta_S} q_S'$,
- $(q_S, q_R, B) \xrightarrow{\ \tau\ }_\delta (q_S, q_R', B)$, if $q_R \xrightarrow{\ \tau\ }_{\delta_R} q_R'$,
- $(q_S, q_R, B + [a]) \xrightarrow{\ \tau\ }_\delta (q_S', q_R, B)$, if $q_S \xrightarrow{\ a\ }_{\delta_S} q_S'$ and $a \in I_S$,
- $(q_S, q_R, B + [a]) \xrightarrow{\ \tau\ }_\delta (q_S, q_R', B)$, if $q_R \xrightarrow{\ a\ }_{\delta_R} q_R'$ and $a \in I_R$,
- $(q_S, q_R, B) \xrightarrow{\ \tau\ }_\delta (q_S', q_R, B + [a])$, if $q_S \xrightarrow{\ a\ }_{\delta_S} q_S'$ and $a \in O_S$, and
- $(q_S, q_R, B) \xrightarrow{\ \tau\ }_\delta (q_S, q_R', B + [a])$, if $q_R \xrightarrow{\ a\ }_{\delta_R} q_R'$ and $a \in O_R$.   ⌐

We compare two state machines S and R by a *simulation relation*, thereby treating τ like any action in $\mathcal{A}$. A binary relation $\varrho \subseteq Q_S \times Q_R$ is a *simulation relation* of S by R if (1) $(\alpha_S, \alpha_R) \in \varrho$, and (2) for all $(q_S, q_R) \in \varrho$, $a \in \mathcal{A} \uplus \{\tau\}$, $q_S' \in Q_S$ such that $q_S \xrightarrow{\ a\ }_S q_S'$, there exists a state $q_R' \in Q_R$ such that $q_R \xrightarrow{\ a\ }_R q_R'$ and $(q_S', q_R') \in \varrho$. If such a ϱ exists, we say that R *simulates* S. A simulation relation ϱ of S by R is *minimal*, if for all simulation relations ϱ' of S by R, $\varrho \subseteq \varrho'$.

We want the composition of two services to be *correct*. As a minimal criterion for correctness, we require deadlock freedom and that every reachable state contains only finitely many pending messages (i.e., the message channels are bounded). We refer to two services that interact correctly as *partners*.

Definition 3 (b-Partner). Let $b \in \mathbb{N}^+$. A state machine R is a b-*partner* of a state machine S if $S \oplus R$ is deadlock free and for all $(q_S, q_R, B) \in \mathcal{R}(S \oplus R)$ and all $a \in I_S \uplus I_R$, $B(a) \leq b$.   ⌐

In Fig. 1, P is a 1-partner of S, but R is not because the composition $S \oplus R$ can deadlock.

If a state machine S has one b-partner, then it has infinitely many b-partners. Lohmann et al. [14] introduce operating guidelines as a way to represent the infinite set of b-partners of S in a finite manner. Technically, an operating guideline is a deterministic state machine T where each state is annotated with a Boolean formula Φ, which specifies the allowed combinations of outgoing transitions. A state machine R is represented by an operating guideline if (1) there exists a minimal simulation relation ϱ of R by T (as T is deterministic, ϱ is uniquely defined); and (2) for every pair of states $(q_R, q_T) \in \varrho$, the outgoing transitions of q_R and the fact whether q_R is a final state must define a satisfying assignment to $\Phi(q_T)$.

Definition 4 (b-Operating Guideline). An *annotated state machine* (T, Φ) consists of a deterministic state machine T and a Boolean annotation Φ, assigning to each state $q \in Q$ of T a *Boolean formula* $\Phi(q)$ over the literals $I \uplus O \uplus \{\tau, \text{final}\}$.

A state machine R *matches* with (T, Φ) if there exists a minimal simulation relation ϱ of R by T such that for all $(q_R, q_T) \in \varrho$, $\Phi(q_T)$ evaluates to *true* for the following assignment β: $\beta(a) = \text{true}$ if $a \neq \text{final} \wedge q_R \xrightarrow{\ a\ }_{\delta_R}$ or $a = \text{final} \wedge q_R \in \Omega_R$, and $\beta(a) = \text{false}$ otherwise.

Let $b \in \mathbb{N}^+$. The *b-operating guideline* $OG_b(S)$ of a state machine S is an annotated state machine such that for all state machines R, R matches with $OG_b(S)$ iff R is a b-partner of S.

Figure 2a depicts $OG_1(S) = (T, \Phi)$ of the service S. The state machine P (Fig. 1c) matches with (T, Φ): The minimal simulation relation of P by T is $\varrho = \{(P_0, T_0), (P_1, T_3), (P_1, T_1), (P_2, T_5), (P_2, T_4), (P_0, T_5), (P_0, T_4), (P_1, T_7), (P_2, T_7), (P_0, T_7)\}$, and the formula Φ is evaluated to true, for all pairs of ϱ. For example, for (P_0, T_0) we have $\Phi(P_0) = (true \vee false) \wedge (true \vee false) = true$, and for (P_0, T_4) we have $\Phi(T_4) = true$. Thus, P is a 1-partner of S. Figure 2b depicts the smallest subgraph G of $OG_1(S)$ such that P is still simulated by G, i.e., the subgraph used for the simulation relation above. In contrast to P, the state machine R (Fig. 1d) does not match with (T, Φ), because (R_1, T_1) violates the simulation relation: We have $R_1 \xrightarrow{!c}$ but $T_1 \not\xrightarrow{!c}$. Thus, R is not a 1-partner of S.

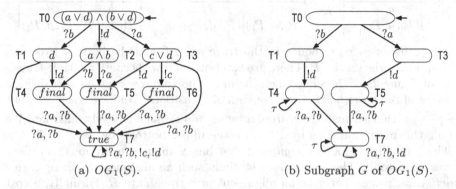

(a) $OG_1(S)$.   (b) Subgraph G of $OG_1(S)$.

Fig. 2. $OG_1(S)$ and its smallest subgraph G such that P is simulated by G. The annotation of a state is depicted inside the state. For $OG_1(S)$, every state has a τ-labeled self-loop and the annotation an additional disjunct τ, which is omitted in the figure for reasons of readability.

In the remainder of the paper, we abstract from the actual bound chosen and use the terms partner and operating guideline rather than b-partner and b-operating guideline.

3.2 Event Logs and Alignments

An *event log* is a multiset of traces. Each trace describes the communication between S and R in a particular case in terms of a sequence of events (i.e., sent and received messages). We describe an event as an action label and abstract from extra information, such as the message content or the timestamp of the message. Formally, a trace $w \in \mathcal{A}^*$ is a sequence of actions, and $L \in \mathcal{B}(\mathcal{A}^*)$ is an event log.

To compare a (discovered) service model R with the given event log L, we use the alignment-based approach described in [4]. This approach relates each trace $w \in L$ to a sequence σ of transitions of R that can be executed from R's initial state by pairing events in w to events of σ.

Formally, a *move* is a pair $(x, y) \in ((\mathcal{A} \uplus \{\gg\}) \times (\delta_R \uplus \{\gg\})) \setminus \{(\gg, \gg)\}$. We call (x, y) a *move in the model* if $x =\gg \wedge y \neq \gg$, a *move in the log* if $x \neq \gg \wedge y =\gg$, a *synchronous move* if $x \neq \gg \wedge y \neq \gg$, and a *silent move* if $x =\gg \wedge y \neq \gg \wedge l(y) = \tau$.

An *alignment* of a trace $w \in L$ to R is a sequence $\gamma = (x_1, y_1) \ldots (x_k, y_k)$ of moves such that the projection of $(x_1 \ldots x_k)$ to $\mathcal{A}$ is w, the projection of $(y_1 \ldots y_k)$ to δ_R is $(\alpha_R, a_1, q_1) \ldots (q_{j-1}, a_j, q_j)$, and transition label $l(y_i)$ and action x_i coincide for every synchronous move (x_i, y_i) of γ. Let $trace(\gamma) \in \mathcal{A}^*$ denote the word $l(y_1) \ldots l(y_k)$ with all τ-labels removed.

Some alignments for L and P in Fig. 1 are:

$$\gamma_1 = \begin{array}{|c|c|} \hline a & c \\ \hline a & \gg \\ \hline (P_0, a, P_1) & \\ \hline \end{array} \quad \gamma_2 = \begin{array}{|c|c|} \hline a & d \\ \hline a & d \\ \hline (P_0, a, P_1) & (P_1, d, P_2) \\ \hline \end{array} \quad \gamma_3 = \begin{array}{|c|c|} \hline b & d \\ \hline b & d \\ \hline (P_0, b, P_1) & (P_1, d, P_2) \\ \hline \end{array}$$

The top row of γ_1 corresponds to the trace $ac \in L$ and the bottom two rows correspond to the service P. There are two bottom rows because multiple transitions of P may have the same label; the upper bottom row consists of transition labels, and the lower bottom row consists of transitions. We have $\alpha_P \xrightarrow{a}{}_{\delta_P^*}$ but $\alpha_P \xcancel{\xrightarrow{ac}}{}_{\delta_P^*}$; that is, ac deviates from a by an additional c-labeled transition. We denote this move in the log by a "$\gg$" in the upper bottom row.

The goal is to find a *best alignment* that has as many synchronous and silent moves as possible. The approach in [4] finds such an alignment by using a *cost function on moves*. Let γ be an alignment of a trace w to R. Formally, a cost function κ assigns to each move (x, y) of an alignment γ a cost $\kappa((x, y))$ such that a synchronous or silent move has cost 0, and all other types of moves have cost > 0. The cost of γ is $\kappa(\gamma) = \sum_{i=1}^{k} \kappa((x_i, y_i))$; γ is a best alignment if, for all alignments γ' of w to R, $\kappa(\gamma') \geq \kappa(\gamma)$. We use the function λ_R to denote, for each trace $w \in L$, a best alignment of w to R.

Finally, we combine the best alignment of each trace of L to R into a weighted automaton AA. A state of AA encodes a sequence of (labels of) transitions of R. We define the weight $\omega(w)$ of each state w as the number of times a trace of L was aligned to w. We shall use AA for the computation of metrics for the two quality dimensions precision and generalization later on.

Definition 5 (Alignment Automaton). The *alignment automaton* $AA(L, R) = (V, v_0, E, \omega)$ of L and R consists of a set of states $V = \mathcal{A}^*$, an initial state $v_0 = \varepsilon$ (ε is the empty trace), a transition relation $E \subseteq V \times \mathcal{A} \times V$ with $v \xrightarrow{a}{}_E va$ iff there exists $w \in L$ such that $va \sqsubseteq trace(\lambda_R(w))$, and a weight function $\omega : V \to \mathbb{N}^+$ such that $\omega(v) = \sum_{w \in L \wedge v \sqsubseteq trace(\lambda_R(w))} L(w)$ for all $v \in V$. ⌟

Figure 3 depicts the alignment automaton $AA(L, P)$ of the event log L and the state machine P. Each trace in L is either aligned to the transition sequence labeled with a, ad or bd (ignoring τ's), as a transition sequence labeled with ac is not present in P. The weight of each state is depicted inside the state; for example, $\omega(a) = 110$ means 110 traces of L can be aligned to a transition sequence of P whose prefix is a.

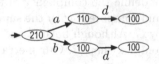

Fig. 3. The alignment automaton $AA(L, P)$

4   Service Discovery from Observed Behavior

Given a state machine S and an event log L, service discovery aims to produce a service R that is (1) a partner of S and (2) of high quality. The first requirement reduces the search space from all composable services to partners of S, and can be achieved by either model checking $S \oplus R$ or checking whether R matches with the operating guideline $OG(S)$ of S. In the following, we discuss the second requirement.

4.1   Incorporating the Quality Dimensions

We are interested in discovering a partner of high quality. Numerous metrics for measuring the four quality dimensions have been developed [4,6,26]. However, we cannot simply apply these metrics but have to adapt them to cope with service models.

Fitness. Let R be a partner of S and L an event log. Fitness indicates how much of the behavior in the event log L is captured by the model R. A state machine with good fitness allows for most of the behavior seen in the event log. We redefine the cost-based fitness metrics from [4] for state machines: We quantify fitness as the total alignment costs for L and R (computed using the best alignments provided by λ_R) compared to the worst total alignment costs. The worst total alignment costs are just moves in the log for the events in the observed trace and no moves in the model, in all optimal alignments.

Definition 6 (Fitness). The *fitness* of L and R is defined by

$$fit(L, R) = 1 - \frac{\sum_{w \in L} \big(L(w) \cdot \kappa(\lambda_R(w)) \big)}{\sum_{w \in L} \big(L(w) \cdot \sum_{x \in w} \kappa((x, \gg)) \big)}.$$

Assume a cost function κ where each synchronous and each silent move has cost 0, and all other types of moves have cost 1. The best alignments given by λ_P are $\gamma_1 - \gamma_3$. We have costs of 1 for γ_1, 0 for γ_2, and 0 for γ_3; therefore, we calculate $fit(L, P) = 1 - \frac{10 \cdot 1 + 100 \cdot 0 + 100 \cdot 0}{10 \cdot 2 + 100 \cdot 2 + 100 \cdot 2} \approx 0.976$. As expected, the fitness value is high because only 10 out of 210 traces are non-fitting traces in L (i.e., the traces ac).

Simplicity. Simplicity refers to state machines minimal in structure, which clearly reflect the log's behavior. This dimension is related to Occam's Razor, which states that "one should not increase, beyond what is necessary, the number of entities required to explain anything." Various techniques exist to quantify model complexity [17]. We define the complexity of the model R by its number of states and transitions, and compare it with the smallest subgraph G of $OG(S)$ such that R is simulated by G. Although both R and G have the same behavior, G is not necessarily less complex than R. Our metric takes this into account.

Definition 7 (Simplicity). Let $OG(S) = (T, \Phi)$. The *simplicity* $sim(L, R)$ of L and R is $\frac{|Q_G| + |\delta_G|}{|Q_R| + |\delta_R|}$ if $|Q_G| + |\delta_G| <= |Q_R| + |\delta_R|$ and 1 otherwise, where G is the smallest subgraph of T such that G simulates R. ⌋

Figure 2b shows the smallest subgraph G of $OG(S)$ such that G simulates P. G consists of 6 states and 14 transitions (including the τ-loops at states T_4, T_5, and T_7). Therefore, $|Q_G| + |\delta_G| = 6 + 14 = 20$ and $|Q_P| + |\delta_P| = 3 + 4 = 7$; thus, $sim(L, P) = 1$. As expected, L and P have a perfect simplicity value, as P is less complex than G.

Precision. Precision indicates whether a state machine is not too general. To avoid "underfitting", we prefer state machines with minimal behavior to represent the behavior observed in the event log as closely as possible. We redefine the alignment-based precision metric from [6] for state machines. This metric relies on building the alignment automaton AA, which relates executed and available actions after an aligned trace of the log.

Definition 8 (Precision). Let $AA(L, R) = (V, v_0, E, \omega)$ be the alignment automaton of L and R. Then the *precision* of L and R is defined by $pre(L, R) = \left(\sum_{v \in V} \left(\omega(v) \cdot |exec(v)| \right) \right) / \left(\sum_{v \in V} \left(\omega(v) \cdot |avail(v)| \right) \right)$, where $exec(v) = en(v)$ in $AA(L, R)$, and $avail(v) = \bigcup_{q \in X} en(q)$ with $X = \{q \mid \alpha_R \xrightarrow{w}_{\delta_R^*} q \wedge w_{|\mathcal{A}} = v\}$ in R. ⌋

Figure 3 shows the alignment automaton $AA(L, P)$, which has been build from the best alignments γ_1–γ_3. We obtain $pre(L, P) = \frac{210 \cdot 2 + 110 \cdot 1 + 100 \cdot 0 + 100 \cdot 1 + 100 \cdot 0}{210 \cdot 2 + 110 \cdot 1 + 110 \cdot 2 + 100 \cdot 1 + 100 \cdot 2} = 0.6$. As expected, L and P have average precision, as P allows for far more behavior than the behavior observed in L.

Generalization. Generalization penalizes overly precise state machines which "overfit" the given log. In general, a state machine should not restrict behavior to just the behavior observed in the event log. Often only a fraction of the possible behavior has been observed, e.g., due to concurrency. For this dimension, we developed a new metric. We combine the generalization metric from [4] with the alignment automaton $AA(L, R)$. The idea is to use the estimated probability $\pi(x, y)$ that a next visit to a state w *of the alignment automaton* will reveal a new trace not observed before: $x = |en(w)|$ is the number of unique activities observed at leaving state w, and $y = \omega(w)$ is the number of times w was visited by the event log. We employ an estimator for $\pi(x, y)$, which is inspired by [9].

Definition 9 (Generalization). Let $AA(L, R) = (V, v_0, E, \omega)$ be the alignment automaton of L and R. The *generalization* of L and R is defined by $gen(L, R) = 1 - \left(\frac{1}{|V|} \sum_{v \in V} \pi(|en(v)|, \omega(v)) \right)$, where π can be approximated [4] by $\pi(x, y) = \frac{x(x+1)}{y(y-1)}$, if $y \geq x + 2$, and $\pi(x, y) = 1$, if $y \leq x + 1$.

We obtain $gen(L, P) = 1 - \frac{1}{5} \left(\frac{2 \cdot 3}{210 \cdot 209} + \frac{1 \cdot 2}{110 \cdot 109} + \frac{1 \cdot 2}{100 \cdot 99} \right) \approx 1$. Given the numbers of traces in L, L and P have nearly perfect generalization as expected, because it is unlikely to reveal a new trace not observed before.

Balancing the Quality Dimensions. As quality refers to the possibly competing quality dimensions fitness, simplicity, precision and generalization [3], we cannot assume the existence of a partner that has the highest value for every dimension. We rather need to balance these dimensions and, therefore, assume that a user specified his requirements using weights ω_{fit}, ω_{sim}, ω_{pre}, and ω_{gen}. With these four weights, we can actually search for the partner of S that has highest quality.

Definition 10 (Quality). Let $\omega_{all} = \omega_{fit} + \omega_{sim} + \omega_{pre} + \omega_{gen}$. The *quality* of R for L is defined by $quality(L, R) = \frac{\omega_{fit}}{\omega_{all}} fit(L, R) + \frac{\omega_{sim}}{\omega_{all}} sim(L, R) + \frac{\omega_{pre}}{\omega_{all}} pre(L, R) + \frac{\omega_{gen}}{\omega_{all}} gen(L, R)$

Using weights of 2 for fitness, precision, and generalization, and a weight of 1 for simplicity (incorporating that the discovered service can be simpler than its simulation subgraph), we obtain $quality(L, P) = \frac{2}{7} \cdot 0.976 + \frac{1}{7} \cdot 1 + \frac{2}{7} \cdot 0.6 + \frac{2}{7} \cdot 1 \approx 0.879$.

4.2   A Finite Abstraction of the Search Space

The actual challenge of service discovery is that the search space is the set partners of S, which is infinite. In the following, we present an abstraction that reduces the search space to a *finite* number of partners. To this end, we restrict ourselves to partners of S that are *valid subgraphs* of $OG(S) = (T, \Phi)$, i.e., subgraphs of T whose states are connected, contain the initial state of T, and that match with $OG(S)$. As T contains only finitely many states, the number of valid subgraphs of $OG(S)$ is finite too. So, instead of investigating any partner of S, we only consider valid subgraphs of $OG(S)$.

However, this finite abstraction comes at a price: Although every valid subgraph is a partner of S, we may have excluded partners of S that have a better quality than any valid subgraph. More precisely, it can be shown that this abstraction only preserves fitness. We do not elaborate on this and refer the interested reader to [22]. The experimental results in Sect. 5 illustrate the appropriateness of the abstraction.

4.3   Algorithm and Implementation

Discovering a partner for a given state machine S and an event log L is challenging because the search space is the infinite set of partners of S. Even the finite abstraction of the search space to valid subgraphs (see Sect. 4.2) may still be too large to search for an optimal candidate exhaustively. Thus, we are using a *genetic algorithm* to find a partner of high but possibly not of highest quality. Genetic algorithms have been successfully applied for discovering workflow models [16,10]. A genetic algorithm evolves a population of candidate solutions (i.e., the *individuals*) step-wise (i.e., in *generations*) toward better solutions of an optimization problem. In our setting, an individual is a state machine R. The quality of a candidate solution is determined by the quality of R (see Def. 10).

Our algorithm employs the general procedure of genetic algorithms, which is depicted in Fig. 4. It creates children through the operations crossover (i.e., randomly exchanging subgraphs between two given individuals), mutation (i.e., randomly adding or removing a transition or a final state from a given individual), and replacement (i.e., replacing a randomly chosen individual by a new, randomly generated individual). We employ a combination of four different termination criteria: A time and a generation limit (i.e., the evolution stops after a given amount of time or generations), a stagnation limit (i.e., the evolution stops if the quality of the high-quality individual stagnates a given number of generations), and a quality limit (i.e., the evolution stops if the high-quality individual meets a specified quality threshold).

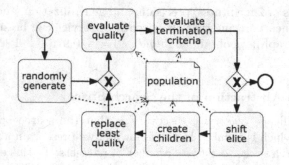

Fig. 4. The different phases of the genetic algorithm

We have implemented the genetic algorithm, with and without the abstraction presented in Sect. 4.2, as a runner-up package in the latest ProM 6.3 release[1].

5   Experimental Results

In this section, we evaluate the feasibility of our approach by discovering partners for eight service models of industrial size. Table 1 gives an overview about the eight service models. The services "Loan Approval" and "Purchase Order" are taken from the WS-BPEL specification [12], all other examples are industrial service models provided by a consulting company.

---

[1] https://svn.win.tue.nl/trac/prom/wiki/rel63:release

Table 1. Size of the service models, the operating guidelines, and event logs

name (abbreviation)	service S		$OG(S)$		event log L	
	$|Q|$	$|\delta|$	$|Q|$	$|\delta|$	cases	events
Car Breakdown (CB)	$11,381$	$39,865$	$1,449$	$13,863$	300	$1,938$
Deliver Goods (DG)	$4,148$	$13,832$	$1,377$	$13,838$	300	$1,938$
Loan Approval (LA)	30	41	21	84	300	$2,537$
Purchase Order (PO)	402	955	169	$1,182$	300	$2,537$
Internal Order (IO)	$1,516$	$4,996$	97	567	300	$1,938$
Ticket Reservation (TR)	304	614	111	731	300	$2,381$
Reservations (RS)	28	33	370	$3,083$	300	$2,671$
Contract Negotiation (CN)	784	$1,959$	577	$4,859$	300	$1,938$

As most services were specified in WS-BPEL, we had to translate them into state machines using the compiler BPEL2oWFN [13]. For each state machine S, we calculated the operating guideline $OG(S)$ using the tool Wendy [15]. Next, we used the underlying state machine T of $OG(S)$ to generate a random event log L using the tool Locretia[2]. Because T is the "most permissive" partner [14] of S, there exists a partner exhibiting the observed behavior in L. Each such event log L is free of noise and consists of 300 cases with about $1,900$–$2,700$ events. Table 1 shows the details. The size of our generated event logs is the size of event logs successfully applied to evaluate the genetic process discovery algorithm in [10]. Finally, we used our implementation to discover a partner of S from $OG(S)$ and L.

As parameters for the genetic algorithm, we used an initial population of 100 individuals, a mutation/crossover/replacement probability of 0.3 with at most 1 crossover point, and elitism of 0.3, i.e., the 30 individuals with the highest quality are directly shifted to the next generation. The computation of a new generation stops after $1,000$ generations, if the highest quality stagnates for 750 generations, if a quality of 0.999 is reached, or if the algorithm ran for 60 minutes. To take into account that a discovered service can be simpler than the subgraph to be compared, we chose a weight of 1 for simplicity and a weight of 2 for all other dimensions. The experiment data is available online[3].

To the best of our knowledge, there does not exist any other service discovery implementation with which we could compare our algorithm. Therefore, we performed two different experiments: discovering a partner from the complete search space (Experiment 1), and discovering a partner from the abstract search space (Experiment 2).

The results in Table 2 show that discovered partners in Experiment 1 are more complex than the ones in Experiment 2; that is, valid subgraphs are smaller than arbitrary partners. This explains the higher computation time in Experiment 1

---

[2] http://svn.gna.org/viewcvs/service-tech/trunk/locretia/
[3] https://u.hu-berlin.de/mueller

by a factor of 1–44 compared to Experiment 2: Smaller candidates enable the algorithm to compute more generations in less time. For the same reason, Experiment 2 produced, in general, partners with higher fitness. The simplicity values are by Def. 6 higher for Experiment 2. In all examples, the discovered partners in Experiment 2 have slightly higher precision values than the partners discovered in Experiment 1. However, in three out of eight examples they have slightly lower generalization values. Restricting the search space to valid subgraphs is an abstraction, which neither preserves precision nor generalization. Therefore, we expected lower precision and generalization values for the partners discovered in Experiment 2. Despite the loss of preservation of the abstraction, the overall quality of the respective partner discovered in Experiment 2 is in all examples better.

Summing up, our experimental results validate that, in general, partner discovery produces better results on a finite abstraction of the search space than on the complete search space. Although the abstraction only preserves fitness, the values of the other three dimensions and the quality are high.

Table 2. Discovery of an ordinary partner (Experiment 1) and a valid subgraph (Experiment 2) using the genetic algorithm (with *quality* and *time*) conducted on a MacBook Pro, Intel Core i5 CPU with 2.4 GHz and 8 GB of RAM.

S	discovered partner in Experiment 1								discovered partner in Experiment 2							
	$|Q|$	$|\delta|$	q	fit	sim	pre	gen	t in s	$|Q|$	$|\delta|$	q	fit	sim	pre	gen	t in s
CB	548	1,180	0.72	0.59	0.59	0.7	0.95	3,744	86	384	0.95	0.87	1	0.99	0.96	3,602
DG	246	829	0.71	0.5	0.94	0.57	0.94	3,689	82	316	0.96	0.91	1	0.98	0.98	1,763
LA	15	19	0.97	0.91	1	0.98	1	3,239	14	30	0.98	0.98	1	0.98	0.97	73
PO	101	248	0.94	0.92	0.89	0.99	0.94	3,605	33	107	0.97	0.9	1	1	1	214
IO	107	106	0.62	0.11	0.19	0.95	1	3,698	9	11	0.87	0.6	1	0.98	0.95	3,021
TR	29	99	0.91	0.93	1	0.82	0.95	3,606	15	48	0.96	0.96	1	0.99	0.92	143
RS	218	671	0.93	0.95	0.98	0.8	1	3,601	176	582	0.97	1	1	0.91	1	207
CN	73	220	0.62	0.7	1	0.61	0.35	3,798	74	201	0.94	0.86	1	0.97	0.94	3,606

6 Related Work

The term "service discovery" describes techniques for finding a service model in a service repository in service-oriented architectures [24], and techniques for producing a service model from observed communication behavior of services [5]. In this paper, we refer to the latter. We investigated the discovery of a service model from observed communication behavior, which corresponds to a particular form of process mining [3]. Process mining research has been focused on workflows (i.e., closed systems) but during the last few years, process mining techniques have also been applied to services resulting in the term "service mining". Paper [2] reviews service mining research and identifies two main challenges regarding the discovery of services: (1) the correlation of instances of a service with instances of another service (e.g., [8,19]) and (2) the discovery of services based on observed behavior (e.g., [11,25,23,7,27,18]). This paper contributes to the second challenge.

In [21], we considered with weak termination a stronger correctness criterion than deadlock freedom but solely focused on the fitness dimension, thus, ignored the three other quality dimensions. To make the discovery efficient, we do not discover a "best" model as in [21] but a model of high quality using a genetic algorithm. The idea of using an genetic algorithm is inspired by the work of Buijs et al. [10] on discovering sound workflow models while balancing the four conflicting quality dimensions. In Sect. 4, we discussed the relation of our metrics for these four quality dimensions and the metrics used in [10]. For the simplicity metric, we used the structure of the operating guideline, which does not exist for workflow models. Correctness in our setting is deadlock freedom of the service composition, a weaker criterion than soundness in [10]. To deal with correctness in the setting of services, we assume a service S to be given and we discover a partner of S from observed behavior of S.

Musaraj et al. [23] correlate messages from an event log without correlation information and use this information in their discovery algorithm. In contrast, we abstract from correlation information and assume cases to be independent. Furthermore, our approach produces a partner of a given service model S and balances the four conflicting quality dimensions guided by user preferences. Motahari-Nezhad et al. [20,18] only consider fitness (referenced as "recall"), simplicity and precision, and ignore generalization of the discovered service. Like Musaraj et al. [23], they do not assume a service model to be given and, thus, they cannot guarantee that their produced service model can interact correctly with its environment. Other approaches discover workflow models from service interaction [11] from interaction patterns [7,27]. Whereas our algorithm produces a complete service model, [11,7,27] can only discover parts of a service.

7   Conclusion and Future Work

We presented a technique to discover a service model from a given service S and observed behavior of a service P interacting with S. Our technique produces a service model for P that can interact correctly (no deadlocks) with S and, in addition, balances the four conflicting quality dimensions (i.e., fitness, simplicity, precision, and generalization). As an additional improvement, we proposed an abstraction technique to reduce the infinite search space to a finite one. As an exhaustive search to find an optimal solution may still be intractable, we implemented our technique as a genetic algorithm. In a prototypical implementation, we experimented with several service models of industrial size. Our results showed that the algorithm finds (nearly) optimal solutions in acceptable time. It is worth mentioning that our approach is not restricted to service models but can discover arbitrary reactive systems.

In future work, we aim to extend our presented approach by improving the simplicity metrics, studying the impact of different weights of the quality dimensions on the quality of the discovered partner, and investigating how the abstraction technique based on valid subgraphs can be improved such that it preserves all metrics. We also plan to extend our approach to stronger correctness criteria than deadlock freedom, e.g., weak termination (i.e., the possibility to always terminate in a service composition).

Acknowledgement. Support from the Basic Research Program of the National Research University Higher School of Economics is gratefully acknowledged.

References

1. van der Aalst, W.M.P.: The application of Petri nets to workflow management. Journal of Circuits, Systems, and Computers 8(1), 21–66 (1998)
2. van der Aalst, W.M.P.: Service mining: Using process mining to discover, check, and improve service behavior. IEEE Transactions on Services Computing (2012)
3. van der Aalst, W.M.P.: Process Mining: Discovery, Conformance and Enhancement of Business Processes. Springer (2011)
4. van der Aalst, W.M.P., Adriansyah, A., van Dongen, B.F.: Replaying history on process models for conformance checking and performance analysis. Wiley Interdisciplinary Reviews: Data Mining and Knowledge Discovery 2(2), 182–192 (2012)
5. van der Aalst, W., et al.: Process mining manifesto. In: Daniel, F., Barkaoui, K., Dustdar, S. (eds.) BPM Workshops 2011, Part I. LNBIP, vol. 99, pp. 169–194. Springer, Heidelberg (2012)
6. Adriansyah, A., Munoz-Gama, J., Carmona, J., van Dongen, B.F., van der Aalst, W.M.P.: Alignment based precision checking. In: La Rosa, M., Soffer, P. (eds.) BPM Workshops 2012. LNBIP, vol. 132, pp. 137–149. Springer, Heidelberg (2013)
7. Asbagh, M., Abolhassani, H.: Web service usage mining: mining for executable sequences. In: WSEAS 2007, vol. 7, pp. 266–271 (2007)
8. Basu, S., Casati, F., Daniel, F.: Toward web service dependency discovery for SOA management. In: SCC 2008, vol. 2, pp. 422–429 (2008)
9. Boender, C., Rinnooy Kan, A.: A bayesian analysis of the number of cells of a multinomial distribution. The Statistician, 240–248 (1983)
10. Buijs, J.C.A.M., van Dongen, B.F., van der Aalst, W.M.P.: On the role of fitness, precision, generalization and simplicity in process discovery. In: Meersman, R., et al. (eds.) OTM 2012, Part I. LNCS, vol. 7565, pp. 305–322. Springer, Heidelberg (2012)
11. Dustdar, S., Gombotz, R.: Discovering web service workflows using web services interaction mining. Int. Journal of Business Process Integration and Management 1(4), 256–266 (2006)
12. Jordan, D., et al.: Web services business process execution language version 2.0. OASIS Standard 11 (2007)
13. Lohmann, N.: A feature-complete Petri net semantics for WS-BPEL 2.0. In: Dumas, M., Heckel, R. (eds.) WS-FM 2007. LNCS, vol. 4937, pp. 77–91. Springer, Heidelberg (2008)
14. Lohmann, N., Massuthe, P., Wolf, K.: Operating guidelines for finite-state services. In: Kleijn, J., Yakovlev, A. (eds.) ICATPN 2007. LNCS, vol. 4546, pp. 321–341. Springer, Heidelberg (2007)
15. Lohmann, N., Weinberg, D.: Wendy: A tool to synthesize partners for services. Fundam. Inform. 113(3-4), 295–311 (2011)

16. Medeiros, A., Weijters, A., van der Aalst, W.M.P.: Genetic process mining: an experimental evaluation. Data Mining and Knowledge Discovery 14, 245–304 (2007)
17. Mendling, J., Neumann, G., van der Aalst, W.M.P.: Understanding the occurrence of errors in process models based on metrics. In: Meersman, R., Tari, Z. (eds.) OTM 2007, Part I. LNCS, vol. 4803, pp. 113–130. Springer, Heidelberg (2007)
18. Motahari-Nezhad, H.R., Saint-Paul, R., Benatallah, B.: Deriving protocol models from imperfect service conversation logs. IEEE Trans. Knowl. Data Eng. 20(12), 1683–1698 (2008)
19. Motahari Nezhad, H.R., Saint-Paul, R., Casati, F., Benatallah, B.: Event correlation for process discovery from web service interaction logs. The VLDB Journal 20(3), 417–444 (2010)
20. Motahari-Nezhad, H., Saint-Paul, R., Benatallah, B., Casati, F.: Protocol discovery from imperfect service interaction logs. In: 2013 IEEE 29th International Conference on Data Engineering (ICDE), pp. 1405–1409 (2007)
21. Müller, R., van der Aalst, W.M.P., Stahl, C.: Conformance checking of services using the best matching private view. In: ter Beek, M.H., Lohmann, N. (eds.) WS-FM 2012. LNCS, vol. 7843, pp. 49–68. Springer, Heidelberg (2013)
22. Müller, R., Stahl, C., van der Aalst, W.M.P., Westergaard, M.: Service discovery from observed behavior while guaranteeing deadlock freedom in collaborations. BPM Center Report BPM-13-12, BPMcenter.org (2013),
    http://bpmcenter.org/wp-content/uploads/reports/2013/BPM-13-12.pdf
23. Musaraj, K., Yoshida, T., Daniel, F., Hacid, M.S., Casati, F., Benatallah, B.: Message correlation and web service protocol mining from inaccurate logs. In: ICWS 2010, pp. 259–266 (2010)
24. Papazoglou, M.: Web Services - Principles and Technology. Prentice Hall (2008)
25. Rouached, M., Gaaloul, W., van der Aalst, W.M.P., Bhiri, S., Godart, C.: Web service mining and verification of properties: An approach based on event calculus. In: Meersman, R., Tari, Z. (eds.) OTM 2006. LNCS, vol. 4275, pp. 408–425. Springer, Heidelberg (2006)
26. Rozinat, A., van der Aalst, W.M.P.: Conformance checking of processes based on monitoring real behavior. Information Systems 33(1), 64–95 (2008)
27. Tang, R., Zou, Y.: An approach for mining web service composition patterns from execution logs. In: WSE 2010, pp. 53–62 (2010)

Priority-Based Human Resource Allocation in Business Processes*

Cristina Cabanillas[1], José María García[2], Manuel Resinas[3],
David Ruiz[3], Jan Mendling[1], and Antonio Ruiz-Cortés[3]

[1] Vienna University of Economics and Business, Austria
{cristina.cabanillas,jan.mendling}@wu.ac.at
[2] STI Innsbruck, University of Innsbruck, Austria
jose.garcia@sti2.at
[3] University of Seville, Spain
{resinas,druiz,aruiz}@us.es

Abstract. In Business Process Management Systems, human resource management typically covers two steps: resource assignment at design time and resource allocation at run time. Although concepts like role-based assignment often yield several potential performers for an activity, there is a lack of mechanisms for prioritizing them, e.g., according to their skills or current workload. In this paper, we address this research gap. More specifically, we introduce an approach to define resource preferences grounded on a validated, generic user preference model initially developed for semantic web services. Furthermore, we show an implementation of the approach demonstrating its feasibility.

Keywords: preference modeling, preference resolution, priority-based allocation, priority ranking, RAL, resource allocation, SOUP.

1 Introduction

Business Process Management System (BPMS) are increasingly used for supporting service composition. Typically, they work with executable process models that define the control flow, data processing, and resource involvement of a specific process. Resources in this context include both automatic services and services provided by human resources. In particular, the appropriate selection of human resources is critical as various factors such as workload or skills have an impact on work performance. While priorities for automatic services are intensively researched, it is surprising that prioritizing human resources has been hardly discussed. In classical workflow management, only two steps of resource management are considered: resource assignment at the level of process specification and resource allocation at run time [1]. *Resource assignment* builds on

* This work was partially supported by the European Union's Seventh Framework Programme (FP7/2007-2013), the European Commission (FEDER), the Spanish and the Andalusian R&D&I programmes (grants 318275 (GET Service), 284860 (MSEE), TIN2009-07366 (SETI), TIN2012-32273 (TAPAS), TIC-5906 (THEOS)).

S. Basu et al. (Eds.): ICSOC 2013, LNCS 8274, pp. 374–388, 2013.

defining for each activity the human resources that are candidates to work on the activity. These are called *potential performers*. At run time, the *resource allocation* step considers these potential performers to select *actual performers* (often a single person) who find the activity in their worklist. For instance, the Yet Another Workflow Language (YAWL) system [2] uses this concept to support various Workflow Resource Patterns (WRPs) [3]. Even though these WRPs identify strategies to balance workload, there is no explicit consideration of prioritizing potential performers to facilitate the selection of the actual performer. This is remarkable, as deriving a set of performers immediately poses the question of who would be the best candidate to pick up the work. Also professional solutions such as Activiti[1], WebSphere MQ[2] or BPEL4People, do not provide means to prioritize performers, but assign priority indicators to activities only.

In this paper, we address this research gap of how prioritization of resources can be integrated in BPMS. More specifically, we provide two contributions: (i) we conceptually define prioritized allocation based on preferences; and (ii) we propose a concrete way in which preferences over resources can be defined such that a resource priority ranking can be automatically generated. Our solution builds on the adaptation of a user preference model that was developed for the discovery and ranking of semantic web services [4] to the domain at hand. As a proof of concept, we have extended the resource management tool Collection of Resource-centrIc Supporting Tools And Languages (CRISTAL)[3][5] with the Semantic Ontology of User Preferences (SOUP) component [6] to support priority-based allocation. In this system, Resource Assignment Language (RAL) [7] is used for resource selection.

The rest of the paper is structured as follows. In Section 2, we conceptually define priority-based allocation based on preferences and describe the requirements to address it based on a motivating scenario. In Section 3, we explain the adaptation of the preference metamodel and its formalization for automated prioritization. In Section 4, we evaluate the approach regarding preference modeling and resolution. Work related to preference modeling and resource prioritization in Business Processes (BPs) is detailed in Section 5, before closing the paper by drawing some conclusions and deriving potential future work in Section 6.

2   Priority-Based Resource Allocation

We define *priority-based resource allocation* as the ability to rank a set of resources according to one or more preferences. The result is thus a prioritized list of resources that can be allocated to a process activity. In the following, we present a real scenario that motivates the problem, and a set of requirements that must be considered in order to deal with it.

---

[1] http://www.activiti.org/

[2] http://www-01.ibm.com/software/integration/wmq/

[3] http://www.isa.us.es/cristal

2.1   Motivating Scenario

The need for resource prioritization is motivated by a real scenario located in the Andalusian Institute of Public Administration (in Spanish IAAP), which serves more than eight million end users. The Business Process (BP) in question represents the procedure to create and process a resolution proposal for hiring people and has a high use frequency in the IAAP. Fig. 1 shows the process in Business Process Model and Notation (BPMN). Once a draft of a resolution proposal is created, it is concurrently sent to the Consultative Board and to the Legal Department for evaluation. The IAAP then analyzes the reports and decides whether an external resolution is required. In that case, a request is sent to an external committee, which must create and send a new resolution. Otherwise, the resolution proposal is reviewed, and changes are applied to the initial one according to the reports received. In any case, the documents generated are signed and archived, and the resolution result is appropriately notified.

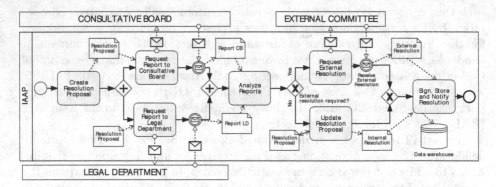

Fig. 1. BP to create and process a resolution proposal for hiring people

The part of the organizational structure of the IAAP related to Administrative Resource Management involved in this BP is hierarchically structured in eight *positions*: Business Manager (BM), Technician of the IAAP (T-IAAP), Assistant of the IAAP (A-IAAP), Secretary (SE), Assistant of the Legal Department (A-LD), Technician of the Legal Department (T-LD), Assistant of the Consultative Board (A-CB) and Technician of the Consultative Board (T-CB). They are occupied by a total of eleven people. Table 1 shows the selection conditions for each activity (positions are acronymized) and the preferences to prioritize the resulting set of potential performers for allocation.

2.2   Requirements for Resource Prioritization

The preferences for priority-based allocation as defined in the example have to yield a partial order relation over the set of potential performers of an activity.

Table 1. Resource selection conditions and resource preferences

Activity	Potential Performers	Preferences
Create Resolution Proposal	T-IAAP	The greatest number of past executions of the activity (*history*)
Request Report to CB/LD	T-IAAP	The best *balance* between low cost (*price*) and short worklist (*availability*), i.e., a person is preferred over another person if his/her cost is lower and his/her worklist is not longer, or *vice versa*
Analyze Reports	T-IAAP	The least average execution time for the activity (*speed*)
Request External Resolution	SE	The best skills on using a specific software application (*expertise*)
Update Resolution Proposal	T-IAAP, T-CB or T-LD	The same person who created the resolution draft (*Binding of Duties (BoD) [8]*)
Sign, Store and Notify Resolution	SE	A person that has been working for the company for at least one year (*experience*). In case of no distinction, the person with shortest worklist (*availability*)

More specifically, we identify a set of requirements that must hold in order to deal with such automated resource prioritization as follows:

- *Resource assignment.* Some mechanism for resource assignment must be put into place to calculate the potential performers before resource prioritization. There are many different approaches for that purpose, e.g., [8–10].
- *Expressive preference modeling.* In this context, there is a need for expressive preferences that range from single-value criteria (e.g., age), to composite preferences where the preferences themselves can be ranked (cf. preference for *Sign, Store and Notify Resolution* in Table 1).
- *Preference resolution.* Some mechanism must enable the automated resolution of preferences at run time based on actual values.
- *Information availability.* In addition, similarly as for resource assignment, specific information (also called *properties*) about the resources needs to be stored, updated, and retrieved, to define and resolve resource preferences. For instance, the following types of properties can be distinguished for our motivating scenario:
  - *Personal and Organizational Data.* From personal data such as the ID number, name or age, to properties related to positions occupied in the company or functional roles being held. This data partially depends on the type of organizational model used in the company.
  - *Skills.* As shown for activity *Request External Resolution* in Table 1, knowledge on specific software applications, technologies, methodologies, *etcetera* may be of interest for resource prioritization.
  - *Professional Information.* Information on the salary of the resource (e.g. in terms of cost/hour) or the years of experience, can be necessary to determine the resource that best meets the needs of the company.

- *Worklist.* The workload of the resources can also be critical to offer or allocate an activity to a specific person. An organization may prefer having balanced workloads rather than very busy people and idle people.
- *History.* For each person, information about the past execution of process activities must be stored, e.g. activities performed, BPs to which they belonged, execution time, number of times executed, *etcetera.*

This list cannot be exhaustive, but has to be adapted for the context of the process at hand. For instance, in other cases it might also be necessary to access calendar data, such as scheduled meetings or holidays, in order to prioritize according to availability on a specific date.

3   Materializing Priority-Based Resource Allocation

As derived from the previous section, the main challenge for resource prioritization is two-fold: (i) to come up with a mechanism to express preferences over resources, and (ii) to develop a way to rank a set of resources according to those preferences. Furthermore, the solution should be as independent as possible from the properties used in the preferences so that they can accommodate the different requirements several organizations may have.

The first challenge is solved by leveraging SOUP, a highly expressive user preference model defined by García et al. [4, 6] that we adapt to the BP domain in this paper. To deal with the second challenge, we have developed a novel algorithm to rank resources according to the preferences expressed in SOUP. Both the preference metamodel and the algorithm are independent of the properties used in the preferences.

3.1   SOUP: A Metamodel to Define Preferences

In SOUP, a preference can be intuitively expressed as "I prefer y rather than x", where x and y are instances of domain concepts that represent properties of the resources to be allocated (e.g., size of the worklist). This relation between concept instances can be mathematically interpreted as a strict partial order. Therefore, in SOUP a preference can be defined as:

Definition 1 (Preference). *Let C be a non-empty set of domain concepts, and* $\mathrm{dom}(C)$ *the set of all possible instances of those concepts. We define a preference as* $\mathcal{P} = (C, <^{\mathcal{P}})$, *where* $<^{\mathcal{P}} \subseteq \mathrm{dom}(C) \times \mathrm{dom}(C)$ *is a strict partial order (irreflexive, transitive and asymmetric), and if $x, y \in \mathrm{dom}(C)$, then $x <^{\mathcal{P}} y$ is interpreted as "I prefer y rather than x".*

Consequently, each preference term instance defines its order depending on the concrete concepts referred (C) and some operand values that determine the evaluation of the $<^{\mathcal{P}}$ relation. Furthermore, if we consider a finite set of concept instance pairs $(x, y) \in <^{\mathcal{P}}$, $\mathcal{P}$ can be represented as a directed acyclic graph, also known as *Hasse diagram* [11], where each node corresponds to a concept instance, and edges represent the preference relation $<^{\mathcal{P}}$.

Fig. 2 shows a UML representation of SOUP preference terms. Atomic preferences can be expressed using different preference terms, whereas composite preferences can be used to compose those terms, defining the relation between previously expressed atomic preferences. Both atomic and composite preferences are handled by ranking mechanisms that implement the ranking process according to the corresponding term definition.

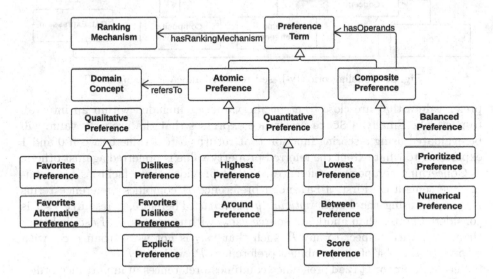

Fig. 2. UML representation of SOUP

In particular, atomic preferences are related to a domain-specific concept that usually represents a property that should be optimized to fulfill the user preference over it. SOUP supports both qualitative and quantitative preferences, depending on the nature of the property referred by the concrete preference. On the one hand, if the property is qualitative, e.g. the skills of a resource, one can use a `Favorites` preference to state that certain values of that property are favored against the rest (e.g., skills on a concrete software application). Conversely, a `Dislikes` preference can be used to enumerate the values that should not be provided for the referred property. A `FavoritesAlternative` allows defining a favorite and an alternative set of property values, meaning that values contained in the former set are the most preferred, but if there is none then values from the latter set can also be considered. A `FavoritesDislikes` preference is a combination of a `Favorites` and a `Dislikes` preference, where preferred values are the ones in the favored set or at least not in the disfavored set. Finally, an `Explicit` preference simply states the preference between two concrete values of a property (e.g. skills on LibreOffice are more preferred than skills on Microsoft Office).

On the other hand, quantitative preferences compare numerical values of the related properties. Thus, a `Highest` (`Lowest`) preference means the user prefers higher (lower) values for the referred property. `Around` and `Between` preferences

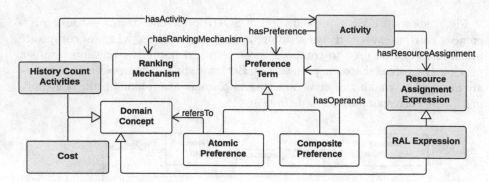

Fig. 3. Modeling priority-based resource allocation using SOUP

prefer values that are close to a specific value, or included within an interval, respectively. Finally, a `Score` preference expresses that the property value will be evaluated using a scoring function that returns a real value between 0 and 1 expressing to what extent the referred property value is preferred against others.

Concerning composite preferences, SOUP provides three facilities for defining the semantics. First, a `Balanced` preference $\mathcal{P}$ combines preference terms $\mathcal{P}_1, \ldots, \mathcal{P}_n$ using the *Pareto-optimality principle*. Therefore, a resource rsc_l is considered better than another resource rsc_m with respect to $\mathcal{P}$ if rsc_l is better than rsc_m with respect to any P_i such that rsc_l is not worse than rsc_m with respect to the rest of the combined preferences $\mathcal{P}_j$ with $i \neq j$.

Second, a `Prioritized` preference combines preferences in importance order. If a list of terms $\mathcal{P}_1, \mathcal{P}_2, \ldots, \mathcal{P}_n$ is combined using this operator, resources will be ranked first in terms of $\mathcal{P}_1$. Those that are equally preferred using $\mathcal{P}_1$ are ranked in terms of $\mathcal{P}_2$, and so forth.

Finally, a `Numerical` preference is the combination of preferences using a real function to obtain a numerical score value for each resource. Resources are ranked in terms of their score values. However, this composite preference can only combine quantitative preferences that can be evaluated to a score value.

3.2   Modeling Priority-Based Resource Allocation with SOUP

Two aspects must be modeled for resource prioritization, namely resource assignments for defining potential performers, and preference modeling for defining their order of priority (cf. Fig. 3).

First, each activity of the BP has a resource assignment expression that defines its set of potential performers. In our case, we use Resource Assignment Language (RAL) [12] as a language to select a set of potential performers. The language is grounded on a consensual organizational metamodel [13] that takes into consideration not only people and roles, but also positions, organizational units and skills. It also allows selecting people based on the performers of previous activities in the process. We have chosen Resource Assignment Language (RAL) for its expressiveness, extensibility, and for its capabilities to automatically resolve RAL expressions [7].

Second, preferences for resource prioritization are formulated using SOUP `Preference Terms`. All such preferences in SOUP must refer to some domain concept that represents the properties used in the preference. Therefore, modeling the preferences specified for each of the activities of the scenario also involves identifying the domain concepts used to prioritize resources. For instance, our scenario requires domain concepts like `Cost` and the number of times a resource has carried out a certain activity (`History Count Activities`). Additionally, a RAL expression can also be used in place of a domain concept. An example of such a preference is *I prefer the resource that is responsible for activity Create Resolution Proposal*, which can be modeled by means of a preference term of type `Favorites` referred to a domain concept of type `RAL Expression` and an operand that specifies the expression: `IS PERSON RESPONSIBLE FOR ACTIVITY Create Resolution Proposal`.

3.3 Ranking Resources According to SOUP Preferences

The prioritization of resources according to preferences is based on ranking mechanisms, which can be defined as follows:

Definition 2 (Ranking mechanism). *We define a ranking mechanism as an algorithm that receives as input a preference and a set of resources to be ranked, and returns as output a partially ordered set of the resources ranked according to the preference.*

Each `Preference Term` has a ranking mechanism that is used to implement the ranking process according to the corresponding term definition. Ranking mechanisms can be shared between different preference terms. In [6], ranking mechanisms for composite preference terms are discussed. However, the authors do not provide details about the ranking mechanisms for atomic preferences because they heavily depend on the characteristics of the knowledge base that contains the information about the domain concepts used in the preferences.

Therefore, in this section we adapt SOUP by providing a formalization of a generic ranking mechanism for atomic preferences, which has been designed to deal with the following characteristics of the knowledge base used for priority-based resource allocation: (1) it is usually distributed in different heterogeneous repositories such as a process log, an organizational model and an Enterprise Resource Planning (ERP) system; (2) it is dynamic in the sense that some of its repositories are continuously changing (e.g., the worklist of each resource); and (3) computing the value of a domain concept for a resource can be a complex operation. For instance, computing the availability of a resource may involve checking his/her agenda, a calendar of the holidays of the country in which s/he works and the worklist of his/her pending tasks.

Reflecting these characteristics, we separate the evaluation of a domain concept for a resource from the ordering of the resources according to this evaluation. The first task is solved by defining a function $eval_P^{KB}$ that is specific for each domain concept and for each knowledge base and can be defined as follows.

Definition 3 (Domain concept evaluation). *Let KB be a knowledge base,* $\mathcal{P} = (\mathcal{C}, <^{\mathcal{P}})$ *be an atomic preference, and* $\mathcal{R}$ *be the set of resources of the organization.*

- *If the domain concept* $\mathcal{C}$ *represents a quantitative property, then we define the evaluation as a function* $eval_{\mathcal{P}}^{KB} : \mathcal{R} \to \mathbb{R}$, *such that it returns a real number that represents the value of the domain concept for the given resource.*
- *If the domain concept* $\mathcal{C}$ *represents a qualitative property, then we define the evaluation as a function* $eval_{\mathcal{P}}^{KB} : \mathcal{R} \to \{false, true\}$, *such that it returns a boolean that represents whether the value of the domain concept belongs to the set specified in the preference.*

For instance, the evaluation of the quantitative concept *size of the worklist* for a resource r is the size of the worklist of resource r. Similarly, the evaluation of the qualitative concept *resource expression* with operand *IS PERSON RESPONSIBLE FOR ACTIVITY Create Resolution Proposal* (which is a RAL expression) for a resource r is true if, according to the organizational model, r is a person responsible for that activity.

The second task that must be performed involves applying the partial order specified by the type of a preference to the result of an evaluation. This is done by defining for each type of preference, a function that compares these results.

Definition 4 (Greater-than comparison). *Let KB be a knowledge base with information about the domain concepts used in the preferences,* P *be an atomic preference such that* $\mathcal{P} = (\mathcal{C}, <^{\mathcal{P}})$, *and D be the range of function* $eval_{\mathcal{P}}^{KB}$ *for such preference. We define a greater-than comparison for partial order* $<^{\mathcal{P}}$ *as a function* $gt_{<^{\mathcal{P}}} : D \times D \to \{false, true\}$ *such that* $gt_{<^{\mathcal{P}}}(d_i, d_j)$ *returns true if* d_i *is greater than* d_j *according to* $<^{\mathcal{P}}$, *i.e., if* d_i *is preferred over* d_j.

The implementation of this function can be straightforwardly derived from the type of the preference it corresponds to. For instance, if $<^{\mathcal{P}}$ corresponds to the type *Higher*, then $gt_{\text{Higher}}(n, n')$ is true iff $n > n'$. The same procedure can be applied to all of the other types of atomic preferences.

Using these two functions it is easy to provide an implementation of a generic ranking mechanism of atomic preferences as depicted in Algorithm 1. The algorithm simply iterates over the list of resources provided to the ranking mechanism and adds an edge $r \to r'$ to the graph if r' is preferred to r according to the preference $\mathcal{P}$ and the information in the knowledge base *KB*. Note that it is possible to provide more efficient implementations by means of domain-specific ranking mechanisms that leverage capabilities of the repositories of the knowledge base. However, a discussion of the different implementations of ranking mechanisms that can be developed is out of the scope of this paper.

Regarding ranking mechanisms for composite preferences, a similar approach could be followed. For instance, a ranking mechanism for composite preference `Prioritized` could be implemented using the same algorithm as Algorithm 1 but changing function $gt_{<^{\mathcal{P}}}$ for a function that uses the ranking mechanisms of its composed preferences to obtain partial results and, then, composes all of them together according to the semantics of `Prioritized`.

Algorithm 1 . Generic ranking mechanism of atomic preferences

---

1: **IN:** A knowledge base KB, an atomic preference $\mathcal{P} = (\mathcal{C}, <^{\mathcal{P}})$ and a set of potential performers $\mathcal{R}$
2: **OUT:** A strict partially ordered set of resources $POSET$
3: add all resources $\mathcal{R}$ as nodes of $POSET$
4: **for all** $r \in \mathcal{R}$ **do**
5:     **for all** $r' \in \mathcal{R} \setminus \{r\}$ **do**
6:         add edge $r \to r'$ to $POSET$ if $gt_{<^{\mathcal{P}}}(eval_{\mathcal{P}}^{KB}(r'), eval_{\mathcal{P}}^{KB}(r))$
7:     **end for**
8: **end for**

Finally, having all of these ranking mechanisms, the priority-based allocation for an activity A of a BP just involves using the appropriate ranking mechanism with the allocation preferences of such an activity and the set of resources selected during the resource assignment as inputs. Then, from the partially ordered set obtained by the ranking mechanism it is easy to derive a total order that is a linear extension of the partial order using well-known topological sorting algorithms [14]. Note that preferences define a strict partial order amongst the resources. This means that given two resources r_1 and r_2 it may not be possible to establish a preference between them. In that case, the resources are randomly ordered.

4   Evaluation

To validate our proposal, we have developed a proof-of-concept implementation[4] for priority-based allocation and we have applied it to the scenario detailed in Section 2.1. The implementation can be divided into a domain-independent part and a domain-specific part. The first part is based on PURI [6], a preference framework that provides the building blocks to implement new ranking mechanisms and also provides an implementation of the ranking mechanisms of all of the composite preferences. For our proof-of-concept, we implemented the generic ranking mechanism for both the atomic preferences and for all gt functions based on the preference types defined in SOUP. The second part involves two steps: (1) identifying the domain concepts used to prioritize resources and modeling the preferences for each activity of the process, and (2) identifying the knowledge base and implementing the $eval$ functions to evaluate the domain concepts. We discuss these two steps in the following.

4.1   Modeling the Preferences

Modeling the preferences specified for each of the activities of the scenario involves identifying the domain concepts used to prioritize resources, and using the SOUP metamodel to express the preferences regarding such domain concepts.

---

[4] Available at http://www.isa.us.es/cristal

```
Request Report to CB/LD: Assigned to persons with position T-IAAP.
The preference is balanced between low cost and short worklist.
iaap:RequestReport a bp:Activity ;
  bp:hasResourceAssignment [
    a ral:Expression ;
    ral:expr "HAS POSITION T-IAAP"
  ] ;
  bp:hasPreference [
    a soup:BalancedPreference ;
    soup:hasOperands
        [ a soup:LowestPreference ; soup:refersTo org:cost ] ,
        [ a soup:LowestPreference ; soup:refersTo worklist:size ]
  ] .

Update Resolution Proposal: Assigned to people with positions T-IAAP,
T-CB or T-LD. The preferred person is that who did the initial proposal.
iaap:UpdateProposal a bp:Activity ;
  bp:hasResourceAssignment [
    a ral:Expression ;
    ral:expr "HAS POSITION T-IAAP OR HAS POSITION T-CB OR
              HAS POSITION T-LD"
  ] ;
  bp:hasPreference [
    a soup:FavoritesPreference ;
    soup:refersTo ral:Expression ;
    soup:hasFavorites "IS PERSON RESPONSIBLE FOR ACTIVITY
                       Create Resolution Proposal Draft"
  ] .
```

Fig. 4. Examples of preferences expressed in RDF/Turtle syntax

Due to space constraints, we illustrate how these two tasks have been done with regard to activities *Request Report to CB/LD* and *Update Resolution Proposal*. The same approach can be used with the remaining activities.

Fig. 4 depicts the resource assignment (`bp:hasResourceAssignment`) and the preferences (`bp:hasPreferences`) for the aforementioned activities expressed in SOUP using RDF/Turtle syntax. For activity *Request Report to CB/LD* the preference is composite because it balances two atomic preferences: lowest cost and shortest worklist. Therefore, the composite preference is represented by means of an element of type `soup:BalancedPreference`, which is the type of composite preference that best suits the intention of the modeler. Regarding the atomic preferences, they are connected with the composite preference by means of relation `soup:hasOperands`. Both atomic preferences are of the same type (soup:LowestPreference). However, the former refers to the domain concept expressed with `org:cost`, which represents the cost of the resource, whereas the latter refers to the domain concept expressed with `worklist:size`, which represents the size of the worklist of the resource. Note that these two domain concepts must have an *eval* function implemented for them so that they can be evaluated for each resource.

The preference for activity *Update Resolution Proposal* is also atomic. However, it refers to the organizational information stored about each resource. In particular, it sets a qualitative preference stating that it prefers the people that fulfill the condition stated by property `soup:hasFavorites`.

4.2   Identifying the KB and Implementing *eval* Functions

In our scenario, there are three repositories that store the values of the properties used for the prioritization of resources. The *organizational repository* stores personal information of all members of the company along with their positions, roles, and units within the organization, information about skills, salary or hiring date, and all the data that is not related to participation in BP activities. The *worklist repository* stores the worklists of all resources in the organization. Finally, the *history repository* stores the event log of past process executions. The organizational repository is manually updated, whereas the worklist repository and the history repository are updated by the BPMS, which in our implementation is Activiti. The *eval* functions can be divided into the following four categories according to the repository they use to evaluate the domain concept:

Quantitative organizational evaluations: They are used to evaluate concepts that represent quantitative properties stored in the organizational repository such as personal (e.g., age) or professional information (e.g., salary).

Qualitative organizational evaluations: They are used to evaluate concepts that represent qualitative properties stored in the organizational repository including organizational information and skills. The implementation of this type of evaluations leverages CRISTAL [5] to resolve RAL expressions and obtain the set of resources.

Worklist evaluations: They are used to evaluate concepts that represent quantitative properties related to the size of the worklist. They interact with the BPMS to obtain the information about them.

History evaluations: They are used to evaluate concepts that represent quantitative properties about the participation of resources in past process activity executions. This evaluation also accesses the history of the BP.

5   Related Work

We next present a summary of the pros and cons of the current approaches for preference modeling in different domains, followed by an analysis of current support for resource prioritization in Business Process Management (BPM).

Preference Modeling. There are several formalisms that can be used to represent preferences in different fields [15]. Quantitative preferences modeled as utility or scoring functions have been widely used in economics and operations research [16, 17], as well as in web systems [18, 19]. This approach solves the multiple criteria decision making by transforming it to aggregated scoring functions. However, these functions are difficult to define by users, and not all the preferences that are strict partial orders can be represented [20]. In artificial intelligence research, solutions have been focused on defining preferences in a qualitative way, easier to understand and more natural to define by humans [21]. These preference models offer facilities to define preferences as a set of statements or terms that are contextually related. In database research, there are also several solutions, for instance, using top-k or skyline algorithms to obtain the best search items according to a stated preference [22, 20]. These preference models usually offer qualitative facilities to define preferences, though their implementation usually leads to large result sets that do not discriminate well between items to be ordered [15]. We have chosen SOUP [4] because it is a hybrid approach, as it combines quantitative and qualitative facilities to define preferences. Furthermore, it is independent of the domain, so it is suitable for resource prioritization. Indeed, the expressiveness of the model is semantically close to BP modeling, which enables its interoperability with other resource allocation solutions.

Resource Prioritization in Business Processes. Regarding the prioritization of resources in BPM, we have studied the support provided by the specifications BPMN 2.0, BPEL4People and WS-HumanTask; the BPMS Activiti and YAWL [10]; and the product suites WebSphere MQ and ARIS systems, concerning preference definition and resource ranking. We find that they neither provide support for preference specification nor for ranking of potential performers in order to prioritize resource allocation. Crowdsourcing systems, which outsource the execution of activities to the crowd, usually rely on a fixed set of features such as skills, location, certification, cost or reputation to implement priotization [23], or they use some auction or competition mechanism to select the best worker [24]. However, the prioritization mechanism is defined in the system for all the activities and cannot be customized according to other criteria.

The importance of ranking resources is also emphasized in other recent work. In [25], the authors define a resource visualization concept that is aimed to support resource allocation using three different metrics to recommend work distribution. The distribution of work is addressed in [26] trying to keep the balance between quality and performance. In [27], six resource allocation mechanisms are compared with regard to suitability, urgency, conformance and availability. Although all of them agree on the need of dynamic work allocation to adapt to the evoluting needs of organizations, they do not deal with preference modeling itself. Some other solutions approach this problem from a process mining perspective, focusing on providing recommendation from information inferred from event logs [28–31]. A resource manager is finally responsible for making the final decisions for allocation. Altogether, the work presented in this paper generalizes and complements the current support in the field of BPM regarding preference modeling. It would be interesting to combine it, e.g., with visualization support as proposed in [25, 31].

6 Conclusions and Future Work

In this paper, we addressed the problem of integrating priorities into resource assignment and allocation. To this end, we extended concepts from preference modeling and combined them with resource management techniques.

The main advantage of our solution is that it provides a mechanism to define a wide variety of different types of preferences while being independent of both the properties used in the preferences and the knowledge base that contains the information about them. These features make it easier to accommodate the different requirements several organizations may have. This is a significant difference with respect to the support provided by current systems, which are defined to deal with a specific set of properties. Furthermore, the expressiveness of the preferences that can be defined with our approach outperforms the current support in the BPM field regarding priority-based allocation.

We plan to extend the preference model to support complex cases involving the agenda of the resources in order to allow expressing and using preferences referring to the expected end time of an activity. We also want to explore how a similar technique could be applied to the distribution of work to resources, i.e., in the opposite direction. Activity priority might be considered in that case.

References

1. Russell, N., van der Aalst, W.M.P., ter Hofstede, A.H.M., Edmond, D.: Workflow Resource Patterns: Identification, Representation and Tool Support. In: Pastor, Ó., Falcão e Cunha, J. (eds.) CAiSE 2005. LNCS, vol. 3520, pp. 216–232. Springer, Heidelberg (2005)
2. van der Aalst, W.M.P., ter Hofstede, A.H.M.: YAWL: Yet Another Workflow Language. Inf. Syst. 30(4), 245–275 (2005)
3. Tan, H., van der Aalst, W.M.P.: Implementation of a YAWL Work-List Handler based on the Resource Patterns. In: CSCWD 2006, pp. 1–6 (2006)
4. García, J.M., Ruiz, D., Ruiz-Cortés, A.: A Model of User Preferences for Semantic Services Discovery and Ranking. In: Aroyo, L., Antoniou, G., Hyvönen, E., ten Teije, A., Stuckenschmidt, H., Cabral, L., Tudorache, T. (eds.) ESWC 2010, Part II. LNCS, vol. 6089, pp. 1–14. Springer, Heidelberg (2010)
5. Cabanillas, C., del Río-Ortega, A., Resinas, M., Ruiz-Cortés, A.: CRISTAL: Collection of Resource-centrIc Supporting Tools And Languages. In: BPM 2012 Demos, vol. 940, pp. 51–56 (2012)
6. García, J.M., Junghans, M., Ruiz, D., Agarwal, S., Ruiz-Cortés, A.: Integrating Semantic Web Services Ranking Mechanisms Using a Common Preference Model. Knowledge-Based Systems 49, 22–36 (2013)
7. Cabanillas, C., Resinas, M., Ruiz-Cortés, A.: Defining and Analysing Resource Assignments in Business Processes with RAL. In: Kappel, G., Maamar, Z., Motahari-Nezhad, H.R. (eds.) ICSOC 2011. LNCS, vol. 7084, pp. 477–486. Springer, Heidelberg (2011)
8. Strembeck, M., Mendling, J.: Modeling process-related RBAC models with extended UML activity models. Inf. Softw. Technol. 53, 456–483 (2011)
9. Awad, A., Grosskopf, A., Meyer, A., Weske, M.: Enabling Resource Assignment Constraints in BPMN. tech. rep., BPT (2009)
10. Adams, M.: The Resource Service. In: Modern Business Process Automation, pp. 261–290 (2010)

11. Davey, B.A., Priestley, H.A.: Introduction to Lattices and Order, 2nd edn. Cambridge University Press (2002)
12. Cabanillas, C., Resinas, M., Ruiz-Cortés, A.: RAL: A high-level user-oriented resource assignment language for business processes. In: Daniel, F., Barkaoui, K., Dustdar, S. (eds.) BPM Workshops 2011, Part I. LNBIP, vol. 99, pp. 50–61. Springer, Heidelberg (2012)
13. Russell, N., ter Hofstede, A., Edmond, D., van der Aalst, W.M.P.: Workflow Resource Patterns. tech. rep., BETA, WP 127, Eindhoven University of Technology (2004)
14. Cormen, T.H., Leiserson, C.E., Rivest, R.L., Stein, C.: Introduction to algorithms. MIT press (2001)
15. Domshlak, C., Hüllermeier, E., Kaci, S., Prade, H.: Preferences in ai: An overview. Artif. Intell. 175(7-8), 1037–1052 (2011)
16. Fishburn, P.C.: Utility theory for decision making. Wiley (1970)
17. Keeney, R.L., Raiffa, H.: Decisions with multiple objectives: Preferences and value tradeoffs. Cambridge Univ Press (1993)
18. Agrawal, R., Wimmers, E.L.: A Framework for Expressing and Combining Preferences. In: SIGMOD Conference, pp. 297–306 (2000)
19. Zeng, L., Benatallah, B., Ngu, A.H.H., Dumas, M., Kalagnanam, J., Chang, H.: QoS-Aware Middleware for Web Services Composition. IEEE Trans. Software Eng. 30(5), 311–327 (2004)
20. Chomicki, J.: Preference formulas in relational queries. ACM Trans. Database Syst. 28(4), 427–466 (2003)
21. Boutilier, C., Brafman, R.I., Domshlak, C., Hoos, H.H., Poole, D.: CP-nets: A Tool for Representing and Reasoning with Conditional Ceteris Paribus Preference Statements. J. Artif. Intell. Res (JAIR) 21, 135–191 (2004)
22. Kießling, W.: Foundations of Preferences in Database Systems. In: VLDB, pp. 311–322 (2002)
23. Vukovic, M.: Crowdsourcing for Enterprises. In: SERVICES, pp. 686–692 (2009)
24. Satzger, B., Psaier, H., Schall, D., Dustdar, S.: Auction-based crowdsourcing supporting skill management. Inf. Syst. 38(4), 547–560 (2013)
25. De Leoni, M., Adams, M., van der Aalst, W.M.P., Ter Hofstede, A.H.M.: Visual support for work assignment in process-aware information systems: Framework formalisation and implementation. Decis. Support Syst. 54(1), 345–361 (2012)
26. Kumar, A., van der Aalst, W.M.P., Verbeek, E.M.W.: Dynamic Work Distribution in Workflow Management Systems: How to Balance Quality and Performance. J. Manage. Inf. Syst. 18(3), 157–193 (2002)
27. Reijers, H.A., Jansen-Vullers, M.H., zur Muehlen, M., Appl, W.: Workflow management systems + swarm intelligence = dynamic task assignment for emergency management applications. In: Alonso, G., Dadam, P., Rosemann, M. (eds.) BPM 2007. LNCS, vol. 4714, pp. 125–140. Springer, Heidelberg (2007)
28. Liu, T., Cheng, Y., Ni, Z.: Mining event logs to support workflow resource allocation. Know.-Based Syst. 35, 320–331 (2012)
29. Liu, Y., Wang, J., Yang, Y., Sun, J.: A semi-automatic approach for workflow staff assignment. Comput. Ind. 59(5), 463–476 (2008)
30. Rinderle-Ma, S., van der Aalst, W.M.P.: Life-Cycle Support for Staff Assignment Rules in Process-Aware Information Systems. Department of Technology Management, Eindhoven University of Technology (2007)
31. Bose, R.P.J.C., van der Aalst, W.M.P.: Process Mining Applied to the BPI Challenge 2012: Divide and Conquer While Discerning Resources. In: La Rosa, M., Soffer, P. (eds.) BPM Workshops 2012. LNBIP, vol. 132, pp. 221–222. Springer, Heidelberg (2013)

Prediction of Remaining Service Execution Time Using Stochastic Petri Nets with Arbitrary Firing Delays

Andreas Rogge-Solti and Mathias Weske

Business Process Technology Group,
Hasso Plattner Institute, University of Potsdam, Germany
{andreas.rogge-solti,mathias.weske}@hpi.uni-potsdam.de

Abstract. Companies realize their services by business processes to stay competitive in a dynamic market environment. In particular, they track the current state of the process to detect undesired deviations, to provide customers with predicted remaining durations, and to improve the ability to schedule resources accordingly. In this setting, we propose an approach to predict remaining process execution time, taking into account *passed time* since the last observed event.

While existing approaches update predictions only upon event arrival and subtract elapsed time from the latest predictions, our method also considers expected events that have *not* yet occurred, resulting in better prediction quality. Moreover, the prediction approach is based on the Petri net formalism and is able to model concurrency appropriately. We present the algorithm and its implementation in ProM and compare its predictive performance to state-of-the-art approaches in simulated experiments and in an industry case study.

Keywords: business process performance, remaining time prediction, stochastic Petri nets, generally distributed durations, conditional probability.

1 Introduction

Organizations provide services to their customers. To provide a high degree of flexibility, these services are implemented by business processes. As a result, business process management (BPM) plays an important role to improve the performance and quality of business processes [22]. Customers and clients compare the range of goods and services of competitors in a world-wide market, increasing the pressure on companies to conduct their business efficiently and effectively. In particular, a company needs to monitor and control its processes in case of delays, or other unexpected events, to meet given service level agreements.

Predicting the remaining process duration and detecting and preventing risks has spawned much interest recently [13,4,8,18]. The motivation is to ensure customer satisfaction by increasing the overall ratio of services that complete within defined thresholds. Accurate prediction methods are essential to prevent exceptionally long service times. Predictions of remaining service times of a running case can be used in other scenarios, as well. One scenario is to provide customers with information about the progress and expected duration of their case. Further, the predicted remaining duration can be used internally, e.g., for resource scheduling.

S. Basu et al. (Eds.): ICSOC 2013, LNCS 8274, pp. 389–403, 2013.
© Springer-Verlag Berlin Heidelberg 2013

Several models exist for prediction purposes. Often, the simplifying assumption of exponentially distributed durations is made [17], because the resulting models can be analyzed efficiently. However, if we also want to capture deterministic time-outs or irregularities like multiple modes of distributions, we need more expressive performance models. Current prediction algorithms proposed in [4,8] only update the predictions upon arrival of events, or are based on exponential distributions [25]. In contrast to this, we take advantage of passed time as an influencing and restricting factor of predictions. In other words, we make use of knowledge about expected events *not observed yet*, and thereby significantly improve the prediction accuracy. To our knowledge, the approach presented in this paper is the first to rely on Petri nets for remaining time prediction of already running cases, which allows us to treat concurrent activities appropriately.

Based on a stochastic model of a business process that can be obtained by expert's knowledge or historical performance information extracted from event logs, this paper introduces a novel prediction algorithm. The prediction algorithm can cope with both non-parametric stochastic models and parametric models of known shape. It is implemented and available as open-source plug-in in the process mining framework ProM [2].

We compare the results of the prediction approach with state-of-the-art approaches [4], and with a model using exponentially distributed durations. As basis for comparison we use a simulated experiment and a case-study based on real container tracking data from a Dutch logistics service provider.

The remainder of this paper is structured as follows. In Sect. 2, we provide preliminary definitions used throughout this work. Subsequently, Sect. 3 describes the proposed method's theoretical background and the implemented solution. Afterwards, in Sect. 4, we evaluate the predictions of different existing approaches to our approach and discuss the findings. In Sect. 5, we compare our work with related methods and highlight conceptual differences. Finally, we conclude in Sect. 6.

2 Preliminaries

In the following, we describe the concepts, on which the prediction algorithm is based. Our goal is to predict the remaining time until completion of a certain business process instance. We use the terms *instance*, and *case* interchangeably in the remainder of the paper.

Basically, the prediction uses historical information (i.e., information on how similar cases have performed in the past), and all the information that we have about the current case. First, the prediction algorithm makes the basic assumption that historical and current process execution information (i.e., the start or end of activities) are stored as events with timestamps. We call a collection of events belonging to a process an *event log*, or simply *log* in the remainder of this paper.

Events are correlated to the activities of a certain case of a process. We group events of a particular case into a *trace* and order the events by the timestamp of occurrence. Note that a trace can be either complete (i.e., the events of a completed case are all in the trace), or still running (i.e., some events are still expected). In order to distinguish these cases and to be able to define the behavior of the process, business process models are widely used in companies [22]. These models serve other purposes as well, e.g., analysis, simulation, ground for common understanding of processes, implementation specification.

In this work, we use business process models to capture performance criteria of a business process. In fact, we use Petri nets as modeling basis in this paper. Petri nets cover the most important control flow constructs of business processes like sequential execution, exclusive choice, parallelism, and synchronization. Furthermore, they have a well-defined semantics and can be verified for correctness [1]. In practice, high-level process modeling languages are common, e.g., the industry standard BPMN, but most of those models can be transformed into Petri nets [15]. We employ an extended Petri net formalism to capture performance aspects, but let us revisit the plain form, first:

Definition 1 (Petri net). *A Petri net is a tuple $PN = (P, T, F, M_0)$ where:*
- *$P = \{p_1, p_2, \ldots, p_m\}$ is a set of places.*
- *$T = \{t_1, t_2, \ldots, t_n\}$ is a set of transitions.*
- *$F \subseteq (P \times T) \cup (T \times P)$ is a set of connecting arcs representing flow relations.*
- *$M_0 \in P \to \mathbb{N}_0^+$ is an initial marking.*

We restrict the Petri net models to be sound WF-nets, i.e., having an input and output place with every transition on a path between these two places and no dead locks or live locks, cf. [1]. Soundness also requires the output place to be reached eventually from all markings, s.t., no tokens remain in the net. The models do not need to be structured or free-choice, because we use a simulation-based approach to prediction. In this work, we enrich this model with additional stochastic timing information to be able to make predictions of remaining durations.

Definition 2 (GDT_SPN). *A stochastic Petri net with generally distributed transitions (GDT_SPN), is a seven-tuple: $GDT\_SPN = (P, T, \mathcal{P}, \mathcal{W}, F, M_0, \mathcal{D})$, where (P, T, F, M_0) is the basic underlying Petri net. Additionally:*
- *The set of transitions $T = T_i \cup T_t$ is partitioned into immediate transitions T_i and timed transitions T_t.*
- *$\mathcal{P} : T \to \mathbb{N}_0^+$ is an assignment of priorities to transitions, where $\forall t \in T_i : \mathcal{P}(t) \geq 1$ and $\forall t \in T_t : \mathcal{P}(t) = 0$.*
- *$\mathcal{W} : T_i \to \mathbb{R}^+$ assigns probabilistic weights to the immediate transitions.*
- *$\mathcal{D} : T_t \to D$ is an assignment of arbitrary probability distributions D to timed transitions, reflecting the durations of the corresponding activities in the real world.*

GDT_SPN models rely on the well-known notion of generalized stochastic Petri nets (GSPN) by Marsan et al. [17]. The key difference to GSPNs is that we do not enforce the Markovian property, i.e., memorylessness, which restricts transition delays to be exponentially distributed in the continuous case. Typically, real world processes exhibit duration distributions, that are not exponential. For instance, services can contain deterministic time-outs, or durations of activities can belong to normal or log-normal classes, e.g., surgery durations are assumed to follow a log-normal distribution [21]. Accordingly, we allow to use *any* parametric or non-parametric distribution, as long as we can draw samples from it. In comparison to GSPNs, which have the convenient property that they are isomorphic to Markov processes, we lose the possibility to calculate expected durations analytically and efficiently, but resort to analysis by Monte Carlo simulation instead [6].

When lifting the Markov assumption, an execution semantics needs to be selected [16]. We use race-semantics with enabling memory, as defined in [16] and used in [25], too. Firing rights between concurrently enabled immediate transitions are resolved probabilistically based on their weights. When immediate and timed transitions are enabled, immediate transitions fire first, due to higher priority. When only timed transitions are enabled, they race for the right to fire first. This allows to model time-outs. The enabling memory semantics specifies that concurrent non-conflicting activities do not lose their progress when another transition fires. However, if a transition gets disabled, it has to restart its work the next time it becomes enabled. The class of GDT_SPN models allows to model most reasonable business processes with their specific timing properties.

Now, how do we obtain GDT_SPN models with duration distributions for every transition? If the process models to be enriched with performance information are not known in advance, algorithms from process mining can be used to infer the Petri net models that capture the observed behavior in the log [5,2].

In previous work [19], we described a method based on replaying event logs on Petri nets using the notion of alignments [3]. By aligning the historical traces to the model and by calculating activity durations for each transition, we gain statistical timing information. Statistical information collected in this way can be used to fit statistical parametric distributions (e.g., normal, log-normal, exponential, phase-type), and non-parametric distributions [11]. Non-parametric techniques might prove more accurate, if the durations contain irregularities, such as two peaks, but are also subject to overfitting.

Preferably, in latter cases, it would help to find the reasons for such irregularities, and thus be able to separate cases belonging to one heap from those belonging to the other heap. Machine learning methods, e.g., classification algorithms, are frequently used for this task. Example applications are described in [7], where the authors used non-parametric regression techniques on case attributes such as the amount of the insurance claim that proved well as indicator for case duration. However, these additional approaches are out of scope of this work, and we focus on the case, where no additional information is present in the log.

3   Prediction during Process Execution

In this section the core contribution of this paper is introduced and the prediction algorithm is presented. Given the preliminaries described in the previous section, we first introduce the key concept that the prediction is based on, i.e., constrained activity durations.

3.1   Constrained Activity Durations

An important assumption for our work is that the system detects process relevant events if they happen—i.e., the events are always recorded in the system—and that the time from occurrence to detection is negligible. This assumption applies especially for processes that are supported by process aware information systems. It allows us to use information that goes beyond the mere detection of observed events. We can use the information that an enabled activity has *not been completed yet* at a given point in time, if the event for completion of the task was not observed yet.

The concept is illustrated with an example. Consider the GDT_SPN model of an insurance claim process in Fig. 1. In this process, there are two options for proceeding after the *Check case* activity. Either the case will be handled with a 70% chance or it will be rejected in the remaining 30% of the cases. In the model, these probabilities are depicted as annotated weights of the immediate transitions, shown as black bars competing for one token. The delay distributions are specified in a parametric form in day units, e.g., the *Check case* transition is exponentially *(exp)* distributed with a firing rate parameter λ=2 days, and the

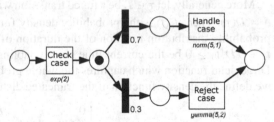

Fig. 1. Model of a simplified insurance process. The current trace contains only the event indicating that activity *Check case* has finished.

Handle case transition is normally *(norm)* distributed with a mean of five days and a standard deviation of one day. After either the handling or the rejection of the case, this simple process is completed, i.e., the token reaches the output place.

In the current situation depicted in Fig. 1, the case was checked and awaits a decision. Without loss of generality, we assume the upper branch was chosen and align the time axis of the density function of the duration of the *Handle case* transition to be zero when it becomes enabled.

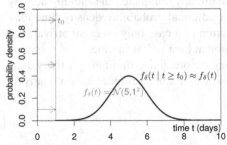
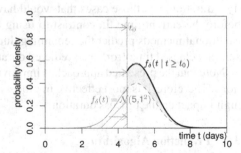

(a) After one day, the truncated density is almost unchanged

(b) After 4.5 days, the truncated density is significantly different from the original density

Fig. 2. Truncated probability density functions of the duration of activity *Handle case*, i.e., constrained to (a) being greater than one day, and (b) being greater than 4.5 days.

Figure 2 shows the resulting distribution of the *Handle case* transition at two *later* points in time. Fig. 2(a) depicts the normally distributed probability density, which is the well-known bell-shaped curve, where after one day, activity *Handle case* was not yet completed. Note that this observation does not change the original distribution significantly, as it is unlikely that the activity is completed earlier than after one day.

Fig. 2(b) shows the the same situation, but more time has passed without detecting the end of the activity. Let $\delta \in \mathcal{D}$ be the duration distribution of the *Handle case* activity. In dashed grey the probability density function of the original duration $f_\delta(t)$ is depicted. The vertical line shows the current time t_0 that advances from left to right, as time proceeds. The thick black curve $f_\delta(t \mid t \geq t_0)$ is the truncated density of the remaining cases. It depicts the conditional probability density of the duration excluding the non-consistent cases (crossed out area left from t_0).

More generally, let $\tau \in T_t$ be a timed transition with the assigned duration distribution $\delta = D(\tau)$. Then, $f_\delta(t)$ is the probability density function and $F_\delta(t) = \int_{-\infty}^{t} f_\delta(t)\mathrm{dt}$ is the probability distribution function of the duration of τ. Let TD be the time domain. Let $t_0 \in TD, t_0 \geq 0$ be the current time since enabling of τ. Let further δ_{Dirac} denote the Dirac delta function which captures the whole probability mass at a single point. Then we define the density function of the truncated distribution as:

$$f_\delta(t \mid t \geq t_0) = \begin{cases} 0 & t < t_0 \quad F_\delta(t_0) < 1 \\ \frac{f_\delta(t)}{1-F_\delta(t_0)} & t \geq t_0, F_\delta(t_0) < 1 \\ \delta_{Dirac}(t-t_0) & F_\delta(t_0) = 1 \end{cases} \tag{1}$$

The part of the density function that is above the threshold t_0 is rescaled such that it integrates to 1, which is a requirement for probability density functions. Note that in the exceptional case that $F_\delta(t_0) = 1$ (i.e., the current time t_0 progressed further than the probability density function's support), we use the Dirac delta function with its peak at t_0. In this case, the activity is expected to finish immediately at t_0.

The intuition is as follows. We base our predictions on a stochastic model describing the distribution of a large amount of cases. From that distribution, we discard the fraction of the cases that is not consistent with our observation for the current activity's duration, i.e., those cases that would have already completed the running activity before the current time. In contrast to using conditional probability density functions, traditional methods predict the remaining duration of a case only on event arrival, and subtract elapsed time from the predicted duration at later points in time.

Note that the presented approach is improving the prediction of running activity durations. Therefore, it is most effective in processes, where some activities have a relatively high impact on the process duration.

3.2 Prediction Algorithm

Besides the already mentioned assumption of immediate detection of events by the prediction framework, we consider each activity duration in isolation, independently from other activities. This is a common simplifying assumption that we share with all analytical approaches to prediction.

In order to make predictions for a single case, the current state of the case and the model that captures experiences about the behavior of the process needs to be known. The prediction algorithm takes four inputs: (1) the *GDT_SPN model* of the business process, cf. Definition 2 in Sect. 2, (2) the current *trace* of the case, i.e., all observed events up to time t_0, (3) the *current time* t_0, and (4) the number of simulation *iterations* indicating the precision of the prediction. Algorithm 1 describes the procedure.

The algorithm is straightforward. It starts by finding the appropriate current state, i.e., the marking, in the model by replaying the available observed events of the case in the model. We assume that a workflow engine is in charge of controlling the process flow, which facilitates replay of observed events in the log. If this is not the case, an extension based on techniques from [3] can be used to align non-fitting traces with the model.

Algorithm 1. Prediction algorithm

```
1: procedure PREDICT(model, trace, current_time, iterations)
2:     currentMarking ← replay(trace, model)        ▷ replay the observed events in the model
3:     times ← new List()                                        ▷ used to collect results
4:     for all i ∈ iterations do
5:         time ← simulateConstrained(model, currentMarking, current_time)
6:         times.add(time)
7:     end for
8:     return getMean(times)                          ▷ the average of the simulated values
9: end procedure
```

As a second step the algorithm collects simulation results, i.e., completion *times*, of a given number of simulation iterations in a list. Each simulation run represents a sample from the possible continuations of the process according to the model. The simulateConstrained method simulates continuations of the trace for the GDT_SPN model, but instead of sampling from the original transition distributions $F_\delta(t)$, it samples from the truncated distributions conditioned on the current time $F_\delta(t \mid t \geq t_0)$, as described in Sect. 3.1. The completion times of all simulated continuations of the case are collected and the algorithm returns the mean of these sample values.

Note that the accuracy of a prediction based on simulated samples depends on both the number of computed samples, as well as the standard deviation within the samples. Therefore, we also support the mode, where instead of a sample size, the user can set required accuracy thresholds. For example, the simulation continues taking samples, until the 99 percent confidence interval on the prediction lies within ± 3 percent of the predicted value.

3.3 Open-Source Implementation

We implemented the prediction algorithm in the process mining framework ProM as a plugin[1]. The method to enrich a Petri net with historical performance data extracted from a log is also available in that plugin. It is possible to learn different kind of parametric models, e.g., normally distributed durations, as well as nonparametric models, e.g., simple histograms, or kernel density estimators. If the learned models are used only for prediction, simple histograms based on the observed samples suffice for making predictions. In this latter case of histograms, the sampling method can simply pick one of the past observations randomly. We exclude the observations that do not meet the constraint of being greater or equal to the current time t_0. There might be cases, when the current instance takes longer for an activity than all previously observed cases. In this cases, the histogram based sampling returns the constraint t_0 itself.

When expert estimates exist and parametric probability distributions are used in the GDT_SPN model, e.g., normal, exponential, or lognormal distributions, we use rejection sampling. Rejection sampling is simple: we draw a sample from the original distribution and check, whether it meets the given constraints. If not, we reject the sample and repeat the process until we get a sample that meets the constraints.

---

[1] Implementation provided open-source in the StochasticPetriNet package of ProM. Available at http://www.processmining.org

In our case, rejection sampling becomes inefficient, if the current time has progressed beyond most of the distribution's probability mass, as almost all samples will be rejected. For such cases, we also implemented a slice sampling method that samples directly from the conditional probability density $f_\delta(t \mid t \geq t_0)$ in Equation 1 by a random walk under the density function. Slice sampling can be used to sample from any distribution as long as we can compute the corresponding density function.

4 Evaluation

In the following evaluation, we analyze the quality and run time of our approach. To assess prediction quality, we compare our approach to the related prediction method described in [4], and an analytical method based on regular GSPNs. We further investigate how the presented approach scales in terms of run time for different model sizes. We start with the evaluation of the prediction quality. Therefore, we use both a simulated model, and real data from a logistics provider in the Netherlands. First, we explain the experimental setup.

4.1 Experimental Setup

The experimental setup is depicted in Fig. 3. In the synthetic cases a GDT_SPN model that contains both the control flow structure definition and the performance specification in form of duration distributions is used. From this model 10000 traces of execution are generated and stored in the simulated log. Besides the simulated log, also the Petri net model (i.e., the underlying Petri net of the GDT_SPN model), is used as input. In real settings, we have a Petri net and a log given as input. To evaluate the prediction quality, a 10-fold cross validation is performed. Therefore, the log is split into ten evenly divided parts and nine of them are used as the training log to learn the performance behavior and the remaining part as test log to test the prediction accuracy. We iterate over these parts, such that each of them is used once as test log. The Petri net is enriched to a GDT_SPN by collecting the performance data of the training log, as described in [19].

We are interested in the different prediction methods' accuracy to predict the remaining duration of a case *any time* during the process. Therefore, we trigger the predictions

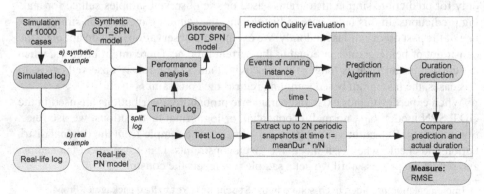

Fig. 3. Experimental setup for evaluating the prediction quality of the algorithm

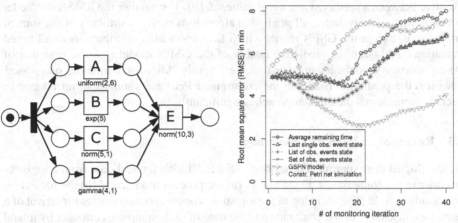

(a) A GDT_SPN process model with four parallel activities A, B, C, D and a final activity E, with annotated duration distributions.

(b) Root mean square errors (RMSE) in minutes at 40 periodic predictions. Mean duration: 17.32 minutes.

Fig. 4. A model with four parallel branches (a) and corresponding prediction errors (b) using 10-fold cross-validation with 40 periodic predictions, s.t. the 20th iteration is at the mean duration

periodically. The length of such a period is based on the mean process duration that is obtained from the training log. More precisely, $2N$ periodic predictions are made for each instance in the test log, such that the Nth snapshot is at the mean duration of the process. This means that while initially all instances still run, some instances will be finished at later prediction iterations. Note that only predictions for still running cases are added to the resulting statistics.

The evaluation proceeds for each trace in the test log as follows. At each iteration of the periodic prediction, we compute the relative time t_0 to the trace start and pass t_0 and the partial trace containing the events of the case with time $\leq t_0$ to the prediction algorithm described in Sect. 3. The predicted duration for different prediction methods are computed and compared to the actual duration of the trace from time t_0. The simplest method for prediction is using the *average remaining time*, which is simply the mean process duration gathered from the training set minus the elapsed time t_0. Additionally, we compare against the state transition systems approach [4] with different configurations. Predictions based on the history sharing (i) the *last observed event only*, (ii) the *list of all previous observed events*, and (iii) the *set of all previous observed events*. Finally, we also compare our approach against a regular GSPN based approach, i.e., an approach where only exponential distributions are allowed in timed transitions of the model.

Note that if any of the methods predicts a negative remaining time, i.e., that the current case should have completed already at time t_0, the predicted duration is set to 0.

4.2 Results of a Simulated Experiment

Figure 4 shows (a) an example model containing four parallel branches that is used for the simulated experiment, and (b) the root mean square error (RMSE), for each of the 40 periodic predictions mentioned above. The RMSE is an error measure for quantifying the error between a predicted and a real value, cf. [9]. The smaller the RMSE, the better is the prediction in average. All prediction algorithms perform similarly at the start of an instance, except the GSPN model which fits exponential distributions to all timed transitions. Although the prediction quality of the GSPN model is worse than that of the comparison models, it can be analyzed efficiently. After some time has progressed, however, the prediction based on the constrained Petri net simulation, introduced in Sect. 3, outperforms the other approaches significantly.

4.3 Results of an Industry Case Study

We conducted the experiment described in Sect. 4.1 also for real data from a logistics provider in the Netherlands. Fig. 5 shows (a) the process model, and (b) the prediction errors side by side. The event log of the logistics process contains entries for arrival of a seavessel, discharge of the container, and the date of picking up the container by inland transport in a sequential order. It contains 784 cases over the year 2011.

In this case study, the different abstraction levels of the comparison method [4] collapse to the same results, cf. Fig. 5(b), because the process is sequential. The GSPN method yields comparable results as the benchmark methods in [4]. But we can observe that our presented approach produces more accurate predictions of the remaining process duration than the benchmarks.

To summarize the results of the evaluation of prediction quality, we highlight the following characteristics of our approach:
- At early prediction periods the approach performs about as well as the benchmarks.
- The improvements become more significant as time proceeds.
- The approach is most valuable for long running cases, which are critical to be detected and avoided.

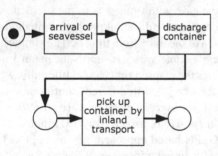

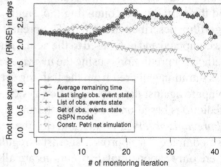

(a) Model of a sequential logistics process capturing the arrival of seavessels, container discharges and further inland shipping.

(b) RMSE in days for the logistics process at 40 periodic predictions. Mean duration: 4.03 days.

Fig. 5. Model (a) and prediction errors (b) for the logistics provider case study using 10-fold cross validation with 40 periodic predictions, s.t. the 20th iteration is at the mean duration.

4.4 Scalability Analysis

We propose to use simulation as means to predict the remaining service execution time for a running case. Therefore, it is interesting to see, how long the prediction approach takes to simulate the remaining behavior of the process. To test for scalability, we conduct the following experiment.

First, we randomly generate structured, acyclic GDT_SPN models of different sizes by iterative insertion of sequential, parallel, and exclusive blocks, until we reach the desired node size of the net. For each timed transition we specify a distribution, i.e., *uniform, normal,* or *lognormal* distributions, or non-parametric *Gaussian kernel* density

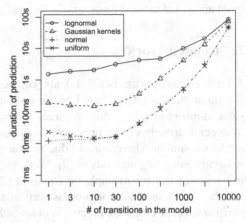

Fig. 6. Prediction durations for differently sized randomly generated, acyclic GDT_SPN models. Axes in log-scale.

estimators based on a random number of observations. In general, the run time of the prediction algorithm depends on multiple factors:

- The *average number of transitions* that need to fire to reach the end of the process, influenced by the size of the net, the progress of the current case, and potential cycles.
- The *kind of transition distributions*, as there exist distributions that are rather costly to draw samples from, e.g., complicated non-parametric models, as well as simple models, e.g., the uniform distribution.
- The *requested accuracy of the prediction*. Besides the fact that computing a narrow confidence interval takes more samples than allowing more sampling error, the variance of the process durations also influences the number of samples required to achieve the requested precision.
- The *computing power* of the system running the simulation.

For our experiments, we fixed the *requested accuracy* to a 99 percent confidence interval within maximum ±3 percent of error of the mean remaining duration. Regarding *computing power*, we used a regular laptop computer with a Pentium i7 620M (2.66 GHz cores) equipped with 8GB of ram. We varied the other two factors, i.e., the *average number of transitions* and the *kinds of distributions* used. Fig. 6 depicts the average time taken for remaining time prediction of acyclic GDT_SPN models based on the number of transitions in the model in log-scale. For example, predicting the duration of a medium sized model (100 transitions) takes around 300 milliseconds for rather expensive non-parametric Gaussian kernel density estimation. Prediction of models with lognormally distributed values takes long because of higher variance. Note that a prediction of a model with 10000 transitions still is feasible in less than 100 seconds with these configurations.

In our experience, most business processes involving human activities take hours, days, or sometimes even months to complete. In these situations, the quality of the prediction is more important than the performance of the prediction approach. If performance is critical however, the approach could be extended to provide a fall back option to an analytical method based on GSPN models, as implemented in [25].

5 Related Work

A lot of related work exists that deals with prediction based on historical observations. Common are predictions based on time-series data, e.g., for the stock market or for sales numbers of a company. Whereas in time series data, the individual values tend to depend strongly on the previous values, in a business process, these dependencies are less common. Therefore and due to space limitations, we refer to the overview of existing forecasting methods in [9]. Work on the analysis of trends and change points in *processes* can for example be found in [23]. However, for this work, we assume that the current model of the process performance is representing the current real world performance. So either the process is in a steady state, or mentioned methods, as in [23], are used to keep the model up to date.

5.1 Process Related Predictions

There has been work on prediction of case durations based on historical observations. In their work, van der Aalst et al. use the available information in logs to predict the remaining duration based in observed durations in the past [4]. They create an annotated state transition system for the logs, which can be calibrated in terms of abstraction, and collect remaining durations for each state from the log. Our approach is similar in the sense that it also abstracts from data and resources, but uses GDT_SPN models instead of transition systems, making our approach more accurate when parallelism exists in the process. The work in [4] serves as one of the benchmarks for our prediction method in the next section.

Building on the work in [4], Folino et al. [8] present an improvement based on predictive clustering. They make use of additional contextual information of a trace, e.g., the current workload, to perform clustering. The idea is to group similar traces and base predictions on such subsets of the log for new ones with similar features. They use the predictions to warn in case of a predicted transgression of a threshold. Our prediction method could substitute the state-transition based method in [8], improving the results for processes with parallelism, and during execution of the instances.

Other work for prediction of performance was presented by Hwang et al. [10] and similarly Zheng et al. [24]. They use formulae to compute quality of service criteria, such as expected durations of compositions. Typically, these works assume the service compositions to be composed of building blocks. The methods proposed can be used for business processes, too. However, the block-structured assumption is lifted in this work, allowing for more complex models, and we also consider already running instances.

The work presented by Leitner et al. [14] considers already running instances, too. They use regressions for durations between two-point measures in the process. The predictions are then used to identify whether a service level agreement will be violated. Similarly, Pika et al. [18] define indicators for the risk of deadline violations. They search for patterns, such as abnormal activity durations, and use that information for predicting whether a case will be late. By contrast, our work includes knowledge of the whole business process model to make predictions and we use the elapsed time since the last event as constraining factor. Kang et al. [13] advocate also business process monitoring in real-time. Their approach is based on classifying historical traces in correct and incorrect traces by inductive data mining techniques, e.g., support vector machines. Similarly as in our motivation, their goal is to predict and classify current instances, e.g., if they are likely to produce failures. However, their approach is only capturing sequential processes, and event's timestamps are not considered in the prediction.

Simulation has also been proposed and used for operational decision making by Rozinat et al. [20]. The idea is to set up a simulation environment capturing the current situation and start a short-term simulation from this state with different simulation parameters. Their use of simulation is for operational decision support and is focused on the overall performance of business processes. In contrast, we use simulation to make a prediction for the current instance only and use the current elapsed time as additional input to the simulation which allows to improve single predictions.

Analysis of stochastic Petri nets with generally distributed firing times, i.e, GDT _SPN models in this paper, has already been done before. Monte Carlo simulation is the preferred choice for analysis, e.g., in [25]. However, those works rather focus on transient analysis, e.g., average throughput and waiting times, instead of predicting remaining durations of single instances with conditional probability densities based on the current prediction time.

5.2 Quality of Service Related Forecasting

Jiang et al. [12] handle time series in business activity monitoring and focus on detecting outliers and change points. Their approach does not consider the process structure, but they only consider specific features of a process, such as customer usage profiles, and within those features they focus on adapting the prediction model to observed trends and changes. Another approach by Zeng et al. [23] applies the ARIMA forecasting method to predict performance criteria for event sequences (corresponding to *traces* in our terminology) and thus support seasonality of changes. They do not use that approach for single instances, but rather for aggregated key performance indicators (KPIs). Their prediction can be mapped to the prediction approach in [4] with the states distinguished as lists of ordered events. Based on that model the values are classified by regression to separate them in those that meet the KPIs, and those that violate them. There is a drawback to using event sequences for prediction in processes with parallelism, as there is a combinatorial state space issue with the interleavings, such that for a single prediction much otherwise useful training data are spread to other interleaving sequences and do not influence the prediction for the current sequence. Compared to that, our work improves on the aspect of prediction of a single case in *real-time* and is less likely to suffer from sparse training data issues in processes with parallelism.

Trend aware forecasting methods are out of scope of this paper, because we assume the process to be in steady state. If the process performance is subject to seasonality or trends, an integration of methods like ARIMA seems promising, however. To the best of our knowledge, the main contribution of this work, i.e., using temporal restrictions to make predictions more accurate, has not been proposed in literature before.

6   Conclusion

We described a relevant and common setting for the prediction of remaining process duration, where a process aware information system is aware of changes in process instances immediately. Based on this setting, we isolated one important aspect, i.e., the conditional duration distributions based on passed time and investigated the effects on prediction accuracy. We compared our results with state-of-the-art approaches devised for similar settings, and with the results of efficiently analyzable GSPN models.

The presented prediction approach is able to capture parallelism in business processes naturally, because it is based on Petri nets, as opposed to techniques based on state transition systems [4,8]. Another advantage of Petri nets is that they are able to capture resources in a native way. As future work, we want to integrate the resource perspective to make the prediction account for dependencies between instances of the process.

Further, we plan to lift the independence assumption and take correlations between activity durations into account. Classification based on case attributes has shown much potential to improve predictions, cf. [8], and we expect similar gains in prediction accuracy when combined with this method. In this paper, we assumed the model to represent the current state accurately, which in reality is often not the case, because the process might be subject to changes, e.g., changes due to seasonality, resource situation or process redesign. The integration of a mechanism to detect such changes and adapt the model accordingly would further increase the accuracy of predictions.

References

1. van der Aalst, W.M.P.: Verification of workflow nets. In: Azéma, P., Balbo, G. (eds.) ICATPN 1997. LNCS, vol. 1248, pp. 407–426. Springer, Heidelberg (1997)
2. van der Aalst, W.M.P.: Process Mining: Discovery, Conformance and Enhancement of Business Processes. Springer (2011)
3. van der Aalst, W.M.P., Adriansyah, A., van Dongen, B.F.: Replaying history on process models for conformance checking and performance analysis. Wiley Interdisciplinary Reviews: Data Mining and Knowledge Discovery 2, 182–192 (2012)
4. van der Aalst, W.M.P., Schonenberg, M.H., Song, M.: Time prediction based on process mining. Information Systems 36(2), 450–475 (2011)
5. Agrawal, R., Gunopulos, D., Leymann, F.: Mining process models from workflow logs. In: Schek, H.-J., Saltor, F., Ramos, I., Alonso, G. (eds.) EDBT 1998. LNCS, vol. 1377, pp. 469–483. Springer, Heidelberg (1998)
6. Bobbio, A., Telek, M.: Computational restrictions for SPN with generally distributed transition times. In: Echtle, K., Powell, D.R., Hammer, D. (eds.) EDCC 1994. LNCS, vol. 852, pp. 131–148. Springer, Heidelberg (1994)
7. van Dongen, B.F., Crooy, R.A., van der Aalst, W.M.P.: Cycle time prediction: When will this case finally be finished? In: Meersman, R., Tari, Z. (eds.) OTM 2008, Part I. LNCS, vol. 5331, pp. 319–336. Springer, Heidelberg (2008)

8. Folino, F., Guarascio, M., Pontieri, L.: Discovering context-aware models for predicting business process performances. In: Meersman, R., et al. (eds.) OTM 2012, Part I. LNCS, vol. 7565, pp. 287–304. Springer, Heidelberg (2012)
9. De Gooijer, J.G., Hyndman, R.J.: 25 years of time series forecasting. International Journal of Forecasting 22(3), 443–473 (2006)
10. Hwang, S.Y., Wang, H., Tang, J., Srivastava, J.: A probabilistic approach to modeling and estimating the QoS of web-services-based workflows. Information Sciences 177(23), 5484–5503 (2007)
11. Härdle, W.: Applied nonparametric regression. Cambridge University Press (1990)
12. Jiang, W., Au, T., Tsui, K.L.: A statistical process control approach to business activity monitoring. IIE Transactions 39(3), 235–249 (2007)
13. Kang, B., Kim, D., Kang, S.H.: Periodic performance prediction for real-time business process monitoring. Industrial Management & Data Systems 112(1), 4–23 (2011)
14. Leitner, P., Wetzstein, B., Rosenberg, F., Michlmayr, A., Dustdar, S., Leymann, F.: Runtime prediction of service level agreement violations for composite services. In: Dan, A., Gittler, F., Toumani, F. (eds.) ICSOC/ServiceWave 2009. LNCS, vol. 6275, pp. 176–186. Springer, Heidelberg (2010)
15. Lohmann, N., Verbeek, E., Dijkman, R.: Petri net transformations for business processes – A survey. In: Jensen, K., van der Aalst, W.M.P. (eds.) ToPNoC II. LNCS, vol. 5460, pp. 46–63. Springer, Heidelberg (2009)
16. Marsan, M.A., Balbo, G., Bobbio, A., Chiola, G., Conte, G., Cumani, A.: The effect of execution policies on the semantics and analysis of stochastic Petri nets. IEEE Transactions on Software Engineering 15(7), 832–846 (1989)
17. Marsan, M.A., Conte, G., Balbo, G.: A class of generalized stochastic Petri nets for the performance evaluation of multiprocessor systems. ACM TOCS 2(2), 93–122 (1984)
18. Pika, A., van der Aalst, W.M.P., Fidge, C.J., ter Hofstede, A.H.M., Wynn, M.T.: Predicting deadline transgressions using event logs. In: La Rosa, M., Soffer, P. (eds.) BPM 2012 Workshops. LNBIP, vol. 132, pp. 211–216. Springer, Heidelberg (2013)
19. Rogge-Solti, A., van der Aalst, W.M.P., Weske, M.: Discovering stochastic Petri nets with arbitrary delay distributions from event logs. In: BPM Workshops. Springer, Heigelberg (to appear)
20. Rozinat, A., Wynn, M.T., van der Aalst, W.M.P., ter Hofstede, A.H.M., Fidge, C.J.: Workflow simulation for operational decision support. Data & Knowledge Engineering 68(9), 834–850 (2009)
21. Strum, D.P., May, J.H., Vargas, L.G.: Modeling the uncertainty of surgical procedure times: Comparison of log-normal and normal models. Anesthesiology 92(4), 1160–1167 (2000)
22. Weske, M.: Business Process Management: Concepts, Languages, Architectures, 2nd edn. Springer (2012)
23. Zeng, L., Lingenfelder, C., Lei, H., Chang, H.: Event-driven quality of service prediction. In: Bouguettaya, A., Krueger, I., Margaria, T. (eds.) ICSOC 2008. LNCS, vol. 5364, pp. 147–161. Springer, Heidelberg (2008)
24. Zheng, H., Yang, J., Zhao, W., Bouguettaya, A.: QoS analysis for web service compositions based on probabilistic QoS. In: Kappel, G., Maamar, Z., Motahari-Nezhad, H.R. (eds.) ICSOC 2011. LNCS, vol. 7084, pp. 47–61. Springer, Heidelberg (2011)
25. Zimmermann, A.: Modeling and evaluation of stochastic Petri nets with TimeNET 4.1. In: 2012 6th International Conference on Performance Evaluation Methodologies and Tools (VALUETOOLS), pp. 54–63. IEEE (2012)

Entity-Centric Search for Enterprise Services

Marcus Roy[1,2,3], Ingo Weber[2,3], and Boualem Benatallah[3]

[1] SAP Research, Sydney, Australia
[2] NICTA, Sydney, Australia*
[3] School of Computer Science and Engineering, Sydney, Australia
{m.roy,ingo.weber,boualem}@cse.unsw.edu.au

Abstract. The consumption of APIs, such as Enterprise Services (ESs) in an enterprise Service-Oriented Architecture (eSOA), has largely been a task for experienced developers. With the rapidly growing number of such (Web)APIs, users with little or no experience in a given API face the problem of finding relevant API operations – e.g., mashups developers. However, building an effective search has been a challenge: Information Retrieval (IR) methods struggle with the brevity of text in API descriptions, whereas semantic search technologies require domain ontologies and formal queries. Motivated by the search behavior of users, we propose an iterative keyword search based on entities. The entities are part of a knowledge base, whose content stems from model-driven engineering. We implemented our approach and conducted a user study showing significant improvements in search effectiveness.

1 Introduction

In many enterprise-level efforts of application development or integration, the search and use of APIs has traditionally been a task performed by internal and experienced developers. However, recently there has been a significant increase in providing publicly available APIs, particularly on the Web[1]. As a consequence, the level of experience a user can have with any given API decreases on average. Thus, finding the desired functionality within an API becomes more challenging. Examples of users who are typically inexperienced in a given API include Mashup developers wanting to create new composite applications; and consultants developing business scenarios on the basis of existing functionality. Hence we expect users to neither be experts in the API-related domain nor to know a specific query language to express their information need. We therefore believe it is crucial to provide such users with a highly effective, ad-hoc keyword search over API operations. In this paper, we consider a specific class of Web APIs, namely Enterprise Services (ESs): enterprise-class Web services [5], as are common in an eSOA. ESs are usually advertised through specific repositories, e.g. SAP's Enterprise Service Workplace and Registry (ESW) [18] or IBM's

---

* NICTA is funded by the Australian Government as represented by the Department of Broadband, Communications and the Digital Economy and the Australian Research Council through the ICT Centre of Excellence program.

[1] http://blog.programmableweb.com/2012/11/26/
8000-apis-rise-of-the-enterprise, accessed 12/12

S. Basu et al. (Eds.): ICSOC 2013, LNCS 8274, pp. 404–412, 2013.
© Springer-Verlag Berlin Heidelberg 2013

WebSphere Service Registry and Repository (WSRR[2]), which can easily contain thousands of services [16].

To understand how users formulate free text queries, we investigated search logs from SAP's ESW. An initial analysis hereby revealed some common search patterns, i.e. users often started their search with a short query text using key business-related entities, e.g., "employee" and actions performed on these entities, e.g. "find employee". Motivated by the observations that users articulate their search needs using a small number of keywords [19] representing business entities or actions, and that they exhibit browsing-like behavior [7], we aim at providing an iterative keyword search over entities linked to ESs.

In this work, we tackle the difficult challenge to support keyword search over ES repositories: linking keywords used by users to concepts used by the service repository infrastructure to index and represent services, for which textual documentation is not always available. The proposed search technique relies on knowledge from model-driven engineering, including business entities consumed or generated by services and service operation patterns (e.g., create and read on business entities). In the following, we refer to the superset of business entities and action expressions as *entities*. In previous work, we presented an approach to automatically extract such entities [16] and learn naming conventions [17] from ES operation names, referred to as signatures. Using service design knowledge as an index over an ESs repository, we propose a ranking based on four different ranking measures related to entities. We implemented and evaluated the proposed keyword search and compared it to a state of the art IR-based search used at SAP, with significantly better results in terms of precision and recall[3]. In summary, the contributions are as follows: (i) an iterative search using entities extracted from service design knowledge, and (ii) an entity ranking using four different ranking measures related to entities.

2   Representing Service Design Knowledge

This section briefly revisits a formal representation of service design knowledge; for more details, we refer to [16]. To summarize the abstract representation of service design principles, we refer to a specific example of service design used in SAP, largely consisting (i) a business meta-data model, (ii) service design patterns and (iii) naming conventions as described hereinafter.

First, the business meta-data model generally defines a model of business entities, e.g. 'Sales Order', 'Customer' etc., used by both business and development departments. We describe this model using the MOF[4] layers from model-driven engineering. The M2-Model refers to metadata objects (and their relationship), e.g., 'Business Object' (BO), which describes corresponding data objects (and their relationship) in the M1-Model, e.g., 'Sales Order' as instances of BO.

Second, service design patterns are used during service development to describe the management of business entities and the behavior of respective ESs.

---

[2] http://www-01.ibm.com/software/integration/wsrr, accessed 08/12.

[3] A detailed description of the evaluation experiment and result can be found in [15]

[4] Meta-Object-Facility (MOF) : http://www.omg.org/mof/, accessed 08/12.

Similar to the business meta-data model, models of service design patterns can be defined on M2-level to describe specific service design patterns on M1-level, e.g. 'Change' as an instance of the 'Operation Pattern' (OP).

In order to make this information usable for an entity ranking, we first abstract meta-data models and data models into *type graphs* and *entity graphs*; with entities referring to data objects and types to meta-data objects respectively. For this, we use directed acyclic graphs (DAGs) to describe entities, types and edges between entities and types representing "belongTo" relationships. We hereby explicitly distinguish between entities and types to facilitate the definition of separate ranking measures (see Section 3). Finally, we define a service advertisement as a set of entities linked to an ES. In the following, we formally describe (a) an entity graph, (b) a type graph, (c) a mapping to link entities to types and (d) a mapping to link signatures to entities.

Definition 1 (Type Graph G_C). *We define a directed acyclic type graph $G_C := (C, R_C)$ with C representing a set of types $c \in C$ and $R_C \subseteq C \times C$ denoting a set of directed edges between types.*

Definition 2 (Entity Graph G_E). *We define a directed acyclic entity graph $G_E := (E, R_E)$ with E representing a set of entities $e \in E$ and $R_E \subseteq E \times E$ denoting a set of directed edges between entities.*

Definition 3 (Entity-Type Mapping Φ). *We define a mapping $\Phi : E \to C$, $\Phi(e) = c$ for $e \in E$, with $\forall e \in E : \exists c \in C : \Phi(e) = c$. Furthermore, for each $c \in C$ we denote the (possibly empty) subset $E_c \subseteq E$ such that $\forall c \in C : \forall e \in E_c : \Phi(e) = c$. Obviously these subsets are distinct for different c, i.e. $\forall c_i, c_j \in C : c_i \neq c_j \Rightarrow E_{c_i} \cap E_{c_j} = \emptyset$*

Definition 4 (Signature-Entity Mapping Ψ). *We define a set of signatures $s \in S$ and a mapping $\Psi : S \to 2^E$, $\Psi(s) = E_D$ for $E_D \subseteq E$.*

Third, service design includes naming conventions for the purpose of consistency: they prescribe in which order(s) the types and entities mentioned above should be assembled when forming ES signatures. We use non-deterministic automata with ε-moves (NFA-ε) to represent naming conventions, describing a language of valid ESs signatures. For instance, the partial naming convention 'BO-BON' expects type BO to be followed by type BON – e.g. 'SalesOrderItem' (rather than 'ItemSalesOrder'). Note that the construction of the NFA-ε can be done automatically by learning it from a sufficiently large set of existing ESs [17]. A formal definition and examples are given in [16].

3   Keyword-Based Search Using Entity Ranking

In this section, we describe the keyword-based search and entity ranking. Fig. 1 shows a flowchart of involved functionalities, i.e. (i) *Entity Detection*, (ii) *Entity Ranking* and (iii) *Entity Suggestion and ES Query* as described in the following.

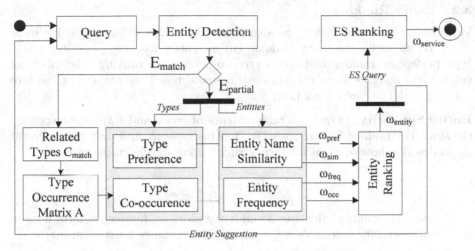

Fig. 1. Entity Suggestion and ES Query using Proposed Entity Ranking

3.1   Entity Detection

The entity detection function analyzes the free text query and identifies a list of completely and partially matched entities from the entity graph G_E. For this, the user input is first pruned to a list of noun and verbs, generally referred to as tokens. Each token is then normalized using the porter stemming algorithm[5]. We hereby understand the user input as a sequence of normalized tokens referred to as term string t. The term string t is then used to determine all possible token n-grams, i.e., token subsequences, using the following notation: $t = abc$, where $a, b,$ and c are tokens. From t, we construct $\tilde{t} := \{\tilde{t}_1, \ldots, \tilde{t}_6\} = \{a, b, c, ab, bc, abc\}$, where the $\tilde{t}_i$ are the n-grams from t. For instance, for $t \equiv \texttt{Sales Order}$ we have $\tilde{t} = \{\texttt{Sales, Order, Sales Order}\}$. In a final step, we check all $\tilde{t}_i \in \tilde{t}$ against the entity graph G_E for complete entity matches $E_{match} \subseteq E$ defined as follows:

$$E_{match}(t) := \{e \in E \mid \exists \tilde{t}_i \in \tilde{t} : \tilde{t}_i = e\} \tag{1}$$

In a second step, we check all n-grams $\tilde{t}_i$ against the entity graph G_E to find partially matching entities. A partial match is a "sufficiently good" match between term n-grams $\tilde{t}_i$ and entity n-grams $\tilde{e}_j$, where $\tilde{e}_j$ is constructed from $e \in E$ as $\tilde{t}_i$ from t. This is expressed in a *entity similarity measure*, $\omega_{sim}(t, e)$, between term string t and entity e, which we formally define in Section 3.2. Roughly speaking, this similarity score is a normalized accumulation of the pairwise similarity of n-grams ($\tilde{t}_i$ and $\tilde{e}_j$), which is, in turn, calculated as the edit distance (or Levenshtein distance) [12] between the respective n-grams. The similarity is sufficiently high if $\omega_{sim}(t, e)$ exceeds a custom threshold ρ_{tr}. The set of partially matching entities $E_{partial}(t)$ for t thus is defined as

$$E_{partial}(t) := \{e \in E \mid \omega_{sim}(t, e) > \rho_{tr}\}. \tag{2}$$

---

[5] Porter Stemmer: `http://tartarus.org/martin/PorterStemmer`, accessed 08/12.

3.2   Entity Ranking

We propose an entity ranking as a combination of four different ranking measures: (i) an entity similarity ranking, (ii) an entity frequency ranking, (iii) a type preference ranking and (iv) a type co-occurrence ranking. The following subsections describe these ranking measures and how they are aggregated into a single ranking score for entities.

Entity Similarity. In order to rank matches of terms and entities, we adopted the similarity ranking for terms used in [3]. This measure first computes a weight ω_q to describe how much of the term string t is covered by an n-gram $\tilde{t}_i \in \tilde{t}$:

$$\omega_q(\tilde{t}_i) := \frac{|\tilde{t}_i|}{|t|}$$

Second, the ranking calculates a similarity score ω_s between a term n-gram $\tilde{t}_i \in \tilde{t}$ and an entity n-gram $\tilde{e}_j \in \tilde{e}$ using the edit distance function $sim(\tilde{t}_i, \tilde{e}_j)$:

$$\omega_s(\tilde{t}_i, \tilde{e}_j) := \frac{1}{sim(\tilde{t}_i, \tilde{e}_j) + 1}(1 - \frac{\min(sim(\tilde{t}_i, \tilde{e}_j), |\tilde{e}_j|)}{|\tilde{e}_j|})$$

The second factor represents the overall similarity of $\tilde{t}_i$ and $\tilde{e}_j$, which returns zero if the edit distance $sim(\tilde{t}_i, \tilde{e}_j)$ exceeds the size of $\tilde{e}_j$. The first factor is used to reduce the weight of high edit distances, thus favouring shorter matches. The similarity value, $\omega_t(t, e)$, over all n-grams $\tilde{t}$ and $\tilde{e}$ is defined as follows:

$$\omega_t(t, e) := \sum_{\tilde{t}_i \in \tilde{t}} \omega_q(\tilde{t}_i) * \sum_{\tilde{e}_j \in \tilde{e}} \omega_s(\tilde{t}_i, \tilde{e}_j)$$

Finally, we normalize the similarity score $\omega_{sim}(t, e)$ over similarity values ω_t:

$$\omega_{sim}(t, e) := \frac{\omega_t(t, e)}{\max(\{\omega_t(t, e_k) | e_k \in E\})} \tag{3}$$

Entity Frequency. Second, we compute an entity frequency ω_{freq}. This is essentially "DF" from the standard TF/IDF ranking used in IR [12]: ω_{freq} disregards TF and basically reverses IDF, to capture how frequently signatures $s \in S$ link to a particular entity $e \in E$. As ES signatures have defined syntax, i.e., the naming conventions, they rarely contain entities of the same kind – making the TF part in TF/IDF obsolete. Also due to the clearly defined vocabulary, redundancy in terms is virtually non-existent – removing the need to prune them with IDF from TF/IDF. In contrast, we assign a higher importance to entities which are often linked to ES signatures. We argue that, for an entity-centric search, it is favorable to rank entities higher if more operations refer to them. We hereby contextualize the frequency of entities according to their type association, i.e. the frequency of an entity e in a corpus of ESs is normalized by the number of all ESs linked to an entity referring to the same type as e. To mitigate the effect of outliers, we apply a logarithm function (as defined in Sec. 2, Φ is the projection of entities to types, and Ψ the projection of signatures to sets of entities). Finally, we normalize the frequency score $\omega_{freq}(e)$ over all ω_f (analog to Eq. 3).

$$\omega_f(e) := \frac{\log(|\{s \in S \mid e \in \Psi(s)\}| + 1)}{\log(|\{s \in S \mid \forall e_i \in E, \Phi(e) = \Phi(e_i) : e_i \in \Psi(s)\}| + 1)}$$

Type Preference. In contrast to previously described, entity-related ranking measures, the type preference uses a probabilistic distribution of preferred types of entities from existing ES search queries. For this, we reuse search logs collected from SAP over a period of three months, from which we identified user queries that contained exact matches of entities as defined in Eq. 1. In the following, we refer to the set of matched query term strings as T_q. Each query term $t_q \in T_q$ hereby contains at least one entity. Using T_q, we extract the matched entities, infer their associated types and aggregate the frequency of identical types. At this stage, we only consider exact matches of entities to reduce the ambiguity of associated types. We then define the type preference $\omega_{pref}(c)$ for a type $c \in C$ as the frequency of entities related to c, divided by total number of entities extracted from T_q. Finally, we use a logarithm function to mitigate outliers. Finally, we normalize the type preference score $\omega_{pref}(c)$ over ω_p (analog to Eq. 3).

$$\omega_p(c) := \frac{\log(|\{e \mid t_q \in T_q, e \in E_{match}(t_q), \Phi(e) = c\}| + 1)}{\log(|\{e \mid t_q \in T_q, e \in E_{match}(t_q)\}| + 1)}$$

Type Co-Occurrence. The type co-occurrence $\omega_{occ}(t, c)$ determines the likelihood of a type c to occur with a set of types matched by the query term string t. Types are referred to by transitions in the corresponding automaton [17]. In that context, a type is considered co-occurring if it appears along an accepting path containing one or more types already matched to the user search query. To rank co-occurring types, we measure the frequency of their occurrence among all accepting paths, weighted by the number of contained matched types. The result of the ranking is a list of types which often appear with types identified in the user input. A detailed description of the type co-occurrence ranking component $\omega_{occ}(t, c)$ can be found in [15].

Combined Ranking Score. To calculate a single ranking score for entities, we use a weighted average over all ranking measures. For this, we refer to the set of ranking measures as $\omega(t, e) \in \Omega(t, e) = \{\omega_{sim}(t, e), \omega_{freq}(e), \omega_{pref}(c = \Phi(e)), \omega_{occ}(t, c = \Phi(e))\}$. We define a weight function $p : \Omega \to \mathbb{R}$ for the ranking measures $\omega(t, e) \in \Omega(t, e)$: increasing the weight means increasing the relative importance of the respective ranking measure. The weighted average score $\omega_{entity}(t, e)$ is then computed for a query term string t and an entity $e \in E$:

$$\omega_{entity}(t, e) := \frac{\sum\limits_{\omega(t,e) \in \Omega(t,e)} p(\omega(t,e)) * \omega(t,e)}{\sum\limits_{\omega(t,e) \in \Omega(t,e)} p(\omega(t,e))} \tag{4}$$

3.3   Entity Suggestions and ES Queries

For the purpose of generating suggestions and querying related ESs, we refer to the workflow as shown in Figure 1. After the entity detection, we receive a (possibly empty) set of complete and partial entity matches E_{match} and $E_{partial}$. With E_{match}, we infer a set of related types and rank any co-occurring types using ω_{occ} and ω_{pref}. With $E_{partial}$, we use entity name similarity ω_{sim} and calculate their entity frequency ω_{freq}. Finally, we calculate the entity ranking score ω_{entity} (cf. Eq. 4) and use the list of ranked entities in two ways: to provide suggestions to the user, i.e., displaying the top-x-ranked entities; and to find and rank ESs. The latter requires an additional ranking score, to derive an ES ranking from the entity ranking. As such, we use the ratio of completely and partially matched entities to all entities associated to an ES. The score for each ES is the accumulation of the ranking scores of entities associated to the ES, divided by the total number of associated entities. Complete matches are counted as 1, partial matches as ω_{entity}, and unmatched entities as 0 (denoted as $val(t, e)$). We define the ranking score for an ES $s \in S$ and a query term t as follows:

$$val(t, e) = \begin{cases} 1, & \text{if } e \in E_{match} \\ \omega_{entity}(t, e), & \text{if } e \in E_{partial} \\ 0, & \text{otherwise} \end{cases}$$

$$\omega_{service}(t, s) := \frac{1}{|\Psi(s)|} * \sum_{e \in \Psi(s)} val(t, e) \tag{5}$$

4   Related Work

The search approach proposed in this paper can be seen as a combination of existing IR methods and additional domain knowledge – see e.g., [10] for an overview. For brevity, we omit some details here, which can be found in the TR. First, keyword-based searches can utilize additional knowledge in form of ontologies and/or linguistic knowledge to refine/expand free text queries and enhance the ranking of different types of documents, e.g., structured documents (e.g., Semantic Web [6,20]) or unstructured documents (e.g., Web [2,4,3]). In contrast to our goals, these approaches require larger documents. However, some ranking measures in our work are inspired by approaches in this category, e.g., entity similarity ranking [3], entity ranking based on lexical or domain knowledge [2,4], entity relationship-based ranking [1]. In a similar context, we consider the relationship defined in automata to rank types of entities and use entity frequency to identify key ESs. Second, our iterative querying paradigm is inspired by [13]. ActiveObjects [11] advocates the learning of actions on entities extracted from Web search logs – intriguing for Web queries, less applicable for service design with a well defined action vocabulary. QueryFeature-Graph [8] links queries to features of a system, e.g., captured from query logs, which could be used to further bridge the gap between user and system terminology. In the area of code search, Portfolio [14] provides a search for API functions using a combination of word similarity and word occurrences. Exemplar [9] describes an approach to enhance code search using API documentation. Neither makes use of models from model-driven engineering.

5   Conclusion and Future Work

We presented an iterative keyword search for ESs based on entities. As such, we proposed an entity ranking combining different ranking measures applied to entities and their associated types. The ranking returns a list of ranked entities, which we use as suggestions to the user as well as to find a set of relevant ESs related to these entities. Based on our user study, we conclude that such an entity-centric keyword search indeed increases the effectiveness of ES search: while the average number of search attempts increases slightly, precision and recall amongst the top ten search results increased steeply over a traditional IR method – for more details on the evaluation, we refer to [15]. In future work, we aim at (i) utilizing ES documentation in the search as another ranking measure; and (ii) deriving additional knowledge from previous searches.

References

1. Aleman-Meza, B., Arpinar, I., Nural, M., Sheth, A.: Ranking Documents Semantically Using Ontological Relationships. In: ICSC 2010 (2010)
2. Burton-Jones, A., Storey, V.C., Sugumaran, V., Purao, S.: A Heuristic-Based Methodology for Semantic Augmentation of User Queries on the Web. In: Song, I.-Y., Liddle, S.W., Ling, T.-W., Scheuermann, P. (eds.) ER 2003. LNCS, vol. 2813, pp. 476–489. Springer, Heidelberg (2003)
3. Brauer, F., Huber, M., Hackenbroich, G., Leser, U., Naumann, F., Barczynski, W.M.: Graph-Based Concept Identification and Disambiguation for Enterprise Search. In: WWW, Raleigh, NC, USA. ACM (2010)
4. Conesa, J., Storey, V.C., Sugumaran, V.: Improving Web-Query Processing Through Semantic Knowledge. DKE 66(1), 18–34 (2008)
5. Curbera, F., Khalaf, R., Mukhi, N., Tai, S., Weerawarana, S.: The Next Step in Web Services. Commun. ACM 46, 29–34 (2003)
6. Ding, L., Finin, T., Joshi, A., Pan, R., Cost, R.S., Peng, Y., Reddivari, P., Doshi, V., Sachs, J.: Swoogle: A Search and Metadata Engine for the Semantic Web. In: Conference on Information and Knowledge Management, CIKM 2004 (2004)
7. Dong, X., Halevy, A.: Indexing dataspaces. In: ACM SIGMOD (2007)
8. Fourney, A., Mann, R., Terry, M.A.: Query-feature graphs: bridging user vocabulary and system functionality. In: UIST, pp. 207–216 (2011)
9. Grechanik, M., Fu, C., Xie, Q., McMillan, C., Poshyvanyk, D., Cumby, C.: A Search Engine for Finding Highly Relevant Applications. In: ICSE 2010 (2010)
10. Hoang, H.H., Tjoa, A.M.: The State of the Art of Ontology-based Query Systems: A Comparison of Existing Approaches. In: ICOCI 2006 (2006)
11. Lin, T., Pantel, P., Gamon, M., Kannan, A., Fuxman, A.: Active Objects: Actions for Entity-centric Search. In: WWW 2012 (2012)
12. Manning, C.D., Raghavan, P., Schtze, H.: Introduction to Information Retrieval. Cambridge Univ. Press (2008)

13. Mass, Y., Ramanath, M., Sagiv, Y., Weikum, G.: IQ: The Case for Iterative Querying for Knowledge. In: CIDR, pp. 38–44 (2011)
14. McMillan, C., Grechanik, M., Poshyvanyk, D., Xie, Q., Fu, C.: Portfolio: finding relevant functions and their usage. In: ICSE 2011 (2011)
15. Roy, M.: Facilitating Enterprise Service Management Using Service Design Knowledge. PhD thesis, CSE, UNSW (under review, 2013)
16. Roy, M., Suleiman, B., Schmidt, D., Weber, I., Benatallah, B.: Using SOA Governance Design Methodologies to Augment Enterprise Service Descriptions. In: Mouratidis, H., Rolland, C. (eds.) CAiSE 2011. LNCS, vol. 6741, pp. 566–581. Springer, Heidelberg (2011)
17. Roy, M., Weber, I., Benatallah, B.: Extending Enterprise Service Design Knowledge Using Clustering. In: Liu, C., Ludwig, H., Toumani, F., Yu, Q. (eds.) Service Oriented Computing. LNCS, vol. 7636, pp. 142–157. Springer, Heidelberg (2012)
18. SAP. Enterprise Services Workplace (August 2012), http://esworkplace.sap.com
19. Spink, A., Wolfram, D., Jansen, M.B.J., Saracevic, T.: Searching the Web: The public and their queries. JASIST 52(3), 226–234 (2001)
20. Toch, E., Gal, A., Reinhartz-Berger, I., Dori, D.: A Semantic Approach to Approximate Service Retrieval. ACM Trans. Inter. Tech. (2007)

Tactical Service Selection with Runtime Aspects

Rene Ramacher and Lars Mönch

Chair of Enterprise-wide Software Systems
Univerity of Hagen, 58084 Hagen, Germany
{Rene.Ramacher,Lars.Moench}@FernUni-Hagen.de

Abstract. The quality of service (QoS) of a service composition is addressed by a QoS-aware service selection. In the presence of sophisticated service charging models a cost-minimized service selection can be obtained related to a number of requests expected for a service composition in a predefined planning horizon. A service selection that is used to execute requests throughout an entire planning horizon is called tactical. The majority of service selection models assume a deterministic service execution and therefore the need for runtime adaptions of a service composition to react on service failures or deviating QoS values is neglected. The challenge that is addressed with this paper is to develop a tactical service selection approach that anticipates runtime adaptions of a service composition. It is shown that the tactical service selection can be efficiently combined with an existing service reconfiguration method to achieve both runtime-related goals and tactical objectives.

Keywords: QoS-aware Service Selection, Uncertain QoS, Distributed Decision Making.

1   Introduction and Related Work

The QoS and the cost of a service composition are addressed by a QoS-aware service selection. In the literature related to service marketing sophisticated service charging models, including subscription-based charging, service bundling, and quantity discounts, are proposed. A QoS-aware service selection model for a cost-minimized service selection in the presence of sophisticated service charging models is presented in [5]. The cost-minimized service selection is related to an expected number of service invocations in a planning horizon to fairly compare a service charged on a subscription base and a service charged on a transaction base. The cost-minimization objective is a tactical objective because it is related to a set of service invocations that occur in the planning horizon. Accordingly, a service selection model that pursues tactical objectives is called tactical.

   The tactical service selection model presented in [5] relies on the assumption of a deterministic service execution which is not realistic because in a real environment service failures occur and some of the QoS attributes are uncertain. Service reconfiguration approaches are proposed to deal with volatile and uncertain execution environments. Canfora et al. [3] propose the reconfiguration of a service composition to react on service failures and on QoS values that

S. Basu et al. (Eds.): ICSOC 2013, LNCS 8274, pp. 413–420, 2013.

deviate from their expected ones. Li et al. [4] propose a service reconfiguration approach that focuses on service failures. The efficiency of an online performed service reconfiguration is addressed. The approach of Canfora et al. is extended by Ramacher and Mönch in [6] to the reconfiguration of time-critical service compositions that suffer from uncertain response times. In contrast to a tactical service selection, a service reconfiguration is called an operative service selection because it is always related to the execution of a certain request. Because of this request-centric point of view, operative service selection models cannot account for tactical objectives as e.g. the cost minimization in the presence of sophisticated service charging models.

This paper proposes a tactical service selection that accounts for a volatile and uncertain environment by anticipating the operatively executed service reconfiguration. Using a general framework for distributed decision making systems [7], the tactical service selection aligns the service reconfiguration to the tactical objectives. This alignment is carried out in terms of restrictions concerning the services that are considered by the service reconfiguration. The generality of the proposed alignment allows the integration of any of the aforementioned service reconfiguration approaches within the proposed tactical service selection.

The remainder of this paper is organized as follows. Section 2 introduces the service selection model. The proposed tactical service selection approach is presented in Section 3. Afterwards, a solution approach for the tactical service selection is developed in Section 4. Section 5 briefly summarizes the experiments performed to evaluate the approach. Finally, Section 6 concludes the paper and provides future research topics.

2   Service Selection Model

The structure of a service composition is defined in terms of a process model that consists of abstract tasks $T = \{t_1, ..., t_n\}$. This paper considers only sequential process models in which the tasks $t_1, ..., t_n$ are executed successively. The execution starts by task t_1 and ends with t_n. The processing of a task t_{i+1} can only be started after the execution of t_i is completed. Extending the ideas of this paper to more general process models that also contain conditional branches and flow constructs is possible by adopting the concepts presented in [6,8].

The functional requirements of a task have to be fulfilled by a concrete service that is used to execute the task. A service class S_i consists of the services that fulfill the functional requirements of t_i. Hence, establishing the service classes corresponds to a service selection with respect to functional requirements. The service classes can be determined manually or by reasoning techniques that rely on semantically enriched service interfaces. The set of all services is denoted as $S = \bigcup_{t_i \in T} S_i$. A service binding b determines the service $b(t_i) \in S_i$ that is used to execute the task t_i. Hence, the service binding b is defined as the mapping:

$$b : T \mapsto S, t_i \to b(t_i) \in S_i. \tag{1}$$

In the remainder, we abbreviate the service $b(t_i)$ that is bound to t_i with b_i.

The cost of a service consists of its invocation-dependent transaction cost and its associated periodic fees. The transaction cost $c(s) \in \mathbb{R}^+$ for a service $s \in S$ is charged each time s is invoked. The periodic fee $S(s) \in \mathbb{R}^+$ is an invocation-independent cost that has to be considered to use a service throughout a period. A service s is charged transaction-based when $c(s) > 0$ and $S(s) = 0$ holds, while a subscription-based charging is applied for $s \in S$ in the case of $c(s) = 0$ and $S(s) > 0$. A reasonable service selection that deals with services that are charged on a transaction base and services that are charged on a subscription base needs to take into account the expected number of service invocations. The quantity Q is the number of requests that are expected for the service composition within a predefined planning horizon.

The actual response time of a service $s \in S$ is $r(s) \in \mathbb{R}^+$. Since this time is only known after a service was executed, an expected response time $\tilde{r}(s) \in \mathbb{R}^+$ is used for an ex-ante performed service selection. In the presence of a globally constrained execution time $\bar{e}$, a service binding b is determined such that the execution time restriction is met by taking into account the expected response times by:

$$\sum_{t_i \in T} \tilde{r}(b_i) \leq \bar{e}. \tag{2}$$

In (2), $\tilde{r}$ represents an expected response time that can be obtained e.g. by a quantil-based measure [6]. A service binding b is called the primary service binding if b is determined prior to the execution of a request. Because it is likely that the actual response time of a service will deviate from the estimated one, a service binding needs to be adjusted by a service reconfiguration during the execution of a request to avoid the violation of the end-to-end constrained execution time. The reconfiguration adjusts the currently applied service binding b to take into account the actual execution process and the realization of the QoS attributes. An adjusted service binding is thus always related to a certain request and is therefore called operational. The operational service binding that is related to the request ρ is denoted with b^ρ. Initially, the operational service binding is the primary service binding.

3   Hierarchical Tactical Service Selection

The integration of the tactical service selection and the operative service reconfiguration is carried out by utilizing the hierarchical architecture of distributed decision making (DDM) systems. According to Schneeweis [7], a two-stage DDM system is divided into a top- and a base-level. The coupling between the top- and base-level is carried out by an instruction. The top-level determines an instruction that influences the base-level's decision. The top-level exploits an anticipation of the base-level to support the decision making. The anticipation is used to represent the characteristics of the base-level that are relevant to the top-level [7]. Top-, base-, and the anticipated base-level are defined in terms of their action space, criterion, and information status.

The tactical service selection (TSS) corresponds to the top-level while the service reconfiguration is represented by an operative service selection (OSS) that corresponds to the base-level. The TSS uses an instruction to align the OSS to the tactical objectives. An instruction is a vector of operational service classes $\widehat{S}_i \subseteq S_i$. The OSS selects the service b_i^ρ from the operational service class $\widehat{S}_i$ that is used to execute the task t_i during request ρ is processed.

The decision making of the TSS is supported by an anticipation of the OSS. The anticipation captures the assumption of the TSS concerning the OSS's service selection for a task in a certain situation. The operational service classes are determined by the TSS such that the periodic cost and the cost expected for Q invocations of the service composition are minimized. In the following, the action space, the criterion, and the information status of the top-, base-, and the anticipated base-level are introduced.

The action space of the TSS is defined as:

$$A^T = P(S_1) \times ... \times P(S_n) \tag{3}$$

where $P(S_i)$ denotes the power set of the service class S_i. According to the definition of the action space, an action $\widehat{S} \in A^T$ is represented by the vector $\widehat{S} = (\widehat{S}_1, ..., \widehat{S}_n)$ of operational service classes. The information status of the TSS at the decision time t_0 is $I_{t_0}^T = Q$ where Q is the number of requests expected for the service composition.

The criterion of the TSS is divided into a private criterion C^{TT} and a bottom-up criterion C^{TB} [7]. The bottom-up criterion represents the influence of the anticipated OSS on the decision making process of the TSS. The private criterion of the TSS is to minimize the periodic cost of the services that are included in the operational service classes. The periodic costs are determined as the sum of the periodic fees of the services selected by an action $\widehat{S}$, i.e.

$$C^{TT}(\widehat{S}) = \sum_{t_i \in T} \sum_{s_{ij} \in \widehat{S}_i} S(s_{ij}). \tag{4}$$

The bottom-up criterion concerns the transaction costs of the service invocations to execute Q requests of the service composition. Since the decision which service $s_{ij} \in \widehat{S}_i$ is actually invoked to execute the task t_i is related to the OSS, an anticipated number of service invocations $\tilde{q}_{ij}$ is considered. Taking into account the anticipation $AF(IN)$ of the OSS with respect to the instruction $IN = \widehat{S}$, the bottom-up criterion is stated as:

$$C^{TB}(AF(IN)) = \sum_{t_i \in T} \sum_{s_{ij} \in \widehat{S}_i} c(s_{ij})\tilde{q}_{ij}. \tag{5}$$

The action space of the OSS is defined as the set of mappings between the tasks T and the operational service classes $\widehat{S}$ identified by the TSS:

$$A^B = Map(T, \widehat{S}) = \left\{ b \mid b : T \mapsto \bigcup_{i=1}^{n} \widehat{S}_i, t_i \to b(t_i) \in \widehat{S}_i, t_i \in T \right\}. \tag{6}$$

The information status $I_\Psi^B = t_{cur}$ of the OSS captures the time Ψ elapsed since the processing of a request has been started and the task $t_{cur} \in T$ to be processed next.

The goal of the OSS is to obtain a service binding $b \in Map(T, \widehat{S})$ that ensures a reliable execution of the service composition with respect to its end-to-end constrained execution time. Considering Ψ and t_{cur}, the service binding b is determined such that the execution time restriction will be met, i.e.

$$\Psi + \sum_{i=cur}^{n} \tilde{r}(b_i) \leq \bar{e}. \tag{7}$$

The OSS applies a cost-minimizing objective concerning the transaction costs. The criterion of the OSS is given by:

$$C_\Psi^B(b) = \sum_{i=cur}^{n} c(b_i). \tag{8}$$

The service selection of the OSS is anticipated by the TSS. The service selection b_i^ρ of the OSS relies on the start time of the task t_i during the execution of the request ρ. The actual start time of t_i is unknown to the TSS because it depends on the actual response times of the services invoked to execute the tasks prior to t_i. Hence, a set of response time scenarios Ω is used to obtain a reasonable anticipation. A scenario $\omega \in \Omega$ represents a certain response time $r^\omega(s_{ij})$ for each $s_{ij} \in S$. The response time $r^\omega(s_{ij})$ is sampled from a response time distribution of the service s_{ij}.

The anticipated information status is given as $\tilde{I}_{t_0}^B = (\Omega, Q)$. The goal of the anticipated OSS is to determine a service binding for each $\omega \in \Omega$ such that the execution time restriction of the service composition is met. Hence, the action space of the anticipated OSS is $Map(T, \widehat{S})^{|\Omega|}$. Let $b \in Map(T, \widehat{S})^{|\Omega|}$ be an action of the anticipated OSS. Then $b^\omega : T \to \bigcup_{i=1}^{n} \widehat{S}_i$ is the operational service binding for scenario ω and $b_i^\omega \in \widehat{S}_i$ is the service used to execute the task t_i in ω.

The anticipated criterion of the OSS considers the transaction cost resulting from the execution of all scenarios. For an action $b \in Map(T, \widehat{S})^{|\Omega|}$, the criterion is stated as:

$$\tilde{C}^B(b) = \sum_{\omega \in \Omega} \sum_{t_i \in T} c(b_i^\omega). \tag{9}$$

Moreover, the execution time restrictions for the scenarios in Ω are state as:

$$\sum_{t_i \in T} r^\omega(b_i^\omega) \leq \bar{e}, \omega \in \Omega. \tag{10}$$

The anticipated number of invocations $\tilde{q}_{ij}$ of the service s_{ij} is derived from the decision of the anticipated OSS as:

$$\tilde{q}_{ij} = \frac{Q}{|\Omega|} \cdot \sum_{\omega \in \Omega} e_{i\omega}(s_{ij}) \tag{11}$$

where $e_{i\omega}(s_{ij}) = 1$ when $b_i^\omega = s_{ij}$ and otherwise 0.

4 Integrated Solution Approach

This section presents a solution approach used to obtain the operational service classes such that the objectives of the TSS, stated by (4) and (5), are achieved. A possible implementation of the OSS is described in [1,6,8].

The scenarios used to capture the uncertainty of the response times are linked together by nonanticipativity constraints [2]. The nonanticipativity constraints ensure that the same decisions are taken in all scenarios that are indistinguishable at the decision time. Two scenarios ω and ω' are indistinguishable in the case of an operational service selection if the difference of the start time of t_i in ω and ω' is less than a threshold τ used to initiate a service reconfiguration. In this situation, the same service has to be selected for task t_i in ω and ω'.

The TSS is implemented as the mixed integer program (MIP) formulated through (12)-(21). In the MIP, the service selection is captured by the binary decision variables e_{ij} and z_{ij}^{ω}. The variables e_{ij} represent the decision of the TSS. The value of e_{ij} is 1 if the service $s_{ij} \in S_i$ is included in the operational service class $\widehat{S}_i$, otherwise it is 0. The operational service selection in scenario $\omega \in \Omega$ is captured by the variables z_{ij}^{ω}. The variable z_{ij}^{ω} is set to 1 if the service s_{ij} is used to execute the task t_i in the scenario ω, otherwise z_{ij}^{ω} is set to 0. The real-valued decision variables $\tilde{q}_{ij}$ represent the expected number of invocations of the service s_{ij} according to (11). The start time of a task t_i in a scenario ω is modeled by the real-valued decision variable a_i^{ω}. The binary decision variables $\sigma_i^{\omega,\omega'}$ are used to implement the nonanticipativity constraints. The value of $\sigma_i^{\omega,\omega'}$ is 1 if the difference of the start time of t_i in the scenarios ω and ω' is larger than the threshold τ, otherwise it is 0. We obtain:

$$\min \sum_{t_i \in T} \sum_{s_{ij} \in S_i} S(s_{ij})e_{ij} + \sum_{t_i \in T} \sum_{s_{ij} \in S_i} c(s_{ij})\tilde{q}_{ij} \tag{12}$$

subject to:

$$\sum_{s_{ij} \in S_i} z_{ij}^{\omega} = 1, \forall \omega \in \Omega, t_i \in T \tag{13}$$

$$a_i^{\omega} \geq 0, \forall \omega \in \Omega, t_i \in T \tag{14}$$

$$a_{i+1}^{\omega} \geq a_i^{\omega} + \sum_{s_{ij} \in S_i} r^{\omega}(s_{ij})z_{ij}^{\omega}, \forall \omega \in \Omega, t_i \in T \setminus \{t_n\} \tag{15}$$

$$\sum_{t_i \in T} \sum_{s_{ij} \in S_i} r^{\omega}(s_{ij})z_{ij}^{\omega} \leq \bar{e}, \forall \omega \in \Omega \tag{16}$$

$$z_{ij}^{\omega} \leq e_{ij}, \forall \omega \in \Omega, i \in T, s_{ij} \in S_i \tag{17}$$

$$\tilde{q}_{ij} = \frac{Q}{|\Omega|} \sum_{\omega \in \Omega} z_{ij}^{\omega}, \forall t_i \in T, s_{ij} \in S_i \tag{18}$$

$$a_i^{\omega} - a_i^{\omega'} - \tau \geq M(\sigma_i^{\omega\omega'} - 1), \forall \omega, \omega' \in \Omega, i \in T \tag{19}$$

$$z_{ij}^{\omega} - z_{ij}^{\omega'} \leq \sigma_i^{\omega,\omega'} + \sigma_i^{\omega',\omega}, \forall \omega, \omega' \in \Omega, t_i \in T, s_{ij} \in S_i \tag{20}$$

$$z_{ij}^{\omega}, e_{ij} \in \{0,1\}, \forall \omega \in \Omega, t_i \in T, s_{ij} \in S_i. \tag{21}$$

The objective function (12) concerns the total cost resulting from the periodic fees of the services that are included in the operational service classes and the transaction costs incurred by Q service invocations according to (4) and (5).

The constraints (13)-(16) account for the operational service selection. First, the equations (13) ensure that exactly one service is selected for each task in each scenario. According to the inequalities (14), the start time of each task has to be non-negative. In addition, the start time of a task t_{i+1} is determined by the completion time of its preceding task t_i which is ensured by the inequalities (15). In (15), the completion time of the preceding task t_i is calculated as the sum of its start time and the scenario-related response time of the service that is selected to execute t_i. The inequalities (16) account for the execution time restriction that has to be fulfilled for each scenario $\omega \in \Omega$ according to (2).

The inequalities (17) and (18) are the constraints to couple the TSS with the action space of the anticipated OSS. According to (17), the service s_{ij} can be selected to execute task t_i only if s_{ij} is element of the operational service class $\widehat{S}_i$. The equations (18) are used to obtain the estimated number of invocations $\tilde{q}_{ij}$ of each service s_{ij}.

The inequalities (19) and (20) are the nonanticipativity constraints. According to (19), the value of $\sigma_i^{\omega,\omega'}$ is 1 only if the difference of the start time of task t_i in the scenarios ω and ω' exceeds the threshold τ. If this is the case then the left-hand side will be positive and $o_i^{\omega,\omega'}$ is set to 1. Otherwise, the value of $\sigma_i^{\omega,\omega'}$ has to be 0. With respect to (20) a different service can be selected in ω and ω' for t_i only if either $\sigma_i^{\omega,\omega'}$ or $\sigma_i^{\omega',\omega}$ takes a value of 1. Otherwise, the right-hand side of (20) is 0 forcing that the same service is selected for t_i in ω and ω'.

5   Computational Experiments

Experiments are conducted to evaluate the TSS model with respect to its computational tractability and the anticipation of the operational service selection. The experiments are performed on randomly generated problem instances. A detailed description of the experiments is not included due to space restrictions. The experiments show that a tactical service selection can be obtained for service compositions containing up to 20 tasks in less than one hour of computing time. An anticipation with 30 scenarios allows a successful execution for almost all requests. In contrast, the number of successfully executed requests decreases dramatically when no anticipation is used by the TSS. The quality of the anticipation with respect to the transaction cost increases with an increasing number of scenarios. However, the number of scenarios is restricted by an increasing computational burden that is required to solve the TSS model.

6 Conclusion

A tactical service selection is presented that addresses a cost-minimized service selection in the presence of sophisticated service charging models. Exploiting the concepts of DDM systems, the proposed tactical service selection integrates an operatively performed service reconfiguration by anticipation to consider uncertain response times and their impact on an end-to-end constrained execution time. The service reconfiguration is aligned to the tactical objectives and a successful service execution is ensured. In future research, an approach based on a metaheuristic will be developed to decrease the computational burden required to solve the TSS model for large scale service compositions.

References

1. Ardagna, D., Pernici, B.: Adaptive service composition in flexible processes. IEEE Trans. Software Engineering 33(6), 369–384 (2007)
2. Birge, J.R., Louveaux, F.: Introduction to Stochastic Programming. Series in Operations Research and Financial Engineering. Springer (1997)
3. Canfora, G., Di Penta, M., Esposito, R., Villani, M.L.: QoS-aware replanning of composite web services. In: Proceedings of the IEEE International Conference on Web Services, pp. 121–129 (2005)
4. Li, J., Ma, D., Mei, X., Sun, H., Zheng, Z.: Adaptive QoS-aware service process reconfiguration. In: Proceedings of the 8th International Conference on Services Computing (SCC), pp. 282–289. IEEE Computer Society, Washington, DC (2011)
5. Ramacher, R., Mönch, L.: Cost-minimizing service selection in the presence of end-to-end QoS constraints and complex charging models. In: Proceedings of the 9th International Conference on Services Computing (SCC), pp. 154–161 (2012)
6. Ramacher, R., Mönch, L.: Reliable service reconfiguration for time-critical service compositions. In: Proceedings of the 10th International Conference on Services Computing (SCC), pp. 184–191 (2013)
7. Schneeweiss, C.: Distributed Decision Making. Springer (2003)
8. Yu, T., Zhang, Y., Lin, K.-J.: Efficient algorithms for web services selection with end-to-end QoS constraints. ACM Transactions on the Web (TWeb) 1(1) (2007)

Online Reliability Time Series Prediction for Service-Oriented System of Systems

Lei Wang[1,2], Hongbing Wang[1,*],
Qi Yu[3], Haixia Sun[1], and Athman Bouguettaya[4]

[1] School of Computer Science and Engineering, Southeast University, China
[2] Dept. of Management Science and Engineering, Nanjing Forestry University, China
{leiwang,hbw,haixiasun}@seu.edu.cn
[3] College of Computing and Information Sciences, Rochester Institute of Tech, USA
qi.yu@rit.edu
[4] School of Computer Science and Information Technology, RMIT, Australia
athman.bouguettaya@rmit.edu.au

Abstract. A Service-Oriented System of System (or SoS) considers system as a service and constructs a value-added SoS by outsourcing external systems through service composition. To cope with the dynamic and uncertain running environment and assure the overall Quality of Service (or QoS), online reliability prediction for SoS arises as a grand challenge in SoS research. In this paper, we propose a novel approach for component level online reliability time series prediction based on Probabilistic Graphical Models (or PGMs). We assess the proposed approach via invocation records collected from widely used real web services and experiment results demonstrate the effectiveness of our approach.

1 Introduction

A SoS pools computing resources together to create a new, value-added, and more complex system. As a new computing paradigm that has attracted significant popularity, Service-Oriented Architecture (SOA) provides a principled mechanism to construct a SoS [1, 5] by dynamically integrating its component systems through service composition. It is anticipated that a service-oriented SoS runs under a complicated and highly dynamic environment. Hence, the runtime QoS assurance is of significant importance for a service-oriented SoS.

Proactive Fault Management (or PFM) offers an effective mechanism to enhance the reliability of software systems [6]. Nonetheless, to achieve PFM in service-oriented SoSs, a central challenge lies in automatic and accurate prediction of the reliability of the SoS. In particular, a self-* (*configuration, healing, optimization, or protection*) SoS demands online reliability prediction that accurately predicts the reliability of the SoS in nearly realtime to deal with the

---

* This work is partially supported by NSFC (No.61232007) and Doctoral Fund of Ministry of Education of China (No.20120092110028) and JSNSF (No.BK2010417) and PSSF of higher education in Jiangsu Prov. (No.2013SJB6300051).

S. Basu et al. (Eds.): ICSOC 2013, LNCS 8274, pp. 421–428, 2013.

highly dynamic running environment. As illustrated in Figure 1, online reliability prediction estimates the system's reliability in the "near future" (i.e., the prediction time period of Δt_p). More specifically, Δt_l is defined as the *leading time*, which starts from t and ends when a user invokes a SoS. Δt_p is defined as the *prediction period*, which corresponds to a future invocation time period. Δt_d is the *data window size* for historic records.

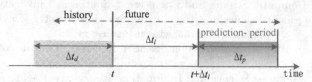

Fig. 1. Schematic View of Online Reliability Prediction

In a service-oriented SoS, the prediction period Δt_p is determined by the execution period of component level systems and the unstable communication links. Hence, the length of invocation is usually uncertain, which makes the length of Δt_p vary from one user's requirement to another [3]. As most existing *online failure prediction* methods are designed for failure probability prediction in a fixed time period, they are not directly applicable for a varied prediction period. In contrast, a viable reliability prediction approach for a service-oriented SoS should capture the changes of reliability during a variable prediction period. Assume that Δt_p is long enough for most user requirements. The key idea of reliability prediction for a service-oriented SoS is to predict the reliability *time series* during the period of Δt_p.

To our best knowledge, this is the first work on *online reliability time series prediction* for service-oriented SoS. It is fundamentally different from relevant existing works, including online failure prediction for traditional computer systems [6] and reliability prediction in service computing [11]. Despite the running environment of a service-oriented SoS is complex and highly dynamic, the reliability of the overall system is mainly affected by several major factors, which include (1) the unstable communication links between the component systems, (2) the internal working status of component systems, and (3) the loading capacity of component systems under the current throughput. It is always difficult and sometimes even impossible to directly collect a outsourced from third-party service providers remote system's performance parameters. Nonetheless, the above factors also significantly affect the throughput and response time of component systems. More importantly, parameters like throughput and response time can be easily obtained via client-side evaluation of the target component systems. This key observation allows us to analyze the component level system's reliability along with its throughput and response time, which provides a holistic view of the system's running state and its surrounding environment.

The major contribution of the paper centers around using Probabilistic Graphical Models (*PGMs*) to analyze historical and current system parameters, including *Reliability, Throughput* and *Response Time*. The Markov chain rules are employed to capture the causal relationships between adjacent time series of the system parameters, which represented as Conditional Probability Tables (*CPTs*). These *CPTs* will be used together with the PGM to make online reliability prediction based on the current system parameters. Experiments conducted over real-world web services justify the effectiveness of our approach.

2   Related Work

It has been discovered that the arrival times of atomic web services reliability follow an *Erlangian* distribution because the failures' arrival times are dependent on the operating states (e.g. idle and active states) [4]. Collaborative filtering based approaches have been widely employed in service computing to predict the QoS (including reliability) of previously unknown services [8–11]. As an example, a matrix factorization based approach is used to predict the missing values in service component's user-item failure probability matrix. With the component level service reliability prediction results, the system level reliability is aggregated by the composition structures [12].

Online failure prediction in traditional computer systems aims to identify during runtime whether a failure will occur in the *near future*. A taxonomy for existing *online failure prediction* approaches mainly include three categories [6], which are *Failure tracking*, *Symptom monitoring* and *Detected error reporting*. All of these methods depend on a directly server side observation on system working status or system log files.

3   Online Reliability Time Series Prediction

In this section, a Probabilistic Graphical Models based Reliability Time Series Online Prediction for component level service-oriented System of Systems (*PGMs-RTSOP*) is proposed.

The typical *PGMs* model supporting dynamic changes of the time, which is Dynamic Bayesian Networks (*DBNs*) model [2]. The changes from adjacent time points of historic system parameters studied in this paper exist no obviously causality, due to the dynamics of the SoS runtime environment. While the regulation of changes from continuous system parameters time series (time series is composed of a plurality of time points) can often reflect a specific event (such as software version upgrade). The continuous change of the SoS system parameters time series satisfy the Markov chain rules.

In this paper, we propose m_DBNs (see Figure 2), an augmentation of the traditional DBNs that uses the Markov chain rule to model the causal relationship between adjacent system parameters (e.g., the current time series t and the near future time series $t+1$). The nodes in the m_DBNs correspond to the system parameters, including *Response Time* (*RT*), *Throughput* (*T*) and *Reliability* (*R*). The parameters are represented by the time series patterns, which are referred to as *motifs* [7], discovered from historical data to facilitate the prediction of future time series.

Since both *Response Time* and *Throughput* are easy to measure, they can be regarded as observed variables for the current time series t. On the other hand, directly measuring *Reliability* is difficult so its state is usually derived based on *Response Time* and *Throughput*. Hence, *Reliability* can be regarded as a hidden variable whose value is affected by both $RT(t)$ and $T(t)$. The dependencies between different nodes are denoted by the arcs in the m_DBNs.

Using the proposed $PGMs\text{-}RTSOP$ for online reliability time series prediction consists of the following four major steps.

1. **Motifs Discovery:** Motifs discovery is to identify the featured patterns of time series from parameters of RT, T and R of a component system. We divide the historic parameter into two different time series. Hence, motifs for each parameter can be divided as two categories: motifs for current time t and motifs for near future $t+1$. To achieve motifs discovery, we group together similar time series in historic parameters (RT, T, R) through a clustering algorithm (e.g., K-means). Consequently, motifs are defined as the centroids of the resultant clusters. We will use RT as an example. Assume that the length of each time series is Δt_p so the n time series of RT is given by $RT_{t-n\Delta t_p}, \cdots, RT_{t-2\Delta t_p}, RT_{t-\Delta t_p}, RT_t$. Specifically, the i-th time series of RT is defined as: $RT(i) = \overrightarrow{RT_{((t-(n-i-1))\Delta t_p,(t-(n-i))\Delta t_p)}}$, where $i = 1, \cdots, n$. We further assume that s is the time interval that RT is collected. Hence, each time series can be represented by a vector with size $\frac{\Delta t_p}{s}$ and the distance between two time series $RT(i)$ and $RT(j)$ can be calculated as

$$dis(RT(i), RT(j)) = \sqrt{\sum_{k=1}^{\frac{\Delta t_p}{s}} (RT(i)_k - RT(j)_k)^2} \qquad (1)$$

   The motifs are calculated as the centroids of the clusters.
   We re-divide the time period for parameter RT and get the near future system parameters. We choose the time period after Δt_l for each $RT(i)$, which is defined as $RT(i)_{t+\Delta t_l}$. We will use the motifs discovery method presented for $RT(i)$ to discover motifs in $RT(i)_{t+\Delta t_l}$.

2. **Motifs based Time Series Representation:** In this step, we label system parameters by the discovered motifs. In particular, each time series of a system parameter will labeled by the nearest motifs discovered in the previous step. Again, we will use RT as an example and the same process applies to other parameters. Given the k motifs for RT, $RT\_motifs(j), j = 1, \cdots, k$. we label $RT(i)$ by $RT\_motifs(m)$. i.e.,

$$RT(i) \leftarrow Label\_of(RT\_motifs(m)), \text{ where} \qquad (2)$$
$$dis(RT(i), RT\_motifs(m)) \leq dis(RT(i), RT\_motifs(j)), \; j \neq m \qquad (3)$$

3. **Conditional Probability Table Construction:** In the proposed m_DBNs, we define its original state B_0 by the motifs of system parameter time series at time t. The m_DBNs captures the transition model of

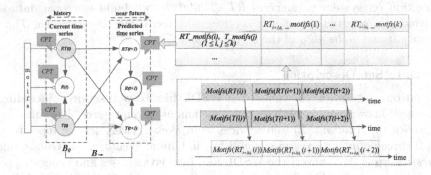

Fig. 2. The Construction Process of the $CPTs$

causal relations for the system parameter time series from time t to time $t+1$, i.e., the state transition $B_\rightarrow$ from current state to the near future.

Each node in the m_DBNs model is associated with a conditional probability table (or CPT). As an example, the CPT for node $RT(t+1)$ is shown in Figure 2. Each row in the CPT corresponds to one possible combinations of values (represented by motifs) taken by its dependent nodes (or conditional nodes) (i.e., $RT(t)$ and $T(t)$). Each column denotes one of the k motifs of $RT(t+1)$, .i.e., $RT_{t+\Delta t_l}\_motifs(1)$, $\cdots$, $RT_{t+\Delta t_l}\_motifs(k)$.

We analyze the labeled historical parameters to gather statistics on historic parameters to construct the $CPTs$ for each node. Let $motifs(RT(i)) = RT\_motifs(\alpha)$, $motifs(T(i)) = T\_motifs(\beta)$ and $motifs(RT_{t+\Delta t_l}(i)) = RT_{t+\Delta t_l}\_motifs(\delta)$. The probability from all of the causal relation satisfies $(RT\_motifs(\alpha), T\_motifs(\beta)) \rightarrow RT_{t+\Delta t_l}\_motifs(\delta)$ will be the value of the cell at the intersection of the row $(RT\_motifs(\alpha), T\_motifs(\beta))$ and column $RT_{t+\Delta t_l}\_motifs(\delta)$.

4. **Online Reliability Time Series Prediction:** The prediction is carried out through the m_DBNs model using the following three steps:
   (a) The real-time system parameters $RT(t), T(t)$ will be labeled by their nearest motifs, which results in $RT(t)\_motifs(\alpha)$ and $T(t)\_motifs(\beta)$.
   (b) The motifs of $RT(t)$ and $T(t)$ will be the conditional item in the CPT of $RT(t+1)$ and $T(t+1)$. Hence, the prediction results for parameter $RT(t+1)$ and $T(t+1)$ will be the motifs holding the maximal probability by the conditional item of $RT(t)\_motifs(\alpha)$ and $T(t)\_motifs(\beta)$.
   (c) The predicted motifs of $RT(t+1)$ and $T(t+1)$ will be substituted into the CPT of $R(t+1)$ as the conditional items to get the cell holding the maximal probability value. The prediction result for reliability time series of $R(t+1)$ will be the motifs of the cell's column name.

4   Experiments

We conduct a set of experiments to assess the effectiveness of the proposed $PGMs\text{-}RTSOP$. Since there is no sizable service dataset that provides continuous observation on system parameters RT, T and R, we build our own dataset by invoking a selected set of web services and recording the *Response Time*, *Throughput* and *Reliability* of the service invocations.

4.1   Data Set Description

To build our dataset, we download the WSDL files of web services, including: (1) the well-known popular web services, such as *bing, SalesForce, PayPal, ebay, Google Search, Amazon*; (2) web services from WebserviceX service repository; and (3) three popular web services published in China: *Weather, QQ Online*, and *DomesticAirline*. We convert the WSDL files into java classes and generate java test files using Axis2. Finally, service invocation requests for a selected API of each web services are sent out every $200ms$ from our PC client and the response time, the size of the returned data (*bit*), and return type of the HTTP message are collected. Let the data size for the returned message from a remote web service be *res_size*. We represent the *Throughput* as the data size successfully transmitted within a unit time from the web service, i.e., $\frac{res\_size}{RT*1000}$ (*kbps*). We set an upper limit for the response time of a service invocation as $1000ms$. If the response time goes beyond the limit, it will be considered as a *timeout* error. We collect the system parameters continuously for 24 hours.

We preprocess to the collected system parameters as follows. We define the time interval for continuous 10 returned messages as a time series point. Since a service request is sent every $200ms$, a time slide is set to $2s$, so each time series contain 10 time points. Then, for a given time point, $RT = (\sum_{i=1}^{10} RT_i)/10$, $T = (\sum_{i=1}^{10} T_i)/10$, $R = e^{-\gamma \cdot t}$. where, RT_i is the *Response Time* and T_i is *Throughput* parameter for each invocation during the time point. γ is the proportion of failure invocations and $t = 2s$. We set $\Delta t_p = 20s$ and $\Delta t_l = 4s$. The historic time series parameters for time t and $t+1$ is built separately. More specifically, the time series for time t: the collected 24-hour *Response Time, Throughput* and *Reliability* system parameters are divided into 4320 ($= 24 * 60 * 3$) continuous time series, which are represented as $RT^j(i)$, $T^j(i)$, $T^j(i)$, where j indexes web services and i indexes time series. To generate the time series for time $t+1$, we move right for two time points (i.e. the time span of Δt_l), also each 10 continuous time points as a time series, represented as $RT^j_{t+\Delta t_l}(i)$, $T^j_{t+\Delta t_l}(i)$, $R^j_{t+\Delta t_l}(i)$.

4.2   Approaches to Compare

We implement four different reliability time series online prediction methods to compare with our approach. Specifically, the four comparison approaches include:

- Average Value of Historic Reliability (*AVHR*): The 10 points of the predicted time series result all equals the historic average reliability value.
- Regression (*Reg*): A least square fitting function is calculated according to historical reliability time series parameter. The fitting function is used to predict the near future reliability time series.

- Similarity based Prediction (SP): Let the real-time observed reliability time series be R_t. $R_{t+\Delta t_l}(i)$ will be the reliability time series prediction result, when $R(i)$ is the nearest historic (in time t) *Reliability* time series to R_t.
- Bayes' Rules (BR): We collect the statistics on the conditional probability of motifs for the historic parameter R, i.e., $P(R(t)_{t+\Delta t_l}\_motifs|R(t)\_motifs)$. With the conditional item of real-time system parameter of R (labeled by its motifs), the motifs will be the prediction result, which makes $R(t)_{t+\Delta t_l}\_motifs$ obtain a maximal probability.

4.3   Performance Comparison

We set the number of motifs as $k=20$ and $k=25$ in *PGMs-RTSOP* and BR and compare the averaged MAE (Mean Absolute Error) [11] of different prediction methods for 10, 50, 100, 200, 300 and 400 number of predictions. The experimental results are shown in Figure 3 (a-b).

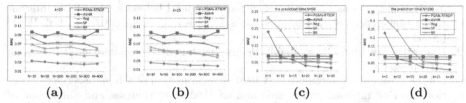

| (a) | (b) | (c) | (d) |

Fig. 3. The Prediction Performance Comparison. (a) *MAE*, $k=20$; (b) *MAE*, $k=25$; (c) *MAE*, $N=50$; (d) *MAE*, $N=200$.

As can be seen from the results, for BR and the proposed *PGMs-RTSOP*, the prediction accuracy increases slightly with the increasing of prediction times, while the approaches of *AVHR*, *Reg* and *SP* change differently as the number of predictions increases. In addition, the curves of the *PGMs-RTSOP* and BR are closer to a straight line whereas those of *AVHR* and *SP* show obvious fluctuations. This observation demonstrates the robustness of prediction performance of *PGMs-RTSOP* and BR. This is mainly due to that the dependency between adjacent motifs have certain patterns as the system parameters change, which makes the proposed *m_DBNs* model more suitable to carry out online reliability time series prediction.

In the second set of experiments, we vary the number of motifs for from 5 to 30. Each method is executed 50 and 200 times, respectively. Also, in the BR method, the number of motifs is the same with our *PGMs-RTSOP* method. As can be seen from Figure 3 (c-d), the motifs number exhibits a significant impact on both *PGMs-RTSOP* and BR. The larger value of k results in a smaller MAE. When $k \geq 20$, the improvement of prediction accuracy slows down. Since the *AVHR*, *Reg* and *SP* do not exploit motifs, their MAE values remain constant over different k values. When $k \geq 20$, the prediction accuracy of *PGMs-RTSOP* significantly outperforms all other four approaches.

5   Conclusion

In this paper, we present an online reliability time series prediction approach, referred to as *PGMs-RTSOP* for service-oriented SoS. The proposed approach integrates motifs into the traditional dynamic Bayesian Networks, resulting in an *m_DBNs* model, to deal with the uncertain SoS runtime environment. We conduct experiments on real-world web services to evaluate the effectiveness of the proposed approach. Four other reliability prediction approaches are implemented for comparison purpose. The experimental results demonstrate the high prediction accuracy and the robust prediction performance of *PGMs-RTSOP*. The proposed online reliability time series prediction approach is instrumental to achieve *online fault removal* and *fault tolerance recovery* mechanisms under a complicated and changing environment.

References

1. Cook, T.S., Drusinksy, D., Shing, M.T.: Specification, validation and run-time monitoring of soa based system-of-systems temporal behaviors. In: IEEE International Conference on System of Systems Engineering, SoSE 2007, pp. 1–6. IEEE (2007)
2. Koller, D., Friedman, N.: Probabilistic graphical models: principles and techniques. MIT press (2009)
3. Lelli, F., Maron, G., Orlando, S.: Client side estimation of a remote service execution. In: 15th International Symposium on Modeling, Analysis, and Simulation of Computer and Telecommunication Systems, MASCOTS 2007, pp. 295–302. IEEE (2007)
4. Mansour, H.E., Dillon, T.: Dependability and rollback recovery for composite web services. IEEE Transactions on Services Computing 4(4), 328–339 (2011)
5. Rothenhaus, K.J., Michael, J.B., Shing, M.T.: Architectural patterns and auto-fusion process for automated multisensor fusion in soa system-of-systems. IEEE Systems Journal 3(3), 304–316 (2009)
6. Salfner, F., Lenk, M., Malek, M.: A survey of online failure prediction methods. ACM Computing Surveys 42(3), 10:1–10:42 (2010)
7. Shellman, E.R., Burant, C.F., Schnell, S.: Network motifs provide signatures that characterize metabolism. Molecular BioSystems 9(3), 352–360 (2013)
8. Yu, Q.: Decision tree learning from incomplete qos to bootstrap service recommendation. In: Proc. 19th IEEE International Conference on Web Services, ICWS 2012, pp. 194–201 (2012)
9. Yu, Q.: Qos-aware service selection via collaborative qos evaluation. World Wide Web Journal (accepted to appear, 2013)
10. Yu, Q., Zheng, Z., Wang, H.: Trace norm regularized matrix factorization for service recommendation. In: Proc. 20th IEEE International Conference on Web Services, ICWS 2013 (2013)
11. Zheng, Z., Lyu, M.R.: Collaborative reliability prediction of service-oriented systems. In: Proceedings of the 32nd ACM/IEEE International Conference on Software Engineering, ICSE 2010, pp. 35–44. ACM (2010)
12. Zheng, Z., Ma, H., Lyu, M., King, I.: Collaborative web service qos prediction via neighborhood integrated matrix factorization (early access articles). IEEE Transactions on Services Computing (2012)

Multi-level Elasticity Control of Cloud Services*

Georgiana Copil, Daniel Moldovan, Hong-Linh Truong, and Schahram Dustdar

Distributed Systems Group, Vienna University of Technology
{e.copil,d.moldovan,truong,dustdar}@dsg.tuwien.ac.at

Abstract. Fine-grained elasticity control of cloud services has to deal with multiple elasticity perspectives (quality, cost, and resources). We propose a cloud services elasticity control mechanism that considers the service structure for controlling the cloud service elasticity at multiple levels, by firstly defining an abstract composition model for cloud services and enabling multi-level elasticity control. Secondly, we define mechanisms for solving conflicting elasticity requirements and generating action plans for elasticity control. Using the defined concepts and mechanisms we develop a runtime system supporting multiple levels of elasticity control and validate the resulted prototype through experiments.

1 Introduction

Cloud services[1] are designed in a fashion that they typically use as many as possible resource capabilities from cloud providers and are distributed on different virtual machines consuming various types of services offered by cloud providers, possibly from different cloud infrastructures. Therefore, requirements for them would differ from the traditional applications, and potentially, they can achieve elasticity not only in terms of resources but also of cost and quality.

1.1 Motivation

In our previous work we have developed SYBL [1], a language for elasticity requirements specification which enables the user to define: (i) *monitoring* specifications for specifying which metrics need to be monitored, (ii) *constraints* for specifying acceptable limits for the monitored metrics, (iii) *strategies* for specifying actions to be taken under certain conditions, and (iv) *priorities* for the previous specifications. Listing 1.1 shows a *cost-related elasticity requirement* specified by, e.g., the service designer, using SYBL, stating that when the total cloud service price is higher than 800 Euro, a scale-in action is needed.

---

* This work was supported by the European Commission in terms of the CELAR FP7 project (FP7-ICT-2011-8 #317790).
[1] In this paper, *cloud service* refers to the whole cloud application, including all of its own software artifacts, middleware and data, that can be deployed and executed on cloud computing infrastructures.

S. Basu et al. (Eds.): ICSOC 2013, LNCS 8274, pp. 429–436, 2013.
© Springer-Verlag Berlin Heidelberg 2013

Listing 1.1. SYBL elasticity directives

```
@SYBL_ServiceUnitLevel(Id="CloudService",strategies=
    "St1: STRATEGY CASE  total_cost>800 Euro : ScaleIn")
@SYBL_CodeRegionLevel(Id="AnalyticsAlgorithm",constraints=
    "C1: CONSTRAINT dataAccuracy>90%;
    C2: CONSTRAINT dataAccuracy>95% WHEN total_cost>400;
    C3: CONSTRAINT total_cost<800;"
priorities="Priority(C2)>Priority(C1);Priority(C3)>Priority(C1);")
```

While elasticity requirements can be specified at different levels, current elasticity control techniques do not support controlling different parts of the cloud service (i.e., elasticity requirement on service unit, on groups of service units) and from a multi-dimensional perspective. Controlling the cloud service at multiple levels enables a finer-grained control according to described elasticity requirements. On the other hand, multiple levels of elasticity requirements could give rise to conflicts on cross-level or even on the same levels. Therefore, we need solutions for overcoming cross-level conflicting elasticity requirements and generating plans for multi-level elasticity control.

1.2   Related Work

Controlling cloud services elasticity in the contemporary view has been targeted by both research and industry. Several authors propose controllers for the automatic scalability/elasticity of entire cloud services [2] or just parts of the cloud service (i.e., cloud service data-end) [3]. Guinea et al. [4] develop a system for multi-level monitoring and adaptation of service-based systems by employing layer-specific techniques for adapting the system in a cross-layer manner. Kranas et al. [2] propose a framework for automatic scalability using a deployment graph as a base model for the application structure and introduce elasticity as a service cross-cutting different cloud stack layers. Cloud providers offer tools for automatic scalability like AutoScale[2] or SmartCloud initiative[3], automatically scaling resources depending on user's detailed resource-level policies. However, these approaches do not control the cloud service on multiple levels taking into consideration the complex service structure, or the multiple dimensions of elasticity (quality, resources, and cost) [5].

1.3   Contributions

In this paper, we propose a system for multi-level cloud services elasticity control by considering the service complex structure and supporting multi-dimensional elasticity. We present the following contributions: (i) a generic composition model of cloud services for enabling the fine-grained control aware of the structure of the cloud service and (ii) a fine-grained, multiple levels automatic elasticity control of cloud services.

---

[2] http://aws.amazon.com/autoscaling/

[3] http://www.ibm.com/cloud-computing/us/en/index.html

The rest of this paper is organized as follows: Section 2 defines our generic composition model. Section 3 presents our techniques supporting multi-level elasticity control while Section 4 presents experiments. Section 5 concludes the paper and outlines our future work.

2   Mapping Service Structures to Elasticity Metrics

2.1   Elasticity Metrics

Cloud service metrics differ on the service type, the service unit targeted by the metric, or the environment in which the service resides. *Resource-level metrics* are the most encountered in cloud IaaS APIs (e.g., IO cost, CPU utilization, disk access, memory usage). *Service unit-level metrics* refer to service units (e.g. web server, or database server) and are used for having a higher level view and being able to determine the unit's health or performance (e.g., request queue length, response time, price). Going higher into the abstraction level, when evaluating the performance of the cloud service one usually considers *cloud service-level metrics* like the whole cloud service response time or number of users per day. In elasticity control, these metrics can be associated to different cloud service parts (e.g., the whole cloud service, service unit or a group of service units), usually, metrics from higher levels (e.g., cloud service level) aggregating metrics from lower levels.

2.2   Abstracting Cloud Services

For obtaining highly granular control of cloud services and being aware of what service unit is being controlled, a model for structuring service-related information is needed. Our proposed model shown in Figure 1 has the form of a graph, with various types of relationships and nodes, representing both static and runtime description of the cloud service and aims at supporting different types of cloud services (e.g. queue-based applications, or web applications):

- *Cloud Service*, e.g., is a web application, or a scientific application. The cloud service represents the entire application/system, and can be further decomposed into service topologies and service units. The term is in accordance with existent architectures and standards (e.g., IBM [6] and TOSCA [7]).
- *Service Unit* [8], e.g., is a database, or a load balancer. The service units are modules or individual services offering computation or data capabilities.
- *Code Region*, e.g., is a data or a computation intensive code sequence. A code region is a code sequence for which the user has elasticity requirements.
- *Service Topology*, e.g., is a business tier, data tier, or a part of a workflow. A cloud service topology represents a group of service units that are semantically connected and that have elasticity capabilities as a group.
- *OS Process*, e.g., is a web server process or any process of the cloud service.
- *Elasticity Metric*, e.g., is cost vs. throughput, or cost vs. availability. Elasticity metrics can be associated with any cloud service part (e.g., service unit, service topology, or code region).

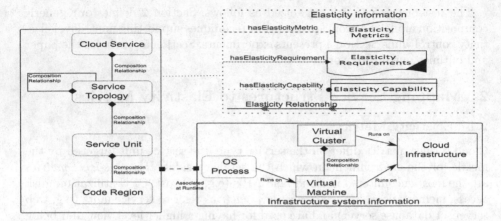

Fig. 1. Cloud service abstraction model

- *Elasticity Requirement*, e.g., is a SYBL directive. They can be specified through any language (e.g. SYBL) and are linked to any cloud service part.
- *Elasticity Capability*, e.g., is the elastic reconfiguration for higher availability, or the creation of new processing jobs for a map-reduce application.
- *Elasticity Relationship*, e.g., is a connection between any two cloud service parts, which can be annotated with elasticity requirements.

In order to describe the cloud service during runtime, a **dependency graph** (Figure 2) is used. The dependency graph is an instantiation of the described model, capturing all the information concerning structure and runtime information like metrics and associated virtual machines.

If we take the example of a Web service (the left side of Figure 2),the cloud user views his/her Web service as a set of services, the metrics targeted in users elasticity requirements being high level metrics. At runtime, the dependency graph is constructed (right part of the figure), service instances being deployed on virtual machines, in different virtual clusters, and the accessible metrics are low level ones. These two views on metrics (cloud user and control system) are mapped by our elasticity control runtime, aggregating low-level metrics for computing higher level ones.

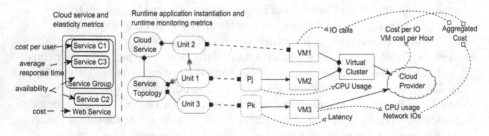

Fig. 2. Constructing runtime dependency graph

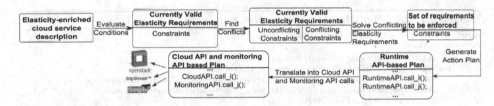

Fig. 3. Elasticity control: from directives to enforced plans

---

Algorithm 1. Solving single-level and cross-level elasticity requirements conflicts

---

1: **function** SOLVESINGLELEVELCONFLICTS($graph_i$)
2:     **for each** l in $cloudServiceAbstractionLevels$ **do**
3:         $confConstraints$= getConflictingConstraints($graph_i,l$)
4:         $graph_i$.removeConstraints($confConstraints$)
5:         **for each** $constraintSet$ in $confConstraints$ **do**
6:             $newGeneratedConstraintsLevel$.add(constraintSolving($confConstraints$))
7:         **end for**
8:         $graph_i$.addConstraints($newGeneratedConstraintsLevel$)
9:     **end forreturn** $graph_o = graph_i$
10: **end function**
11: **function** SOLVECROSSLEVELCONFLICTS($graph_i$)
12:     **for each** $level1$ in $cloudServiceAbstractionLevel$ **do**
13:         **for each** $level2$ in $cloudServiceAbstractionLevel$ **do**
14:             **if** $level1 \neq level2$ **then**
15:                 $conflictingConstraints$.add(getConflictingConstraints($level1,level2$))
16:             **end if**
17:         **end for**
18:         $graph_i$.removeConstraints($conflictingConstraints$)
19:         $graph_i$.addConstraints(translateToHigherLevel($conflictingConstraints$))
20:     **end forreturn** $graph_o$=SolveSingleLevelConflicts($graph_i$)
21: **end function**

---

3   Multi-level Elasticity Control Runtime

Considering the model of the cloud service described through the abstract model
presented in the previous section, we enable multiple levels elasticity control of
cloud services, based on the flow shown in Figure 3. The elasticity requirements
are evaluated and conflicts which may appear among them are resolved. After
that, an action plan is generated, consisting of actions which would enable the
fulfillment of specified elasticity requirements.

3.1   Resolving Elasticity Requirements Conflicts

We identify two types of conflicts: (i) conflicts between elasticity requirements
targeting the same abstraction level, and (ii) conflicts which appear between
elasticity requirements targeting different abstraction levels. For the first type,
as shown in function *SolveSingleLevelConflicts* from Algorithm 1, sets of conflicting constraints are identified and a new constraint overriding previous set is
added to the dependency graph for each level (lines 3-10). In the second type of
conflicts (see Algorithm 1, function *SolveCrossLevelConflicts*) the constraints
from a lower level (i.e., service unit level) are translated into the higher constraint's level (i.e., service topology level), by aggregating metrics considering

---

Algorithm 2. Generating the action plan enforcing the constraints

---

Input: *graph* - Cloud Service Dependency Graph
Output: *ActionPlan*
```
1: while getNumberOfViolatedConstraints(graph) > 0 do
2:     for each level in cloudServiceAbstractionLevel do
3:         actionSet=evaluateEnabledActions(graph, getViolatedConstraints(graph,level)
4:         Action=findAction(actionSet) with max(constraints fulfilled - violated)
5:         addAction(ActionPlan,Action)
6:     end for
7: end whilereturn ActionPlan
```

---

the dependency graph. Since the problem is reduced to same-level conflicting directives, we use the approach for the same-level conflicting directives and compute a new directive from overlapping conditions. In both (i) and (ii) it can be the case of conflict for directives that are targeting different metrics which influence each other (i.e., cost and availability- when availability increases, the cost increases as well). However, knowing how one metrics' evolution affects the other is a research problem itself which we envision as future work.

3.2   Generating Elasticity Control Plans

For generating the action plan, we formulate the planning problem as a maximum coverage problem: we need the minimum set of actions which help fulfilling the maximum set of constraints. Since maximum coverage problem is an NP-hard problem, and our research does not target finding the optimal solution for it, we choose the greedy approach which offers an $1 - \frac{1}{e}$ approximation. The greedy approach shown in Algorithm 2 takes as input the dependency graph and returns the action plan for enforcing the constraints. The main step of the plan generation loop (lines 2-9) consists of finding each time the action for fulfilling the most constraints. For evaluating this, each action has associated the metrics affected and the way in which it affects them (i.e., scale out with VM of type x increases the cost with 200 Euro). The number of fulfilled constraints through action enforcement is defined as the difference between the number of constraints enforced and the number of constraints violated.

4   Experiments

We have implemented elasticity control as a service based on SYBL engine [1] for supporting multi-level, cloud service model aware elasticity control of cloud services[4]. Figure 4 shows the elasticity requirements and the experimental cloud service which is a data-oriented application with two main topologies: a data servicing oriented topology and a data analytics oriented topology. For the YCSB [5] client we generate the workload as a continuous alternation of combinations

---

[4] Prototype, full paper and further details: http://www.infosys.tuwien.ac.at/research/viecom/SYBL/index.html

[5] https://github.com/brianfrankcooper/YCSB/wiki

Table 1. Cost and execution time for Data Service Topology units

Configuration	Controllers	DB Nodes	Total execution time	Cost
Config1	1	3	578.4 s	0.48
Config2	1	6	472.1 s	0.91
Config3	2	2	382.4 s	0.42
Config4	3	7	372.2 s	0.72

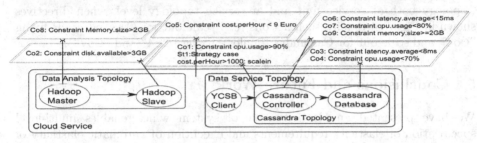

Fig. 4. Current cloud service structure and elasticity directives

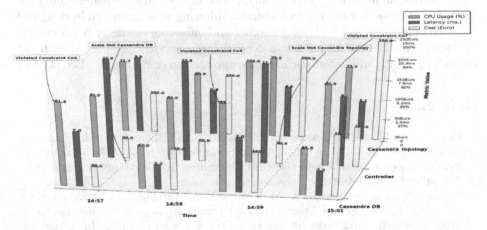

Fig. 5. Metrics (CPU usage, cost and latency) and elasticity actions for service units in Data Service Topology

of the enumerated types of workloads run in parallel. The Hadoop cluster to processes large data-sets using Mahout machine learning library[6].

For reflecting the importance of higher level elasticity control in addition to the obvious low level one, Table 1 presents performance and cost data on different Data Service Topology configurations. We assume each virtual machine costs 1 EUR/hour. Although scale out actions at service unit level do manage to increase performance (i.e., Config2 vs. Config1 increase in performance of 18.37%), they also enable a considerable cost increase (90 % increase in costs for Config2 vs Config1). In contrast with this action level, a scale out action on Cassandra topology (Config3) offers a performance improvement in time of 33.88% over Config1, and a cost improvement of 12.03%. This is due to

---

[6] http://mahout.apache.org/

the fact that more controllers also increase the parallelism of requests, eliminate bottlenecks and facilitate the workload to finish in less time. However, when considering the difference of performance and cost between configurations 3 and 4, it is obvious that the dimension of the cluster and the number of clusters necessary are strongly dependent on the workload characteristics.

Figure 5 shows how the elasticity control engine can scale the Data Service Topology both at service unit and at service topology level, when directives shown in Figure 4 require such actions (e.g. scale out for Cassandra DB fixing "Co4" and scale out for Cassandra topology fixing "Co4" and "Co7").

5   Conclusions and Future Work

We have presented an elasticity control system which enables multi-level specification of elasticity requirements and execution of automatic elasticity of cloud services.

With cross multi-level elasticity control capabilities, cloud providers could sell elasticity as a service to cloud consumers, allowing application code designers to specify elasticity in a high level manner and enforcing elasticity requirements for them while cloud consumers can deploy elastic services pre-packed with our techniques, which will automatically scale application components when needed.

References

1. Copil, G., Moldovan, D., Truong, H.L., Dustdar, S.: SYBL: an Extensible Language for Controlling Elasticity in Cloud Applications. In: 13th IEEE/ACM International Symposium on Cluster, Cloud and Grid Computing (CCGrid), pp. 112–119. IEEE Computer Society (2013)
2. Kranas, P., Anagnostopoulos, V., Menychtas, A., Varvarigou, T.: ElaaS: An Innovative Elasticity as a Service Framework for Dynamic Management across the Cloud Stack Layers. In: 2012 Sixth International Conference on Complex, Intelligent and Software Intensive Systems (CISIS), pp. 1042–1049 (July 2012)
3. Tsoumakos, D., Konstantinou, I., Boumpouka, C., Sioutas, S., Koziris, N.: Automated, Elastic Resource Provisioning for NoSQL Clusters Using TIRAMOLA. In: 2013 13th IEEE/ACM International Symposium on Cluster, Cloud and Grid Computing (CCGrid), pp. 34–41. IEEE Computer Society (2013)
4. Guinea, S., Kecskemeti, G., Marconi, A., Wetzstein, B.: Multi-layered monitoring and adaptation. In: Kappel, G., Maamar, Z., Motahari-Nezhad, H.R. (eds.) ICSOC 2011. LNCS, vol. 7084, pp. 359–373. Springer, Heidelberg (2011)
5. Dustdar, S., Guo, Y., Satzger, B., Truong, H.L.: Principles of Elastic Processes. IEEE Internet Computing 15(5), 66–71 (2011)
6. IBM: IBM Cloud Computing Reference Architecture v3.0
7. OASIS Group: TOSCA Specification, v1.0 (2013)
8. Tai, S., Leitner, P., Dustdar, S.: Design by Units: Abstractions for Human and Compute Resources for Elastic Systems. IEEE Internet Computing 16(4), 84–88 (2012)

Reasoning on UML Data-Centric Business Process Models

Montserrat Estañol[1], Maria-Ribera Sancho[1,2], and Ernest Teniente[1]

[1] Universitat Politècnica de Catalunya, Barcelona, Spain
[2] Barcelona Supercomputing Center, Barcelona, Spain
{estanyol,ribera,teniente}@essi.upc.edu

Abstract. Verifying the correctness of data-centric business process models is important to prevent errors from reaching the service that is offered to the customer. Although the semantic correctness of these models has been studied in detail, existing works deal with models defined in low-level languages (e.g. logic), which are complex and difficult to understand. This paper provides a way to reason semantically on data-centric business process models specified from a high-level and technology-independent perspective using UML.

1   Introduction

Modeling business processes correctly from their early stages is key to the success of an organization, in order to avoid the propagation of errors to the final service that is offered to the customer. At the same time, these models should be easy to understand for the people involved in the process. One way of modeling business processes is by means of the data-centric approach, in which data plays a key role. In a nutshell, business artifacts model key business-relevant entities which are updated by a set of services that implement the business process tasks.

Automated reasoning on data-centric BPM has attracted a lot of research in recent years and several promising techniques have been proposed [2, 5, 8]. However, all these proposals specify the business process model in some variant of logic, resulting in a specification that is low-level and complex, and therefore difficult to understand and unpalatable for business people.

Our work in this paper is aimed at providing semantic reasoning on data-centric business process models specified from a technology-independent and high-level perspective using UML/OCL [7]. We then translate the UML specification into a data-centric dynamic system (DCDS) [2] which can be reasoned with in order to determine the correctness of the original specification.

2   Basic Concepts

This section presents briefly presents the UML models that we use for the initial specification and the target language that provides the reasoning capabilities.

S. Basu et al. (Eds.): ICSOC 2013, LNCS 8274, pp. 437–445, 2013.

2.1   UML Data-Centric Business Process Models

We assume that each dimension of the BALSA framework used to model a data-centric BPM is represented by means of UML and OCL, as proposed in [7].

Business Artifacts. *Business artifacts* are intended to hold all the information needed to complete business process execution. We represent business artifacts by means of UML class diagrams. Figure 1 shows the UML class diagram of our running example which summarizes a generic process of lending a book from a library. *CopyRequest* is the key business artifact in this process since it records the information regarding copies of books requested by the users. A *CopyRequest* may be either a *Reservation* or a *Loan*. The rest of the classes in the diagram are those business artifacts required to hold all the information necessary to request a copy of a book: *User*, *Book* and *Copy* (of a book).

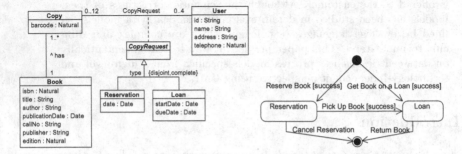

Fig. 1. Class diagram for a library   **Fig. 2.** State machine diagram of *CopyRequest*

The additional integrity constraints for Figure 1 are shown below.

```
1. Key constraints: Book -> ISBN, User -> id, Copy -> barcode.
2. A Copy may not be in more than three CopyRequests of subtype Reservation.
3. A Copy may not be in more than one CopyRequests of subtype Loan.
```

Lifecycle. The *lifecycle* of a business artifact states the key, business-relevant, stages in the possible evolution of the artifact. We represent lifecycles through UML state machine diagrams. Figure 2 shows the lifecycle of the main artifact in our example, *CopyRequest*. A *CopyRequest* is created as a *Reservation* or as a *Loan*, depending on whether the user has asked to reserve a copy of a book or to get it on a loan. When a *Reservation* is picked up by the user, then the *CopyRequest* becomes a *Loan*. Finally, a *CopyRequest* is deleted when the reservation is canceled or the book on loan is returned.

Associations. Transitions in the UML state machine diagram are decomposed into several tasks that must be performed in order for the transition to take place. *Associations* are used to establish the conditions under which these tasks can be executed and we represent them in activity diagrams. Therefore, we will have one such diagram for each transition. Figure 3 shows the activity diagram

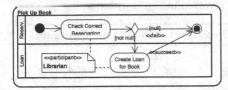

```
action CreateLoanForBook (r: Reservation)
localPost: r.oclIsTypeOf(Loan) and
     r.startDate=today() and
     r.dueDate=getDueDate() and not
     r.oclIsTypeOf(Reservation)
```

Fig. 3. Activity diagram of *Pick Up Book*

Listing 1. Code for service *CreateLoanForBook*

corresponding to *PickUpBook*. First of all, it must be checked whether the *Reservation* provided by the user is correct and that the copy is available. If it is, the *Loan* for the book is created and the transition ends successfully. Otherwise, the transition cannot take place.

Services. A *service* (or *task*) encapsulates an atomic unit of work meaningful to the business process. The execution of services makes business artifacts evolve. We use OCL operation contracts (defined by means of a precondition and a postcondition) to state their effect. Listing 1 shows the OCL operation contract for *CreateLoanForBook*, stating how the *Reservation* becomes a *Loan*.

2.2 Data-Centric Dynamic Systems

A relational data-centric dynamic system (DCDS) is a tuple $S = \langle D, P \rangle$, where D corresponds to the *data layer* and P to the *process layer*. More specifically, the data layer D is defined as a tuple $D = \langle C, R, E, I_0 \rangle$, such that C is a set of *values*, R is a *database schema* containing a finite set of tables, E is a finite set of *equality constraints* and I_0 represents the *initial instance* of the database schema.

On the other hand, the process layer is a tuple $P = \langle F, A, \varrho \rangle$ such that:

- F is a finite set *functions*. They represent the interface to external services.
- A is a finite set of *actions*. They are in charge of evolving the data layer. They are executed sequentially and are atomic. An action $\alpha \in A$ has the form $\alpha(p_1, ..., p_n) : \{e_1, ..., e_m\}$, where:
  - α is the *action's name* and $p_1, ..., p_n$ represent *input parameters*.
  - $\{e_1, ...e_m\}$ is a set of *effects*. They take place simultaneously.
- ϱ is a finite set of *condition-action rules*, defined as $Q \mapsto \alpha$. Q is a *first-order query* over R. Its free variables are the parameters of α. α is an *action* in A.

3 Translating a UML Data-Centric BPM to a DCDS

This section presents the translation process from an initial model defined in UML/OCL into a Data-centric Dynamic System (DCDS). As it may be seen in Table 1, each of the UML models (columns) is translated into one or more elements in the DCDS (rows). Notice that the database schema is used to hold static information, not only from the class diagram, but also from the state machine and the activity diagram. Condition-action rules are used to represent the dynamic evolution in both the state machine and the activity diagram, whereas actions are the ones in charge of making the actual changes in the system.

Table 1. Overview of the elements involved in the translation

	Class Diagr.	State Mach. Diagr.	Act. Diagr.	Op. Contracts
DB Schema	DB_o	DB_i	DB_f	
CA Rules		CA_o	CA_i	CA_f
Actions			A_o	A_f

3.1   Business Artifacts in a Class Diagram

As the business artifacts hold static information and are represented in a class diagram, we will translate the diagram into a database schema, and the remaining integrity constraints will be translated into equality constraints. This translation is performed according to well-known techniques of database design [12].

Figure 4 shows the database schema corresponding to the class diagram in Figure 1. There is one table for each class; class identifiers correspond to the primary key[1] of the corresponding tables. Associations are represented by adding attribute(s) to the linked tables or by creating an additional table for the association itself. Finally, the class hierarchy between *CopyRequest* with *Reservation* and *Loan* in the original example has been implemented through foreign keys from the subclasses to the superclass. The remaining constraints (*disjoint* and *complete*, shown in the class diagram, and textual constraints numbers 2 and 3), should be translated into equality constraints. Due to space limitations, we cannot show their translation here.

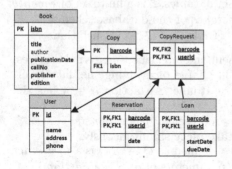

Fig. 4. Translation of the class diagram into a database schema

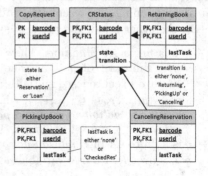

Fig. 5. Keeping track of the status of *CopyRequest* and *Pick Up Book*

3.2   Lifecycles in a State Machine Diagram

The translation of the state machine diagram into a DCDS requires the following: adding a table to the database schema, defining CA rules, and specifying the details of the actions in the previously defined CA rules. The table that is added

---

[1] Primary and foreign keys should be defined as equality constraints in the DCDS. However, for the sake of understanding, we show them graphically in the figure.

to the database schema is used to keep track of the status of the artifact BA associated to the state machine diagram. It will contain the primary keys of BA and two attributes: *state* and *transition*. Attribute *state* represents the current state of the artifact, and *transition* indicates, if any, the transition whose effects the artifact is under. Attribute *transition* is used to prevent the execution of two transitions simultaneously. See Figure 5 for an example.

For each transition in the state machine diagram we will define a CA rule. These rules will indicate the actions which *may* be carried out when the artifact is in a certain state by referring to the *BAStatus* table. As transitions that create the artifact have no source state, the left-hand side of the corresponding rules will indicate that they can be executed anytime using condition *true*. The action's parameters will be the primary key of the business artifact for which the state machine diagram is defined, except for actions that create the business artifact, which will have none.

For instance, rule 1 states that *GetBookOnALoan* can be executed anytime. Rule 2 states that, to execute the action *PickUpBook*, the artifact must be in state *Reservation* and it cannot be undergoing any transition.

$$true \mapsto GetBookOnALoan() \qquad (1)$$
$$CRStatus(bc, id, `Reservation', `none') \mapsto PickUpBook(bc, id) \qquad (2)$$

3.3   Associations in an Activity Diagram

In order to translate the associations, for each activity diagram we will need to define an additional DB schema table and several CA rules. The table will be used to keep track of the last task (or service) that has been executed in the activity diagram by means of attribute *lastTask*. In addition, it will reference *BAStatus* and will include *BAStatus*'s primary key. Figure 5 shows the additional tables we require in our example.

Now that we have added these tables, we are able to specify the effect of the DCDS actions required by the condition-action rules that we defined for the state machine diagram. First of all, they need to insert a new element in the table corresponding to the activity diagram of its transition to indicate that the execution of the activity diagram can begin. They should also update the information in *BAStatus* to indicate that a transition is taking place. Lastly, they should copy the rest of the contents of every table, as the semantics of the DCDS establish that content that is not explicitly copied is lost [2]. Action *PickUpBook(bc,id)* is specified below. Although not shown, it would also copy the contents of all tables except *CRStatus* with barcode bc and userId id:

$$true \rightsquigarrow PickingUpBook(bc, id, `none')$$
$$CRStatus(bc, id, `Res.', `none') \rightsquigarrow CRStatus(bc, id, `Res.', `PickingUp')$$

Finally, condition-action rules will be used to establish when a service can be executed. The condition of each rule will indicate the service that must have been executed for the next service to take place (referencing the table created earlier) and will include the precondition of the service that may be executed (a service cannot be executed if the precondition is false).

Moreover, activity diagrams may include decision nodes and guard conditions that restrict the execution of the next service. We will only deal with decision nodes that depend on the result of the previous service and in which one of the conditions causes the end of the execution of the diagram so that they do not require additional conditions on the CA rule.

According to these rules, the translation of transition *PickUpBook* results in the CA rules below. The two actions correspond to the atomic tasks of the activity diagram. The first rule indicates that no task has been performed yet, while the second one will only fire if the reservation has been correctly checked.

$$PickingUpBook(bc, id, \text{`none'}) \mapsto CheckCorrectReservation(bc, id)$$

$$PickingUpBook(bc, id, \text{`CheckedRes'}) \mapsto CreateLoanForBook(bc, id)$$

3.4   Services (Tasks) in Operation Contracts

The evolution of business artifacts in our framework is driven by the specification of the atomic services (tasks) that are carried out in an activity diagram, while this is achieved by actions in DCDS. Therefore, it naturally follows that we should translate our tasks into DCDS actions.

A DCDS action α has the form $\alpha(p_1, ..., p_n) : \{e_1, ..., e_m\}$. In our translation, $p_1, ..., p_n$ will correspond to the primary keys of the main business artifact which is being modified. DCDSs use functions to represent input from a user and they can only be a part of e_i. Because of this, we do not include the operation's input parameters as part of the action's parameters p_i. For instance, for service *CreateLoanForBook*, the action's signature will be the following: *CreateLoanForBook(barcode, id)*.

$e_1, ..., e_m$ are the effects of the DCDS action. Each e_i has the form $q_i^+ \wedge Q_i^- \leadsto E_i$. $q_i^+ \wedge Q_i^-$ represents the information that must be in the database schema in order for the E_i to take place. Those changes that are made regardless of any condition will have *true* as their $q_i^+ \wedge Q_i^-$.

In order to translate the OCL postconditions into logic we will base our work on [10]. The authors identify a set of OCL constructs that indicate when a class, relationship or attribute is created, deleted or modified. Bearing this in mind, the translation of these constructs into a set of effects e_i has the following form:

- **Insertion:**
  $true \leadsto Table_{INS_i}(...)$
- **Deletion:**
  $Table_i(pk_i', ...) \wedge \neg(pk_i = pk_i') \leadsto Table_i(pk_i', ...)$
  $Table_{REL_j}(pk_j', ...) \wedge \neg(pk_j = pk_j') \leadsto Table_{REL_j}(pk_j', ...)$, where $Table_{REL}$ refers to tables which are affected by the deletion of an element.

– **Attribute change:**

$Table_{ATT_i}(pk, ..., x_j) \rightsquigarrow Table_{ATT_i}(pk, ..., y_j)$

$Table_{ATT_i}(pk', ...) \wedge \neg(pk = pk') \rightsquigarrow Table_{ATT_i}(pk', ...)$

If any of the attributes/columns in these tables are given the value of input parameters in the operation contract, then the translated action will include the corresponding call to a function in their translation. We also need to make additional changes to the tables to reflect the evolution through the activity diagram. There are two cases: either the service is the last one in the activity diagram, or not.

If it is the last service in the activity diagram AD, it will delete the row in the table that corresponds to the activity diagram AD with the primary key of the artifact that has been manipulated. It will also change table $BAStatus$: $BAStatus(pk, oldState, x) \rightsquigarrow BAStatus(pk, newState, \text{'none'})$. If it is not the last service in the activity diagram AD, it will change the corresponding row in the table that corresponds to activity diagram AD, indicating that the service has already been executed.

Finally, we need to add rules to copy the contents of all non-modified tables. In our example, the translation of service $CreateLoanForBook$ results in:

$$true \rightsquigarrow Loan(barcode, id, today(), dueDate()) \tag{3}$$

$$Reservation(barcode', id', x_1) \wedge \neg(barcode = barcode' \wedge id = id')$$
$$\rightsquigarrow Reservation(barcode', id', x_1) \tag{4}$$

$$CRStatus(barcode, id, x_1, x_2) \rightsquigarrow CRStatus(barcode, id, \text{'Loan'}, \text{'none'}) \tag{5}$$

$$CRStatus(barcode', id', x_1, x_2 \wedge \neg(barcode = barcode' \wedge id = id')$$
$$\rightsquigarrow CRStatus(barcode', id', x_1, x_2) \tag{6}$$

$$PickingUpBook(barcode', id', x) \wedge \neg(barcode = barcode' \wedge id = id')$$
$$\rightsquigarrow PickingUpBook(barcode', id', x) \tag{7}$$

First of all, the translated action deletes the $Reservation$ (4) and turns it into a $Loan$ (3). Moreover, as $CreateLoanForBook$ is the last service in its activity diagram it updates $CRStatus$ (eqs. (5) and (6)) and deletes the corresponding row in $PickingUpBook$ (7). Due to space limitations, we do not show the rules that copy the content of the rest of tables.

4   Reasoning on a UML Data-Centric BPM

After obtaining the DCDS, it can be used to reason semantically (i.e. check if the model satisfies the business requirements) about the original UML/OCL specification. Comparing the answers provided by the DCDS with those expected will help ensure that the model represents the required behavior. We assume that the model is structurally correct.

Given a DCDS $\mathcal{S} = \langle \mathcal{D}, \mathcal{P} \rangle$, with a data layer $\mathcal{D} = \langle \mathcal{C}, \mathcal{R}, \mathcal{E}, \mathcal{I}_0 \rangle$ (notice that it includes an initial database instance $\mathcal{I}_0$) and a process layer $\mathcal{P} = \langle \mathcal{F}, \mathcal{A}, \varrho \rangle$, and a property Φ expressed in $\mu\mathcal{L}_P$ (a variant of μ-calculus), we can check whether $\mathcal{S}$ satisfies Φ by using the technique in [2]. For instance, in our example, we could check if a user is forbidden to have two simultaneous reservations of different copies of the same book. Formally[2]:

$$\nu X.(\forall bc_1, bc_2, id, isbn_1, isbn_2.Reservation(bc_1, id) \wedge Reservation(bc_2, id)\wedge$$
$$Copy(bc_1, isbn_1) \wedge Copy(bc_2, isbn_2) \wedge (bc1 \neq bc2)$$
$$\rightarrow (isbn_1 \neq isbn_2)) \wedge [-]X$$

In this case, we would get a negative answer, because the property is not guaranteed in the process's specification. Therefore, the designer should make the necessary corrections (he has probably forgotten to add an integrity constraint).

5   Related Work

When it comes to semantic reasoning on data-centric BPM, many of the existing approaches are close to [2], our target system of representation. The distinctive characteristic of [1] is that it uses a Knowledge and Action Base defined in a variant of Description Logic to represent the artifacts. [3] maps an ontology, representing the artifacts, to a DCDS in order to verify certain properties expressed in a variant of μ-calculus. [5] uses variables to represent artifacts, which are updated by services defined in first-order logic. The properties that the model should fulfill are defined in LTL-FO. [8] goes as far as to define a specification language, ABSL, based on CTL, to specify the artifacts' lifecycle behavior and checks the fulfillment of properties defined in ABSL. In contrast to our work, none of these proposals provide a higher level of representation for the dynamic aspects of the DCDS, and CTL and LTL-FO are not as powerful as μ-calculus.

On the subject of reasoning on UML diagrams, research has either focused on one particular type of diagram or on the consistency between some of them. Examples of approaches that fall in the first category are [10, 11] for the class diagram, [4] for the state-machine diagram or [6] for the activity diagram.

[9] reviews approaches in the second category. About half of the analyzed works deal with semantic consistency across different UML models; however, none of them deal with class, activity, state machine diagrams and operation specifications at the same time.

In summary, existing data-centric BPM proposals that deal with reasoning do not use high-level languages to represent the models. On the other hand, none of the proposals that reason on UML diagrams are able to handle at the same time the different diagrams we need for modeling the four BALSA dimensions.

6   Conclusions

Starting from the UML models we used in [7] to represent business process models from a data-centric perspective, in this paper we have shown a way

---

[2] In order to simplify the definition of the properties we have abused notation and included only the minimum number of variables representing each table's attributes.

to translate them into a data-centric dynamic system (DCDS) [2] in order to determine their semantic correctness before they are put into practice. UML is a standard, high-level and widely used language, and consequently it is easier to understand than logic. DCDSs, on the other hand, are grounded on logic, and therefore it is possible to perform automatic reasoning on them in order to check the correctness of the model. Moreover, DCDSs are able to represent and deal with the static and dynamic components, including non-deterministic services.

To the best of our knowledge, our proposal is the first to show a way to reason with data-centric process models defined at a high level of abstraction. Therefore, it bridges the gap between specifications defined in a high-level language but which are not possible to verify, and specifications which can be checked but are low-level and difficult to understand.

Acknowledgments. This work has been partially supported by the Ministerio de Ciencia e Innovación under projects TIN2011-24747 and TIN2008-00444, Grupo Consolidado, the FEDER funds and Universitat Politècnica de Catalunya.

References

1. Bagheri Hariri, B., Calvanese, D., Montali, M., De Giacomo, G., De Masellis, R., Felli, P.: Description logic knowledge and action bases. J. Artif. Intell. Res (JAIR) 46, 651–686 (2013)
2. Bagheri Hariri, B., et al.: Verification of relational data-centric dynamic systems with external services. In: PODS, pp. 163–174. ACM (2013)
3. Calvanese, D., De Giacomo, G., Lembo, D., Montali, M., Santoso, A.: Ontology-based governance of data-aware processes. In: Krötzsch, M., Straccia, U. (eds.) RR 2012. LNCS, vol. 7497, pp. 25–41. Springer, Heidelberg (2012)
4. Choppy, C., Klai, K., Zidani, H.: Formal verification of UML state diagrams: a Petri net based approach. ACM SIGSOFT Soft. Eng. Notes 36(1), 1–8 (2011)
5. Damaggio, E., Deutsch, A., Vianu, V.: Artifact systems with data dependencies and arithmetic. ACM Transactions on Database Systems 37(3), 1–36 (2012)
6. Eshuis, R.: Symbolic model checking of UML activity diagrams. ACM Trans. Softw. Eng. Methodol. 15(1), 1–38 (2006)
7. Estañol, M., Queralt, A., Sancho, M.-R., Teniente, E.: Artifact-centric business process models in UML. In: Yao, S.B., Weldon, J.L., Navathe, S., Kunii, T.L. (eds.) Data Base Design Techniques 1978. LNCS, vol. 132, pp. 292–303. Springer, Heidelberg (1982)
8. Gerede, C.E., Su, J.: Specification and verification of artifact behaviors in business process models. In: Krämer, B.J., Lin, K.-J., Narasimhan, P. (eds.) ICSOC 2007. LNCS, vol. 4749, pp. 181–192. Springer, Heidelberg (2007)
9. Lucas, F.J., Molina, F., Álvarez, J.A.T.: A systematic review of UML model consistency management. Information & Software Technology 51(12), 1631–1645 (2009)
10. Queralt, A., Teniente, E.: Reasoning on UML conceptual schemas with operations. In: van Eck, P., Gordijn, J., Wieringa, R. (eds.) CAiSE 2009. LNCS, vol. 5565, pp. 47–62. Springer, Heidelberg (2009)
11. Queralt, A., Teniente, E.: Verification and validation of UML conceptual schemas with OCL constraints. ACM Trans. Softw. Eng. Methodol. 21(2), 13 (2012)
12. Teorey, T., Lightstone, S., Nadeau, T.: Database Modeling and Design, 4th edn. Morgan Kaufmann, San Francisco (2006)

QoS-Aware Multi-granularity Service Composition Based on Generalized Component Services

Quanwang Wu, Qingsheng Zhu, and Xing Jian

Computer College, Chongqing University, Chongqing, China
{wqw,qszhu,jx}@cqu.edu.cn

Abstract. QoS-aware service composition aims to maximize overall QoS values of the resulting composite service. Traditional methods only consider service instances that implement one abstract service in the composite service as candidates, and neglect those that fulfill multiple abstract services. To overcome this shortcoming, we present the concept of generalized component services to expand the selection scope to achieve a better solution. The problem of QoS-aware multi-granularity service composition is then formulated and how to discover candidates for each generalized component service is elaborated. A genetic algorithm based approach is proposed to optimize the resulting composite service instance. Empirical studies are performed at last.

1 Introduction

Service composition is staged at two phases: at first, the abstract composite service, consisting of a collection of abstract services orchestrated by kinds of workflow patterns, is defined, and then at running time, it is instantiated and executed by binding abstract services to concrete ones. Since many service instances could provide equivalent functionality with different Quality of Service (QoS) values, an efficient optimization approach for automatic service composition is required to optimize the overall QoS and meet global QoS constraints. This so-called QoS-aware service composition problem is a hot research topic and a lot of efforts have been devoted to it in recent years. Zeng *et al.* [1] use integer programming to find the optimal solution but the approach suffers from poor scalability due to its exponential computational complexity. Canfora *et al.* [2] present a genetic algorithm based approach to enhance the efficiency. The overall QoS reflected by the fitness value of the genome increases from generation to generation and the best one is returned as the solution. Other technologies are also applied to tackle this problem such as skyline query [3] and ant colony optimization [4].

However, current methods mostly lack flexibility of selection. That is, they only consider service instances that implement one abstract service in the composite service as candidates, and neglect those that fulfill multiple abstract services. To illustrate, consider a composite service consisting of three abstract services s_1, s_2 and s_3, which are executed in sequence. Assume there are service instances si_1, si_2 and si_3 which fulfill the functionality of services s_1, s_2 and s_3, respectively, and meanwhile there exists another service instance si_4, which implements the functionalities of s_1 and s_2 in sequence. Current composition approaches will limit candidates to si_1, si_2

S. Basu et al. (Eds.): ICSOC 2013, LNCS 8274, pp. 446–455, 2013.

and si_3, but not consider si_4 even if its QoS is better than the aggregated QoS of si_1 and si_2, as the process definition of the composite service does not contain a single service that can accommodate si_4.

To the best of our knowledge, only a few works have tried to overcome this shortcoming. Barakat *et al.* [5] utilize the planning knowledge hierarchy to allow the expression of multiple decompositions of tasks, but how to construct the hierarchy among tasks automatically is not mentioned. Zhou *et al.* [6] present the problem of QoS-based multi-granularity service selection, and propose an integer programming based method. They only consider composite services orchestrated in the sequence pattern and do not explain how to discover candidates in various granularities. Feng *et al.* [7] study how to produce a new service composition plan with better QoS, while preserving its original behaviors, by replacing the service with another service or a set of services of finer or coarser grain.

In this paper, we present the concept of generalized component services (GCSs) to expand selection scope for service composition to achieve a better solution. The GCS is defined in a semantic manner, and the QoS-aware multi-granularity service composition model is formulated on the basis of this concept. In this model, any service instance which can fulfill partial functionality of the composite service with the same execution sequence can be discovered and employed for composition. A genetic algorithm based approach is presented to tackle this optimization problem and how the proposed approach outperforms the traditional one is described.

2   QoS-aware Multi-granularity Service Composition Model

2.1   Preliminaries

The functionality description of a semantic service can be denoted as a quadruple (I, O, P, E), such as in OWL-S[1], where:

(1)   I and O are the inputs and outputs of the service. I and O consist of one or multiple parameter types and a parameter type is associated to a concept of a shared ontology. Two types C_1 and C_2 can either be equal ($C_1 \equiv C_2$), in a subclass relationship ($C_1 \sqsubseteq C_2$) or not related.

(2)   P is the precondition which must hold before service execution and E is the effect which holds after service execution. P and E can be expressed by rule syntaxes such as SWRL[2].

Apart from the functional description, a service instance[3] owns a non-functional description: QoS. QoS attributes can be classified into two categories: positive and negative (denoted as Q^+ and Q^-). For the former, larger values indicate better performance (e.g. reliability and availability) while for the latter, smaller values indicate better performance (e.g. price and response time).

---

[1]   http://www.w3.org/Submission/OWL-S
[2]   http://www.w3.org/Submission/SWRL
[3]   In our discussion the term service refers to the abstract functionality and the term service candidate or instance refers to a concrete service provided to be consumed (e.g. web service).

Definition 1: Composite Service. A composite service is a value-added service, formed as a number of component services orchestrated according to a set of control-flow and data-flow dependencies.

From the view of process orchestration, a composite service can be represented as a directed acyclic graph (V_G, E_G), where, V_G is the set of vertices including services, gateways, the source and sink vertices, and E_G is the set of edges including control edges and data edges. Gateways encode the routing logic of control-flow dependencies. A split gateway has a single incoming control edge and multiple outgoing control edges, while a join gateway has multiple incoming control edges and a single outgoing control edge. We assume the process orchestration is structured, i.e., for each split gateway, there exists a corresponding join gateway merging the forked flows (e.g. XOR-join to XOR-split, AND-join to AND-split).

Control edges represent logical dependencies between services by specifying the order of interactions, and together with gateways, control edges determine the execution flow of the composite service. At the same time, data edges represent data dependencies between services and a data edge is a 3-tuple (s_{from}, s_{to}, C) meaning that the service s_{from} supplies the concept C to s_{to}. This supply relation holds, iff:

$$(\exists o \in s_{from}.O,\ o \sqsubseteq C) \wedge (\exists i \in s_{to}.I,\ C \sqsubseteq i)$$

To ensure uniqueness of traversal sequence on the vertices V_G in the following sections, let τ be a topological ordering of V_G, which should always be followed during traversing. Fig. 1 depicts the process orchestration of a composite service for illustration and the topological ordering τ can be as follows: $s_1 \oplus s_2 s_3 \oplus s_4 \otimes s_5 s_6 \otimes$ (the source and sink vertices are omitted here).

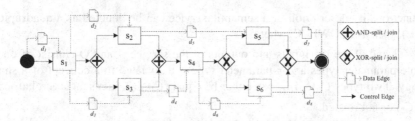

Fig. 1. Process orchestration of a composite service

Meanwhile, from the view of the functional description, a composite service can also be represented as (I, O, P, E) like a common service. Each element of the quadruple can be deduced from component services and the process orchestration. The data in data edges from the source vertex are the inputs, and the data in data edges to the sink vertex are the outputs. P can be deduced by aggregating the preconditions of the first-executed services in the composite service, and E can be deduced by aggregating the effects of the last-executed services. For a concrete composite service instance, it also has the non-functional attribute QoS and the QoS values are determined by QoS values of its concrete components and orchestration patterns. The detailed aggregation functions can be found in [2, 8, 9].

2.2   Granularity Model for Service Composition

Definition 2: Generalized Component Service (GCS). A generalized component service represents the functionality of a well-formed substructure in the composite service and in turn it can be used to compose this composite service as a component. The substructure can contain one or more services and it is well-formed if:

(1) all the services in it are connected via gateways and control edges;

(2) for each service, all its data edges are included;

(3) for any split gateway contained by the substructure, its corresponding join gateway is also included and vice versa; furthermore, all the vertices between them are included as well.

The first two requirements are intuitive and the reason to add the third one is to obviate GCSs that can not be used to compose the original composite service due to the violation of the control-flow dependencies. Take the substructure of s_1 and s_2 executed in sequence in Fig. 1 as an example: because of lack of s_3, which is also between the split & join gateways like s_2, this substructure is not well-formed.

GCS can also be expressed as (I, O, P, E), and each element can be deduced from the included services and the process orchestration. For example, if the source (sink) vertex is in the substructure, the data in data edges from the source (sink) vertex are the inputs (outputs). Otherwise, the data in data edges which have no starting (ending) vertices are the inputs (outputs).

For two GCSs from a specific composite service, if their included services are exactly the same, their functionality will be also completely the same according to the definition and requirements of GCSs. Thus, for a GCS, its set of services can be utilized as its identity and representation. Examples of GCSs in Fig. 1 are as follows: $gcs_1 = \{s_2, s_3\}$, $gcs_2 = \{s_1, s_2, s_3\}$, $gcs_3 = \{s_4, s_5, s_6\}$, $gcs_4 = \{s_1\}$. There are always many ways to decompose a composite service into multiple GCSs. For example, the composite service in Fig. 1 can be decomposed into gcs_2 and gcs_3, or into gcs_4, gcs_1 and gcs_3, and so on.

Definition 3: GCS Granularity. The granularity of a GCS is defined as the number of services it contains and it is denoted as $gra(GCS)$. For example, $gra(gcs_1) = 2$, $gra(gcs_2) = 3$, $gra(gcs_4) = 1$. A GCS is called fine-grained if its granularity is equal to 1, and otherwise it is called coarse-grained.

2.3   Problem Formulation

The target for QoS-aware service composition is to optimize overall QoS of the resulting composite service. The simple additive weighting (SAW) is adopted as the QoS utility function to facilitate ranking of composite service instances in terms of QoS. According to SAW, the QoS utility of a composite service instance csi_k can be calculated in Eq. 1, where, w_t is the preference weight and $q_t(csi_k)$ is the aggregated value of the tth QoS attribute of csi_k, and $q_{t,max}$, $q_{t,min}$ denote the minimal and maximal possible aggregated values of the tth QoS attribute, respectively.

$$U(csi_k) = \sum_{q_t \in Q^-} \frac{q_{t,max} - q_t(csi_k)}{q_{t,max} - q_{t,min}} . w_t + \sum_{q_t \in Q^+} \frac{q_t(csi_k) - q_{t,min}}{q_{t,max} - q_{t,min}} . w_t \qquad (1)$$

Besides, users may impose global constraints on QoS attributes, e.g., the reliability should be larger than 95%. Hence, the QoS-aware multi-granularity service composition problem can be summarized as a two-step process:

1. When the user request for a specific composite service is received, the composition engine first identifies all the GCSs of the composite service, and then starts to discover instances for each GCS through the service registry using functional matching based on semantic descriptions;

2. With a number of service instances available for each GCS, the composition engine instantiate the composite service to a concrete one who is the optimal in terms of QoS utility and satisfies user's global QoS constraints.

In this context, the traditional QoS-aware service composition problem can be regarded as a special kind of our problem, where, granularity of GCSs is limited to 1.

3   Identification of GCSs and Discovery of Service Instances

In order to discover service instances in various granularities for the composite service CS, all its generalized component services should be first identified. Since in a GCS the set of services can be utilized as its indicator, an intuitive method is to enumerate all the combinations of services in CS and check whether requirements of GCSs are satisfied. However, the time complexity of this method is exponential, as the number of all the combinations is 2^n provided that the number of services is n.

```
Algorithm 1 constructGCS(CS,startId,endId,GCSSet)
for i=startId; i≤endId; i++ do
    v₁=CS.V_G.get(i,τ);
    if(isService(v₁)) then
        constructRest(CS,i+1,endId,GCSSet,v₁);
    else if(isSplit(v₁)) then
        nestDepth=0; branchStart=i+1; SComb.clear();
        for i=i+1; i≤ endId; i++ do
            v₂=CS.V_G.get(i,τ);
            if(isService(v₂)) then
                SComb.append(v₂);
                if(nestDepth==0 && pointToJoin(v₂)) then
                    constructGCS(CS,branchStart,i,GCSSet);
                    branchStart=i+1;
                end if
            else if(isSplit(v₂)) then
                ++nestDepth;
            else if(isJoin(v₂) && nestDepth--==0) then
                break;
            end if
        end for
        constructRest(CS,i+1,endId,GCSSet,SComb);
    end if
end for
```

Hence, we use the three requirements to construct GCSs, which is shown in Algorithm 1. *constructGCS* is a recursive function, *startId* and *endId* represent the indexes of the first and last vertex in *CS*, respectively, and *GCSSet* stores the constructed GCSs. The function first traverses vertices of *CS* from *startId* to *endId* successively following the topological ordering τ. If the vertex v_i is a service, the function *constructRest* is invoked, which constructs GCSs whose initial part is fixed to v_i. If it is a split gateway, the traverse of vertices is continued in order to find each branch between this pair of split & join gateways. Inside this pair of gateways there may be nested with other split gateways, and thus *nestDepth* is used to measure the depth of nesting. It ascends when another split gateway is encountered and descends when the join gateway is encountered. A branch is determined when the outgoing control edge from the vertex v_2 points to a join gateway and *nestDepth* is equal to 0, and then the function recurs for each branch. When the corresponding join gateway to this split gateway is found, this inner traverse breaks. For all the services between this pair of split & join gateways, stored in *SComb*, *constructRest* is also invoked.

The function *constructRest(CS, startId, endId, GCSSet, SComb)* focuses on how to construct the rest part of a GCS when its initial part is fixed to the service combination *SComb*. Since the current *SComb* is a well-formed GCS itself, it is added into *GCSSet* first. Then vertex traverse is started from *startId* to *endId* successively, also following τ. When the vertex is a service, it is appended into *SComb*, and when the depth of nest is equal to 0 and the vertex is a join gateway or a service, *SComb* is added to *GCSSet* as a well-formed GCS.

After *GCSSet* is identified, the composition engine looks up for instances from the registry for each GCS in it. A service instance *si* is categorized as a candidate of a *gcs*, if its functionality exactly matches *gcs* with respect to logic-based equivalence of their formal semantics [10]. The matching in terms of inputs and outputs exploits defined semantics of the associated concepts as values of service parameters and the exact matching between *si* and *gcs* is formally expressed as:

$$\forall i_1 \in si.I, \ \exists i_2 \in gcs.I : i_1 \equiv i_2 \ \wedge \ \forall o_1 \in gcs.O, \ \exists o_2 \in si.O : o_1 \equiv o_2$$

The relaxed matching levels in terms of inputs and outputs such as subsuming and plugging in can be considered depending on the application requirement. Besides, the matching in terms of the precondition and effect can also be performed if necessary [11]. After service discovery, each GCS has a list of service candidates and $cnd(gcs_i)$ is used to denote all the discovered instances of gcs_i.

4   Genetic Algorithm for Optimizing Service Composition

Ahead of optimization, we first present the concept of generalized candidates to associate instances for GCSs in various granularities to services in the composite service.

Definition 4: Generalized candidates. Let $gs(s_i)$ denote the set of GCSs in *GCSSet*, whose first-traversed service is s_i. The generalized candidates $gcnd(s_i)$ of s_i represents the union set of $cnd(gcs_k)$ whose GCS gcs_k belongs to $gs(s_i)$. Formally, it is defined as:

$$gcnd(s_i) = \bigcup_{gcs_k \in gs(s_i)} cnd(gcs_k)$$

Therefore, $gcnd(s_i)$ contains candidates in varying granularities for s_i and the granularity of the candidate determines how many services from s_i in the composite service it can fulfill. Let $s_{i,j}$ represent the jth candidate in $gcnd(s_i)$. For example, if $gra(s_{i,1}) = 1$, it indicates $s_{i,1}$ can only fulfill the functionality of s_i, and if $gra(s_{i,1}) = 3$, $s_{i,1}$ can fulfill not only the functionality of s_i, but also that of s_{i+1} and s_{i+2}. Fig. 2 depicts services in Fig. 1 associated with their generalized candidates.

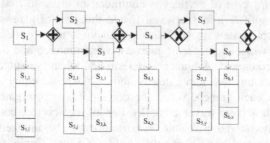

Fig. 2. Services and their generalized candidates

4.1   Genetic Encoding and Fitness Function

A concrete composite service instance is encoded as a genome for our problem. The genome is represented by an array with its length equal to the number of component services and the ith entry in the array refers to the selection result of the ith service. That is to say, given that the value of the ith entry is j, it indicates that $s_{i,j}$ is selected to execute s_i.

When a coarse-grained instance $s_{i,j}$ from $gcnd(s_i)$ with the granularity of k is selected for s_i, it can not only fulfill the functionality of s_i, but also fulfill the functionality of $s_{i+1}, s_{i+2}, \ldots, s_{i+k-1}$. In this case, it is not necessary to select instances for those services, and the corresponding genes in the genome are filled with the pound sign "#" to indicate that these services have been implemented. Based on this representation rule, each service in the composite service is implemented by and only by one service instance in the composite service instance represented by a valid genome. Fig. 3 depicts an example of the genome. In the composite service instance represented by this genome, there are five service instances: $s_{1,3}, s_{2,9}, s_{4,2}, s_{5,5}, s_{6,4}$, where $s_{2,9}$ implements the tasks of s_2 and s_3, and $s_{6,4}$ implements the tasks of s_6, s_7 and s_8.

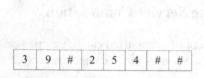

Fig. 3. An example of the genome

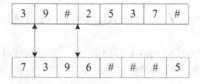

Fig. 4. An example of crossover

The fitness function measures the fitness of the represented solution. As clarified in Subsection 2.3, the fitness of a composite service instance csi_k relies on its QoS utility, and if QoS constraints are satisfied. Thus, it is defined as the sum of QoS utility value and penalty for violations of QoS constraints. Eq. 2 is the fitness function, where *pnl* is negative, representing the penalty value for one violation, and x_t is a binary value defined in Eq. 3, denoting whether the tth QoS constraint qc_t is satisfied.

$$F(csi_k) = U(csi_k) + \sum_{t=1}^{|Q|} pnl \times x_t \qquad (2)$$

$$x_t = \begin{cases} 1 & if \ q_t \in Q^+ \ and \ q_t(csi_k) \le qc_t \ or \ q_t \in Q^- \ and \ q_t(csi_k) \ge qc_t \\ 0 & else \end{cases} \qquad (3)$$

4.2   Genetic Operators

To guarantee that the representation rule of coarse-grained instances is always followed during the evolution of GA (i.e., to keep the genome valid), we extend each genetic operator with special adaptation.

Initialization Operator: An empty array with the length equal to the number of services is initialized and the random assignment is performed from the first gene to the last. An instance c from the generalized candidates $gcnd(s_l)$ of s_l is randomly selected and bound to the first gene. If $gra(c) \ge 2$, the following $gra(c)$-1 genes are assigned with "#". Then the ith gene ($i = 1 + gra(c)$) is selected to be assigned and this process loops until the last gene is assigned.

Crossover Operator: For a genome with a length of n, there are totally n-1 splitting points. However, choosing some of them as splitting points will render the resulting genome invalid after crossover, and thus in a genome, the genes belonging to the same coarse-grained service instance should not be split. Let sp_1 be the set of feasible splitting points in $parent_1$, and sp_2 for $parent_2$. The splitting points the crossover operator can use are limited to the intersection of sp_1 and sp_2. For instance, in Fig. 4, sp_1 is {1, 3, 4, 5, 6}, sp_2 is {1, 2, 3, 7}, and thus feasible splitting points is {1, 3}.

Mutation Operator: Traditionally, each gene in the genome is selected and mutated with the same probability and in this case, coarse-grained service instances will be more likely to be replaced. Therefore, instead, a service instance is randomly selected with the same probability from all the service instances contained in the represented solution. The corresponding genes of the selected instance are then reassigned while complying with the representation rule.

4.3   Empirical Studies

A composite service with n abstract services is simulated and there are m_1/n service instances for each fine-grained GCS in it, m_2 instances totally for all coarse-grained GCSs of various granularities. Let λ represent the ratio that the number of course-grained candidates divided by that of fine-grained candidates, i.e., $\lambda = m_2/m_1$. The QWS dataset [12] is adopted to associate the service candidates. For a candidate with the granularity of k, k pieces of QoS data randomly selected from QWS dataset are first aggregated and then the aggregated datum is associated to the candidate.

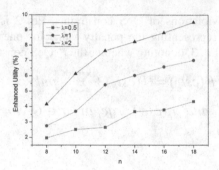

Fig. 5. Enhanced utility w.r.t. n

We evaluate the effectiveness of the proposed GA by comparing it with the traditional GA from [2], which only considers instances of fine-grained GCSs as candidates. The effectiveness is measured by using the enhanced percentage of the QoS utility value in the best solution and it is defined as $1 - u_{traditionalGA} / u_{GA}$. Figure 5 depicts values of enhanced utilities in three case of λ=0.5, 1 and 2, with n growing from 8 to 18 and m_1 set to 5*n. When λ becomes larger, i.e., the number of service instances for coarse-grained GCSs grows, the enhanced utility ascends. This value also goes up with the increase of n. Our approach outperforms the traditional one because the selection scope for service composition is expanded.

5   Conclusions

Traditional approaches for QoS-aware service composition lacks flexibility of selection, as only service instances which have corresponding functionality specified in the composite service via a single service are considered as candidates. This paper presents the concept of generalized component services to expand the choice space for QoS-aware service composition, and then proposes GA to solve the problem. The effectiveness is shown at last via empirical studies.

References

1. Zeng, L., et al.: QoS-aware middleware for Web Services Composition. IEEE Transactions on Software Engineering 30(5), 311–327 (2004)
2. Canfora, G., et al.: An approach for QoS-aware service composition based on genetic algorithms. In: Proceedings of GECCO 2005, pp. 1069–1075 (2005)
3. Alrifai, M., Skoutas, D., Risse, T.: Selecting skyline services for QoS-based web service composition. In: Proceedings of WWW 2010, pp. 11–20 (2010)
4. Wu, Q., Zhu, Q.: Transactional and QoS-aware dynamic service composition based on ant colony optimization. Future Generation Computer Systems 29(4), 1112–1119 (2013)
5. Barakat, L., Miles, S., Poernomo, I., Luck, M.: Efficient multi-granularity service composition. In: 2011 IEEE International Conference on Web Services, ICWS (2011)
6. Zhou, B., Yin, K., Jiang, H., Zhang, S., Kavs, A.J.: QoS-based selection of multi-granularity web services for the composition. Journal of Software 6(3), 366–373 (2011)

7. Feng, Z., et al.: QoS-aware and multi-granularity service composition. Information Systems Frontiers 15(4), 553–567 (2013)

8. Jaeger, M.C., et al.: Qos aggregation for web service composition using workflow patterns. In: International Enterprise Distributed Object Computing Conference, pp. 149–159 (2004)

9. Xia, Y., Luo, X., Li, J., Zhu, Q.: A Petri-Net-Based Approach to Reliability Determination of Ontology-Based Service Compositions. IEEE Transactions on Systems, Man, and Cybernetics: Systems 43(5), 1240–1247 (2013)

10. Klusch, M., Fries, B., Sycara, K.: OWLS-MX: A hybrid Semantic Web service matchmaker for OWL-S services. Web Semantics: Science, Services and Agents on the World Wide Web 7(2), 121–133 (2009)

11. Bartalos, P., Bieliková, M.: Qos aware semantic web service composition approach considering pre/postconditions. In: IEEE International Conference on Web Services (ICWS), pp. 345–352 (2010)

12. Al-Masri, E., Mahmoud, Q.H.: Investigating web services on the world wide web. In: Proceeding of WWW 2008, pp. 795–804 (2008)

Evaluating Cloud Services Using a Multiple Criteria Decision Analysis Approach

Pedro Costa[1], João Carlos Lourenço[2], and Miguel Mira da Silva[1]

[1] Department of Computer Science and Engineering, Instituto Superior Técnico,
Universidade de Lisboa, Lisbon, Portugal
[2] Centre for Management Studies of IST (CEG-IST), Instituto Superior Técnico,
Universidade de Lisboa, Lisbon, Portugal
{pedro.c.costa,joao.lourenco,mms}@ist.utl.pt

Abstract. The potential of Cloud services for cost reduction and other benefits has been capturing the attention of organizations. However, a difficult decision arises when an IT manager has to select a Cloud services provider because there are no established guidelines to help make that decision. In order to address this problem, we propose a multi-criteria model to evaluate Cloud services using the MACBETH method. The proposed method was demonstrated in a City Council in Portugal to evaluate and compare two Cloud services: Google Apps and Microsoft Office 365.

Keywords: Cloud Services, IT Services, Multiple Criteria Decision Analysis, MACBETH, Service Quality.

1 Introduction

IT industry is evolving and there is a new business model, which is revolutionizing and changing it: Cloud services. Organizations can now contract services from the Cloud rather than owning the assets to provide those services [1-2]. However, despite the growing adoption of Cloud services, most decision-makers continue to express some concerns [3], because these services are still in their beginning and quite far from maturity. In fact, decision-makers have doubts about what, when, and how they should migrate to the Cloud, because there are no clear guidelines in this area [4]. In addition to this, decision-makers may not have the knowledge about the real benefits, risks, and costs associated with Cloud solutions, which may lead them to postpone the decision to migrate to Cloud. Therefore, organizations need a systematic tool to evaluate and review their business needs and weigh the potential gains and opportunities by the Cloud against the challenges and risks, to make a well-planned and understood strategy [4].

In this paper we study how to help a decision-maker (DM) to evaluate Cloud solutions. To address this problem we propose a Multiple Criteria Decision Analysis (MCDA) approach [5], based on the MACBETH method [6-7], to build a multi-criteria value model [8-9] to evaluate Cloud services. Complementary, our proposal

S. Basu et al. (Eds.): ICSOC 2013, LNCS 8274, pp. 456–464, 2013.

should also: *(i)* clarify DMs doubts and fears about Cloud Computing; *(ii)* be easy to apply and not requiring specialized expertise; *(iii)* be able to provide understandable results; and *(iv)* be less expensive than current solutions.

This paper describes the building process of the proposed multi-criteria evaluation model that was demonstrated in a Portuguese City Council that wanted to migrate their productivity software (mail and office) to the Cloud. The Cloud services evaluated and compared were Google Apps and Microsoft Office 365. At the end of the process we obtained an overall value score for each of these options, which depicted their overall attractiveness for the City Council. We used the feedback of the DM during the process and the Moody and Shanks Framework [10] to evaluate our proposal, which showed that it is suitable for evaluating Cloud services.

This study was conducted by using Design Science Research Methodology (DSRM) that aims at creating a commonly accepted framework for research in Information Systems (IS) as well as creating and evaluating artefacts to solve relevant organization problems [11]. The steps of DSRM that were used to organize the paper are: problem identification and motivation; objectives of a solution definition; design and development; demonstration; evaluation; and communication [12].

2   Related Work

A decision problem typically involves balancing multiple, and often conflicting, criteria. MCDA consists in "a collection of formal approaches which seek to take explicit account of multiple criteria in helping individuals or groups explore decisions that matter" [5]. In this section we are going to explain briefly some of the most used MCDA methods.

Outranking Methods. Outranking methods are applied directly to partial preference functions, which are defined for each criterion. These preference functions may correspond to natural attributes on a cardinal scale, or may be constructed in some way, as ordinal scales, and do not need to satisfy all of the properties of value functions, only the ordinal preferential independence would still necessary. In outranking methods, for two options a and b, where $z_i(a) \geq z_i(b)$ for all criteria i, we can say that option a outranks option b if there is sufficient evidence to justify a conclusion that a is least as good as b, taking all criteria into account [5].

Analytical Hierarchy Process (AHP). AHP is a method based on evaluating options in terms of an additive preference function. The initial steps in using the AHP are to develop a hierarchy of criteria (value tree) and to identify options. AHP uses pairwise comparisons of options to score the options on each criterion and uses pairwise comparison of criteria to weight the criteria, assuming ratio scales for all judgments. The overall score of an option is obtained by the weighted summation of its scores on the different criteria [5], [13].

MACBETH. MACBETH (Measuring Attractiveness by a Categorical Based Evaluation Technique) is an approach for multi-criteria value measurement [8-9]. It uses semantic judgments about the differences in attractiveness of several stimuli to help a

DM quantify the relative attractiveness of each option. It employs an initial, iterative, questioning procedure that compares two elements at a time, requesting only a qualitative preference judgment. As the answers are entered into the MACBETH decision support system [14] it automatically verifies their consistency. It subsequently generates a numerical scale, by solving a linear programming problem, which is representative of the DM's judgments. Through a similar process it permits the generation of weighting scales for criteria [7].

Outranking methods differ from the others in that there is no underlying aggregative value function, so they do not produce an overall preference scale for the options. AHP generates global scores to represent the overall preference upon the options, which is a wanted feature. However, there are known issues regarding this method concerning, for example, the appropriateness of the conversion from the semantic to the numeric scale used in AHP [15-16]. A MACBETH advantage over other methods for multi-criteria value measurement is that it only requires qualitative judgments to score options and to weight criteria. Furthermore, its decision support system (M-MACBETH) is able to compute the overall value scores of the options by applying the additive model, and to make extensive sensitivity and robustness analysis.

3   Proposal

To address the problem specified in Section 1 multiple independent criteria must be taken into account to evaluate the Cloud services. In our proposal, we use the MACBETH method to evaluate the options against the criteria previously approved by the DM. Our method consists in three main steps summarized below:

A) Structuring the Model. The decision-making process begins by structuring the problem, which consists in identifying the issues of concern for the DM. The DM's fundamental points of view should be taken as evaluation criteria. Each criterion should be associated with a (qualitative or quantitative) descriptor of performance, to measure the extent to which the criterion can be satisfied. Two reference levels (e.g. "neutral" and "good") must be defined on each descriptor of performance. Then, other performance levels may be added to the descriptor, if needed. We created a template with the reference levels of performance for all Cloud services evaluation criteria presented in [17] (see Table 1). In any case, a DM may always select other evaluation criteria or descriptors of performance in order to meet specific organization's needs.

B) Evaluating the Options. In the second step the DM is asked about his preferences in order to build a value function for each criterion and to weight the criteria. To build a value function for a criterion the DM is asked to judge the differences in attractiveness between each two levels of performance by choosing one (or more) of the MACBETH semantic categories: *very weak*, *weak*, *moderate*, *strong*, *very strong*, or *extreme*. Then, M-MACBETH uses a linear programming problem [7] to generate a numerical value scale compatible with the DM's judgments, which should be validated in terms of the proportions of the resulting scale intervals.

Table 1. Evaluation criteria with their respective reference levels

Criteria	Reference Levels	
	Good	Neutral
Client Support	The service provider has defined methods to support the client but is not able to communicate and report service failures	The service provider has no defined methods to support the client but is able to communicate and report service failures
Compliance with Standards	The service provider follows all the standards, processes and policies	The service provider follows some of the standards, processes, and policies
Data Ownership	90% of levels of rights	50% of levels of rights
Service Level Agreements Capacity	The service provider is able to negotiate all terms of the SLAs	The service provider is able to negotiate some terms of the SLAs
Adaptability to Client Requirements	The service provider is able to include core or important client requirements in the service	The service provider is able to include client requirements if they not require any modification in the service
Elasticity	100% of level of added resources	50% of level of added resources
Portability	The service can be ported to other service provider without disruption	The service can be ported to other service provider but can not move all the data
Availability	99% amount of time without interruptions per day	97% amount of time without interruptions per day
Maintainability	The service maintenance does not affect the service up time	The service maintenance stops the service
Reliability	The service can operate without failures under common unfavorable conditions (e.g. power failure)	The service can operate under unfavorable conditions but some components may not work
Risks	The service provider has an effective risk identification and treatment but no contingency plan	The service provider has o risk identification, no risk treatment, and no contingency plan
Acquisition and Transaction Cost	€0	€1000
Cost	€10	€20
Laws and Regulations	The service is subject to laws and regulations to protect clients against all kind of irregularities in the provider's country	The service is subject to laws and regulations only to protect clients against data losses in the provider's country
Innovation	The service is able to make all updates to new technologies and to include innovative features automatically	The service is able to make updates to new technologies but not automatically
Interoperability	The service is able to interact with other services	The service is able to interact only with services from the same service provider
Service Response Time	0.5 seconds	2 seconds
Confidentiality and Data Loss	The information is restricted to authorized people and a failure is promptly detected but no reported	The information is restricted to authorized people but there is no detection and reported failures
Data Integrity	The data stored is accurate and valid and backups are updated to the second	The data stored is accurate and valid and backups are updated monthly

To weight the criteria, the DM ranks the neutral–good swings of the criteria by their overall attractiveness. Afterwards, the DM is asked to judge the difference in attractiveness between each two neutral–good swings using the MACBETH semantic categories, and his answers are used by M-MACBETH to create a weighting scale. Finally, the DM should validate the proposed weights and adjust them if necessary.

C) **Analysing the results.** In this step the performances of the options (factual data) are converted into value scores, using the value functions previously built for the criteria, and an overall value score is calculated for each option by weighted summation of its value scores. A final ranking of the options is then achieved using their overall scores. Before giving a selection recommendation it is wise to perform sensitivity and robustness analyses, to know how sensitive or robust is the ranking obtained to "small" changes in the parameters of the model.

4   Demonstration

The main objective of this proposal is to construct a tool that enables any organization to evaluate Cloud services options. Based on this, we have selected a City Council in Portugal, whose CIO (the DM in this case) had doubts about what Cloud service he should purchase. Due to the advantages of Cloud Computing, the DM wished to migrate some services (e-mail and productivity) to the Cloud. However, he did not know how to choose the most adequate service option for the City Council. Only two services covered the City Council needs: Google Apps and Microsoft Office 365. We acted as a decision analyst guiding the decision process in order to help the DM. The M-MACBETH decision support system was used to display the model being developed.

A) **Structuring the Model.** This first step began with some meetings with the City Council's DM in order to understand the decision context and to identify the evaluation criteria that should be used in the model. The DM accepted all criteria listed in Table 1 as the essential criteria to their problem. Then the DM was asked to validate for each criterion a "neutral" reference level (i.e. a performance that would be neither positive nor negative in the linked criterion) and a "good" reference level (i.e. a performance level considered significantly attractive in the light of the criterion). For example, the "neutral" and "good" reference levels defined for the criterion "Availability" were 97% and 99%, respectively (Table 1). Afterwards, more performance levels were added such that each criterion had at least three performance levels equally spaced.

B) **Evaluating the Options.** A value function was built for each criterion by asking the DM to judge the differences in attractiveness between each two levels of performance, choosing one of the MACBETH semantic categories. Figure 1a presents the DM's judgments matrix for the criterion "Availability", where we can see, for example, that the difference in attractiveness between 100% and 99% amount of time without interruptions per day was judged "weak", whereas the differences between 99% and 98%, 98% and 97%, and 97% and 96% were deemed "moderate", which means that the DM values less the difference between 100% and 99% than the other mentioned differences. The numerical value scale was anchored on the reference levels "neutral" and "good" to which were assigned the value scores 0 and 100, respectively. The M-MACBETH decision support system proposed a numerical value scale based on the set of qualitative judgments inputted in the matrix of judgments using linear programming. The proposed MACBETH scale was then subjected to DM analysis in terms of proportions of the resulting scale intervals. Figure 1b presents the value function obtained for criterion "Availability". The value functions for the other 18 criteria were built in a similar manner.

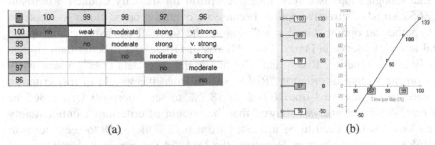

	100	99	98	97	96
100	nn	weak	moderate	strong	v. strong
99		no	moderate	strong	v. strong
98			no	moderate	strong
97				no	moderate
96					no

(a)   (b)

Fig. 1. MACBETH judgements matrix (a) and value function (b) for criterion "Availability"

Afterwards, the relative weights for the 19 criteria were assessed using the MACBETH weighting procedure. The DM was first asked to rank the criteria neutral-good swings by their overall attractiveness. We started by asking the question: "From the 19 criteria, if you could choose just one to move from a neutral performance to a good performance which criterion would you select?" The DM's answer identified the criterion with the highest weight. The questioning procedure continued until the final ranking of neutral-good swings was achieved. Next, the DM was asked to judge the difference in attractiveness between each two neutral-good swings. With the DM's judgments inputted in the weighting matrix M-MACBETH generated the weights shown in Figure 2. Then the DM validated the proposed MACBETH scale. For example, he was asked if the neutral-good swing on criterion "Integrity" is worth two times the neutral–good swing on criterion "Confidentiality and Data Loss", which the DM agreed.

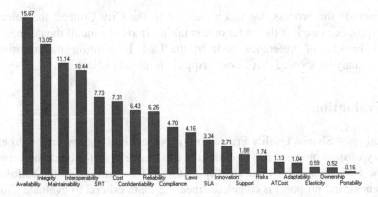

Fig. 2. Weighting scale obtained for the evaluation criteria

C) **Analysing the Results.** The performances of the Google Apps and Microsoft Office 365 upon each of the criteria were inputted in M-MACBETH. The software transformed the performances into the value scores, presented in Figure 3, using the value functions previously built, and calculated the overall scores for the options (see column "Overall" in Figure 3). Google Apps ranked first with 102.08 overall units and Microsoft Office 365 ranked second with 81.21 overall units. Only Google Apps obtained an overall score higher than the score of the hypothetical option "Good at all" (i.e. a fictitious options that has a good performance in all the criteria), which shows that Google Apps is a very attractive option for the City Council. Microsoft Office 365 also is an attractive option, because its overall score is closer to the score of the hypothetical option "Good at all" than to the score of the hypothetical option "Neutral at all". Observe in Figure 3 that Microsoft Office 365 is better than Google Apps only in two criteria: "Risks" and "Confidentiality and Data Loss". A sensitivity analysis on the weight of criterion "Risks" showed that the weight of this criterion would need to be increased from 1.74% to 18.7% to see Microsoft Office 365 be ranked first. A similar analysis showed that the weight of criterion "Confidentiality and Data Loss" would need to be increased from 6.43% to 13.6% to see Microsoft Office 365 as the winner option. However, the DM did not consider plausible these changes on the weights. A robustness analysis made with M-MACBETH considering simultaneous variations of ±3% on the weights of all criteria, though not allowing negative weights, revealed that Google Apps continued to be the most attractive option.

Options	Overall	Compliance	Ownership	SLA	Support	Adaptability	Elasticity	Portability	Availability	Maintainability
Google	102.08	100.00	125.00	-133.00	200.00	-100.00	37.00	0.00	129.70	100.00
[Good at all]	100.00	100.00	100.00	100.00	100.00	100.00	100.00	100.00	100.00	100.00
Microsoft	81.21	100.00	125.00	-133.00	200.00	-100.00	37.00	0.00	129.70	0.00
[Neutral at all]	0.00	0.00	0.00	0.00	0.00	0.00	0.00	0.00	0.00	0.00
Weights :		0.0470	0.0052	0.0334	0.0188	0.0104	0.0059	0.0016	0.1567	0.1114

Reliability	Risks	ATCost	Cost	Laws	Innovation	Interoperability	SRT	Confidentiability	Integrity
233.00	100.00	100.00	160.00	150.00	100.00	100.00	67.00	0.00	100.00
100.00	100.00	100.00	100.00	100.00	100.00	100.00	100.00	100.00	100.00
100.00	200.00	100.00	77.00	150.00	0.00	0.00	67.00	250.00	100.00
0.00	0.00	0.00	0.00	0.00	0.00	0.00	0.00	0.00	0.00
0.0626	0.0174	0.0113	0.0731	0.0416	0.0271	0.1044	0.0773	0.0643	0.1305

Fig. 3. Overall value scores of the options

To conclude the process, we recommended to the City Council the selection of Google Apps, because it is the better option taking into account all the defined criteria and the judgments of preference made by the DM. In addition, the sensitivity and robustness analyses showed that Google Apps is a robust choice.

5   Evaluation

The Moody and Shanks Quality Framework propose eight quality factors to evaluate the quality of data models [10]. We applied this framework to the demonstration by asking the DM about these eight quality factors. The results were the following: *(i)* **completeness**: the proposal is complete since the main criteria to evaluate Cloud services are present; *(ii)* **integrity**: there is no business rule that prevents errors defining the criteria and their descriptors of performance of the proposal since it relies on interviews and observations; *(iii)* **flexibility**: a DM can add or remove criteria to adjust the evaluation model to his organization's businesses and strategies; *(iv)* **understandability**: the proposal is easy to understand since their language is close to the traditional usage in Cloud services, but the DM do not know the decision analysis process and this phase is more difficult without a guide; *(v)* **correctness**: the proposal is correct and valid for their intentions; *(vi)* **simplicity**: the proposal is simple to follow and we verified that is simple to apply; *(vii)* **integration**: the proposal is consistent with the problem and help organizations to make the best decision; and *(viii)* **implementability**: the proposal implementability is dependent on the law and policies in each organization. The City Council's CIO admitted to use it as an auxiliary tool.

This demonstration allowed us to test our proposal in the research problem stated. The City Council suffered from the same problem, as we found in literature, and our proposal helped them to overcome it. The field case revealed that the method developed is a suitable tool for evaluating Cloud services.

6   Conclusion

The research literature and publications from consulting enterprises consider that Cloud Computing has benefits, risks, challenges and issues. But all agree that organizations suffer when choosing which Cloud services they would contract, which reveals a generic and important problem: typically, DMs are not prepared to evaluate Cloud services. To address this problem, we propose to evaluate Cloud services with an MCDA method called MACBETH that simplifies the decision-making process in organizations adopting Cloud services.

This paper has a particular focus on the multi-criteria evaluation process and its application to a City Council in Portugal, where two Cloud services (Google Apps and Microsoft Office 365) were evaluated. With this demonstration we conclude that our proposal is suitable and can be applied to evaluate Cloud services. The Moody and Shanks evaluation we performed supports this conclusion, as almost all quality factors were accomplished.

Regarding future work, more research effort related to the different Cloud models could be used in order to create criteria catalogues that could be applied to different Cloud models, such as SaaS, PaaS, and IaaS. In addition, our proposal can be further improved by developing a software tool specific for Cloud services evaluation.

References

1. Willcocks, L., Lacity, M.: The New IT Outsourcing Landscape – From Innovation to Cloud Services. Palgrave Macmillan, Basingstoke (2012)
2. McAfee, A.: What Every CEO Needs to Know About the Cloud. Harv. Bus. Rev. 89, 124–132 (2011)
3. IDC Portugal: Situação Actual e Tendências de Adopção de Serviços Cloud Computing em Portugal (in Portuguese), IDC Survey (2012)

4. Conway, G., Curry, E.: Managing Cloud Computing: A Life Cycle Approach. In: 2nd International Conference on Cloud Computing and Services Science (CLOSER), Porto, Portugal (2012)
5. Belton, V., Stewart, T.J.: Multiple Criteria Decision Analysis: An Integrated Approach. Kluwer Academic Publishers, Boston (2002)
6. Bana e Costa, C.A., Vansnick, J.C.: The MACBETH approach: Basic Ideas, Software, and an Application. In: Meskens, N., Roubens, M.R. (eds.) Advances in Decision Analysis, vol. 4, pp. 131–157. Kluwer Academic Publishers, Dordrecht (1999)
7. Bana e Costa, C.A., De Corte, J.M., Vansnick, J.C.: MACBETH. Int. J. Inf. Technol. Decis. Mak. 11, 359–387 (2012)
8. Keeney, R.L., Raiffa, H.: Decisions with Multiple Objectives: Preferences and Value Tradeoffs. John Wiley & Sons, New York (1976)
9. von Winterfeldt, D., Edwards, W.: Decision Analysis and Behavioral Research. Cambridge University Press, Cambridge (1986)
10. Moody, D.L., Shanks, G.G.: Improving the Quality of Data Models: Empirical Validation of a Quality Management Framework. Inf. Syst. 28, 619–650 (2003)
11. Hevner, A.R., March, S.T., Park, J.: Design Science in Information Systems Research. MIS Q. 28, 75–105 (2004)
12. Peffers, K., Tuunamen, T., Rothenberger, M.A., Chatterjee, S.: A Design Science Research Methodology for Information Systems Research. J. Manage. Inf. Syst. 24, 45–77 (2008)
13. Saaty, T.L.: The Analytic Hierarchy Process: Planning, Priority Setting, Resource Allocation. McGraw-Hill (1980)
14. Bana e Costa, C.A., De Corte, J.M., Vansnick, J.C: M-MACBETH Version 1.1 User's Guide (2005), http://www.m-macbeth.com/ (retrieved)
15. Bana e Costa, C.A., Vansnick, J.C.: A Critical Analysis of the Eigenvalue Method used to Derive Priorities in AHP. Eur. J. Oper. Res. 187, 1422–1428 (2008)
16. Dyer, J.S.: Remarks on the Analytic Hierarchy Process. Manage. Sci. 36, 249–258 (1990)
17. Costa, P., Santos, J., Mira da Silva, M.: Evaluation Criteria for Cloud Services. In: IEEE 6th International Conference on Cloud Computing, Santa Clara Marriott, CA, USA (2013)

An Approach for Compliance-Aware Service Selection with Genetic Algorithms

Fatih Karatas[1] and Dogan Kesdogan[2]

[1] Chair for IT Security Management, University of Siegen, D-57072 Siegen, Germany
[2] Chair for Management Information Systems IV, University of Regensburg,
D-93055 Regensburg, Germany
karatas@wiwi.uni-siegen.de, kesdogan@ur.de

Abstract. Genetic algorithms are popular for service selection as they
deliver good results in short time. However, current approaches do not
consider compliance rules for single tasks in a process model. To address
this issue, we present an approach for compliance-aware service selection
with genetic algorithms. Our approach employs the notion of compliance distance to detect and recover violations and can be integrated into
existing genetic algorithms by means of a repair operation. As a proof-
of-concept, we present a genetic algorithm incorporating our approach
and compare it with related state-of-the-art genetic algorithms lacking
this kind of check and recovery mechanism for compliance.

Keywords: Service-oriented Computing, Service Selection, Compliance,
Multi-objective Optimization, Genetic Algorithms.

1 Introduction

Service-oriented computing (SOC) is a favored approach for developing distributed applications by orchestrating loosely coupled services according to a
process model [1]. Each service realizes a well-defined task at a certain Quality-
of-Service (QoS) level. In this regard, service selection algorithms are employed
to determine service compositions for given process models. Mathematically this
problem is usually represented as Multidimensional Multiple-choice Knapsack
Problem (MMKP) [2]. As MMKP is NP-hard [3], heuristic approaches (e.g. genetic algorithms, GAs) are favored to find near-optimal solutions in short time.

Processes need to be compliant with rules originating from sources such as the
Health Insurance Portability and Accountability Act (HIPAA) and ISO 27001.
These issues are usually considered to be part of process definition and execution
[4]. However, certain aspects of compliance such as location of execution can be
compromised by heuristic service selection (see section 3.1). Proposed approaches
for service selection based on GAs such as [5–7] do not address this issue.

This paper contributes the following: 1) To our best knowledge the first discussion which compliance aspects (see section 2) might be violated by heuristic
service selection, 2) a method to detect and recover compliance violations in
heuristically determined service compositions utilizing the notion of compliance

S. Basu et al. (Eds.): ICSOC 2013, LNCS 8274, pp. 465–473, 2013.

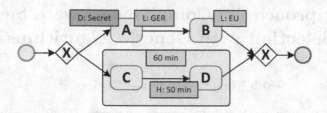

Fig. 1. Sample workflow with compliance annotations

distance as introduced by Sadiq et al. [8] and 3) a GA called COMPAGA based on NSGA-II which incorporates our method by means of a repair operation. This algorithm is tested against several state-of-the-art GAs (see section 4).

The remainder of this paper is structured as follows. Section 2 motivates the presented work. Our approach is presented in Section 3 and evaluated in Section 4. Section 5 covers related works. Finally, the paper is concluded in Section 6.

2 Motivation

Fig. 1 shows a sample process model which is the starting point for service composition. The aim of QoS-aware service selection is to determine compositions which fulfill the QoS constraints of a process model. While for small and medium size problems exact solutions can be determined, it is not feasible for real-world problems. GAs (see e.g. [5–7]) proved to deliver good results in short time.

Processes might also be subject to semantic constraints arising from e.g. standards and regulations. Semantic constraints are called *compliance rules* and can refer to one or more *compliance aspects* (see below). A process is called *compliant* if it does not violate any of its compliance rules [9]. In the following we will introduce the five compliance aspects differentiated in the literature (e.g. [9–11]), name the primary question which each addresses and cite and example from either HIPAA or the *German Federal Data Protection Act* (BDSG):

– **Activities:** Which tasks are performed in which sequence? (BDSG:4) requires user agreement to personal data collection prior to any such action.
– **Data:** What data objects are produced and consumed and which management rules are applied? (BDSG:3a) requires anonymization or psudonymization of personal data if there is no need to access such data in plain.
– **Location:** Where are tasks performed? (BDSG:4b) requires that personal data might be transferred to 3rd parties outside of Germany only if an appropriate level of protection can be assured by the 3rd party.
– **Resources:** By whom are tasks performed? (HIPAA:164.530.a.1.ii) requires that institutions implementing HIPAA must appoint a person or office responsible for receiving privacy complaints.
– **Time limits:** Within which time constraints are tasks being performed? (HIPAA:164.524.a.1; HIPAA:164.524.b.2.i) empowers patients to be informed about their stored protected health infomration (PHI) within 30 days.

3   Approach

In this section we first discuss which compliance aspects might be violated by heuristic service selection. Next we present our approach for detecting compliance violations and finally our algorithm for recovering compliance.

3.1   Impact of Compliance Aspects on Heuristic Service Selection

Activities: The sequence of tasks is defined by the process modeler. As service selection algorithms take process models as input to determine suiting compositions, this aspect is out of scope for service selection. A number of approaches exist to ensure the compliance of process models during design time (see section 5). Thus in the following we assume process models to be compliant regarding the sequence of activities when service selection is performed.

Data: Depending on the type of data, services might be required to fulfill a minimum of security measures (e.g. encryption strength). This leads to the necessity to consider these requirements as local constraints. Thus this aspect needs to be considered by service selection algorithms.

Location: Depending on the type of data, processing might be restricted to certain countries and/or regions. This usually applies to single tasks and thus needs to be considered as local constraint in service selection.

Resources: Ensuring that certain tasks are restricted to certain entities can be achieved e.g. utilizing credentials. This assignment of entities to tasks needs to be performed by the process modeler. Restricting invocation of services to authorized entities is mainly a question of configuration and thus out of scope.

Time limits: Processes might contain non-human as well as human tasks. For human tasks, process designers usually allot a certain amount of time for completion. Thus, service selection for sub-processes subject to time limits needs to consider the time limit as well as alloted times for human tasks.

3.2   Detecting Compliance Violations

Compliance of service compositions is measured utilizing compliance distance as introduced by Sadiq et al. [8]. Compliance distance is a quantitative measure which in its basic form counts the number of compliance violations in a process instance. Here it is adapted for service selection and counts the number of violations caused by selected services in a composition. This basic view assumes that consequences of compliance violations are equally bad. Sadiq at al. pointed out that a more sophisticated approach is to associate a cost with each violation and to define compliance distance as the sum of violation costs [8]. For the sake of simplicity we will use the basic measure in the following.

Data and *location* violations can be detected locally. *Time limit* scopes may be nested and be composed of human as well as non-human tasks. Thus a data structure *timeScopes* is defined containing one list *scope* per time scope in a process model as well as its *time limit*. Given a process model P and a service composition SC, the compliance distance of SC can be determined in two steps. First, for each task $p \in P$ it is checked if the selected service in SC fulfills *data* and *location* requirements defined in P. If this is not the case, the index of p is stored in a list V. In case that p is part of one or several time scopes, the index of p is stored in all respective lists $scope \in timeScopes$. Secondly, all lists $scope \in timeScopes$ are iterated to sum up times allotted to human tasks as well as response times of selected services in SC. If a sum is greater than the *time limit* assigned to *scope*, all elements $p \in scope . p \notin V \wedge \neg p.isHumanTask$ are added to V. The compliance distance of SC then equals $|V|$. Algorithm 1 shows the pseudo-code for this operation.

3.3 Recovering Compliance

In order to replace services efficiently in logarithmic time, the set of service alternatives is clustered with three levels. The first level clusters services according to service class S_i, the second to *data* class and the third to *location* where the latter two are interchangeable (see fig. 2).

Given such a clustering, P, V, and a non-compliant SC, the repair operation works as follows. For each violation $v \in V$ the corresponding service class S_v as well as the set C of *data* and *location* constraints are determined. Then the clustering is searched for a service of class S_v which has a) at least the required

---

Algorithm 1. Detect Compliance Violations(P, SC)

```
 1  V := empty list;
 2  timedScopes := data structure with one list per time scope and its time limit;
 3  foreach p ∈ P do
 4      C := p.getConstraints;
 5      foreach c ∈ C do
 6          if c.isDataAnnotation ∨ c.isLocationAnnotation then
 7              Check if SC[p] meets compliance requirement c;
 8              if SC[p] does not meet c then add p to V
 9          else if c.isTimeConstraint then
10              Add p to all corresponding lists in timedScopes;
11          end
12      end
13  end
14  foreach scope ∈ timedScopes do
15      if Σ human processing times + Σ response times > scope.timeLimit then
16          foreach p ∈ scope . p ∉ V ∧ ¬p.isHumanTask do
17              Add p to V;
18          end
19      end
20  end
21  return V;
```

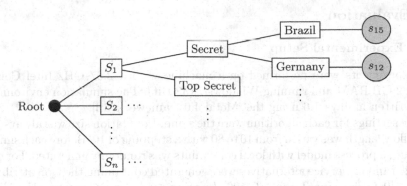

Fig. 2. Service clustering

data class, b) the required *location* and c) minimum response time. If such as candidate exists, it replaces the old service of class S_v in SC (see algorithm 2).

The success of the repair operation depends on the existence of suiting service alternatives. As such it cannot be guaranteed that a non-compliant SC becomes compliant afterwards. *Time limit* constraints are addressed implicitly by picking services with minimum response time. Explicit addressing would again require a two-step approach as in algorithm 1. Our approach will lead to a compliant SC in terms of *time limits* if suiting service alternatives exist. Otherwise *time limit* constraints cannot be met without violating another local constraint. Therefore a more sophisticated approach is not necessary.

To test our repair operation, we implemented a GA based on NSGA-II [12] called COMPliance-Aware GA (COMPAGA). COMPAGA first generates a random initial population and then iteratively performs selection, crossover and mutation operators on this population. Next it calculates the compliance distance of the new offspring with algorithm 1. If the compliance distance of the offspring is ≥ 1, the repair operation (see algorithm 2) is performed with a probability of p_{rep}. Experiments with different values for p_{rep} showed 75% to be a good compromise between runtime and average compliance distance of obtained solutions (see section 4.2).

Algorithm 2. Repair operation(P, SC, V)

1 *Clustering* := Three-level clustering of service alternatives;
2 **foreach** $v \in V$ **do**
3   S_v := service class of v;
4   C := *data* and *location* constraints for S_v in P;
5   *cand* := *Clustering*.pick($s \in S_v$. $s.data \geq C.data \wedge s.location = C.location$
6                          $\wedge$ *s.responseTime* = *min*);
7   **if** *cand* $\neq \emptyset$ **then**
8 | $SC[S_v]$:= *cand*;
9   **end**
10 **end**
11 **return** SC;

---

4 Evaluation

4.1 Experimental Setup

All experiments were performed on a machine with a 2.67 GHz Intel Core i5 CPU, 2 GB RAM and running Windows 7 (32 Bit). The simulation environment was written in Java 1.6 using the jMetal 4.0 framework [13].

The settings for each algorithm were the same. Population size was always 100. Workflow length was varied from 10 to 80 with a stepping of 10. Before each simulation run, a process model with local constraints was randomly generated. For each task 20 random service alternatives were generated containing the QoS attributes $price \in]0,5]$, $responseTime \in]0,500]$, $location \in \{Brazil, Germany, USA\}$ and $encryption \in \{None, AES-64, AES-128, AES-256\}$. Next, this service set was clustered as discussed in section 3.3. After that, each algorithm performed optimization on this setting 100 times with an allowed maximum of 25,000 evaluations. The algorithms had to minimize a total of three objectives: Price, Response Time and Compliance Distance.

We selected a number of state-of-the-art GAs (IBEA [14], NSGA-II [12] and SPEA2 [15]) which provide overall good results for most optimization problems. Besides, a random approach was utilized to obtain an approximate baseline for our experiments. These algorithms are shipping with jMetal.

4.2 Results

In our experiments we investigated the influence of workflow length on the runtime of each algorithm as well as the average compliance distance, response time and price of determined solutions (see fig. 3).

Runtime: The random approach was naturally the fastest and IBEA the slowest. The runtime of SPEA2 was roughly the median of the random approach and IBEA. Second fastest was NSGA-II. The runtime of COMPAGA was slightly higher than NSGA-II due to the additional repair operation. This difference increased with increasing workflow length due to higher repair efforts.

Compliance distance: Average compliance distance generally increased for increasing workflow length except of COMPAGA which delivered significantly better results. IBEA, NSGA-II and SPEA2 yielded similar results with IBEA being slightly better than the other. The random approach performed worst.

Response time: Again, the random approach performed worst. IBEA, NSGA-II and SPEA performed similar with IBEA delivering slightly better solutions. COMPAGA outperformed the remaining algorithms increasingly for increasing workflow length. The reason seams obvious as time constraints are a compliance aspect addressed by the repair operation. Therefore the reduced response time is considered as a side effect of minimizing compliance distance.

Price: The random approach performed worst while the GAs delivered similar results. COMPAGA performed slightly better for workflow lengths ≥ 40. This seems odd as the price of each service alternative is random. Our explanation

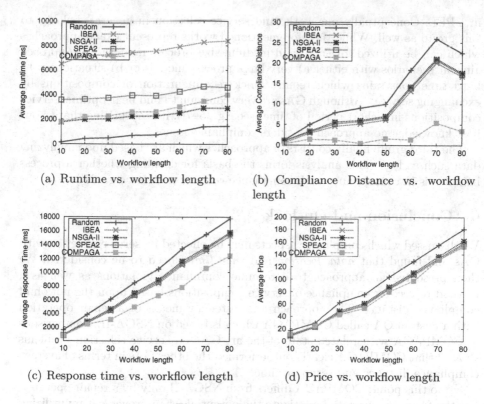

(a) Runtime vs. workflow length

(b) Compliance Distance vs. workflow length

(c) Response time vs. workflow length

(d) Price vs. workflow length

Fig. 3. Evaluation results

is that solutions with lower compliance distance also had a lower price than the other solutions. Therefore we do not attribute this to COMPAGA.

5   Related Work

Approaches for checking process compliance can roughly be divided into three categories: 1) design time approaches for process models, 2) approaches that check compliance during or after system configuration and 3) approaches to verify the compliance of process instances during and after execution. The first group ranges from guiding approaches based upon compliant process patterns (e.g. [16]) to methods for statically checking properties of process models, e.g. based on rule Petri nets (RPNs) (e.g. [17]). Governatori et al. provide a framework which produces a detailed report whether a process model (partly) fulfills compliance rules expressed using the Formal Contract Language (FCL) [18].

Approaches of the second group include formal methods for compliance-aware service composition such as [19]. Another research direction are approaches for verification of service compositions such as [20, 21]. [20] focuses on reachability, liveness and deadlocks. The authors of [21] propose a specification language for compliance properties as well as a verification framework for service compositions in BPEL. Conceptually our work (and service selection in general) belongs to this group as well. While the aforementioned works represent exact approaches which can be utilized for small and medium-size process models, our approach aims at scenarios with either a) very large process models or b) situations with hard time constrains which require quick reconfiguration of compositions by exchanging services. Although GAs are very common to find near-optimal service compositions in a short period of time (see e.g. [5–7]), it is surprising that to our best knowledge no approach considers compliance issues.

The third group finally consists of approaches which are based upon analyzing data such as logs. This analysis forms the basis for deciding whether a process instance is in conformance with compliance rules or not (see e.g. [22]).

6   Conclusion and Outlook

We discussed which compliance aspects may be effected by service selection with GAs and found that *data*, *location* and *time limits* need to be considered. We then presented an approach to determine compliance violations as well as a method to recover compliance of service compositions based upon the notion of compliance distance. The approach was tested by means of a repair operation with a custom GA called COMPAGA which is based on NSGA-II. Comparisons of COMPAGA with related state-of-the-art GAs on service selection problems showed that COMPAGA clearly outperformed the other GAs in terms of average compliance distance and response time.

Up to this point, COMPAGA differs from NSGA-II only by a repair operator. For the future we want to investigate the potential for improvement by utilizing customized genetic operators that leverage domain-specific knowledge regarding compliance. Since the runtime of COMPAGA increases faster than the runtime of other GAs, increasing the performance of COMPAGA is essential for dealing with workflow lengths $>> 80$ efficiently. Another important field of future research is the question of guaranteeing compliance or to conclude that no compliance is possible for given process models and service alternatives.

Acknowledgments. This work is supported by the German Federal Ministry of Education and Science (BMBF) under grant no. 13N10964 in the project ReSCUeIT. We particularly thank Marcel Heupel and the anonymous reviewers for informative and thorough reviews.

References

1. Papazoglou, M.P., Traverso, P., Dustdar, S., Leymann, F.: Service-oriented computing: State of the art and research challenges. Computer 40(11), 38–45 (2007)
2. Yu, T., Lin, K.J.: Service selection algorithms for web services with end-to-end qos constraints. In: Proc. IEEE Intl. Conf. on E-Commerce Tech., pp. 129–136 (2004)
3. Kellerer, H., Pferschy, U., Pisinger, D.: Knapsack Problems. Springer, Heidelberg (2004)
4. Kharbili, M.E., de Medeiros, A.K.A., Stein, S., van der Aalst, W.M.P.: Business process compliance checking: Current state and future challenges. In: Loos, P., Markus, Nüttgens, et al (eds.) MobIS. LNI, vol. 141, pp. 107–113. GI (2008)

5. Canfora, G., Di Penta, M., Esposito, R., Villani, M.L.: An approach for qos-aware service composition based on genetic algorithms. In: Proc. Conference on Genetic and Evolutionary Computation (GECCO), pp. 1069–1075 (2005)
6. Jaeger, M.C., Mühl, G.: Qos-based selection of services: The implementation of a genetic algorithm. In: Communication in Distributed Systems (KiVS), 2007 ITG-GI Conference, pp. 1–12 (2007)
7. Ye, Z., Zhou, X., Bouguettaya, A.: Genetic algorithm based qoS-aware service compositions in cloud computing. In: Yu, J.X., Kim, M.H., Unland, R. (eds.) DASFAA 2011, Part II. LNCS, vol. 6588, pp. 321–334. Springer, Heidelberg (2011)
8. Sadiq, S., Governatori, G., Namiri, K.: Modeling control objectives for business process compliance. In: Alonso, G., Dadam, P., Rosemann, M. (eds.) BPM 2007. LNCS, vol. 4714, pp. 149–164. Springer, Heidelberg (2007)
9. Reichert, M., Weber, B.: Enabling Flexibility in Process-Aware Information Systems. Springer (2012)
10. Curtis, B., Kellner, M.I., Over, J.: Process modeling. Communications of the ACM 35(9), 75–90 (1992)
11. Stohr, E.A., Zhao, J.L.: Workflow automation: Overview and research issues. Information Systems Frontiers 3(3), 281–296 (2001)
12. Deb, K., Pratab, A., Agarwal, S., Meyarivan, T.: A fast and elitist multiobjective genetic algorithm: NSGA-II. IEEE Trans. Evol. Comp. 6(2), 182–197 (2002)
13. Durillo, J.J., Nebro, A.J.: jMetal: A java framework for multi-objective optimization. Advances in Engineering Software 42(10), 760–771 (2011)
14. Zitzler, E., Künzli, S.: Indicator-based selection in multiobjective search. In: Yao, X., et al. (eds.) PPSN VIII, vol. 3242, pp. 832–842. Springer, Heidelberg (2004)
15. Zitzler, E., Laumanns, M., Thiele, L.: SPEA2: Improving the strength pareto evolutionary algorithm for multiobjective optimization. In: Giannakoglou, K.C., et al. (eds.) Evolutionary Methods for Design, Optimisation, and Control, CINME, Barcelona, Spain, pp. 95–100 (2002)
16. Ghose, A., Koliadis, G.: Auditing business process compliance. In: Krämer, B.J., Lin, K.-J., Narasimhan, P. (eds.) ICSOC 2007. LNCS, vol. 4749, pp. 169–180. Springer, Heidelberg (2007)
17. Accorsi, R., Lowis, L., Sato, Y.: Automated certification for compliant cloud-based business processes. BISE 3(3), 145–154 (2011)
18. Governatori, G., Hoffmann, J., Sadiq, S., Weber, I.: Detecting regulatory compliance for business process models through semantic annotations. In: Ardagna, D., Mecella, M., Yang, J. (eds.) RGU 1974. LNBIP, vol. 17, pp. 5–17. Springer, Heidelberg (1974)
19. Bernardi, G., Bugliesi, M., Macedonio, D., Rossi, S.: A theory of adaptable contract-based service composition. In: Proc. 2008 10th Intl. Symp. on Symbolic and Numeric Algorithms for Scientific Computing. SYNASC 2008, pp. 327–334. IEEE Computer Society, Washington, DC (2008)
20. Narayanan, S., McIlraith, S.A.: Simulation, verification and automated composition of web services. In: Proc. 11th Intl. Conf. on World Wide Web (WWW), pp. 77–88 (2002)
21. Yu, J., Manh, T.P., Han, J., Jin, Y., Han, Y., Wang, J.: Pattern based property specification and verification for service composition. In: Aberer, K., Peng, Z., Rundensteiner, E.A., Zhang, Y., Li, X. (eds.) WISE 2006. LNCS, vol. 4255, pp. 156–168. Springer, Heidelberg (2006)
22. Rozinat, A., van der Aalst, W.M.P.: Conformance checking of processes based on monitoring real behavior. Information Systems 33(1), 64–95 (2008)

Decomposing Ratings in Service Compositions

Icamaan da Silva[1] and Andrea Zisman[2]

[1] Department of Computer Science, City University London, United Kingdom
icamaan.silva.1@city.ac.uk
[2] Computing Department, The Open University, United Kingdom
Andrea.Zisman@open.ac.uk

Abstract. An important challenge for service-based systems is to be able to select services based on feedback from service consumers and, therefore, to be able to distinguish between good and bad services. However, ratings are normally provided to a service as a whole, without taking into consideration that services are normally formed by a composition of other services. In this paper we propose an approach to support the decomposition of ratings provided to a service composition into ratings to the participating services in a composition. The approach takes into consideration the rating provided for a service composition as a whole, past trust values of the services participating in the composition, and expected and observed QoS aspects of the services. A prototype tool has been implemented to illustrate and evaluate the work. Results of some experimental evaluation of the approach are also reported in the paper.

Keywords: Rating decomposition, rating propagation, trust values, feedback.

1   Introduction

In a highly competitive environment where anyone can become a service provider and the number of similar services available increases quickly, it is crucial for a system to be capable of choosing the most suitable service for a particular user. Trust and reputation have been the focus of research in several open systems such as e-commerce, peer-to-peer, and multi-agent systems [5][10][11]. Some trust and reputation approaches have also been suggested for web-service systems [7][13][14], and have been used in several e-marketplaces applications such as eBay [2], GooglePlay [4], and Amazon [1]. In general, trust and reputation web-services based approaches are limited and immature [14]. For example, these approaches (i) assume that information given by service providers can be trusted; (ii) assume that feedbacks provided can always be trusted; (iii) demand a large number of interactions or non-intuitive information from users; and (iv) do not properly handle the existence of malicious users when considering their feedback.

An important feature of service-based systems is the fact that services are formed by the composition of other services and in many situations the existence of several services is transparent for service consumers; i.e., service consumers do not know if they are using a single service or a composition of services. In this context, service consumers normally provide feedback to the composition as a whole without

S. Basu et al. (Eds.): ICSOC 2013, LNCS 8274, pp. 474–482, 2013.

considering that the service is composed of several resources. The participating services in a composition, and the way they interact with each other, may influence the feedback associated with the composition. When creating new service compositions it is necessary to distinguish between "good" and "bad" services and to consider the reputation of the individual services. In a competitive market, service providers should also know about the reputation of their services to improve them.

It is essential to have ways to decompose provided ratings and trust values of a composition to the individual services in the composition. However, an approach in which a rating given for a composition is replicated to, or averaged with, the services participating in the composition is not appropriate since it will not provide fair ratings to the participating services. For example, some participating services that performed well may be penalised by other services in the composition that performed badly.

In this paper we present a framework to support the decomposition of service ratings to individual services participating in a service composition. The framework uses a rating decomposition approach that considers (i) rating provided by a user to a service composition as a whole, (ii) previous trust values associated with the individual services in the composition, (iii) the values of QoS aspects that the individual services took to perform their tasks (observed QoS values), and (iv) the QoS values specified for the services in the composition by their respective service providers (expected QoS values). The previous trust values associated with individual services are calculated based on a trust model that we have previously proposed [12].

Motivating Example. As an experiment to illustrate how the decomposition process impacts on the trust values of the services in a composition, we present in Table 1 an example in which a user provides ratings (R) in different intervals to a service composition with two services $s1$ and $s2$. Assume the initial trust values associated with $s1$ and $s2$ as 0.7 and 0.3 respectively. We run the experiment for 25 interactions. Table 1 shows the final trust values associated with $s1$ and $s2$ after the 25 interactions using an approach as the one we are suggesting and an approach in which the ratings are replicated. The results presented in the table show that replicating the ratings provided to the service composition to the participating services tend to penalize the services with higher trust values and favour the services with lower trust values. After the 25th interaction the trust values associated with $s1$ and $s2$ are nearly the same when we replicate the ratings provided to the service composition. This is not the case when using the approach described in this paper, since the different rating values calculated to the individual services provide distinct new trust values to the services.

Table 1. Trust values of services with s1 and s2 for different decomposition approaches

Ratings provided	Our approach		Replication of R	
	Trust Values – $s1$	Trust Values – $s2$	Trust Values – $s1$	Trust Values – $s2$
[0.0, 2.5[	0.20	0.09	0.14	0.12
[2.5, 5.0[	0.53	0.23	0.39	0.36
[5.0, 7.5[	0.86	0.37	0.59	0.57
[7.5, 10.0]	0.98	0.61	0.85	0.82

The rest of this paper is structured as follows. In Section 2 we present our rating decomposition process. In Section 3 we discuss implementation and evaluation aspects. In Section 4 we give an account of related work. In Section 5 we present final remarks.

2   Rating Decomposition

In this section, we describe the mechanisms used to decompose a rating R, provided by a user, to a service composition, into ratings associated with individual services participating in the composition. We also present a trust model to calculate trust values of individual services participating in a composition.

Our framework deals with service compositions that are transparent to the users. This means that users of a particular service composition do not distinguish whether they are accessing a composition of services or only a single service component. The users are not able to provide ratings to the individual services in a composition or to specify different levels of importance to the individual services in a composition.

The rating decomposition approach used in our framework considers (i) the rating provided by a user U to a service composition, (ii) the previous trust values associated with the participating services, (iii) the observed QoS values of the participating services, and (iv) the expected QoS values specified for the participating services by their respective service providers. For illustrative purpose, in this paper we concentrate on response times QoS values. In the approach, the values for ratings associated with services in a composition are within the interval [0.0, 10.0], as are the ratings provided for a service composition by the users. More specifically, the decomposed rating for a service s_i in a composition is given by the equation below:

$$r(s_i) = R \times \frac{T(s_i)}{\frac{\sum_{l=1}^{n} T(s_l)}{n}} + \frac{\sum_{j=1}^{m} p(s_i, t_j, t'_j)}{m} \tag{1}$$

with

$$p(s,t,t') = \begin{cases} 0.0 & if \quad -0.1 \leq \dfrac{t'-t}{t'} \leq 0.1 \\[2mm] -1.0 & else\ if \quad \dfrac{t'-t}{t'} \leq -0.5 \\[2mm] 1.0 & else\ if \quad \dfrac{t'-t}{t'} \geq 0.5 \\[2mm] \dfrac{t'-t}{t'} \times 2 & otherwise \end{cases} \tag{2}$$

where:

- s_i: is a service participating in a service composition;
- $r(s_i)$: is the final rating calculated for service s_i;
- R: is the rating provided by a user for the service composition;
- $T(s_i)$: is the trust value calculated for service s_i;
- n: is the number of component services in the service composition;
- l: is an index representing all the services in the composition ($1 <= l <= n$);
- $p(s, t, t')$: is a recompense function (penalty score) calculated for a service s based on the QoS value of s to perform its task and the QoS value specified for s;
- t': is the QoS specified for s_i by the service provider (expected);
- t: is the actual QoS value that s_i took to perform its task (observed);

- m: is the number of considered QoS values;
- j: is an index representing all the considered QoS values $(1 <= j <= m)$.

We use trust values of the participating services in a composition to calculate the individual ratings of the services in order to analyse how well a service has performed when compared to the other services participating in the composition. We assume that a service with a high trust value has performed well in the past, while a service with a low trust value has performed poorly. Nepal, *et al.* [9] believes that taking into consideration past trust values of participating services when decomposing a rating offers a certain level of consistency. In his view, when a service has performed better than other services in the past, then this service tends to continue to perform better.

As shown in equation (1), the approach considers a *recompense function* $(p(s,t,t'))$ during the rating decomposition process. As the name suggests, the *recompense function* is intended to reward a service in case its performance is better than what it was stated by its service provider (in terms of QoS values), or penalize the service otherwise. For a service s_i, the function has as input parameters the QoS values stated by the service provider, and the actual QoS value that the service took to perform a task when it was invoked. Positive values for the recompense function signify a reward to the service, while negative values signify a penalty to the service.

Given that several aspects may cause variations on the QoS values of a service (e.g., number of requests at a time, quality of the network connection), we have limited the possible result values for this function. This is to prevent the recompense function to cause a high influence in the rating decomposition process, since the function is only intended to reward or penalize a participating service. For example, the highest possible value as output is 1.0 (similarly a penalty of -1.0) when the difference between the actual QoS value is at least 50% lower than the QoS value stated by the service provider (similarly when the actual QoS value is at least 50% higher than the one stated by the provider). We also consider that small variations between the actual QoS value of a service and the QoS value stated by the service provider should not be rewarded or penalized. In this case, we consider a difference of 10% between the actual and given QoS values as being a small variation. The values above were identified after running some experiments with different variations.

Trust Value Calculation. The decomposition of ratings relies on trust values associated with the services in a composition. In the approach, trust values are calculated based on past ratings identified for the participating services. The trust values associated with a service are values in the interval [0.0, 1.0]. In the case in which a service s does not have associated past ratings to calculate the trust value of s, the approach assumes a trust value of 0.5 for s. This value represents the average of possible rating values. The trust model used to calculate the trust values associated with the participating services is based on the trust model we have described in [12].

The calculation of trust values is based on the Dirichlet probability distribution expected value [8]. The ratings given to the composition and decomposed into the participating services are continuous values between 0.0 and 10.0. Each rating calculated for a service is mapped into a 5-component variable $(v_1, \dots, v_5)$ based on the calculation of the level of membership $(m(c, v_i))$ of a continuous rating, according to the equation described by Josang *et al.* [6]. The levels of memberships of the 5-component variable are represented as a vector of size five $(\vec{V})$. For example, consider the situation in which the decomposed rating of a service is 7.0. In this case, the membership vector ($\vec{V}$) would be calculated as [0, 0, 0.2, 0.8, 0].

To calculate the trust value associated with a particular service the membership vectors are aggregated through a weighted sum. In order to weight each rating (membership vector) an aging factor component is used. The aging factor is intended to give more importance to recent ratings than old ones. As defined in [5], the trust value of a service based on ratings is calculated by the function below:

$$T(s) = \sum_{j=1}^{k} \rho_j \delta_j \qquad \text{with} \tag{3}$$

$$\rho_j = \frac{(j-1)}{(k-1)} \qquad \delta_j = \frac{\vec{R}[j]+C}{\sum_{m=1}^{k}(\vec{R}[m]+C)} \qquad \vec{R} = \sum_{l=1}^{n}\vec{V}_l \alpha^{\Delta t} \tag{4}$$

where:

- $\vec{R}$: is the aggregated vector calculated by the weighted sum of all the vectors $\vec{V}_l$;
- $\vec{V}_l$: is the membership vector mapping a decomposed rating to a service s;
- n: is the total number of ratings decomposed for the participating service s;
- k: is the size of $\vec{V}$ ($k=5$);
- ρ_j: is a value assigned to each component $v1,...,vk$ to give a value in an interval;
- C: is a constant used to ensure that all values in the elements of the vector are greater than 0, to allow a posterior analysis of the Dirichlet distribution;
- $\alpha^{\Delta t}$: is the aging factor, where α is a constant and Δt is the difference in terms of time between the available ratings for s ($\Delta t \in \mathbb{N}$, $\mathbb{N}$ is the set of natural numbers).

In order to illustrate, consider the scenario in which a participating service has three available ratings to calculate its level of trust: 7.0, 8.0, and 6.0. The membership vectors for the three ratings are $\vec{V}_1 = [0, 0, 0.2, 0.8, 0]$, $\vec{V}_2 = [0, 0, 0, 0.8, 0.2]$, and $\vec{V}_3 = [0, 0, 0.6, 0.4, 0]$. Then, applying equations (4) the aggregated vector is $\vec{R} = [0, 0, 0.8, 2.0, 0.2]$ (considering $\Delta t = 0$, which means all received ratings were received in the same period of time). Finally, the trust value associated with the participating services is $T(s) = 0.67$ (considering $C = 0.1$).

3   Implementation Aspects and Evaluation

A prototype tool has been implemented in order to evaluate the main aspects of the approach. The tool has two main modules, namely (i) rating decomposition module and (ii) trust calculation module. To evaluate the approach, we also implemented a simulator to generate ratings for the evaluation. The prototype and simulator were implemented using Java. The proposed approach has been evaluated in terms of two different cases: *case (1) - the impact that the ratings provided for a composition have in the rating decomposition process; case (2) - the impact that the observed QoS values of the services have in the rating decomposition process.*

Case (1): In this case we want to evaluate the effects that the trust values associated with the participating services in a composition have in the rating decomposition process, as well as the impact that the ratings provided for the composition have in the rating decomposition process. More specifically, we want to analyse how the rating decomposition process considers services with different trust values and different given service composition ratings. This experiment is important because service compositions may be formed by services with different trust values, which need to be considered when decomposing a rating provided for a whole composition.

In the experiments we considered a service composition with four services (*s1*, *s2*, *s3*, and *s4*) with trust values of 0.26, 0.50, 0.74, and 0.98, respectively. These values provide an average trust value of 0.62. We assumed that the trust values were calculated based on a history of ten ratings previously decomposed for each of the participating services. In the experiments we also considered 25 units of times (time-steps), and that the service composition received ratings are based on a uniform distribution in every time-step. We also considered response times as the QoS aspects and that the difference between the expected and observed response times of a service is less than or equal to 10% (i.e., recompense function $p = 0.0$, as per equation (2)).

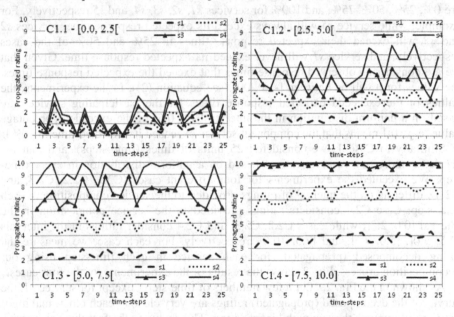

Fig. 1. Propagated ratings to participating services (Case (1))

We executed the experiments for four different cases (C1.1, C1.2, C1.3, and C1.4), differing on the interval of ratings provided to the service composition in each time-step. Case C1.1 considers ratings provided to the service composition in the interval [0.0, 2.5[; while cases C1.2, C1.3, and C1.4 consider ratings in the intervals [2.5, 5.0[, [5.0, 7.5[, and [7.5, 10.0], respectively. We measure the rating decomposed (propagated) for each service in each time-step using our decomposition process. Fig. 1 shows the results of the experiments for the four cases C1.1 to C1.4 above.

As shown in Fig. 1, in all cases, there is an oscillation in the ratings decomposed for the services. The results also show that in cases C1.2 and C1.3 the curves for the decomposed ratings have a similar behaviour for all the four services. In case C1.4, the values of the decomposed ratings for services *s3* and *s4* are similar since the services cannot have ratings higher than 10.0. In case C1.1, when the rating provided for the composition is close to 0.0, the decomposed ratings are also quite similar.

Case (2): In this case we want to analyze the effect of the recompense function in the rating decomposition process. More specifically, we are interested in the comparison on how the expected and observed QoS values for services participating in a composition can influence the ratings decomposed to these services. This experiment is important because service compositions may be formed by services that performed in different ways and, therefore, these services need to be penalised or rewarded.

In the experiments we considered a service composition with five services (*s1, s2, s3, s4,* and *s5*) and the response time as the QoS aspect. We assume that all the participating services have not received previous ratings and, therefore, they have the same trust values (0.5) in the first time-step. We consider the five services with different probabilities of exceeding the expected response times. These probabilities are 0%, 25%, 50%, 75%, and 100% for services *s1, s2, s3, s4,* and *s5* respectively. For example, while service *s5* will always exceed its expected response time, services *s2* and *s3* will exceed their expected response times in 25% and 50% of the cases respectively, and service *s1* will never exceed its expected response time. Given that we are considering observed response times that exceed the expected response times, the values for p will be between $[-1.0, 00]$ (see equation (2)). In the experiments, the values of the exceeded expected response times for the participating services are based on a uniform distribution in the interval $[0.1, 0.5]$ of the exceeded percentage value (e.g., 0.1 means that the component service exceeded its expected time in 10%).

Similarly to Case 1, we considered 25 units of times (time-steps), and that the service composition receives ratings based on a uniform distribution in every time-step. We executed the experiments for four different cases (C2.1, C2.2, C2.3, and C2.4), differing on the interval of ratings provided to the service composition in each time-step. Case C2.1 considers ratings provided to the service composition in the interval $[0.0, 2.5[$; while cases C2.2, C2.3, and C2.4 consider ratings in the intervals $[2.5, 5.0[, [5.0, 7.5[$, and $[7.5, 10.0]$, respectively. For each case, we measure the rating decomposed (propagated) for each service in each time-step using our decomposition process. Fig. 2 shows the results of the experiments for the four cases.

As shown in the Fig. 2, after a few numbers of time-steps, except for service *s1*, the curves of the decomposed (propagated) ratings are very close to each other, making it hard to differentiate the one with higher rating. This is due to the fact that any service can get a higher decomposed rating since, in this experiments, (a) we do not differentiate the past trust values of the services and (b) the probability of a service exceeding its response time does not interfere with the differences between the observed and expected response times. For example, although *s5* is always exceeding its expected response time, the difference between the expected response time and the observed response time can be small; while service *s2* that exceeds its expected response time in only 25% of the cases could have an observed response time much higher than its expected one, which will cause *s5* to have a higher decomposed rating than *s2*. Even service *s1* could receive decomposed ratings similar to the other services, as it is in case C2.1 for the first and second time-steps, in which services *s1, s2,* and *s3* have the same decomposed ratings.

Another point to be highlighted is the fact that the results in the experiments in Case 2 show that the differences between the decomposed ratings of the services are smaller than the differences of the decomposed ratings of the services in Case 1. This is due to the fact that in Case 2 the trust values of the services are not being considered - all the services have the same past values of 0.5. Moreover, the trust values of the services have a bigger impact in the decomposed ratings than the penalty (or reward) given for the expected and observed response times.

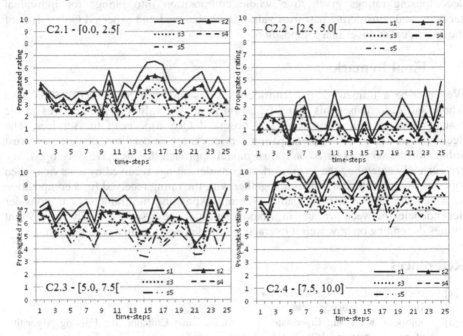

Fig. 2. Propagated ratings to participating services (Case (2))

4 Related Work

Several approaches have been proposed to support service selection, trust, and reputation management over the last years [5][9][10][11]. Most of these approaches focus on reputation management aspects [5][10][11]. Very few approaches consider the fact that services are composed by other individual resources (services) and reputation scores need to be reflected in the individual services [9].

Although rating decomposition is an area that has been investigated in different disciplines such as Business, Cognitive Psychology, Mathematics, and Computer Science, there are few approached that supports rating decomposition in service-based systems [3][9]. Nepal et. al. [9] propose a methodology to propagate ratings provided to a service composition into participating services. Similarly, the approach takes into account the trust values of the participating services. However, it assumes that service consumers are aware of the participating services in a composition. Goldberg et. al. [3] propose an approach based on Singular Value Decomposition (SVD) technique in which rated objects are represented as latent variables that allow discriminating between positive and negative ratings. This technique is effective to predict the user appreciation of an object, but it does not provide ways of discriminating the resource that affects the rating of the whole object. Srivastava and Sorenson [13] describe an approach to service selection based on user's perception of the QoS attributes, rather than the actual attribute values. They propose an interactive approach to find out the most appropriate values for each QoS attribute. The framework and process described in this paper complement existing trust-based approaches by providing a way of decomposing ratings given to a whole composition into ratings for individual services, and considering past trust values, and observed and expected QoS values of the individual services in a composition.

5   Final Remarks

We describe a framework that considers ratings provided for a composition as a whole and decomposes this rating based on past trust values of the services in the composition, as well as expected and observed QoS aspects of the services. The decomposed ratings of the participating services are also used to calculate new trust values for the services based on a trust model approach that we have developed. We are currently extending the framework to consider ratings received by a service when this service is invoked in isolation, together with the rating received for a composition in which the service is participating. We are expanding the framework to consider dependencies between services in a composition, since a service can have different ratings depending on how well it interacts with other services in a composition.

References

[1]   Amazon, http://amazon.com
[2]   eBay, http://ebay.com
[3]   Goldberg, K., et al.: Eigentaste: A Constant Time Collaborative Filering Algorithm Information retrieval 4(2) (2001)
[4]   GooglePlay, http://googleplay.com
[5]   Josang, A., Haller, J.: Dirichlet Reputation Systems. In: 2nd International Conference on Availability, Reliability and Security (ARES 2007), Vienna (April 2007)
[6]   Josang, A., Luo, X., Chen, X.: Continuous Ratings in Discrete Bayesian Reputation Systems. In: Proceedings of the IFPIM (2008)
[7]   Liu, Y., Ngu, A., Zheng, L.: QoS computation and policing in dynamic web service selection. In: Proc. of World Wide Web Conference (2004)
[8]   Marden, J.I.: Mathematical Statistics: Old School. University of Illinois (2012)
[9]   Nepal, S., Malik, Z., Bouguettaya, A.: IEEE Int. Conf. on Web Services ICWS (2009)
[10]   Ruohomaa, S., Kutvonen, L.: Trust management survey. In: Herrmann, P., Issarny, V., Shiu, S.C.K. (eds.) iTrust 2005. LNCS, vol. 3477, pp. 77–92. Springer, Heidelberg (2005)
[11]   Schafer, J.B., Frankowski, D., Herlocker, J., Sen, S.: Collaborative Filtering Recommender Systems. In: Brusilovsky, P., Kobsa, A., Nejdl, W. (eds.) The Adaptive Web. LNCS, vol. 4321, pp. 291–324. Springer, Heidelberg (2007)
[12]   da Silva, I., Zisman, A.: A framework for trusted services. In: Liu, C., Ludwig, H., Toumani, F., Yu, Q. (eds.) ICSOC 2012. LNCS, vol. 7636, pp. 328–343. Springer, Heidelberg (2012)
[13]   Srivastava, A., Sorenson, P.G.: Service Selection based on customer Rating of Quality of Service Attributes. In: IEEE International Conference on Web Services (2010)
[14]   Wang, Y., Vassileva, J.: Towards Trust and Reputation Based Web Service Selection: A Survey. International Transaction Systems Science and Applications 3(2) (2007)

Automatic Generation of Test Models for Web Services Using WSDL and OCL

Macías López[1], Henrique Ferreiro[1],
Miguel A. Francisco[2], and Laura M. Castro[1]

[1] MADS Group, University of A Coruña, Spain
{macias.lopez,henrique.ferreiro,laura.castro}@madsgroup.org
[2] Interoud Innovation S.L, Spain
miguel.francisco@interoud.com

Abstract. Web services are a very popular solution to integrate components when building a software system, or to allow communication between a system and third-party users, providing a flexible, reusable mechanism to access its functionalities.

To ensure these properties though, intensive testing of web services is a key activity: we need to verify their behaviour and ensure their quality as much as possible, as efficiently as possible. In practise, the compromise between effort and cost leads too often to smaller and less exhaustive testing than it would be desirable.

In this paper we present a framework to test web services based on their WSDL specification and certain constraints written in OCL, following a black-box approach and using property-based testing. This combination of strategies allows us to face the problem of generating good quality test suites and test cases by automatically deriving those from the web service formal description. To illustrate the use of our framework, we present an industrial case study: a distributed system which serves media contents to customers' TV screens.

Keywords: Property-Based Testing, Web Services, WSDL, OCL.

1 Introduction

The need to provide access to different kind of systems across the web has become critical. The usual way to do it is through web services, which aim to provide a means for interaction among software systems, or systems and final users over the network. There are multiple ways for describing these interactions, one commonly used being WSDL (Web Services Description Language) [5], an XML-based language to specify the operations offered by a web service. The WSDL standard operates at the syntactic level and does not represent the requirements or operational constraints of the web service. Thus, in order to add semantic information to web service description, the WSDL description must be completed. A number of choices have been proposed to do this, such as WSDL-S (Web Services Semantics) [6], SWRL (Semantic Web Rule Language) [4], or OCL (Object Constraint Language) [2].

S. Basu et al. (Eds.): ICSOC 2013, LNCS 8274, pp. 483–490, 2013.
© Springer-Verlag Berlin Heidelberg 2013

To ensure the quality of a web service [13], we need to guarantee that the operations work as their specification require, this is, that the semantic information is not violated. Based on previous work [16] which used UML descriptions together with OCL properties to perform automatic testing of software components, we propose to apply property-based testing (PBT) [12] to perform automatic testing of web services. When using PBT, testers have to write properties that the system under test (SUT) needs to satisfy, rather than specific test cases. From the properties description, tools can produce the specific test cases automatically. Using this technique, we have a black-box model which describes the functional properties of the SUT and use it for testing purposes. In particular, given a WSDL description of a web service and its OCL semantic definition, we generate the model instead of writing it manually.

2   Property-Based Testing and QuickCheck

As an alternative to manually producing tests from a high-level natural-language specification, or writing a formal model to describe a system or component, PBT uses declarative statements to specify properties that the software needs to satisfy according to its specification. Using this approach, test cases can then be generated from those properties, a process that can be automated, allowing to run many tests for each written property.

In our work, we have used QuickCheck, a PBT tool that automates generation, execution and evaluation of test cases. This allows us to run lots of tests with very little effort, checking whether the defined properties hold or not.

For testing complex systems, however, isolated properties are not expressive nor powerful enough. Instead of sequences of independent test cases, we want to test sequences of calls which modify the *state* of the service, checking that some conditions hold before and after each interaction, and that the global state of the service remains coherent with its expected behaviour call after call.

3   Test Approach: From WSDL+OCL to Properties

The requirements of a system represent the needs that it must fulfil, and they are usually specified in an abstract way, without technical details. As we want to use PBT to test the web services behind the WSDL specification, we need to have the appropriate properties which describe the requirements of the SUT. To do that, we get information both from the WSDL and the OCL constraints, and the combination of both allows us to automatically build our test model, composed by properties. Depending on the requirements of the web service, the test model can differ: for stateless web services, universally quantified properties are generated; for stateful ones, the requirements are modelled into a state machine. Either from the properties or from the state machine modelling the web service, QuickCheck derives the specific test cases, and then, using an HTTP adapter (generated from the WSDL specification), we feed the SUT. Thus, using our framework, the testers do not need to know any specific details about web services implementation languages.

In addition, if the same API is pre-served, different implementations of a web service can be tested with the same test properties. The general architecture of our framework is shown in Figure 1.

Firstly, we need to retrieve informa-tion from the WSDL file, so a WSDL parser has been developed. We decided to implement our own because we need to integrate the semantic information pro-vided as OCL constraints, writing it as an easy-to-manage structure to transform into properties. For instance, from the WSDL for a calculator we need: the name of the web service from the `service` tag; the name of each operation from the `operation` tag, contained in `interface`; the name of `input` and `output` tags for each operation; the `types` referred by each

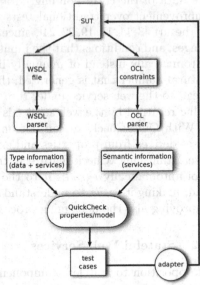

Fig. 1. Proposed testing architecture

input and output elements; the `endpoint` and the `operation` from the `binding` tag to get the URL; and the `modelReference` attribute referring the OCL file.

Then, we have to parse the referred OCL file and check if there is semantic information associated to any of the operations retrieved in the second item before. As in the previous case, we found several tools to parse OCL files, but in all cases the parsing functionality has to be executed associating a UML model to the OCL. This led us to develop our own OCL parser, taking advantage from the work made by the OCLNL project [3]: a labelled BNF grammar [15] for OCL. This grammar was fed to the BNF compiler (BNFC) [1] to produce the abstract syntax tree, lexer and parser which we used.

Finally, when the required information from the WSDL and OCL file is re-trieved, it is time to build the properties for testing.

3.1   Stateless web Services

Stateless services or systems do not have an internal state that affects the out-come of a sequence of calls to their API, so the response returned by a specific call is independent of the specific moment when it is executed. In this case, the name of the operation to be tested and the type of its result and arguments is parsed from the WSDL file; in turn, the test oracle is built out of the constraints specified in the OCL file.

For the calculator example, we could generate the following property:

```
prop_pow() ->
  ?FORALL({A, B}, {ocl_gen:int(), ocl_gen:nat()},
      mathUtils:pow(A, B) == ocl_seq:iterate(fun (I, Acc) -> Acc * A end, 1, ocl_seq:new(1, B))).
```

QuickCheck can run this property and produce specific test cases; this way, instead of specifying input data manually, data generators are used to generate data of the corresponding data type. This approach leads to a significant improvement over traditional tests [21] and most of the research in the state of the art [8–11, 17, 19, 22, 24], since instead of specific values, we define types, ranges, and conditions that the input data has to meet, which are then produced automatically instead of manually listed. So, for each pair of an integer and a natural number that is generated, they are used by the HTTP adapter to make a call to the web service under test, getting the URL from the WSDL file. The value returned by the web service is finally checked in the property body.

With QuickCheck we can not only generate a large amount of specific test cases derived from properties and executed against the real SUT. Another very interesting QuickCheck feature is that, when a failing test case is found, the tool automatically *shrinks* it to the smallest equivalent counterexample it can find, making it easier to understand the reason of the failing case [23], and thus improving also the debugging process.

3.2   Stateful Web Services

In opposition to stateless components, in which each action is independent of each other, many systems have a behaviour that depends on which actions were previously performed. In order to test these systems, the internal state has to be taken into account in the test process. QuickCheck has support for testing this kind of systems by using state machines. Instead of specifying general properties, the state machine behaviour is specified by defining an initial state and a state transition function. Additionally preconditions and postconditions are used to verify state-related properties in each step. The generated tests cases consist in random sequences of state transitions where, at each state, both pre- and postconditions are checked [7]. Our case study, explained in the next section, falls in this category of stateful web services.

4   Case Study: VoDKATV

VoDKATV is an IPTV/OTT middleware that provides end-users access to different services on a TV screen, tablet, smartphone, PC, etc., allowing an advanced multi-screen media experience. Architecturally, it is a distributed system composed by several components, which are integrated through web services.

Among other things, VoDKATV stores information about the users and devices that can access the system. Devices are identified by a MAC address, and they are associated to a household (*room*, in VoDKATV nomenclature). Thus, when a new user is registered, a new household must be created and the devices of that user must be registered to that household. This particular subset of VoD-KATV functionalities is offered by one single administration web service, which we have chosen as case study. The web service offers, among others, operations to create, modify, update and delete households and devices.

The operation used to create a new household is specified in WSDL as:

```
<wsdl:operation name="CreateRoom"
    pattern="http://www.w3.org/ns/wsdl/in-out"
    style="http://www.w3.org/ns/wsdl/style/iri" wsdlx:safe="true">
    <wsdl:input element="msg:createRoomParams"/>
    <wsdl:output element="msg:createRoomResponse"/>
</wsdl:operation>
```

where `createRoomParams` specifies the parameters received by the web service (roomId and `description`):

```
<xsd:element name="createRoomParams">
    <xsd:complexType>
        <xsd:sequence>
          <xsd:element name="roomId" type="xsd:string" />
          <xsd:element name="description" type="xsd:string" minOccurs="0" maxOccurs="1"/>
        </xsd:sequence>
    </xsd:complexType>
</xsd:element>
```

and `createRoomResponse` is the response returned by the web service:

```
<xsd:element name="createRoomResponse">
    <xsd:complexType>
        <xsd:sequence>
          <xsd:element name="roomId" type="xsd:string" />
          <xsd:element name="description" type="xsd:string" minOccurs="0" maxOccurs="1"/>
          <xsd:element name="error" type="tns:error" minOccurs="0" maxOccurs="1" />
        </xsd:sequence>
    </xsd:complexType>
</xsd:element>

<xsd:complexType name="error">
    <xsd:sequence>
        <xsd:element name="code" type="xsd:string" />
        <xsd:element name="params" type="tns:errorParams" minOccurs="0" maxOccurs="1"/>
        <xsd:element name="description" type="xsd:string" />
    </xsd:sequence>
</xsd:complexType>

<xsd:complexType name="errorParams">
    <xsd:sequence>
      <xsd:element name="param" type="tns:errorParam" minOccurs="1" maxOccurs="unbound"/>
    </xsd:sequence>
</xsd:complexType>

<xsd:complexType name="errorParam">
    <xsd:attribute name="name" type="xsd:string" />
    <xsd:attribute name="value" type="xsd:string" />
</xsd:complexType>
```

Our approach requires to specify the behaviour of the web service so that the test cases can be generated automatically. The specification of the `CreateRoom` operation is:

- if the specified household identifier (`roomId`) is empty, the web service must return a `required` error;
- if the specified household identifier (`roomId`) already exists in the VoDKATV system, the web service must return a `duplicated` error;
- otherwise, the household must be created, and its identifier (`roomId`) and description (`description`) must be returned by the web service.

This specification is written using OCL pre- and postconditions. For instance, the specification for the `CreateRoom` operation can be written in OCL with the following code, where `state_rooms` represents the internal test state:

```
context VoDKATVInterface::CreateRoom(roomId:String, description:String): CreateRoomResponse
post CreateRoom:
  if ((roomId = '') or (roomId = null)) then
    (self.state_rooms = self.state_rooms@pre and
        result.errors->size() = 1 and
        result.errors->at(0).code = 'required')
  else if (self.state_rooms->select(room | room.roomId = roomId)->notEmpty()) then
    (self.state_rooms = self.state_rooms@pre and
        result.errors->size() = 1 and
        result.errors->at(0).code = 'duplicated')
    else self.state_rooms = self.state_rooms@pre->including(
        Tuple {
          roomId:String = roomId,
          description:String = description
        }) and
            result.roomId = roomId and
            result.description = description
    endif
  endif
```

This OCL specification, together with the WSDL, is used by our framework to generate QuickCheck properties. To do that, we use the same approach described in [16], but using WSDL and OCL to generate QuickCheck code. In addition, during test execution, the newly generated QuickCheck model uses the HTTP adapter, which is also generated by our tool from the WSDL. Thus, when an operation is executed, the corresponding web service operation will be invoked, and the result is analysed by the corresponding postcondition. For example, this is part of the code generated to check that a `required` error is returned when the household identifier is empty:

```
postcondition(PreState, AfterState,
            {call, vodkaTV, createRoom, [RoomId, Description]}, Response) ->
  case RoomId of
    "" ->
      ocl_seq:eq(AfterState#state_rooms, PreState#state_rooms)
          andalso ocl_string:eq(ocl_datatypes:get_property(code, Response), "required")
  end;
```

where `ocl_seq`, etc. are ancillary modules that implement utility functions.

Therefore, as a result, we have a QuickCheck test model automatically generated by our tool from the WSDL and the OCL constraints. This test model checks that the web service described by the WSDL satisfies the constraints specified with OCL.

4.1   Analysis of Results

QuickCheck generates specific test cases from the generated test model, i.e., random sequences of commands with random parameter values that satisfy the preconditions. As a second step, QuickCheck executes these commands, invoking the corresponding operations of the web service, and checks if the SUT fulfils the postconditions.

Although we have not found any errors in the web service used as case study (which, considering the system has been in production for a number of years, was to be expected), we have introduced a number of errors to empirically verify the effectiveness of our methodology. We have real error reports of VODKATV as source of inspiration, thus demonstrating that all of them were exposed immediately using the generated QuickCheck model and proposed test architecture. Besides, thanks to QuickCheck shrinking capabilities, the counterexamples found were qualified, when shown to the developers who fixed the error corresponding reports, as very valuable, had it been in place when they had to diagnose them.

5   Conclusions and Future Work

In this paper we have presented a test framework to build test models for web services using a PBT tool, where semantics are added to WSDL using OCL constraints. Using this black-box approach, properties are automatically generated from one WSDL specification, and specific test cases are automatically generated and executed. Our framework can generate properties for both stateless and stateful web services, using declarative statements in the first case and state machines models in the second. In all cases, the test model produced by the framework can be used as an updated specification of the SUT with the shape of an executable model.

One of the main advantages of our approach is the use a PBT tool like QuickCheck to generate and run the test cases, because it automatically generates complex testing sequences which stress-test the real system in a more objective and efficient way than any human tester could [14, 18, 20]. We remove the need to think of specific test cases, rather the general behavioural properties. Another important aspect of QuickCheck is its shrinking and counterexample capabilities, a very valuable asset to fault debugging.

We have used a standard specification language, OCL, so testers need not learn a specification language to write test cases, because properties are automatically generated from the OCL specification. Another advantage of using PBT instead of hand-written tests is that properties are independent of the implementation details of the SUT. This means that an evolving code base does not force rewriting the test model, maintaining an intact, updated and executable specification of the SUT.

As future work, we should be able to trace back the conditions that have failed when QuickCheck generates a counterexample, showing the specific piece of OCL code that has produced the error. Furthermore, nowadays a particular kind of web services is most popular: RESTful web services; we plan to extend our framework to adapt specifically to the intrinsic properties of these web services.

References

1. BNFC, http://bnfc.digitalgrammars.com/
2. Object Constraint Language (OCL), http://www.omg.org/spec/OCL/2.3.1/

3. OCLNL, http://www.key-project.org/oclnl/
4. Semantic Web Rule Language (SWRL), http://www.w3.org/Submission/SWRL/
5. Web Services Description Language (WSDL), http://www.w3.org/TR/wsdl/
6. Web Services Semantics (WSDL-S), http://www.w3.org/Submission/WSDL-S/
7. Arts, T., Hughes, J., Johansson, J., Wiger, U.: Testing telecoms software with Quviq QuickCheck. In: ACM SIGPLAN Workshop on Erlang., pp. 2–10 (2006)
8. Askarunisa, A., Abirami, A., Mohan, S.: A test case reduction method for semantic based web services. In: International Conference on Computing, Communication and Networking Technologies, pp. 1–7 (2010)
9. Bai, X., Lee, S., Tsai, W., Chen, Y.: Ontology-based test modeling and partition testing of web services. In: IEEE International Conference on Web Services, pp. 465–472 (2008)
10. Bartolini, C., Bertolino, A., Marchetti, E., Polini, A.: WS-TAXI: A WSDL-based testing tool for web services. In: International Conference on Software Testing, Verification, and Validation, pp. 326–335 (2009)
11. Bertolino, A., Inverardi, P., Pelliccione, P., Tivoli, M.: Automatic synthesis of behavior protocols for composable web-services. In: ACM SIGSOFT Symposium on the Foundations of Software Engineering, pp. 141–150 (2009)
12. Derrick, J., Walkinshaw, N., Arts, T., Benac Earle, C., Cesarini, F., Fredlund, L.-A., Gulias, V., Hughes, J., Thompson, S.: Property-based testing - the ProTest project. In: de Boer, F.S., Bonsangue, M.M., Hallerstede, S., Leuschel, M. (eds.) FMCO 2009. LNCS, vol. 6286, pp. 250–271. Springer, Heidelberg (2010)
13. Emmerich, W.: Managing web service quality. In: International Workshop on Software Engineering and Middleware, pp. 1–1 (2006)
14. Fink, G., Bishop, M.: Property-based testing: a new approach to testing for assurance. SIGSOFT Software Engineering Notes 22(4), 74–80 (1997)
15. Forsberg, M., Ranta, A.: Labelled BNF: a highlevel formalism for defining well-behaved programming languages. Estonian Academy of Sciences: Physics and Mathematics 52, 356–377 (2003)
16. Francisco, M.A., Castro, L.M.: Automatic generation of test models and properties from UML models with OCL constraints. In: International Workshop on OCL and Textual Modelling, pp. 49–54 (2012)
17. Lampropoulos, L., Sagonas, K.F.: Automatic WSDL-guided test case generation for proper testing of web services. In: International Workshop on Automated Specification and Verification of Web Systems, vol. 98, pp. 3–16 (2012)
18. Mouchawrab, S., Briand, L.C., Labiche, Y., Di Penta, M.: Assessing, comparing, and combining state machine-based testing and structural testing: A series of experiments. IEEE Transactions Software Engineering 37(2), 161–187 (2011)
19. Noikajana, S., Suwannasart, T.: An improved test case generation method for web service testing from WSDL-S and OCL with pair-wise testing technique. In: International Computer Software and Applications Conference, pp. 115–123 (2009)
20. Farrell-Vinay, P.: Managing Software Testing. Auerbach Publishers (2008)
21. Petrenko, A.: Why automata models are sexy for testers (Invited talk). In: Virbitskaite, I., Voronkov, A. (eds.) PSI 2006. LNCS, vol. 4378, pp. 26–26. Springer, Heidelberg (2007)
22. Timm, J., Gannod, G.: Specifying semantic web service compositions using UML and OCL. In: IEEE International Conference on Web Services, pp. 521–528 (2007)
23. Zeller, A., Hildebrandt, R.: Simplifying and isolating failure-inducing input. IEEE Trans. Softw. Eng. 28(2), 183–200 (2002)
24. Zheng, Y., Zhou, J., Krause, P.: An automatic test case generation framework for web services. Journal of Software 2(3), 64–77 (2007)

An Incentive Mechanism
for Game-Based QoS-Aware Service Selection

Puwei Wang* and Xiaoyong Du

Key Laboratory of Data Engineering and Knowledge Engineering of Ministry
of Education, Renmin University of China
School of Information, Renmin University of China
Beijing, China, 100872
wangpuwei@ruc.edu.cn

Abstract. QoS-aware service selection deals with choosing the service
providers from the candidates which are discovered to fulfill a requirement, while meeting specific QoS constraints. In fact, the requester and
its candidate service providers usually are autonomous and self-interested.
In the case, there is a private information game of the service selection
between a requester and its candidate providers. An ideal solution of the
game is that the requester selects and reaches agreement about the interest allocation with the high-QoS and low-cost service providers. This
paper proposes an approach to design a novel incentive mechanism to
get the ideal solution of the game. The incentive mechanism design is
solved as a constrained optimization problem. Finally, the experiments
are performed to show the effectiveness of the incentive mechanism.

Keywords: QoS-aware Service Selection, Game Theory, Incentive
Mechanism, Contract.

1 Introduction

Service-Oriented Computing (SOC) is a computing paradigm that utilizes
self-contained and platform-independent services as computational elements for
developing software applications distributed within and across organizational
boundaries. Currently, QoS-aware service selection is an important problem. Existing approaches of QoS-aware service selection usually focuses on the development of various QoS metrics. The work [1] proposes the QoS ontology for
annotating service with QoS data, and finds optimal services by matching QoS
constraints against candidate services' QoS data. In their views, the requester that
offers an application requirement is considered a controller that could choose the
service providers using QoS constraints and command the selected providers to realize the requirement. In fact, the requester and the service provider usually are
autonomous, rational and self-interested in nature. In the case, the requester publishes an application requirement and the service provider actively discovers the
requester's requirement. The requester gets a benefit while its requirement is realized under the QoS constraints by the service providers. To motivate the service
providers to realize the requirement, a part of the benefit should be regarded as a

---

* Corresponding author.

S. Basu et al. (Eds.): ICSOC 2013, LNCS 8274, pp. 491–498, 2013.
© Springer-Verlag Berlin Heidelberg 2013

transfer payment to the service providers. Generally, the requester prefers to pay little transfer payment to its service providers, while each service provider prefers to get high transfer payment. Thus, in the scenario, the requester and its candidate provider have a common interest for realizing the requirement, but they have a conflicting interest over the transfer payment.

By relying on the game theory [2], this scenario could be modeled as a game. For a candidate service provider, its profit is the difference between the transfer payment and its service cost. In the game, its strategy explicitly is for maximizing its profit. For a requester, its profit is the difference between the benefit from its satisfied requirement and the transfer payment to its service providers. Considering the service providers which could gain same profit, the requester could pay less transfer payment to the service providers which have lower cost. Moreover, the higher QoS constraints, such as short response time and high availability, could bring the more benefit to the requester. The strategy of the requester thus is to find such service providers that could have high QoS and relatively low service cost (called the efficient service providers in this paper). Obviously, the QoS and service cost are the critical information in the game. Because that the QoS of a service provider is verifiable at run time, we suppose that the service provider will report its actual QoS to the requester. So, the QoS is the open information for the requester and its providers. However, the service cost of a service provider is not verifiable by the requester at any time, and the service provider definitely is not willing to expose its actual cost. Hence, there is a private information game between a requester and its candidate providers.

This paper proposes an approach to design an incentive mechanism to get an ideal solution of the private information game. We propose that the ideal solution is: 1) the requester and the efficient providers among the candidate providers could reach agreement about the QoS constraints and transfer payments; 2) in the service providers which reach agreement with the requester, the efficient provider gets more profit than that the relatively inefficient provider gets and 3) the more efficient the candidate providers are, the more profit the requester could get. The solution ensures that the efficient providers are willing to participate in the game and inefficient ones are motivated to improve their efficiency. The requester also is willing to offer their requirements in the game.

2   The Game of Service Selection

In the set up game, there involves two kinds of players: i) a requester and ii) the candidate service provider. The requester publishes a functional requirement, and the candidate service providers, which meet the functional requirement, have different QoS and different service costs. The basic model of the requester and the service provider are given as follows.

2.1   Requester and Service Provider

The functional requirement F_r is described as a finite set of desired state transitions $F_r = \{t_i | i \in [1, n]\}$. For different desired state transition, the requester could have different QoS constraints, such as response time and availability, etc. The work [3] proposes using a single QoS value to be a measurement of the QoS constraints. Based on the work, we could use a single QoS value to represent the QoS constraints of a desired state transition. The benefit that the requester r could get from a desired state transition t is described as $O_t(q)$, in which $q \in (0, +\infty)$ is the QoS of executing the desired state transition t.

The functional description of a service provider $s \in S$ also is given as a finite set of state transitions F_s. We suppose that the provider discovers the requester's functional requirement F_r while it could meet the requirement $(F_s = F_r)$, and its QoS is configurable, such as the work [6], i.e., the provider is able to adjust its QoS to meet the requester's QoS constraint. According to economics, besides the QoS, the cost also depends on another factor, marginal cost. The marginal cost, an economic concept, depicts the change in cost that arises while the quality improves by one unit [4]. In other words, the smaller the marginal cost is, the service cost increases less, while the QoS improves by one unit. It could be concluded that the efficient providers, i.e., those have high QoS and low cost, have small marginal cost. Thus, it is the marginal cost of service provider that the requester wants to know in the game. In the paper, the marginal cost is called the type of service provider. Without loss of generality, we suppose that the fixed cost of a service provider is zero. The cost function of a provider for executing a state transition has two parameters: QoS and type of the provider. Formally, for a state transition $t \in F_s$, the cost function of the provider s is described as $C_t(q, \theta)$, in which q is the QoS of executing the state transition t and θ is the type of the provider s.

Generally, although the requester does not know the exact service costs of its candidate providers, the requester still could find out that the type of service provider follows a kind of probability distribution. Formally, the type of service provider follows a continuous probability distribution Γ over the interval $(0, +\infty)$, with a probability function $f(\theta) > 0$. For an interval $[\theta_{i-1}, \theta_i] \subset (0, +\infty)$, a cumulative probability function is $P[\theta_{i-1}, \theta_i] = \int_{\theta_{i-1}}^{\theta_i} f(\theta)d\theta$.

2.2   Procedure of the Private Information Game

In the procedure of the QoS-aware service selection, as shown in Fig.1, there is a set of candidate providers whose types follows a continuous probability distribution Γ over the interval $(0, +\infty)$. There is a requester whose functional requirement is described as a set of desired state transitions F_r. The requester could know the benefit and cost functions of the desired state transitions in F_r, but is not aware of the exact types of the candidate providers. Based on the distribution Γ and the benefit and cost functions of F_r, the requester makes and offers a set of contracts for its desired state transitions F_r (step 1). The contracts are made to create the mutuality of obligation concerning the QoS constraints and the promised transfer payments about the desired state transitions. The candidate providers accept or reject the contracts by using a proposed contracting process (step 2). If all contracts are accepted by some of the candidate providers,

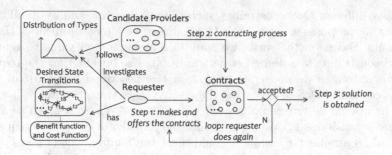

Fig. 1. Procedure of the Private Information Game

a solution of the service selection is obtained (*step 3*). A solution of the game of service selection thus is a situation where each contract offered by the requester is accepted by at least a candidate provider. If the contracts are not accepted, there exists a loop where the requester revises and offers the contracts again. The loop continues until that the revised contracts are accepted by some of the candidate providers.

3   Incentive Mechanism

In the incentive mechanism, we propose a two-phase contracting process between requester and provider. A requester r has a functional requirement F_r. Given m candidate providers $S = \{s_1, ..., s_m\}$, the requester r does not know the candidate provider's type, but it knows that the provider's type follows a probability distribution Γ.

3.1   Two-Phase Contracting

First Phase. The requester firstly makes a set of contracts for its desired sate transitions according to the benefit and cost functions of the desired state transitions and the probability distribution of the provider's type. Concretely, the requester decides a set of partition points $\Theta = \{\theta_0, \theta_1, ..., \theta_n\}$, and gets the intervals of provider's type $\{(\theta_0, \theta_1], ..., (\theta_{n-1}, \theta_n]\}$. The requester makes a set of contracts $\{\langle t(\theta_1), q(\theta_1), \delta(\theta_1)\rangle, ..., \langle t(\theta_n), q(\theta_n), \delta(\theta_n)\rangle\}$ based on the intervals. In a contract $\langle t(\theta_i), q(\theta_i), \delta(\theta_i)\rangle$, $\delta(\theta_i)$ denotes a transfer payment to the service provider whose type is in $(\theta_{i-1}, \theta_i]$ (the provider is also called the $(\theta_{i-1}, \theta_i]$ provider in this paper) which executes the desired state transition $t(\theta_i) \in F_r$ at the QoS $q(\theta_i) \in (0, +\infty)$.

The requester does not know its candidate provider's type, but it could figure out the probability that the provider's type is in a given interval based on the probability distribution. Let $P(\cdot, \cdot)$ be the cumulative probability function of the distribution. For a contract $\langle t(\theta_i), q(\theta_i), \delta(\theta_i)\rangle$, the profit that the requester could get from the contract is $V(\theta_i) = O_{t(\theta_i)}(q(\theta_i)) - \delta(\theta_i)$. The probability that there exists at least a provider whose type is in the interval $(\theta_{i-1}, \theta_i]$ among the

m providers is denoted as $\rho(\theta_i)$. The expected profit in the phase is described as $E_{\text{first}}(V(\theta_i)) = \rho(\theta_i) \cdot V(\theta_i)$. In the phase, a service provider is permitted to choose and accept a contract. If a provider accepts a $(\theta_{i-1}, \theta_i]$ contract, the requester then knows that the provider's type is in $(\theta_{i-1}, \theta_i]$. In this way, the requester could know the scope of the most efficient candidate provider's type.

Second Phase. While there are the contracts which are not accepted in the first phase, there is a second phase. Since the requester knows the scope of the most efficient provider's type, the requester could revise the remanent unaccepted contracts to the most efficient provider. Concretely, while the $(\theta_{k-1}, \theta_k]$ provider does not exist among the candidates and the $(\theta_{i-1}, \theta_i]$ provider is the most efficient provider among the candidates in the first phase (the probability of the situation is described as $\rho(\theta_k, \theta_i)$), the requester revises the contract $\langle t(\theta_k), q(\theta_k), \delta(\theta_k) \rangle$ to be $\langle t(\theta_k), q_{\theta_k}(\theta_i), \delta_{\theta_k}(\theta_i) \rangle$ in the second phase. The revised contract $\langle t(\theta_k), q_{\theta_k}(\theta_i), \delta_{\theta_k}(\theta_i) \rangle$ promises that if the $(\theta_{i-1}, \theta_i]$ provider realizes the desired state transition $t(\theta_k)$ at the QoS $q_{\theta_k}(\theta_i)$, the provider will get the transfer payment $\delta_{\theta_k}(\theta_i)$. The requester could get the profit from the revised contract as $V_{\theta_k}(\theta_i) = O_{t(\theta_k)}(q_{\theta_k}(\theta_i)) - \delta_{\theta_k}(\theta_i)$. The expected profit in the phase then is described as $E_{\text{second}}(V_{\theta_k}(\theta_i)) = \rho(\theta_k, \theta_i) \cdot V_{\theta_k}(\theta_i)$.

Expected Profit Function of Requester. By adding the expected profits in the two phases, the expected profit of the requester r is described as $F_{\Phi, \Gamma}$.

3.2   Constraints in the Mechanism

Participation Constraint. A service provider will quit the game, if it will get a negative profit from the contract. Thus, a contract is acceptable at least provider could get a non-negative profit. Formally, given a contract $\langle t(\theta_i), q(\theta_i), \delta(\theta_i) \rangle \in \Phi$, the participation constraint that ensures the $(\theta_{i-1}, \theta_i]$ provider participates in the game is described as follows: $U(\theta_i) = \delta(\theta_i) - C_{t(\theta_i)}(q(\theta_i), \theta_i) \geqslant 0$. A requester will quit the game, if it will get a negative expected profit. The participation constraint that ensures the requester to participate in the game is described as follows: $F_{\Phi, \Gamma} \geqslant 0$.

Incentive Compatibility Constraint. The requester makes a contract based on an interval of provider's type. While the requester does not know the provider's type, the incentive compatibility constraint is to ensure that the provider whose type is in the interval is willing to accept the contract and the other providers whose types are out of the interval are unwilling to do so.

Constrained Optimization Problem. A set of contracts is feasible if it satisfies both participation and incentive compatibility constraints. The problem to make a feasible set of contracts that bring the requester a maximum profit becomes a constrained optimization problem. The constrained optimization problem to maximize the expected profit $F_{\Phi, \Gamma}$ under the constraint (7) is given.

$$\max_{\{\langle t(\theta_i), q(\theta_i), \delta(\theta_i) \rangle | i \in [1, n]\}} F_{\Phi, \Gamma} \tag{1}$$

subject to the set of contracts is feasible

The solution of the optimization problem is an optimal feasible set of contracts Φ. The requester offers the optimal feasible set of contracts to its candidate providers. If the contracts are accepted, a solution of the game is obtained.

4   Experimental Results

A prototype system of the QoS-aware service selection using the incentive mechanism is implemented in Java. Matlab is a numerical computing environment and the interior point algorithm [5] that is proposed for solving the constrained nonlinear optimization problem has been realized in the Matlab environment. The interior point algorithm in the Matlab is directly used for solving the optimization problem (5) to make an optimal feasible set of contracts.

A repository of 100,000 state transitions and their benefit and cost functions are generated randomly and the cost functions are sensitive to the provider's type. In real world, the most efficient and inefficient service providers usually are very few and there are many average service provider. Thus, we use the gamma distribution to imitate the probability distribution of the provider's type. As the experimental data, the requester's requirement is generated randomly as a set of desired state transitions from the repository. Each requester has 30 candidate providers whose types are generated randomly from the gamma distribution.

The gamma distribution has a shape parameter. The smaller the parameter is, the more efficient providers there exist in the candidates. The number of desired state transitions of a requester is set to be 10. Fig.2(a) plots the average expected profit of 100 requesters, while the shape parameter of the gamma distribution is set to be from 6.5 to 5.5. The result shows that the more efficient the candidate providers are, the more profit the requester could get.

We also compare our approach with a service selection without using the incentive mechanism. In this kind of service selection, the requester and its candidate providers still follow our proposed two-phase contracting process. But the expected profit function of a requester is figured out without consideration of the incentive compatibility constraint. The contracts also are made by solving the problem to maximize the expected profit. In the experiments, the shape parameter of the gamma distribution is set to be 6 and the number of desired state transitions in an requester is set to be from 1 to 25. Fig.2(b) plots the average expected profit of 100 requesters. The result shows that it is clearly better while the mechanism is employed and the expected profit increases while the number of desired transitions increases. In the game of service selection, Fig.2(c) plots the average actual profit of the 100 requesters. The result shows that the actual profit are mainly in accord with the expected profit. The selected providers of the 100 requesters also get their profits in the game. Fig.2(d) plots the average actual total profit of the selected providers. The result shows that the actual total profit of the selected providers also is better while the mechanism is employed.

The reason is that the incentive mechanism motivates the efficient providers to contract with the requester. The desired state transitions of the requester could be fulfilled at the high QoS by the efficient providers which have relatively

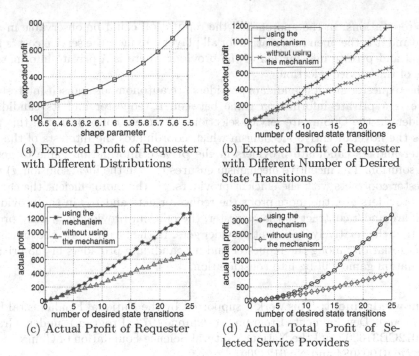

(a) Expected Profit of Requester with Different Distributions

(b) Expected Profit of Requester with Different Number of Desired State Transitions

(c) Actual Profit of Requester

(d) Actual Total Profit of Selected Service Providers

Fig. 2. Expected and Actual Profit of Requester and Selected Service Providers

low cost. As a result, the requester and its selected service providers both are benefited from our proposed incentive mechanism.

5 Related Work and Conclusion

The QoS in Web services is an important research issue. Various QoS models are proposed for capturing non-functional features of Web services [3]. The service selection then relys on that the services are differentiated based on the well-defined QoS attributes. Zeng [6] proposes a planning algorithm for the Web service selection with QoS constraints. But, with more and more services are deployed, the requirement begin to have the computational burden to get a solution satisfying the QoS constraints. Serhani [7] proposes the third-party broker for service registry which helps the requester conveniently knowing the services. The broker balances the burden of the requester.In the approaches, the requester takes the responsibility to choose services based on QoS constraints and command the selected services to realize its requirement. Considering the service provider's autonomy, agent-based approach is proposed. Tang [8] proposes that service providers, acting as agents, collaborate with requesters on their own initiative. The work does not focus on the incentives for requester and service provider. Recently, some incentive mechanisms are designed relying on monetary rewards. Jurca et al. [9] design the incentives for the participants according to their reputations. In the approaches, the reputation could be observable in advance and it is the open information for all players. In fact, the service cost is the critical and private information of the provider, there is a private information game of the service selection.

The requester and its candidate providers are autonomous and self-interested. There is a private information game between a requester and its candidate providers in the QoS-aware service selection. The main contribution of this paper is the novel incentive mechanism which coordinates the interests of the requester and its candidate providers in the private information game to get a ideal solution. The incentive mechanism ensures that in the ideal solution, i) the requester contracts with the efficient providers, ii) the more efficient the candidate providers are, the more profit the requester gets and iii) in the providers which are under contract to the requester, the efficient provider gets more profit than that the relatively inefficient provider gets. In the future work, the multilateral negotiation among the requester and its candidate providers in the private information game will be into consideration.

Acknowledgement. This work is supported by the National Fundamental Research and Development Program of China (973 Program) under Grant No.2012CB316205 and the National Natural Science Foundation of China under grant No.61003084 and No.61232007.

References

1. Wang, X., Vitvar, T., Kerrigan, M., Toma, I.: A QoS-Aware Selection Model for Semantic Web Services. In: Dan, A., Lamersdorf, W. (eds.) ICSOC 2006. LNCS, vol. 4294, pp. 390–401. Springer, Heidelberg (2006)
2. Conitzer, V.: Computing game-theoretic solutions and applications to security. In: The Conference on Artificial Intelligence (AAAI 2012), pp. 2106–2112 (2012)
3. Liu, Y., Ngu, A.H., Zeng, L.Z.: QoS Computation and Policing in Dynamic Web Service Selection. In: International World Wide Web Conference (WWW 2004), pp. 66–73 (2004)
4. Laffont, J.J., Martimort, D.: The Theory of Incentives: The Principal-Agent Model. Princeton University Press (2001)
5. Nesterov, Y., Nemirovskii, A.: Interior-Point Polynomial Algorithms in Convex Programming. Society for Industrial and Applied Mathematics (1995)
6. Zeng, L., Benatallah, B., Ngu, A.H.H., et al.: QoS-aware middleware for Web services composition. IEEE Transactions on Software Engineering 30(5), 311–327 (2004)
7. Serhani, M.A., Dssouli, R., Hafid, A., et al.: A QoS broker based architecture for efficient web services selection. In: ICWS 2005, pp. 113–120 (2005)
8. Tang, J., Jin, Z.: Assignment Problem in Requirement Driven Agent Collaboration and its Implementation. In: AAMAS 2010, pp. 839–846 (2010)
9. Zhang, Y., van der Schaar, M.: Reputation-based incentive protocols in crowdsourcing applications. In: INFOCOM 2012, pp. 2140–2148 (2012)

Goal Oriented Variability Modeling
in Service-Based Business Processes

Karthikeyan Ponnalagu[1,3], Nanjangud C. Narendra[2], Aditya Ghose[3],
Neeraj Chiktey[1,4], and Srikanth Tamilselvam[1]

[1] IBM Research India, Bangalore, India
{pkarthik,srikanth.tamilselvam}@in.ibm.com
[2] IBM India Software Lab, Bangalore, India
narendra@in.ibm.com
[3] University of Wollongong, Australia
aditya.ghose@gmail.com
[4] International Institute of Information Technology, Hyderabad, India
chikteyneeraj@yahoo.co.in

Abstract. In any organization, business processes are designed to adhere to specified business goals. On many occasions, however, in order to accommodate differing usage contexts, multiple variants of the same business process may need to be designed, all of which should adhere to the same goal. For business processes modeled as compositions of services, automated generation of such *goal preserving* process variants is a challenge. To that end, we present our approach for generating all goal preserving variants of a service-based business process. Our approach leverages our earlier works on semantic annotations of business processes and service variability modeling. Throughout our paper, we illustrate our ideas with a realistic running example, and also present a proof-of-concept prototype.

Keywords: Business Process, SOA, service variability modeling, goal semantics.

1 Introduction

In general, a business process is derived based on a specified business goal. However, there are many occasions , where multiple variants of the business process need to be derived to address different usage contexts. At the same time, however, each such variant needs to adhere to the same business goal [7]. We call such variants *goal-preserving* variants of a business process. In existing business process design approaches [11], business processes are usually designed and stored separately from the goals from which they were derived. As a result, derivation of multiple goal-preserving variants becomes a costly and time-consuming exercise. To that end, in this paper, we present a novel approach by which variability modeling and subsequent derivation of goal preserving variants is completely driven

S. Basu et al. (Eds.): ICSOC 2013, LNCS 8274, pp. 499–506, 2013.

by goal decomposition models. In this paper, we assume the following inputs:
(a) a goal model (e.g., as depicted in Fig. 2) with goals and associated decomposition of sub goals (AND, OR) represented as a collection of boolean conditions
in conjunctive normal form (CNF) [6]; (b) a capability library containing a set
of services with semantically annotated *effects* [11]; and (c) a semantically annotated process design created with the composition of such services, said process
design adhering to the goal model. Our proposed approach works as follows.
First, an initial business process is generated from the goals as per our earlier
work [8]. Second, based on the effect annotations, we derive the goal-based *variability analysis model (VAM)* for the services participating in a business process.
This model extends our earlier work on service variation modeling [14], to determine all possible variants of the services that adhere to their mapped goals.
Third, using the VAM, we generate the required goal-preserving variants for the
original process.

This paper is organized as follows. We present related work in Section 2. Section 3 discusses our running example, which is drawn from the insurance domain.
In Section 4 we provide some basic definitions and also show how goals can be
established as a foundation for variability analysis. We present and discuss our
prototype implementation in Section 5, and conclude the paper with suggestions
for future work in Section 6.

2   Related Work

In Product Line Engineering (PLE) based approaches [2,4], variability of products is systematized in terms of variability identification, modeling, conflict resolution and finally instantiation. But in SOA, a custom developed SOA based
application could comprise services and processes developed by different organizations [5]. These services and processes need to be modified for supporting
different user contexts, using valid variations that satisfy the corresponding organization goals. Approaches for process variability support such as Provop [9], focus on managing large collections of process variants of a single process model.On
similar lines, the citation [13] describes an approach to quantitatively calculate
similarity between any two variants of a business process, so that activities such
as process reuse, analysis and discovery can be facilitated. This is done via the
modeling of process constraints on tasks, such as which tasks should (or should
not) execute together. Such methods undoubtedly possess effective variability
management techniques, but without alignment between the goal model and
business process model. In works such as [10], the process goals are proposed as
a collection of tasks with specific input and output parameters, and are matched
against existing tasks in a capability library; the matching is accomplished via AI
planning techniques. In declarative workflow based approaches [16], constraint
satisfaction is employed to address the different types of process flexibility such
as differing a modeling decision to a later phase of the process life cycle, accommodating changes to the process design or deviating the process execution from

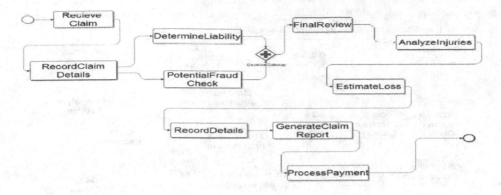

Fig. 1. Insurance Claims Process - Solution `Pr1`

modeling time decisions. It requires the constraints to be specified in a declarative language such as DecSerFlow [17], leading to challenges such as management of large collection of process variants in the repository [1]. Our proposed work, on the other hand, provides a more realistic and practical approach wherein we provide the necessary facility for the business analyst to specify process and service goals at a level of abstraction comfortable for him/her. We then provide an approach to decompose the goals into sub-goals until there is an ontological match between them and the semantically annotated effects of services in the capability library. Subsequently the goal-linked process and services are subjected to variability analysis for checking and generating valid variations that continue to preserve the goals but satisfy changing user requirements.

3   Running Example

Our running example depicts a goal decomposition model for an organization dealing with different types of insurance claims as illustrated in Fig. 2. The Goal `Process Accident Claims` is primarily decomposed into four mandatory sub-goals `Receive Claim`, `Verify Claim`, `Record Claim` and `Analyze Injuries`. Each of these sub goals, contains both mandatory and optional leaf level sub-goals that the organization expects to be addressed by different insurance claim business processes. Let us consider an accident claim process `Pr1` as illustrated in Fig. 1. The inputs to this process are the details of the customer requesting the claim, and the details of the claim. The outputs of this process are the acceptance/rejection of the claim, along with the claim amount to be paid to the customer (which will be zero in case of rejection). `Pr1` consists of four major sub-processes - (i) `Record Claim` (RC), (ii) `Verify Claim` (VC), (iii) `Analyze Injuries` (AC) and (iv) `Report` (RP). In `Verify Claim` sub-process, the *DetermineLiability (DL)* and *PotentialFraudCheck (PF)* services are first executed in parallel, and then their results are combined and sent to *ClaimInvestigation (CI)* service. A final review of the verified claim is then implemented by *FinalReview (FR)* service. A variant of `Pr1`, adhering to the goal model in Fig. 2

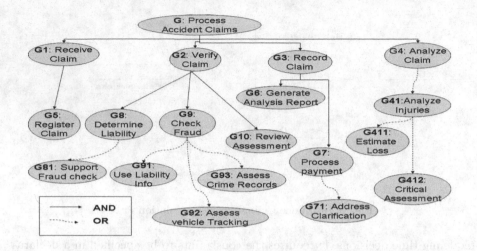

Fig. 2. Insurance Claims Process - Goal Model

by satisfying all the mandatory sub-goals (along with a different combination of optional sub-goals) as Pr1, could be Pr2.The process Pr2 contains the following differences from Pr1: DL and PF services are serialized (satisfying the optional sub-goal G81); PF service is modified (satisfying the optional sub-goal G91) to also consider the extent of liability from the service DL along with the customer and claim details to determine the possibility of occurrence of fraud. In the rest of this paper, we discuss how our variability analysis model can help generate the goal-preserving variants of Pr1, such as Pr2.

4   A Goal-Oriented Approach to Variability Analysis

In this section, we argue for the centrality of goals in variability analysis.

In our earlier paper [8], we proposed a goal refinement procedure based on the KAOS methodology [3]. With this procedure, we asserted that the set of sub-goals for a goal will achieve the goal (entailment); it will be the smallest set of sub-goals to achieve the goal (minimality); and it will never be incorrect (consistency). In our proposed approach in this paper, we leverage such a refined goal model as illustrated in Fig. 2 to identify the set of minimally required sub-goals to entail the overall process goal.

Let us consider the process Pr1 from our running example. The goal model for G depicted in Fig. 2 can be expressed in CNF form as $G = G5 \wedge G8 \wedge G9 \wedge G10 \wedge G6 \wedge G7 \wedge G4$. Let us assume the mapping of the services in Pr1 with the goal model as follows: $Pr1 \vdash G, RC \vdash G5, VC \vdash G2, RP \vdash G3, AI \vdash G4, DL \vdash G8, PF \vdash G9, FR \vdash G10, CI \vdash G411$. Now as an illustration, leveraging these variability mappings, the following variability analysis for the services DL and PF can be established: The service DL can have both interface and implementation level variations that could preserve either the Goals $G8$ or $G81$. Similarly the service PF can have both interface and implementation level variations preserving either of goals $G9$, $G91$, $G92$ and $G93$. For example to support the variant Pr2 of Pr1, we can leverage the variations satisfying $G81$ and $G91$ respectively by the services DL and PF. This enables generation of goal-preserving variants.

We therefore establish that a service or process variant is goal preserving only if it eventually adheres to the same goal that the base service adheres to. We discuss the different scenarios in which this goal adherence can be verified. We assume that the existing variant(s) of the service are also available in the capability library and are semantically annotated with end effect scenarios.

Let us consider a service s_j to be a variant of s_i. Let e_i and e_j be the corresponding effect annotations of s_i and s_j respectively. Let $e_i = \{c_1, c_2, ..., c_m\}$ and $e_j = \{c_{j1}, c_{j2}, ..., c_{jn}\}$. Let $G_i == \{c_a, c_b, ..., c_k\}$ be a sub goal of G. Let the service s_i entail G_i. Then the following condition needs to be met: $\{c_a, c_b, ..., c_k\} \in e_i$. This can be illustrated using our running example as follows: consider the Goal $G8$, which contains the following literal: DetermineLiability = 'yes'. Now to establish that the service DL satisfies the goal $G8$, we expect the above literals to be part of the end effects of DL such that DL = DetermineLiability = 'yes', match-past record = 'yes' . Now to establish that s_j is a goal-preserving variant of s_i, one of the three following scenarios have to be met:

1. The service s_i satisfies the AND sub-goal G_i and G_i does not contain a disjunctive clause. In this case, the service s_j can be established as a goal preserving variant of s_i, only if the following condition is satisfied: $\{c_a, c_b, ..., c_k\} \in e_j$. This also implies $G_i \in \{e_i \cap e_j\}$. To illustrate, let us assume a variant DL' of service DL, which has the end effects as follows: DL' = DetermineLiability = 'yes',examine-vehicle= 'yes'. We can establish that DL' also entails the goal $G8$ and hence DL' is a goal preserving variant of DL.
   Now for the remaining two scenarios, let us assume an AND sub-goal G_i, such that G_i can be expressed as $\{G_{i1} \vee G_{i2}\}$. Let $G_i = \{c_a, c_b, ..., c_k\}$, $G_{i1} = \{c_a, c_b, ..., c_k, c_{k+1}...c_m\}$ and $G_{i2} = \{c_i, c_j, ..., c_k, c_{k+1}...c_n\}$.

2. Let the service s_i satisfy the AND sub-goal G_i, which contains a disjunctive clause. Then the service s_j can be established as a goal preserving variant of s_i, only if at least one of the following conditions is satisfied: $\{c_i, c_j, ..., c_k\} \in e_j$, $\{c_i, c_j, ..., c_k, c_{k+1}...c_m\} \in e_j$, $\{c_i, c_j, ..., c_k, c_{k+1}...c_m\} \in e_j$. This also implies $G_i \in \{e_i \cap e_j\}$ like the previous condition. This can be again illustrated from the running example using the service PF and the goal $G9$. We observe that $G9$ can be expressed as $\{G91 \vee G92 \vee G93\}$. Let the service $PF =$ Determine Fraud = 'yes', Spot Investigation = 'yes' entail the goal $G9$ = Determine Fraud = 'yes'. Let a service PF' = Determine Fraud = 'yes', Utilize Liability = 'yes', Inspect Vehicle = 'yes' be a variant of service PF, that uses the liability information to check for fraud in process Pr2. We see that PF' entails the goal $G91$ = Determine Fraud = 'yes', Utilize Liability = 'yes', as it satisfies the above condition.

3. Let a service s_i satisfy the OR sub-goal G_{i1}. Then the service s_j can be established as a goal preserving variant of s_i, only if at least one of the

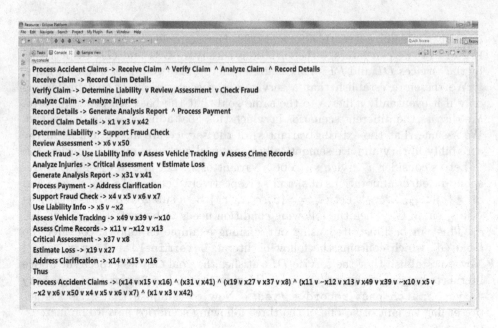

Fig. 3. The Generation of Process `Pr1` in CNF

following conditions is satisfied: $\{c_a, c_b, ..., c_k\} \in e_j$, $\{c_a, c_b, ..., c_k, c_{k+1}...c_m\} \in e_j$, $\{c_a, c_b, ..., c_k, c_{k+1}...c_n\} \in e_j$. This implies $\{G_{i1} \vee G_i\} \in \{e_i \cap e_j\}$. This can be illustrated similarly using the services PF' and PF. Now given that PF' preserves the OR sub-goal $G91$, we can establish that PF is a goal preserving variant of PF', as it satisfies $G9$.

5   Implementation and Experimentation

For running the experiment to demonstrate goal driven variability analysis, we have developed an Eclipse plugin[1] that helps represent the goal model as a goal-graph. The goal model of the business process depicted in Fig. 2 can be refined as $G = \{G5, G8, G9, G10, G6, G7, G4\}$ using our goal refinement procedure. The CNF form that we have generated from this goal model using our tool is expressed as $G \rightarrow G4 \wedge G5 \wedge G6 \wedge G7 \wedge G8 \wedge G9 \wedge G10$. Let $X = \{xi \mid i = 1, 2...50\}$ be a list of Boolean literals. Each of these sub goals of G are defined as $G4 \rightarrow x1 \vee x3 \vee x42$, $G5 \rightarrow x4 \vee x5 \vee x6 \vee x7$, $G6 \rightarrow x5 \vee \neg x2 \vee \neg x6$, $G7 \rightarrow \neg x10 \vee x49 \vee x39$, $G8 \rightarrow x11 \vee \neg x12 \vee x13$, $G9 \rightarrow x14 \vee x15 \vee x16$ and $G10 \rightarrow \neg X28$. Similarly we represent the process `Pr1` with semantic end effect annotations. We can also observe from the CNF expressions of G and `Pr1`, that `Pr1` satisfies G as illustrated in Fig. 3. In addition to illustrating the implementation with our running example, we also ran an additional experiment with increasing scale of complexity as follows: let us express a process P as

---

[1] Demo video accessible from `http://variabilitymodelling.wordpress.com`

$P \to T1 \wedge T2 \wedge T3 \wedge T4 \wedge T5 \wedge T6$. The tasks are defined as : $T1 \to x1 \wedge x10 \wedge \neg x50$, $T2 \to x20 \wedge \neg x12 \wedge x39$, $T3 \to x14 \wedge \neg x50 \wedge x34$, $T4 \to x7 \wedge \neg x19 \wedge x45$, $T5 \to \neg x2 \wedge x34 \wedge x15$, $T6 \to \neg x28$. We ran the CNF form of G using the WinSat tool [15]. We observed that there were 36 different solutions that could satisfy G. Now for each service $T1$ through $T6$, we derived the following mappings to the sub-goals of G: $T1 \vdash G4$, $T2 \vdash G7$, $T3 \vdash G9$, $T4 \vdash G5$, $T5 \vdash G6$, $T6 \vdash G10$. We can conclude from this that $P \vdash G$. Now for each of the services associated with a sub-goal of G, we can perform the variability analysis. For example, for $T1$, the respective goal preserving variants that can be derived are as follows: $T11 \to x42$, $T12 \to x3$, $T13 \to x1$, $T14 \to x1 \wedge x42$, $T15 \to x42 \wedge x3$, $T16 \to x1 \wedge x3$. We can see that each of the variants of $T1$ still satisfy the sub goal $G4$. Similarly we could have goal preserving variants for the other services as well. Similarly, the variants for $T2$ are : $T21 \to x39 \wedge \neg x12$; $T22 \to \neg x10 \wedge x11$. And the variants for $T3$ are: $T31 \to x15 \wedge \neg x27$; $T32 \to x15 \wedge x16$, while the variants for $T4$ are: $T41 \to x4 \wedge x5$; $T42 \to x7$. The variants for T5 are : $T51 \to \neg x6$; $T52 \to x5 \wedge \neg x2$. Hence these variants still preserve their mappings with the sub goals and thus the process $P \vdash G$. Now given all the goal preserving variants for each of these services, we could generate goal preserving variants of P. This addresses the first objective of our proposed approach, which is goal driven variability analysis. Now suppose we already have existing candidate variants, we can validate whether these variants satisfy the respective goal or not. For example suppose we have an existing variant of T3, $T32 \to x20 \vee x31$. Since $T3$ entails $G9$ ($G9 \to x14 \vee x15 \vee x16$), we could infer that $T32$ is not a valid variant of $T3$ as $T32$ could not satisfy the mapping $T3 \vdash G9$. This addresses the second objective of our proposed approach, which is validating existing variants for their goal preserving nature. Let process P' be a variant of P and be defined as: $P' \to (x1 \vee x3) \wedge (x20 \vee \neg x12 \vee x39) \wedge (x15 \vee \neg x27) \wedge (x7 \vee \neg x19 \vee x45) \wedge (\neg x2 \vee x34 \vee x15)$. From the list of goal preserving variants and the original services, we can establish that $P' \to T16 \wedge T2 \wedge T31 \wedge T4 \wedge T5$. Since each of the service variants are goal preserving we can infer that $P' \vdash G$.

6   Conclusions

In this paper, we have looked at variability in service-based business processes through a goal-oriented lens. In particular, we have shown how, given a business processs, its goal model, and a set of services (and variants thereof) as part of a capability library, all goal-preserving variants of the business process can be generated. Generating such variants is crucial in cases when organizations need to generate multiple variants of the same business process in order to cater to varying user requirements. We have also presented the conditions under which such goal-preserving variants can be generated. As part of future work, we will address co-evolution of goal models and business process models by integrating ideas from this paper with those from an earlier work [12].

References

1. Ayora, C., Torres, V., Reichert, M., Weber, B., Pelechano, V.: Towards run-time flexibility for process families: Open issues and research challenges. In: La Rosa, M., Soffer, P. (eds.) BPM 2012 Workshops. LNBIP, vol. 132, pp. 477–488. Springer, Heidelberg (2013)
2. Chen, L., Babar, M.A., Ali, N.: Variability management in software product lines: a systematic review. In: Proceedings of the 13th International Software Product Line Conference, pp. 81–90. Carnegie Mellon University (2009)
3. Darimont, R., van Lamsweerde, A.: Formal refinement patterns for goal-driven requirements elaboration. SIGSOFT Software Engineering Notes 21, 179–190 (1996)
4. Deelstra, S., Sinnema, M., Nijhuis, J., Bosch, J.: Cosvam: A technique for assessing software variability in software product families. In: ICSM, pp. 458–462 (2004)
5. Thomas Erl. Service-oriented Architecture: Concepts, Technology, and Desing. Pearson Education India (2006)
6. Carbonell, J., et al.: Context-based machine translation. In: Proceedings of the 7th Conference of the Association for Machine Translation in the Americas, pp. 19–28 (2006)
7. Ghose, A.K., Koliadis, G.: Auditing business process compliance. In: Krämer, B.J., Lin, K.-J., Narasimhan, P. (eds.) ICSOC 2007. LNCS, vol. 4749, pp. 169–180. Springer, Heidelberg (2007)
8. Ghose, A.K., Narendra, N.C., Ponnalagu, K., Panda, A., Gohad, A.: Goal-driven business process derivation. In: Kappel, G., Maamar, Z., Motahari-Nezhad, H.R. (eds.) ICSOC 2011. LNCS, vol. 7084, pp. 467–476. Springer, Heidelberg (2011)
9. Hallerbach, A., Bauer, T., Reichert, M.: Capturing variability in business process models: the provop approach. J. Softw. Maint. Evol. 22, 519–546 (2010)
10. Heinrich, B., Bolsinger, M., Bewernik, M.: Automated planning of process models: The construction of exclusive choices. In: ICIS, page Paper 184 (2009)
11. Hinge, K., Ghose, A., Koliadis, G.: Process seer: A tool for semantic effect annotation of business process models. In: Proceedings of the 2009 IEEE International Enterprise Distributed Object Computing Conference, EDOC 2009, pp. 54–63. IEEE Computer Society, Washington, DC (2009)
12. Hoesch-Klohe, K., Ghose, A.K., Dam, H.K.: Maintaining motivation models (in BMM) in the context of a (WSDL-S) service landscape. In: Liu, C., Ludwig, H., Toumani, F., Yu, Q. (eds.) ICSOC 2012. LNCS, vol. 7636, pp. 582–590. Springer, Heidelberg (2012)
13. Lu, R., Sadiq, S.W., Governatori, G.: On managing business processes variants. Data Knowl. Eng. 68(7), 642–664 (2009)
14. Narendra, N.C., Ponnalagu, K.: Towards a variability model for soa-based solutions. In: IEEE SCC, pp. 562–569 (2010)
15. Qasem, M., Prügel-Bennett, A.: Learning the large-scale structure of the max-sat landscape using populations. Trans. Evol. Comp. 14(4), 518–529 (2010)
16. Reichert, M., Weber, B.: Enabling flexibility in process-aware information systems. Springer (2012)
17. van der Aalst, W.M.P., Pesic, M.: DecSerFlow: Towards a truly declarative service flow language. In: Bravetti, M., Núñez, M., Zavattaro, G. (eds.) WS-FM 2006. LNCS, vol. 4184, pp. 1–23. Springer, Heidelberg (2006)

A Cooperative Management Model for Volunteer Infrastructure as a Service in P2P Cloud

Jiangfeng Li and Chenxi Zhang[*]

School of Software Engineering, Tongji University, Shanghai, P.R. China
lijf@tongji.edu.cn, zhangcx2000@163.com

Abstract. IaaS model in the Cloud Computing provides infrastructure services to users. However, the provider of such centralized Cloud requires notable investments to maintain the infrastructures. P2P Cloud, whose infrastructures are provided by multiple volunteer nodes in the P2P network, gives a low cost option to the provision of Cloud Computing. In this paper, a decentralized P2P infrastructure cooperative management model is proposed to offer autonomic infrastructure management and on-demand resource allocation as a service. The model supports nodes to manage complex and various computational resources in P2P infrastructure. Overlay self-configuration service is proposed to dynamically configure the connectivity of nodes in decentralized environments. Task assignment service is designed to allocate resources to run tasks submitted by individual users. Moreover, on-demand resource aggregation mechanism provides service of resource aggregation under user-defined criteria.

Keywords: Decentralized Cooperative Management, Volunteer IaaS, Virtualized Resource Aggregation, Resource Allocation, P2P Cloud System.

1 Introduction

Cloud Computing has attracted interest from both the research community and commercial world. It relies on sharing of resources that can be rapidly provisioned and released with minimal management effort or service provider interaction [1]. In a Cloud system, on-demand self-service allows users to obtain, configure and deploy cloud services.

The three main services are provided by the Cloud computing architecture according to the needs of customers [2]. Firstly, Software as a Service (SaaS) provides access to application software as a service, such as Customer Relationship Management (CRM) [3]. Secondly, Platform as a Service (PaaS) provides a platform for developing applications on top of it, such as the Google App Engine (GAE) [4]. Finally, Infrastructure as a Service (IaaS) provides computers (physical or virtual), and other resources, such as Amazon EC2 [5]. Technically, IaaS offers incremental scalability of computing resources and on-demand storage [6].

---

[*] Corresponding author.

S. Basu et al. (Eds.): ICSOC 2013, LNCS 8274, pp. 507–514, 2013.
© Springer-Verlag Berlin Heidelberg 2013

In industry, a lot of services have been provided by Cloud systems from plenty of companies. However, for the reason that data centers of a Cloud system belong to a single company, it has the possibility that the company go bankrupt, which makes "single point of failure" for customers. In addition to, the centralized Cloud may cost too much to maintain and manage. The Cloud provider needs to effort a lot not only in notable investments of maintaining a cloud center, but also in managing the complex and large size of cloud components.

In this paper, we propose a P2P Infrastructure Cooperative Management (P2PICM) model to manage resources in the P2P infrastructure. The P2PICM model is a fully decentralized model without any server to provide central services. It supports multiple resource providers, which is different from the feature of single resource provider in the IaaS Cloud architecture. On the other hand, it is different from models in Volunteer Computing. Firstly, our proposed model can be used in both local and geographic scale, while the Volunteer Computing is only used in geographic scale. Moreover, there is no central repository of tasks in our proposal while it exists in the Volunteer Computing systems.

The rest of this paper is organized as follows. In Section 2 we briefly review the related works. The system model and proposed services are presented in Section 3. Section 4 evaluates the simulation results. Conclusions and future works are discussed in Section 5.

2   Related Works

In recent years, several authors have recognized the potential benefits of P2P architectures. In [7], the authors proposed an autonomic cooperative model to find the available resources in grid systems. The model is based on P2P unstructured architecture. [8] used P2P hybrid architecture to discover useful grid resources inside or outside the domain. However, resources in those proposals are physical resources instead of virtualized resources. Moreover, different resources cannot be aggregated to run one task.

A different distributed paradigm is Volunteer Computing. In the Volunteer Computing, volunteers donate resources for running scientific projects with significant computational requirements. BONIC[9], SETI@home[10], Folding@home[11] are some of the popular projects running on Volunteer Computing systems. In [12], the authors developed a proximity-aware resource discovery architecture for peer-to-peer based volunteer computing systems. The proposed resource discovery algorithm selects resources based on the requested quality of service, current load of peers, and communication delay.

P2P Cloud system [13], a fully distributed decentralized system, provides infrastructure services without any centralized problems that the Cloud is facing. Infrastructures in a P2P Cloud system come from the volunteer nodes in the network. Cloud@Home [14][15] is a hybrid system which combines features from the Volunteer Computing model and Cloud Computing paradigm. Cloud@Home architecture relies on centralized components, while allowing end users to contribute additional resources.

3   Proposed Model and Services

3.1   System Model

We construct a P2P Infrastructure Cooperative Management (P2PICM) model to manage resources in the P2P infrastructure. The model can allocate on-demand resources to run tasks submitted by users. Such resources may be CPU, memory, hard disk, bandwidth, or a combination of them. Fig. 1 shows the P2PICM model.

The P2PICM model is a two-level model. The P2P Infrastructure Level stores resources of P2P infrastructures. The Peer Manager Level, which consists of several Peer Managers (PMs), deals with the requests from individual users through the User Interface. In this sense, a node contains two main parts, 1) infrastructure resources, and 2) PM that manages the infrastructure resources.

A PM is composed of components of Local Resource, Neighbor Table, Cache, and Task List. Local Resource includes both the individual and summarized information of resources that the PM manages. Neighbor Table holds the IDs of neighbor PMs. Cache preserves system-wide PM information. Task List contains tasks that are waiting for being executed and tasks that are being executed.

Concentrating on CPU-intensive applications, PMs are interested in resources with high CPU processing power. Fig. 2 shows an example of PM structure used in a CPU-intensive application. In the CPU-intensive environment, the ith Resource Capacity is the speed of the ith CPU. The value of the ith Free Resource is defined by Equation (1). In the Equation, a weight of 0.01 is used to make the two measurements comparable.

$$Value_i = \begin{cases} CPU_{SPEED} \times (1 - CPU_{UTILIZATION}) & if\ CPU_{UTILIZATION} < 100\% \\ CPU_{SPEED}\ /\ CPU_{LOAD} \times 0.01 & otherwise \end{cases} \quad (1)$$

3.2   Overlay Self-configuration Service

The Overlay Self-configuration Service is able to dynamically configure the connectivity of PMs in the network under preferences of the PMs. According to the cache information, a PM selects the best n PMs which have the largest free resource, nearest location, and connects them as neighbors. Every unit time, each PM updates Cache by exchanging information of Local Resource and Cache with all the neighbors. Thus, the overlay will reconfigure after each PM changes neighbors.

In order to prevent PM from consuming too much resource in communicating with its neighbors, the number of a PM's neighbors has an upper bound. The upper bound of PM_i's neighbor number is defined by Equation (2).

$$Upper\_Bound_i = p_i \times Capacity\_PM_i / rc \quad (2)$$

where p_i is the max percentage of resources that PM_i allows to use in communication with neighbors, $Capacity\_PM_i$ is the PM Total Resource Capacity, and rc is the resource consumption of communicating with one neighbor.

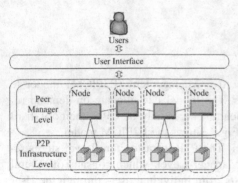

Fig. 1. The structure of the P2PICM model.

Fig. 2. An example of PM structure in a CPU-intensive application

Peer Manager				
Local Information				
PM ID	Resource ID	Resource Capacity	Free Resource	Location
PM001	R01	820	0	
	R02	680	68	LA
PM Total Resource Capacity	1500			
PM Total Free Resource	68			
Cache				
PM ID	Resource ID	Free Resource	Time Stamp	Location
PM002	R01	612	2	LB
	R02	210		
PM003	R01	66	1	LC
	R03	20		
	R01	310		
PM004	R02	200	2	LB
	R04	22		
PM016	R03	20	0	LD
...	...	...	...	...

Neighbor Table			
PM002	PM003	PM004	...
Task List			
Waiting Queue			
Task 003	Task 036	Task 062	Task 166 ...
Running List			
Task ID	SubCloud ID	Resource ID	
Task001	SC001	PM001R01	
Task001	SC001	PM002R03	
Task033	SC002	PM016R02	
Task033	SC002	PM018R01	
Task033	SC002	PM020R03	
Task068	SC006	PM016R01	
Task068	SC006	PM004R03	
Task068	SC006	PM020R02	
...	...	...	

In the processes of information exchange in a PM and one of its neighbor, merging caches of the PM (LocalPM) and the neighbor (NeighborPM) is the main function. In the merge operation, a temporary cache is used for the LocalPM to store information of NeighborPM and other PMs which are stored in NeighborPM's Cache. The LocalPM selects a number of PMs in the temporary cache according to its preference. It stores the information of PMs having closer Time Stamps to the current time and larger Free Resources in its cache.

3.3   Task Assignment Service

Task Assignment Service allocates resources to run tasks submitted by the users. As each task has two resource requirements: 1) *Least Resource Capacity (LRC)*, and 2) *Least Resource Number (LRN)*, the PM will allocate resources that satisfy the requirements of both *Least Resource Capacity* and *Least Resource Number*.

Suppose there are m resources whose Free Resources are larger than *LRC* in the a PM's Local Resource. If m is no less than *LRN*, the task will be run in the PM. However, it has a high probability that m is less than *LRN*. At this time, the PM requests other PMs to provide at least *LRN-m* resources to run the task.

Firstly, the requested PM searches for the additional resources according to resource information stored in its Cache. Those m' $(>=LRN\text{-}m)$ resources that satisfy the requirement of least resource capacity are marked as candidates. Then, the PM checks whether the information of each candidate stored in the Cache is accurate, by the assistant from the PM that manages the candidate. Next, if the candidate information is correct, those $m+m'$ resources (m resources managed the requested PM and m' resources provided by other PMs) will be aggregated together and formed as a Sub-Cloud by On-demand Resource Aggregation Service, which will be introduced in section 4.3.

Contrarily, if some candidate information is incorrect, it means currently there are not enough resources to run the task. The PM will continue finding suitable resources for the task. The finding process will be terminated when either suitable resources are found or there is no suitable resource for the task.

Finally, the task will be run using resources in the SubCloud, or go on staying in the Waiting Queue, and be assigned after a given time.

3.4   On-Demand Resource Aggregation Service

The On-demand Resource Aggregation Service is used to request SubClouds of the whole P2P Cloud to some user-defined criteria, e.g., a group of resources belong to 10 different nodes, the top 3 nearest nodes. When a task requests the allocation of some resources according to a specific metric, the resource aggregation ranks the resources according to that metric, and returns the set of resources matching the query. Next, the selected resources are bound together by linking all nodes that own the resources with a separate overlay (separate from the overlay of PMs). Such resources and the overlay form a SubCloud in the P2P Cloud. We use a ring overlay to link the nodes in the Sub-Cloud. Each node of the SubCloud has a direct link to its predecessor and successor.

Every SubCloud elects a node as the coordinator using bully election algorithm. To keep the robustness of the SubCloud, the coordinator is used to maintain the ring overlay of the SubCloud. So, a task can be running in the resources in the SubCloud, even if nodes in the SubCloud leave the network or fail. Too many nodes leave or fail may cause suspension of running the task because the number of resources in the SubCloud is less than *LRN*. At this time, the coordinator will ask the requested PM allocate additional more resources. To prevent the task from being suspended because of resource shortage frequently, the number of resources in the SubCloud is set as $(1 + p) \times LRN$. p is a parameter between 0 and 1. It is adjusted according to the average probability of nodes leave from the network.

4   Simulation Evaluation

We use Peersim [16] to simulate the P2PICM model. The simulation runs a cycle every unit time. Four different task arrival rates are used to conduct four loading environments – low, medium, high and very high, in which 25%, 50%, 80%, and 90% of resources were loaded. Table 1 shows the parameters of the simulation.

Table 1. Parameters of simulations

Parameters	Values	Parameters	Values
Cycles	100	CacheSize	200, 600, 1024, 2048
PM Number	2048	NeighborNumber	2, 5, 10, 20
Task Running Time	$\dfrac{tasksize}{\sum freeresource}$	Resource Number managed by a PM	1-15
Task LRN	1-8	Resource Capacity	10-300
Task LRC	1-300	Tasksize Distribution	*Poisson Distribution*
Task Size	32-4096	Task Arrival Rate (number per unit time)	400, 1000 , 2000, 3000

Since every PM uses its cache information to select new neighbors and assign tasks, the accuracy of information in every cache influences on the performance of the system. Fig. 3 shows the average percentage of correct elements per cache. The figure indicates that smaller cachesize has higher percentage of correct elements. This results from the fact that information in a cache is sorted by the time stamp. The information which has a higher time stamp is put into a toper element in the cache. So, no matter how large a cachesize is, the upper elements have higher accuracy than the lower elements. On the other hand, information stored in the bottom of the cache has higher possibility that the information is out of date, which reduces the information accuracy.

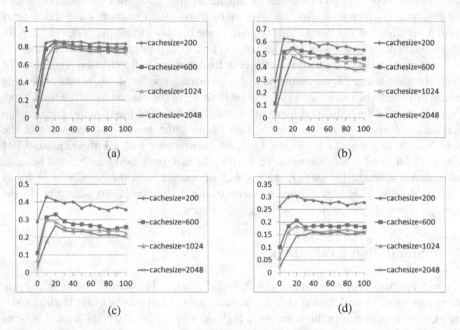

Fig. 3. Average percentages of correct elements per cache. The simulation runs in four loading environments – low (a), medium (b), high (c) and very high (d).

Fig. 4 shows the Task Execution Response Time and Fig. 5 shows the Task Wrongly Assign Number of the P2PICM model in the simulation. In the figure, 200 cachesize has the highest Task Execution Response Time, and the lowest Task Wrongly Assign Number, in the four loading environments. It is attributed to the fact that smaller cachesize makes a cache has higher percentage of correct elements, which is confirmed by the above simulation result (Fig. 3). The higher percentage of correct elements means that a task is less likely assigned to a wrong PM, so the Task Wrongly Assign Number reduces. However, the lower cachesize makes tasks, especially those tasks which require large resources to run, have less chance to be assigned. Such a task needs to wait for a long time before it is assigned, so it increases the Task Execution Response Time.

Besides the cachesize, the number of a PM's neighbors significantly impact on the performance through the accuracy of the information in cache. Fig. 6 shows the average accuracy rate of the information in cache (Cachesize is 200). In the figure, the more neighbor number is, the higher accuracy is. The accuracies when the neighbor number is more than 5 have little difference, but much higher than when neighbor number is 2.

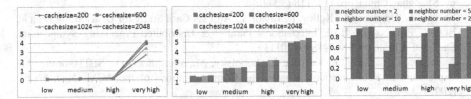

Fig. 4. Task execution response time

Fig. 5. Task wrongly assign number

Fig. 6. Average accuracy rate of the information per cache

5   Conclusion and Future Work

We present a P2P Infrastructure Cooperative Managements model. In the model, cache information is used for a PM to select a number of best PMs as neighbors under its preference. The overlay self-configures every unit time by PMs changing their neighbors. A PM allocates a group of suitable resources which satisfy the task requirements to run the task. Those resources are aggregated as a SubCloud for running the task. The future work aims to solving multi-resources in P2P Cloud system, while restrictions on the order of running tasks are considered.

Acknowledgments. The research is supported by National Basic Research Program of China (No. 2010CB328106).

References

1. Panzieri, F., Babaoglu, O., Ferretti, S., Ghini, V., Marzolla, M.: Distributed Computing in the 21st Century: Some Aspects of Cloud Computing. In: Jones, C.B., Lloyd, J.L. (eds.) Dependable and Historic Computing. LNCS, vol. 6875, pp. 393–412. Springer, Heidelberg (2011)
2. Buyya, R., Yeo, C., Venugopal, S., Broberg, J., Broberg, I.: Cloud Computing and Emerging IT Platforms: Vision, Hype, and Reality for Delivering Computing as the 5th Utility. Future Generation Computer Systems 25(6), 599–616 (2009)
3. Cusumano, M.: Cloud Computing and SaaS as New Computing Platforms. Communications of the ACM 53(4), 27–29 (2010)
4. Ciurana, E.: Developing with Google App Engine. Apress, Berkeley (2009)
5. Varia, J.: Best Practices in Architecting Cloud Applications in the AWS Cloud. In: Cloud Computing: Principles and Paradigms, pp. 459–490. Wiley Press (2011)

6. Garg, S.K., Versteeg, S., Buyya, R.: A Framework for Ranking of Cloud Computing Services. Future Generation Computer Systems 29(4), 1012–1023 (2013)

7. Li, J., Zhang, C.: A Domain Based Two-Layer Autonomic Management Model in Grid Systems. In: 2nd International Conference on Computational Intelligence and Software Engineering, Wuhan, China, pp. 1–4 (2009)

8. Li, J., Zhang, C.: A Decentralized Cooperative Autonomic Management Model in Grid Systems. In: 4th International Conference on Frontier of Computer Science and Technology, Shanghai, China, pp. 112–118 (2009)

9. Elwaer, A., Harrison, A., Kelley, I., Taylor, I.: Attic: A Case Study for Distributing Data in BOINC Projects. In: IEEE International Parallel & Distributed Processing Symposium, Shanghai, China, pp. 1863–1870 (2011)

10. Anderson, D.P., Cobb, J., Korpela, E., Lebofsky, M., Werthimer, D.: SETI@home: An Experiment in Public-resource Computing. Communications of the ACM 45(1), 56–61 (2002)

11. Beberg, A.L., Ensign, D.L., Jayachandran, G., Khaliq, S., Pande, V.S.: Folding@home: Lessons from Eight Years of Volunteer Distributed Computing. In: IEEE International Symposium on Parallel and Distributed Processing, Rome, Italy, pp. 1–8 (2009)

12. Ghafarian, T., Deldari, H., Javadi, B., Yaghmaee, M.H., Buyya, R.: CycloidGrid: A Proximity-Aware P2P-based Resource Discovery Architecture in Volunteer Computing Systems. Future Generation Computer Systems 29(6), 1583–1595 (2013)

13. Babaoglu, O., Marzolla, M., Tamburini, M.: Design and Implementation of a P2P Cloud System. In: 27th ACM Symposium on Applied Computing, Trento, Italy (2012)

14. Cunsolo, V.D., Distefano, S., Puliafito, A., Scarpa, M.: Cloud@Home: Bridging the Gap between Volunteer and Cloud Computing. In: Huang, D.-S., Jo, K.-H., Lee, H.-H., Kang, H.-J., Bevilacqua, V. (eds.) ICIC 2009. LNCS, vol. 5754, pp. 423–432. Springer, Heidelberg (2009)

15. Cunsolo, V.D., Distefano, S., Puliafito, A., Scarpa, M.: Volunteer Computing and Desktop Cloud: the Cloud@Home Paradigm. In: IEEE International Symposium on Network Computing and Applications, Los Alamitos, CA, USA, pp. 134–139 (2009)

16. Peersim, http://peersim.sourceforge.net

Process Refinement Validation and Explanation with Ontology Reasoning

Yuan Ren[1], Gerd Gröner[2], Jens Lemcke[3], Tirdad Rahmani[3], Andreas Friesen[3],
Yuting Zhao[1], Jeff Z. Pan[1], and Steffen Staab[4]

[1] University of Aberdeen
[2] PALUNO – University of Duisburg-Essen
[3] SAP AG
[4] University of Koblenz-Landau

Abstract. In process engineering, processes can be refined from simple ones to more and more complex ones with decomposition and restructuring of activities. The validation of these refinements and the explanation of invalid refinements are non-trivial tasks. This paper formally defines process refinement validation based on the execution set semantics and presents a suite of refinement reduction techniques and an ontological representation of process refinement to enable reasoning for the validation and explanation of process refinement. Results show that it significantly improves efficiency, quality and productivity of process engineering.

1 Introduction

It is germane in process management to represent processes at different levels of abstraction, ranging from abstract processes (coarse description) to specific processes (fine-grained characterisation). Due to the different levels of abstractions, it is not obvious to determine whether or not a refined process reflects the intended behaviour of the original process. This makes the validation of refinements and the explanation of sources for invalidity crucial issues. Manual validation is usually error-prone, time-consuming and increases the cost of process engineering. Existing (semi-) automatic methods still limit the flexibility in process refinement. In this paper, we make the following contributions to the automatic validation of process refinement.[1]

- Based on the classic execution set semantics, we propose a formal and intuitive semantics of process refinement (Sec. 2).
- Based upon the above semantics, we propose a novel approach to automatically validate and explain process refinements (Sec. 3) by combining graph-based transformation and ontology reasoning.
- We implemented our approach and conducted evaluations in terms of performance and usefulness (Sec. 4). Experiments show that realistic refinement scenarios can be validated below one minute and average-sized problems in a split second. This significantly improves the quality and productivity of process engineering.

---

[1] Detailed proofs of all theorems can be found in our online technical report:
  http://homepages.abdn.ac.uk/jeff.z.pan/pages/pub/ProcessRefinement.pdf

S. Basu et al. (Eds.): ICSOC 2013, LNCS 8274, pp. 515–523, 2013.
© Springer-Verlag Berlin Heidelberg 2013

2 Problem Description

A *process* (or *process model*) is a directed graph $P = \langle V, E \rangle$ without multiple edges between two vertices. Vertices (V) include activities and gateways (A, G $\subseteq$ V). The start and end events ($v^S, v^E \in A$) are two special activities, e.g., process P_1 in Fig. 1 consists of two activities A and B between the start and end events. No activity is allowed twice in a process model.

A gateway is either opening or closing ($G^O, G^C \subseteq G$), and either exclusive or parallel ($G^\circledast, G^\oplus \subseteq G$). Process P_3 contains parallel gateways and exclusive gateways. Exclusive gateways can be used to construct loops, e.g., in P_1, A and B can be repeatedly executed. The set of edges (E) is a binary relation on V. For each $v_1 \in V$, we know its *direct predecessors (successors)* $pre(v_1) := \{v_2 \in V \mid (v_2, v_1) \in E\}$ ($suc(v_1) := \{v_3 \in V \mid (v_1, v_3) \in E\}$). Given a valid process model $P = \langle V, E \rangle$ with $|pre(v^S)| = |suc(v^E)| = 0$, $|suc(v^S)| = |pre(v^E)| = 1$; $\forall o \in G^O$ ($c \in G^C$), $|pre(o)|(= |suc(c)|) = 1$; $\forall a \in A \setminus \{v^S, v^E\}$, $|pre(a)| = |suc(a)| = 1$, we define gateway-free predecessor as $PS(v_1) := \{v_2 \in A \setminus \{v^S\} \mid v_2 \in pre(v_1) \text{ or } \exists u \in G, u \in pre(v_1) \text{ and } v_2 \in PS(u)\}$ and successor as $SS(v_1) := \{v_3 \in A \setminus \{v^E\} \mid v_3 \in suc(v_1) \text{ or } \exists u \in G, u \in suc(v_1) \text{ and } v_3 \in SS(u)\}$. These two definitions make gateways "transparent", e.g., in P_2, $SS(A_1) = \{A_2, B_1\}$. In the following, we refer to elements of PS (SS) as predecessors (successors) for short.

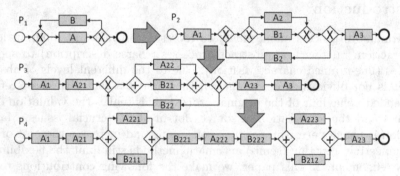

Fig. 1. A chain of process refinements

A *process refinement* is a transformation from an abstract process into a more specific one. An example of a chain of several process refinements is depicted in Fig. 1, in which P_2 refines P_1 by decomposing activity A into A_1, A_2 and A_3, B into B_1 and B_2. P_2 is further refined by P_3, in which A_2 is further decomposed into A_{21}, A_{22} and A_{23}, B_2 into B_{21} and B_{22} and so on.

The semantics of a process is based on its *executions*. An execution is a *proper sequence* of activities $a_i \in A$: $[a_1 a_2 \ldots a_n]$. It starts from one of the successors of v^S and continues with subsequent activities. The ordering relations among activities must be obeyed, i.e., an activity a must be appended to the sequence before all $SS(a)$ and after all $PS(a)$. When it comes to an exclusive gateway ($\circledast$), a proper sequence can go through exactly one exclusive branch. For example in

P_1, after appending A, a sequence can be either terminated by v^E, or continued by B. When it comes to a parallel gateway ($\oplus$), a proper sequence must go through all parallel branches. For example in P_3, after appending A_{21}, a sequence must append both A_{22} and B_{21} before making a choice between B_{22} and A_{23}. The ordering between A_{22} and B_{21} can be arbitrary. The result is a proper sequence of activities—an execution:

Definition 1 (Execution Set). *The execution set of a process P, denoted by ES_P, is the (possibly infinite) set of all executions of P.*

For example, ES_{P_1} for process P_1 in Fig. 1 is $\{[A], [ABA], [ABABA], \dots\}$. Process P_3 contains parallel gateways to express that some activities can be executed in any order: $ES_{P_3} = \{[A_1 A_{21} A_{22} B_{21} A_{23} A_3], [A_1 A_{21} B_{21} A_{22} A_{23} A_3], \dots\}$.

The MIT business process handbook [1] characterises the behaviour of a process in terms of its execution set semantics, and the refinement is specified by the comparison of the execution sets of an abstract and a specific process. A process P subsumes another process Q under the maximal execution set semantics *iff* $ES_Q \subseteq ES_P$. However, architects might use different activity names in abstract and specific processes. Thus, the process architect has to declare which activities of the specific process refine which activity of the abstract process. This is denoted by the *orig*-function, e.g., $orig(A_1) = orig(A_2) = A.$, The *orig*-function is extended to executions and execution sets, e.g., applying this to P_2 yields $orig(ES_{P_2}) = orig(\{[A_1 A_2 A_3], [A_1 A_2 B_2 A_2 A_3], \dots\}) = \{[AAA], [AABAA], \dots\}$. Furthermore, an activity of the abstract process might be *decomposed* into multiple activities in the specific process. Even if we discard the different names, the specific activities still outnumber their origins. For example, process P, consisting of a single activity A, is refined into a process Q with consecutive subactivities $A_1, \dots, A_n$. Intuitively, Q is a valid refinement of P but the execution of P has length 1 and the execution of Q has length n. To resolve this, we define the *decomposable process* P^D of P that is constructed from P by constructing a loop around every activity of P, except the start and end event.

3   Validation and Explanation with Ontologies

The definition of valid refinement is intuitive without parallel gateways since all orderings are explicitly stated. Accordingly, we first present the validation of parallel-free process refinements. Afterwards, we extend our approach to incorporate parallel gateways.

3.1   Validating Parallel-Free Process Refinement

For parallel-free refinements, we use (Description Logics) ontologies and reasoning to validate and explain refinements. A Description Logics (DL) ontology consists of a terminology box (TBox) and an assertion box (ABox). The TBox describes the schematic knowledge with concepts and roles. In this paper, the ontology will be built in the DL fragment $\mathcal{ALC}$. Concepts are inductively defined by the following constructs: $\top \mid \bot \mid A \mid \neg C \mid C \sqcap D \mid C \sqcup D \mid \exists r.C \mid \forall r.C$, in which $\top$ denotes the universal set of the domain, $\bot$ denotes the empty set, A is a named concept, C and D are arbitrary concept expressions. R and S are roles. $\neg C$ is the negation of C, $\sqcap$ and $\sqcup$ the conjunction and disjunction. $\exists r.C$ and $\forall r.C$ represent the set of individuals who have an r relation to some instance of C, or r relations only to instances of C. The subsumption between two concepts C and D is depicted as $C \sqsubseteq D$. Two concepts are disjoint if $C \sqcap D \sqsubseteq \bot$. We write $Disjoint(C_1, C_2, \ldots, C_n)$ to denote that any two C_i, C_j $(1 \leq i, j \leq n, i \neq j)$ are mutually disjoint with each other. If an axiom α can be inferred from an ontology $\mathcal{O}$, we say $\mathcal{O}$ entails α, denoted by $\mathcal{O} \models \alpha$. We mainly use the subsumption checking reasoning service, i.e., checking if $\mathcal{O} \models C \sqsubseteq D$.

The abstract process restricts the set of "allowed" predecessors and successors, while the specific process states the "existing" predecessors and successors after the refinement. We restrict predecessor and successor relations in the abstract process by universal restrictions ($\forall$), and existential quantifications ($\exists$) describe predecessors and successors of activities from the specific process. For both process models, we use the same roles to and $from$ for successor and predecessor relationships. Formally, the ontology $\mathcal{O}$ is built as follows:

Definition 2 (Refinement Ontology). *Let S be a set of predecessors or successors, respectively, we define four operators for translations as follows:*

- *Pre-refinement-from operator $\mathbf{Pr}_{from}(S) = \forall from. \bigsqcup_{x \in S} x$*
- *Pre-refinement-to operator $\mathbf{Pr}_{to}(S) = \forall to. \bigsqcup_{y \in S} y$*
- *Post-refinement-from operator $\mathbf{Ps}_{from}(S) = \bigsqcap_{x \in S} \exists from.x$*
- *Post-refinement-to operator $\mathbf{Ps}_{to}(S) = \bigsqcap_{y \in S} \exists to.y$*

For conciseness, we always have one abstract process P and one specific process Q. In order to detect invalid refined activities, we introduce the concept *Invalid*. Then, we construct an ontology $\mathcal{O}_{P \to Q}$ with the following patterns. The refinement from P_1 to P_2 in Fig. 1 is used as an example.

1. For each activity $X \in A_Q$ with $orig(X) = Z$, we use $X \sqsubseteq Z$ to represent the composition of activities, which covers the *activity origin*.
2. For each activity $X \in A_P$, we use $X \sqsubseteq Invalid \sqcup \mathbf{Pr}_{from}(PS_{PD}(X))$, $X \sqsubseteq Invalid \sqcup \mathbf{Pr}_{to}(SS_{PD}(X))$ to describe the activities in the pre-refinement process. Due to possible decompositions of activities, we use the decomposable process to characterise the predecessor and successor sets, e.g., $A \sqsubseteq Invalid \sqcup \forall from.(Start \sqcup A \sqcup B)$, $A \sqsubseteq Invalid \sqcup \forall to.(End \sqcup B \sqcup A)$, $B \sqsubseteq Invalid \sqcup \forall from.(B \sqcup A)$, $B \sqsubseteq Invalid \sqcup \forall to.(A \sqcup B)$. The pre-refinement process restricts allowed predecessor and successor activities. Thus, the *Invalid* concept is added as an alternative, implying that if any component of X does not satisfy the ordering constraints of X, it will become *Invalid*.
3. For each activity $X \in A_Q$, we use $X \sqsubseteq \mathbf{Ps}_{from}(PS_Q(X))$, $X \sqsubseteq \mathbf{Ps}_{to}(SS_Q(X))$ to represent predecessor and successor sets of it in the specific process.
4. $Disjoint(X|X \in A_Q)$, $orig(X) = Z$ (for $X \in A_Q$). These axioms represent the uniqueness of all activities with the same origin, e.g., $Disjoint(A_1, A_2, A_3)$.

5. $Disjoint(X|X \in A_P)$. This axiom represents the uniqueness of all the activities in the abstract process, e.g., $Disjoint(Start, End, A, B)$.

With the above axioms, ontology $\mathcal{O}_{P \to Q}$ is a representation of the refinement from P to Q. All executions of Q can be represented by some existential restrictions ($\exists$). Given the subsumption of activities, these $\exists$ chains must satisfy the universal restrictions ($\forall$) in $\mathcal{O}_{P \to Q}$ to fulfill the executions of P^D. Due to the uniqueness of concepts, an invalid refinement between P^D and Q will make invalid refined activities to be subsumed by $Invalid$. This helps to pinpoint the source of an invalid refinement.

Theorem 1. *For any parallel-free refinement from P to Q, the refinement is invalid due to activity $A \in A_Q$, iff $\mathcal{O}_{P \to Q} \models A \sqsubseteq Invalid$.*

3.2   Extending Processes with Parallel Gateways

The presence of parallel gateways requires some pre-processing steps on the abstract and/or specific processes before building the refinement ontology.

If the *specific process* contains parallel gateways, e.g., the refinement from P_2 to P_3 in Fig. 1, we observe that parallel branches implicitly describe different possible executions among activities in sibling branches. E.g., in P_3, there are two parallel branches, each of them contains one activity (A_{22} or B_{21}). The implicit executions of the parallel sibling activities A_{22} and B_{21} are $[A_{22}B_{21}]$ and $[B_{21}A_{22}]$, i.e., either activity A_{22} is executed before B_{21} or B_{21} before A_{22}. For the validation, we have to take all these implicit executions of parallel branches into account. To remedy this, we replace all parallel gateways with exclusive gateways and connect the input and output of all previously parallel activities (with the help of exclusive gateways). Fig. 2 illustrates a replacement of P_3.

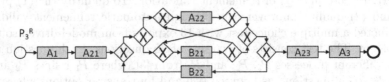

Fig. 2. P_3^R: Replaced process P_3

If the *abstract process* contains parallel gateways, as in the refinement from P_3 to P_4, we observe: (i) Activities A_{22} and B_{21} of the abstract process P_3 are in parallel. According to the execution set semantics, activities A_{22} and B_{21} can be executed in any order. (ii) The decomposition principle allows for an infinite repetition of activities. Thus, in the specific process P_4, this implies that the ordering relations between decompositions of A_{22} and B_{21}, e.g., A_{221}, B_{211}, etc. in P_4, do not affect the validity of the refinement from P_3 to P_4. To remedy this, the sibling parallel activities A_{22} and B_{21} can be regarded as "transparent" to each other in the refinement checking. Activities of parallel sibling branches (e.g., A_{22} or B_{21}) are removed in the abstract process, and their corresponding decomposed activities are removed in the specific process, respectively. Thus, execution relations of activities in parallel sibling branches are neglected in the abstract process. We refer to this reduction as *parallel branch break-down*.

4   Evaluation

The technical performance of our approach is influenced by the run-time of DL reasoning. We implemented a generator that simulates arbitrarily complex refinement scenarios with different characteristics. We used a standard laptop with a 2.67 GHz dual core, four-threads CPU with 8 GB RAM using Java 1.6 and TrOWL v0.5.1 (http://trowl.eu). Fig. 3 suggests that the reasoning time of arbitrary parallel-free refinements (dotted graph in the left figure) grows less than exponentially (less than a straight line on a logarithmic scale) compared to the number of activities. The parallel branch break-down contributes most to performance degradation. We generated sequences where each sequential step consists of two parallel activities. As the combination of all branches has to be considered separately, the left figure shows exponentially growing run-times.

To estimate the performance in practice, we generated processes with 25% parallel flow, 50% exclusive flow, and 25% loops because that ratio appeared most natural. The validation run-times are plotted on the right of Fig. 3. In [2], IBM examined 735 industrial business processes from different domains. The processes contained 17 activities on average. The maximum was 118. Thus, a realistic refinement scenario would contain about 34 activities on average and 236 at maximum. As can be seen from the figure, the corresponding run-times of our approach would be 0.062s for the average and about 40s for the largest process.

In addition to the technical performance, we also assessed the business value (productivity and quality) of refinement validation. To quantify the (1) productivity and (2) quality improvements through automatic refinement validation, we conducted a multiple choice test with 13 experts from model-driven software development. The test consists of two sets of 20 questions. Each question refers to three different processes P_1, P_2, and P_3 from [3], where P_1 refines P_2 and P_2 refines P_3. Each question has between two and four answer options where none or multiple answers can be correct. For the one set of 20 questions, denoted by S for "support", the result of the refinement validation is highlighted in the process models. The other set, denoted by N for "no support", has to be answered without support. We measured the number of correct and wrong answers per set (C_S, W_S, C_N, W_N) and the times for each set (t_S, t_N). The whole test took about 1.5 hours. We calculate each person's quality of answers as $Q_x = C_x/(C_x + W_x)$ and productivity as $P_x = C_x/t_x$, where $x \in \{S, N\}$. In order to abstract from personal work styles and experiences, we calculate the per-person improvement in quality as $QI = \frac{Q_S}{Q_N} - 1$ and in productivity as $PI = \frac{P_S}{P_N} - 1$. Our test reveals an average per-person improvement in quality of $\overline{QI} = 70\%$ and in productivity of $\overline{PI} = 378\%$, which shows the potential cost savings through our approach.

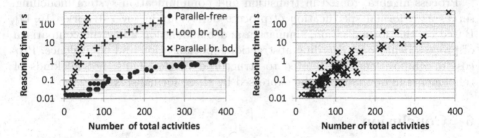

Fig. 3. Reasoning times on logarithmic scale

5 Related Work

The business process management community investigates the analysis of interaction properties [4], the difference analysis between process models [5], the recognition of equivalent fragments [6] and the validation of consistency-aware changes of a process model with respect to a process template [7]. However, none of these approaches considers the problem of process refinement given an abstract and a specific process.

Behavioural profiles [8] describe processes by characteristic relations. They are used for measuring the compliance of process executions, which are given by logs, with respect to their models [9]. Behavioural profiles offer an alternative representation compared to our predecessor and successor relationships. However, according to our notion of refinement, there are some particular cases like the occurrence of two exclusive activities in the same branch of a loop, which is differently handled in our loop break-down compared to the behavioural profiles.

A bunch of works [10–12] considers process model abstraction. A process model abstraction provides a more abstract and higher-level view by aggregating and eliminating activities of the original (more detailed) process model. In contrast to our work, several rules are used to preserve the execution order, while we allow for an arbitrary refinement and check the validity afterwards. Refinement of actions is modelled by operators in [13]. These operators preserve the semantic correctness by taking the relations into account. Our refinement notion differs in two aspects. First, we do not use refinement operators and therefore, we cannot ensure correctness by construction. Thus, a key part of our contribution is the validation of refinements. Second, our semantics rather refers to the interleaving semantics, where the behaviour is given by sequences of activities, while in [13] the causal semantics is used.

Work on process equivalence is faced with a related problem of formalising and comparing the behaviour of processes. A formalisation of equivalence for BPMN like process models is presented in [14]. The equivalence of process models, e.g., of a reference and a specific process, is analysed in [15], where equivalence is expressed by a degree of similarity between two processes.

Process algebra, rooted in transition and communication system modelling, serves as a formal specification of process behaviour in several works [16, 17]. Based on this formalisation, simulation and bisimulation allow the comparison of process behaviour regarding abstraction, specialisation and equivalence. Process decompositions, are limited to structured blocks. Thus, not all kinds of refinements in our work can be expressed by these formalisms.

6   Conclusion

In this paper, we have defined a formal semantics of process refinement based on the execution set semantics and presented an ontological solution to a process refinement problem and several reduction techniques to enable the refinement validation and explanation using standard reasoning services. The evaluation shows that our approach significantly improves the efficiency and correctness of process engineering.

Acknowledgement. This work was partially supported by the European Union's Seventh Framework Programme under grant agreement 604123 (FIspace).

References

1. Wyner, G.M., Lee, J.: Defining specialization for process models. In: Organizing Business Knowledge: The MIT Process Handbook, pp. 131–174. MIT Press (2003)
2. Fahland, D., Favre, C., Jobstmann, B., Koehler, J., Lohmann, N., Völzer, H., Wolf, K.: Instantaneous Soundness Checking of Industrial Business Process Models. In: Dayal, U., Eder, J., Koehler, J., Reijers, H.A. (eds.) BPM 2009. LNCS, vol. 5701, pp. 278–293. Springer, Heidelberg (2009)
3. Curran, T.A., Ladd, T., Ladd, A.: SAP R/3 Business Blueprint: Understanding Enterprise Supply Chain Management, 2nd edn. Prentice Hall International (1999)
4. Lohmann, N., Massuthe, P., Stahl, C., Weinberg, D.: Analyzing Interacting WS-BPEL Processes using Flexible Model Generation. DKE 64, 38–54 (2008)
5. Dijkman, R.: Diagnosing differences between business process models. In: Dumas, M., Reichert, M., Shan, M.-C. (eds.) BPM 2008. LNCS, vol. 5240, pp. 261–277. Springer, Heidelberg (2008)
6. Gerth, C., Luckey, M., Küster, J.M., Engels, G.: Detection of Semantically Equivalent Fragments for Business Process Model Change Management. In: IEEE International Conference on Services Computing, pp. 57–64 (2010)
7. Sadiq, S., Orlowska, M., Sadiq, W.: Specification and Validation of Process Constraints for Flexible Workflows. Information Systems 30(5), 349–378 (2005)
8. Weidlich, M., Mendling, J., Weske, M.: Efficient Consistency Measurement Based on Behavioral Profiles of Process Models. IEEE Trans. Software Eng. 37(3), 410–429 (2011)
9. Weidlich, M., Polyvyanyy, A., Desai, N., Mendling, J., Weske, M.: Process Compliance Analysis based on Behavioural Profiles. Inf. Syst. 36(7), 1009–1025 (2011)
10. Smirnov, S., Reijers, H., Weske, M., Nugteren, T.: Business Process Model Abstraction: A Definition, Catalog, and Survey. Distributed and Parallel Databases, 1–37 (2012)

11. Eshuis, R., Grefen, P.: Constructing Customized Process Views. Data & Knowledge Engineering 64(2), 419–438 (2008)
12. Liu, D., Shen, M.: Workflow Modeling for Virtual Processes: An Order-preserving Process-view Approach. Information Systems 28(6), 505–532 (2003)
13. van Glabbeek, R., Goltz, U.: Refinement of Actions and Equivalence notions for Concurrent Systems. Acta Inf. 37(4/5), 229–327 (2001)
14. Lam, V.: Equivalences of BPMN Processes. Service Oriented Computing and Applications 3, 189–204 (2009)
15. van der Aalst, W.M.P., de Medeiros, A.K.A., Weijters, A.J.M.M.: Process Equivalence: Comparing Two Process Models Based on Observed Behavior. In: Dustdar, S., Fiadeiro, J.L., Sheth, A.P. (eds.) BPM 2006. LNCS, vol. 4102, pp. 129–144. Springer, Heidelberg (2006)
16. Milner, R.: Communication and Concurrency. Prentice Hall (1989)
17. Sangiorgi, D.: Bisimulation for Higher-Order Process Calculi. Information and Computation 131, 141–178 (1996)

Automated Service Composition
for on-the-Fly SOAs

Zille Huma[1], Christian Gerth[1], Gregor Engels[1], and Oliver Juwig[2]

[1] Department of Computer Science, University of Paderborn, Germany*
{zille.huma,gerth,engels}@upb.de
[2] HRS-Hotel Reservation Service, Germany
Oliver.Juwig@hrs.de

Abstract. In the service-oriented computing domain, the number of available software services steadily increased in recent years, favored by the rise of cloud computing with its attached delivery models like Software-as-a-Service (SaaS). To fully leverage the opportunities provided by these services for developing highly flexible and aligned SOA, integration of new services as well as the substitution of existing services must be simplified. As a consequence, approaches for automated and accurate service discovery and composition are needed. In this paper, we propose an automatic service composition approach as an extension to our earlier work on automatic service discovery. To ensure accurate results, it matches service requests and available offers based on their structural as well as behavioral aspects. Afterwards, possible service compositions are determined by composing service protocols through a composition strategy based on labeled transition systems.

1 Introduction

Service-oriented computing (SOC) has emerged as a promising trend to enable the vision of large-scale, heterogeneous and flexible software systems at enterprise level through service-oriented architecture (SOA). For this purpose, a SOA developer defines a *service request* to discover and compose the services that are developed and published on service markets by service providers in terms of *service offers*.

With the advent of cloud computing, the growing plethora of available services provides enormous opportunities for the development of future *On-The-Fly* SOAs that are highly flexible and can be aligned more easily to meet constantly changing requirements. To make this vision come true, accurate and automated service discovery and composition mechanisms are needed that have to face several challenges.

First of all, to enable an efficient and precise identification, services must be described in a suitable way by rich service specifications that comprise structural as well as behavioral aspects of requested and offered services.

* This work was partially supported by the German Research Foundation (DFG) within the Collaborative Research Centre "On-The-Fly Computing" (SFB 901)

S. Basu et al. (Eds.): ICSOC 2013, LNCS 8274, pp. 524–532, 2013.

Secondly, service discovery and composition mechanisms must deal with the existing multifaceted heterogeneity of the involved service partners, such as their independent domain ontologies, selection of different languages/notations to specify service descriptions, and different granularity levels of the service descriptions as a result of their independent domain knowledge, etc. To overcome these challenges, we proposed a UML-based rich service description language (RSDL) [6] and an automatic service discovery mechanism for RSDL-based service descriptions [5]. An application scenario for our proposed approach came from our industrial partners Hotel Reservation Service (HRS)[1]. In this scenario, potential new hotel services shall be automatically discovered and connected to provide end users with booking facilities for these hotels.

In this paper, we extend our approach by a service composition mechanism, which enables the composition of *multiple* services each offering various operations in order to fulfill a service request. Our proposed mechanism ensures precise service composition results as it comprehensively covers different elements in service offers and requests, such as operation signatures, operation semantics (pre- and post-conditions), and service protocols to discover and compose potential service offers that satisfy a request.

In the next section, we briefly introduce our proposed language for comprehensive service specifications and our service discovery mechanism. In Section 3, we describe our service composition mechanism in detail. Section 4 briefly introduces our tool support. In Section 5, we discuss related work and finally, we conclude the paper and give an outlook on future work in Section 6.

2 Foundations

To realize our vision of a comprehensive service specification, we proposed a UML-based rich service description language (RSDL) [6]. Our RSDL provides notations to describe the structure and the behavior of service requests and offers. Figure 1(a) shows a RSDL-based *service request* of HRS consisting of three parts. *(A)* specifies operation signatures, i.e., *findRoom()*, *viewDetails()*, *bookRoom()*, ..., using the Web Service Description Language (WSDL) [17]. *(B)* specifies operation semantics in terms of pre- and post-conditions for individual operations specified using UML-based visual contracts (VC) [9]. A VC describes the system state before and after the invocation of an operation in terms of UML object diagrams that are typed over the ontologies of the service partners. Finally, a desired invocation sequences is specified in *(C)* in terms of a requestor protocol as UML sequence diagram. Similarly, Figure 1(b) shows a RSDL-based *service offer* of the hotel service *HotelX*. The specification consists of *(A)*: operation signatures *searchRoom()*, *makeRoomReservation()*, ... , *(B)*: VCs typed over the ontology of HotelX, and *(C)*: a provider protocol as UML statechart diagram. In case of a service offer, multiple invocation sequences of provided operations shall be possible, which we specify using a UML statechart diagram. A more detailed description of our RSDL is given in [7].

---

[1] http://www.hrs.com

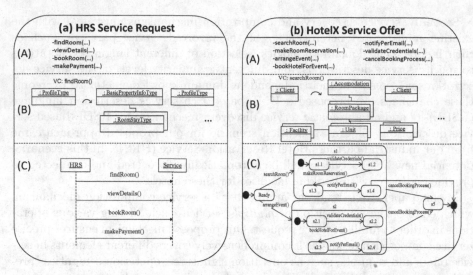

Fig. 1. (a) RSDL-based Service Request of HRS and (b) RSDL-based Service Offer of HotelX

To enable an automated service discovery and composition for such RSDL-based service requests and offers, we proposed a multi-step approach, whose overview is given in [7]. Here it is important to mention that the first three steps are part of our earlier work and the details of these steps along with examples are provided in [5,7]. In this paper, our main focus is on service composition, which we will discuss in detail in the next section.

After operation matching phase (Step 3), the result is a set of $1 : 1$, $1 : n$, $n : 1$ and (partially) $n : m$ mappings between requested operations in a service request and offered operations in available service offers. A mapping in this set is represented as (m_r, m_o), where m_r is an operation or a sequence of operations in the service request r, which is mapped to m_o, which is an operation or a sequence of operations in a service offer o.

As an example, the operation mappings obtained by matching the service request of *HRS* and the service offer of *HotelX* and two further service offers of *HotelY* and *PayOnline* are shown in Figure 2. One mapping for HRS is the $n : 1$ operation mapping $(findRoom() \rightarrow viewDetails(), searchRoom())$ that maps the sequence of requested operations to an offered operation of *HotelX*. Based on the operation mappings, we compose the operations of the service offers to satisfy the service request in the next section.

3   Automated Service Composition

To compose service offers, our approach compares and composes the protocol of a service request and the protocols of service offers that contain matched operations. For that purpose, we evaluate whether the mapped operations of the offered service can be invoked in the desired order resulting in valid service

Providers Requestor HRS	HotelX	HotelY	PayOnline
findRoom() → viewDetails	searchRoom() (n:1)	getAvailableRoom() (n:1)	-
bookRoom()	validateCredentials() → makeRoomReservation() → notifyPerEmail() (1:n)	reserve() (1:1)	-
makePayment()	-	-	signIn() → payDues()→ generateReceipt()→ signOut() (1:n)

Fig. 2. Operation Mappings between the HRS Request and three available Service Offers

compositions. The *service composition* consists of three main tasks: Translation of the protocols to labeled transition systems (LTS), composition of LTSs, and an analysis of the composed LTS. Due to space constraints, the details of the first task are described in [7]. Its outcome are LTSs for the service protocols that are shown in Figure 3. In the following sections, we discuss the last two tasks in detail.

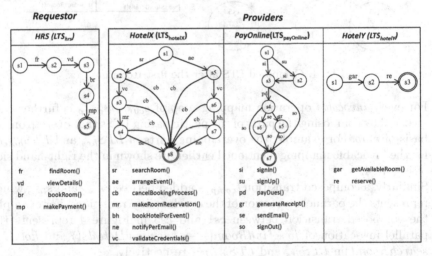

Fig. 3. LTSs for the Service Partners in our Running Example

LTS Composition: In order to automatically detect possible service compositions, we compose the LTSs of a service request and service offers by overlapping them on the basis of the operation mappings determined earlier. As output our algorithm returns a set of possible service compositions or a failure notification in case of no possible service composition. In this case, the requestor is provided with suggestions to restructure his/her request based on identified partial compositions. In the following, we describe our algorithm given in Listing 1.

1. A composed state s_{comp}, i.e, a composition of the initial states of all participating LTSs, is created and added to the yet empty composed LTS lts_{comp}.

Figure 4 shows a partially composed lts_{comp} for our running example with $cs1$ as its initial state.

2. Next, the `while`-loop traverses over the states of the composed LTS lts_{comp} and constructs it further until there are no more states to be traversed.

3. For every currently traversed state s_{cur}, the *invocable* operation mappings from $OpMap_r$ are determined. An operation mapping is *invocable* in a composed state s, if its comprising operation sequences can be directly invoked in s. For instance, for $cs1$ in Figure 4, one of the two invocable mappings in $OpMap_{hrs}$ is ($hrs.findRoom() \rightarrow hrs.viewDetails()$, $hotelX.searchRoom()$) as $hrs.findRoom() \rightarrow hrs.viewDetails()$ can be invoked from $hrs.s1$ and $hotelX.searchRoom()$ can be invoked from $hotelX.s1$.

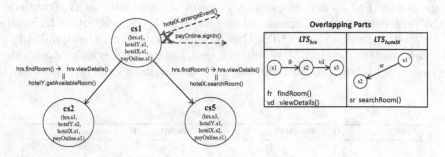

Fig. 4. Composed LTS after the first Iteration

4. For every *invocable* operation mapping map of s_{cur}, lts_{comp} is further constructed by composing the parts of the participating LTSs that overlap on the basis of map. For example, the overlapping parts of LTS_{hrs} and LTS_{hotelX} for the invocable mapping mentioned earlier are shown in the right-hand side of Figure 4.

5. Similarly, a composed transition t_{comp} is added between s_{cur} and s_{tar}, which represents the parallel invocation of the overlapping transitions. For example, the composed transition between $cs1$ and $cs5$ in Figure 4 represents the parallel invocation of $hrs.findRoom() \rightarrow hrs.viewDetails()$ and $hotelX.searchRoom()$ in LTS_{hrs} and LTS_{hotelX}, respectively.

6. Analogously, the composed states $cs2$ and $cs5$ are traversed and as a result, lts_{comp} is further constructed until there are no more states to be traversed. Figure 5 shows the completely composed LTS lts_{comp} of our running example, which is analyzed to determine any possible service compositions in the next subsection.

A salient feature of the proposed algorithm is its *selective composition* strategy where the LTS composition is moderated through the LTS of the requested service protocol. That means, only those parts of the LTSs of offered service protocols are considered that overlap with the LTS of requested protocol and hence are *relevant* for the requestor based on the identified operation mappings. As a result, the composed LTS is smaller in size and easier to analyze as compared

Listing 1. Algorithm to compose LTSs of the service partners

Input: LTS of Service Request lts_r
Input: Set of LTSs of selected offers $\{lts_{o_1}, ..., lts_{o_k}\}$
Input: Set of operation mappings $OpMap_r$ for r
Output: Set of possible service compositions $Result_{comp}$ OR Failure
    Notification

findServiceCompositions($lts_r, \{lts_{o_1}, ..., lts_{o_k}\}, OpMap_r$)

  define s_{comp}:$(r.s_0, o_1.s_0, ..., o_k.s_0)$;   // ①
  add s_{comp} as initial state to the composed LTS lts_{comp};

  while $lts_{comp}.hasMoreStates()$ **do**   // ②
    $s_{cur}=lts_{comp}.\text{nextState}()$, where s_{cur}:$(r.s_c, o_1.s_c, ... o_k.s_c)$;

    while $s_{cur}.hasInvocableMappings()$ **do**   // ③

      $map=s_{cur}.nextInvocableMapping()$, where $map : (m_r, m_o)$ AND
      $o \in \{o_1, ..., o_k\}$;   // ④

      add s_{tar}:$(r.s_t, o_1.s_t, ... o_k.s_t)$ to lts_{comp}, where $r.s_c \xrightarrow{m_r} r.s_t$ AND
      $o.s_c \xrightarrow{m_o} o.s_t$;   // ⑤

      add t_{comp} to lts_{comp}, where $t_{comp}=s_{cur} \xrightarrow{m_r \| m_o} s_{tar}$;   // ⑥

    end
  end

  if $lts_{comp}.hasCompleteTraces()$ **then**   // ⑦
    | $Result_{comp}= lts_{comp}.completeTraces()$ **return** $Result_{comp}$
  end
  else return Failure_Notification
end

to a conventionally composed LTS. For example, a conventional LTS composition mechanism may include some other transitions in the composed LTS, e.g., from $cs1$, some other possible transitions are $hotelX.arrangeEvent()$ or $payOnline.signIn()$.

Analysis of the Composed LTS: In our given example, $cs1 \rightarrow cs2 \rightarrow cs3 \rightarrow cs4$ and $cs1 \rightarrow cs5 \rightarrow cs6 \rightarrow cs7$ represent two possible service compositions (see Figure 5). Based on these results, a service requestor (e.g. HRS) may decide for a particular composition based on quality attributes of the provided services, which can be easily added by extending our rich service specification language.

The algorithm notifies a failure in finding a valid service composition, if lts_{comp} does not have any complete trace. In this case, the service requestor gets feedback in terms of the partially composed LTS and the particular points where a composition failed. On the basis of this feedback, the requestor may restructure his/her service request. A detailed example for such a failure scenario is specified in [7]. Finally, a set of possible service compositions is obtained that satisfy the service request or a failure notification with feedback for a requestor is returned.

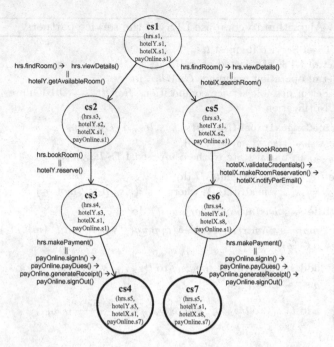

Fig. 5. Completely Composed LTS of our running Example

4   Tool Support

We have implemented a tool, called RSDL Workbench as a part of the service computing platform developed at the Collaborative Research Center (CRC 901) "On-The-Fly Computing"[2]. It provides an editor and matcher for service partners to specify and automatically match their RSDL-based service descriptions.

The RSDL Workbench has been realized as an Eclipse plugin and is implemented using EMF, GMF, and Henshin[3]. For more detailed information, the interested reader is referred to [7].

5   Related Work

For this section, our particular focus is on the *workflow-based* approaches for automatic service composition[14].

Concerning service request and offer matching, none of these approaches [2,8,11,1,3,15,13] are comprehensive enough. Some [2,8,11] examine operation signatures and operation semantics assuming that the requested/offered service consist of a single operation and hence, do not consider service protocols. Similar to our approach, [11] specifies the operation semantics in terms of visual contracts. On the contrary, METEOR-S [1], which allows service discovery

---

[2] http://sfb901.uni-paderborn.de

[3] http://www.eclipse.org/modeling/emft/henshin/

and composition of WSDL-S-based [10] service descriptions, only considers a requested service protocol and offered services are assumed to provide only a single operation. Similarly, [3,15,13] propose service composition mechanisms for OWL-S [12] and UML-based service descriptions based on the operation signatures and service protocols but do not consider operation semantics. In this context, [16] comprehensively matches OWL-S-based service specifications but has certain shortcomings in terms of heterogeneity resolution features, which we will discuss shortly.

Concerning the resolution of the multifaceted heterogeneity of service partners, some approaches [2,1,4] realizes the need for ontological heterogeneity resolution and come up with mechanism for this purpose. For instance, in [1] semantic annotation for WSDL elements are described, which can support an ontological heterogeneity resolution mechanism, whereas an elaborate mediator-based mechanism is used in [4]. The resolutions of linguistic heterogeneity is considered in [15]. Other service composition approaches either do not address the underlying heterogeneity [11,16] or they [8,3,13] assume the existence of a resolution mechanism and therefore avoid major complexities of the problem at hand.

We claim that our approach overcomes the weaknesses of most of the approaches discussed here and hence is a promising approach for On-The-Fly SOAs.

6   Conclusion and Future Work

To enable the vision of *On-The-Fly* SOAs, we proposed an automated composition mechanism based on our earlier work on rich service descriptions and automatic service discovery [5,6]. Our proposed mechanism ensures accurate results as it relies on comprehensive matching and composition of the service request and offers based on their structural as well as behavioral features. We have implemented the RSDL Workbench and evaluated our approach on a real-world case study of our industrial partner HRS.

In future, we aim to evaluate the effectiveness of our approach more extensively through further case studies in the CRC environment. We also aim to further strengthen our heterogeneity resolution mechanism with features, such as, complex mappings between ontologies.

References

1. Aggarwal, R., Verma, K., Miller, J.A., Milnor, W.: Constraint Driven Web Service Composition in METEOR-S. In: IEEE International Conference on Services Computing (SCC 2004), pp. 23–30. IEEE Computer Society (2004)
2. Bartalos, P., Bieliková, M.: QoS Aware Semantic Web Service Composition Approach Considering Pre/Postconditions. In: Proceedings of IEEE Int. Conf. on Web Services (ICWS 2010), pp. 345–352. IEEE Comp. Soc. (2010)
3. Brogi, A., Corfini, S., Popescu, R.: Semantics-based Composition-oriented Discovery of Web Services. ACM Trans. Internet Technol. 8(4), 19:1–19:39 (2008)

4. Haller, A., Cimpian, E., Mocan, A., Oren, E., Bussler, C.: WSMX - A Semantic Service-Oriented Architecture. In: IEEE International Conference on Web Services (ICWS 2005), pp. 321–328. IEEE Computer Society (2005)

5. Huma, Z., Gerth, C., Engels, G., Juwig, O.: Towards an Automatic Service Discovery for UML-based Rich Service Descriptions. In: France, R.B., Kazmeier, J., Breu, R., Atkinson, C. (eds.) MODELS 2012. LNCS, vol. 7590, pp. 709–725. Springer, Heidelberg (2012)

6. Huma, Z., Gerth, C., Engels, G., Juwig, O.: UML-based Rich Service Description and Discovery in Heterogeneous Domains. In: Proceedings of the Forum at the Conference on Advanced Information Systems Engineering (CAiSE 2012). CEUR Workshop Proceedings, vol. 855, pp. 90–97. CEUR-WS.org (2012)

7. Huma, Z., Gerth, C., Engels, G., Juwig, O.: Automated Service Discovery and Composition for On-the-Fly SOAs. Tech. Rep. TR-RI-13-333, University of Paderborn, Germany (2013),
   http://is.uni-paderborn.de/uploads/tx_sibibtex/tr-ri-13-333.pdf

8. Kona, S., Bansal, A., Blake, M.B., Gupta, G.: Generalized Semantics-Based Service Composition. In: IEEE International Conference on Web Services (ICWS 2008), pp. 219–227. IEEE Computer Society, Washington, DC (2008)

9. Lohmann, M.: Kontraktbasierte Modellierung, Implementierung und Suche von Komponenten in serviceorientierten Architekturen. Ph.D. thesis, University of Paderborn (2006)

10. LSDIS Lab: Web Service Semantics,
    http://lsdis.cs.uga.edu/projects/WSDL-S/wsdl-s.pdf

11. Naeem, M., Heckel, R., Orejas, F., Hermann, F.: Incremental Service Composition based on Partial Matching of Visual Contracts. In: Rosenblum, D.S., Taentzer, G. (eds.) FASE 2010. LNCS, vol. 6013, pp. 123–138. Springer, Heidelberg (2010)

12. OWL-S Coalition: OWL-based Web Service Ontology (2006),
    http://www.ai.sri.com/daml/services/owl-s/1.2/

13. Pathak, J., Basu, S., Honavar, V.: Modeling Web Service Composition using Symbolic Transition Systems. In: Proceedings of AAAI Workshop on AI-Driven Technologies for Service-Oriented Computing. AAAI Press, California (2006)

14. Rao, J., Su, X.: A Survey of Automated Web Service Composition Methods. In: Cardoso, J., Sheth, A.P. (eds.) SWSWPC 2004. LNCS, vol. 3387, pp. 43–54. Springer, Heidelberg (2005)

15. Spanoudaki, G., Zisman, A.: Discovering Services during Service-Based System Design Using UML. IEEE Trans. on Softw. Eng. 36(3), 371–389 (2010)

16. Vaculin, R., Neruda, R., Sycara, K.: The process mediation framework for semantic web services. Int. J. Agent-Oriented Softw. Eng. 3(1), 27–58 (2009)

17. W3C: Web Service Description Language (WSDL) (2007),
    http://www.w3.org/TR/wsdl20/

Deriving Business Process Data Architectures from Process Model Collections

Rami-Habib Eid-Sabbagh, Marcin Hewelt, Andreas Meyer, and Mathias Weske

Hasso Plattner Institute at the University of Potsdam
{rami.eidsabbagh,marcin.hewelt,andreas.meyer,
mathias.weske}@hpi.uni-potsdam.de

Abstract. The focus in BPM shifts from single processes to process interactions. Business process architectures were established as convenient way to model and analyze such interactions on an abstract level focusing on message and trigger relations. Shared data objects are often a means of interrelating processes. In this paper, we extract hidden data dependencies between processes from process models with data annotations and their object life cycles. This information is used to construct a business process architecture, thus enabling analysis with existing methods. We describe and validate our approach on an extract from a case study that demonstrates its applicability to real world use cases.

1 Introduction

The last decade has seen widespread adaptation of business process management resulting in large process model collections. Although process models often need to interact to deliver services or produce goods, they generally are elicited in isolation, prone to miss the interdependencies with other processes. Business process architectures (BPAs) have been proposed to provide an abstracted view on interrelated process models (see [1] for a survey of BPA approaches). Our BPA approach [2,3] relates processes by trigger and message flows, allows for multiple process instances, n-to-m communication, and offers formal verification.

While previous work dealt with modeling and verification of BPAs, this contribution extracts data dependencies between processes. Even if the interaction of processes is not modeled explicitly, process relations can be deduced by looking at the data objects and how processes manipulate them. If one process produces a certain data object which another process consumes, then those processes have to be carried out in sequence. We summarize identified dependencies for several data objects in a *process data dependency matrix (PDM)* and use it to construct a *business process data architecture (data BPA)*, which reveals and depicts hidden data-related interdependencies and thus eases the management of process model collections. The resulting data BPA can be verified with the method presented in [3] unveiling erroneous process interaction due to data.

Aside BPAs, several techniques have been introduced to depict business process interactions, e.g., choreography diagrams in BPMN [4], service interaction patterns [5], or Proclets [6]. The mentioned alternatives focus on the interaction behavior between processes or services by modeling the message exchange. A BPA represents relations between processes giving them a partial ordering with respect to process execution.

S. Basu et al. (Eds.): ICSOC 2013, LNCS 8274, pp. 533–540, 2013.

In contrast to all aforementioned techniques, we utilize relations between data objects utilized in multiple processes to determine the relations between these processes. This naturally leads to the object-centric process modeling paradigm, e.g., [7], where a process is modeled by the involved data objects and synchronization follows from data state changes represented in object life cycles. This synchronization between multiple object life cycles induces the partial ordering of all data object changes and therefore the execution. Although architectures can be build based on this paradigm by synchronizing object life cycles, no approach exists describing this procedure. Additionally, the control flow view is only provided implicitly, whereas the combination of our approach and our earlier work shows both perspectives. A first step towards integration of control flow and data was presented by Fahland et al. [8], who utilize Proclets to model object-centric processes.

2   Scenario

Throughout the paper, we will use the following scenario taken from a case study on order and delivery processes. Figures 1 to 3 present the five process models of our scenario. Process p_1 (Fig. 1) first analyses a verified order and checks if the ordered products are in stock. If this is the case, they are shipped, the invoice is sent, and the payment is received. Otherwise the products are built. Process p_2 (Fig. 2a) is similar to process p_1 in Fig. 1, except that it sends the product only after the payment was received and allows to reject an unconfirmed order. Process p_3 (Fig. 2b) archives a processed order. Process p_4 (Fig. 3a) verifies the customer and may reject his order. Finally, process p_5 (Fig. 3b) handles invoicing and payment.

These processes utilize the two data objects "order" and "product". Hence two object life cycles (OLCs) are required. An OLC describes the manipulations allowed to be performed upon the corresponding data object. The utilized OLCs will be presented as part of the description of our approach in Section 4. All process models satisfy the notion of weak conformance [9] with respect to the utilized data objects, i.e., process models and OLCs do not contradict.

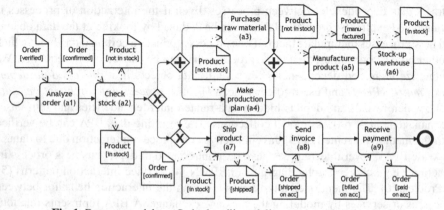

Fig. 1. Process model p_1: Order handling, delivery on account (on acc.)

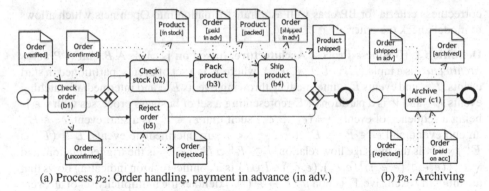

(a) Process p_2: Order handling, payment in advance (in adv.)   (b) p_3: Archiving

Fig. 2. Process models p_2 and p_3

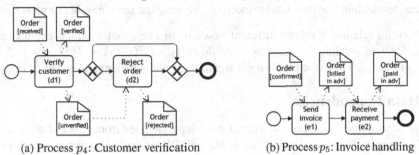

(a) Process p_4: Customer verification   (b) Process p_5: Invoice handling

Fig. 3. Process models p_4 and p_5

3 Foundations

Data in process models can be represented by a set of data objects and their states. A data object is an entity processed during process execution and is characterized by states and state transitions. At any point in time, a data object is in exactly one state which constitutes a business situation. We formalize data objects as *object life cycles* (OLCs) which consist of a set of states S, a set of state transitions $T \subseteq S \times S$, an initial, and a final state. Note, that we consider only *acyclic* OLCs for now.

A process model consists of a set of control flow nodes and a relation defining the partial ordering of activities performed during process execution. Further, activities can be annotated with data objects, which represent pre- and postconditions for activities and determine when an activity is enabled (in addition to control flow) as well as their expected outcome. For each process model, we assume that it is structurally sound and that it weakly conforms to all utilized data objects [9], i.e., for each data object modification by an activity there exists a corresponding path in the OLC of this object. We assume that all activities' data object accesses are modeled and that no activity writes a data object it has not read before.

BPA describe all processes of an organization and their interdependencies. Each process is understood as a sequence of events, which are interconnected by message and trigger flows, depicting process interaction on an abstract level. BPAs allow to model *multiplicities*, a term subsuming the sending and receiving of variably many messages and triggers to and from multiple process instances of several processes. [3] proposed correctness criteria for BPAs as well as a transformation into Open nets which allows to model check the criteria.

Definition 1 (Business Process Architecture, based on [2, 3]). A *Business Process Architecture* is a tuple $(E, V, L, I, \chi, \mu, =)$, where E is a set of events, partitioned in start events, E^S, end events E^E, intermediate throwing events E^T, and intermediate catching events E^C and V is a partition of E representing a set of business processes with $v \in V$ being a sequence of events $v = \langle e_1, ..., e_n \rangle$ such that $e_1 \in E^S$ is a start event, $e_n \in E^E$ an end event, and $e_i \in E^C \cup E^T$ for $1 < i < n$ are intermediate events. $L \subseteq (E^T \cup E^E) \times E^C$ is the message flow relation, $I \subseteq (E^T \cup E^E) \times E^S$ is the trigger relation, and $\chi \subseteq \{((e, e_1), (e, e_2)) \mid (e, e_1), (e, e_2) \in L \cup I\}$ is a conflict relation indicating flows that are mutually exclusive. Function $\mu : E \to \mathcal{P}(\mathbb{N}_0)$ denotes the multiplicity set of an event and $= \subseteq (E^T \times E^C) \cup (E^C \times E^T)$ is an equivalence relation between events of the same process demanding that they send respectively receive the same number of messages. $\diamond$

The conflict relation χ relates different flows from one event e which exclude each other. Assume sending event e has three flows $(e, e_1), (e, e_2) \in L, (e, e_3) \in I$ and $(e, e_1) \chi (e, e_2)$. Then it sends a trigger signal to e_3 and a message to either e_1 or e_2.

4 Data Dependencies

In this section, we show how to extract data dependencies from process models and OLCs, derive the *Process Data Relation Matrix (PDM)*, and construct a *Business Process Data Architecture (data BPA)*.

4.1 Deriving the Process Data Relation Matrix

Annotating the Object Life Cycle. Activities in process models can read or modify data objects. A modifying access changes the state of the data object, corresponding to a state transition in the OLC. We label the state transitions with pairs of process and activity to record their originator. This defines a relation $map \subseteq (S \times \mathcal{P} \times \mathcal{A} \times S)$, where $\mathcal{P}$ and $\mathcal{A}$ are sets of process models and activities. The map is visualized as arc inscriptions, e.g., the modifying access is reflected by the inscription $p_2[b_3]$ on the arc between states "in stock" and "packed" in Fig. 4. The modifications performed by activities are not limited to directly succeeding data states, but can comprise multiple state transitions, as long as there exists a path in the OLC. Activity $p_1[a_7]$ for example transforms data object "product" from state "in stock" to state "shipped" omitting the intermediary state "packed". In this case an additional dashed arc is added to the annotated OLC. Activities which only read data object state are also annotated, depicted by an arc originating from the read state. For example Fig. 4 indicates that state "not in stock" is read by activities a_3 and a_4 of process p_1.

From the annotated OLC, one can deduce direct data dependencies between activities by looking at consecutive state transitions. Two activities from two different processes are dependent $(p[a_i] \dashrightarrow p'[a_j])$ if one activity $p'[a_j]$ reads or modifies a data object that another activity $p[a_i]$ has modified before. For example the transition "unverified" $\xrightarrow{p_4[d_2]}$ "rejected" of data object "order" is followed by the transition "rejected" $\xrightarrow{p_3[c_1]}$ "archived". Because c_1 modifies a state written by d_2 it can only occur afterwards.

Additionally, we define the conflict relation ⊗. Two annotated state transitions ∈ *map* are in conflict, when they originate in the same source state and belong to different processes. In the OLC of "product" both $p_2[b_3]$ and $p_1[a_7]$ originate in state "in stock" and hence are in conflict.

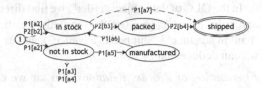

Fig. 4. Annotated product object life cycle

Deriving Process Relations. The two base relations ⟶ and ⊗ on activity level are lifted to process level, as follows. To determine the relation between two processes, all direct relations between their activities need to be considered along all paths of the OLC of shared data objects because different paths might show contradicting relations.

To determine *exclusive processes* it suffices that one pair of activities be in conflict relation. The OLC in Fig. 5 implies $p_1[a_2] \otimes p_2[b_2]$ (because both originate in the same state) and hence processes p_1 and p_2 are exclusive ($p_1\#p_2$). The exclusive relation is dominant, in the sense that it overrules other relations in ambiguous situations. Two processes p and p' are called *completely exclusive* ($p[\#]p'$) if a conflict relation involving their activities occurs along each path of the OLC.

Process p' *sequentially* depends on process p with respect to a particular data object D (written as $p \to_D p'$), if all data accesses of p happen before p' accesses D for the first time on any path of the corresponding OLC. Additionally, there must exist at least one direct data dependency $p[x] \twoheadrightarrow p'[y]$. Regarding the data object "order" process p_3 sequentially depends on p_4 as can be seen from Fig. 5.
We define two variants of the sequential relation. Two processes p and p' are *sequentially overlapping* ($\overset{1}{\to}$) if $p \to p'$ and additionally p reads the last state it has modified in parallel with process p' on handover. A process p' *follows* ($\overset{111}{\to}$) a process p, if p' only reads the modifications performed on a data object by process p, i.e. if there are activities $x_1,\ldots,x_k$ of p and $y_1,\ldots,y_l$ of p' such that $p[x_i] \twoheadrightarrow p'[y_j]$ for some $1 \leq i \leq k, 1 \leq j \leq l$ and each y_j has only reading access.

Two processes p, p' are *interacting* ($\rightleftarrows$) if on some path of an OLC direct data dependencies between activities of p and p' occur and vice versa, i.e. $p[x_i] \twoheadrightarrow p'[y_j]$ and $p'[y_k] \twoheadrightarrow p[x_l]$ for some activities x_i, x_l of p and y_j, y_k of p'. Additionally $x_i < x_l$ and $y_j \leq y_k$ have to hold regarding the behavioral profiles of p and p'. Because process p induces the first data dependency on the path it is the initiator of the interaction. If the condition for interacting processes holds on different paths of an OLC the initiator has to be the same process on each path. Otherwise the processes are considered *contradicting* ($\perp$). Generally, interacting means that two processes take turns operating on a data object.

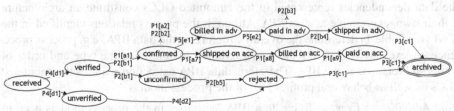

Fig. 5. Annotated order object life cycle

In the OLC of data object "order", we find direct data dependencies $p_2[b_1] \dashrightarrow p_5[e_1]$ and $p_5[e_2] \dashrightarrow p_2[b_3]$ (on the top path "verified"–"confirmed"–"billed in advance"–"paid in advance"–"shipped in advance"), and $b_1 < b_3$ as well as $e_1 < e_2$ hold. Therefore we can deduce that $p_2 \leadsto p_5$.

Aggregation of Process Relations. So far we considered only single data objects to determine process relations. However, as processes might be related via several data objects we need to consider the cases in which the determined relations differ.

If the sequential relations for two processes agree in regard to all data objects they both accesss, the processes are said to be sequentially dependent ($\rightarrow$). Similarly, this applies for sequentially overlapping and following relations. If, on the other hand, the sequential relation differs for data objects D and D', e.g. $p \rightarrow_D p'$ and $p' \rightarrow_{D'} p$, then processes p, p' are interacting, except when their behavioral profiles contradict. This happens for example, when $p[a] \dashrightarrow p'[b_1]$ in the OLC of D, $p'[b_2] \dashrightarrow p[a]$ in the OLC of D' and $b_1 < b_2$ in the behavioral profile of p' all hold.

Two processes are *contradicting*, if they are contradicting for at least one data object. A PDM with contradicting processes when turned into a data BPA will fail to terminate, because of deadlocks during execution. If two processes p and p' are exclusive in regard to one data object, while the other data objects yield different relations, we assume their overall relation to be contradicting. However, processes we identified as contradicting might succeed for some process traces, because activities causing the contradiction were not executed in this trace. In such ambiguous cases, process traces need to be considered which will be part of future work.

Table 1 shows the PDM for the running example, which defines the coarse structure of the data BPA that must conform to the identified relations. As processes p_3, p_4, and p_5 only access the data object "order", their relations are determined by this data object. Processes p_1, p_2 and p_3 sequentially depend on process p_4, process p_3 additionally is sequentially dependent on both p_1 and p_2. Processes p_1 and p_2 use both data objects, but because their relation is exclusive for both, we can unambiguously identify their overall relation as exclusive in the PDM. Processes p_1 and p_5 are also exclusive because of $p_1.[a_7] \otimes p_5.[e_1]$ in the OLC of the data object "order".

Table 1. PDM for scenario

Processes	p1	p2	p3	p4	p5
p1	–	#	→	←	#
p2	#	–	→	←	$\leadsto$
p3	←	←	–	←	–
p4	→	→	→	–	–
p5	#	$\leftsquigarrow$	–	–	–

4.2   Extracting the Business Process Data Architecture

The data dependencies represented in the annotated OLCs constitute an architecture of their own, expressible as *data BPA*. Although the process relations identified in the PDM (see Table 1) determine the overall structure of the data BPA, e.g. process precedence, or exclusivity, they are too coarse-grained to determine the type and order of events and relations in the BPA. Therefore, data BPA extraction requires the annotated OLCs as well as behavioral profiles [10] of the process models.

From Activities to Events. To create a BPA, activities in the process models need to be mapped onto events, $\beta : A \mapsto E$. However, there is no one-to-one mapping because internal activities are ignored. Only those activities are mapped, that occur in the data dependency relation $(domain(\beta) = \{x \mid x \dashrightarrow y \text{ or } y \dashrightarrow x\})$. Each pair $x \dashrightarrow y$ becomes a sending event $\beta(x)$ and a receiving event $\beta(y)$, which are related in the BPA. Consider the annotated OLC of data object "order" in Fig. 5. Activity $p_2[b_1]$ modifies the state from "verified" to "confirmed", a state which is read by activity $p_5[e_1]$. Processes p_2 and p_5 have further data dependencies $p_2[b_1] \dashrightarrow p_5[e_1]$, $p_5[e_2] \dashrightarrow p_2[b_3]$ and $p_5[e_2] \dashrightarrow p_2[b_4]$, which each turn into a pair of a sending and a receiving event. Activity $p_2[b_4]$ is furthermore in data dependency with $p_3[c_1]$, meaning that $\beta(b_4)$ and $\beta(c_1)$ are in relation. Since in the BPA formalism no event can be both sending and receiving, a second event is introduced for b_4 such that technically $\beta : A \mapsto 2^E$.

The Order of Events. To determine the types of relations and events and to order the events inside BPA processes, we employ behavioral profiles [10]. If according to the behavioral profile an activity a is minimal, i.e. it is the first activity in the process model, $\beta(a)$ is a start event. If a is maximal, i.e. the last activity, $\beta(a)$ is an end event, otherwise it is an intermediary event. The type of relation is now easy to decide, as all flows ending in a start event are trigger flows, and otherwise are message flows. In the running example, d_1 is the last activity in p_4 and hence $\beta(d_1)$ becomes an end event. Activity a_1 is minimal and hence mapped to a start event. The flow $(\beta(d_1), \beta(a_1))$ therefore is a trigger flow $\in I$. Since receiving event $\beta(b_3)$ is neither the first nor the last activity of p_2, it becomes an intermediate catching event $\in E^C$ and $(\beta(e_2), \beta(b_3))$ becomes a message flow $\in L$.

The data BPA process p_2 contains several events, start event $\beta(b_1)$, intermediate throwing event $\beta(b_2)$, intermediate catching events $\beta(b_3)$ and $\beta(b_4)$ and the end event $\beta(b_4)$. To determine the order of the events we consult the behavioral profile and get $b_1 < b_2 < b_3 < b_4$. This order on the activities translates into an order on the BPA events.

Conflicting Processes. The conflict relation $\otimes$ affects the creation of the data BPA in the following way. In Fig. 5, activities $p_1[a_1]$ and $p_2[b_1]$ both transform data object "order" from state "verified" to "confirmed". Hence, those activities are conflicting and the data BPA must prevent the processes, to which $\beta(a_1)$ and $\beta(b_1)$ belong, to be instantiated at the same time. To achieve this, the trigger flows which instantiate exclusive processes need to be in the BPA conflict relation χ. In the running example both $\beta(a_1)$ and $\beta(b_1)$ are the start events of their respective processes and are both triggered by $\beta(d_1)$, because of $d_1 \dashrightarrow a_1$ and $d_1 \dashrightarrow b_1$. For the data BPA, this means that trigger flows $(\beta(d_1), \beta(a_1)), (\beta(d_1), \beta(b_1)) \in \chi$. Graphically, this is depicted as a XOR gateway in the resulting data BPA in Fig. 6.

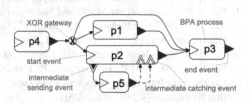

Fig. 6. Resulting data BPA

Multiplicity. As described in Section 3, an activity a might have several data objects as its precondition, e.g. data object "D" in state "s" and data object "E" in state "t". Assume that "D[s]" is written by $p_1[b]$ and "E[t]" is written by $p_2[c]$ and that p_1 and p_2 are non-exclusive, hence implying data dependencies $b \dashrightarrow a$ and $c \dashrightarrow a$. In the BPA this translates into sending events $\beta(b)$ and $\beta(c)$ both in flow relation with receiving event $\beta(a)$. Since a needs data objects from both b and c, also $\beta(a)$ needs messages from both $\beta(b)$ and $\beta(c)$. To express this condition, the multiplicity of $\beta(a)$ is set to the total number of activities on which a depends, in this case $\mu(\beta(a)) = \{2\}$.

However, the situation looks different if a has "D" in state "s" and "D" in state "t" as its precondition. Because now either state would suffice to enable a, the receiving event $\beta(a)$ would need a message from either p_1 or p_2, and the multiplicity would be trivial.

5 Conclusion

In this contribution, we presented an approach to extract data interdependencies between a set of process models and vizualize them as business process data architecture (data BPA). Our approach assumes that process models are annotated with data objects and that weakly conforming object life cycles (OLCs) for this objects are given.

The data modifications performed by process activities are annotated in the OLCs to derive direct data dependencies ($\rightarrow$ and $\otimes$) between activities. Based on that, we extract relations between processes for single and multiple data objects and summarize them in the process data dependency matrix (PDM). Another result is the data BPA, which visualizes found interdependencies and allows formal analysis.

To unambiguously determine some process relations it is required to consider execution traces of process models, which was not part of this contribution. In future work we will also work on lifting the restriction of acyclic OLCs. Our next goal is to combine the data BPAs from this contribution with control flow based BPAs and check their conformance, to accurately represent interdependencies in process model collections.

References

1. Dijkman, R., Vanderfeesten, I., Reijers, H.A.: The Road to a Business Process Architecture: an Overview of Approaches and their Use. Technical Report WP-350, Eindhoven University of Technology (2011)
2. Eid-Sabbagh, R.-H., Dijkman, R., Weske, M.: Business Process Architecture: Use and Correctness. In: Barros, A., Gal, A., Kindler, E. (eds.) BPM 2012. LNCS, vol. 7481, pp. 65–81. Springer, Heidelberg (2012)
3. Eid-Sabbagh, R.-H., Hewelt, M., Weske, M.: Business Process Architectures with Multiplicities: Transformation and Correctness. In: Daniel, F., Wang, J., Weber, B. (eds.) BPM 2013. LNCS, vol. 8094, pp. 227–234. Springer, Heidelberg (2013)
4. OMG: Business Process Model and Notation (BPMN), Version 2.0 (2011)
5. van der Aalst, W.M.P., Mooij, A.J., Stahl, C., Wolf, K.: Service Interaction: Patterns, Formalization, and Analysis. In: Bernardo, M., Padovani, L., Zavattaro, G. (eds.) SFM 2009. LNCS, vol. 5569, pp. 42–88. Springer, Heidelberg (2009)
6. van der Aalst, W.M.P., Barthelmess, P., Ellis, C.A., Wainer, J.: Proclets: A Framework for Lightweight Interacting Workflow Processes. International Journal of Cooperative Information Systems 10(4), 443–481 (2001)
7. Cohn, D., Hull, R.: Business Artifacts: A Data-centric Approach to Modeling Business Operations and Processes. IEEE Data Engineering Bulletin 32(3), 3–9 (2009)
8. Fahland, D., de Leoni, M., van Dongen, B.F., van der Aalst, W.M.P.: Conformance Checking of Interacting Processes with Overlapping Instances. In: Rinderle-Ma, S., Toumani, F., Wolf, K. (eds.) BPM 2011. LNCS, vol. 6896, pp. 345–361. Springer, Heidelberg (2011)
9. Meyer, A., Polyvyanyy, A., Weske, M.: Weak Conformance of Process Models with respect to Data Objects. In: Services and their Composition (ZEUS), pp. 74–80 (2012)
10. Weidlich, M., Mendling, J., Weske, M.: Efficient Consistency Measurement Based on Behavioral Profiles of Process Models. IEEE Trans. Software Eng. 37(3), 410–429 (2011)

A Case Based Approach to Serve Information Needs in Knowledge Intensive Processes

Debdoot Mukherjee[1], Jeanette Blomberg[2], Rama Akkiraju[2], Dinesh Raghu[1],
Monika Gupta[1], Sugata Ghosal[1], Mu Qiao[2], and Taiga Nakamura[2]

[1] IBM Research – India
{debdomuk,diraghu1,monikgup,gsugata}@in.ibm.com
[2] IBM Almaden Research Center, USA
{blomberg,akkiraju,taiga,mqiao}@us.ibm.com

Abstract. Case workers who are involved in knowledge intensive business processes have critical information needs. When dealing with a case, they often need to check how similar case(s) were handled and what best practices, methods and tools proved useful. In this paper, we present our Solution Information Management (SIM) system developed to assist case workers by retrieving and offering targeted and contextual content recommendations to them. In particular, we present a novel method for intelligently weighing different fields in a case when they are used as context to derive recommendations. Experimental results indicate that our approach can yield recommendations that are approximately 15% more precise than those obtained through a baseline approach where the fields in the context have equal weights. SIM is being actively used by case workers in a large IT services company.

1 Introduction

Case Management [23] has emerged as the discipline for supporting flexible and knowledge intensive business processes, which may require significant human judgment and decision making. Unlike traditional Business Process Management (BPM), which has focused on automating process workflows, Case Management is aimed at equipping *knowledge workers*[1] efficiently steer processes toward completion. Since, knowledge workers add significant economic value to an enterprise and their contributions are especially critical in growing the services economy, the demand for Case Management tools has been growing [1]—especially in domains such as customer relationship management, IT service management, healthcare, legal, insurance and citizen services. When knowledge workers begin to work with a case they often ask—*Did we handle such a case before? If so, how? What best practices are available to solve similar cases?* To get answers to such questions, they often search in enterprise repositories. However, knowledge workers are frustrated with the inability of the available knowledge management tools in finding the information they need, when they need it, due to the poor state of the art of enterprise search. Studies report that they may spend 15% to 35% of their time

---

[1] The term, *knowledge worker*, was first coined by Peter Drucker to denote those who develop or apply knowledge in the workplace. [16] discusses different roles of knowledge workers.

S. Basu et al. (Eds.): ICSOC 2013, LNCS 8274, pp. 541–549, 2013.
© Springer-Verlag Berlin Heidelberg 2013

Key Case Fields (by Type)	
Categorical	Win/Loss Outcome, Industry, Country, Offerings, Contract Type, Service Line, Risk Rating, Delivery Center
Numeric	Total Contract Value, Governance Cost, Transition Cost, Onsite / Offshore ratio, Resource Mix
Text	Client Name, Opportunity title & overview, Scope, Solution Summary, Competition Analysis, Win Themes, Value Proposition, Governance, Transition methodology, Risks, Assumptions, Cost Case, Architecture, Legal Terms & Conditions, Project plan, SLA - Support Model

Fig. 1. Sample Fields from SIM's Case Model

searching for information and are successful in finding relevant information less than 50% of the time [7,5]. In practice, what works better is reaching out to subject matter experts in the organization through informal networks. But, identifying the right person often requires numerous phone calls and email exchanges, which takes up precious, productive time of knowledge workers. Our study of knowledge workers at a large IT services organization reveals that a multitude of technical and organizational challenges currently make it extremely difficult for case workers to find the information necessary for their daily work. Clearly, developing technologies for effectively aggregating and disseminating case knowledge is a strong business imperative for next generation Case Management [13,20,22] and Social BPM [21] products.

In this paper, we describe how information retrieval guided by the context of the case-at-hand and the semantics of the case domain generates useful content recommendations for the knowledge workers. We discuss a knowledge management application called Solution Information Management (SIM), which was developed to serve information needs arising in the *Opportunity-To-Order* process (*i.e.,* the sales lifecycle) at an IT services company. SIM mines contextual and targeted information by searching a federated set of repositories. The repositories store solution design documents created during past opportunities as well as best-practice reference materials about offerings, delivery capabilities, lessons learned and engagement processes. A *case* in SIM uniquely identifies an IT service deal that was pursued in the past. For each case, we catalog all information related to the deal as fields in a *case model*; Figure 1 shows a sample of fields in SIM's case model. We apply an array of information extractors to resolve contents of different case fields from the unstructured documents created in a deal. Then, the richly fielded case models are indexed such that one can execute targeted semantic queries and not just full text keyword search. Suppose, a case worker is looking for existing prior assets or lessons learned on "low cost data center consolidation solutions in financial service industry in Western Europe". In SIM, one can create a complex query to address such a requirement—*Geography* : "Western Europe", *Offering* : "data center consolidation", *Win-Theme* : "Low Cost", *Industry* : "Financial Services". The results obtained from a such a query are much more precise than what a keyword search would yield. Further, the SIM system can generate content recommendations for the information needs in different process steps based on the already known fields in the case or the *context* of the case. An interesting question that arises is how to weigh the affect of different fields in the context. In the above example, suppose the case worker is now interested in recommendations for potential risks underlying the solution. How do we weigh the four query clauses as we look to retrieve cases with *Risks* that can be of interest? Do we weigh the clause on *Offering* more than the others or is a match of the *Industry* more important to fetch relevant *Risks*? Resolving an appropriate weighting of the different query clauses is crucial in order to maximize the relevance of recommendations. It is a complex problem since there are hundreds of fields in industrial case repositories and manually specifying weighting schemes is infeasible. We propose an automated approach, named *Correspondence Analysis*, which infers how one case field can influence recommendations for another case field. Correspondence scores dictate the weights of different query clauses in generating recommendations.

We conduct experiments where we assess the relevance of recommendations on two different case fields, obtained from a corpus of 715 cases. The relevance of recommendations obtained through our approach is significantly better than that from a baseline approach which assumes equal weights for all fields in context. Improvement observed in standard IR metrics like *Precision@K* and *nDCG* is as high as 15%.

2   System Overview: Solution Information Management

In this section, we describe Solution Information Management (SIM), a tool that assembles content from a variety of data sources relevant to case domain, indexes the information after converting it into a semantic format, and then delivers relevant information to the case worker depending upon the context of a case. Figure 3 shows the different stages in the knowledge engineering pipeline in SIM. Here, we briefly outline the function of each stage. Refer to our technical report [25] for a detailed overview.

Crawl & Parse: We configure crawlers in SIM that periodically download the contents of the different repositories. The crawlers output files in their native, binary formats, *e.g., .pdf, .ppt, .xls, .doc*. The next step is to *parse* formatted text from such files. Also, we export pages and slides as images; these images show up alongside search results to enable a preview feature.

Annotate: The *Annotate* stage creates semi-structured case models with information extracted from dense, unstructured documents associated with historical cases. The *Segmenter* module takes as input the formatted text parsed from the documents. It distinguishes the headings in the documents from any other text based on their special formatting or font-styles. Next, it feeds the words in an inferred heading to a trained text classifier model which predicts the case semantic implied by that heading. Once we determine the case semantic for a heading, we extract the text from the region following the heading into a field in a case model. Additionally, we compute a *Quality Score* and a *Summary* for every text field. The *Quality Score* assesses the amount of information present in the case field relative to that present in the same field in other cases in the corpus. Such a score helps penalize sparse fields as we generate recommendations. A *Summary* for a case field is obtained by applying the Maximal Marginal Relevance technique [4] to choose a small number of sentences that convey the maximum information. Summaries help users do a quick evaluation of case fields.

Index: The case models created in the *Annotate* stage are imported into a full text index of a search engine. SIM uses Apache Solr as the foundation for indexing and search.

Query & Search: To generate recommendations for a field of a case being worked upon, SIM creates an OR-ed construct of query clauses, where each clause is generated from the contents of a known field in the case. A key question that arises is how do we

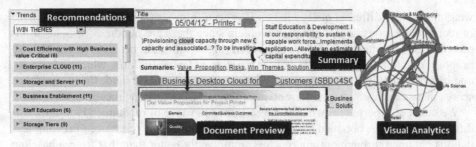

Fig. 2. Visualizing Results in SIM

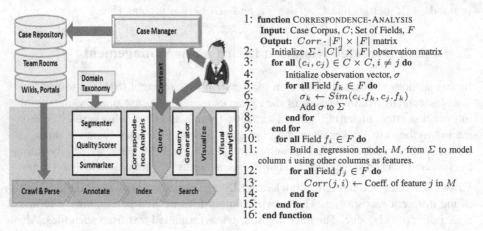

1: **function** CORRESPONDENCE-ANALYSIS
   Input: Case Corpus, C; Set of Fields, F
   Output: $Corr$ - $|F| \times |F|$ matrix
2:     Initialize Σ - $|C|^2 \times |F|$ observation matrix
3:     **for all** $(c_i, c_j) \in C \times C, i \neq j$ **do**
4:         Initialize observation vector, σ
5:         **for all** Field $f_k \in F$ **do**
6:             $\sigma_k \leftarrow Sim(c_i.f_k, c_j.f_k)$
7:             Add σ to Σ
8:         **end for**
9:     **end for**
10:    **for all** Field $f_i \in F$ **do**
11:        Build a regression model, M, from Σ to model column i using other columns as features.
12:        **for all** Field $f_j \in F$ **do**
13:            $Corr(j, i) \leftarrow$ Coeff. of feature j in M
14:        **end for**
15:    **end for**
16: **end function**

Fig. 3. Knowledge Engineering Pipeline in SIM   **Fig. 4.** Correspondence Analysis

weigh the matches of the different query clauses to maximize relevance of recommendations. To address this issue, we develop *Correspondence Analysis*, a technique that helps us ascertain the weight of each query clause. We discuss it in detail in Section 2.1. Further, the relevance score for any result is boosted based on different factors such as users' rating, document age, the number of previous hits on the result, *Quality Score* for the result field and others domain specific rules (*e.g.,* boost if the deal was won).

Visualize: Figure 2 illustrates how recommendations are visualized in the SIM tool. On the left-hand pane, one finds a list of key topics that are obtained by clustering the recommendations generated for a particular case field. In the middle pane, we present the recommended case models as well as relevant reference materials. For each result, one can view the *summaries* of different case fields. Also, one may open up a *document preview* for a case field, which shows snapshots of the document regions where the field is documented. SIM also helps users visually discover interesting associations within selected cases through interactive graph visualizations.

2.1 Correspondence Analysis

As we derive content recommendations for a certain field of a case (henceforth referred to as the *target* field), it is important to understand what other fields in the case can serve as *context*. For instance, as we seek recommendations on the case field, *Risks,* does it make sense to search for *Risks* in cases from the same *Industry* or cases with the same *Solution Offering*? If both *Industry* and *Solution Offering* appear to lend *context* to *Risks*, then how does one weigh the influence of each of these fields? Turns out that even domain experts are unable to conclusively answer such questions. Again, assigning equal weights to the affect of each field in the context does not appear to be ideal (See Section 3). Moreover, since there could be hundreds of fields in case repositories, manually defining weighting schemes may not be feasible. Here, we describe *Correspondence Analysis*[2], an automated approach that analyzes the case corpus to infer how similarities in different case fields correlate with each other. The correspondence output can be used for defining preferential weighting for fields in SIM queries.

For each pair of case fields, say α and β, we define *Correspondence*, $Corr(\alpha, \beta)$, as the degree to which similarity in α corresponds to similarity in β across pairs of cases. A high value for $Corr(\alpha, \beta)$ suggests that α is a good candidate to serve as *context* for β because if we are able to retrieve cases with similar α, then it is likely that the contents of β in those cases may recur in the current case. For the above example, if our analysis of the case corpus shows that cases with the same *Offering* often exhibit similar *Risks*, then a case worker would be interested to find *Risks* in past cases that have the current *Offering*. Thus, it may be worthwhile to assign a high weight for the query clause with *Offering*. Now, when deriving recommendations for a target field, it is important to have the "right" relative weighting for all other fields in the context. We use multiple linear regression as a tool to determine the relative impact that fields in the context can have upon the target field.

Figure 4 discusses the algorithm for correspondence analysis. We sample pairs of cases from the case corpus to observe how the different fields are similar across the case pairs. For each pair of cases, we create an observation vector where each observation measures the similarity of a particular field across the two cases. The similarity function, Sim, depends on the type of field. We use boolean similarity for categorical fields, cosine similarity[3] for text fields and inverse of euclidean distance[4] for numeric fields. Next, in order to assess how similarity of a target field may be influenced by similarities in other fields, we regress the observations from all other fields against the corresponding observations for the target field. The coefficients obtained from a linear regression model can be indicative of how similarities in different fields influence similarity in the target field.

3   Experiments on Contextual Search

In this section, we report experiments conducted to assess the efficacy of our proposed approach in finding the "right" context in order to maximize relevance of recommendations. As discussed in Section 2, when seeking recommendations for a *target* case field, we weigh the query clauses created from the contents of other fields by their respective

---

[2] Not to be confused with the multi-variate statistical technique with the same name that summarizes categorical data in a two dimensional graphical format

[3] http://en.wikipedia.org/wiki/Cosine_similarity

[4] http://en.wikipedia.org/wiki/Euclidean_distance

Correspondence scores with the target case field. Our experiments measure the usefulness of such a weighting in improving relevance of recommendations over a baseline approach where equal weights are assigned to each clause in the contextual query.

3.1 Experimental Set-Up

In our experiments, we use a case corpus of 715 case models cataloged from information created during sales engagements at a large IT services company. Each case model was created by aggregating information about a single deal from three different databases within the company. The schema for our integrated case models consisted of 314 fields of different types (*e.g.,* categorical, text, numeric, dates). However, not all case models had all 314 fields; in fact most of them were sparsely populated. For the purposes of our experiments, we choose *Risks* and *Assumptions* as the two target fields for which we generate recommendations. Both of these fields are free text fields; often their contents are organized as a bulleted list of items, sometimes even over a hundred items in a single case. Such lists of *Risks* and *Assumptions* are particularly useful to conduct quality assurance reviews and are a necessary input for crafting clauses in the legal contract when closing a deal.

Competing Approaches: We investigate the efficacy of two approaches of leveraging context in deriving relevant recommendations for a target field. First, we evaluate a *baseline approach* where we construct query clauses out of the contents all non-empty fields in a case model except the target field. In this approach, the matches for all the query clauses are weighed equally while generating recommendations. Second, we apply the *weighted approach*, where we create query clauses from a select set of fields that have a high correspondence score with the target fields. Further, the query clauses are weighed in proportion to the correspondence scores of the respective fields.

Generating Recommendations: We randomly select 8 case models from the case corpus where the fields, *Risks* and *Assumptions* are non-empty. For each case, we construct two queries following the two approaches described above. We execute the queries with Apache Lucene to obtain a ranked list of case models in the corpus with similar contexts. Finally, we retrieve the contents of the target fields in the result case models and present them to an expert who assigns relevance judgments as described below.

Judging Relevance: Judging relevance of a recommendation is hard for anyone who is not actually involved in the case and getting time from case workers to run controlled experiments is always a challenge. However, we manage to work around this issue in the following manner. Note that the case models from which queries were created already have the target fields filled up, so we can use their contents as *ground truth*. Now, the task of comparing two items is much easier than deciding the relevance of a recommendation to a given context. Thus, we ask an expert user who understands the vocabulary of the case domain to compare the recommendation results obtained for a query with its ground truth. The expert chooses one of the 3 labels for each recommendation—*0 : "Not Related"; 1 : "Somewhat Related", 2 : "Related"*. If there is an exact match of any *Risk* or *Assumption* item listed in the recommendation to any item in the ground truth, then it is labeled as "2". If there is some topical match, then the recommendation

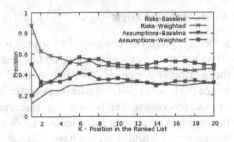

Field	Baseline		Weighted	
	nDCG	P@20	nDCG	P@20
Risks	0.504	0.312	0.668	0.456
Assumption	0.57	0.325	0.688	0.49
Overall	0.535	0.318	0.678	0.473

Fig. 5. Summary of Results   **Fig. 6.** Precision@K

is marked as "1". Such a labeling strategy helped us collect relevance judgments for each of the top 20 recommendation results derived for the two competing approaches across eight queries for the two chosen target fields; totaling to 640 judgments.

Collecting Metrics: The relevance judgments are used to compute two metrics: *Precision@K* and *Normalized Discounted Cumulative Gain (nDCG)*. For computing precision, a relevance label of 0 is considered irrelevant, labels of 1 and 2 are considered relevant. Now, *Precision@K* is defined as the fraction of relevant results for the top-K ranked recommendations. *nDCG* [8] is often used as a measure for evaluating a ranked list with multiple relevance levels. The premise behind Discounted Cumulative Gain (DCG) is that highly relevant documents appearing lower in a search result list should be penalized as the graded relevance value is reduced logarithmically proportional to the position of the result. For a judgment vector of length p, we compute DCG_p as follows:

$$DCG_p = \sum_{i=1}^{p} \frac{2^{rel_i} - 1}{log_2(i + 1)}$$

Next, we re-compute DCG_p after sorting the judgment vector and call it Ideal DCG ($IDCG_p$). Finally, $nDCG$ for the judgment vector is defined as DCG_p expressed as a fraction of $IDCG_p$.

3.2 Experimental Results

Figure 5 summarizes the metrics *nDCG* and *Precision@20* as observed for the two competing approaches on our dataset. For *Risks*, the *weighted* approach records an improvement of 16.4% in *nDCG* and 14.4% in Precision@20 over the *baseline* approach. For *Assumptions*, we find increases of 11.8% and 16.5% in *nDCG* and Precision@20 respectively. Thus, on average, across the two case fields, both metrics show an improvement of $\approx$ 15%. Figure 6 plots the values of *Precision@K* for K = 1 through 20 for the two approaches, *baseline* and *weighted*. For the recommendations on *Risks*, the values of *Precision@K* for the *weighted* approach are are consistently higher than those recorded by the *baseline* approach. For *Assumptions*, the curve for the weighted approach is seen to be lagging at K=1,2 but then it surges ahead and thereafter leads the baseline's curve. These results clearly indicate that an intelligent weighting of the different fields in context can improve the relevance of recommendations and that *Correspondence Analysis* can be a viable approach for choosing the weights.

4   Related Work

Recently, there has been a lot of research on Adaptive Case Management and Social BPM technologies for handling ad hoc business processes [23,13,22,21,10]. However, these efforts have largely focused on developing better case modeling techniques to enhance the level of collaboration between case workers in order to increase the throughput of case processing. We believe that research in case management should also attend to the problem of serving information needs of case workers since cases often get stalled because case workers do not have adequate information. Our work is a first step in this direction.

In the past, reuse of business process information, including formal models and implementation artifacts; has found interest in the BPM community [24]. RepoX [19] and MIT Process Handbook [11] allow storage of business process models with free text search and structured search capabilities. Our past work [6] introduced the notion of contextual search and demonstrated its benefit for requirement gathering activities in SAP engagements. This paper improves upon [6] in the following ways. Unlike the work in [6] that only dealt with textual artifacts, the approach presented in this paper can infer an appropriate weighting of context with different types of fields—text, numeric and categorical. Further, the computation of the strength of an associative relationship between two fields in [6] ignored the influence of other case fields; we address this limitation through the multi-variate modeling in *Correspondence Analysis*. Moreover in [6], the results were not evaluated with the help of relevance judgments from experts. Related work in other academic communities include the literature on Knowledge Management [14,12,3] and research on *Case Based Reasoning* [2,17].

5   Conclusions and Future Work

The SIM tool is being actively used in the *Opportunity-To-Order* process at a large IT Services company and has received positive feedback from its users. They believe that this domain-specific knowledge management system delivers much more precise and contextual results than the enterprise-wide search system they used before. The users suggest that the tool reduces dependencies on personal networks and and yields significant productivity improvements as it jump-starts the case work with relevant information. In this paper, we present a controlled experiment to evaluate the efficacy of a key aspect of our system–generating preferentially weighted contextual queries. Future work can look at design of experiments to study the holistic effect of SIM on knowledge worker productivity. Also, we are currently extending our solution along a number of dimensions to deliver more precise recommendations and enrich the user experience for case workers. Our on-going efforts include: construction of large graphs that link information from different sources, development of stocastic graph inference techniques to answer queries on the graphs and a cognitive system to parse natural language queries.

References

1. Case Management - Combining Knowledge with Process, http://bit.ly/cErahE (accessed: May 29, 2013)
2. Aamodt, A., Plaza, E.: Case-based reasoning: Foundational issues, methodological variations, and system approaches. AI Communications 7(1), 39–59 (1994)

3. Alavi, M., Leidner, D.E.: Knowledge management and knowledge management systems: Conceptual foundations and research issues. MIS Quarterly 25(1), 107–136 (2001)
4. Carbonell, J., Goldstein, J.: The use of mmr, diversity-based reranking for reordering documents and producing summaries. In: Proceedings of the 21st Annual International ACM SIGIR Conference on Research and Development in Information Retrieval, pp. 335–336. ACM (1998)
5. Feldman, S., Sherman, C.: The high cost of not finding information. Information Today Inc. (2004)
6. Gupta, M., Mukherjee, D., Mani, S., Sinha, V.S., Sinha, S.: Serving information needs in business process consulting. In: Rinderle-Ma, S., Toumani, F., Wolf, K. (eds.) BPM 2011. LNCS, vol. 6896, pp. 231–247. Springer, Heidelberg (2011)
7. IDC. Quantifying Enterprise Search (2002)
8. Järvelin, K., Kekäläinen, J.: Cumulated gain-based evaluation of ir techniques. ACM Trans. Inf. Syst. 20(4), 422–446 (2002)
9. Kim, J., Xue, X., Croft, W.B.: A probabilistic retrieval model for semistructured data. In: Boughanem, M., Berrut, C., Mothe, J., Soule-Dupuy, C. (eds.) ECIR 2009. LNCS, vol. 5478, pp. 228–239. Springer, Heidelberg (2009)
10. Liptchinsky, V., Khazankin, R., Truong, H.-L., Dustdar, S.: A novel approach to modeling context-aware and social collaboration processes. In: Ralyté, J., Franch, X., Brinkkemper, S., Wrycza, S. (eds.) CAiSE 2012. LNCS, vol. 7328, pp. 565–580. Springer, Heidelberg (2012)
11. Malone, T.W., Crowston, K., Herman, G.A.: Organizing business knowledge. MIT Press (2003)
12. McDermott, R.: Why information technology inspired but cannot deliver knowledge management. California Management Review 41(4), 103–117 (1999)
13. Motahari-Nezhad, H.R., Bartolini, C., Graupner, S., Spence, S.: Adaptive case management in the social enterprise. In: Liu, C., Ludwig, H., Toumani, F., Yu, Q. (eds.) ICSOC 2012. LNCS, vol. 7636, pp. 550–557. Springer, Heidelberg (2012)
14. Nonaka, I.: A dynamic theory of organizational knowledge creation. Organization Science
15. Osiriski, S., Stefanowski, J., Weiss, D.: Lingo: Search results clustering algorithm based on singular value decomposition. In: Proceedings of the Intelligent Information Processing and Web Mining, IIPWM, vol. 4, pp. 359–368 (2004)
16. Reinhardt, W., Schmidt, B., Sloep, P., Drachsler, H.: Knowledge Worker Roles and Actions: Results of Two Empirical Studies. Knowledge and Process Management 18(3), 150–174 (2011)
17. Rissland, E.L., Daniels, J.J.: A hybrid cbr-ir approach to legal information retrieval. In: Proceedings of the Fifth International Conference on Artificial Intelligence and Law (ICAIL)
18. Robertson, S., Zaragoza, H., Taylor, M.: Simple bm25 extension to multiple weighted fields. In: Proceedings of the Thirteenth ACM International Conference on Information and Knowledge Management, pp. 42–49. ACM (2004)
19. Song, M., Miller, J.A., Arpinar, I.B.: Repox: An xml repository for workflow designs and specifications. PhD thesis, Citeseer (2001)
20. Swenson, K.D.: Mastering the Unpredictable. Meghan-Kiffer Press (2010)
21. Swenson, K.D., Palmer, N., Kemsley, S., et al.: Social BPM. Future Strategies Inc. (2011)
22. Swenson, K.D., Palmer, N., et al.: How Knowledge Workers Get Things Done. Future Strategies Inc. (2012)
23. Van der Aalst, W.M., Weske, M., Grünbauer, D.: Case handling: a new paradigm for business process support. Data & Knowledge Engineering 53(2), 129–162 (2005)
24. Yan, Z., Dijkman, R., Grefen, P.: Business process model repositories–framework and survey. Information and Software Technology 54(4), 380–395 (2012)
25. Mukherjee, D., et al.: A Case Based Approach to Serve Information Need. Knowledge Intensive Processes. IBM Technical Report (2013)

Patience-Aware Scheduling for Cloud Services: Freeing Users from the Chains of Boredom[*]

Carlos Cardonha[1], Marcos D. Assunção[1], Marco A.S. Netto[1],
Renato L.F. Cunha[1], and Carlos Queiroz[2]

[1] IBM Research Brazil
[2] IBM Research Australia

Abstract. Scheduling of service requests in Cloud computing has traditionally focused on the reduction of pre-service wait, generally termed as waiting time. Under certain conditions such as peak load, however, it is not always possible to give reasonable response times to all users. This work explores the fact that different users may have their own levels of tolerance or patience with response delays. We introduce scheduling strategies that produce better assignment plans by prioritising requests from users who expect to receive results earlier and by postponing servicing jobs from those who are more tolerant to response delays. Our analytical results show that the behaviour of users' patience plays a key role in the evaluation of scheduling techniques, and our computational evaluation demonstrates that, under peak load, the new algorithms typically provide better user experience than the traditional FIFO strategy.

1 Introduction

Traditionally, job schedulers do not take into account how users interact with services. They optimise system metrics, such as resource utilisation and energy consumption, and user metrics such as response time. However, understanding interactions between users and a service provider over time allows for custom optimisations that bring benefits for both parties.

In this article we propose scheduling strategies that take into account users' expectations regarding response time and their patience when interacting with Cloud services. Such strategies are relevant mainly to handle peak load conditions without the need to allocate additional resources for the service provider. Although elasticity is common in a Cloud setting, resources may not be available quickly enough and their allocation can incur additional costs that may be avoidable. The main contributions of this paper are: (i) a **Patience-Aware Scheduling (PAS)** strategy and an **Expectation-Aware Scheduling (EAS)** strategy for Cloud systems; (ii) Analytical comparisons between the **EAS** strategy and the traditional **First-In, First-Out (FIFO)** scheduling strategy; (iii) Evaluation of the proposed strategies and a discussion on when they bring benefits for users and service providers.

---

[*] Extended version of this paper is available at `arxiv.org`

S. Basu et al. (Eds.): ICSOC 2013, LNCS 8274, pp. 550–557, 2013.

2   Proposed Scheduling Strategies

This work considers Cloud services that support applications running on mobile devices and desktops, most of which are highly interactive and iterative. Service performance over time usually shapes the users' expectations on how it is likely to perform in the future. The provider stores information on how its service responded to user requests and uses this information to gauge her expectations and patience.

PAS and **EAS** utilise user expectation to schedule service requests. Both strategies share the following common goals: (i) minimise the number of users abandoning the service; (ii) maximise the users' level of happiness with the service; and (iii) perform such optimisations without adding new resources to the service. An incoming job request will be directly assigned if there are available resources in the service provider. Therefore, choosing among **FIFO**, **PAS**, and **EAS** becomes more crucial during peak load.

PAS has the goal of serving first users whose patience levels are the lowest when interacting with the Cloud service. When new requests arrive, the algorithm sorts the tasks in its waiting queue according to the *Patience* of their users (in ascending order), and when a new resource is freed, the request positioned in the head of the waiting list is assigned to it. An adequate estimate of how the user's happiness level and the user's tolerance curves behave is very important for the evaluation of the proposed strategies. In our implementation of **PAS** and in our computational evaluation, we employed the definition of Brown *et al.* [6], where patience is given by the ratio of the time a user expects to wait for results to the time the user actually waits for them.

EAS has the goal of serving first requests from users whose response time expectations are translated into "soft" deadlines that are positioned earlier in time. The difference between **EAS** and traditional deadline-based algorithms lies in the nature of the "buffer" adding to the minimum response time, as it changes over time and is related to users' patience. **EAS** sorts service requests in the waiting queue according to their users' expectation, which is the sum of arrival time and expected response time, where *arrival time* is the time at which the job arrived on the waiting queue and *expected response time* is the time that the service provider need to complete the task. **EAS**, then, schedules the job with the least *expectation* when a new resource is freed.

2.1   Analytical Investigation of the EAS Strategy

Let $\mathcal{U}$ be the set of users of a service provider. Let $\mathcal{T}$ denote the sequence of job requests being submitted, where each $t \in \mathcal{T}$ arrives at time $a(t) \in \mathbb{R}^+$ and has processing time $\Delta(t) \in \mathbb{R}$. Task t is submitted by user $u(t)$, who is expecting to wait an amount of time $w(u(t)) \in \mathbb{N}$ in addition to $\Delta(t)$, *i.e.*, $w(u)$ denotes u's tolerance with response delays. The service provider has a dispatching algorithm responsible for the assignment of each incoming task to one of its m processors.

Let us denote by $s(t) \in \mathbb{R}^+$ the time at which task t starts to be processed. The response time for task t is given by $r(t) = (s(t) - a(t)) + \Delta(t)$, and $e(u(t), t) =$

$r(t) - (\Delta(t) + w(u(t)))$ denotes the amount of time by which the response time differs from $u(t)$'s original expectation.

We denote user u's level of happiness by $h(u) \in [0, 1]$, a linear scale where $h(u) = 0$ and $h(u) = 1$ indicates that u is absolutely discontent and happy, respectively. We assume that u stops sending requests as soon as $h(u)$ is below some critical value $c(u)$ in $[0, 1]$. User u is active if $h(u) > c(u)$. The impact that $e(u, t)$ has on $h(u)$ is formulated by function $i : \mathcal{U} \times \mathbb{R} \to \mathbb{R}$, and the impact that $e(u, t)$ has on $w(u)$ is described by some function $j : \mathcal{U} \times \mathcal{T} \times \mathbb{R} \to \mathbb{R}$. If we assume that $i(u, e(u, t))$ and $j(u, t, e(u, t))$ are addictive factors, then, after the computation of some task t, the happiness level of user $u(t)$ will be given by $h(u) + i(u, e(u, t))$, while $u(t)$'s patience level becomes $w(u(t)) + j(u(t), t, e(u(t), t))$.

Optimisation Criteria. Let Z denote the closed interval $[0, 1] \subset \mathbb{R}$. We say that a vector $s \in Z^{|\mathcal{U}|}$ denotes a service provider's *user happiness state* if $s_x = h(u_x)$ $\forall u_x \in \mathcal{U}$, $1 \le x \le \mathcal{U}$. In order to evaluate and compare different scheduling strategies, we have to define a cost function $c : Z^{|\mathcal{U}|} \to \mathbb{R}$. The definition of a proper cost function depends on the optimisation criteria one wants to establish. We will consider two optimisation goals. The first one is the *maximisation of the overall happiness of users*, where service providers should try to reach states $s \in Z^{|\mathcal{U}|}$ of maximal L^1-norm. The other criteria consists of the *maximisation of active users*, where service providers try to keep as many active users as possible. Formally, a state $s \in Z^{|\mathcal{U}|}$ satisfying this second goal is associated to a vector $s' \in Z^{|\mathcal{U}|}$ such that $s'_x = s_x$ if $s_x \ge c(u_x)$, $s'_x = 0$ otherwise, and $\|s'\|_0$ is maximal.

Batch Requests. We consider initially how scheduling strategies affect the user happiness states when we take into account a single batch of job requests. We assume here that each user submits a single request, and therefore we do not investigate variations of $w(u)$. The optimisation criteria in this section will be the L^1-norm of the user happiness state vector. Let us consider the family of scenarios where each task in $\mathcal{T}$ consumes time Δ, and let $t_x, t_y \in \mathcal{T}$ be such that $x + m < y$ and $a(t_x) + w(u_x) > a(t_y) + w(u_y)$.

If **FIFO** is employed, the scheduling plan P will have each request t serviced according to arriving time $a(t)$. In particular, t_x will be processed before t_y according to P and in different moments in time (i.e., they will not be serviced in parallel).

For the same sequence $\mathcal{T}$, because $a(t_x) + w(u_x) > a(t_y) + w(u_y)$, **EAS** would invert the order in which tasks t_x and t_y are processed, so let us consider the plan P' that is almost equal to P, having only the positions of t_x and t_y exchanged. Because all the tasks consume the same amount of time, it is clear that we can transform plan P into plan P^* that would be generated by **EAS** if we apply the same exchange technique sequentially until every pair of requests is positioned accordingly.

Let s and s' be the user happiness state vectors of p after the execution of plans P and P', respectively, and let f_x and f_y be the times at which t_x and t_y have their processing tasks finished according to plan P, respectively (*i.e.*, $f_x < f_y$). Let us refer to $e(t_x)$ and $e(t_y)$ as $e^1(t_x)$ and $e^1(t_y)$ for **FIFO**, respectively, and as $e^2(t_x)$ and $e^2(t_y)$ for **EAS**, respectively.

Finally, let $q_{x,y} : \mathbb{R} \times \mathbb{R} \to \mathbb{R}$ be the function parameterized by $e(t_x)$ and $e(t_y)$ denoting the sum of the changes in the happiness levels of users u_x and u_y after tasks t_x and t_y have been serviced, respectively. It is clear that $q_{x,y}$ depends on the behaviour of i.

Proposition 1. *If $q_{x,y}$ is always the same $\forall x, y \in \mathcal{U}$, is monotonic, and respects exactly one of the following scenarios, then it is possible to decide if either* **EAS** *or* **FIFO** *yields a plan resulting in a user happiness state s with maximal* $||s||_1$:

- $f_{x,y}(a,b) \geq f_{x,y}(c,d)$ *whenever* $|a| + |b| \geq |c| + |d|$; *or*
- $f_{x,y}(a,b) \leq f_{x,y}(c,d)$ *whenever* $|a| + |b| \geq |c| + |d|$; *or*
- $f_{x,y}(a,b) = f_{x,y}(c,d)$ *whenever* $|a| + |b| \geq |c| + |d|$.

Proof. Simple inspection shows that $a(t_x)+\Delta+w(u_x)$, $a(t_y)+\Delta+w(u_y)$, f_x, and f_y can appear in six different relative ordering schemes (e.g., $a_y + \Delta + w(u_y) < a_x+\Delta+w(u_x) < f_x < f_y$ is one of them)[1]. Moreover, one can also see that $e^1(t_x)+e^1(t_y) = e^2(t_x) + e^2(t_y)$ and that $max(e^1(t_x), e^1(t_y)) > max(e^2(t_x), e^2(t_y))$ in each of these cases. Therefore, we have $|e^1(t_x)| + |e^1(t_y)| \geq |e^2(t_x)| + |e^2(t_y)|$.

Based on these observations and on our hypothesis, we have the following situations:

- if $f_{x,y}(a,b) \geq f_{x,y}(c,d)$ whenever $|a| + |b| \geq |c| + |d|$, then $c(s) \geq c(s')$;
- if $f_{x,y}(a,b) \leq f_{x,y}(c,d)$ whenever $|a| + |b| \geq |c| + |d|$, then $c(s) \leq c(s')$; and
- if $f_{x,y}(a,b) = f_{x,y}(c,d)$ whenever $|a| + |b| \geq |c| + |d|$, then $c(s) = c(s')$.

Therefore, P' is better than, equal to, or worse than P if $f_{x,y}$ has the first, the second, or the third property, respectively.

Finally, if we assume that $f_{x,y}$ is always the same $\forall x, y$ in $\mathcal{U}$, the resulting user happiness state associated to P^* is better than, equal to, or worse than P if $f_{x,y}$ has the first, the second, or the third property, respectively. $\square$

Other propositions comparing the proposed and **FIFO** strategies are presented in the extended version of the paper [7].

3   Evaluation

A discrete event simulator was used to evaluate the performance of the scheduling strategies. To model the load of a Cloud service, we crafted three types of workloads with variable numbers of users over a 24-hour period: normal day, flat day, and peaky day. More detail on the workloads is given in the extended version of this work [7].

For each workload we vary the number of resources used by the Cloud service, thus allowing for evaluating the system under different stress levels. When using the system, a user makes a request and waits for its results before making a new

---

[1] Recall that $a(t_x) + \Delta + w(u_x)$ is already defined as greater than $a(t_y) + \Delta + w(u_y)$.

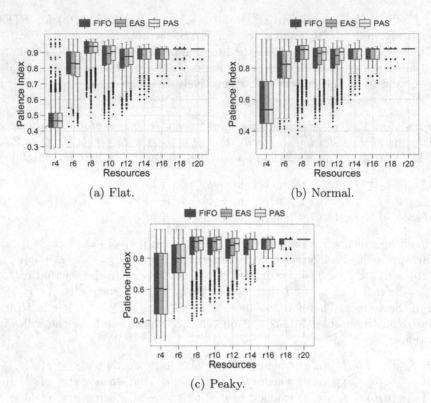

(a) Flat.

(b) Normal.

(c) Peaky.

Fig. 1. Patience index under different workloads

request, with a think time between receiving results and making another request uniformly distributed between 0 and 100 seconds. To facilitate the analysis and comparison among the techniques, the length of jobs is constant (10 seconds).

Previous interactions with the service are used to build a user's expectation on how the service should respond, and how quickly a request should be processed. The model that defines a user's expectation on the response time of a request uses two moving averages, (i) an Exponential Weighted Moving Average (EWMA) of the previous 20 response times, with $\alpha = 0.8$; and (ii) an average of the past 4 response times, used to eliminate outliers. When a request completes, if the response time is 30% below the average of the past 4 response times, then the EWMA is not updated, though the value is considered in future iterations. In essence, this model states that the user expects the service to behave similar to previous interactions, with a higher weight to more recent requests. Even though changes in response time affect the user's perception of the service, she disregards large deviations in service quality; unless they become common. As we believe that in real conditions, users would not correctly average their past response times (*i.e.* they may not recall past experiences well) we add a tolerance of 20% to the estimate of response time provided by the model.

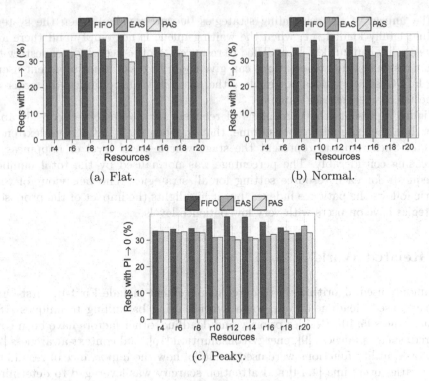

(a) Flat.   (b) Normal.

(c) Peaky.

Fig. 2. Percentage of requests whose patience index tends to 0

Users patience thresholds—*i.e.* the maximum response time that she considers acceptable—is randomly selected between 40 seconds and 60 seconds. The provider tracks how it served previous requests made by a user and users the same model described above to compute an estimate of what it believes the user's expectation to be. 60 seconds is also what the provider considers to be the maximum acceptable response time that satisfies the service users. However, for **EAS** and **PAS**, if a request's response is above 60 seconds, the EWMA is updated with 40 seconds, which may give the user priority the next time she submits a request. It is a way the scheduler finds to penalise itself for yielding a response time too far from what it believes the user's expectation to be.

Figure 1 depicts the Patience Indexes (as defined in Section 2) of requests when below 1.0 for flat, normal, and peaky workloads. The lower the values the more unhappy the users. We observe that for high and low system load (*i.e.* r4–6 and r16–20), all strategies perform similarly, whereas for the other loads **PAS** and **EAS** produce higher Patience Indexes than **FIFO**. Under high loads, most requests are completed after the expected response time, thus not allowing the scheduler to exchange the order of the requests in the waiting queue in subsequent task submissions. On the other hand, a very light system contains a short (or empty) waiting queue; hence not having requests to be sorted.

The impact of the scheduling strategies becomes evident when the system is almost fully loaded, *i.e.* when the waiting queue is not empty and there are requests that can quickly be assigned to resources. In this scenario, requests with longer response time expectations can give room to tasks from impatient users. The **FIFO** strategy does not explore the possibility of modifying the order of requests considering user patience.

Figure 2 presents the percentage of requests that were served considerably later than the expected response time, that is, when their Patience Index tends to zero. Such requests represent the stage where users' level of happiness is decreasing considerably. The percentage was normalised by the total number of requests for each resource setting for all strategies. The behaviour of this metric follows the patience indexes, but it highlights the impact of the proposed strategies have on users with very low patience levels.

4   Related Work

Commonly used algorithms in resource management include First-In First-Out, priority-based, deadline-driven, some hybrids using backfilling techniques [18], among others [5,10]. Besides priority and deadline, other factors have been considered, such as fairness [9], energy-consumption [16], and context-awareness [2]. Moreover, utility functions were used to model how the importance of results to users varies over time [4,14] and attention scarcity was leveraged to determine priority of service requests in the Cloud [15].

User behaviour has been explored for optimising resource management in the context of Web caching and page pre-fetching [1,3,8,11]. The goal is to understand how users access web pages, investigate their tolerance level on delays, and pre-fetch or modify page content to enhance user experience. Techniques in this area focus mostly on web content and minimising response time of user requests.

Service research has also investigated the impact of delays on users' behaviour. For instance, Taylor [17] described the concept of delays and surveyed passengers affected by delayed flights to test their hypotheses. Brown et al. [6] and Gans et al. [12] investigated the impact of service delays in call centres. In behavioural economics, Kahneman and Tversky [13] introduced prospect theory to model how people make choices in situations that involve risk or uncertainty.

5   Conclusions

We presented **PAS** and **EAS** that use estimates on users' level of tolerance or patience to define the order in which resources are assigned to requests. Our analysis identified that it is not trivial to choose between **EAS** and **FIFO** as the quality of their schedules depends strongly on users' happiness with a service and tolerance to delays. Our computational evaluation shows that both **PAS** and **EAS** perform better than **FIFO** under peak load scenarios, and that **PAS** is slightly better than **EAS**.

References

1. Alt, F., Sahami Shirazi, A., Schmidt, A., Atterer, R.: Bridging waiting times on web pages. In: 14th Int. Conf. on Human-computer Interaction with Mobile Devices and Services (MobileHCI 2012), pp. 305–308. ACM, New York (2012)
2. Assunção, M.D., et al.: Context-aware job scheduling for cloud computing environments. In: 5th IEEE Int. Conf. on Utility and Cloud Computing, UCC (2012)
3. Atterer, R., Wnuk, M., Schmidt, A.: Knowing the user's every move: user activity tracking for website usability evaluation and implicit interaction. In: 15th Int. Conf. on World Wide Web (WWW 2006), pp. 203–212. ACM, New York (2006)
4. AuYoung, A., et al.: Service contracts and aggregate utility functions. In: 15th IEEE Int. Symp. on High Performance Distributed Computing, HPDC 2006 (2006)
5. Braun, T.D., Siegel, H.J., Beck, N., Bölöni, L.L., Maheswaran, M., Reuther, A.I., Robertson, J.P., Theys, M.D., Yao, B., Hensgen, D., et al.: A comparison of eleven static heuristics for mapping a class of independent tasks onto heterogeneous distributed computing systems. Journal of Parallel and Distributed Computing 61(6), 810–837 (2001)
6. Brown, L., Gans, N., Mandelbaum, A., Sakov, A., Shen, H., Zeltyn, S., Zhao, L.: Statistical analysis of a telephone call center: A queueing-science perspective. Journal of the American Statistical Association 100, 36–50 (2005)
7. Cardonha, C., et al.: Patience-aware scheduling for cloud services: Freeing users from the chains of boredom. arXiv preprint cs/1308.4166 (2013)
8. Cunha, C.R., Jaccoud, C.F.B.: Determining www user's next access and its application to pre-fetching. In: 2nd IEEE Symp. on Computers and Communications (ISCC 1997), Washington, DC, USA, p. 6 (1997)
9. Doulamis, N.D., Doulamis, A.D., Varvarigos, E.A., Varvarigou, T.A.: Fair scheduling algorithms in grids. IEEE Transactions on Parallel and Distributed Systems 18(11), 1630–1648 (2007)
10. Feitelson, D.G., Rudolph, L., Schwiegelshohn, U., Sevcik, K.C., Wong, P.: Theory and practice in parallel job scheduling. In: Feitelson, D.G., Rudolph, L. (eds.) IPPS-WS 1997 and JSSPP 1997. LNCS, vol. 1291, pp. 1–34. Springer, Heidelberg (1997)
11. Galletta, D.F., Henry, R.M., McCoy, S., Polak, P.: Web site delays: How tolerant are users? Journal of the Association for Information Systems 5(1), 1–28 (2004)
12. Gans, N., Koole, G., Mandelbaum, A.: Telephone call centers: Tutorial, review, and research prospects. Manufacturing & Service Operations Management 5(2), 79–141 (2003)
13. Kahneman, D., Tversky, A.: Prospect theory: An analysis of decision under risk. Econometrica: Journal of the Econometric Society, 263–291 (1979)
14. Precise and Realistic Utility Functions for User-Centric Performance Analysis of Schedulers (2007)
15. Netto, M.A.S., Assunção, M.D., Bianchi, S.: Leveraging attention scarcity to improve the overall user experience of cloud services. In: Proceedings of the IFIP 9th International Conference on Network and Service Management, CNSM 2013 (2013)
16. Pineau, J.F., Robert, Y., Vivien, F.: Energy-aware scheduling of bag-of-tasks applications on master–worker platforms. Concurrency and Computation: Practice and Experience 23(2), 145–157 (2011)
17. Taylor, S.: Waiting for service: the relationship between delays and evaluations of service. The Journal of Marketing, 56–69 (1994)
18. Tsafrir, D., Etsion, Y., Feitelson, D.G.: Backfilling using system-generated predictions rather than user runtime estimates. IEEE Transactions on Parallel and Distributed Systems 18(6), 789–803 (2007)

MaxInsTx: A Best-Effort Failure Recovery Approach for Artifact-Centric Business Processes

Haihuan Qin, Guosheng Kang, and Lipeng Guo

School of Computer Science, Fudan University, China
{09110240015,12110240015,10110240002}@fudan.edu.cn

Abstract. Process instances may overlap and interweave with each other. This significantly complicates the failure recovery issue. Most of existing mechanisms assume a one-to-one relationship between process instances, which will cause unnecessary recovery in such context. Artifact-centric business process models give equal consideration on both data and control flow of activities, thus facilitate addressing this issue. In this paper, we propose a best-effort failure recovery approach MaxInsTx: a transactional artifact-centric business process model with complex cardinality relationships and correlations considered; a recovery mechanism to resolve the impact of the failed process on concurrent processes meanwhile protect maximal instances involved in failures from failure impact.

1   Introduction

Business processes (BPs) have become a necessity for modern organizations to stay competitive. In real life, instances of one BP may be split or merged into instances of another BP due to business needs [1-3]. For example, an online shop, acting as a broker, may divide its orders into multiple purchase orders, one pur supplier, and merge items of (different) orders from the same supplier into one purchase order for bulk purchases, as shown in Fig.1. The cardinality between order process and purchase order process is many-to-many and correlations among their instances are complex. We call such scenarios relevant business scenarios. The fabric instances complicates problems and attracts increasing attention [1-3]. No works has been done on the recovery issue yet.

Most of existing workflow transactions simply assume a one-to-one relationship between BP instances (e.g., [4]), and resolve the impact of a failed BP on concurrent BPs through handling dirty reads and dirty writes [5]. Once a failed BP is recovered, all side effects of its committed tasks are semantically undone. However, in the context of relevant business scenario, such recovery is an "over-recovery" and no longer applicable.

Fig.2 illustrates a relevant business scenario for an online store represented by artifact-centric BP models. This modeling language is used since business data and runtime data gathered in artifacts facilitate modeling instance level correlation [3].

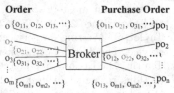

Fig. 1. A relevant business scenario

S. Basu et al. (Eds.): ICSOC 2013, LNCS 8274, pp. 558–566, 2013.

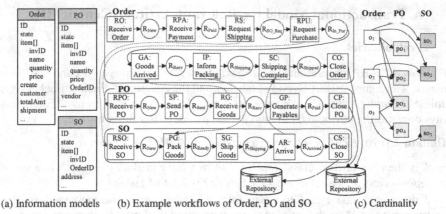

(a) Information models   (b) Example workflows of Order, PO and SO   (c) Cardinality

Fig. 2. Workflows involved in the online store example and cardinality between them

Three (key) artifacts are involved: *Order*, *Purchase Order (PO)* and *Ship Order (SO)*. Fig. 2(a) shows their information models and Fig. 2(b) their workflows. Attributes of an artifact can be simple or relation-typed (denoted by "[]") with nested attributes. Once receiving a customer order, the store initiates an *Order*. After receiving payment, the *Order* create a *PO* by sending a message to *RPO*, and its task *GA* cannot be initiated until receives the message from *PO*, i.e., there exist creation and synchronization (sync for short) dependencies between instances of *Order* and *PO*. An *Order* may create multiple *POs*, one pur supplier, meanwhile multiple *Orders* may be merged into one *PO* for bulk purchases. Similar splitting and merge exist among *Orders* and *SOs*. The relationships between these artifacts are m-to-m, as shown in Fig. 2(c), and nested attribute *OrderID* contained in *PO* (or *SO*) indicates correlations among them.

Several issues are worthy of attention. First, creation dependencies cannot be covered by traditional transactions. For example, an *Order* o_1 creates a *PO* po_1, po_1 should be rolled back when o_1 is canceled, which is similar to dirty reads problem [5]. However, if po_1 is rolled back for items are out of stock, o_1 also needs to be recovered for it cannot be accomplished. Second, it is too costly to recover all dependent artifacts of a failed artifact when dependencies can be m-to-m. For example, if o_1 is canceled, po_1, po_2 and po_3 will be affected and recovered, however, the entire recovery of po_2 and po_3 will further cause other normal cases o_2 and o_3 to be affected and recovered. To avoid such over-recovery, the affected parts of po_2 and po_3 need to be identified, and fixed (i.e., partially rolled back) without affecting o_2 and o_3 as well as their purchases.

To solve above questions, we propose a best-effort failure recovery approach *MaxInsTx* and make two contributions: (1) we develop a transactional artifact-centric BP model with creation dependencies considered and cardinality types of dependencies distinguished; (2) we propose an approach to resolve the impact of the failed BP on concurrent BPs, avoiding unnecessary recoveries through overlap evaluation.

This paper is organized as follows. The transactional model and the failure recovery mechanism are presented in Section 2 and 3 (resp.). Section 4 discusses effectiveness and feasibility. Section 5 discusses related work and Section 6 concludes this paper.

2   A Transactional Model for Relevant Artifact-Centric BPs

2.1   Preliminaries

In EZFlow [6], a BP is represented by *artifact classes*, *tasks*, *repositories* and *workflow schemas*, with a core artifact carrying both data and the enactment. Each artifact class is a tuple $A = (name, Atts)$, where *name* is its name, *Atts* is a set of attributes. Each class always contains the attribute *ID* to hold the unique identifier of its instances.

Definition 2.1: An *EZFlow* schema is a tuple $(C, \Gamma, R, M, T, F, G)$, where

- C is the *core* artifact class, Γ is a set of *auxiliary* artifact classes; R is a set of repositories; M is a set of message types; T is a set of tasks;
- F maps each task t in T to a pair $(m_i; M_o)$, where m_i is the message type that triggers t and M_o is the set of message types produced by t. Each message type is produced by at most one task and can be used to trigger at most one task;
- G is a set of triples (u, v, g) where (1) either $u \in R$ and $v \in T$ or $u \in T$ and $v \in R$; and (2) g is a guard on the edge (u, v).

EZFlow uses *snapshots* to represent the system state of a workflow at time instants, which contains tables for artifact classes, workflow enactments, etc. A workflow moves from one *snapshot* to another when an external message arrives or a triggered task completes its execution, evolving the artifact along its lifecycle. The enactment of a workflow is an alternating sequence of system states and tasks $s_0 t_0 s_1 t_1 .. t_{n-1} s_n$ such that s_0 is the initial state and each s_{i+1} is derived from s_i through t_i $(0 \le i < n)$.

2.2   Correlations and Dependencies of Artifacts

Correlations combine individual BPs into relevant business scenarios. We use a *correlation graph* to present correlations between artifacts. Correlation conditions are defined by projection operation π and intersection predicate $\sqcap$. The projection $\pi_{A_1,...,A_n}(\alpha)$ restricts artifact α to its attributes set $\{A_1, ..., A_n\}$. The predicate $\sqcap$ checks whether two input sets have overlap. If overlap exists, the expression will be true. An atomic correlation condition is an intersection expression applied to projection expressions.

Definition 2.2: A *correlation graph* G is a tuple $(\mathcal{A}, E, \Phi, \kappa)$, where

- $\mathcal{A}$ is a nonempty set of artifacts closed under references (through attributes). Artifacts in $\mathcal{A}$ are called nodes of the graph;
- $E \subseteq \mathcal{A} \times \mathcal{A}$ is a set of edges which denotes correlations among artifacts;
- $\Phi: E \to Con$ is a mapping that assigns each edge a correlation condition, i.e., a set (conjunction) of atomic conditions; and
- $\kappa: E \to Card$ is a mapping from E to $\{1:1, 1:m, m:1, m:m\}$ specifying cardinality relationship between artifacts of source node and end node of an edge.

Above definition adapts the correlation graph in [3] to support *m-to-m* cardinality relationship. Instances of two correlated artifacts are correlated if the correlation condition is true on these instances. For example, suppose correlation condition of *Order* and PO is $con = \pi_{ID,item.invID}(Order) \sqcap \pi_{item.OrderID,item.invID}(PO)$, o_l and po_l are instances of $Order$ and PO, resp., o_l is correlated with po_l if con is true on o_l and po_l.

Only correlated artifacts may exchange messages. Thus, we define messages among artifacts with respect to correlation graph, using "ext" to denote external environment.

Definition 2.3: Given a correlation graph $G = (\mathcal{A}, E, \Phi, \kappa)$, a message type msg among artifacts wrt G is a tuple $(N, Atts, \alpha_s, \alpha_r, \vdash)$, where

- N is a distinct message name; $Atts$ is a set of attributes of the message;
- α_s and α_r denotes the sender and receiver (resp.), satisfying at most one of them can be "ext", and if both are artifacts, they must be correlated;
- $\vdash$ indicates whether the sender creates an instance of the receiving artifact when a message instance arrives, "yes" means creation, "no" means no creation.

Correlated artifacts along with these $msgs$ form a relevant business scenario.

Definition 2.4: A relevant artifact-centric BPs schema RW is a tuple (G, Msg), where G is a correlation graph, and Msg is a set of message types wrt G.

Dependencies exist between two artifacts α_i and α_j if they are correlated. Basically, there are two categories of dependencies: creation dependency and sync dependency. α_j has creation dependency on α_i if α_i contributes to the creation of α_j (i.e., α_i sends a message whose $\vdash$ is "yes" to α_j). α_j has sync dependency on α_i if α_j cannot proceed until the message from α_i arrives (i.e., α_i sends a message whose $\vdash$ is "no" to α_j).

Instance level dependencies are created at runtime. Given instances $I_{\alpha i}$ of α_i and $I_{\alpha j}$ of α_j, we use notations $\alpha_j < I_{\alpha i} >$ and $\alpha_i \ll I_{\alpha j} \gg$ to denote the instances of α_j which are created by $I_{\alpha i}$ and the instances of α_i which contribute to the creation of $I_{\alpha j}$, resp; and $Rv(I_{\alpha i}, msg)$ and $Sd(I_{\alpha j}, msg)$ to denote the instances which receive the message msg sent from $I_{\alpha i}$ and the instances which send the message msg received by $I_{\alpha j}$, resp. Instance level dependencies are defined as follows.

Definition 2.5: Given artifacts α_i and α_j and their instances $I_{\alpha i}$ of α_i and $I_{\alpha j}$ of α_j, $I_{\alpha j}$ is creation dependent on $I_{\alpha i}$ if α_j is creation dependent on α_i and $I_{\alpha j} \in \alpha_j < I_{\alpha i} >$. Cardinality type of this dependency is: 1-to-1 if $|\alpha_j < I_{\alpha i} >|=|\alpha_i \ll I_{\alpha j} \gg |=1$; 1-to-m if $|\alpha_j < I_{\alpha i} >| >1$ and $|\alpha_i \ll I_{\alpha j} \gg |=1$; m-to-1 if $|\alpha_j < I_{\alpha i} >|=1$ and $|\alpha_i \ll I_{\alpha j} \gg|>1$; or m-to-m if $|\alpha_j < I_{\alpha i} >|>1$ and $|\alpha_i \ll I_{\alpha j} \gg|>1$.

Definition 2.6: Given artifacts α_i and α_j and their instances $I_{\alpha i}$ of α_i and $I_{\alpha j}$ of α_j, $I_{\alpha j}$ is sync dependent on $I_{\alpha i}$ if α_j is sync dependent on α_i and $I_{\alpha j} \in Rv(I_{\alpha i}, msg)$. Cardinality type of this dependency is: 1-to-1 if $|Rv(I_{\alpha i}, msg)| =|Sd(I_{\alpha j}, msg)|=1$; 1-to-m if $|Rv(I_{\alpha i}, msg)| >1$ and $|Sd(I_{\alpha j}, msg)|=1$; m-to-1 if $|Rv(I_{\alpha i}, msg)|=1$ and $|Sd(I_{\alpha j}, msg)|>1$; or m-to-m if $|Rv(I_{\alpha i}, msg)| >1$ and $|Sd(I_{\alpha j}, msg)|>1$.

2.3   EZFlow-Tx: A Transactional Artifact-Centric BP Model

To avoid unnecessary recovery, we relax the atomicity property: besides "all" or "nothing", we allow an artifact be in a new state "fixed committed", i.e., the artifact is fixed by eliminating its error parts and preserving other parts.

In detail, we define the following transactional states of an artifact: *initial*, *active*, *committed*, *compensated*, *fixed-running*, and *fixed committed*. An artifact can correctly evolve to state *committed*, or to state *compensated* via rolling back operation. Especially, an artifact reaches state *fixed-running* if some parts of it fail and are fixed. After its execution resumes, it will finally reach state *fixed committed*. At the same time, we define two transactional states for the relation-typed attributes of an artifact: *normal* and *compensated*, representing whether sub-tuples of the attribute is affected by certain errors. Consequently, we add attribute *txState* to an artifact, and *rstate* to each relation-type attribute to record their transactional state resp.

Definition 3.7: A transactional artifact-centric BP schema W is a tuple (EZ, Tx), where EZ is an *EZFlow*, and

- *Tx* defines transactional attributes, it maps each task t in T to a tuple (rec, comp, fix) where *rec=trivial | compensatable*, *trivial* means t has no need to be recovered; and *compensatable* means the side effects of t can be semantically undone by its compensating task *comp* or its partial side effects corresponded to the failed parts can be semantically undone through its error fixing task *fix* after its completion.

In normal execution, the enactment of the transactional workflow is similar to that of EZFLow. The sequence of tasks in the enactment $t_0t_1..t_{n-1}$ forms a workflow transaction, wherein each task is a sub-transaction that keeps CID properties. When a task t fails, backward recovery will be initiated unless task t is *trivial*.

Now we describe the recovery procedure. When an artifact I_f fails and is recovered, its dependent artifacts will be identified. Suppose artifact I_r depends on I_f with the cardinality type of m-to-1 or m-to-m, i.e., I_f only contributes to parts of I_r, we will (1) invoke the fixing task *fix* of I_r to fix the parts affected by I_f and preserve unaffected parts. After fixing, sub-transaction of fixed tasks are set to *fixed committed*, *rstate* of the fixed sub-tuples are set to *compensated*, and *txState* of I_r is set to *fixed-running*; then (2) resume the execution of I_r to handle its normal parts upon recovery completion. If the executions of rest tasks of I_r are successfully committed, *txState* of I_r will be set to *fixed committed*. Note that cardinality and correlations are used to determine the failure parts of I_r. If an artifact is entirely affected, it will be wholly compensated, the *txState* of the artifact together with the *rstate* of all its sub-tuples will be set to *compensated*.

The transaction of a relevant scenario is **correct** if every failed transaction has been semantically undone or fixed, and artifacts, which have creation/created or sync dependency on it, have also been semantically undone or fixed.

3   A Recovery Mechanism for Relevant BPs

Here, we outline a creation/sync dependency discovery method and a recovery mechanism for keeping data consistency of relevant business scenario when failure occurs.

3.1   Creation/Sync Dependency Discovery and Overlaps

To discover dependencies among artifacts, we design two relations: (1) instances creation record *InstCre(cre, cred, msg, pdT, rvT, ts)* where *cre* is an artifact which sends the message *msg* through task *pdT*, *cred* is an artifact created by task *rvT* at the time the *msg* arrives, *ts* represent the execution time of *rvT*; (2) instances sync record *SynDepd* (*sd, syn, msg, pdT, rvT, ts*) where *sd* and *syn* are artifacts that sends and receives the message *msg* resp. When a task is triggered by a message *msg*, a tuple will be added into *InstCre* if *msg* has "yes" as value of ⊢, otherwise, a tuple will be added into *SynDepd*.

When an instance I_i of artifact α_i fails and is recovered, its dependent artifacts can be derived as follows: (1) artifacts with creation dependency: $\pi_{cred}(\sigma_{cre=I_i}(InstCre))$; (2) artifacts with created dependency: $\pi_{cre}(\sigma_{cred=I_i}(InstCre))$; and (3) artifacts with sync dependency: $\pi_{syn}(\sigma_{sd=I_i}(SynDepd))$. For every dependent instance I_x, we can similarly compute the number of artifacts on which it is creation/created or sync dependent, thus, the cardinality type of dependency between I_i and I_x can be determined.

When cardinality type of dependency between I_x and I_i is not 1-to-1, we need to fix the error parts of I_x which overlap I_i rather than wholly roll back. The error parts can be computed by $\sigma_\varphi(\alpha_x)$, where α_x is the artifact class of I_x, and φ is constructed as follows. First, get correlation condition between α_x and α_i from correlation graph G, construct an equation expressions for each pair of projection attributes of each intersection expression in turn. Then construct two equation expressions $\alpha_x.ID = I_x$ and $\alpha_i.ID = I_i$ to filter the result. φ is a conjunction of all these equation expressions.

For example, when the *Order* instance o_3 in Fig. 2(c) fails, po_3 will need to be fixed for $po_3 \in PO < o_3 >$ and cardinality type of the dependency is m-to-1. Suppose *Order* and *PO* are correlated and the correlation condition is $\pi_{ID,\ item.invID}(Order) \sqcap \pi_{item.OrderID,\ item.invID}(PO)$. The failed parts of po_3 can be computed by $\sigma_{PO.ID=po_3 \wedge PO.item.OrderID=Order.ID \wedge PO.item.invID=Order.item.invID \wedge Order.ID=o_3}(PO)$.

3.2   A Mechanism for Handling Cascaded Recovery

Cascaded recovery needs to be considered because isolation is relaxed. When an instance I_i fails, its dependent instances I_D will be identified. However, dependencies do not necessarily indicate being affected. To avoid over-recovery, we use overlaps to determine if an instance $I_d \in I_D$ is really affected. Different overlap degrees have different recovery strategies: (1) no overlap: resume its execution; (2) complete overlap: entirely recover it; (3) partial overlap: fix the parts that overlap the failed instance, then resu- me its execution to handle the rest normal parts upon recovery completion. When I_d needs to be recovered, it may cause its dependent instances to be cascaded recovered.

We construct a directed acyclic graph Artifact Dependency Graph (ADG) for I_i, containing all its dependent instances which overlap its failed parts. Each node in an ADG represents an artifact. Its structure contains: (1) *cID*: artifact identifier, denoted by I_i; (2) *deFrom<cID, type>*: a list records artifacts that directly cause I_i to be recovered and corresponding affecting type; (3) *failedPart*: the failed parts of I_i; and (4) *bkRecCmd*: recovery command for I_i, which can be "compensate" or "fix". Each edge represents dependency between nodes with solid line for creation dependency and dash line for sync dependency. If a node I_x depends on node I_y, there will be an edge from I_x to I_y. The structure of an edge is a tuple *e=(source, target, type)* where *type* describes dependency type between *source* and *target* nodes, i.e., "create", "created" or "sync".

When building an ADG for the failed instance I_f, instances with creation/created or sync dependency on I_f are identified, and those ones overlap its failed parts are added into the graph. For a creation dependent instance I_{cd}, only instances that have sync or creation dependencies on it meanwhile overlap its failed parts are affected and need to be added. For a created dependent instance I_c, only instances which have sync or created dependencies on it meanwhile overlap its failed part need to be added. The recovery of a sync dependent instance I_{sd} is similar to that of the failed instance.

If I_i is affected by one instance, its *failedPart* is the intersection between I_i and the *failedPart* of that instance. If I_i is affected by multiple instances, overlaps between I_i and these instances will be computed resp., and the *failedPart* is the union of these overlaps. With regard to instances that may depend on each other, we use the following rules to avoid creating a cycle. Given two nodes I_x and I_y, I_y is dependent on I_x and overlaps its *failedPart*. I_y will be added as a dependent instance of I_x if I_y has not existed in the ADG. Otherwise, missing nodes affected by I_y should be added, and *failedPart* should be adjusted for I_y and all instances derived from it. For each derived instance I_z with creation type, if overlap between *failedPart* of I_y and I_z contains I_z's *failedPart*, similar *failedpart* adjustment should be done for I_z. The overlap adjustment is iteratively handled until there is no change to the intersection or there is no overlap with other instances. In this way, cycling dependency is avoided, and the recovery of I_y does not miss any affected parts since the impact of I_x's failure on I_y has been handled.

The ADG construction algorithm builds an ADG for the failed instance I_f. The algorithm has two inputs: I_f and its fail parts *failedPart*. An ADG is represented by a set of nodes N and a set of edges E. The algorithm is outlined as follows.

1. Create two assisting lists: (1) *affLi<aff, deFrom, dp>* to store affected instances and iterate through different level of a ADG, where *aff* is derived from *deFrom* with dependency type *dp*; (2) *tempLi* to temporarily store the affected instances of instances in *affLi*.
2. Construct a node for I_f and add it into *affLi* to start ADG construction.
3. For each element *el* in *affLi*,
   3.1. If *el.aff* does not exist in N, add an edge from *el.deFrom* to *el.aff* into E, add every affected instances of *el.aff* into *tempLi*.
   3.2. Else retrieve *el.aff* into I_m (affected by multiple instances. No cycle). If NotContain (I_m*.deFrom.type, el.dp*) or NotEmptyDifferenceSet(*el.aff.failedPart*, I_m*.failedPart*), add missing instances affected by *el.aff* into *tempLi*, adjust *failedpart* of all affected instances.
4. After processing all elements of *affLi*, empty *affLi* and move instances from *tempLi* to *affLi* to start next level construction. If *affLi* is not empty, repeat step 3.

Fig.3 shows a sample ADG_1 for I_f containing ten concurrent BPs I_1-I_{10}.

The ADG is used to conduct cascaded recovery. When a BP I_f fails, its dependent BPs will be identified and suspended for overlap evaluation, while independent BPs keep running. Then the recovery procedure invokes the ADG construction algorithm to construct an ADG for I_f, with failed parts of each affected instance computed, and finally traverse the ADG to recover each affected instance I_a according to its recovery command *bkRecCmd*, which is set to "compensate" when its failed parts equal to its contents, or set to "fix" when its failed parts are a proper subset of its contents. Due to space limit, algorithm details are ignored here.

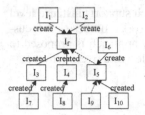
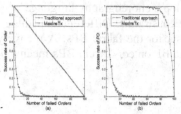
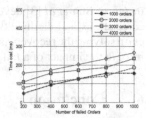

Fig. 3. Sample ADG_1 for I_f **Fig. 4.** Success rate comparison   **Fig. 5.** Time cost

4   Evaluation of Effectiveness and Feasibility

To evaluate the effectiveness, we compare the BP success rate of *MaxInsTx* with that of traditional approach (all or nothing). Experiment is conducted on m *Orders* and n *POs*, where $m=100$, $n=20$. We assign $[1,5]$ items to each *Order* with uniform distribution. The probability that an item in an *Order* belongs to a certain *PO* is $1/n$.

Fig. 4 shows the success rate of *Orders* and *POs*. In Fig. 4(a), the success rate of *Orders* of *MaxInsTx* decrease linearly because only the failed *Orders* will fail. In Fig. 4(b), the success rate of *POs* of *MaxInsTx* shows no impact when the number of failed *Orders* varies from 1 to 54, because *POs* will fail only when they become empty due to the failed *Orders*. After that, the *SRPO* decreases gradually for a while and then decreases dramatically in the last period. However, both the success rate of *Orders* and *POs* of traditional approach decrease dramatically, since other *Orders* and all the *POs* correlated with the failed *Orders* will fail. Obviously, *MaxInsTx* has much better performance, which verifies its effectiveness.

Next, we analyze the time cost of *MaxInsTx*. In this experiment, the number of failed *Orders* varies from 200 to 1000, the number of total *Orders* varies from 1000 to 4000, and the number of *POs* is fixed to 20. The configuration of our microcomputer is as follows: 3.2 GHz Dual Core processor, 2 GB memory, Windows XP OS.

Fig. 5 shows that the time cost is affected by both the number of failed *Orders* and total *Orders*. The time cost curve increases slowly with the increasing of the number of failed *Orders*. The overall time cost is very small. Hence *MaxInsTx* is feasible.

5   Related Work

Many works have addressed the issue of long-live transaction coordination through ACID relaxation. One of the representative approaches is proposed in [4] which allows relaxing any attributes of ACID through introducing a "pre-commit" phase and a "negotiation" phase. Xiao *et al* [5] further address the issue of concurrency control. They propose a rule-based approach to resolve the concurrency issue through analyzing write dependency and potential read dependency among BPs.

None of the above works take the impact of complex cardinality relationships into consideration. In practice, the existing of m-to-m relationships among BPs complicates many problems and attracts increasing attention. Fahland *et al* [1] address the behavioral conformance checking problem complicated by the fabric of BP instances. Zhao *et al* [2] focus on managing instance correspondence through correlations attached to each instance. Sun *et al* [3] develop a choreography language which supports instance level correlations and cardinality constraints. Different from these works, our research focuses on solving the recovery issue for the fabric BPs. A recovery approach is proposed to resolve the impact of a failed BP on concurrent BPs meanwhile avoid over-recovery.

6   Conclusion

This paper proposed a best-effort failure recovery approach *MaxInsTx* for relevant business scenarios, supporting complex dependencies between artifacts. We relax the atomicity property of transactions, allowing an artifact be partially fixed such that its unaffected parts are preserved as much as possible. A failure recovery mechanism is proposed with the advantage of avoiding unnecessary recoveries.

Acknowledgment. This work is partially supported by NSFC grant 60873115.

References

1. Fahland, D., de Leoni, M., van Dongen, B.F., van der Aalst, W.M.P.: Conformance Checking of Interacting Processes with Overlapping Instances. In: Rinderle-Ma, S., Toumani, F., Wolf, K. (eds.) BPM 2011. LNCS, vol. 6896, pp. 345–361. Springer, Heidelberg (2011)
2. Zhao, X., Liu, C., Yang, Y., Sadiq, W.: Handling instance correspondence in inter-organisational workflows. In: Krogstie, J., Opdahl, A.L., Sindre, G. (eds.) CAiSE 2007. LNCS, vol. 4495, pp. 51–65. Springer, Heidelberg (2007)
3. Sun, Y., Xu, W., Su, J.: Declarative Choreographies for Artifacts. In: Liu, C., Ludwig, H., Toumani, F., Yu, Q. (eds.) ICSOC 2012. LNCS, vol. 7636, pp. 420–434. Springer, Heidelberg (2012)
4. Khachana, R.T., James, A., Iqbal, R.: Relaxation of acid properties in AuTra, the adaptive user-defined transaction relaxing approach. Future Gener. Comput. Syst. 27(1), 58–66 (2011)
5. Xiao, Y., Urban, S.D.: Using rules and data dependencies for the recovery of concurrent processes in a service-oriented environment. IEEE Transactions on Services Computing 5(1), 59–71 (2012)
6. Xu, W., Su, J., Yan, Z., Yang, J., Zhang, L.: An Artifact-Centric Approach to Dynamic Modification of Workflow Execution. In: Meersman, R., et al. (eds.) OTM 2011, Part I. LNCS, vol. 7044, pp. 256–273. Springer, Heidelberg (2011)

Extending WS-Agreement to Support Automated Conformity Check on Transport and Logistics Service Agreements*

Antonio Manuel Gutiérrez[1], Clarissa Cassales Marquezan[2], Manuel Resinas[1], Andreas Metzger[2], Antonio Ruiz-Cortés[1], and Klaus Pohl[2]

[1] School of Computer Engineering
University of Seville
{amgutierrez,resinas,aruiz}@us.es
[2] Paluno - University of Duisburg-Essen, Essen, Germany
{clarissa.marquezan,andreas.metzger,klaus.pohl}@paluno.uni-due.de

Abstract. Checking whether the agreed service quality attributes are fulfilled or maintained during the service life-cycle is a very important task for SLA (Service Level Agreement) enforcement. In this paper, we leverage conformance checking techniques developed for computational services to automate the conformity checking of transport & logistics services. Our solution extends the WS-Agreement metamodel to support the definition of frame and specific SLAs. With this extension, we define a new validation operation for the conformity check of transport & logistics SLAs based on CSPs solvers. The key contribution of our work is that, as far as we know, it is the first definition of an automated conformity check solution for long term agreements in the transport & logistics domain. Nonetheless, other domains in which similar SLAs are defined can also benefit from our solution.

1 Introduction

Service Level Agreements (SLAs) are essential in service provision because they define the quality attributes of services meeting consumers and providers preferences. These quality attributes or SLOs (Service Level Objectives) describe in a measurable way how the service should behave during its life-cycle or what the basic requirements for its execution are. Checking whether the agreed SLOs are fulfilled or maintained is a very important task for SLA enforcement.

In transport & logistics services, one type of SLA commonly used by large companies establishes an interval of time in which multiple executions of the same service will be requested by the Logistic Service Client (LSC) and executed by the Logistic Service Provider (LSP). This type of SLA comprises one

* This work was partially supported by the European Union's Seventh Framework Programme (FP7/2007-2013), the European Commission (FEDER), the Spanish and the Andalusian R&D&I programmes (grant agreements 215483 (S-Cube), 285598 (FInest) and 604123 (FIspace), TIN2012-32273 (TAPAS), TIC-5906 (THEOS)).

S. Basu et al. (Eds.): ICSOC 2013, LNCS 8274, pp. 567–574, 2013.

frame agreement document and multiple "child" agreements, *i.e.*, for each LSC request a new agreement will be created eventually containing the same SLOs from its parent frame agreement. Currently, a manual process is used to check whether the SLOs of "child" agreements (called specific agreements) conform with the SLOs of the frame agreement. Numbers from a large company from the transport & logistics domain [8] show that in a random month approximately 100,000 transportations happen. We can say that each transportation might be associated with a specific agreement. This means that the number of specific agreements to be checked by a large company could reach up to 100,000 documents per month. Thus, our goal is to automate this checking by proposing a conformity check solution for SLAs in the transport & logistics domain.

Conformity checks in SLAs of computational services, like Cloud services and SBAs (Service Based Applications), have been extensively proposed. Two main groups of proposals can be found: One group aims at checking whether the execution of a service conforms with the SLOs on the SLA document [2]. The other group focuses on supporting consistent SLA definition, avoiding errors or inconsistent terms between documents [10,4]. Nevertheless, when it comes to SLAs of real physical services like shipment of goods in the transport & logistics domain, the current conformity check solutions lack a proper handling of this type of SLAs. The main reason for this are the differences between SLAs in the transport & logistics and computational SLAs: the existence of two levels of agreements and the need to aggregate information between these levels to perform conformity check. Current works fall short on addressing these differences.

In this paper, we propose a solution able to handle the aforementioned differences and provide the automated conformity check of SLAs in transport & logistics domain. Our proposal is based on WS-Agreement which is a standard that is widely used and that has been successfully applied in the computational domain [10]. However, it currently lacks the necessary formalization to represent the relationship among the two levels of SLAs in transport & logistics, *i.e.*, frame and specific agreements. Therefore, we extend the WS-Agreement metamodel to fill this gap. With these extensions, we can define a new validation operation for the conformity check of transport & logistics SLAs. This new operation extends previous work [10,9] which were targeted only at computational SLAs. In that work, SLOs are mapped to Constraints Satisfaction Problems (CSPs) and the conformity check is achieved using CSP solvers. We validate our proposal with the implementation of a tool[1]. The key contribution of our work is that, as far as we know, it is the first definition in the literature of an automated conformity check solution for SLAs in the transport & logistics domain. Furthermore, since our conformity checking is domain independent, other domains in which similar long-term agreements are defined can also benefit from our solution.

The remaining of this paper is organized as follows. In Section 2 we describe the related work. Section 3 presents the WS-Agreement extension proposed in this paper. Section 4 presents the new operations defined in order to perform the conformity check. In Section 5 we discuss the conclusions and future work.

---

[1] http://www.isa.us.es/tlcc

2   Related Work

In the past years, there has been an increasing amount of research efforts trying to bring into the transport & logistics domain technical solutions based on Service Oriented Computing[2]. Nevertheless, when it comes to SLAs and conformity check in this domain, there is a limited amount of work. The solution of Augenstein et al. [1] introduce a platform based on a service-oriented approach for managing contracts on 4PL business[3]. The proposed solution itself is mainly focused on coordinating the business process conducted among these different partners. Another example is the work introduced by Bing and Zhongying [3]. They use mathematical terms to define the parameters of a contract in transport & logistics collaborative business process. Mai and Teo [7] also followed a mathematical approach to define and analyze contracts in the collaborative business process in transport & logistics. Nevertheless, none of the aforementioned solutions focus on the conformity check of the agreements among the partners.

As previously discussed, the major differences between services in transport & logistics to computational services are the existence of two levels of agreements and the need to aggregate and compare information between these levels to perform conformity check. In this section, we show how current works on conformity check fall short on addressing these differences. The work proposed by Leitner et al. [6] aims at predicting SLA violations in business process. The authors consider two types of SLOs: instance-level, associated with each instance of a business process in isolation; and aggregated, representing the execution of several instances of the same type of business process. The violation prediction of aggregated SLOs is performed on values at the same SLA level, *i.e.*, the same type of document describing the SLOs of a business process. In our case, we need to aggregate information at the same level, but in contrast, we need to compare this information to a different level of SLA document. This will be discussed in detail in the next section.

Bartoline et al. [2] proposed to monitor the QoS attributes of service choreographies to detect violations on the choreography SLA. The authors present a new approach to annotate the BPMN Choreography Diagram with functional and non-functional constraints that need to be fulfilled by a service entering the choreography. At design time, these constraints are analyzed and translated into monitoring rules to be used during runtime. Goel et al. [5] use temporal logics of safety (DSF - Deterministic Safety Formula) to formalize the SLOs and model checking to support the monitoring conformance of SLAs. Their solution is able to detect and present to the user the occurrence of violations of the specified SLA. The aforementioned approaches do not deal with the conformance checking between frame and specific agreements and they have limited support for expressing aggregate information in SLOs.

---

[2] http://www.finest-ppp.eu/files/deliverables/d08/finest_d8_1_final.pdf

[3] 4PL business (4th Party Logistics) or 3PL (3rf Party Logisitcs) are types of business processes that result in a supply chain with collaborative tasks executed by different logistics partners.

3   Modelling Long Term Transport and Logistics Agreements

The first step towards supporting automated checks is to model frame and specific agreements so that their constraints can be checked by a software component. A limitation of the AS-IS situation in transport & logistics is that there is no explicit mechanism to represent the aggregation of specific agreements by the frame agreement. However, as introduced in Section 1, some types of SLO values defined in the specific agreements are actually constrained by the SLOs defined in the frame agreement and the SLOs of the specific agreements that have been already signed. This is the case of, e.g., an SLO "maximum containers" specified in a frame agreeement to limit the total amount of containers transported in a time period. This SLO affects to SLOs related to number of containers transported in every specific agreement under the frame agreement context.

We propose modelling the relationship between the SLOs of frame agreements and specific agreements by clearly defining the existence of what we called: atomic and aggregated SLOs. The SLO type defines which kind of constraints have to be applied during the conformity check and this allows to identify and create the explicit link between frame and specific agreement. All types of contracts have atomic attributes. Values are assigned to these attributes at the contracting phase of the service and do not change over time unless they are explicitly renegotiated by the parties. In contrast, aggregated attributes are only associated with frame agreements and their values depend on the values of atomic attributes from specific agreements associated with the frame agreement.

WS-Agreement specification provides an agreement document schema so it can be used to define frame and specific agreement. Specific agreements and atomic SLOs can be directly defined with this model. For instance, Figure 1 depicts an specific agreement modelled in WS-Agreement. However, there is no mechanism to model which specific agreements are associated with the frame agreement nor to define aggregated SLOs so frame agreements cannot be directly modelled with WS-Agreement. Therefore, in this proposal we extend WS-Agreement to be able to model frame agreements.

First, we extend the WS-Agreement context with one additional section (cf. Figure 1) to include all the specific agreements validated in the frame agreement

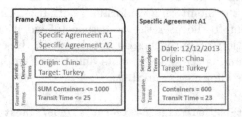

Fig. 1. WS-Agreement modelling of Frame Agreements and Specific Agreements

context. Second, in order to define aggregated SLOs, accumulative operators are introduced. Thus, the example "maximum containers" SLO could be defined as:

```
Guarantee Terms: Maximum Containers: Provider guarantees
                      SUM (SpecificAgreement.Containers) < 1000
```

where SpecificAgreement refers to the specific agreements whose conformity with this frame agreement has been evaluated and SUM is the summation operator. A set of aggregation operators such as COUNT, MAX and MIN could be used. These extensions enable the definition of the aggregation SLOs (Figure 1).

4   Automated Validation of Specific Agreements

The validation of a specific agreement in the context of a frame agreement involves checking their conformity. Automating conformity checking between frame agreement and specific agreement makes possible to detect errors in early stages. So, once a frame agreement has started its validity period, each time a new specific agreement is signed, the conformity between its SLA terms and frame agreement can be checked. This check operation is described in this section.

Two types of conformance issues may appear between specific and frame agreements. On one hand, specific agreements may include atomic SLOs that violate atomic SLOs defined in the frame agreement (e.g. if the frame agreement determines a transit time limit of 25 days, a transit time of 30 days in specific agreement would not be conform). On the other hand, specific agreements may also violate aggregated SLOs (e.g. if the frame agreement defines an aggregation SLO "maximum containers = 100", specific agreements with SLO "containers" are not conform to the frame agreement if its atomic SLO "containers" plus the atomic SLO "containers" from previous specific agreements is more than 100).

From this discussion, we conclude that valid values for any service property used in specific agreement SLOs have to be *also* valid for frame agreement SLOs (not the opposite). Consequently, the conformance between a specific and a frame agreement conformity can be informally defined as follows: *"a specific agreement conforms to a frame agreement if the set of possible values for the service properties used in its SLOs is a subset of the possible values for the service properties used in the SLOs in the frame agreement"*.

CSP Mapping. Following this notion of conformance, we follow an approach similar to [10] to automate its checking. The procedure involves mapping both the frame agreement and the specific agreement into a Constraint Satisfaction Problem (CSP) and use a CSP solver to check the conformance between them. The difference being that, in our case, it is necessary to take the aggregated SLOs and previous specific agreements into account.

There are several reasons for choosing CSPs to automate this checking. First, an important part of the agreement (SDT and GT) are described as constraints

```
INPUT: A specific agreement SA, a  frame agreement FA
OUTPUT: A CSP (V, D, C)

FOR each Specific Agreement SA' created in the context of FA
  FOR each Service Property SP in SA' Service Property Section
    IF SP is in FA Aggregated SLOs
       V  ←  V  ∪  μ(SP)
       D  ←  D  ∪  domain(SP)
    FOR each Guarantee Term GT in SA' Guarantee Terms Section
      SLO  ←  SLO of guarantee term GT
      IF SP in SLO is in FA Aggregated SLOs
        C  ←  C  ∧  μ(SLO)

FOR each Service Property SP in SA Service Property Section
   V  ←  V  ∪
   D  ←  D  ∪  domain(SP)
FOR each Guarantee Term GT in SA Guarantee Terms Section
   SLO  ←  SLO of guarantee term GT
   C  ←  C  ∧  SLO
```

Fig. 2. Algorithm for mapping specific agreements into CSPs

on properties and attributes so it can be described as CSP constraints in a straight way. Second, similar mappings have been successfully used to automate conformance tasks between agreement offer and templates [10]. Finally, there is a plethora of off-the-shelf CSP solvers that can be used to automate this checking[4].

The mapping step of the procedure involves two different mappings to CSP. One for the specific agreement whose conformance is being checked and the previous specific agreements that have been created in the context of the same frame agreement and another one for the frame agreement itself.

The mapping for specific agreements is depicted in Figure 2. The variables of the CSP are the service properties specified in the agreements and their domains are the domains of the service properties. Regarding the constraints, they are the content of the SLOs of the specific agreements (in the case of previous specific agreements, only of those SLOs that include service properties used in aggregated SLOs in the frame agreement). Note that variables are processed by function $\mu(X)$, which renames service properties according to the agreement it belongs (i.e.: $\mu(transittime <= 30)$ in specific agreement 1 returns '$transittime_1 <= 30'$) to avoid collisions of names between the different specific agreements.

The algorithm depicted in Figure 3 applies the same mapping, but now to the elements of the frame agreement. However, in this case, if the SLO uses the aggregation operation, then it is previously processed by a function $\alpha(SLO)$, which unfolds aggregation operations in SLOs according to the specific agreements related to the service property used in the SLO (i.e.: $\alpha(SUM containers < 1000)$ returns $containers_1 + containers_2 + ... < 1000)$).

The CSPs obtained applying both mappings to example specific agreements and frame agreement is displayed in Table 1. Finally, with these CSP mappings, conformance between specific and frame agreement can be defined as follows:

Definition 1. *Let SA be a specific agreement, FA a frame agreement, (V_s, D_s, C_s) the CSP obtained after mapping SA and previous specific agreements created in the*

---

[4] http://www.emn.fr/z-info/choco-solver/

```
INPUT: A frame agreement FA
OUTPUT: A CSP (V, D, C)

FOR each Service Property SP in FA Service Property Section
   V  ←  V ∪ SP
   D  ←  D ∪ domain(SP)
FOR each Guarantee Term GT in FA Guarantee Term Section
   SLO  ←  SLO of guarantee term GT
   IF SLO uses Aggregation operation
      C  ←  C ∧ α(GT)
   ELSE
      C  ←  C ∧ SLO
```

Fig. 3. Algorithm for mapping frame agreements into CSPs

Table 1. Mapping for Example

Agreement	CSP Mapping
Specific Agreements (Current and A1)	$V \leftarrow A1Containers, Containers, TransitTime$ $D \leftarrow [0, 1000], [0, 1000], [0, 365]$ $C \leftarrow A1Containers = 500 \land Containers = 600 \land TransitTime = 23$
Frame Agreement	$V \leftarrow Containers, TransitTime,$ $D \leftarrow [0, 1000], [0, 365]$ $C \leftarrow TransitTime < 30 \land A1Containers + Containers <= 1000$

context of FA, and (V_f, D_f, C_f) the CSP obtained after mapping FA. The current specific agreement conforms with the frame agreement if:

$$conforms(SA, FA) \Leftrightarrow \neg sat(V_s \cup V_f, D_s \cup D_f, C_s \land \neg C_f)$$

The rationale for this definition is as follows. According to the intuitive definition stated above, a specific agreement conforms to a frame agreement if the set of possible values for the service properties used in the SLOs in the specific agreement is a *subset* of the possible values for the service properties used in the SLOs in the frame agreement. In terms of CSP this can be expressed as:

$$conforms(SA, FA) \Leftrightarrow \forall \vec{x} \in V_s \cup V_f \cdot satisfies(x, C_s) \Rightarrow satisfies(x, C_f)$$

which can be rewritten as:

$$conforms(SA, FA) \Leftrightarrow \neg \exists \vec{x} \in V_s \cup V_f \cdot \neg(\neg satisfies(x, C_s) \lor satisfies(x, C_f))$$

Finally, as satisfiability operation holds if exists solution for a boolean formula, we can write:

$$conforms(SA, FA) \Leftrightarrow \neg sat(V_s \cup V_f, D_s \cup D_f, C_s \land \neg C_f)$$

With this definition, the result of validation for the example in Table 1 is *false* since $\neg(A1Containers + Containers <= 1000) \equiv 600 + 500 > 1000$ is satisfiable. Therefore, $conforms(SA, FA) \equiv false$.

These operations have been implemented in the ADA (Agreement Document Analyser) Framework using JAVA language and CHOCO solver. The prototype can be accessed in the project URL: http://www.isa.us.es/tlcc.

5   Conclusions

In this paper, the Transport & Logistics compliance checking has been automated using computational service model, as WS-Agreement specification, and techniques as CSP transforming and solvers. However, the complex artifacts in scenario, as frame agreements, which define rules for consequent specific agreements, require extending WS-Agreement specification with enhanced models to support frame agreements and specific agreements. As new models are defined, new mappings have been introduced to solve the compliance checking with CSP solvers. This proposal supports conformity checking for frame agreement and specific agreement in Transport & Logistics but as these artifacts appear naturally in other computational and non-computational scenarios. Therefore the enriched model can be the basis to solve other two-level SLA scenarios.

References

1. Augenstein, C., Ludwig, A., Franczyk, B.: Integration of service models - preliminary results for consistent logistics service management. In: 2012 Annual SRII Global Conference (SRII), pp. 100–109 (2012)
2. Bartolini, C., Bertolino, A., De Angelis, G., Ciancone, A., Mirandola, R.: Apprehensive qos monitoring of service choreographies. In: Proceedings of the 28th Annual ACM Symposium on Applied Computing, SAC 2013, pp. 1893–1899. ACM, New York (2013)
3. Bing, W., Zhongying, L.: Decision-making in optimizing the contract of third party logistic. In: 6th International Conference on Service Systems and Service Management, ICSSSM 2009, pp. 444–449 (2009)
4. Braga, C., Chalub, F., Sztajnberg, A.: A formal semantics for a quality of service contract language. Electronic Notes in Theoretical Computer Science 203(7), 103–120 (2009)
5. Goel, N., Kumar, N., Shyamasundar, R.K.: SLA monitor: A system for dynamic monitoring of adaptive web services. In: 2011 Ninth IEEE European Conference on Web Services (ECOWS), pp. 109–116 (2011)
6. Leitner, P., Ferner, J., Hummer, W., Dustdar, S.: Data-driven and automated prediction of service level agreement violations in service compositions. Distributed and Parallel Databases 31(3), 447–470 (2013)
7. Hua Mai, Y., Xin Miao, L., Teo, C.P., Qingqing, X.: Geometric approach for logistics outsoursing contracting. In: 2010 8th International Conference on Supply Chain Management and Information Systems (SCMIS), pp. 1–7 (2010)
8. Metzger, A., Franklin, R., Engel, Y.: Predictive monitoring of heterogeneous service-oriented business networks: The transport and logistics case. In: Service Research and Innovation Institute Global Conference (SRII 2012). Conference Publishing Service (CPS). IEEE Computer Society (2012)
9. Müller, C., Resinas, M., Ruiz-Cortés, A.: Automated analysis of conflicts in ws-agreement. IEEE Transactions on Services Computing PP(99), 1 (2013)
10. Müller, C., Resinas, M., Ruiz-Cortés, A.: Explaining the non-compliance between templates and agreement offers in WS-agreement. In: Baresi, L., Chi, C.-H., Suzuki, J. (eds.) ICSOC-ServiceWave 2009. LNCS, vol. 5900, pp. 237–252. Springer, Heidelberg (2009)

Automatic Composition of Form-Based Services in a Context-Aware Personal Information Space

Rania Khéfifi[1], Pascal Poizat[2], and Fatiha Saïs[1]

[1] LRI, CNRS and Paris Sud University
{rania.khefifi,fatiha.sais}@lri.fr
[2] LIP6, CNRS and Paris Ouest University
pascal.poizat@lip6.fr

Abstract. Personal Information Spaces (PIS) help in structuring, storing, and retrieving personal information. Still, it is the users' duty to sequence the basic steps in different online procedures, and to fill out the corresponding forms with personal information, in order to fulfill some objectives. We propose an extension for PIS that assists users in achieving this duty. We perform a composition of form-based services in order to reach objectives expressed as workflow of capabilities. Further, we take into account that user personal information can be contextual and that the user may have personal information privacy policies. Our solution is based on graph planning and is fully tool-supported.

Keywords: Service Composition, Ontologies, Contextual Data, Personal Information, Privacy, Graph Planning.

1 Introduction

Personal Information Spaces (PIS) support users in structuring, storing, and retrieving their personal information. However, with regards to online procedures, *e.g.*, administrative processes, users are left alone to find out which services can be used to achieve parts of the procedures, how to sequence parts of these services, and how to fill the service forms using their personal information. Service composition [8,2] supports the realization of business processes out of the automatic assembly of online services. Still, a first issue is to deal with data at the *good level of abstraction*. Service composition algorithms that support data do it at the type level. If some service requires a data of type d, any value will be ok. This is not realistic in a PIS where data is contextual. Depending on a context of interest, not all possible values for data type d are equivalent and/or valid to be used as a service input. A second issue is that personal information is *sensitive*. Users should be able to specify access policies to be endorsed while passing data to the composed services.

Contributions. We present in this paper a service composition approach for the *realization of online procedures that are expressed as workflows*. This approach is *context-aware*. It considers the contextual usability of user personal information that are to be transmitted in online service forms. Further, it supports personal

S. Basu et al. (Eds.): ICSOC 2013, LNCS 8274, pp. 575–583, 2013.

information *access policies* while computing the compositions. Our approach is *automatic* and *tool-supported* through the use of semantic annotations, the encoding of the composition requirements into an AI planning problem, and an extension of a state-of-the-art graph planning algorithm.

Related Work. Several service composition approaches have used context information, *e.g.,* [9,13,10]. Most of them consider context with a technical perspective (*e.g.,* device type, battery charge, GPS information) that is used to select functionality (services). We consider contexts in a more general sense, together with possible relations (subsumption, disjointness) between them that enable contextual reasoning. We do not only use contexts to select services but also to select the best (in terms of usability) data to give to these services. Some approaches [5,1,4] take into account policies in the composition process. While [5] supports them after composition generation and [1,4] at execution time, we consider policies directly in the composition process. In a previous work [11] we have developed a service composition approach based on graph planning. The work we present here can be seen as an extension of it that supports contexts and access policies.

Outline. After giving preliminaries on graph planning in Section 2, our models are introduced in Section 3. The description of the way the composition issue can be solved using an extension of graph planning is presented in Section 4. We end with conclusions and perspectives in Section 5. Due to lack of room, it was not possible to put all details in this paper. An extended version that includes a detailed example is available online in the authors' Web pages.

2   Preliminaries

Planning is *"the task of coming up with a sequence of actions that will achieve a goal"* [12]. A (propositional) *planning problem* can be modeled by a tuple $\Pi = (\mathbf{P}, \mathbf{A}, \mathbf{I}, \mathbf{G})$, where $\mathbf{P}$ is a set of propositions, $\mathbf{A}$ is a set of actions, each action $\mathbf{a} \in \mathbf{A}$ with a set of preconditions $\mathbf{Pre(a)} \subseteq \mathbf{P}$, a set of negative effects $\mathbf{Eff^-(a)} \subseteq \mathbf{P}$, and a set of positive effects $\mathbf{Eff^+(a)} \subseteq \mathbf{P}$ such that $= \mathbf{Eff^-(a)} \cap \mathbf{Eff^+(a)} = \emptyset$, also denoted with $\mathbf{a} = (\mathbf{Pre(a)}, \mathbf{Eff^-(a)}, \mathbf{Eff^+(a)})$, $\mathbf{I} \subseteq \mathbf{P}$ is the input, or initial state, of the problem, and $\mathbf{G} \subseteq \mathbf{P}$ is the goal of the problem.

Two actions $\mathbf{a}$ and $\mathbf{b}$ are *independent* iff $\mathbf{Eff^-(a)} \cap (\mathbf{Pre(b)} \cup \mathbf{Eff^+(b)}) = \emptyset$ and $\mathbf{Eff^-(b)} \cap (\mathbf{Pre(a)} \cup \mathbf{Eff^+(a)}) = \emptyset$. A set of actions is independent when its actions are pairwise independent.

Among the different techniques to solve planning problems, Graphplan [3] is a technique that yields a compact representation of relations between actions and represent the whole problem world. It has proven to be very efficient and has been applied with success to Web service composition [11] and to composition repair [14]. The Graphplan algorithm is based on the computation of a *planning graph* (Fig. 1), which is a directed acyclic graph composed of interleaved layers called proposition layers $\mathbf{PL}_i \subseteq \mathbf{P}$ and actions layers $\mathbf{AL}_i \subseteq \mathbf{A}$.

The first proposition layer, $\mathbf{PL}_0$, is made up of the propositions in $\mathbf{I}$. The Graphplan algorithm then performs *graph expansion*. Given a proposition layer

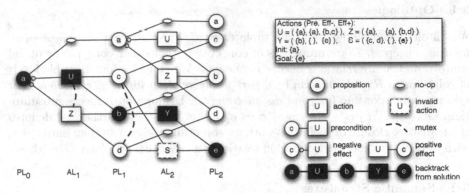

Fig. 1. Graphplan example

PL_i, an action **a** is added in AL_i if its preconditions and negative effects are in PL_i. If so, all positive effects of **a** are added in PL_i, and **a** is connected with precondition arcs (resp. negative effect arcs) to its preconditions (resp. negative effects) in PL_{i-1} and with positive effect arcs to its positive effects in PL_i. Specific actions (no-ops) are used to keep propositions from one layer to the next one. Graph planning also introduces the concept of mutual exclusion (mutex) between non independent actions. Mutual exclusion is reported from a layer to the next one while building the graph.

The expansion phase stops either when the objective is reached, *i.e.*, if **G** is included in PL_i, without mutex between elements in **G**, or with a fix-point, *i.e.*, if $PL_i = PL_{i-1}$. In second case there is no solution to the planning problem. In the first case, the Graphplan algorithm then performs a *backtrack* from the goal propositions in PL_i to the initial proposition layer PL_0. Planning graphs whose computations have stopped at level k enable to retrieve all solutions up to this level. Additionally, planning graphs enable to retrieve solutions in a concise form, taking benefit of actions that can be done in parallel (denoted ‖).

An example is given in Figure 1. The extraction phase gives plans **U**; **Y**, **Z**; **Y**, and (**U**‖**Z**); **S**. However, **U** and **Z** are in mutual exclusion. Accordingly, since there is no other way to obtain **c** and **d** than with exclusive actions, these two propositions are in exclusion in the next proposition layer, making **S** impossible. The only possible solution plans are therefore **U**; **Y** and **Z**; **Y**. Note that other nodes are indeed in mutual exclusion but we have not represented this for clarity.

3   Modeling of the Composition Problem

In this section, we formalize the problem of composing form-based services in context-aware personal information spaces. We will present the different inputs of this composition problem. In Section 4 we will then address how this problem can be solved automatically using an extension of graph planning.

3.1   Ontologies

An ontology can be denoted by a tuple $\mathcal{O} = (\mathcal{C}, \mathcal{P}, \mathcal{R})$ where $\mathcal{C}$ are classes (semantic concepts), $\mathcal{P}$ are properties of concepts (either other concepts or literal values), and $\mathcal{R}$ are relations between concepts. We consider four possible kinds of relations in $\mathcal{R}$: *subsumption* ($\preceq$), *part-whole relationship* ($\sqsubset$), *equivalence*, or *synonymy relationship* ($\equiv$), and *disjunction* ($\perp$). Disjunction respects subsumption, *i.e.*, $\forall c_1, c_1', c_2, c_2' \in \mathcal{C}, c_2 \preceq c_1, c_2' \preceq c_1', c_1 \perp c_1' \Rightarrow c_2 \perp c_2'$. Further, $\preceq^*$ denotes the transitive closure of $\preceq$. In this work we sometimes rely on simpler ontologies, with only classes and a subsumption relation. In such a case we have $\mathcal{O} = (\mathcal{C}, \preceq)$.

3.2   Semantic Structures

In [6], we have developed the notion of semantic context-aware PIS based on three principles: modeling, contextualization, and instantiation of personal information. Modeling is achieved using an ontology, $\mathcal{O} = (\mathcal{C}, \mathcal{P}, \mathcal{R})$, that describes the personal information types (PIT), their properties, and relations. Contexts are also described with an ontology, $\mathcal{O}_{\text{Cont}} = (\mathcal{C}_{\text{Cont}}, \preceq_{\text{Cont}})$. Given two contexts c_1 and c_2, $c_2 \preceq c_1$ means that all property values that are valid for c_1 are also valid for c_2. To instantiate the user's personal information we have considered that a property value for a property p is defined by a tuple $pv = (v, c, \delta)$ where v is the value, c is a context of the context ontology, and δ is a real number in $[0..1]$ that represents the usability of value v for property p in context c.

To foster automation of the composition process, we further assume that the user structures the PIS with reference to categories of personal information using an ontology $\mathcal{O}_{\text{Info}} = (\mathcal{C}_{\text{Info}}, \preceq_{\text{Info}})$. On the other side, within the context of a research project[1], we are working with an SME partner that develops services for administrations and enterprises. Each service is semantically annotated with semantic information for the forms fields, for the outputs it can produce, and with the set of functionalities, or capabilities, it achieves. The first two correspond to the PIT ontology. For the later we rely on an ontology of capabilities, $\mathcal{O}_{\text{Cap}} = (\mathcal{C}_{\text{Cap}}, \preceq_{\text{Cap}})$. Finally, services can be organized in categories too. For this we assume an ontology of service categories, $\mathcal{O}_{\text{Serv}} = (\mathcal{C}_{\text{Serv}}, \preceq_{\text{Serv}})$

3.3   Policies

The user may express policies on the use of the personal information to be given to services. Given a personal information category x (from $\mathcal{C}_{\text{Info}}$) and a service category y (from $\mathcal{C}_{\text{Serv}}$), a policy authorization (or authorization for short) is a couple (x, y), also denoted by $x \triangleright y$. Its meaning is that any personal information of a category that is x or subsumes it can be given to any service of a category that is y or subsumes it. A policy set, or policy for short, is a set of authorizations.

---

[1] Personal Information Management through Internet
http://genibeans.com/cgi-bin/twiki/view/Pimi/WebHome

3.4   Workflows and Procedures

Workflows capture the behavioral aspects of online procedures. Given a set of names A, used to label the basic activities, a simple (yet expressive) kind of workflow over A, WF^A, can be modeled following [7] by a tuple $(N, \rightarrow, \lambda)$. N is the set of workflow nodes. It can be further divided into disjoint sets $N = N_A \cup N_{SO} \cup N_{SA} \cup N_{JO} \cup N_{JA}$, where N_A are basic activities of the workflow, N_{SO} are XOR-split nodes, N_{SA} are AND-split nodes, N_{JO} are XOR-join nodes, and N_{JA} are AND-join nodes. XOR-split and XOR-join nodes enable to model exclusive choice, while AND-split and AND-join nodes enable to model parallelism. $\rightarrow \subseteq N \times N$ denotes the control flow, and $\lambda : N_A \rightarrow A$ is a function assigning names to activity nodes. We note $\bullet x = \{y \in N \mid y \rightarrow x\}$ and $x \bullet = \{y \in N \mid x \rightarrow y\}$. We require that workflows are well-structured and without loop. A signicant feature of well-structured workflows is that the XOR-splits and the OR-Joins, and the AND-splits and the AND-splits appear in pairs. Moreover, we require $|\bullet x| \leq 1$ for each x in $N_A \cup N_{SA} \cup N_{SO}$ and $|x \bullet| \leq 1$ for each x in $N_A \cup N_{JA} \cup N_{JO}$.

A procedure is the specification of functionalities that should be achieved to reach some goal. These functionalities correspond to capabilities that will be realized through the use of one or several form-based services. We may then model a procedure by a workflow labelled by capabilities, *i.e.*, defined over $\mathcal{C}_{\text{Cap}}$.

3.5   Services

Services require a set of inputs in order to produce outputs and achieve their capabilities. They are organized in categories. Given the ontologies introduced in 3.2, we model services as a tuple $w = (u, I, O, K, C)$ where u is the service URI (address of the service form), $I \subseteq \mathcal{P}$ are the service inputs, $O \subseteq \mathcal{P}$ are the service outputs, $K \subseteq \mathcal{C}_{\text{Cap}}$ are the service capabilities, and $C \in \mathcal{C}_{\text{Serv}}$ is the service category. In the sequel we suppose a set of services W being available to the user. Services may not have capabilities. These correspond for example to transformational services (*e.g.*, to retrieve a postal code from a city name).

3.6   Composition Requirement

The requirement of composition is to find out a correct sequence of groups of services, possibly executed in parallel, *i.e.*, a plan in the sense of planning, that altogether are able to achieve some procedure using only the data they produce and the personal information the user agrees to provide them with. Further, one may precise a specific context in which the procedure is to be executed and a minimal usability value for contextualized information (below this threshold information is not relevant). Given the ontologies introduced in 3.2, a composition requirement is a tuple $Req = (Proc, \underline{c}, \epsilon, W, PIS, Pol)$ where $Proc$ is the procedure one wants to achieve, $\underline{c} \in \mathcal{C}_{\text{Cont}}$ is the context in which we apply the procedure ($\top$ for none), $\epsilon \in [0..1]$ is the minimal acceptable usability degree, W are the available services, PIS is the user PIS (*i.e.*, the set of contextualized property values it contains), and Pol is the user policy set.

4   Automatic Encoding and Resolution of the Composition Problem

In Section 3, we have formalized the composition problem that we address. In this section, we present how it can be automatically solved using a planning problem encoding and by extending the Graphplan algorithm. The approach we follow is first to encode the procedure and the services as planning actions.

4.1   Procedure Encoding

We reuse here a transformation from workflows to Petri nets defined in [7] that has been modified to map planning actions in [11]. The behavioral constraints underlying the workflow semantics (*e.g.*, an action being before/after another one) are supported through two kinds to propositions: $r_{x,y}$ and $c_{x,y}$. We also have a proposition $\sharp$ for initial states, and a proposition $\sqrt{}$ for correct termination states. We may then define actions:

- for each $x \in N_{SA}$, we have an action $\mathbf{a} = \oplus x$, for each $x \in N_{JA}$, we have an action $\mathbf{a} = \overline{\oplus}x$, and for each $x \in N_A$, we have an action $\mathbf{a} = [\lambda(x)]x$. In all three cases, we set:
  $\mathbf{Pre(a)} = \mathbf{Eff^-(a)} = \bigcup_{y \in \bullet x}\{r_{x,y}\}$, and $\mathbf{Eff^+(a)} = \bigcup_{y \in x\bullet}\{c_{x,y}\}$.
- for each $x \in N_{SO}$, for each $y \in x\bullet$, we have an action $\mathbf{a} = \otimes x, y$ and we set:
  $\mathbf{Pre(a)} = \mathbf{Eff^-(a)} = \bigcup_{z \in \bullet x}\{r_{x,z}\}$, and $\mathbf{Eff^+(a)} = \{c_{x,y}\}$.
- For each $x \in N_{JO}$, for each $y \in \bullet x$, we have action $\mathbf{a} = \overline{\otimes}x, y$ and we set:
  $\mathbf{Pre(a)} = \mathbf{Eff^-(a)} = \{r_{x,y}\}$ and $\mathbf{Eff^+(a)} = \bigcup_{z \in \bullet x}\{c_{x,z}\}$
- for each $x \to y$, we have an action $\mathbf{a} = \leadsto x, y$ and we set:
  $\mathbf{Pre(a)} = \mathbf{Eff^-(a)} = \{c_{x,y}\}$ and $\mathbf{Eff^+(a)} = \{r_{y,x}\}$.
- additionally, for any initial action $\mathbf{a}$ we add $\sharp$ in $\mathbf{Pre(a)}$ and $\mathbf{Eff^-(a)}$.
- additionally, for any final action $\mathbf{a}$ we add $\sqrt{}$ in $\mathbf{Eff^+(a)}$.

The procedure and the services are inter-related by ordering constraints over the capabilities. Let us suppose a simple procedure with two capabilities in a sequence $k_1 \to k_2$, a service w_1 with capability k_1, and a service w_2 with capability k_2. w_1 should not be put in an action layer before capability k_1 is enabled. This is achieved after putting the action corresponding to step k_1 in the encoding of the procedure in an action layer. In turn, the actions encoding the following steps of the procedure (here only the $\leadsto$ action, that will enable the action for k_2 later on) should be blocked until capability k_1 has been planned, *i.e.*, here, w_1 has been put in an action layer. For this we propose to rely on two propositions for each capability k in $\mathcal{C}_{\mathrm{Cap}}$: $\mathbf{enabled_k}$ and $\mathbf{done_k}$. In the encoding of the procedure workflow, we then replace any action $a = [k]x$ by two actions a' and $\bar{a}'$ and we set $\mathbf{Pre(a')} = \mathbf{Pre(a)}$, $\mathbf{Eff^-(a')} = \mathbf{Eff^-(a)}$, $\mathbf{Eff^+(\bar{a}')} = \mathbf{Eff^+(a)}$, $\mathbf{Eff^+(a')} = \{\mathbf{enabled_k}, \mathbf{link}_x\}$, and $\mathbf{Eff^-(\bar{a}')} = \{\mathbf{done_k}, \mathbf{link}_x\}$, with $\mathbf{link}_x$ ensuring the correct ordering between a' and $\bar{a}'$.

4.2 Service Encoding

A service can be executed only if all its inputs are available and if its capacities are enabled by the current state of execution of the procedure. The service then generates its outputs and indicates that the capacities have been achieved. Each service $w = (u, I, O, K, C)$ is therefore encoded as an action $\mathbf{a} = (\mathbf{Pre}(\mathbf{a}), \mathbf{Eff}^-(\mathbf{a}), \mathbf{Eff}^+(\mathbf{a}))$ with $\mathbf{Eff}^-(\mathbf{a}) = \bigcup_{k \in K} \{\mathbf{enabled_k}\}$, $\mathbf{Eff}^+(\mathbf{a}) = O \cup \bigcup_{k \in K} \{\mathbf{done_k}\}$, and $\mathbf{Pre}(\mathbf{a}) = I \cup \mathbf{Eff}^-(\mathbf{a})$.

4.3 Resolution of the Composition Problem

Once we have encoded the procedure and the services as planning actions, we can apply the 2-step Graphplan algorithm: graph expansion and then backtracking (see Sect. 2). The second step is the same as in the original algorithm [3]. However, due to the contextualization of data and the use of policies, the first step has to be modified as follows.

Contextual Propositions. As far as the encoding of personal information is concerned, we replace basic propositions by tuples $(p, \underline{c}, \delta)$ corresponding to the PIS property values. Such a tuple denotes that some value for property p in known for context $\underline{c}$ (the context used in the composition requirements) with usability degree δ. Other propositions, *e.g.*, corresponding to the encoding of the procedure, are regular with reference to graph planning.

Filtering Out. A preliminary optimizing step is to filter out any proposition corresponding to personal information p for which there is no enabling policy (some $x' \rhd \_ \in Pol$ where x, $x \preceq_{\text{Info}}{}^* x'$, denotes the category of p). We also remove actions corresponding to services that are not allowed to use some of their inputs, *i.e.*, a service w with at least an input $p \in I(w)$ such that there is no $x' \rhd y' \in Pol$, with x, $x \preceq_{\text{Info}}{}^* x'$, being the category of p and y, $y \preceq_{\text{Serv}}{}^* y'$, being the category of w.

Initialization - $\mathbf{PL_0}$. The first proposition layer contains the initial proposition for the procedure, $\sharp$, together with propositions for the contextual property values in the PIS. For the later, for each property value (v, c, δ) for p, we compute a contextual proposition $(p, \underline{c}, \delta')$ where δ' is equal to $\delta \times \Delta_{c,\underline{c}}^{\mathcal{O}_{\text{Cont}}}$ with $\delta \times \Delta_{c,\underline{c}}^{\mathcal{O}_{\text{Cont}}}$ being the semantic similarity measure between two concepts in the ontology $\mathcal{O}_{\text{Cont}}$ (see [6] for the way we compute this for contextual data querying). We put in $\mathbf{PL_0}$ all the $(p, \underline{c}, \delta')$ where δ' is maximal.

Expansion Basic Step. What changes here with reference to [3] is the condition and effect of adding an action $\mathbf{a}$ related to some service w in an action layer. First w should be authorized to use its input data. This is ensured by the filtering step, above. Second, all inputs required for w should be available in the current proposition layer with a degree higher than the threshold, *i.e.*, for each p in $I(w)$, there is some $(p, \underline{c}, \delta)$ in $\mathbf{PL_{i-1}}$ such that $\delta \geq \epsilon$. If so, for each p in $O(w)$, we add $(p, \underline{c}, \delta')$ in $\mathbf{PL}_i$, where δ' is the minimal value of δ for all the inputs of w in $\mathbf{PL}_{i-1}$. Further, for every k in $K(w)$, we require $\mathbf{enabled_k} \in \mathbf{PL}_{i-1}$ and we add $\mathbf{done_k}$ in $\mathbf{PL}_i$. Since several services may produce the same data, at each step of the expansion we perform a cleaning by keeping in $\mathbf{PL}_i$ only the tuples with the maximal δ, i.e., if we have $(p, \underline{c}, \delta_1)$ and $(p, \underline{c}, \delta_2)$ in $\mathbf{PL}_i$, with $\delta_1 \geq \delta_2$, we keep only the first one.

Nothing changes for actions related to the procedure encoding. Given such an action $\mathbf{a}$, we should have $\mathbf{Pre(a)} \subseteq \mathbf{PL}_{i-1}$, $\mathbf{Eff^-(a)} \subseteq \mathbf{PL}_{i-1}$, and then we add $\mathbf{Eff^+(a)}$ in $\mathbf{PL}_{i-1}$. Non independent actions are treated as in [3], using mutex.

Expansion Termination. Expansion stops with a fix point or with success. The later is reached when there is the $\sqrt{}$ proposition in the current proposition layer, which means that we have successfully completed the procedure. In such as case a solution can be obtained using backtrack. Fix point is if the current proposition layer $\mathbf{PL}_i$ add no new proposition with reference to $\mathbf{PL}_{i-1}$. In order to support data contextualization, we consider a tuple $(p, \underline{c}, \delta_i)$, $\delta_i \geq \epsilon$, to be a new proposition either if there is no tuple $(p, \underline{c}, \_)$ in $\mathbf{PL}_{i-1}$ or if there is a tuple $(p, \underline{c}, \delta_{i-1})$ such that $\delta_{i-1} < \epsilon$. This is because having a new contextual value with a degree above the requirement threshold may yield new possibilities for service-related actions.

4.4   Tool Support

We have defined an Eclipse Modeling Framework model for the models presented in this paper, namely composition requirements with their constituents, and planning problems. Using an ATL model-to-model transformation, we transform the former into the later and then dump the planning problem into a text file using an Acceleo model-to-text transformation. We have implemented our modifications to the graph planning expansion structure in a Java implementation of the Graphplan algorithm[2]. This operates on the textual planning problem file to retrieve solution plans. We are currently packaging our tool support to make it freely available.

5   Conclusion

In this paper we have presented a service composition approach that supports the contextualization of personal information and related user policies. This is achieved using an encoding as a planning problem and the extension of a graph planning technique, which provides full automation of the process. As future work, we plan to study the joint use of several contexts and the contextualization of services, i.e., enabling context-oriented constraints for input and output data in online services. The usability degree we use can be seen as a form of non-functional information used in composition. We plan to study the combination of it with user-specific preferences over non-functional service attributes.

---

[2] http://sourceforge.net/projects/jplan/

Acknowledgement. This work is supported by project "Personal Information Management through Internet" (PIMI-ANR 2010 VERS 0014-03) of the French National Agency for Research.

References

1. Anand, P., Vladimir, K., Lalana, K., Anupam, J.: Enforcing policies in pervasive environments. In: Proc. of MobiQuitous (2004)
2. Bartalos, P., Bieliková, M.: Automatic Dynamic Web Service Composition: A Survey and Problem Formalization. Computing and Informatics 30(4), 793–827 (2012)
3. Blum, A., Furst, M.L.: Fast Planning Through Planning Graph Analysis. Artificial Intelligence 90(1-2), 281–300 (1997)
4. Dulay, N., Damianou, N., Lupu, E.C., Sloman, M.: A policy language for the management of distributed agents. In: Wooldridge, M.J., Weiß, G., Ciancarini, P. (eds.) AOSE 2001. LNCS, vol. 2222, pp. 84–100. Springer, Heidelberg (2002)
5. Hutter, D., Volkamer, M.: Information Flow Control to Secure Dynamic Web Service Composition. In: Clark, J.A., Paige, R.F., Polack, F.A.C., Brooke, P.J. (eds.) SPC 2006. LNCS, vol. 3934, pp. 196–210. Springer, Heidelberg (2006)
6. Khéfifi, R., Poizat, P., Saïs, F.: Modeling and Querying Context-Aware Personal Information Spaces. In: Liddle, S.W., Schewe, K.-D., Tjoa, A.M., Zhou, X. (eds.) DEXA 2012, Part II. LNCS, vol. 7447, pp. 103–110. Springer, Heidelberg (2012)
7. Kiepusewski, B.: Expressiveness and suitability of languages for control flow modelling in workflows. Queensland University of Technology, Brisbane (2003)
8. Marconi, A., Pistore, M.: Synthesis and Composition of Web Services. In: Bernardo, M., Padovani, L., Zavattaro, G. (eds.) SFM 2009. LNCS, vol. 5569, pp. 89–157. Springer, Heidelberg (2009)
9. Mostéfaoui, S.K., Hirsbrunner, B.: Towards a Context-Based Service Composition Framework. In: Proc. of ICWS (2003)
10. Mrissa, M., Benslimane, D., Maamar, Z., Ghedira, C.: Towards a semantic- and context-based approach for composing web services. IJWGS 1(3/4), 268–286 (2005)
11. Poizat, P., Yan, Y.: Adaptive Composition of Conversational Services through Graph Planning Encoding. In: Margaria, T., Steffen, B. (eds.) ISoLA 2010, Part II. LNCS, vol. 6416, pp. 35–50. Springer, Heidelberg (2010)
12. Russell, S.J., Norvig, P., Canny, J.F., Malik, J.M., Edwards, D.D.: Artificial Intelligence: A Modern Approach. Prentice hall, Englewood Cliffs (1995)
13. Sheshagiri, M., Sadeh, N., Gandon, F.: Using Semantic Web Services for Context-Aware Mobile Applications. In: Proc. of MobiSys (2004)
14. Yan, Y., Poizat, P., Zhao, L.: Repair vs. Recomposition for Broken Service Compositions. In: Maglio, P.P., Weske, M., Yang, J., Fantinato, M. (eds.) ICSOC 2010. LNCS, vol. 6470, pp. 152–166. Springer, Heidelberg (2010)

Synthesizing Cost-Minimal Partners for Services

Jan Sürmeli and Marvin Triebel

Humboldt-Universität zu Berlin, Institut für Informatik,
Unter den Linden 6, D-10099 Berlin, Germany
{suermeli,triebel}@informatik.hu-berlin.de

Abstract *Adapter synthesis* bridges incompatibilites between loosely
coupled, stateful services. Formally, adapter synthesis reduces to *partner
synthesis*. Beside an adapter, a partner could be a configurator or serve as
an ingredient in solutions for discovery and substitution. We synthesize a
cost-minimal partner for a given service based on additional behaviorial
constraints. We consider the worst case total costs, specifying individual
transition costs as natural numbers. In this paper, we sketch our formal
approach, and briefly discuss our implementation.

Keywords: Service-orientation, partner synthesis, controller synthesis,
adaptation, non-functional properties, cost-optimization, formal methods.

1 Introduction

A *stateful service* [1] implements a complex task involving interaction with other
services. We study loosely coupled, asynchronously interacting stateful services
and their composition. In this setting, two services N and P do not necessarily
cooperate *optimally*: N and P may have incompatible data types, run into a
deadlock, or cause unnecessarily high costs. *Adapter synthesis* addresses this
problem: An automatically constructed *adapter* A for N and P is a a a service
ensuring that the composition of N, A and P is *optimal*.

Adapter synthesis reduces to *partner synthesis* [2]. Partner synthesis is the
task to automatically construct a *partner service* P for a service N, such that
their composition $N \oplus P$ satisfies given requirements and is optimal regarding
given preferences. Partner synthesis may additionally be applied in other settings,
such as *service configuration* [3], *service discovery* [4] and *service substitution* [5].
As sketched above, requirements and preferences may be defined on different
levels [6], such as syntax, behavior and non-functional properties. There exist
solutions for partner synthesis for selected behavioral [7] and non-functional
requirements [8].

We tackle partner synthesis for the non-functional requirement of
cost-boundedness and the preference of *cost-minimality*. A cost-bounded (cost-
minimal) partner P of a service N ensures finite (minimal) costs in $N \oplus P$
regarding N. In the setting of adaptation, a cost-minimal adapter may reduce
the adaptation costs, the costs of each adapted service, or overall costs. In our
cost model, we consider *worst case total costs*; that is, the supremum of the

S. Basu et al. (Eds.): ICSOC 2013, LNCS 8274, pp. 584–591, 2013.

caused costs in all runs. We aim at modeling non-functional aspects such as execution costs, energy consumption, execution time, carbon dioxide emissions or labor costs. Therefore, we formalize costs as natural numbers.

We explain all core concepts by means of examples in Sect. 2. Based thereon, we sketch our approach to synthesize a cost-minimal partner in Sect. 3 and briefly evaluate our prototypical implementation thereof in Sect. 4. Finally, we discuss related work in Sect. 5 and conclude our work in Sect. 6.

2   Cost-Minimal Partners for Services

We formally model services as *weighted nets* [8]: A weighted net is a Petri net [9], modeling the behavioral aspects, augmented with a cost function, modeling the non-functional aspects. We omit a formal description of weighted net syntax and semantics, but informally introduce the core concepts by means of examples. For more detailed definitions, we kindly point the reader to [10].

Figure 1 shows the five weighted nets N, P_0, P_1, P_2 and $N \oplus P_0$. A circle represents a *buffer* which may hold *tokens*, modeling the state of the service. A token represents a message or other information. As we do not distinguish between individual tokens, we represent each token as a black dot. A rectangle represents a *transition* that consumes from and produces tokens on buffers according to the arrows. If considered, we inscribe a transition with its *costs*. A dashed line marks the *interface*, which consists of one buffer for each exchanged message type.

Figure 1(a) shows a model of a buyer service N with the interface {!Order, ?COD, ?Parcel}; that is, N *sends* messages of type Order and *receives* messages of types COD and Parcel. Initially, N may either terminate causing costs of 3 or may place an order by sending a message Order. In the latter case, N waits for an incoming message which may either be COD or Parcel. Thereby, COD and Parcel mean that the product will be sent by *cash on delivery* and *parcel post*, respectively. Receiving a COD-message or Parcel-message yields the initial state and causes costs of 2 or 0, respectively. The idea is that *cash on delivery* carries a fee whereas *parcel post* does not.

Figure 1(b) shows service P_0 with interface {?Order, !COD, !Parcel}: An online shop that non-deterministically chooses between answering an Order-message with either a COD-message or a Parcel-message. Figure 1(c) shows P_1 which differs from P_0 in the possible answers to an Order-message: P_1 only answers with Parcel. Figure 1(d) shows another variation P_2 of P_0, which may choose COD only twice. We only consider the costs of N and omit costs in P_0, P_1 and P_2.

We observe that the interfaces of N and P_0 match. Therefore, we may *compose* N and P_0, resulting in the weighted net $N \oplus P_0$ shown in Fig. 1(e). Regarding *behavior*, we observe that $N \oplus P_0$ satisfies the behavioral requirements of *weak termination* with message bound 1 (wt_1); that is, $N \oplus P_0$ is free of deadlocks and livelocks, and for each message type, there is always at most one pending message. Thus, we call P_0 a wt_1-*partner* of N. Inspecting the compositions $N \oplus P_1$ and $N \oplus P_2$, we additionally observe that both P_1 and P_2 are wt_1-partners of N. In the remainder, we write *partner* instead of wt_1-partner to increase readability.

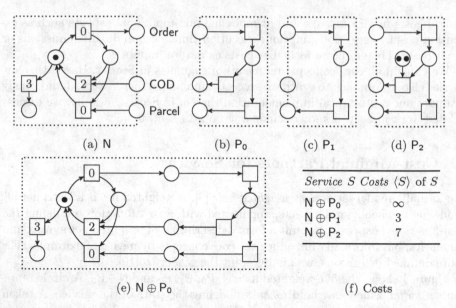

(a) N   (b) P_0 (c) P_1 (d) P_2

(e) $N \oplus P_0$

Service S	Costs $\langle S \rangle$ of S
$N \oplus P_0$	∞
$N \oplus P_1$	3
$N \oplus P_2$	7

(f) Costs

Fig. 1. A service N, three partners $P_0, \ldots, P_2$ of N; the composition $N \oplus P_0$ of N and P_0, and the costs of the composition of N with its depicted partners

We switch from the behavioral to the *non-functional* perspective. In this paper, we apply the model of *worst case total costs*: We define the *costs* $\langle N \oplus P \rangle$ of a weighted net $N \oplus P$ by *totaling* the costs along each *run*, and then selecting the *supremum* of those values. Thereby, a run is a finite sequence of consecutive transitions. As we only consider costs as natural numbers, each run causes finite costs. As there are generally infinitely many runs of arbitrary length, the supremum of the costs of all runs may either be a natural number or infinite. In the case $\langle N \oplus P \rangle$ is finite, we call $N \oplus P$ *cost-bounded*.

Table 1(f) in Fig. 1 summarizes the costs of the aforementioned compositions. Based on these values, we illustrate the concepts of *cost-bounded controllability* and *k-cost-bounded controllability*. Additionally, we introduce the term *cost-minimal partner*. We start with $N \oplus P_1$. Regardless of the number of sent Order-messages, only Parcel-messages are received. As the reception of Parcel does not cause costs, $\langle N \oplus P_1 \rangle$ is finite. Thus, we call N *cost-boundedly controllable*, because there exists a partner causing finite costs. More specifically, it holds $\langle N \oplus P_1 \rangle = 3$, caused by the termination of N with costs of 3. Consequently, we call N also *k-cost-boundedly controllable* for $k = 3$. Because these costs of 3 are inevitable, for all partners P, we find $\langle N \oplus P \rangle \geq 3$. Thus, P_1 is a *cost-minimal partner* of N. Although $\langle N \oplus P_2 \rangle$ is finite as well, we find that P_2 is no cost-minimal partner of N: In contrast to P_1, P_2 may send a COD-message up to two times, thus rising the supremum from 3 to $2 + 2 + 3 = 7$. Inspecting $N \oplus P_0$, we find $\langle N \oplus P_0 \rangle$ is infinite; that is, costs may rise arbitrarily in $N \oplus P_0$: N may send arbitrarily many Order-messages and P_0 may answer arbitrarily many of them with COD. Summarizing, a service N is (1) *k-cost boundedly controllable*, if there exists a partner P, such that $\langle N \oplus P \rangle \leq k$, and (2) cost-bounded controllable, if there is some k, such that N is k-cost-boundedly controllable. A partner P is cost-minimal, if for all partners P' it holds $\langle N \oplus P \rangle \leq \langle N \oplus P' \rangle$.

Imagine a variation N′ of N, where receiving Parcel inflicts costs of 1. Every partner of N′ causes unbounded costs and thus N′ is *not* cost-boundedly controllable: In order to avoid deadlocks, a partner must answer each Order-message. If a high level of abstraction is the reason for such a lack of cost-bounded controllability, we propose to regard *use case costs* instead of total costs. Regarding our example, consider sending Order and receiving either Parcel or COD as the use case. The *use case costs* are the costs of the most expensive complete occurrence of the use case, ignoring all costs outside the use case. If the use case is acyclic, the use case costs are always finite, and we also may reduce partner synthesis w.r.t. use case costs to partner synthesis w.r.t. total costs. Regarding the example, a cost-minimal partner always answers Parcel, yielding use case costs of 1.

3 Synthesizing Cost-Minimal Partners

In this section, we merely sketch our synthesis approach. For a more detailed, formal description, we kindly point the reader to [10]. We synthesize a cost-minimal partner for a given service N in two steps: First, we compute the *minimal cost bound* of N, second, we synthesize a partner for N based thereon. The *minimal cost bound* $\mathrm{mb}(N)$ of N is the least k, such that N is k-cost-boundedly controllable. Formally, we define $\mathrm{mb}(N) \in \mathbb{N}_0 \cup \{\infty\}$ by

$$\mathrm{mb}(N) := \min(\{\langle N \oplus P \rangle \mid P \text{ is a partner of } N\}). \tag{1}$$

We observe that $\mathrm{mb}(N)$ is finite iff N is cost-boundedly controllable. If $\mathrm{mb}(N)$ is known, synthesizing a cost-minimal partner either reduces to synthesizing an arbitrary partner (if $\mathrm{mb}(N)$ is infinite) or a k-cost bounded partner for $k = \mathrm{mb}(N)$ (if $\mathrm{mb}(N)$ is finite). Both problems are solvable: The synthesis of an arbitrary partner is decribed in [7]; for $k = \mathrm{mb}(N)$ the synthesis of an k-cost-bounded partner may be solved by applying the synthesis procedure in [8]. We sketch our computation strategy for $\mathrm{mb}(N)$. First, we decide cost-bounded controllability. In order to decide cost-bounded controllability, we reduce cost-bounded controllability to the decidable problem of k-cost bounded controllability [8]. The reduction is non-trivial, as cost-bounded controllability only implies k-cost-bounded controllability for all $k \geq \mathrm{mb}(N)$. Our idea is to find a canonical k, such that N is cost-bounded controllable iff N is k-cost-bounded controllable. Finally, we find $\mathrm{mb}(N)$ in the interval $0, \ldots, k$.

To this end, we analyze the composition of N and its *most-permissive partner* $\mathrm{mp}(N)$. Intuitively, $\mathrm{mp}(N)$ yields the maximal behavior of N in the composition with an arbitrary partner. A computation procedure for $\mathrm{mp}(N)$ is given in [7]. The *cost discriminant* $\mathrm{dis}(N) \in \mathbb{N}_0$ of N equals the supremum of the costs of all acyclic runs of $N \oplus \mathrm{mp}(N)$. In our running example P₀ (Fig. 1(b)) is the most-permissive partner of N (Fig. 1(a)). The only acyclic run of their composition (Fig. 1(e)) is the run where N directly terminates, which costs 3: All other runs visit the initial state at least twice. Thus, we conclude $\text{dis}(\mathsf{N}) = 3$. We omit a formal definition of $\text{dis}(N)$ in this paper. Instead, we repeat its most important property in the following proposition.

Proposition 1 ([10]). *If* $\text{mb}(N)$ *is finite, then* $\text{mb}(N) \leq \text{dis}(N)$.

That is, $\text{dis}(N)$ is an upper bound for $\text{mb}(N)$ if N is cost-boundedly controllable. Please note that the inverse trivially holds, because then $\text{mb}(N)$ is infinite and thus $\text{dis}(N) < \text{mb}(N)$. Based on Proposition 1, we may conclude that N is cost-boundedly controllable iff N is k-cost-boundedly controllable with $k = \text{dis}(N)$.

Theorem 1. *Let* $k = \text{dis}(N)$. *Then, k-cost-bounded controllability of N coincides with cost-bounded controllability of N.*

Proof. If N is k-cost-boundedly controllable for any $k \in \mathbb{N}_0$, then N is obviously also cost-boundedly controllable. If N is not k-cost-boundedly controllable with $k = \text{dis}(N)$, then $\text{mb}(N) > \text{dis}(N)$. By Proposition 1, $\text{mb}(N)$ is infinite.   □

In previous work [8], we have shown that k-cost-bounded controllability is decidable. Then, by Theorem 1, cost-bounded controllability is decidable as well. Because either $\text{mb}(N) \in \{0, \ldots, \text{dis}(N)\}$ or $\text{mb}(N)$ is infinite, $\text{mb}(N)$ is computable. In our running example, N is k-cost-boundedly controllable for $k = 3$: $\mathsf{P_1}$ is a partner yielding costs of 3 (Table 1(f)). However, N is not k-cost-boundedly controllable for $k = 2$, because no partner could prevent N from terminating with costs of 3. Therefore, $\text{mb}(\mathsf{N}) = 3$ and $\mathsf{P_1}$ is a cost-minimal partner of N.

4   Implementation and Experimental Results

With our tool TARA[1] we synthesize a cost-optimal partner for a given weighted net following our approach from Sect. 3. Thereby, we compute (1) $\text{mp}(N)$, (2) $\text{dis}(N)$, (3) $\text{mb}(N)$, (4) a cost-optimal partner of N. We solve (1) by calling the partner synthesis tool WENDY [11]. For task (2), we first construct the state space of $N \oplus \text{mp}(N)$ applying the state space analyzer LOLA [12]. Then, we compute an over-approximation $k \geq \text{dis}(N)$ from the state space, because computing the exact cost discriminant $\text{dis}(N)$ is very expensive. Task (3) begins with deciding cost-bounded controllability as explained in Theorem 1, applying techniques from [8]. If N is not cost-boundedly controllable, we conclude that $\text{mb}(N)$ is infinite. Otherwise, we find $\text{mb}(N)$ in the discrete interval $[0, \ldots, k]$. There, we apply a binary search, reducing the number of probes to $\log(k)$. Finally, we solve task (4) applying techniques from [8].

The implementation is prototypical and lacks an elaborate evaluation until now. We present some experimental results in Table 1. We obtained Petri net models from given BPEL models with BPEL2oWFN [13] and some mostly academic examples from literature. We added randomly determined cost functions

[1] In order to try TARA, please visit: http://service-technology.org/tara

Table 1. Experimental results of TARA

Weighted net	Origin	|state space|	time (sec)
Beverage machine	Literature [4]	37	< 0.01
Loan approval	BPEL specification [14]	43	0.04
Olive oil ordering	Literature [15]	50	< 0.01
Online shop 2	Literature [13]	77	0.12
Online shop 1	Literature [13]	137	0.10
Travel service 1	BPEL specification [14]	192	0.06
3 Dining philosophers	Literature [16]	499	0.06
Purchase order	BPEL specification [14]	1032	0.31
SMTP	Communication protocol	1042	0.84
Travel service 2	BPEL specification [14]	1440	0.90
Registration (abstract)	Consultant company	2239	2.37
Registration	Consultant company	27372	10.20
5 Dining philosophers	Literature [16]	43848	24.07

to formerly unweighted models. For each model N, column |state space| shows the number of reachable states of the composite $N \oplus mp(N)$, respectively. Column *time (sec)* shows the computation time for synthesizing a cost-optimal partner. As TARA delivered results in less than a second for most of our test cases, we believe that our approach is valid in principal. However, there were also results with computation times of over ten seconds for a real world service, namely **Registration**. Thus, we believe that there is much room for optimization targeting models with large state spaces. Here, we plan to evaluate the applicability of existing approaches, in particular techniques from the field of process analysis.

5   Related Work

We extend our previous work [8] by synthesizing cost-minimal partners instead of k-cost-bounded partners for a given k. Weighted nets are inspired by *weighted automata* [17,18] over arbitrary semirings. We restrict ourselves to a cost model similar to the semiring known as max plus algebra. In general, our techniques can be applied for any semiring which is isomorphic to the max plus algebra. *Weighted timed automata* extend weighted automata by clocks and costs for staying inside one state. Weighted timed automata are a very complex model class (see for instance [19]) and we are not aware of partner synthesis approaches for this formalism. *Q-Automata* [20] constitute another model to capture non-functional requirements in behavioral models. Here, the focus is on composition of component models, making the setting very similar to ours. The approaches deviate in the communication model: Interaction of Q-Automata means synchronization of concurrent actions. Asynchronous communication between Q-automata may be realized by a buffer system in between. We compose open systems by means of asynchronous message exchange without a buffer system. The aim of

Q-Automata is enabling analysis of compositions of open systems. To our knowledge, there does not exist a partner synthesis approach for Q-Automata.

In the area of service-oriented architectures, Oster et al. [21] present a framework to synthesize service compositions regarding non-functional preferences by applying model checking. In contrast to our approach, the composite is built from existing services. We consider the case where only one service is known beforehand. Zeng et al. [22] find an optimal composition of non-interacting atomic tasks each implemented by a web service. We consider interacting systems. In [23], the authors extend timed Petri nets with a cost model. The authors study the issue of minimal cost reachability and coverability. The formalism considers closed systems in contrast to our research of open systems.

6   Summary and Future Work

In this paper, we addressed the problems of (1) *deciding cost-bounded controllability* of and (2) *synthesizing a cost-minimal partner* for a given service. We reduced (1) and (2) to the solvable problems of deciding k-cost-bounded controllability and of synthesizing a k-cost-bounded partner, respectively. We considered transitions costs modeled by natural numbers and studied the worst case total costs of a service composite. We presented some first experimental results of our prototypical implementation.

For future work, we plan to investigate cost models concerned with average costs. To this end, we plan to adopt algorithms from the field of mean-payoff games [24,25]. Another promising direction is to combine our techniques with timed or probabilistic models. Additionally, we would like to evaluate our approach with more realistic examples. In particular, we aim at checking the feasibility of our approach in the field of adaptation and substitutability. We believe that the runtime of the synthesis approach could be improved by developing a new synthesis algorithm for our problem class, instead of reducing our problem to another problem class.

References

1. Papazoglou, M.P.: Web Services: Principles and Technology. Pearson - Prentice Hall, Essex (2007)
2. Gierds, C., Mooij, A.J., Wolf, K.: Reducing adapter synthesis to controller synthesis. IEEE T. Services Computing 5(1), 72–85 (2012)
3. van der Aalst, W.M.P., Lohmann, N., Rosa, M.L.: Ensuring correctness during process configuration via partner synthesis. Inf. Syst. 37(6), 574–592 (2012)
4. Lohmann, N., Massuthe, P., Wolf, K.: Operating guidelines for finite-state services. In: Kleijn, J., Yakovlev, A. (eds.) ICATPN 2007. LNCS, vol. 4546, pp. 321–341. Springer, Heidelberg (2007)
5. Stahl, C., Massuthe, P., Bretschneider, J.: Deciding substitutability of services with operating guidelines. In: Jensen, K., van der Aalst, W.M.P. (eds.) ToPNoC II. LNCS, vol. 5460, pp. 172–191. Springer, Heidelberg (2009)

6. Papazoglou, M.P.: What's in a Service? In: Oquendo, F. (ed.) ECSA 2007. LNCS, vol. 4758, pp. 11–28. Springer, Heidelberg (2007)
7. Wolf, K.: Does my service have partners? In: Jensen, K., van der Aalst, W.M.P. (eds.) ToPNoC II. LNCS, vol. 5460, pp. 152–171. Springer, Heidelberg (2009)
8. Sürmeli, J.: Service discovery with cost thresholds. In: ter Beek, M.H., Lohmann, N. (eds.) WS-FM 2012. LNCS, vol. 7843, pp. 30–48. Springer, Heidelberg (2013)
9. Reisig, W.: Petri Nets: An Introduction. Monographs in Theoretical Computer Science. An EATCS Series, vol. 4. Springer (1985)
10. Sürmeli, J., Triebel, M.: Cost-optimizing compositions of services - analysis and synthesis. Informatik-Berichte 242, Humboldt-Universität zu Berlin (2013)
11. Lohmann, N., Weinberg, D.: Wendy: A tool to synthesize partners for services. Fundam. Inform. 113(3-4), 295–311 (2011)
12. Wolf, K.: Generating petri net state spaces. In: Kleijn, J., Yakovlev, A. (eds.) ICATPN 2007. LNCS, vol. 4546, pp. 29–42. Springer, Heidelberg (2007)
13. Lohmann, N., Massuthe, P., Stahl, C., Weinberg, D.: Analyzing interacting ws-bpel processes using flexible model generation. Data Knowl. Eng. 64(1), 38–54 (2008)
14. Alves, A., et al.: Web services business process execution language version 2.0 (2007)
15. Fisteus, J.A., Fernández, L.S., Kloos, C.D.: Applying model checking to bpel4ws business collaborations. In: Proceedings of the 2005 ACM Symposium on Applied Computing, SAC 2005, pp. 826–830. ACM, New York (2005)
16. Dijkstra, E.W.: Hierarchical ordering of sequential processes. Acta Inf. 1, 115–138 (1971)
17. Droste, M., Kuich, W., Vogler, H.: Handbook of Weighted Automata, 1st edn. Springer Publishing Company, Incorporated (2009)
18. Buchholz, P., Kemper, P.: Model checking for a class of weighted automata. Discrete Event Dynamic Systems 20, 103–137 (2010)
19. Bouyer, P., Brihaye, T., Markey, N.: Improved undecidability results on weighted timed automata. Information Processing Letters 98(5), 188–194 (2006)
20. Chothia, T., Kleijn, J.: Q-automata: Modelling the resource usage of concurrent components. Electronic Notes in Theoretical Computer Science 175(2), 153–167 (2007); Proceedings of the Fifth International Workshop on the Foundations of Coordination Languages and Software Architectures (FOCLASA 2006)
21. Oster, Z.J., Ali, S.A., Santhanam, G.R., Basu, S., Roop, P.S.: A service composition framework based on goal-oriented requirements engineering, model checking, and qualitative preference analysis. In: Liu, C., Ludwig, H., Toumani, F., Yu, Q. (eds.) ICSOC 2012. LNCS, vol. 7636, pp. 283–297. Springer, Heidelberg (2012)
22. Zeng, L., Benatallah, B., Ngu, A.H.H., Dumas, M., Kalagnanam, J., Chang, H.: QoS-Aware Middleware for Web Services Composition. IEEE Trans. Software Eng. 30(5), 311–327 (2004)
23. Abdulla, P.A., Mayr, R.: Minimal Cost Reachability/Coverability in Priced Timed Petri Nets. In: de Alfaro, L. (ed.) FOSSACS 2009. LNCS, vol. 5504, pp. 348–363. Springer, Heidelberg (2009)
24. Zwick, U., Paterson, M.: The complexity of mean payoff games on graphs. Theoretical Computer Science 158, 343–359 (1996)
25. Brim, L., Chaloupka, J., Doyen, L., Gentilini, R., Raskin, J.F.: Faster algorithms for mean-payoff games. Form. Methods Syst. Des. 38(2), 97–118 (2011)

An Architecture to Provide Quality of Service in OGC SWE Context

Thiago Caproni Tavares, Regina Helenna Carlucci Santana,
Marcos José Santana, and Júlio Cezar Estrella

Institute of Mathematics and Computer Science, ICMC/USP,
Avenida Trabalhador São Carlense, 400 - São Carlos, Brasil
{thiagocp,rcs,mjs,jcezar}@icmc.usp.br
http://www.icmc.usp.br

Abstract. The aim of this paper is to describe an architecture named
SWARCH (Sensor Web Architecture) that provides quality of service in
the context of Sensor Web Enablement (SWE) standards. Sensor Web
Enablement is a set of standards proposed by OGC (OpenGis Consortium). These standards provide a transparent and interoperable way to
access data measured by sensors. Thus, SWARCH adds to these features
of the SWE standard ways of service selection that meet several quality
requirements such as response time, availability of sensors, measurement
reliability, among others. Quality requirements are defined by users and
a broker in the architecture. This broker allows appropriate selection of
the sensor network that matches to the QoS parameters. To validate our
results, a case study showing reductions up to 50% and 25% in access
times to SOS and SES services are presented.

Keywords: Web service, Sensor Networks, Performance Evaluation.

1 Introduction

A sensor network is composed of sensors that monitors one or a set of phenomena,
and whose results are sent to an application or a final user [1,11]. A challenge
in sensor networks utilization is in the feasibility of managing and provision the
necessary information use in different applications. On the one side, we have the
infrastructure composed by the sensors and the use of these sensors and strategies
of the information obtained through them. On the other side, some applications
or observers need to receive and process the information. Thus, sensor networks
must have an infrastructure for communication, between sensors and between
network and its observers. Middlewares that provides tools to manage these
communications can be developing to facilitate the use of sensor networks [10].

An approach that has been proposed in the literature considers the sensor
network as a Web Service [4]. Besides, middlewares using the concepts of service
oriented architecture (SOA) have been widely discussed in the literature [6,5].
The Open Geospatial Consortium (OGC) has been working on the definition
of standards and programming frameworks [7]. In this context, SWE (Sensor

S. Basu et al. (Eds.): ICSOC 2013, LNCS 8274, pp. 592–599, 2013.
© Springer-Verlag Berlin Heidelberg 2013

Web Enablement) was proposed. It consists in a set of standards, protocols and interfaces that provides a framework to create sensor system following the principles of service-oriented architectures. Nevertheless, a gap in studies of sensor networks exposed as a service-oriented architecture was found. Mechanisms of Quality of Service are underexplored. Thus, this work presents architecture, named SWARCH, which allows the quality of service provisioning to the context of SWE standards.

This paper is organized as follows. Section 2 shows the SWE standards and a gap regard to quality of service. Section 3 presents the architecture to guarantee QoS in the SWE context. Section 4 discusses a case study to validate the SWARCH. Finally, Section 5 shows conclusion and future work which can be developed from the present work.

2   Background

The SWE defines sensor as devices discovered and accessed by means of a standardization of protocols and interfaces. It can be defined as an infrastructure that enables the integration of sensing resources. Applications or users can discover, access, modify and register sensing and alert services through a standardized way using sensor Web infrastructure. In [2], it is presented an overview of these patterns that are divided in two models. The information model comprises a set of standards that defines data models. These data models are used for the encoding of sensor observations as well as for its metadata. Two patterns are highlighted in information model: Observation & Measurements ((O&M)) and Sensor Model Language (SensorML). The SensorML determines a XML encoding to the description of sensors. It defines the location, input and output data, and the phenomena that is observed by the sensors. In turn, O&M standard defines a schema for the description of observations carried out by sensors. The interface models are used to provide an access mechanism to measured data from sensors through Web service interfaces. Thus, four main services are defined in SWE. The Sensor Observation Service (SOS) is a service that allows to insert and to retrieve sensing data. The Sensor Event Service (SES) is service that allows the registration of users and/or applications in an alert system. The Sensor Planning Service (SPS) is used to modify settings of the sensors into the sensor network. Finally, the Web Notification Service (WNS) is a service that provides an asynchronous notification mechanism between SWE services and clients or between other SWE services.

Additionally, it is being discussed by the community a standard of sensor discovery, which are referred to as SOR (Sensor Observation Registry) and SIR (Sensor Instance Registry). These registry services still have not become SWE standards. A gap found in the SWE specifications refers to QoS constraints. SWE standards do not treat this question in their specifications. The OGC itself assumes this gap considering it as a challenge to be achieved. "OGC standards provide an important framework for addressing semantics, but more work needs to be done to enable fusion of data from diverse sensor types. Data quality and quality of service are important issues to be addressed in sensor web standards development activities" [8]. In [4], it is presented a survey of abstraction mechanisms of sensor networks. The authors conclude that QoS treatments are still little explored in this area.

A work considering QoS criteria in the context of the standards SWE is presented in [9]. The authors provide a search service that take into account non-functional and functional requirements in service selection. The search engine used by the authors does not perform a direct association with the services specifications provided by SWE such as SIR, SOS, and SES. The authors propose an abstract registry that is used to store the functional and nonfunctional requirements. The approach to provide quality of service presented in this paper differs in various aspects in relation to the proposal presented in [9]. Section 3 describes the architecture for QoS provision in the sensor network context and details each component of SWARCH.

3   SWARCH Description

The reference architecture of SWE standards follows a model where there are a client, a registry, and a server. In this model, the client searches a sensor system in the registry. So, the registry returns the sensors that can meet it, functionally. In turn, the client, after discovering service, performs some interaction with it. The aim of the proposed architecture in this work adds the features already implemented in the standard SWE architecture with the selection of services through QoS criteria. The SWARCH, presented in Figure 1, is composed by four components: Client, Broker, Registry, and Services. In short, clients send requests to the Broker that has the responsibility to find services with a specific QoS provisioning. A set of messages that are mostly defined by the SWE standards is used in SWARCH. The exception occurs only for the message 2 that is a composition of the SIR search message where is added an element of quality of service. Therefore, regarding other messages we can highlight the message 1 that represents a request to insert the sensor system description, and it must be held by the service provider. Additionally, message 3 corresponds to a search message that is submitted to the service registry. The Broker in SWARCH extracts message 3 from the message 2. Messages 4 and 5 are messages that carry measurements and alert notifications of sensors, respectively.

The Broker is divided into four major modules. The first interaction is made between Client and WSModule on Broker (message 2). The Client sends a SOAP message that contains two information. The first one sets the search message that will be used for the query in the SIR. In turn, the second information defines the QoS parameters that will be used in the selection of the service. The WSModule receives the SOAP message from the Client. So, WS-Module extracts the encapsulated information and forwards to SearchModule. After, the SearchModule uses the message to make the search query in the SIR, and returns the response message sent by the registry in an array. This array contains the sensor system descriptions (SensorML) of services found in SIR. In sequence, the SearchModule

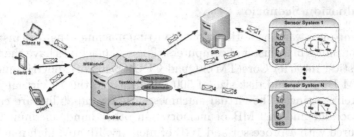

Fig. 1. Swarch Components

updates the array with descriptions of sensors that are cached in the TestModule. The TestModule, upon receiving this query, updates the information from sensors that were not yet inserted into the cache. However, the TestModule returns only the sensors that were present in the cache prior to accepting this new update, and this must be done due to the fact that there is no time to return QoS information of sensors that are not in the cache. The returned array cannot have sensor descriptions, i.e. the size of array is zero. Furthermore, array with size higher than zero means that there is quality of service information to at least one sensor in cache. In this way, the SearchModule prompts the SelectionModule to return the service that best meets the QoS parameters specified by the Client. In contrast, there is a random service selection, since no QoS information is registered in cache. However, the Broker will contain information of quality of service of these services in the next search. Finally, the SearchModule encapsulates service description document in a SOAP response message and sends it to the Client. The architecture presented in this Section is implemented in a prototype to validate the idea in inserting a QoS Broker in SWE context. The prototype has been implemented using the software components provided by 52° North Initiative. Section 4 presents a validation of this prototype.

4   Case Study

The use of a mechanism that supports service discovery based on quality of service criteria is justified for the following scenario. Several companies provide sensing data over the Web using the standards of the SWE. These companies offer a natural disaster sensing service that monitors water level concentration in a specific city. Thus, developers can implement several types of applications that may have different restrictions regarding quality of service. In this case, the architecture proposed in this work selects not only functional aspects of sensing system, but also nonfunctional aspects. The validation of proposal architecture in this work is developed by simulating a scenario where 12 companies (each one offering the same service and data types) provide sensing information of level of water concentration to a particular region. The Section 4.1 presents the evaluation scenario used to validate our approach.

4.1   Evaluation Scenario

The 12 companies were instantiated on 12 virtual machines that are instantiated on 3 real machines in a cluster of computers. The real machines have the following characteristics: Intel(R) Core(TM)2 Quad CPU Q9400 of 2.66GHz, memory of 8 GB RAM DDR 3, and disk size of 500 GB. In turn, the 12 virtual machines have different settings. The virtual machines with low capability are configured with 1 processor and 512 MB of memory. On other hand, medium machines are configured with 1 processor and 1GB of memory. Finally, high machines are configures with 2 processor and 2 GB of memory.

The SOS services configured on virtual machines contain a data base with the levels of concentration of water. The insertion of the observations in the data base mimics the behavior of sensor networks that sends an observation to the service every 5 minutes to SOS during one month. In this validation it is used an observation filter that restricts the observation period into 3 days. It is considered two factors in validation: Broker utilization and amount of threads (clients). The response time is the metric utilized in experiments. Two types of experiments were performed. The first experiment accesses SWE services (SOS and SES) without Broker intermediation, i.e. the search of the sensors is sent directly to the SIR. It is important to note that the client searches for observable properties that are registered in all virtual machines configured for the implementation of validation. In first experiment, the SIR service returns a list of 12 possibilities of services to the clients. Then, the threads select a service to submit requests randomly. Otherwise, the second experiment takes into account Broker utilization in the service discovery process. In this case, a QoS parameter is sent together with the search message, and unlike the first experiment, the return message from the Broker reports only one service. The Broker returns only the service that meets client QoS criteria. Twenty experiments were executed considering ten amounts of threads and versions with and without Broker. Each experiment is replicated 30 times to obtain a statistical validity. It is important to note that obtained response times in the experiments consider interaction between clients and providers, after the service selection. Section 4.2 discusses the obtained results.

4.2   Results

The results obtained for the completion of the validation presented in this section are represented in two types of charts. Response time charts present the variation of average response times in relation to increasing of workloads. The confidence intervals are calculated using an alpha of 0.05 (95% confidence interval). In turn, Pareto charts show the influences of each of the factors in the tests. In contrast to response time charts, the Pareto charts show an analysis considering a workload only to 10 and 100 threads. This analysis consists in calculating a linear regression model that considers two factors with two levels, such as: **Broker utilization** (with and without Broker) and **workload** (10 and 100 threads). The method of calculation is presented in [3].

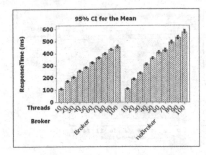

Fig. 2. SES: Response Times

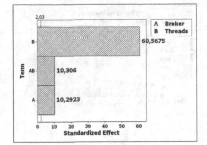

Fig. 3. SES: Factor Influence

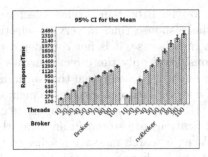

Fig. 4. SOS: Response Times

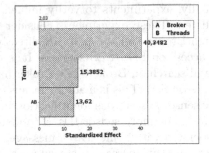

Fig. 5. SOS: Factor Influence

The chart in Figure 2 shows the results of experiments conducted on the SES service. The Broker intermediation improves response times for up to 21.6% on experiments of SES service. The Figure 3 shows a Pareto chart that defines the number of threads as the most influential factor in the tests, followed by the Broker factor. The use of the threads has significant influence in experiments since the values for the Broker in Pareto chart overtook vertical line. So, the experiments demonstrate that the Broker provides better performance when there is an increase on workload service. In the experiments conducted on the SOS service (Figure 4), it is also possible to observe that the improvement in response times, using the Broker intermediation, is higher regarding SES services. Furthermore, the Broker, used as an intermediary in the selection of the SOS service, decreases response times in approximately 46% compared to its non-use. Regarding to the influence, demonstrated in Figure 5, it is noticeable that amount of threads is the most influential factor. However, the Broker intermediation has a considerable influence. Thus, important information that must be highlighted for both SOS and SES services is related to the confidence interval obtained on Broker experiments. The standard deviation of the experiments without the Broker is higher when compared to the standard deviation of the experiment including the Broker. So, these results show that the use of the Broker makes the service access more stable.

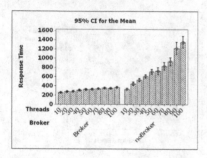
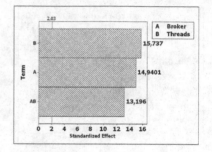

Fig. 6. Broker: Response Times   **Fig. 7.** Broker: Factor Influence

Finally, experiments to verify influence of the Broker in service select were conducted. These experiments consider the response time in service selection through Broker and through SIR directly. In this case, it is not considered the time access on SOS/SES services. It is considered only the direct searches on SIR and search on Broker. The Broker has another cache system that optimizes searches on SIR. This is made by means of a storing search messages in memory. Every sensor system has identification in SIR service. So, a search message can return one or more sensor IDs. The identifications are stored in an array that is associated with some search message. When a search message reaches to the Broker, and this message is stored in cache, the Broker changes this message for a search by ID. ID searches are faster than searches by other criteria. However, we considered in the Broker experiments a cache hit rate of 40%. The chart of Figure 6 demonstrates the response times for the selection service. It can be observed that response times in Broker experiments are lower and more stable. Additionally, Pareto chart presented in Figure 7 shows the broker with almost the same influence of the amount of threads. That is, the Broker impacts significantly on response times of service selection. Section 5 presents the conclusion and future work of our approach.

5   Conclusion and Future Work

This paper presents architecture to provide QoS support in SWE context, highlighting specifically the SOS and SES services. Therefore, the proposed architecture has, as a main element, a Broker that periodically monitors the QoS parameters on SWE services. The QoS provisioning was implemented by means of an insertion of a quality of service element in a SIR search message, and this QoS element is used to guide the Broker in a service selection that meets application with quality of service constraints. The validation of the architecture presented in this paper evaluates response times on service access using a Broker as intermediary component in SWE services selection. Furthermore, it also evaluates response times in service access through experiments planning that indicates statically the architecture efficiency. Additionally, the insertion of the Broker in the process of service selection improves significantly the response times in access to the considered services.

Future work should add functionality to improve the specifications of quality of service parameters. Thus, the implementation of this feature may be used more formal mechanism for the determination of QoS parameters such as WSLA (Web Service Level Agreement). The use of this type of specification can assist in maintaining interoperability of SWARCH with the protocols and languages defined in SWE. In addition, it is intended to extend the tool for use in cloud computing. In this case, the Broker would have function to check the QoS parameters to manage the elasticity of the resources available in the processing of the SWE services configured in a cloud infrastructure.

Acknowledgements. The authors would like to thank the financial support of FAPESP (São Paulo Research Foundation), FAPEMIG (Minas Gerais Research Foundation), and IFSULDEMINAS/Campus Inconfidentes (Federal Institute of Education, Science and Technology of Southern of Minas Gerais).

References

1. Akyildiz, I., Vuran, M.C.: Wireless Sensor Networks. John Wiley & Sons, Inc., New York (2010)
2. Bröring, A., Echterhoff, J., Jirka, S., Simonis, I., Everding, T., Stasch, C., Liang, S., Lemmens, R.: New generation sensor web enablement. Sensors 11(3), 2652–2699 (2011), http://www.mdpi.com/1424-8220/11/3/2652
3. Jain, R.K.: The Art of Computer Systems Performance Analysis: Techniques for Experimental Design, Measurement, Simulation, and Modeling. Wiley (April 1991)
4. Laukkarinen, T., Suhonen, J., Hännikäinen, M.: A survey of wireless sensor network abstraction for application development. IJDSN 2012 (2012), http://dblp.uni-trier.de/db/journals/ijdsn/ijdsn2012.html#LaukkarinenSH12
5. Mohamed, N., Al-Jaroodi, J.: Service-oriented middleware approaches for wireless sensor networks. In: 2011 44th Hawaii International Conference on System Sciences (HICSS), pp. 1–9 (2011)
6. Neto, F.C., Ribeiro, C.M.F.A.: Dynamic change of services in wireless sensor network middleware based on semantic technologies. In: International Conference on Autonomic and Autonomous Systems, pp. 58–63 (2010)
7. OGC: Ogc standards and specifications (December 2013), http://www.opengeospatial.org/standards (last access: May 06, 2013)
8. OGC: Why is the ogc involved in sensor webs? (2013), http://www.opengeospatial.org/domain/swe (last access: May 09, 2013)
9. Parhi, M., Acharya, B.M., Puthal, B.: Discovery of sensor web registry services for wsn with multi-layered soa framework. In: 2011 2nd International Conference on Computer and Communication Technology (ICCCT), pp. 524–530 (2011)
10. Wang, M., Cao, J., Li, J., Das, S.K.: Middleware for wireless sensor networks: A survey. J. Comput. Sci. Technol. 23(3), 305–326 (2008)
11. Yick, J., Mukherjee, B., Ghosal, D.: Wireless sensor network survey. Comput. Netw. 52(12), 2292–2330 (2008)

Verification of Semantically-Enhanced Artifact Systems*

Babak Bagheri Hariri, Diego Calvanese, Marco Montali,
Ario Santoso, and Dmitry Solomakhin

KRDB Research Centre for Knowledge and Data, Free University of Bozen-Bolzano
lastname@inf.unibz.it

Abstract. Artifact-Centric systems have emerged in the last years as a suitable framework to model business-relevant entities, by combining their static and dynamic aspects. In particular, the Guard-Stage-Milestone (GSM) approach has been recently proposed to model artifacts and their lifecycle in a declarative way. In this paper, we enhance GSM with a Semantic Layer, constituted by a full-fledged OWL 2 QL ontology linked to the artifact information models through mapping specifications. The ontology provides a conceptual view of the domain under study, and allows one to understand the evolution of the artifact system at a higher level of abstraction. In this setting, we present a technique to specify temporal properties expressed over the Semantic Layer, and verify them according to the evolution in the underlying GSM model. This technique has been implemented in a tool that exploits state-of-the-art ontology-based data access technologies to manipulate the temporal properties according to the ontology and the mappings, and that relies on the GSMC model checker for verification.

1 Introduction

In the last decade, the marriage between processes and data has been increasingly advocated as a key objective towards a comprehensive modeling and management of complex enterprises [10]. This requires to go beyond classical (business) process specification languages, which largely leave the connection between the process dimension and the data dimension underspecified, and to consider data and processes as "two sides of the same coin" [21]. In this respect, artifact-centric systems [19,16] have lately emerged as an effective framework to model business-relevant entities, by combining in a holistic way their static and dynamic aspects. Artifacts are characterized by an "information model", which maintains the artifact data, and by a lifecycle that specifies the allowed ways to progress the information model. Among the different proposals for artifact-centric process modelling, the Guard-Stage-Milestone (GSM) approach has been recently proposed to model artifacts and their lifecycle in a declarative, flexible way [17]. GSM is equipped with a formal execution semantics [13], which unambiguously characterizes the artifact progression in response to external events. Several key constructs of the OMG standard on Case Management and Model Notation [1] have been borrowed from GSM.

---

* This research has been partially supported by the EU under the ICT Collaborative Project ACSI (Artifact-Centric Service Interoperation), grant agreement n. FP7-257593.
[1] http://www.omg.org/spec/CMMN/

S. Basu et al. (Eds.): ICSOC 2013, LNCS 8274, pp. 600–607, 2013.

Despite the tight integration between the data and process component, the artifact information model typically relies on relatively simple structures, such as (nested) lists of key-value pairs. This causes an abstraction gap between the high-level, conceptual view that business stakeholders have of domain-relevant entities and relations, and the low-level representation adopted inside artifacts. To overcome this problem, in [9] it is proposed to enhance artifact systems with a Semantic Layer, constituted by a full-fledged ontology linked to the artifact information models through mapping specifications. On the one hand, the ontology allows one to understand the evolution of the artifact system at a higher level of abstraction. On the other hand, mapping specifications allow one to connect the elements present in the Semantic Layer with the concrete data in the artifact information models, relying on the Ontology-Based Data Access (OBDA) [6].

We follow here an approach similar to [9], and which is based on specifying in terms of the Semantic Layer dynamic/temporal laws that the system should obey, and that need to be verified according to the evolution in the underlying artifact layer. Differently from [9], in which the Semantic Layer is mainly used to *govern* the progression of artifacts, by forbidding the execution of actions that would lead to violation of the constraints in the ontology, here we are primarily interested in exploiting the Semantic Layer to ease the specification of the dynamic/temporal laws. In this light, we extend the technique provided in [9] by relying on a more expressive verification formalism, which supports first-order epistemic queries embedded into an expressive temporal language, the first-order μ-calculus [15], while allowing for quantification across states. The latter makes it possible to predicate over the temporal evolution of individuals, an enhancement that is fundamental for capturing many practical scenarios. To specify the ontology constituting the Semantic Layer, we adopt the OWL 2 QL profile [18] of the standard Web Ontology Language (OWL) [4], since it enjoys so-called *first-order rewritability* of query answering [8], which guarantees that conjunctive queries posed over the ontology can be rewritten into first-order queries that incorporate the ontological constraints, and thus do not require further inference for query answering.

This framework has led to the development of a tool called OBGSM, which relies on GSM as the artifact model, and on state of the art technologies for dealing with the ontology and the mappings, and for performing verification. We refer to an extended version of this paper [3] for proofs and the application of OBGSM on a real case study.

2 Preliminaries

OWL 2 QL is a profile of the Web Ontology Language OWL 2 standardized by the W3C. OWL 2 QL is specifically designed for building an ontology layer to wrap possibly very large data sources. Technically, OWL 2 QL is based on the description logic *DL-Lite$_\mathcal{R}$*, which is a member of the *DL-Lite* family [8], designed specifically for effective ontology-based data access, and which we adopt in the following.

In description logics (DLs) [1], the domain of interest is modeled by means of *concepts*, representing classes of objects, and *roles*, representing binary relations between objects.[2] In *DL-Lite$_\mathcal{R}$*, concepts C and roles U obey to the following syntax:

---

[2] Without loss of generality, we do not distinguish between roles (OWL 2 object properties), and attributes (OWL 2 data properties) - see [6].

$$B ::= N \mid \exists U \qquad\qquad C ::= B \mid \exists U.B \qquad\qquad U ::= P \mid P^-$$

P denotes a *role name*, and P^- an *inverse role*, which swaps the first and second components of P. N denotes a *concept name*, and B a *basic concept*, which is either simply a concept name, or the projection of a role P on its first component ($\exists P$) or its second component ($\exists P^-$). In the concept $\exists U.B$, the projection on the first (resp., second) component of U can be further qualified by requiring that the second (resp., first) component of U is an instance of the basic concept B.

In DLs, the domain knowledge is split into an intensional part (*TBox*), and an extensional part (*ABox*). Specifically, a *DL-Lite$_\mathcal{R}$ ontology* is a pair (T, A), where the TBox T is a finite set of (concept and role) *inclusion assertions* of the forms $B \sqsubseteq C$ and $U_1 \sqsubseteq U_2$, and of *disjointness assertions* of the forms disjoint(B_1, B_2) and disjoint(U_1, U_2). The ABox A is a finite set of *facts* (membership assertions) of the forms $N(c_1)$ and $P(c_1, c_2)$, where N and P occur in T, and c_1 and c_2 are constants.

The semantics of a *DL-Lite$_\mathcal{R}$* ontology is given in terms of first-order *interpretations* $\mathcal{I} = (\Delta^\mathcal{I}, \cdot^\mathcal{I})$, where $\Delta^\mathcal{I}$ is the interpretation domain and $\cdot^\mathcal{I}$ is an interpretation function that assigns to each concept C a subset $C^\mathcal{I} \subseteq \Delta^\mathcal{I}$ and to each role U a binary relation $U^\mathcal{I} \subseteq \Delta^\mathcal{I} \times \Delta^\mathcal{I}$, capturing the intuitive meaning of the various constructs (see [8] for details). An interpretation that satisfies all assertions in T and A is called a *model* of the ontology (T, A), and the ontology is said to be *satisfiable* if it admits at least one model.

Queries. As usual (cf. OWL 2 QL), answers to queries are formed by terms denoting individuals explicitly mentioned in the ABox. The *domain of an ABox A*, denoted by ADOM(A), is the (finite) set of terms appearing in A. A *union of conjunctive queries* (UCQ) q over a KB (T, A) is a FOL formula of the form $\bigvee_{1 \leq i \leq n} \exists \vec{y_i}.conj_i(\vec{x}, \vec{y_i})$ with free variables $\vec{x}$ and existentially quantified variables $\vec{y}_1, \ldots, \vec{y}_n$. Each $conj_i(\vec{x}, \vec{y_i})$ in q is a conjunction of atoms of the form $N(z)$, $P(z, z')$, where N and P respectively denote a concept and a role name occurring in T, and z, z' are constants in ADOM(A) or variables in $\vec{x}$ or $\vec{y_i}$, for some $i \in \{1, \ldots, n\}$. The *(certain) answers* to q over (T, A) is the set $ans(q, T, A)$ of substitutions σ of the free variables of q with constants in ADOM(A) such that $q\sigma$ evaluates to true in every model of (T, A). If q has no free variables, then it is called *boolean* and its certain answers are either true or false.

We compose UCQs using ECQs, i.e., queries of the query language *EQL-Lite*(UCQ) [7], which is the FOL query language whose atoms are UCQs. An *ECQ* over T and A is a possibly open formula of the form

$$Q := [q] \mid \neg Q \mid Q_1 \wedge Q_2 \mid \exists x.Q$$

where q is a UCQ. The *answer to Q over (T, A)* is the set ANS(Q, T, A) of tuples of constants in ADOM(A) defined by composing the certain answers $ans(q, T, A)$ of UCQs q through first-order constructs, and interpreting existentials as ranging over ADOM(A).

Finally, we recall that *DL-Lite$_\mathcal{R}$* enjoys the *FO rewritability* property, which states that for every UCQ q, $ans(q, T, A) = ans($REW$(q), \emptyset, A)$, where REW(q) is a UCQ computed by the reformulation algorithm in [6]. Notice that this algorithm can be extended to ECQs [7], and that its effect is to "compile away" the TBox. Similarly, ontology satisfiability is FO rewritable for *DL-Lite$_\mathcal{R}$* TBoxes [6], which states that for every

TBox T, there exists a boolean first-order query $\mathsf{q}_{unsat}(T)$ such that for every non-empty ABox A, we have that (T, A) is satisfiable iff $ans(\mathsf{q}_{unsat}(T), T, A) = \mathsf{false}$.

Ontology-Based Data Access (OBDA). In an OBDA system, a relational database is connected to an ontology representing the domain of interest by a mapping, which relates database values with values and (abstract) objects in the ontology (cf. [6]). In particular, we make use of a countably infinite set $\mathcal{V}$ of values and a set $\varLambda$ of function symbols, each with an associated arity. We also define the set $\mathcal{C}$ of constants as the union of $\mathcal{V}$ and the set $\{f(d_1, \ldots, d_n) \mid f \in \varLambda \text{ and } d_1, \ldots, d_n \in \mathcal{V}\}$ of *object terms*.

Formally, an OBDA system is a structure $\mathcal{O} = \langle R, T, \mathcal{M} \rangle$, where: *(i)* $R = \{R_1, \ldots, R_n\}$ is a database schema, constituted by a finite set of relation schemas; *(ii)* T is a *DL-Lite$_\mathcal{R}$* TBox; *(iii)* $\mathcal{M}$ is a set of mapping assertions, each of the form $\Phi(\vec{x}) \rightsquigarrow \Psi(\vec{y}, \vec{t})$, where: (a) $\vec{x}$ is a non-empty set of variables, (b) $\vec{y} \subseteq \vec{x}$, (c) $\vec{t}$ is a set of object terms of the form $f(\vec{z})$, with $f \in \varLambda$ and $\vec{z} \subseteq \vec{x}$, (d) $\Phi(\vec{x})$, which also called as *source query*, is an arbitrary SQL query over R, with $\vec{x}$ as output variables, and (e) $\Psi(\vec{y}, \vec{t})$, which also called as *target query*, is a CQ over T of arity $n > 0$ without non-distinguished variables, whose atoms are over the variables $\vec{y}$ and the object terms $\vec{t}$.

Given a database instance $\mathcal{I}$ (made up of values in $\mathcal{V}$ and conforming to schema R) and a mapping assertion $m = \Phi(x) \rightsquigarrow \Psi(y, t)$, the *virtual ABox* generated from $\mathcal{I}$ by m is $m(\mathcal{I}) = \bigcup_{v \in eval(\Phi, \mathcal{I})} \Psi[x/v]$, where $eval(\Phi, \mathcal{I})$ denotes the evaluation of the SQL query Φ over $\mathcal{I}$, and where we consider $\Psi[x/v]$ to be a set of atoms (as opposed to a conjunction). The ABox generated from $\mathcal{I}$ by the mapping $\mathcal{M}$ is $\mathcal{M}(\mathcal{I}) = \bigcup_{m \in \mathcal{M}} m(\mathcal{I})$. As for ABoxes, the active domain $\mathrm{ADOM}(\mathcal{I})$ of a database instance $\mathcal{I}$ is the set of values occurring in $\mathcal{I}$. Given an OBDA system $\mathcal{O} = \langle R, T, \mathcal{M} \rangle$ and a database instance $\mathcal{I}$ for R, a *model* for $\mathcal{O}$ wrt $\mathcal{I}$ is a model of the ontology $(T, \mathcal{M}(\mathcal{I}))$. We say that $\mathcal{O}$ wrt $\mathcal{I}$ is satisfiable if it admits a model wrt $\mathcal{I}$.

A UCQ q over an OBDA system $\mathcal{O} = \langle R, T, \mathcal{M} \rangle$ and a relational instance $\mathcal{I}$ for R is simply an UCQ over $(T, \mathcal{M}(\mathcal{I}))$. To compute the certain answers of q over $\mathcal{O}$ wrt $\mathcal{I}$, we follow the standard three-step approach [6]: *(i)* q is *rewritten* to compile away T, obtaining $q_r - rew(q, T)$; *(ii)* the mapping $\mathcal{M}$ is used to *unfold* q_r into an SQL query over R, denoted by $\mathrm{UNFOLD}(q_r, \mathcal{M})$ [20]; *(iii)* such a query is executed over $\mathcal{I}$, obtaining the certain answers. For an ECQ, we can proceed in a similar way, applying the rewriting and unfolding steps to the embedded UCQs. It follows that computing certain answers to UCQs/ECQs in an OBDA system is FO rewritable. Applying the unfolding step to $\mathsf{q}_{unsat}(T)$, we obtain also that satisfiability in $\mathcal{O}$ is FO rewritable.

3   Semantically-Enhanced Artifact Systems

In this section we introduce Semantically-enhanced Artifact Systems (SASs), taking inspiration from the semantic governance framework introduced in [9]. Intuitively, SAS models systems in which artifacts progress according to their lifecycles, and in which the evolution of the entire system is understood through the conceptual lens of an OWL 2 QL ontology. In accordance with the literature [14], it is assumed that artifacts are equipped with a relational information model. More specifically, a SAS is constituted by: *(i)* A *Relational Layer*, which account for the (relational) information models of the artifacts, and which employs a global transition relation to abstractly capture the

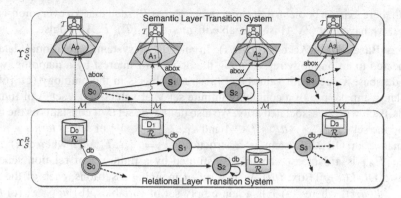

Fig. 1. Sketch of the Relational and Semantic Transition System of a SAS

step-by-step evolution of the system as a whole. *(ii)* A *Semantic Layer*, which contains an OWL 2 QL ontology that conceptually accounts for the domain under study. *(iii)* A set of *mapping assertions* describing how to virtually project data concretely maintained at the Relational Layer into concepts and relations modeled in the Semantic Layer, thus providing a link between the artifact information models and the ontology.

In the following, we assume a countably infinite set of values $\mathcal{V}$. Formally, a SAS $\mathcal{S}$ is a tuple $\mathcal{S} = \langle R, \mathcal{I}_0, \mathcal{F}, T, \mathcal{M} \rangle$, where: *(i)* R is a database schema that incorporates the schemas of all artifact information models present in the Relational Layer; *(ii)* $\mathcal{I}_0$ is a database instance made up of values in $\mathcal{V}$ and conforming to R, which represents the initial state of the Relational Layer,; *(iii)* $\mathcal{F} \subseteq \Gamma \times \Gamma$ is the transition relation that describes the overall progression mechanism of the Relational Layer, where Γ is the set of all instances made up of values in $\mathcal{V}$ and conforming to R; *(iv)* T is a *DL-Lite*$_\mathcal{R}$ TBox; *(v)* $\mathcal{M}$ is a set of mapping assertions that connect R to T, following the approach described in Section 2. The triple $\langle R, T, \mathcal{M} \rangle$ constitutes, in fact, an OBDA system. Thus, $\mathcal{S}$ can be seen as an OBDA system equipped with a transition relation that accounts for the dynamics of the system at the level of R, starting from $\mathcal{I}_0$.

3.1 Execution Semantics

The execution semantics of a SAS $\mathcal{S}$ is provided by means of transition systems. While the temporal structure of such systems is fully determined by the transition relation of $\mathcal{S}$, the content of each state in the system depends on whether the dynamics of SASs is understood directly at the Relational Layer, or through the conceptual lens of the Semantic Layer ontology. In the former case, each state is associated to a database instance that represents the current snapshot of the artifact information models, whereas in the latter case each state is associated to an ABox that represents the current state of the system, as understood by the Semantic Layer.

Following this approach, the execution semantics of $\mathcal{S}$ is captured in terms of two transition systems, one describing the allowed evolutions at the Relational Layer (*Relational Transition System - RTS*), and one abstracting them at the Semantic Layer (*Semantic Transition System - STS*). Figure 1 provides a graphical intuition about the RTS and STS, and their interrelations.

RTS. Given a SAS $\mathcal{S} = \langle R, \mathcal{I}_0, \mathcal{F}, T, \mathcal{M} \rangle$, its RTS $\mathcal{T}_\mathcal{S}^R$ is defined as a tuple $\langle R, \Sigma, s_0, db, \Rightarrow \rangle$, where: *(i)* Σ is a set of states, *(ii)* $s_0 \in \Sigma$, *(iii)* db is a function that, given a state in Σ, returns a corresponding database instance (conforming to R), *(iv)* $\Rightarrow \subseteq \Sigma \times \Sigma$ is the transition relation. The components Σ, $\Rightarrow$ and db of $\mathcal{T}_\mathcal{S}^R$ are defined by simultaneous induction as the smallest sets satisfying the following conditions:

- $db(s_0) = \mathcal{I}_0$;
- for every databases instance $\mathcal{I}'$ such that $\langle db(s), \mathcal{I}' \rangle \in \mathcal{F}$:
  - if there exists $s' \in \Sigma$ such that $db(s') = \mathcal{I}'$, then $s \Rightarrow s'$;
  - otherwise, if $\mathcal{O} = \langle R, T, \mathcal{M} \rangle$ is *satisfiable* wrt $\mathcal{I}'$, then $s' \in \Sigma$, $s \Rightarrow s'$ and $db(s') = \mathcal{I}'$, where s' is a fresh state.

The satisfiability check done in the last step of the RTS construction accounts for the semantic *governance* (cf. Section 1): a transition is preserved in the RTS only if the target state does not violate any constraints of the Semantic Layer, otherwise it is rejected [9].

STS. Given a SAS $\mathcal{S} = \langle R, \mathcal{I}_0, \mathcal{F}, T, \mathcal{M} \rangle$, its STS $\mathcal{T}_\mathcal{S}^S$ is defined as a tuple $\langle R, \Sigma, s_0, db, \Rightarrow \rangle$, which is similar to an RTS, except from the fact that states are attached to ABoxes, not database instances. In particular, $\mathcal{T}_\mathcal{S}^S$ is defined as a "virtualization" of the RTS $\mathcal{T}_\mathcal{S}^R = \langle R, \Sigma, s_0, db, \Rightarrow \rangle$ at the Semantic Layer: it maintains the structure of $\mathcal{T}_\mathcal{S}^R$ unaltered, reflecting that the progression of the system is determined at the Relational Layer, but it associates each state to a virtual ABox obtained from the application of the mapping specification $\mathcal{M}$ to the database instance associated by $\mathcal{T}_\mathcal{S}^R$ to the same state. Formally, the transition relation $\mathcal{M}$ is equivalent to the one of the $\mathcal{S}$, and the *abox* function of $\mathcal{T}_\mathcal{S}^S$ is defined as follows: for each $s \in \Sigma$, $abox(s) = \mathcal{M}(db(s))$.

4   Verification of Semantically-Enhanced Artifact Systems

Given a SAS $\mathcal{S}$, we are interested in studying verification of semantic dynamic/temporal properties specified over the Semantic Layer, i.e., to be checked against the STS $\mathcal{T}_\mathcal{S}^S$. As verification formalism, we consider a variant of first-order μ-calculus [15,22], called $\mu\mathcal{L}_A^{EQL}$ [2,11]. We observe that μ-calculus is one of the most powerful temporal logics: it subsumes LTL, PSL, and CTL* [12]. The logic $\mu\mathcal{L}_A^{EQL}$ supports querying the states of the STS through the first-order epistemic queries introduced in Section 2. In $\mu\mathcal{L}_A^{EQL}$, first-order quantification is restricted to objects present in the current ABox, and can be used to relate objects across states. The syntax of $\mu\mathcal{L}_A^{EQL}$ is as follows:

$$\Phi ::= Q \mid \neg\Phi \mid \Phi_1 \wedge \Phi_2 \mid \exists x.\text{LIVE}(x) \wedge \Phi \mid \langle - \rangle \Phi \mid Z \mid \mu Z.\Phi$$

Where Q is an ECQ over T, Z is a second-order variable denoting a 0-ary predicate, μ is the least fixpoint operator, and the special predicate $\text{LIVE}(x)$ is used to indicate that x belongs to the current active domain, i.e., it is mentioned in some concept or role of the current ABox. For a detailed semantics of $\mu\mathcal{L}_A^{EQL}$, refer to [2,11].

Given a SAS $\mathcal{S}$, we show that verification of $\mu\mathcal{L}_A^{EQL}$ properties over the STS $\mathcal{T}_\mathcal{S}^S$ can be reduced to verification of $\mu\mathcal{L}_A$ [10] properties over the RTS $\mathcal{T}_\mathcal{S}^R$, where $\mu\mathcal{L}_A$ is a logic similar to $\mu\mathcal{L}_A^{EQL}$, except for the local formula Q, which is an (open) first-order query over the database schema in the Relational Layer.

Theorem 1. *For every SAS $\mathcal{S}$ and $\mu\mathcal{L}_A^{EQL}$ property Φ, there exists a $\mu\mathcal{L}_A$ property Φ' such that $\mathcal{T}_\mathcal{S}^R$ satisfies Φ if and only if $\mathcal{T}_\mathcal{S}^S$ satisfied Φ'.*

5 SAS Instantiation: The OBGSM Tool

The formal framework of SASs has led to the development of the OBGSM tool. OBGSM assumes that the RTS is obtained from artifacts, specified using the Guard-Stage-Milestone (GSM) approach. The main task accomplished by the tool is the reformulation of temporal properties expressed over the ontology in terms of the underlying GSM information model. In particular, OBGSM adopts: *(i)* The state of the art OBDA system -ONTOP-[3] to efficiently rewrite and unfold the epistemic queries embedded in the temporal property to verify. *(ii)* the recently developed GSMC model checker for GSM [5] to accomplish the actual verification phase. GSMC is currently the only model checker able to verify temporal formulae over artifact systems.

Since the temporal formalism supported by GSMC is a variant of the first-order branching time logic CTL [12] with a restricted form of quantification across states, the $\mu\mathcal{L}_A^{EQL}$ has been restricted accordingly in the tool [4]. This, in turn, required to suitably accommodate the mapping language so as to ensure that temporal formulae over the Semantic Layer correspond, once rewritten and unfolded, to properties that can be processed by GSMC. Furthermore, in accordance to -ONTOP-, both the temporal properties and the mappings rely on the SPARQL query language to query the Semantic Layer.

For a more comprehensive description of the tool, and its application to a real-world case study in the energy domain, developed within the ACSI Project, please refer to [3].

6 Discussion

The OBGSM tool works under the assumption that the Semantic Layer is used to enhance GSM, but not to govern it. In fact, the construction of the RTS is handled internally by GSMC, it is not possible (at least for the time being) to prune it so as to remove inconsistent states. Hence, OBGSM must assume that all the states in the RTS are consistent with the constraints of the Semantic Layer. This can be trivially achieved by, e.g., avoiding to use negative inclusion assertions in the TBox, which are the only source of inconsistency for OWL 2 QL. If inconsistent states can be generated by the GSM specification, the strategy of delegating the verification to GSMC as a black box cannot be followed directly. One possible solution to this is to minimally change the GSMC implementation by introducing a test to detect states that should not be added to the RTS during the construction, then implementing it as a satisfiability check wrt the ontology. The other possible solution is to consider fragments of the verification logic, and investigate whether the check for consistency can be embedded in the formula to verify, so as to avoid any impact on GSMC. These scenarios provide us with interesting problems for future investigation.

References

1. Baader, F., Calvanese, D., McGuinness, D., Nardi, D., Patel-Schneider, P.F. (eds.): The Description Logic Handbook: Theory, Implementation and Applications. Cambridge University Press (2003)
2. Bagheri Hariri, B., Calvanese, D., Montali, M., De Giacomo, G., De Masellis, R., Felli, P.: Description logic Knowledge and Action Bases. J. of Artificial Intelligence Research (2013)

---

[3] http://ontop.inf.unibz.it/

[4] Notice that CTL can be expressed in the alternation-free fragment of the μ-calculus [15].

3. Bagheri Hariri, B., Calvanese, D., Montali, M., Santoso, A., Solomakhin, D.: Verification of semantically-enhanced artifact systems (extended version). CoRR (2013)
4. Bao, J., et al.: OWL 2 Web Ontology Language document overview, 2nd edn. W3C Recommendation. World Wide Web Consortium (2012)
5. Belardinelli, F., Lomuscio, A., Patrizi, F.: Verification of GSM-based artifact-centric systems through finite abstraction. In: Liu, C., Ludwig, H., Toumani, F., Yu, Q. (eds.) ICSOC 2012. LNCS, vol. 7636, pp. 17–31. Springer, Heidelberg (2012)
6. Calvanese, D., De Giacomo, G., Lembo, D., Lenzerini, M., Poggi, A., Rodriguez-Muro, M., Rosati, R.: Ontologies and databases: The *DL-Lite* approach. In: Tessaris, S., Franconi, E., Eiter, T., Gutierrez, C., Handschuh, S., Rousset, M.-C., Schmidt, R.A. (eds.) Reasoning Web 2009. LNCS, vol. 5689, pp. 255–356. Springer, Heidelberg (2009)
7. Calvanese, D., De Giacomo, G., Lembo, D., Lenzerini, M., Rosati, R.: EQL-Lite: Effective first-order query processing in description logics. In: Proc. of IJCAI 2007, pp. 274–279 (2007)
8. Calvanese, D., De Giacomo, G., Lembo, D., Lenzerini, M., Rosati, R.: Tractable reasoning and efficient query answering in description logics: The *DL-Lite* family. J. of Automated Reasoning 39(3), 385–429 (2007)
9. Calvanese, D., De Giacomo, G., Lembo, D., Montali, M., Santoso, A.: Ontology-based governance of data-aware processes. In: Krötzsch, M., Straccia, U. (eds.) RR 2012. LNCS, vol. 7497, pp. 25–41. Springer, Heidelberg (2012)
10. Calvanese, D., De Giacomo, G., Montali, M.: Foundations of data aware process analysis: A database theory perspective. In: Proc. of PODS 2013 (2013)
11. Calvanese, D., Kharlamov, E., Montali, M., Santoso, A., Zheleznyakov, D.: Verification of inconsistency-tolerant knowledge and action bases. In: Proc. of IJCAI 2013 (2013)
12. Clarke, E.M., Grumberg, O., Peled, D.A.: Model checking. The MIT Press (1999)
13. Damaggio, E., Hull, R., Vaculín, R.: On the equivalence of incremental and fixpoint semantics for business artifacts with Guard-Stage-Milestone lifecycles. Information Systems (2013)
14. Deutsch, A., Hull, R., Patrizi, F., Vianu, V.: Automatic verification of data-centric business processes. In: Proc. of ICDT 2009, pp. 252–267 (2009)
15. Emerson, E.A.: Model checking and the Mu-calculus. In: Immerman, N., Kolaitis, P. (eds.) Proceedings of the DIMACS Symposium on Descriptive Complexity and Finite Models. DIMACS Series in Discrete Mathematics and Theoretical Computer Science, pp. 185–214. American Mathematical Society Press (1996) ISBN 0-8218-0517-7
16. Hull, R.: Artifact-centric business process models: Brief survey of research results and challenges. In: Meersman, R., Tari, Z. (eds.) OTM 2008, Part II. LNCS, vol. 5332, pp. 1152–1163. Springer, Heidelberg (2008)
17. Hull, R., Damaggio, E., De Masellis, R., Fournier, F., Gupta, M., Heath III, F.T., Hobson, S., Linehan, M., Maradugu, S., Nigam, A., Sukaviriya, P.N., Vaculin, R.: Business artifacts with Guard-Stage-Milestone lifecycles: Managing artifact interactions with conditions and events. In: Proc. of the 5th ACM Int. Conf. on Distributed Event-Based Systems, DEBS 2011 (2011)
18. Motik, B., Cuenca Grau, B., Horrocks, I., Wu, Z., Fokoue, A., Lutz, C.: OWL 2 Web Ontology Language profiles, 2nd edn. Tech. rep., W3C Recommendation (2012)
19. Nigam, A., Caswell, N.S.: Business artifacts: An approach to operational specification. IBM Systems J. 42(3), 428–445 (2003)
20. Poggi, A., Lembo, D., Calvanese, D., De Giacomo, G., Lenzerini, M., Rosati, R.: Linking data to ontologies. In: Spaccapietra, S. (ed.) Journal on Data Semantics X. LNCS, vol. 4900, pp. 133–173. Springer, Heidelberg (2008)
21. Reichert, M.: Process and data: Two sides of the same coin? In: Meersman, R., et al. (eds.) OTM 2012, Part I. LNCS, vol. 7565, pp. 2–19. Springer, Heidelberg (2012)
22. Stirling, C.: Modal and Temporal Properties of Processes. Springer (2001)

A Framework for Cross Account Analysis

Vugranam C. Sreedhar*

IBM TJ Watson Research Center,
Yorktown Heights, NY, 10598, USA
vugranam@us.ibm.com

Abstract. A key challenge of Strategic Outsourcing (SO) from a service delivery perspective is trying to understand one key question: Why two SO accounts that seemingly looks the same have very different cost structure? In this article we present a parameterized framework for modeling and analysis of cross account behavior. We abstract certain key account features as parameters and construct models for answering behavioral characteristics of SO accounts. We use spectral graph clustering for detecting similar accounts, and also develop parameterized clustering for detecting coherent behavior of accounts. We have implemented a prototype of the approach and we discuss some preliminary empirical result of cross account analysis.

Keywords: Data mining, spectral graphs, clusterning, Workload, Effort, Service Delivery.

1 Introduction

Strategic Outsourcing (SO) occurs when a company transfers the control of one or more its business unit or Information Technology (IT) infrastructure management to another company, so that it can focus on its core business. A service provider, such as IBM, provides SO IT services for multiple different customer accounts. A service provider focuses on two main business objectives when delivering IT services: (1) Profit maximization by cutting cost of IT service management, and (2) Service quality in par or better than what is negotiated during contract phase via service level agreements (SLAs).

Large service providers, such as IBM, often put in place a process, such as the lean process, to eliminate wastage, improve productivity and improve quality. They often organize service delivery by creating one or more delivery center. Each delivery center is further split into a set of delivery pools. A pool is made of set of system administrators (SAs) who focus on one or two kinds of work types, such as "Backup and Restore" or "Performance and Capacity". Even with in each work type one can identify complexity features, such as high, medium and low. For instance, a pool may contain only SAs that do high complexity "Security and Compliance" work type.

---

* I would like thank D. Rosu, M. Surendra, A. Paradkar, and K. Christiance for helping me understand SO Delivery.

S. Basu et al. (Eds.): ICSOC 2013, LNCS 8274, pp. 608–615, 2013.

One question that is often asked by service provider executives is why does it costs more to manage one account compared another "seemingly similar" account. To answer such a question requires an understanding on the behavior of different kinds of account. There are human, process, policy, technology, location, and other characteristics that makes one account more cost effective and productive compared to another account. In this article we present a framework, called CAAF (Cross Account Analysis Framework), to compare coherent behavioral characteristics of accounts. We have identified certain key characteristics that can be parameterized for modeling and analysis of account behavior. Given a set of accounts and a set of features of the accounts, we identify a sub-set of features and sub-set of accounts that exhibit coherent behavior. Using CAAF project executives or other stakeholders can compare and contrast accounts that are similar with respect to a sub-set of features. In other words, CAAF can parameterized with respect to a set of accounts and features that exhibit a coherent behavior. We have prototyped an implementation of CAAF and we will highlight some preliminary empirical results.

The rest of the article is organized as follow: Section 2 describes cross account modeling that forms the basis for CAAF. Section 3 describes cross account analysis based on similarity and difference analysis. Section 4 presents preliminary empirical results. Section 5 highlights some of the related work. Finally we conclude in Section 6.

2   Cross Account Modeling

Let $A = \{a_1, a_2, \ldots, a_N\}$ be a set of N accounts. Each account a_i has a set of features $F = \{f_1, f_2, \ldots f_M\}$. Let H and H' be two sub-sets of features of F. We say that the two sub-sets of features are similar, denoted as, $H \sim H'$, if the distance $\Delta(H, H') \leq \epsilon$, where $\epsilon \in \Re$. We can use any of the classical distance/similarity functions for Δ, such as Jaccard coefficient, cosine distance, etc. We say two accounts a_i and a_j are similar, denoted as $[a_i \sim a_j]|H$ if $H(a_i) \sim H(a_j)$, where $H(a_i)$ is the set of features of a_i.

2.1   Feature Modeling

We identify two main kinds of features: (1) nominal or categorical features, such as geographies and sectors and (2) continuous features such as the number of tickets per servers. For continuous features we can use counts or total values such as total number tickets or servers. We can also use (normalized) ratio such as "tickets per server". When we discuss ticket related features we usually mean total number of Severity 1 Tickets or total number of Incident Tickets per Server. Assume that two accounts a_i and a_j are similar with respect to the total number of Incident Tickets, but when we look at severity feature, say Severity 1 Tickets, it is possible that the accounts may have two different number of Severity 1 Tickets. We convert continuous variables into nominal or categorical variables using binning by focusing on a range of values. For instance, we create a ranges such as $\{0 - 0.24, 0.25 - 0.49, 0.5 - 0.74, \ldots\}$ for the feature "tickets per server per month". Once such range of values are created by binning, we can say that two accounts are similar with respect to the feature "tickets per server per month" if they both belong to the same bin. In the rest of the article we only deal with nominal or categorical values. In our implementation when we bin, we also keep track of several statistics for each bin, such as mean, standard deviation, median, first quartile, third quartile, maximum value, and the minimum value. Often when we look for similarity between accounts within a bin, we sometimes compare them with the statistics of the bin to obtain more insights into their characteristics.

2.2 Cross Account Graph

Given the notion of maximal similarity and difference relation between accounts, we represent them as a graph, called the Cross Account Graph (CAG), $G = (A, E_s, E_d, W, F)$, where A is the set of nodes representing accounts, E_s is set edges representing similarity relations between accounts, E_d is a set of edges representing difference relations between accounts, $W \in \Re$ is the set of edge weights, and F is set of all relevant features across all accounts. For nominal values one can use either Jaccard coefficient or Cosine coefficient for similarity measure. The Jaccard coefficient between two feature sets H_i and H_j is given by

$$\Delta_{JC}(H_i, H_j) = \frac{|H_i \cap H_j|}{|H_i \cup H_j|} \tag{1}$$

We insert a similarity edge between accounts a_i and a_j only if $\Delta_{JC}(H_i, H_j) > \epsilon$, where H_i and H_j are the feature sets of a_i and a_j, respectively. We use a threshold $\epsilon = 0.15$ for inserting a similarity edge between two account nodes.

3 Cross Account Analysis

Recall that our goal is to be able to answer some cross account differential questions such as: Given two accounts that looks similar, why does it cost more to manage one account compared to managing the other account? It is important to keep in mind that we insert a similarity edge between two accounts a_i and a_j only if the Jaccard coefficient between the feature sets of the two accounts is greater than some threshold ϵ (which in our case is about 0.15). We label the similarity edge between two accounts with the set $\sigma(a_i, a_j) = H_i \cap H_j$ and label the difference edge with the label the set $\delta(a_i, a_j) = ((H_i \cup H_j) - (H_i \cap H_j))$, where H_i and H_j are the feature sets of accounts a_i and a_j, respectively. In our implementation of CAAF we do not have explicit similarity and difference edges, we simply label edges using a triple (σ, δ, w) where σ is the similarity set, δ is the difference set and w is the Jaccard coefficient.

We use spectral graph analysis for clustering CAG [1], where we represent CAG using normalized Laplacian matrix. Let $G = (A, E_s, W)$ be an undirected graph with nodes A, E_s the set of labeled edges denoting similarity relation, and $W \in \Re$ is the set of weights associated with similarity edges. For our purpose

AccountID	Geography	Sector	ITPSBin	CTPSBin	HPSCBin
A001	SAmerica	Finance	ITPSB1	CTPSB1	HPSCB1
A002	NAmerica	Retail	ITPSB1	CTPSB1	HPSCB2
A003	SAmerica	Finance	ITPSB1	CTPSB1	HPSCB3
A004	NAmerica	Retail	ITPSB1	CTPSB1	HPSCB3
A005	SAmerica	Finance	ITPSB1	CTPSB1	HPSCB3
A006	NAmerica	Retail	ITPSB1	CTPSB1	HPSCB2
A007	NAmerica	GB	ITPSB2	CTPSB1	HPSCB2
A008	NAmerica	Retail	ITPSB2	CTPSB2	HPSCB2
A009	SAmerica	Finance	ITPSB2	CTPSB2	HPSCB2
A010	NAmerica	Finance	ITPSB2	CTPSB2	HPSCB2
A011	Europe	Finance	ITPSB1	CTPSB1	HPSCB1
A012	AP	Retail	ITPSB1	CTPSB1	HPSCB2
A013	Europe	Finance	ITPSB1	CTPSB2	HPSCB3
A014	AP	Retail	ITPSB1	CTPSB1	HPSCB3
A015	Europe	Finance	ITPSB1	CTPSB2	HPSCB3
A016	AP	Retail	ITPSB2	CTPSB1	HPSCB2
A017	AP	GB	ITPSB2	CTPSB1	HPSCB2
A018	Europe	Retail	ITPSB2	CTPSB2	HPSCB2
A019	Europe	Finance	ITPSB2	CTPSB2	HPSCB2
A020	AP	Finance	ITPSB2	CTPSB2	HPSCB2

Fig. 1. An example with 20 accounts and 5 features

we use Jaccard coefficient for weights. Let $a, b \in A$, and let $a \xrightarrow{s} b \in E_s$, and $w(a, b) \in W_s$ be the weight of the edge $a \xrightarrow{s} b$. The degree $d(a)$ of a node a is the sum of edge weights incident on node a. The normalized Laplacian matrices is defined as follows:

$$\mathcal{L}(a, b) = \begin{cases} 1 - \frac{w(a,a)}{d(a)} & \text{if } a = b \text{ and } d(a) \neq 0; \\ -\frac{w(a,b)}{\sqrt{d(a) \times d(a)}} & \text{if } (a, b) \in E_s; \\ 0 & \text{otherwise} \end{cases} \tag{2}$$

The eigenvalues of normalized Laplacian $\mathcal{L}$ are non-negative and real, and in fact $0 \leq \lambda \leq 2$. We can use the eigenvalues and eigenvectors of $\mathcal{L}$ to cluster the cross account graph [2]. A key aspect of our approach for cross account analysis is the parameterization of the feature domain for clustering. In other words, given a CAG and a feature set H that is of interest we calculate clusters for the CAG with respect to the feature set H.

Example: Consider the example shown in Figure 1 that consists of 20 accounts with 5 features. The feature ITPSBin corresponds to number of the number of "incident tickets per server" that has been binned into two buckets. Similarly the feature CTPSBin corresponds to binned number of "change tickets per server". The feature HPSCBin is the binned number of "effort per server". Figure 2 illustrates the CAG for the accounts that are in NAmerica and SAmerica. Using spectral graph clustering algorithm, we identify two clusters made of $\{A001, A003, A004, A005\}$ and $\{A002, A006, A007, A008, A009, A010\}$.

Consider the example shown in Figure 1. Figure 2(b) illustrates the CAG for the last 10 accounts. The nodes colored in blue (nodes A011, A013, A015, and A019) are accounts that are in Europe and belong to Finance sector. One can see that for these accounts, which incidentally forms a nice cluster (spectral clustering algorithm will create one cluster for these nodes), have different "effort per server" as indicated by the feature HPSCBin.

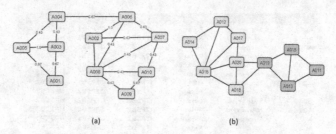

(a)   (b)

Fig. 2. CAG representation for (a) the first 10 accounts and (b) the last 10 accounts shown in Figure 1. The edge weights are Jaccard's coefficients, with threshold $\epsilon = 0.15$. As an example the similarity set for the edge A001 → A003 is {SAmerica, Finance, ITPSB1, CTPSB1} and the difference set is {HPSCB1}.

Next consider the set of nodes made of A012, A014, and A016. All these accounts are very similar with respect to all features, except HPSCBin. A service delivery executive would want to know why account A014 has a different effort compared to the other two similar accounts. We will come back to this point later in Section 4.

4   Empirical Result

In this section we present some preliminary empirical result using data from over 60 accounts for Intel and Unix server management from the year 2009 and 2010.[1] We identified over 80 different features by working closely with the delivery team. Since much of the account specific information are business sensitive, we can only provide some high level empirical results. For the 60 accounts, we selected about 30 different features for the prototype. We used binning to convert continuous values to nominal values.

We implemented spectral clustering using Jaccard coefficient using 30 features and generated 12 clusters. We then calculated Cramer's V coefficient for accounts in each cluster and identified features that provide Cramer's V coefficient of over 0.4. We used these sets of feature for parameterizing clusters to highlight accounts that are similar but have cost differentials (see Figure 2).

Our results for cross account analysis are illustrated in Figure 3 and 4. We identified three kinds of efforts: (1) Management effort that relate to project management, attending meetings, etc. (2) Operational effort that relate to resolving tickets, investigating defects, etc. and (3) Claimed Effort that an SA can claim. It is important to keep in mind that an SA can claim more or less than the time spent working on various activities. There is a claiming process that is put in place to charge the client for various tasks that are performed in an account.

---

[1] To protect the sensitive nature of the customer account data we have normalized and anonymized the data and the result discussed in this section.

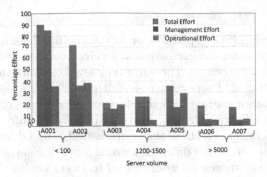

Fig. 3. Cross account comparison. Y axis is the percentage effort in hours per SA per week, and X axis is the binning of server count or volume.

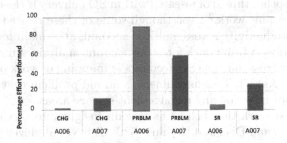

Fig. 4. Problem tickets differentials between to similar accounts

The results are based on 2009/2010 data that was anonymized as accounts A001 to A007. The X-axis shows server volume or count in different buckets or bins. Y-axis is the effort in hours per week per SA as a percentage of the total across various activities.

The accounts A003, A004, and A004 have different cost structures with in the same bin of server volume. Working with the account team, we identified few important reasons why the cost structure were different for these accounts. For instance, focusing on operational effort, we found out that not all tickets are routed to data repository where we collected the data for analysis in the case of A004 account. In the case of A003 we found out that the account team had put in place a better quality improvement programs in terms resolving tickets and other activities. Finally, the difference between account A001 and A002 with respect to management effort is that this effort was not fully tracked and logged for account A002, and so not all management claims were fully recorded. Notice that for accounts A006 and A007 the two sets of bar graphs are quite similar for the features illustrated in Figure 3. But when we drilled down to "tickets per server" across problem and change tickets, we found differences. This is illustrated in Figure 4. We found that significantly more effort is spent in dealing with change tickets within A007, compared to A006. Also A007 had fewer problem tickets and shorter resolution time per ticket.

5 Related Work

Strategic Outsourcing (SO) especially for Infrastructure Technology (IT) server management is a complex services business. Service providers, such as IBM, manage a large number of accounts. There are very few literature that provide some deeper understanding of IT services across multiple different accounts. To the best of our knowledge ours is the first work that focuses on cross account analysis. Lechner et al. describe a Service Delivery Portal (SDP) for IT infrastructure service management [3]. The main focus of that work is design and development of SDP that has been deployed across different account environment, and not cross account analysis. There are several work related to ticket analysis, where the main focus is on identifying and reducing the number of tickets, or performing ticket to server linkage via text analytics [4–6]. In our implementation we rely on ticket to server linkage to obtain features related to effort performed in a service delivery environment. Another thread of research within SO delivery is the automation for eliminating repeatable work.[2] Even though some of these related work focus on improving the productivity across multiple accounts, the main focus once again is not on developing a framework for cross account analysis. Another line of research that cuts across multiple SO accounts is mapping of work order to system administrators (SAs) [7]. Task assignment is an old problem that has been very well studied in optimization and management science areas.

Two other past work that helped us to gain insight into service delivery are that of Buco et al. and Diao and Heching [8, 9]. Buco et al. developed a methodology for instrumenting service delivery pools to get a fine grain effort spent by SAs for improving IT delivery quality. We use the result of their work in capturing some of the features related to effort performed and how much time SA spend across different work order characteristics [8]. Diao and Heching discuss analysis methods that were performed using service delivery operational data into order understand managerial insight into a complex service delivery system [9]. In particular they collected service delivery data to develop metrics and measures of interest to improve service delivery. We use some of their data, especially data related to activity time that SAs spend on different kinds of activities for our feature sets.

6 Conclusion

In this article we described a framework, called CAAF, for cross account analysis. SO account executives and project executives can parameterize to obtain a fine-grain result for cross account comparison. Our approach uses a combination of clustering techniques and sub-set features to extract relevant information for cross account analysis. We are currently working on to deploy the framework into service delivery environment so that projective executives and delivery managers can compare and contrast productivity and efficiency of several different SO accounts.

---

[2] http://www.ca.com/7media/Files/technologybriefs/
automate-service-delivery-techbrief.pdf

References

1. Chung, F.: Spectral Graph Theory. CBMS Reg. Conf. Ser. Math., vol. 92. American Mathematical Society (1997)
2. Luxburg, U.: A tutorial on spectral clustering. Statistics and Computing 17(4), 395–416 (2007)
3. Lenchner, J., Rosu, D., Velasquez, N.F., Guo, S., Christiance, K., DeFelice, D., Deshpande, P.M., Kummamuru, K., Kraus, N., Luan, L.Z., Majumdar, D., McLaughlin, M., Ofek-Koifman, S., Perng, D.P.C.-S., Roitman, H., Ward, C., Young, J.: A service delivery platform for server management services. IBM J. Res. Dev. 53(6), 792–808 (2009)
4. Marcu, P., Grabarnik, G., Luan, L., Rosu, D., Shwartz, L., Ward, C.: Towards an optimized model of incident ticket correlation. In: Proceedings of the 11th IFIP/IEEE International Conference on Symposium on Integrated Network Management, IM 2009, pp. 569–576. IEEE Press, Piscataway (2009)
5. Khan, A., Jamjoom, H., Sun, J.: Aim-hi: a framework for request routing in large-scale it global service delivery. IBM J. Res. Dev. 53(6), 820–829 (2009)
6. Symonenko, S., Rowe, S., Liddy, E.D.: Illuminating trouble tickets with sublanguage theory. In: Proceedings of the Language Technology Conference of the NAACL, Companion Volume: Short Papers. NAACL-Short 2006, pp. 169–172. Association for Computational Linguistics, Stroudsburg (2006)
7. Loewenstern, D., Pinel, F., Shwartz, L., Gatti, M., Herrmann, R.: A learning method for improving quality of service infrastructure management in new technical support groups. In: Liu, C., Ludwig, H., Toumani, F., Yu, Q. (eds.) ICSOC 2012. LNCS, vol. 7636, pp. 599–606. Springer, Heidelberg (2012)
8. Buco, M.J., Rosu, D., Meliksetian, D.S., Wu, F., Anerousis, N.: Effort instrumentation and management in service delivery environments. In: [10], pp. 257–260
9. Diao, Y., Heching, A.: Analysis of operational data to improve performance in service delivery systems. In: [10], pp. 302–308
10. 8th International Conference on Network and Service Management, CNSM 2012, October 22-26. IEEE, Las Vegas (2012)

DataSheets: A Spreadsheet-Based Data-Flow Language

Angel Lagares Lemos, Moshe Chai Barukh, and Boualem Benatallah

SOC Group, University of New South Wales, Australia
{angell,moshe,boualem}@cse.unsw.edu.au

Abstract. We are surrounded by data, a vast amount of data that has brought about an increasing need for combining and analyzing it in order to extract information and generate knowledge. A need not exclusive of big software companies with expert programmers; from scientists to bloggers, many end-user programmers currently demand data management tools to generate information according to their discretion. However, data is usually distributed among multiple sources, hence, it requires to be integrated, and unfortunately, this process is still available just for professional developers. In this paper we propose DataSheets, a novel approach to make the data-flow specification accessible and its representation comprehensible to end-user programmers. This approach consists of a spreadsheet-based data-flow language that has been tested and evaluated in a service-centric composition framework.

Keywords: Data-Flow, End-User Programming, Spreadsheets.

1 Introduction

During the next minute approximately 640,000Gb of global IP data will be transferred; by 2016, the annual global Internet traffic will surpass the zettabyte threshold, which means a growth rate of 29% yearly [1]. In 2013, the total digital data created (and replicated) will reach 4ZB[1]. Data is getting ever vaster more rapidly, yet data in turn may be combined to generate usable information. At the same time, 8% of all U.S. jobs require programming skills often needed to analyze data and generate reports relying just on simple personal productivity software [2], involving many data transferring tasks (e.g., parse and reformat strings passed between Web services) [3]. However since data is often distributed over a multitude of systems in many different formats, these tasks often remain complex requiring the ability of expert programmers.

For instance, data integration often demands the use of transformation functions, which must be defined in the data-flow. However, (i) existing techniques rely on languages such as XSLT[2] or XQuery[3], which are too complex for end-user programmers [4], and (ii) while there had been multiple attempts to simplify data

---

[1] http://goo.gl/9Ps63
[2] http://www.w3.org/TR/xslt20/
[3] http://www.w3.org/TR/xquery/

S. Basu et al. (Eds.): ICSOC 2013, LNCS 8274, pp. 616–623, 2013.

transformation languages, they have never been integrated in service composition languages, where creating a data flow to manipulate data sets still requires a user to engage in some form of programming [5]. E.g., specifying data transformation in BPEL is, in general, programmed using native BPEL expressions.

End-users require simple, easy to use and learn visual environments for data-flow management. To address this we introduce the application of spreadsheets which brings unrivalled advantages: (i) they are naturally tidy and uncluttered, as opposed to data-flow visual languages [6], (ii) they offer a simple, but effective formula language using spatial relationships that masks users from the low-level details of traditional programming [7], (iii) a spreadsheet-user only needs to master two concepts, namely cells as variables and functions for expressing relations between cells. The benefits of using spreadsheet-based data-flow languages have been proven and its suitability to EUP is undeniable. In fact, spreadsheet is the most common EUP environment [8].

In light of the aforementioned, we propose DataSheets, a spreadsheet-based data-flow language that aims to remove the complexity of expressing data-flows, allowing users to design data integration and data quality processes without having expertise in the underlying languages. The main contributions of this paper are as follows:

- A spreadsheet-based data-flow language designed for specifying mappings between different web services in a service composition environment. Unlike traditional approaches which calls the need for programmers to be proficient in complex data-flow and transformational languages such as XSLT, XPath, etc., we have been motivated to choose a spreadsheet language since it is already familiar to a vast majority of end-user programmers.
- The implementation and evaluation of a prototype that realizes the proposed data-flow language.

2 Spreadsheet-Based Data-Flow

The specification of data-flow is a two-step process: schema matching and data transformation. Schema matching requires a target and a set of sources and data transformation demands transformation functions, both notions are included in spreadsheets, where the cells can be either sources or targets and spreadsheet functions can be applied to them. We rely on the notion of representing services as forms based on our previous work [9], whereby we adopt the following: a list of services corresponds to a sheet, where each service message (input and output) corresponds to a column, and each field corresponds to a cell. A cell accepts the following data types: integer, float, boolean, string, one-dimensional array (e.g. {1,2,A7}) and two-dimensional array (e.g. {1,2,3;A1:A3}). In contrast to spreadsheets, array values are not expanded along rows or columns; in our approach a single cell can encapsulate these types.

The specification of the data-flow is performed per service, meaning just one service message at a time, from where the data-flow for every target field is specified (for short we call this service message "target message" and the service

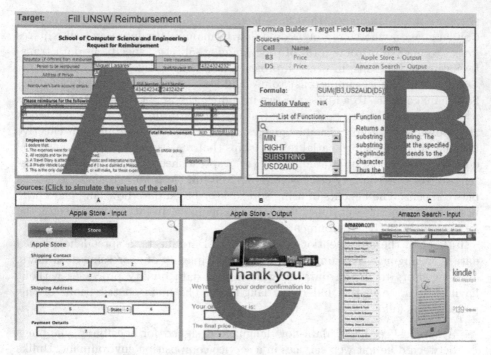

Fig. 1. Data-Flow Specification - Main Areas

that contains it "target service"). The target message has to be one of the input messages (by definition an output message cannot play this role) of the services in the composition. The sources consist of all the service message fields belonging to the services that precede the target service within the control flow. The target fields are editable cells, where the user can enter data-flow formulas. The source fields are cells grouped by messages; each message is located in a column; and the messages are grouped by services.

An example is depicted in Fig. 1, where the input message of the service "Fill UNSW Reimbursement" is the target service (section A) and three messages are shown as sources (section C). "Apple Store" service is one of the sources represented in the spreadsheet, where column "A" contains the fields of the input message and column "B" the fields of the output message. The fields are the cells of the spreadsheet and can be identified in the same manner as cells are in regular spreadsheet editors, for instance "B3" corresponds to the field "Price" of the output message of "Apple Store" service.

2.1   Formulas

Formulas describe the operations that place the result in the target field. The data-flow for target fields is to be specified by entering a formula the same way as one would do it in a spreadsheet. Formulas can contain:

- Constant Values, such as " 'some text' ", "5", "7.3";
- References to single fields, such as "C7", or to a range of fields, e.g., "B2:D5"

– 1-D and 2-D arrays, such as "{1,2;3,4}"
– Functions, such as "SUM", "INDEX" (e.g. INDEX({1,2;3,4},2,1)).

While references in spreadsheets are absolute, here the references to source fields are always relative. If the position of a service is modified in the control flow, the fields of that service that were acting as sources and all the formulas where they are used are updated automatically. As an example, let us consider the formula for the field "Total" shown in Fig. 1 (Section B) that contains the reference "B3" (field "Price" of "Apple Store" Output). If the service "Apple Store", previously preceding the service "Amazon Search", swaps the position with "Amazon Search", the "Apple Store" service will change the position into the list of sources and its output message will be in the column "D"; in consequence, the reference "B3" would be automatically converted into "D3".

To help the user in the task of building the formulas and maintain the consistency with the spreadsheet analogy, this approach includes the concept of a formula builder, where the user: (i) is presented a list of the sources used in the formula with all the information to clearly identify them, (ii) is entitled to edit the formula using a list of available functions and obtain feedback through tooltips, and (iii) is able to simulate the result of the formula.

3   DataSheets Implementation

DataSheets has been implemented and integrated in an EUP process composition platform, namely FormSys [9], as a proof-of-concept. The architecture presented here shows the modules related to DataSheets (Fig. 2).

Their interaction occurs as follows: A user selects a set of Web services and defines the control-flow. Then, the user specifies the data-flow via the *Spreadsheet Data-Flow* interface, which is generated by the *Spreadsheet Generator*. The *Formula Parser* evaluates the formulas by generating a tree of tokens from the

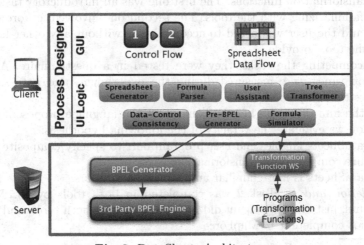

Fig. 2. DataSheets Architecture

functions, references and constants extracted; if an error is found, it will be indicated by the *User Assistant*. *Data-Control Consistency* maintains the coherence between the control and data flow by means of a combined control and data-flow directed graph that is evaluated using the Tarjan's strongly connected components algorithm [10]: in case a strongly connected component is detected, there is an inconsistency and the user is warned. The *Formula Simulator* permits the user to simulate the data-flows at the design time by means of consuming the *Transformation Function WS* with testing values. Once the data-flow is defined, the system translates it into a proprietary XML document using the *Pre-BPEL Generator* and then into BPEL using the *BPEL Generator*. Finally the BPEL code is deployed using a *3rd Party BPEL Engine*.

Regarding the technologies used for the implementation, the system can be split in two different parts: (i) the *Process Designer* and *BPEL Generator*, which include all the modules for process modeling and BPEL code generation, has been implemented in Symfony, a MVC framework for PHP, and jQuery; and (ii) the *3rd Party BPEL Engine*, which deploys and executes BPEL code, the engine used is Intalio|Server.

4   Evaluation

We have conducted a user study, where we collected the participants' experience using DataSheets techniques, which were integrated in FormSys, and we compared it with a state-of-the-art third party tool, Altova MapForce[4] (MapForce for short). We chose MapForce since it offers an interface, based on connecting elements through arrows, which is considered an EUP technique. A total of 14 participants took part in the study, of which none of them knew how to program in BPEL or any other process composition language.

Participants were required to use the tools by performing two tasks, both required the specification of complex data-flows, including the application of nested transformation functions. The first one was an introductory task to help them in familiarizing with the tools. The second one involved a more complex scenario and the user was asked to accomplish it without any other help than the one the tools provide.

After competing the tasks, they were tested in a questionnaire. Also task completion times were measured during the experiment, and notes gathered from users thinking aloud.

With the aim of evaluating the benefits of the language proposed, through this section we evaluate the veracity of the following hypothesis:

H_1: DataSheets enables end-user programmers to specify composite services that require complex data transformation.

H_2: DataSheets is more familiar and expressive to users.

Completion and H_1 Task 2 was completed in both tools by 85.7% of the participants, just one participant did not complete it in both tools, and another one did not complete it in MapForce.

---

[4] http://www.altova.com/mapforce.html

Table 1. Completion

Completed	Second Att.	FormSys			MapForce		
		f	%	%*	f	%	%*
	No	4	28.6	30.8	2	14.3	16.7
Yes	Yes	9	64.3	69.2	10	71.4	83.3
	Total	13	92.9	100.0	12	85.7	100.0
No		1	7.1		2	14.3	
Total		14	100.0		14	100.0	

f=frequency, %=percent, %*=percent over completed

To evaluate H_1 we carried out a binomial test using the one-tailed p-value. We consider that if the tool succeeds by an average greater than 50%, H_1 should be considered true (hence, $H_1 : p > 0.5$). The null hypothesis is $H_0 : p \leq 0.5$.

The value obtained from the binomial test was $p - 0.00085$. Considering a standard criterion of $\alpha = 0.05$, p is less than α, in consequence, H_0 can be rejected, which confirms that the results support H_1.

Usability and H_2 We consider that the combination of the results obtained by the user interface and functionality questions gives a reasonable measure of the tool usability. The comparison of the opinions from participants about the tools is to be used to evaluate H_2. The Wilcoxon signed rank sum test for paired samples has been applied to test H_0. The results are shown in table 2.

Table 2. Usability Comparison - Wilcoxon Signed Ranks Test

		Ranks			Test Statistics	
		N	Mean Rank	Sum of Ranks	FormSys - MapForce	
	Negative Ranks	22^a	51.89	1141.50	Z	-8.512^d
FormSys - MapForce	Positive Ranks	124^b	77.33	9589.00	p-value (2-t)	.000
	Ties	88^c				
	Total	234				

a: FormSys(FS)<MapForce(MF). b: FS>MF. c: FS=MF. d: Based on negative ranks

The resulting p-value (0.000) is less than the significance level, it indicates a difference statistically significant between the two groups and implies the rejection of H_0. The evidences extracted from the test results support H_2.

Discussion

The results reveal a number of positive trends in the current research and pointed out enhancements to consider for future directions:

– DataSheets facilitates defining and understanding data-flows. Quite significantly, we note that, in fact, 92.9% of the participants solved task 2 without any additional help provided; more so, even the two participants who had never programmed before were able to solve the task.
– The spreadsheet-like representation has been proved to be more familiar to end users. At the same time, the users found that the proposed language allowed them to express formulas seamlessly.
– As to matters of improvement: the participants pointed out the excessive use of vertical scrolling, which at times caused them to loose focus on the task; as well as some participants felt the types of errors and their description we not meaningful enough.

5   Related Work

Process-centric composition languages, amongst which BPEL4WS (collectively known as BPEL) is considered the prevailing standard, are intended for professional programmers (e.g., business process developers) and beyond the scope of non-programmers. Support tools for process management (e.g., Intalio BPM[5], Oracle BPEL Process Manager[6]) often provide a graphical interface from which BPEL code is generated. While these graphical aids improve the productivity of programmers, these tools remain complex for non-programmers.

Recently, authoritative research have argued for the need to integrate EUP techniques and tools in BPM/SOA platforms [11] and slowly they are emerging, specifically, business process composition platforms [12]. The most successful EUP tools for Web service composition can be found in the area of mashups. In this area, Marmite [5], introduced a linked data-flow/spreadsheet view, where formulas are column references and transformation functions are represented as new services, hence, the spreadsheet abstraction, opposite to DataSheets, is applied rather loosely. Furthermore, (i) mashups are oriented to data aggregation and they lack in techniques to provide a complete process-centric composition environment, and (ii) they still require the understanding of data-flow related programming concepts such as data and message passing [13].

In spite of the fact that spreadsheets are the most common EUP environment and they have been applied in an ample number of EUP systems [14], to the best of our knowledge, DataSheets is the first spreadsheet-based data-flow language integrated in a BPM/SOA composition environment.

6   Conclusion

In this paper we focused on the problem of data-flow modeling for EUP. Based on an approach using spreadsheets, we implemented and evaluated the approach. The key contributions are: (i) an integrated data-flow tool, which, during the

---

[5] http://www.intalio.com/bpm

[6] http://www.oracle.com/technetwork/middleware/bpel/overview/index.html

design time, gives the user the faculty to specify expressions to be used at run-time, that determine the value of a target field from values of source fields using a language similar to the one used to specify a cell formula in spreadsheets, and (ii) a user study conducted to evaluate the effectiveness of the proposed language, which results demonstrate that the research prototype where we applied the proposed techniques can compete and even outperform state-of-the-art tools on data-flow specification and representation.

References

1. Cisco Visual Networking Index: Forecast and methodology, 2009-2014. White paper, CISCO, vol. 2 (June 2010)
2. Ko, A.J., Myers, B.A., Aung, H.H.: Six learning barriers in end-user programming systems. In: IEEE Symposium on Visual Languages and Human Centric Computing, pp. 199–206 (2004)
3. Asavametha, A., Ayyavu, P., Scaffidi, C.: No application is an island: Using topes to transform strings during data transfer. In: International Conference on Information Science and Applications (ICISA), pp. 1–10. IEEE (2011)
4. Rahm, E., Bernstein, P.: A survey of approaches to automatic schema matching. The VLDB Journal 10(4), 334–350 (2001)
5. Wong, J., Hong, J.I.: Making mashups with marmite: towards end-user programming for the web. In: Proceedings of the SIGCHI Conference on Human Factors in Computing Systems, pp. 1435–1444. ACM (2007)
6. Nunez, F., Blake, E.: Vissh: A data visualisation spreadsheet. In: Joint Eurographics-IEEE TCVG Symposium on Visualization (VisSym), pp. 209–218. The Eurographics Association (2000)
7. Jones, S., Blackwell, A., Burnett, M.: A user-centered approach to functions in excel. In: Proceedings of the 8th ACM SIGPLAN International Conference on Functional Programming, pp. 165–176. ACM Press (2003)
8. Panko, R.: Spreadsheet errors: What we know. What we think we can do. Arxiv preprint arXiv:0802.3457 (2008)
9. Weber, I., Paik, H., Benatallah, B., Gong, Z., Zheng, L., Vorwerk, C.: Formsys: form-processing web services. In: Proceedings of the 19th International Conference on World Wide Web, pp. 1313–1316. ACM (2010)
10. Tarjan, R.: Depth-first search and linear graph algorithms. In: 12th Annual Symposium on Switching and Automata Theory, pp. 114–121. IEEE (1971)
11. Casati, F.: How end-user development will save composition technologies from their continuing failures. In: Piccinno, A. (ed.) IS-EUD 2011. LNCS, vol. 6654, pp. 4–6. Springer, Heidelberg (2011)
12. Mehandjiev, N., Namoune, A., Wajid, U., et al.: End user service composition: Perceptions and requirements. In: Proceedings of the 8th IEEE European Conference on Web Services, pp. 139–146. IEEE Computer Society (2010)
13. Namoun, A., Nestler, T., De Angeli, A.: Service composition for non-programmers: Prospects, problems, and design recommendations. In: 8th European Conference on Web Services (ECOWS), pp. 123–130. IEEE (2010)
14. Ko, A.J., Abraham, R., Beckwith, L., Blackwell, A., Burnett, M., et al.: The state of the art in end-user software engineering. ACM Computing Surveys (CSUR) 43(3), 21 (2011)

Decision Making in Enterprise Crowdsourcing Services

Maja Vukovic and Rajarshi Das

IBM T.J. Watson Research Center, Yorktown Heights, NY 10598, USA
{maja,rajarshi}@us.ibm.com

Abstract. Enterprises are increasingly employing crowdsourcing to engage employees and public as part of their business processes, given a promising, low cost, access to scalable workforce online. Common examples include harnessing of crowd expertise for enterprise knowledge discovery, software development, product support and innovation. Crowdsourcing tasks vary in their complexity, required level of business support and investment, and most importantly the quality of outcome. As such, not every step in a business process can successfully lend itself to crowdsourcing. In this paper, we present a decision-making and execution service, called CrowdArb[1], operating on crowdsourcing tasks in the large global enterprise. The system employs decision theoretic methodology to assess whether to crowdsource or not a selected step of the knowledge discovery process. The system addresses the challenges of trade-off between the quality and time of the crowdsourcing responses, as well as the trade-off between the cost of crowdsourcing experts and time required to complete the entire campaign. We present evaluation results from simulations of CrowdArb in enterprise crowdsourcing campaign that engaged over 560 client representatives to obtain actionable insights. We discuss how proposed solution addresses the opportunity to close the gap of semi-automated task coordination in crowdsourcing environments.

Keywords: Enterprise, Organizational Services, Crowdsourcing.

1 Introduction

Crowdsourcing aims to outsource tasks that are traditionally performed by designated human agents to an often, undefined large group of humans online. Enterprise domain is thriving with examples of innovative and successful examples of crowdsourcing, by engaging both external and internal contributors. Models of crowdsourcing can be found along the different stages of product and service lifecycle [1]: innovation [2], design [3], development [4], quality management [5], and testing [6] to name a few.

Crowdsourcing appeals to enterprises due to the promise of low cost, access to scalable workforce online. The focus of our work is on enterprise crowdsourcing model where only in-house experts participate, as opposed to the "open-call" model where tasks are open for contribution to external participants. We seed the crowdsourcing campaign by selecting participants based on their expertise and enable them to further route knowledge requests within their social work networks.

---

[1] CrowbArb is short for Crowd Arbitrage.

S. Basu et al. (Eds.): ICSOC 2013, LNCS 8274, pp. 624–638, 2013.
© Springer-Verlag Berlin Heidelberg 2013

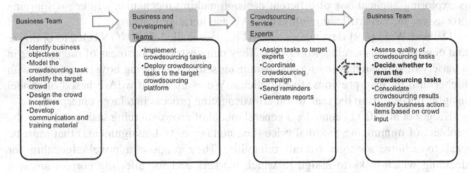

Fig. 1. Enablement of crowdsourcing capabilities in business processes

Figure 1. shows key actors and activities in setting up a crowdsourcing campaign. The business team designs crowdsourcing tasks, identifies target crowd, and designs the incentives. Business and development teams deploy the crowdsourcing tasks onto the service of choice. Crowdsourcing service automates crowd management and coordination of tasks and response consolidation. Business teams analyze the responses, evaluate their quality and decide whether to re-approach the crowd.

Cost of crowdsourcing, aside from crowd engagement (incentives), includes task design, campaign management, and quality assurance. The decision of whether the tasks meet the quality expectations and whether to rerun the crowdsourcing task is challenging and complex. Even when there are no tangible incentives involved, expert's time (away from their main job) is affected, and cost of re-engagement increases over the time of crowdsourcing campaign; and at the same time it impacts experts' productivity in the on-going operational processes.

In this paper we present a decision-making service CrowdArb, which automates the process of identifying whether a given activity should be crowdsourced or not.

The main contributions of this paper are:

1. Novel application of enterprise crowdsourcing to strategic insights.
2. The model for decision making for crowdsourcing service.
3. Evaluation results from the CrowdArb simulation with model parameters derived from real-world enterprise crowdsourcing effort engaging over 560 experts.

Next section puts our work in the context of state of the art of decision-making applications for crowdsourcing. Section 3 describes the business scenario, from which we derive model parameters for CrowdArb. Section 4 presents the core functions of the crowdsourcing service. Section 5 details the design of CrowdArb and evaluation results from simulation runs, and discusses the expected utility of crowdsourcing campaign. We conclude and outline future work in Section 6.

2   Related Work

Different parameters may affect the decision to crowdsource: availability of skilled workers, budget, task complexity, time, contribution quality, etc. Research community is exploring applications of different decision-making mechanisms in crowdsourcing processes, such as artificial intelligence (AI) and iterative learning.

Dai and Weld [8,9] develop a novel AI planner, called TURKONTOL, to optimize and control crowdsourcing workflows. They demonstrate robustness of the planner in a variety of simulated scenarios and parameter settings, showing how it performs with higher utilities than previous, fixed policies. We evaluate CrowdArb based on model insights derived from the real-world crowdsourcing process in a large enterprise.

Karger et al. [10,11] consider a general model of crowdsourcing tasks, and pose the problem of minimizing the total price (i.e., number of task assignments) that must be paid to achieve a target overall reliability. They propose a novel algorithm for deciding which tasks to assign to which workers and for inferring correct answers from the workers' answers. Their algorithm, which is a based on based on low-rank matrix approximation, outperforms majority voting and, in fact, is asymptotically optimal through comparison to an oracle that knows the reliability of every worker.

Kittur et al. [12] present CrowdForge, a general-purpose framework for solving complex problems through micro-task markets. CrowdForge manages the coordination between workers so that complex artifacts can be effectively produced by individuals contributing only small amounts of time and effort. The framework provides a systematic and dynamic way to break down tasks into subtasks and manage the flow and dependencies between them. The focus of this work is more on the system support for crowdsourcing workflow management, and less on support for time, quality and price tradeoff in the crowdsourcing process.

Other researchers [13,14] have looked into the relationship between financial incentives and performance by marshalling ideas and methodologies available in economic theory and social science. Mason and Watts [13] demonstrate that the increased incentives incerased the quantity, but not the quality of work. They studied the effect of financial incentives on performance in Amazon Mechanical Turk (AMT) [15]. Crowd members who were paid more considered that their work was valued more. As a result they were no more motivated to work harder than the crowd members who were paid less. Mason and Watson suggest that the structure of the incentives could result in better work for less pay.

Horton and Chilton [14] extend the work in [13] by developing a simple rational model of labor supply in crowdsourcing systems. The model factors out the reservation wage—the key parameter in a labor supply model—by making it invariant with respect to the experimental parameters. In experiments in AMT, they find mixed evidence for the rational model. Despite being sensitive to the price incentives workers seemed to be insensitive to the magnitude of the task-completion time. The authors explain the divergence between the theoretical predictions and experimental results by showing that some of the workers followed a suboptimal strategy of aiming to reach salient target earnings instead of maximizing their total earnings.

Decision making in crowdsourcing is a complex problem, necessarily incorporating economic, social and AI mechanisms to capture crowd behavior, incentives and crowdsourcing process targets (in terms of time, quality, etc.). One challenge that remains is effective inference of parameters required for decision-making in the context of the crowdsourcing task.

3   Business Context

Knowledge about clients, their infrastructure and processes is in the collective possession of business and technical teams working with a client. Sales and technical teams collaborate with client to understand their requirements and propose technical solutions. As a result different experts possess the knowledge about one or more aspects of client profile (e.g. product and services that they have purchased, how these are configured and customized to client's needs, client industry knowledge, etc.).

In order to capture client's pain points and potential sales opportunities, we employ crowdsourcing to engage sales and technical to uncover details about the client, such as their existing infrastructure. This data is the key input into decision-making process for strategy discussion at the client-level. Once the data is collected, a team of analysts performs quality assurance. Submitted data that doesn't meet quality expectations may be returned to experts for improvement. Once the data is of acceptable quality, business team will decide whether to host an in-person workshop engaging multiple client representatives. The outcome of the workshop is a set of client strategies. Figure 2 captures the main steps in our scenario.

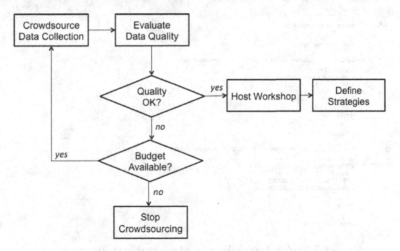

Fig. 2. Scenario: Client assessments using crowdsourcing

Client assessments were formed as a questionnaire consisting of 15 sections, ten of which captures details about the workloads (types of software and services) that clients are using, and the other five captured details about the infrastructure hosting them. Workload section consisted of 15 questions capturing the details about the offerings, and infrastructure section captured 10 questions about the infrastructure. All questions were mandatory. To meet the minimum quality requirements users had to enter five workloads and one data center section. Business analysts evaluated the results daily and for the responses that did not meet the quality expectations would have to manually reopen the task and reach back to the client team, requesting more details. Once all the client teams returned assessments that met quality expectations, a workshop would be scheduled to further discuss strategies for supporting each client.

Figure 3. shows a snippet of a knowledge request for workloads (crowdsourcing task). Each expert has a number of controls available at their hand, shown on top of the figure. They can save draft of the knowledge request at any point in time, or submit it once all mandatory questions have been answered. They can delegate all or selected questions, where checkboxes next to the question indicate if the question is selected for delegation. Asterisks next to the question number indicate that the question is mandatory. A knowledge request can also include optional questions. If two users are simultaneously working on the same task, they will be notified when the other user has made a change and will be asked to refresh their form using the "Refresh page" button. Administrator can cancel and delete any knowledge requests. View button offers insights into the collaboration graph and delegation and response history.

Fig. 3. Sample knowledge request for workload discovery

4   Enterprise Crowdsourcing Service

To implement principles of collaborative knowledge discovery we employ system BizRay [7], a general-purpose, cloud-enabled, enterprise crowdsourcing self-service that expedites delivery of crowdsourcing campaigns to discover critical tacit business knowledge that is in collective possession of the experts. Knowledge requests are captured as a distributed questionnaire, which consists of one or more sections, each containing one or more questions. BizRay manages its lifecycle, similar to a workflow system and facilitates delegation of requests. More than one expert can complete each questionnaire instance. If the information gathered is incomplete or unidentified, the user can forward the request to another expert, asking for their help.

As experts contribute their knowledge, the system keeps track of their identity resulting in the formation of communities around the object of that inquiry. Crowdsourcing is an effective mechanism to engage multiple team members concurrently to discover different pieces of a knowledge request. Furthermore it allows for team members to engage others (Figure 4.), which is a useful feature if the target client representative may have left the organization or moved to a different role.

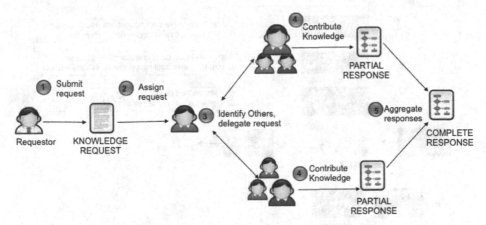

Fig. 4. Collective Intelligence Approach to Knowledge Discovery [7]

Figure 5. shows the typical flow of operations in BizRay enterprise crowdsourcing including the extensions for automated decisions (steps 5-7), which are the contributions of this work. The operation starts with a system administrator developing a questionnaire (step 1a), which entails design of a knowledge request template consisting of questions that can be grouped into multiple sections. Questionnaire is designed around a given entity, in our case that is a "client". In step 1b, the system administrator assigns tasks to the initial expert crowd. In our scenario the experts include client representatives and technical sales experts. In step 1c, BizRay automatically sends a notification with a task assignment to target expert group. At that point, experts either work and complete their tasks (step 2a), or if they are unable to complete the request on their own they may delegate one or more questions to team members in their social work network (step 2b). During the lifetime of the crowdsourcing campaign system will periodically trigger reminders for pending tasks, and escalations to management where appropriate (step 3). Administrator can pull the reports with the current status and responses to evaluate the results (step 4).

In order to automate the decision-making process about the quality of the responses and whether to engage crowd members again, we have extended BizRay to support steps 5-7, which is one of the contributions of this paper. In step 5, CrowdArb computes the quality of the responses received. Before the deployment system administrator defines the quality rules (e.g. which questions have to be answered, or count of completed questions or sections). These rules are used to identify low quality contributions. In step 6, low quality contributions and the cost of crowdsourcing are used as parameters into the decision theoretic model. In step 7, selected tasks are resent to the crowd for further refinement in order to improve the quality levels.

BizRay is implemented as a Web-based service. It interfaces with LDAP-based enterprise directory service to authenticate enterprise experts, and to obtain organizational data. BizRay exposes REST-based APIs allowing for integration with other systems and services. APIs allow for full task and questionnaire management and reporting capabilities, including e-mail and notification triggers.

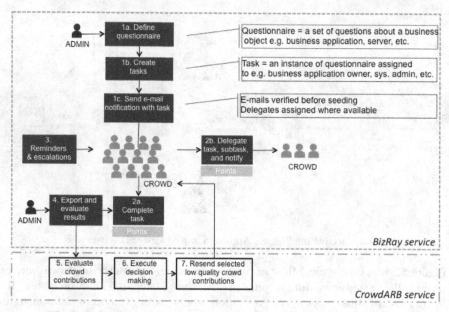

Fig. 5. Extension of BizRay using CrowdArb service for decision-making

5   Decision-Theoretic Approach and Evaluation Results

This section outlines the probabilistic graphical model we employ in CrowdArb service for decision making in enterprise crowdsourcing service. The aim of the CrowdArb is to solve the following decision problem. At the start of any decision interval, the administrator is unsure about the state or the readiness of each of the client representatives (agents) for inclusion in the workshop. The state of each client representative evolves on its own every week as each agent works independently with his or her client. If in any decision interval, the administrator believes that a sufficient number of agents are ready for the workshop she can invite that subset of the agents to the workshop. While inviting agents who are ready adds utility to the overall business process, including agents to the workshop who are not ready has its own costs. To reduce the uncertainty about the state of the agents, the administrator can choose to run an email campaign in each decision cycle to contact the agents to get a better understanding of their state of readiness. Since the email campaign has its own costs, the campaign has to be limited only to a subset of the agent population.   It is also worth noting that the email campaign itself may also change the state of the contacted agents who may be more motivated to work expeditiously with his client. Thus, given the cost of the email campaign, the problem for the administrator is to determine which subset of client representatives to contact in each decision cycle so as to maximize the overall expected utility.

CrowdArb models the above scenario as follows. In a given decision interval, the administrator models the readiness of each client representative in completing a questionnaire as a random variable $X = \{s1, s2, s3\}$.   In total, an agent has to complete 15 sections of which 10 are related to workloads and 5 are related to data centers. In this model, the state $s1$ (= poor) indicates that the agent is unable to enter four sections on workload and less than one section on data centers. An agent is in state $s2$ (= fair) when she is able to provide information on at least four workloads and one data center (5 sections completed). The state $s3$ (= good) equates to an agent being able to complete sections on more than four workloads and more then one data center (or cumulatively, complete more five sections).   As noted earlier, the administrator is uncertain about the value of X for each agent and maintains a probability distribution over $\{s1, s2, s3\}$.

Table 1. Utility function U(X,A)

		Actions	
		a1	a2
	s1	0	-15
States	s2	0	10
	s3	0	40

We define the administrator's action (decision) space for each agent by variable A = $\{a1, a2\}$, where $a1$ denotes that the agent is not included in the workshop, and $a2$ denotes that the agent will be included the workshop. Agents who are in good state $s3$ or fair state $s2$ are in better position to contribute to the workshops than agents who are in state $s1$.   This is reflected in the systems utility function, which is given by $U(X,A)$ in Table 1. Costs in Table 1 are tied to cost of running of the workshop, but have been anonymized so as not to expose directly underlying business model.

Based on historical data, our prototype records how the state of each agent evolves over time as each agent works independently with her client. An agent who is in state s_i proceeds to s_j with a small probability in each time interval between successive decision periods. A sample time-evolution matrix, TE, which can be used in our CrowdArb prototype is given in Table 2.

Table 2. Time-evolution matrix

		States(t+1)		
		s1	s2	s3
	s1	0.85	0.1	0.05
States(t)	s2	0.05	0.85	0.1
	s3	0.1	0.05	0.8

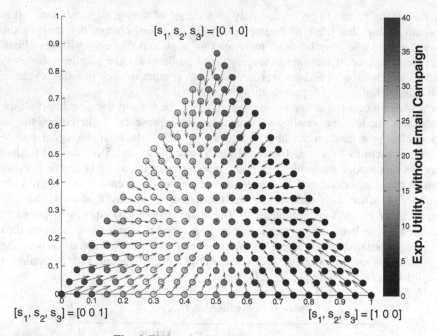

Fig. 6. Expected utility without email campaign

The dynamics of the state of each agent between two successive decision intervals can be represented as a vector field overlaid on a simplex as shown in Figure 6. The color of each of the sampled X in the simplex represents the maximum expected utility for the optimal action in that X: MEU[D[a*]] = Sum_a* ($P(X|A)$ $U(X,A)$). For example, for an agent with $X = [1,0,0]$, that administrator can opt to not invite him to the workshop, resulting in a maximum expected utility of zero. Instead, inviting an

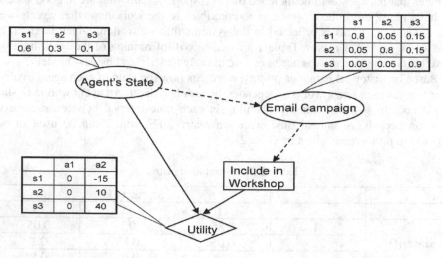

Fig. 7. Influence Diagram

agent with $X = [0,0,1]$ results in a maximum expected utility of 40. The vector field shows that due to the time-evolution matrix, the administrator's uncertainty over X grows over time even if there is absolute certainty of the initial value of X. Consequently, the expected utility per agent also decreases over time.

Figure 7 shows the administrator's decision problem as an influence diagram (but without the dashed arrows). If the administrator can avail of the Email Campaign, then the influence diagram is extended to include the dashed arrows in Figure 7. As noted earlier, the importance of the email campaign is twofold. First, agents who are contacted via the email campaign are motivated to work with their respective clients and improve their state of readiness. Second, if the agent then responds to the email campaign, then the administrator has a better estimate of the readiness of the agent for possible inclusion in the workshop. Based on historical data, the administrator can define CPT_ec, a conditional probability table of an agent's state after the email campaign given the agent's state before the email campaign. An example of CPT_ec is given in Table 3.

Table 3. Conditional probability table for agent's state after email campaign

		States(t+1)		
		s1	s2	s3
States(t)	s1	0.8	0.05	0.15
	s2	0.05	0.8	0.15
	s3	0.05	0.15	0.9

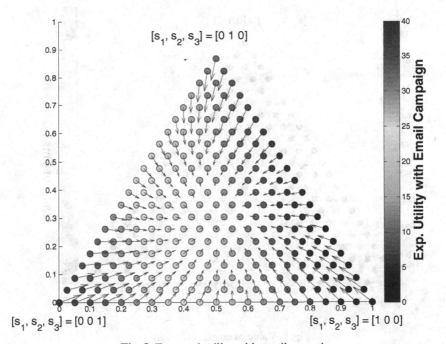

Fig. 8. Expected utility with email campaign

Given a conditional probability table CPT_ec, the administrator computes a new maximum expected utility MEU_ec[D[a*]] for each agent if she were to include the agent in the email campaign. The distribution of MEU_ec over the unit simplex of X is shown in Figure 8. The value of the email campaign, V_ec, can now be quantified as the difference between MEU_ec and MEU without the email campaign. The administrator can opt to contact the agent if the agent's V_ec exceeds the cost of running the email campaign for that agent.

Figure 9 shows the distribution of V_ec over the unit simplex of states. Note that V_ec is close to zero if the administrator is fairly certain about the state of the agent. For example, for an agent with X is close to [0,0,1], the administrator knows that given the time-evolution matrix, the agent's state X is not going to change dramatically away from [0,0,1]. Since the agent's MEU at X = [0,0,1] is already near the maximum value, and contacting the agent via the email campaign is not going to result in a significantly higher MEU_ec. Similarly, when X is very close to [1,0,0], the administrator finds that given the agent's extremely poor state of readiness, the agent is unlikely to increase to significant increase in MEU_ec following an email campaign. On the other hand, when the agent's state is less certain, for example X = [0.66,0,0.33], V_ec is high as information gained through the email campaign is most likely to impact the administrator's decision of whether to include the agent in the workshop or not. Cost of email campaign per agent. C_ec was set to 3 utility units, and an agent was contacted only if V_ec > C_ec.

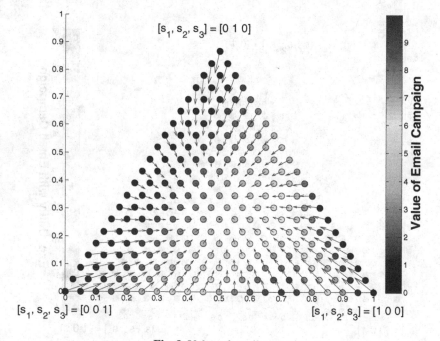

Fig. 9. Value of email campaign

In practice, we find that not all agents who are contacted through the email campaign are able to respond. Based on historical data, the response rate is typically 0.2. In our prototype, for agent's who do not respond to the email campaign (i.e., in addition to those agent's who are not enrolled in the email campaign), the administrator updates the states of the agents using the time-evolution matrix.

To quantify the efficacy of CrowdArb, we have performed simulations with model parameters derived from real-world BizRay use-cases. In particular, CrowdArb simulated 560 client representatives with known initial states as follows: 60% in poor state of readiness ($X = [1,0,0]$), 30% in fair state of readiness ($X = [0,1,0]$), and 10% in good state ($X = [0,0,1]$).   We applied CrowdArb to decide whether to include each agent in the email campaign each week for 20 consecutive weeks beginning at the start of a financial quarter, and then decide whether or not to hold a workshop.

Figure 10. compares the sorted distribution of maximum expected utility (MEU) of all the 560 agents obtained at the 20th decision cycle (to take one example) from two cases: (a) when no email campaign was used, and (b) when CrowdArb determined which agents to include in the email campaign based on the criterion V_ec > C_ec. As expected, most of the additional utility derived from the email campaign arises not from agents who are already having very high (or very low) expected utility, but from those whose expected utility is 15 (corresponding to $X = [0,1,0]$) or less.

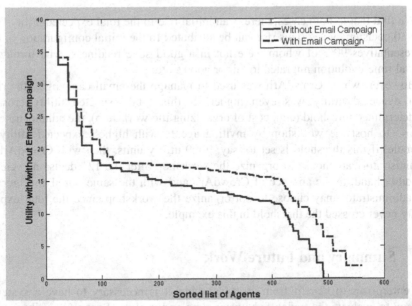

Fig. 10. Sorted distribution of maximum expected utility at 20th decision cycle

Instead of focusing only on one decision cycle Figure 11. compares the time series of total expected utility obtained in the same two cases (i.e., without email campaign and with email campaign) starting from the same initial configurations.

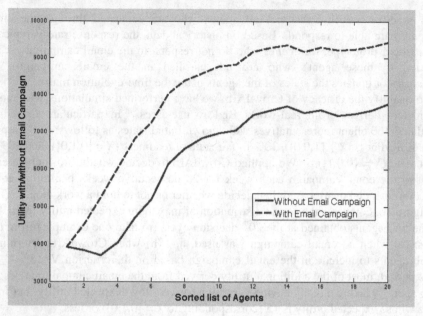

Fig. 11. Time-series based comparison of total expected utility

We find that in both cases, there is an initial rise in the total expected utility for the first 10 decision cycles. This rise can be attributed to the initial configuration of client representatives 90% of whom were not in a good state readiness, who through the natural time-evolution migrated to fair or good state.

However, when CrowdArb was used to manage the email campaign, the rise in total expected utility was even higher. If this total expected utility crosses a predetermined threshold (e.g., cost of organizing the workshop), the administrator can choose to host the workshop by inviting agents with highest expected utility. For example, if this threshold is set to, say, 9000 utility units, then with CrowdArb, the administrator can choose to organize the workshop after the 12th decision cycle. On the other hand, in the absence of CrowdArb and with the same initial configuration, the administrator may choose to not organize the workshop since the total expected utility never crossed the threshold in this example.

6   Summary and Future Work

For enterprises to benefit from crowdsourcing it is necessary to have a systematic method to evaluate the tradeoffs between time and quality of crowd contributions and available budget to execute crowdsourcing campaigns. In this paper we presented a CrowdArb service for decision-making integrated with the enterprise crowdsourcing service, which assesses whether to crowdsource a specific stage of business process or not given a set of parameters. CrowdArb employs decision-theoretic methodology that computes the expected utility for a decision problem D, given an action a; action being execution of crowdsourcing. CrowdArb takes into account probability of achieving high-quality crowd contributions over a time period.

We demonstrated the effectiveness of CrowdArb in addressing the challenges of trade-off between the quality of crowdsourcing tasks and the cost of engaging crowdsourcing experts. We presented results from CrowdArb simulation based on the model parameters derived from enterprise crowdsourcing campaign that engaged over 560 client representatives. Crowdsourcing tasks took the form of a complex knowledge request, which was assigned to one or more team members working with a client. We discussed how proposed solution addresses the opportunity to close the gap of semi-automated task coordination in crowdsourcing environments.

Business processes are collections of activities with a defined flow of execution. As process steps are considered for crowdsourcing, enterprises need to be able decide whether to make an investment or not. Applications of the proposed approach go beyond use case described in paper. For example, on-Cloud migration is one process that can benefit of workflows of crowdsourcing campaigns and networks for experts. By engaging network and system admins, application and business process owners, business analysts and deployment teams we can efficiently discover the infrastructure and financial characteristics of existing workloads and the underlying topology to facilitate move of legacy applications to Cloud infrastructures.

Our future work will focus on a method for automatically identifying the parameters required for decision-making in the context of generic crowdsourcing services, irrespective of the crowdourcing task type and complexity.

References

1. Vukovic, M.: Crowdsourcing for Enterprises. In: SERVICES, pp. 686–692 (2009)
2. Bayus, B.L.: Crowdsourcing New Product Ideas over Time: An Analysis of the Dell IdeaStorm Community. Management Science 59, 226–244 (2013) (published online before print November 5, 2012), doi:10.1287/mnsc.1120.1599
3. Brabham, D.C.: Moving the crowd at Threadless: Motivations for participation in a crowdsourcing application. Information, Communication & Society 13(8), 1122–1145 (2010)
4. Lakhani, K., Garbin, D., Lonstein, E.: TopCoder (A), Developing Software through Crowdsourcing. Harvard Business School Case 610-032 (2009)
5. Vukovic, M., Natarajan, A.: Collective Intelligence for Enhanced Quality Management of IT Services. In: Liu, C., Ludwig, H., Toumani, F., Yu, Q. (eds.) Service Oriented Computing. LNCS, vol. 7636, pp. 703–717. Springer, Heidelberg (2012)
6. Smith, R.: Using games to improve productivity in software engineering. In: Proceedings of the ACM SIGKDD Workshop on Human Computation, HCOMP 2010 (2010)
7. Laredo, J., Vukovic, M., Rajagopal, S.: Service for Crowd-Driven Gathering of Non-Discoverable Knowledge. In: Pallis, G., et al. (eds.) ICSOC 2011 Workshops. LNCS, vol. 7221, pp. 283–294. Springer, Heidelberg (2012)
8. Dai, P., Mausam, Weld, D.S.: Decision-Theoretic Control of Crowd-Sourced Workflows. In: AAAI 2010 (2010)
9. Weld, D.S., Mausam, Dai, P.: Execution control for crowdsourcing. In: Proceedings of the 24th Annual ACM Symposium Adjunct on User Interface Software and Technology (UIST 2011 Adjunct), pp. 57–58. ACM, New York (2011)

10. Karger, D.R., Oh, S., Shah, D.: Iterative Learning for Reliable Crowdsourcing Systems. In: Neural Information Processing Systems, pp. 1953–1961 (2011)
11. Karger, D.R., Oh, S., Shah, D.: Budget-optimal Crowdsourcing Using Low-rank Matrix Approximations. In: 49th Annual Allerton Conference on Communication, Control, and Computing (Allerton), pp. 284–291 (2011)
12. Kittur, A., Smus, B., Khamkar, S., Kraut, R.E.: CrowdForge: crowdsourcing complex work. In: Proceedings of the 24th Annual ACM Symposium on User Interface Software and Technology (UIST 2011). ACM, New York (2011)
13. Mason, W., Watts, D.: Financial Incentives and the "Performance of Crowds". In: Proceedings of ACK SIGKDD Workshop on Human Computation, HCOMP (2009)
14. Horton, J., Chilton, L.: The Labor Economics of Paid Crowdsourcing. In: Proceedings of the 11th ACM Conference on Electronic Commerce (2010)

Towards Optimal Risk-Aware Security Compliance of a Large IT System

Daniel Coffman[1], Bhavna Agrawal[2], and Frank Schaffa[2]

[1] Walker Digital LLC, Stamford, CT, USA
DanielMark.Coffman@walkerdigital.com
[2] IBM T. J. Watson Research Center, Yorktown Heights, NY, USA
{bhavna,schaffa}@us.ibm.com

Abstract. A modern information technology (IT) system may consist of thousands of servers, software components and other devices. Operational security of such a system is usually measured by the compliance of the system with a group of security policies. However, there is no generally accepted method of assessing the risk-aware compliance of an IT system with a given set of security policies. The current practice is to state the fraction of non-compliant systems, regardless of the varying levels of risk associated with violations of the policies and their exposure time windows. We propose a new metric that takes into account the risk of non-compliance, along with the number and duration of violations. This metric affords a risk-aware compliance posture in a single number. It is used to determine a course of remediation, returning the system to an acceptable level of risk while minimizing the cost of remediation and observing the physical constraints on the system, and the limited human labor available. This metric may also be used in the course of the normal operation of the IT system, alerting the operators to potential security breaches in a timely manner.

Keywords: Risk-aware compliance, cloud computing, compliance metrics, compliance optimization.

1 Introduction

Modern information technology (IT) systems are large, and disparate. They may consist of thousands of servers, software components, networks, and other devices. They may be located in one or several data centers. An IT system may contain resources owned by a number of different organizations or individuals, but managed by a single entity. Increasingly, the server systems may not even be physical systems themselves, but may be hosted on a number of cloud servers; we designate the server systems as endpoints to distinguish them from the cloud servers. Fig. 1 illustrates an IT system consisting of n_s endpoints, under the control of n_o operators. Additionally, there might be a hierarchy of endpoints belonging to different clusters or clients in a complex delivery center.

The proper operation of an IT system may be interrupted for a number of reasons. Among them are hardware and software failures, resource limitations and malicious

S. Basu et al. (Eds.): ICSOC 2013, LNCS 8274, pp. 639–651, 2013.

attacks. The former will be addressed through the adoption of monitoring and best practices, but the latter problems related to a system's security, require special scrutiny. Most often, the managing entity will enumerate the potential threats to the system and will develop and implement a set of policies as a first step of protection from malicious attacks. Such policies may be common to all endpoints or unique to a particular set of endpoints.

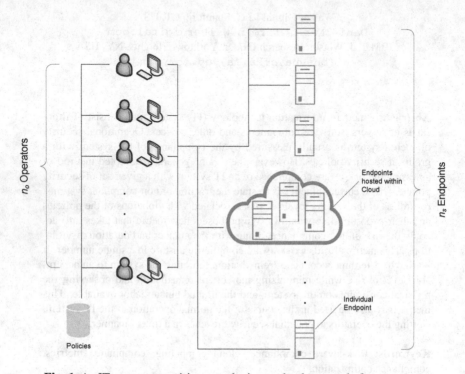

Fig. 1. An IT system comprising n_s endpoints under the control of n_o operators

It is the duty of the operators to ensure that each policy is respected on each relevant endpoint. Evidently, not all endpoints will simultaneously be in compliance with each policy. Frequently, there will be a contractual obligation that obliges the managing entity to maintain the endpoints at a certain level of compliance. However, there is no generally adopted method for measuring this level of compliance as also pointed out by authors in [1] and [2]. There are still more definitions available on the security metrics [3,4] but not many for compliance. Savola [5] defines the compliance metrics as a set of different factors, like number of policy exceptions requested/granted, cost of control, number of security incidence, elapsed time from incident identification to remediation etc., but it is not a single number.

The current practice for measuring compliance is for the operators to report the fraction of the endpoints not in compliance with one or more policies [1,6]. This approach, however, has at least three significant weaknesses. It ignores the fact that some violations of policy may be of a much more serious nature than others. Further it ignores the time-dependence of such a violation: some violations are initially not terribly serious, but become much more serious as they are left unrepaired. Finally, some policies may yield only a single result on a single endpoint, whereas others may yield many results; this must be accounted for properly.

An example will prove illustrative. Consider the case of two policies: (i) that passwords must expire after 90 days; and (ii) that on a UNIX system, only the root user may write to the /sbin directory. Obviously, violations of policy ii are potentially much more serious than violations of policy i. However, checking all accounts on an endpoint according to policy i will yield Q_i responses where Q_i is the number of user accounts with one response per account. On the other hand, checking an endpoint for compliance with policy ii will yield only a single response. Finally, a password being unchanged for a short time after its expiration date will probably cause no harm, but the longer it remains unchanged, the greater the threat it represents that the endpoint's security will be compromised.

Once some violations of the policies have been observed, the system must be brought back into as compliant a state as possible. Again, there is no generally accepted way to accomplish this and only a few accounts of this in the literature. Levi [7] presents a method for generating a prioritized list of vulnerabilities, but he does not take into account the aggregation impact, which is when a large number of slightly lower risk vulnerabilities might pose a higher risk than a single high risk vulnerability. Additionally, he does not account for the impact of time for which these vulnerabilities are exposed as explained in the example above. Taraz [8] presents a method of computing the vulnerability score of a single device, but not for a large group of devices.

In the subsequent sections of this paper, we present a compliance metric that addresses these weaknesses. We develop a methodology using this metric for restoring the IT system to maximal compliance within given constraint of resources and cost. In addition, we show how this metric is used in the daily operations of the IT system.

2   Risk-Aware Compliance Metric

When calculating the rate of compliance of an IT system, the current practice ignores the different risks associated with different types of violations. However, such violations may be of very different characters in the risks they pose to the IT system. Evidently, some violations may be much more serious if they are left uncorrected for a substantial length of time. We propose a metric which takes these factors into account.

Consider a single policy k and a single endpoint l. We define $P(N_{kl}, Q_{kl}, R_k)$ as the probability that the endpoint is safe according to policy k. P is given by the binomial distribution:

$$P(N_{kl}, Q_{kl}, R_k) = \sum_{n=0}^{N_{kl}} \binom{Q_{kl}}{n} R_k^n (1 - R_k)^{Q_{kl}-n} \qquad (1)$$

Where

N_{kl} = number of responses indicating compliance with policy k on endpoint l
Q_{kl} = Total number of responses from checking policy k on endpoint l

R_k = Risk factor associated with policy k (also a probability of compromise for a single violation of policy k)

Here, $\binom{Q_{kl}}{n}$ are the usual binomial coefficients. The risk factors, R_k, are assigned values between 0 (lowest risk) & 1 (highest risk) based on the risk associated with the policy. For the paper, we do ad hoc assignment, but in practice they are assessed by the area specialists familiar with the various risks and policies. As an example, if the policy requires "password never expires box should be unchecked", there might be 10 user id's which are compliant, and 5 that are not, then the value of N will 10, and Q will be 15 for this endpoint and this policy. Note that for $Q=1$, $P(0,1,R)=1-R$, that is the probability of being safe (not being at risk) after the detection of a single violation.

Once we determine the probability of being safe from one policy violation on one endpoint, we can combine these to determine the compliance metric for a larger system of endpoints, governed by a number of policies. We define the risk-aware compliance metric, Λ, as the product of these probabilities for all endpoints, and all policies:

$$\Lambda = \prod_{k=1}^{n_p} \prod_{l=1}^{n_s} P(N_{kl}, Q_{kl}, R_k) \tag{2}$$

where n_p is the total number of policies being checked on each endpoint, and n_s is the total number of endpoints. This metric evaluates to 1 when all the endpoints are compliant with all the policies, and tends to zero with a large number of violations. Additionally, we note that Λ falls very rapidly with the number of detected violations (=Q-N, non-compliant messages) from its maximum value of 1, particularly for high risk violations. This is illustrated in Fig. 2, where this compliance metric is plotted against the number detected violations for policies with different risk factors.

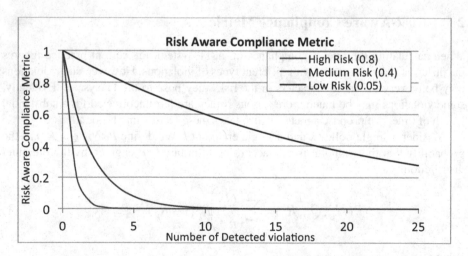

Fig. 2. Risk-aware Compliance Metric as a function of the number of detected violations for three different risk factors

The metric may be extended to incorporate the duration of a detected violation, that is, the time elapsed since the violating condition was first observed. We do this by modifying the risk factors associated with the policies to include this duration

$$R_k(t_i) = R_k + (1-R_k)(1-e^{-t_i/\tau_k}) \qquad (3)$$

where t_i is the time for which the detected violation has remained unrepaired, and τ_k is the criticality time constant for this policy. Once again, the area specialists will be able to specify the criticality time constants based on their experience and knowledge. As we would expect, the risk factor increases from its original value to a maximum of 1 as the elapsed time increases, as depicted in Fig. 3a. Fig. 3b shows the corresponding change of Λ, which slowly goes to zero from its original value as time goes by. The results are plotted for a single detected violation for clarity of presentation, however, behavior is similar for multiple violations of multiple policies.

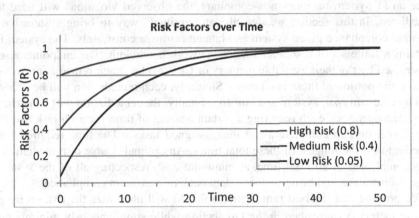

Fig. 3a. Risk factors as a function of time, for a time constant $\tau = 10$ in arbitrary units

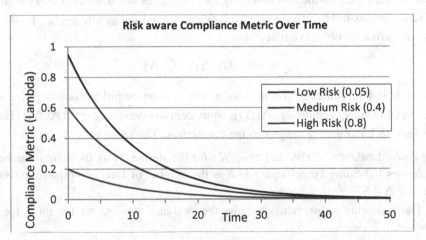

Fig. 3b. Compliance Metric as a function of time, for a single detected violation and three different risk factors

The risk-aware compliance metric is used in several different ways. It functions first as a "tripwire"; the metric is calculated periodically and a message is sent to the operators when the value of the metric falls below some predefined value. This typically indicates that some high risk violation has just been detected. Further, with the incorporation of the duration of observed violations, the value of the metric will degrade even if no new violations are reported. Finally, by observing the pattern of the measured values of the metric over time, it is possible to detect problems in the configuration of the IT system: e.g. if the metric exhibits considerable scatter and discontinuous behavior rather than varying smoothly over time, it is indicative of systematic problems.

3   Optimal Risk-Aware Compliance

Once an IT system becomes non-compliant, the observed violations will need to be remediated. In this section we describe an "optimal" way to bring system back to maximal compliance given system and human resource constraints. The system itself contains a finite set of resources such as network bandwidth. The endpoints also are constrained by say their available memory or CPU cycles. Each remediation will consume some portion of these resources. Similarly, each remediation will be accompanied by a certain *cost,* system and human. Finally, the remediation will be performed by human operators, each requiring a certain amount of time for each task and therefore a total time to complete all of their assigned tasks. The time required for the remediation is the longest of these total times. An optimal course of remediation will be accomplished in allowed time, at minimum cost, respecting all of the system resource constraints, and bringing the system back to maximum compliance.

We propose that the best remediation solution will maximize the risk-aware compliance metric, Λ, described in the last section while simultaneously minimizing the costs of such remediation and observing the constraints noted above. Let Δ be the set of remediations to be performed, and if Λ can be written as a function of Δ, then we can define the objective function as

$$\chi = -\alpha \ln(\Lambda(\Delta)) + C(\Delta) \tag{4}$$

where C is the total cost of remediation and α is an empirical, non-negative scale factor. Obviously *maximizing* $\Lambda(\Delta)$ is equivalent to *minimizing* $-\ln(\Lambda(\Delta))$. Hence, we seek to minimize χ subject to the constraints. The value of α is used to adjust the desired balance of risk and cost. We further define $\overline{N}$ as the initial number of responses indicating compliance and N is the number of final compliance messages. Hence, $\Delta = N - \overline{N}$.

The following subsections describe the cost and constraints for this objective function.

3.1   Cost

We use a linear approximation for defining cost, $C(\Delta)$,

$$C(\Delta) = \sum_{k=1}^{n_p} C_k \Delta_k \tag{5}$$

where n_p = number of policies, C_k is the cost to repair one violation of policy k and Δ_k is the total number remediations performed according to policy k, which can be further defined as:

$$\Delta_k = \sum_{j=1}^{n_o} \sum_{l=1}^{n_s} \Delta_{jkl} \tag{6}$$

where n_o is the number of operators, n_s is the number of endpoints, and Δ_{jkl} is the number of remediations performed by operator j according to policy k on endpoint l.

While we use a linear approximation of cost, this is not a strict requirement, and can be generalized without impacting the formulation and solution of the problem

The optimal system performance then consists in finding that set $\Delta = \{\Delta_{jkl}\}$ which maximizes $\Lambda(\Delta)$ while simultaneously minimizing $C(\Delta)$ subject to the constraints.

3.2   Constraints

For each of the system resource, *e.g.* CPU, memory, disk space, etc., there is a constraint on the maximum amount available. The performance of all remediations on a particular endpoint can never consume more than this amount. Furthermore, assuming that there is a maximum time allowed for all remediation work to be completed (e.g. total amount of time across all operators), the time required to perform the remediation must not exceed this maximum. We defined these two constraints below.

Resource Constraints

On endpoint l, there will be an amount of a resource of type m, say G_{ml}. The amount must be greater than the amount required by all of the desired remediations. That is

$$G_{ml} \geq \sum_{k=1}^{n_p} F_{km} \Delta_{kl} \tag{7}$$

$$\Delta_{kl} = \sum_{j=1}^{n_o} \Delta_{jkl} \tag{8}$$

where here, F_{km} is the amount of a resource of type m to required for one remediation according to policy k.

Time Constraints

Operator j will require a time t_j to complete his or her work. With the assumption that the individual tasks are completed sequentially, without interruption or overlap, this time is given by

$$t_j = \sum_{l=1}^{n_s} \sum_{k=1}^{n_p} T_k \Delta_{jkl}$$ (9)

where T_k is the time required to work on policy k.

The amount of time to complete all the remediations is obviously given by the longest such time. If the maximum allowable time for all remediations is T then we require

$$T \geq \max_j (t_j)$$ (10)

3.3 Optimization Function

Using the definition of cost and constraint functions defined above, the objective (minimization) function in Eq (4) can be re-written as (employing the standard technique of combining constraints with objective function using Lagrange multipliers):

$$\chi = -\alpha \ln(\Lambda(\Delta)) + \sum_{k=1}^{n_p} C_k \Delta_k + \sum_{m=1}^{n_R} L_m \sum_{l=1}^{n_s} (G_{ml} - \sum_{k=1}^{n_p} F_{km} \Delta_{kl}) + \sum_{j=1}^{n_o} \mu_j (T - \sum_{l=1}^{n_s} \sum_{k=1}^{n_p} T_k \Delta_{jkl})$$ (11)

Where n_R is the number of resource types, and L_m and μ_j are Lagrange multipliers. For computational tractability, we approximate the first term. First, by definition (dropping subscripts for simplicity of presentation)

$$\ln(\Lambda) = \ln(\prod P(N, Q, R)) = \sum \ln(P(N, Q, R))$$ (12)

Now consider

$$\ln(P(N, Q, R)) = \ln(\sum_{n=0}^{N} \binom{Q}{n} R^n (1 - R)^{Q-n}).$$ (13)

In order to make the objective function more tractable, we approximate P by $\hat{P}$ (a quadratic function) where

$$-\ln(\hat{P}(N, Q, R)) = C(Q - N)^2.$$ (14)

We fix the value of C by requiring

$$-\ln(\hat{P}(0, Q, R)) = -\ln(P(0, Q, R)).$$ (15)

Now

$$-\ln(\hat{P}(N,Q,R)) = \frac{-\ln(1-R)}{Q}(Q-N)^2 \tag{16}$$

The good agreement between the exact and approximate values is illustrated in Fig. 4. We also note that even with larger values of Q, the difference between the exact and approximate values is larger, but the agreement still holds.

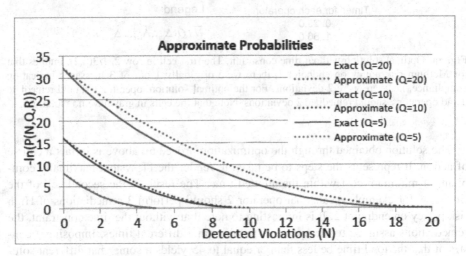

Fig. 4. Exact and Approximate probabilities for a range of Q values

With this approximation, the objective function is quadratic in Δ and may be minimized as an integer programming problem using any of the several optimizer packages including CPLEX [9] and Gurobi [10].

4   Discussion

The optimization problem described above is an integer programming (IP) problem with a quadratic objective function. It is well-known that such a problem is difficult to solve exactly. However, for rather small sets of policies, and endpoints with only a few operators, the problem is computationally tractable.

We present results first using an exact IP optimization for a system with two operators ($n_o = 2$), three policies ($n_p = 3$) and four endpoints ($n_s = 4$). Further, violations of the policies are of high, medium and low risk, respectively. The costs are taken to be 10, 5 and 5 for remediations of these policies, with each remediation taking a time of 8, 5 and 2, respectively; these values are obviously arbitrary, but can easily be mapped to a real values. This system will require the determination of 24 values for its complete optimization. These values are given in Fig. 5a for an optimization with roughly equal weights given to the risk-aware metric and the cost function and no constraint on the total time.

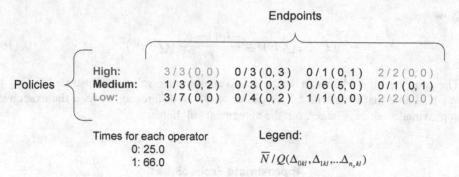

Fig. 5a. Optimal solution without time constraint. The first cell in row 2, 1/3(0,2), implies that for Medium risk policy on endpoint 1, there were originally 1 out of 3 messages indicating compliance, i.e. there were 2 deviations. For the optimal solution, operator 1 should remediate 0 and operator 2 should remediate 2 deviations. Note that the cells in gray have no violations.

The solution obtained through the optimization procedure above is in fact a course of action. It represents the steps to be taken to render the IT system maximally compliant at minimum cost within the allotted time. The result in the second cell of the first row, for example means that operator 2 should perform 3 remediations of High risk policy on endpoint 2. It is interesting to note that without the time constraint, the remediations assigned to the operators require quite different times. Imposing a constraint that the total time be less than or equal to 45 yields a somewhat different solution, as illustrated in Fig. 5b. Now, the effort required of both operators is almost exactly the same, whereas one fewer low risk violation can now be remediated.

This simple model may be explored further to reveal the dependence of the risk-aware metric on the allotted time. Naturally, as less time is available to complete the work, less can be done to bring the system into compliance and the metric will achieve a lower value at the optimum point.   This is shown in Fig. 6.

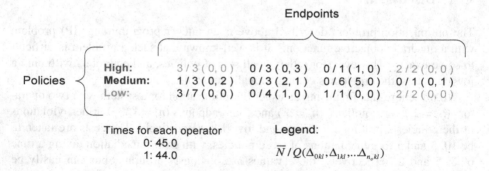

Fig. 5b. Optimal solution with total time required to be less than 45

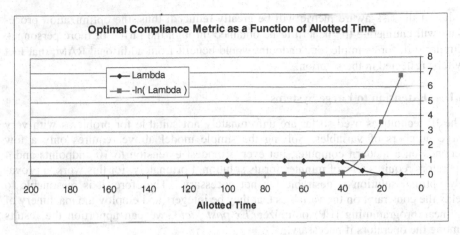

Fig. 6. Value of Risk-aware Compliance Metric at Optimum Point as a function of the time allotted for remediation. Also shown is the negative logarithm of this quantity. Note that if all violations were remediated by a single operator, this would require a time of 108, on this scale.

Also of interest is the appropriate value of α, the relative weight of the risk-aware metric and the cost function in the objective function. Again, we can examine the simple model here for some guidance. Let $\alpha = \max(C)/\max(-\ln(\Lambda))*w$; clearly w, the *weight* factor, should be of order unity. We optimize our model for a number of values of this weight factor, with results presented in Fig. 7. At values greater than one, the risk-aware metric dominates the objective function, while for values less than one, the cost function is dominant; In this latter regime, the metric's value plummets as it is no longer cost-effective to remediate even high risk violations. We assert that value of about 4 offers a good balance of cost and risk for this simple model.

The optimal solution pinpoints the resource or resources that constrain the performance of the system overall. As noted above, if there is inadequate time available, the

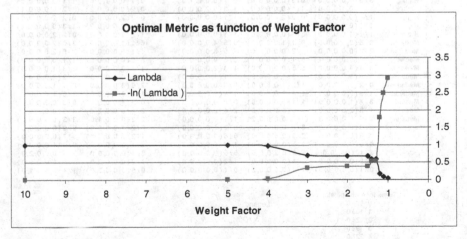

Fig. 7. Value of the Risk-aware Compliance Metric at the optimum point, as a function of the weight factor, $w = \alpha \max(-\ln(\Lambda))/\max(C)$

value of the risk-aware metric will be greatly reduced; thus, the optimization procedure will enumerate the benefit to be obtained through the hiring of more personnel. Similarly if, for example, one endpoint would benefit from additional RAM, that fact will be reflected in the solution.

4.1   Extension to Large Systems

The IP techniques used so far are unfortunately not suitable for problems with very large numbers of variables. Solving the simple model above requires only a few seconds on a modern computer, but even a modest extension to 10 endpoints and 4 operators requires tens of minutes for its solution. Fortunately, for this work, a provably optimal solution is desirable but not necessary. Therefore, it is reasonable to relax the constraint on the variables that they be integers and employ the machinery of a linear programming (LP) optimizer. *Ex post facto*, we can apportion the results among the operators if necessary.

Consider a model with 5 operators, 5 policies for high risk violations, 10 for medium risk and 6 for low risk, and altogether 1000 endpoints. Using the same objective function and constraints, this model may be optimized in just a few seconds with LP. In this first investigation, we relax the time constraints. The results are shown in Fig. 8, in the same format used for the smaller model, solved through IP. We note that the results are sensible --- the high risk violations are remediated in preference to the lower risk violations --- and so on.

The difficulty with using LP techniques comes exactly when imposing the constraints. When the time constraint comes into play, the solution will sometimes favor equal division of the work among the operators, say each being assigned 20% of a task. Thus, we cannot adopt the LP solution without further work in parceling out the work. However, this is not a worrisome state of affairs since the number of

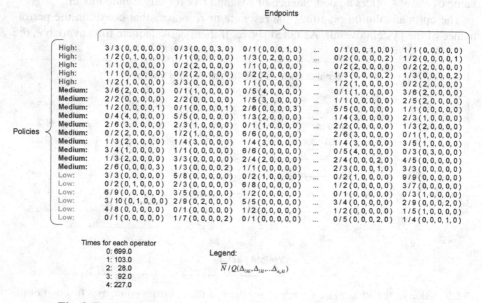

Fig. 8. Extract of optimal results for a large model, solved using LP techniques

remediations required is normally quite large, in the tens of thousands, so that the exact distribution of tasks is immaterial. The LP solution will, however, provide reliable guidance on the exact mixture of tasks, that is remediations of high, medium and low risk violations, that will lead to an optimally compliant system.

5   Further Work

There are several facets of this work which will be explored further. As mentioned above, this work approximates the total cost of remediation with a simple linear function of the number of remediations performed. We wish to examine how this may be relaxed without compromising the numerical properties desired for the optimization.

As mentioned above, we will examine techniques for apportioning the results from LP optimization and adopt one which is numerically tractable and theoretically defensible. Further, we will employ this technique on real data collected from data centers to aid in the improvement of the compliance of the systems they support.

References

1. Jansen, W.: Directions in security metrics research. National Institute of Standards and Technology, NISTIR 7564 (2010)
2. Julisch, K.: Security compliance: the next frontier in security research. In: Proceedings of the 2008 Workshop on New Security Paradigms, pp. 71–74. ACM (2009)
3. First.org. A Complete Guide to the Common Vulnerability Scoring System Version 2.0 - CVSS, http://www.first.org/cvss/cvss-guide
4. Pironti, J.P.: Developing Metrics for Effective Information Security Governance. INTEROP, New York (September 2008), http://www.interop.com/newyork/2008/presentations/conference/rc10-pironti.pdf
5. Savola, R.: Towards a security metrics taxonomy for the information and communication technology industry. In: International Confernce on Software Engineering Advances, ICSEA, Cap Estrel, France (August 2007)
6. Herrmann, D.S.: Complete guide to security and privacy metrics: measuring regulatory compliance, operational resilience, and ROI. CRC Press (2007)
7. Levi, E.: Device, Method and Program Product for Prioritizing Security Flaw Mitigation Tasks in a Business Service. U.S. Patent Application 12/361,279, Filed (January 28, 2009)
8. Taraz, R.: Method and apparatus for rating a compliance level of a computer connecting to a network. U.S. Patent Application 11/289,740, Filed (November 29, 2005)
9. Cplex, IBM ILOG. 12.5 User's Manual (2010), ftp://public.dhe.ibm.com/software/websphere/ilog/docs/optimization/cplex/ps_usrmancplex.pdf
10. Optimization, Gurobi. Gurobi optimizer reference manual (2012), http://www.gurobi.com

Behavioral Analysis of Service Delivery Models

Gargi B. Dasgupta, Renuka Sindhgatta, and Shivali Agarwal

IBM Research India
{gdasgupt,renuka.sr,shivaaga}@in.ibm.com

Abstract. Enterprises and IT service providers are increasingly challenged with the goal of improving quality of service while reducing cost of delivery. Effective distribution of complex customer workloads among delivery teams served by diverse personnel under strict service agreements is a serious management challenge. Challenges become more pronounced when organizations adopt ad-hoc measures to reduce operational costs and mandate unscientific transformations. This paper simulates different delivery models in face of complex customer workload, stringent service contracts, and evolving skills, with the goal of scientifically deriving design principles of delivery organizations. Results show while Collaborative models are beneficial for highest priority work, Integrated models works best for volume-intensive work, through up-skilling the population with additional skills. In repetitive work environments where expertise can be gained, these training costs are compensated with higher throughput. This return-on-investment is highest when people have at most two skills. Decoupled models work well for simple workloads and relaxed service contracts.

1   Introduction

Service-based economies and business models have gained significant importance over the years. The clients and service providers exchange value through service interactions with the goal of achieving their desired outcomes. Given the focus on the individual customer's value and uniqueness of the customer's needs, the service providers need to meet a large variety of expectations set by the customers. This is the primary reason for the service delivery to be labor-intensive where human intervention and interaction is unavoidable.

Service providers aim to maintain the quality of service by structuring their service delivery (SD) operations as service systems (SS). A SS is an organization of resources and processes that support and drive the service interactions so that the outcomes meet customer expectations [22][19]. The size, complexity, and uniqueness of the technology installations require specialists at provider's end to support customer needs. In addition, customers require multiple business functions, applications and technologies to be supported. Hence their workload tends to be complex and dynamic. The specialized service workers (SW) or human resources of a SS are teamed together in order to serve the service requests (SR) or work of the customer.

We motivate the study by presenting the IT Service Management SS where a service provider maintains complex systems and infrastructure of the customer as described in detail by authors in [21]. When system interruption or degradation occurs

S. Basu et al. (Eds.): ICSOC 2013, LNCS 8274, pp. 652–666, 2013.
© Springer-Verlag Berlin Heidelberg 2013

i.e., a server goes down or a network link is broken, the customers request for service to be restored in the form of tickets or service requests (SR). In a typical IT infrastructure set up, there are several dependencies between the supporting systems. Hence, a ticket resolution often requires multiple systems to be analyzed and rectified. Fig 1. depicts the dependencies between such systems. A single SR stating "Unresponsive and slow Web server" would require service workers to check the web server, the database server and the storage space to identify root cause and resolve the SR.

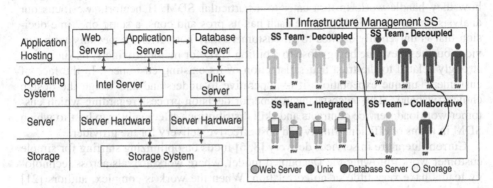

Fig. 1. Sample of IT Service Management Dependencies and Service Delivery Models

The SS team in a delivery organization can be arranged based on their skills and competencies. We use SS team and team interchangeably in the paper. Each team has skills in the domain of specialization. The customer work then gets delivered out of one or more SS teams. We classify customer work as complex when it requires support of more than one skill domain or technology for its resolution. As complex customer SR arrives at the delivery organization, it requires the different teams supporting it to work towards its resolution. Depending on how the SS teams have been organized, the following structures are imposed on the SR resolution workflows.

- Decoupled Workflow: When multiple teams work independently on a complex customer SR, with each team only responsible for partial resolution of the issue, it imposes a Decoupled structure on the SR resolution flow. No single team has ownership of the SR and the work is completed sequentially by teams working on parts of it. This often results in complex work taking longer to resolve as it traverses multiple teams. The structure is prevalent when complex SR is handled by different teams as shown in Figure 1.
- Collaborative Workflow: When the complex SR is handled by experts from multiple teams, working on the SR simultaneously, it imposes a Collaborative structure on the SR resolution flow. In this case effort of multiple people is locked in parallel but the quality of work improves. As indicated in Figure 1, experts from teams work together to complete the SR.
- Integrated Workflow: In cases where a team is composed of multiple skill specializations, the SR may be handled by multiple skills within the same team. Here the SS team owns the SR and one or more multi-skilled people work towards its resolution. This imposes an Integrated structure on the resolution flow. While customer satisfaction is highest in this model due to tightly synchronized

workflow, the cost to the provider is higher from perspective of supporting multiple skills. Figure 1 depicts an integrated workflow where the team has both database server skill and storage system skill required for resolving an SR.

The above workflows form the basic building blocks of any complex delivery environment and define a Service Delivery Model (SDM) followed by the Service System to meet the customer expectations. The choice of a particular SDM influences SLA performance, costs, work completion times and learning. The teams, depending on how they handle work, in turn cater to a particular SDM. Henceforth we focus our analysis on the three SDMs. Since each has its pros and cons, a static one-time decision that is universally applied to all customers may not suffice. Especially with services business revenue being close to a billion USD for major providers, its success is strongly related to the trust and satisfaction of its existing customers. In the face of customers' unique expectations it is imperative to understand and weigh the design choices at hand. This necessitates a superior decision process regarding which customer workload, service contracts and skill distributions effectively map best to which SDM in terms of efficient, timely and cost effective delivery for the provider.

Current literature in services delivery [8, 6] focus on optimizing staffing for simple customer work following the Decoupled model, where work arrivals across technology teams have very little or no correlation. When the work is complex, authors [21] focus on improving SLA performance for higher priority work using the Collaborative model, but the throughput of the high volume work noticeably suffers.

Contributions: In this paper, we aim to analyze different SDMs from the perspective of performing complex work and focus on multiple performance parameters of SLA, throughput and utilization. Learning is modeled in workers as they perform repeated activities. The cost versus performance tradeoff for training on additional skills is analyzed to understand the optimal number of skills workers should be trained on. Different rework scenarios are studied that can lead to quality degradation. We define the best SDM as one that: (a) has the best SLA performance, throughput and resource utilization across all priorities of work (b) has least amount of degradation in the performance parameters in the event of high rework (c) has the least cost of delivery. The goal of this work is to establish insights into the best SDM under specific workload, SLA and learning environments and discern the improvements (if-any) that can be achieved by adopting a hybrid model. To the best of our knowledge this is the first work that addresses the above perspectives of service delivery design to this detail, and offers key insights.

This paper is organized as follows: Section 2 describes the different aspects of complex work and how they are affected by the SDMs. Section 3 introduces our simulation model and the various parameters of interest. Section 4 presents the experimental analysis and section 5 presents a review of the related work.

2   Complex Work in Service Systems

We now cover the background on the generalized service operations and present different aspects of delivery models for complex work resolution in service systems. Depending on the teaming principles in place, a customer's work could be supported by one or multiple teams following different delivery models. An SS is typically characterized by:

- A finite set of customers, denoted by C, supported by the service system.
- A finite set of shifts, denoted by A, across which the W service workers (SW) are distributed.
- A finite set of skill domains, denoted by D, with L levels in each skill.
- A finite set of priority levels, denoted by the set P.
- A finite set of service requests (SR) raised by the customer that arrives as work into the SS

We next discuss the work arrivals, SLAs of the SR, and service times and skills of workers in context of supporting complex customer work.

2.1 Work Arrivals

According to existing body of literature in the area of Service Delivery systems [86, 8], work arrives into a SS at a finite set of time intervals, denoted by T, where during each interval the arrivals stay stationary. Arrival rates are specified by the mapping $\alpha : C \times T \to \Re$, assuming that each of the SR arrival processes from the various customers C_i are independent and Poisson distributed with $\alpha(C_i, T_j)$ specifying the rate parameter. When there is a correlation between the work arrivals across different teams supporting a customer, it denotes a complex SR from the customer that requires attention from multiple skill domains. In this case, the independence property still holds for the first team where work is performed.

2.2 Service Level Agreements

SLA constraints, given by the mapping $\gamma : C \times P \to (r_1, r_2), r_i \in \Re, i = 1,2$ is a map from each customer-priority pair to a pair of real numbers representing the SR resolution time deadline (time) and the percentage of all the SRs that must be resolved within this deadline in a month. For example, $\gamma(Customer_1, P_1) = \langle 4,95 \rangle$, denotes that 95% of all SRs from customer$_1$ with priority P_1 in a month must be resolved within 4 hours. Note that the SLAs are on the entire SR itself, which means for complex work the targets apply to resolution across multiple SS teams.

2.3 Skill

In a multi-skill environment, given D domains of skills, let the vector $Sr = (s_r(d_0), s_r(d_1),..., s_r(d_i))$ denote the required skill levels required for a SR r, $d_i \in D, 0 \le i \le |D|$, where $s_r : D \to [0,1], r \in SR$ denotes the required skill function that returns the level of skill required in each of the domains to complete the service request r. Similarly, the possessed skill defined for each worker w is given by $Sw = (s_w(d_0), s_w(d_1),..., s_w(d_i))$, where $s_w : D \to [0,1], w \in W$, returns a real number between 0 and 1 representing the level of skill that agent w possesses, relative to each domain element. Further, 0 denotes no skill and 1 denotes perfect skill. Assuming at least two levels of expertise, $L : D \rightarrow N >= 2$ returns the number of discrete levels defined for each domain (minimum two levels). Work assignment via dispatching looks at the vectors Sr and Sw while deciding the best match between work and resources. Fig. 2 shows two existing skills in the domain $= \{D_1, D_2\}$, each with two levels of skill = {High, Low}.

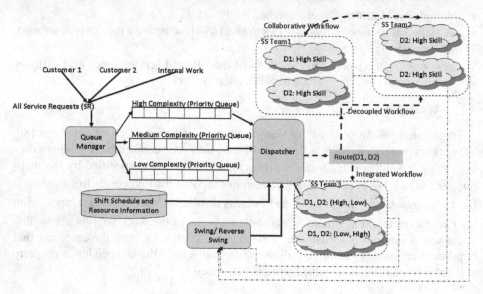

Fig. 2. An operational model of service systems (SS)

2.4 Cost

The cost of delivery is directly related to the cost of the resources working in the SS. Let C_{DC-l} be the base cost of the resource in Decoupled model with single skill expertise at level l. The base cost is assumed to be higher for higher skilled people (i.e., $C_{DC-l1} > C_{DC-l2}, \forall l1 > l2$). In contrast, the Integrated model has multi-skilled people who would need to be trained on each additional skill. Let l_H be the highest skill level of a resource in the Integrated model. We assume that the base cost of a multi-skilled resource is dominated by the base cost of her highest expertise. (S)he also has N additional skills, out of which n_i skills are at level l_i. Let δ_{l_i} the cost for training for each skill to level l_i. Assuming a linear cost model of skills, the cost incurred by the Integrated model for training a multi-skilled resource is then given by:

$$C_{INT} = C_{DC-l_H} + \sum_i n_i * \delta_{l_i}, where \sum_i n_i = N \qquad (1)$$

Since $C_{DC-l} > \delta_l$, i.e., the base cost is higher than the training cost, at lower values of N, it makes sense to train the same resource on an additional skill rather than hire a new resource. For higher N, it becomes more beneficial to hire a new SW.

2.5   Service Time

The time taken by a SW to complete an SR is stochastic and follows a lognormal distribution for a single skill, where the parameters of the distribution are learned by conducting time and motion exercises described in [6]. Service time distributions are characterized by the mapping $\tau : P \times D \to \langle \mu_1, \sigma_1 \rangle$, where μ_1 and σ_1 are the mean and standard deviation parameters of the lognormal distribution and represent the time a worker usually takes to do this work. The distribution varies by the priority of a SR as well as the minimum skill-level required to service it. For complex work requiring multiple skills $(D_1, \ldots D_i)$ the total service time is an additive component of the individual work completions and follows a shifted lognormal distribution [16].

Since complex work takes more time to complete, for the sake of maintaining throughput, it becomes imperative to assign some work to people skilled below the minimum skill-level. When lower skilled people (s_w) do higher skilled work (s_r), where $s_r > s_w$, the service times become longer. This increase in service time is obtained from an adaptation of the LFCM algorithm (Narayanan et al. 2012), where the service time $\mu_n(s_w, s_r)$ to finish the nth repetition of work requiring skill s_r by worker with skill level s_w is given by:

$$\mu_n(s_w, s_r) = \mu_1 n^{\left(-\beta\left(1 - \frac{\log\left(1 + \gamma / t_n\right)}{\log n}\right)\right)}$$

(2)

where μ_1 is the mean service time to execute the higher skilled work for the *first* time, β is the learning factor, γ is the skill gap between levels s_w and s_r, t_n is the time spent by worker at level s_r. Higher the gap γ, and lower the time spent t_n, higher is μ_n. μ_1 represents the longest time to do this type of work, but with work repetitions, expertise is gained and μ_n decreases [13]. In practice we bound the minimum value of μ_n at μ_{min}, which is the lowest service time work s_r can take. The parameters $\langle \mu_1, \beta, \gamma, \mu_{min} \rangle$ are learned by conducting time and motion studies [16] in real SS to measure the exclusive time spent by a SW on a SR. As given by Eqn. (2), slower learning rates and bigger gaps in the skill required of a SR and skill possessed by a SW, both contribute to longer service times.

2.6   Dispatching

The Dispatcher is responsible for diagnosis of the faulty component(s) as well as work assignment to a suitable worker. For fault diagnosis the dispatcher intercepts the complex SR to determine the most likely faulty component(s) and maps them to skill domains that must be consulted (in sequence) for resolution. The SR then traverses through the diagnosed list of teams. In Fig. 2, a SR dispatched with the tag

Route $\{D_1, D_2\}$, needs to traverse through teams that support D_1 and D_2 . When multiple domains of customers are supported, solving the fault-diagnosis without ambiguity is non-trivial [24]. Dispatching errors are commonly termed as *misroutes* and may result in wasted time and cause customer dissatisfaction. With more number of supported components, the risk of misrouting is higher. This is exacerbated in the Decoupled model. The Integrated model avoids this to some extent with multi-skilled resources being able to handle complex issues within the team.

During work assignment, SWs are to SRs of the matching skill-level requirements. When matching skills are not available higher or lower skilled SW may be utilized for servicing a SR. This is referred to as *swing* and *reverse swing* respectively. Fig. 2 shows the Dispatcher routes complex customer work either through the Decoupled, Integrated or Collaborative models and decides to turn on swing/reverse-swing policies based on feedback information from the system.

3   Simulation Based Evaluation

There are many challenges in real-life Service delivery operations that make analytical modeling of a SS a cumbersome exercise [6]. These include the aggregate SLAs specified by customers, the inter-dependence of work queues, the variation of service time distributions with the skill level of the worker, the random breaks taken by resources and the complex preemption rules on the ground. Hence, we resort to simulation as a tool to model the operational characteristics of SS and estimate the performance of systems pertaining to the three SDM. There have been other comparisons of analytical and simulation-based models that corroborate our choice of simulation as a tool [11]. We propose a discrete-event simulation model for a SS according to its definitions in Section 2 and the parameters defined below. The model is similar to the one proposed in [6, 8] with the main that exception that both work and people can have multiple skills. All our experiments have been conducted with data from SS in server support area in the data-center management domain. The data is collected over multiple years using tools [6] defined for IT service management.

Simulation Parameters
The SS simulated extend the definitions in Section 2 with the following specializations.

- T contains one element for each hour of week. Hence, |T| = 168.
- P = {P1, P2, P3, P4}, where, P1 > P2 > P3 > P4.
- We assume $|D| = 3, L = 3$. The three different levels of expertise simulated are {Low, Medium, High}, where, High > Medium > Low. Each level of expertise has a least service time distribution $(\mu_{min}, \sigma_{min})$ associated with it (as in Table 1), which characterizes the minimum time this work type could take. The estimates are obtained from real life time and motion studies [6].

- *Swing:* Swing is invoked when Low queue length>10, where low skilled work is assigned to a high skilled resource. Service times remain same in this case.
- *Reverse Swing:* Reverse Swing is invoked when High and Medium queue length>10, where high skilled work is assigned to a low skilled resource. Service times become longer (Eqn. 2) in this case.
- *Preemption:* Preemption relation $\Rightarrow$ is the transitive closure of the tuples $P_1 \Rightarrow P_2$, $P_2 \Rightarrow P_3$, $P_2 \Rightarrow P_4$.
- *Transfer:* In case of work requiring multiple skills and a Decoupled work structure, the work gets handed over from one team to another. The teams could be geographically co-located (transfer time ~30min) or dispersed (> 30min). There are no transfer rates in Integrated since multiple skills can be found in single team. Collaborative has no transfer times.
- *Lead Time:* The time taken to synchronize the availability of multiple workers in Collaborative flow.
- *Rework:* A percentage of the work is re-opened due to bad quality fixes. Occurs when low skilled workers work on high skilled requests.
- *Dispatching:* Assigns work to resource with matching skill requirements if available. If not available, route to the worker with the lowest skill gap.
- *Learning Factor:* We assume a default moderate learning rate of $\beta = 0.1$ for each SW. Table 1 shows the mean and standard deviation (μ_1, σ_1) for the maximum service times taken by a resource at each skill level, when the work is executed the *first* time. These estimates are obtained from the time and motion studies reported in [6].
- *Misroutes:* Dispatching errors cause misroutes and are associated with wasted effort in addition to the transfer-times. Thus they map to longer completion times.
- *Utilization of SW:* This is related to the productive hours or busy time spent in work resolution.

The interplay of the above parameters and their combined effect is addressed in the experimental analysis.

4   Experimental Analysis

In this section, we describe our experimental evaluation based on data from four real-life SS in the server support area. The four skill domains supported include Operating Systems, Storage, Database and Web Middleware. The Decoupled, Collaborative and Integrated models of delivery are simulated with work arrivals, priority distributions and SLA target times as shown in Table 1(left). In Decoupled and Collaborative models, we create 4 teams, each supporting one skill domain. The resources in these models predominantly possess medium and higher skill levels, as shown in Table 1(right), while in Integrated model the reverse is true. Every SR is dispatched with multiple skill requirements. In the Decoupled model, complex work starts at the first faulty component and transferred sequentially from one team to another. In the Collaborative model people from all teams work in parallel to solve the issue. In the Integrated model, one team is created containing all the 4 skills. The skills are distributed among the workers based on whether they have (2, 3 or 4) skills each. We assume a SW in an Integrated team has only one skill in the highest level, and rest at low or medium levels. Service times follow lognormal distribution for each skill and the means get lower with repetitions according to Eqn. 2. Table 1(right) shows the minimum and maximum service times at each level.

We employ the AnyLogic Professional Discrete Event simulation toolkit [4] for the experiments. Up to 40 weeks of runs were simulated with measurements taken at end of each week. No measurements were recorded during the warm up period of first four weeks. In steady state the parameters measured include:

- SLA measurements at each priority level
- Completion times of work (includes queue waiting times, transfer times, and service times)
- Throughput of the SS (work completed/week)
- Resource utilization (captures the busy-time of a resource)

For all the above parameters the observation means and confidence intervals are reported. Whenever confidence intervals are wider, the number of weeks in simulation is increased and reported values in the paper are within 95% confidence intervals. We seed the simulation with a good initial staffing solution from the Optimizer kit [15] which returned the optimal number of staff to handle the work.

Table 1. Experimental Parameters (Workload, Skills, Service Times)

Workload	Arrival SR/week	1575
Priority	% Distribute	Target Time (hours)
P1	10	4
P2	20	6
P3	40	12
P4	30	24

Number of resources = 38	SDM		Min, Max Service Times	
Distribution of Skill Level (L)	% Distribute (COLLAB, DECOUP)	% Distribute (INTEGRATED)	Min ST $<\mu_{min}, \sigma_{min}>$	Max ST $< \mu_1, \sigma_1>$
Low	40	70	30,20	60,20
Medium	40	20	15,15	40,15
High	20	10	10,10	30, 10

4.1   Complex Multi-skill Work

We investigate the scenario of work requiring multiple skills and correlated ticket arrivals across teams with experimental parameters given by Table1. First we handle complex work that requires 2 skills and resources are either single skilled (Decoupled, Collaborative) or have 2 skills (Integrated). The experiment assumes 10% misroutes and 5-10% rework in the environment. The results in Fig. 3 show that mean values for SLA performance with 95% confidence levels. The following observations stand-out: (a) Collaborative model works well in terms of SLA performance for higher priority work. This re-confirms the assumptions by authors [21]. The fact that experts simultaneously work on the multiple skills, and their service times are also the lowest reflects in the good performance of low volume, high priority work. However in case of high volume lower priority work, the Collaborative model does not do well.

As multiple people's effort is locked on higher priority work, lower priority work gets queued up and ultimately affects SLA performance. (b) Decoupled does better than Collaborative in case of P3 and P4 work. This is because Decoupled has the least synchronization overhead among multiple skills, which works well for high volume work. But this lack of tight integration in work resolution workflow, affects the P1, P2 SLA performance. (c) Integrated does the best across all severities, and clearly has the right balance between tight synchronization of critical work and decoupling of larger volume work. Interestingly, while people have lower skill levels in Integrated, and may initially take longer to service; overall SLA performance is not affected as long as there is some learning in the environment.

Fig. 4 presents performance of all the three models as the rework % increases. Only the P3 performance plot is presented as a representative case, but similar trends are observed at other priorities. The performance degradation in the Integrated model is the least, as rework increases. This shows that this model has the best appetite to absorb additional work in case of error situations, without affecting performance. In theory it can be argued that rework may be inherently higher in the Integrated model as people have lower level of expertise that may result in poor quality of work and higher rework % than the counterpart models. Fig. 4 shows that even if the rework in Integrated model is higher by as much as 10% than the other two models, the SLA performance of the highest volume P3 bucket is still better.

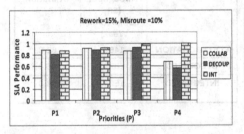 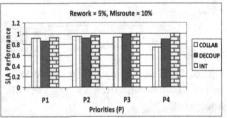

(a) Rework = 5%, Misroute=10%   (b) Rework = 10%, Misroute=10%

Fig. 3. SLA Performance in different Service Delivery Models

In Fig. 5, we repeat the similar experimentation with misroutes, while keeping the rework at 10%. However as misroutes increase beyond 10%, the performance of all models degrade uniformly. Since misrouting is related to dispatching errors, we conclude that beyond 10% of misrouting in the environment, no SDM performs well and alternative methods for error diagnosis [24] are needed. Table2 presents the throughput and resource utilizations of the different models. At 5% rework and 10% misroute, the mean throughputs of Collaborative are the lowest, while Decoupled and Integrated are comparable. This is because in the Collaborative model multiple people's efforts are simultaneously blocked and the effort/SR is much higher.

Fig. 6 shows the drop in throughput for the different models as rework increases which shows that beyond 15%, the drop in Decoupled throughput is more pronounced. To understand the consistently lower throughput of Collaborative model, we look at how long the work took to complete in the different models. Recall that completion time measure both the queue waiting times as well as the service times. Fig. 7 shows that at lower severities the completion times are comparable across all models, while higher severities see an exponential increase in the completion times for Collaborative. Completion times of Integrated are marginally higher than Decoupled at all priorities. This can be attributed to the higher service times for multi-skilled resources. But it does not translate to any obvious throughput disadvantages.

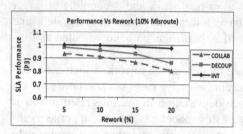

Fig. 4. Performance as Rework increases

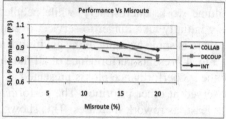

Fig. 5. Performance as Misroute increases

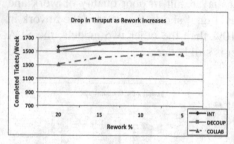

Fig. 6. Drop in Throughput as Rework increases Utilizations (Rework = 5%, Misroute=10%)

Table 2. Weekly Throughput and Resource

	Mean Throughput (SR Completed/ Week)	Resource Utilization
COLLABORATION	1457	62.8
DECOUPLED	1620	46.4
INTEGRATED	1624	53.0

Table 2 also shows higher resource utilizations for Collaborative for a lower net throughput that can be attributed to the longer completion times. Fig. 8 plots the change in utilization as rework in the SS increases. Decoupled has the best utilizations which is because of the lowest completion times. Integrated is slightly higher in terms of utilization at a comparable throughput. Overall, Fig. 8 shows that even across higher rework %, the utilizations of decoupled remains the best, with the Integrated model following closely. A hybrid model that is Collaborative for (P1, P2) work and Integrated for (P3, P4) achieves best of both and requires only partial upskilling of the population. Based on above results we summarize the following:

Observation 1: The Integrated model works well in terms of SLA performance, throughput and resource utilization across all reasonable rework scenarios. With some moderate learning in the environment, the higher service times in Integrated have a lower impact on SS performance than the transfers in Decoupled. If the higher priority work have tight SLAs and continues to be < 10% of the pool's work, having a hybrid model, can achieve best of both worlds: Collaborative for high priority complex work enables high SLA performance for critical issues. For high volume, low *priority work, an Integrated model that up-skills only 20% of the population with an additional low level skill can significantly improve performance and throughput of lower priorities.*

4.2   Skills and Learning

Having established the Integrated model with the most uniform performance across the parameters of interest, we now experiment with some of the learning aspects of it.

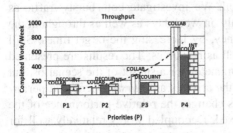
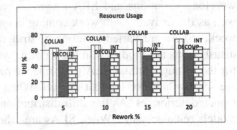

Fig. 7. Completion Time across Priorities   **Fig. 8.** Increase in Utilization with Rework

The biggest drawback of the Integrated scenario is the higher costs it entails, especially if the need to up-skill grows. Our next set of experiments investigates the benefits of up-skilling a resource beyond 2 skills. Table 3 presents the SS parameters as the work coming in becomes more complex (i.e. requires 3-4 skills and resources possess (2, 3 or 4) skills. Results are shown in Table3. Rows 1 and 3 show that for complex work, having SW with more skills does improve P1, P2 performance marginally. Also since work now takes longer to complete, we expect throughputs to drop uniformly in this scenario. Instead we notice that throughput drops are greater when skills per SW are more. This interesting observation can be explained by the fact that the people with more skills are now busier for longer, since the work resolution takes more time. With certain skills being more in-demand, it results in unique skills in the environment being tied up for too long, while incoming work in the queue waits for a suitable SW to become available. This is confirmed by the higher resource utilizations for lower throughput, when people have > 2 skills. Interestingly, the drop in throughput is lowest, when people have only 2 skills. It is therefore more beneficial to split highly complex work (requiring 3-4 skills) among multiple resources, than have one multi-skilled SW do all aspects of it. The cost implications of having multi-skilled SW are shown in the last column of Table3, computed as per Eqn. (1). A blended rate (across skill levels) of 80K₹ per SW per month and an up-skilling cost of 20K₹ per skill is assumed. We argue that since SLA performance at the higher priorities can be independently improved by having a Collaborative model for the critical work, the higher costs of multi-skilling a person beyond two skills has limited returns, especially since it comes with the risk of lowering throughput.

The sensitivity of the learning factor (β) on the performance of the Integrated model is shown in Table 4. Even with a small amount of learning in the system (0.07-0.1), the performance of the SDM is good. With close to no learning in the system (< 0.03), however the deterioration in service times is pronounced and this affects the SS parameters of throughput and utilization.

Observation 2: For complex work the return on investment for up-skilling is the maximum when resources have at most two skills. Up-skilling beyond that may result in little or no benefit in performance. An Integrated SDM works well in most cases, given that there is some amount of learning in the environment.

4.3   Workload and SLA variations

Our final set of results in Table 5 show that all previous observations hold for other workload variations and SLA ranges as well. We investigate both bursty traffic as well as flat arrivals, with work coming in only on weekdays as well as throughout the week. SLAs are varied in terms of stringency, by increasing the target times. Skill distributions are modified in the work as well as resources. The results are presented for the throughput and SLA performance parameter for a subset of the scenarios, but are seen to hold for the rest as well. When the arrivals are *bursty* Decoupled performance deteriorates. As the skill distributions change, the relative performance of the models remains same. When SLAs are relaxed, Decoupled works relatively well for P1 performance. However as seen from Table 5, Integrated continually performs better than its counterparts across variations in arrival patterns, skill distribution and SLA stringency.

Table 3. Complex Work requiring >=2 skills

(Skills Required, Skills Possessed)	SLA Perf (P1)	SLA Perf (P2)	Mean Thruput (SR/wk)	Util (%)	Cost ₹ / SW/Month
SR = 3, SW= 3	81%	89%	1173	70%	140K
SR = 3, SW= 2	77%	86%	1188	70%	120K
SR = 4, SW= 4	77%	86%	510	87%	160K
SR = 4, SW= 3	75%	81%	507	87%	140K
SR = 4, SW= 2	74%	80%	704	75%	120K

Table 4. Learning factor sensitivity

INTEGRATED	Mean Thruput (SR/week)	Completion Time (min)	Util (%)
With Learning Model (β=0.1)	1624	110.44	54.8%
With Learning Model(β=0.07)	1608	140.54	65.9%
With Learning Model(β=0.03)	1282	173.81	80.1%
With No Learning Model	1191	377.63	83.3%

Observation 3: The Integrated model consistently outperforms the others under a reasonable set of workload arrivals, SLA targets and skill distributions.

Table 5. Performance comparison, with workload, SLA and skill distribution variations

	Throughput (SR/week)				P1 SLA Attainment	
	Arrival (Flat)	Arrival (Bursty)	Skills Equal Dist	Skills Skewed to Higher Levels	SLA Stringent	SLA Relaxed
COLLABORATION	1418	1370	1360	1318	80	90.1
DECOUPLED	1635	1551	1400	1428	73.2	88.3
INTEGRATED	1638	1616	1505	1611	79.8	89.4

5   Related Work

The concept of shared service has existed for a long time, for e.g., multiple departments within an organization shared services like HR, finance, IT etc. However, its extension to shared delivery models for IT services has been gaining momentum from the last decade [5]. A recent study [23] of global service delivery centers revealed that shared services not only reduces costs, but also improves quality. A body of work exists on organizational design principles underlying an effective service delivery system [1] and resource hiring and training in such models [20]. However there is no work on generalizing the service delivery models and evaluating the pros and cons when presented with different kinds of workloads and work arrival patterns. This is the gap that this work addresses. Learning and forgetting curves in production and manufacturing industry [13] has received a lot of attention. The service delivery work, being repetitive in nature can benefit from these results in modeling the effect of learning and forgetting on service times. There is another line of work that studies the effects of task assignment on long term resource productivity. This is because the task assignment impacts mean learning rate, mean forgetting rate, mean prior expertise, variance of prior expertise etc and thus has a direct consequence on productivity. This paper incorporates some of the manufacturing domain results. The work in [18] presents a heuristic approach for assigning work by taking into account all these factors. How to staff, cross-train them and utilize multi-skill resources has also received adequate attention in the past in the context of call-centers [79]. The work in [12] advocates that a flexible worker should process a task s/he is uniquely qualified for before helping others in shared tasks. This is advocated in work-in-process constrained flow-lines staffed with partially cross-trained workers with hierarchical skill sets. Experimental results from our simulation are in agreement with many of the suggested best practices for multi-skilled resources. The effect of collaboration between teams has also been studied in work in [21] which proposes the concept of social compute unit. We have used this structure in the collaborative work flow model in this paper. The paper [10] theorizes how task/team familiarity interact with team coordination complexity to influence team performance.

6   Conclusion

We perform behavioral analysis of the different SDMs and present insights on their performance for changing workload patterns, SLAs, learning and skill distribution parameters. These insights have critical implications on optimized service delivery and can be used to transform service providers' work organization by helping determine which customer(s) work fits best into which SDM. In future we plan to create a platform where these insights are used for automated transformation.

References

1. Agarwal, S., Reddy, V.K., Sengupta, B., Bagheri, S., Ratakonda, K.: Organizing Shared Delivery Systems. In: Proc. of 2nd International Conference on Services in Emerging Markets, India (2011)

2. Agarwal, S., Sindhgatta, R., Sengupta, B.: SmartDispatch: enabling efficient ticket dispatch in an IT service environment. In: Proc. of the 18th ACM SIGKDD International Conference on Knowledge Discovery and Data Mining, KDD 2012 (2012)
3. Alter, S.: Service System Fundamentals: Work System, Value Chain, and Life Cycle. IBM Systems Journal 47(1), 71–85 (2008)
4. Anylogic Tutorial 2008, How to build a combined agent based/system dynamics model in Anylogic. System Dynamics Conference (2008),
   http://www.xjtek.com/anylogic/articles/13/
5. Assembly Optimization: A Distinct Approach to Global Delivery, IBM White Paper (2010)
6. Banerjee, D., Dasgupta, G.B., Desai, N.: Simulation-based evaluation of dispatching policies in service systems. In: Winter Simulation Conference 2011 (2011)
7. Cezik, M.T., L'Ecuyer, P.: Staffing multi-skill call centers via linear programming and simulation. Management Science Journal (2006)
8. Diao, Y., Heching, A., Northcutt, D., Stark, G.: Modeling a complex global service delivery system. In: Winter Simulation Conference 2011 (2011)
9. Easton, F.F.: Staffing, Cross-training, and Scheduling with Cross-trained Workers in Extended-hour Service Operations. Manuscript, Robert H. Brethen Operations Management Institute (2011)
10. Espinosa, J.A., Slaughter, S.A., Kraut, R.E., Herbsleb, J.D.: Familiarity, Complexity, and Team Performance in Geographically Distributed Software Development. Organization Science 18(4), 613–630 (2007)
11. Franzese, L.A., Fioroni, M.M., de Freitas Filho, P.J., Botter, R.C.: Comparison of Call Center Models. In: Proc. of the Conference on Winter Simulation Conf. (2009)
12. Gel, E.S., Hopp, W.J., Van Oyen, M.P.: Hierarchical cross-training in work-in-process-constrained systems. IIE Transactions 39 (2007)
13. Jaber, M.Y., Bonney, M.: A comparative study of learning curves with forgetting. In: Applied Mathematical Modelling, vol. 21, pp. 523–531 (1997)
14. Kleiner, M.M., Nickelsburg, J., Pilarski, A.: Organizational and Individual Learning and Forgetting. Industrial and Labour Relations Review 65(1) (2011)
15. Laguna, M.: Optimization of complex systems with optquest. OptQuest for Crystal Ball User Manual, Decisioneering (1998)
16. Lo, C.F.: The Sum and Difference of Two Lognormal Random Variables. Journal of Applied Mathematics 2012, Article ID 838397, 13 pages (2012)
17. Narayanan, C.L., Dasgupta, G., Desai, N.: Learning to impart skills to service workers via challenging task assignments. IBM Technical Report. Under Review (2012)
18. Nembhard, D.A.: Heuristic approach for assigning workers to tasks based on individual learning rates. Int. Journal. Prod. Res. 39(9) (2001)
19. Ramaswamy, L., Banavar, G.: A Formal Model of Service Delivery. In: Proc. of the 2008 IEEE International Conference on Service Computing (2008)
20. Subramanian, D., An, L.: Optimal Resource Action Planning Analytics for Services Delivery Using Hiring, Contracting & Cross-Training of Various Skills. In: Proc. of IEEE SCC (2008)
21. Sengupta, B., Jain, A., Bhattacharya, K., Truong, H.-L., Dustdar, S.: Who do you call? Problem Resolution through Social Compute Units. In: Liu, C., Ludwig, H., Toumani, F., Yu, Q. (eds.) ICSOC 2012. LNCS, vol. 7636, pp. 48–62. Springer, Heidelberg (2012)
22. Spohrer, J., Maglio, P.P., Bailey, J., Gruhl, D.: Steps Toward a Science of Service Systems. IEEE Computer 40(1), 71–77 (2007)
23. Shared Services & Outsourcing Network (SSON) and The Hackett Group, "Global service center benchmark study" (2009)
24. Verma, A., Desai, N., Bhamidipaty, A., Jain, A.N., Barnes, S., Nallacherry, J., Roy, S.: Automated Optimal Dispatching of Service Requests. In: Proc. of the SRII (2011)

A Novel Service Composition Approach
for Application Migration to Cloud

Xianzhi Wang[1,2], Xuejun Zhuo[1], Bo Yang[1], Fan Jing Meng[1], Pu Jin[1], Woody Huang[3], Christopher C. Young[3], Catherine Zhang[3], Jing Min Xu[1], and Michael Montinarelli[4]

[1] IBM Research – China, Beijing, P.R. China
{wxianzhi,zhuoxuej,yangbbo,mengfj,jinpubj,xujingm}@cn.ibm.com
[2] Harbin Institute of Technology, Harbin, Heilongjiang, P.R. China
xianzhi.wang@hit.edu.cn
[3] IBM Research – Watson, Yorktown, NY, US
{ywh,ccyoung,cxzhang}@us.ibm.com
[4] IBM Global Technology Services, Rochester, NY, US
mmonti@us.ibm.com

Abstract. Migrating business applications to cloud can be costly, labor-intensive, and error-prone due to the complexity of business applications, the constraints of the clouds, and the limitations of existing migration techniques provided by migration service vendors. However, the emerging software-as-a-service offering model of migration services makes it possible to combine multiple migration services for a single migration task. In this paper, we propose a novel migration service composition approach to achieve a cost-effective migration solution. In particular, we first formalize the migration service composition problem into an optimization model. Then, we present an algorithm to determine the optimal composition solution for a given migration task. Finally, using synthetic trace driven simulations, we validate the effectiveness and efficiency of the proposed optimization model and algorithm.

Keywords: Cloud computing, modeling, migration, service composition.

1   Introduction

The increasingly wide adoption of cloud computing has witnessed huge demands for migrating business applications to cloud. In 2012, IDC reported that more than 50% of European larger companies stated that they have a strategy for IT infrastructure refactoring to benefit from cloud economics, of which the cloud migration investment is forecast to grow at 30.6% Compound Annual Growth Rate in the next 5 years [1].

In response to the huge migration demands, many migration service vendors have emerged to offer diverse migration services. They can be categorized into three major types: *image-based migration*, *application-centric migration*, and *migration to virtualized containers*. The image-based migration technique, such as Racemi® [2] and CohesiveFT [3], converts source serves into virtual images and imports them into target cloud after necessary adjustments. Application-centric migration, such as

S. Basu et al. (Eds.): ICSOC 2013, LNCS 8274, pp. 667–674, 2013.

AppZero [4] and CliQr™ [5], provisions a new application deployment environment on the target by extracting and migrating the application artifacts, configurations, and resources from the source. The migration to virtualized containers method, such as Ravello [6] and CohesiveFT Software Defined Networking [3], migrates the source VM without any modification to run in a virtualized container inside the target cloud.

However, migrating business applications to cloud is considered costly, labor-intensive, and error-prone due to the complexity of the applications, the constraints of the clouds, and the limitations of existing migration techniques provided by migration service vendors[7]. It is extremely difficult or even impossible for single vendor to migrate a complex application entirely on its own. Fortunately, the emerging software-as-a-service model makes it possible to combine multiple migration services to accomplish a single migration task. By consolidating the diverse migration capabilities provided by multiple vendors, a more comprehensive and flexible migration service can be provided. For example, Racemi® can provide server migration services to the IBM® SmartCloud® Enterprise (SCE)[8] but cannot remediate middleware and application configurations (e.g. hostname, IP address) after migration; whereas the CohesiveFT can close the gap with the network virtualization service. As can be seen, the application can be successfully migrated to IBM® SCE by composing the services provided by the two vendors.

In this paper, we propose a novel service composition approach to provide an application migration solution with a wide-spectrum of capabilities, by consolidating diverse migration techniques offered by different vendors. The main contributions of the paper are two-fold: 1) We formalize the migration service composition problem into an optimization model; 2) We provide an algorithm to solve the optimization problem and validate it using simulations.

The remainder of this paper is organized as follows. Section 2 introduces the modeling of the basic concepts and the problem. The matching and optimization algorithm is presents in Section 3 and evaluated in Section 4. Section 5 investigates related work. Section 6 concludes the paper and discusses the future works.

2   Problem Definition and Modeling

In migration context, a business application can be modeled as state with a hierarchy of components with valued configuration attributes and interdependencies. The problem of determining an optimal cost-effective migration solution can be considered as a state transition problem, aiming to find an optimal subset of vendor services and their operation sequence so that they can collaboratively transform the application from its initial state to a cloud-acceptable state.

2.1   Problem Definition

In this section, we consider scenarios where applications are migrated into a single given cloud and formalize the basic concepts as follows.

$c(a_1, a_2,...,a_k)$: denotes an application component which can be migrated separately as an individual unit, where $\forall a_i, i \in \{1,...,k\}$ are the detailed configuration attributes attached to the component.

$\tilde{c}(a_1 = x_1, a_2 = x_2,..., a_k = x_k)$: denotes an instance of component c in which $\forall a_i, i \in \{1,...,k\}$ have been set with specific values.

$C = \{c_1, c_2,..., c_l\}$: denotes all the components to be migrated in the application.

$S(C^*) = (\tilde{C}^*, D)$: denotes a state of a set of application components $C^* \subseteq C$. $\tilde{C}^* = \{\tilde{c}_1^*, \tilde{c}_2^*,..., \tilde{c}_g^*\}$, which represents an instance of this set of components where each component is attached with valued configuration attributes. $D = \{(type, c_{from} \rightarrow c_{to}, \{c_{from}.a_x \rightarrow c_{to}.a_y\})\}$, which denotes the dependency relations between components. The first parameter indicates the dependency type, e.g., *runsOn*, *connectsTo*, *includes*, etc. The second parameter indicates the two components related to this dependency. The last parameter indicates the detailed mapping relations between the attributes of the corresponding components, if any.

Based on above definition, the problem-specific concepts are formalized as below:

$S_{ini}(C) = (\tilde{C}_{ini}, D_{ini})$: denotes the initial state of the application to be migrated.

$\mathbf{S}_{tgt}(C) = \{S_{tgt}^1(C), S_{tgt}^2(C),..., S_{tgt}^k(C)\}$: denotes a collection of all possible acceptable target states of the application in the cloud, where $S_{tgt}^i(C) = (C_{tgt}^i, D_{tgt}^i)$ is an individual state in it.

$V = [v_1, v_2,..., v_n]$: denotes a collection of migration services provides by vendors.

$\mathbf{M} = [M_1, M_2,..., M_n]$: denotes vendors' migration capability. More specifically, the capability of each vendor $v_j (\in V)$ is represented by its enabled state transition $M_j = (S_j^{cond}(C_j^{cond}), S_j^{in}(C_j^{mig}), S_j^{out}(C_j^{mig}))$, where C_j^{mig} is the component to be migrated by v_j, $S_j^{in}(C_j^{mig})$ and $S_j^{out}(C_j^{mig})$ are the input and output states of C_j^{mig}, respectively, while $S_j^{cond}(C_j^{cond})$ is the requirements imposed by v_j as prerequisites on components other than $C_j^{mig} (\neq C_j^{cond})$. Note that a vendor can be matched to multiple components within single migration task. For example, a vendor which performs server-based migration may possibly be mapped to two separate servers (regarded as different components), respectively.

$\mathbf{Cost} = [Cost(v_1), Cost(v_2),..., Cost(v_n)]$: denotes vendor-specific functions for calculating migration cost, which are specific to the number of migrated components plus operational cost.

$\mathbf{H} = [H(v_1), H(v_2),..., H(v_n)]$: denotes the quantified measurement of human efforts required by vendor services per usage based on historical experiences.

$\mathbf{T} = [T(v_1), T(v_2),..., T(v_n)]$: denotes the predicted time consumed by each vendor to perform migration per usage based on benchmark.

H_{max} : denotes the maximal human effort acceptable for application migration

T_{max} : denotes the maximal migration time acceptable for application migration

$\mathbf{G} = (\mathbf{N}, \mathbf{E})$: is a directed acyclic graph which denotes a migration solution. $\mathbf{N} = [N_1 v_1, N_2 v_2, ..., N_n v_n]$ is a set of nodes, i.e., a repetitive set of vendors which are selected to collaboratively accomplish the migration task, $N_i \in \{0, 1, ..., n\}$. $\mathbf{E} = \{(v_x, v_y, P_{x,y})\}$ is a set of edges, i.e., directed links (e.g., from v_x to v_y) representing their precedent order in migration, and context information $P_{x,y}$.

2.2   Problem Modeling

The objective of the migration problem is to determine an optimal migration solution denoted as a graph $\mathbf{G}$ which minimizes the overall migration and time-framed operational cost under user specified constrains on time and human efforts. The optimization problem is formally formulized as follows:

$$\arg \min_{\mathbf{G}} \sum_{i=1}^{n} N_i Cost(v_i) \tag{1}$$

$$s.t. \ \ f(S_{ini}(C), \mathbf{S}_{tgt}(C), \mathbf{M}, \mathbf{G}) = 1 \tag{2}$$

$$\sum_{i=1}^{n} N_i H(v_i) \leq H_{max} \tag{3}$$

$$t_{max}(\mathbf{G}, \mathbf{T}) \leq T_{max} \tag{4}$$

In Eq (2), $f = 1$ if and only if $\mathbf{G}$ is a feasible migration solution, i.e., it is able to transform application state from S_{ini} to an acceptable target state in $\mathbf{S}_{tgt}$, by collaboratively utilizing vendors' migration capability represented by $\mathbf{M}$. In Eq (4), $t_{max}(\mathbf{G}, \mathbf{T})$ is the maximum migration time for solution $\mathbf{G}$ estimated based on $\mathbf{T}$.

3   The Algorithm

The migration problem defined in the last section can be reduced to the Subset Sum problem with exponential set size which is proved to be NP-Hard. In this paper, we propose an algorithm based on A-star algorithm with effective pruning strategies to significantly reduce the solution space.

Firstly, we will introduce how to calculate Lower-Bound of Potential Cost (LBPC) for each intermediate state. In particular, given any intermediate state S and a target state S_{tgt}^i , the corresponding LBPC is calculated as the maximum LBPC estimated for each attribute of each component of the given application. Suppose A is a set of all attributes of the application, $x(a)$ and $x_{tgt}(a)$ are the current and target values of $a (\in A)$ specified in $S(C)$ and $S_{tgt}^i(C)$, respectively. We define:

$$Cost^*(S(C), S_{tgt}^i(C)) = \max_{a \in A} Cost^*(a : x \to x_{tgt}) \tag{5}$$

where $Cost^*(x(a) \to x_{tgt}(a))$ is the estimated LBPC for transforming the value of a single attribute a into a given target value, which can be further calculated as the minimum value among the minimal cost of value-change achieved directly by a single vendor, and minimal cost achieved by multiple vendors.

$$Cost^*(a : x \rightarrow x_{tgt}) = \min(Cost_{idc}(a : x \rightarrow x_{tgt}), Cost_{dc}(a : x \rightarrow x_{tgt})) \quad (6)$$

$Cost_{idc}$ contains at least two parts, the minimal cost for any vendor that accepts the given attribute value, and the minimal cost for any vendor that can transform the attribute into target value.

$$Cost_{idc}(a) = Cost_{fromX} + Cost_{toTgt} \quad (7)$$

For the value-change performed by single vendor, the LBPC is the minimal cost of all vendors that enables the value-change, i.e.,

$$Cost_{dc}(a) = \min\{Cost(v) \mid v \text{ enables } a : x \rightarrow x_{tgt}\} \quad (8)$$

Also $Cost*(S, S_{tgt}^i)$ should be set $+\infty$ when any target value is unreachable.

The input are the initial and target states: S_{ini} and $\mathbf{S}_{tgt}$, registered vendors V represented with $(\mathbf{M}, \mathbf{Cost}, \mathbf{H}, \mathbf{T})$, and user specified constraints: H_{max} and T_{max} . The output is the $\mathbf{G} = (\mathbf{N}, \mathbf{E})$ as defined above. The detail procedure is as follows.

(1)	*Preprocessing stage*
1	**Identify all cloud-compatible target states** $\mathbf{S}_{tgt}$ and **filter vendors**
2	Calculate $Cost^*(S_{ini}, S_{tgt}^i)$ for each $S_{tgt}^i \in \mathbf{S}_{tgt}$
3	$\mathbf{S}_{tgt} \leftarrow \mathbf{S}_{tgt} / \{S_{tgt}^i \mid S_{tgt}^i \in \mathbf{S}_{tgt} \wedge Cost^*(S_{ini}, S_{tgt}^i) = +\infty\}$ // Remove unreachable state
	// Heuristic 1: preordering and pruning target states
4	Sort the target states of $\mathbf{S}_{tgt}$ in ascending order according to $Cost^*(S_{ini}, S_{tgt}^i)$
(2)	*Iteration stage*
5	**FOR** the first element S_{tgt}^i of sorted $\mathbf{S}_{tgt}$ elements // get target states in order
6	Initialize $OL \leftarrow \{S_{ini}\}$, $CL \leftarrow \varnothing$, $Cost(S_{ini}) \leftarrow 0$, $SFB \leftarrow +\infty$, $G(S_{ini}) \leftarrow \varnothing$
7	**IF** $OL = \varnothing$, **CONTINUE** // this target state has been fully exploited
8	$S \leftarrow$ Get the first element of OL
9	$OL \leftarrow OL / \{S\}$, $CL \leftarrow CL \cup \{S\}$ // Move S from OL to CL
10	**FOR** each vendor $v_j (\in V)$
11	**IF** C_j^{mig} cannot be tackled individually, **CONTINUE** // try next vendor
12	**IF** S does not support $S_j^{cond}(C_j^{cond})$ or $S_j^{in}(C_j^{mig})$,**CONTINUE** // try next vendor
13	$S' \xleftarrow{M_j} S$ // generate new state from current state by v_j
	// Initialize S''s cost and corresponding (partial) solution as S's duplicate
14	$G(S') \leftarrow G(S)$, $Cost(S') \leftarrow Cost(S) + Cost(v_j)$
	// Heuristic 2: pruning recurring ineffective states
15	**IF** $\exists S^e \in OL \cup CL \wedge S^e = S' \wedge Cost(S^e) \leq Cost(S')$,**CONTINUE** // try next vendor
16	Calculate $Cost^*(S', S_{tgt})$
	// Heuristic 3: pruning by so-far-the-lowest feasible cost as upper-bound
17	**IF** $Cost(S') + Cost^*(S', S_{tgt}) \geq SFB$, **CONTINUE** // try next vendor
	// Build corresponding solution of S', i.e., (partial) solution from S_{ini} to S'

18	$N(S') \leftarrow N(S') \cup \{v_j\}$ // add v_j into $G(S')$'s node set
19	$V^{ilo} \leftarrow$ Find the vendors directly support $S_j^{in}(C_j^{mig})$ in v_j's matching with S
20	**FOR** each $v_x \in V^{ilo}$
21	$E(S') \leftarrow E(S') \cup \{(v_j, v_x)\}$ // Add link to $G(S')$'s edge set
22	$C_G \leftarrow C_G \cup \{I/O, (v_j, v_x), S_{x,j}\}$ // Add to Global Context
	// $S_{x,j}$ is a mediating state between v_x and v_j, satisfying
	$(S_{x,j} \subseteq S_x^{out} \cap S_j^{in}(C_j^{mig})) \wedge (\bigcup_{v_x \in V^{ilo}} S_{x,j} = S_j^{in}) \wedge (\bigcap_{v_x \in V^{ilo}} S_{x,j} = \varnothing)$
	END FOR
23	$V^c \leftarrow$ Find the vendors directly support $S_j^{cond}(C_j^{cond})$ in v_j's matching with S
24	**FOR** each $v_y \in V^c$
25	**IF** $(v_j, v_y) \notin E(S')$, $E(S') \leftarrow E(S') \cup \{(v_j, v_y)\}$
	END FOR
26	**FOR** each $d = (type, c_{from} \rightarrow c_{to}, \{c_{from}.a_x \rightarrow c_{to}.a_y\}) \in D$
27	**IF** $\{v_x \mid C_{from} \subseteq C_x'^{mig}\} \neq \{v_y \mid C_{from} \subseteq C_y'^{mig}\}, v_x, v_y \in N(S')$
28	$E(S') \leftarrow E(S') \cup \{(v_x, v_y)\}$
29	$C_G \leftarrow C_G \cup \{dependency, (v_x, v_y), d\}$
	END FOR/* End of solution building */
30	**IF** $S' = S_{tgt}$ // have reached the target state
31	$SFB \leftarrow Cost(S')$ // now there must be $Cost^*(S', S_{tgt}) = 0$
32	$G \leftarrow G(S')$ // this solution is currently the best
	CONTINUE //try next vendor
33	$OL \leftarrow OL \cup \{S'\}$ // Insert S' to OL, make sure it is still sorted after insertion
	CONTINUE //try next vendor
	END FOR
	END FOR
34	**RETURN** SFB and G // when all target states have been explored

4   Implementation and Evaluation

In this section, we validated our approach via synthetic trace driven simulations. The settings of key parameters are shown in Table 1. Based on the parameter settings, we randomly generated a cloud profile from which two target states are identified. We evaluated the performance of the algorithm in term of computation time consumed to obtain the optimal solution under different conditions.

Table 1. Parameter settings for performance evaluation

Type	Parameter	(range of) value
variable	# of heterogeneous servers per application (*NoHS*)	1~16
variable	# of components per server (*NoC*)	6~14
variable	# of vendors per component type (*NoV*)	5, 10, 15

Fig.1(a) shows the computation time of the algorithm with respect to *NoHS* and *NoV*, under *NoC*=10. As can be seen, by adopting multiple effective pruning strategies, the computation time of the algorithm is controlled within a reasonable scale. Although the increasing speed of computation time tends to increase as scale of the synthetic trace grows, the algorithm is proved to be able to handle scenarios with a sufficiently large problem scale efficiently, i.e., 15*(1+12+12*10)=1995 vendors when *NoV*=15, which is far more than existing vendors in realistic market. Under this large scale scenario, our algorithm managed to find the optimal composition solution within 25 minutes. This performance is apparently affordable in practical uses, given that a real migration planning could usually take several hours or even days.

Fig.1(b) shows the computation time with respect to *NoC* and *NoV*, where *NoHS* is set to 10. The results show that the computation time with respect to *NoC* increases much slower than that w.r.t *NoHS*. Within certain scope, the curves are nearly linear, e.g., when *NoC* varying between 8 and 12 with *NoV* =15, and *NoC* varying between 10 and 14 with *NoV* =10. These results reveal the fact that *NoHS* is inherently more influential to the performance of the algorithm, since each new heterogeneous server is likely to bring much more new types of intra-server components, which further increases the complexity of the problem.

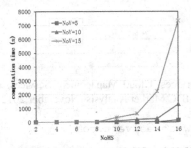
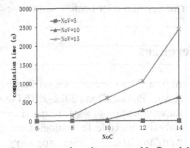

(a) computation time w.r.t. *NoHS* and *NoV*   (b) computation time w.r.t. *NoC* and *NoV*

Fig. 1. Algorithm performance w.r.t. *NoHS*, *NoC* and *NoV*

Based on the above performance analysis with the simulated representative synthetic data, we can conclude that the optimization model and algorithm are both effective and efficient to be applied in the real business application migration cases.

5   Related Work

Migrating application to cloud has been widely studied from different perspectives, which include frameworks and tools for migration execution [9], toolkits and models to support decision making of migration feasibility [10], frameworks for target cloud selection [11], techniques to discover application configuration for migration [12], and etc. Specifically, in [9] the authors introduced the Darwin framework which integrates set of tools that can enable smooth workload migration to cloud or non-cloud environment. In [10], the authors proposed Cloud Transformation Advisor which recommends an optimal application transformation solution based on transforming patterns definition. However, all of these works only focused on particular application types, software stacks or target clouds and are hardly applied in migrating applications with complicated topologies and software stacks individually.

Though service composition has been widely studied in services computing, being orthogonal with these existing works, in this paper, we apply service composition to solve the realistic and urgent challenges in cloud migration. To our best knowledge, this is the first work proposing to solve the cloud migration problem by consolidating different vendor services.

6   Conclusion and Future Work

In this paper, we presented a novel service composition based approach for business application migration to cloud to accomplish the complicated migration tasks at lower cost, which consolidates diverse capabilities offered by different migration vendors. By capturing and formalizing the key concepts involved in cloud migration, we formally modeled the problem and provided an efficient algorithm to solve its optimal problem. Through synthetic trace driven simulations, the effectiveness and efficiency of the modeling and algorithm have been validated. Besides the cost issue during consolidating vendor services, we plan to conduct more factors such as network performance and user preference in the future.

References

[1] Ahorlu, M.: European Cloud Professional Services, Cloud Management Services, and Hosted Private Cloud 2012–2016 Forecast. In: IDC Market Analysis (November 2012)

[2] Racemi, http://www.racemi.com/

[3] Cohesive Flexible Technologies, http://www.cohesiveft.com/

[4] AppZero, http://www.appzero.com/

[5] CliQr Technologies, http://www.cliqr.com/

[6] Ravello Systems, http://www.ravellosystems.com/

[7] Frey, S., Hasselbring, W.: Model-Based Migration of Legacy Software Systems to Scalable and Resource-Efficient Cloud-Based Applications: The CloudMIG Approach. In: Intl Conf. on Cloud Computing, GRIDs, and Virtualization (November 2010)

[8] IBM SmartCloud Enterprise, http://www-935.ibm.com/services/us/en/cloud-enterprise/

[9] Ward, C., et al.: Workload Migration into Clouds – Challenges, Experiences, Opportunities. In: Proc. of Intl. Conf. on Cloud Computing, pp. 164–171 (June 2010)

[10] Chee, Y., Zhou, N., Meng, F.J., Bagheri, S., Zhong, P.: A Pattern-Based Approach to Cloud Transformation. In: Proc. of Intl. Conf. on Cloud Computing, pp. 388–395 (2011)

[11] Khajeh-Hosseini, A., Sommerville, I., Bogaerts, J., Teregowda, P.: Decision Support Tools for Cloud Migration in the Enterprise. In: Intl Conf. on Cloud Computing, pp. 541–548 (June 2011)

[12] Menzel, M., Ranjan, R.: CloudGenius: Decision Support for Web Server Cloud Migration. In: Intl World Wide Web Conference, pp. 979–988 (April 2012)

PPINOT Tool Suite: A Performance Management Solution for Process-Oriented Organisations*

Adela del-Río-Ortega, Cristina Cabanillas,
Manuel Resinas, and Antonio Ruiz-Cortés

Universidad de Sevilla, Spain
{adeladelrio,resinas,aruiz}@us.es, cristina.cabanillas@wu.ac.at

Abstract. A key aspect in any process-oriented organisation is the measurement of process performance for the achievement of its strategic and operational goals. Process Performance Indicators (PPIs) are a key asset to carry out this evaluation, and, therefore, the management of these PPIs throughout the whole BP lifecycle is crucial. In this demo we present PPINOT Tool Suite, a set of tools aimed at facilitating and automating the PPI management. The support includes their definition using either a graphical or a template-based textual notation, their automated analysis at design-time, and their automated computation based on the instrumentation of a Business Process Management System.

1 Defining and Analysing PPIs with PPINOT

Performance requirements on business processes (BPs) are usually specified in terms of Process Performance Indicators (PPIs), which are quantifiable metrics that can be measured directly by data that is generated within the process flow and are aimed at evaluating the efficiency and effectiveness of business process.

The management of those PPIs is, thus, an important part of the BP lifecycle that includes at least the definition of PPIs, their analysis to find relationships between them, the instrumentation of the information systems that support the BPs in order to take the measures that are necessary to calculate the PPIs, the actual calculation of the PPIs during process execution, and the monitoring of the PPIs fulfillment.

The PPINOT Metamodel [1] provides a foundation on which an automated support for these activities can be built. It identifies the concepts that are necessary for defining Process Performance Indicators (PPIs) such as the different types of measures that can be used to compute the PPI value. It was defined to address the challenge of providing PPI definitions that are unambiguous and

---
* This work was partially supported by the European Commission (FEDER), the Spanish and the Andalusian R&D&I programmes (grants TIN2009-07366 (SETI), TIN2012-32273 (TAPAS), TIC-5906 (THEOS)). The authors thank the PPINOT development team at the ISA group, for their development work; concretely Ana Belén Sánchez and Edelia García.

S. Basu et al. (Eds.): ICSOC 2013, LNCS 8274, pp. 675–678, 2013.

complete, traceable to the business process elements used in their definition, independent of the language used to model business processes (BP) and amenable to automated analysis.

Two notations have been developed on top of the PPINOT Metamodel, namely a graphical notation and a template-based textual notation [2]. The former extends BPMN to allow the graphical definition of PPIs together with their corresponding BPs. The latter provides a template for PPIs and a set of linguistic patterns the user must follow to make the PPI definition easier [2]. Figure 1 shows an example of a PPI defined using PPINOT. The left hand side corresponds to a template-based definition, the right hand side depicts the corresponding XML serialisation of the PPINOT Metamodel.

PPI-009	Average lifetime of an RFC
Process	Request for change (RFC)
Goals	• BG-014: Reduce RFC time-to-response
MeasureDefinition	The PPI is defined as *the average of the duration between time instants when event Receive RFC is triggered and when process RFC management becomes completed*
Target	The PPI value must be less than or equal to *3 working days*
Scope	The process instances considered for this PPI are those in Monthly period (S-2)
Source	Event logs
Responsible	*Planning and quality manager*
Informed	*CIO*
Comments	*Most RFCs are created after 12:00.*

Fig. 1. An example of a PPI defined with PPINOT

The PPINOT Metamodel is also provided with formal semantics based on Description Logics (DL). This enables leveraging reasoning operations implemented by off-the-shelf DL reasoners to automatically extract information from the relationships between PPIs and BP elements. This information can be used to assist process analysts in the definition and instrumentation of PPIs [1].

In this paper, we give an overview of the PPINOT Tool Suite, which is a set of tools based on the PPINOT Metamodel that automate or facilitate some of the aforementioned PPI management activities.

2 PPINOT Tool Suite Overview

Figure 2 overviews the tools that compose the PPINOT Tool Suite. Rectangles depict tools, their inputs and outputs are represented by documents linked with dashed arrows, and the possible interconnections between tools is done by using solid arrows. The tools can be used separately or sequentially, depending on the user purposes. In the following we describe a possible way to use it.

Design. The PPINOT Tool Suite offers two different ways to define PPIs. On the one hand, we can define them graphically together with the BPMN representation of the BP using the PPINOT Graphical Editor, which is a web editor that has been implemented as an extension of the Oryx platform [3]. On the other hand, we can use the PPINOT Templates Editor to define PPIs using the template-based textual notation. The tool guides the user by providing linguistic patterns according to the selection performed in the different fields. In both

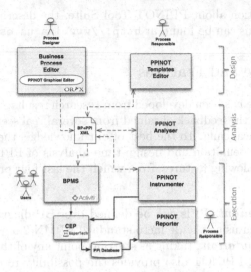

Fig. 2. PPINOT Tool Suite Overview

cases, an XML document with the PPI information together with the BP model is obtained as output.

Analysis. After defining the PPIs, the PPINOT Analyser can be used. It uses the DL formalisation of PPINOT metamodel to implement the analysis operations that obtain information about the way PPIs and BP elements influence each other. Concretely, two kinds of analysis operations are currently supported: (I) *BPElements involved*, which allows answering the question *Given a PPI, Which are the process model's elements involved?*. This information is useful for instance when a PPI must be replaced with others (maybe because it is very costly to obtain its value) and it is necessary to assure that every element of the BP that was measured before is measured in the new case; and (II) *PPIs associated to BPElement*, which allows answering the question *Given a BPElement, Which are the PPIs associated or applied to it?*. This information can assist during the evolution of BPs (e.g., an activity is deleted) to identify which PPIs will be affected and should be updated.

Execution. The last set of tools that can be used are those focused on the execution of the BP. Before execution, the PPINOT Instrumenter configures Activiti (an open source BPMS[1]) to send events to a Complex Event Processor (CEP) and also configures the CEP to compute the values of the defined PPIs from the events generated by Activiti during BP execution. The computed values of the PPIs are stored in a PPI Database. Finally, the PPINOT Reporter can be used to present the user these values[2].

---

[1] http://activiti.org.

[2] In its current version this tool provides a simple list of values. An extension to provide a proper report is planned.

Further information about PPINOT Tool Suite, the description of the tools and user instructions can be found at http://www.isa.us.es/ppinot.

3   Significance and Features

PPINOT Tool Suite has been developed from research results, and validated and extended thanks to the feedback obtained from several real scenarios, both from organisations and academia. To the best of our knowledge, there not exists any similar tool for the definition and design-time analysis of PPIs. Concretely, we can highlight the following features, from which the last four provide the novelty to our proposal:

BPMN 2.0 compliant. PPIs can be defined over BP diagrams (BPDs) previously modelled using the de facto standard BPMN 2.0.

PPI values computation Taking as starting point any of the aforementioned PPI definitions, PPINOT also provides the possibility to extract the information required to calculate PPI values from Activiti, an open source BP management platform, and to create reports with these values.

Graphical definition of PPIs. PPINOT Tool Suite supports the graphical definition of PPIs using a graph-based graphical notation that is easily understandable by non-technical users, at the same time that it is supported by a metamodel that assures the precise and complete definition of PPIs.

Template-based definition of PPIs. PPIs can be defined by fulfilling templates written in structured natural language, where the user only has to properly introduce the missing information, assisted by linguistic patterns.

PPI definition mapping Graphical definition of PPIs can be mapped to their corresponding templates in natural language.

Automated analysis of PPIs. The aforementioned analysis operations can be automatically performed on PPI definitions.

References

1. del Río-Ortega, A., Resinas, M., Cabanillas, C., Ruiz-Cortés, A.: On the Definition and Design-time Analysis of Process Performance Indicators. Information Systems 38(4), 470–490 (2012)
2. del-Río-Ortega, A., Resinas Arias de Reyna, M., Durán Toro, A., Ruiz-Cortés, A.: Defining process performance indicators by using templates and patterns. In: Barros, A., Gal, A., Kindler, E. (eds.) BPM 2012. LNCS, vol. 7481, pp. 223–228. Springer, Heidelberg (2012)
3. Decker, G., Overdick, H., Weske, M.: Oryx - an open modeling platform for the bpm community. In: Dumas, M., Reichert, M., Shan, M.-C. (eds.) BPM 2008. LNCS, vol. 5240, pp. 382–385. Springer, Heidelberg (2008)

SYBL+MELA: Specifying, Monitoring, and Controlling Elasticity of Cloud Services*

Georgiana Copil, Daniel Moldovan, Hong-Linh Truong, and Schahram Dustdar

Distributed Systems Group, Vienna University of Technology
{e.copil,d.moldovan,truong,dustdar}@dsg.tuwien.ac.at

Abstract. One of the major challenges in cloud computing is to simplify the monitoring and control of elasticity. On the one hand, the user should be able to specify complex elasticity requirements in a simple way and to monitor and analyze elasticity behavior based on his/her requirements. On the other hand, supporting tools for controlling and monitoring elasticity must be able to capture and control complex factors influencing the elasticity behavior of cloud services. To date, we lack tools supporting the specification and control of elasticity at multiple levels of cloud services and multiple elasticity metrics. In this demonstration, we will showcase a system facilitating the multi-level and cross-layer monitoring, analysis and control of cloud service elasticity.

1 Motivation

Simplifying the requirements specification and providing rich features for controlling and monitoring elasticity is crucial for several stakeholders, e.g. software service developers and providers, for exploiting the benefits of cloud systems. So far, existing frameworks or tools demonstrate limited, still complex, elasticity specification and controls, e.g., considering cost, or quality when deciding for control actions for cloud services [1–3], without considering the multi-dimensional nature of elasticity, and the fact that the cloud service developer or provider would be interested in describing requirements for different parts of his/her service, and at a high level, without worrying about virtual machine level information. Moreover, there is a lack of elasticity monitoring tools that support cross-layered, multi-dimensional elasticity of complex cloud services. In our work, we overcome some of the above-mentioned limitations by developing a system that performs multi-level monitoring data aggregation, analysis, and control of cloud services, paving the way for truly elastic cloud services.

By demonstrating our system, we could show that, on the one hand, the service providers or developers of the cloud services can easily monitor and specify elasticity requirements for their services at different levels and perspectives. On the other hand, we can discuss with other researchers how our control service takes automatic decisions for adapting the cloud service, in order to meet specified

---

* This work was supported by the European Commission in terms of the CELAR FP7 project (FP7-ICT-2011-8 #317790).

S. Basu et al. (Eds.): ICSOC 2013, LNCS 8274, pp. 679–682, 2013.

elasticity requirements. Such a demonstration, therefore, will be useful for us to understand the complexity to develop novel solutions to simplify the specification and support rich features for elasticity monitoring and control.

2   System Overview

The system to be demonstrated supports an integrated environment for specifying, controlling and monitoring elasticity of cloud services. Depicted in Figure 1, our system receives the cloud service description together with its elasticity requirements which are specified in SYBL [4]. When the cloud service is executed, the *Elasticity Control Service* manages an internal representation of the cloud service, which decomposes the cloud service into service topologies (parts of the cloud service) which can be further decomposed into service units. Each cloud service entity (e.g. service unit, service topology, virtual machines) is associated with various runtime elasticity metrics and elasticity requirements. The elasticity metrics are provided by the *MELA Service* which monitors the elasticity behavior of service entities and conducts elasticity analysis. Based on service structure, elasticity metrics and elasticity requirements, the *Elasticity Control Service* decides suitable elasticity control actions in order to fulfill the requirements.

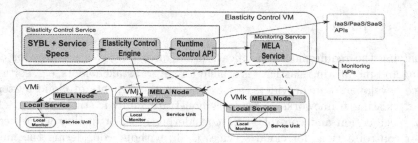

Fig. 1. Monitoring and controlling elastic cloud services

Controlling Elasticity of Cloud Services: For the specification of elasticity requirements we use SYBL language [4], which is a directive-based language enabling the description of high-level elasticity requirements and for the control of elasticity we use the control mechanism detailed in [5]. SYBL has three types of directives: monitoring, constraints and strategies, which can target different levels of the cloud service. The *Elasticity Control Service* analyses the elasticity requirements which can be conflicting or even contradicting, and produces new elasticity requirements on the basis of which it generates action plans for elasticity control of cloud services. For example, elasticity requirements at service topology level could be Co1: CONSTRAINT costPerClientPerHour < 5 euro or Co2: CONSTRAINT responseTime < 0.5 s. The *Elasticity Control Service* would evaluate these requirements, and in case one of them, let's say Co1, is violated, it would generate a new action plan consisting of a

scaleout for a service unit inside the service topology, and a reconfigure(''
highPerformance'') for the service topology. For evaluating whether or not
the requirements are fulfilled and what would be the result of enforcing an action
the *Elasticity Control Service* uses information coming from the *MELA Service*.

Monitoring and Analyzing Elasticity: Our system collects monitoring data
from existing monitoring sources for different types of metrics, from virtual machine level metrics like memory, CPU, to application level metrics like response
time or throughput. It aggregates the monitored metrics into higher level metrics, composing metrics associated with different levels of the cloud service (e.g.
cloud service, service topology or service unit). A service unit can be deployed
over several virtual machine instances, and therefore metrics targeting this level
have be aggregated from metrics at virtual machine level. In the same manner, a cloud service is composed of several service topologies which in turn are
composed of several service units and therefore metrics at cloud service level
need to be aggregated from metrics at service topology level, which are in turn
aggregated from service unit level. Moreover, we can have complex metrics as
is the case for the metric targeted in constraint Co1 which is aggregated by
dividing cost per hour at service topology level and number of clients for the
service topology. The cost at service level is the sum of the cost at service unit
level, which in turn can be aggregated from, e.g. cost per virtual machine, cost
for I/O operations or cost for network interface. The monitored metrics are analyzed for detecting whether or not the cloud service is in elastic behavior (i.e.
fulfills all elasticity requirements), what could be the trend for the evolution of
the metrics and what is the correlation among them. All this information is fed
into the *Elasticity Control Service* for generating elasticity control action plans
in case the cloud service, or parts of the cloud service do not expose the expected
behavior, defined through elasticity requirements.

3   Demonstrating Cloud Services

We use a pilot, but realistic, Data-as-a-Service in an M2M (Machine-to-Machine)
cloud platform as the cloud service in our demonstration. Figure 2 shows a snapshot of our demonstration[1] in which detailed service cloud structures together
with their runtime elasticity behaviors and elasticity control actions are analyzed
and presented to the developer/provider. Via a rich interface, the demonstration will show how elasticity requirements are described, how the cloud service
provider can view in real-time complex high level monitoring metrics understanding their values and impact upon the cloud service and how the cloud service is
automatically controlled for elasticity using all this information.

The user can specify SYBL elasticity requirements at different levels, e.g.
in source code using Java annotations for service units, or in XML for service
topologies. After being started, the *Elasticity Control Service* processes information from the monitoring service and takes elasticity control actions when the

---

[1] The demo video can be found at dsg.tuwien.ac.at/research/
viecom/prototypes/demo/syblmelaicsoc.wmv

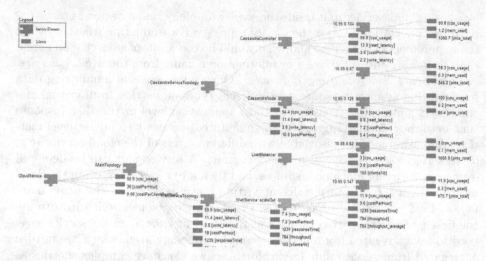

Fig. 2. Example of monitoring and controlling elasticity

requirements are not fulfilled. The user (e.g. cloud service provider) can view the monitoring interface during the application execution, for checking if the behavior is the expected one, for seeing how metrics are aggregated from lower to higher levels, and for learning how the application behaves under different circumstances (e.g. how does adding more resources impact quality?).

References

1. Kazhamiakin, R., Wetzstein, B., Karastoyanova, D., Pistore, M., Leymann, F.: Adaptation of service-based applications based on process quality factor analysis. In: ICSOC/ServiceWave 2009. LNCS, vol. 6275, pp. 395–404. Springer, Heidelberg (2010)
2. Guinea, S., Kecskemeti, G., Marconi, A., Wetzstein, B.: Multi-layered monitoring and adaptation. In: Kappel, G., Maamar, Z., Motahari-Nezhad, H.R. (eds.) ICSOC 2011. LNCS, vol. 7084, pp. 359–373. Springer, Heidelberg (2011)
3. Tsoumakos, D., Konstantinou, I., Boumpouka, C., Sioutas, S., Koziris, N.: Automated, Elastic Resource Provisioning for NoSQL Clusters Using TIRAMOLA. In: 2013 13th IEEE/ACM International Symposium on Cluster, Cloud and Grid Computing (CCGrid), pp. 34–41. IEEE Computer Society (2013)
4. Copil, G., Moldovan, D., Truong, H.L., Dustdar, S.: SYBL: an Extensible Language for Controlling Elasticity in Cloud Applications. In: 2013 13th IEEE/ACM International Symposium on Cluster, Cloud and Grid Computing (CCGrid), pp. 112–119. IEEE Computer Society (2013)
5. Copil, G., Moldovan, D., Truong, H.-L., Dustdar, S.: Multi-level Elasticity Control of Cloud Services. In: Basu, S., Pautasso, C., Zhang, L., Fu, X. (eds.) ICSOC 2013. LNCS, vol. 8274, pp. 429–436. Springer, Heidelberg (2013)

Modeling and Monitoring Business Process Execution

Piergiorgio Bertoli[1], Mauro Dragoni[2], Chiara Ghidini[2], Emanuele Martufi[1],
Michele Nori[1], Marco Pistore[1,2], and Chiara Di Francescomarino[2]

[1] SAYservice, Trento, Italy
{bertoli,martufi,nori,pistore}@sayservice.it
[2] FBK—IRST, Trento, Italy*
{dragoni,ghidini,pistore,dfmchiara}@fbk.eu

Abstract. The growing adoption of IT systems to support business activities has
made available huge amount of data, that can be used to monitor the actual execution of business processes. However, in many real settings, due to the different
degrees of abstraction between business and technological layers and to information hiding, the potentiality of this data cannot be fully exploited. The PROMO
tool, grounded on reasoning services, aims at reconciling the technical and the
business layer, in order to enable the effective monitoring and analysis of business process instances in the face of abovementioned issues.

1 Introduction

Nowadays, huge quantities of data are made available by the growing capability of Information Technology (IT) systems to trace and store business service and application
execution information. The potentiality of this data is enormous from a business point
of view, as it makes it possible (i) to observe the current evolution of ongoing processes; (ii) to provide statistical analysis on past executions; (iii) to detect deviations of
real process executions from ideal process models (as envisaged in [1]); (iv) to identify
performance-specific or instance-specific problems; and hence also to improve business process models based on analyses, deviations, bottlenecks and problems detected
inspecting real process executions. Indeed, a variety of Business Intelligence tools have
been proposed, even by major vendors, that aim at supporting business activity monitoring (BAM) to different extent; for instance, Engineering's eBAM [5], Microsoft's
BAM suite in BizTalk [4], Oracle's BAM [6], Polymita, WebSphere [7], to name a few.

However, business activity monitoring must deal with a significant difficulty, i.e.,
the gap existing between the business and the technological (IT) level. Indeed a perfect
mapping between modeled and IT-traced processes does not exist in the vast majority
of cases. For example, observation of process execution often brings (e.g., because of
manual activities or paper-based documentation) only partial information in terms of
which process activities have been executed and what data or artifacts they have produced so far. Moreover, even when IT information exists, it is not easy to associate it to

* This work is supported by "ProMo - A Collaborative Agile Approach to Model and Monitor
Service-Based Business Processes", funded by the Operational Programme "Fondo Europeo
di Sviluppo Regionale (FESR) 2007-2013" of the Province of Trento, Italy.

S. Basu et al. (Eds.): ICSOC 2013, LNCS 8274, pp. 683–687, 2013.

a specific process instance execution. Indeed, IT-services can be shared among several process classes and instances, and the traced information can be hard to disambiguate. To the best of our knowledge, none of the aforementioned current approaches has completely tackled the above issues, rather relying on the strong simplifying assumption that the business analyst can link directly IT information to business process activities.

In this demo we present PROMO[1], a software tool which, exploiting reasoning services, aims at reconciling the technical layer and the business one to enable the effective monitoring, analysis and querying of business processes.

2 PROMO Approach and Tool

PROMO aims at providing a collaborative (involving *domain experts* and *IT experts*) approach to model, monitor and analyze business processes, filling the unavoidable gap existing between business and IT layers. To this purpose PROMO introduces an intermediate layer (see Figure 1), which enables the communication between the business and the technological one through an intermediate model. Such a model, able to formalize the relationships between the business models and the information extracted at IT level, relies on the integrated representation of all the information collected about the process execution (named *IT-trace*).

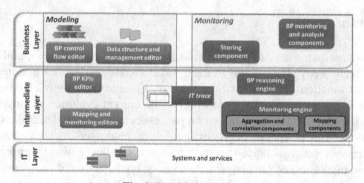

Fig. 1. PROMO overview

To accomplish its goal, PROMO integrates a modeling component and a monitoring component. At the business level, the **modeling component** provides MOKIPRO, a customized version of the MediaWiki-based[2] tool MOKI [3] for the process and ontology editing, which allows *domain experts* to design the business process control flow, as well as the associated data representation and manipulation (by the process activities). MOKIPRO (i) customizes the ORYX editor[3] for the BPMN modeling of business processes and related data structures (see Figure 2); (ii) allows *domain experts* to specify the data structure and, for each process activity, the data that it creates or shows.

---

[1] A video of the demo is downloadable from
https://dkmtools.fbk.eu/moki/icsocVideoDemo.zip
[2] http://www.mediawiki.org
[3] http://bpt.hpi.uni-potsdam.de/Oryx/

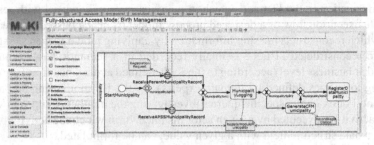

Fig. 2. Process modeling in PROMO

At the IT-level PROMO provides (i) mapping and monitoring editors that allow *IT experts* (taking advantage of the *domain experts* modeling) to specify, respectively, aggregation/monitoring rules and the relationships between business models and the information extracted at IT level; and (ii) a KPI-editor for the definition of interesting KPIs to be monitored. In detail, the DomainObject language [2] is used for defining mapping properties, an ad-hoc rule language for the monitoring rules, while business KPIs are defined as SPARQL [8] queries. It is possible for example to monitor how many times process instances deviate from the "prescribed" behavior or a specific branch of the model is executed, as well as the average time required for the process execution.

Event List	
Event: municipalityLogging - Creation Timestamp: **Tue Jul 02 17:55:30 CEST 2013**	
Key	Value
municipalityUId	Trento
protocolNumber	C888
timestamp	Tue Jul 02 15:39:51 CEST 2013

Event: municipalityLogging - Creation Timestamp: **Tue Jul 02 17:55:32 CEST 2013**	
Key	Value
municipalityUId	Rovereto
protocolNumber	A111
timestamp	Tue Jul 02 21:39:51 CEST 2013

Event: registerDataMunicipality - Creation Timestamp: **Tue Jul 02 17:57:59 CEST 2013**	
Key	Value
municipalityUId	Trento
protocolNumber	C888
timestamp	Thu Jul 04 11:00:51 CEST 2013

Event: municipalityRegistrationCompleted - Creation Timestamp: **Tue Jul 02 17:57:59 CEST 2013**	
Key	Value
municipalityUId	Trento
protocolNumber	C888

Fig. 3. Monitoring IT events in PROMO

At run-time, whenever an IT-level event occurs, the **monitoring component** captures and takes care of it. In detail, the event is managed by the monitoring engine, which, based on the specification and rules defined at design-time, correlates and aggregates events, produces new control events, monitors and maps the events to the corresponding one(s) at the business layer and eventually produces the IT-trace. Figure 3 shows a list of events monitored (and produced) by the monitoring engine in a specific scenario, which will be used in the demo.

The information in the IT-trace, which in many cases is only partial with respect to a complete execution flow of a designed process model, is hence passed to a reasoning engine, which reconstructs missing information by applying model-driven satisfiability rules. The reconstructed IT-trace is finally recorded in a semantic-based store to be monitored at business level (according to the KPIs defined at designed time), or queried (according to queries defined by *domain experts*), by the BP monitoring and analysis component. For example, specific queries investigating the number of times in which a business activity is executed by a given actor instance, or in which the activity provides as output a data structure field with a given value, can be formulated.

3   PROMO Application

The PROMO tool has been applied, among other case studies, to an e-government one: the Italian *Birth Management* procedure, characterized by a process containing 4 pools, 18 activities, 21 gateways, and 13 data structures (including in total 75 distinct fields). Our demo will showcase PROMO on this case study.

At design time, *domain experts* and *IT experts* model the control flow (Figure 2 depicts the initial part of the Municipality pool), data structure and manipulation by activities, as well as mapping definition and monitoring rules for the case study.

As an example, consider when, at run-time, a *MunicipalityLogging* event is registered by the services at the IT layer, captured and analyzed by the monitoring engine. Then, when another event related to the same process instance (e.g., *RegisterDataMunicipality*) occurs (see Figure 3), the monitoring engine correlates and aggregates them, generating a new IT event (*MunicipalityRegistrationCompleted*), used for IT-level monitoring. Further, the (partial) IT-trace is generated and passed to the reasoning engine, which tries to reconstruct missing information according to the process model. For instance, the reasoning engine, aware of the process model control flow, can infer that the execution went through either the *ReceiveParentMunicipalityRecord* or the *ReceiveAPSSMunicipalityRecord* activity. Moreover, knowing the data associated with the two received events (the data structure associated to the *MunicipalityLogging* activity does not contain the *Fiscal Code CF*, while the one associated to the *RegisterMunicipalityData* activity does), as well as the activities in charge to create or show them, the reasoning engine can infer that the process execution actually went through the *GenerateCFMunicipality* activity. The reconstructed trace is finally recorded by the storing component and the related KPIs updated. Among the predefined KPIs of this case study, for instance, there is the number of times in which the *CF* field has been filled by the Municipality rather than by another actor of the procedure and the average time required to complete the whole birth practice.

References

1. van der Aalst, W.M.P.: Process Mining: Discovery, Conformance and Enhancement of Business Processes, 1st edn. Springer Publishing Company, Incorporated (2011)
2. Bertoli, P., Kazhamiakin, R., Nori, M., Pistore, M.: Smart: Modeling and monitoring support for business process coordination in dynamic environments. In: Abramowicz, W., Domingue, J., Węcel, K. (eds.) BIS 2012 Workshops. LNBIP, vol. 127, pp. 243–254. Springer, Heidelberg (2012)

3. Ghidini, C., Rospocher, M., Serafini, L.: Conceptual Modeling in Wikis: a Reference Architecture and a Tool. In: eKNOW 2012, Valencia, Spain, pp. 128–135 (2012)
4. Biztalk team: biztalk, biztalk server,
   https://www.microsoft.com/en-us/biztalk/default.aspx
5. Eclipse team: ebam, extended business activity monitoring,
   http://www.eclipse.org/ebam
6. Oracle team: Oracle bam, oracle business activity monitoring (oracle bam),
   http://www.oracle.com/technetwork/
   middleware/bam/overview/index.html
7. Websphere team: Websphere software, ibm,
   http://www-01.ibm.com/software/websphere/
8. Prud'hommeaux, E., Seaborne, A.: SPARQL query language for RDF (2008), Latest version available as http://www.w3.org/TR/rdf-sparql-query/

A Tool for Business Process Architecture Analysis

Rami-Habib Eid-Sabbagh, Marcin Hewelt, and Mathias Weske

Hasso Plattner Institute at the University of Potsdam
{rami.eidsabbagh,marcin.hewelt,mathias.weske}@hpi.uni-potsdam.de

Abstract. Business Process Architectures (BPA) are used for structuring and managing process collections. For optimising business processes a high level view on their interdependencies is necessary. BPAs allow to capture message and trigger flow relations between processes and their multiple process instances within a process collection. However, tools that allow analysis of BPAs besides visualization do not exist. This contribution presents a novel tool to model and to analyse the correctness of a BPA by transforming it into open nets, translate the correctness criteria into CTL formula and model check those using LoLA.

1 Introduction

With the advent of process model collections (PMC), their organisation and management came into focus. Modeling guidelines were introduced to improve and harmonise the quality of process models created by different process modelers in an organisation [1,2]. For single processes several tool-supported approaches exist which allow to check structural, behavioral, and linguistic properties. Lately, these were also incorporated into modeling tools, e.g. the Signavio BPM tool[1].

Similar approaches, taking a holistic view for assuring quality on a higher abstraction level do not yet exist. In practice, often many processes of PMC interact to deliver a service, or produce a good. Business Process Architectures (BPA) and their correctness criteria present a novel approach to organize business processes in a PMC and analyse them [3]. A BPA groups processes into different subsets of which each is responsible for handling one specific business case. Each BPA subset contains a set of processes together with trigger and message flow relations. To model BPAs and to decide the correctness of such an interaction is not supported by business process modeling tools.

In this contribution we present a novel and innovative tool to visually model BPAs and analyse them for correctness. The tool consists of a BPA core module that integrates existing applications, which we extended for our purpose of BPA analysis. We plan to extend the tool to serve as the basis for PMC management, so that business processes are abstracted into BPAs and visualized, allowing to navigate to the actual process models. The analysis of BPAs provides a first step

---

[1] http://signavio.com

S. Basu et al. (Eds.): ICSOC 2013, LNCS 8274, pp. 688–691, 2013.

for assuring further correctness and consistency properties on a more detailed
process layer.

The remainder of this paper is structured as follows, Section 2 presents the
architecture of the tool, Section 3 provides insights on the maturity of the tool
development, and Section 4 explains details of the planned tool demo.

2   BPA Tool Architecture

Our BPA tool extends and composes functionality of existing tools as depicted
in Fig. 1. The user interface for modeling BPAs and visualizing found errors is
provided by an extension to the Signavio Core Components (SCC)[2]They are the
open source components of the Signavio editor, a web based business process
modeling tool widely used for teaching in academia[3] (BPM Academic Initiative)
and as commercial BPM tool[4]. Our extension introduced a new stencil set for
BPAs, which contains visual shapes and connections rules to draw BPA diagrams.
The Signavio Core Components were selected because they provide a web-based
editor, that is easy to extend and allows to export BPA diagrams as xml files.

The main program logic is implemented as a module for promnicat[5], a tool
developed to perform analysis on large process model collections [4]. This BPA
module consists of a data model, the BPA Analyzer, and two transformation
modules. The data model defines the structure of a BPA, its processes, events,
and the trigger and flow relations between the events. The JsonToBPA transformer imports the xml file output by Signavio Core Components and creates
a BPA data structure to be used by the BPA Analyzer. This data structure is
the input for the BpaToPNML Transformer. It transforms the BPA into a set of
open nets according to the approach presented in [3]. Afterwards, the nets are
composed and the resulting net is serialized using the PNML standard[6]. This
module also generates a set of CTL formulae which express the correctness criteria for the given BPA and are to be checked by LoLA[7]. The CTL formulae
are derived by examining the pre- and postsets of all events in the BPA, e.g.
if an end event has an empty postset, the event is considered part of the final
marking.

In addition we use the Petri net simulator RENEW[8]to convert the PNML
file into the file format that LoLA requires for analysis and to visualize the
transformed net.The Renew module also provides a built-in LoLA integration
for the analysis. To this end it calls LoLA with the CTL formulae specified for
the correctness analysis. The result of the model checker is finally interpreted
and visualized in the Signavio module.

---

[2] http://code.google.com/p/signavio-core-components
[3] http://bpmai.org
[4] http://signavio.com
[5] http://code.google.com/p/promnicat
[6] pnml.org
[7] Low Level Petri net Analyzer, http://service-technology.org/lola
[8] renew.de

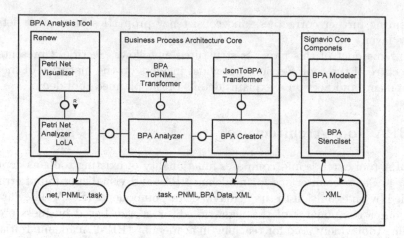

Fig. 1. BPA Tool Architecture

3   Maturity

The proposed tool is in a prototypic stage. The interaction with the integrated tools, Signavio Core Components, Renew, and the LoLA model checker works via files and command line calls. The BPA modeler is based on a widely used web browser editor from Signavio, which itself is used as commercial application. Our extension of the editor to allow the modeling of BPAs uses existing functionality and adds visual shapes and connections rules for BPA elements. The export feature was used as is. The Renew module used to transform BPAs into the file format required for LoLA was already presented in [5]. Model checking the correctness properties is performed by LoLA.

All core functionalities are implemented in the prototype. Our tool supports modeling BPAs in a Web Browser, transforming them into open nets, analysing their correctness, and visualizing the errors found. This version of the BPA tool realizes the BPA analysis approach presented in [3,6].

We plan to extend the next version of the BPA tool with the feature to (semi-)automatically extract BPAs from process model collections. Furthermore we are working on the creation of BPAs from data annotated BPMN process models and object life cycles.

4   Script

The demo showcases the features of our BPA tool beginning with the modeling of BPA diagrams, continuing with their transformation into open nets, the analysis with LoLA, and ending with the display of the results. Especially the possibility to analyse multi-instance and multi-communication, which is novel and is not supported by existing tools so far, will be a major focus of the demonstration. The demo will consist of three steps in which we explain the capabilities of the tool.

1. First a small use case from the public administration, e.g. the founding of an enterprise, will be modeled as BPA with the extended BPA Signavio Core Components. The BPA diagram shows the trigger and message flow relations between the involved processes, compare Fig. 2(a). Importantly, we will highlight the visualization of multi-instances and multi-communication according to the multiplicities depicted in the BPA model.
2. The modeled BPA diagram is transformed into an open net which is visualized in a separate window, compare Fig. 2(b). This step implements the algorithm presented in [6], and extended for BPAs with multiplicities in [3]. All the processes together with trigger and message flow relations are mapped to open net constructs, which are then composed into one net.
3. The resulting open net is the basis for the correctness analysis. Each correctness criterion from [3] (terminating run, no livelocks, no dead processes) translates into a CTL formulae which is model checked by LoLA. If all formulae yield a positive result, we know, that the BPA is correct. Otherwise found errors are displayed in the BPA diagram.

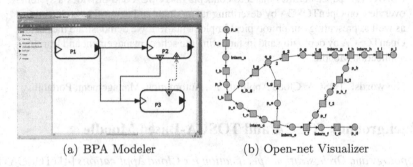

(a) BPA Modeler   (b) Open-net Visualizer

Fig. 2. Screenshots from the BPA Tool

References

1. Mendling, J.: Metrics for Process Models: Empirical Foundations of Verification, Error Prediction, and Guidelines for Correctness. LNBIP, vol. 6. Springer, Heidelberg (2008)
2. Mendling, J., Reijers, H., van der Aalst, W.: Seven Process Modeling Guidelines (7PMG). Qut eprint. Queensland University of Technology (2008)
3. Eid-Sabbagh, R.-H., Hewelt, M., Weske, M.: Business Process Architectures with Multiplicities: Transformation and Correctness. In: Daniel, F., Wang, J., Weber, B. (eds.) BPM 2013. LNCS, vol. 8094, pp. 227–234. Springer, Heidelberg (2013)
4. Eid-Sabbagh, R.-H., Kunze, M., Meyer, A., Weske, M.: A Platform for Research on Process Model Collections. In: Mendling, J., Weidlich, M. (eds.) BPMN 2012. LNBIP, vol. 125, pp. 8–22. Springer, Heidelberg (2012)
5. Hewelt, M., Wagner, T., Cabac, L.: Integrating verification into the PAOSE approach. In: Duvigneau, M., Moldt, D., Hiraishi, K. (eds.) Petri Nets and Software Engineering, PNSE 2011. CEUR Workshop Proceedings, vol. 723, pp. 124–135. CEUR-WS.org (2011)
6. Eid-Sabbagh, R.-H., Weske, M.: Analyzing Business Process Architectures. In: Salinesi, C., Norrie, M.C., Pastor, Ó. (eds.) CAiSE 2013. LNCS, vol. 7908, pp. 208–223. Springer, Heidelberg (2013)

OpenTOSCA – A Runtime
for TOSCA-Based Cloud Applications

Tobias Binz[1], Uwe Breitenbücher[1], Florian Haupt[1], Oliver Kopp[1,2],
Frank Leymann[1], Alexander Nowak[1], and Sebastian Wagner[1]

[1] IAAS, University of Stuttgart, Germany
[2] IPVS, University of Stuttgart, Germany
firstname.lastname@informatik.uni-stuttgart.de

Abstract TOSCA is a new standard facilitating platform independent description of Cloud applications. OpenTOSCA is a runtime for TOSCA-based Cloud applications. The runtime enables fully automated plan-based deployment and management of applications defined in the OASIS TOSCA packaging format CSAR. This paper outlines the core concepts of TOSCA and provides a system overview on OpenTOSCA by describing its modular and extensible architecture, as well as presenting our prototypical implementation. We demonstrate the use of OpenTOSCA by deploying and instantiating the school management and learning application Moodle.

Keywords: TOSCA, Cloud Applications, Automation, Management, Portability.

1 Background: TOSCA and TOSCA-Based Moodle

The *Topology and Orchestration Specification for Cloud Applications* [4] (TOSCA) is a new OASIS standard to describe Cloud-based applications in a portable and interoperable way. TOSCA standardizes the description of the structure and management aspects (i. e., deployment, operation, termination) of applications. The structure of TOSCA-based applications is defined by a *topology*—a graph of typed nodes and directed typed edges. Nodes represent components forming an application and edges define the relations and dependencies between them. For instance, the topology of the *Moodle* application (www.moodle.org) consists of the actual PHP module, an Apache Web Server, a MySQL database, two operating systems (one for the Web server and one for the MySQL database), and two virtual machines (Fig. 1). The relationships in this topology define, for instance, that the Moodle application is "hosted on" a Web server and that the application "connects to" the MySQL database. The types of nodes and relationships specify their properties and management operations. The type "Apache Web Server" defines properties, such as "port" or "version", and management operations, such as "start" or "deploy". The actual implementation of a node is provided by one or many *Deployment Artifacts*, e. g., a Linux VM image, an operating system package for the Apache Web Server, or an archive containing the PHP files of Moodle. In addition, types may define *Implementation Artifacts* that implement the management operations for the respective element. The TOSCA topology and related artifacts are bundled into a *Cloud Service ARchive* (CSAR), the standardized packaging format for TOSCA applications.

S. Basu et al. (Eds.): ICSOC 2013, LNCS 8274, pp. 692–695, 2013.

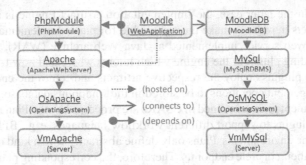

Fig. 1. Moodle Application Topology modeled using *Vino4TOSCA* [2]

TOSCA topologies can be processed by a TOSCA runtime in an imperative or declarative way [5]: *Imperative processing* relies on the implementation of management plans that can be executed fully automated to perform the desired management task, e. g., to instantiate, backup, upgrade, or terminate an application. These high-level management tasks are implemented by orchestrating low-level management operations provided by Implementation Artifacts of nodes and relationships. Because management plans are typically implemented by the application developer, they enable operators to manage the application by running pre-defined plans without the need to understand all the technical details of the management task [1]. Technically, management plans are implemented as workflows. Thus, they inherit properties of workflow technology such as traceability, recoverability, human interaction, and portability. *Declarative processing*, on the other hand, shifts the deployment and management logic from plans to the runtime. To perform the aforementioned high-level management tasks, the runtime has to know the operations that have to be called and their order. Declarative processing is well suited for the deployment of simple applications but is not able to facilitate complex management tasks for various kinds of application structures. For more details, including the TOSCA role model, we recommend the TOSCA specification [4] and TOSCA primer [5].

In summary, TOSCA provides means to describe procedures for managing applications in a standardized way that enable automated and portable processing. With more and more applications described in TOSCA it will enable more and more applications to be hosted in the Cloud.

2   OpenTOSCA: Architecture and Demonstration

OpenTOSCA is a runtime supporting imperative processing of TOSCA applications. Imperative means that the deployment and management logic is provided by plans. The key tasks of OpenTOSCA, addressed by the architecture depicted in Fig. 2, are to operate management operations, run plans, and manage state. Requests to the Container API are passed to the Control component, which orchestrates the different components, tracks their progress, and interprets the TOSCA application. The Core component offers common services to other components, e. g., managing data or validating XML.

Management operations of nodes and relationships are either provided by running (Web) services, e. g., the Amazon EC2 API, or by Implementation Artifacts contained in the CSAR. In the latter case, the Implementation Artifact Engine is responsible to run these artifacts in order to make them available for plans. Implementation Artifacts, e. g., a SOAP Web service implemented as Java Web archive (WAR), are processed by a corresponding plugin of the engine which knows where and how to run this kind of artifact. The plugins deploy the respective artifacts and return the endpoints of the deployed management operations to be stored in the Endpoints database.

The management plans contained in CSARs are processed by the Plan Engine, which also employs plugins to support different workflow languages, e. g., BPMN or BPEL, and their runtime environments. Plans only define abstractly which kind of service they require but not their concrete endpoints. Therefore, the corresponding plan plugin binds each service invoked by the plan to the endpoint of the management operation before it deploys the plan to the respective workflow runtime. The service's endpoint was added to the endpoint database before by the Implementation Artifact Engine. This way of binding workflows ensures portability of management plans between different environments and runtimes [1]. By using the Plan Portability API, management plans can access the topology and instance information, e. g., the property values of nodes and relationships.

The plugin architecture of the Implementation Artifact Engine and Plan Engine ensure extensibility. Portability is ensured by the two engines working together when binding management plans. Strict separation of architectural components through well-defined OSGi interfaces enables the replacement of implementations of components. This also allows each component to be scaled independently.

Demonstration. In the following, we demonstrate how the OpenTOSCA runtime deploys CSARs and how instances of Cloud applications are created. After uploading the CSAR to OpenTOSCA, the deployment of the TOSCA application follows three steps: (i) First, the CSAR is unpacked and the files are put into the Files store, which is backed either by the local file system or Amazon S3. (ii) Then, the TOSCA XML files are loaded, resolved, validated, and processed by the Control component, which calls the Implementation Artifact Engine and the Plan Engine. The Implementation Artifact Engine deploys the referenced Implementation Artifacts (cf. (a) in Fig. 2) and

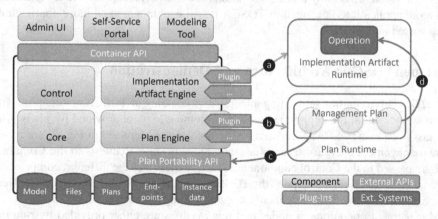

Fig. 2. OpenTOSCA Architecture Overview and Processing Sequence

stores their endpoints in the Endpoints database. (iii) Finally, the Plan Engine binds and deploys the application's management plans (cf. (b) in Fig. 2). The endpoints of the Moodle management plans are stored in the Plans database.

The deployed application can be instantiated by executing the build plan of the application. This plan is either started through the Self-Service Portal, which provides an UI for end user access to the deployed applications, or by sending a SOAP message to it. Credentials (e. g., for Amazon EC2) or configurations (e. g., machine size) are passed as input message to the workflow. The Plan Portability API acts as access point for the plans to the container. By using this API, the topology model, endpoints, and instance data, such as properties of nodes (e. g., the port of a Web server) and relationships, can be read and written (cf. (c) in Fig. 2). Having these data available, the build plan orchestrates the management operations of nodes and relationships to provision and configure the Cloud application (cf. (d) in Fig. 2). To instantiate Moodle, the build plan first starts two virtual machines with a Linux operating system and installs Apache Web Server and MySQL on them. Then, it uses the respective management operations to install the PHP application, import the database schema, and establish the database connection. After completion, a build plan may return certain information, for example, the Web address of the deployed application instance. The Moodle build plan returns the URL of the running Moodle instance, which includes the public URL of the virtual machine running the Apache Web Server. This demonstration is also featured in the *OpenTOSCA demo video* (online at demo.opentosca.org).

Currently, OpenTOSCA is used together with the modeling tool "Winery" [3] in the German government-funded projects *CloudCycle* and *Migrate!* as well as in industry and research cooperations of our institute.

Next Steps. To deploy simple applications without the need to model build plans we plan to add declarative processing of applications to OpenTOSCA. We are also working on building a community around OpenTOSCA at www.opentosca.org.

Acknowledgments. This work was partially funded by the BMWi projects CloudCycle (01MD11023) and Migrate! (01ME11055). We thank Christian Endres, Matthias Fetzer, Markus Fischer, Nedim Karaoğuz, Kálmán Képes, Rene Trefft, and Michael Zimmermann for their help with the implementation of OpenTOSCA.

References

1. Binz, T., Breiter, G., Leymann, F., Spatzier, T.: Portable Cloud Services Using TOSCA. IEEE Internet Computing 16(3), 80–85 (2012)
2. Breitenbücher, U., Binz, T., Kopp, O., Leymann, F., Schumm, D.: Vino4TOSCA: A Visual Notation for Application Topologies based on TOSCA. In: Meersman, R., et al. (eds.) OTM 2012, Part I. LNCS, vol. 7565, pp. 416–424. Springer, Heidelberg (2012)
3. Kopp, O., Binz, T., Breitenbücher, U., Leymann, F.: Winery – Modeling Tool for TOSCA-based Cloud Applications. In: Basu, S., Pautasso, C., Zhang, L., Fu, X. (eds.) ICSOC 2013. LNCS, vol. 8274, pp. 702–706. Springer, Heidelberg (2013)
4. OASIS: OASIS Topology and Orchestration Specification for Cloud Applications (TOSCA) Version 1.0 Committee Specification 01 (2013)
5. OASIS: Topology and Orchestration Specification for Cloud Applications (TOSCA) Primer Version 1.0 (January 2013)

iAgree Studio: A Platform to Edit and Validate WS–Agreement Documents*

Carlos Müller, Antonio Manuel Gutiérrez, Manuel Resinas,
Pablo Fernández, and Antonio Ruiz-Cortés

University of Seville, LSI
ISA research group, http://www.isa.us.es/, Seville, Spain
{cmuller,amgutierrez,resinas,pablofm,aruiz}@us.es

Abstract. The widespread use of SLA-regulated Cloud services, in which the violation of SLA terms may imply a penalty for the parties, have increased the importance and complexity of systems supporting the SLA lifecycle. Although these systems can be very different from each other, ranging from service monitoring platforms to auto-scaling solutions according to SLAs, they all share the need of having machine-processable and semantically valid SLAs. In this paper we present iAgree studio, the first application, up to our knowledge, that is able to edit and semantically validate agreement documents that are compliant with the WS–Agreement specification by checking properties such as its consistency, and the compliance between templates and agreement offers. In addition, it reports explanations when documents are not valid. Moreover, it allows users to combine the validation and explanation operations by means of a scenarios developer.

1 Overview and Motivation

SLAs are widely used nowadays as a means to regulate the terms and conditions under which a service is provided. As the use of SLAs in Cloud services and applications in which the violation of SLA terms may imply a penalty for the parties increases, the complexity and demand of systems supporting the SLA lifecycle also increases. These systems include service monitoring platforms that use SLAs to decide which service metrics should be monitored, auto-scaling solutions that automates the provisioning or deprovisioning of resources according to the SLA, and billing components that calculate the penalties incurred during the use of a service, amongst others. Although very different from each other, all of these systems require having semantically valid SLAs (i.e., without semantic errors) and defined in a machine processable manner.

WS–Agreement [1] is arguably the most widespread recommendation for defining machine processable SLAs. It specifies a template-based agreement creation protocol and an XML Schema that defines the basic structure of an SLA and the other documents

---

* This work was partially supported by the European Commission (FEDER), the Spanish and the Andalusian R&D&I programmes (grants TIN2009–07366 (SETI), TIN2012–32273 (TAPAS), TIC–5906 (THEOS)).

S. Basu et al. (Eds.): ICSOC 2013, LNCS 8274, pp. 696–699, 2013.

```
Template AmazonS3 version 1.0
    Provider Amazon as Responder;

AgreementTerms
    Service AWS–S3 available at. aws.amazon.com/s3   //Service reference in iAgree
        Global description:   //Service description term in iAgree
            Interface;                      //either SOAP or REST
            RRS = False;                    //Reduced Redundancy Storage (RRS)
            StorageSize;                    //StorageSize in TB
            FirstProject;                   //Denotes if it is the first customer project
            TotalPrice, StoragePrice, SupportPlanPrice;

    Monitorable Properties   //Service properties in iAgree
        global:
            MUP;   //Monthly Uptime Percentage, a kind of AmazonS3 service availability
            TransferredGb; ResponseTime; ReadRequests, WriteRequests;
            OnlineReportingSupport, PhoneSupport;   //Customer support facilities
            TurnAroundTime;                         //Minutes to solve problems

    Guarantee Terms
        G1: Provider guarantees MUP >= 99.9;
        G2: Consumer guarantees TransferredGb < StorageSize * 100
                                AND ReadRequests > WriteRequests;
        G3: Provider guarantees ResponseTime < 1000; onlyIf (Interface = SOAP);
        G4: Provider guarantees ResponseTime < 700; onlyIf (Interface = REST);
        G5: One or More between:
            G5.1: Provider guarantees OnlineReportingSupport = true;
            G5.2: Provider guarantees TurnAroundTime = 15;
            G5.3: Provider guarantees PhoneSupport = true;

Creation Constraints:
    C1: StoragePrice = 0.05 * StorageSize; onlyIf RRS = true;
    C2: StoragePrice = 0.12 * StorageSize; onlyIf RRS = false;
    C3: StorageSize <= 5000 TB;
    C4: TotalPrice = StoragePrice + SupportPlanPrice;
        onlyIf (FirstProject = false or StorageSize > 5);
```

Fig. 1. Template of AmazonS3 service scenario in iAgree

used in the agreement creation protocol like agreement templates and agreement offers. However, WS–Agreement leaves open how the different elements of a WS–Agreement document such as a Service Level Objective (SLO) must be specified.

iAgree [4] is a fully-fledged WS–Agreement-compliant language that completes the WS–Agreement schema with a set of languages to describe all WS–Agreement elements. Figure 1 shows an iAgree template inspired in the Amazon Simple Storage Service (AmazonS3) including: terms to describe the service (see service AWS-S3, and Monitorable Properties) and guarantees (see G1-G5), terms compositors to combine the terms (see G5), and creation constraints (see C1-C4). Moreover, iAgree supports expressive arithmetic-logic expressions within the service level objectives (SLOs) (see G2), qualifying conditions (QCs) of conditional terms (see G3-G4), and creation constraints (CCs) (see C2). In addition, an advantage of iAgree is that its validity criteria has been extensively researched [2,3,4] and algorithms for checking and explaining the validity of iAgree documents have also been developed.

Based on those results, in this paper we present *iAgree studio*[1], a web application to edit and validate iAgree documents. In particular, it supports the kinds of conflicts between terms and creation constraints presented in [3,4], and the non-compliance situations between templates and agreement offers exposed in [2].

---

[1] Available at www.isa.us.es/iagreestudio/, including a screencast.

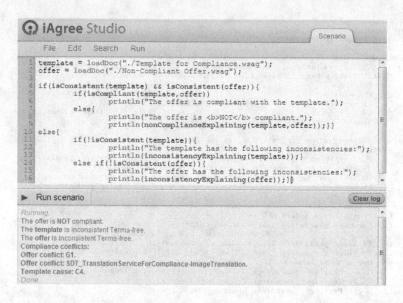

Fig. 2. Scenario to check and explain compliance problems

2 Novelties and Functions

The novelty of iAgree Studio is given by the following features[2]:

High WS–Agreement Compliance. iAgree studio supports to edit and validate WS–Agreement documents with expressive terms including arithmetic-logic expressions relating several service properties inside the SLOs, QCs, and CCs, and supporting terms compositors defining agreement variants inside an agreement. Other WS–Agreement-based solutions studied in [4] do not support these agreement elements that are in the specification limiting their usefulness in real scenarios in which many of these elements are commonly used.

Document Validation. iAgree studio is able to validate iAgree documents by checking that they do not contain semantic errors, supporting the kinds of conflicts between terms and creation constraints presented in [3,4], and the non-compliance situations between templates and agreement offers exposed in [2]. Depending on the kind of document, the validation comprise different properties.

Semantic Errors Explanations. iAgree studio provides an explanation report after the documents validations when semantic errors are detected. Such reports include the terms and creation constraints that are involved in the detected semantic error. For instance, a contradiction between terms, or a non-compliance between offers and template terms that make them non-compliant.

Scenarios Developer. iAgree studio incorporates a *Scenarios developer* that allows users to combine the validation operations and explanation reports to obtain advanced and customisable validation scenarios. For instance, an interesting scenario

---

[2] Note that iAgree studio is an ongoing work and it will be extended in a nearby future with more features.

may be to check the validity of agreement offers and templates before checking the compliance between them. Such scenario is included in Figure 2 for a specific pair of documents including the explanation reports if semantic errors are detected.

In addition, iAgree studio has been tested by our M.Sc students in an SLA learning course and they suggested a number of user-friendly facilities that have been incorporated in current iAgree studio version such as: menus structure organised as in google docs, coloured syntax to highlight iAgree keywords, undo-redo functions, documents can be downloaded in iAgree or a serialised XML-based syntax, several samples presented in [3] are preloaded to try the iAgree studio functionality, etc.

3   Internal Structure

The automated checking and explanation for semantic errors included within iAgree documents is performed by a Constraint Satisfaction Problems [5] (CSP)-based technique implemented within an iAgree Document Analyser (ADA) (cf. Figure 3). Such an automated technique helps the parties involved in achieving an agreement during the whole SLA-lifecycle as follows: when the documents are edited their validity can be assured because the possible semantic errors are reported in the iAgree studio to be solved; when the documents are interchanged at negotiation time, the validity of documents is also assured and the compliance between them can also be checked to ensure their compliance; afterwards, the deployment of valid SLAs is granted.

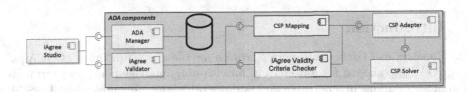

Fig. 3. Structure of our approach

References

1. Andrieux, et al.: Web Services Agreement Specification (WS-Agreement) (v. gfd-r.192). OGF - Grid Resource Allocation Agreement Protocol WG (2011)
2. Müller, C., Resinas, M., Ruiz-Cortés, A.: Explaining the Non-Compliance between Templates and Agreement Offers in WS-Agreement. In: Baresi, L., Chi, C.-H., Suzuki, J. (eds.) ICSOC-ServiceWave 2009. LNCS, vol. 5900, pp. 237–252. Springer, Heidelberg (2009)
3. Müller, C., Resinas, M., Ruiz-Cortés, A.: Automated Analysis of Conflicts in WS–Agreement Documents. IEEE Transactions on Services Computing (2013),
   http://dx.doi.org/10.1109/TSC.2013.9
4. Müller, C.: On the Automated Analysis of WS-Agreement Documents. Applications to the Processes of Creating and Monitoring Agreements. International Dissertation, Universidad de Sevilla (2013),
   http://www.isa.us.es/sites/default/files/muller-Phd-PTB.pdf
5. Tsang, E.: Foundations of Constraint Satisfaction. A. Press (1995)

Winery – A Modeling Tool for TOSCA-Based Cloud Applications

Oliver Kopp[1,2], Tobias Binz[2], Uwe Breitenbücher[2], and Frank Leymann[2]

[1] IPVS, University of Stuttgart, Germany
[2] IAAS, University of Stuttgart, Germany
lastname@informatik.uni-stuttgart.de

Abstract TOSCA is a new OASIS standard to describe composite applications and their management. The structure of an application is described by a topology, whereas management plans describe the application's management functionalities, e. g., provisioning or migration. Winery is a tool offering an HTML5-based environment for graph-based modeling of application topologies and defining reusable component and relationship types. Thereby, it uses TOSCA as internal storage, import, and export format. This demonstration shows how Winery supports modeling of TOSCA-based applications. We use the school management software Moodle as running example throughout the paper.

Keywords: Cloud Applications, Modeling, TOSCA, Management, Portability.

1 Introduction

The *Topology and Orchestration Specification for Cloud Applications* (TOSCA [6]) is an OASIS standard for automating provisioning, management, and termination of applications in a portable and interoperable way. To enable this, TOSCA employs two concepts: (i) application topologies and (ii) management plans. An application topology describes software and hardware components involved and relationships between them. It is a graph consisting of nodes and relationships, where each of them has a type: a node type or a relationship type. These types offer management functionality, which is collected in node type and relationship type implementations. Concrete implementations, such as shell scrips or WAR files, are bundled through artifact templates, which can be referenced by multiple implementations making them reusable. Management plans capture knowledge to deploy and manage an application and are typically modeled as BPMN or BPEL workflows. The topology, management plans, and all required software artifacts such as installables, business logic, and management logic are condensed in an application package called TOSCA Cloud Service ARchive (CSAR for short). As TOSCA is standardized, CSARs are portable across different TOSCA-compliant runtime environments of different vendors.

To enable modeling of TOSCA-based applications in a tailored environment, we have developed Winery, which supports Web-based creation of CSARs using standard Chrome and Firefox browsers. Therefore, no additional software

S. Basu et al. (Eds.): ICSOC 2013, LNCS 8274, pp. 700–704, 2013.

installation is required to use the tool on client side. Winery's main features are type management and graphical topology modeling where the defined types are instantiated and interlinked. To facilitate collaboration, Winery not only supports sharing of TOSCA topologies, but also supports sharing of all related elements such as types or templates, which all are uniquely identified and accessible by URLs. This allows sharing information through passing simple references rather than exchanging entire documents.

Winery itself does not include a TOSCA-compliant runtime environment. One possible runtime environment is the OpenTOSCA system presented by Binz et al. [1].

2   Winery System Overview and Use Case

The TOSCA meta model defines 45 elements in total which can be used to model applications (cf. [4]). We subdivided this set into two classes: The first one contains seven elements that are directly related to visual topology modeling—namely relationship template, relationship constraint, node template, deployment artifact, requirement, capability, and policy. These elements are used in the Topology Modeler. The second class contains all remaining elements that are used to define semantics and configurations such as types, implementations, and policy templates. These elements can be created, modified, and deleted exclusively by using the Element Manager. This way, Winery separates concerns: The Topology Modeler eases modeling of application topologies by depicting elements and combinations thereof visually. On the one hand, this helps architects, application developers, and operators to understand and model applications without the need for technical insight into the type implementations and configurations. On the other hand, technical experts are able to provide and configure node types and relationship types by using the Element Manager. Thus, Winery enables collaborative development of TOSCA-based applications. As a consequence, Winery conceptually consists of three parts: (1) the Topology Modeler, (2) the Element Manager, and (3) the Repository, where all data is stored (see Fig. 1).

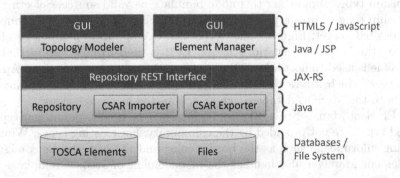

Fig. 1. Components of Winery

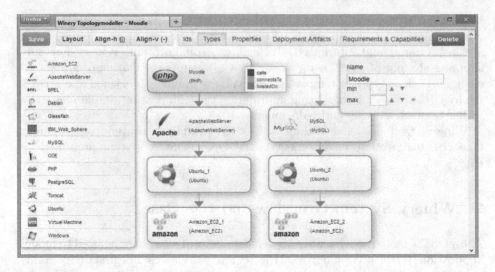

Fig. 2. Moodle Application Topology. Adhering Vino4TOSCA [3], node templates are depicted as rounded rectangles and relationship templates as arrows between the rectangles. The possible relationship types starting from a PHP node template are depicted in the white box.

To create a TOSCA-based application, the first step is to create a new service template that contains an application topology by using the Topology Modeler. Therefore, Winery offers all available node types in a palette. From there, the user drags the desired node type and drops it into the editing area. There, the node type becomes a node template: a node in the topology graph. Node templates can be annotated with requirements and capabilities, property values, and policies. Most importantly, nodes may define deployment artifacts, which provide the actual implementation of the node template, e. g., a VM image, an operating system package for the Apache Web Server, or an archive containing a PHP application's files. Relations between node templates are called relationship templates. They can be created by clicking on a node template, which offers possible relationship types supporting this node template as valid source. Selecting one relationship type creates a new relationship template that has to be connected to the desired target. Figure 2 shows the TOSCA application topology of our use case—the Moodle[1] scenario. Amazon EC2 is used to host two virtual machines: One is used to host a MySQL database, the other one to host an Apache Web Server, which serves the Moodle PHP application. The PHP application connects to the MySQL database, which is depicted as orange arrow.

The Element Manager (Fig. 3) may, for instance, be used to define new types if required types are not provided by the community. For existing types, Winery's rendering information such as the border color and the icon can be configured. The Element Manager also handles the management of artifact templates and

---

[1] http://www.moodle.org

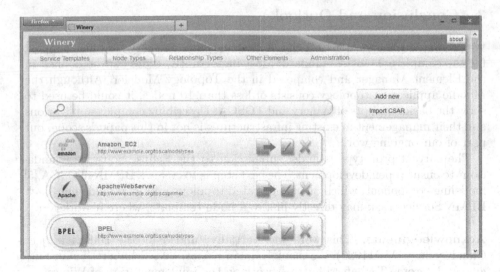

Fig. 3. Element Manger Showing Available Node Types

related components: Files can be associated with an artifact template, which in turn are referenced from implementations as concrete implementation.

Having the topology ready, the next step is to model management plans. Winery does not support plan modeling by itself, but relies on other modeling tools to create plans. We usually use the Eclipse BPEL Designer[2] to model plans and compress the workflow and related files into one archive. In the service template, for each management plan, a plan element is created and the corresponding archive is uploaded. For deployment, we attach a BPEL workflow that provisions the Moodle application on Amazon EC2 virtual machines. The workflow installs the applications as defined in the topology and establishes the "connectsTo" relation by assigning the IP address of the MySQL instance to the Moodle configuration on the Apache Web Server.

After finishing modeling, the backend allows for exporting a CSAR file containing all required definitions. The resulting CSAR file can be deployed on a TOSCA-compliant runtime, which in turn deploys the implementation artifacts and the management plans to appropriate runtime environments. Finally, the user can start a build plan to instantiate an application instance. For more details, we recommend the detailed overview by Binz et al. [2], the TOSCA specification [6], and the TOSCA primer [7].

The Repository itself stores TOSCA models and enables managing their content. It offers importing existing CSARs into the Repository, which, for instance, makes community-defined node types and relationship types available for topology modeling. Winery is built to be integrated into other tool chains and projects which can reuse Winery's type repository, graphical modeling capabilities, or export functionality.

---

[2] http://www.eclipse.org/bpel/

3   Conclusion and Outlook

We presented the open source TOSCA modeling tool "Winery". It offers support for the complete TOSCA standard: Most importantly, types can be defined in the Element Manager and composed in the Topology Modeler. Although the Moodle application topology consists of less than 10 nodes, it could be used to show the basic concepts of Winery and TOSCA. Describing complex applications and their management in existing infrastructures is not in this paper's scope, but part of our ongoing work.

The current prototype is under submission to the Eclipse Software Foundation[3] to ensure open development. The next step is to create a BPMN4TOSCA [5] modeling component, which offers integrated topology and plan modeling: Each BPMN Service Task may directly link to a node template, where it works on.

Acknowledgments. This work was partially funded by the BMWi project CloudCycle (01MD11023). We thank Kálmán Képes, Yves Schubert, Timur Sungur, and Jerome Tagliaferri for their work on the implementation of Winery.

References

1. Binz, T., Breitenbücher, U., Haupt, F., Kopp, O., Leymann, F., Nowak, A., Wagner, S.: OpenTOSCA – A Runtime for TOSCA-based Cloud Applications. In: Basu, S., Pautasso, C., Zhang, L., Fu, X. (eds.) ICSOC 2013. LNCS, vol. 8274, pp. 694–697. Springer, Heidelberg (2013)
2. Binz, T., Breitenbücher, U., Kopp, O., Leymann, F.: TOSCA: Portable Automated Deployment and Management of Cloud Applications. In: Advanced Web Services, pp. 527–549. Springer (2014)
3. Breitenbücher, U., Binz, T., Kopp, O., Leymann, F., Schumm, D.: Vino4TOSCA: A Visual Notation for Application Topologies based on TOSCA. In: Meersman, R., et al. (eds.) OTM 2012, Part I. LNCS, vol. 7565, pp. 416–424. Springer, Heidelberg (2012)
4. Kopp, O.: TOSCA v1.0 as UML class diagram (2013), http://www.opentosca.org/#tosca
5. Kopp, O., Binz, T., Breitenbücher, U., Leymann, F.: BPMN4TOSCA: A Domain-Specific Language to Model Management Plans for Composite Applications. In: Mendling, J., Weidlich, M. (eds.) BPMN 2012. LNBIP, vol. 125, pp. 38–52. Springer, Heidelberg (2012)
6. OASIS: OASIS Topology and Orchestration Specification for Cloud Applications (TOSCA) Version 1.0 Committee Specification 01 (2013)
7. OASIS: Topology and Orchestration Specification for Cloud Applications (TOSCA) Primer Version 1.0 (January 2013)

All links were last followed on August 26, 2013.

---

[3] http://www.eclipse.org/proposals/soa.winery/

Barcelona: A Design and Runtime Environment for Declarative Artifact-Centric BPM

Fenno (Terry) Heath, III[1], David Boaz[2], Manmohan Gupta[3],
Roman Vaculín[1], Yutian Sun[4,*], Richard Hull[1], and Lior Limonad[2]

[1] IBM T.J. Watson Research Center, USA
{theath,vaculin,hull}@us.ibm.com
[2] IBM Haifa Research Lab, Israel
{davidbo,lliori}@il.ibm.com
[3] IBM Global Business Services, India
manmohan.gupta@in.ibm.com
[4] University of California, Santa Barbara, USA
sun@cs.ucsb.edu

A promising approach to managing business operations is based on business artifacts, a.k.a. business entities (with lifecycles) [8, 6]. These are key conceptual entities that are central to guiding the operations of a business, and whose content changes as they move through those operations. A business artifact type is modeled using (a) an information model, which is intended to hold all business-relevant data about entities of this type, and (b) a lifecycle model, which is intended to hold the possible ways that an entity of this type might progress through the business. In 2010 a declarative style of business artifact lifecycles, called Guard-Stage-Milestone (GSM), was introduced [4, 5]. GSM has since been adopted [7] to form the conceptual basis of the OMG Case Management Model and Notation (CMMN) standard [1]. The Barcelona component of the recently open-sourced [2] ArtiFact system supports both design-time and run-time environments for GSM. Both of these will be illustrated in the proposed demo.

The GSM approach will be illustrated in the demo using a simplified *OrderToCash* scenario. Figure 1 shows a screen shot from Barcelona that provides a view of the design editor for this scenario. The focus is on a single artifact type, called `CustomerOrder`. The information model, which is essentially a record with scalar and nested relation fields, is not illustrated in the figure, but is accessible from the tree on the left side. The example focuses on the steps of *Drafting* a (customized) product based on an incoming order; *Submitting* the draft for approval; and then *Processing* the order. These activities are captured as top-level stages in the GSM schema for this example, which is illustrated in the right-hand portion of Figure 1. Stages may contain a single task (as is the case with *Drafting* and *Submitting*), and may be nested (as is the case with *Processing* and inside that, with *Preparing*). Stages may be executed once or repeatedly, and may execute in parallel.

Launching of a stage execution is controlled by rules-based *guards*, designated using blue diamonds on the right edge of the stage. These may be triggered by an external event (in which case a yellow lightening bolt is included), or by internal events.

---

* This author supported in part by NSF grant IIS-0812578.

S. Basu et al. (Eds.): ICSOC 2013, LNCS 8274, pp. 705–709, 2013.
© Springer-Verlag Berlin Heidelberg 2013

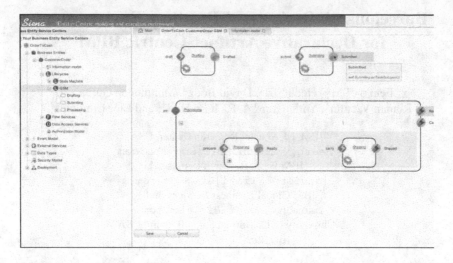

Fig. 1. Illustration of Barcelona graphical schema editor

Completion of a stage execution is controlled by rules-based *milestones*, indicated by orange disks on the right-hand boundaries of stages. These, too, may be triggered by external or internal events.

The Barcelona engine can support GSM schemas with multiple artifact types, and can support large numbers of artifact instances. In typical applications the instances are created programmatically, and progress through their lifecycles through responses to automatic and manual steps. However, to illustrate the run-time operation of Barcelona, and to inspect the status of artifact instances, we use the run-time editor, illustrated in Figure 2. That figure shows a single instance of the CustomerOrder artifact type, at some point in its progression through the business. The central area in the screen shows the data currently held in the information model of this order. Both scalar and nexted values are supported. On the right hand side is a schematic representation of the status of stage executions for this artifact instance. This indicates that both the *Drafting* and *Submitting* stage have executed once, and that the *Processing* stage is currently executing, with substage *Preparing* and inside that subsubstage *Collecting* all executing, and that one occurrence of *ResearchingOrdering* has completed inside. This representation supports hierarchy, to reflect the nesting of stages. If a stage is executed multiple times, then it is listed multiple times in this listing.

The gray buttons at the upper right of the screen are used to simulate the arrival of external events, so that the user can manually progress the artifact instance through its lifecycle, for testing purposes.

The high-level architecture of Barcelona is shown in Figure 3. The following summarizes the major features of the respective components.

Execution engine: Provides support for (1) management of business artifact instances; instances stored in the relational database; (2) management of artifact lifecycles & interactions (by means of service invocations or event subscriptions); (3) interaction

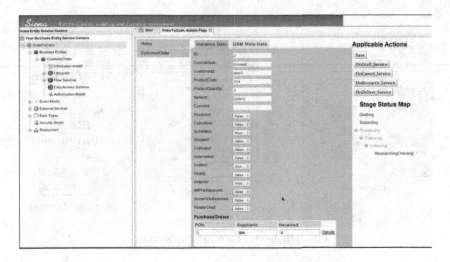

Fig. 2. Illustration of Barcelona runtime

with external environment via REST and WSDL service APIs; (4) management of access control; (5) basic support for execution monitoring.

Solution Designer Editor: Provides functions for easy authoring of artifact-centric business processes, including (1) design of information models (nested relational structures); (2) design of artifact lifecycles, supporting both GSM and Finite-State-Machine lifecycle models (in GSM supporting two condition languages, one based on JEXL, and the other one based on extended OCL); (3) design of data services: serve for providing access to arbitrary data queries over information model of artifact instances; (4) design of flow services, which are complex flows based on flowcharts.

Default Runtime GUI: Supports execution of artifact-centric business processes including (1) step through BOM executions; (2) inspection of the artifact instances states (information model, lifecycle model). The tool is intended for testing, debugging and support of rapid prototyping. In contrast, the Solution Builder application [10] incorporates a special-purpose UI working on top of the Barcelona runtime engine.

Additional Components: There are repositories for (1) Artifact Schemas, (2) Artifact Instances, and (3) External Service specifications (which link to external REST and WSDL services)

As noted above, Barcelona forms one component of the ArtiFact system. The other components are Siena (which supports Finite-State-Machine lifecycles for artifacts), and the ACSI Interoperation Hub (which supports interoperation between enterprises). The ArtiFact system originated with the Siena system, developed at IBM Research starting in 2006. The Barcelona component was added in the early 2010s, with several extensions in the past 2 years. A substantial portion of the Barcelona component, and all of the Interopration Hub, were developed as part of the EU-funded Artifact-Centric Services Interoperation (ACSI) project [9]. The ACSI project studied the artifact-centric

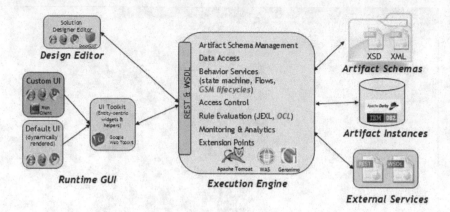

Fig. 3. High-level Barcelona architecture

approach from a variety of perspectives, including conceptual modeling, verification, process mining, systems, services interoperation, access controls, and practical applications; GSM was a starting point for most of these investigations.

The GSM model was used as a basis for the recently released OMG CMMN standard. While there are significant differences between GSM and CMMN, the Barcelona component of the ArtiFact system can be used as a lightweight, open-source tool for studying the basic approach underlying modern case management.

A preliminary version of Barcelona was demonstrated at the BPM 2011 conference. The most important advances since that time include (a) the development of a graphical design editor, (b) the development of the OCL-based condition language (which brings the power of full first-order logic), and (c) the implementation of the operational semantics as described in [3]. (That semantics has certain desirable properties, including conformance to intuitive principles and equivalence to a fixpoint characterization.)

A demo video is available at this URL: http://goo.gl/YAvxd.

References

1. Boaz, D., Limonad, L., Gupta, M.: BizArtifact: Artifact-centric Business Process Management (June 2013), http://sourceforge.net/projects/bizartifact/
2. Damaggio, E., Hull, R., Vaculín, R.: On the equivalence of incremental and fixpoint semantics for business artifacts with guard-stage-milestone lifecycles
3. Hull, R., et al.: Introducing the guard-stage-milestone approach for specifying business entity lifecycles. In: Bravetti, M., Bultan, T. (eds.) WS-FM 2010. LNCS, vol. 6551, pp. 1–24. Springer, Heidelberg (2011)
4. Hull, R., et al.: Business artifacts with guard-stage-milestone lifecycles: Managing artifact interactions with conditions and events. In: ACM Intl. Conf. on Distributed Event-Based Systems, DEBS (2011)
5. Kumaran, S., Nandi, P., Terry Heath III, F.F., Bhaskaran, K., Das, R.: Adoc-oriented programming. In: SAINT, pp. 334–343 (2003)

6. Marin, M., Hull, R., Vaculín, R.: Data centric BPM and the emerging case management standard: A short survey. In: La Rosa, M., Soffer, P. (eds.) BPM 2012 Workshops. LNBIP, vol. 132, pp. 24–30. Springer, Heidelberg (2013)
7. Nigam, A., Caswell, N.S.: Business Artifacts: An Approach to Operational Specification. IBM Systems Journal 42(3) (2003)
8. Vaculín, R., Hull, R., Heath, T., Cochran, C., Nigam, A., Sukavirirya, P.: Declarative business artifact centric modeling of decision and knowledge intensive business processes. In: The Fifteenth IEEE International Enterprise Computing Conference (EDOC 2011), pp. 151–160. IEEE Computer Society (2011)

Author Index